D1092841

THE NEW RAND McNALLY COLLEGE WORLD ATLAS

THE NEW RAND McNALLY COLLEGE WORLD ATLAS

RAND McNALLY & COMPANY
Chicago / New York / San Francisco

Contents

Library of Congress Catalog Card Number: 83-60218
Printed in the United States of America by Rand McNally & Company
SBN 528-83133-X *First printing, 1983*

Flags of the World

Reference Maps of the World

Historical Maps of the United States

Travel Maps of the United States

Tables, Charts, and Facts

Reference Map Index

Thematic Maps of the World

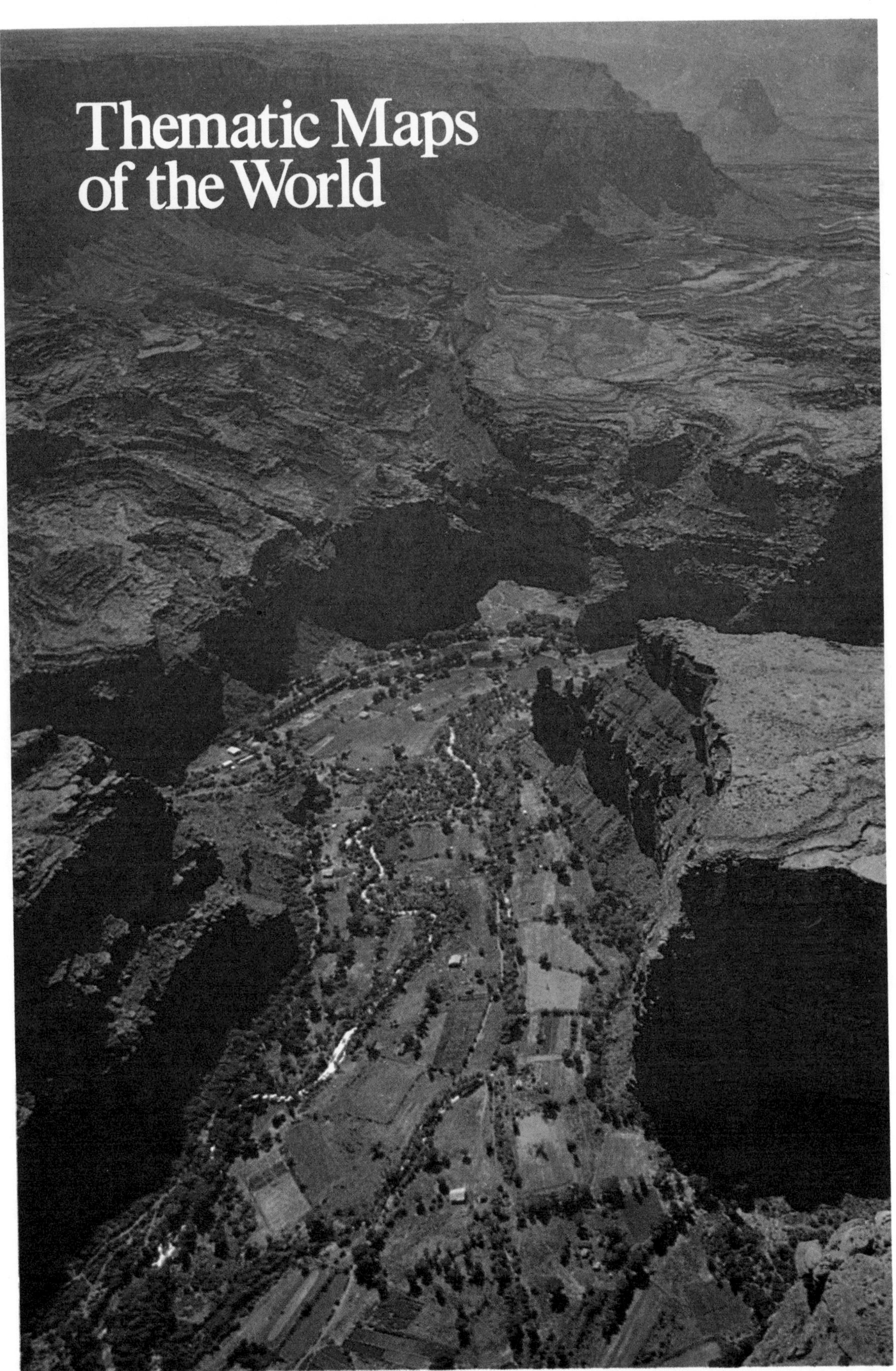

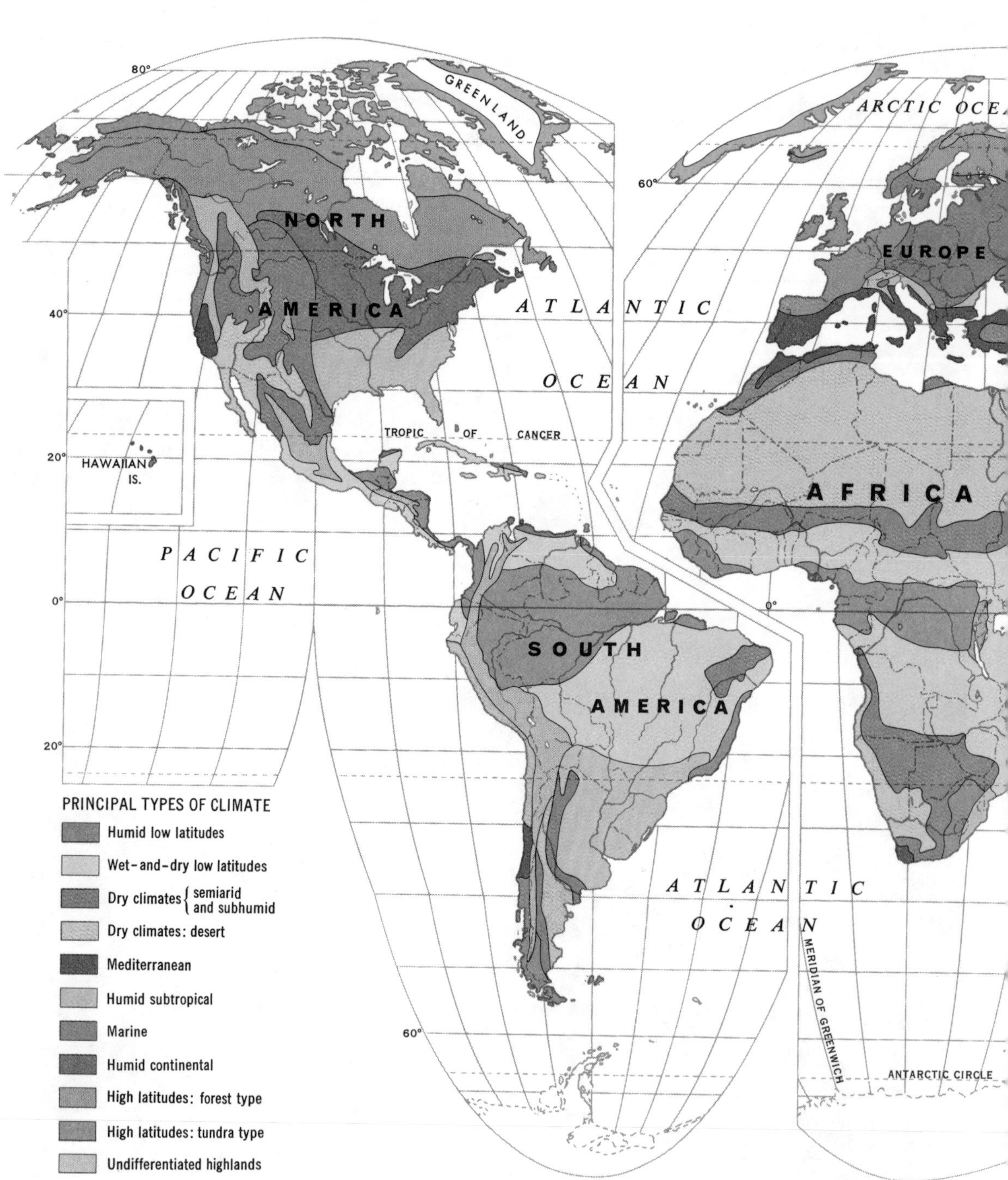

80°
GREENLAND
ARCTIC OCE
60°
NORTH
AMERICA
EUROPE
40°
ATLANTIC
OCEAN
TROPIC OF CANCER
20°
HAWAIIAN IS.
AFRICA
PACIFIC
OCEAN
0°
0°
SOUTH
AMERICA
20°
ATLANTIC
OCEAN
MERIDIAN OF GREENWICH
60°
ANTARCTIC CIRCLE
PRINCIPAL TYPES OF CLIMATE
Humid low latitudes
Wet-and-dry low latitudes
Dry climates { semiarid and subhumid
Dry climates: desert
Mediterranean
Humid subtropical
Marine
Humid continental
High latitudes: forest type
High latitudes: tundra type
Undifferentiated highlands

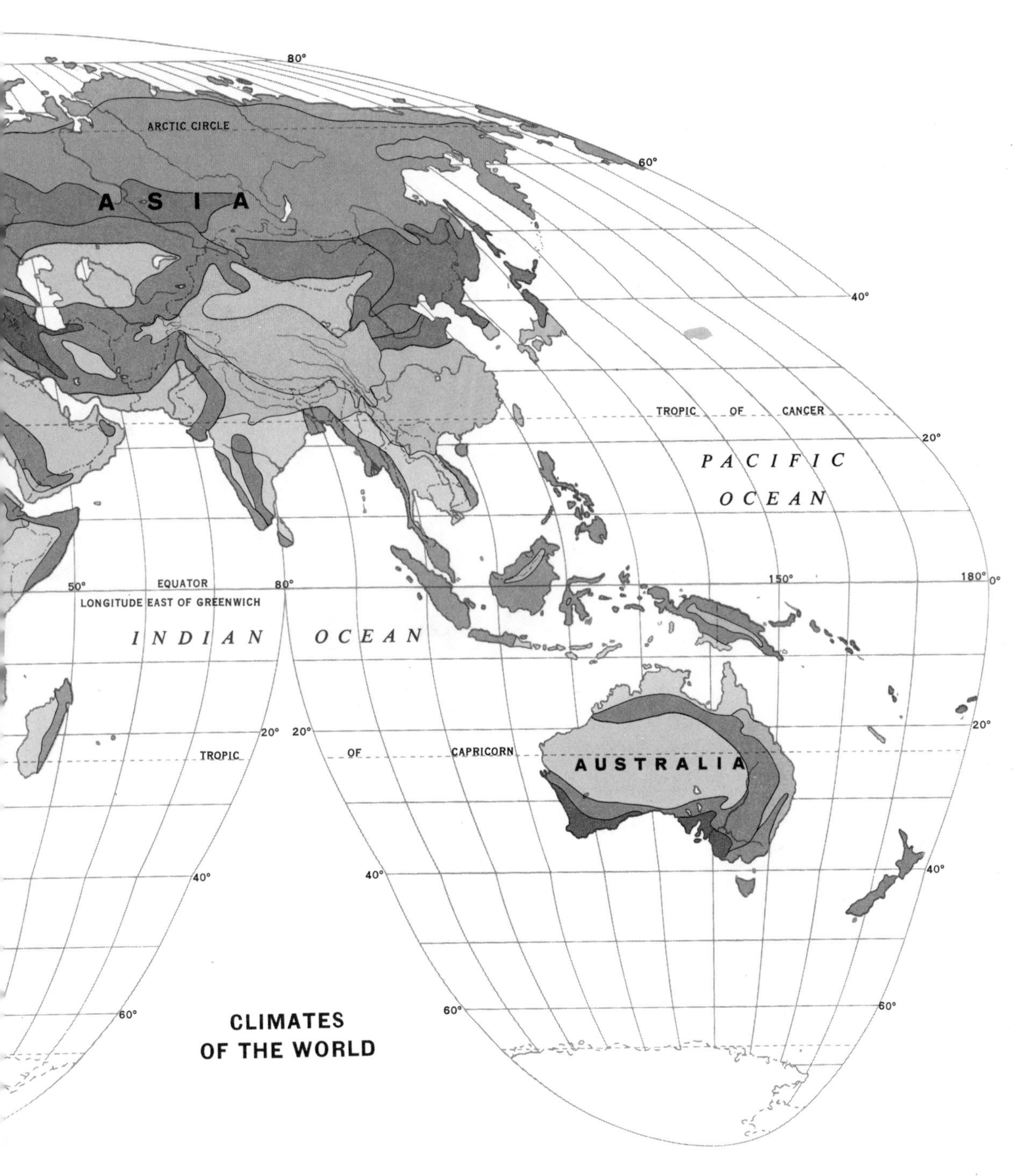
80°
ARCTIC CIRCLE
60°
A S I A
40°
TROPIC OF CANCER
20°
PACIFIC
OCEAN
50°
EQUATOR
80°
150°
180°
0°
LONGITUDE EAST OF GREENWICH
INDIAN OCEAN
20°
20°
TROPIC
OF
CAPRICORN
AUSTRALIA
20°
40°
40°
40°
60°
60°
60°
CLIMATES
OF THE WORLD

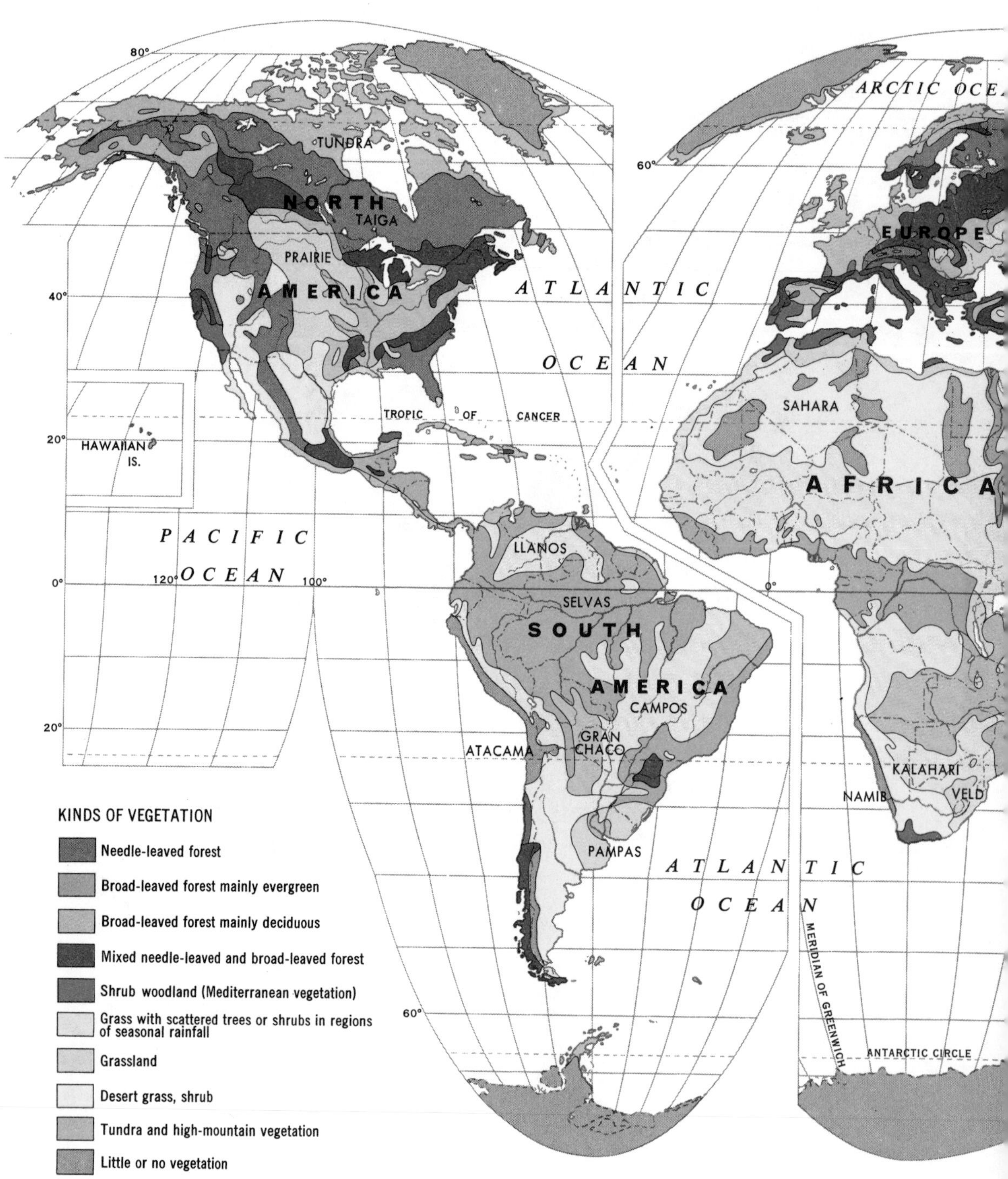

KINDS OF VEGETATION

- Needle-leaved forest
- Broad-leaved forest mainly evergreen
- Broad-leaved forest mainly deciduous
- Mixed needle-leaved and broad-leaved forest
- Shrub woodland (Mediterranean vegetation)
- Grass with scattered trees or shrubs in regions of seasonal rainfall
- Grassland
- Desert grass, shrub
- Tundra and high-mountain vegetation
- Little or no vegetation

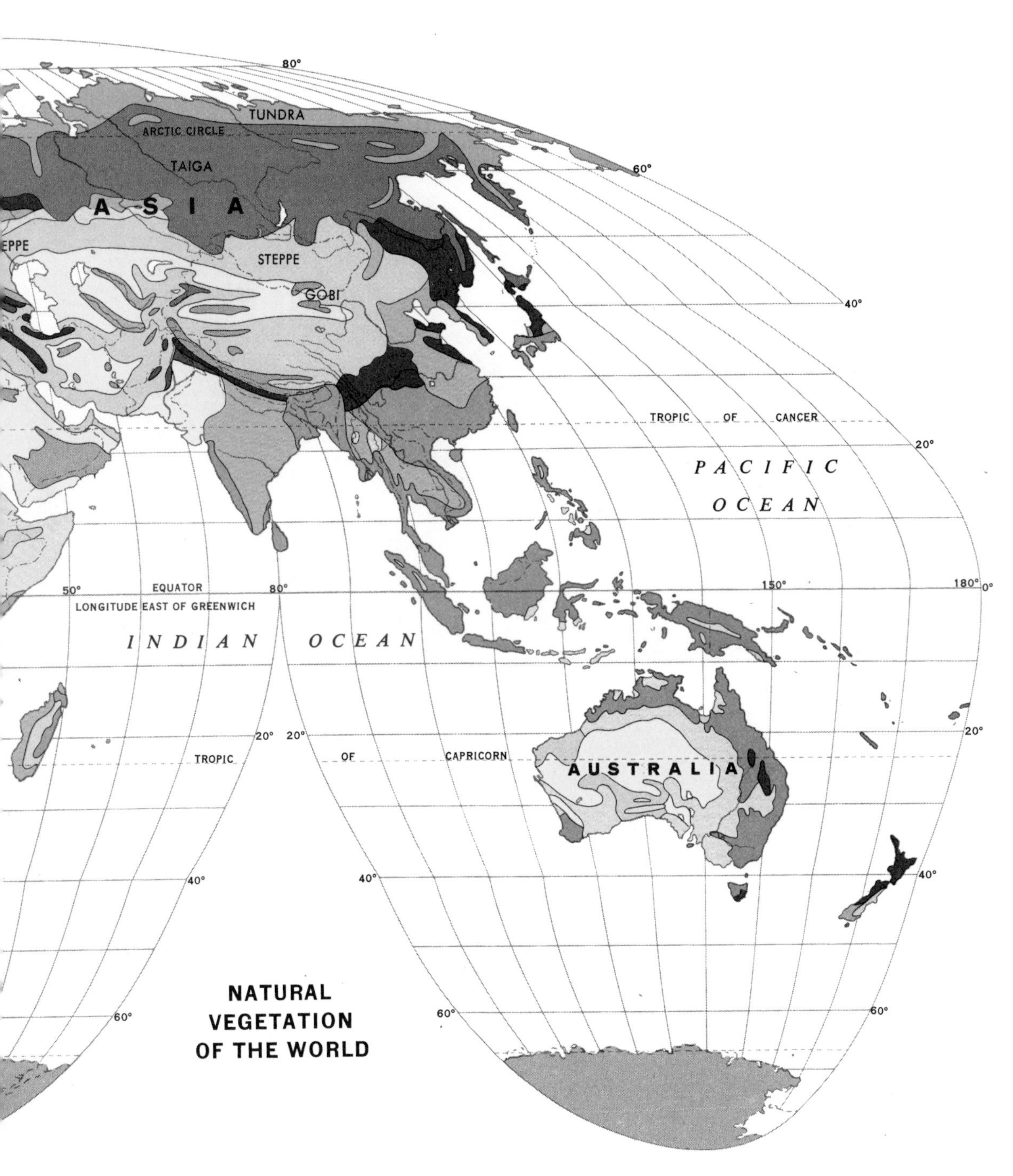

80°
TUNDRA
ARCTIC CIRCLE
TAIGA
A S I A
EPPE
STEPPE
GOBI
60°
40°
TROPIC OF CANCER
20°
PACIFIC
OCEAN
50°
EQUATOR
80°
150°
180°
0°
LONGITUDE EAST OF GREENWICH
INDIAN OCEAN
20°
20°
TROPIC
OF
CAPRICORN
AUSTRALIA
20°
40°
40°
40°
60°
60°
60°
NATURAL
VEGETATION
OF THE WORLD

180°
150°
120°
90°
60°
30°
0°
60°
30°
0°
30°
60°
180°
150°
120°
90°
60°
30°
0°

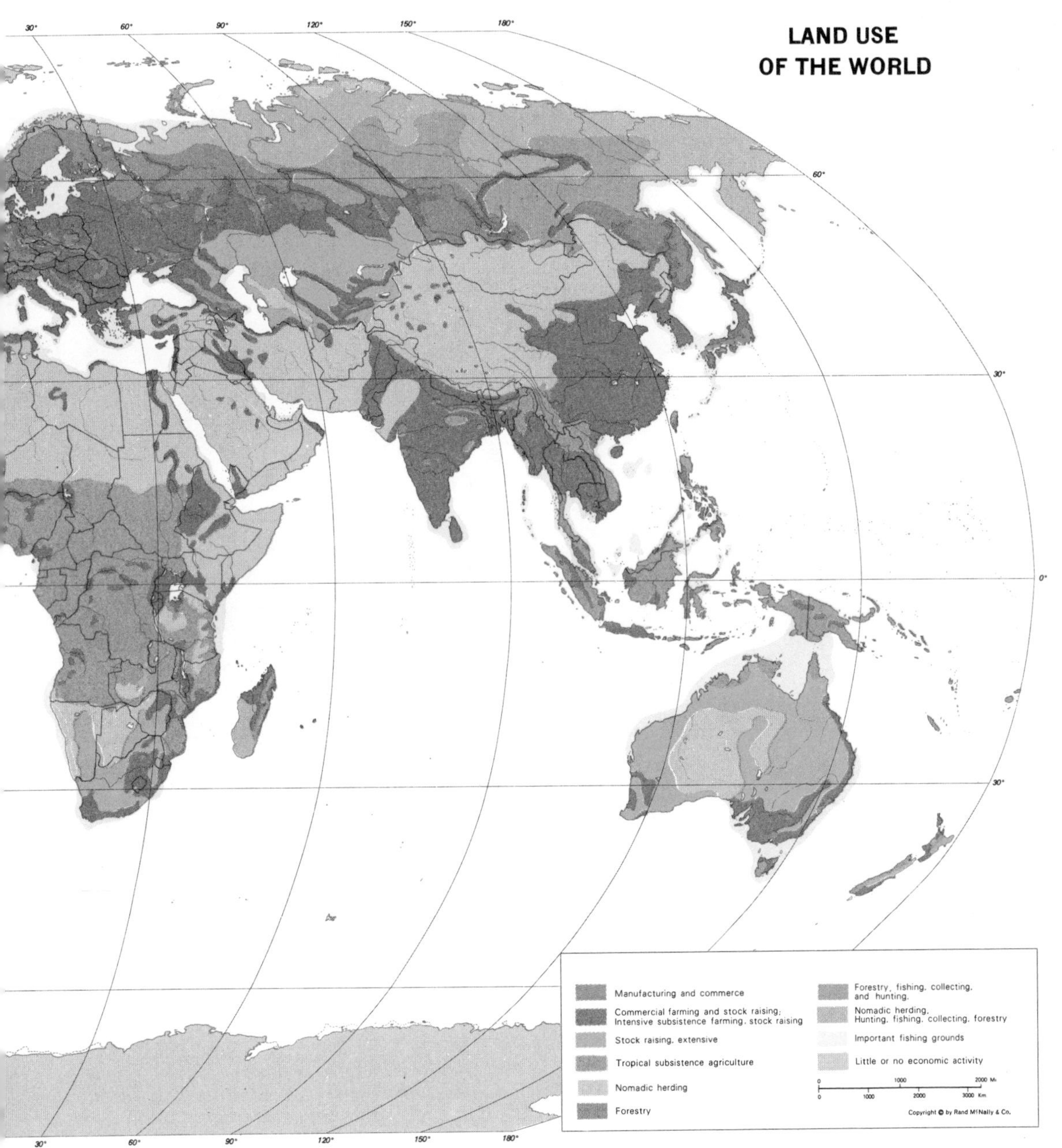
LAND USE
OF THE WORLD
30°
60°
90°
120°
150°
180°
60°
30°
0°
30°
Manufacturing and commerce
Commercial farming and stock raising;
Intensive subsistence farming, stock raising
Stock raising, extensive
Tropical subsistence agriculture
Nomadic herding
Forestry
Forestry, fishing, collecting,
and hunting.
Nomadic herding,
Hunting, fishing, collecting, forestry
Important fishing grounds
Little or no economic activity
0 1000 2000 Mi
0 1000 2000 3000 Km
Copyright © by Rand McNally & Co.

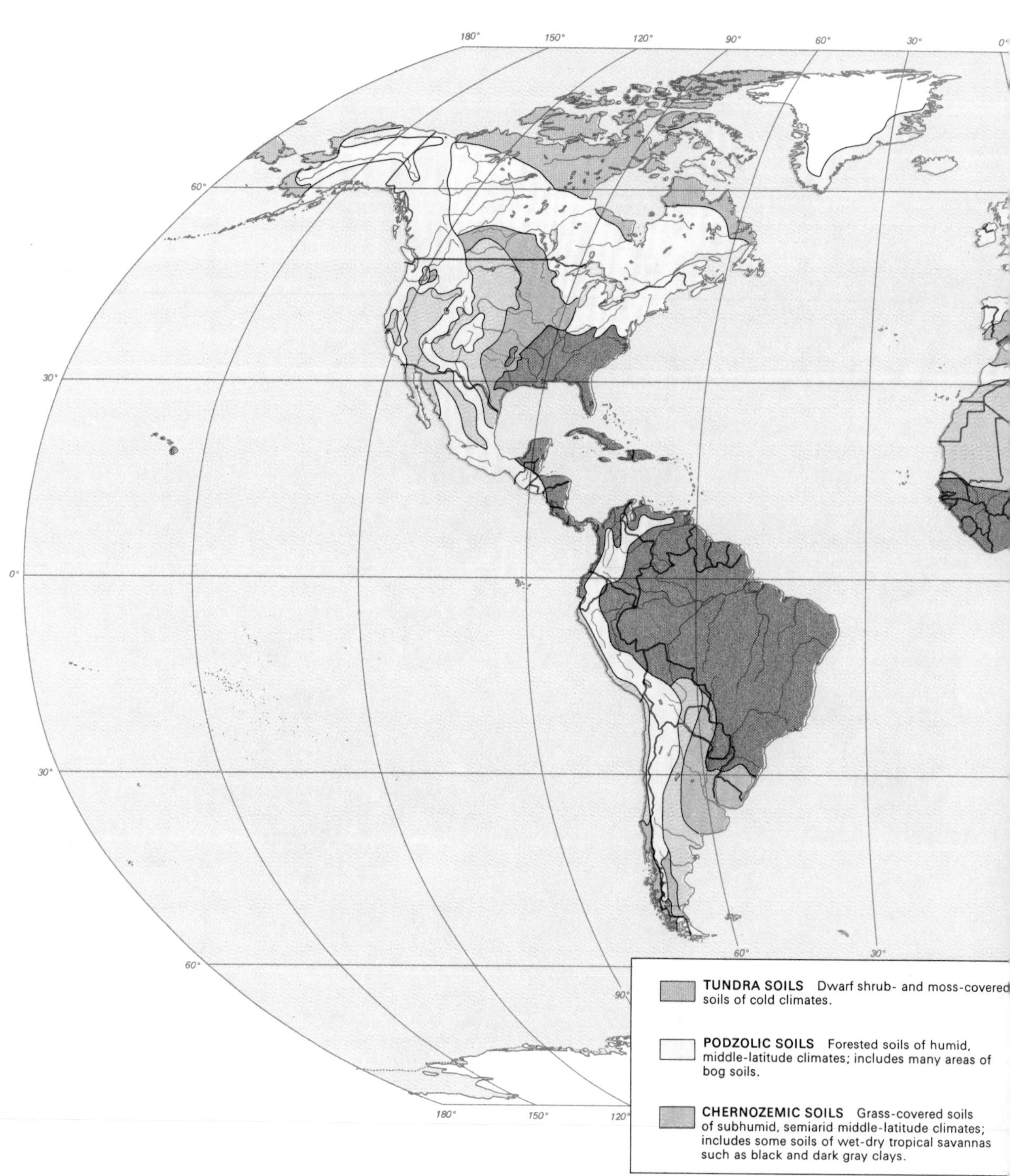

TUNDRA SOILS Dwarf shrub- and moss-covered soils of cold climates.

PODZOLIC SOILS Forested soils of humid, middle-latitude climates; includes many areas of bog soils.

CHERNOZEMIC SOILS Grass-covered soils of subhumid, semiarid middle-latitude climates; includes some soils of wet-dry tropical savannas such as black and dark gray clays.

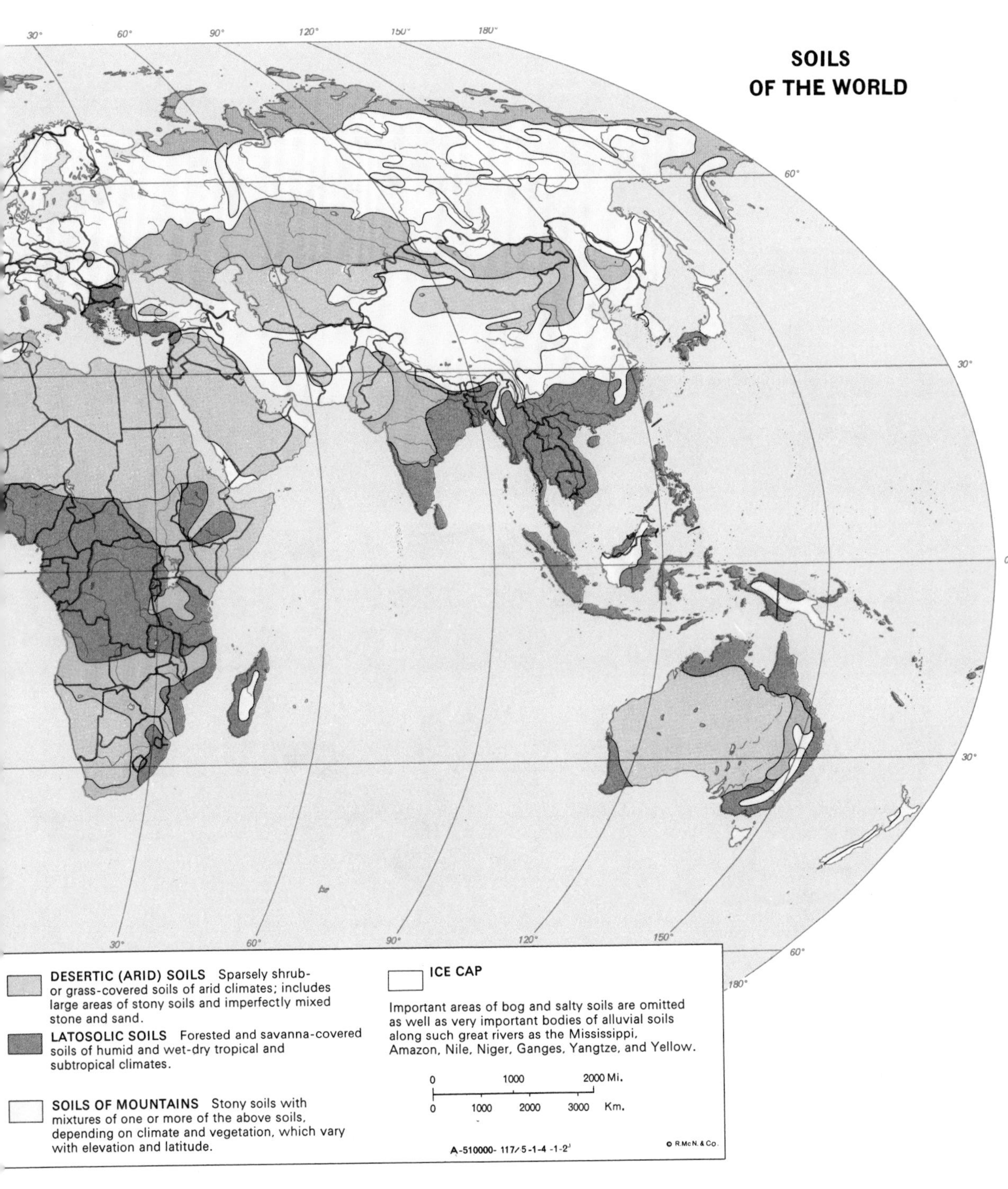
SOILS
OF THE WORLD
30°
60°
90°
120°
150°
180°
60°
30°
0°
30°
60°
180°
DESERTIC (ARID) SOILS Sparsely shrub- or grass-covered soils of arid climates; includes large areas of stony soils and imperfectly mixed stone and sand.
LATOSOLIC SOILS Forested and savanna-covered soils of humid and wet-dry tropical and subtropical climates.
SOILS OF MOUNTAINS Stony soils with mixtures of one or more of the above soils, depending on climate and vegetation, which vary with elevation and latitude.
ICE CAP
Important areas of bog and salty soils are omitted as well as very important bodies of alluvial soils along such great rivers as the Mississippi, Amazon, Nile, Niger, Ganges, Yangtze, and Yellow.
0 1000 2000 Mi.
0 1000 2000 3000 Km.
A-510000- 117/5-1-4 -1-2
© R.McN. & Co.

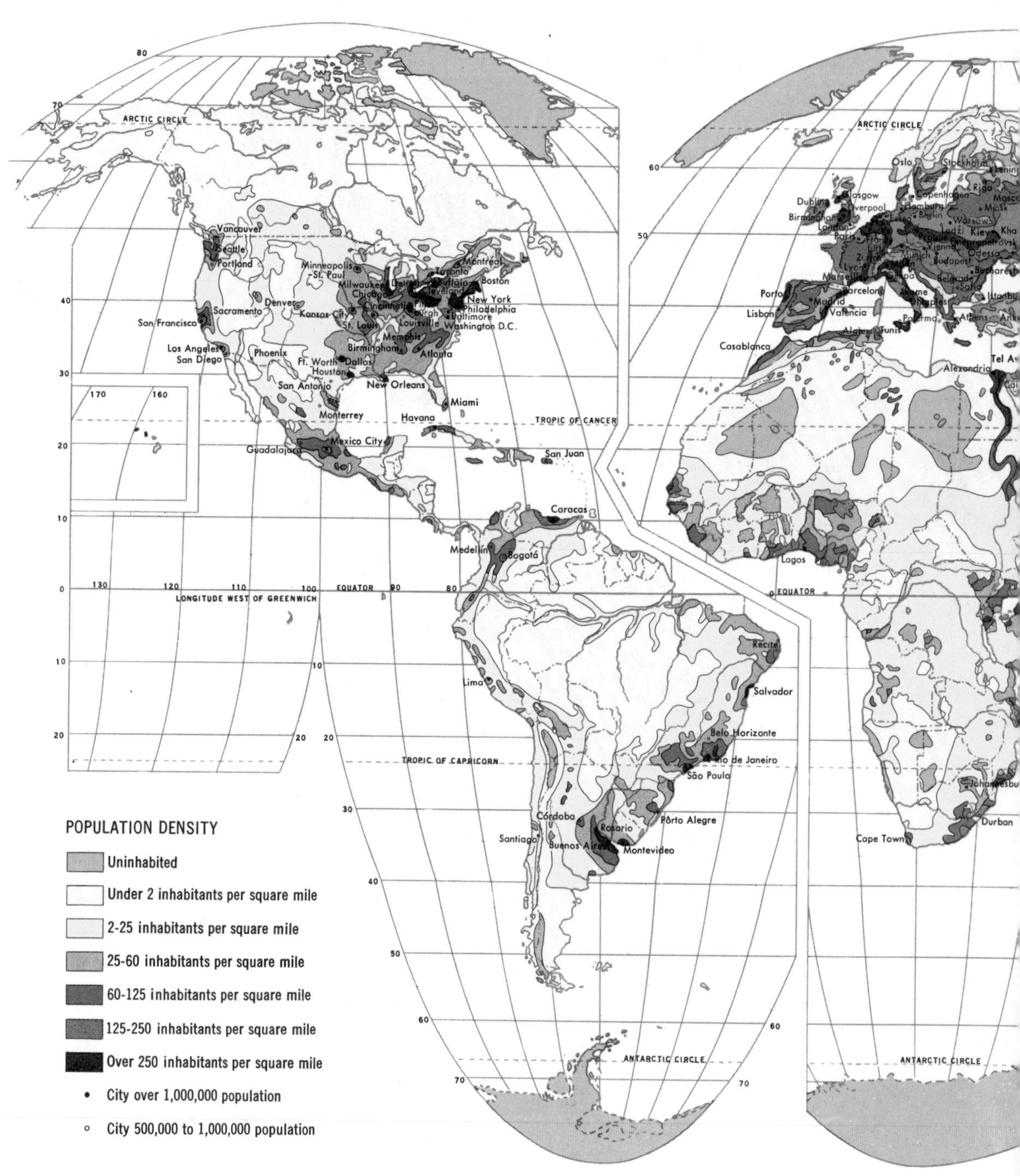
ARCTIC CIRCLE
TROPIC OF CANCER
EQUATOR
LONGITUDE WEST OF GREENWICH
TROPIC OF CAPRICORN
ANTARCTIC CIRCLE
Vancouver
Seattle
Portland
Sacramento
San Francisco
Los Angeles
San Diego
Phoenix
Denver
Minneapolis-St. Paul
Milwaukee
Chicago
Detroit
Toronto
Buffalo
Cleveland
Montréal
Boston
New York
Philadelphia
Baltimore
Washington D.C.
Kansas City
St. Louis
Cincinnati
Louisville
Memphis
Birmingham
Atlanta
Ft. Worth
Dallas
Houston
San Antonio
New Orleans
Miami
Monterrey
Havana
Mexico City
Guadalajara
San Juan
Caracas
Medellín
Bogotá
Lima
Recife
Salvador
Belo Horizonte
Rio de Janeiro
São Paulo
Pôrto Alegre
Córdoba
Rosario
Santiago
Buenos Aires
Montevideo
Oslo
Dublin
Glasgow
Liverpool
Birmingham
London
Paris
Copenhagen
Hamburg
Berlin
Warsaw
Minsk
Riga
Kiev
Odessa
Prague
Vienna
Munich
Budapest
Zurich
Lyon
Milan
Marseille
Barcelona
Madrid
Valencia
Porto
Lisbon
Rome
Naples
Palermo
Athens
Belgrade
Sofia
Algiers
Tunis
Casablanca
Alexandria
Lagos
Cape Town
Durban
POPULATION DENSITY
Uninhabited
Under 2 inhabitants per square mile
2-25 inhabitants per square mile
25-60 inhabitants per square mile
60-125 inhabitants per square mile
125-250 inhabitants per square mile
Over 250 inhabitants per square mile
City over 1,000,000 population
City 500,000 to 1,000,000 population

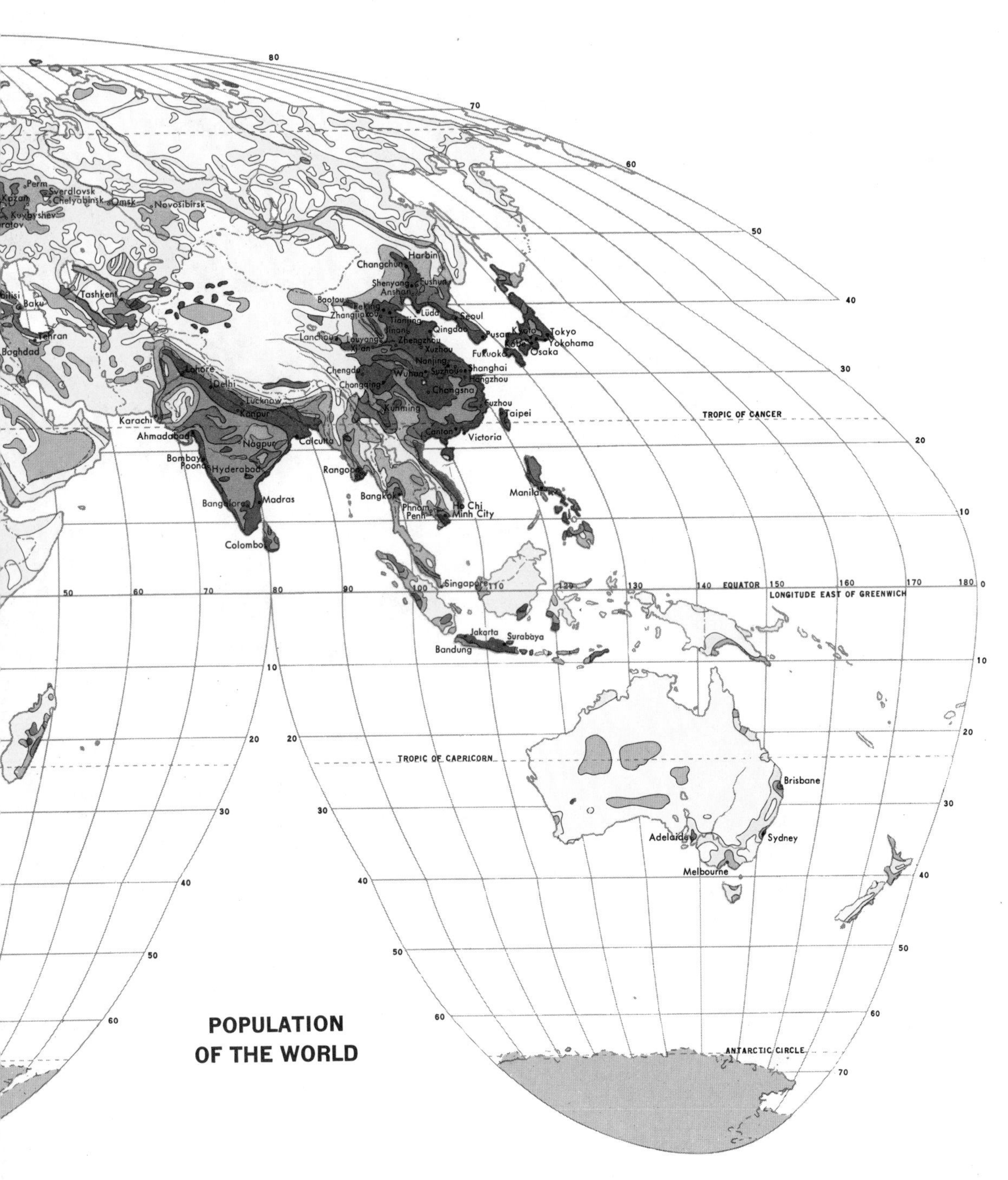
Perm
Sverdlovsk
Chelyabinsk
Omsk
Novosibirsk
Tashkent
Baku
Tehran
Baghdad
Karachi
Ahmadabad
Bombay
Poona
Hyderabad
Bangalore
Madras
Colombo
Lahore
Delhi
Lucknow
Kanpur
Nagpur
Calcutta
Rangoon
Bangkok
Phnom Penh
Ho Chi Minh City
Singapore
Jakarta
Bandung
Surabaya
Manila
Harbin
Changchun
Shenyang
Fushun
Anshan
Baotou
Peking
Zhangjiakou
Tianjing
Lüda
Jinan
Qingdao
Seoul
Lanchou
Luoyang
Xi'an
Zhengzhou
Xuzhou
Nanjing
Chengdu
Chongqing
Wuhan
Suzhou
Shanghai
Hangzhou
Changsha
Kunming
Canton
Victoria
Fuzhou
Taipei
Pusan
Fukuoka
Kyoto
Kobe
Osaka
Tokyo
Yokohama
Brisbane
Sydney
Adelaide
Melbourne
TROPIC OF CANCER
TROPIC OF CAPRICORN
EQUATOR
LONGITUDE EAST OF GREENWICH
ANTARCTIC CIRCLE
POPULATION
OF THE WORLD

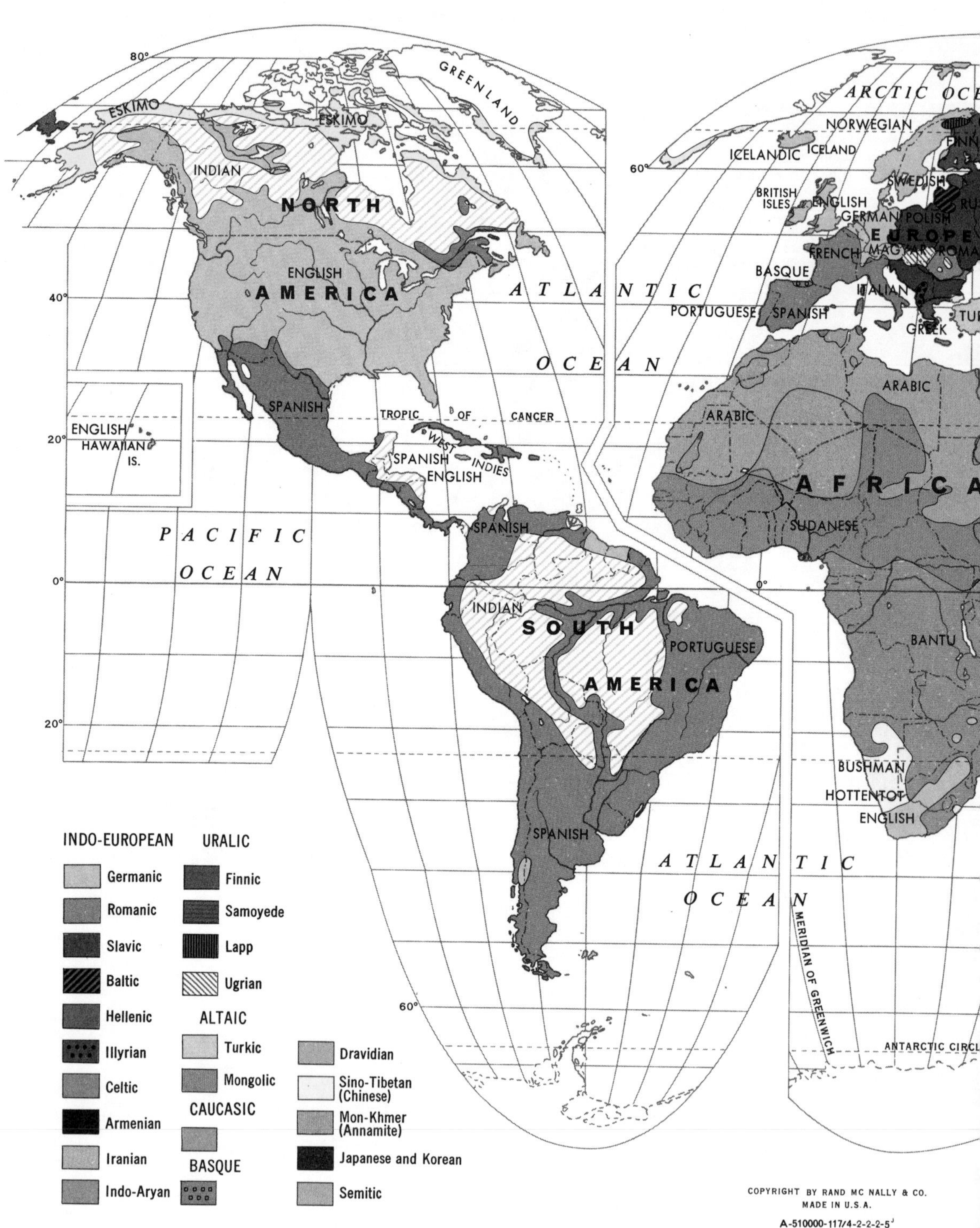
GREENLAND
ARCTIC OCE
ESKIMO
ESKIMO
INDIAN
NORTH
AMERICA
ENGLISH
NORWEGIAN
ICELANDIC
ICELAND
BRITISH ISLES
ENGLISH
SWEDISH
GERMAN
POLISH
EUROPE
FRENCH
MAGYAR
BASQUE
ITALIAN
PORTUGUESE
SPANISH
GREEK
ATLANTIC
OCEAN
SPANISH
TROPIC OF CANCER
ENGLISH
HAWAIIAN IS.
SPANISH
WEST INDIES
ENGLISH
ARABIC
ARABIC
AFRICA
SUDANESE
PACIFIC
OCEAN
SPANISH
INDIAN
SOUTH
AMERICA
PORTUGUESE
BANTU
BUSHMAN
HOTTENTOT
ENGLISH
SPANISH
ATLANTIC
OCEAN
MERIDIAN OF GREENWICH
ANTARCTIC CIRCL
80°
60°
40°
20°
0°
20°
60°
0°
INDO-EUROPEAN
Germanic
Romanic
Slavic
Baltic
Hellenic
Illyrian
Celtic
Armenian
Iranian
Indo-Aryan
URALIC
Finnic
Samoyede
Lapp
Ugrian
ALTAIC
Turkic
Mongolic
CAUCASIC
BASQUE
Dravidian
Sino-Tibetan (Chinese)
Mon-Khmer (Annamite)
Japanese and Korean
Semitic

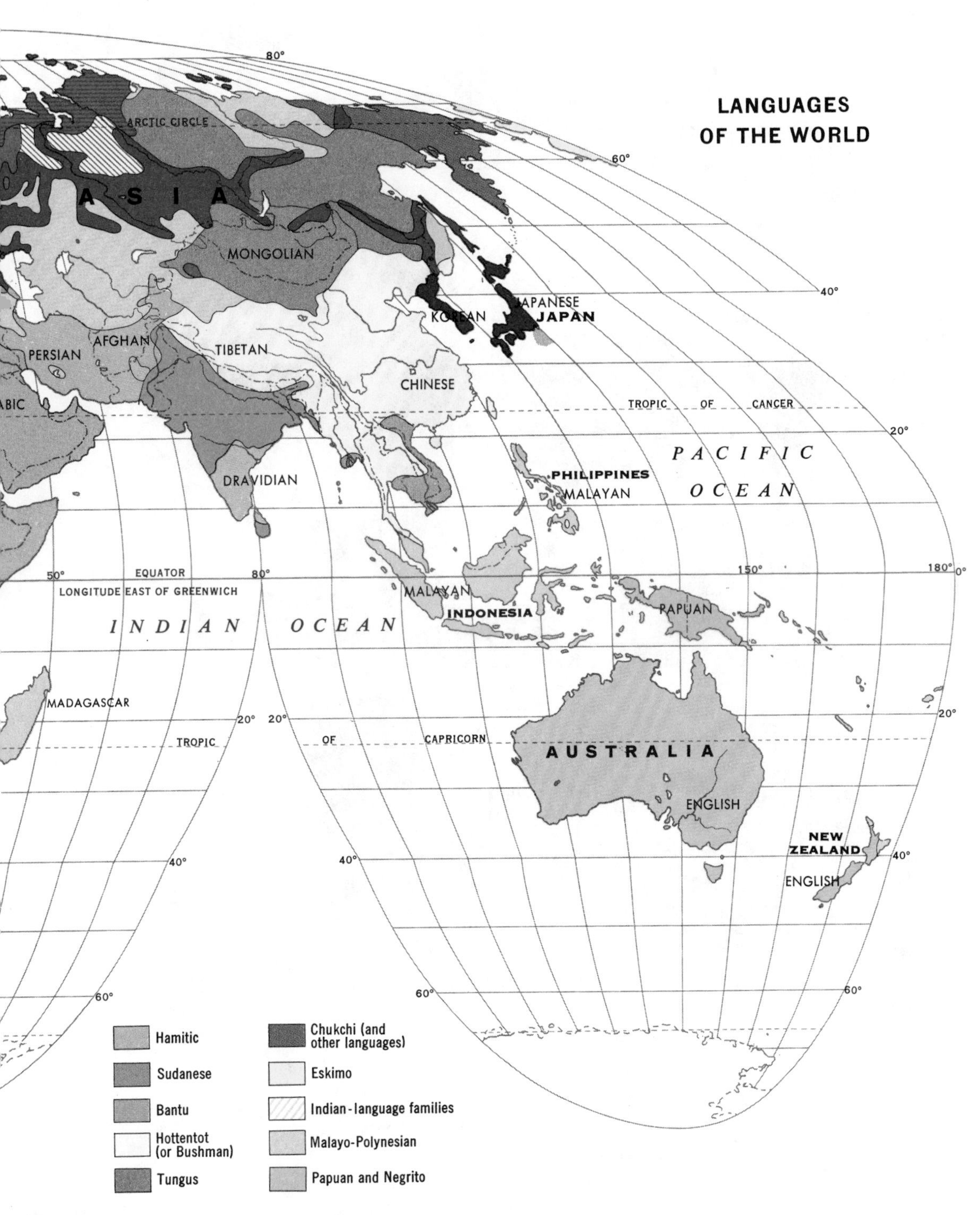
LANGUAGES
OF THE WORLD
80°
ARCTIC CIRCLE
60°
ASIA
MONGOLIAN
40°
JAPANESE
KOREAN
JAPAN
PERSIAN
AFGHAN
TIBETAN
CHINESE
ABIC
TROPIC OF CANCER
20°
PACIFIC
OCEAN
PHILIPPINES
MALAYAN
DRAVIDIAN
50°
EQUATOR
80°
150°
180°
0°
LONGITUDE EAST OF GREENWICH
MALAYAN
INDONESIA
PAPUAN
INDIAN OCEAN
MADAGASCAR
20°
20°
TROPIC
OF
CAPRICORN
20°
AUSTRALIA
ENGLISH
NEW
ZEALAND
ENGLISH
40°
40°
40°
60°
60°
60°
Hamitic
Sudanese
Bantu
Hottentot
(or Bushman)
Tungus
Chukchi (and
other languages)
Eskimo
Indian-language families
Malayo-Polynesian
Papuan and Negrito

Environment Maps
of the World

Introduction

The environment maps show the natural environment and how it has been modified by humans. Ten major environments are depicted, and these categories are identified and described in the legend below.

Classification is based upon the appearance and the general activity of an area. In mapping any distribution, however, it is necessary to limit the number of categories. Therefore, some gradations of meaning exist within each category. For example, "Grassland, grazing land" identifies the lush pampas of Argentina and the savannas of Africa as well as the steppes of the Soviet Union. Furthermore, certain enclaves that are not cropland may fall within the boundaries of cropland areas. Tracts such as these are included as part of the dominant environment surrounding them. Finally, boundaries on these maps, as on all maps, are never absolute but mark the center of transitional zones between categories.

The actual shapes of large metropolitan areas are shown. A red dot indicates concentrated urban development where a shape would be indistinguishable at the map scale. Black dots are used to locate places important as locational reference points.

From these maps, comprehensive observations may be made about major world environments. For example, the maps show that the world's urban areas are limited in extent, and relatively small portions of the earth's surface are made up of cropland. Vast areas show the limited influence of humanity upon the environment.

Environment Map Legend

• URBAN
Major areas of contiguous residential, commercial, and industrial development.

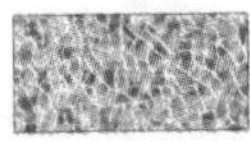

CROPLAND
Cultivated land predominates (includes pasture, irrigated land, and land in crop rotation).

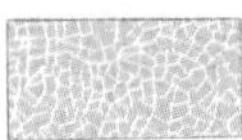

CROPLAND AND WOODLAND
Cultivated land interrupted by small wooded areas.

CROPLAND AND GRAZING LAND
Cultivated land with grassland and rangeland.

GRASSLAND, GRAZING LAND
Extensive grassland and rangeland with little or no cropland.

• OASIS
Important small areas of cultivation within grassland or wasteland.

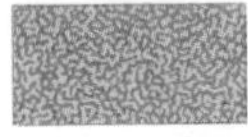

FOREST, WOODLAND
Extensive wooded areas with little or no cropland.

SWAMP, MARSHLAND
Extensive wetland areas (includes mangroves).

TUNDRA
Areas of lichen, shrubs, small trees, and wetland.

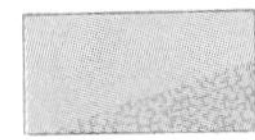

SHRUB, SPARSE GRASS; WASTELAND
Desert shrub and short grass, growing singly or in patches. Wasteland includes sand, salt flats, etc. (Extensive wastelands shown by pattern).

BARREN LAND
Icefields, glaciers, permanent snow, with exposed rock.

• Selected cities as points of reference.

Urban
Cropland
Cropland & Woodland
Cropland & Grazing Land
Grassland, Grazing Land
Forest, Woodland
Swamp, Marshland
Tundra
Shrub, Sparse Grass, Wasteland (pattern)
Barren Land
Oasis
ATLANTIC OCEAN
North Sea
Baltic Sea
Gulf of Bothnia
Bay of Biscay
Mediterranean Sea
Tyrrhenian Sea
Adriatic Sea
Aegean Sea
Reykjavik
Narvik
Trondheim
Bergen
Oslo
Helsinki
LENINGRAD
Tallinn
Stockholm
Göteborg
Riga
Copenhagen
Kaliningrad
Minsk
Glasgow
Belfast
MANCHESTER
Dublin
LONDON
Amsterdam
Hamburg
BERLIN
Elbe
Oder
Warsaw
Antwerp
Essen
Leipzig
Frankfurt
Brest
PARIS
Seine
Loire
Strasbourg
Rhine
Prague
Kraków
L'vov
Munich
Danube
VIENNA
CARPATHIANS
Zürich
ALPS
BUDAPEST
Tisza
La Coruña
Bordeaux
Garonne
Lyon
Rhône
MILAN
Zagreb
Sava
Venice
Bilbao
PYRENEES
Douro
Ebro
Genoa
Belgrade
Bucharest
Lisbon
MADRID
Marseille
BARCELONA
CORSICA
ROME
Sofia
Sevilla
SARDINIA
Naples
Tirane
ISLAS BALEARES
Tanger
Algiers
Oran
Palermo
Tunis
SICILY
Athens
Casablanca
ATLAS MOUNTAINS
MALTA
CRETE
Longitude West of Greenwich 0° Longitude East of Greenwich
Conic Projection
0 50 100 200 300 400 500 Miles
0 100 200 400 600 800 Kilometers

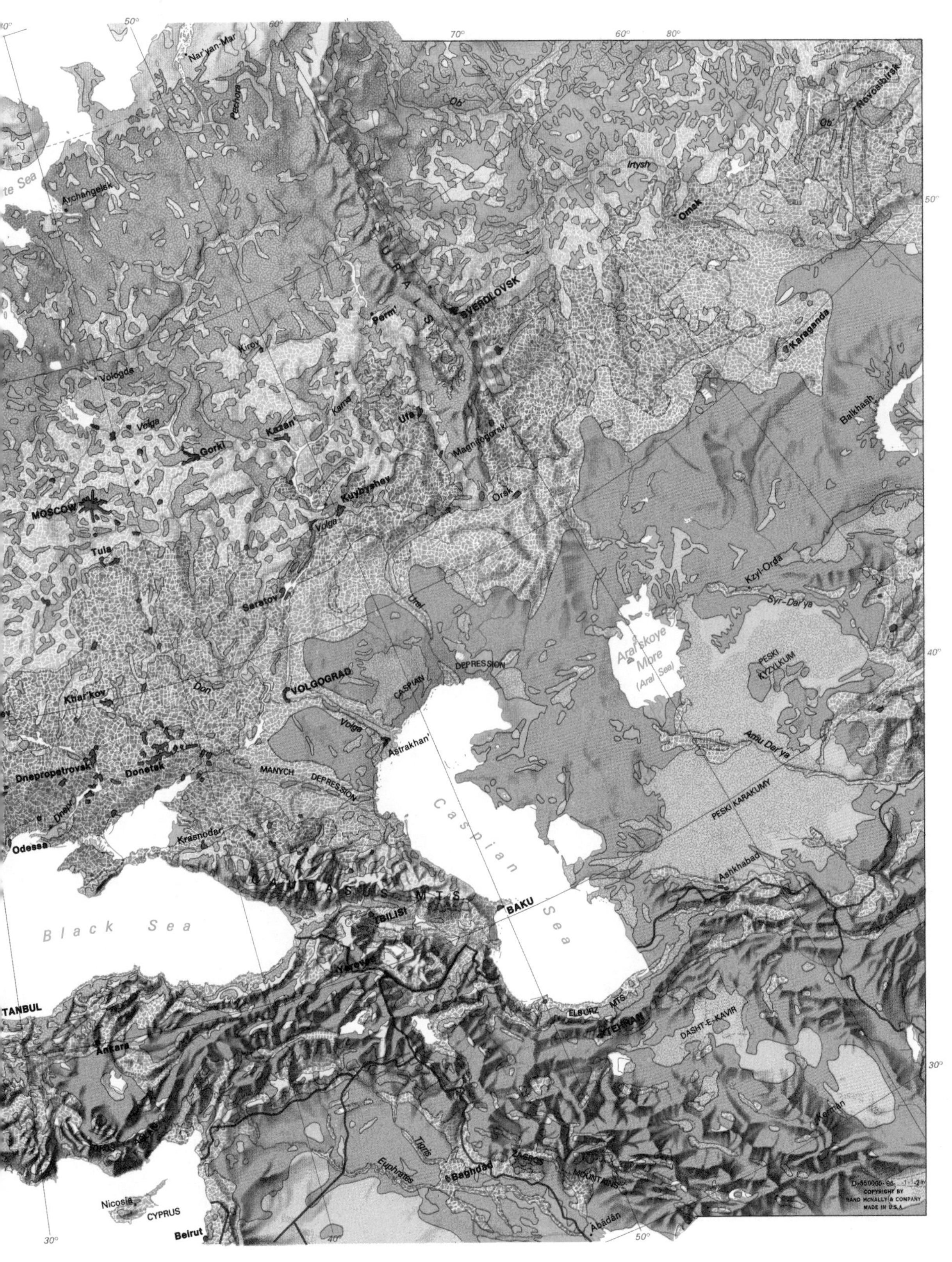

Nar'yan-Mar
Pechora
Archangelsk
Ob'
Novosibirsk
Irtysh
Omsk
URALS
SVERDLOVSK
Perm'
Kirov
Karaganda
Vologda
Kama
Ufa
Balkhash
Volga
Kazan'
Gorki
Magnitogorsk
MOSCOW
Kuybyshev
Orsk
Volga
Tula
Kzyl-Orda
Saratov
Ural
Syr-Dar'ya
Aral'skoye More
(Aral Sea)
PESKI KYZYLKUM
DEPRESSION
VOLGOGRAD
CASPIAN
Kharkov
Don
Volga
Astrakhan'
Amu Dar'ya
Dnepropetrovsk
Donetsk
MANYCH DEPRESSION
Dnepr
Caspian Sea
PESKI KARAKUMY
Odessa
Krasnodar
Ashkhabad
CAUCASUS MTS.
Black Sea
TBILISI
BAKU
Yerevan
ISTANBUL
ELBURZ MTS.
TEHRAN
DASHT-E-KAVIR
Ankara
Kerman
Tigris
Euphrates
Baghdad
ZAGROS MOUNTAINS
Nicosia
CYPRUS
Beirut
Abādān
COPYRIGHT BY RAND MCNALLY & COMPANY MADE IN U.S.A.

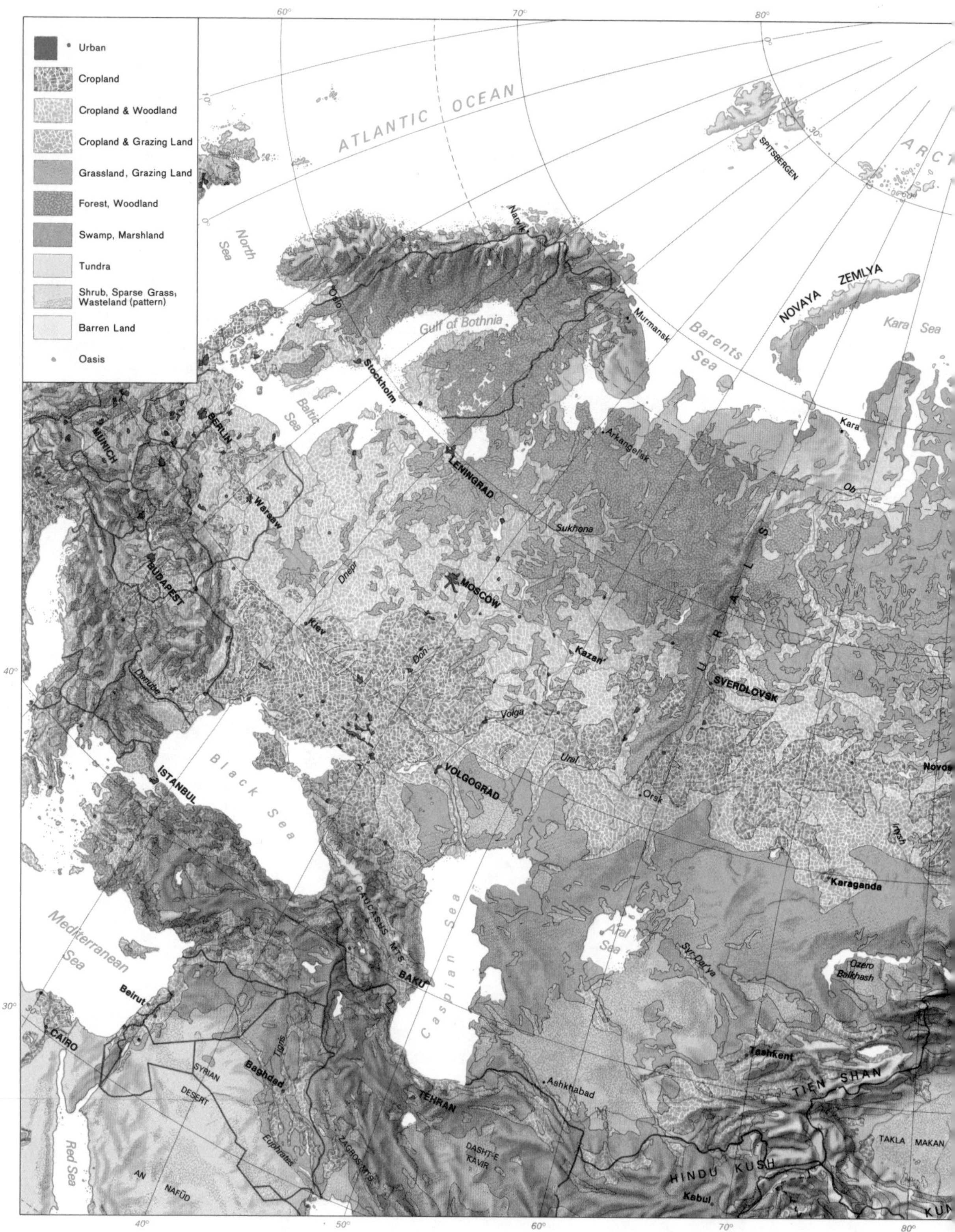
Urban
Cropland
Cropland & Woodland
Cropland & Grazing Land
Grassland, Grazing Land
Forest, Woodland
Swamp, Marshland
Tundra
Shrub, Sparse Grass, Wasteland (pattern)
Barren Land
Oasis
ATLANTIC OCEAN
SPITSBERGEN
North Sea
Narvik
Oslo
Gulf of Bothnia
Stockholm
Baltic Sea
Murmansk
Barents Sea
NOVAYA ZEMLYA
Kara Sea
Kara
Arkangel'sk
LENINGRAD
BERLIN
MUNICH
Warsaw
Ob
Sukhona
U R A L S
Dnepr
MOSCOW
BUDAPEST
Kiev
Don
Kazan'
SVERDLOVSK
Danube
Volga
Ural
VOLGOGRAD
Orsk
ISTANBUL
Black Sea
Irtysh
Karaganda
CAUCASUS MTS.
Caspian Sea
Aral Sea
Syr-Dar'ya
Ozero Balkhash
Mediterranean Sea
BAKU
Beirut
CAIRO
Tigris
SYRIAN DESERT
Baghdad
Tashkent
TIEN SHAN
Ashkhabad
TEHRAN
Euphrates
ZAGROS MTS.
DASHT-E KAVIR
TAKLA MAKAN
Red Sea
AN NAFŪD
HINDU KUSH
Kabul
Novos
60°
70°
80°
40°
50°
30°
10°
0°

Lambert Azimuthal Equal-Area Projection

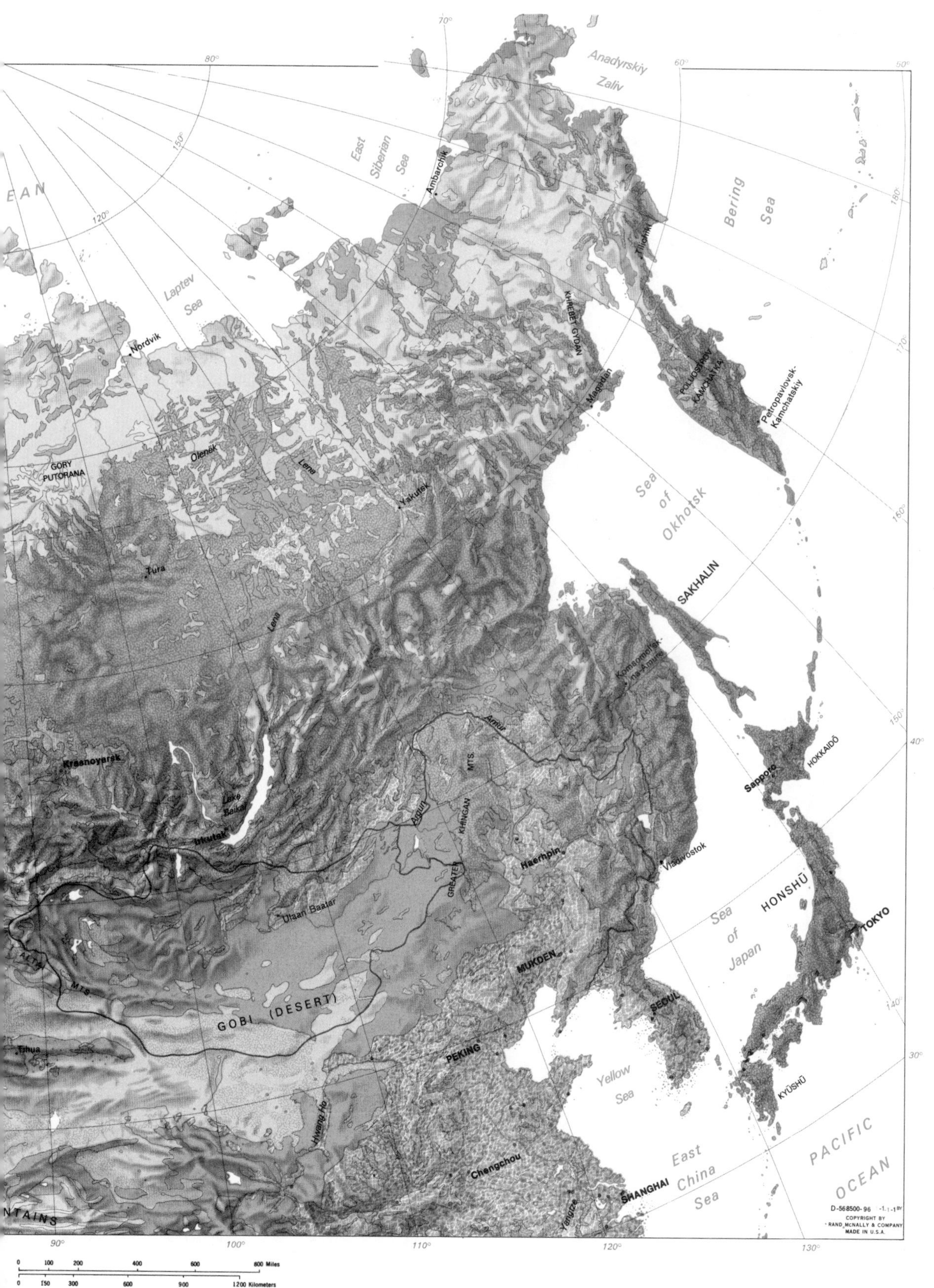
East Siberian Sea
Laptev Sea
Anadyrskiy Zaliv
Bering Sea
Sea of Okhotsk
Sea of Japan
Yellow Sea
East China Sea
PACIFIC OCEAN
Ambarchik
Nordvik
Tilichiki
KHREBET GYDAN
Magadan
POLUOSTROV KAMCHATKA
Petropavlovsk-Kamchatskiy
GORY PUTORANA
Olenëk
Lena
Yakutsk
Tura
SAKHALIN
Komsomol'sk-na-Amure
Amur
HOKKAIDŌ
Sapporo
Krasnoyarsk
Lake Baikal
Irkutsk
MTS.
KHINGAN
GREATER
Argun
Haerhpin
Vladivostok
HONSHŪ
TOKYO
Ulaan Baatar
ALTAI MTS.
GOBI (DESERT)
MUKDEN
SEOUL
PEKING
KYŪSHŪ
Tihua
Hwang Ho
Chengchou
SHANGHAI
Yangtze
D-568500-96
COPYRIGHT BY RAND McNALLY & COMPANY MADE IN U.S.A.
800 Miles
1200 Kilometers

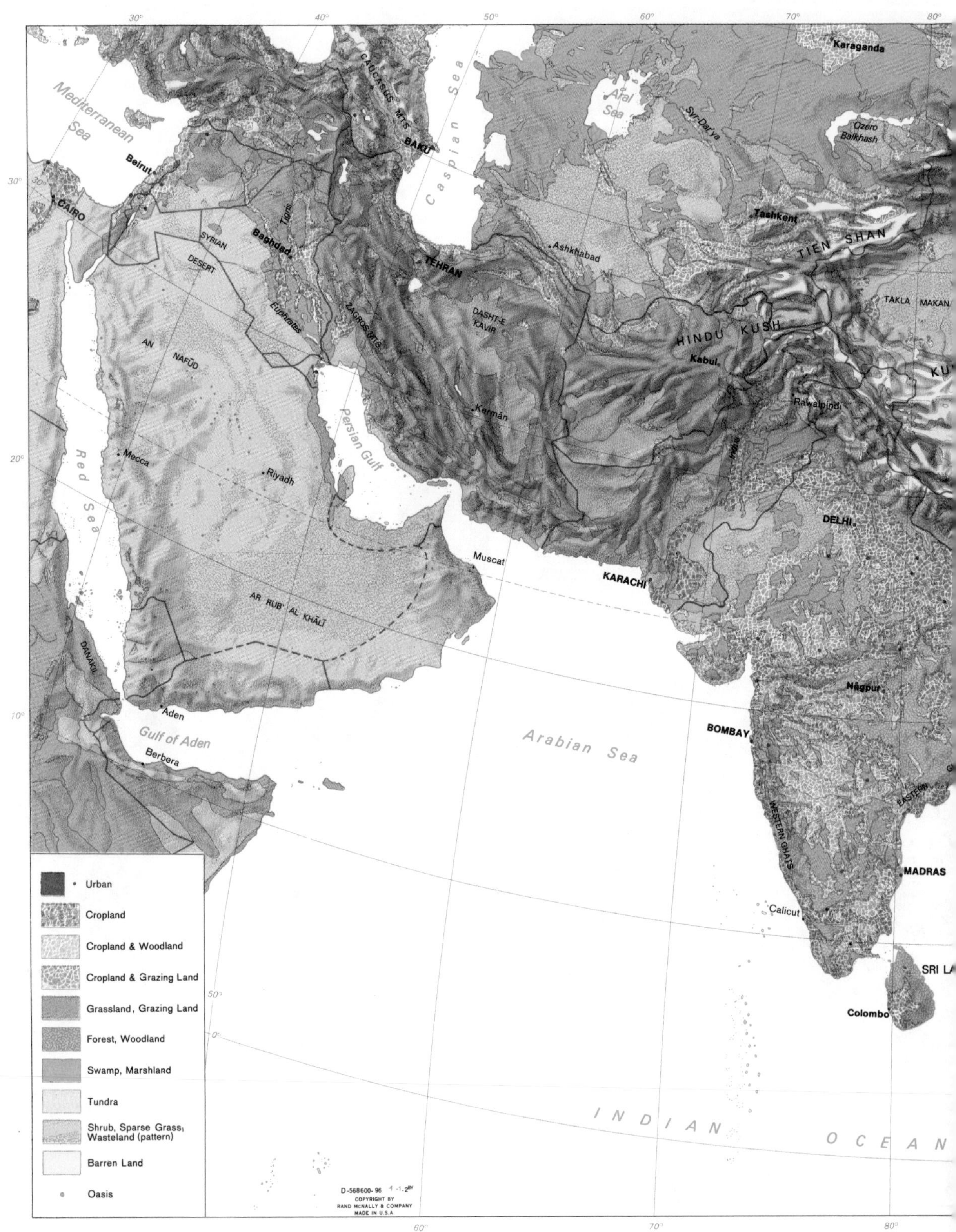

Mediterranean Sea
Beirut
CAIRO
CAUCASUS MTS.
BAKU
Caspian Sea
Aral Sea
Syr-Dar'ya
Karaganda
Ozero Balkhash
Tashkent
TIEN SHAN
TAKLA MAKAN
Baghdad
Tigris
SYRIAN DESERT
Euphrates
TEHRAN
Ashkhabad
ZAGROS MTS.
DASHT-E KAVIR
HINDU KUSH
Kabul
Rawalpindi
AN NAFŪD
Kermān
Persian Gulf
Indus
Mecca
Riyadh
Red Sea
DELHI
Muscat
KARACHI
AR RUB' AL KHĀLĪ
DANAKIL
Aden
Gulf of Aden
Berbera
Nāgpur
BOMBAY
Arabian Sea
WESTERN GHATS
EASTERN
MADRAS
Calicut
SRI LA
Colombo
INDIAN OCEAN
Urban
Cropland
Cropland & Woodland
Cropland & Grazing Land
Grassland, Grazing Land
Forest, Woodland
Swamp, Marshland
Tundra
Shrub, Sparse Grass, Wasteland (pattern)
Barren Land
Oasis
D-568600-96
COPYRIGHT BY RAND McNALLY & COMPANY MADE IN U.S.A.
Lambert Azimuthal Equal-Area Projection

Vladivostok
Haerhpin
GREATER KHINGAN MTS
Ulaan Baatar
ALTAI MTS
GOBI (DESERT)
Tihua
MUKDEN
SEOUL
HONSHŪ
TOKYO
Sea of Japan
PEKING
Yellow Sea
KYŪSHŪ
Hwang Ho
Chengchou
East China Sea
SHANGHAI
PACIFIC OCEAN
NTAINS
WUHAN
TIBET
Mekong
CHUNGKING
T'aipei
Tropic of Cancer
TAIWAN
MALAYAS
Brahmaputra
K'unming
CANTON
Philippine Sea
Hanoi
HAINAN TAO
CUTTA
Mandalay
Salween
MANILA
Mekong
Bay of Bengal
Rangoon
Cebu
MINDANAO
BANGKOK
South China Sea
HO CHI MINH CITY
Gulf of Thailand
Andaman Sea
Kota Kinabalu
Celebes Sea
Manado
Medan
Kuching
SINGAPORE
BORNEO
CELEBES
SUMATRA
Equator
Ujung Pandang
Java Sea
JAKARTA
JAVA
0 100 200 400 600 800 Miles
0 150 300 600 900 1200 Kilometers

Lambert Azimuthal Equal-Area Projection

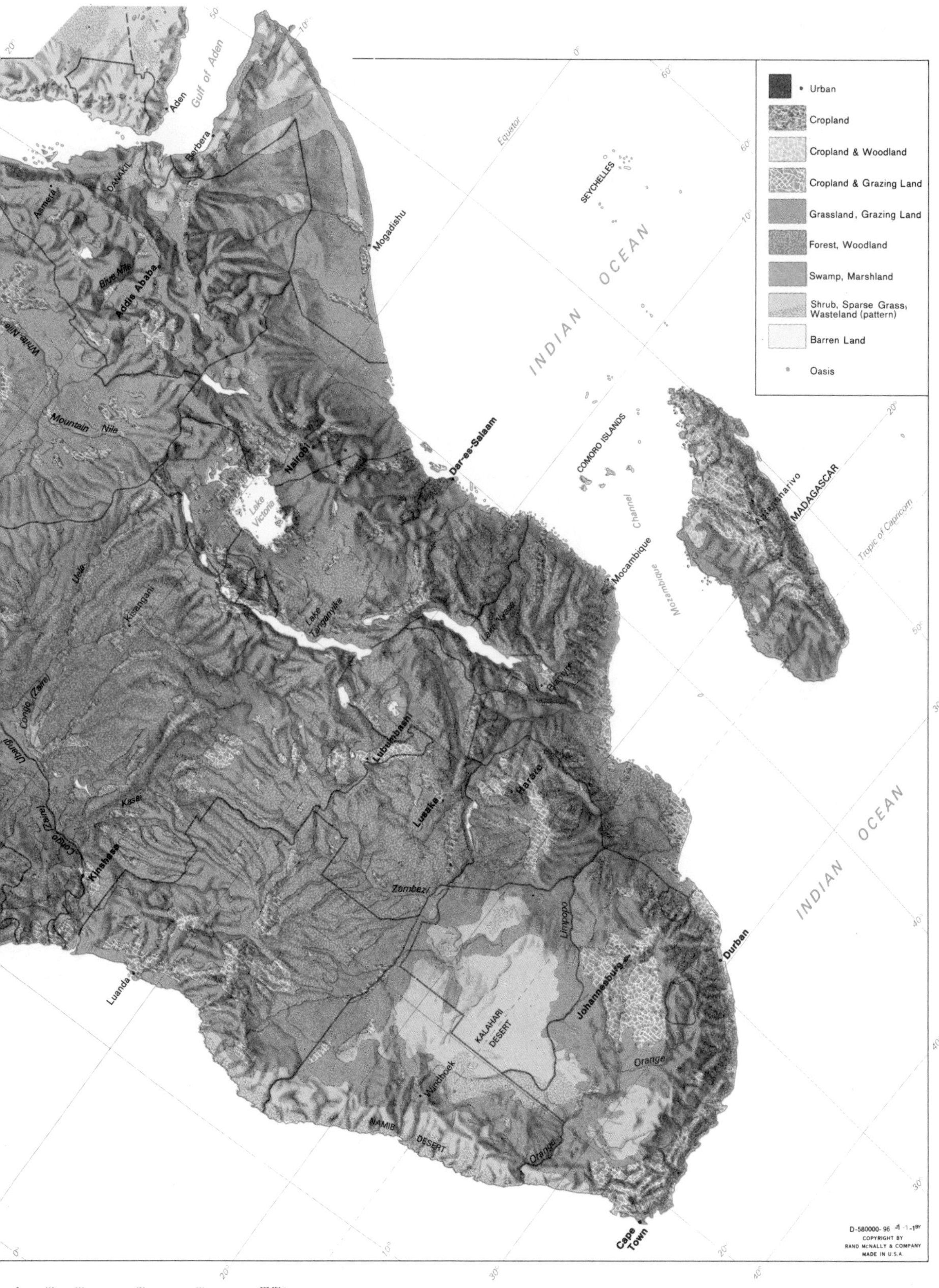
Urban
Cropland
Cropland & Woodland
Cropland & Grazing Land
Grassland, Grazing Land
Forest, Woodland
Swamp, Marshland
Shrub, Sparse Grass, Wasteland (pattern)
Barren Land
Oasis
Gulf of Aden
Aden
Berbera
DANAKIL
Asmera
Addis Ababa
Blue Nile
White Nile
Mountain Nile
Mogadishu
Equator
SEYCHELLES
INDIAN OCEAN
Nairobi
Lake Victoria
Dar-es-Salaam
COMORO ISLANDS
Mozambique Channel
Mocambique
MADAGASCAR
Antananarivo
Tropic of Capricorn
Uele
Kisangani
Lake Tanganyika
Lake Nyasa
Blantyre
Congo (Zaire)
Ubangi
Lubumbashi
Harare
Lusaka
Kasai
Kinshasa
Zambezi
Limpopo
Durban
Johannesburg
Luanda
KALAHARI DESERT
Windhoek
Orange
NAMIB DESERT
Cape Town
INDIAN OCEAN
D-580000-96
COPYRIGHT BY RAND McNALLY & COMPANY MADE IN U.S.A.
0 100 200 400 600 800 Miles
0 150 300 600 900 1200 Kilometers

BORNEO
SUMATRA
Palembang
Banjarmasin
CELEBES
SERAM
Java Sea
Ujung Pandang
JAKARTA
Surabaya
JAVA
SUMBA
TIMOR
Arafura Sea
Timor Sea
Darwin
Gulf of Carpentaria
Daly
INDIAN OCEAN
KIMBERLEY PLATEAU
Victoria
Broome
Fitzroy
Mount Isa
GREAT SANDY DESERT
Alice Springs
GIBSON DESERT
SIMPSON DESERT
Tropic of Capricorn
Carnarvon
GREAT VICTORIA DESERT
Lake Eyre
Kalgoorlie
NULLARBOR PLAIN
Lake Gairdner
FLINDERS RANGES
Broken Hill
DARLING RA.
Great Australian Bight
Perth
Adelaide
Urban
Cropland
Cropland & Woodland
Cropland & Grazing Land
Grassland, Grazing Land
Forest, Woodland
Swamp, Marshland
Shrub, Sparse Grass, Wasteland (pattern)
Barren Land
INDIAN OCEAN
Lambert Azimuthal Equal-Area Projection

150°
160°
170°
180°
Equator
KIRIBATI
UINEA
NEW BRITAIN
SOLOMON ISLANDS
PACIFIC
OCEAN
esby
Coral Sea
rns
VANUATU
(NEW HEBRIDES)
SAMOA ISLANDS
Pago Pago
Townsville
FIJI
ISLANDS
Suva
NEW
CALEDONIA
ÎLES
LOYAUTÉ
Nouméa
Rockhampton
RANGE
TONGA ISLANDS
Brisbane
RANGE
SYDNEY
anberra
DIVIDING
Tasman Sea
BOURNE
Auckland
NORTH ISLAND
PACIFIC
OCEAN
TASMANIA
Hobart
Wellington
SOUTHERN ALPS
Christchurch
SOUTH ISLAND
STEWART
ISLAND
Dunedin
D-590200-96
COPYRIGHT BY
RAND McNALLY & COMPANY
MADE IN U.S.A.
0°
10°
20°
30°
40°
150°
160°
170°
180°
170°
160°
0 100 200 400 600 800 Miles
0 150 300 600 900 1200 Kilometers

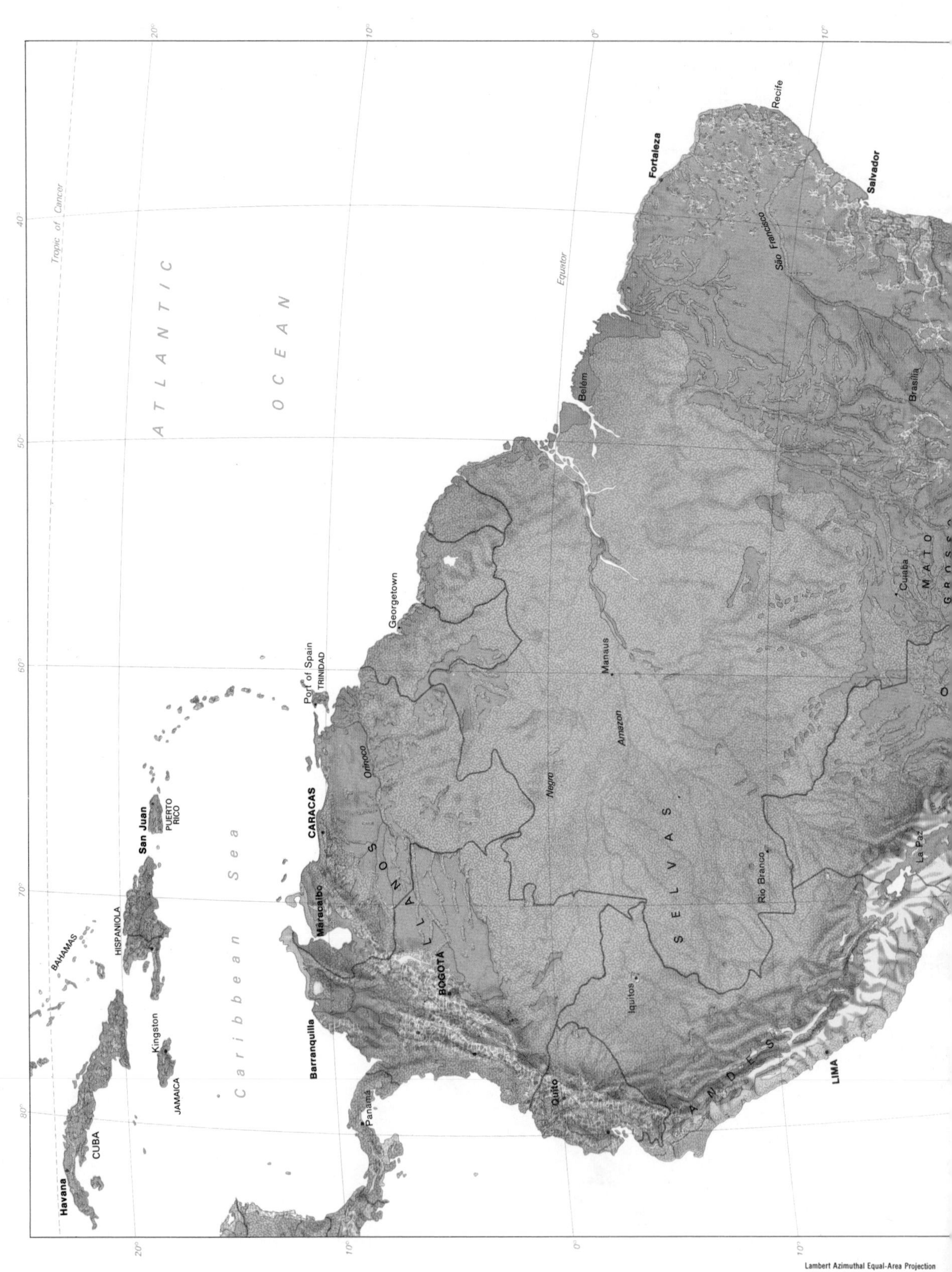

Lambert Azimuthal Equal-Area Projection

Tropic of Capricorn
ANDES
GRAN
Asunción
SÃO PAULO
RIO DE JANEIRO
Paraná
San Miguel de Tucumán
Porto Alegre
Córdoba
PACIFIC
OCEAN
SANTIAGO
BUENOS AIRES
Montevideo
ATLANTIC
OCEAN
PAMPAS
Bahía Blanca
Puerto Montt
PATAGONIA
FALKLAND ISLANDS
Punta Arenas
TIERRA DEL FUEGO
SOUTH GEORGIA
Drake Passage
ANTARCTIC PENINSULA
D-540000-96 -1-1-1
COPYRIGHT BY
RAND McNALLY & COMPANY
MADE IN U.S.A.
Urban
Cropland
Cropland & Woodland
Cropland & Grazing Land
Grassland, Grazing Land
Forest, Woodland
Swamp, Marshland
Shrub, Sparse Grass, Wasteland (pattern)
Barren Land
0 100 200 400 600 800 Miles
0 150 300 600 900 1200 Kilometers

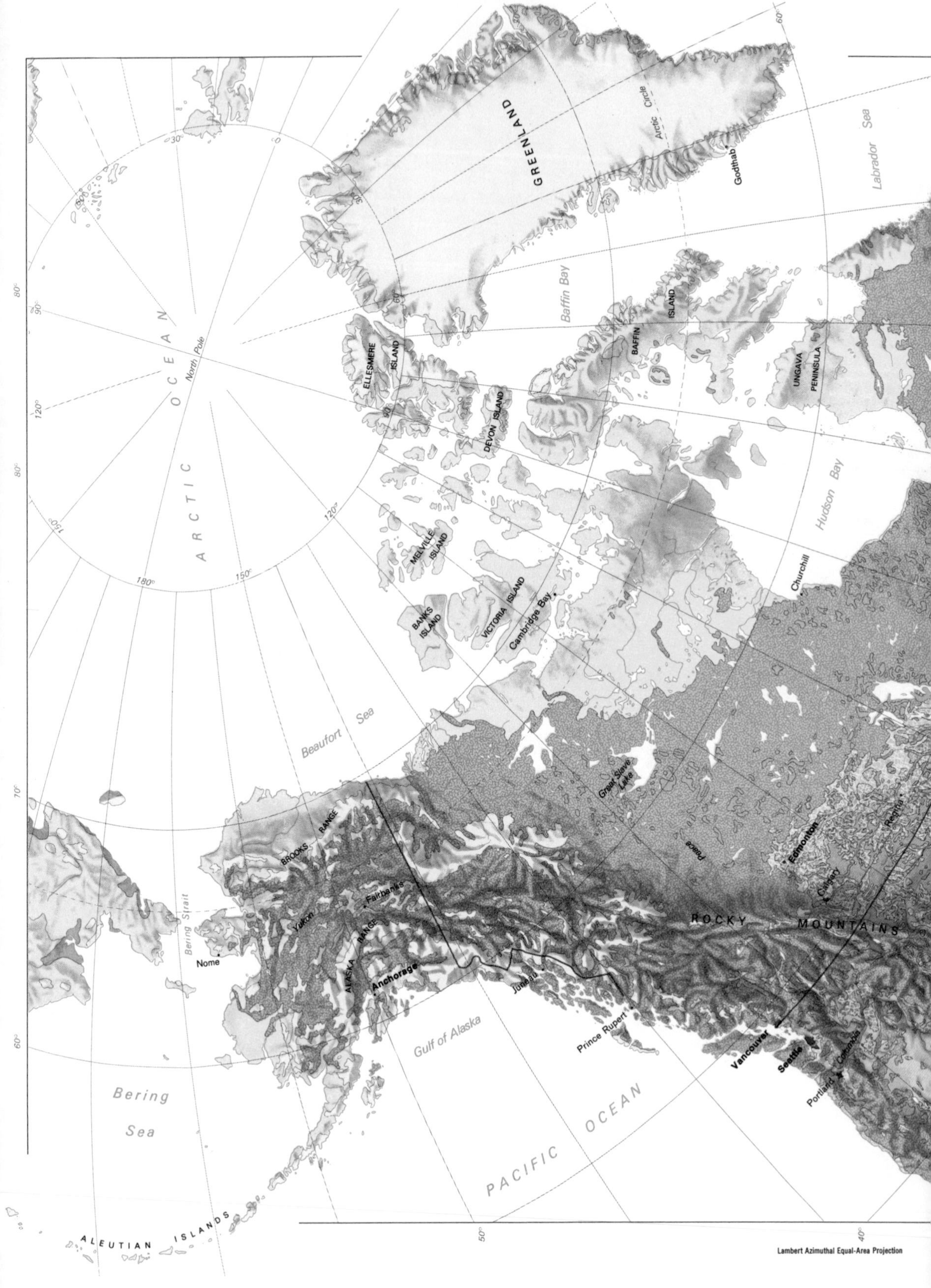
GREENLAND
Arctic Circle
Godthab
Labrador Sea
Baffin Bay
BAFFIN ISLAND
UNGAVA PENINSULA
ELLESMERE ISLAND
DEVON ISLAND
North Pole
ARCTIC OCEAN
Hudson Bay
MELVILLE ISLAND
VICTORIA ISLAND
BANKS ISLAND
Cambridge Bay
Churchill
Beaufort Sea
Great Slave Lake
Peace
Edmonton
Regina
Calgary
BROOKS RANGE
Fairbanks
Yukon
ALASKA RANGE
Bering Strait
Nome
Anchorage
Juneau
Prince Rupert
ROCKY MOUNTAINS
Vancouver
Seattle
Columbia
Portland
Gulf of Alaska
Bering Sea
PACIFIC OCEAN
ALEUTIAN ISLANDS
Lambert Azimuthal Equal-Area Projection

ATLANTIC
OCEAN
Gulf of Mexico
Caribbean Sea
PACIFIC OCEAN
Tropic of Cancer
Golfo de California
ROCKY MOUNTAINS
APPALACHIAN MOUNTAINS
SIERRA MADRE ORIENTAL
SIERRA MADRE OCCIDENTAL
SIERRA MADRE DEL SUR
Lake Superior
Lake Michigan
Lake Huron
Lake Erie
Lake Ontario
St. Lawrence
Mississippi
Missouri
Ohio
Rio Grande
Colorado
St. John's
Halifax
BOSTON
NEW YORK
PHILADELPHIA
WASHINGTON
MONTREAL
TORONTO
DETROIT
CHICAGO
Pittsburgh
Cincinnati
Nashville
Atlanta
Jacksonville
Miami
ST. LOUIS
Kansas City
Minneapolis
Omaha
Rapid City
Denver
Dallas
Houston
New Orleans
Albuquerque
Phoenix
LOS ANGELES
NEVADA
Lake City
Chihuahua
Monterrey
MEXICO CITY
Guadalajara
Mazatlán
La Paz
Mérida
Havana
CUBA
Nassau
BAHAMA ISLANDS
JAMAICA
Kingston
Port au-Prince
HISPANIOLA
San Juan
PUERTO RICO
TRINIDAD
CARACAS
Maracaibo
Panama
San José
Managua
San Salvador
Urban
Cropland
Cropland & Woodland
Cropland & Grazing Land
Grassland, Grazing Land
Forest, Woodland
Swamp, Marshland
Tundra
Shrub, Sparse Grass, Wasteland (pattern)
Barren Land
D-520000- 96 -1-1-1
COPYRIGHT BY RAND McNALLY & COMPANY MADE IN U.S.A.
0 100 200 400 600 800 Miles
0 150 300 600 900 1200 Kilometers

ROCKY MOUNTAINS
Calgary
Lake Winnipeg
Vancouver
PACIFIC OCEAN
Regina
Seattle
Spokane
CASCADE RANGE
Portland
Columbia
Bismarck
Billings
Medford
Boise
Rapid City
Missouri
Casper
Great Salt Lake
Salt Lake City
Reno
GREAT BASIN
SAN FRANCISCO
SIERRA NEVADA
Denver
Fresno
Las Vegas
Wichita
LOS ANGELES
Albuquerque
Amarillo
Oklahoma City
Colorado
San Diego
Phoenix
Red
El Paso
Odessa
PACIFIC OCEAN
Hermosillo
Gulf of California
Rio Grande
San Antonio
SIERRA MADRE OCCIDENTAL
Chihuahua
SIERRA MADRE ORIENTAL
Torreon
Monterrey
Rio Grande

50° 45° 40° 35° 30° 25°
125° 120° 115° 110° 105° 100°

James Bay
Moosonee
Gulf of St. Lawrence
St. Lawrence
Quebec
Halifax
Thunder Bay
Lake Superior
Duluth
Sudbury
MONTREAL
Bangor
Lake Huron
Lake Michigan
Lake Ontario
TORONTO
BOSTON
Buffalo
Milwaukee
DETROIT
Lake Erie
Cleveland
CHICAGO
NEW YORK
PHILADELPHIA
Pittsburgh
WASHINGTON
Indianapolis
Cincinnati
Mississippi
Missouri
ST. LOUIS
Ohio
Norfolk
Roanoke
APPALACHIAN MOUNTAINS
OZARK PLATEAU
Nashville
Charlotte
Memphis
Arkansas
Little Rock
Atlanta
Birmingham
Charleston
ATLANTIC OCEAN
Red
Jacksonville
Tallahassee
New Orleans
Tampa
Gulf of Mexico
Miami
Nassau
Urban
Cropland
Cropland & Woodland
Cropland & Grazing Land
Grassland, Grazing Land
Forest, Woodland
Swamp, Marshland
Shrub, Sparse Grass, Wasteland (pattern)
Barren Land
Polyconic Projection
0 50 100 200 300 400 Miles
0 75 150 300 450 600 Kilometers
90° 85° 80° 75° 70° 65°
40° 35° 30° 25°

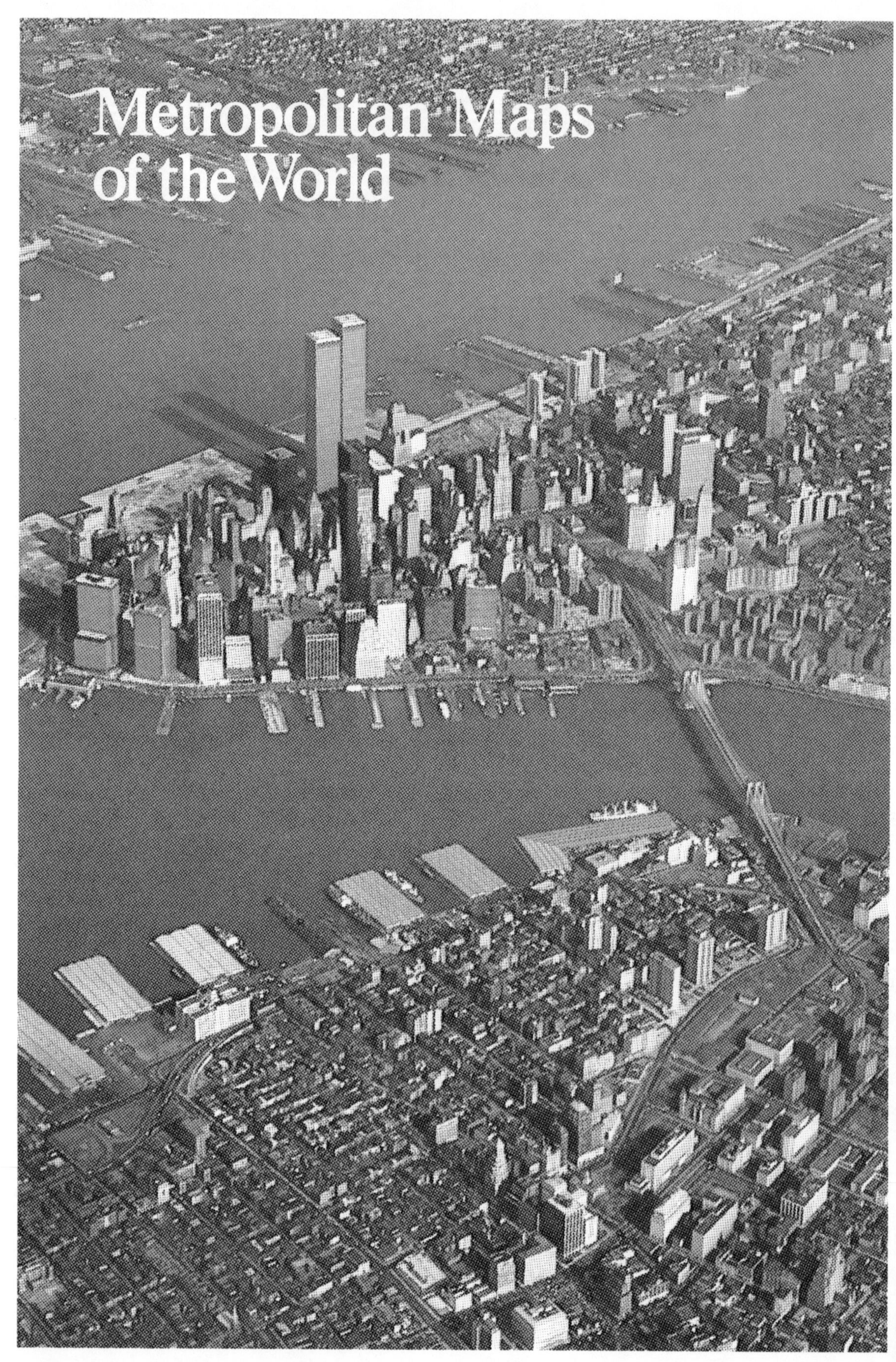
Metropolitan Maps
of the World

Metropolitan Map Legend

Inhabited Localities

The symbol represents the number of inhabitants within the locality

- • 0—10,000
- ○ 10,000—25,000
- ◉ 25,000—100,000
- ▣ 100,000—250,000
- ▣ 250,000—1,000,000
- ■ >1,000,000

The size of type indicates the relative economic and political importance of the locality

Écommoy
Trouville
Lisieux
St.-Denis
PARIS

Hollywood ■ Section of a City,
Westminster Neighborhood
Northland Center ■ Major Shopping Center

Urban Area (area of continuous industrial, commercial, and residential development)

Major Industrial Area

Wooded Area

Political Boundaries

International (First-order political unit)

Demarcated, Undemarcated, and Administrative

Demarcation Line

Internal

State, Province, etc. (Second-order political unit)

County, Oblast, etc. (Third-order political unit)

Okrug, Kreis, etc. (Fourth-order political unit)

City or Municipality (may appear in combination with another boundary symbol)

Capitals of Political Units

BUDAPEST	Independent Nation
Recife	State, Province, etc.
White Plains	County, Oblast, etc.
Iserlohn	Okrug, Kreis, etc.

Transportation

Road

PASSAIC EXPWY. (I-80)
BERLINER RING

Primary
Secondary
Tertiary

Railway

CANADIAN NATIONAL

Primary
Secondary
Rapid Transit

Airport

LONDON (HEATHROW) AIRPORT

Rail or Air Terminal

SÜD BAHNHOF

REICHS-BRÜCKE — Bridge

GREAT ST. BERNARD TUNNEL — Tunnel

Houston Ship Channel — Shipping Channel

Canal du Midi — Navigable Canal

TO MALMÖ — Ferry

Hydrographic Features

Shoreline

Undefined or Fluctuating Shoreline

Amur — River, Stream

Intermittent Stream

SALTO ANGEL — Rapids, Falls

Canal du Midi — Navigable Canal

Irrigation or Drainage Canal

Los Angeles Aqueduct — Aqueduct

Pier, Breakwater

GREAT BARRIER REEF — Reef

L. Victoria — Lake, Reservoir

Intermittent Lake

The Everglades — Swamp

Miscellaneous Cultural Features

PARQUE NACIONAL LANÍN — National or State Park or Monument

FORT DIX — Military Installation

GREENWOOD CEMETERY — Cemetery

SORBONNE — Point of Interest (Battlefield, museum, temple, university, etc.)

STEPHANSDOM — Church, Monastery

UXMAL — Ruins

WINDSOR CASTLE — Castle

Lighthouse

ASWĀN DAM — Dam <> Lock

Crib — Water Intake Crib

Quarry or Surface Mine

Subsurface Mine

Topographic Features

Mt. Kenya 5199 △ Elevation Above Sea Level

Elevations are given in meters

⋆ Rock

A N D E S KUNLUNSHANMAI — Mountain Range, Plateau, Valley, etc.

BAFFIN ISLAND — Island

POLUOSTROV KAMČATKA, CABO DE HORNOS — Peninsula, Cape, Point, etc.

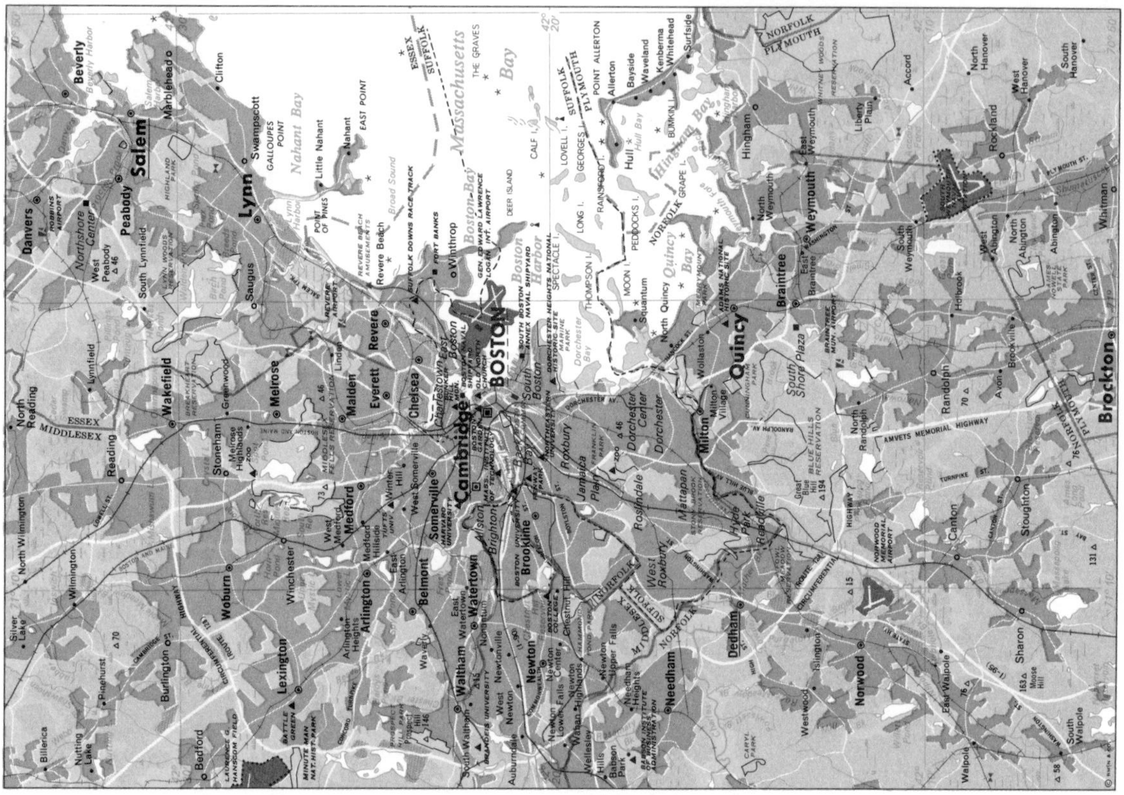

0 5 10 Miles

0 5 10 Kilometers

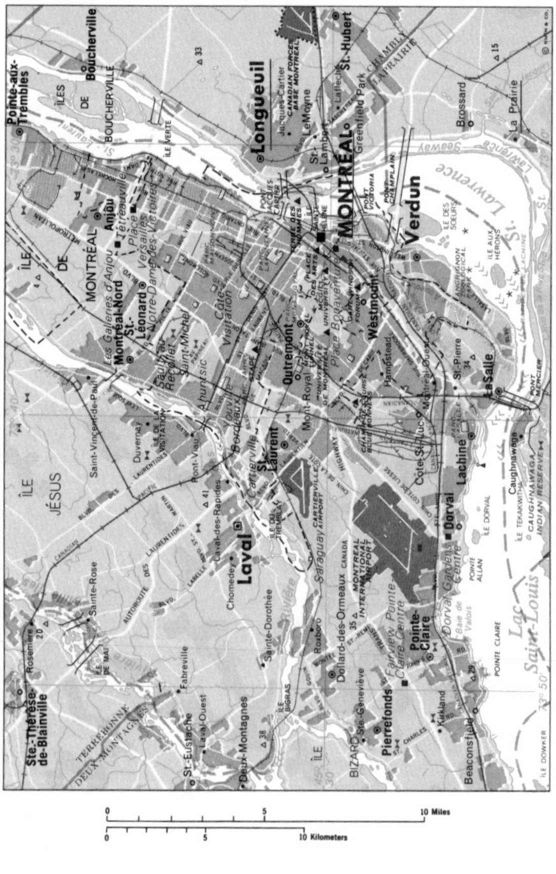

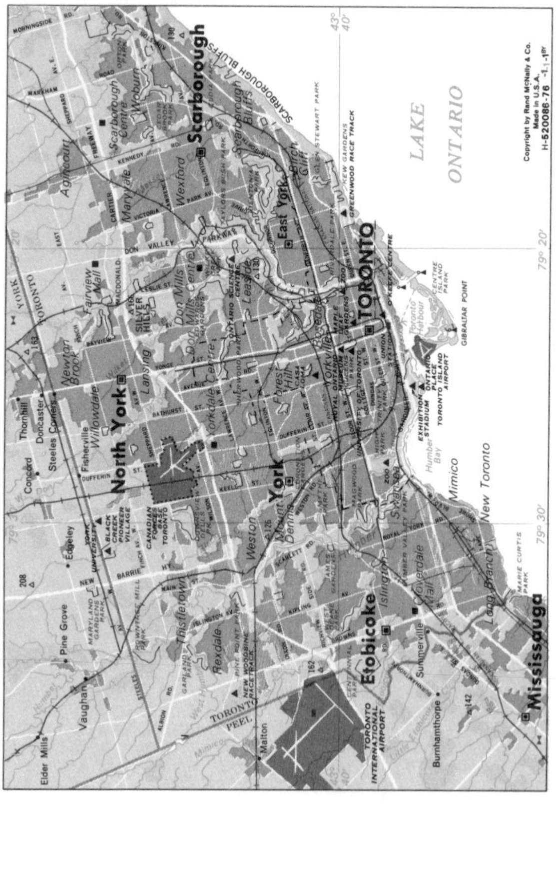

NEW YORK
Jersey City
Newark
Elizabeth
Paterson
Passaic
Hackensack
Paramus
Yonkers
Mount Vernon
New Rochelle
Hempstead
Hicksville
Plainview
Levittown
Bethpage
East Meadow
Freeport
Merrick
Baldwin
Oceanside
Long Beach
Rockville Centre
Valley Stream
Garden City
New Hyde Park
Glen Cove
Bayonne
Union City
Hoboken
West New York
North Bergen
Kearny
Bloomfield
Montclair
Nutley
Belleville
Clifton
Irvington
East Orange
Orange
West Orange
Livingston
Union
Linden
Rahway
Westfield
Cranford
Perth Amboy
Wayne
Ridgewood
Fair Lawn
Teaneck
Englewood
Bergenfield
Long Island Sound
LONG ISLAND
STATEN ISLAND
ATLANTIC OCEAN
Lower New York Bay
Upper New York Bay
Rockaway Point
Jamaica Bay
Brooklyn
Queens
Bronx
Flushing
Jamaica
CONN.
NEW YORK
NEW JERSEY
SUFFOLK
NASSAU
QUEENS
KINGS
RICHMOND
HUDSON
ESSEX
UNION
MIDDLESEX
BERGEN
PASSAIC
MORRIS
Copyright by Rand McNally & Co.
Made in U.S.A.
H-520060-76
0 5 10 Miles
0 5 10 Kilometers

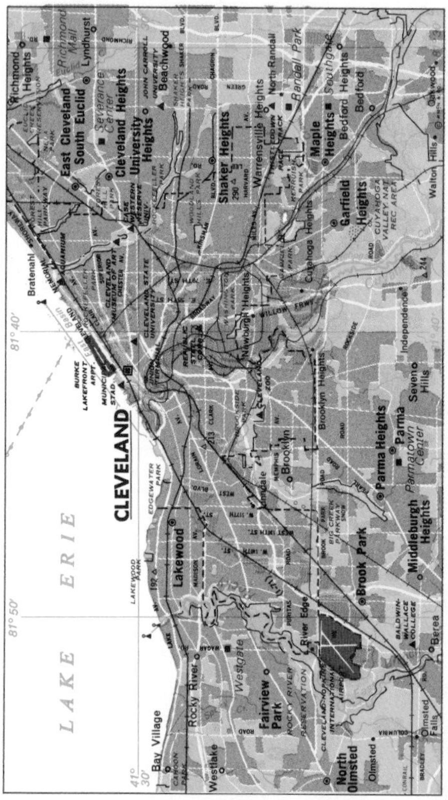

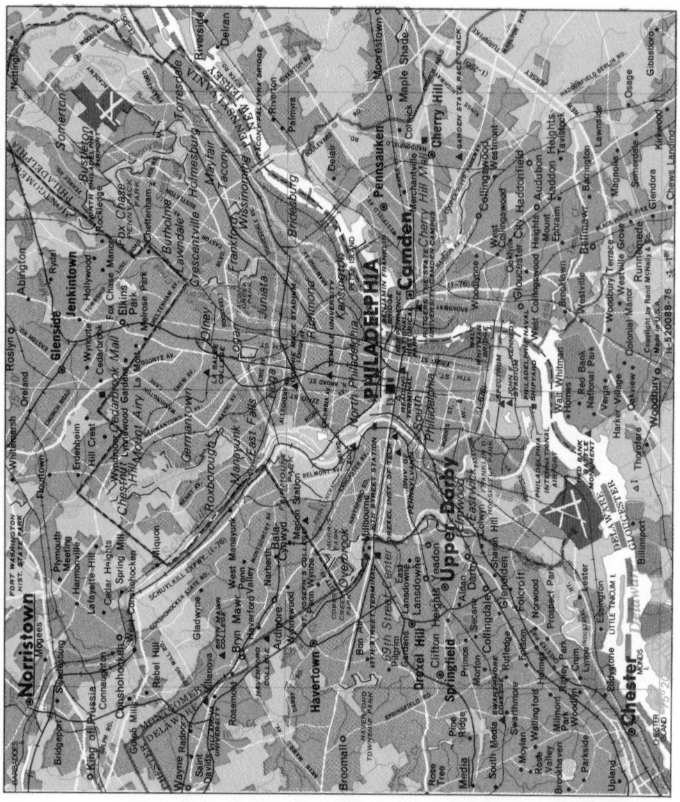

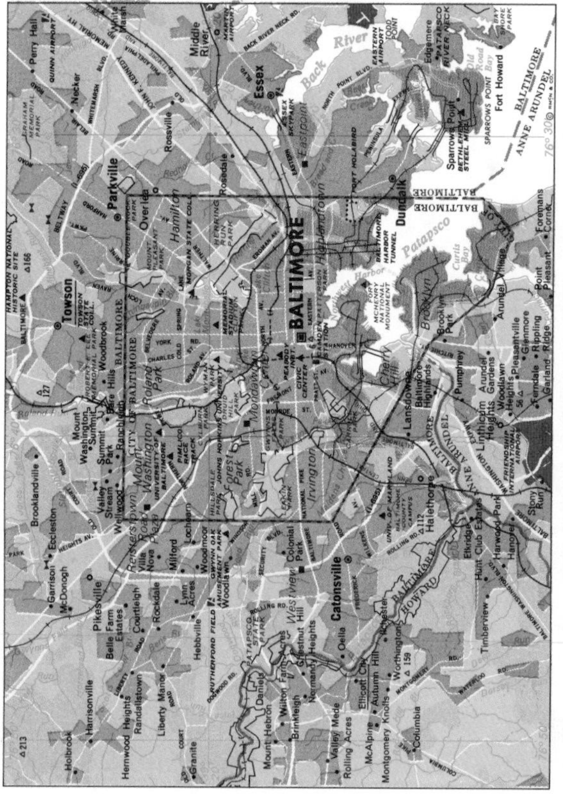

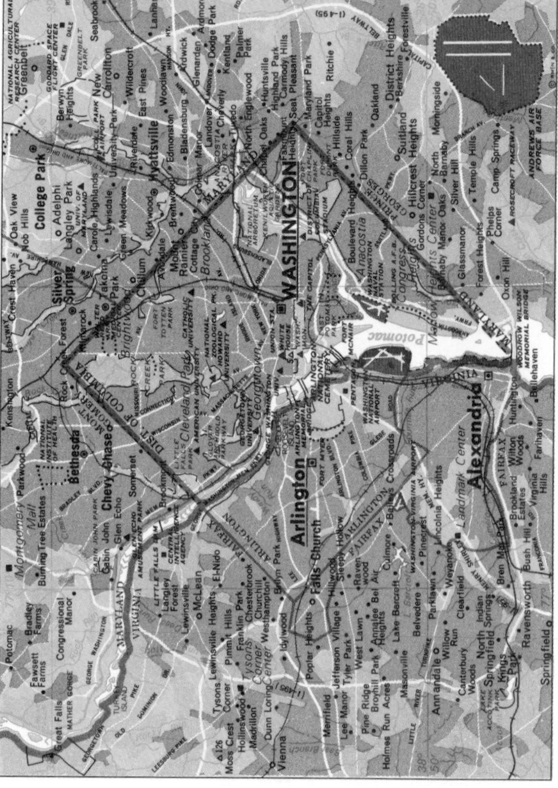

0 5 10 Miles

0 5 10 Kilometers

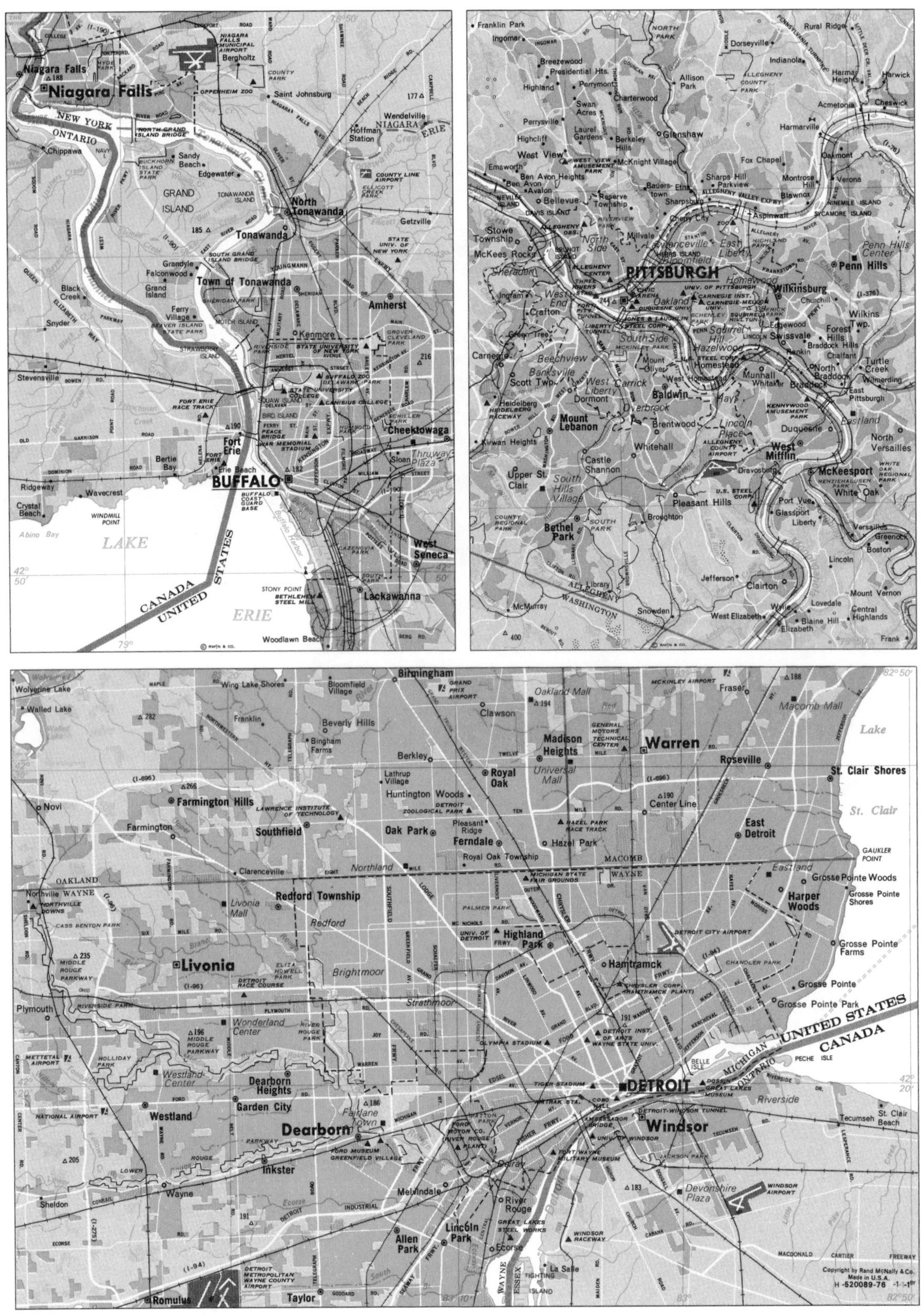
Niagara Falls
Grand Island
Tonawanda
North Tonawanda
Town of Tonawanda
Amherst
Kenmore
Cheektowaga
BUFFALO
Lackawanna
West Seneca
LAKE ERIE
PITTSBURGH
Wilkinsburg
Penn Hills
McKeesport
Mount Lebanon
Bethel Park
Warren
Livonia
Farmington Hills
Southfield
Redford Township
Dearborn
Dearborn Heights
Westland
DETROIT
Windsor
Highland Park
Hamtramck
St. Clair Shores
Copyright by Rand McNally & Co.
Made in U.S.A.
0 5 10 Miles
0 5 10 Kilometers

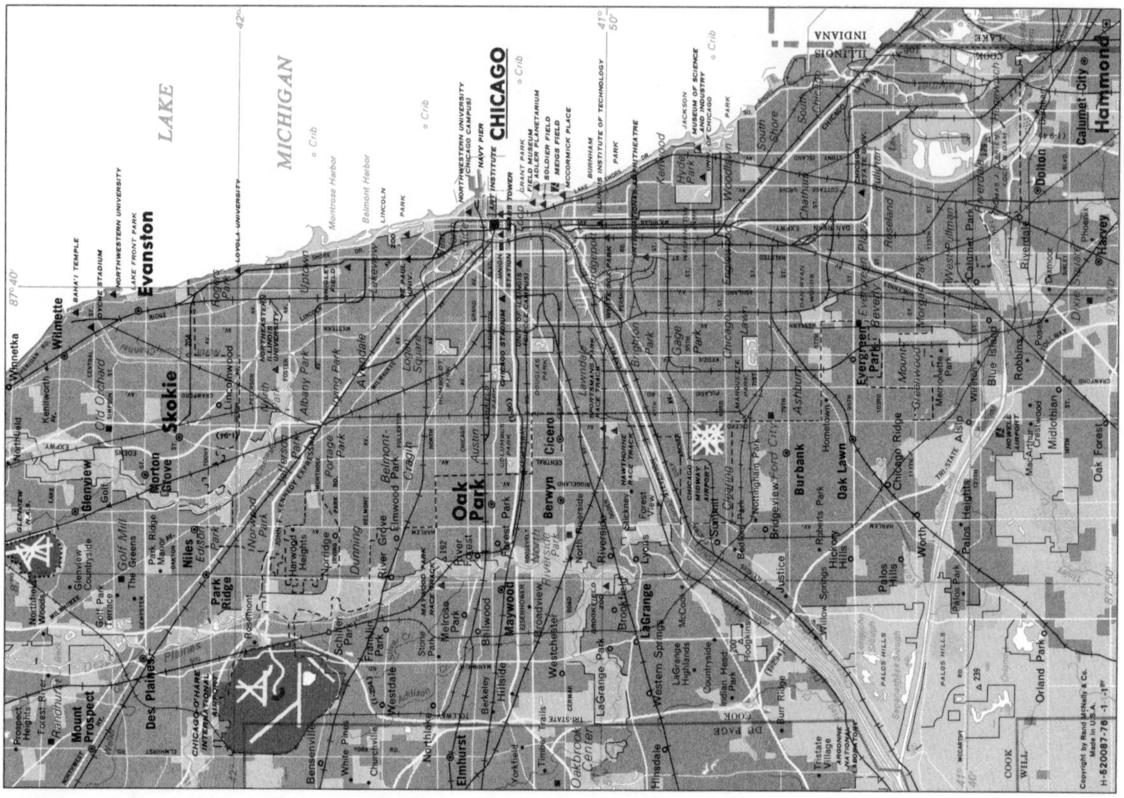

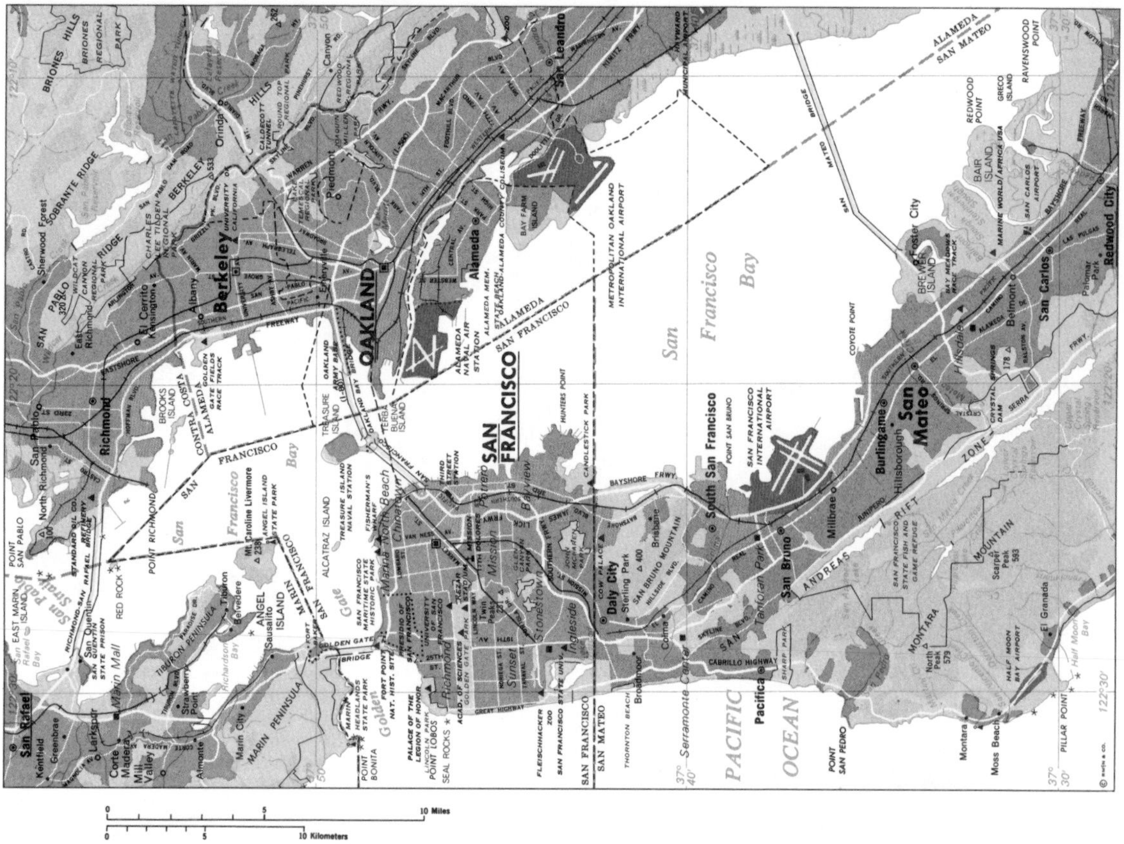

0 5 10 Miles

0 5 10 Kilometers

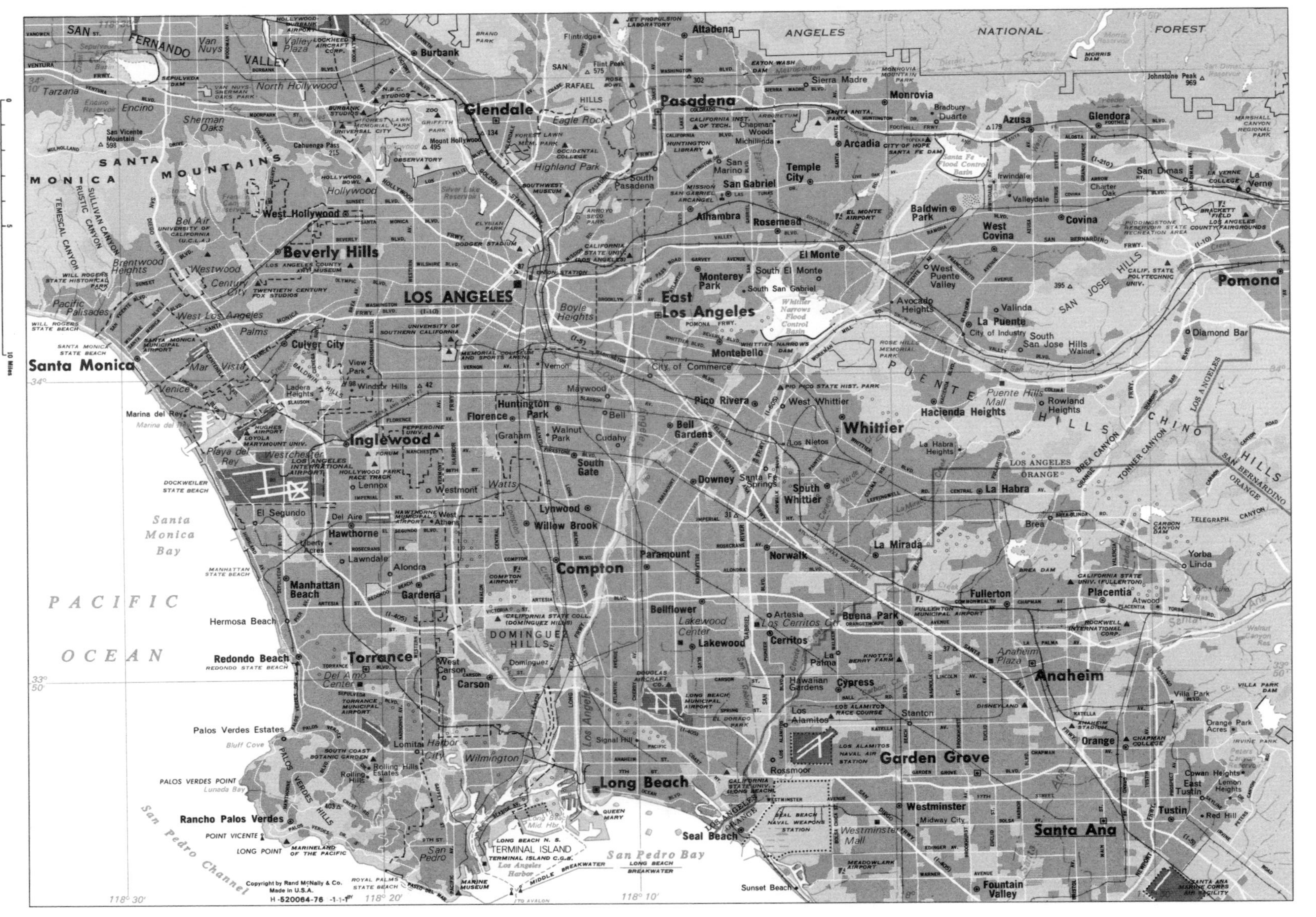

SAN FERNANDO VALLEY
Van Nuys
Burbank
Altadena
ANGELES NATIONAL FOREST
Sierra Madre
Monrovia
Glendora
La Verne
Tarzana
Encino
North Hollywood
Sherman Oaks
Glendale
Pasadena
Eagle Rock
Azusa
San Dimas
SANTA MONICA MOUNTAINS
Highland Park
South Pasadena
San Marino
Arcadia
Temple City
San Gabriel
Baldwin Park
West Covina
Covina
West Hollywood
Bel Air
Beverly Hills
Alhambra
Rosemead
El Monte
Westwood
Century City
LOS ANGELES
Monterey Park
East Los Angeles
South El Monte
Pomona
Pacific Palisades
West Los Angeles
Boyle Heights
La Puente
Diamond Bar
Santa Monica
Culver City
Montebello
Vernon
City of Commerce
PUENTE HILLS
CHINO HILLS
Marina del Rey
Venice
Huntington Park
Maywood
Pico Rivera
Whittier
Hacienda Heights
Rowland Heights
Inglewood
Florence
Bell
Bell Gardens
Westchester
Walnut Park
Cudahy
South Gate
Downey
Santa Fe Springs
South Whittier
La Habra
Lennox
Westmont
Watts
Lynwood
Willow Brook
El Segundo
Hawthorne
Brea
Santa Monica Bay
Lawndale
Compton
Paramount
Norwalk
La Mirada
Manhattan Beach
Gardena
Fullerton
Placentia
Yorba Linda
PACIFIC OCEAN
Hermosa Beach
Bellflower
Lakewood
Cerritos
Buena Park
Redondo Beach
Torrance
Carson
Anaheim
Cypress
Orange
Palos Verdes Estates
Wilmington
Long Beach
Garden Grove
Rancho Palos Verdes
San Pedro
Seal Beach
Westminster
Santa Ana
Tustin
San Pedro Bay
San Pedro Channel
Fountain Valley
Copyright by Rand McNally & Co. Made in U.S.A. H-520064-76
0 5 10 Miles
0 5 10 Kilometers

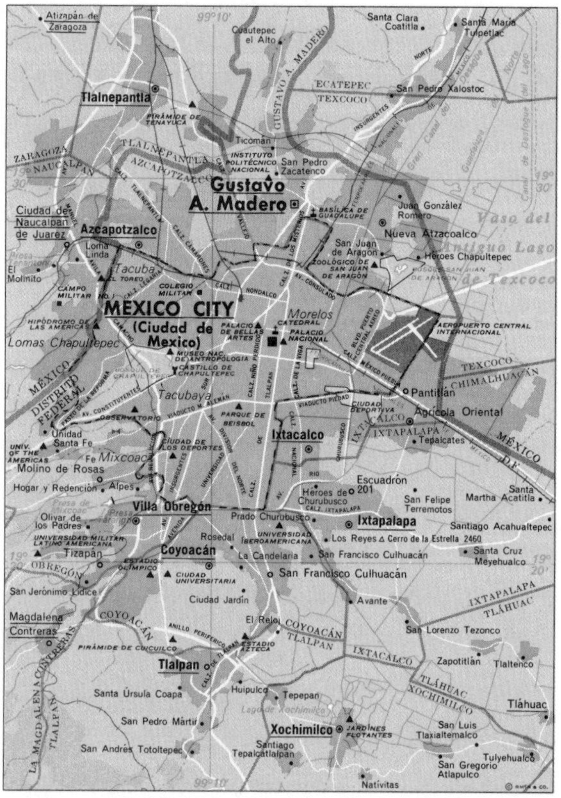

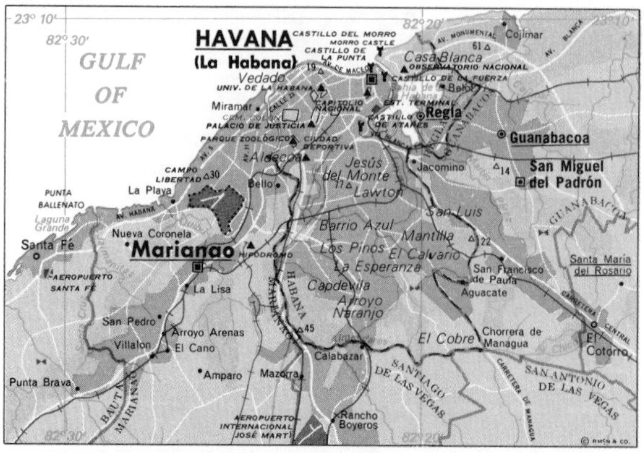

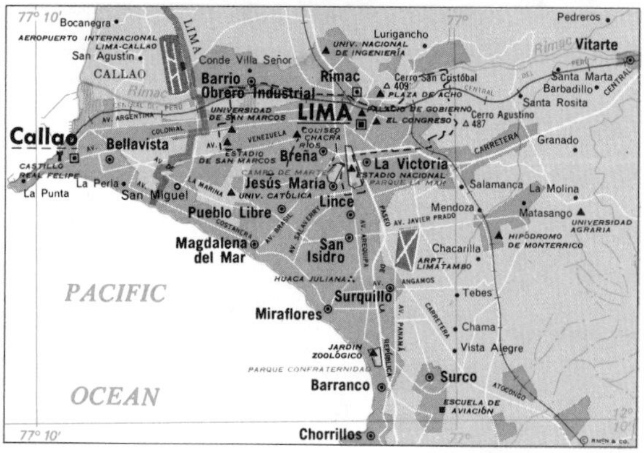

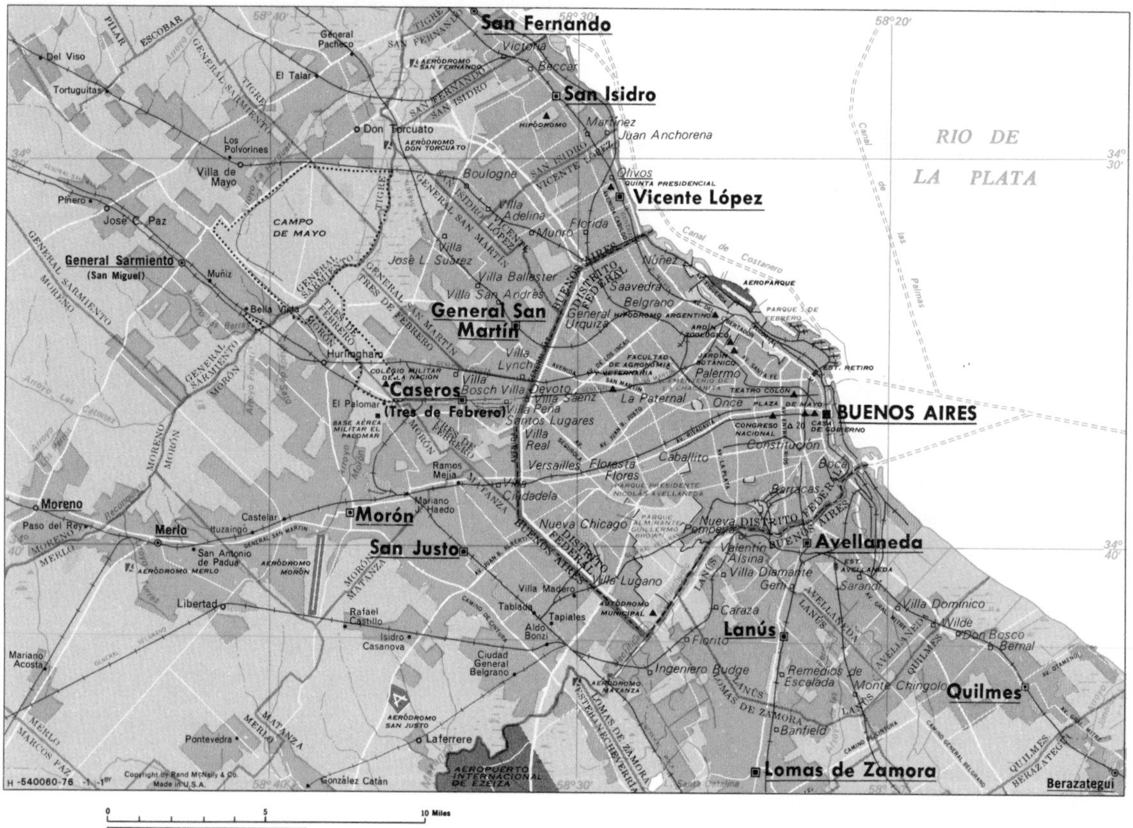

MEXICO CITY (Ciudad de Mexico)

HAVANA (La Habana)

LIMA

BUENOS AIRES

H-540060-76 -1 -1-8Y

0 5 10 Miles

0 5 10 Kilometers

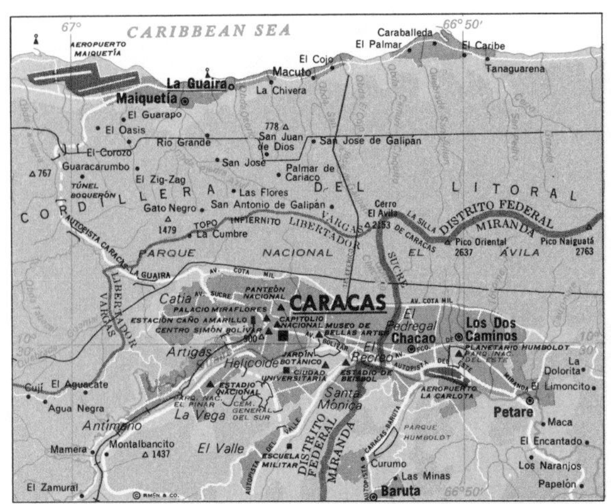

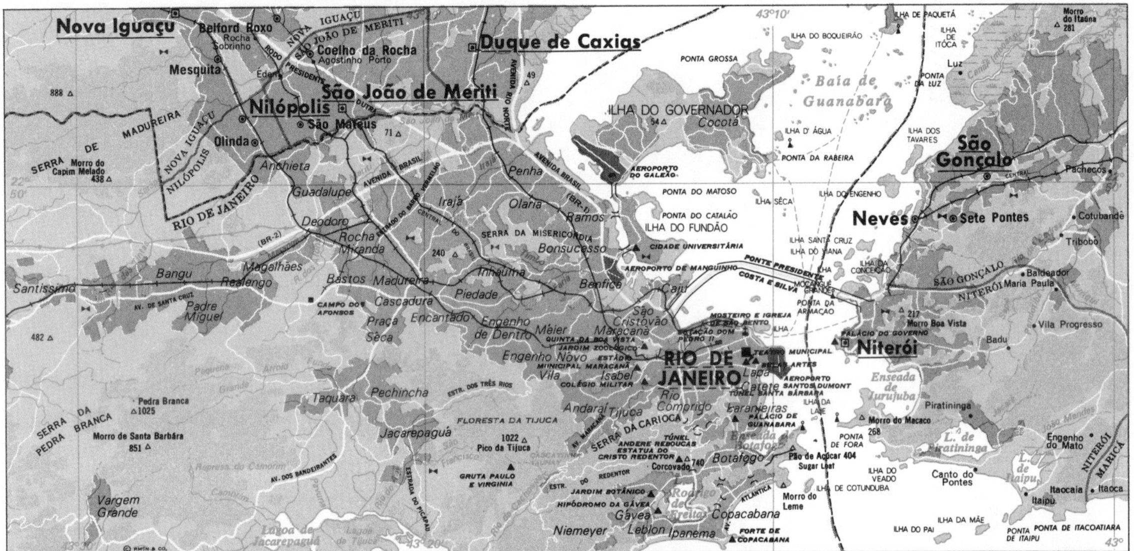

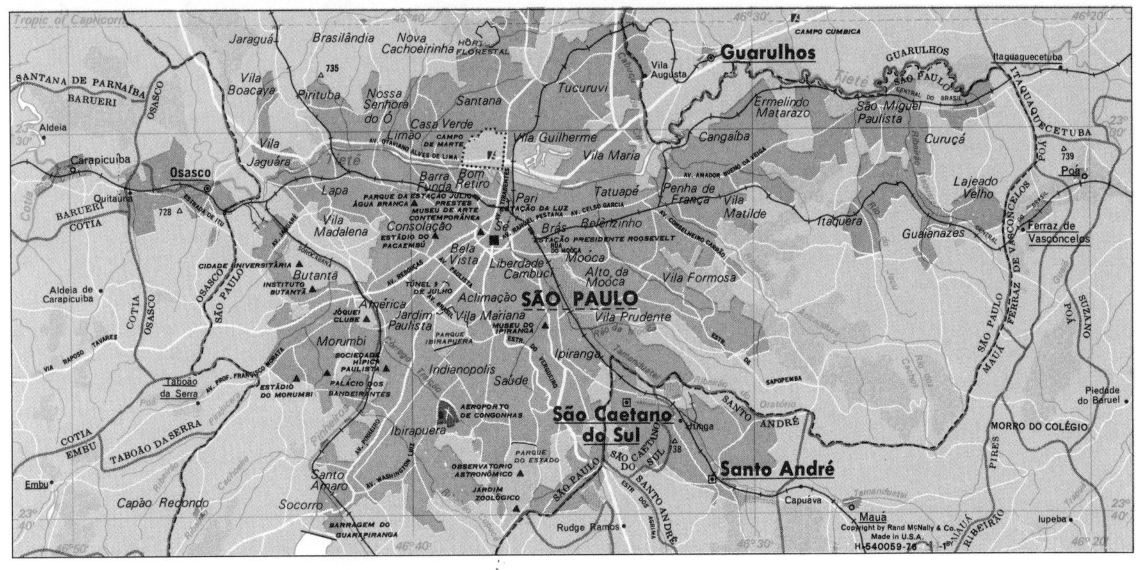

0 5 10 Miles
0 5 10 Kilometers

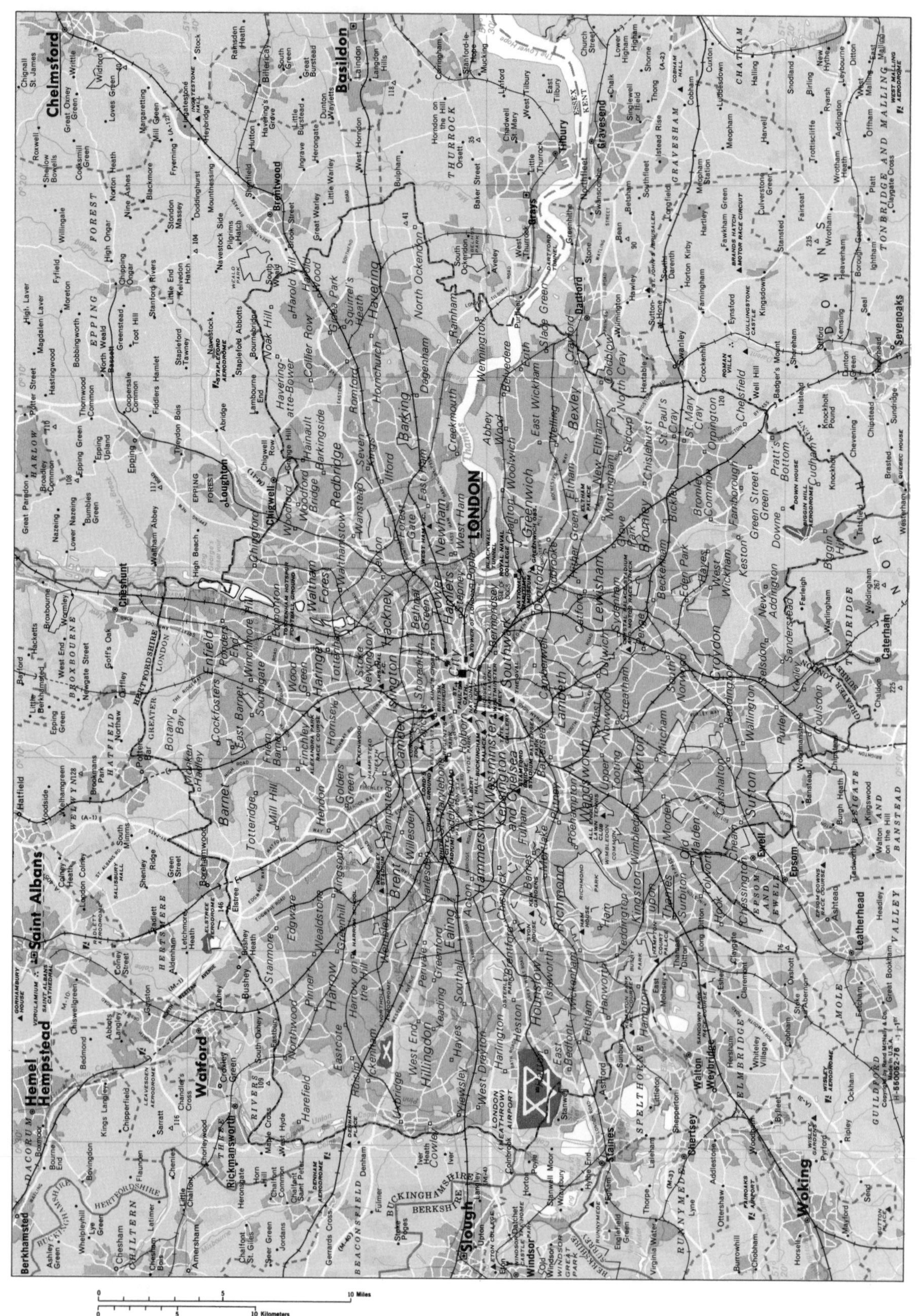

0 5 10 Miles

0 5 10 Kilometers

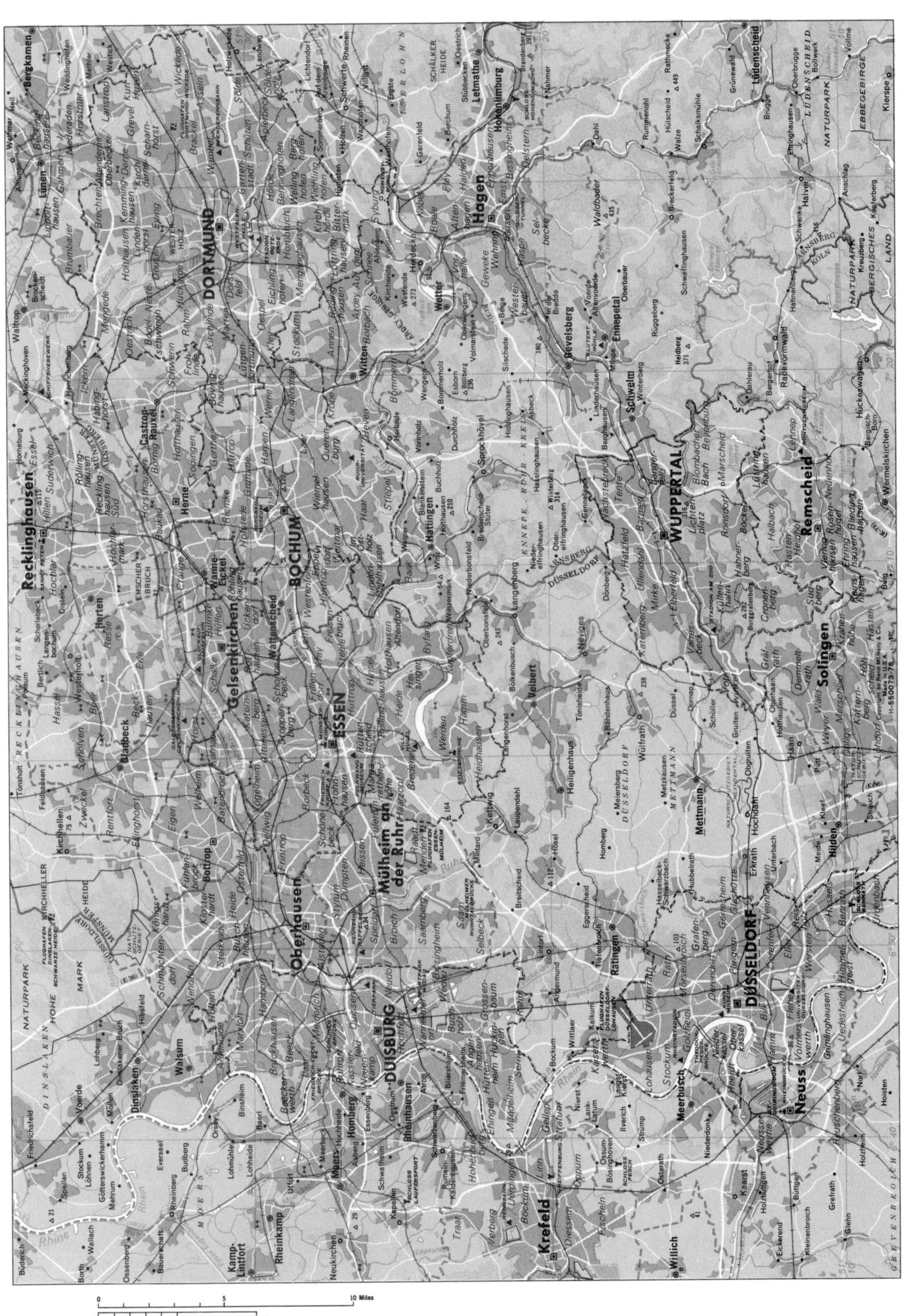
Recklinghausen
Dortmund
Bochum
Essen
Gelsenkirchen
Herne
Castrop-Rauxel
Lünen
Bergkamen
Waltrop
Herten
Gladbeck
Bottrop
Oberhausen
Mülheim an der Ruhr
Duisburg
Dinslaken
Voerde
Walsum
Moers
Kamp-Lintfort
Rheinkamp
Rheinhausen
Homberg
Krefeld
Willich
Meerbusch
Neuss
Düsseldorf
Ratingen
Mettmann
Hilden
Solingen
Remscheid
Wuppertal
Velbert
Hattingen
Witten
Wetter
Hagen
Hohenlimburg
Letmathe
Lüdenscheid
Gevelsberg
Schwelm
Ennepetal
Wanne-Eickel
Wattenscheid
Rhein
Ruhr
0 5 10 Miles
0 5 10 Kilometers

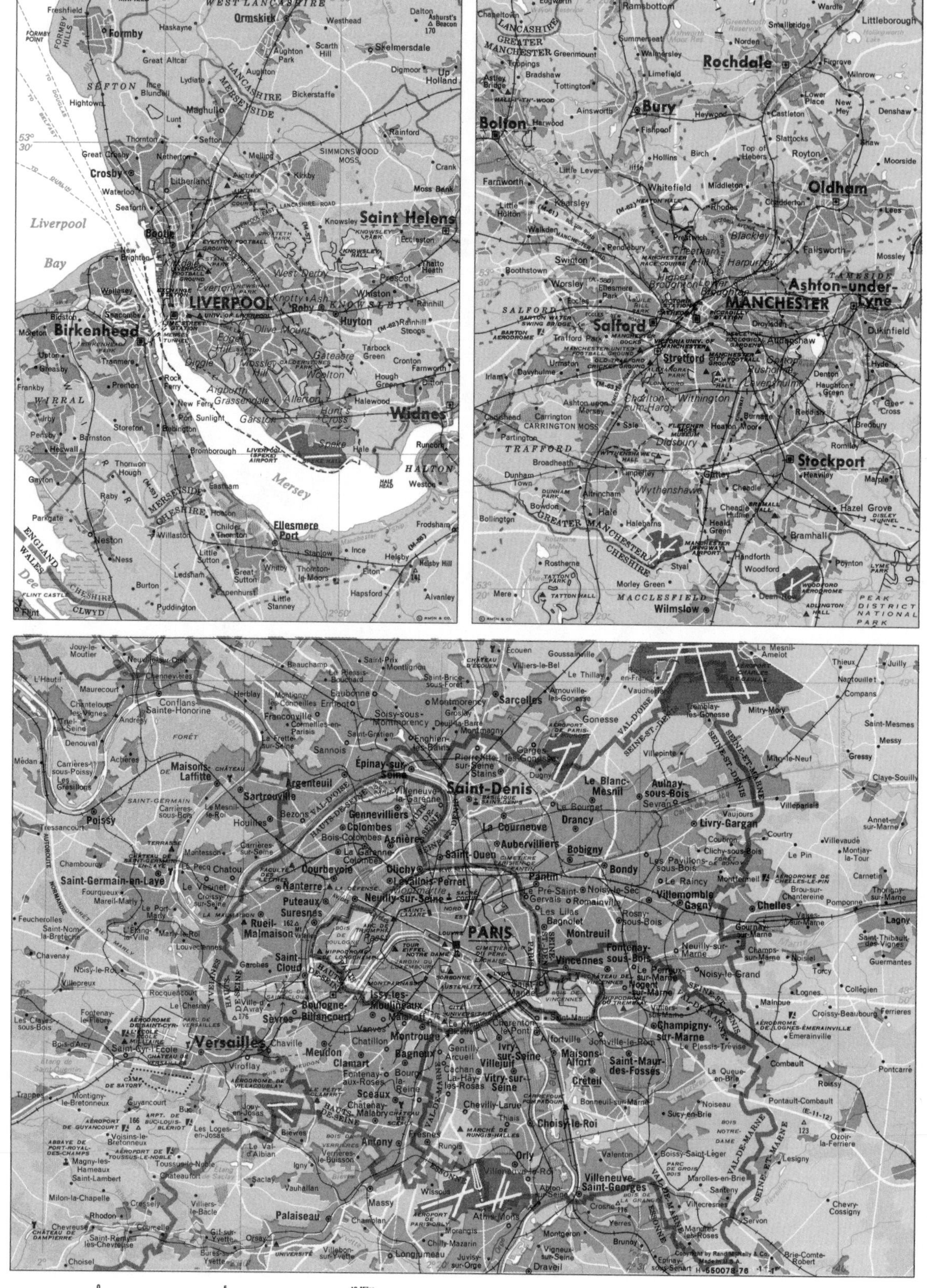

0 5 10 Miles

0 5 10 Kilometers

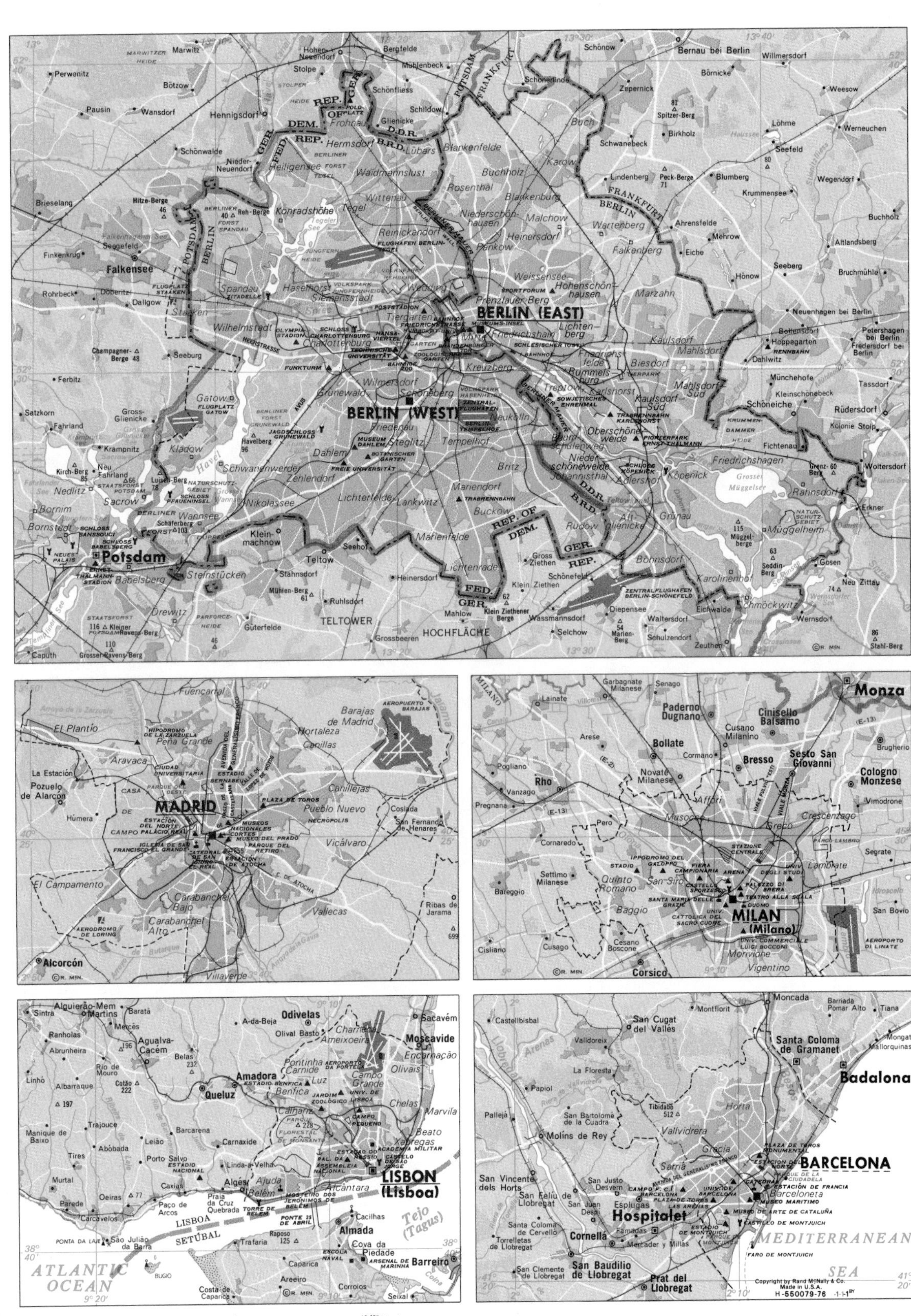
BERLIN (EAST)
BERLIN (WEST)
GER. DEM. REP.
FED. REP. GER.
D.D.R.
B.R.D.
Potsdam
Falkensee
Spandau
Charlottenburg
Tiergarten
Kreuzberg
Neukölln
Tempelhof
Schöneberg
Wilmersdorf
Steglitz
Zehlendorf
Wannsee
Köpenick
Grosser Müggelsee
Teltow
TELTOWER HOCHFLÄCHE
Bernau bei Berlin
Hennigsdorf
MADRID
Barajas de Madrid
AEROPUERTO BARAJAS
Alcorcón
Pozuelo de Alarcón
Carabanchel Alto
Vallecas
Monza
Cinisello Balsamo
Sesto San Giovanni
Bollate
Bresso
Cologno Monzese
Rho
MILAN (Milano)
Corsico
AEROPORTO DI LINATE
LISBON (Lisboa)
Odivelas
Sacavém
Moscavide
Amadora
Queluz
Almada
Barreiro
Tejo (Tagus)
ATLANTIC OCEAN
BARCELONA
Badalona
Santa Coloma de Gramanet
San Cugat del Vallés
Hospitalet
Cornellá
San Baudilio de Llobregat
Prat del Llobregat
MEDITERRANEAN SEA
Copyright by Rand McNally & Co.
Made in U.S.A.
H-550079-76
0 5 10 Miles
0 5 10 Kilometers

Udel'naja
Ručji
Lesnoj
Graždanka
Rybackaja
Lachta
Staraja Derevn'a
Ržovka
Novoje Koval'ovo
Poľustrovo
Malaja Neva
OSTROV VOL'NYJ
Gulf
OSTROV VASILJEVSKIJ
of
Finland
LENINGRAD
Bol'šaja Ochta
Malaja Ochta
GOROD LENINGRAD
Neva
OSTROV KANONERSKIJ
OSTROV GUTUJEVSKIJ
Kudrovo
Ves'olyj Pos'olok
Avtovo
30° 10'
Chimki (Khimki)
Mytishchi
Novoarchangel'skoje
MOSKVA
GOROD MOSKVA
Kurkino
Lianozovo
Družba
Medvedkovo
Novočhovrino
Beskudnikovo
Babuškin (Babuškin)
Putilkovo
Bratcevo
Degunino
Vladykino
Chimki-Chovrino
Tušino (Tushino)
Petrovsko-Razumovskoje
Ostankino
Abramcevo
Strogino
Pokrovsko-Strešnevo
Bogorodskoje
Goljanovo
Mjakino
Sokol'niki
Izmajlovo
Trojce-Lykovo
Serebr'anyj Bor
Chorošovo
Mnevniki
Tatarovo
Fili
Reutov
Novogirejevo
Krylatskoje
MOSCOW (Moskva)
Mazilovo
Perovo
Kunc'ovo (Kuntsevo)
Kuskovo
Lužniki
Vešn'aki
Nemčinovka
Kosino
Vychino
Očakovo
Tekstil'ščiki
Kuz'minki
Ramenka
Čer'omuški
Zarečje
Nagatino
Kolomenskoje
L'ublino (Lyublino)
Meščerskij
Nikulino
Jugo-Zapad
Tropar'ovo
Volchonka-Zil
Z'uzino
Solncevo
Djakovo
Orlovo
Rum'ancevo
Saburovo
Kapotn'a
Bratejevo
Dzerzinskij
Salarjovo
Uzkoje
Čertanovo
Lenino
Borisovo
T'oplyj Stan
Pokrovskoje
Besedy
Nikolo-Chovanskoje
Jasenevo
Mamonovo
Krasnyj Stroitel'
Bir'ul'ovo (Biryulevo)
Aščerino
Baturino
Ostrov
Letovo
Michajlovskoje
Sosenki
Kommunarka
Misailovo
Bitca
CAMPAGNA DI ROMA
Tomba di Nerone
Ottavia
Sant' Onofrio
Tor di Quinto
Settecamini
Monte Mario
ROME (Roma)
VATICAN CITY
CITTÀ DEL VATICANO
Tor Sapienza
Montespaccato
Valcanuta
Centocelle
Monteverde Nuovo
Tor Pignatara
Torre Gaia
Corviale
Garbatella
Quadraro
Magliana
Cecchignola
Petroúpolis
Néa Liósia
Amaroúsion
Iráklion
Néa Ionía
Paralía Aspropírgos
Kólpos
Elevsínos
Dháfni
Khaïdhárion
Peristérion
Néa Filadhélfia
Khalándrion
Galátsion
Skaramagás
ATTIKÍ
AIGÁLEOS
PIRAIÉVS
Ayía Varvára
Aiyáleo
ATHENS (Athínai)
Khólargós
Koridhallós
Níkaia
Zográfos
Pérama
Keratsínion
Kaisarianí
Kallithéa
Piraeus (Piraiévs)
Víron
Imittós
Dhrapetsóna
Néa Smírni
Áyios Dhimítrios
Ilioúpolis
PSITTÁLIA
Palaión Fáliron
Saronikós Kólpos
Kalamákion
Ayiroúpolis
WIENERWALD
Weidling
Jedlesee
Weidlingbach
Kahlenberg
Leopoldau
NIEDER-ÖSTERREICH
WIEN
Neustift am Walde
Nussdorf
Floridsdorf
Donaufeld
Sievering
Grinzing
Kagran
Breitenlee
Pötzleinsdorf
Döbling
Hirschstetten
Hadersdorf
Neuwaldegg
Dornbach
Währing
Donaustadt
Kaisermühlen
Hernals
Leopoldstadt
Stadlau
Essling
Mariabrunn
Ottakring
Aspern
Weidlingau
Hütteldorf
VIENNA (Wien)
Ober Sankt Veit
Hietzing
Favoriten
Simmering
Meidling
Hetzendorf
Speising
Atzgersdorf
Mauer
Kalksburg
Rodaun
Mannswörth
Schwechat
Boyacıköy
Kanlıca
Rumelihisarı
Anadoluhisarı
Kâğıthane
Bebek
Kandilli
Küçükköy
Balmumcu
Vaniköy
Atışalan
Kuruçeşme
Çengelköy
Şişli
Esenler
Beylerbeyi
Topkapı
Güngören
İSTANBUL
Ümraniye
Üsküdar
Yeniköy
Samatya
Yedikule
Zeytinburnu
Kadıköy
Kızıltoprak
Bakırköy
Marmara Denizi (Sea of Marmara)
Erenköy
Bostancı
Copyright by Rand McNally & Co. Made in U.S.A.
H-550080-76
Solymár
Újpest
Rákospalota
Óbuda
Csömör
Kerepes
Pesthidegkút
Angyalföld
Pestújhely
Kistarcsa
Rákosszentmihály
Zugló
Sashalom
Cinkota
Nagytarcsa
PEST
Budakeszi
Buda
Pest
Mátyásföld
BUDAPEST
Rákosliget
Kőbánya
Ferencváros
Rákoskeresztúr
Rákoscsaba
Kelenföld
Rákoshegy
Rákoskert
Budaörs
Kispest
Albertfalva
Ecser
Pesterzsébet
Pestlőrinc
10 Miles
10 Kilometers

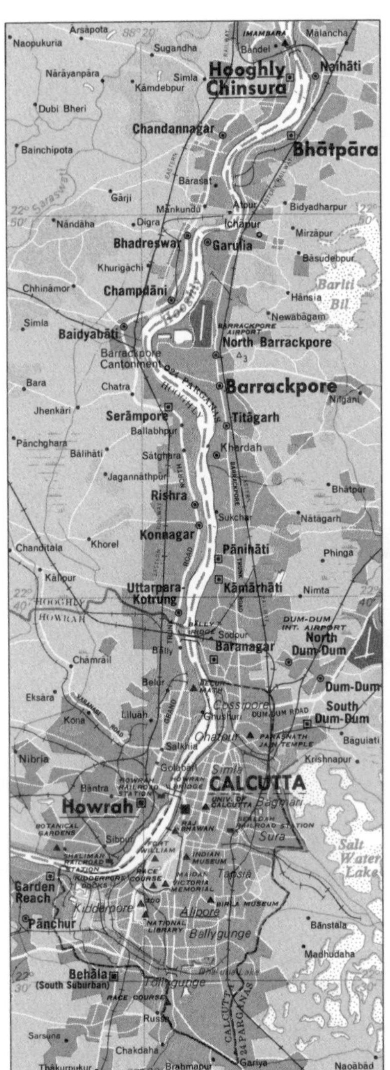

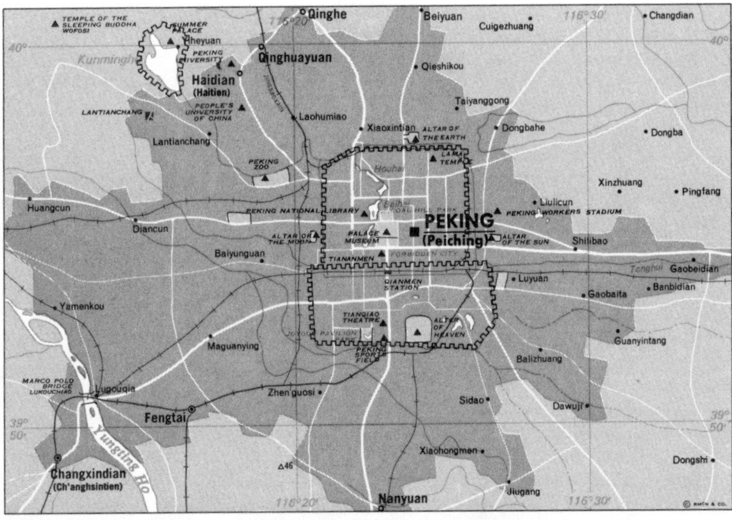

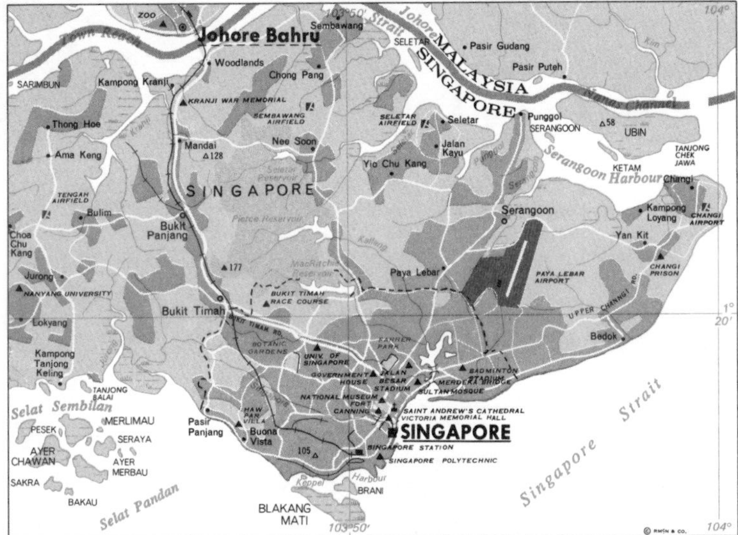

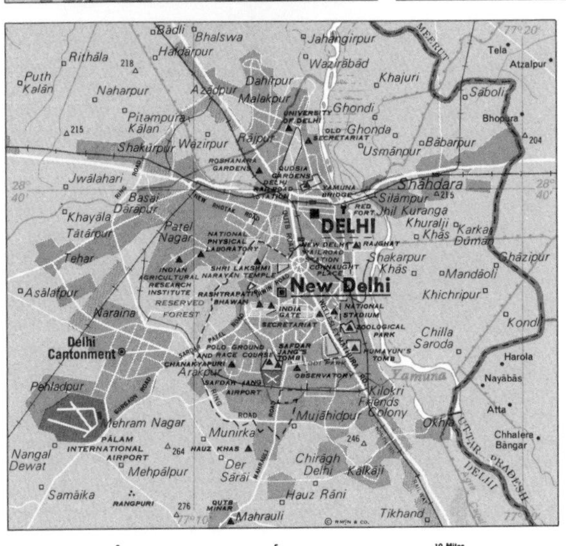

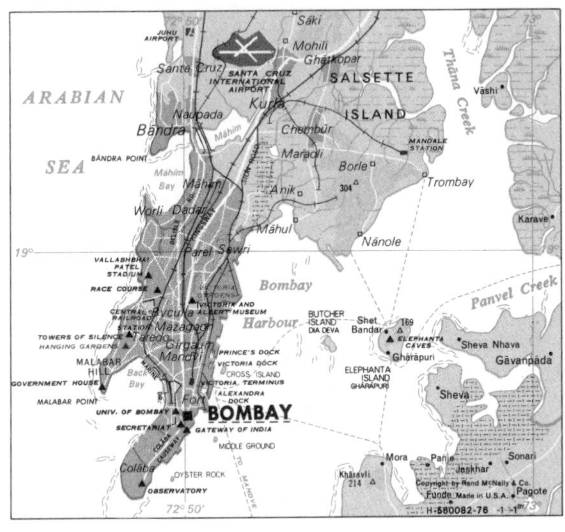

0 5 10 Miles

0 5 10 Kilometers

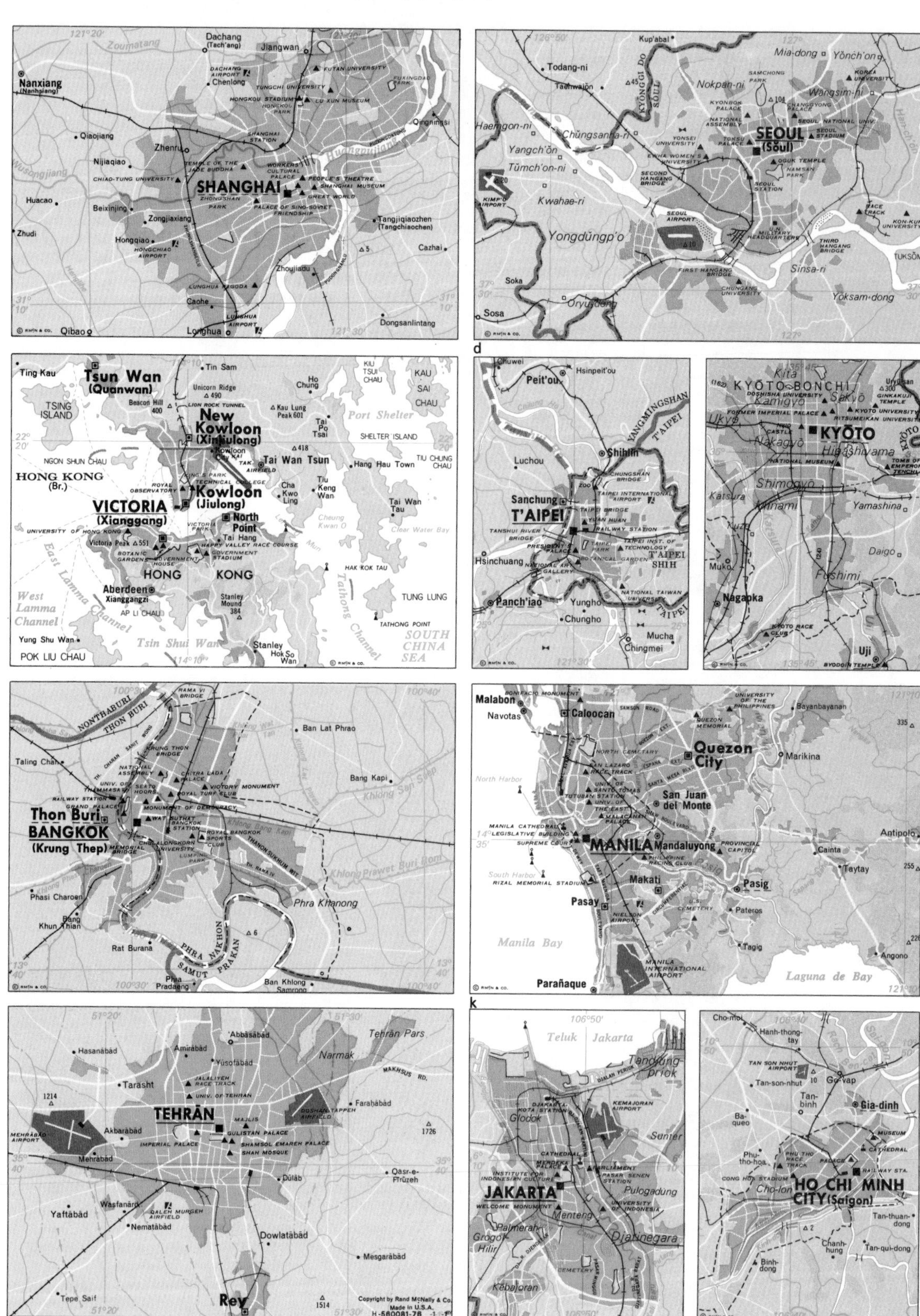

SHANGHAI
SEOUL (Sŏul)
VICTORIA (Xianggang)
HONG KONG
New Kowloon (Xinjiulong)
Kowloon (Jiulong)
Tsun Wan (Quanwan)
T'AIPEI
KYŌTO
Thon Buri
BANGKOK (Krung Thep)
MANILA
Quezon City
TEHRĀN
JAKARTA
HO CHI MINH CITY (Saigon)
Copyright by Rand McNally & Co. Made in U.S.A.
0 5 10 Miles
0 5 10 Kilometers

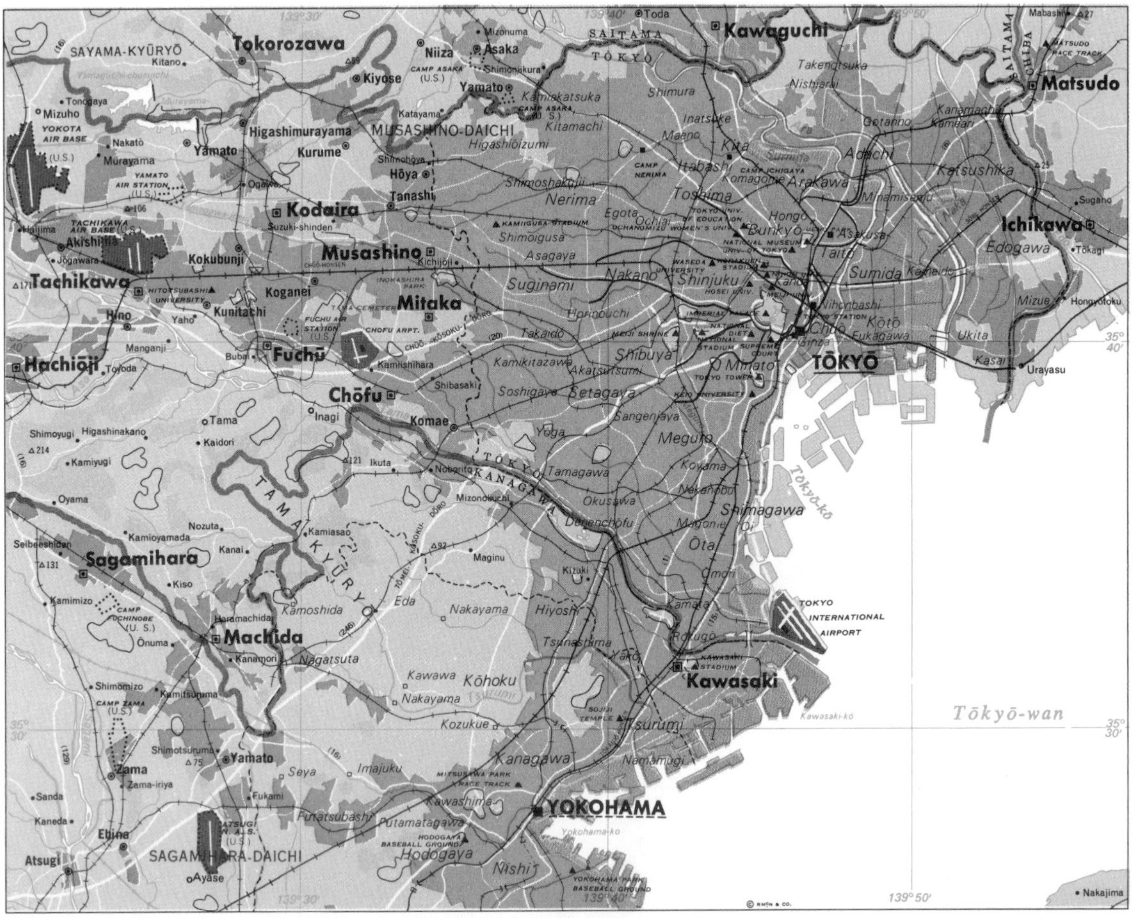

Tokorozawa
Kawaguchi
Matsudo
SAYAMA-KYŪRYŌ
Niiza
Asaka
Kiyose
Yamato
MUSASHINO-DAICHI
Higashimurayama
Kurume
Kodaira
Hōya
Tanashi
Musashino
Tachikawa
Akishima
Kokubunji
Koganei
Kunitachi
Mitaka
Hino
Fuchū
Hachiōji
Chōfu
Komae
Inagi
Tama
TAMA-KYŪRYŌ
Sagamihara
Machida
Zama
Yamato
Ebina
Atsugi
SAGAMIHARA-DAICHI
Ayase
Nerima
Suginami
Setagaya
Shibuya
Shinjuku
Nakano
Toshima
Itabashi
Kita
Arakawa
Adachi
Katsushika
Ichikawa
Edogawa
Sumida
Bunkyō
Taitō
Chiyoda
Chūō
Kōtō
Minato
TŌKYŌ
Meguro
Shinagawa
Ōta
Urayasu
Tōkyō-kō
TOKYO INTERNATIONAL AIRPORT
Kawasaki
Kawasaki-kō
Tsurumi
Kōhoku
Kanagawa
YOKOHAMA
Yokohama-kō
Hodogaya
Nishi
Tōkyō-wan
139°50′
135°30′
35°40′
35°30′

Takatsuki
Ibaraki
Hirakata
Kawanishi
Minō
Ikeda
Takarazuka
Toyonaka
Itami
Settsu
Suita
Neyagawa
ROKKŌ-SANCHI
SETO-NAIKAI-KOKURITSU-KŌEN
Nishinomiya
Ashiya
Amagasaki
Moriguchi
Kadoma
Daitō
Higashiyodogawa
ŌSAKA-HEIYA
KŌBE
Kōbe-kō
Nada
Higashinada
Fukiai
Ikuta
Nagata
Suma
WADA-MISAKI
Ōsaka-Wan
ŌSAKA
Konohana
Minato
Taishō
Nishinari
Abeno
Higashisumiyoshi
Sumiyoshi
Sakai
Higashiōsaka
Yao
Kashiwara
Matsubara
IKOMA-SANCHI
Copyright by Rand McNally & Co.
Made in U.S.A.
H-560080-76
0 5 10 Miles
0 5 10 Kilometers

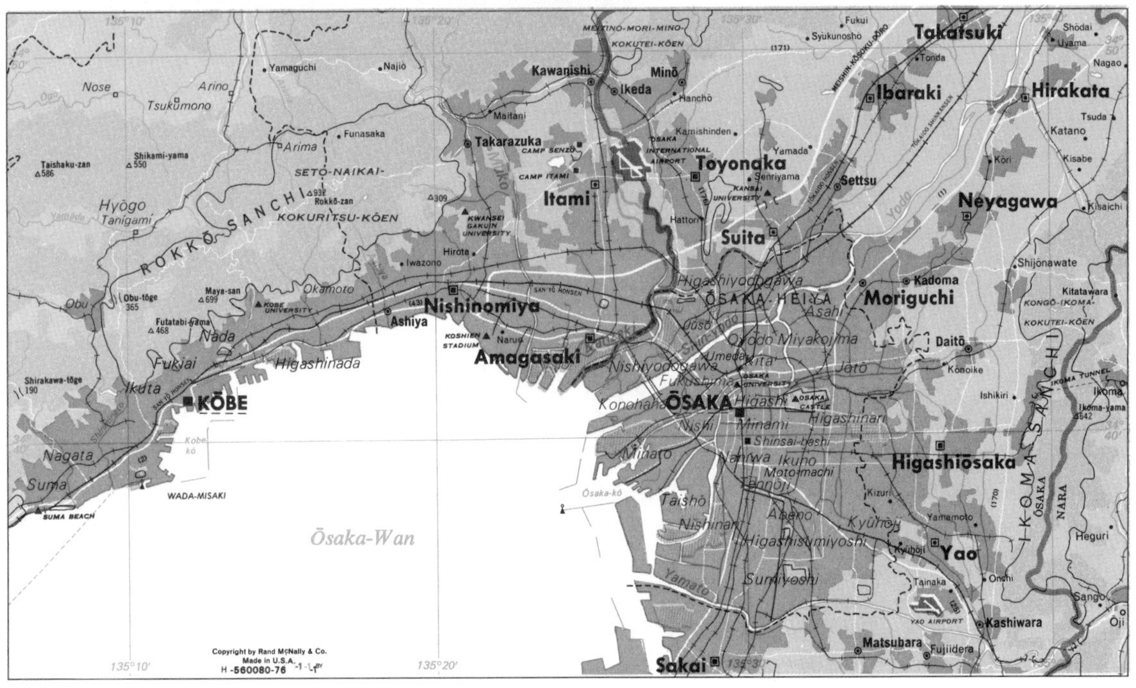

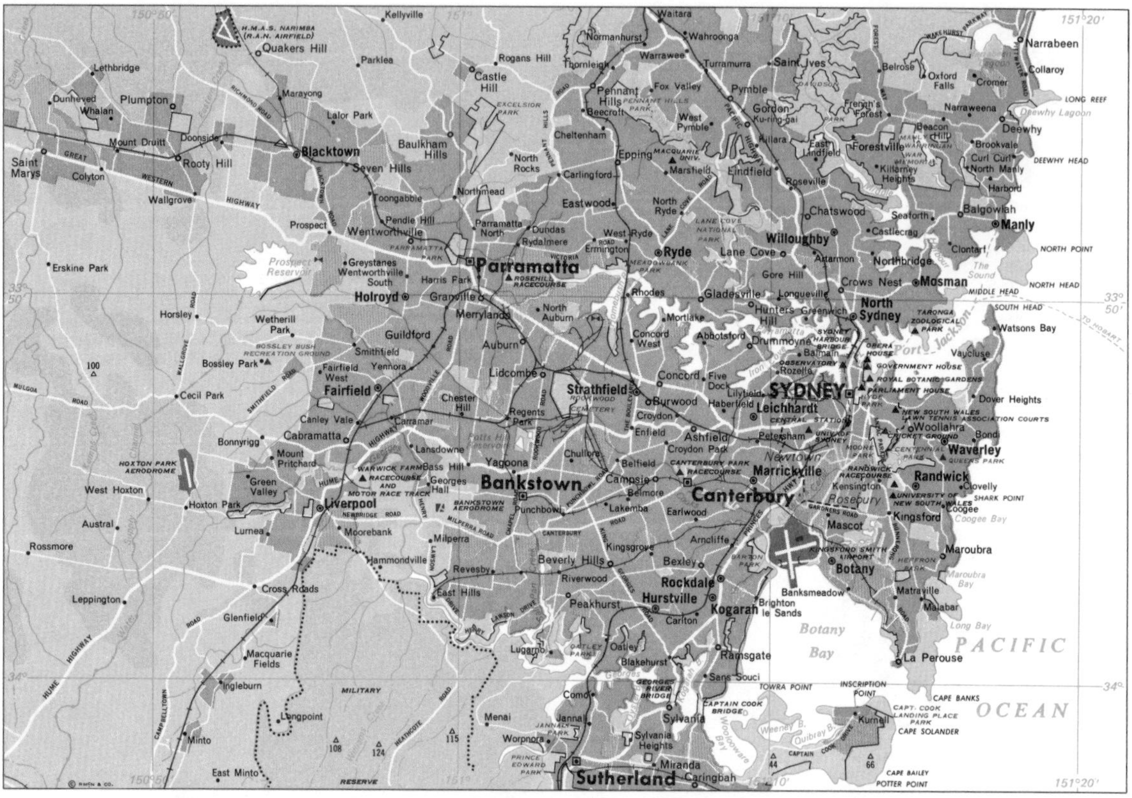

0 5 10 Miles

0 5 10 Kilometers

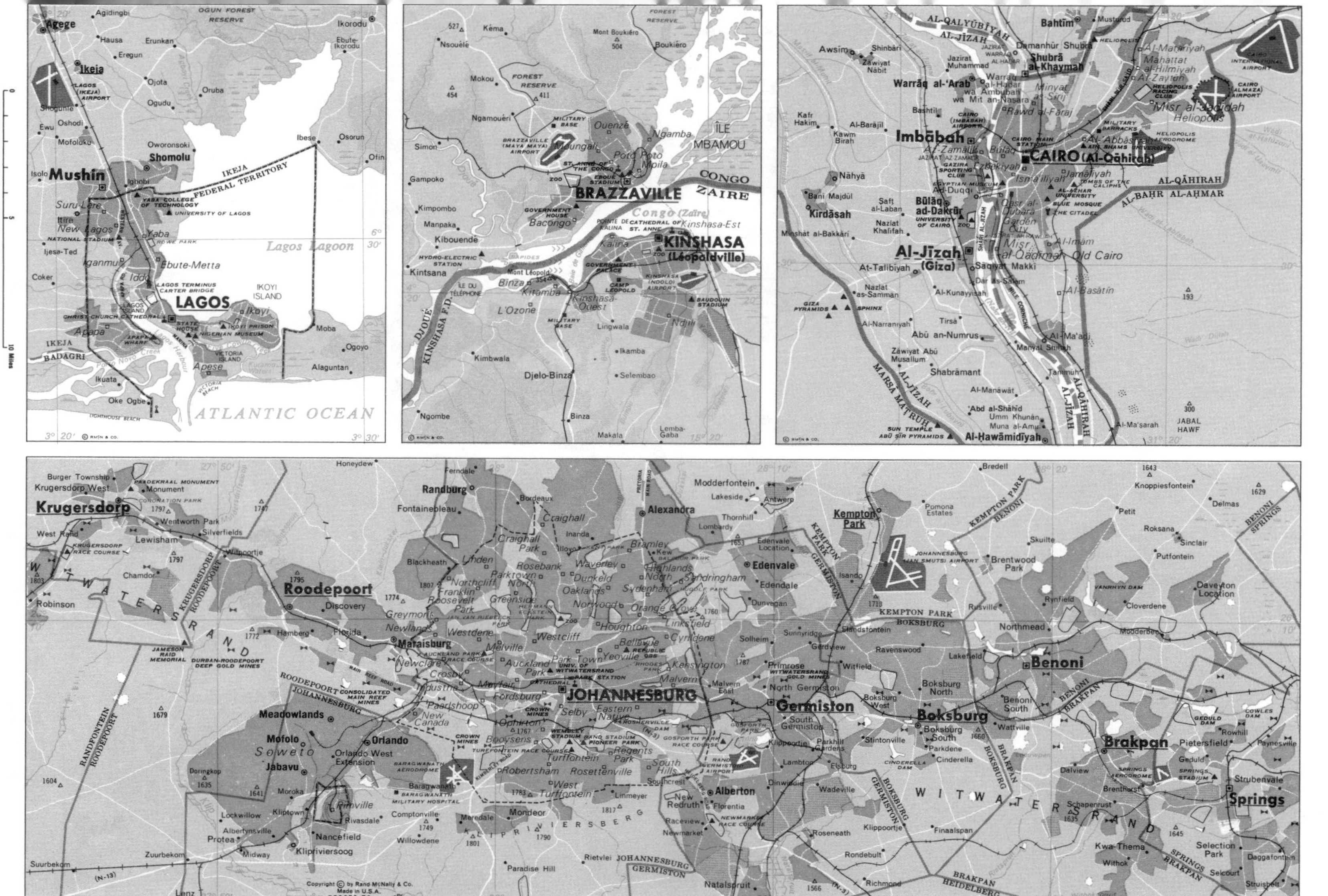

LAGOS
Mushin
Ikeja
Shomolu
Lagos Lagoon
IKEJA FEDERAL TERRITORY
ATLANTIC OCEAN
BRAZZAVILLE
KINSHASA (Léopoldville)
CONGO
ZAIRE
CAIRO (Al-Qāhirah)
Al-Jīzah (Giza)
Imbābah
JOHANNESBURG
Krugersdorp
Roodepoort
Randburg
Alexandra
Edenvale
Kempton Park
Germiston
Boksburg
Benoni
Brakpan
Springs
Alberton
Soweto
W I T W A T E R S R A N D
10 Miles
10 Kilometers
Copyright © by Rand McNally & Co. Made in U.S.A.

Historical Maps of the World

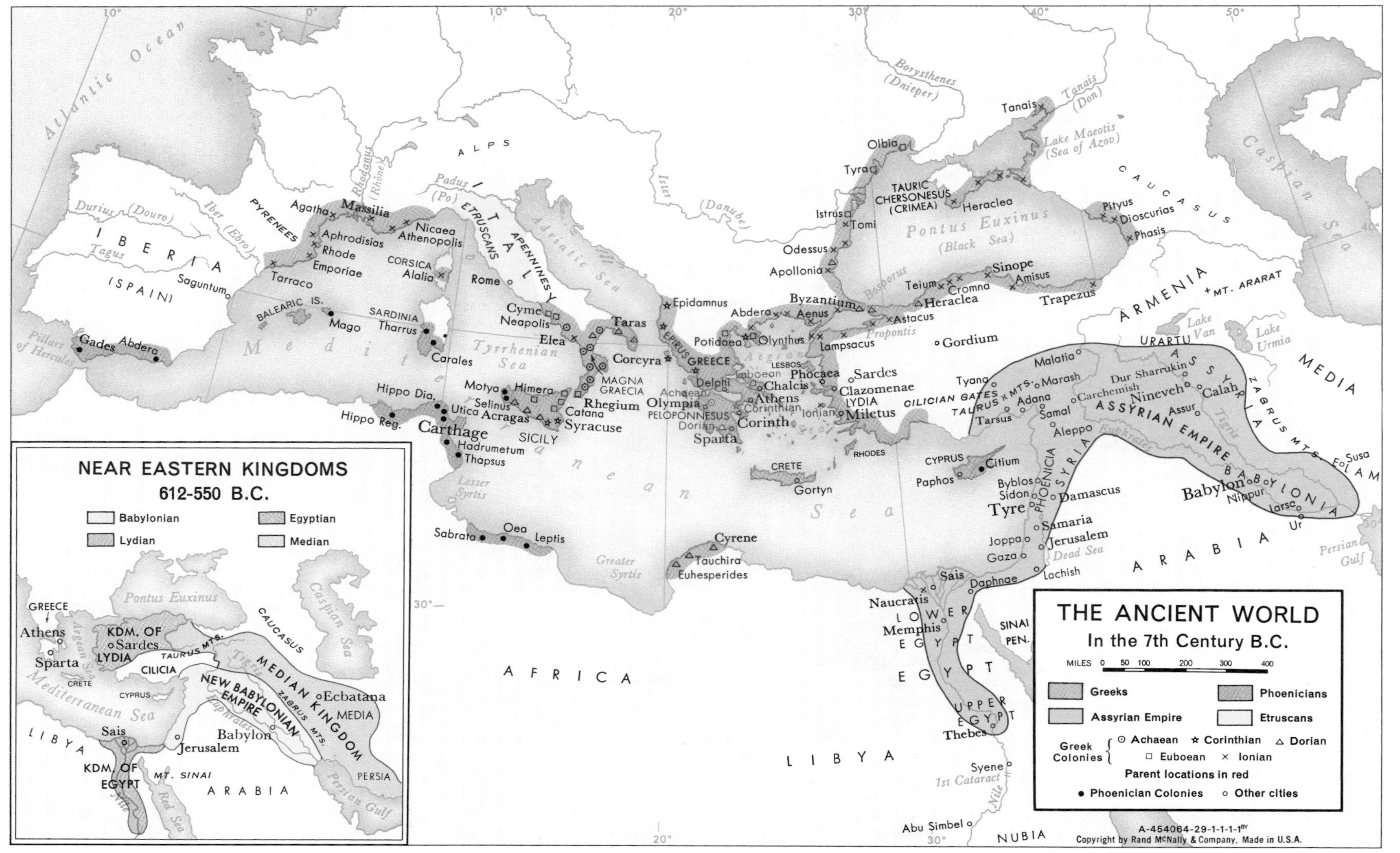
THE ANCIENT WORLD
In the 7th Century B.C.
MILES 0 50 100 200 300 400
Greeks
Phoenicians
Assyrian Empire
Etruscans
Greek Colonies
⊙ Achaean
★ Corinthian
△ Dorian
□ Euboean
× Ionian
Parent locations in red
• Phoenician Colonies
○ Other cities
A-454064-29-1-1-1
Copyright by Rand McNally & Company, Made in U.S.A.
NEAR EASTERN KINGDOMS
612-550 B.C.
Babylonian
Egyptian
Lydian
Median
KDM. OF LYDIA
Sardes
CILICIA
MEDIAN KINGDOM
Ecbatana
MEDIA
PERSIA
NEW BABYLONIAN EMPIRE
Babylon
Jerusalem
KDM. OF EGYPT
Sais
ARABIA
LIBYA
GREECE
Athens
Sparta
Atlantic Ocean
IBERIA
(SPAIN)
PYRENEES
ALPS
ITALY
ETRUSCANS
APENNINES
Rome
Massilia
Carthage
SICILY
Syracuse
GREECE
Athens
Corinth
Sparta
Olympia
Delphi
CRETE
CYPRUS
RHODES
Byzantium
Pontus Euxinus (Black Sea)
Caspian Sea
CAUCASUS
ARMENIA
MT. ARARAT
URARTU
MEDIA
ASSYRIAN EMPIRE
Nineveh
Calah
Assur
ZAGRUS MTS.
BABYLONIA
Babylon
ELAM
Susa
SYRIA
PHOENICIA
Tyre
Sidon
Damascus
Jerusalem
LOWER EGYPT
UPPER EGYPT
Memphis
Thebes
NUBIA
SINAI PEN.
ARABIA
AFRICA
LIBYA
Mediterranean Sea

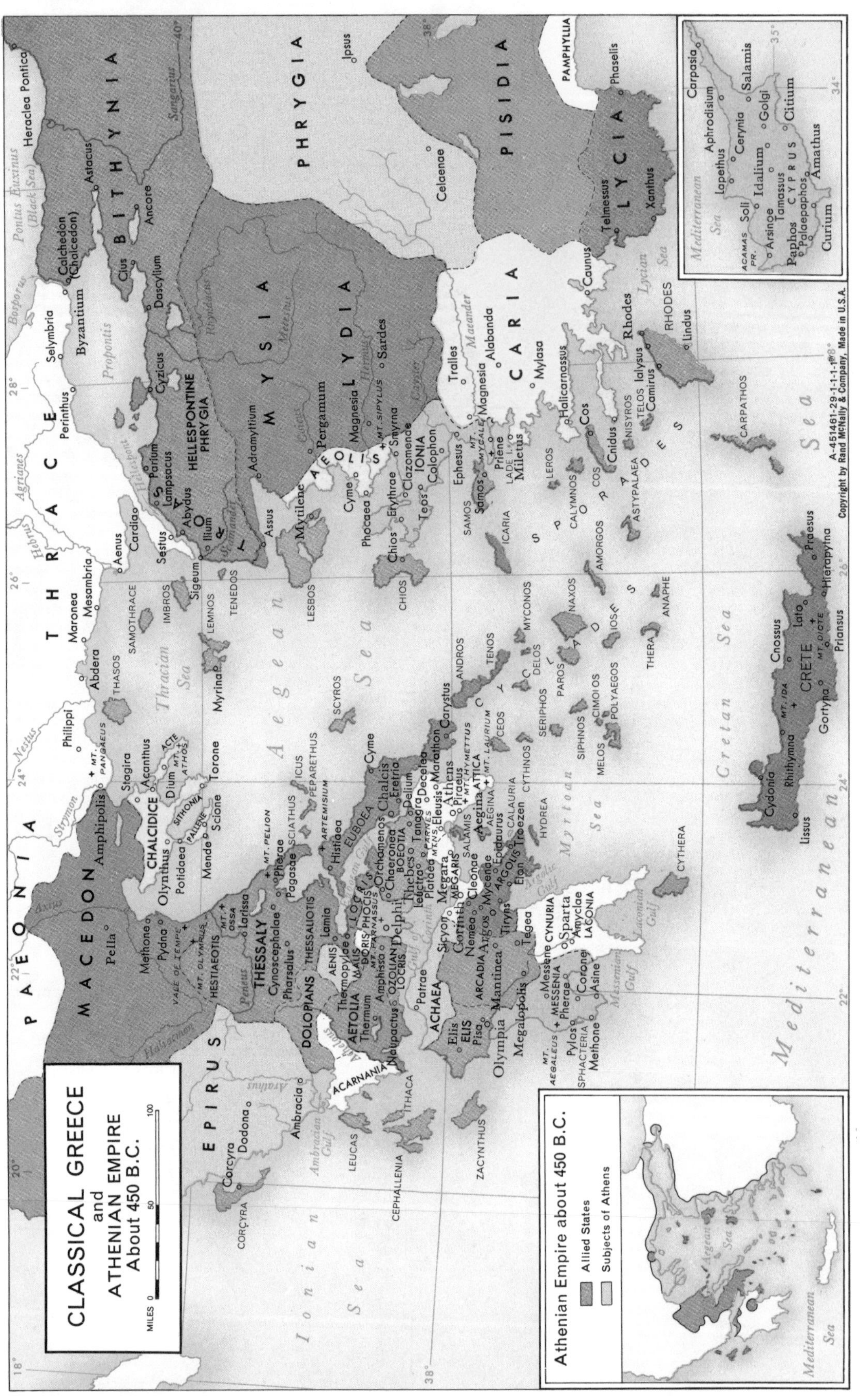
CLASSICAL GREECE
and
ATHENIAN EMPIRE
About 450 B.C.
MILES 0 50 100
Athenian Empire about 450 B.C.
Allied States
Subjects of Athens
PAEONIA
THRACE
MACEDON
BITHYNIA
PHRYGIA
MYSIA
LYDIA
CARIA
PISIDIA
LYCIA
PAMPHYLIA
EPIRUS
THESSALY
CHALCIDICE
HELLESPONTINE PHRYGIA
TROAS
AEOLIS
IONIA
Aegean Sea
Ionian Sea
Thracian Sea
Myrtoan Sea
Cretan Sea
Mediterranean Sea
Pontus Euxinus (Black Sea)
Propontis
CRETE
CYPRUS
Athens
Sparta
Corinth
Byzantium
A-451461-29-1-1-1-8
Copyright by Rand McNally & Company, Made in U.S.A.

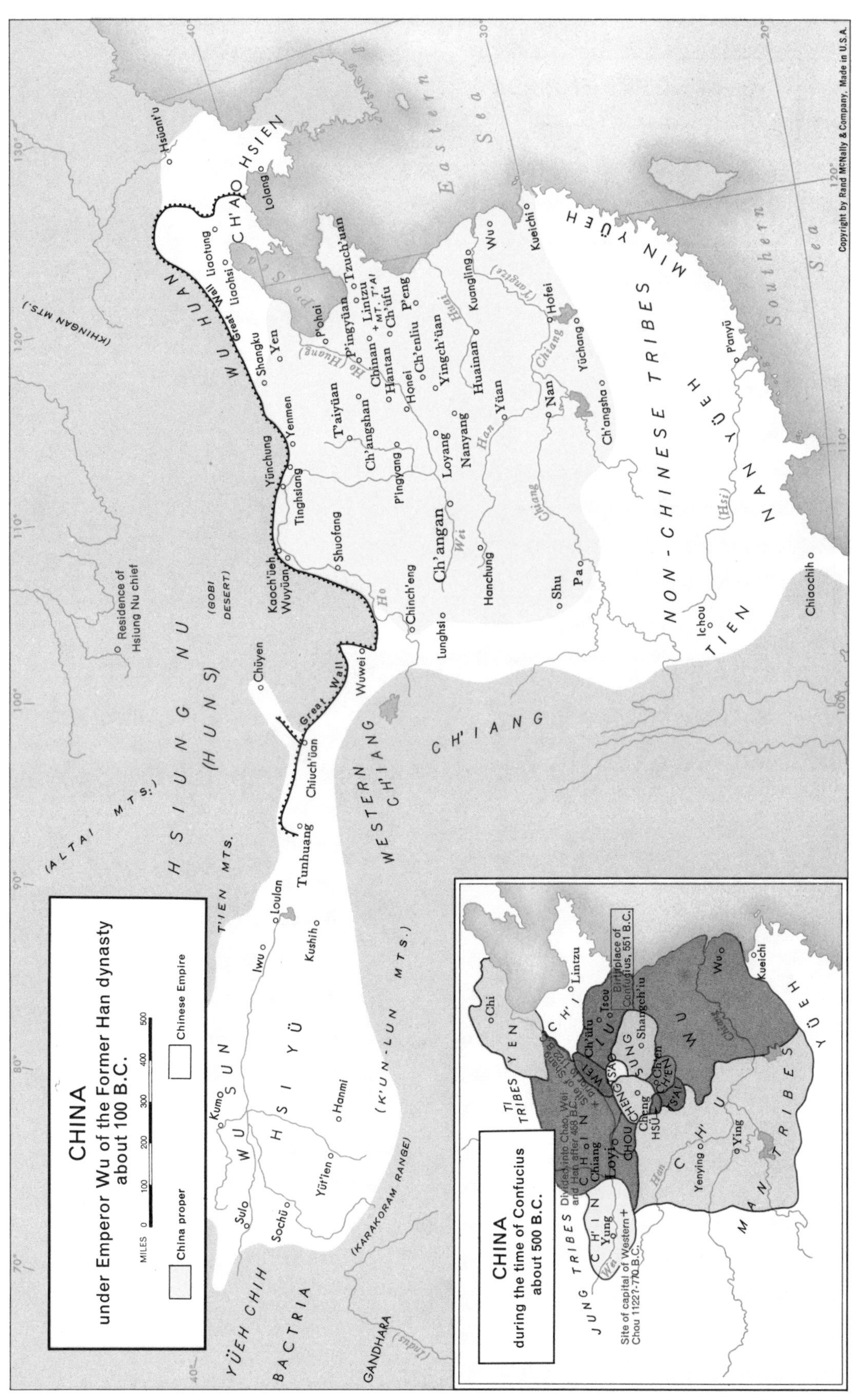
CHINA
under Emperor Wu of the Former Han dynasty
about 100 B.C.
MILES 0 100 200 300 400 500
China proper
Chinese Empire
HSIUNG NU
(HUNS)
(ALTAI MTS.)
(KHINGAN MTS.)
(GOBI DESERT)
Residence of Hsiung Nu chief
T'IEN MTS.
WU SUN
HSI YÜ
YÜEH CHIH
BACTRIA
GANDHARA
(Indus)
(KARAKORAM RANGE)
(K'UN-LUN MTS.)
WESTERN CH'IANG
CH'IANG
NON-CHINESE TRIBES
TIEN
NAN YÜEH
MIN YÜEH
WU HUAN
CH'AO HSIEN
Eastern Sea
Southern Sea
Great Wall
Kumo
Sulo
Sochü
Yüt'ien
Hanmi
Kushih
Iwu
Loulan
Tunhuang
Chiuch'üan
Chüyen
Wuwei
Lunghsi
Chinch'eng
Kaoch'üeh
Wuyüan
Shuofang
Tinghsiang
Yünchung
Yenmen
Shangku
Yen
Liaohsi
Liaotung
Lolang
Hsüant'u
T'aiyüan
Ch'angshan
P'ingyang
Ch'angan
Wei
Ho
Ho (Huang)
P'ohai
P'ingyüan
Tzuch'uan
Chinan
Lintzu
MT. T'AI
Ch'üfu
Hantan
Honei
Ch'enliu
P'eng
Yingch'üan
Loyang
Nanyang
Huainan
Huai
Kuangling
Wu
Kueichi
Hofei
Yüchang
Ch'angsha
Nan
Yüan
Han
Hanchung
Shu
Pa
Chiang
Chiang (Yangtze)
Ichou
Chiaochih
P'anyü
(Hsi)
CHINA
during the time of Confucius
about 500 B.C.
JUNG TRIBES
TI TRIBES
CH'IN
Yung
Site of capital of Western Chou 1122?-770 B.C.
CHIN
Chiang
Divided into Chao, Wei and Han after 458 B.C.
Site of Chao capital
WEI
Loyi
CHOU
CHENG
Cheng
HSÜ
YEN
Chi
CH'I
Lintzu
LU
Ch'üfu
Tsou
Birthplace of Confucius, 551 B.C.
SUNG
Shangch'iu
TSAO
Ch'en
CH'EN
TSAI
WU
Wu
Kueichi
YÜEH
CH'U
Ying
Yenying
Han
MAN TRIBES
Copyright by Rand McNally & Company, Made in U.S.A.

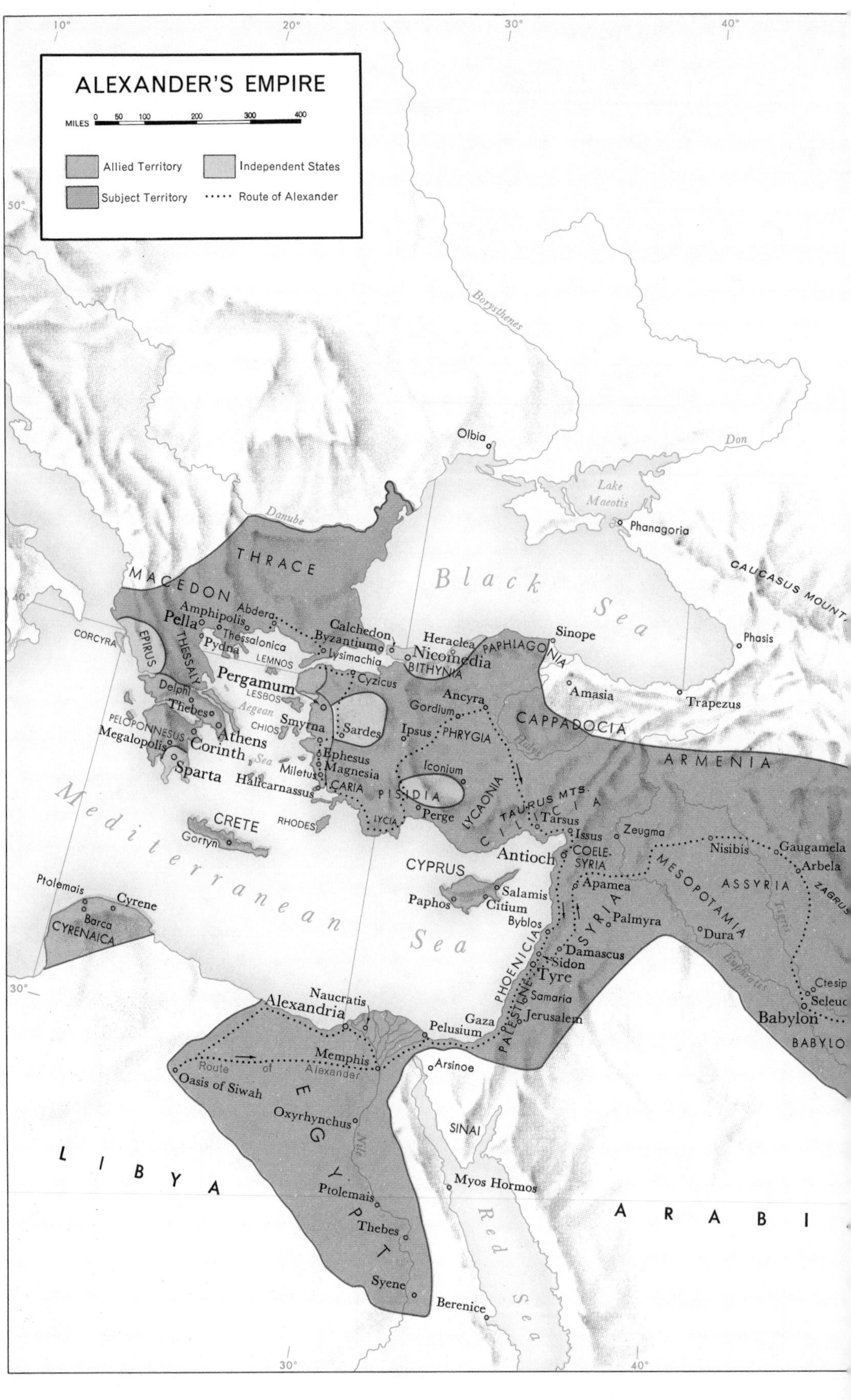

ALEXANDER'S EMPIRE
MILES 0 50 100 200 300 400
Allied Territory
Independent States
Subject Territory
Route of Alexander
Borysthenes
Olbia
Don
Lake Maeotis
Phanagoria
CAUCASUS MOUNT
Danube
THRACE
MACEDON
Black Sea
Abdera
Amphipolis
Pella
Thessalonica
Pydna
EPIRUS
THESSALY
CORCYRA
Calchedon
Byzantium
Lysimachia
LEMNOS
Heraclea
Nicomedia
BITHYNIA
PAPHLAGONIA
Sinope
Phasis
Amasia
Trapezus
Pergamum
Cyzicus
LESBOS
Delphi
Thebes
Aegean Sea
CHIOS
Smyrna
Sardes
Ancyra
Gordium
Ipsus
PHRYGIA
CAPPADOCIA
Halys
ARMENIA
PELOPONNESUS
Megalopolis
Athens
Corinth
Sparta
Ephesus
Magnesia
Miletus
Halicarnassus
CARIA
Iconium
PISIDIA
LYCAONIA
TAURUS MTS.
CILICIA
Tarsus
Mediterranean Sea
CRETE
Gortyn
RHODES
LYCIA
Perge
Issus
Zeugma
Antioch
COELE-SYRIA
Nisibis
Gaugamela
Arbela
MESOPOTAMIA
ASSYRIA
ZAGROS
CYPRUS
Salamis
Paphos
Citium
Apamea
Byblos
SYRIA
Palmyra
Dura
Tigris
Ptolemais
Cyrene
Barca
CYRENAICA
PHOENICIA
Damascus
Sidon
Tyre
Euphrates
Samaria
Ctesip
Seleuc
Naucratis
Alexandria
Gaza
Jerusalem
PALESTINE
Babylon
BABYLO
Pelusium
Memphis
Route of Alexander
Arsinoe
Oasis of Siwah
EGYPT
Oxyrhynchus
SINAI
Nile
LIBYA
Myos Hormos
Ptolemais
ARABI
Thebes
Red Sea
Syene
Berenice
10°
20°
30°
40°
50°

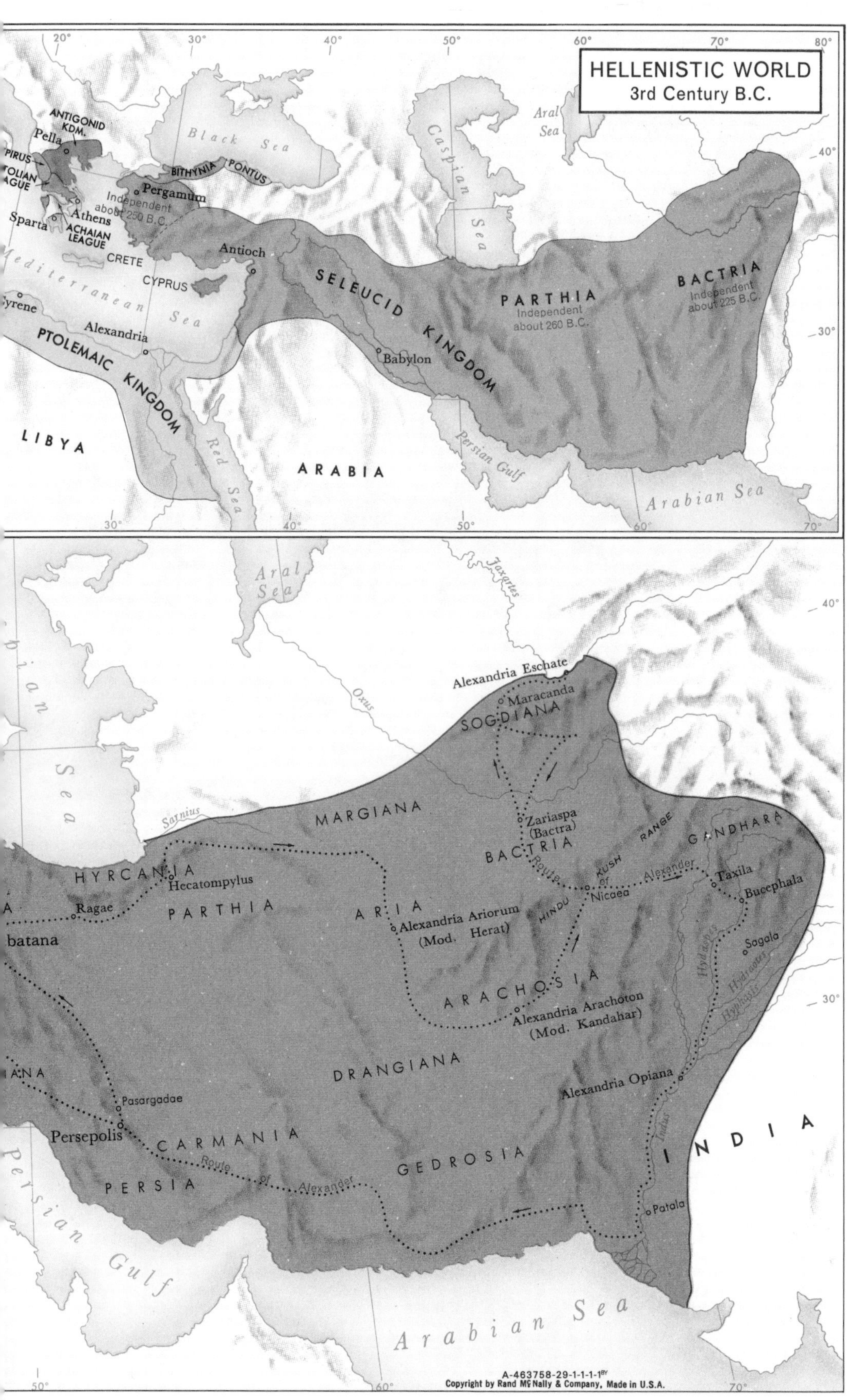
HELLENISTIC WORLD
3rd Century B.C.
ANTIGONID KDM.
Pella
Black Sea
BITHYNIA
PONTUS
Pergamum
Independent about 250 B.C.
Athens
Sparta
ACHAIAN LEAGUE
CRETE
CYPRUS
Antioch
Mediterranean Sea
Alexandria
PTOLEMAIC KINGDOM
LIBYA
SELEUCID KINGDOM
Babylon
Caspian Sea
Aral Sea
PARTHIA
Independent about 260 B.C.
BACTRIA
Independent about 225 B.C.
Red Sea
ARABIA
Persian Gulf
Arabian Sea
Aral Sea
Jaxartes
Oxus
Alexandria Eschate
Maracanda
SOGDIANA
Sarnius
MARGIANA
Zariaspa (Bactra)
BACTRIA
HINDU KUSH RANGE
GANDHARA
Route of Alexander
Taxila
Bucephala
Nicaea
HYRCANIA
Hecatompylus
Ragae
PARTHIA
ARIA
Alexandria Ariorum (Mod. Herat)
batana
Sagala
Hydaspes
Hydraotes
Hyphasis
ARACHOSIA
Alexandria Arachoton (Mod. Kandahar)
DRANGIANA
Alexandria Opiana
Pasargadae
Persepolis
CARMANIA
Route of Alexander
GEDROSIA
INDIA
Indus
PERSIA
Patala
Persian Gulf
Arabian Sea
A-463758-29-1-1-1-1
Copyright by Rand McNally & Company, Made in U.S.A.

ROMAN REPUBLIC
In the Time of Caesar and Cicero
MILES 0 50 100 200 300 400
Roman Provinces
Parthian Empire
Client Kingdoms and Dependencies
Battlefields
North Sea
Atlantic Ocean
BRITANNIA
English Channel
NERVII
BELGAE
TREVERI
Sequana
Lutetia
(Seine)
GAUL
VENETI
Liger
Alesia
Rhenus
(Rhine)
HELVETII
CELTAE
AEDUI
SEQUANI
Garumna
ARVERNI
Rhodanus
AQUITANI
PYRENEES
TRANSALPINE GAUL
Narbo
Massilia
Aquae Sextiae
ALPS
Vercellae
Trebia
Verona
CISALPINE GAUL
Mutina
Rubicon
Lucca
Sarsina
L. Trasimene
APENNINES
Adriatic
Amiternum
ITALY
Corfinium
Rome
Tusculum
Ostia
Formiae
Arpinum
Suessa
Capua
Cannae
Rudiae
Neapolis
Beneventum
Heraclea
ILLYRICUM
CORSICA
SARDINIA
BALEARIC ISLANDS
Durius
Iberus
Numantia
HITHER SPAIN
Tagus
(Ebro)
(Guadiana)
Anas
FARTHER SPAIN
Saguntum
Italica
Gades
Munda
Strait of Gibraltar
New Carthage
Mediterranean
Tyrrhenian Sea
Mylae
Messana
Lilybaeum
SICILY
Agrigentum
Gela
Syracuse
Cirta
Utica
Carthage
Zama
Thapsus
AFRICA
NUMIDIA
MAURETANIA
ATLAS MTS.

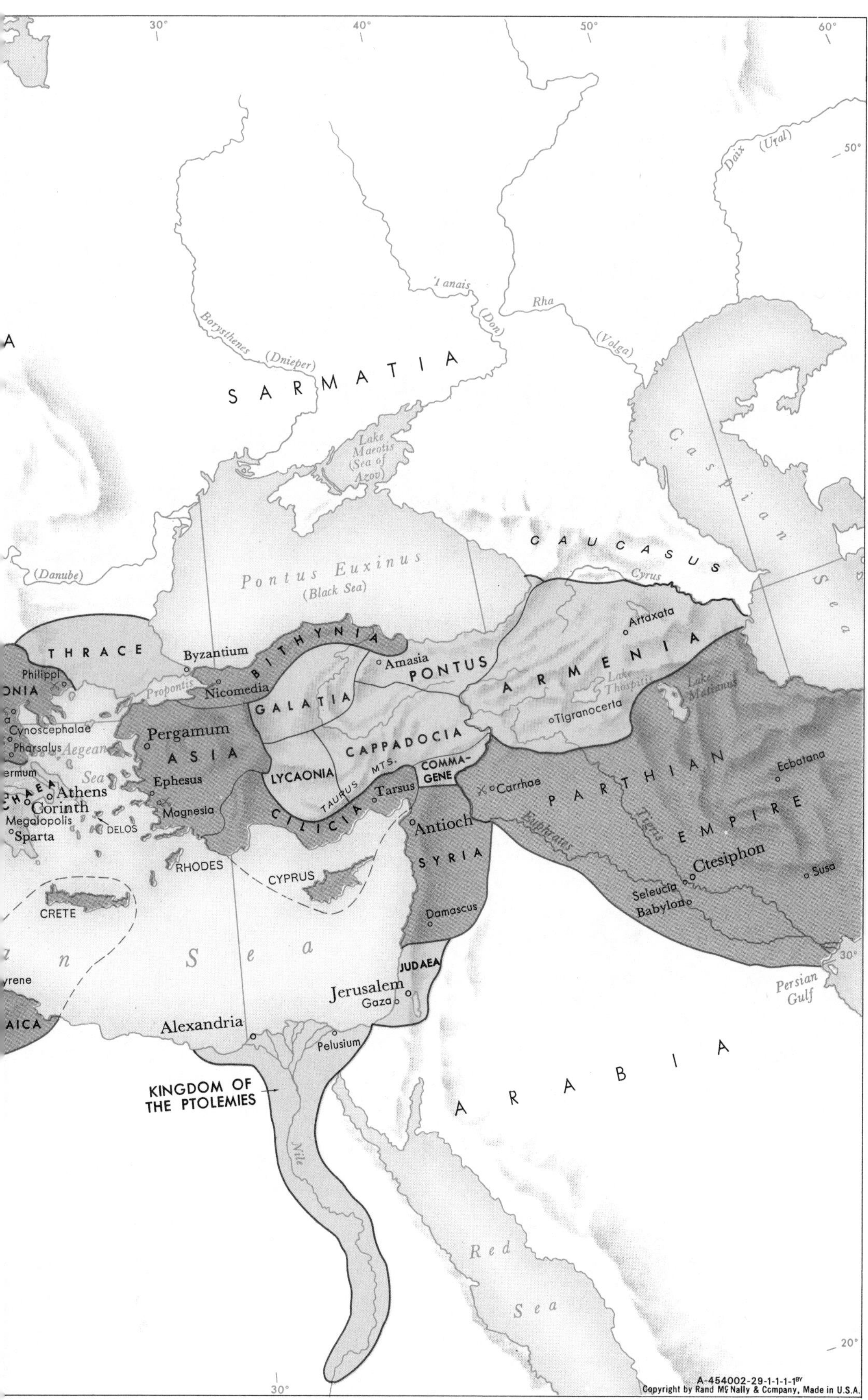

SARMATIA
Borysthenes (Dnieper)
Tanais (Don)
Rha (Volga)
Daix (Ural)
Lake Maeotis (Sea of Azov)
Caspian Sea
CAUCASUS
Cyrus
Pontus Euxinus (Black Sea)
(Danube)
THRACE
Byzantium
BITHYNIA
Nicomedia
Propontis
Amasia
PONTUS
ARMENIA
Artaxata
Lake Thospitis
Lake Matianus
Tigranocerta
GALATIA
CAPPADOCIA
LYCAONIA
TAURUS MTS.
COMMAGENE
CILICIA
Tarsus
Pergamum
ASIA
Ephesus
Magnesia
Philippi
Cynoscephalae
Pharsalus
Aegean Sea
Athens
Corinth
Megalopolis
Sparta
DELOS
RHODES
CYPRUS
CRETE
Carrhae
PARTHIAN EMPIRE
Euphrates
Tigris
Ecbatana
Ctesiphon
Seleucia
Babylon
Susa
Antioch
SYRIA
Damascus
JUDAEA
Jerusalem
Gaza
Alexandria
Pelusium
KINGDOM OF THE PTOLEMIES
Nile
ARABIA
Red Sea
Persian Gulf
30°
40°
50°
60°
50°
30°
20°
30°
A-454002-29-1-1-1-1BY
Copyright by Rand McNally & Company, Made in U.S.A.

North Sea
Atlantic Ocean
Bay of Biscay
Mediterranean
Tyrrhenian Sea
PICTS
SCOTIA
SCANDIA
DIOCESE OF BRITAIN
DIOCESE OF GAUL
DIOCESE OF SPAIN
DIOCESE OF ITALY
DIOCESE OF ROME
DIOCESE OF AFRICA
York
Chester
Lincoln
Caerleon
St. Albans
Colchester
London
Tournay
Cologne
Cambray
Soissons
Rouen
Reims
Treves
Mainz
Paris
Metz
Chalons
Orleans
Tours
Poitiers
Autun
Bordeaux
Lyon
Milan
Pavia
Aquileia
Salzburg
Genoa
Bologna
Ravenna
Ancona
Pisa
Spoleto
Rome
Naples
Toulouse
Arles
Narbonne
Pamplona
Braga
Saragossa
Barcelona
Tarragona
Tortosa
Lisbon
Toledo
Merida
Valencia
Seville
Cadiz
Cartagena
Ceuta
Hippo Regius
Carthage
Tripoli
Palermo
Syracuse
CORSICA
SARDINIA
BALEARIC ISLANDS
PYRENEES
ALPS
Rhine
Weser
Elbe
Oder
Danube
Seine
Loire
Garonne
Rhone
Duero
Ebro
Tagus
Guadiana
Guadalquivir
VISIGOTHS
OSTROGOTHS
ANGLO-SAXONS
FRANKS
BURGUNDIANS
HUNS
VANDALS
547
367-550
C. 450
C. 500
C. 449
358
486
507
443
451
452
412-507
415
409-429
429
568
489
410
455
Routes of the Barbarians
Huns
Visigoths
Vandals
Franks
Lombards
Ostrogoths
Burgundians
Anglo-Saxons
375 – date people passed through region
200-375 – stop in region
507 – final occupation of region

ROMAN EMPIRE ABOUT 400 A.D.
and The Barbarian Invasions
MILES 0 50 100 200 300 400 500
Prefecture of Gaul
Prefecture of Illyricum
Prefecture of Italy
Prefecture of the East
SLAVS
HUNS
100-372
375
150 A.D.
CARPATHIANS
200-375
200-375
340-481
OSTROGOTHS
CHAZARS
CAUCASUS
Caspian Sea
Volga
Don
Dnieper
Dniester
Bug
Vistula
Danube
Cherson
Black Sea
Odessus
DIOCESE OF DACIA
Naissus
DIOCESE OF THRACE
Nicopolis
Philippopolis
Adrianople
DIOCESE OF MACEDONIA
Dyrrhachium
376-395
Constantinople
Propontis
Thessalonica
Heraclea
Nicomedia
Nicaea
Trebizond
ARMENIA
DIOCESE OF PONTUS
Caesarea
SASSANIAN OR NEW PERSIAN EMPIRE
Tigris
Euphrates
Edessa
Dura
Aegean Sea
LESBOS
CHIOS
ANDROS
SAMOS
Pergamum
Smyrna
Ephesus
Antiochia
DIOCESE OF ASIA
Athens
Corinth
Antioch
Apamea
Emesa
DIOCESE OF THE EAST
RHODES
CYPRUS
Damascus
Tyre
Caesarea
Jerusalem
CRETE
Sea
Cyrene
Berenice
Alexandria
DIOCESE OF EGYPT
Memphis
Nile
Red Sea
40° 50° 50° 40° 30° 20° 30° 40°

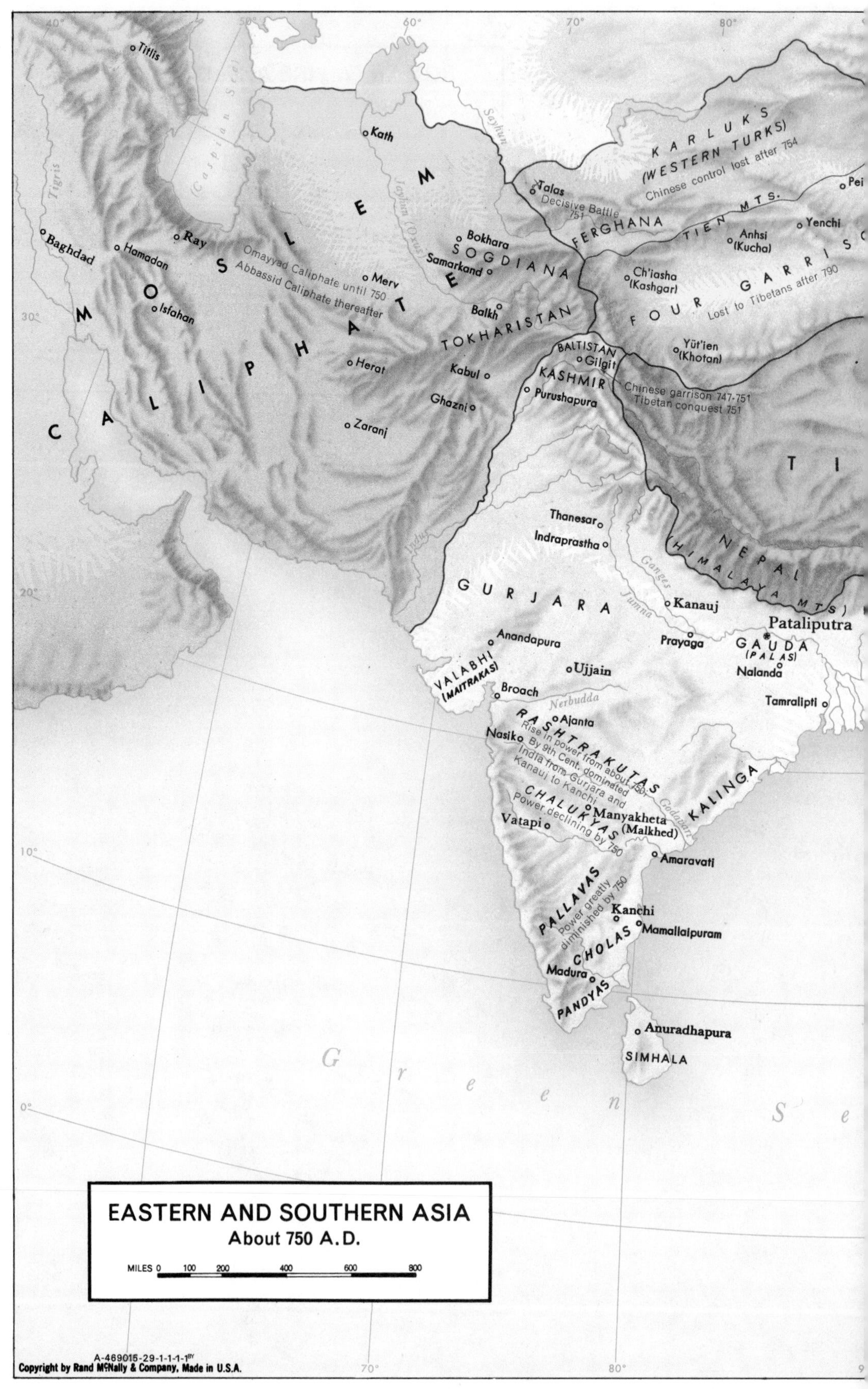
EASTERN AND SOUTHERN ASIA
About 750 A.D.
MILES 0 100 200 400 600 800
MOSLEM CALIPHATE
Omayyad Caliphate until 750
Abbassid Caliphate thereafter
Tiflis
Baghdad
Hamadan
Ray
Isfahan
Merv
Herat
Zaranj
Kath
Bokhara
Samarkand
SOGDIANA
Balkh
TOKHARISTAN
Kabul
Ghazni
Talas
Decisive Battle 751
FERGHANA
KARLUKS (WESTERN TURKS)
Chinese control lost after 754
TIEN MTS.
Pei
Yenchi
Anhsi (Kucha)
Ch'iasha (Kashgar)
FOUR GARRISONS
Lost to Tibetans after 790
Yüt'ien (Khotan)
BALTISTAN
Gilgit
KASHMIR
Purushapura
Chinese garrison 747-751
Tibetan conquest 751
NEPAL
HIMALAYA MTS.
Thanesar
Indraprastha
GURJARA
Kanauj
Prayaga
Pataliputra
GAUDA (PALAS)
Nalanda
Tamralipti
Anandapura
VALABHI (MAITRAKAS)
Ujjain
Broach
Nerbudda
Ajanta
Nasik
RASHTRAKUTAS
Rise in power from about 750
By 9th Cent. dominated India from Gurjara and Kanauj to Kanchi
CHALUKYAS
Power declining by 750
Manyakheta (Malkhed)
Vatapi
KALINGA
Godavari
Amaravati
PALLAVAS
Power greatly diminished by 750
Kanchi
Mamallaipuram
CHOLAS
Madura
PANDYAS
Anuradhapura
SIMHALA
Tigris
Caspian Sea
Jayhun (Oxus)
Sayhun
Indus
Ganges
Jumna
Green Se

Uighur Capital
UIGHURS (EASTERN TURKS)
(GOBI DESERT)
KHITANS
P'O HAI
Capital
Liaotung
SILLA
Hanchow
Capital
JAPAN
Heian
Nara
Capital from 794
Capital from 710-784
Great Wall
Tunhuang
T'UYÜHUNS
LUNG YU
Shan
KUANNEI
HO TUNG
T'aiyüan
HOPEI
Weichow
Yün
HONAN
Loyang
TUCHI
Pien
Sung
Grand Canal
Yangchow
Eastern Sea
CHINGCHI
Ch'angan
SHANNAN HSI
SHANNAN TUNG
HUAINAN
Hsüan
Soochow
Yüeh
Hangchow
Chiangling
CHINA
Ch'engtu
CHIENNAN
CH'IENCHUNG
CHIANGNAN HSI
CHIANGNAN TUNG
Ch'üanchow
LINGNAN
Kwangchow
Tali
NAN CHAO (T'AI)
Southern Sea
ANNAM
Chiaochow
(HAINAN)
PYU
MONS
Thaton
UPPER (LAND) CHENLA
CHAMPA
Amaravati
LOWER (MARITIME) CHENLA
KAUTHARA
Virapura
PANDURANGA
DVARAVATI
TAMBRALINGA
LANGKASUKA
KEDAH
(SUMATRA)
(BORNEO)
Malayu
BANKA
SRIVIJAYA
Srivijaya
(JAVA)
SAILENDRAS
Borobodur Built 772?
TARUMA
MATARAM
The Srivijayan Empire, perhaps under a Sailendran ruler, probably included more of Sumatra and Java and even portions of the Malay peninsula and Borneo by the end of the 8th Century

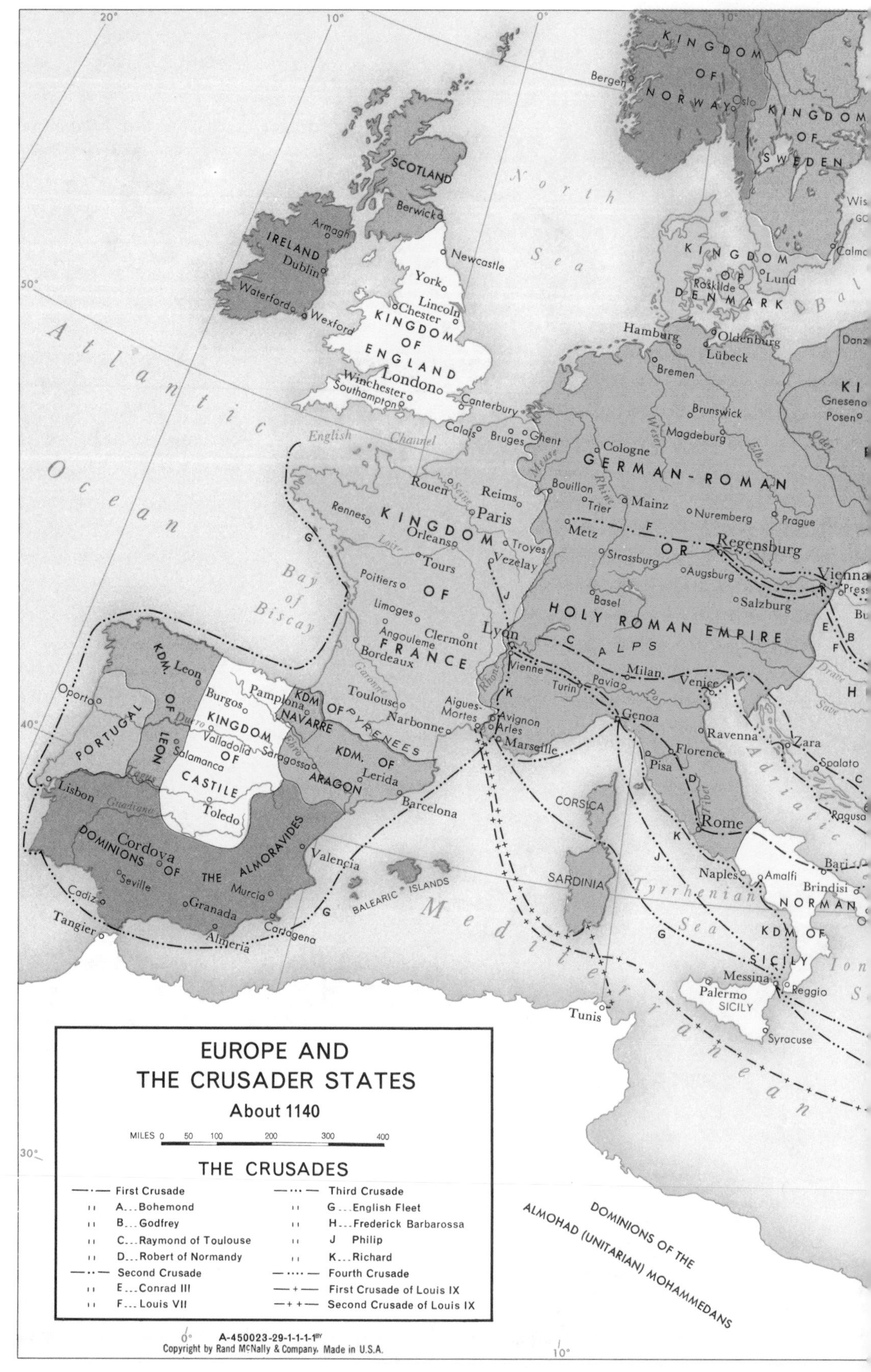
EUROPE AND
THE CRUSADER STATES
About 1140
MILES 0 50 100 200 300 400
THE CRUSADES
First Crusade
A...Bohemond
B...Godfrey
C...Raymond of Toulouse
D...Robert of Normandy
Second Crusade
E...Conrad III
F...Louis VII
Third Crusade
G...English Fleet
H...Frederick Barbarossa
J Philip
K...Richard
Fourth Crusade
First Crusade of Louis IX
Second Crusade of Louis IX
KINGDOM OF NORWAY
KINGDOM OF SWEDEN
KINGDOM OF DENMARK
SCOTLAND
IRELAND
KINGDOM OF ENGLAND
KINGDOM OF FRANCE
GERMAN-ROMAN OR HOLY ROMAN EMPIRE
KDM. OF LEON
PORTUGAL
KINGDOM OF CASTILE
KDM OF NAVARRE
KDM. OF ARAGON
DOMINIONS OF THE ALMORAVIDES
DOMINIONS OF THE ALMOHAD (UNITARIAN) MOHAMMEDANS
NORMAN KDM. OF SICILY
North Sea
Atlantic Ocean
Bay of Biscay
English Channel
Mediterranean
Tyrrhenian Sea
Adriatic
ALPS
PYRENEES
CORSICA
SARDINIA
SICILY
BALEARIC ISLANDS
Bergen
Oslo
Berwick
Armagh
Dublin
Waterford
Wexford
Newcastle
York
Lincoln
Chester
London
Winchester
Southampton
Canterbury
Calais
Bruges
Ghent
Roskilde
Lund
Hamburg
Oldenburg
Lübeck
Bremen
Brunswick
Magdeburg
Gneseno
Posen
Cologne
Bouillon
Trier
Mainz
Nuremberg
Prague
Metz
Regensburg
Strassburg
Augsburg
Vienna
Basel
Salzburg
Rouen
Reims
Paris
Rennes
Orleans
Troyes
Vezelay
Tours
Poitiers
Limoges
Clermont
Angouleme
Bordeaux
Lyon
Vienne
Milan
Pavia
Turin
Venice
Genoa
Toulouse
Narbonne
Aigues-Mortes
Avignon
Arles
Marseille
Ravenna
Zara
Spalato
Florence
Pisa
Rome
Ragusa
Leon
Burgos
Pamplona
Oporto
Valladolid
Saragossa
Salamanca
Lerida
Barcelona
Lisbon
Toledo
Cordova
Valencia
Seville
Murcia
Cadiz
Granada
Cartagena
Almeria
Tangier
Tunis
Naples
Amalfi
Bari
Brindisi
Messina
Reggio
Palermo
Syracuse
Loire
Seine
Meuse
Rhine
Weser
Elbe
Oder
Garonne
Rhone
Po
Tiber
Ebro
Duero
Tagus
Guadiana
Drave
Save
A-450023-29-1-1-1-1BY
Copyright by Rand McNally & Company. Made in U.S.A.

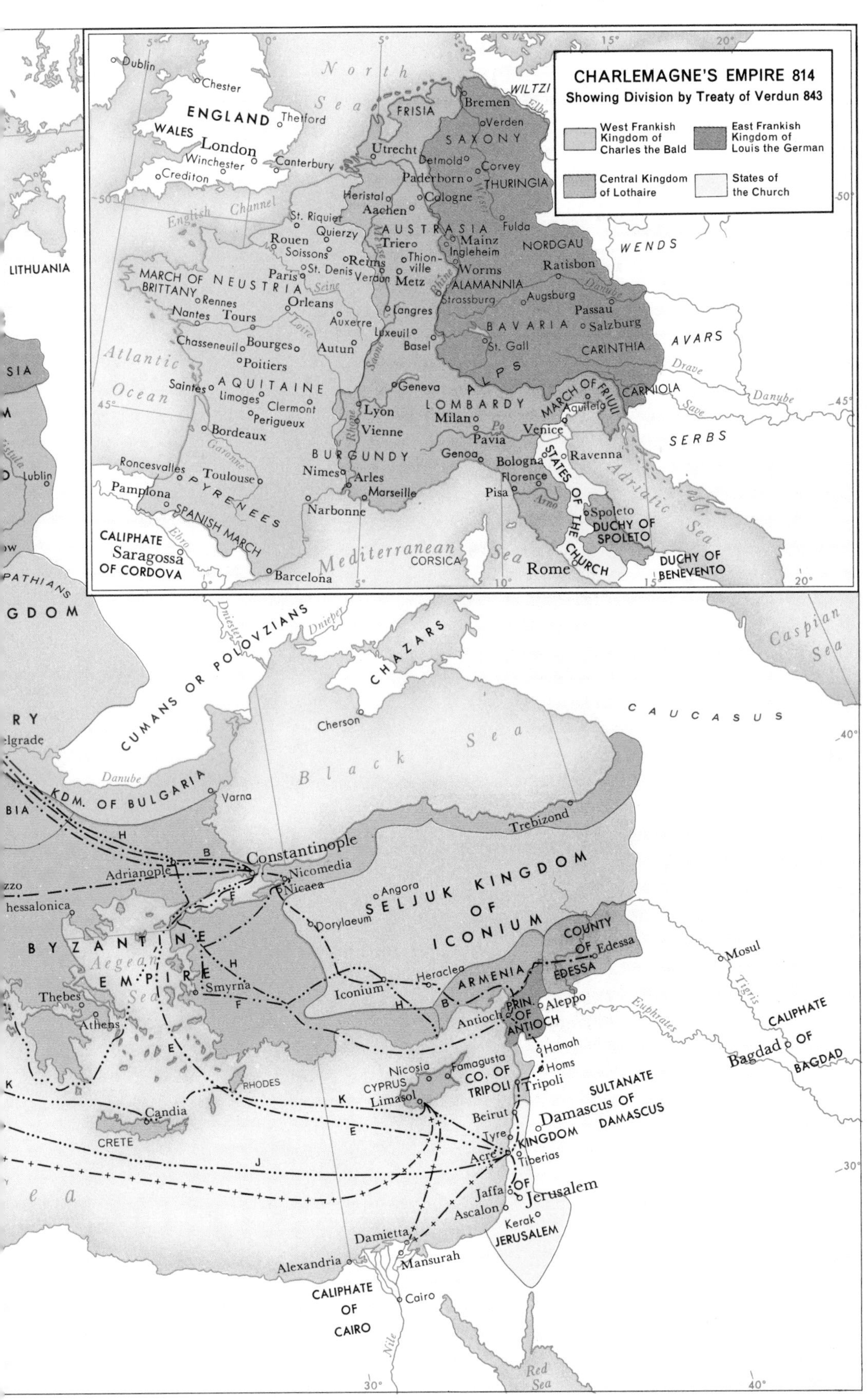
CHARLEMAGNE'S EMPIRE 814
Showing Division by Treaty of Verdun 843
West Frankish Kingdom of Charles the Bald
East Frankish Kingdom of Louis the German
Central Kingdom of Lothaire
States of the Church
ENGLAND
WALES
London
FRISIA
SAXONY
THURINGIA
AUSTRASIA
NEUSTRIA
AQUITAINE
BURGUNDY
LOMBARDY
BAVARIA
ALAMANNIA
NORDGAU
CARINTHIA
AVARS
WENDS
SERBS
CALIPHATE OF CORDOVA
SPANISH MARCH
DUCHY OF SPOLETO
DUCHY OF BENEVENTO
Mediterranean Sea
Adriatic Sea
Atlantic Ocean
North Sea
Black Sea
Caspian Sea
CAUCASUS
CUMANS OR POLOVZIANS
CHAZARS
KDM. OF BULGARIA
Constantinople
SELJUK KINGDOM OF ICONIUM
BYZANTINE EMPIRE
COUNTY OF EDESSA
ARMENIA
PRIN. OF ANTIOCH
CO. OF TRIPOLI
KINGDOM OF JERUSALEM
SULTANATE OF DAMASCUS
CALIPHATE OF BAGDAD
CALIPHATE OF CAIRO
CYPRUS
CRETE
RHODES
Red Sea

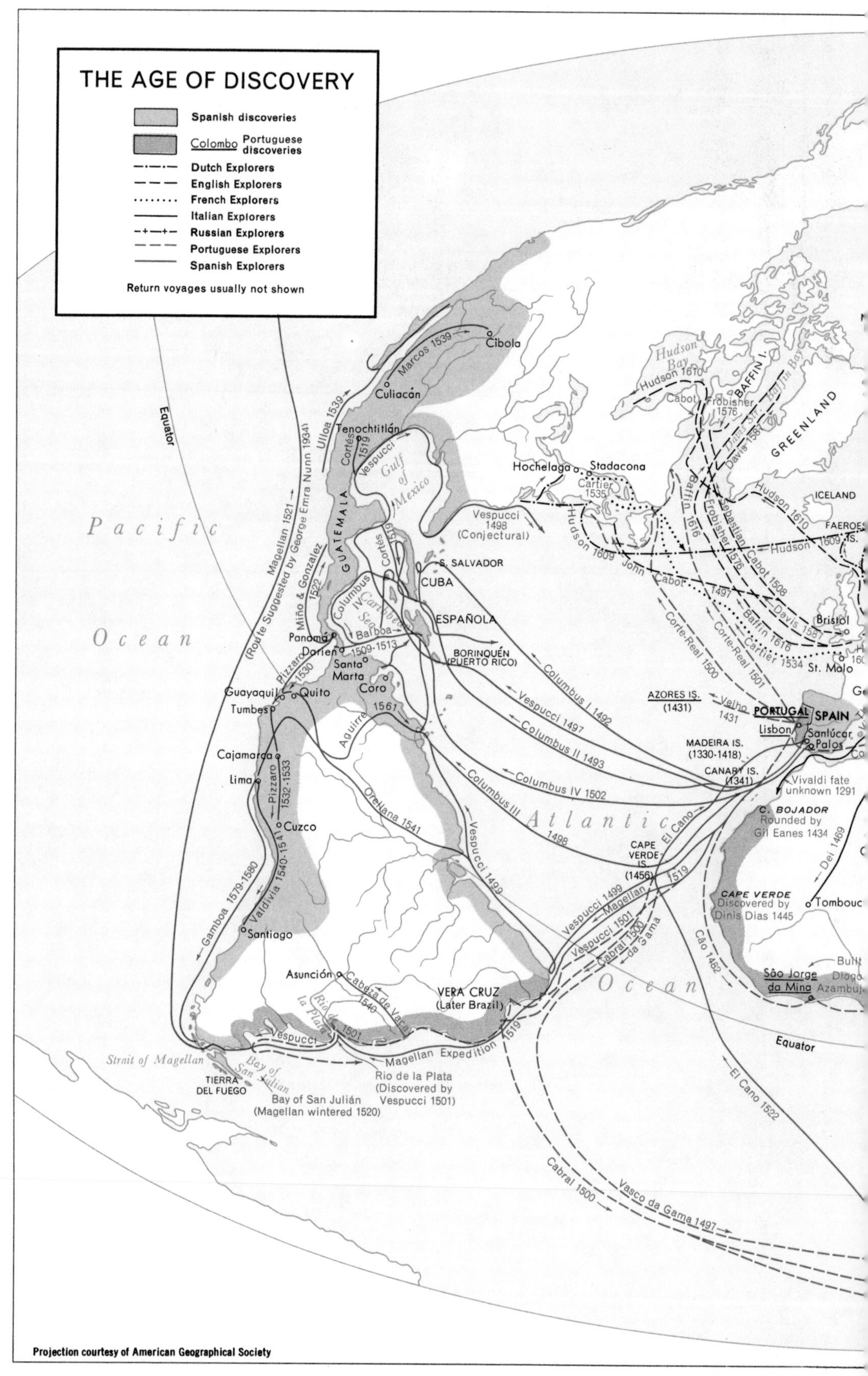
THE AGE OF DISCOVERY
Spanish discoveries
Colombo Portuguese discoveries
Dutch Explorers
English Explorers
French Explorers
Italian Explorers
Russian Explorers
Portuguese Explorers
Spanish Explorers
Return voyages usually not shown
Pacific
Ocean
Atlantic
Ocean
Equator
Gulf of Mexico
Caribbean Sea
Hudson Bay
GREENLAND
ICELAND
FAEROES
BAFFIN I.
Cibola
Culiacán
Tenochtitlán
GUATEMALA
S. SALVADOR
CUBA
ESPAÑOLA
BORINQUÉN (PUERTO RICO)
Panamá
Darien
Santa Marta
Coro
Guayaquil
Quito
Tumbes
Cajamarca
Lima
Cuzco
Santiago
Asunción
VERA CRUZ (Later Brazil)
Strait of Magellan
TIERRA DEL FUEGO
Bay of San Julián (Magellan wintered 1520)
Rio de la Plata (Discovered by Vespucci 1501)
Hochelaga
Stadacona
Bristol
St. Malo
AZORES IS. (1431)
PORTUGAL
SPAIN
Lisbon
Sanlúcar
Palos
MADEIRA IS. (1330-1418)
CANARY IS. (1341)
Vivaldi fate unknown 1291
C. BOJADOR Rounded by Gil Eanes 1434
CAPE VERDE IS. (1456)
CAPE VERDE Discovered by Dinis Dias 1445
Tombouc
São Jorge da Mina
Marcos 1539
Ulloa 1539
Cortés 1519
Vespucci
Magellan 1521
(Route Suggested by George Emra Nunn 1934)
Miño & Gonzalez 1522
Columbus IV
Balboa 1509-1513
Pizzaro 1530
Aguirre 1561
Pizzaro 1532-1533
Valdivia 1540-1541
Gamboa 1579-1580
Orellana 1541
Cabeza de Vaca 1540
Vespucci 1501
Magellan Expedition 1519
Vespucci 1498 (Conjectural)
Cartier 1535
Hudson 1609
Hudson 1610
John Cabot 1497
Cabot
Frobisher 1576
Davis 1585
Baffin 1616
Sebastian Cabot 1508
Cartier 1534
Corte-Real 1500
Corte-Real 1501
Columbus I 1492
Vespucci 1497
Columbus II 1493
Columbus IV 1502
Columbus III 1498
Vespucci 1499
Velho 1431
El Cano
Magellan 1519
Vespucci 1501
Cabral 1500
da Gama
Cão 1482
Dei 1469
El Cano 1522
Cabral 1500
Vasco da Gama 1497
Projection courtesy of American Geographical Society

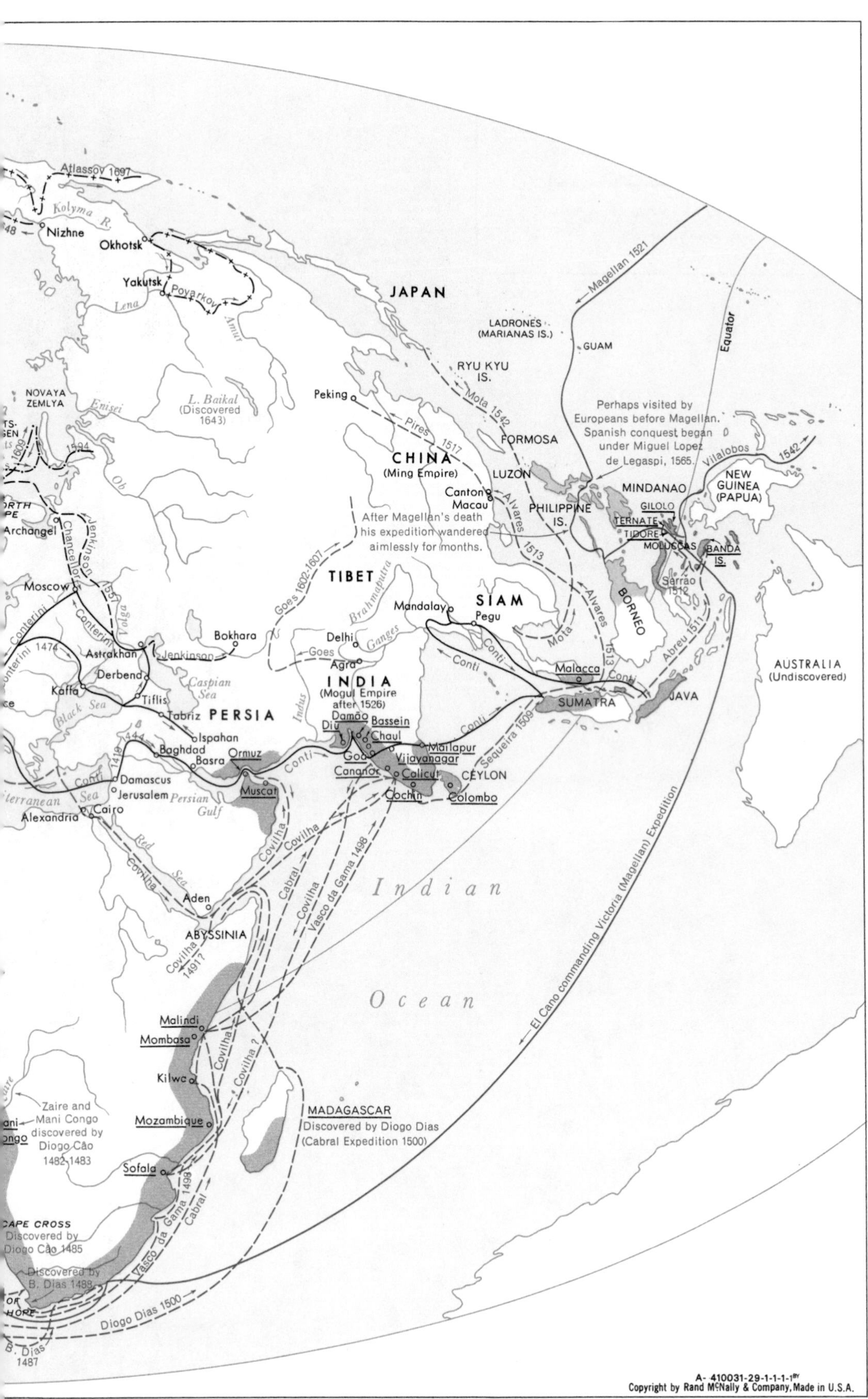
Atlassov 1697
Kolyma R.
Nizhne
Okhotsk
Yakutsk
Poyarkov
Lena
Amur
JAPAN
Magellan 1521
LADRONES
(MARIANAS IS.)
GUAM
Equator
RYU KYU
IS.
NOVAYA
ZEMLYA
Enisei
L. Baikal
(Discovered
1643)
Peking
Pires 1517
Mota 1542
FORMOSA
Perhaps visited by
Europeans before Magellan.
Spanish conquest began
under Miguel Lopez
de Legaspi, 1565.
Vilalobos
1542
1609
1594
Ob
CHINA
(Ming Empire)
LUZON
MINDANAO
NEW
GUINEA
(PAPUA)
Canton
Macau
Alvares
PHILIPPINE
IS.
GILOLO
TERNATE
TIDORE
MOLUCCAS
BANDA
IS.
Archangel
Jenkinson
Chancellor
After Magellan's death
his expedition wandered
aimlessly for months.
1513
Moscow
1557
Volga
Goes 1602-1607
TIBET
Brahmaputra
Mandalay
SIAM
Pegu
Serrao
1512
BORNEO
Conterini
Conterini 1474
Bokhara
Astrakhan
Jenkinson
Delhi
Goes
Ganges
Agra
Mota
Alvares
1513
Abreu 1511
Conti
AUSTRALIA
(Undiscovered)
Derbend
Caspian
Sea
INDIA
(Mogul Empire
after 1526)
Malacca
Kaffa
Tiflis
Black Sea
Tabriz
PERSIA
Indus
Damão
Diu
Bassein
Chaul
SUMATRA
JAVA
Ispahan
1444
Baghdad
Basra
Ormuz
Goa
Mailapur
Vijayanagar
Sequeira 1509
1419
Damascus
Jerusalem
Conti
Sea
Persian
Gulf
Muscat
Cananor
Calicut
CEYLON
Cairo
Alexandria
Cochin
Colombo
Red
Sea
Covilha
Cabral
Vasco da Gama 1498
Indian
El Cano commanding Victoria (Magellan) Expedition
Aden
ABYSSINIA
Covilha 1491?
Ocean
Malindi
Mombasa
Covilha ?
Kilwa
Zaire and
Mani Congo
discovered by
Diogo Cão
1482-1483
Mozambique
MADAGASCAR
Discovered by Diogo Dias
(Cabral Expedition 1500)
Sofala
Vasco da Gama 1499
CAPE CROSS
Discovered by
Diogo Cão 1485
Discovered by
B. Dias 1488
Diogo Dias 1500
B. Dias
1487
A- 410031-29-1-1-1-1
Copyright by Rand McNally & Company, Made in U.S.A.

EUROPE IN 1721
After the treaty of Utrecht, 1713, and Associated Treaties
Miles 0 50 100 200 300
Boundary of Holy Roman Empire
× × Dutch Barrier Forts
SHETLAND ISLANDS
ORKNEY ISLANDS
HEBRIDES
SCOTLAND
Aberdeen
KINGDOM OF GREAT BRITAIN
Edinburgh
Glasgow
Belfast
IRELAND
Dublin
York
Liverpool
Cork
Nottingham
WALES
ENGLAND
Norwich
Cambridge
Oxford
Bristol
London
Thames
Plymouth
Portsmouth
BEACHY HEAD
North Sea
Atlantic Ocean
Bergen
Stavanger
(To Hanover 17
THE UNITED NETHERLANDS
Amsterdam
The Hague
Utrecht
Ryswick
Dunkirk
Antwerp
Neerwinden
Aachen
Oudenarde
Ramillies
Lille
Fontenoy
Malplaquet
AUSTRIAN NETHERLANDS (1714)
English Channel
LA HOGUE
Rouen
Reims
Brest
St. Malo
Paris
Seine
Nancy
LORRAINE
Strassburg
Lorient
Orléans
Loire
Nantes
Tours
Besançon
Basel
FRANCE
Bay of Biscay
Rochefort
Limoges
Angoulême
Lyon
Geneva
SAVOY
Turin
Bordeaux
Garonne
Rhone
CAPE FINISTERRE
Bayonne
Toulouse
Montpellier
Avignon
(To the Pope)
Marseille
Toulon
PYRENEES
Oporto
Valladolid
Burgos
Ebro
Duero
CATALONIA
Saragossa
Barcelona
PORTUGAL
Tagus
Madrid
SPAIN
Alcantara
Toledo
(To Bourbons, 1713)
Valencia
Lisbon
Guadiana
Guadalquivir
BALEARIC ISLANDS
MAJORCA
MINORCA
(To Great Britain 1713)
SARDINIA
(To Hapsburgs 17
(To Savoy 1720)
CORS
CAPE ST. VINCENT
Seville
Granada
Cartagena
Cadiz
CAPE TRAFALGAR
Gibraltar
(To Great Britain 1713)
Algiers
Medit
20°
10°
0°
50°
40°

KINGDOM OF SWEDEN
FINLAND
Nystad
Abo
Helsingfors
Viborg
KARELIA
L. Ladoga
St. Petersburg
INGRIA
Narva
Gulf of Finland
Novgorod
Uppsala
Stockholm
ESTONIA
LIVONIA
(To Russia 1721)
Riga
Moscow
GOTLAND
COURLAND
RUSSIAN EMPIRE
Dvina
Calmar
Baltic Sea
Memel
LITHUANIA
Vitebsk
Smolensk
Niemen
Vilna
Minsk
Copenhagen
Lund
Königsberg
PRUSSIA
Grodno
(To Prussia 1720)
Danzig
Dnieper
Hamburg
Stettin
Prussia
Thorn
POLAND
BRANDENBURG
Elbe
Zorndorf
Posen
Warsaw
Vistula
Kiev
Kharkov
Poltava
Hanover
Berlin
Oder
Lublin
SAXONY
Glogau
Breslau
Cassel
Leipzig
Dresden
SILESIA
HOLY ROMAN EMPIRE
Lemberg
Bar
Targovitza
Cracow
Bug
Dniester
Prague
BOHEMIA
MORAVIA
Czernowitz
Prut
Cherson
AUSTRIA
KINGDOM OF HUNGARY
MOLDAVIA
BAVARIA
Munich
Vienna
Danube
Buda
Pest
Theiss
BESSARABIA
CRIMEA
Salzburg
Innsbruck
TRANSYLVANIA
Drave
TYROL
Temesvar
Zenta
BANAT
(To Hapsburgs 1718)
WALLACHIA
Bucharest
Black Sea
Laibach
Agram
Trieste
Karlowitz
CROATIA
SLAVONIA
Silistria
Verona
Venice
Po
REPUBLIC OF VENICE
Belgrade
Passarowitz
(To Hapsburgs 1718-1739)
Danube
Modena
Bologna
BOSNIA
Sarajevo
BULGARIA
SERBIA
Nish
Sofia
Florence
TUSCANY
PAPAL STATES
Tolentino
Adriatic Sea
Ragusa
MONTENEGRO
OTTOMAN EMPIRE
Adrianople
Constantinople
Tiber
Rome
KINGDOM OF NAPLES
(To Hapsburgs 1714-1735)
Bari
Salonika
Naples
Otranto
Tyrrhenian Sea
CORFU (CORCYRA)
Aegean Sea
Smyrna
Athens
MOREA
(To Ottoman Empire 1718)
Palermo
Reggio
Syracuse
SICILY
(To Savoy 1714)
(To Hapsburgs 1720-35)
Mediterranean Sea
CRETE
20°
30°
40°
50°
10°
A-450035-29-1-2-1-1
Copyright by Rand McNally & Company, Made in U.S.A.

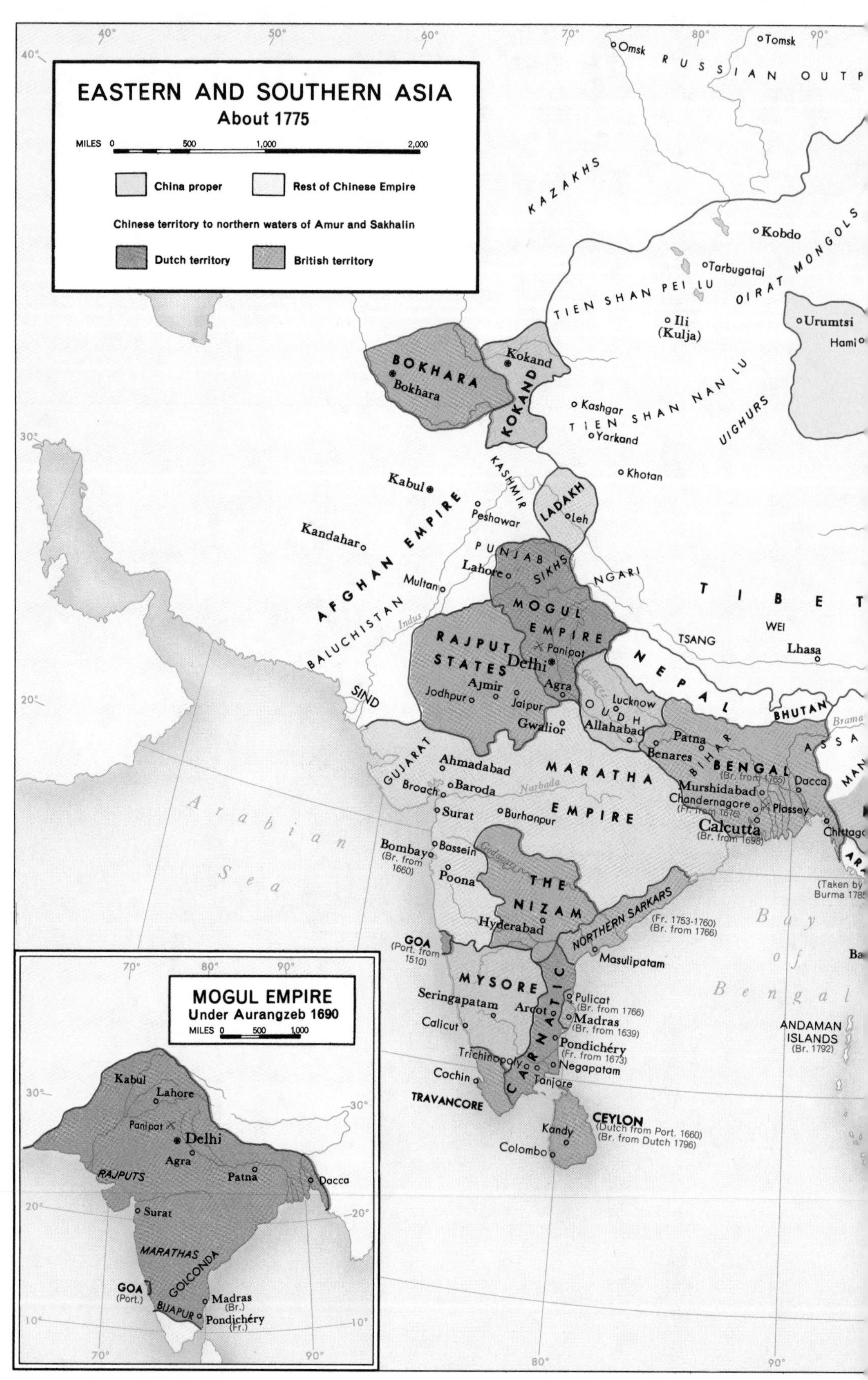
EASTERN AND SOUTHERN ASIA
About 1775
MILES 0 500 1,000 2,000
China proper
Rest of Chinese Empire
Chinese territory to northern waters of Amur and Sakhalin
Dutch territory
British territory
RUSSIAN OUTP
Omsk
Tomsk
KAZAKHS
Kobdo
OIRAT MONGOLS
Tarbugatai
TIEN SHAN PEI LU
Ili (Kulja)
Urumtsi
Hami
BOKHARA
Bokhara
Kokand
KOKAND
Kashgar
TIEN SHAN NAN LU
Yarkand
UIGHURS
Khotan
KASHMIR
Kabul
LADAKH
Leh
Peshawar
Kandahar
AFGHAN EMPIRE
PUNJAB
Lahore
SIKHS
NGARI
TIBET
Multan
BALUCHISTAN
Indus
MOGUL EMPIRE
Panipat
Delhi
RAJPUT STATES
Ajmir
Jodhpur
Jaipur
Agra
TSANG
WEI
Lhasa
NEPAL
BHUTAN
SIND
Ganges
Lucknow
OUDH
Allahabad
Gwalior
Patna
Benares
BIHAR
BENGAL
(Br. from 1765)
Dacca
ASSAM
Brama
GUJARAT
Ahmadabad
Broach
Baroda
Narbada
MARATHA EMPIRE
Murshidabad
Chandernagore (Fr. from 1676)
Plassey
Surat
Burhanpur
Calcutta (Br. from 1698)
Chittago
Arabian Sea
Bombay (Br. from 1660)
Bassein
Godavari
Poona
THE NIZAM
Hyderabad
(Taken by Burma 1785)
NORTHERN SARKARS
(Fr. 1753-1760) (Br. from 1766)
Bay of Bengal
GOA (Port. from 1510)
Masulipatam
MYSORE
Seringapatam
Arcot
Pulicat (Br. from 1766)
Madras (Br. from 1639)
Calicut
CARNATIC
Pondichéry (Fr. from 1673)
Trichinopoly
Negapatam
Tanjore
Cochin
TRAVANCORE
ANDAMAN ISLANDS (Br. 1792)
CEYLON (Dutch from Port. 1660) (Br. from Dutch 1796)
Kandy
Colombo
MOGUL EMPIRE
Under Aurangzeb 1690
MILES 0 500 1,000
Kabul
Lahore
Panipat
Delhi
Agra
RAJPUTS
Patna
Dacca
Surat
MARATHAS
GOLCONDA
GOA (Port.)
Madras (Br.)
BIJAPUR
Pondichéry (Fr.)

Nerchinsk
Irkutsk
BURIAT MONGOLS
Kiakhta
Tsitsihar
MANCHURIA
Urga
Kirin
MANCHUS
FORTY NINE MONGOL BANNERS OF INNER MONGOLIA
KHALKHA MONGOLS
TORGUT MONGOLS
CHAHAR MONGOLS
Jehol
Shengching (Mukden)
Kalgan
Peking
Great Wall
Paoting
CHIHLI
Taiyüan
SHANSI
KANSU
Tsinan
SHANTUNG
Grand Canal
KIANGSU
Lanchow
SHENSI
Sian
Kaifeng
HONAN
ANWEI
Chiangning
Hangchow
Anking
HUPEH
Wuchang
Chengtu
SZECHWAN
Yangtze
Nanchang
CHEKIANG
KIANGSI
Changsha
HUNAN
FUKIEN
Foochow
Kweiyang
KWEICHOW
Kweilin
Yünnan
YUNNAN
KWANGSI
KWANGTUNG
Kwangchow (Canton)
Macao (Port. trading post from 1557)
Bhamo
KOREA
Seoul
JAPAN
YEZO
HONSHU
Yedo
Kyoto
Osaka
Sakai
SHIKOKU
KYUSHU
Nagasaki (Dutch trading post of Deshima from 1641)
LIUCHIU
Pacific Ocean
Zelandia Castel (Dutch, 1624-1662)
FORMOSA
TONGKING
Hanoi
Luang Prabang
Thanh Hoa
(Tongking, Annam and Cochin-China formed Vietnam Empire 1802)
China Sea
Chiengsen
Toungoo
Chiengmai
Vientiane
(Laos states of Luang Prabang and Vientiane, under Siamese Suzerainty from 1778)
Sukhotai
SIAM
Martaban
Lopburi
Ayuthia (Destroyed by Burmese in 1767)
Tavoy
Bangkok (Built 1780's)
Mergui
ANNAM
Hué
Mekong
Siemreap
CAMBODIA
Phnom Penh
COCHIN-CHINA
Saigon (Taken by Annam 1776)
Manila
PHILIPPINE ISLANDS (Spain)
Ligor
Patani
KEDAH
PERAK
PAHANG
Penang (Br. from 1786)
SELANGOR
SUMATRA
Malacca
JOHORE
(Dutch 1641-1795, 1818-1824) (Br. 1795-1818, since 1824)
RIAU ARCH (Center of Bugis power)
Siak
MINANGKABAU
Padang
Jambi
Palembang
BANGKA
BILLITON
BRUNEI
BORNEO
Succadana
Banjermassin
CELEBES
Macassar
Menado
HALMAHERA
MOLUCCAS
CERAM
Amboina
A-469036-29-1-1-1
Copyright by Rand McNally & Company, Made in U.S.A.

BRITISH NORTH AMERICA
UNITED STATES OF AMERICA
Atlantic Ocean
Tropic of Cancer
Gulf of Mexico
Caribbean Sea
Pacific
CAPTAINCY-GENERAL OF LOUISIANA
VICEROYALTY OF NEW SPAIN
INTENDANCY OF YUCATAN
CAPTAINCY-GENERAL OF CUBA
CAPTAINCY-GENERAL OF SANTO DOMINGO
Ceded to France 1795
PUERTO RICO
JAMAICA
Br. 1655
CAPTAINCY-GENERAL (AUDIENCIA) OF GUATEMALA
CAPTAINCY-GENERAL OF CARACAS
VICEROYALTY OF NEW GRANADA
Established 1717, Restored 1740
AUDIENCIA OF SANTA FÉ
PRESIDENCY (AUDIENCIA)
TRINIDAD
Ceded to Great Britain, 1802
DUTCH GUIANA
FRENCH GUIANA
GALAPAGOS IS.
Claimed by Spain, but unoccupied
Disputed by Spain, Russia, and England
Claimed by Spain, but unoccupied
Disputed with U.S. 1783-1795
WEST FLORIDA
EAST FLORIDA
INTENDANCY OF NUEVA CALIFORNIA
INTENDANCY OF VIEJA CALIFORNIA
WESTERN INTERIOR PROVINCES
EASTERN INTERIOR PROVINCES
INTENDANCY OF NUEVO MEXICO
INTENDANCY OF SONORA
INTENDANCY OF DURANGO
INTENDANCY OF SAN LUIS POTOSI
INTENDANCY OF ZACATECAS
INTENDANCY OF GUADALAJARA
INTENDANCY OF VALLADOLID
INTENDANCY OF MEXICO
INTENDANCY OF VERA CRUZ
INTENDANCY OF OAXACA
CHIAPAS
Mexico City
Habana
Santo Domingo 1496
Port au Prince 1749
San Juan 1511
Caracas 1567
Bogotá
Quito
Panama 1519
Cartagena 1533
New Orleans 1718
St. Augustine 1565
Pensacola 1698
St. Louis 1764
San Antonio 1718
Santa Fé 1609
San Francisco 1776
Los Angeles 1781
San Diego 1769
La Paz 1535
Stabroek (Georgetown)
Paramaribo 1640
Cayenne 1664
Belem

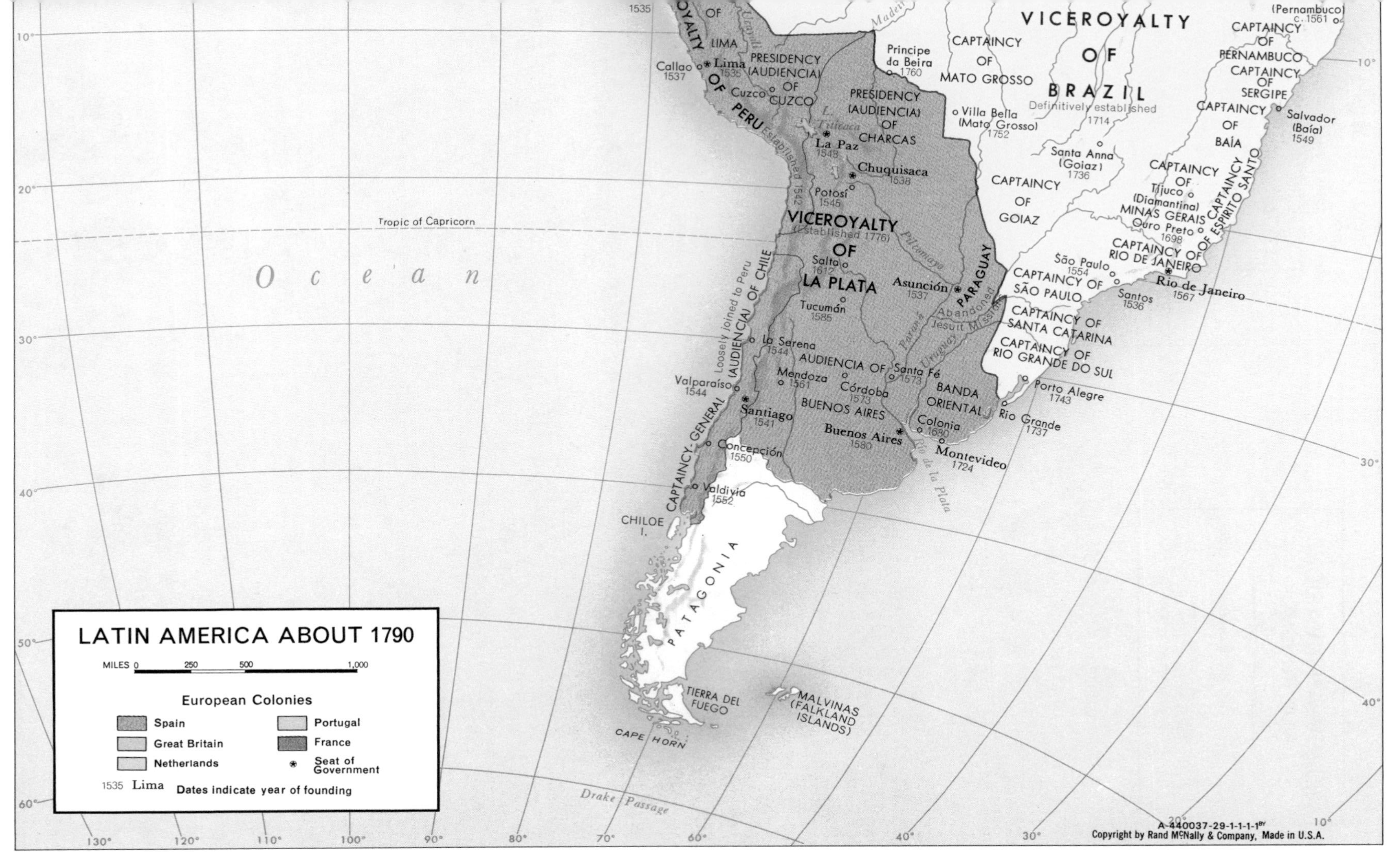
LATIN AMERICA ABOUT 1790
MILES 0 250 500 1,000
European Colonies
Spain
Great Britain
Netherlands
Portugal
France
Seat of Government
1535 Lima Dates indicate year of founding
VICEROYALTY OF BRAZIL
Definitively established 1714
CAPTAINCY OF MATO GROSSO
CAPTAINCY OF GOIAZ
CAPTAINCY OF PERNAMBUCO
(Pernambuco) c. 1561
CAPTAINCY OF SERGIPE
CAPTAINCY OF BAÍA
Salvador (Baía) 1549
CAPTAINCY OF ESPIRITO SANTO
CAPTAINCY OF MINAS GERAIS
Tijuco (Diamantina)
Ouro Preto 1698
CAPTAINCY OF RIO DE JANEIRO
Rio de Janeiro 1567
CAPTAINCY OF SÃO PAULO
São Paulo 1554
Santos 1536
CAPTAINCY OF SANTA CATARINA
CAPTAINCY OF RIO GRANDE DO SUL
Porto Alegre 1743
Rio Grande 1737
Principe da Beira 1760
Villa Bella (Mato Grosso) 1752
Santa Anna (Goiaz) 1736
VICEROYALTY OF PERU
Established 1542
LIMA
Lima 1535
Callao 1537
PRESIDENCY (AUDIENCIA) OF CUZCO
Cuzco
PRESIDENCY (AUDIENCIA) OF CHARCAS
L. Titicaca
La Paz 1548
Chuquisaca 1538
Potosí 1545
VICEROYALTY OF LA PLATA
(Established 1776)
Salta 1612
Tucumán 1585
Asunción 1537
PARAGUAY
Abandoned Jesuit Missions
Paraná
Uruguay
Pilcomayo
AUDIENCIA OF BUENOS AIRES
Santa Fé 1573
Córdoba 1573
Mendoza 1561
Buenos Aires 1580
BANDA ORIENTAL
Colonia 1680
Montevideo 1724
Río de la Plata
CAPTAINCY-GENERAL (AUDIENCIA) OF CHILE
Loosely joined to Peru
La Serena 1544
Valparaíso 1544
Santiago 1541
Concepción 1550
Valdivia 1552
CHILOE I.
PATAGONIA
TIERRA DEL FUEGO
CAPE HORN
MALVINAS (FALKLAND ISLANDS)
Drake Passage
Ocean
Tropic of Capricorn
A-440037-29-1-1-1
Copyright by Rand McNally & Company, Made in U.S.A.

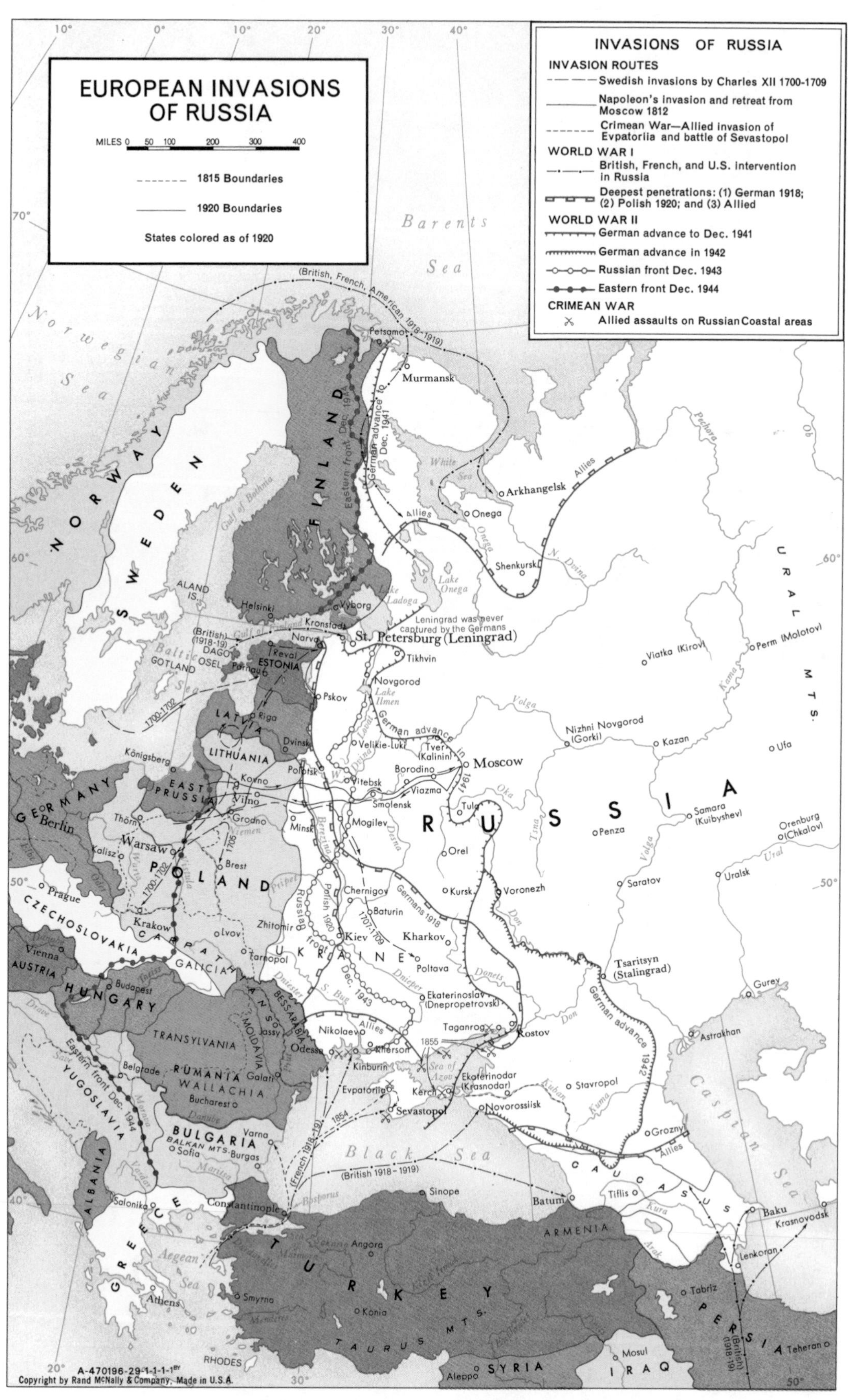
EUROPEAN INVASIONS OF RUSSIA
MILES 0 50 100 200 300 400
1815 Boundaries
1920 Boundaries
States colored as of 1920
INVASIONS OF RUSSIA
INVASION ROUTES
Swedish invasions by Charles XII 1700-1709
Napoleon's invasion and retreat from Moscow 1812
Crimean War—Allied invasion of Evpatoriia and battle of Sevastopol
WORLD WAR I
British, French, and U.S. intervention in Russia
Deepest penetrations: (1) German 1918; (2) Polish 1920; and (3) Allied
WORLD WAR II
German advance to Dec. 1941
German advance in 1942
Russian front Dec. 1943
Eastern front Dec. 1944
CRIMEAN WAR
Allied assaults on Russian Coastal areas
Barents Sea
Norwegian Sea
(British, French, American 1918-1919)
Petsamo
Murmansk
NORWAY
SWEDEN
FINLAND
Eastern front Dec. 1944
German advance to Dec. 1941
Gulf of Bothnia
White Sea
Arkhangelsk
Allies
Onega
Shenkursk
N. Dvina
Pechora
Ob
URAL MTS.
ALAND IS.
Helsinki
Vyborg
Lake Ladoga
Lake Onega
Kronstadt
Leningrad was never captured by the Germans
St. Petersburg (Leningrad)
Tikhvin
(British) (1918-19)
DAGO
OSEL
GOTLAND
Narva
Reval
ESTONIA
Parnau
Baltic Sea
Pskov
Novgorod
Lake Ilmen
1700-1702
LATVIA
Riga
Dvinsk
Königsberg
LITHUANIA
Velikie-Luki
Tver (Kalinin)
German advance 1941
Moscow
Viatka (Kirov)
Perm (Molotov)
Nizhni Novgorod (Gorki)
Kazan
Ufa
Volga
Kama
EAST PRUSSIA
Kovno
Polotsk
Vitebsk
Borodino
Viazma
Smolensk
Tula
Oka
GERMANY
Berlin
Thorn
Vilno
Grodno
Niemen
Minsk
Mogilev
Berezina
RUSSIA
Penza
Samara (Kuibyshev)
Orenburg (Chkalov)
Warsaw
Kalisz
Brest
1706
POLAND
Pripet
Orel
Kursk
Voronezh
Saratov
Uralsk
Ural
Prague
1700-1702
Chernigov
Baturin
Germans 1918
Polish 1920
Russian front
CZECHOSLOVAKIA
Krakow
CARPATHIAN
Lvov
Zhitomir
Kiev
1707-1709
Kharkov
Vienna
AUSTRIA
Tarnopol
GALICIA
UKRAINE
Poltava
Dec. 1943
Tsaritsyn (Stalingrad)
Gurev
HUNGARY
Budapest
Dniester
S. Bug
Dnieper
Donets
Ekaterinoslav (Dnepropetrovsk)
Don
BESSARABIA
MOLDAVIA
Iassy
TRANSYLVANIA
Nikolaev
Allies
Taganrog
Rostov
German advance 1942
Astrakhan
Odessa
Kherson
1855
Kinburn
Sea of Azov
RUMANIA
WALLACHIA
Galati
Belgrade
Eastern front Dec. 1944
YUGOSLAVIA
Bucharest
Danube
Evpatoriia
Kerch
Ekaterinodar (Krasnodar)
Stavropol
Kuban
Kuma
Sevastopol
1854
Novorossiisk
Caspian Sea
Grozny
Allies
BULGARIA
Varna
BALKAN MTS.
Sofia
Burgas
Maritsa
(French 1918-19)
Black Sea
(British 1918-1919)
CAUCASUS
ALBANIA
Salonika
Constantinople
Bosporus
Sinope
Batum
Tiflis
Kura
Baku
Krasnovodsk
GREECE
Aegean Sea
Angora
ARMENIA
Arak
Lenkoran
TURKEY
Athens
Smyrna
Konia
Tabriz
PERSIA
TAURUS MTS.
(British) (1918-19)
Teheran
RHODES
Aleppo
SYRIA
Mosul
IRAQ
A-470196-29-1-1-1

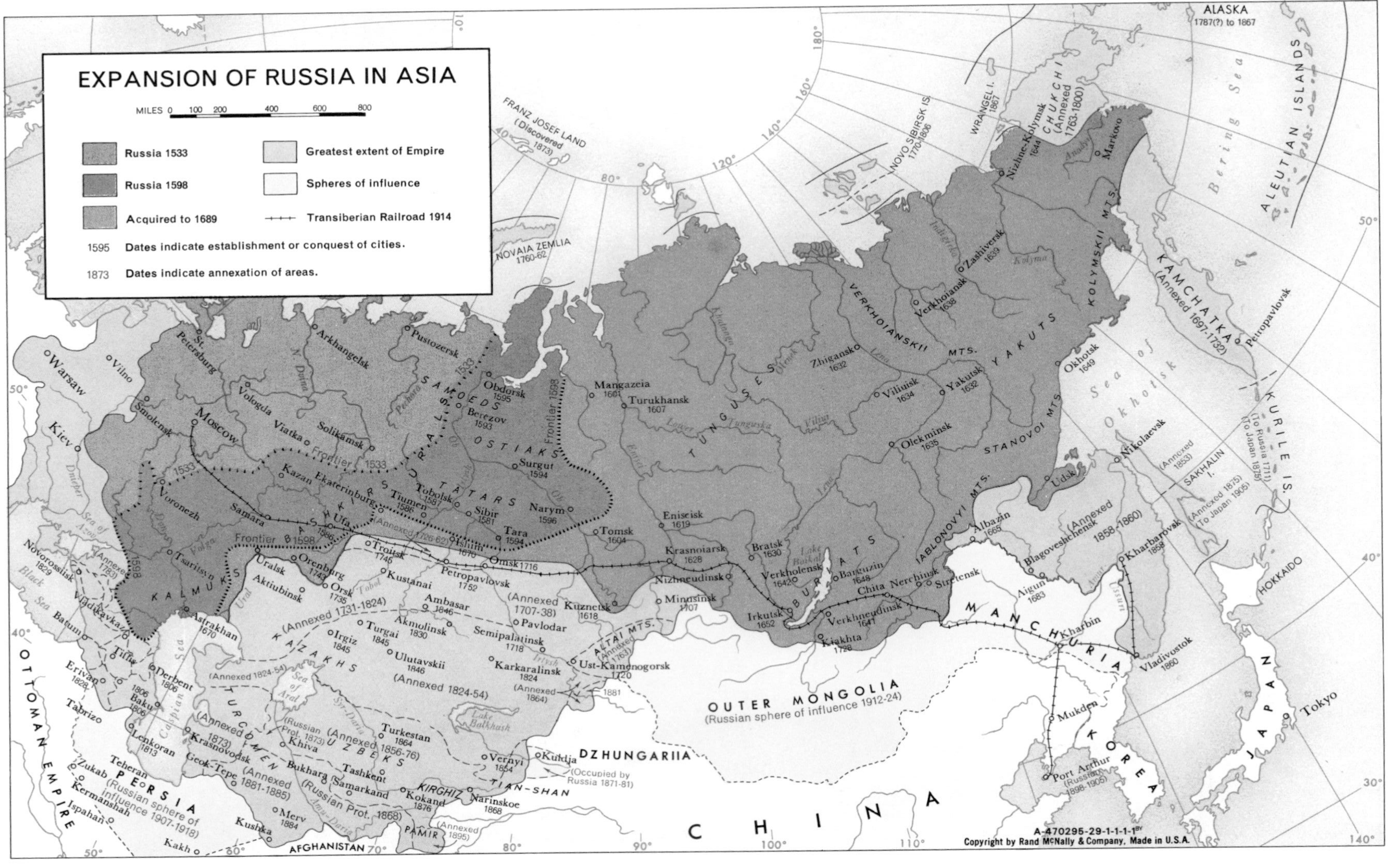
EXPANSION OF RUSSIA IN ASIA
MILES 0 100 200 400 600 800
Russia 1533
Russia 1598
Acquired to 1689
Greatest extent of Empire
Spheres of influence
Transiberian Railroad 1914
1595 Dates indicate establishment or conquest of cities.
1873 Dates indicate annexation of areas.
ALASKA 1787(?) to 1867
ALEUTIAN ISLANDS
Bering Sea
KAMCHATKA (Annexed 1697-1732)
Petropavlovsk
KURILE IS. (To Russia 1711) (To Japan 1875)
SAKHALIN I. (Annexed 1853) (Annexed 1875) (To Japan 1905)
Sea of Okhotsk
HOKKAIDO
JAPAN
Tokyo
KOREA
Vladivostok 1860
Kharbarovsk 1858
Nikolaevsk
CHUKCHI (Annexed 1763-1800)
Markovo
KOLYMSKII MTS.
Nizhne-Kolymsk 1644
WRANGEL I. 1867
NOVO SIBIRSK IS. 1770-1806
Okhotsk 1649
Udsk
STANOVOI MTS.
YAKUTS
Yakutsk 1632
Verkhoiansk 1638
Zashiversk 1639
VERKHOIANSKII MTS.
Olekminsk 1635
Viliuisk 1634
Zhigansk 1632
IABLONOVYI MTS.
Albazin 1665
Blagoveshchensk (Annexed 1858-1860)
Aigun 1683
Kharbin
MANCHURIA
Mukden
Port Arthur (Russian 1898-1905)
Stretensk
Nerchinsk
Chita
Barguzin 1648
Verkhneudinsk 1647
Kiakhta 1728
Irkutsk 1652
Verkholensk 1642
Bratsk 1630
BURIATS
Lake Baikal
TUNGUSES
OUTER MONGOLIA (Russian sphere of influence 1912-24)
CHINA
Krasnoiarsk 1628
Nizhneudinsk
Minusinsk 1707
Eniseisk 1619
Turukhansk 1607
Mangazeia 1601
Tomsk 1604
Kuznetsk 1618
Ust-Kamenogorsk 1720
ALTAI MTS.
DZHUNGARIIA
Kuldja (Occupied by Russia 1871-81)
TIAN-SHAN
Vernyi 1854
Narinskoe 1868
FRANZ JOSEF LAND (Discovered 1873)
NOVAIA ZEMLIA 1760-62
Frontier 1598
OSTIAKS
Surgut 1594
Narym 1596
Obdorsk 1595
Berezov 1593
SAMOEDS
Pustozersk
TATARS
Tara 1594
Omsk 1716
Tobolsk 1587
Sibir 1581
Tiumen 1586
Petropavlovsk 1752
Pavlodar
Semipalatinsk 1718
Karkaralinsk 1824
Ambasar 1846
Akmolinsk 1830
Ulutavskii 1846
KAZAKHS (Annexed 1824-54)
Kustanai
Troitsk 1745
Turgai 1845
Irgiz 1845
Orsk 1735
Orenburg 1743
Aktiubinsk
Uralsk
Ufa 1586
Ekaterinburg
Kazan
Viatka
Solikamsk
Arkhangelsk
N. Dvina
Vologda
Moscow
St. Petersburg
Smolensk
Vilno
Warsaw
Kiev
Dnieper
Voronezh
Samara
Frontier 1533
Frontier 1598
Tsaritsyn
Astrakhan 1670
KALMUKS
Sea of Azov
Black Sea
Novorossiisk 1829
Vladikavkaz
Batum
Tiflis
Erivan 1828
Tabrizo
Baku 1806
Derbent 1806
Lenkoran 1813
Caspian Sea
Krasnovodsk
Geok-Tepe
TURCOMEN (Annexed 1881-1885)
Merv 1884
Kushka
Sea of Aral
Khiva
Bukhara
Samarkand
Tashkent
Turkestan 1864
UZBEKS (Annexed 1856-76)
Kokand 1876
KIRGHIZ
PAMIR (Annexed 1895)
AFGHANISTAN
PERSIA (Russian sphere of influence 1907-1918)
Teheran
Zukab
Kermanshah
Ispahan
Kakh
OTTOMAN EMPIRE
A-470295-29-1-1-1-
Copyright by Rand McNally & Company, Made in U.S.A.

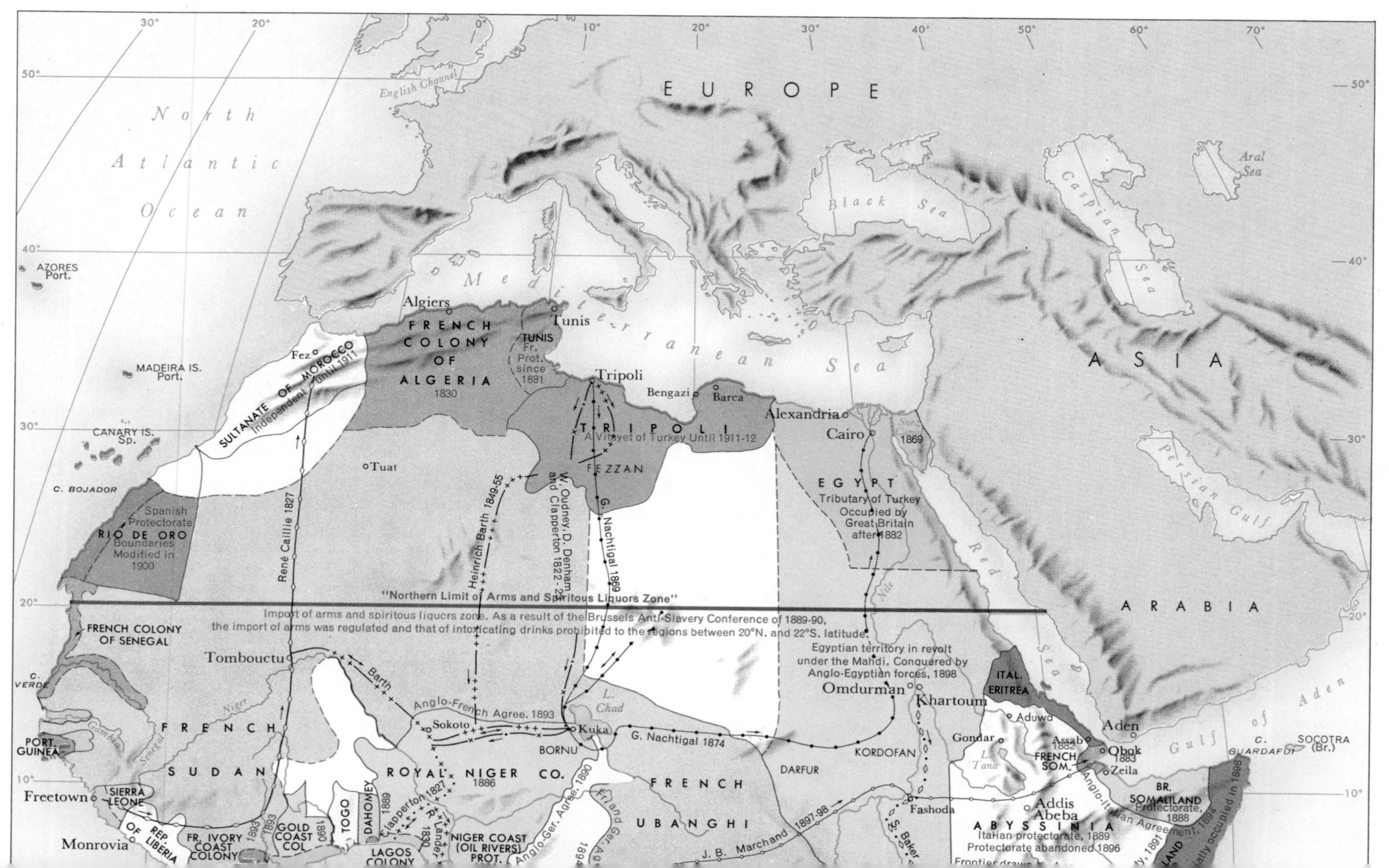
EUROPE
North Atlantic Ocean
English Channel
Mediterranean Sea
Black Sea
Caspian Sea
Aral Sea
ASIA
Persian Gulf
Red Sea
ARABIA
Gulf of Aden
AZORES Port.
MADEIRA IS. Port.
CANARY IS. Sp.
C. BOJADOR
C. VERDE
Spanish Protectorate RIO DE ORO Boundaries Modified in 1900
SULTANATE OF MOROCCO Independent until 1911
Fez
Algiers
FRENCH COLONY OF ALGERIA 1830
Tunis
TUNIS Fr. Prot. since 1881
Tuat
Tripoli
TRIPOLI A Vilayet of Turkey Until 1911-12
FEZZAN
Bengazi
Barca
Alexandria
Cairo
Suez Canal 1869
EGYPT Tributary of Turkey Occupied by Great Britain after 1882
Nile
René Caillié 1827
Heinrich Barth 1849-55
W. Oudney, D. Denham and Clapperton 1822-25
G. Nachtigal 1869
"Northern Limit of Arms and Spiritous Liquors Zone"
Import of arms and spiritous liquors zone. As a result of the Brussels Anti-Slavery Conference of 1889-90, the import of arms was regulated and that of intoxicating drinks prohibited to the regions between 20°N. and 22°S. latitude.
FRENCH COLONY OF SENEGAL
Tombouctu
Barth
Egyptian territory in revolt under the Mahdi, Conquered by Anglo-Egyptian forces, 1898
Omdurman
Khartoum
ITAL. ERITREA
Aduwa
Aden
Gondar
L. Tana
Assab 1882
FRENCH SOM.
Obok 1883
Zeila
C. GUARDAFUI
SOCOTRA (Br.)
BR. SOMALILAND Protectorate, 1888
Addis Abeba
ABYSSINIA
Italian protectorate, 1889
Protectorate abandoned 1896
Anglo-Italian Agreement, 1894
Anglo-French Agree. 1893
L. Chad
Sokoto
Kuka
G. Nachtigal 1874
BORNU
KORDOFAN
DARFUR
Niger
Gambia
Senegal
PORT. GUINEA
FRENCH SUDAN
ROYAL NIGER CO. 1886
FRENCH UBANGHI
Freetown
SIERRA LEONE
REP. OF LIBERIA
Monrovia
FR. IVORY COAST COLONY 1893
GOLD COAST COL. 1890
TOGO
DAHOMEY 1889
Clapperton 1827
Lander 1830
LAGOS COLONY
NIGER COAST (OIL RIVERS) PROT.
Anglo-Ger. Agree. 1890
Fr. and Ger. Agr. 1894
J. B. Marchand 1897-98
Fashoda
S. Baker
30° 20° 0° 10° 20° 30° 40° 50° 60° 70°
50° 40° 30° 20° 10°

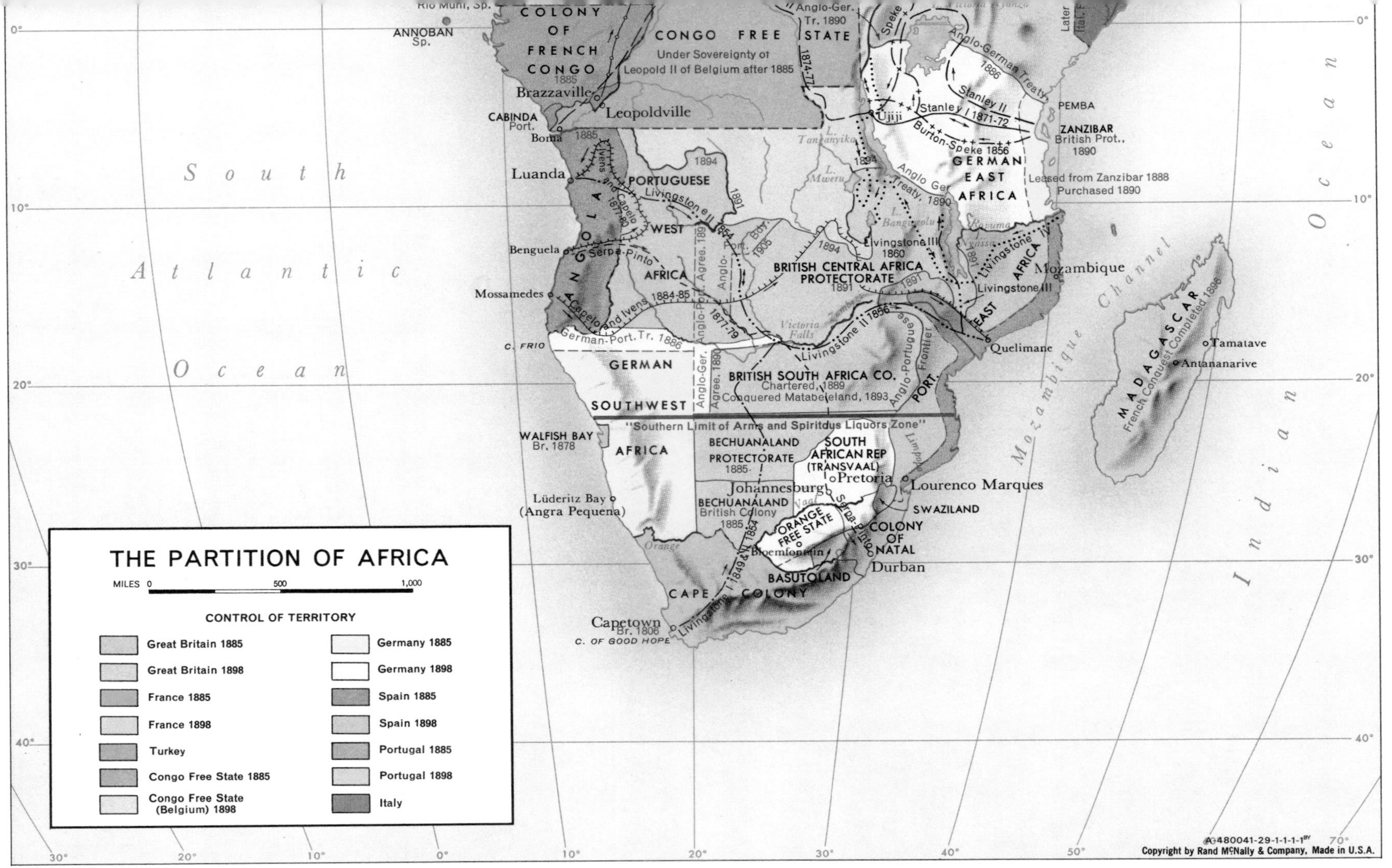
THE PARTITION OF AFRICA
MILES 0 500 1,000
CONTROL OF TERRITORY
Great Britain 1885
Great Britain 1898
France 1885
France 1898
Turkey
Congo Free State 1885
Congo Free State (Belgium) 1898
Germany 1885
Germany 1898
Spain 1885
Spain 1898
Portugal 1885
Portugal 1898
Italy
South Atlantic Ocean
Indian Ocean
Mozambique Channel
MADAGASCAR
French Conquest Completed 1896
Tamatave
Antananarive
CONGO FREE STATE
Under Sovereignty of Leopold II of Belgium after 1885
COLONY OF FRENCH CONGO 1885
Brazzaville
Leopoldville
CABINDA Port.
Boma
Luanda
Benguela
Mossamedes
PORTUGUESE WEST AFRICA
ANGOLA
GERMAN SOUTHWEST AFRICA
WALFISH BAY Br. 1878
Lüderitz Bay (Angra Pequena)
C. FRIO
Capetown Br. 1806
C. OF GOOD HOPE
CAPE COLONY
BASUTOLAND
ORANGE FREE STATE
Bloemfontein
COLONY OF NATAL
Durban
SWAZILAND
Lourenco Marques
SOUTH AFRICAN REP (TRANSVAAL)
Pretoria
Johannesburg
BECHUANALAND PROTECTORATE 1885
BECHUANALAND British Colony 1885
BRITISH SOUTH AFRICA CO. Chartered, 1889 Conquered Matabeleland, 1893
"Southern Limit of Arms and Spiritus Liquors Zone"
BRITISH CENTRAL AFRICA PROTECTORATE 1891
PORT. EAST AFRICA
Mozambique
Quelimane
GERMAN EAST AFRICA
ZANZIBAR British Prot., 1890
PEMBA
Leased from Zanzibar 1888 Purchased 1890
Anglo-German Treaty 1886
Anglo Ger. Treaty, 1890
Anglo-Portuguese Frontier
Anglo-Port. Agree. 1891
Anglo-Ger. Agree. 1890
Anglo-Ger. Tr. 1890
German-Port. Tr. 1886
Stanley I 1871-72
Stanley II
Burton-Speke 1856
Livingstone I 1849 & 1854
Livingstone II 1856
Livingstone III
Serpa-Pinto
Capelo and Ivens 1884-85
Ivens and Capelo 1877-80
Ujiji
L. Tanganyika
L. Mweru
L. Bangweolu
Victoria Falls
Limpopo
Vaal
Orange
ANNOBAN Sp.
Rio Muni, Sp.
A480041-29-1-1-1
Copyright by Rand McNally & Company, Made in U.S.A.

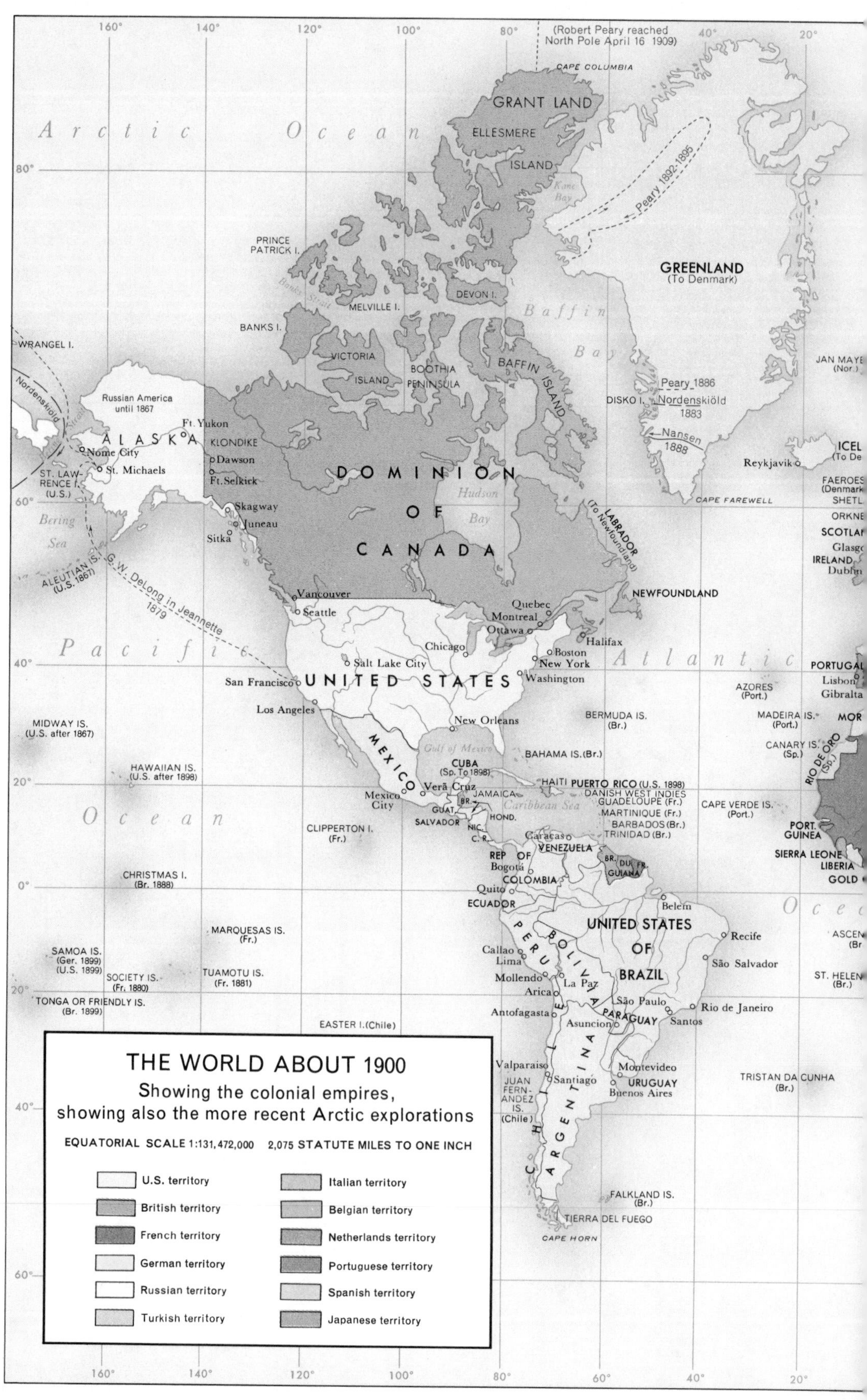
THE WORLD ABOUT 1900
Showing the colonial empires,
showing also the more recent Arctic explorations
EQUATORIAL SCALE 1:131,472,000 2,075 STATUTE MILES TO ONE INCH
U.S. territory
British territory
French territory
German territory
Russian territory
Turkish territory
Italian territory
Belgian territory
Netherlands territory
Portuguese territory
Spanish territory
Japanese territory
(Robert Peary reached North Pole April 16 1909)
CAPE COLUMBIA
GRANT LAND
ELLESMERE ISLAND
Kane Bay
Peary 1892-1895
Arctic Ocean
PRINCE PATRICK I.
MELVILLE I.
DEVON I.
BANKS I.
Banks Strait
VICTORIA ISLAND
BOOTHIA PENINSULA
BAFFIN ISLAND
Baffin Bay
GREENLAND (To Denmark)
Peary 1886
DISKO I.
Nordenskiöld 1883
Nansen 1888
CAPE FAREWELL
Reykjavik
JAN MAYEN (Nor.)
WRANGEL I.
Nordenskiöld
Russian America until 1867
ALASKA
Ft. Yukon
KLONDIKE
Dawson
Ft. Selkirk
Nome City
St. Michaels
ST. LAWRENCE I. (U.S.)
Bering Sea
Skagway
Juneau
Sitka
ALEUTIAN IS. (U.S. 1867)
G.W. DeLong in Jeannette 1879
DOMINION OF CANADA
Hudson Bay
LABRADOR (To Newfoundland)
NEWFOUNDLAND
Vancouver
Seattle
Quebec
Montreal
Ottawa
Halifax
Boston
New York
Washington
Chicago
Salt Lake City
San Francisco
UNITED STATES
Los Angeles
New Orleans
Pacific Ocean
Atlantic Ocean
MIDWAY IS. (U.S. after 1867)
HAWAIIAN IS. (U.S. after 1898)
BERMUDA IS. (Br.)
AZORES (Port.)
PORTUGAL
Lisbon
Gibraltar
MADEIRA IS. (Port.)
CANARY IS. (Sp.)
RIO DE ORO (Sp.)
MEXICO
Gulf of Mexico
BAHAMA IS. (Br.)
CUBA (Sp. To 1898)
HAITI
PUERTO RICO (U.S. 1898)
DANISH WEST INDIES
GUADELOUPE (Fr.)
MARTINIQUE (Fr.)
BARBADOS (Br.)
TRINIDAD (Br.)
Verã Cruz
Mexico City
JAMAICA
Caribbean Sea
GUAT.
SALVADOR
HOND.
NIC.
C. R.
CAPE VERDE IS. (Port.)
PORT. GUINEA
SIERRA LEONE
LIBERIA
CLIPPERTON I. (Fr.)
Caracas
VENEZUELA
BR. DU. FR. GUIANA
REP OF COLOMBIA
Bogotá
Quito
ECUADOR
CHRISTMAS I. (Br. 1888)
Belém
UNITED STATES OF BRAZIL
Recife
São Salvador
PERU
BOLIVIA
Callao
Lima
Mollendo
La Paz
Arica
Antofagasta
São Paulo
Rio de Janeiro
Santos
PARAGUAY
Asuncion
MARQUESAS IS. (Fr.)
SAMOA IS. (Ger. 1899) (U.S. 1899)
SOCIETY IS. (Fr. 1880)
TUAMOTU IS. (Fr. 1881)
TONGA OR FRIENDLY IS. (Br. 1899)
EASTER I. (Chile)
Valparaiso
Santiago
JUAN FERNANDEZ IS. (Chile)
Montevideo
URUGUAY
Buenos Aires
CHILE
ARGENTINA
TRISTAN DA CUNHA (Br.)
FALKLAND IS. (Br.)
TIERRA DEL FUEGO
CAPE HORN
160° 140° 120° 100° 80° 60° 40° 20°
80° 60° 40° 20° 0° 20° 40° 60°

Arctic Ocean
Fridtjof Nansen in Fram 1893-1896
Duke of Abruzzi in Stella Polare 1900
Abruzzi 1900
FRANZ JOSEF LAND OR FRIDTJOF NANSEN LAND (Russia 1928)
NORTHERN LAND (NICHOLAS II)
SPITSBERGEN (Norway 1920)
Baron Adolf Erik Nordenskiöld in Vega 1878-1879
Nansen 1893 - 1896
NEW SIBERIAN ISLANDS
DE LONG IS.
DeLong 1879-1881
TAIMYR PENINSULA
NOVAYA ZEMLYA
Barents Sea
Kara Sea
BEAR I. (Nor.)
1893-1896
1879-1879
NORTH CAPE
Hammerfest
Vardö
WRANGEL I.
De Long Strait
Yenisei
Lena
KDM. OF SWEDEN AND NORWAY
SWEDEN
GR. DUCHY OF FINLAND
Russian Tsar Grand Duke since 1809
Archangel
RUSSIAN EMPIRE
Yakutsk
Christiania
Stockholm
St. Petersburg
Tobolsk
Tomsk
Krasnoyarsk
Moscow
Ufa
Kurgan
Omsk
Trans-Siberian Railway
Samara
Irkutsk
Lake Baikal
Chita
Blagoveyshchensk
Sea of Okhotsk
SAKHALIN (Russia 1875)
Petropavlovsk
Nordenskiöld 1879
KURILE IS.
Khabarovsk
MANCHURIA
MONGOLIA
Urga
Hamburg
Berlin
Warsaw
Vienna
AUS.
HUNG.
Budapest
Odessa
RUM.
SERB.
BUL.
Black Sea
ITALY
Naples
Constantinople
TURKISH EMPIRE
GREECE
MALTA (Br.)
CRETE (Gr. 1898)
CYPRUS (Br. 1878)
Don
Volga
Aral Sea
Lake Balkhash
Irtysh
Caspian Sea
KULJA (Russia 1871-1881)
EMPIRE OF CHINA
Harbin
Moukden
Vladivostok
SINKIANG
Kashgar
Peking
Port Arthur (Russia 1898)
Weihaiwei (Br. 1898)
KOREA
EMPIRE OF JAPAN
Tokyo
Yokohama
Merv (1885)
Teheran
Kabul
AFG.
Bagdad
PERSIA
BALUCH. (Br. 1876)
TIBET
Lhasa
China, Manchu Dynasty since 1644
Tsing Tao (Ger. 1897)
Shanghai
Pacific Ocean
Huang Ho
TRIPOLI (Turk.)
EGYPT
Alexandria
ARABIA
Delhi
NEPAL
BHUTAN
CHINA PROPER
RYUKYU IS. (Jap. 1879)
OGASAWARA IS. (BONIN IS.) (Jap. 1878)
BRITISH INDIAN EMPIRE
also many semiautonomous Indian states
INDIA
Yangtze
Macao (Port.)
Hong Kong (Br.)
FORMOSA (Jap. since 1895)
MARCUS I. (Jap. 1899)
OMAN
Muscat
Calcutta
BURMA
Mandalay
Mecca
Kwangchawwan (Fr. 1898)
SUDAN
ERIT.
KURIA MURIA IS. (Br.)
GOA (Port.)
Bombay
Rangoon
FR. INDO-CHINA
SIAM
MARIANAS (Ger. 1899)
WAKE I. (U.S. 1898)
Lake Chad
ADEN
SOCOTRA (Br. 1886)
Mahé (Fr.)
Madras
ANDAMAN IS. (Br.)
PHILIPPINE IS. (U.S. 1899)
GUAM (U.S. 1898)
ABYSSINIA
LACCADIVE IS. (Br.)
Pondichéry
Bangkok
MARSHALL IS. (Ger. 1899)
CAROLINES (Ger. 1899)
FR. SOM.
BR. SOM.
CEYLON
KAMERUN
MALDIVE IS. (Br.)
NICOBAR IS. (Br.)
STRAITS SETTLEMENTS
SARAWAK (Br. 1888)
N. BORNEO (1888)
PELEW IS. (Ger. 1899)
GILBERT IS. (Br. 1899)
CONGO FREE STATE
Ruled by Leopold II of Belgium
E. AFR.
IT. SOM.
Singapore
SUMATRA
BORNEO
MOLUCCA
NEW GUINEA
(Neth. 1901)
(Ger. 1884)
(Br. 1884)
NEW MECKLENBURG
BISMARCK IS. (Ger. 1884)
ELLICE IS. (Br. 1892)
GER. E. AFR.
ZANZIBAR (Br. 1890)
SEYCHELLES (Br.)
CELEBES
NEW POMERANIA
SOLOMON IS. Div. between Br. and Ger. 1899
ANGOLA
RHODESIA
COMORO IS. (Fr.)
JAVA
(Port.) TIMOR (Neth.)
Indian Ocean
COCOS IS (Br. 1876)
Darwin
NEW HEBRIDES
FIJI IS. (Br. 1874)
Mozambique
PORT. E. AFR.
MADAGASCAR (Fr. 1896)
MAURITIUS (Br.)
NORTHERN TERRITORY
REUNION (Fr.)
GER. S.W. AFR.
BECHUANA-LAND
TRANS-VAAL
Lourenço Marques
NATAL
COMMONWEALTH OF AUSTRALIA
(including Tasmania formed in 1901)
WESTERN AUSTRALIA
QUEENSLAND
SOUTH AUSTRALIA
NEW CALEDONIA (Fr.)
LOYALTY IS. (Fr. 1864)
Brisbane
ORANGE STATE
CAPE COLONY
Capetown
Perth
Adelaide
NEW SOUTH WALES
Sydney
VICTORIA
Melbourne
TASMANIA
Wellington
NEW ZEALAND
Organized as a Dominion in 1907
20° 40° 60° 80° 100° 120° 140° 160°
80° 60° 40° 20° 0° 20° 40° 60°
A-410041-29-1-1-1-1

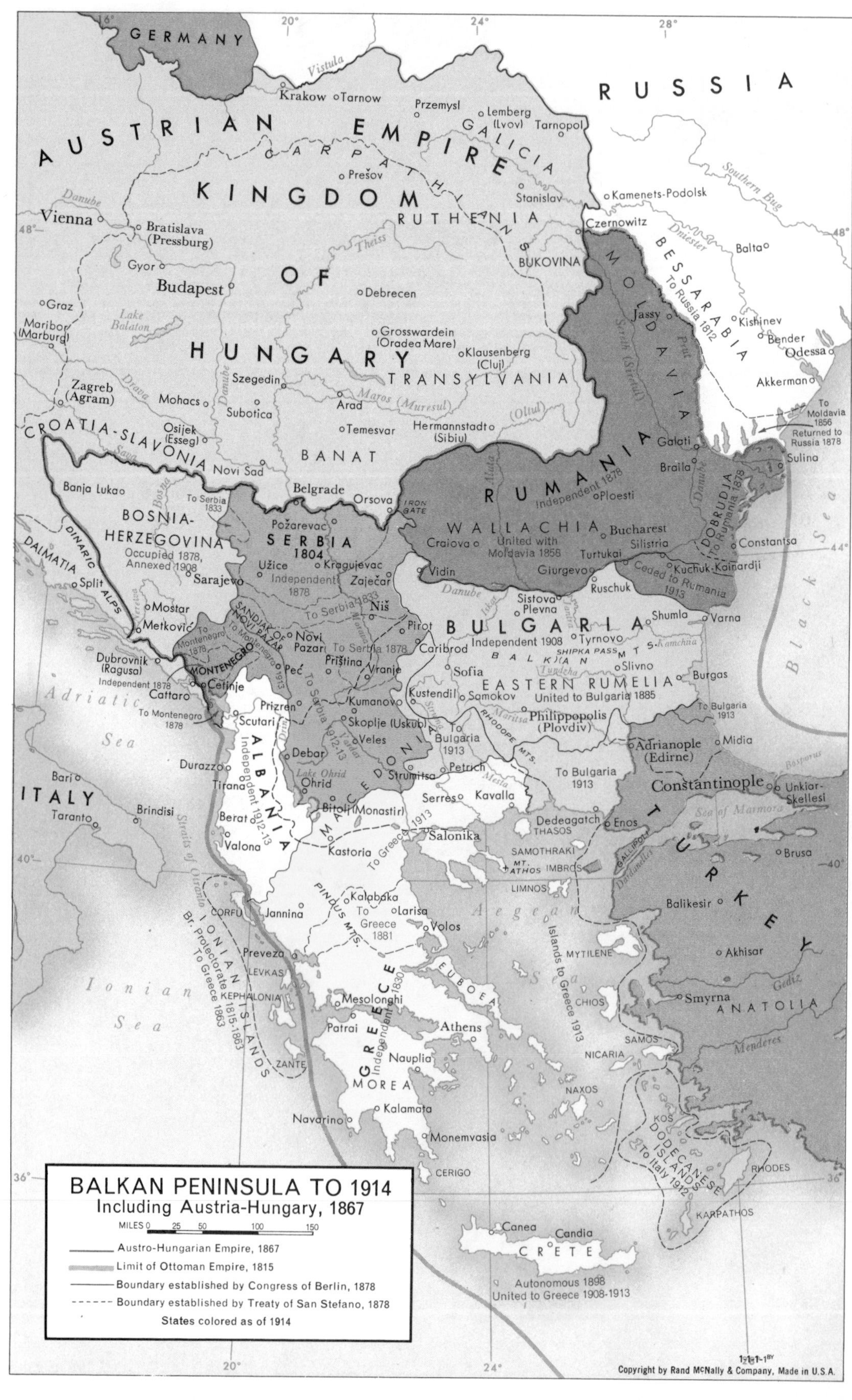
BALKAN PENINSULA TO 1914
Including Austria-Hungary, 1867
MILES 0 25 50 100 150
Austro-Hungarian Empire, 1867
Limit of Ottoman Empire, 1815
Boundary established by Congress of Berlin, 1878
Boundary established by Treaty of San Stefano, 1878
States colored as of 1914
GERMANY
RUSSIA
AUSTRIAN EMPIRE
KINGDOM OF HUNGARY
CARPATHIANS
GALICIA
RUTHENIA
BUKOVINA
TRANSYLVANIA
BANAT
CROATIA-SLAVONIA
MOLDAVIA
BESSARABIA
To Russia 1812
RUMANIA
Independent 1878
WALLACHIA
United with Moldavia 1856
DOBRUDJA
To Rumania 1878
Ceded to Rumania 1913
To Moldavia 1856
Returned to Russia 1878
BOSNIA-HERZEGOVINA
Occupied 1878, Annexed 1908
SERBIA 1804
Independent 1878
To Serbia 1833
To Serbia 1878
SANDJAK OF NOVI PAZAR
To Montenegro 1913
To Serbia 1912-13
MONTENEGRO
To Montenegro 1878
DALMATIA
DINARIC ALPS
BULGARIA
Independent 1908
BALKAN MTS.
EASTERN RUMELIA
United to Bulgaria 1885
RHODOPE MTS.
To Bulgaria 1913
MACEDONIA
To Greece 1913
ALBANIA
Independent 1912-13
GREECE
Independent 1830
To Greece 1881
PINDUS MTS.
EUBOEA
MOREA
IONIAN ISLANDS
Br. Protectorate 1815-1863
To Greece 1863
TURKEY
ANATOLIA
DODECANESE ISLANDS
To Italy 1912
CRETE
Autonomous 1898
United to Greece 1908-1913
Islands to Greece 1913
ITALY
Adriatic Sea
Ionian Sea
Aegean Sea
Black Sea
Sea of Marmora
Vienna
Bratislava (Pressburg)
Budapest
Krakow
Tarnow
Przemysl
Lemberg (Lvov)
Tarnopol
Prešov
Stanislav
Kamenets-Podolsk
Czernowitz
Balta
Kishinev
Bender
Odessa
Akkerman
Jassy
Galati
Braila
Sulina
Ploesti
Bucharest
Silistria
Turtukai
Giurgevo
Constantsa
Kuchuk-Kainardji
Ruschuk
Craiova
Vidin
Debrecen
Grosswardein (Oradea Mare)
Klausenberg (Cluj)
Hermannstadt (Sibiu)
Arad
Temesvar
Szegedin
Subotica
Mohacs
Osijek (Esseg)
Novi Sad
Belgrade
Orsova
IRON GATE
Gyor
Graz
Maribor (Marburg)
Zagreb (Agram)
Banja Luka
Sarajevo
Split
Mostar
Metković
Dubrovnik (Ragusa)
Independent 1878
Cattaro
Cetinje
Požarevac
Užice
Kragujevac
Zaječar
Niš
Pirot
Novi Pazar
Priština
Peć
Vranje
Prizren
Kumanovo
Skoplje (Uskub)
Veles
Debar
Ohrid
Lake Ohrid
Bitolj (Monastir)
Kastoria
Scutari
Durazzo
Tirana
Berat
Valona
Caribrod
Sofia
Samokov
Kustendil
Strumitsa
Petrich
Sistova
Plevna
Shumla
Varna
Tyrnovo
SHIPKA PASS
Slivno
Burgas
Philippopolis (Plovdiv)
Adrianople (Edirne)
Midia
Constantinople
Unkiar-Skellesi
Enos
GALLIPOLI
Dardanelles
Bosporus
Brusa
Balikesir
Akhisar
Smyrna
Serres
Kavalla
Dedeagatch
THASOS
Salonika
SAMOTHRAKI
MT. ATHOS
IMBROS
LIMNOS
MYTILENE
CHIOS
SAMOS
NICARIA
NAXOS
KOS
RHODES
KARPATHOS
CERIGO
Canea
Candia
Jannina
Kalabaka
Larisa
Volos
CORFU
Preveza
LEVKAS
KEPHALONIA
ZANTE
Mesolonghi
Patrai
Athens
Nauplia
Kalamata
Navarino
Monemvasia
Bari
Brindisi
Taranto
Straits of Otranto
Danube
Vistula
Southern Bug
Dniester
Theiss
Lake Balaton
Drava
Sava
Maros (Muresul)
Oltul
Prut
Sereth (Siretul)
Maritsa
Struma
Vardar
Drin
Menderes
Gediz
48°
44°
40°
36°
16°
20°
24°
28°
Copyright by Rand McNally & Company, Made in U.S.A.

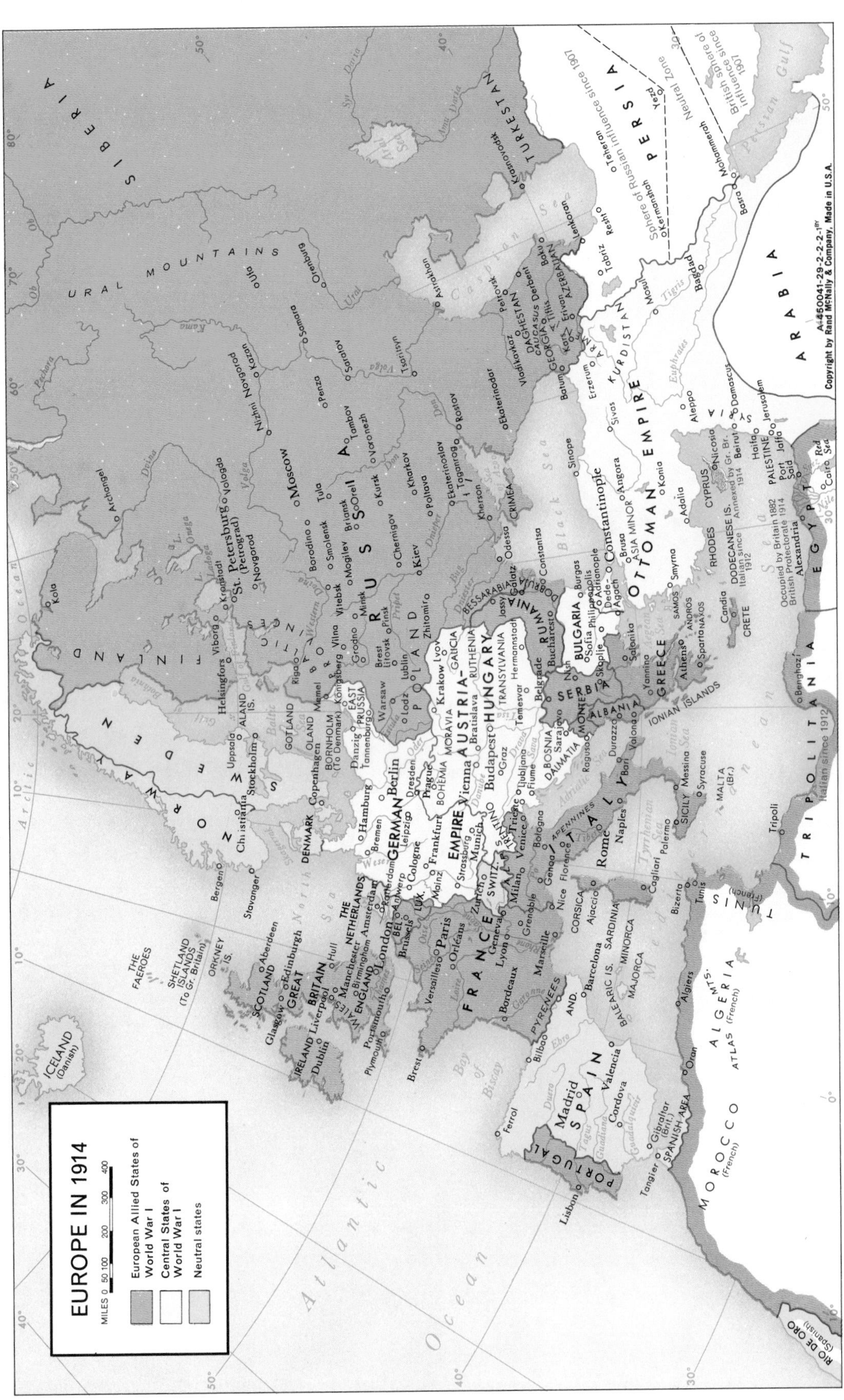
EUROPE IN 1914
MILES 0 50 100 200 300 400
European Allied States of World War I
Central States of World War I
Neutral states
A-450041-29-2-2-1
Copyright by Rand McNally & Company, Made in U.S.A.

ICELAND
NORWAY
Occupied by Germany 1940
SWEDEN
DENMARK
Occupied by Germany 1940
GREAT BRITAIN
IRISH FREE STATE
SCOTLAND
WALES
ENGLAND
NETHERLANDS
Occ. by Ger. 1940
BEL.
Occ. by Ger. 1940
LUX.
GERMANY
FRANCE
Occupied by Germany 1940
VICHY FRANCE 1940
SPAIN
PORTUGAL
SWITZERLAND
AUSTRIA
To Germany Anschluss 1938
CZECHOSLOVAKIA
HUNGARY
YUGOSLAVIA
ITALY
ALBANIA
GREECE
EAST PRUSSIA
MEMELAND To Ger. 1939
Nazi-Soviet Pact Annexed by Germany 1939
Atlantic Ocean
North Sea
Bay of Biscay
Mediterranean
MOROCCO To France
ALGERIA To France
TUNIS French Protectorate
TRIPOLITANIA To Italy
CYRENAICA To Italy
LIBYA
AFRICA
A-450043-29-1-1-2-2
Copyright by Rand McNally & Company, Made in U.S.A.

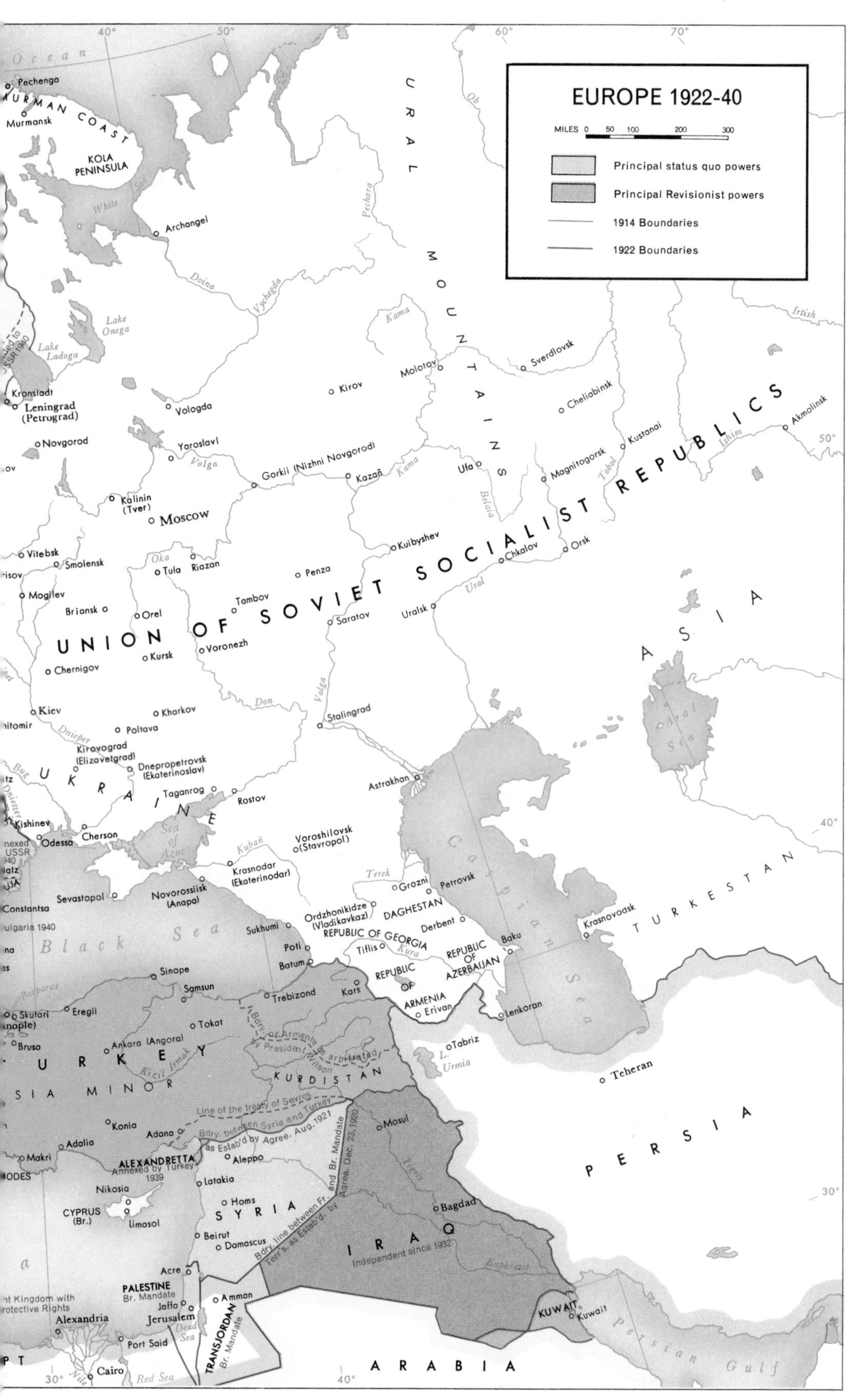

EUROPE 1922-40
MILES 0 50 100 200 300
Principal status quo powers
Principal Revisionist powers
1914 Boundaries
1922 Boundaries
UNION OF SOVIET SOCIALIST REPUBLICS
URAL MOUNTAINS
KOLA PENINSULA
MURMAN COAST
Pechenga
Murmansk
White Sea
Archangel
Dvina
Vychegda
Pechora
Ob
Irtish
Kama
Lake Onega
Lake Ladoga
Kronstadt
Leningrad (Petrograd)
Vologda
Kirov
Molotov
Sverdlovsk
Cheliabinsk
Akmolinsk
Kustanai
Ishim
Tobol
Magnitogorsk
Novgorod
Yaroslavl
Volga
Gorkii (Nizhni Novgorod)
Kazan
Ufa
Belaia
Kalinin (Tver)
Moscow
Kuibyshev
Chkalov
Orsk
Ural
Vitebsk
Smolensk
Oka
Tula
Riazan
Penza
Mogilev
Briansk
Orel
Tambov
Saratov
Uralsk
ASIA
Voronezh
Kursk
Chernigov
Don
Kiev
Kharkov
Stalingrad
Aral Sea
Poltava
Dnieper
Kirovograd (Elizavetgrad)
Dnepropetrovsk (Ekaterinoslav)
UKRAINE
Taganrog
Rostov
Astrakhan
Bug
Dniester
Kishinev
Odessa
Cherson
Sea of Azov
Kuban
Voroshilovsk (Stavropol)
Caspian Sea
Krasnodar (Ekaterinodar)
Terek
Grozni
Petrovsk
Sevastopol
Novorossiisk (Anapa)
Constantsa
Ordzhonikidze (Vladikavkaz)
DAGHESTAN
Krasnovodsk
TURKESTAN
Black Sea
Sukhumi
REPUBLIC OF GEORGIA
Derbent
Poti
Tiflis
Kura
REPUBLIC OF AZERBAIJAN
Baku
Batum
REPUBLIC OF ARMENIA
Sinope
Samsun
Trebizond
Kars
Erivan
Lenkoran
Bosporus
Skutari
Eregli
Tokat
Bdry. of Armenia by President Wilson as arbitrated
L. Urmia
Tabriz
Teheran
Brusa
Ankara (Angora)
Kizil Irmak
TURKEY
ASIA MINOR
KURDISTAN
Line of the treaty of Sevres
Bdry. between Syria and Turkey as Estab'd by Agree. Aug. 1921
Bdry. between Fr. and Br. Mandate Agree. Dec. 23, 1920
Mosul
Tigris
PERSIA
Konia
Adana
Adalia
Makri
ALEXANDRETTA Annexed by Turkey 1939
Aleppo
Latakia
Nikosia
CYPRUS (Br.)
Limasol
Homs
SYRIA
Bagdad
Beirut
Damascus
Bdry. line between Fr. and Br. Terr's. as Estab'd by Agree.
IRAQ
Independent since 1932
Euphrates
Acre
PALESTINE Br. Mandate
Jaffa
Jerusalem
Amman
TRANSJORDAN Br. Mandate
Dead Sea
KUWAIT
Kuwait
Persian Gulf
Alexandria
Port Said
Cairo
Nile
Red Sea
ARABIA
Kingdom with Protective Rights
Ceded to USSR 1940
Annexed USSR 1940
Bulgaria 1940
30°
40°
50°
60°
70°

EUROPE
AFTER WORLD WAR II
Showing changes to 1950
MILES 0 50 100 200 300 400 500
North Atlantic Treaty Organization (NATO)
Soviet Russia and People's Democracies
Major Neutral Powers
Yugoslavia-Communist State but Neutral
A-450045-29-1-2-1
Copyright by Rand McNally & Company, Made in U.S.A.

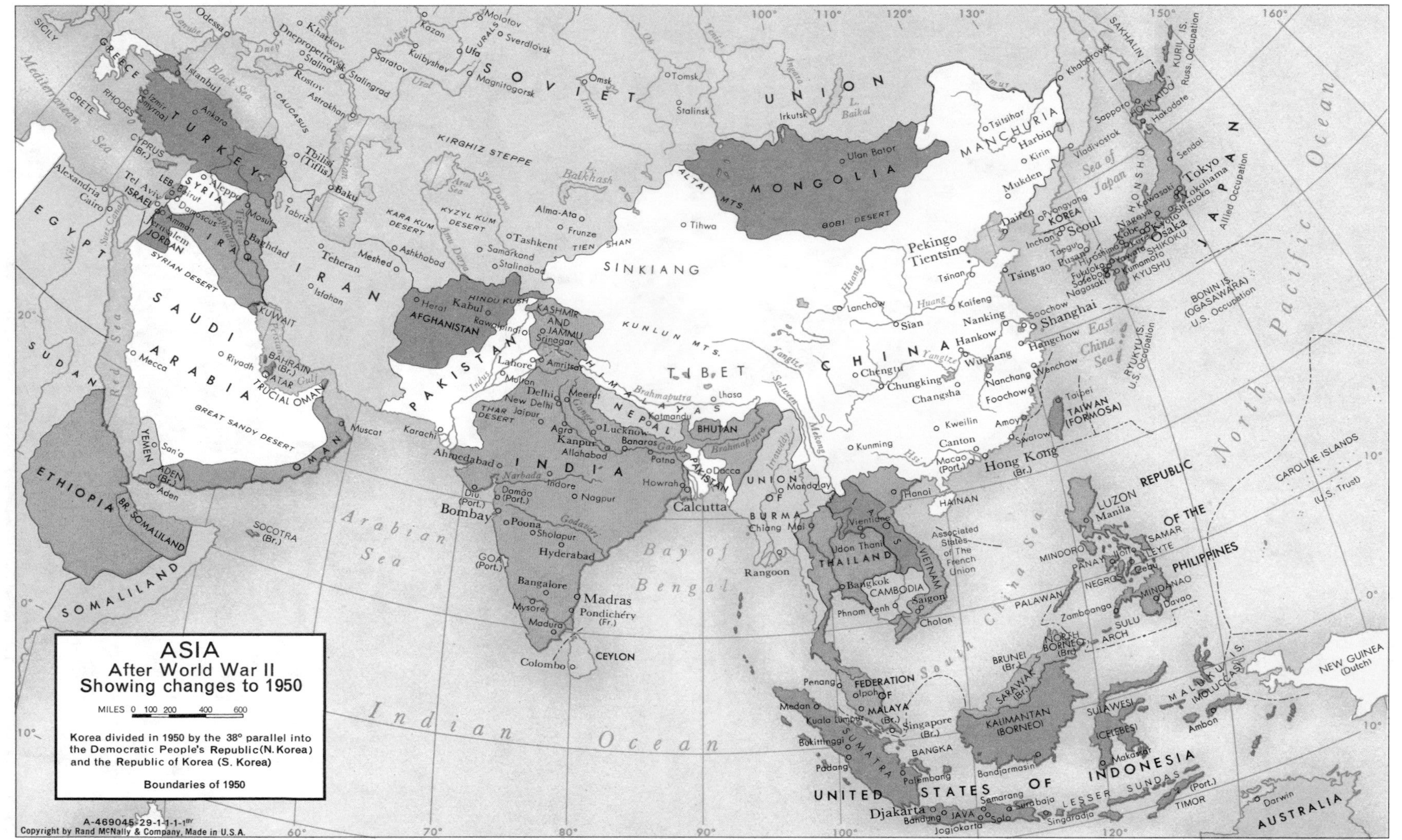
ASIA
After World War II
Showing changes to 1950
MILES 0 100 200 400 600
Korea divided in 1950 by the 38° parallel into the Democratic People's Republic (N. Korea) and the Republic of Korea (S. Korea)
Boundaries of 1950
A-469045-29-1-1-1
Copyright by Rand McNally & Company, Made in U.S.A.
SOVIET UNION
MONGOLIA
MANCHURIA
SINKIANG
TIBET
CHINA
KOREA
JAPAN
TURKEY
SYRIA
LEB.
ISRAEL
JORDAN
IRAQ
IRAN
KUWAIT
SAUDI ARABIA
YEMEN
ADEN (Br.)
OMAN
TRUCIAL OMAN
AFGHANISTAN
PAKISTAN
INDIA
NEPAL
BHUTAN
CEYLON
UNION OF BURMA
THAILAND
CAMBODIA
VIETNAM
FEDERATION OF MALAYA
TAIWAN (FORMOSA)
REPUBLIC OF THE PHILIPPINES
UNITED STATES OF INDONESIA
EGYPT
SUDAN
ETHIOPIA
BR. SOMALILAND
SOMALILAND
AUSTRALIA
NEW GUINEA (Dutch)
Indian Ocean
North Pacific Ocean
Arabian Sea
Bay of Bengal
South China Sea

Flags of the World

AFGHANISTAN
ALBANIA
ALGERIA
ANDORRA
ANGOLA
ANTIGUA
ARGENTINA
AUSTRALIA
AUSTRIA
BAHAMAS
BANGLADESH
BARBADOS
BELGIUM
BELIZE
BENIN
BHUTAN
BOLIVIA
BOTSWANA
BRAZIL
BRUNEI
BULGARIA
BURMA
BURUNDI
BYELORUSSIAN SOVIET SOCIALIST REPUBLIC
CAMBODIA (Kampuchea)
CAMEROON
CANADA
CAPE VERDE
CENTRAL AFRICAN REPUBLIC
CHAD
CHILE
CHINA
COLOMBIA
COMOROS
CONGO

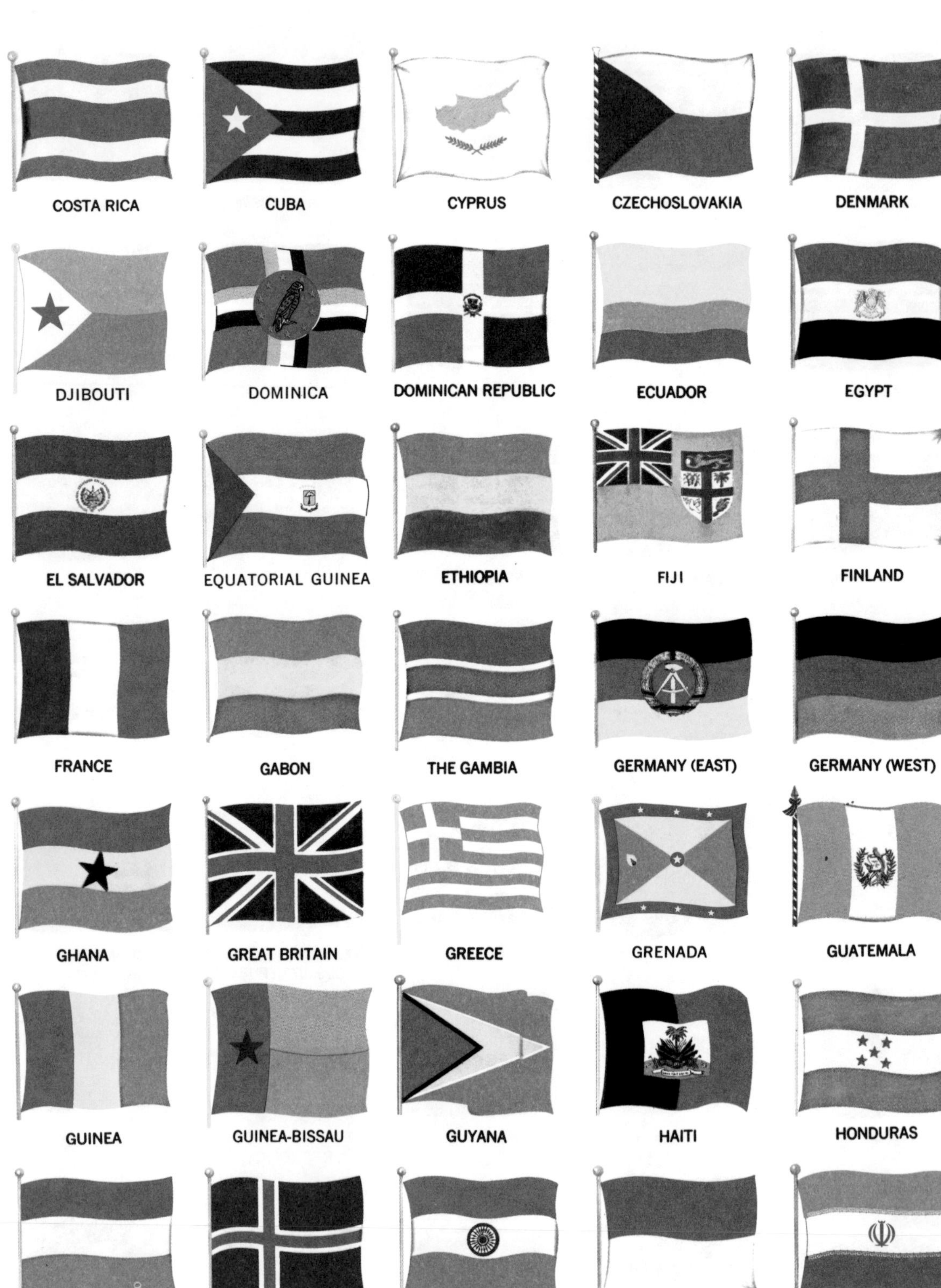
COSTA RICA
CUBA
CYPRUS
CZECHOSLOVAKIA
DENMARK
DJIBOUTI
DOMINICA
DOMINICAN REPUBLIC
ECUADOR
EGYPT
EL SALVADOR
EQUATORIAL GUINEA
ETHIOPIA
FIJI
FINLAND
FRANCE
GABON
THE GAMBIA
GERMANY (EAST)
GERMANY (WEST)
GHANA
GREAT BRITAIN
GREECE
GRENADA
GUATEMALA
GUINEA
GUINEA-BISSAU
GUYANA
HAITI
HONDURAS
HUNGARY
ICELAND
INDIA
INDONESIA
IRAN

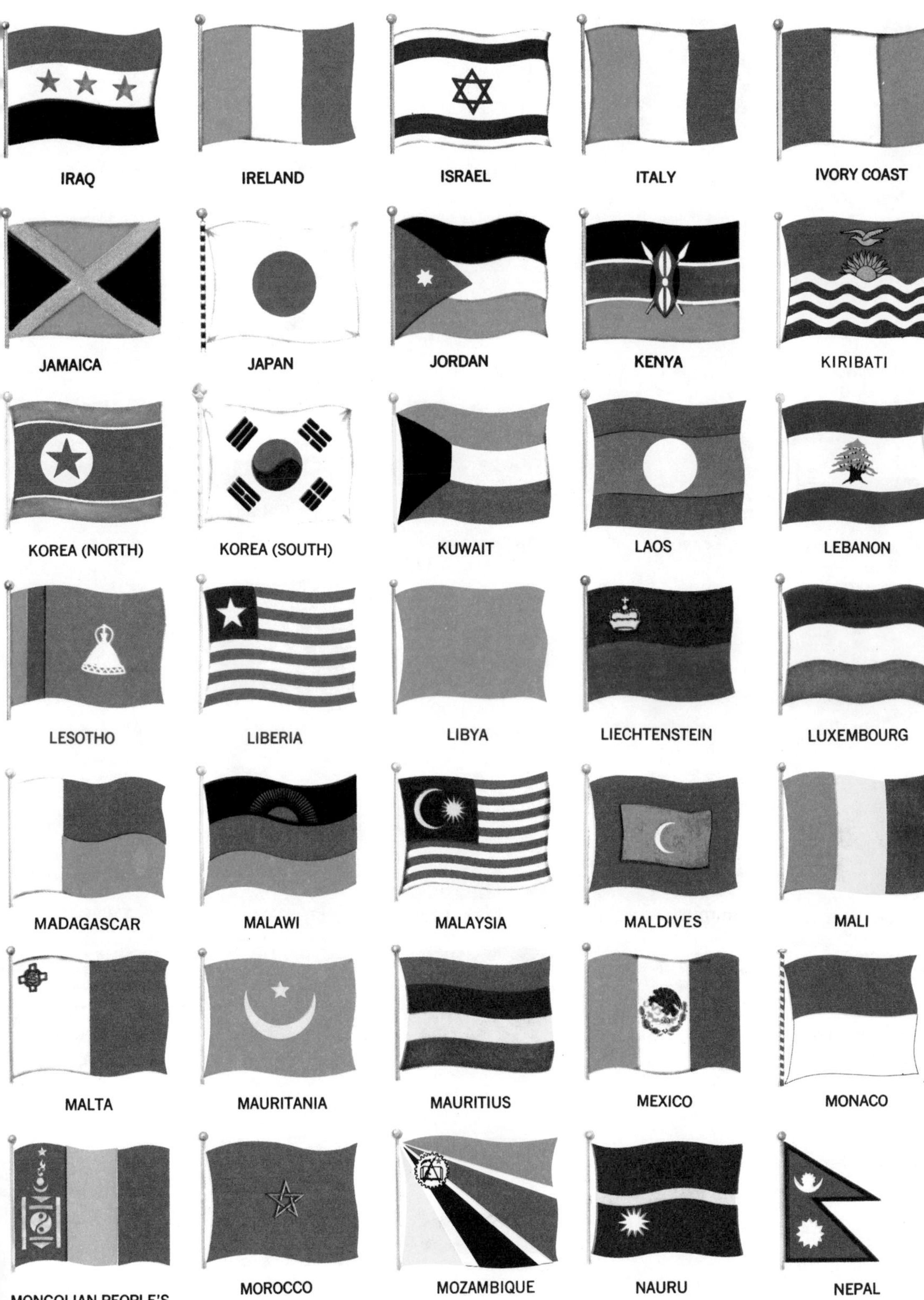
IRAQ
IRELAND
ISRAEL
ITALY
IVORY COAST
JAMAICA
JAPAN
JORDAN
KENYA
KIRIBATI
KOREA (NORTH)
KOREA (SOUTH)
KUWAIT
LAOS
LEBANON
LESOTHO
LIBERIA
LIBYA
LIECHTENSTEIN
LUXEMBOURG
MADAGASCAR
MALAWI
MALAYSIA
MALDIVES
MALI
MALTA
MAURITANIA
MAURITIUS
MEXICO
MONACO
MONGOLIAN PEOPLE'S REPUBLIC
MOROCCO
MOZAMBIQUE
NAURU
NEPAL

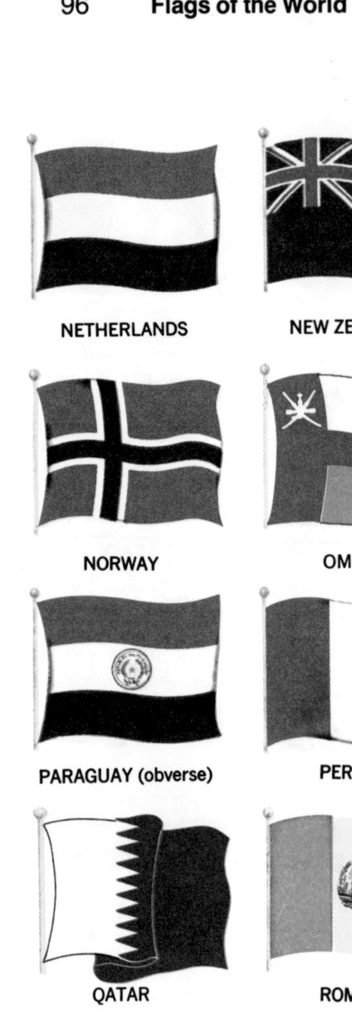

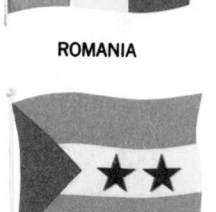

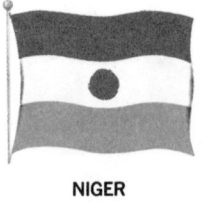

NETHERLANDS NEW ZEALAND NICARAGUA NIGER NIGERIA

NORWAY OMAN PAKISTAN PANAMA PAPUA-NEW GUINEA

PARAGUAY (obverse) PERU PHILIPPINES POLAND PORTUGAL

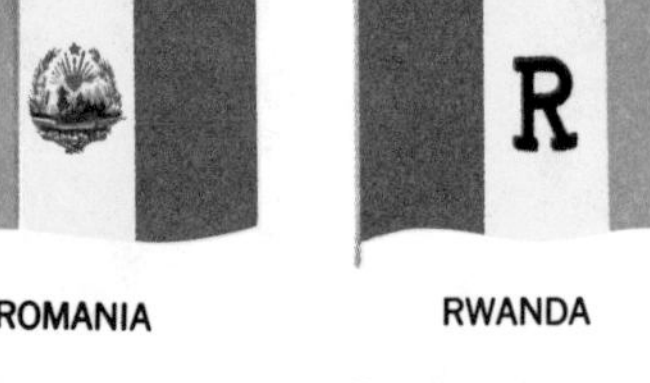

QATAR ROMANIA RWANDA SAINT LUCIA ST. VINCENT

SAN MARINO SAO TOME AND PRINCIPE SAUDI ARABIA SENEGAL SEYCHELLES

SIERRA LEONE SINGAPORE SOLOMON ISLANDS SOMALIA SOUTH AFRICA

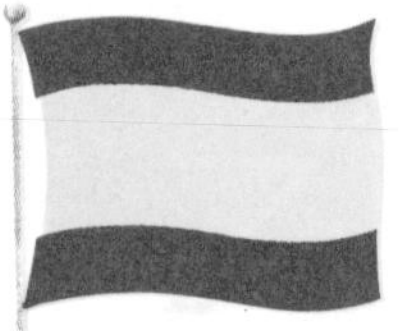

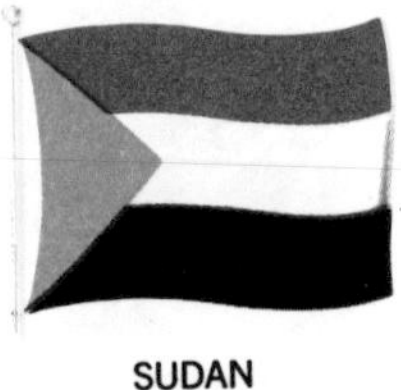

SPAIN SRI LANKA SUDAN SURINAME SWAZILAND

SWEDEN
SWITZERLAND
SYRIA
TANZANIA
THAILAND
TOGO
TRINIDAD AND TOBAGO
TUNISIA
TURKEY
TUVALU
UGANDA
UKRAINIAN SOVIET SOCIALIST REPUBLIC
UNION OF SOVIET SOCIALIST REPUBLICS
UNITED ARAB EMIRATES
UNITED STATES
UPPER VOLTA
URUGUAY
VANUATU
VATICAN CITY
VENEZUELA
VIETNAM
WESTERN SAMOA
YEMEN
PEOPLE'S DEMOCRATIC REPUBLIC OF YEMEN
YUGOSLAVIA
ZAIRE
ZAMBIA
ZIMBABWE
UNITED NATIONS
ORGANIZATION OF AFRICAN UNITY
ORGANIZATION OF AMERICAN STATES
COUNCIL OF EUROPE
RED CROSS
RED CRESCENT (Most Muslim countries)
RED MOGEN DAVID (Israel)

Reference Maps of the World

Reference Map Legend

CULTURAL FEATURES

Political Boundaries

- International
- Secondary (State, province, etc.)
- County

Populated Places

Cities, towns, and villages

Symbol size represents population of the place

Chicago
Gary
Racine
Glenview
Edgewood

Type size represents relative importance of the place

Corporate area of large U.S. and Canadian cities and urban area of other foreign cities

Major Urban Area
Area of continuous commercial, industrial, and residential development in and around a major city

- Community within a city
- Capital of major political unit
- Capital of secondary political unit
- Capital of U.S. state or Canadian province
- County Seat
- Military Installation
- Scientific Station

Miscellaneous

- National Park
- National Monument
- Provincial Park
- Indian Reservation
- Point of Interest
- Ruins
- Buildings
- Race Track
- Railroad
- Tunnel
- Underground or Subway
- Dam
- Bridge
- Dike

LAND FEATURES

Passes =

Point of Elevation above sea level + 8,520 FT.

WATER FEATURES

- Coastlines and Shorelines
- Indefinite or Unsurveyed Coastlines and Shorelines
- Lakes and Reservoirs
- Canals
- Rivers and Streams
- Falls and Rapids
- Intermittent or Unsurveyed Rivers and Streams
- Directional Flow Arrow
- Rocks, Shoals and Reefs

TYPE STYLES USED TO NAME FEATURES

A S I A	Continent
DENMARK CANADA	Country, State, or Province
BÉARN	Region, Province, or Historical Region
CROCKETT	County
PANTELLERIA (ITALY)	Country of which unit is a dependency in parentheses
SRI LANKA (CEYLON)	Former or alternate name
Rome (Roma)	Local or alternate city name
Naval Air Station	Military Installation
MESA VERDE SAN XAVIER	National Park or Monument, Provincial Park, Indian Res.,
UINTA DESERT	Major Terrain Features
MT. MORIAH	Individual Mountain
STROMBOLI NUNIVAK	Island or Coastal Feature
Ocean Lake River Canal	Hydrographic Features

Note: Size of type varies according to importance and available space. Letters for names of major features are spread across the extent of the feature.

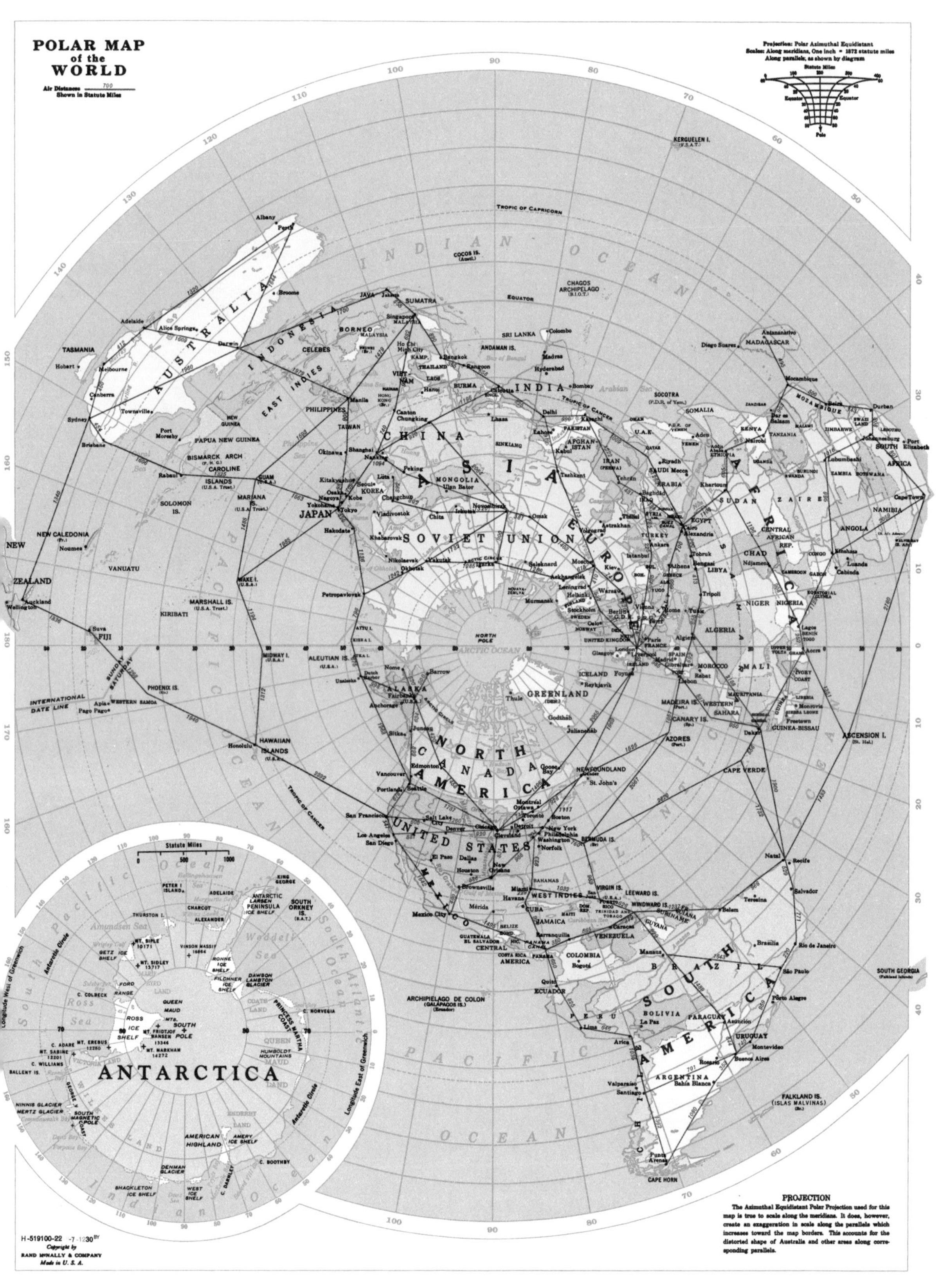
POLAR MAP
of the
WORLD
Air Distances 700 Shown in Statute Miles
Projection: Polar Azimuthal Equidistant
Scales: Along meridians, One inch = 1872 statute miles
Along parallels, as shown by diagram
Statute Miles
Equator
Pole
INDIAN OCEAN
TROPIC OF CAPRICORN
EQUATOR
AUSTRALIA
INDONESIA
EAST INDIES
ASIA
CHINA
SOVIET UNION
EUROPE
AFRICA
NORTH AMERICA
CANADA
UNITED STATES
MEXICO
SOUTH AMERICA
BRAZIL
GREENLAND
NORTH POLE
ARCTIC OCEAN
PACIFIC OCEAN
ATLANTIC OCEAN
INTERNATIONAL DATE LINE
TROPIC OF CANCER
KERGUELEN I.
MADAGASCAR
SRI LANKA
INDIA
JAPAN
PHILIPPINES
NEW ZEALAND
TASMANIA
FIJI
HAWAIIAN ISLANDS
ALASKA
ICELAND
WEST INDIES
FALKLAND IS.
(ISLAS MALVINAS)
SOUTH GEORGIA
CAPE HORN
ANTARCTICA
SOUTH POLE
Statute Miles
Ross Sea
Weddell Sea
Amundsen Sea
Antarctic Circle
Longitude West of Greenwich
Longitude East of Greenwich
PROJECTION
The Azimuthal Equidistant Polar Projection used for this map is true to scale along the meridians. It does, however, create an exaggeration in scale along the parallels which increases toward the map borders. This accounts for the distorted shape of Australia and other areas along corresponding parallels.
H-519100-22
Copyright by RAND McNALLY & COMPANY
Made in U. S. A.

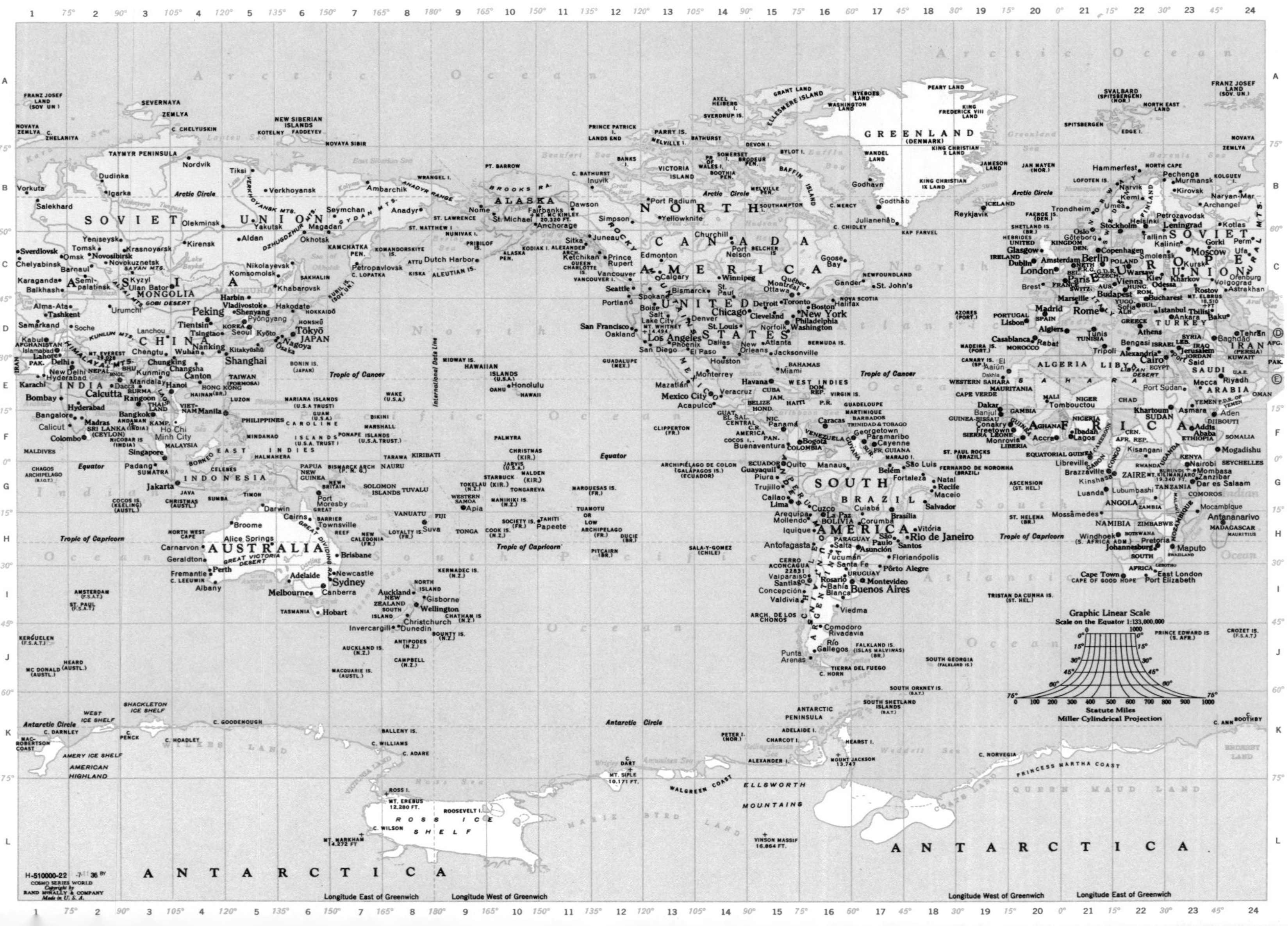
Arctic Ocean
NORTH AMERICA
CANADA
UNITED STATES
GREENLAND (DENMARK)
ALASKA
SOUTH AMERICA
BRAZIL
EUROPE
SOVIET UNION
ASIA
CHINA
INDIA
MONGOLIA
JAPAN
INDONESIA
AFRICA
AUSTRALIA
ANTARCTICA
Arctic Circle
Tropic of Cancer
Equator
Tropic of Capricorn
Antarctic Circle
International Date Line
Graphic Linear Scale
Scale on the Equator 1:133,000,000
Statute Miles
Miller Cylindrical Projection
Longitude East of Greenwich
Longitude West of Greenwich
H-510000-22
COSMO SERIES WORLD
Copyright by RAND McNALLY & COMPANY
Made in U. S. A.

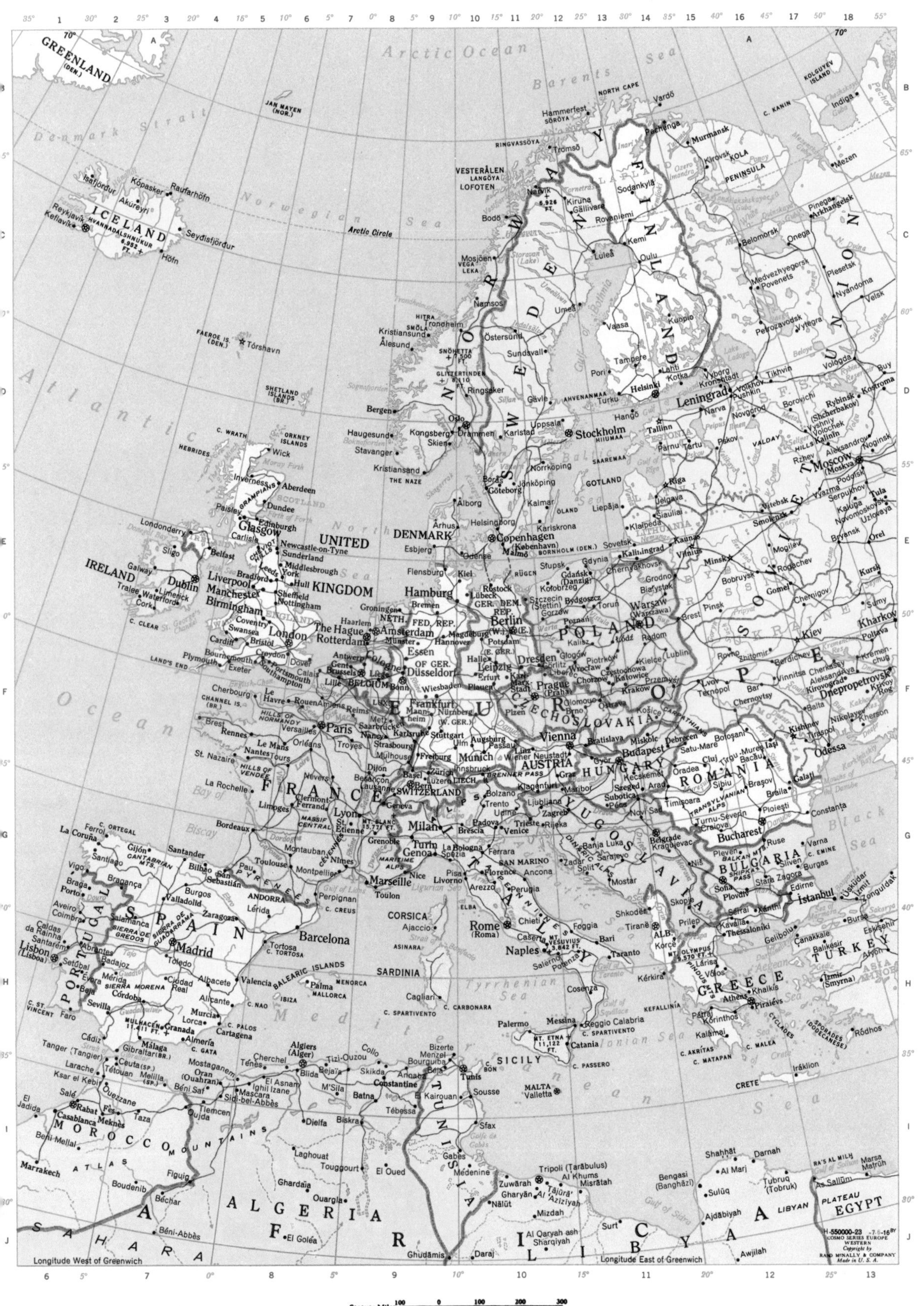

Conic Projection

Statute Miles 100 0 100 200 300
Kilometers 100 0 100 200 300 400

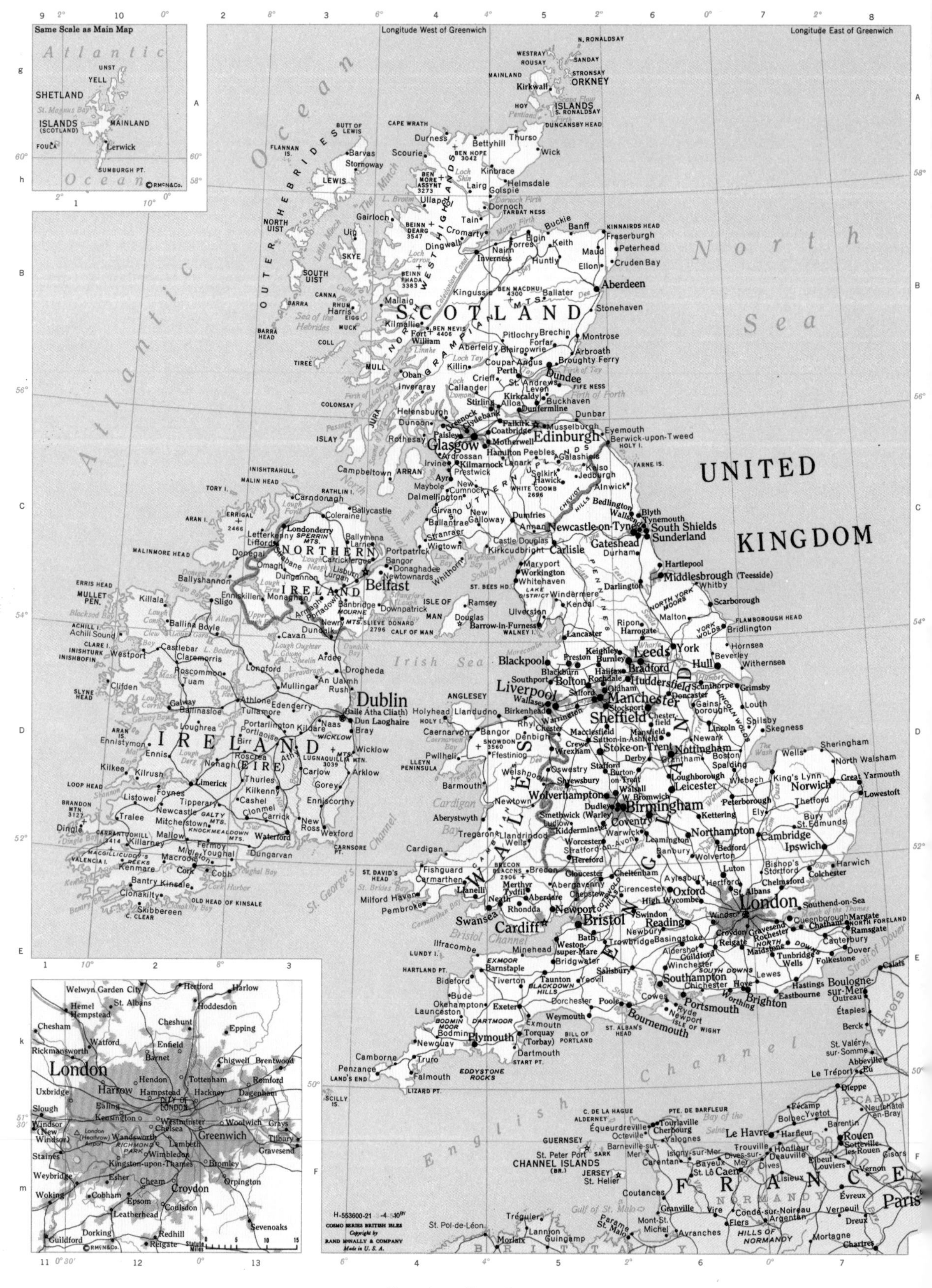

Statute Miles 25 0 25 50 75
Kilometers 25 0 25 50 100

Conic Projection

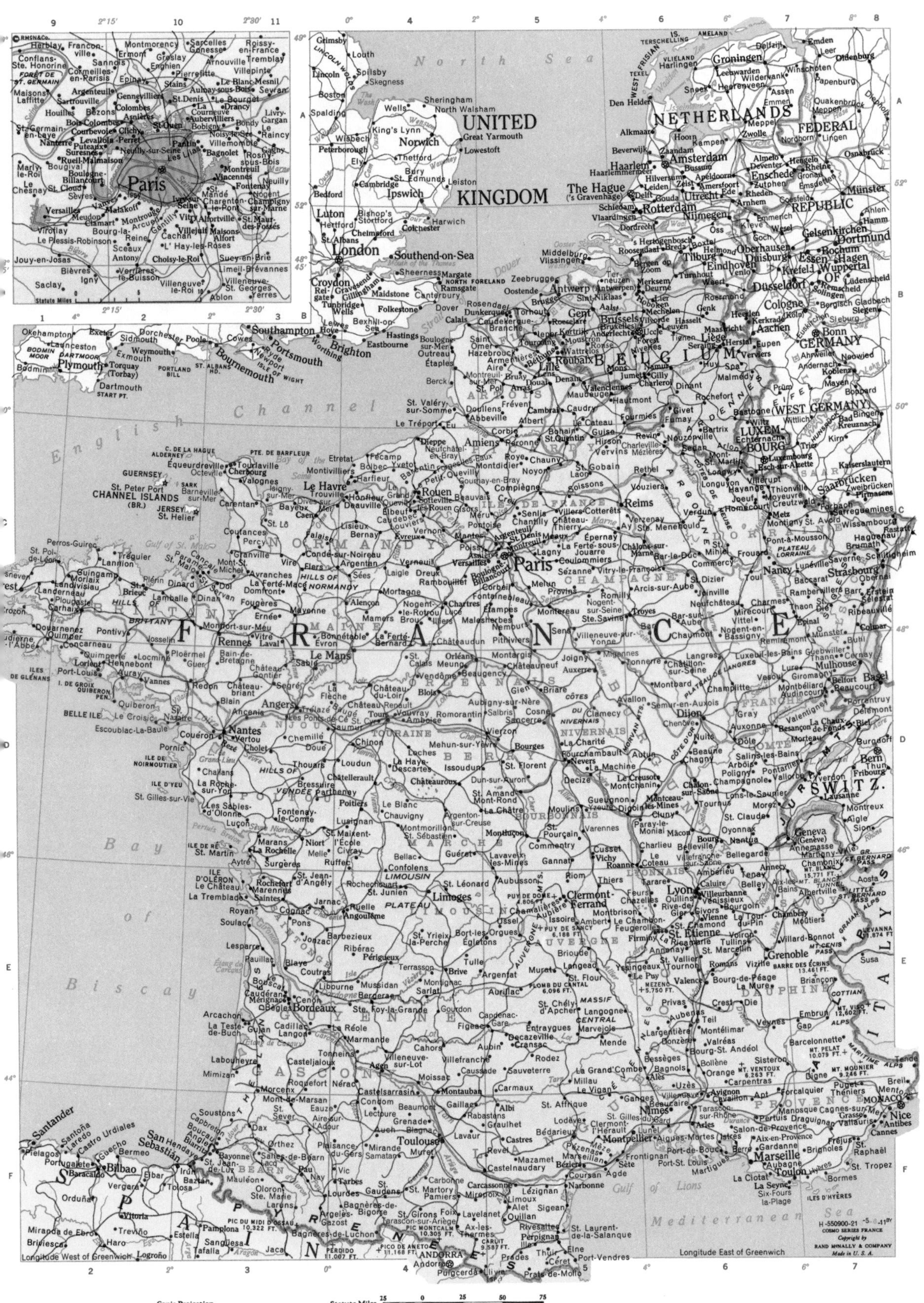
North Sea
UNITED KINGDOM
NETHERLANDS
FEDERAL REPUBLIC OF GERMANY
(WEST GERMANY)
BELGIUM
LUXEMBOURG
FRANCE
SWITZ.
ITALY
SPAIN
ANDORRA
MONACO
English Channel
Bay of Biscay
Gulf of Lions
Mediterranean Sea
CHANNEL ISLANDS (BR.)
GUERNSEY
JERSEY
Paris
London
Amsterdam
Brussels
The Hague ('s Gravenhage)
Rotterdam
Antwerp (Antwerpen)
Luxembourg
Bern
Geneva (Genève)
Lyon
Marseille
Bordeaux
Toulouse
Nantes
Nice
Strasbourg
Lille
Le Havre
Rouen
Reims
Dijon
Grenoble
Montpellier
Limoges
Clermont-Ferrand
Orléans
Tours
Le Mans
Rennes
Brest
Bilbao
San Sebastián
Santander
Andorra
MASSIF CENTRAL
NORMANDY
BRITTANY
CHAMPAGNE
ÎLE-DE-FRANCE
BOURGOGNE
AUVERGNE
PROVENCE
GUYENNE
GASCONY
PYRENEES
ALPS
JURA MTS.
Longitude West of Greenwich
Longitude East of Greenwich
H-550900-21 -5-8-11
COSMO SERIES FRANCE
Copyright by RAND McNALLY & COMPANY
Made in U. S. A.
Conic Projection
Statute Miles 25 0 25 50 75
Kilometers 25 0 25 50 100

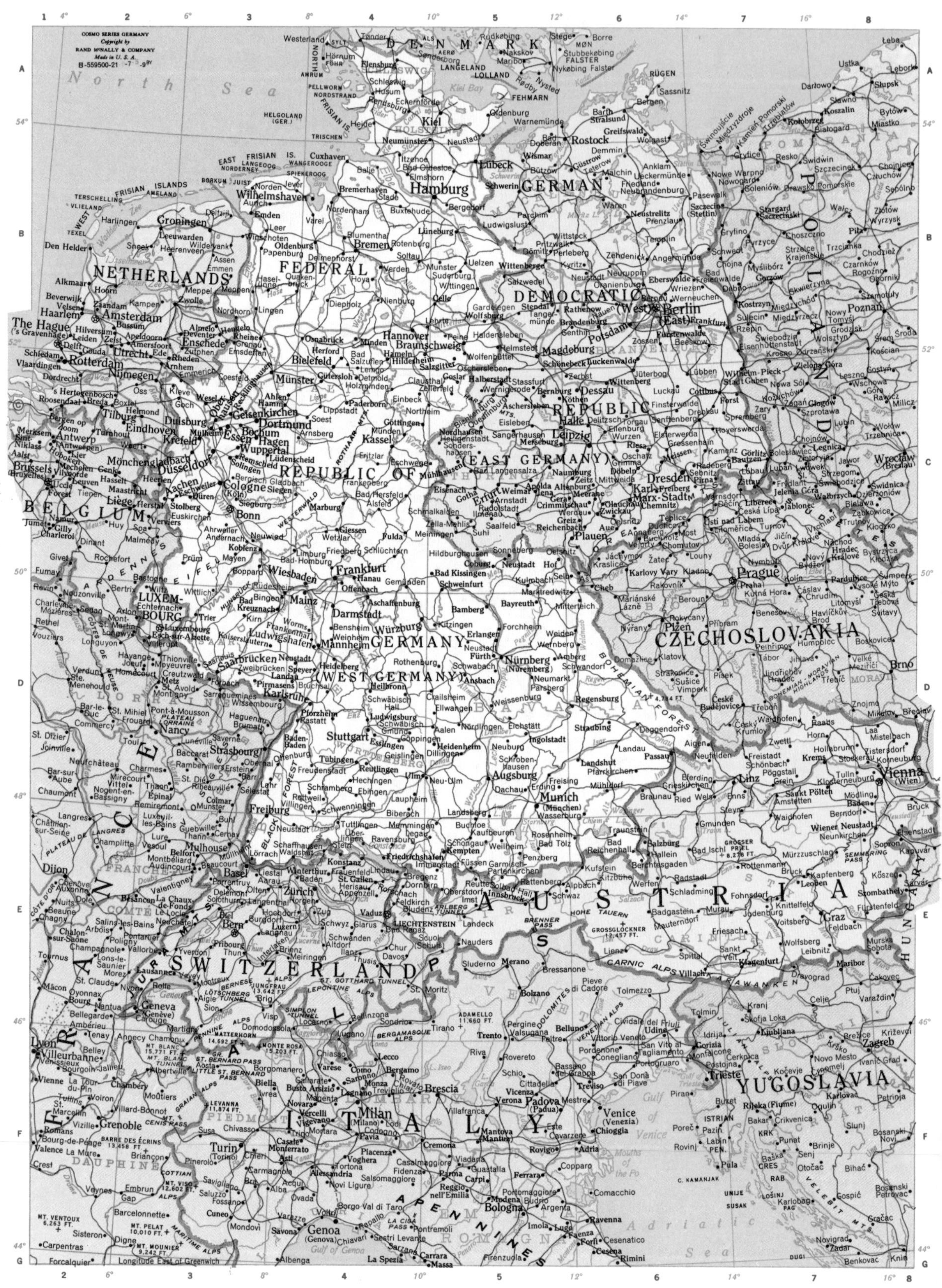

Statute Miles 25 0 25 50 75

Kilometers 25 0 25 50 100

Conic Projection

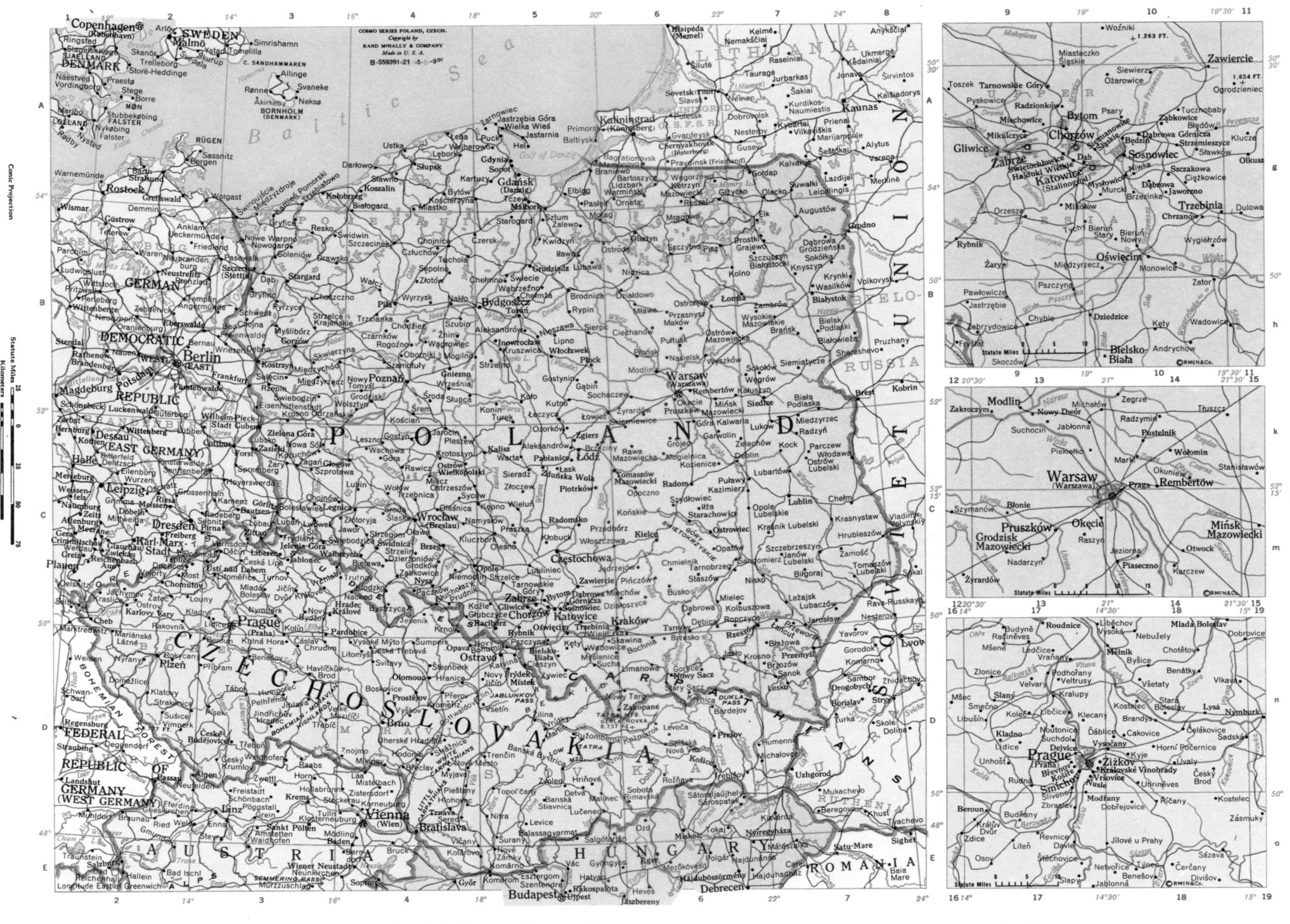
COSMO SERIES POLAND, CZECH.
Copyright by
RAND McNALLY & COMPANY
Made in U. S. A.
POLAND
CZECHOSLOVAKIA
Baltic Sea
Conic Projection
Statute Miles 25 0 25 50 75
Kilometers 25 0 25 50 100

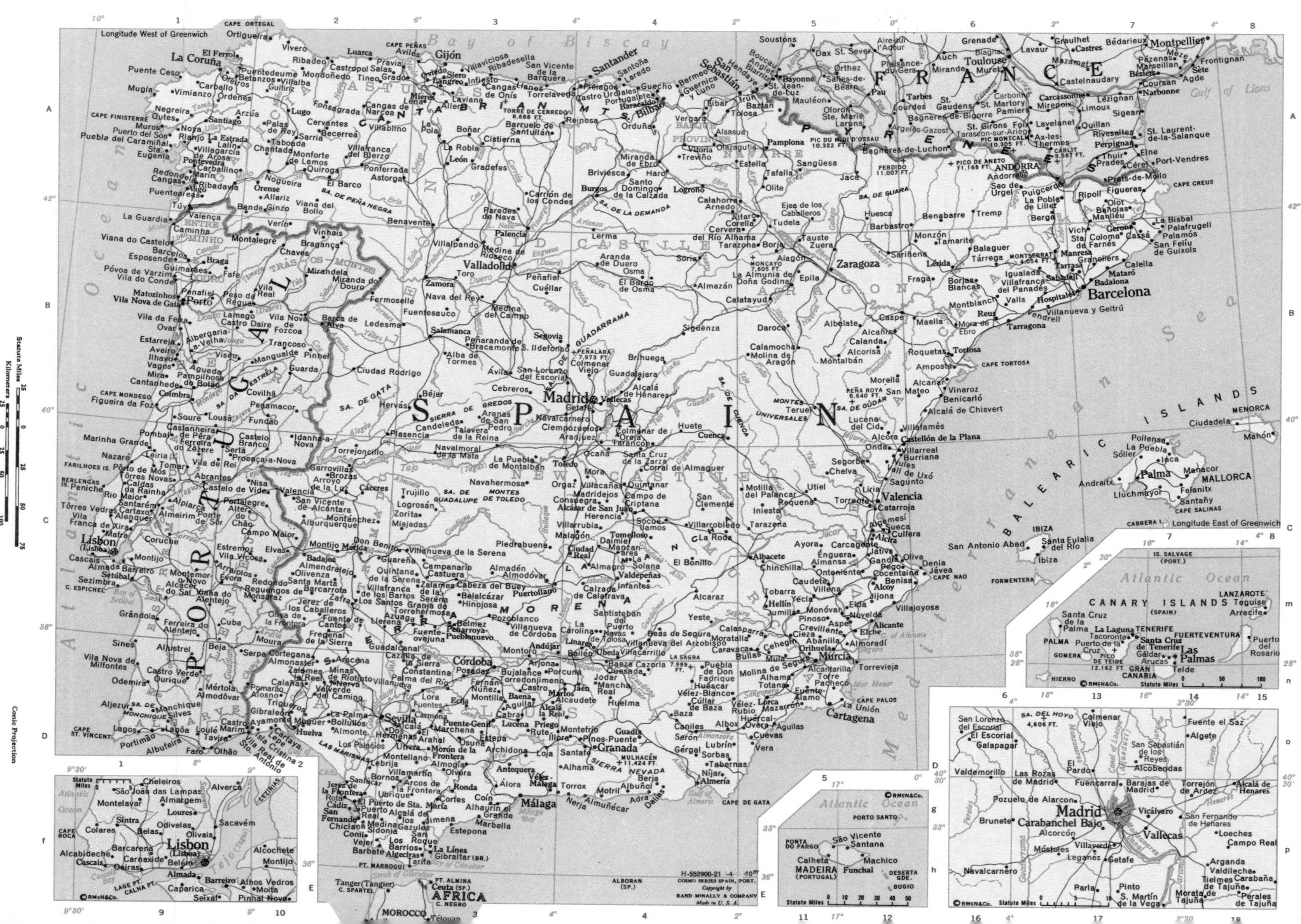

Statute Miles 25 0 25 50 75

Kilometers 25 0 25 50 100

Conic Projection

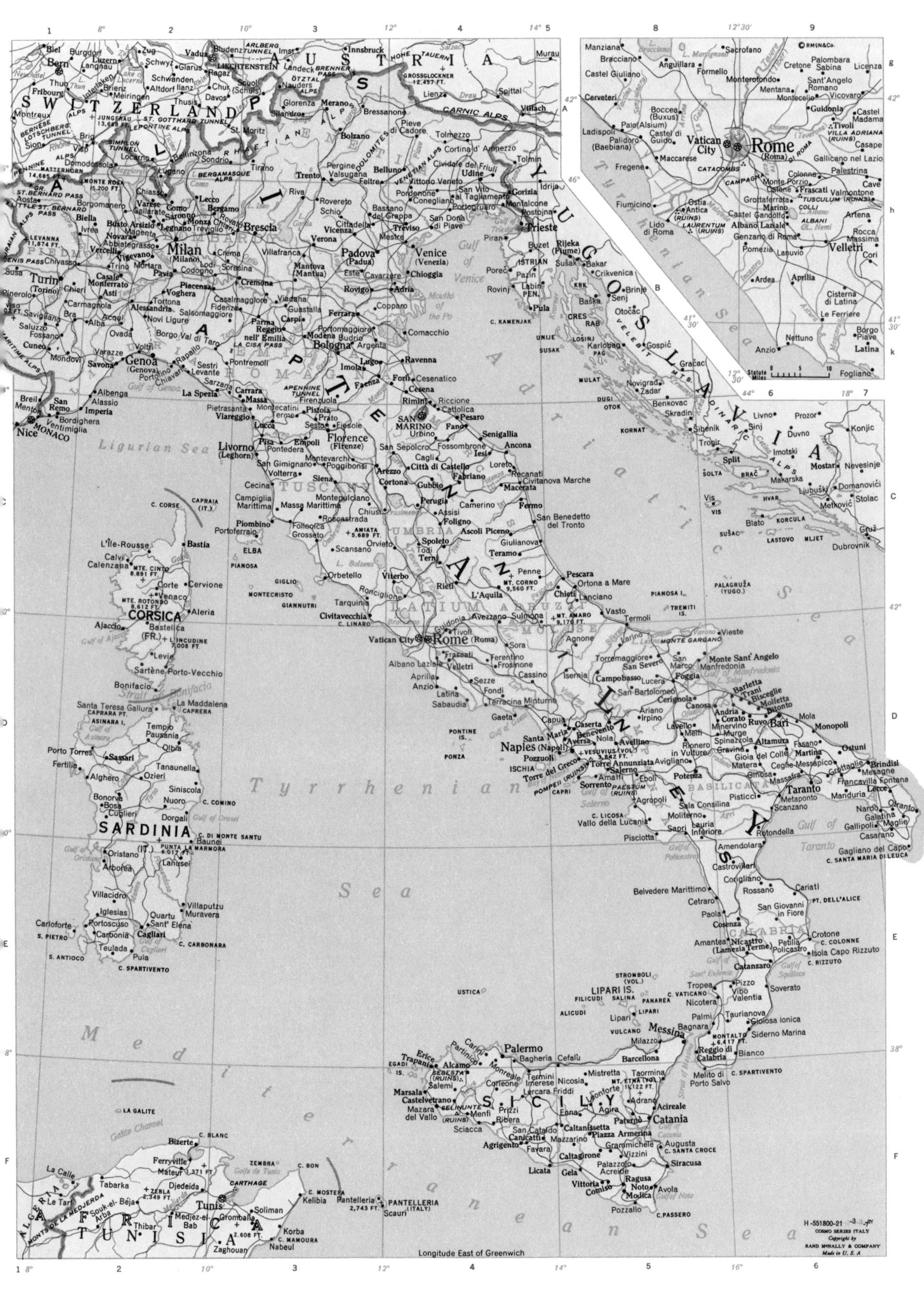
SWITZERLAND
AUSTRIA
LIECHTENSTEIN
YUGOSLAVIA
ALPS
APENNINES
CORSICA (FR.)
SARDINIA (IT.)
SICILY
TUNISIA
ALGERIA
AFRICA
SAN MARINO
MONACO
Adriatic Sea
Ligurian Sea
Tyrrhenian Sea
Mediterranean Sea
Milan
Turin
Genoa
Venice
Bologna
Florence
Rome
Naples
Bari
Palermo
Messina
Catania
Cagliari
Tunis
Vatican City
Longitude East of Greenwich
H-551800-21
COSMO SERIES ITALY
RAND McNALLY & COMPANY
Made in U. S. A.
Conic Projection
Statute Miles
Kilometers

SOVIET UNION
ROMANIA
HUNGARY
YUGOSLAVIA
BULGARIA
ALBANIA
AUSTRIA
CZECHOSLOVAKIA
GREECE
TURKEY
ITALY
Black Sea
Adriatic Sea
Budapest
Belgrade (Beograd)
Bucharest (București)
Sofia (Sofiya)
Vienna (Wien)
Zagreb
Sarajevo
Skopje
Tiranë
Istanbul
Thessaloníki (Salonika)
Kishinev
Chernovtsy
Cluj
Timișoara
Debrecen
Szeged
Plovdiv
Varna
Constanța
Split
Trieste
Statute Miles 25 0 25 50 75
Kilometers 25 0 25 50 100
Conic Projection
Longitude East of Greenwich

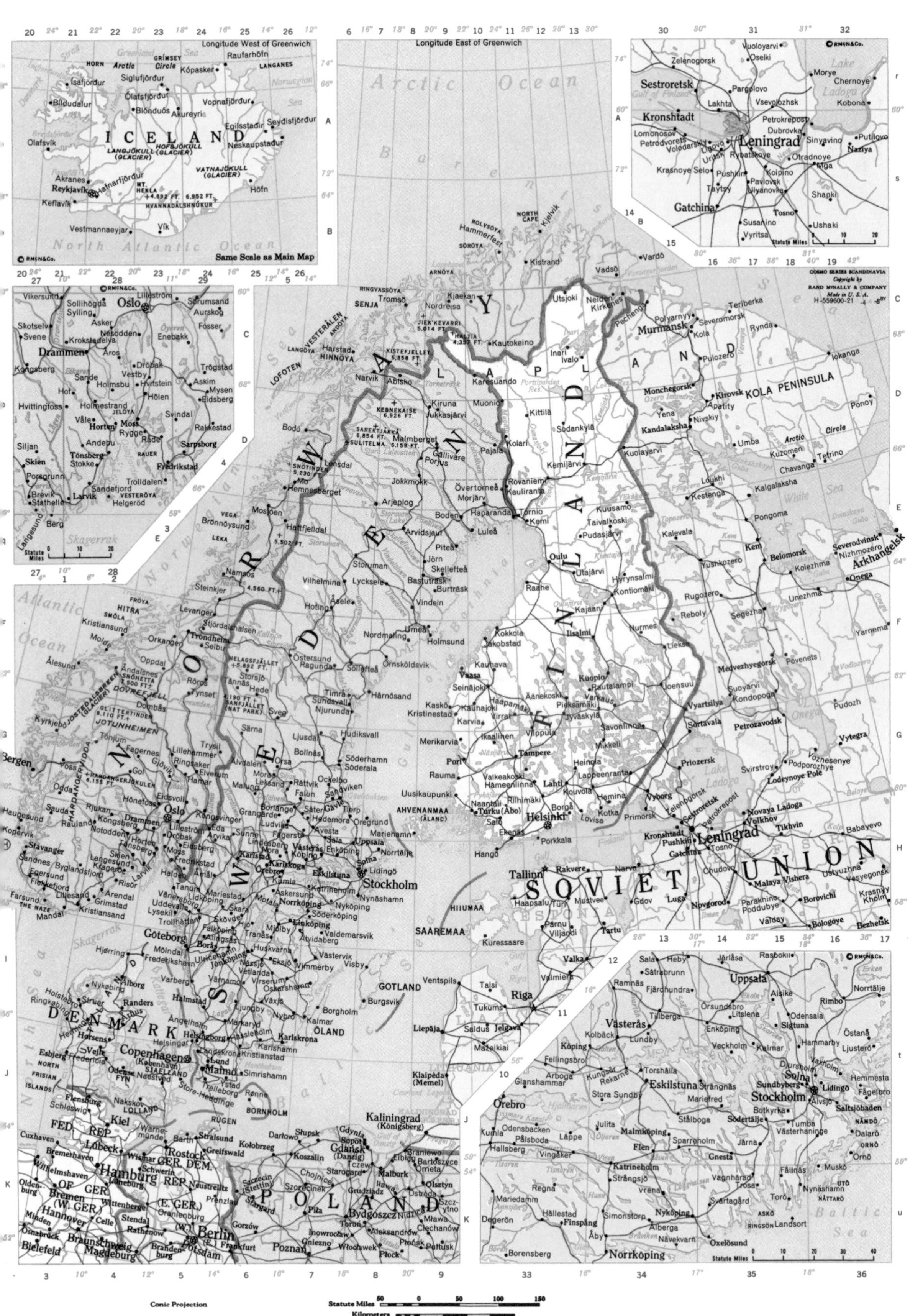
Longitude West of Greenwich
Longitude East of Greenwich
ICELAND
Same Scale as Main Map
Arctic Ocean
North Atlantic Ocean
NORWAY
SWEDEN
FINLAND
LAPLAND
SOVIET UNION
DENMARK
POLAND
KOLA PENINSULA
Oslo
Stockholm
Helsinki
Leningrad
Copenhagen
Reykjavík
Riga
Tallinn
Berlin
Hamburg
Göteborg
Bergen
Trondheim
Murmansk
Arkhangelsk
Uppsala
GOTLAND
ÖLAND
BORNHOLM
SAAREMAA
HIIUMAA
AHVENANMAA (ÅLAND)
COSMO SERIES SCANDINAVIA
Copyright by RAND McNALLY & COMPANY
Made in U. S. A.
Conic Projection
Statute Miles
Kilometers

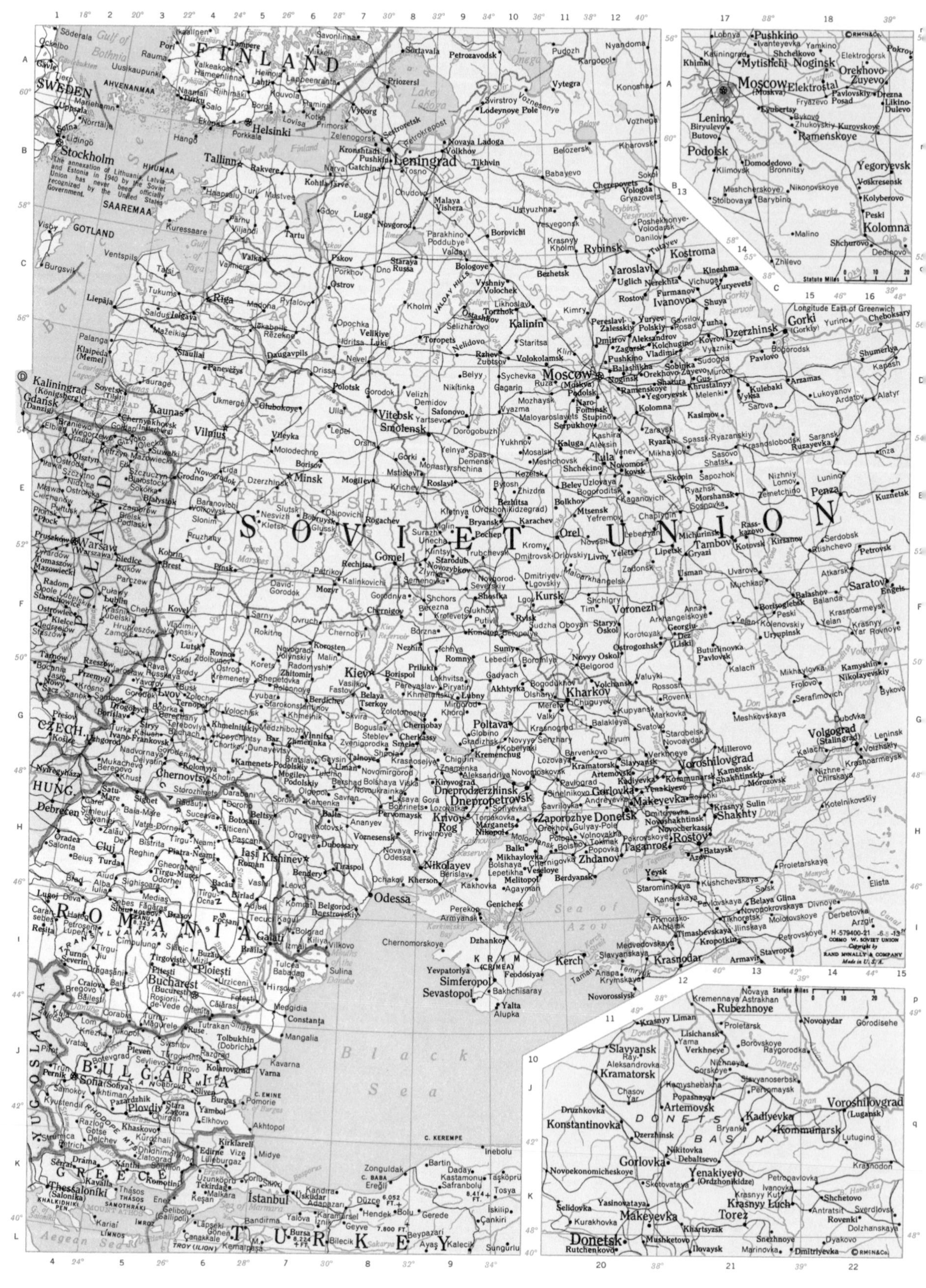
FINLAND
SWEDEN
SOVIET UNION
POLAND
ROMANIA
BULGARIA
TURKEY
GREECE
Black Sea
Sea of Azov
Moscow
Leningrad
Kiev
Helsinki
Stockholm
Warsaw
Bucharest
Sofia
Istanbul
Odessa
Kharkov
Minsk
Riga
Tallinn
Gorki
Volgograd
Voroshilovgrad
Donetsk
Rostov
The annexation of Lithuania, Latvia, and Estonia in 1940 by the Soviet Union has never been officially recognized by the United States Government.
Longitude East of Greenwich
Statute Miles
Kilometers
Conic Projection

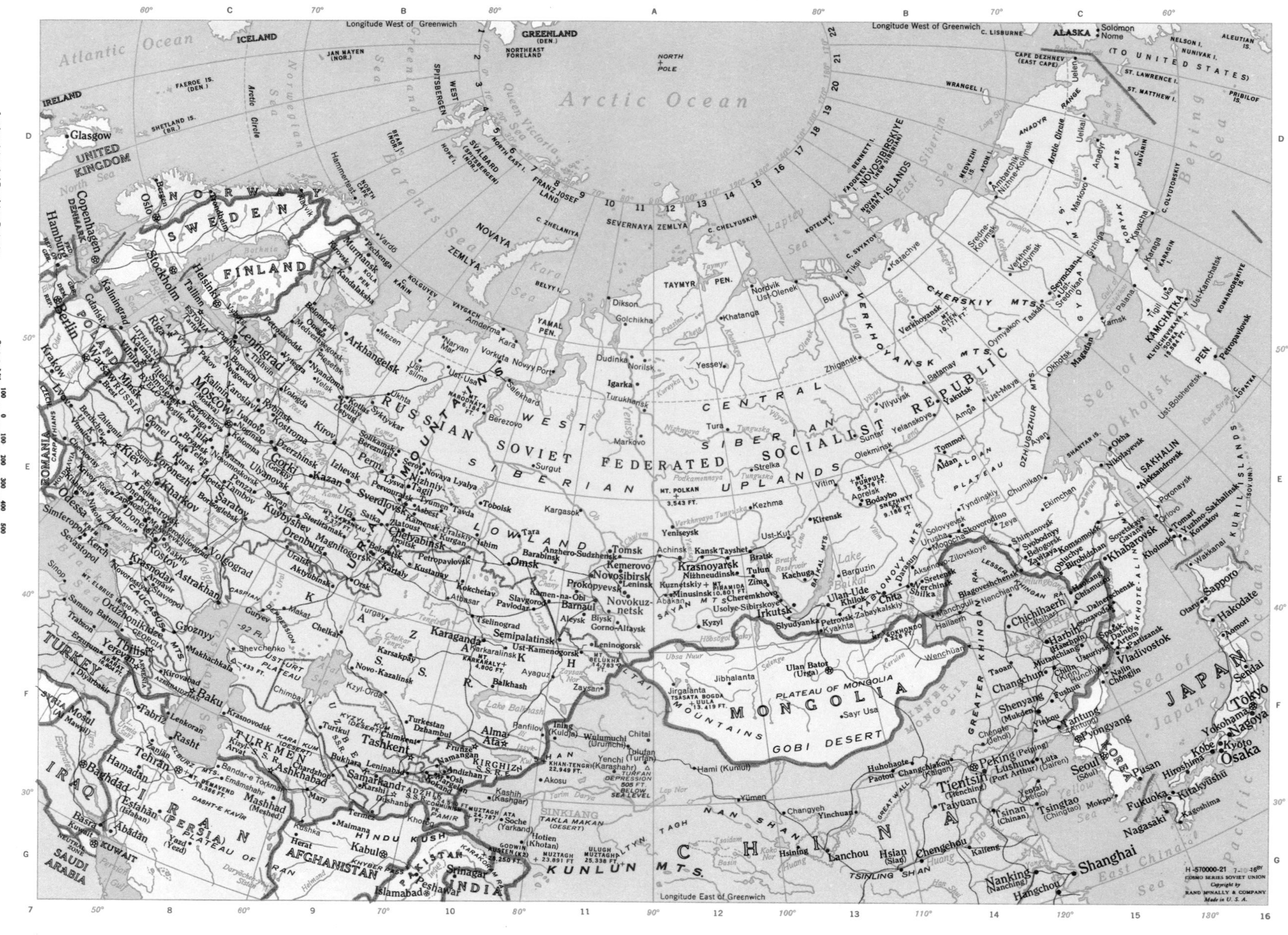

Lambert Azimuthal Equal Area Projection

Statute Miles 100 0 100 200 300 400 500

Kilometers 100 0 100 300 500 700

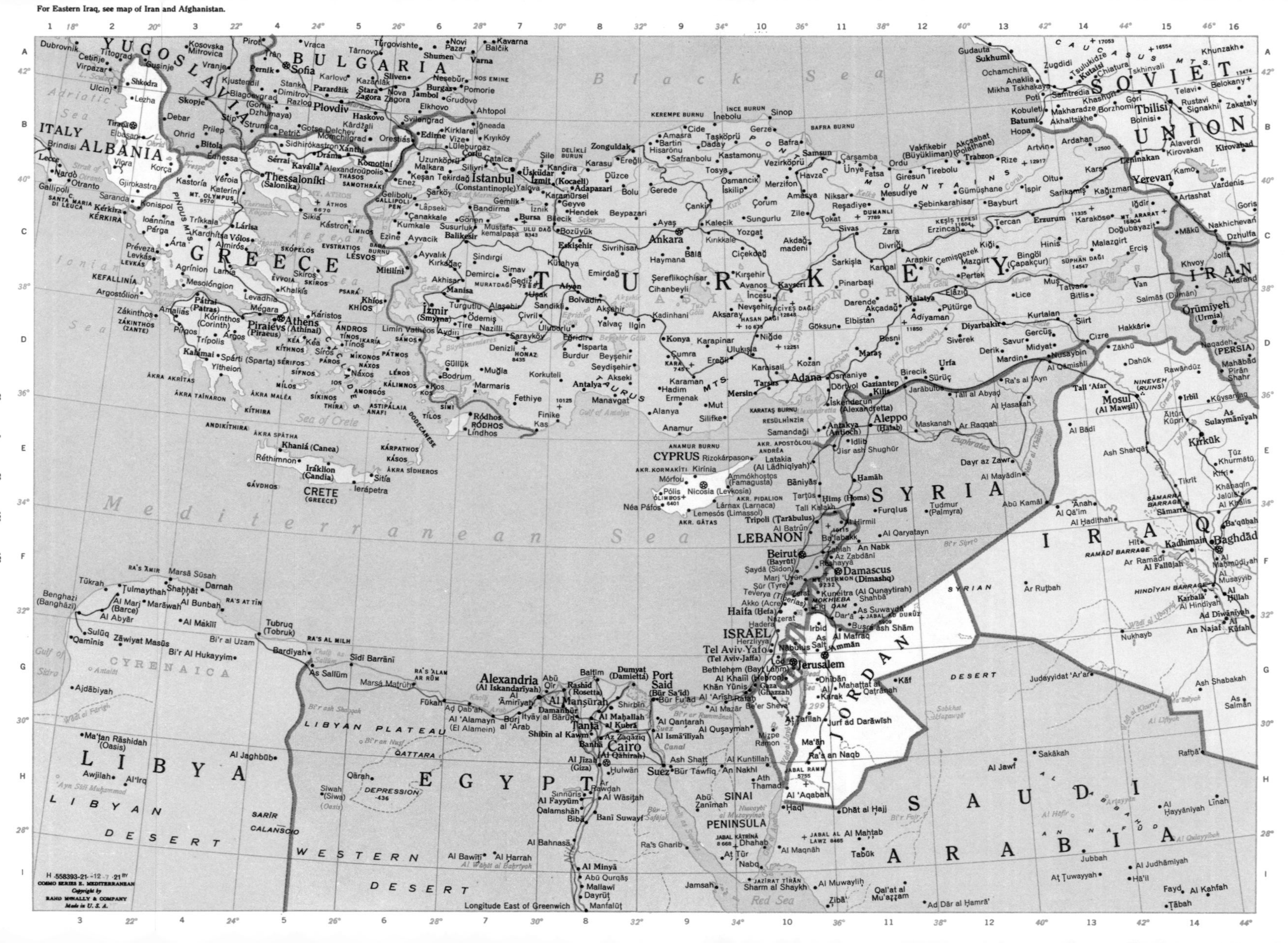
For Eastern Iraq, see map of Iran and Afghanistan.
SOVIET UNION
TURKEY
SYRIA
IRAQ
IRAN
LEBANON
ISRAEL
JORDAN
SAUDI ARABIA
EGYPT
LIBYA
GREECE
BULGARIA
YUGOSLAVIA
ALBANIA
ITALY
CYPRUS
CRETE (GREECE)
SINAI PENINSULA
Black Sea
Mediterranean Sea
Ionian Sea
Aegean Sea
Sea of Crete
Red Sea
LIBYAN PLATEAU
LIBYAN DESERT
WESTERN DESERT
SYRIAN DESERT
QATTARA DEPRESSION
CAUCASUS MTS.
TAURUS MTS.
PINDUS MTS.
PONTIC MOUNTAINS
ASIA MINOR
CYRENAICA
Ankara
Istanbul (Constantinople)
Athens (Athínai)
Beirut (Bayrūt)
Damascus (Dimashq)
Jerusalem
'Ammān
Baghdād
Cairo (Al Qāhirah)
Alexandria (Al Iskandarīyah)
Nicosia (Levkosía)
Sofia
Tbilisi
Yerevan
Tiranë
Longitude East of Greenwich
Statute Miles
Kilometers
Lambert Conformal Conic Projection
H-558393-21-12-7-21 BY
COSMO SERIES E. MEDITERRANEAN
Copyright by RAND McNALLY & COMPANY
Made in U. S. A.

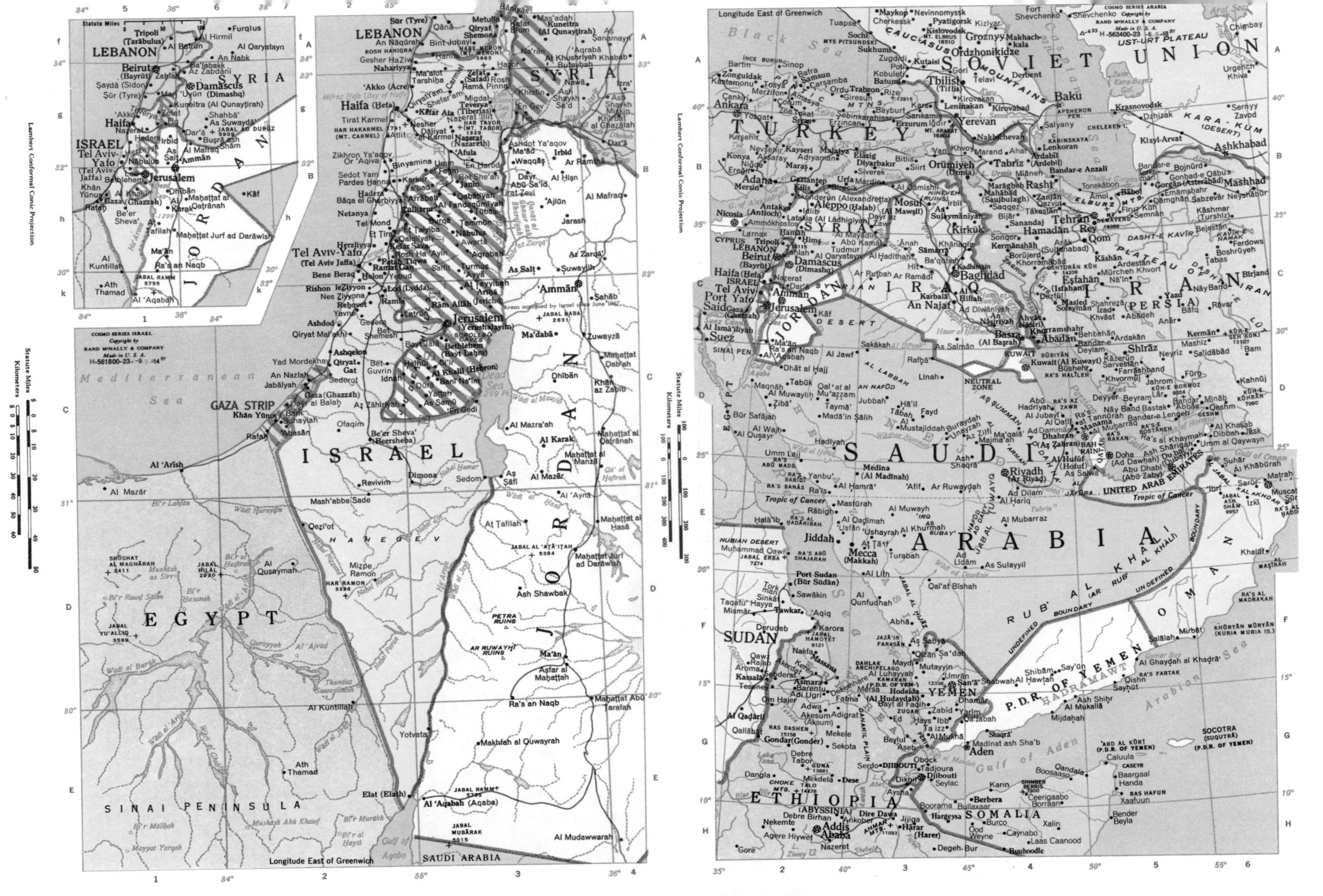
COSMO SERIES ISRAEL
Copyright by
RAND McNALLY & COMPANY
Made in U. S. A.
H-561800-23
LEBANON
SYRIA
ISRAEL
JORDAN
EGYPT
SINAI PENINSULA
SAUDI ARABIA
GAZA STRIP
Mediterranean Sea
Dead Sea
Gulf of Aqaba
Jerusalem (Yerushalayim)
Tel Aviv-Yafo (Tel Aviv Jaffa)
Haifa (Hefa)
'Ammān
Damascus (Dimashq)
Beirut (Bayrūt)
Areas occupied by Israel since June 1967
Longitude East of Greenwich
Lambert Conformal Conic Projection
Statute Miles 5 0 5 10 20 30 40 50
Kilometers 5 0 5 10 20 30 40 50 60
COSMO SERIES ARABIA
Copyright by
RAND McNALLY & COMPANY
Made in U. S. A.
H-563400-23
SOVIET UNION
TURKEY
SYRIA
IRAQ
IRAN (PERSIA)
SAUDI ARABIA
KUWAIT
QATAR
UNITED ARAB EMIRATES
OMAN
YEMEN
P.D.R. OF YEMEN
SUDAN
ETHIOPIA
SOMALIA
Black Sea
Caspian Sea
Arabian Sea
Gulf of Aden
Tropic of Cancer
Longitude East of Greenwich
Lambert Conformal Conic Projection
Statute Miles 100 0 100 200 300
Kilometers 100 0 100 200 300 400

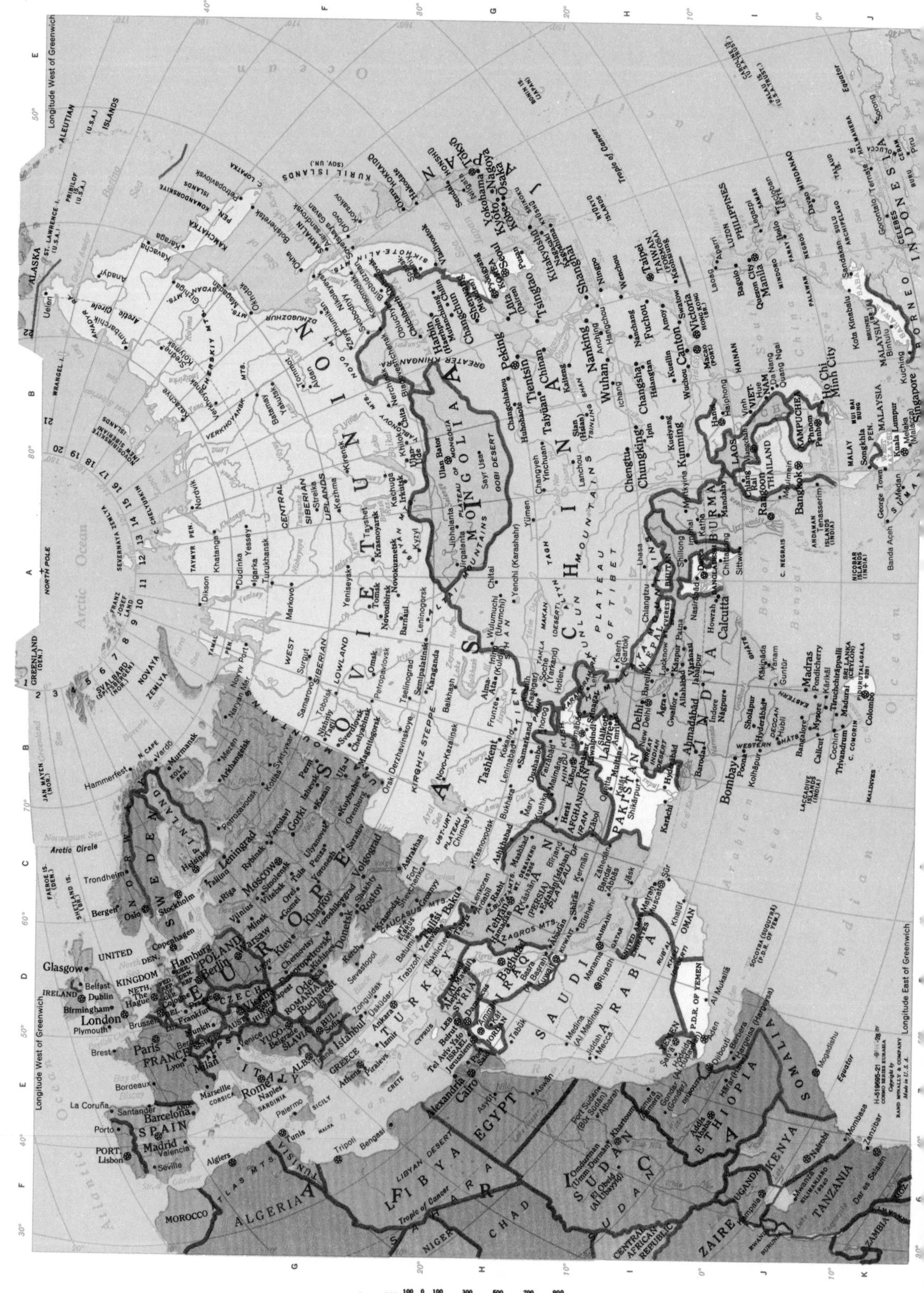

Statute Miles 100 0 100 300 500 700 900

Kilometers 100 0 100 300 700 1100

Lambert Azimuthal Equal Area Projection

Polyconic Projection
Statute Miles 100 0 100 200 300
Kilometers 100 0 100 200 300 400
Longitude East of Greenwich
Tropic of Cancer
H-560793-21 -3-10
COSMO SERIES E. ASIA
Copyright by
RAND McNALLY & COMPANY
Made in U. S. A.
SOVIET UNION
MONGOLIA
CHINA
JAPAN
NORTH KOREA
SOUTH KOREA
TAIWAN (FORMOSA) (NATIONALIST CHINA)
VIETNAM
LAOS
BURMA
INDIA
BHUTAN
BANGLADESH
THAILAND
HOKKAIDO
HONSHŪ
SHIKOKU
KYŪSHŪ
SAKHALIN
Sea of Japan
Yellow Sea
East China Sea
South China Sea
Pacific Ocean
Lake Baykal
GOBI DESERT
PLATEAU OF MONGOLIA
ALTAY MOUNTAINS
KUNLUN MOUNTAINS
HIMALAYA MTS.
GREATER KHINGAN RA.
SIKHOTE ALIN
YUNNAN PLATEAU
Shanghai
Tokyo
Peking
Nanking
Canton
Seoul
Hanoi
Lhasa (Lasa)
Urumchi (Wulumuchi)
Ulan Bator (Urga)

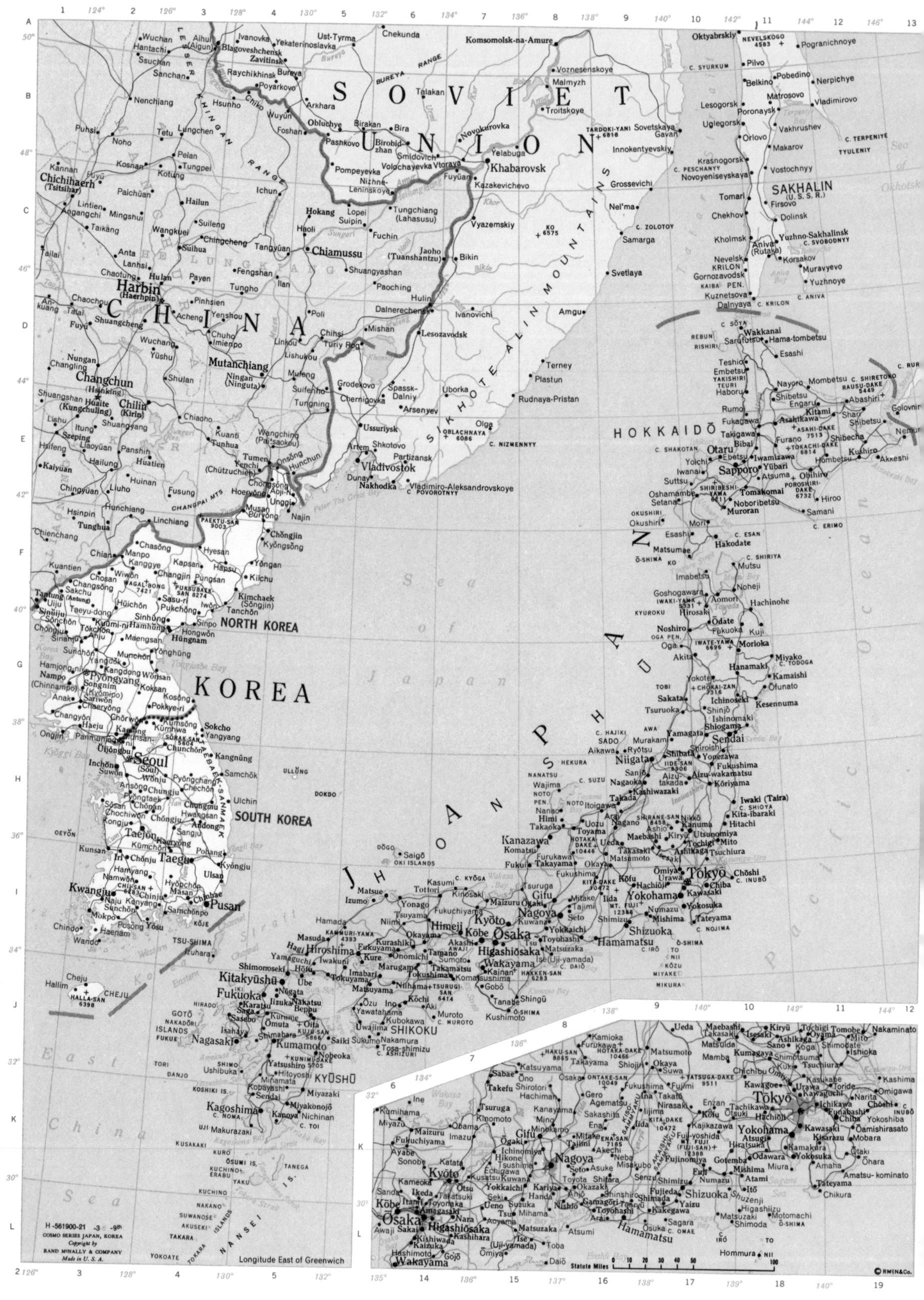

Statute Miles 50 0 50 100 150
Kilometers 50 0 50 100 200

Lambert Conformal Conic Projection

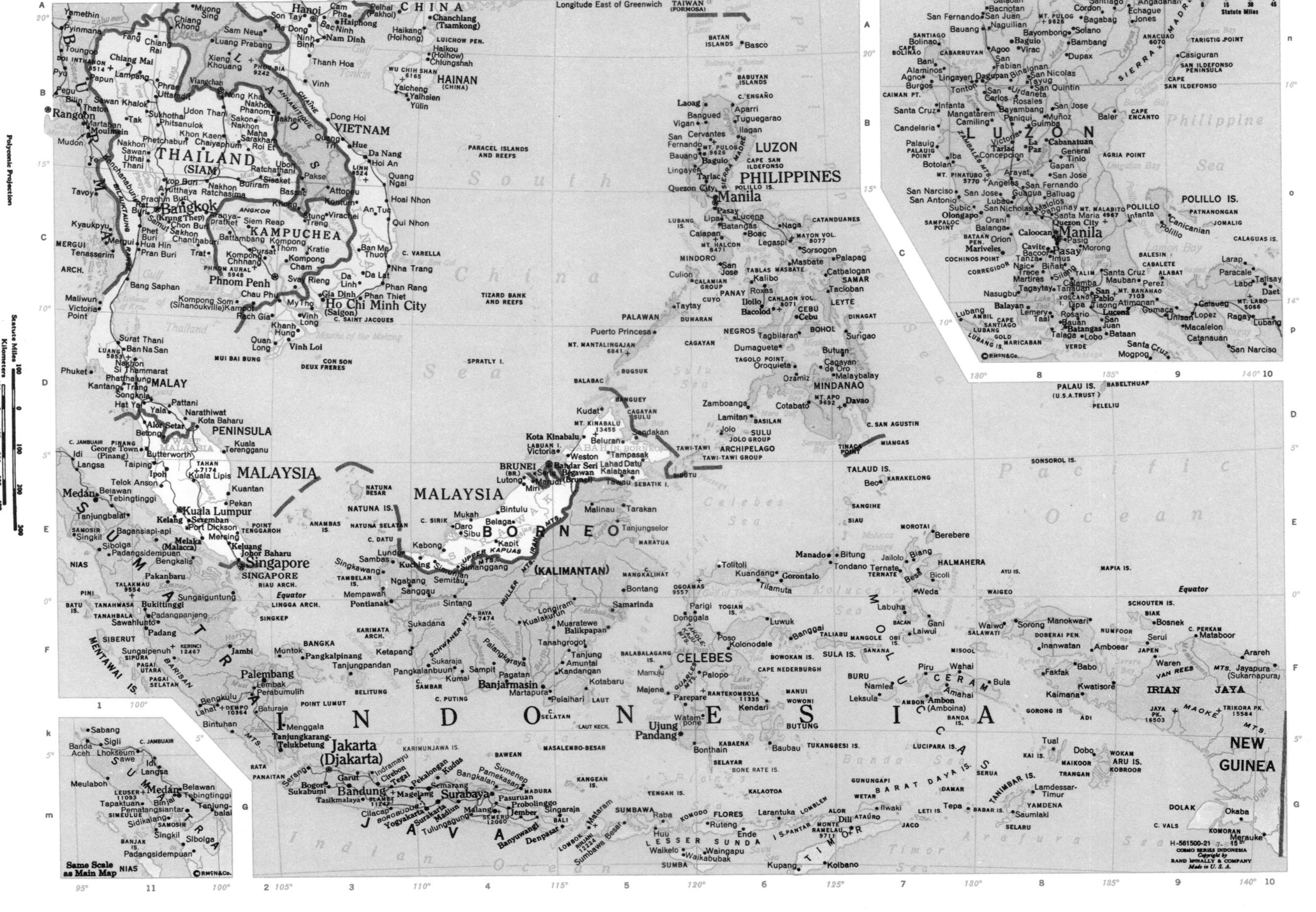
Longitude East of Greenwich
CHINA
VIETNAM
THAILAND (SIAM)
KAMPUCHEA
LAOS
BURMA
PHILIPPINES
LUZON
MINDANAO
MALAYSIA
MALAY PENINSULA
BORNEO (KALIMANTAN)
CELEBES
INDONESIA
SUMATRA
JAVA
MOLUCCAS
IRIAN JAYA
NEW GUINEA
South China Sea
Pacific Ocean
Indian Ocean
Manila
Singapore
Jakarta (Djakarta)
Bangkok
Ho Chi Minh City (Saigon)
Phnom Penh
Kuala Lumpur
Hanoi
Rangoon
Polyconic Projection
Statute Miles
Kilometers
Same Scale as Main Map
H-561500-21
COSMO SERIES INDONESIA
Copyright by RAND McNALLY & COMPANY
Made in U. S. A.

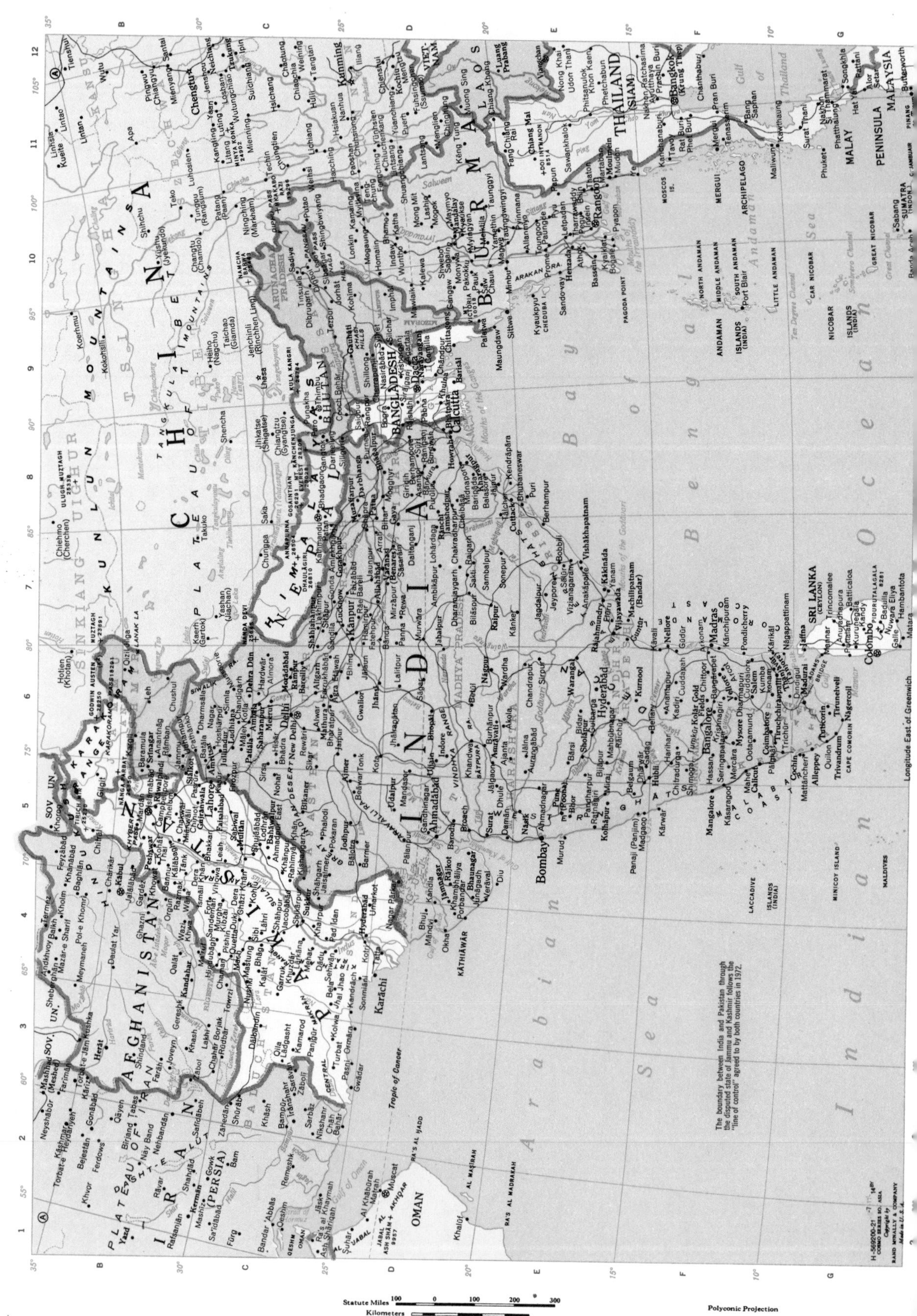

Statute Miles 100 0 100 200 300

Kilometers 100 0 100 200 300 400

Polyconic Projection

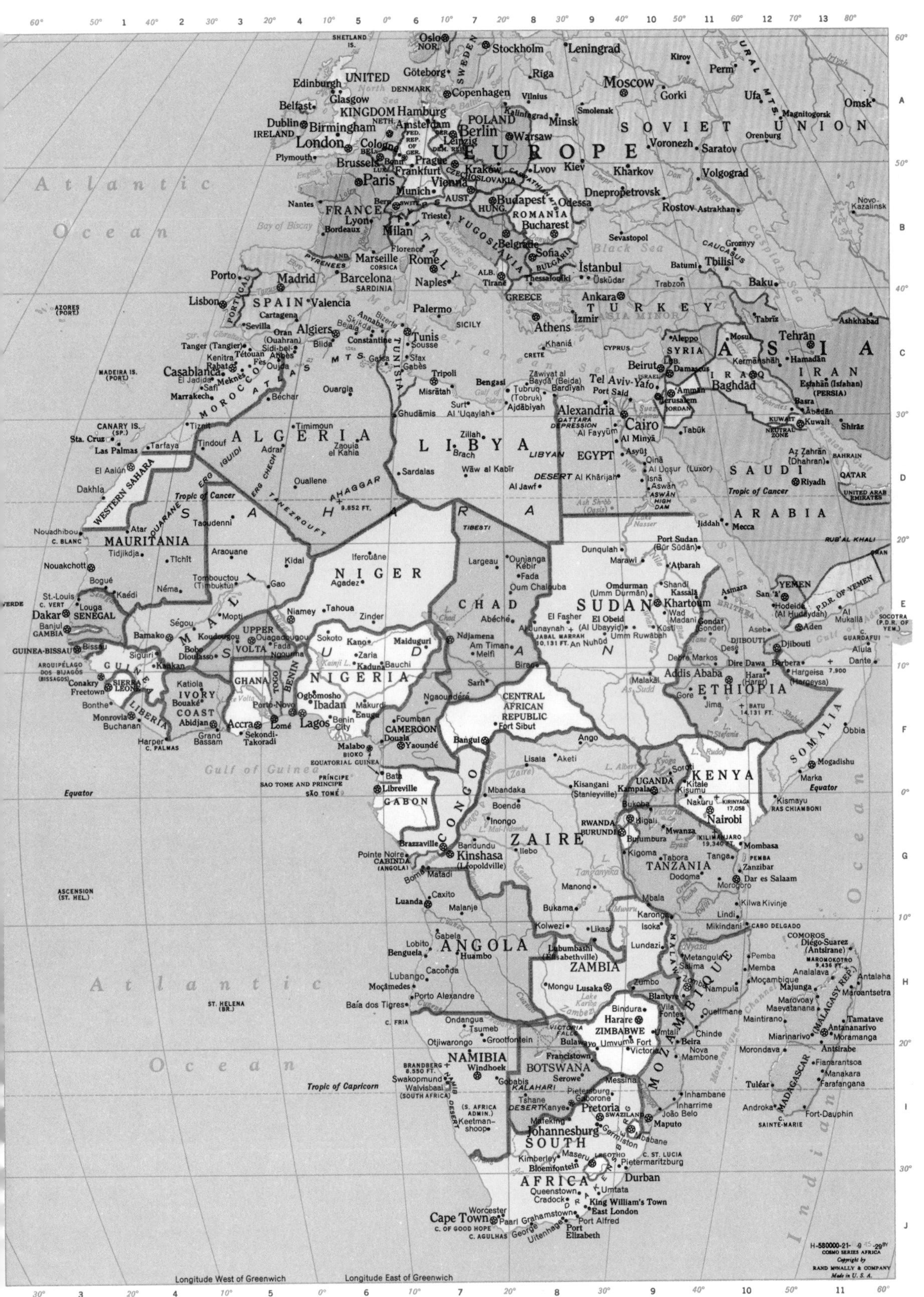
EUROPE
SOVIET UNION
ASIA
Atlantic Ocean
Indian Ocean
Gulf of Guinea
Black Sea
Caspian Sea
Red Sea
Mediterranean Sea
Equator
Tropic of Cancer
Tropic of Capricorn
UNITED KINGDOM
IRELAND
FRANCE
SPAIN
PORTUGAL
ITALY
YUGOSLAVIA
ROMANIA
BULGARIA
GREECE
TURKEY
SYRIA
IRAQ
IRAN
SAUDI ARABIA
YEMEN
P.D.R. OF YEMEN
MOROCCO
ALGERIA
TUNISIA
LIBYA
EGYPT
SUDAN
ETHIOPIA
SOMALIA
KENYA
UGANDA
TANZANIA
WESTERN SAHARA
MAURITANIA
MALI
NIGER
CHAD
SENEGAL
GAMBIA
GUINEA-BISSAU
GUINEA
SIERRA LEONE
LIBERIA
IVORY COAST
UPPER VOLTA
GHANA
TOGO
BENIN
NIGERIA
CAMEROON
CENTRAL AFRICAN REPUBLIC
EQUATORIAL GUINEA
GABON
CONGO
ZAIRE
RWANDA
BURUNDI
ANGOLA
ZAMBIA
MALAWI
MOZAMBIQUE
ZIMBABWE
BOTSWANA
NAMIBIA
SOUTH AFRICA
SWAZILAND
LESOTHO
MADAGASCAR (MALAGASY REP.)
SAHARA
London
Paris
Madrid
Lisbon
Rome
Berlin
Warsaw
Moscow
Leningrad
Stockholm
Oslo
Copenhagen
Istanbul
Ankara
Athens
Cairo
Alexandria
Tripoli
Tunis
Algiers
Casablanca
Dakar
Bamako
Niamey
Lagos
Accra
Abidjan
Monrovia
Freetown
Conakry
Khartoum
Addis Ababa
Nairobi
Mogadishu
Kinshasa
Brazzaville
Luanda
Lusaka
Harare
Pretoria
Johannesburg
Durban
Cape Town
Baghdad
Tehrān
Beirut
Damascus
Jerusalem
Mecca
Jiddah
Riyadh
Aden
Djibouti
Dar es Salaam
Kampala
Ndjamena
Bangui
Yaoundé
Libreville
Maputo
Windhoek
Antananarivo
Longitude West of Greenwich
Longitude East of Greenwich
H-580000-21
COSMO SERIES AFRICA
Copyright by RAND McNALLY & COMPANY
Made in U. S. A.
Sinusoidal Projection
Statute Miles 100 0 100 300 500 700 900
Kilometers 100 0 100 300 500 700 900 1100 1300

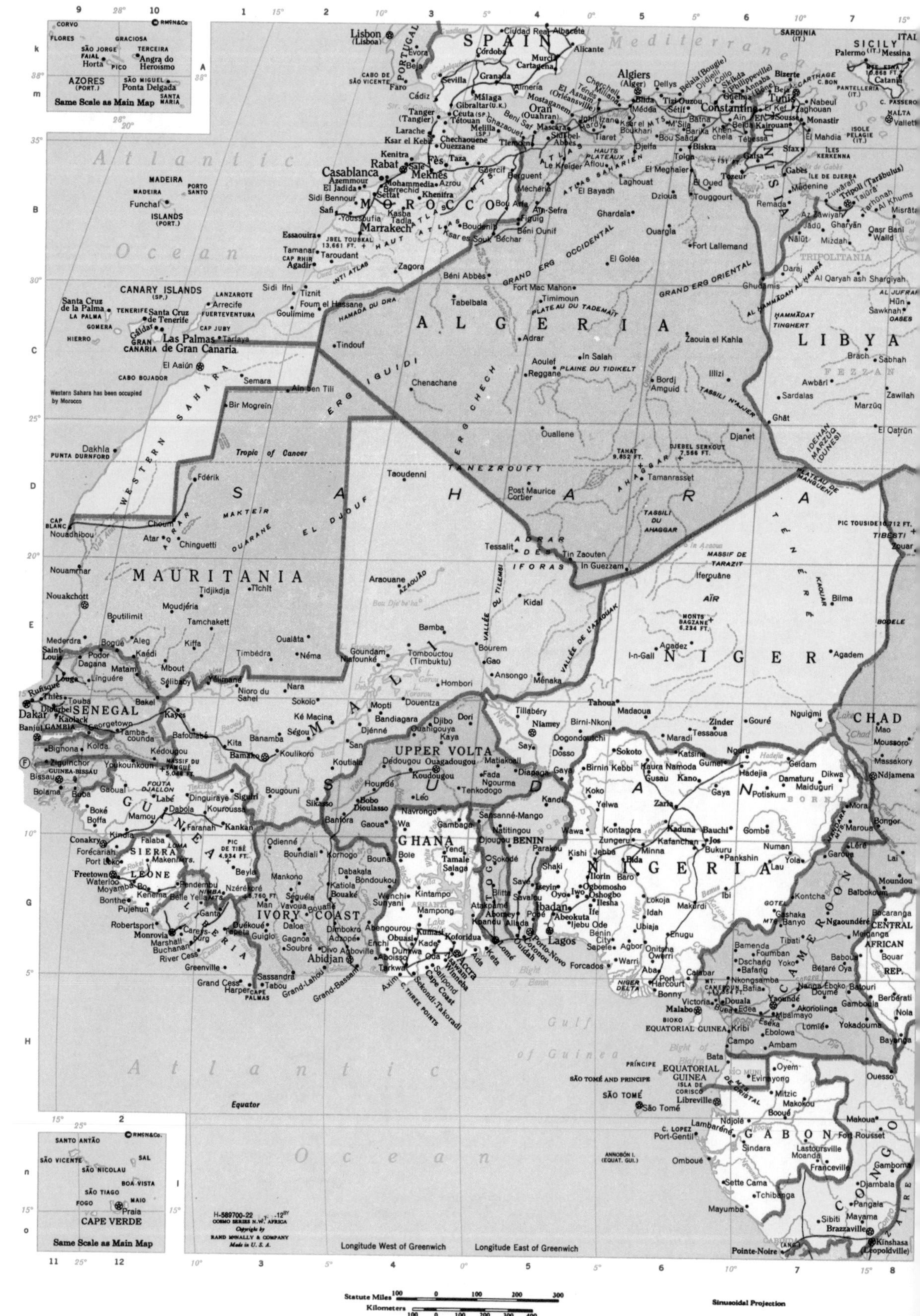
AZORES (PORT.)
Same Scale as Main Map
CORVO
FLORES
GRACIOSA
SÃO JORGE
TERCEIRA
FAIAL
Horta
Angra do Heroísmo
PICO
SÃO MIGUEL
Ponta Delgada
SANTA MARIA
Atlantic Ocean
MADEIRA ISLANDS (PORT.)
MADEIRA
PORTO SANTO
Funchal
CANARY ISLANDS (SP.)
LANZAROTE
Arrecife
FUERTEVENTURA
TENERIFE
Santa Cruz de Tenerife
Santa Cruz de la Palma
LA PALMA
GOMERA
HIERRO
Gáldar
GRAN CANARIA
Las Palmas de Gran Canaria
CAP JUBY
Tarfaya
CABO BOJADOR
El Aaiún
Western Sahara has been occupied by Morocco
WESTERN SAHARA
Semara
Bir Mogreïn
Dakhla
PUNTA DURNFORD
Tropic of Cancer
CAP BLANC
Nouadhibou
Fdérik
Choum
Atar
Chinguetti
ADRAR
MAKTEÏR
OUARANE
EL DJOUF
Nouamghar
MAURITANIA
Nouakchott
Tidjikdja
Tichît
Moudjéria
Boutilimit
Tamchakett
Kiffa
Aleg
Kaédi
Mederdra
Rosso
Saint-Louis
Podor
Dagana
Matam
Bogué
Louga
Linguère
Mbout
Sélibaby
Timbédra
Oualâta
Néma
Yélimané
Rufisque
Thiès
Touba
Diourbel
Kaolack
Dakar
SENEGAL
Bakel
Kayes
Banjul
GAMBIA
Georgetown
Tambacounda
Kolda
Bignona
Ziguinchor
GUINEA-BISSAU
Bissau
Bolama
Kédougou
MASSIF DU TANGUÉ 5,046 FT.
Youkounkoun
FOUTA DJALLON
Gaoual
Boké
Boffa
Labé
Mamou
Dabola
Dinguiraye
Siguiri
Kouroussa
Faranah
Kankan
Kindia
Conakry
Forécariah
Falaba
SIERRA LEONE
Port Loko
Makeni
Freetown
Waterloo
Moyamba
Bo
Kenema
Bonthe
Pujehun
Pendembu
Beyla
PIC DE TIBÉ 4,934 FT.
Nzérékoré
Robertsport
Monrovia
Marshall
Buchanan
River Cess
Greenville
Harper
LIBERIA
Ganta
Tapeta
CAPE PALMAS
Grand Cess
Tabou
Sassandra
Grand-Lahou
Grand-Bassam
Abidjan
IVORY COAST
Man
Duékoué
Guiglo
Daloa
Gagnoa
Soubré
Divo
Agboville
Abengourou
Dimbokro
Adzopé
Bouaké
Katiola
Séguéla
Vavoua
Bouaflé
Mankono
Odienné
Boundiali
Korhogo
Dabakala
Bondoukou
Bouna
Ferkessédougou
GHANA
Bole
Yendi
Tamale
Salaga
Wa
Gambaga
Navrongo
Wenchi
Sunyani
Kintampo
Mampong
Kumasi
Obuasi
Koforidua
Kade
Dunkwa
Enchi
Aboisso
Tarkwa
Axim
Sekondi-Takoradi
Cape Coast
Saltpond
Winneba
Accra
Ada
Keta
Lomé
Ouidah
Cotonou
Porto-Novo
CAPE THREE POINTS
TOGO
Sokodé
Atakpamé
Kpandu
Aného
Abomey
BENIN
Djougou
Natitingou
Parakou
Kandi
Savé
Savalou
Sansanné-Mango
UPPER VOLTA
Ouagadougou
Koudougou
Dédougou
Ouahigouya
Kaya
Djibo
Dori
Fada Ngourma
Tenkodogo
Diapaga
Bobo Dioulasso
Houndé
Gaoua
Léo
Banfora
Sikasso
Bougouni
Koutiala
San
Djenné
Mopti
Bandiagara
Douentza
Ségou
Bamako
Koulikoro
Kita
Bafoulabé
Banamba
Kolokani
Nioro du Sahel
Nara
Sokolo
Ké Macina
Niafounké
Goundam
Tombouctou (Timbuktu)
Bourem
Gao
Ansongo
Ménaka
Hombori
Kidal
Araouane
Taoudenni
Tessalit
ADRAR DES IFORAS
VALLÉE DU TILEMSI
VALLÉE DE L'AZAOUAK
MALI
SUDAN
Tin Zaouten
In Guezzam
Tillabéry
Niamey
Say
Dosso
Dogondoutchi
Birni-Nkoni
Tahoua
Madaoua
Maradi
Tessaoua
Zinder
Gouré
Nguigmi
Agadez
I-n-Gall
NIGER
AÏR
Iferouâne
MONTS BAGZANE 6,234 FT.
MASSIF DE TARAZIT
TÉNÉRÉ
Bilma
KAOUAR
Agadem
BODELE
TIBESTI
PIC TOUSIDE 10,712 FT.
Zouar
CHAD
Mao
Moussoro
Massakory
Ndjamena
Bongor
Lai
Moundou
Sokoto
Gusau
Kaura Namoda
Katsina
Kano
Birnin Kebbi
Gaya
Hadejia
Nguru
Gumel
Geidam
Potiskum
Damaturu
Maiduguri
Dikwa
BORNU
Gombe
Bauchi
Jos
Bukuru
Pankshin
Numan
Yola
Zaria
Kaduna
Kafanchan
Kontagora
Zungeru
Minna
Bida
Kishi
Jebba
Ilorin
Baro
Lokoja
Idah
Makurdi
Ibi
Lau
NIGERIA
Shaki
Oyo
Iseyin
Ogbomosho
Oshogbo
Ilesha
Iwo
Ife
Ibadan
Abeokuta
Ijebu Ode
Lagos
Benin City
Sapele
Forcados
Warri
Agbor
Onitsha
Owerri
Enugu
Aba
Port Harcourt
Bonny
Calabar
Ubiaja
NIGER DELTA
Bight of Benin
Gulf of Guinea
Bight of Biafra
CAMEROON
Garoua
Maroua
Mora
Kontcha
Gashaka
Banyo
Ngaoundéré
Tibati
Foumban
Bamenda
Dschang
Bafang
Nkongsamba
Bafia
MT. CAMEROON
Victoria
Buea
Douala
Edea
Yaoundé
Nanga-Eboko
Batouri
Doumé
Mbalmayo
Akonolinga
Kribi
Ebolowa
Lomié
Yokadouma
Ambam
Campo
CENTRAL AFRICAN REP.
Bocaranga
Meiganga
Bouar
Baboua
Bétaré Oya
Berbérati
Gamboula
Nola
Bayanga
Malabo
BIOKO
EQUATORIAL GUINEA
PRÍNCIPE
SÃO TOMÉ AND PRINCIPE
SÃO TOMÉ
São Tomé
Bata
RÍO MUNI
ISLA DE CORISCO
Libreville
Oyem
Evinayong
Mitzic
Makokou
Booué
Ndjolé
Lambaréné
C. LOPEZ
Port-Gentil
GABON
Sindara
Omboué
Lastoursville
Moanda
Franceville
Makoua
Fort Rousset
Ouesso
Sette Cama
Tchibanga
Mayumba
CONGO
Djambala
Gamboma
Pangala
Mayama
Sibiti
Brazzaville
Kinshasa (Léopoldville)
Pointe-Noire
ANNOBÓN I. (EQUAT. GUI.)
Equator
Lisbon (Lisboa)
PORTUGAL
Évora
Beja
Faro
CABO DE SÃO VICENTE
SPAIN
Ciudad Real
Albacete
Córdoba
Murcia
Cartagena
Alicante
Sevilla
Granada
Almería
Cádiz
Málaga
Gibraltar (U.K.)
Str. of Gibraltar
Tanger (Tangier)
Ceuta (SP.)
Tétouan
Melilla (SP.)
Larache
Chechaouene
Ouezzane
Ksar el Kebir
Kenitra
Rabat
Salé
Fès
Taza
Meknès
Casablanca
Azemmour
El Jadida
Mohammedia
Berrechid
Settat
Azrou
Khenifra
Sidi Bennour
Safi
Youssoufia
Kasba Tadla
Marrakech
MOROCCO
Essaouira
JBEL TOUBKAL 13,661 FT.
HAUT ATLAS
MOYEN ATLAS
ANTI ATLAS
Tamanar
CAP RHIR
Agadir
Taroudant
Tiznit
Sidi Ifni
Foum el Hassane
Goulimime
Zagora
Boudenib
Ksar es Souk
Guercif
Figuig
Béchar
Oujda
Mediterranean Sea
Algiers (Alger)
Oran (Ouahran)
Mostaganem
El Asnam (Orléansville)
Ténès
Cherchell
Miliana
Blida
Médéa
Dellys
Tizi Ouzou
Bejaïa (Bougie)
Djidjelli
Collo
Skikda (Philippeville)
Annaba (Bône)
Constantine
Sétif
M'Sila
Batna
Biskra
Khenchela
Tébessa
Guelma
Aïn Beïda
Beni Saf
Ghazaouet
Mascara
Tlemcen
Sidi bel Abbès
Saïda
Tiaret
Bou Saâda
Boukhari
Djelfa
Laghouat
Aflou
Le Kreider
HAUTS PLATEAUX
ATLAS SAHARIEN
Méchéria
Aïn Sefra
Bou Arfa
Beni Ounif
Berguent
El Bayadh
Ghardaïa
Touggourt
El Oued
Ouargla
El Meghaier
Tolga
Dzioua
Fort Lallemand
El Goléa
GRAND ERG OCCIDENTAL
GRAND ERG ORIENTAL
Béni Abbès
Fort Mac Mahon
Timimoun
Tabelbala
PLATEAU DU TADEMAÏT
HAMADA DU DRA
Tindouf
ALGERIA
Adrar
Aoulef
In Salah
Reggane
PLAINE DU TIDIKELT
ERG IGUIDI
ERG CHECH
Chenachane
Bordj Amguid
Illizi
Zaouia el Kahla
TASSILI N'AJJER
Djanet
Ouallene
TANEZROUFT
TAHAT 9,852 FT.
DJEBEL SERKOUT 7,566 FT.
AHAGGAR
Tamanrasset
TASSILI DU AHAGGAR
Post Maurice Cortier
SAHARA
TUNISIA
Tunis
Bizerte
Béja
Le Kef
Kairouan
Sousse
Monastir
El Mahdia
Gafsa
Sfax
Tozeur
Gabès
Médenine
ÎLE DE DJERBA
ÎLES KERKENNA
C. BON
Nabeul
Zaghouan
PANTELLERIA (IT.)
SARDINIA (IT.)
SICILY (IT.)
Palermo
Messina
Catania
MT. ETNA 10,868 FT.
MALTA
Valletta
ISOLE PELAGIE (IT.)
LIBYA
Tripoli (Tarābulus)
Zuwārah
Tājūrā
Az Zawiyah
Tarhūnah
Al Khums
Misrātah
Gharyān
Jādū
Nālūt
Mizdah
Qasr Banī Walīd
TRIPOLITANIA
Ghadāmis
Darāj
Al Qaryah ash Sharqiyah
AL HAMMĀDAH AL HAMRĀ
HAMMĀDAT TINGHERT
Hūn
Sawknah
Brach
Sabhah
FEZZAN
Awbārī
Sardalas
Marzūq
Zawilah
Ghāt
IDEHAN MARZŪQ (DUNES)
El Qatrūn
PLATEAU DE MANGUENI
Longitude West of Greenwich
Longitude East of Greenwich
CAPE VERDE
Same Scale as Main Map
SANTO ANTÃO
SÃO VICENTE
SÃO NICOLAU
SAL
BOA VISTA
SÃO TIAGO
MAIO
FOGO
Praia
H-589700-22
COSMO SERIES N.W. AFRICA
Copyright by RAND McNALLY & COMPANY
Made in U. S. A.
Statute Miles 100 0 100 200 300
Kilometers 100 0 100 200 300 400
Sinusoidal Projection

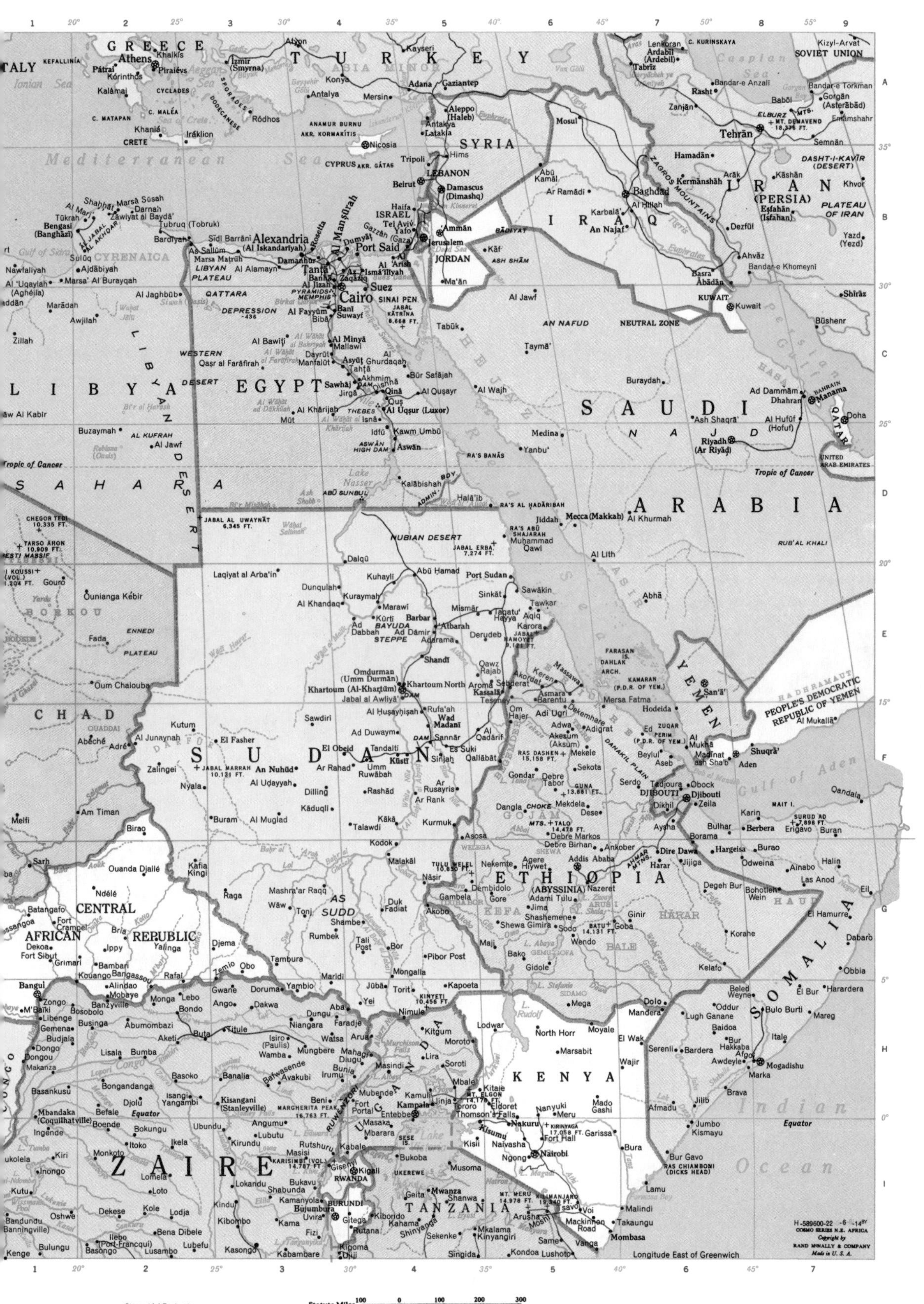
GREECE
Athens
Piraiévs
Pátrai
Kórinthos
Kalámai
Khaniá
Iráklion
CRETE
CYCLADES
DODECANESE
Ródhos
TURKEY
İzmir (Smyrna)
Kayseri
Konya
Antalya
Adana
Gaziantep
Mersin
ASIA MINOR
CYPRUS
Nicosia
Mediterranean Sea
SYRIA
Aleppo (Haleb)
Antakya
Latakia
Hims
Tripoli
LEBANON
Beirut
Damascus (Dimashq)
Haifa
ISRAEL
Tel Aviv-Yafo
Jerusalem
'Ammān
JORDAN
Ma'ān
Gaza
IRAQ
Mosul
Baghdad
Al Hillah
Karbalā'
An Najaf
Basra
Ar Ramādi
Abū Kamāl
KUWAIT
Kuwait
NEUTRAL ZONE
IRAN (PERSIA)
Tehrān
Rasht
Zanjān
Hamadān
Kermānshāh
Esfahān (Isfahan)
Dezfūl
Ahvāz
Ābādān
Bandar-e Khomeyni
Būshehr
Shīrāz
Yazd (Yezd)
Kāshān
Semnān
Qom
DASHT-I-KAVIR (DESERT)
PLATEAU OF IRAN
ZAGROS MOUNTAINS
ELBURZ MTS.
MT. DEMAVEND 18,376 FT.
Caspian Sea
SOVIET UNION
Lenkoran
Ardabil (Ardebil)
Tabriz
Bandar-e Anzali
Babol
Gorgān (Asterābād)
Bandar-e Torkman
Emāmshahr
Kizyl-Arvat
Khvor
Persian Gulf
Ad Dammām
Dhahran
BAHRAIN
Manama
QATAR
Doha
Al Hufūf (Hofuf)
UNITED ARAB EMIRATES
SAUDI ARABIA
Riyadh (Ar Riyāḍ)
NAJD
Buraydah
Ash Shaqrā'
Medina
Yanbu'
Mecca (Makkah)
Jiddah
Al Khurmah
Al Lith
Abhā
Taymā'
Tabūk
Al Jawf
AN NAFUD
RUB' AL KHALI
Tropic of Cancer
Red Sea
YEMEN
San'ā'
Hodeida
PEOPLE'S DEMOCRATIC REPUBLIC OF YEMEN
Aden
Al Mukallā
Shuqrā'
Gulf of Aden
LIBYA
Bengasi (Banghāzī)
Tubruq (Tobruk)
Al Jaghbūb
Ajdābiyah
Marsa' Al Burayqah
Zillah
Buzaymah
Al Jawf
AL KUFRAH
SAHARA
LIBYAN DESERT
EGYPT
Alexandria (Al Iskandarīyah)
Rosetta
Al Manṣūrah
Port Said
Dumyāṭ
Ismā'īlīyah
Suez
Cairo
Al Jīzah
Ṭanṭā
Damanhūr
Marsa Maṭrūḥ
Sidi Barrānī
As Sallūm
Al Alamayn
LIBYAN PLATEAU
QATTARA DEPRESSION -436
Al Fayyūm
Banī Suwayf
Al Minyā
Mallawī
Asyūṭ
Sawhāj
Qinā
Al Uqṣur (Luxor)
Isnā
Idfū
Kawm Umbū
Aswān
ASWAN HIGH DAM
Lake Nasser
Al Khārijah
Al Bawīṭī
Qaṣr al Farāfirah
WESTERN DESERT
Al Ghurdaqah
Būr Safājah
Al Quṣayr
SINAI PEN.
JABAL KATRĪNA 8,668 FT.
Kalābishah
Ḥalā'ib
NUBIAN DESERT
JABAL ERBA 7,274 FT.
JABAL AL UWAYNĀT 6,345 FT.
SUDAN
Khartoum (Al-Kharṭūm)
Omdurman (Umm Durmān)
Khartoum North
Port Sudan
Sawākin
Abū Ḥamad
Atbarah
Shandī
Wad Madanī
Kassalā
El Obeid
Kūstī
Sinnār
El Fasher
An Nuhūd
JABAL MARRAH 10,131 FT.
Nyala
Kādugli
Malakāl
Juba
Wāw
SUDD
Dunqulah
Laqiyat al Arba'īn
CHAD
Abéché
Adré
Am Timan
Ounianga Kébir
ENNEDI PLATEAU
BORKOU
Fada
Oum Chalouba
TIBESTI MASSIF
EMI KOUSSI
CENTRAL AFRICAN REPUBLIC
Bangui
Bria
Ndélé
Yalinga
Rafaï
Zémio
Obo
Birao
ETHIOPIA (ABYSSINIA)
Addis Ababa
Asmara
Massawa
Mekele
Gondar
Dese
Dire Dawa
Harar
Jima
Gambela
Nekemte
RAS DASHEN 15,158 FT.
DANAKIL PLAIN
DJIBOUTI
Djibouti
SOMALIA
Mogadishu
Berbera
Hargeisa
Kismayu
Marka
Brava
KENYA
Nairobi
Mombasa
Nakuru
Kisumu
Eldoret
Malindi
Lamu
L. Rudolf
UGANDA
Kampala
Entebbe
Jinja
Gulu
Lake Victoria
RWANDA
Kigali
BURUNDI
Bujumbura
TANZANIA
Mwanza
Arusha
Moshi
KILIMANJARO 19,340 FT.
Tanga
Kigoma
Ujiji
ZAIRE
Kisangani (Stanleyville)
Mbandaka (Coquilhatville)
Equator
Indian Ocean
Longitude East of Greenwich
H-589600-22 -6 -14
COSMO SERIES N.E. AFRICA
Copyright by RAND McNALLY & COMPANY
Made in U. S. A.
Sinusoidal Projection
Statute Miles 100 0 100 200 300
Kilometers 100 0 100 200 300 400

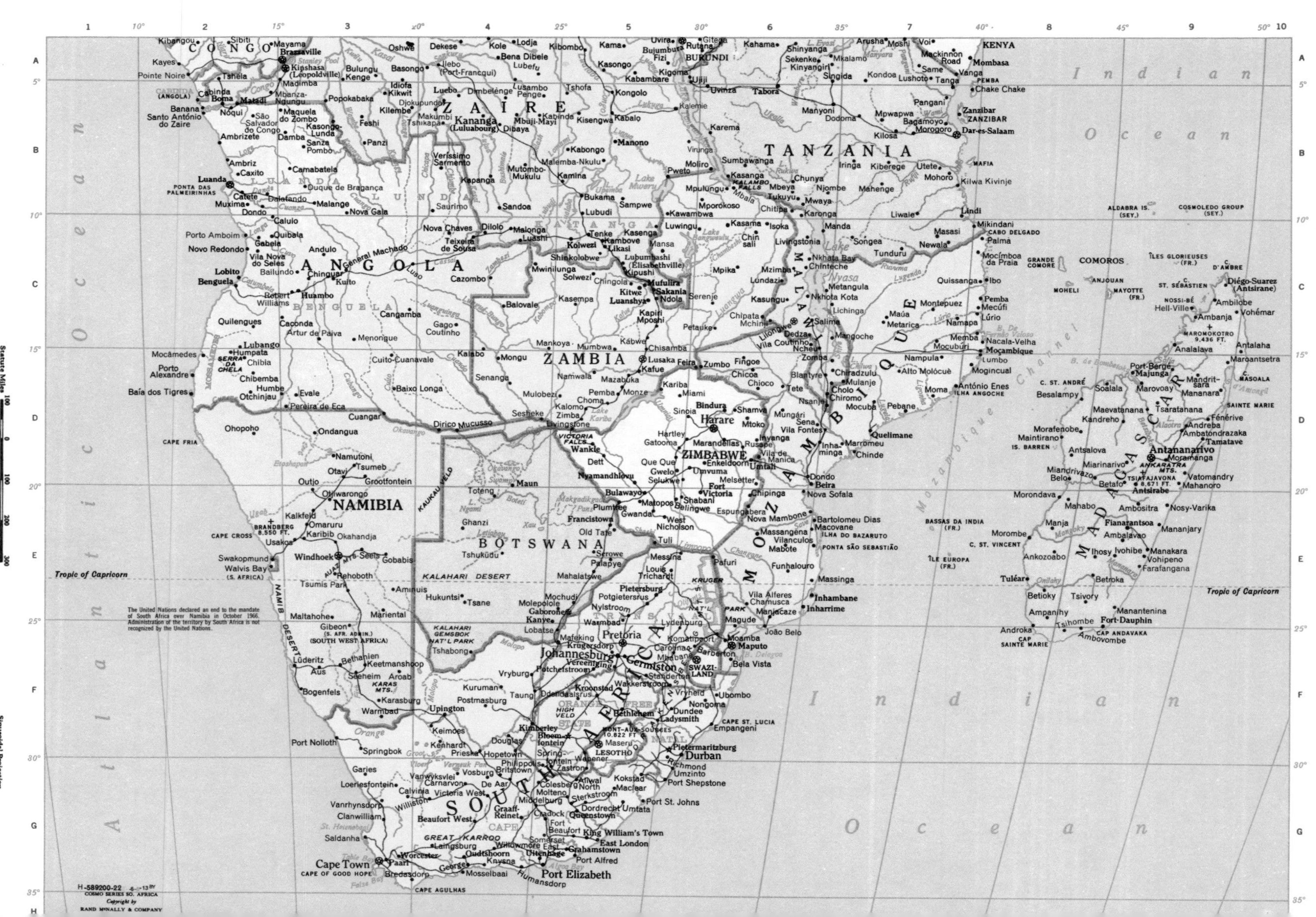
Indian Ocean
Atlantic Ocean
Mozambique Channel
KENYA
TANZANIA
BURUNDI
ZAIRE
CONGO
ANGOLA
ZAMBIA
MALAWI
MOZAMBIQUE
ZIMBABWE
BOTSWANA
NAMIBIA
SOUTH AFRICA
LESOTHO
SWAZILAND
MADAGASCAR
COMOROS
KALAHARI DESERT
NAMIB DESERT
Tropic of Capricorn
The United Nations declared an end to the mandate of South Africa over Namibia in October 1966. Administration of the territory by South Africa is not recognized by the United Nations.
Statute Miles 100 0 100 200 300
Kilometers 100 0 100 200 300 400
Sinusoidal Projection

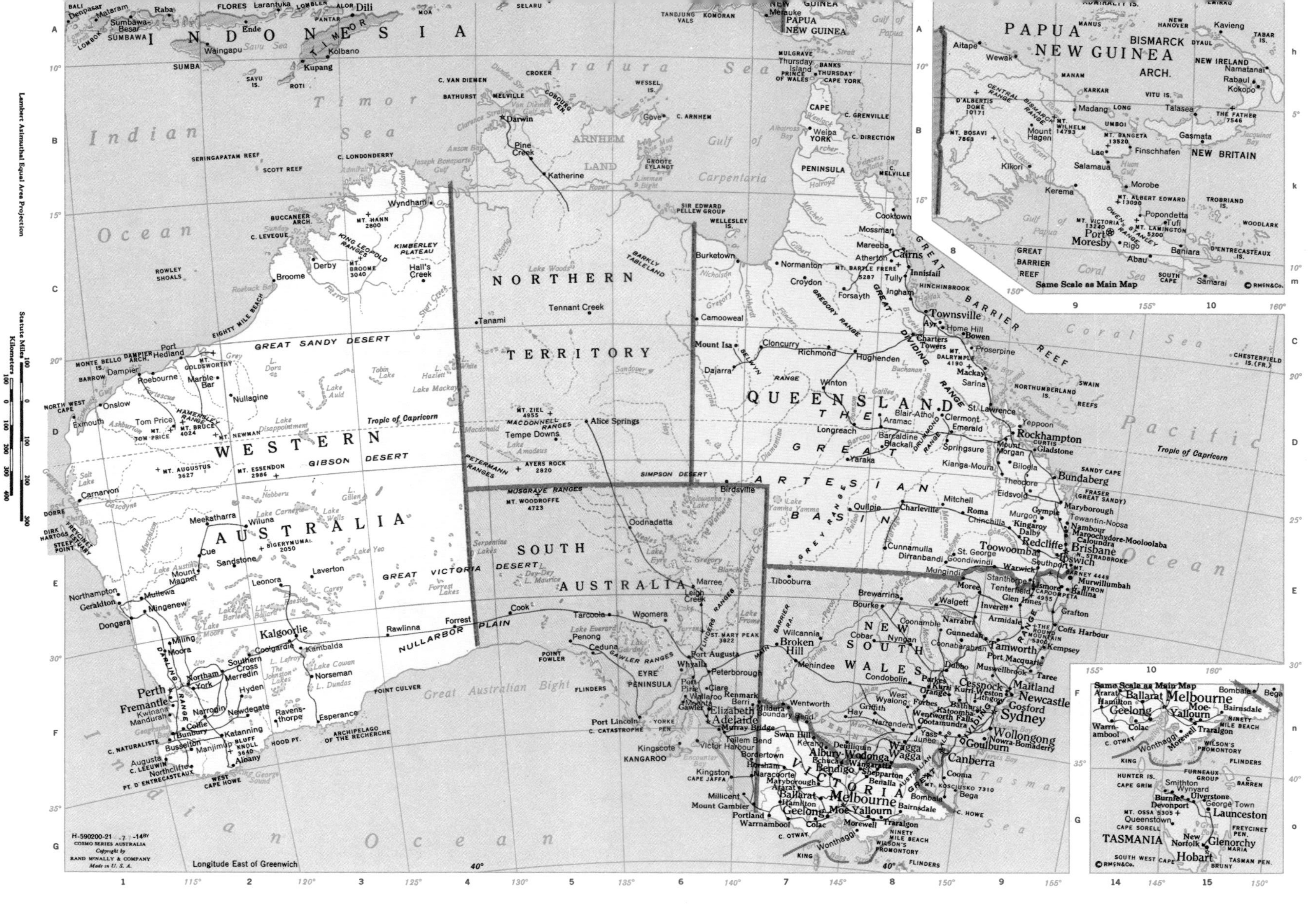
INDONESIA
PAPUA NEW GUINEA
BISMARCK ARCH.
NEW BRITAIN
NEW IRELAND
WESTERN AUSTRALIA
NORTHERN TERRITORY
SOUTH AUSTRALIA
QUEENSLAND
NEW SOUTH WALES
VICTORIA
TASMANIA
Indian Ocean
Timor Sea
Arafura Sea
Gulf of Carpentaria
Coral Sea
Pacific Ocean
Tasman Sea
Great Australian Bight
GREAT BARRIER REEF
GREAT DIVIDING RANGE
THE GREAT ARTESIAN BASIN
GREAT SANDY DESERT
GIBSON DESERT
GREAT VICTORIA DESERT
NULLARBOR PLAIN
SIMPSON DESERT
ARNHEM LAND
CAPE YORK PENINSULA
Tropic of Capricorn
Darwin
Perth
Adelaide
Melbourne
Sydney
Brisbane
Canberra
Hobart
Port Moresby
Alice Springs
Kalgoorlie
Same Scale as Main Map
Longitude East of Greenwich
H-590200-21 -7 -14BY
COSMO SERIES AUSTRALIA
Copyright by
RAND McNALLY & COMPANY
Made in U. S. A.
Lambert Azimuthal Equal Area Projection
Statute Miles
Kilometers

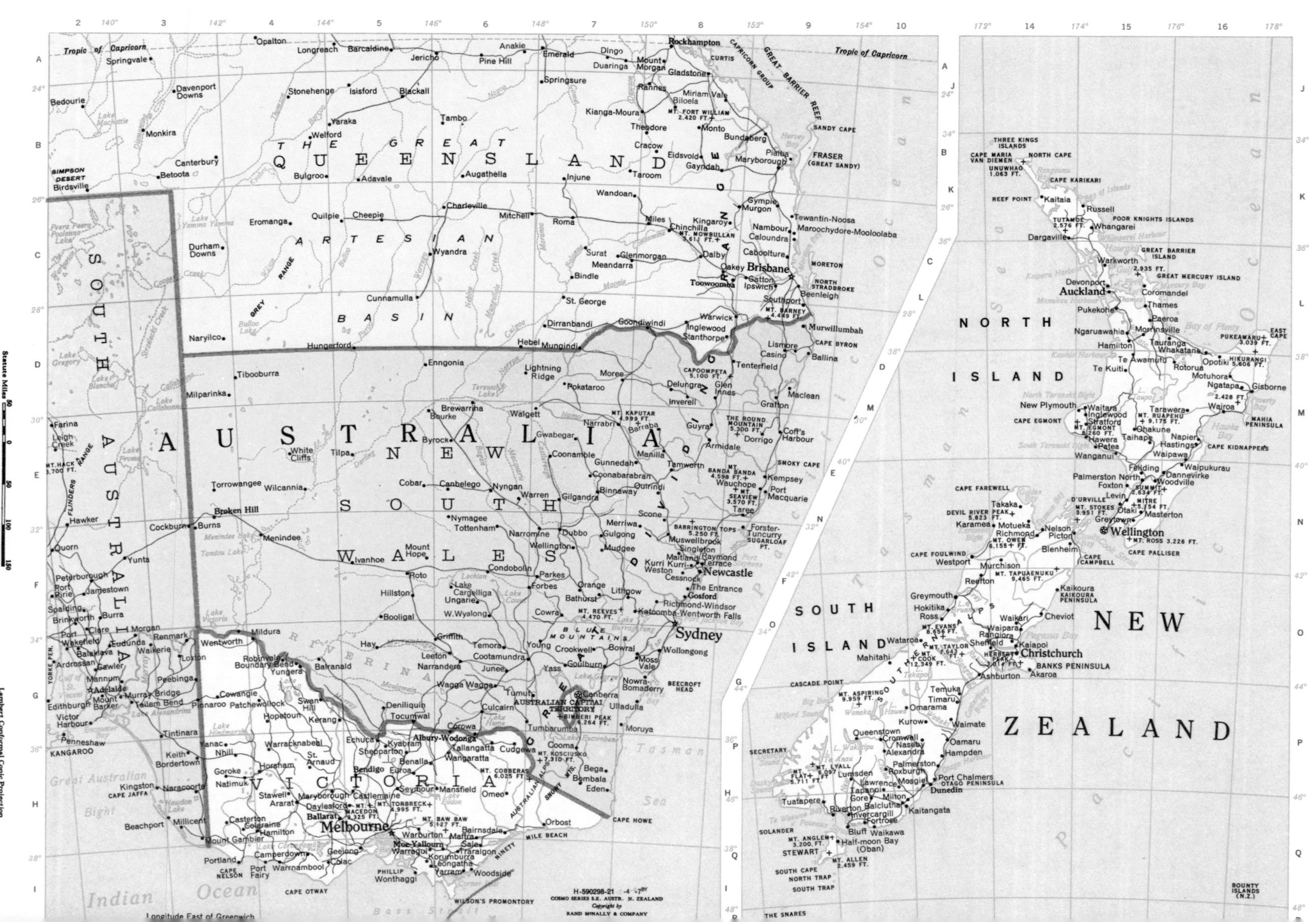
AUSTRALIA
THE GREAT QUEENSLAND
ARTESIAN BASIN
NEW SOUTH WALES
VICTORIA
SOUTH AUSTRALIA
AUSTRALIAN CAPITAL TERRITORY
BLUE MOUNTAINS
RIVERINA
Tropic of Capricorn
GREAT BARRIER REEF
CAPRICORN GROUP
FRASER (GREAT SANDY)
SIMPSON DESERT
Rockhampton
Brisbane
Toowoomba
Sydney
Newcastle
Wollongong
Canberra
Melbourne
Ballarat
Bendigo
Geelong
Adelaide
Broken Hill
Mildura
Albury-Wodonga
Wagga Wagga
Tamworth
Armidale
Dubbo
Bathurst
Orange
Goulburn
MT. KOSCIUSKO 7,310 FT.
CAPE HOWE
WILSON'S PROMONTORY
CAPE OTWAY
Indian Ocean
Great Australian Bight
Bass Strait
Tasman Sea
NEW ZEALAND
NORTH ISLAND
SOUTH ISLAND
Auckland
Wellington
Hamilton
Rotorua
Napier
Gisborne
New Plymouth
Palmerston North
Christchurch
Dunedin
Invercargill
Nelson
Blenheim
Greymouth
Timaru
Queenstown
MT. RUAPEHU 9,175 FT.
MT. EGMONT 8,260 FT.
MT. COOK 12,349 FT.
CAPE EGMONT
CAPE PALLISER
BANKS PENINSULA
Pacific Ocean
BOUNTY ISLANDS (N.Z.)
Longitude East of Greenwich
H-590298-21 -4 -7[BY]
COSMO SERIES S.E. AUSTR. N. ZEALAND
Copyright by RAND McNALLY & COMPANY
Statute Miles 50 0 50 100 150
Kilometers 50 0 50 100 200
Lambert Conformal Conic Projection

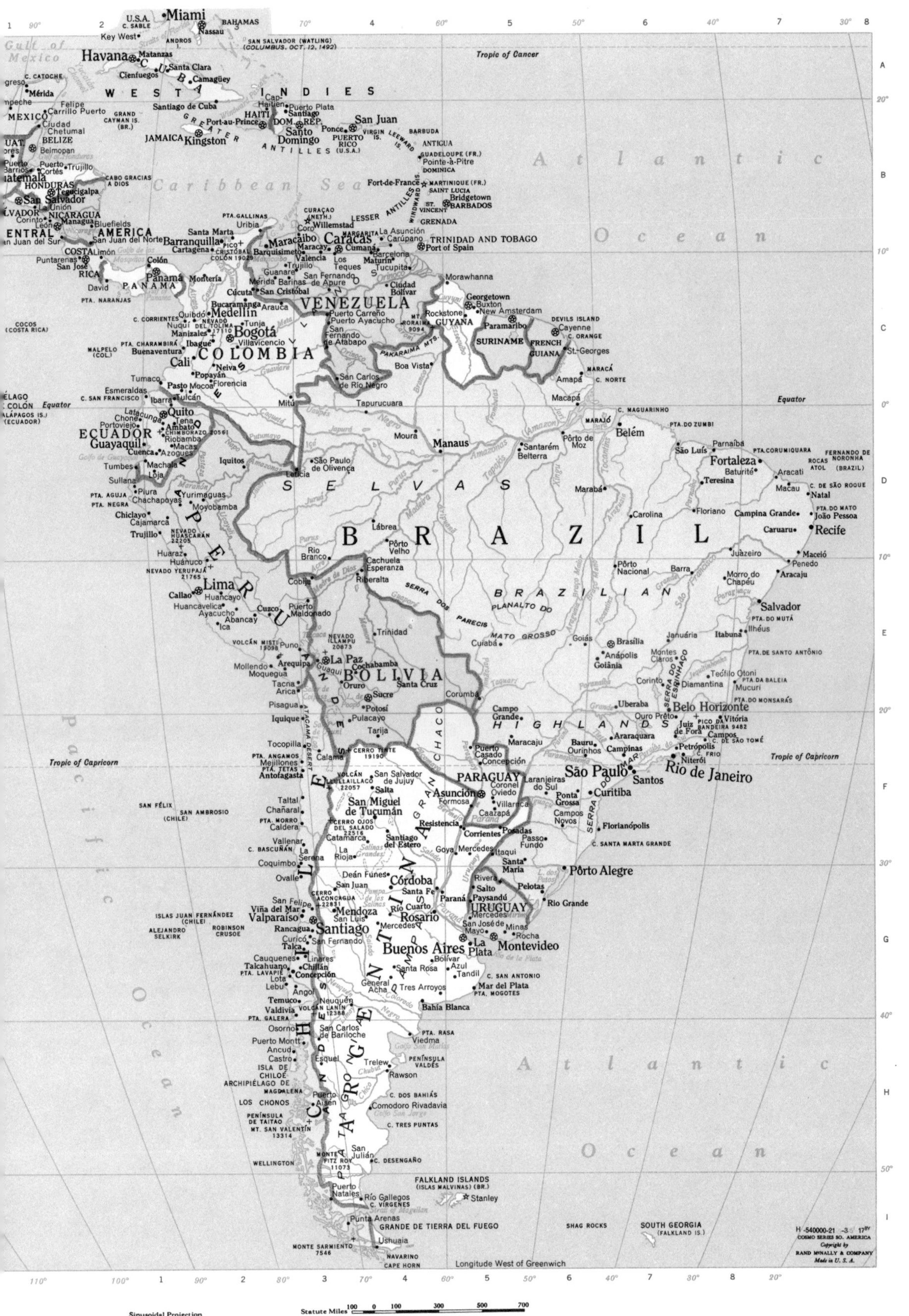
Tropic of Cancer
Gulf of Mexico
Miami
U.S.A.
C. SABLE
Key West
BAHAMAS
Nassau
ANDROS
SAN SALVADOR (WATLING)
(COLUMBUS, OCT. 12, 1492)
Havana
Matanzas
CUBA
Santa Clara
Cienfuegos
Camagüey
C. CATOCHE
Mérida
W E S T   I N D I E S
Felipe Carrillo Puerto
MEXICO
GRAND CAYMAN IS. (BR.)
Santiago de Cuba
Cap-Haïtien
Puerto Plata
Santiago
HAITI
DOM. REP.
Port-au-Prince
Santo Domingo
San Juan
Ponce
PUERTO RICO (U.S.A.)
VIRGIN IS.
LEEWARD IS.
BARBUDA
ANTIGUA
GREATER ANTILLES
JAMAICA
Kingston
Ciudad Chetumal
BELIZE
Belmopan
Puerto Cortés
Trujillo
HONDURAS
Tegucigalpa
San Salvador
La Unión
NICARAGUA
Managua
Bluefields
Corinto
León
AMERICA
San Juan del Norte
COSTA RICA
Limón
Puntarenas
San José
CABO GRACIAS A DIOS
Caribbean Sea
GUADELOUPE (FR.)
Pointe-à-Pitre
DOMINICA
Fort-de-France
MARTINIQUE (FR.)
SAINT LUCIA
Bridgetown
BARBADOS
ST. VINCENT
WINDWARD IS.
LESSER ANTILLES
GRENADA
CURAÇAO (NETH.)
Willemstad
PTA. GALLINAS
Uribia
Santa Marta
Barranquilla
Cartagena
PICO CRISTÓBAL COLÓN 19029
Maracaibo
Coro
Caracas
MARGARITA
La Asunción
Carúpano
Cumaná
Barquisimeto
Maracay
Valencia
Barcelona
Maturín
TRINIDAD AND TOBAGO
Port of Spain
Tucupita
Trujillo
Guanare
Los Teques
San Fernando de Apure
Mérida
Barinas
Ciudad Bolívar
Colón
Panamá
PANAMA
David
PTA. NARANJAS
Montería
Cúcuta
San Cristóbal
Bucaramanga
Arauca
VENEZUELA
Morawhanna
Georgetown
Buxton
New Amsterdam
Rockstone
GUYANA
Paramaribo
SURINAME
FRENCH GUIANA
DEVILS ISLAND
Cayenne
C. ORANGE
St.-Georges
Quibdó
Medellín
NEVADO DEL TOLIMA 17110
Tunja
Manizales
Ibagué
Bogotá
Villavicencio
Puerto Carreño
Puerto Ayacucho
San Fernando de Atabapo
MT. RORAIMA 9094
PAKARAIMA MTS.
C. CORRIENTES
COCOS (COSTA RICA)
MALPELO (COL.)
PTA. CHARAMBIRÁ
Buenaventura
Cali
COLOMBIA
Neiva
Popayán
Boa Vista
San Carlos de Río Negro
MARACÁ
C. NORTE
Amapá
Tumaco
Esmeraldas
C. SAN FRANCISCO
Pasto
Mocoa
Florencia
Tulcán
Ibarra
Quito
Mitú
Tapurucuara
Macapá
Equator
C. MAGUARINHO
MARAJÓ
PTA. DO ZUMBI
Belém
Latacunga
Chone
Tena
Portoviejo
Ambato
CHIMBORAZO 20561
Riobamba
ECUADOR
Guayaquil
Macas
Cuenca
Azogues
Moura
Manaus
Santarém
Belterra
Pôrto de Moz
São Luís
Parnaíba
PTA. CORUMIQUARA
FERNANDO DE NORONHA (BRAZIL)
ROCAS ATOL
Fortaleza
Baturité
Aracati
Macau
Natal
C. DE SÃO ROQUE
Tumbes
Machala
Loja
Iquitos
São Paulo de Olivença
Leticia
Sullana
Piura
PTA. AGUJA
PTA. NEGRA
Chachapoyas
Yurimaguas
Moyobamba
S E L V A S
Marabá
Teresina
Carolina
Floriano
Campina Grande
PTA. DO MATO
João Pessoa
Chiclayo
Cajamarca
Trujillo
NEVADO HUASCARÁN 22205
Lábrea
B R A Z I L
Caruaru
Recife
Huaraz
Huánuco
NEVADO YERUPAJÁ 21765
PERU
Pôrto Velho
Rio Branco
Cachuela Esperanza
Riberalta
Juàzeiro
Maceió
Penedo
Aracaju
Pôrto Nacional
Barra
Morro do Chapéu
Lima
Callao
Huancayo
Huancavelica
Ayacucho
Abancay
Ica
Cuzco
Puerto Maldonado
Cobija
SERRA DOS PARECIS
B R A Z I L I A N
PLANALTO DO MATO GROSSO
Salvador
PTA. DO MUTÁ
Ilhéus
Trinidad
NEVADO ILLAMPU 20873
VOLCÁN MISTI 19098
Puno
Arequipa
La Paz
Cochabamba
BOLIVIA
Santa Cruz
Oruro
Sucre
Potosí
Cuiabá
Goiás
Brasília
Anápolis
Goiânia
Januária
Itabuna
Montes Claros
PTA. DE SANTO ANTÔNIO
Teófilo Otoni
Mollendo
Moquegua
Tacna
Arica
Pisagua
Iquique
Corumbá
Corinto
Diamantina
SERRA DO ESPINHAÇO
PTA. DA BALEIA
Mucuri
PTA. DO MONSARÁS
Uberaba
Belo Horizonte
Ouro Prêto
PICO DA BANDEIRA 9482
Vitória
Juiz de Fora
Campos
C. DE SÃO TOMÉ
C. FRIO
Campo Grande
H I G H L A N D S
Araraquara
Campinas
Petrópolis
Niterói
Rio de Janeiro
Pulacayo
Tarija
CHACO
ATACAMA DESERT
Tocopilla
CERRO TINTE 19190
Calama
Maracaju
Bauru
Ourinhos
PTA. ANGAMOS
Mejillones
PTA. TETAS
Antofagasta
Puerto Casado
Concepción
Tropic of Capricorn
VOLCÁN LLULLAILLACO 22057
San Salvador de Jujuy
Salta
PARAGUAY
Coronel Oviedo
Laranjeiras do Sul
São Paulo
Santos
Curitiba
Ponta Grossa
Asunción
Formosa
Villarrica
Caazapá
SAN FÉLIX
SAN AMBROSIO (CHILE)
Taltal
Chañaral
PTA. MORRO
Caldera
San Miguel de Tucumán
CERRO OJOS DEL SALADO 22615
Resistencia
Corrientes
Posadas
Campos Novos
SERRA DO MAR
Florianópolis
Vallenar
C. BASCUÑÁN
La Serena
Coquimbo
Catamarca
Santiago del Estero
La Rioja
Goya
Mercedes
Itaqui
Passo Fundo
Santa Maria
C. SANTA MARTA GRANDE
Pôrto Alegre
Ovalle
Deán Funes
Córdoba
Santa Fe
Rivera
Salto
Pelotas
Paysandú
URUGUAY
Rio Grande
San Juan
San Felipe
CERRO ACONCAGUA 22831
Paraná
Río Cuarto
ISLAS JUAN FERNÁNDEZ (CHILE)
ALEJANDRO SELKIRK
ROBINSON CRUSOE
Viña del Mar
Valparaíso
Mendoza
San Luis
Rosario
Mercedes
San José de Mayo
Minas
Rocha
Montevideo
Rancagua
Santiago
Curicó
San Fernando
Talca
Linares
Buenos Aires
La Plata
Cauquenes
Chillán
Talcahuano
PTA. LAVAPIÉ
Concepción
Lota
Lebu
Angol
Bolívar
Santa Rosa
Azul
Tandil
C. SAN ANTONIO
General Acha
Tres Arroyos
Mar del Plata
PTA. MOGOTES
Temuco
Valdivia
Neuquén
VOLCÁN LANÍN 12388
Bahía Blanca
PTA. GALERA
Osorno
San Carlos de Bariloche
PTA. RASA
Viedma
Puerto Montt
Ancud
Castro
Esquel
Trelew
Rawson
PENÍNSULA VALDÉS
ISLA DE CHILOÉ
ARCHIPIÉLAGO DE MAGDALENA
LOS CHONOS
Puerto Aisén
C. DOS BAHÍAS
Comodoro Rivadavia
PENÍNSULA DE TAITAO
MT. SAN VALENTÍN 13314
C. TRES PUNTAS
San Julián
MONTE FITZ ROY 11073
C. DESENGAÑO
WELLINGTON
ARGENTINA
PATAGONIA
GRAN CHACO
PAMPA
ANDES
CHILE
FALKLAND ISLANDS (ISLAS MALVINAS) (BR.)
Stanley
Puerto Natales
Río Gallegos
C. VÍRGENES
Strait of Magellan
Punta Arenas
GRANDE DE TIERRA DEL FUEGO
MONTE SARMIENTO 7546
Ushuaia
NAVARINO
CAPE HORN
SHAG ROCKS
SOUTH GEORGIA (FALKLAND IS.)
Atlantic Ocean
Pacific Ocean
Longitude West of Greenwich
H-540000-21 -3-5-17
COSMO SERIES SO. AMERICA
Copyright by RAND McNALLY & COMPANY
Made in U. S. A.
Sinusoidal Projection
Statute Miles 100 0 100 300 500 700
Kilometers 100 0 100 300 500 700 900 1100

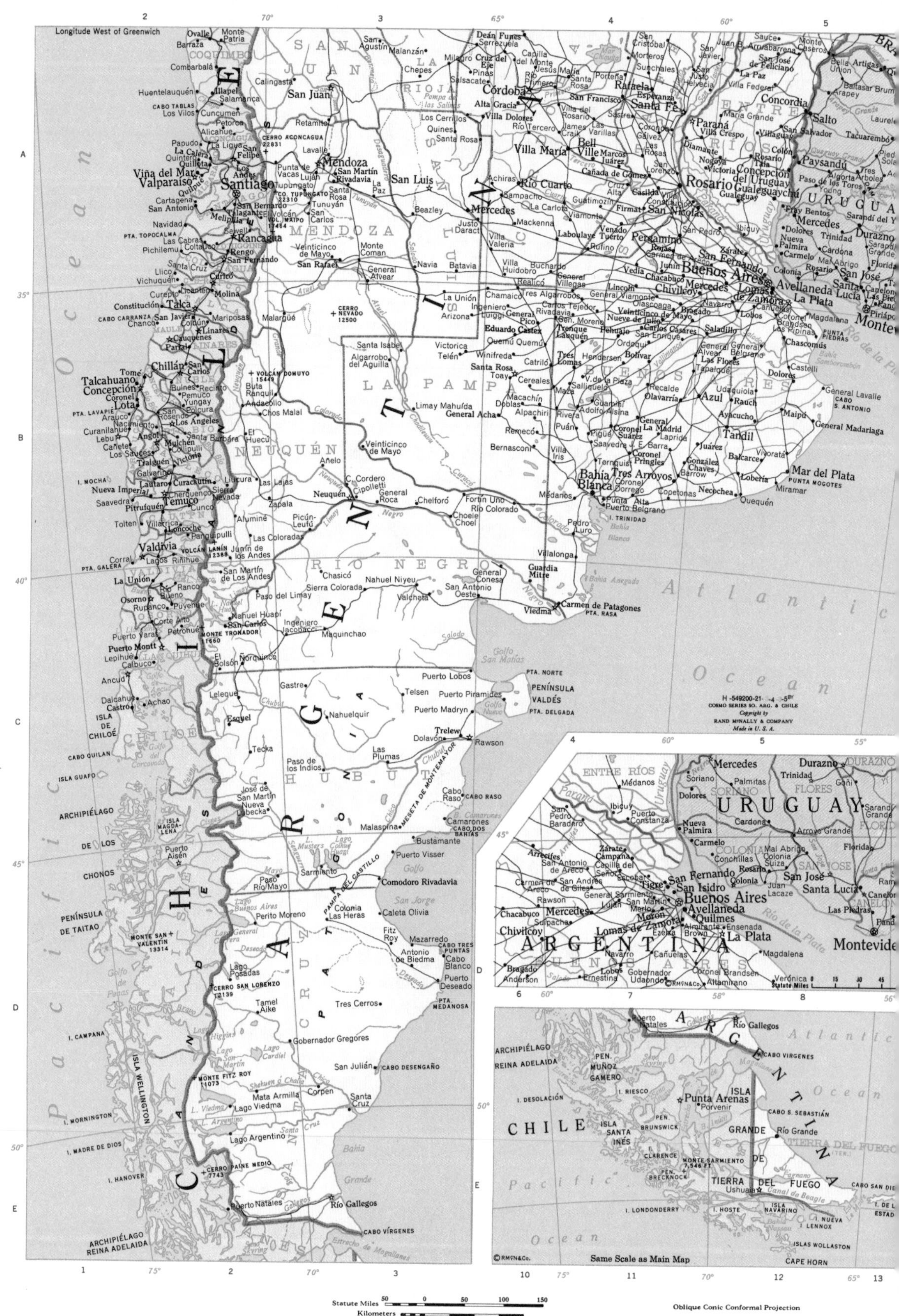
Longitude West of Greenwich
SAN JUAN
LA RIOJA
MENDOZA
SAN LUIS
LA PAMPA
NEUQUÉN
RÍO NEGRO
CHUBUT
SANTA CRUZ
BUENOS AIRES
ENTRE RÍOS
URUGUAY
CHILE
ARGENTINA
PATAGONIA
Pacific Ocean
Atlantic Ocean
Santiago
Valparaíso
Viña del Mar
Concepción
Talcahuano
Temuco
Valdivia
Osorno
Puerto Montt
Castro
Chillán
Talca
Rancagua
Mendoza
San Juan
San Luis
Córdoba
Santa Fe
Rosario
Paraná
Buenos Aires
La Plata
Mar del Plata
Bahía Blanca
Neuquén
Santa Rosa
Río Cuarto
Tandil
Azul
Viedma
Carmen de Patagones
Trelew
Rawson
Puerto Madryn
Esquel
Comodoro Rivadavia
Puerto Deseado
San Julián
Santa Cruz
Río Gallegos
Puerto Natales
Montevideo
Paysandú
Salto
CERRO ACONCAGUA 22831
CO. TUPUNGATO 22310
VOL. MAIPO 17464
CERRO NEVADO 12500
VOLCÁN DOMUYO 15449
VOLCÁN LANÍN 12388
MONTE TRONADOR 11660
MONTE SAN VALENTÍN 13314
CERRO SAN LORENZO 12139
MONTE FITZ ROY 11073
CERRO PAINE MEDIO 7743
ISLA DE CHILOÉ
ARCHIPIÉLAGO DE LOS CHONOS
PENÍNSULA DE TAITAO
ISLA WELLINGTON
ARCHIPIÉLAGO REINA ADELAIDA
Golfo San Matías
PENÍNSULA VALDÉS
Golfo San Jorge
Bahía Grande
Río de la Plata
CABO VÍRGENES
H-549200-21
COSMO SERIES SO. ARG. & CHILE
Copyright by RAND McNALLY & COMPANY
Made in U. S. A.
ISLA GRANDE DE TIERRA DEL FUEGO
Punta Arenas
Ushuaia
Río Grande
Porvenir
ISLA SANTA INÉS
CAPE HORN
ISLAS WOLLASTON
Same Scale as Main Map
Statute Miles 50 0 50 100 150
Kilometers 50 0 50 100 150 200
Oblique Conic Conformal Projection

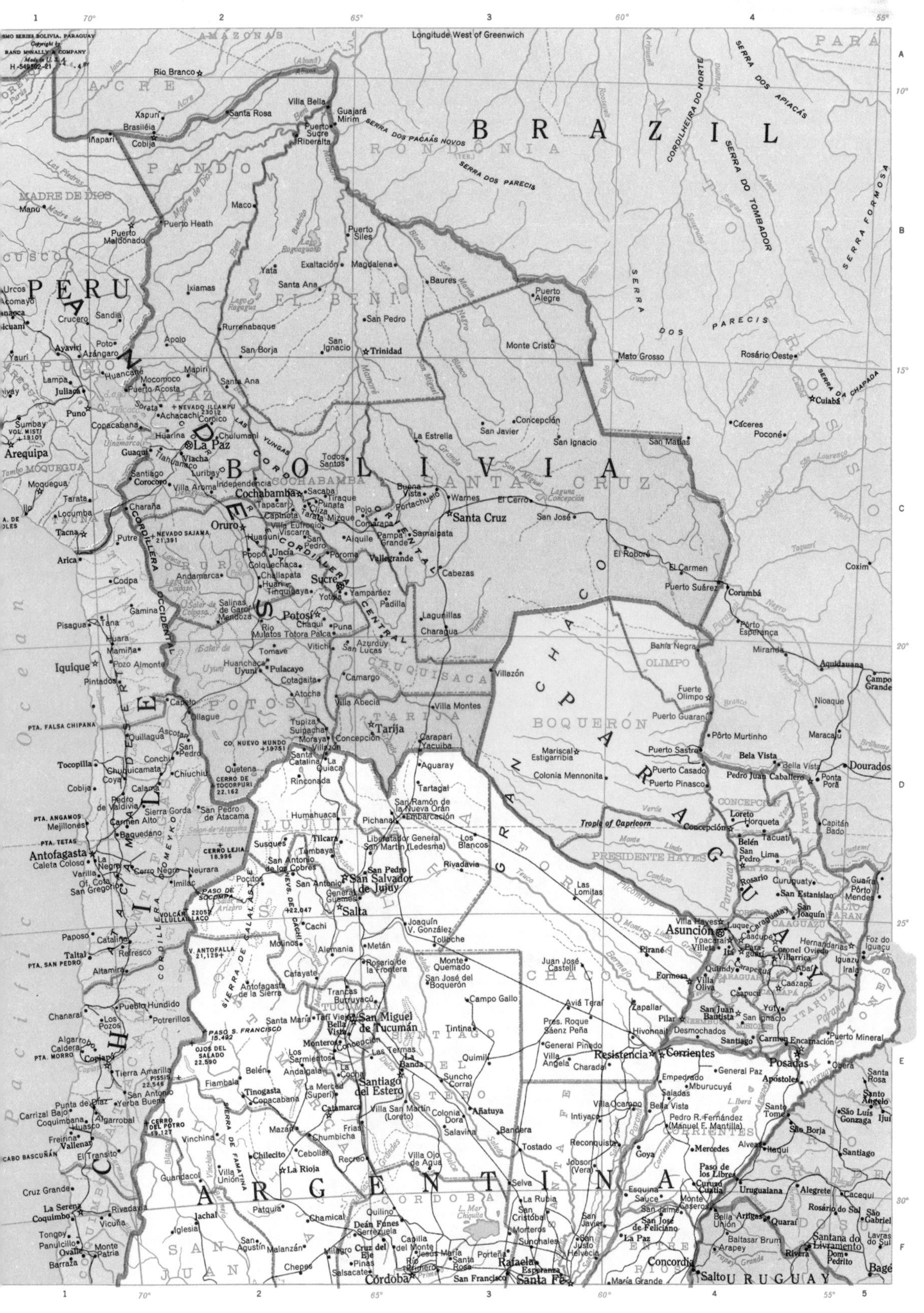

Oblique Conic Conformal Projection

Statute Miles 50 0 50 100 150

Kilometers 50 0 50 100 150 200

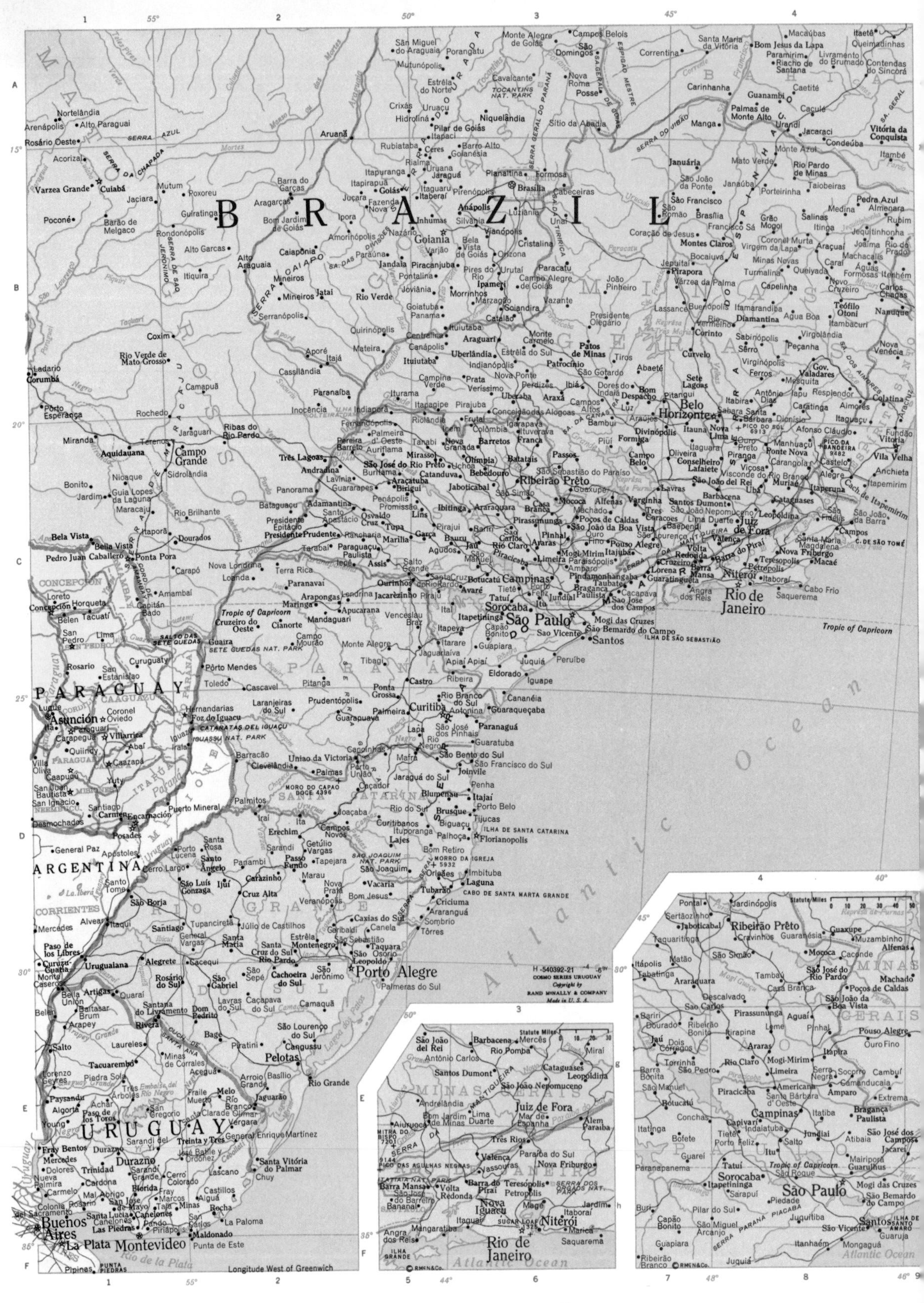

Statute Miles 50 0 50 100 150
Kilometers 50 0 50 100 150 200

Oblique Conic Conformal Projection

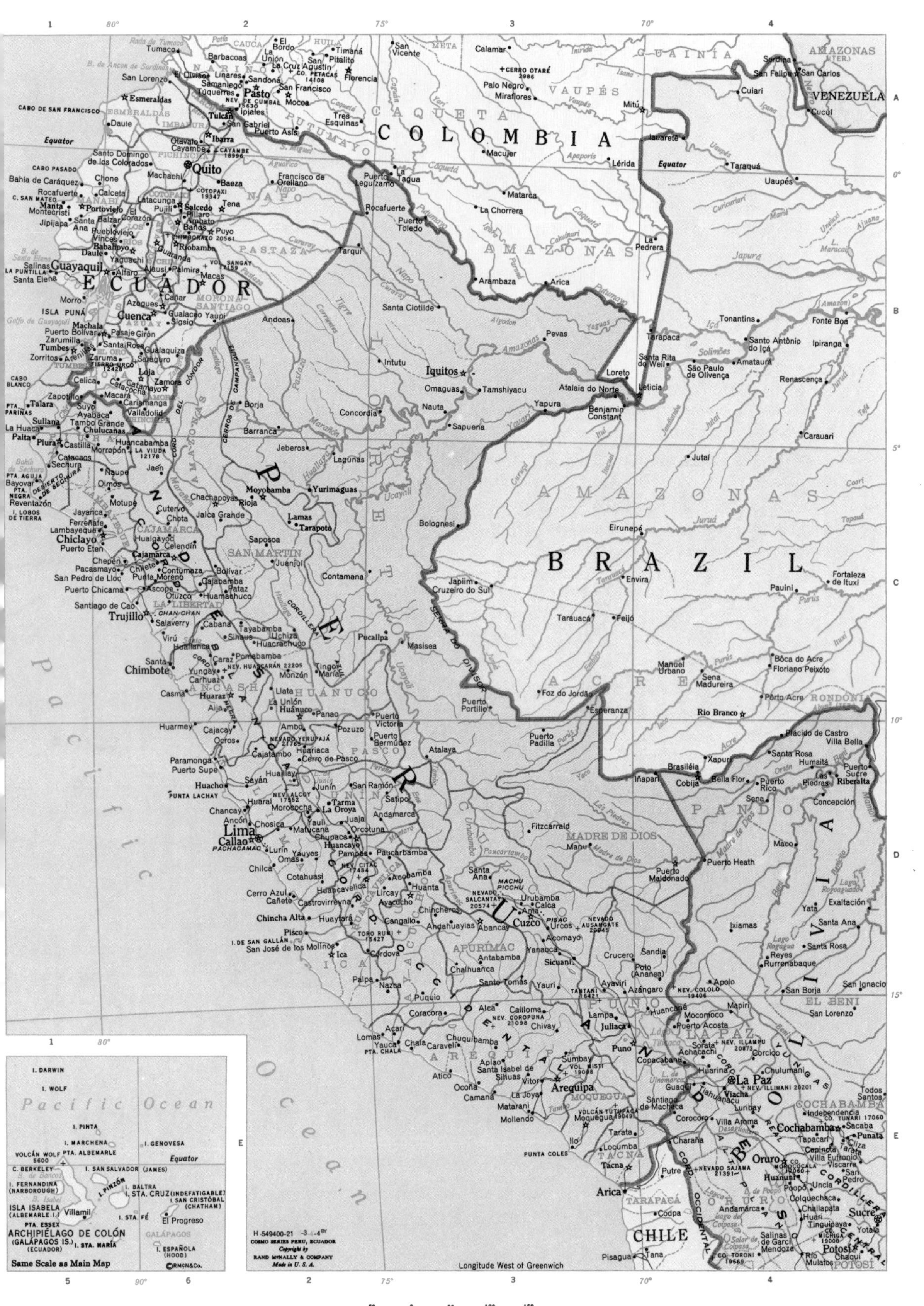

Oblique Conic Conformal Projection

Statute Miles 50 0 50 100 150

Kilometers 50 0 50 100 150 200

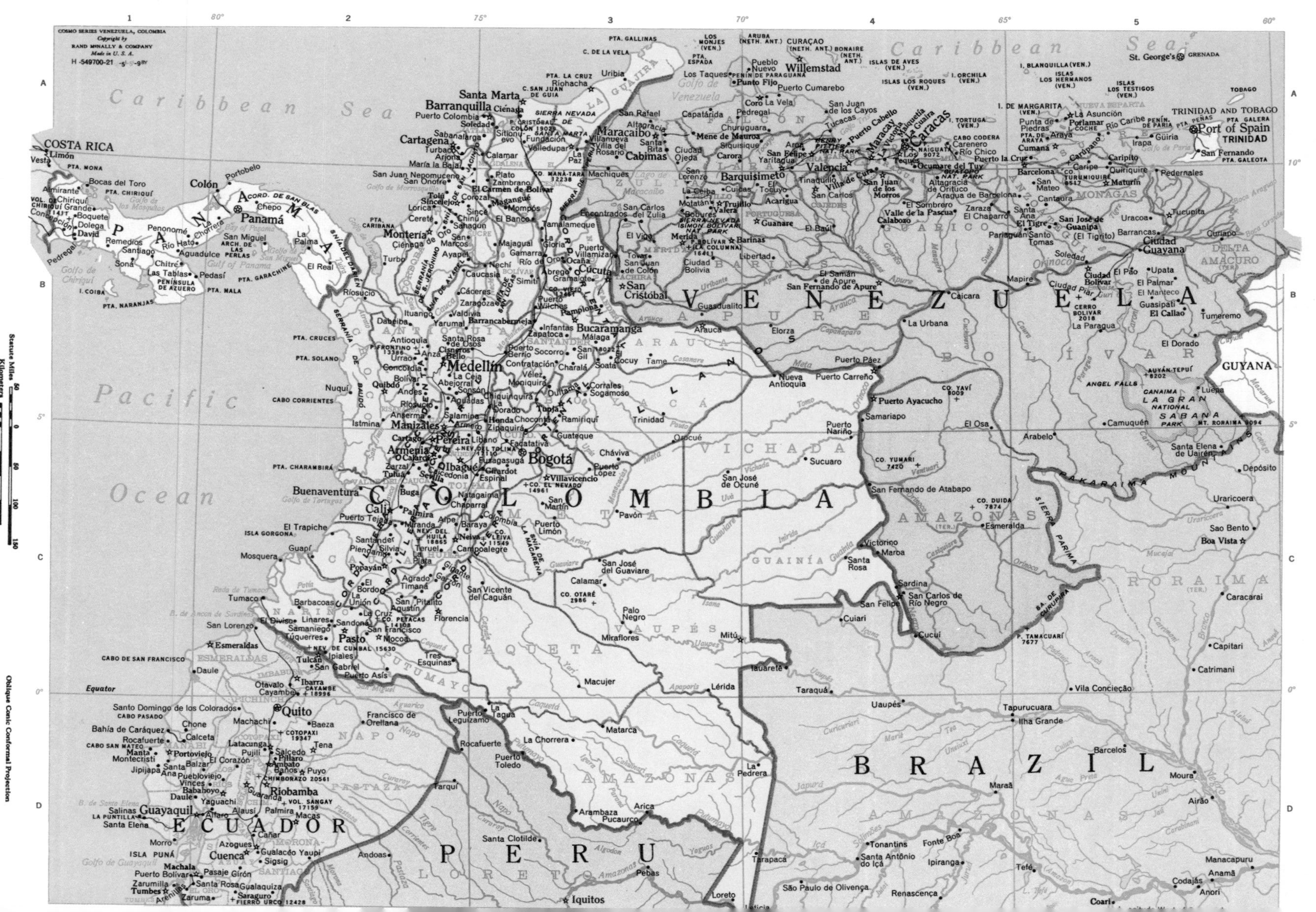
Caribbean Sea
Pacific Ocean
COLOMBIA
VENEZUELA
BRAZIL
PERU
ECUADOR
PANAMA
GUYANA
COSTA RICA
TRINIDAD AND TOBAGO
Bogotá
Caracas
Quito
Panamá
Port of Spain
Medellín
Cali
Barranquilla
Cartagena
Maracaibo
Guayaquil
Iquitos
COSMO SERIES VENEZUELA, COLOMBIA
Copyright by RAND McNALLY & COMPANY
Made in U. S. A.
Statute Miles 50 0 50 100 150
Kilometers 50 0 50 100 150 200
Oblique Conic Conformal Projection

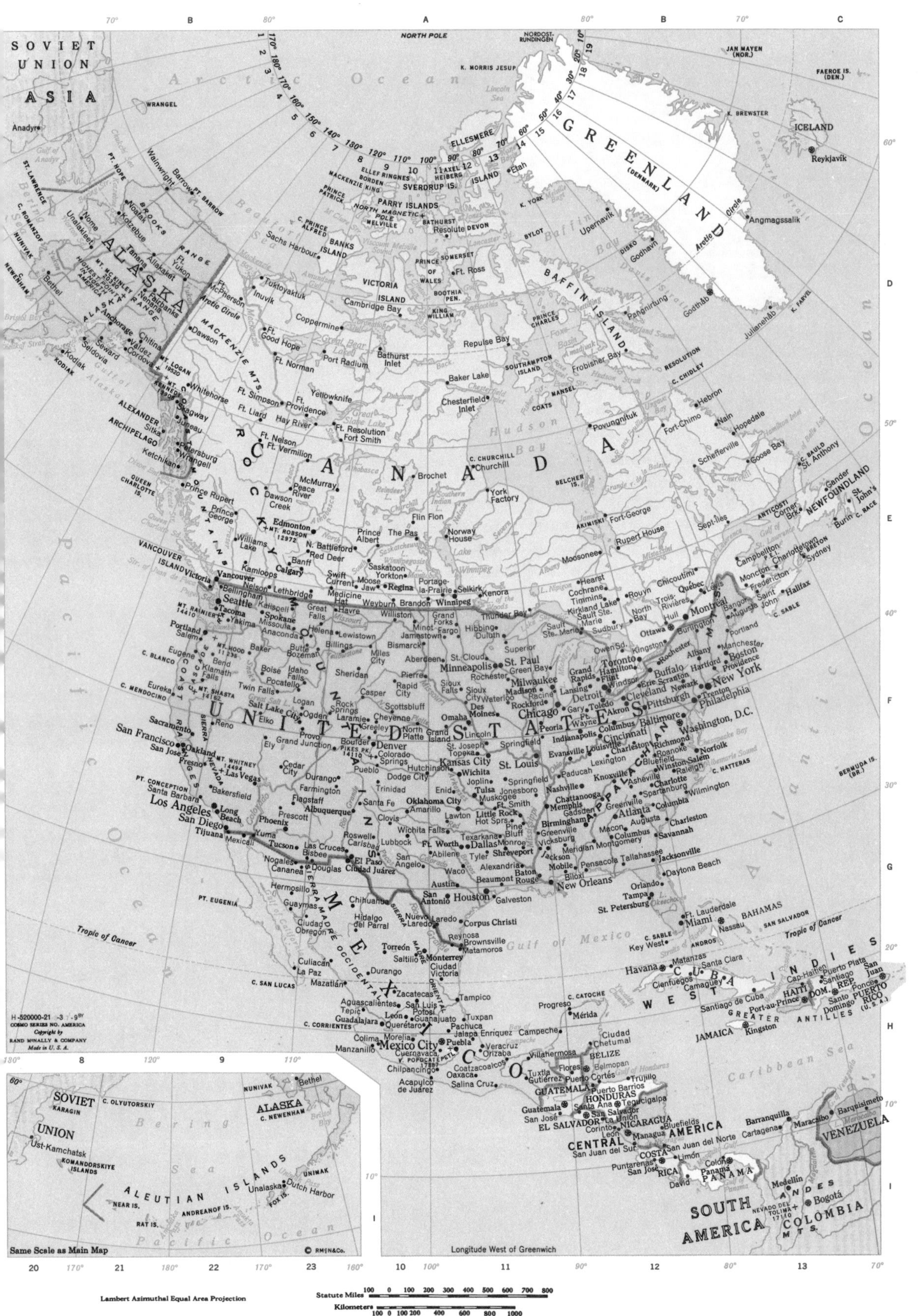
NORTH POLE
Arctic Ocean
SOVIET UNION
ASIA
GREENLAND (DENMARK)
ICELAND
Reykjavík
ALASKA
CANADA
UNITED STATES
MEXICO
ROCKY MOUNTAINS
APPALACHIAN MTS.
SIERRA MADRE OCCIDENTAL
SIERRA MADRE ORIENTAL
BROOKS RANGE
ALASKA RANGE
MACKENZIE MTS.
BAFFIN ISLAND
VICTORIA ISLAND
BANKS ISLAND
ELLESMERE
PARRY ISLANDS
SOUTHAMPTON ISLAND
NEWFOUNDLAND
Hudson Bay
Beaufort Sea
Baffin Bay
Gulf of Alaska
Gulf of Mexico
Caribbean Sea
Pacific Ocean
Atlantic Ocean
Tropic of Cancer
Arctic Circle
Anchorage
Fairbanks
Juneau
Whitehorse
Yellowknife
Edmonton
Calgary
Vancouver
Victoria
Regina
Winnipeg
Churchill
Ottawa
Montréal
Québec
Toronto
Halifax
St. John's
Seattle
Portland
San Francisco
Los Angeles
San Diego
Las Vegas
Phoenix
Salt Lake City
Denver
Minneapolis
St. Paul
Chicago
Detroit
St. Louis
Kansas City
Dallas
Houston
New Orleans
Atlanta
Miami
Washington, D.C.
Philadelphia
New York
Boston
Mexico City
Guadalajara
Monterrey
Havana
CUBA
BAHAMAS
WEST INDIES
GREATER ANTILLES
JAMAICA
HAITI
DOM. REP.
PUERTO RICO (U.S.A.)
BELIZE
GUATEMALA
HONDURAS
EL SALVADOR
NICARAGUA
COSTA RICA
PANAMA
CENTRAL AMERICA
SOUTH AMERICA
COLOMBIA
VENEZUELA
BERMUDA IS. (BR.)
ALEUTIAN ISLANDS
Bering Sea
Same Scale as Main Map
Longitude West of Greenwich
H-520000-21 -3 -9BY
COSMO SERIES NO. AMERICA
Copyright by RAND McNALLY & COMPANY
Made in U. S. A.
Lambert Azimuthal Equal Area Projection
Statute Miles 100 0 100 200 300 400 500 600 700 800
Kilometers 100 0 100 200 400 600 800 1000

Statute Miles 50 25 0 50 100 150 200 250

Kilometers 50 0 100 200 300

Oblique Conic Conformal Projection

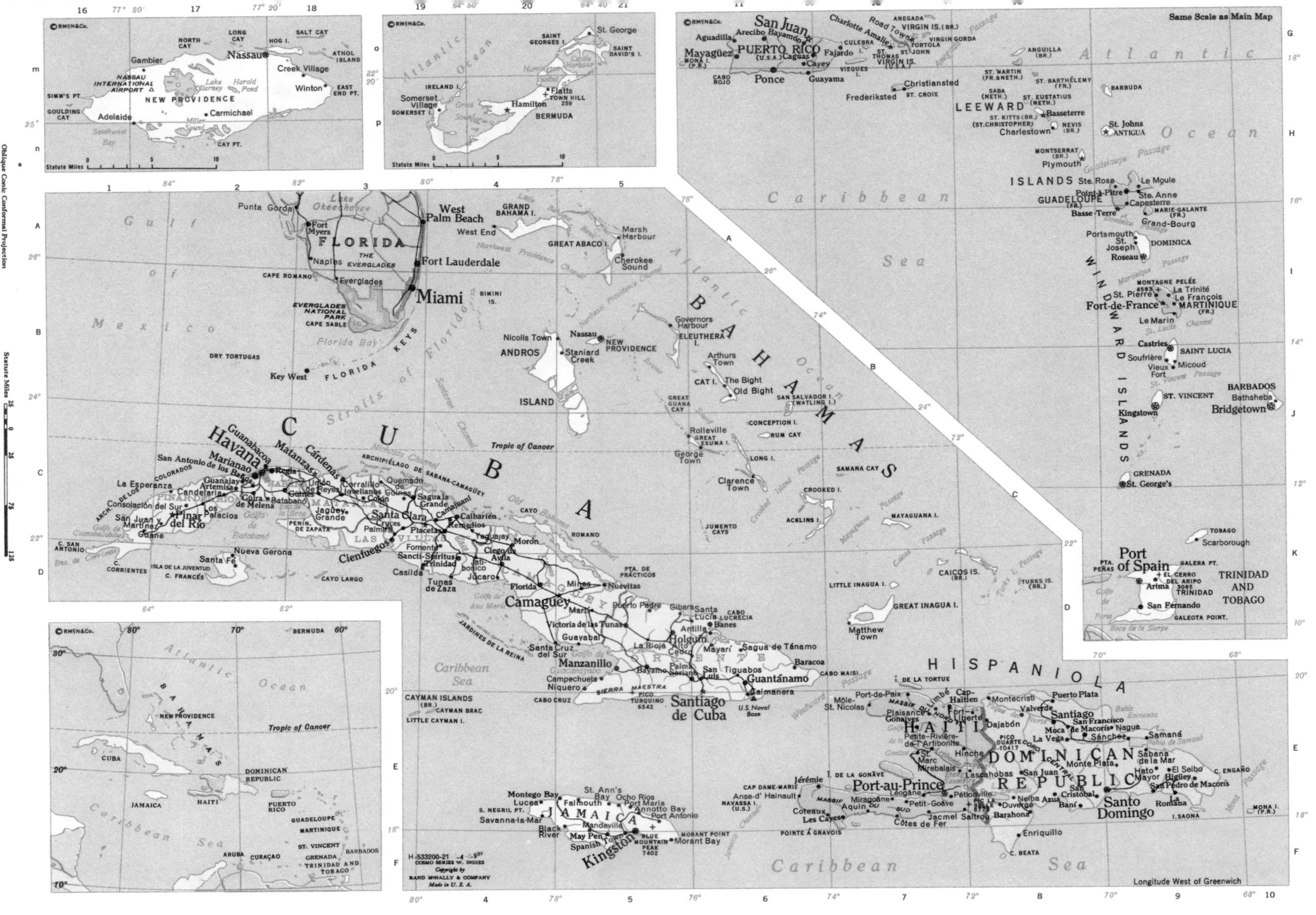
Same Scale as Main Map
Atlantic Ocean
Caribbean Sea
Gulf of Mexico
CUBA
BAHAMAS
HISPANIOLA
HAITI
DOMINICAN REPUBLIC
JAMAICA
PUERTO RICO
LEEWARD ISLANDS
WINDWARD ISLANDS
TRINIDAD AND TOBAGO
BARBADOS
FLORIDA
BERMUDA
NEW PROVIDENCE
Havana
Santiago de Cuba
Camagüey
Cienfuegos
Matanzas
Cárdenas
Pinar del Río
Guantánamo
Manzanillo
Holguín
Santa Clara
Kingston
Montego Bay
Port-au-Prince
Santo Domingo
San Juan
Ponce
Nassau
Miami
Key West
West Palm Beach
Fort Lauderdale
Port of Spain
Bridgetown
Castries
Kingstown
St. George's
Roseau
Fort-de-France
Basse-Terre
St. Johns
Charlotte Amalie
Hamilton
Tropic of Cancer
Longitude West of Greenwich
Oblique Conic Conformal Projection
Statute Miles
Kilometers
H-533200-21
COSMO SERIES W. INDIES
Copyright by RAND McNALLY & COMPANY
Made in U. S. A.

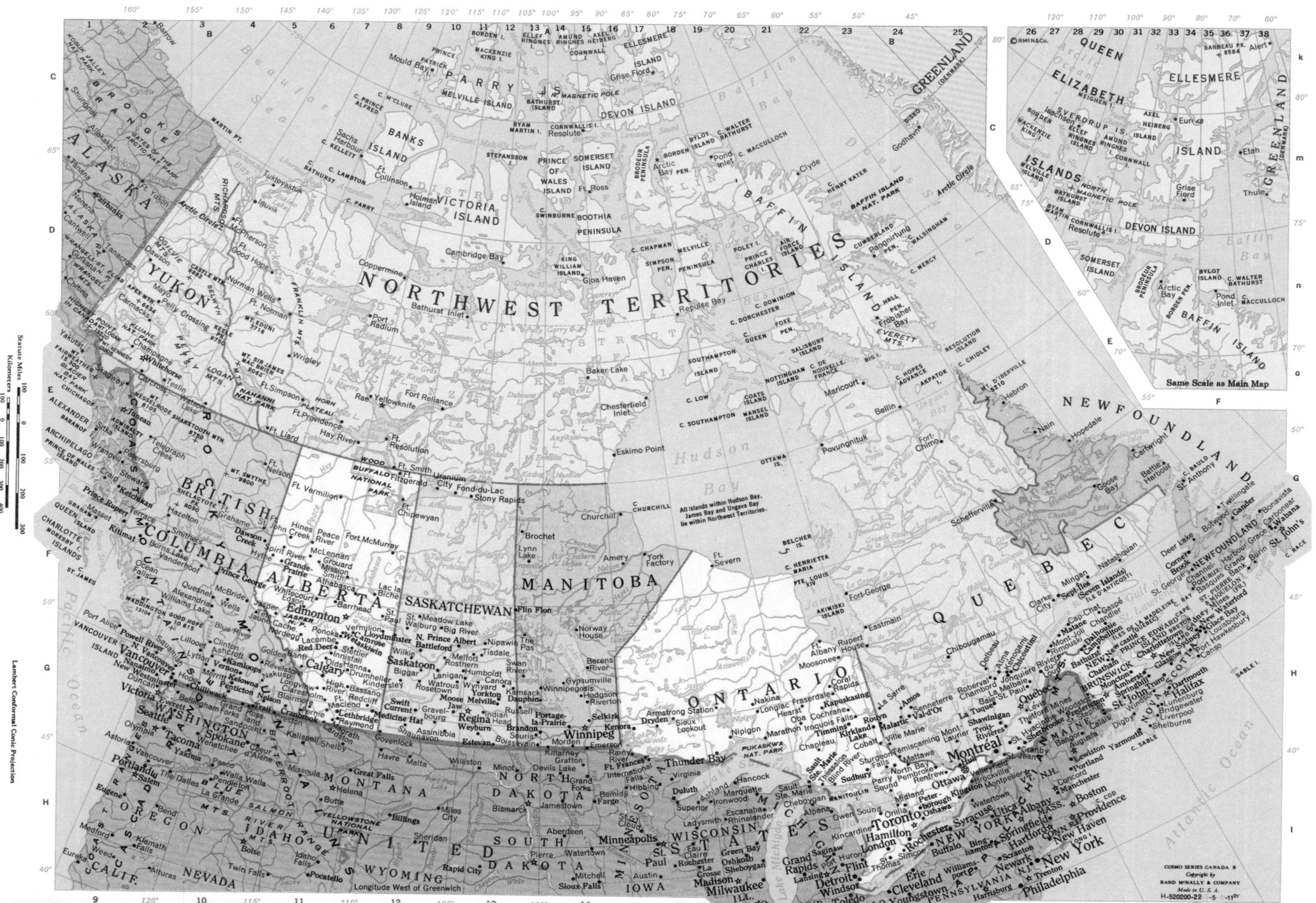

Statute Miles 100 0 100 200 300

Kilometers 100 0 100 200 300 400

Lambert Conformal Conic Projection

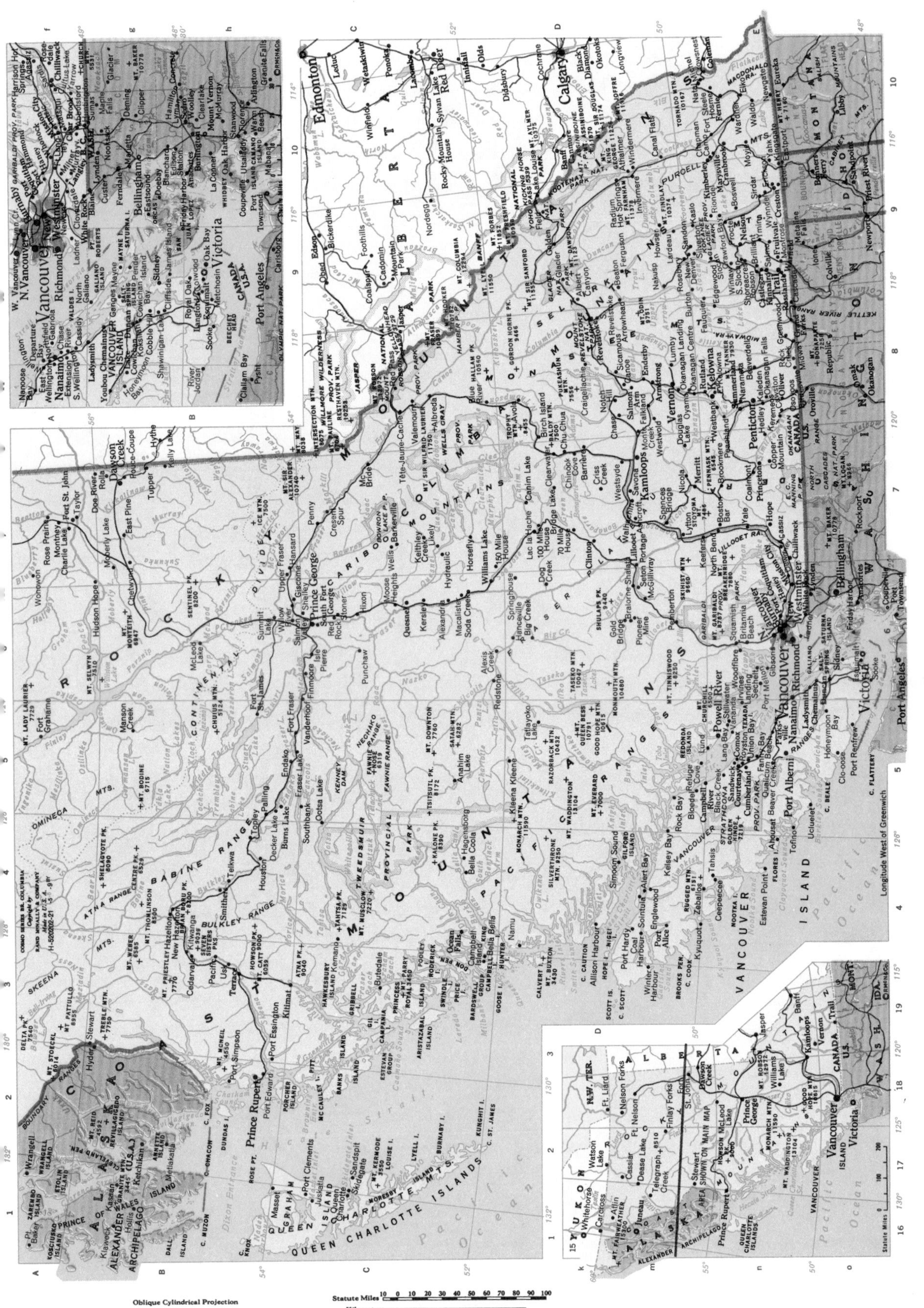
Oblique Cylindrical Projection
Statute Miles
Kilometers
Longitude West of Greenwich

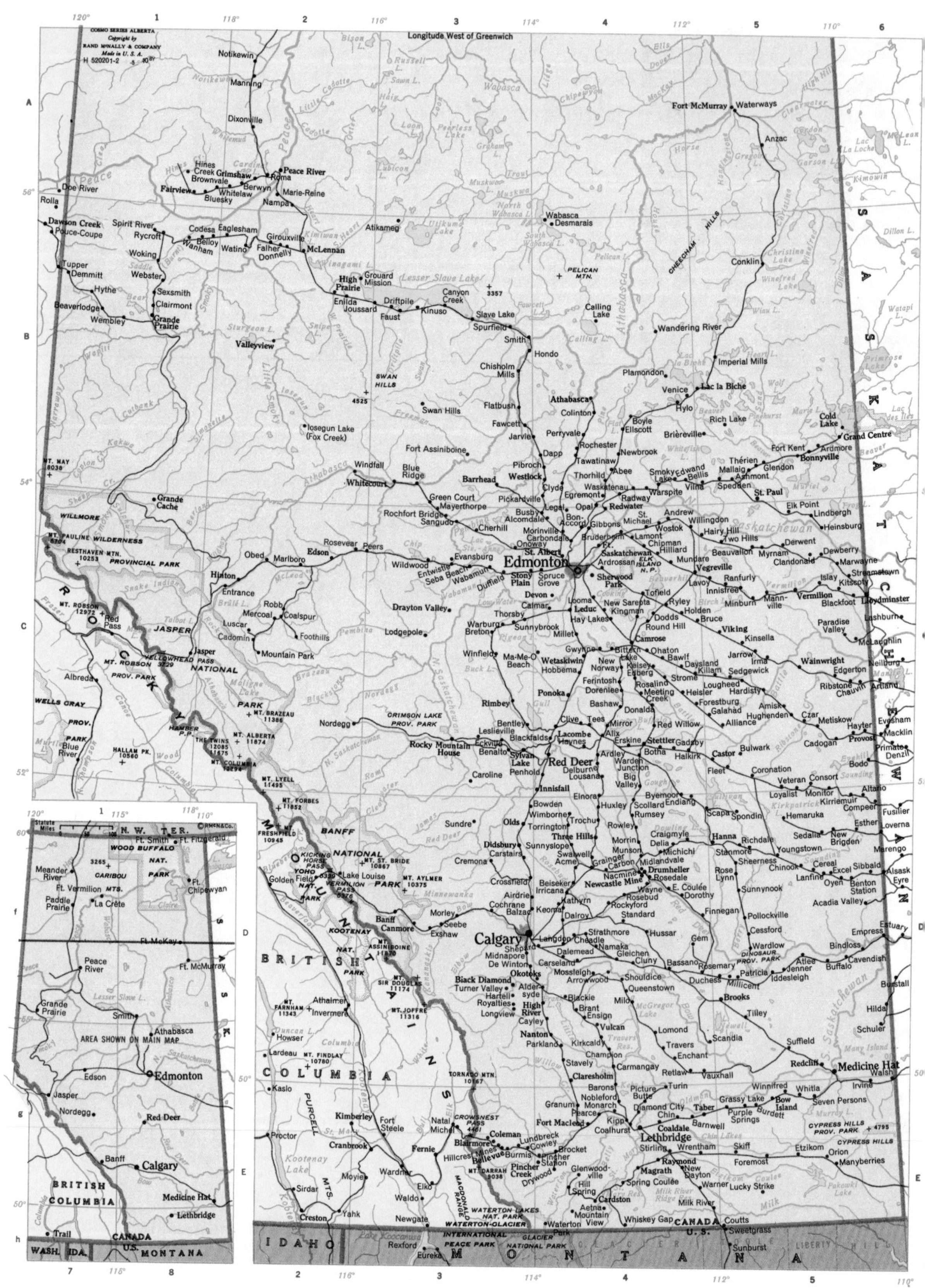
COSMO SERIES ALBERTA
Copyright by
RAND McNALLY & COMPANY
Made in U. S. A.
H 520201-2
Longitude West of Greenwich
Edmonton
Calgary
Red Deer
Lethbridge
Medicine Hat
Fort McMurray
Peace River
Grande Prairie
Athabasca
Lesser Slave Lake
Banff
Jasper
JASPER NATIONAL PARK
BANFF NATIONAL PARK
WILLMORE WILDERNESS PROVINCIAL PARK
ELK ISLAND N. P.
WATERTON LAKES NAT. PARK
WATERTON-GLACIER INTERNATIONAL PEACE PARK
GLACIER NATIONAL PARK
CYPRESS HILLS PROV. PARK
DINOSAUR PROV. PARK
CRIMSON LAKE PROV. PARK
BRITISH COLUMBIA
IDAHO
MONTANA
CANADA
U.S.
AREA SHOWN ON MAIN MAP
N. W. TER.
WOOD BUFFALO NAT. PARK
Statute Miles 10 0 10 20 30 40 50 60 70
Kilometers 10 0 10 20 40 60 80 100
Oblique Cylindrical Projection

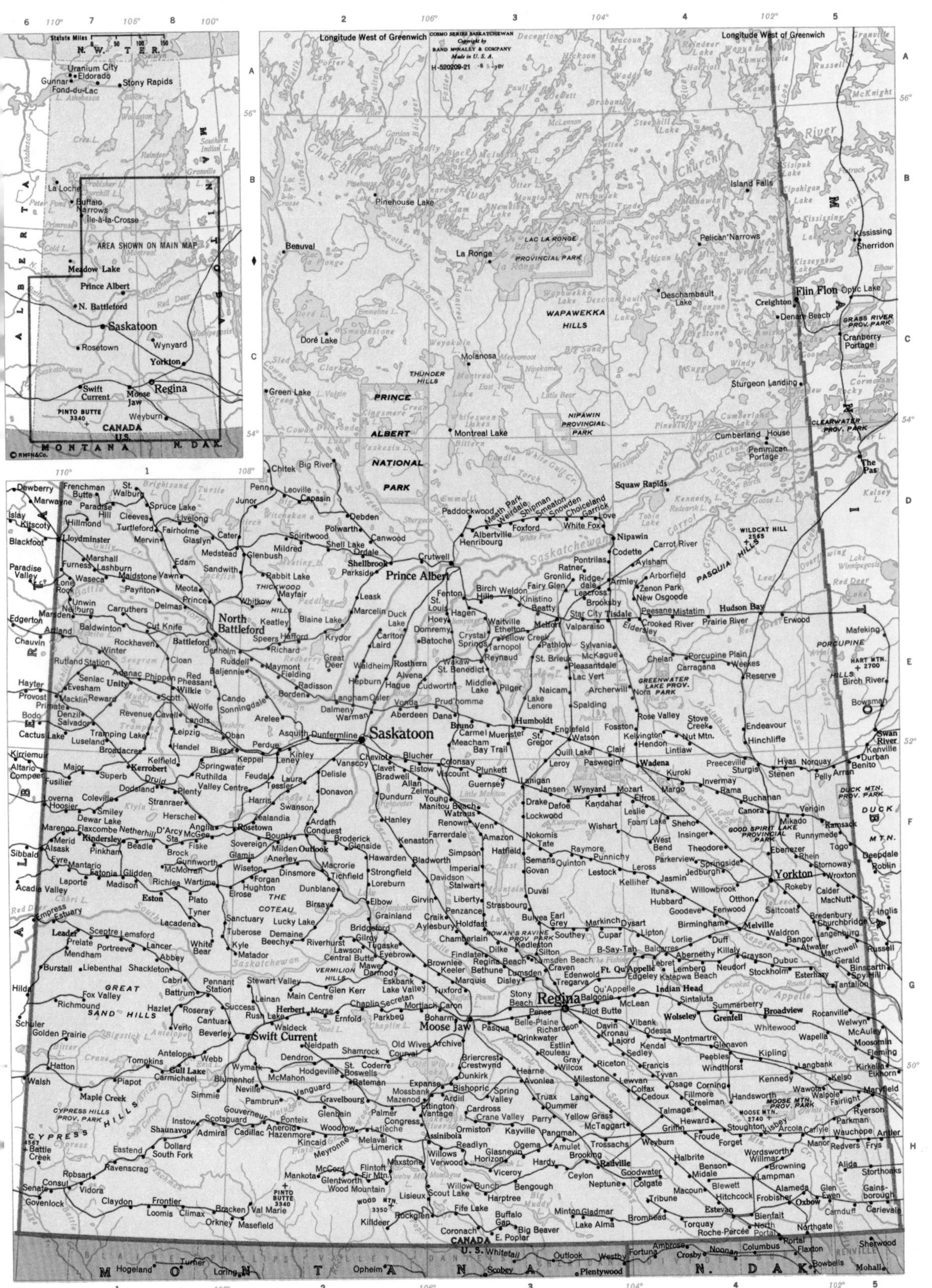
Longitude West of Greenwich
COSMO SERIES SASKATCHEWAN
Copyright by
RAND McNALLY & COMPANY
Made in U. S. A.
H-520209-21
N. W. TER.
Uranium City
Eldorado
Gunnar
Fond-du-Lac
Stony Rapids
L. Athabasca
La Loche
Buffalo Narrows
Île-à-la-Crosse
AREA SHOWN ON MAIN MAP
Meadow Lake
Prince Albert
N. Battleford
Saskatoon
Rosetown
Wynyard
Yorkton
Regina
Swift Current
Moose Jaw
Weyburn
PINTO BUTTE 3340
CANADA
U.S.
MONTANA
N. DAK.
ALBERTA
MANITOBA
Beauval
Pinehouse Lake
La Ronge
LAC LA RONGE PROVINCIAL PARK
Doré Lake
Green Lake
Molanosa
THUNDER HILLS
PRINCE ALBERT NATIONAL PARK
Montreal Lake
NIPAWIN PROVINCIAL PARK
WAPAWEKKA HILLS
Deschambault Lake
Pelican Narrows
Island Falls
Flin Flon
Creighton
Denare Beach
Kississing
Sherridon
Cranberry Portage
GRASS RIVER PROV. PARK
Sturgeon Landing
Cumberland House
Pemmican Portage
The Pas
CLEARWATER PROV. PARK
Squaw Rapids
Nipawin
Codette
Carrot River
WILDCAT HILL 2565
PASQUIA HILLS
Hudson Bay
Erwood
Mafeking
PORCUPINE HILLS
HART MTN. 2700
Birch River
Bowsman
Swan River
Kenville
Durban
Benito
DUCK MTN. PROV. PARK
Chitek
Big River
Penn
Leoville
Capasin
Debden
Dewberry
Marwayne
Frenchman Butte
St. Walburg
Paradise Hill
Spruce Lake
Islay
Kitscoty
Hillmond
Lloydminster
Blackfoot
Marshall
Lashburn
Paradise Valley
Waseca
Maidstone
Paynton
North Battleford
Battleford
Unity
Wilkie
Macklin
Kerrobert
Kindersley
Prince Albert
Shellbrook
Rosthern
Saskatoon
Humboldt
Melfort
Tisdale
Wadena
Kamsack
Canora
Yorkton
Melville
Watrous
Lanigan
Wynyard
Outlook
Rosetown
Biggar
Regina
Moose Jaw
Swift Current
Indian Head
Wolseley
Grenfell
Broadview
Moosomin
Fort Qu'Appelle
Estevan
Weyburn
Assiniboia
Gravelbourg
Shaunavon
Maple Creek
Radville
Oxbow
Carnduff
Leader
GREAT SAND HILLS
THE COTEAU
CYPRESS HILLS PROV. PARK
CYPRESS HILLS
MOOSE MTN. PROV. PARK
MOOSE MTN. 2740
GOOD SPIRIT LAKE PROVINCIAL PARK
GREENWATER LAKE PROV. PARK
ROWAN'S RAVINE PROV. PARK
VERMILION HILLS
WOOD MTN. 3350
PINTO BUTTE 3340
Saskatchewan
South Saskatchewan
CANADA
U.S.
MONTANA
N. DAK.
Hogeland
Turner
Loring
Opheim
Scobey
Whitetail
Outlook
Westby
Plentywood
Fortuna
Ambrose
Crosby
Noonan
Columbus
Flaxton
Portal
Bowbells
Sherwood
Mohall
Oblique Cylindrical Projection
Statute Miles 10 0 10 20 30 40 50 60
Kilometers 10 0 10 20 40 60 80

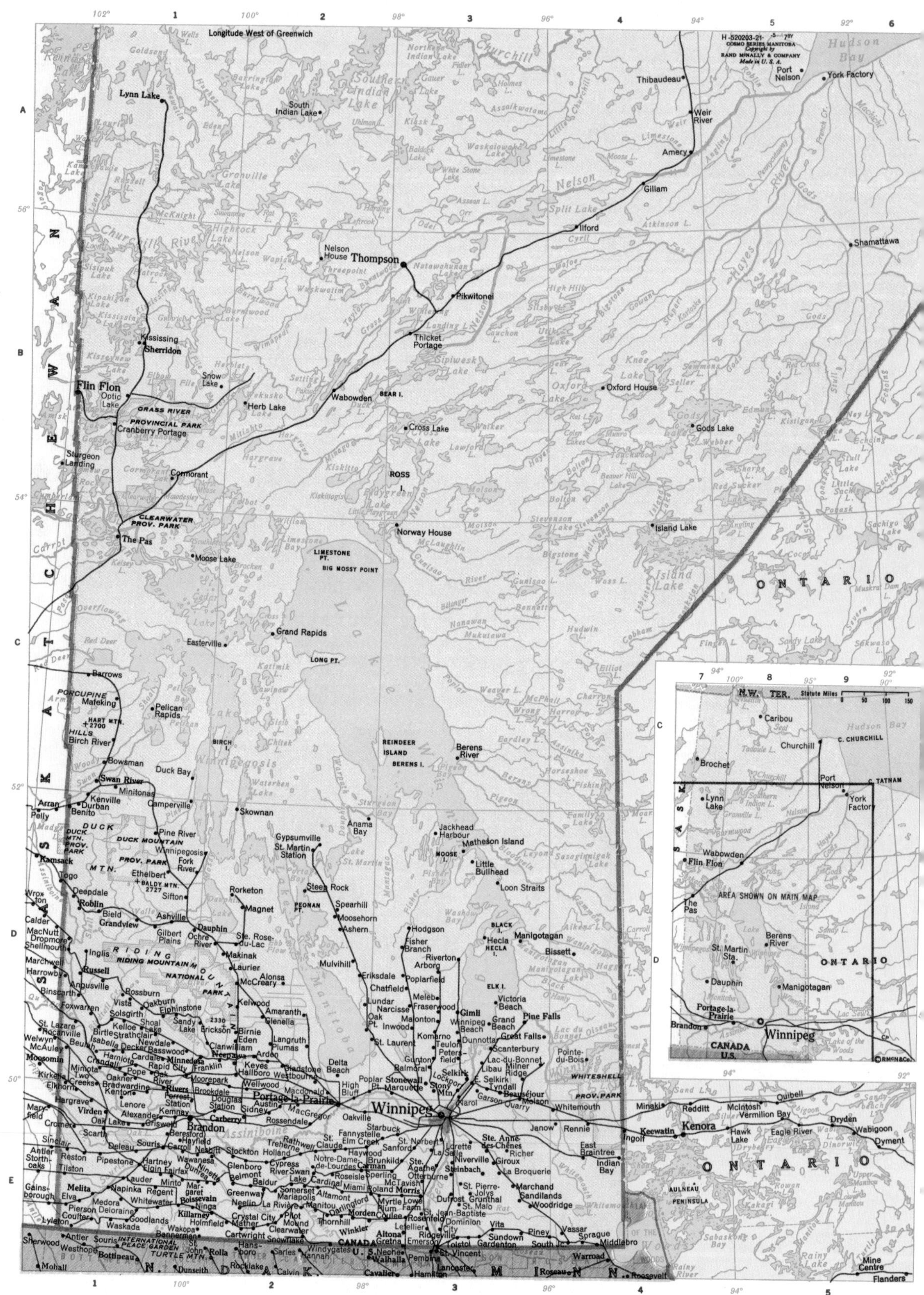

Longitude West of Greenwich
Winnipeg
Thompson
Brandon
Flin Flon
The Pas
Churchill
Hudson Bay
ONTARIO
AREA SHOWN ON MAIN MAP
Statute Miles 10 0 10 20 30 40 50 60 70
Kilometers 10 0 10 20 40 60 80 100
Oblique Cylindrical Projection

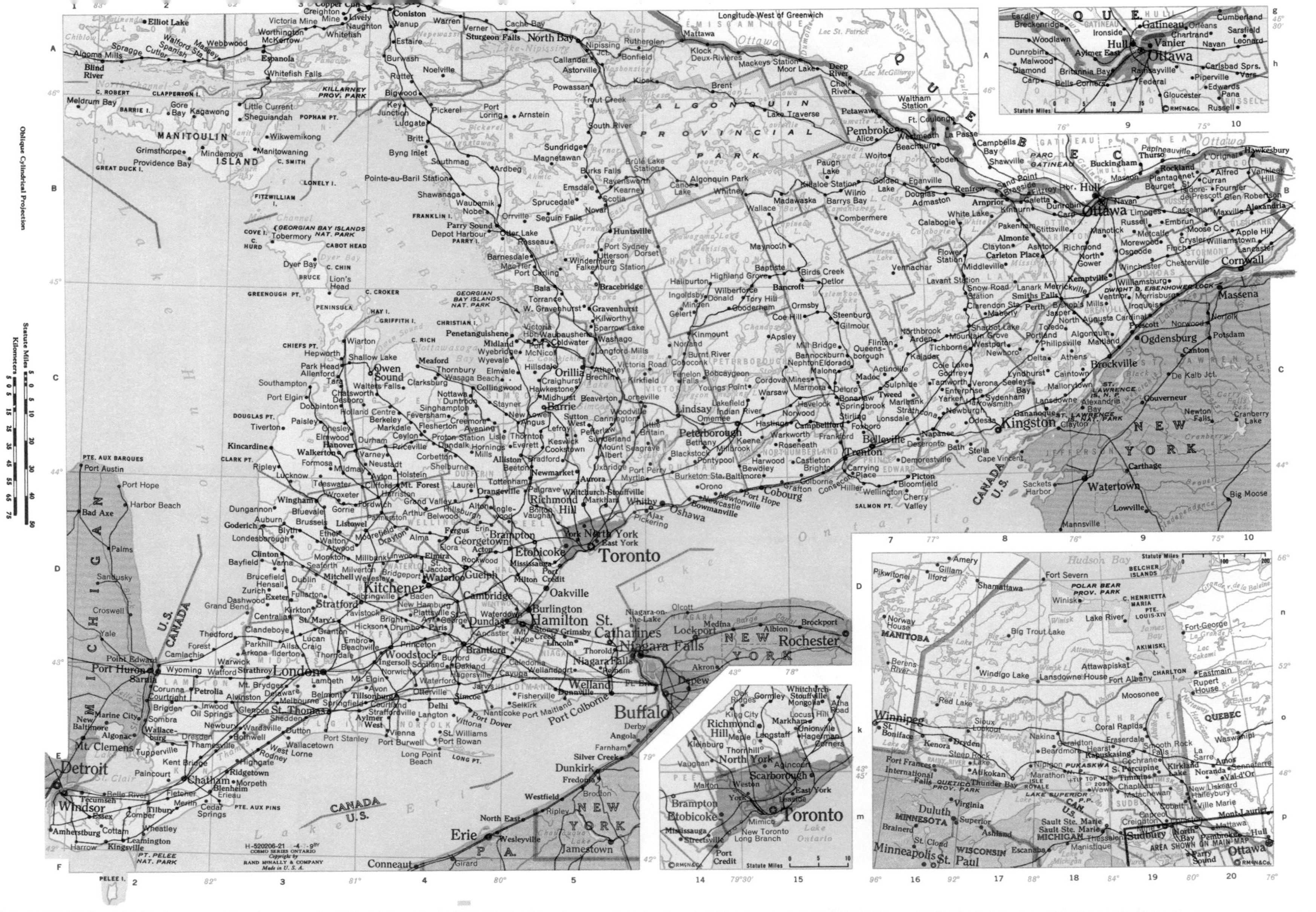
Oblique Cylindrical Projection
Statute Miles 5 0 5 10 20 30 40 50
Kilometers 5 0 5 15 25 35 45 55 65 75
H-520206-21 COSMO SERIES ONTARIO
Copyright by RAND McNALLY & COMPANY
Made in U. S. A.

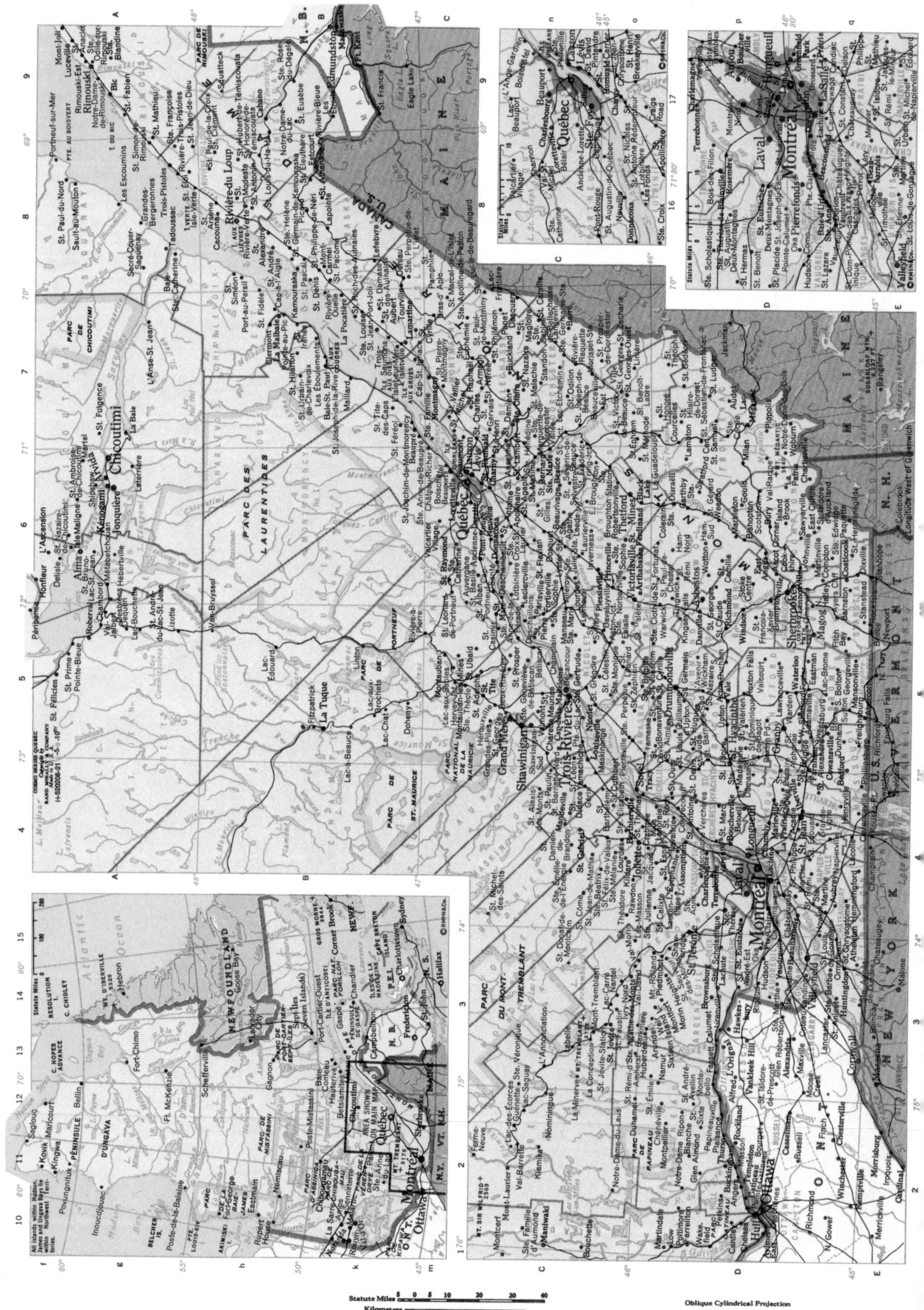
Statute Miles
Kilometers
Oblique Cylindrical Projection
PARC DES LAURENTIDES
NEWFOUNDLAND
MAINE
NEW YORK
VERMONT
N. H.

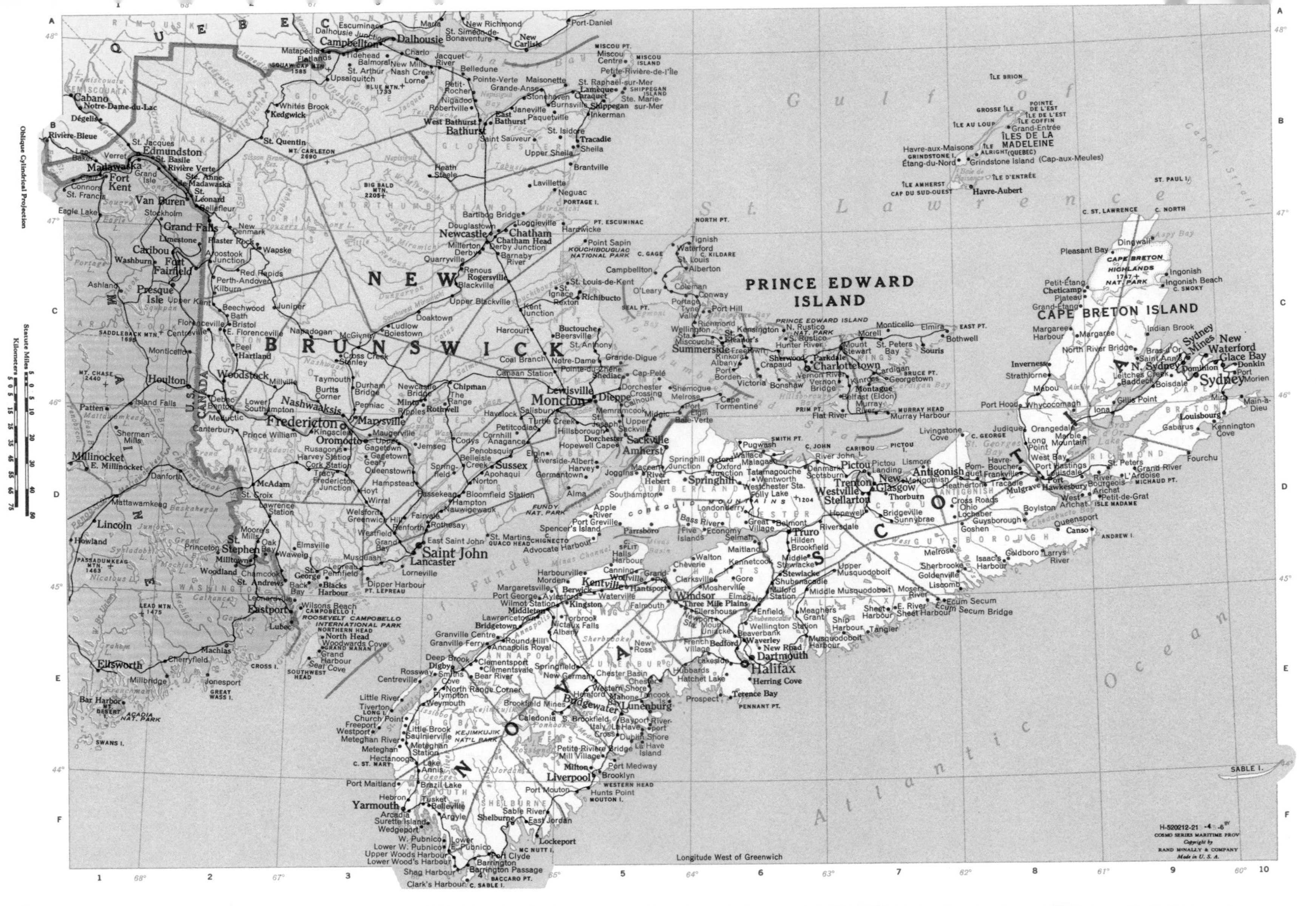
QUEBEC
NEW BRUNSWICK
PRINCE EDWARD ISLAND
CAPE BRETON ISLAND
NOVA SCOTIA
MAINE
Gulf of St. Lawrence
Atlantic Ocean
Bay of Fundy
Cabot Strait
ÎLES DE LA MADELEINE
SABLE I.
Halifax
Dartmouth
Saint John
Moncton
Fredericton
Charlottetown
Summerside
Sydney
Truro
Yarmouth
Bathurst
Campbellton
Dalhousie
Edmundston
Chatham
Newcastle
Amherst
Sackville
New Glasgow
Antigonish
Liverpool
Bridgewater
Lunenburg
Kentville
Windsor
Digby
Woodstock
Presque Isle
Caribou
Houlton
Millinocket
Lincoln
Ellsworth
Eastport
St. Stephen
Longitude West of Greenwich
H-520212-21
COSMO SERIES MARITIME PROV
Copyright by RAND McNALLY & COMPANY
Made in U. S. A.
Oblique Cylindrical Projection
Statute Miles
Kilometers

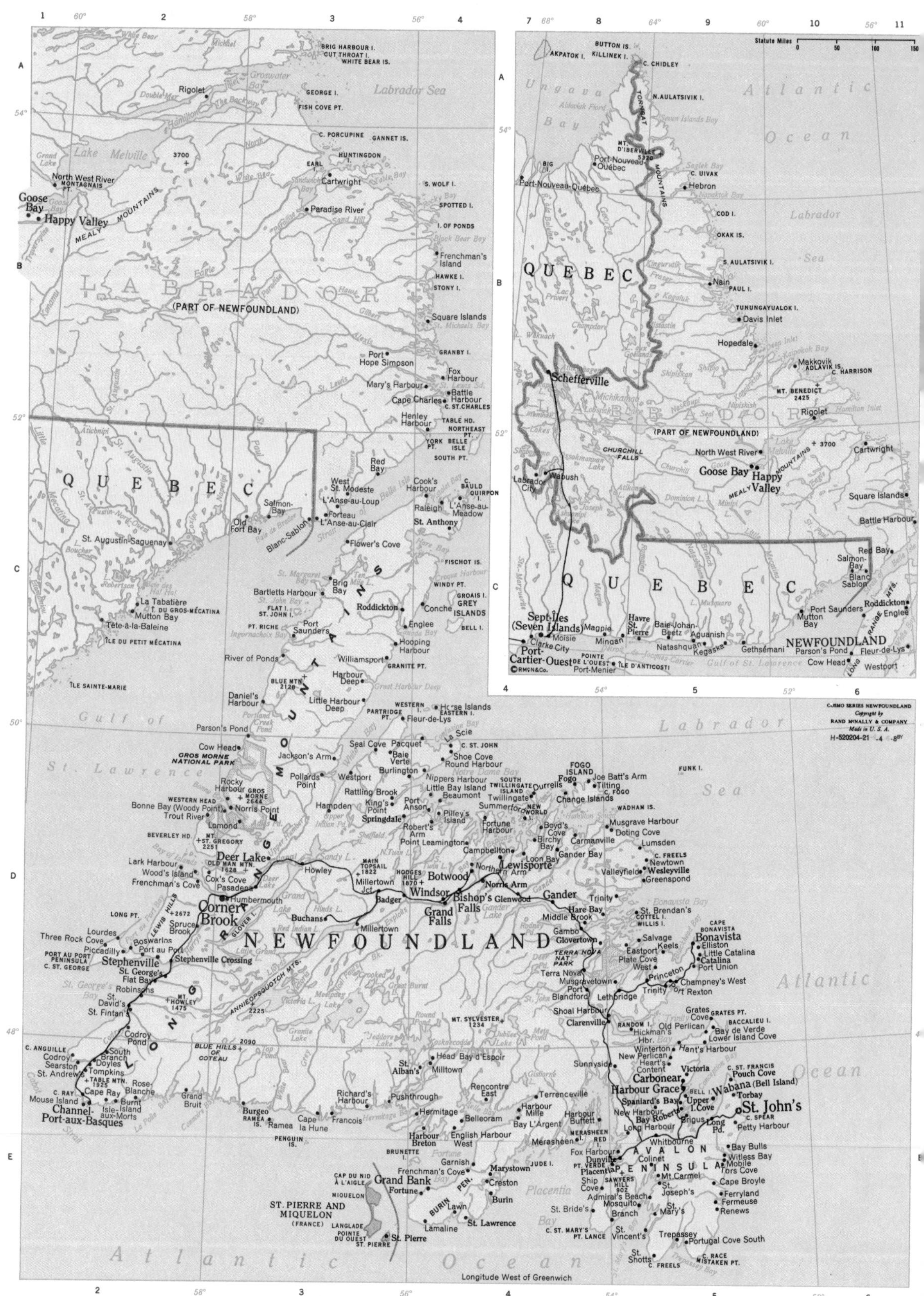
Labrador Sea
LABRADOR
(PART OF NEWFOUNDLAND)
QUEBEC
NEWFOUNDLAND
Gulf of St. Lawrence
Atlantic Ocean
Longitude West of Greenwich
Lambert Conformal Conic Projection

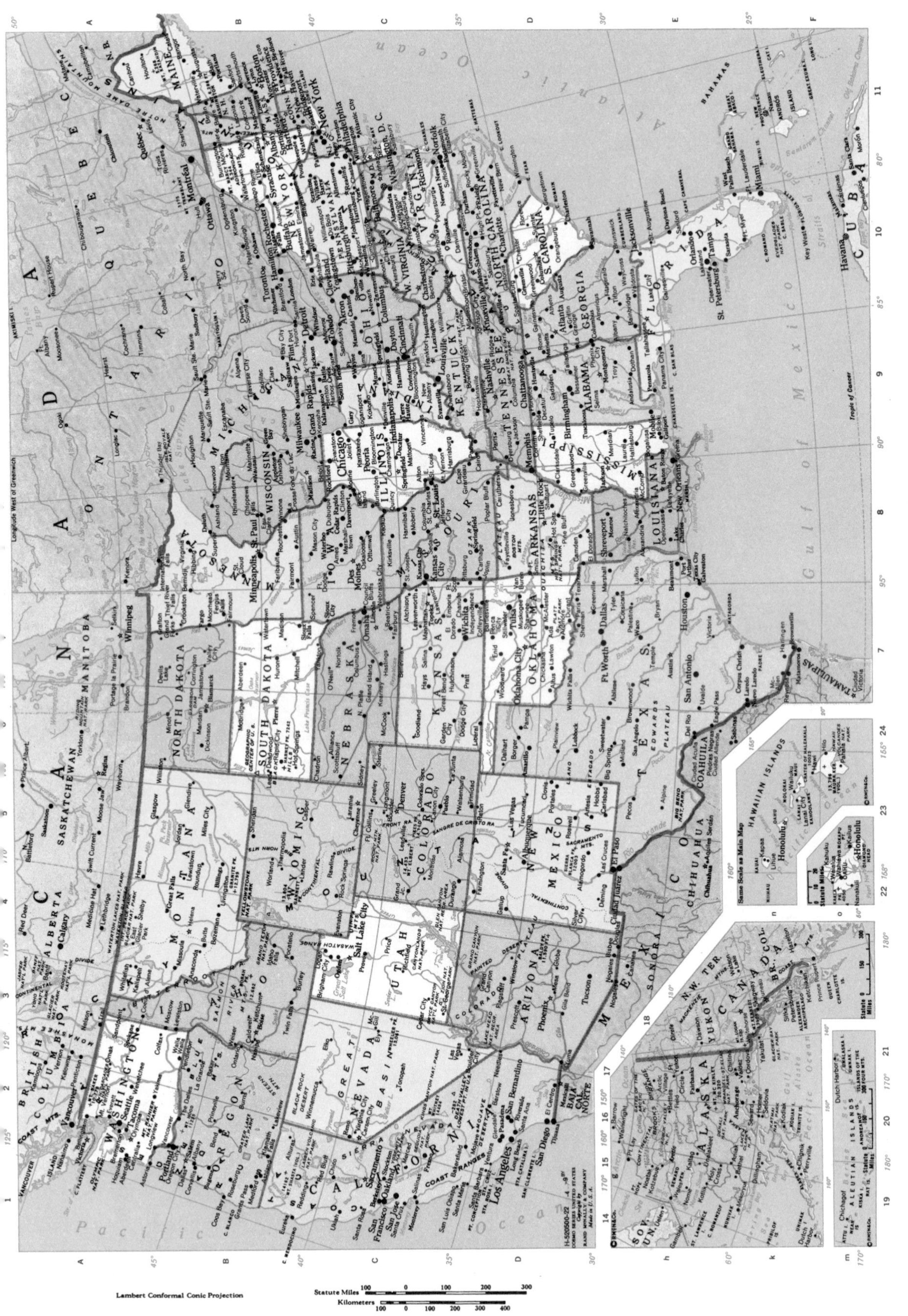
Lambert Conformal Conic Projection
Statute Miles 100 0 100 200 300
Kilometers 100 0 100 200 300 400

Statute Miles 5 0 5 10 20 30 40

Kilometers 5 0 5 15 25 35 45 55

Lambert Conformal Conic Projection

Arctic Ocean
Pacific Ocean
Bering Sea
Gulf of Alaska
Bristol Bay
CANADA
UNITED STATES
YUKON
BRITISH COLUMBIA
U.S.S.R.
U.S.
BROOKS RANGE
ALASKA RANGE
ALEUTIAN ISLANDS
SEWARD PENINSULA
ALASKA PENINSULA
ALEXANDER ARCHIPELAGO
Anchorage
Fairbanks
Nome
Juneau
Barrow
Kodiak
Sitka
Ketchikan
Whitehorse
Prince Rupert
Anadyr
Providenіya
Longitude West of Greenwich
Polyconic Projection
Statute Miles
Kilometers
H-520502-21
COSMO SERIES ALASKA
Copyright by RAND McNALLY & COMPANY
Made in U. S. A.

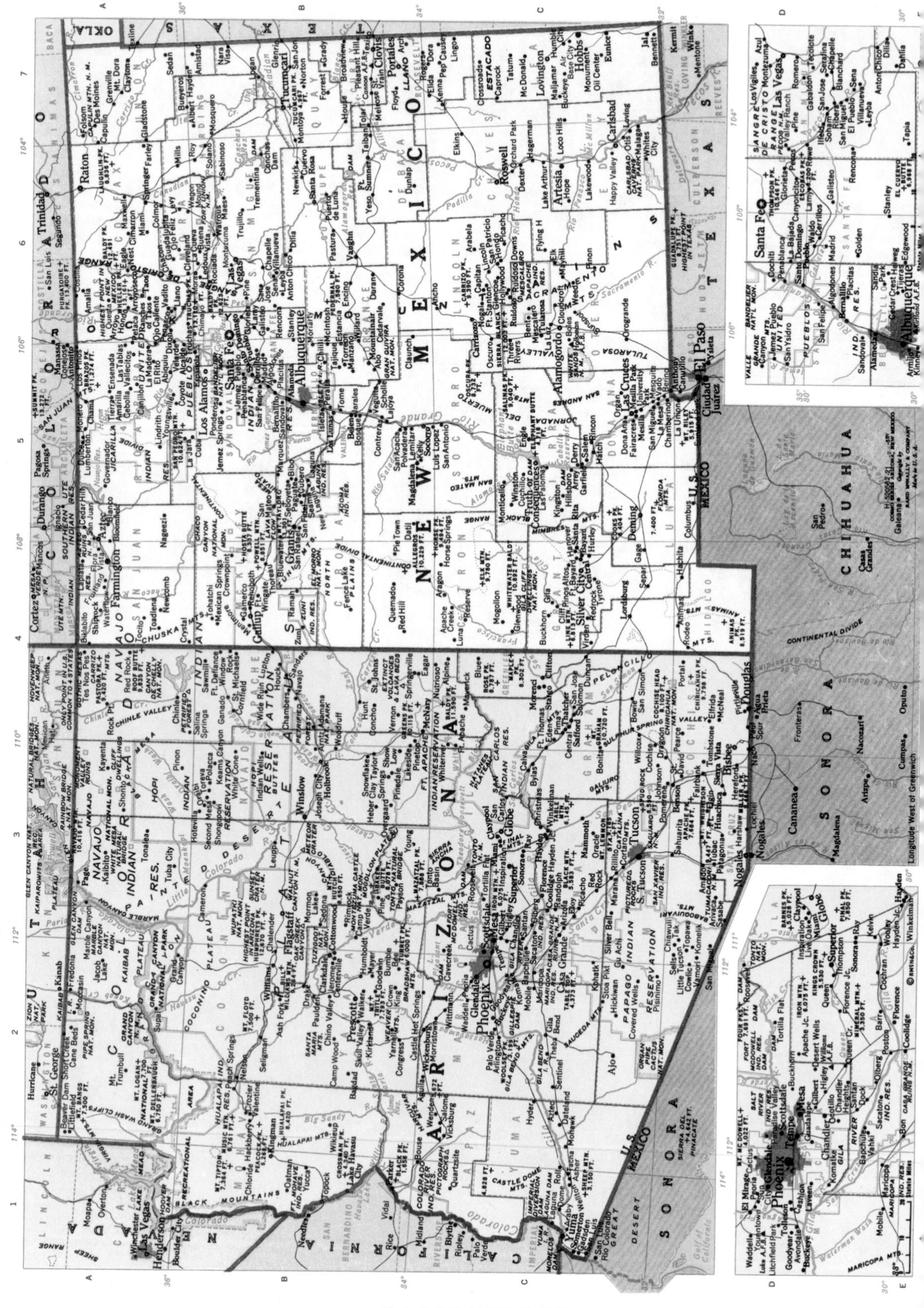

Statute Miles 10 0 10 20 30 40 50 60 70 80 90

Kilometers 10 0 10 20 40 60 80 100 120

Lambert Conformal Conic Projection

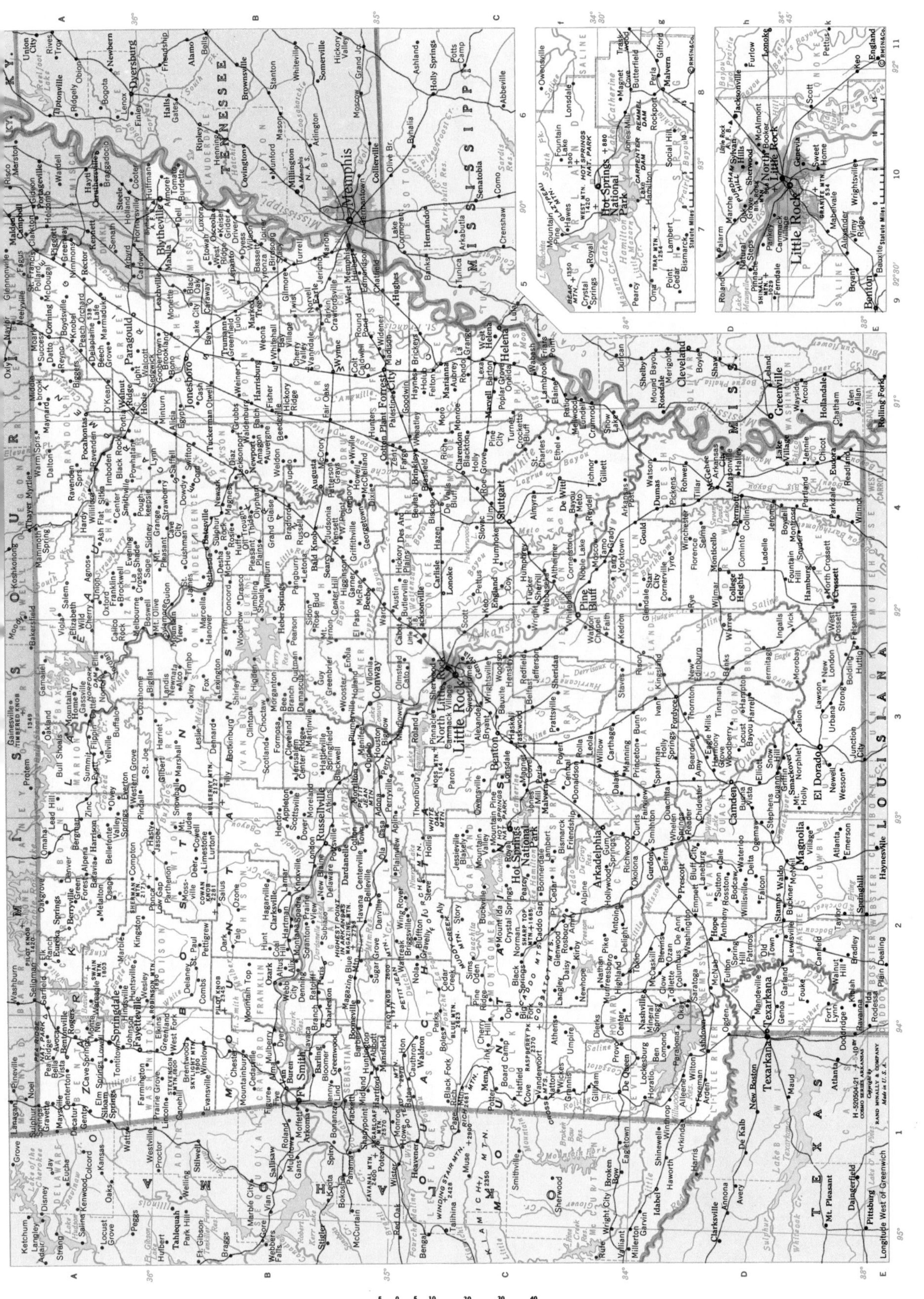

Lambert Conformal Conic Projection

Statute Miles 5 0 5 10 20 30 40

Kilometers 5 0 5 15 25 35 45 55

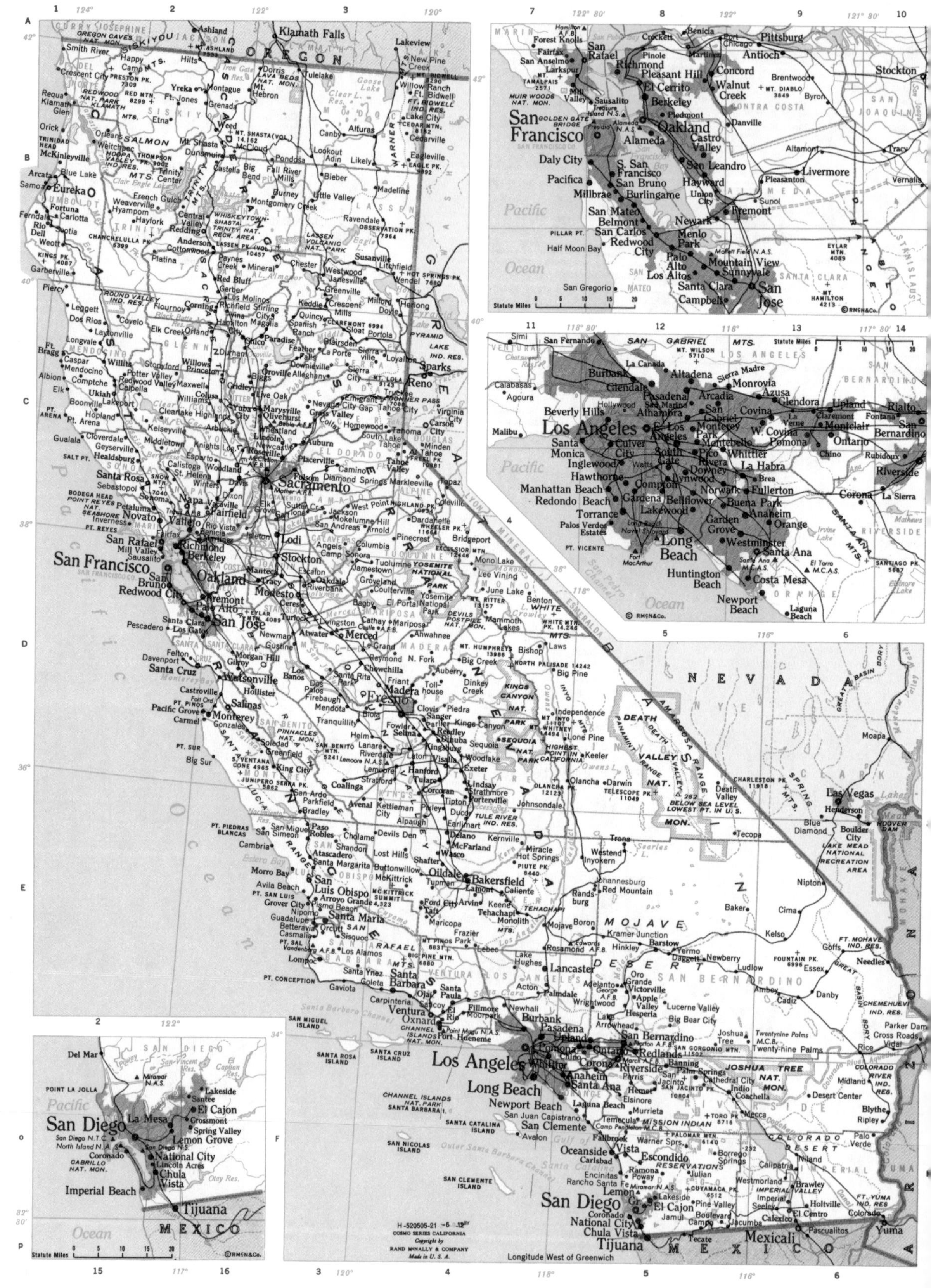

Statute Miles 10 0 10 20 30 40 50 60 70 80 90

Kilometers 10 0 10 20 40 60 80 100 120

Lambert Conformal Conic Projection

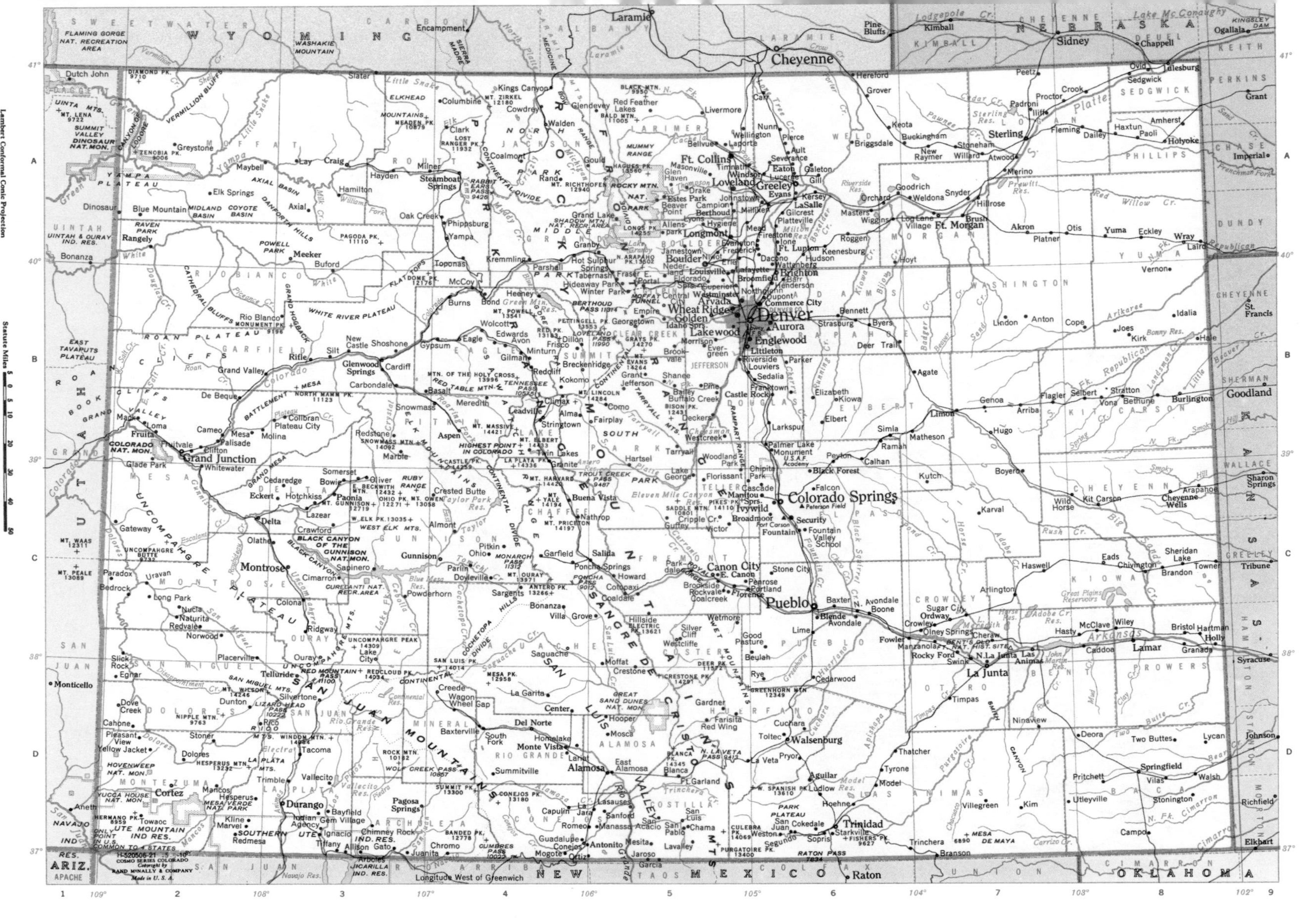

WYOMING
NEBRASKA
KANSAS
OKLAHOMA
NEW MEXICO
UTAH
ARIZ.
Cheyenne
Laramie
Sidney
Denver
Colorado Springs
Pueblo
Boulder
Ft. Collins
Greeley
Loveland
Longmont
Golden
Aurora
Englewood
Lakewood
Arvada
Wheat Ridge
Grand Junction
Montrose
Durango
Cortez
Trinidad
Walsenburg
Alamosa
La Junta
Lamar
Sterling
Ft. Morgan
Burlington
Limon
Canon City
Leadville
Aspen
Glenwood Springs
Steamboat Springs
Craig
Gunnison
Salida
Raton
Goodland
SAN JUAN MOUNTAINS
SANGRE DE CRISTO MTS.
CONTINENTAL DIVIDE
SAN LUIS VALLEY
UNCOMPAHGRE PLATEAU
WHITE RIVER PLATEAU
MESA VERDE NAT. PARK
Lambert Conformal Conic Projection
Statute Miles 5 0 5 10 20 30 40 50
Kilometers 5 0 5 15 25 35 45 55 65 75
Longitude West of Greenwich

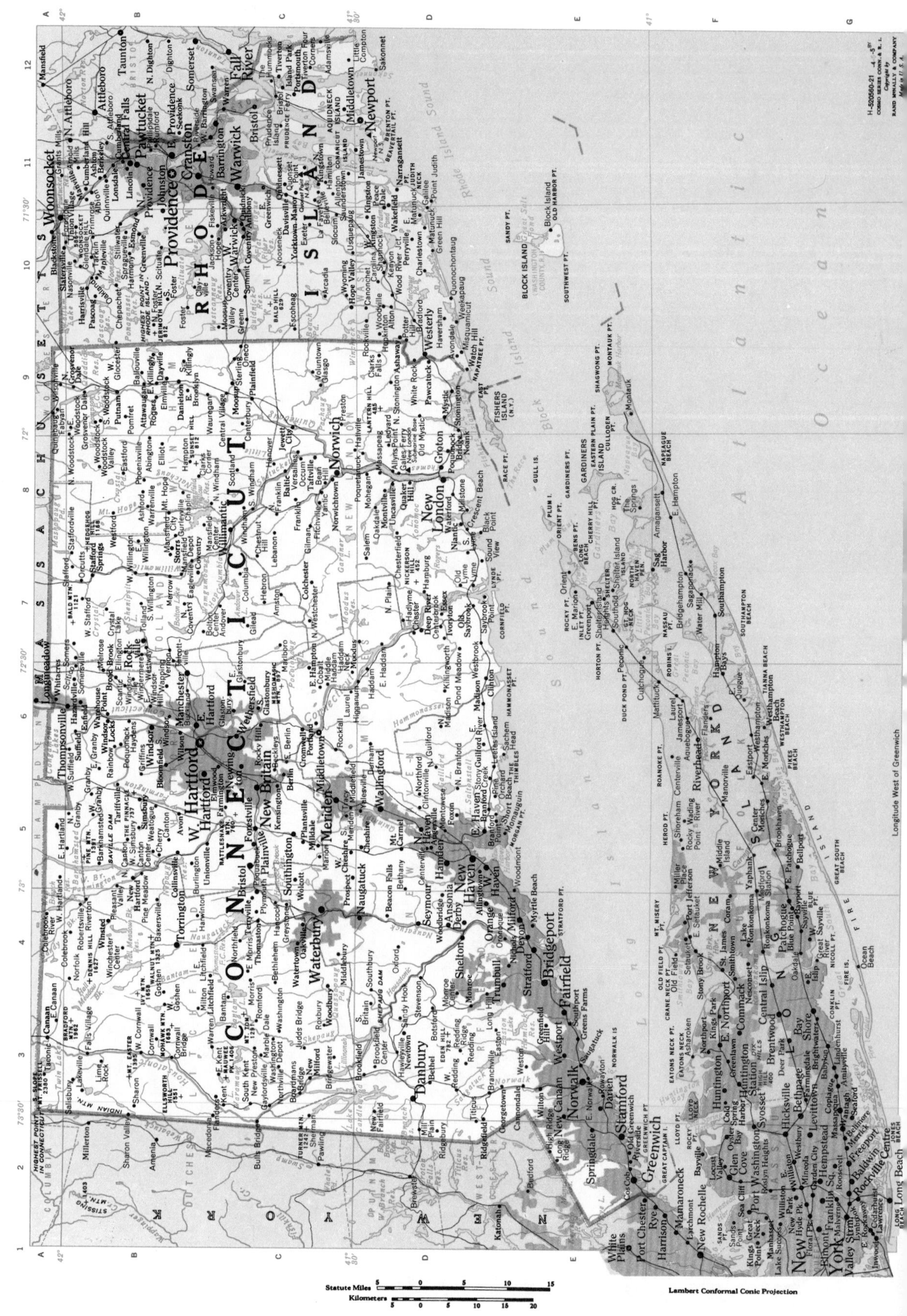
CONNECTICUT
RHODE ISLAND
MASSACHUSETTS
NEW YORK
Long Island Sound
Block Island Sound
Atlantic Ocean
Longitude West of Greenwich
Statute Miles
Kilometers
Lambert Conformal Conic Projection

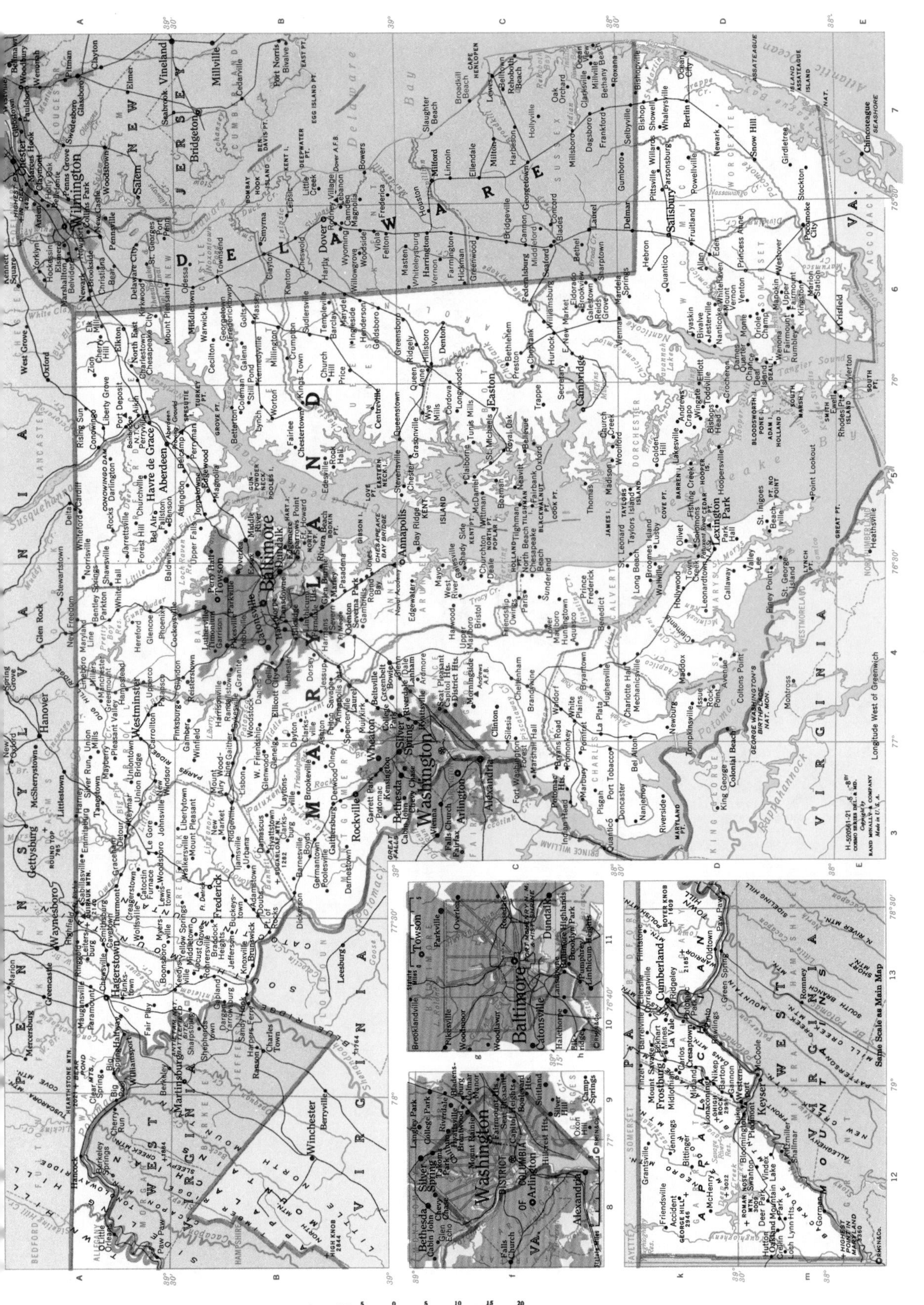

Lambert Conformal Conic Projection

Statute Miles 5 0 5 10 15 20

Kilometers 5 0 5 10 15 20 25 30

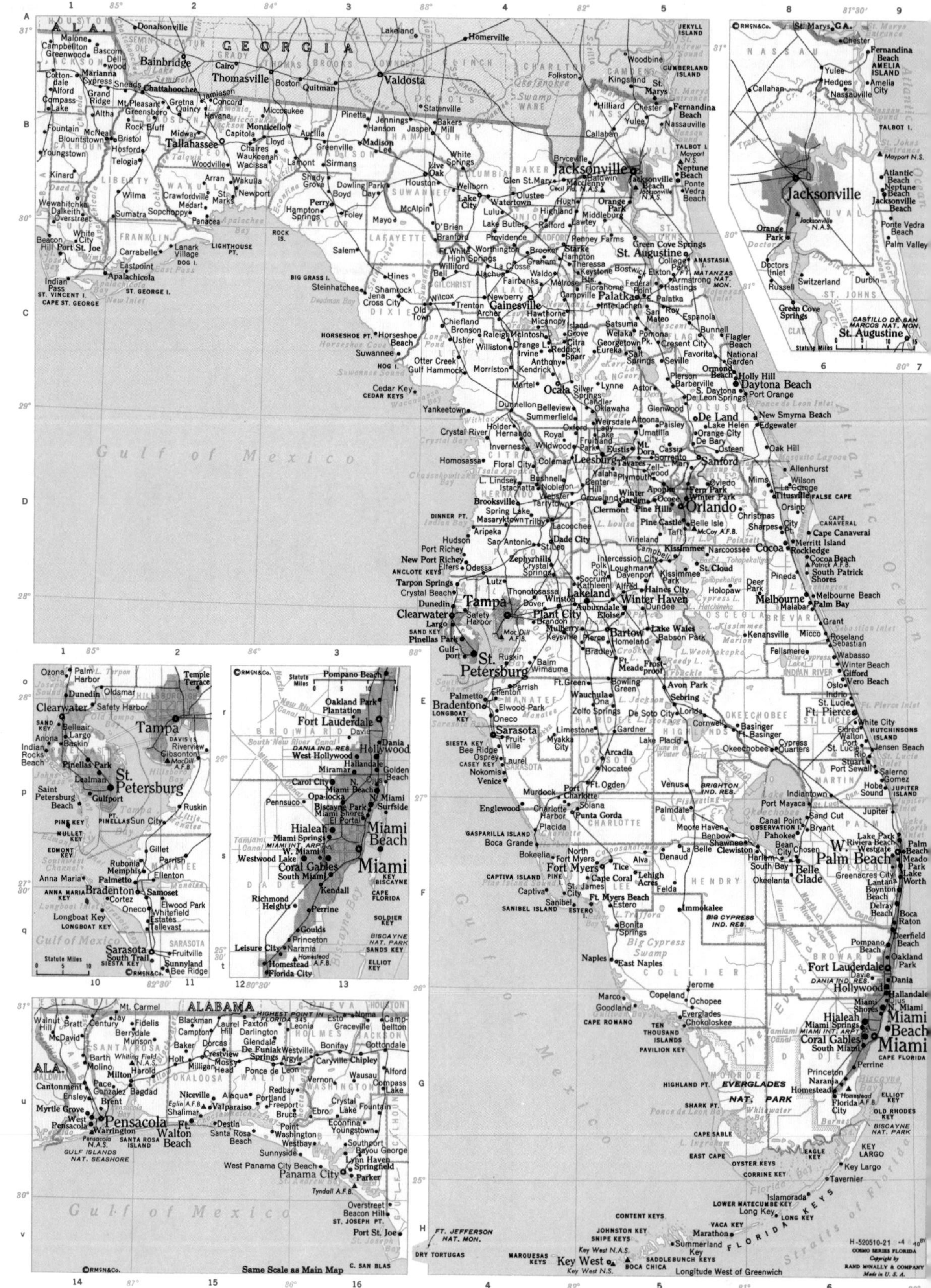

Statute Miles 5 0 5 10 20 30 40 50

Kilometers 5 0 5 15 25 35 45 55 65

Lambert Conformal Conic Projection

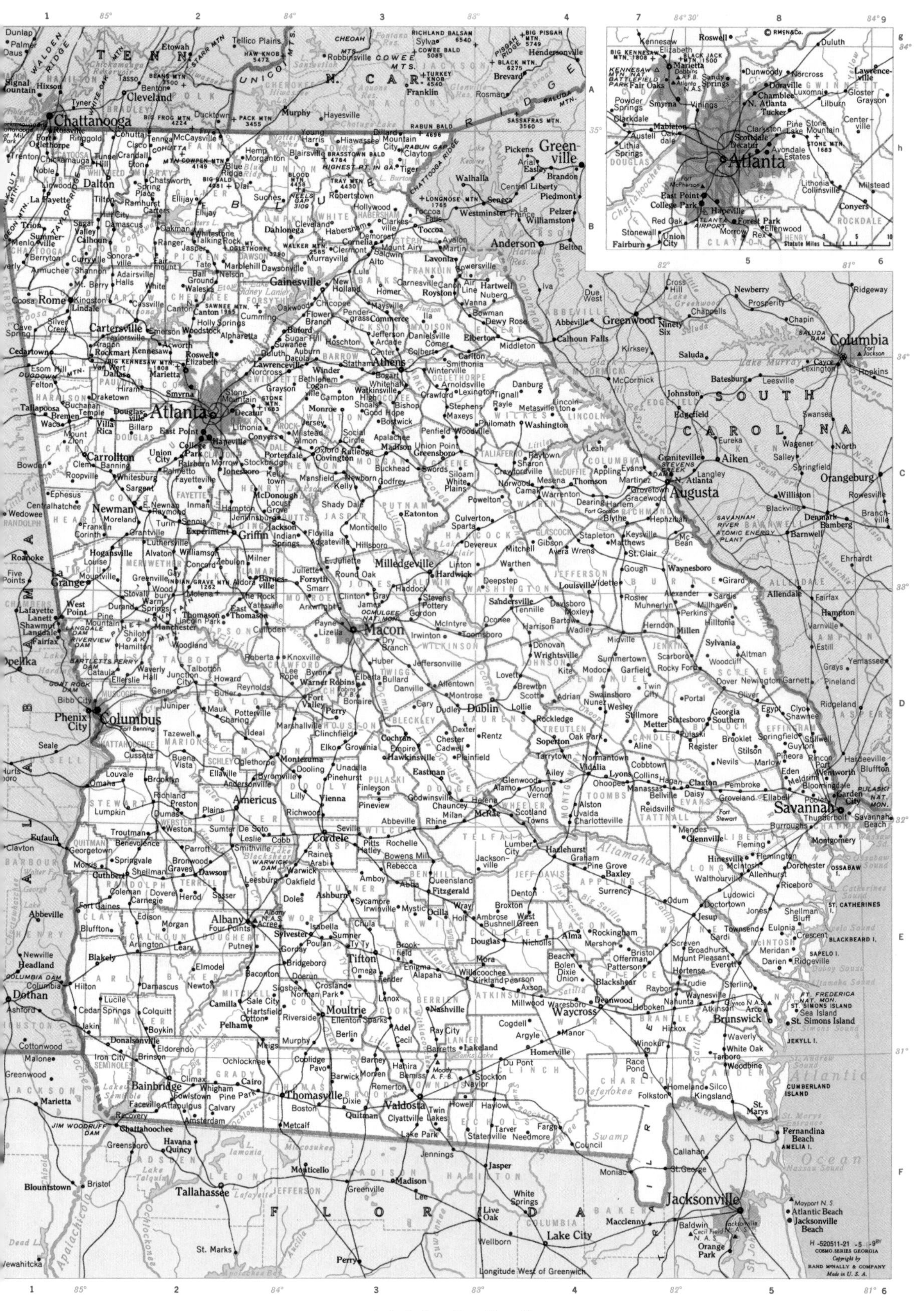

Lambert Conformal Conic Projection

Statute Miles 5 0 5 10 20 30 40

Kilometers 5 0 5 15 25 35 45 55

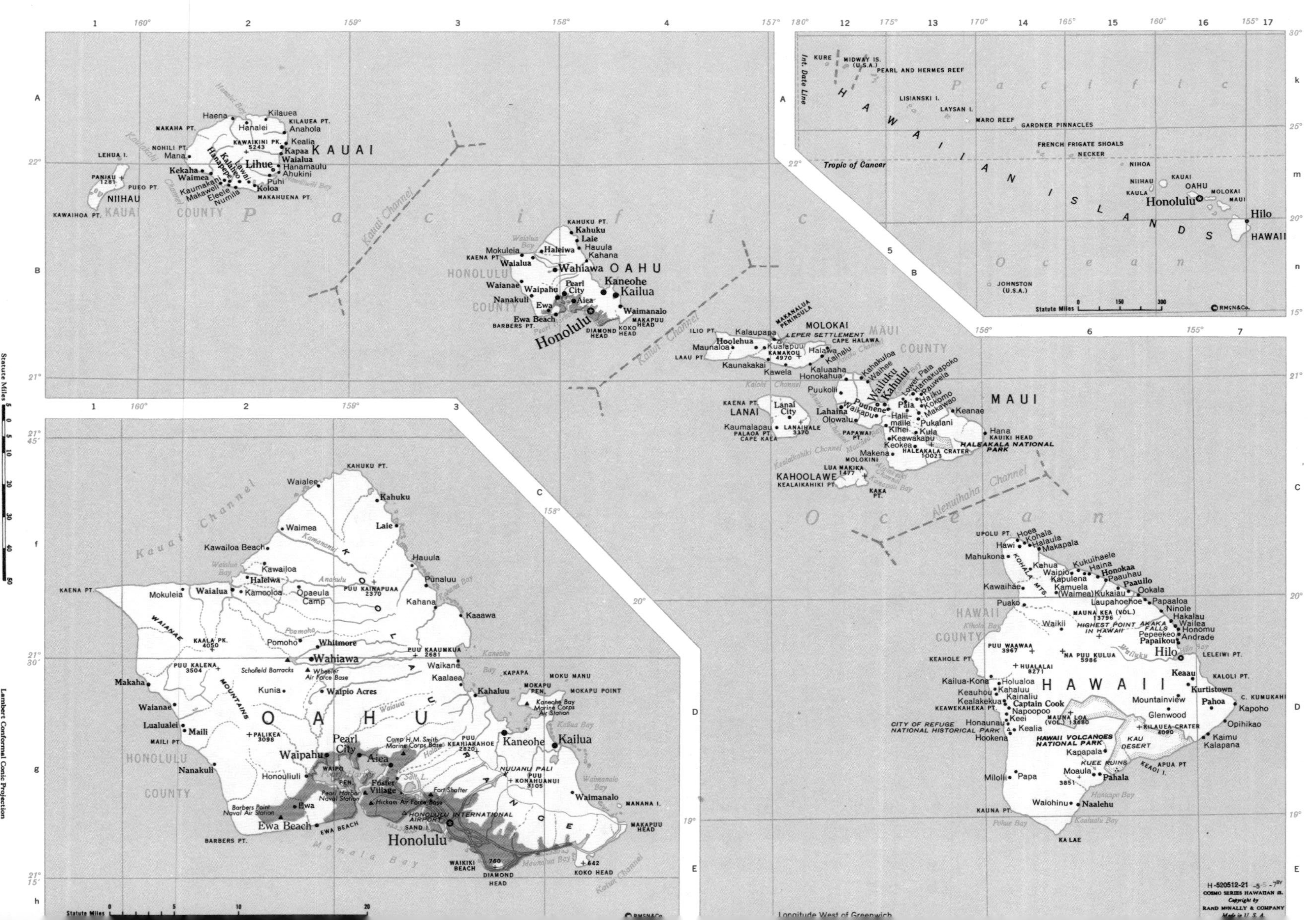
KAUAI
NIIHAU
Lihue
Hanalei
Haena
Kilauea
Anahola
Kealia
Kapaa
Waialua
Hanamaulu
Ahukini
Puhi
Koloa
Kekaha
Waimea
Mana
Kaumakani
Makaweli
Eleele
Numila
Kalaheo
Hanapepe
Lawai
KAUAI COUNTY
Kauai Channel
OAHU
Honolulu
Kaneohe
Kailua
Waimanalo
Wahiawa
Haleiwa
Waialua
Mokuleia
Kahuku
Laie
Hauula
Kahana
Waianae
Waipahu
Pearl City
Aiea
Ewa
Ewa Beach
Nanakuli
HONOLULU COUNTY
Kaiwi Channel
MOLOKAI
LEPER SETTLEMENT
Kalaupapa
Hoolehua
Maunaloa
Kaunakakai
Kualapuu
Kamalo
Halawa
Kawela
Kaluaaha
Honokahua
LANAI
Lanai City
Kaumalapau
MAUI
MAUI COUNTY
Wailuku
Kahului
Lahaina
Olowalu
Puunene
Waikapu
Paia
Haiku
Makawao
Pukalani
Kula
Kihei
Makena
Hana
Keanae
HALEAKALA NATIONAL PARK
KAHOOLAWE
Alenuihaha Channel
HAWAII
Hilo
Hawi
Kohala
Mahukona
Kawaihae
Puako
Waimea (Kamuela)
Honokaa
Paauilo
Laupahoehoe
Pepeekeo
Papaikou
Keaau
Kurtistown
Mountainview
Glenwood
Pahoa
Kapoho
Kalapana
Kailua-Kona
Holualoa
Kealakekua
Captain Cook
Napoopoo
Honaunau
Hookena
Milolii
Papa
Pahala
Naalehu
Waiohinu
HAWAII VOLCANOES NATIONAL PARK
CITY OF REFUGE NATIONAL HISTORICAL PARK
MAUNA KEA (VOL.) 13796
HIGHEST POINT IN HAWAII
MAUNA LOA (VOL.) 13680
HUALALAI 8271
KILAUEA CRATER 4090
KAU DESERT
HAWAII COUNTY
KA LAE
Pacific Ocean
HAWAIIAN ISLANDS
Int. Date Line
Tropic of Cancer
KURE
MIDWAY IS. (U.S.A.)
PEARL AND HERMES REEF
LISIANSKI I.
LAYSAN I.
MARO REEF
GARDNER PINNACLES
FRENCH FRIGATE SHOALS
NECKER
NIHOA
JOHNSTON (U.S.A.)
Statute Miles 0 150 300
Statute Miles 0 5 10 20
Longitude West of Greenwich
H-520512-21
COSMO SERIES HAWAIIAN IS.
Copyright by RAND McNALLY & COMPANY
Made in U.S.A.
Statute Miles 5 0 5 10 20 30 40 50
Kilometers 5 0 5 10 20 30 40 50 60
Lambert Conformal Conic Projection

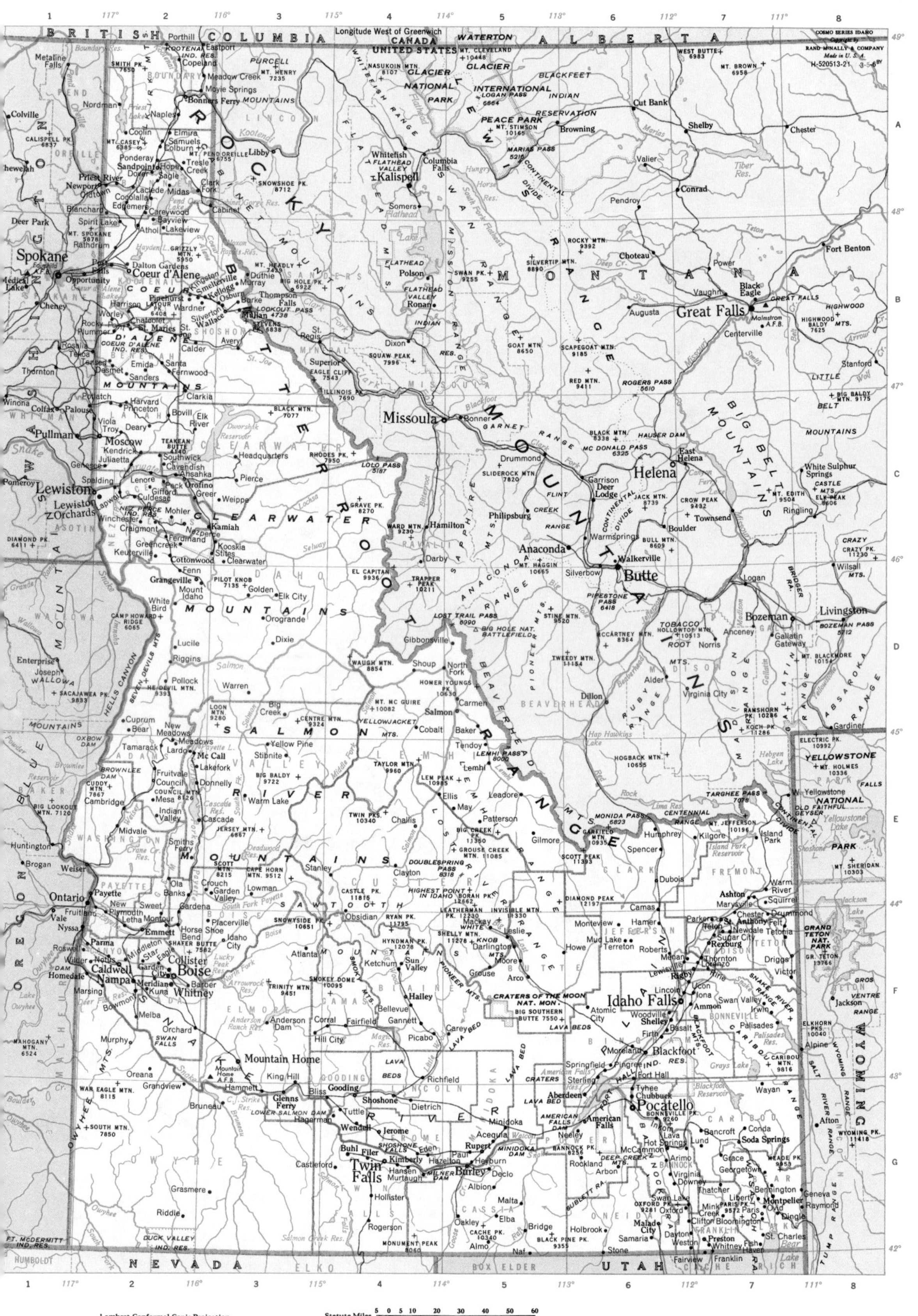

Lambert Conformal Conic Projection

Statute Miles 5 0 5 10 20 30 40 50 60

Kilometers 5 0 5 15 25 35 45 55 65 75

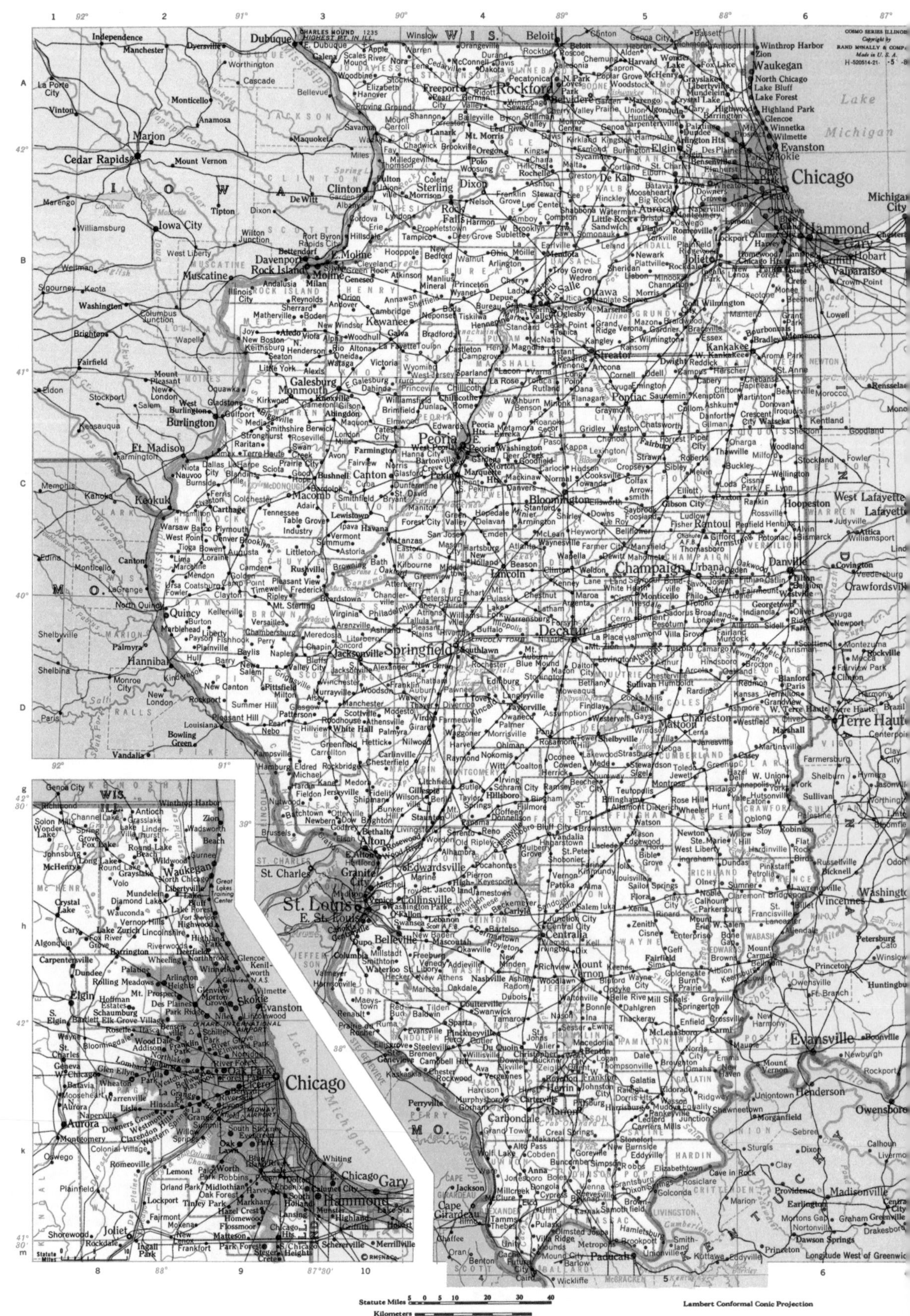
COSMO SERIES ILLINOIS
Copyright by RAND McNALLY & COMPANY
Made in U. S. A.
CHARLES MOUND 1235
HIGHEST PT. IN ILL.
I O W A
W I S.
M O.
Lake Michigan
Chicago
Rockford
Peoria
Springfield
Decatur
Champaign
Bloomington
Galesburg
Quincy
St. Louis
E. St. Louis
Cedar Rapids
Iowa City
Davenport
Dubuque
Burlington
Keokuk
Hannibal
Terre Haute
Evansville
Paducah
Cairo
Hammond
Gary
Waukegan
Elgin
Aurora
Joliet
Kankakee
Danville
Statute Miles 5 0 5 10 20 30 40
Kilometers 5 0 5 15 25 35 45 55
Lambert Conformal Conic Projection
Longitude West of Greenwich

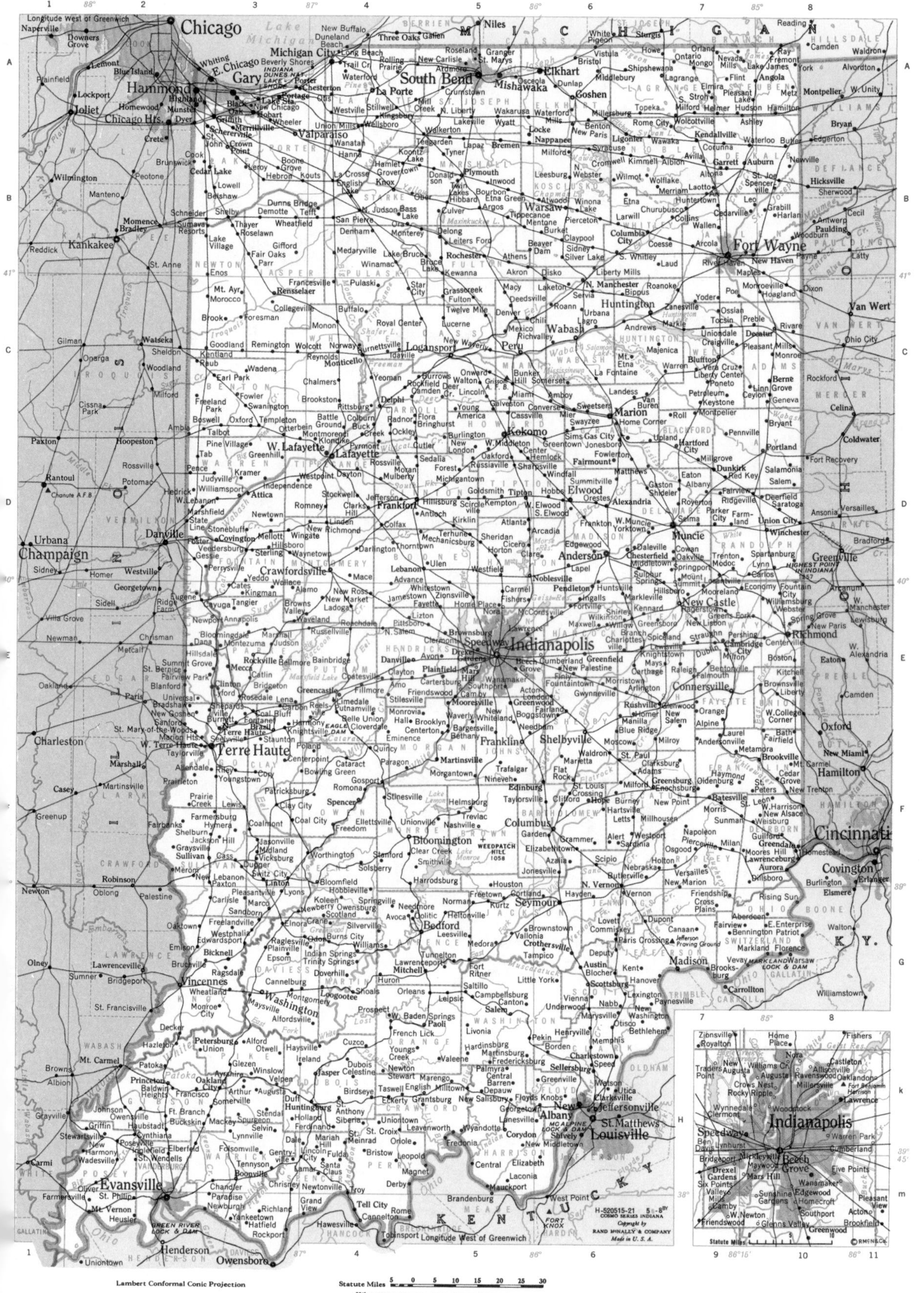
Longitude West of Greenwich
Chicago
Gary
Hammond
South Bend
Elkhart
Fort Wayne
Kokomo
Lafayette
Muncie
Anderson
Indianapolis
Richmond
Terre Haute
Bloomington
Columbus
Evansville
Louisville
Cincinnati
Kankakee
Champaign
Danville
Vincennes
Washington
New Albany
Jeffersonville
Lake Michigan
M I C H I G A N
O H I O
K E N T U C K Y
WEEDPATCH HILL 1058
HIGHEST POINT IN INDIANA 1257
H-520515-21
COSMO SERIES INDIANA
Copyright by RAND McNALLY & COMPANY
Made in U. S. A.
Lambert Conformal Conic Projection
Statute Miles 5 0 5 10 15 20 25 30
Kilometers 5 0 5 15 25 35

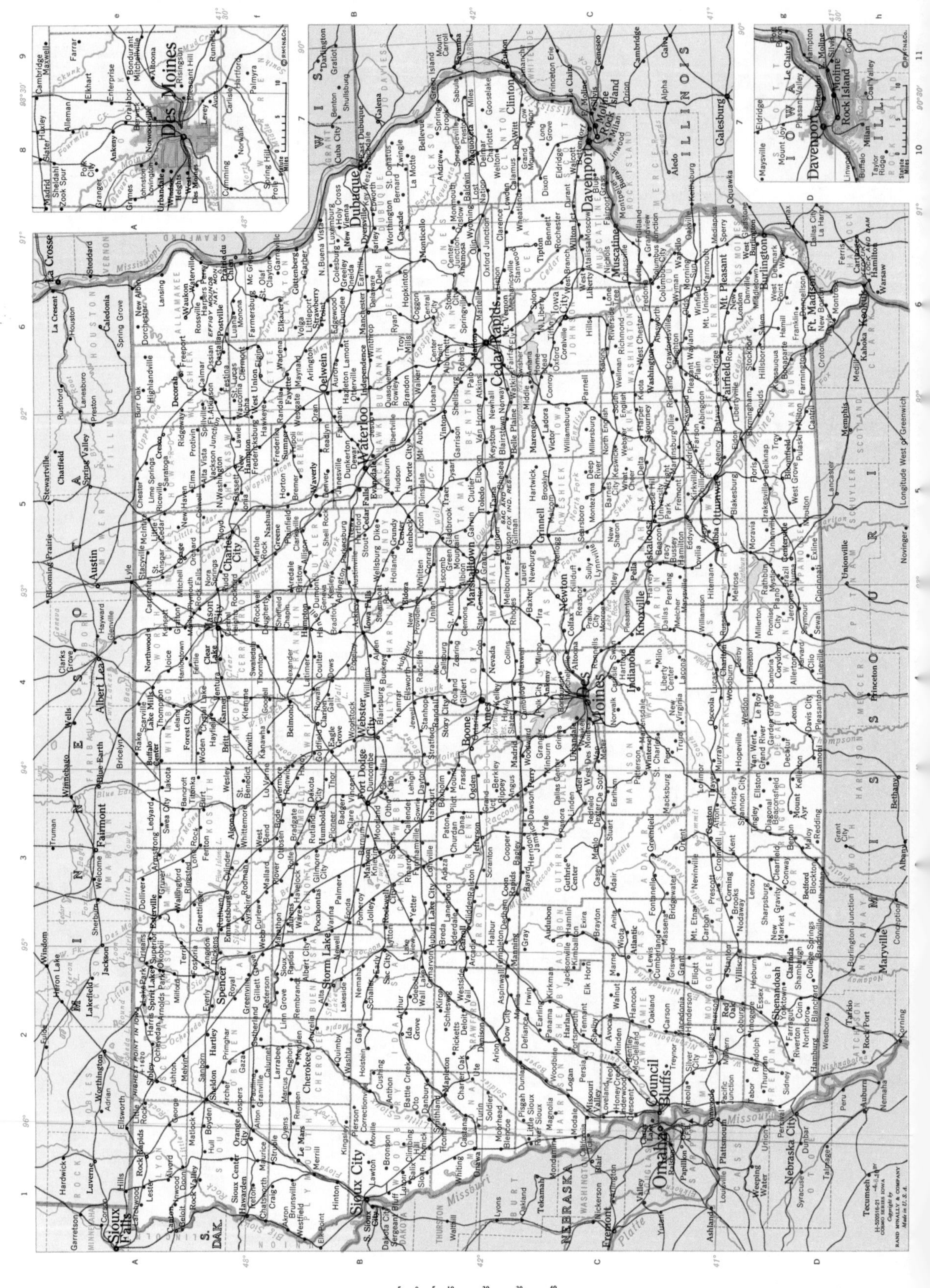

Statute Miles 5 0 5 10 20 30 40

Kilometers 5 0 5 15 25 35 45 55

Lambert Conformal Conic Projection

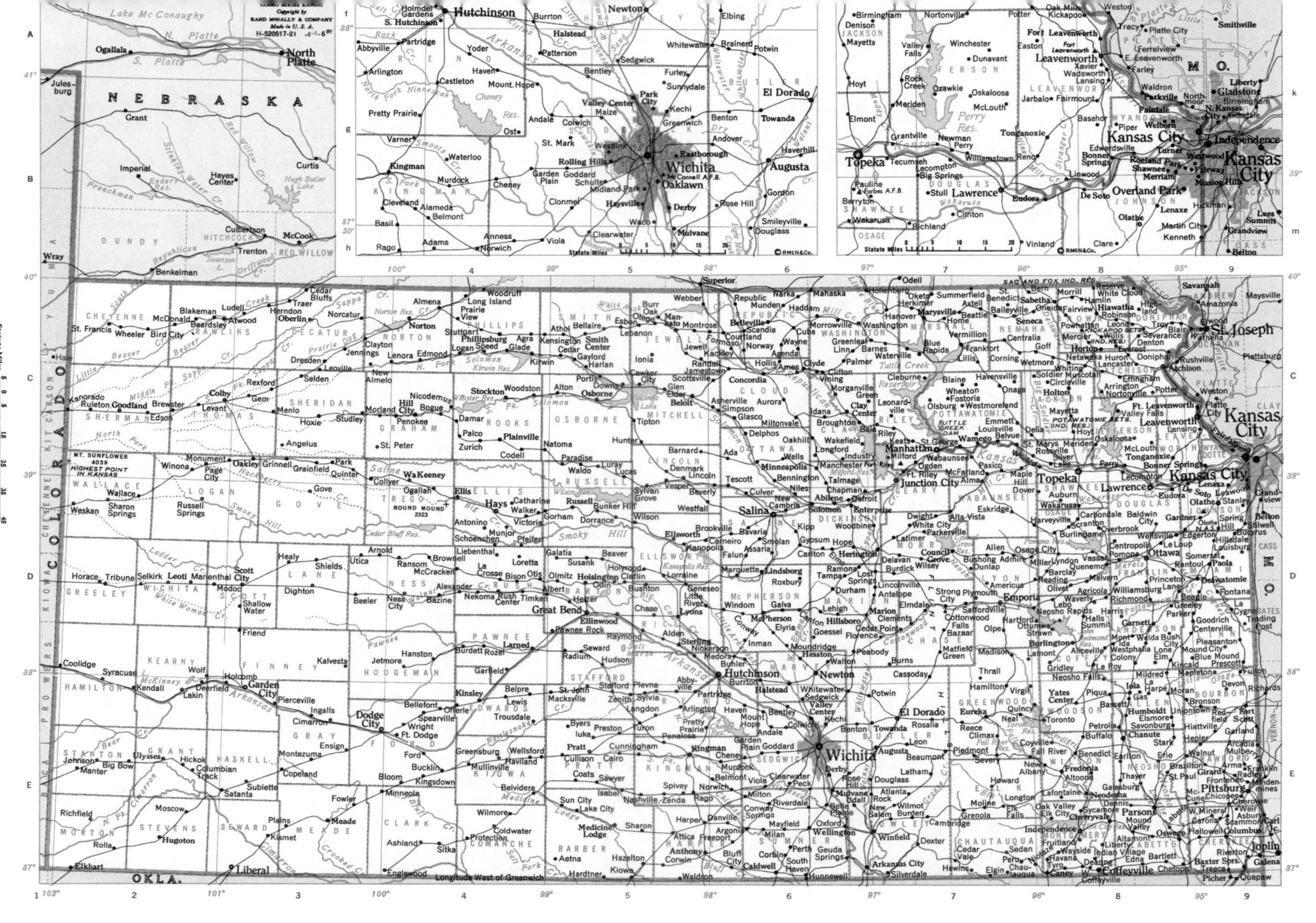

Lambert Conformal Conic Projection

Statute Miles 5 0 5 15 25 35 45

Kilometers 5 0 5 15 25 35 45 55 65

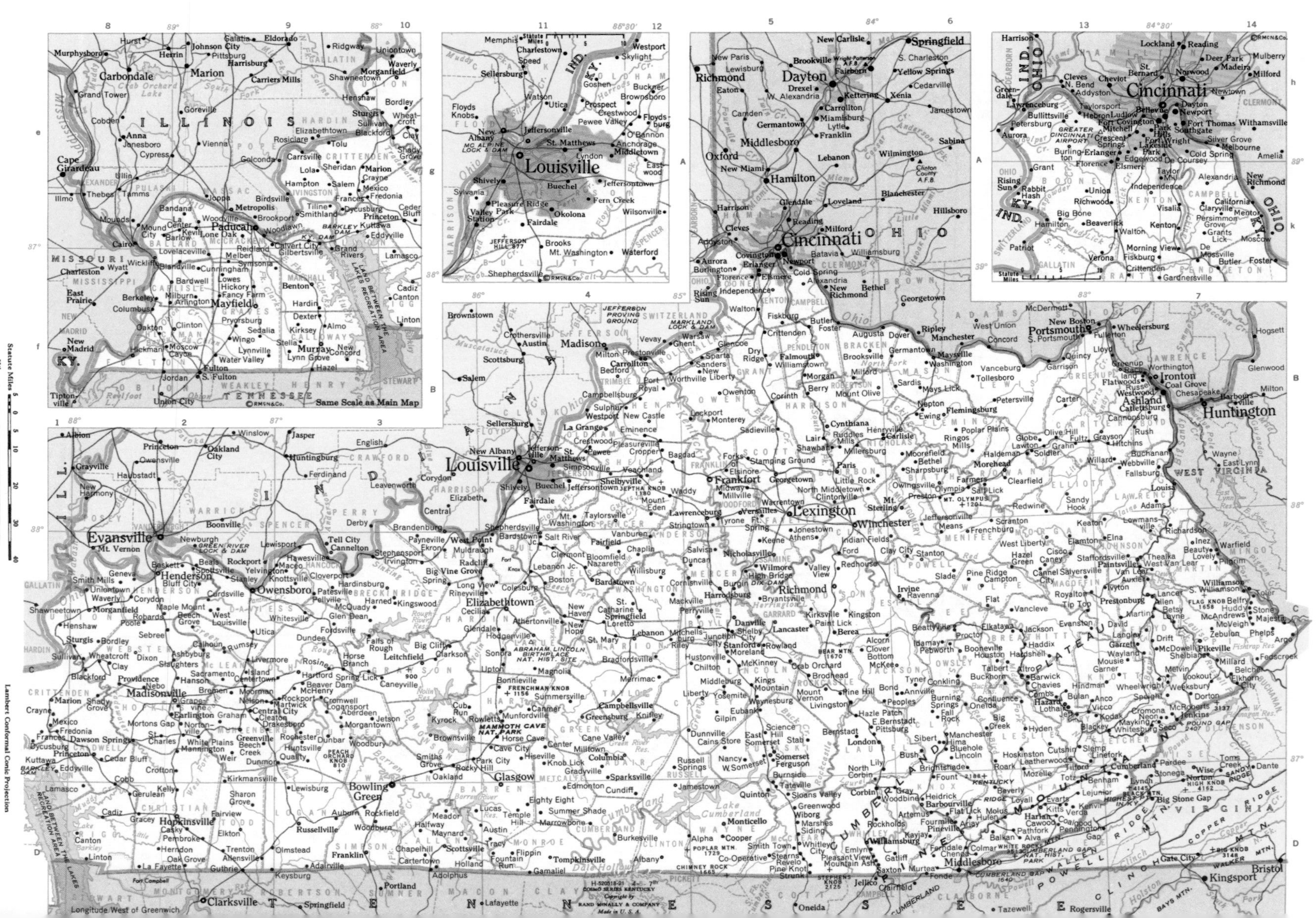

Statute Miles 5 0 5 10 20 30 40
Kilometers 5 0 5 10 20 30 40 50 60
Lambert Conformal Conic Projection
Same Scale as Main Map
Longitude West of Greenwich
ILLINOIS
MISSOURI
TENNESSEE
OHIO
INDIANA
WEST VIRGINIA
VIRGINIA
Louisville
Lexington
Frankfort
Cincinnati
Dayton
Evansville
Owensboro
Bowling Green
Paducah
Huntington
Ashland
Covington
Henderson
Hopkinsville
Elizabethtown
Richmond
Middlesboro
Clarksville
Kingsport
H-520518-21
COSMO SERIES KENTUCKY
Copyright by RAND McNALLY & COMPANY
Made in U. S. A.

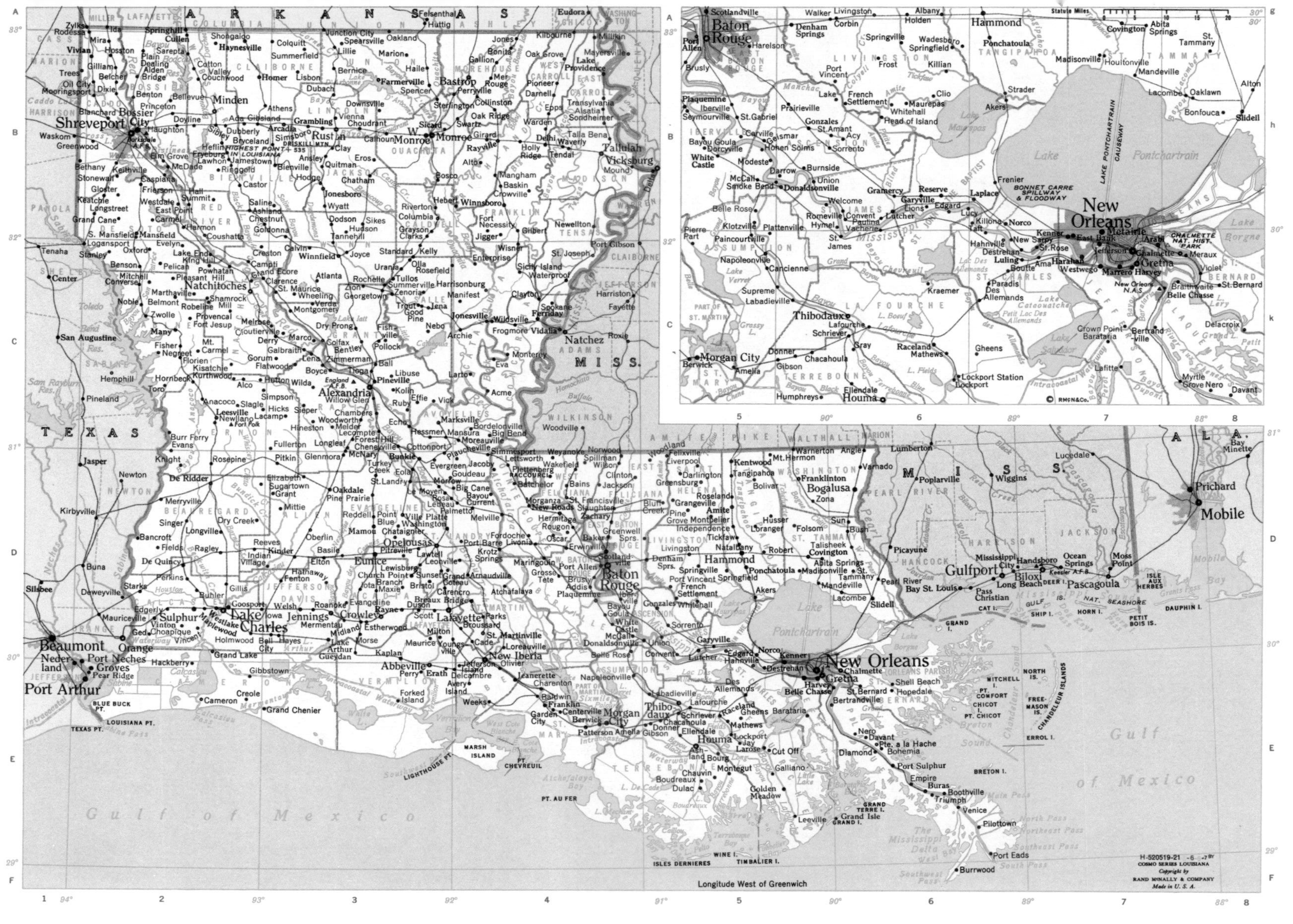

Lambert Conformal Conic Projection

Statute Miles 5 0 5 10 20 30 40

Kilometers 5 0 5 15 25 35 45 55

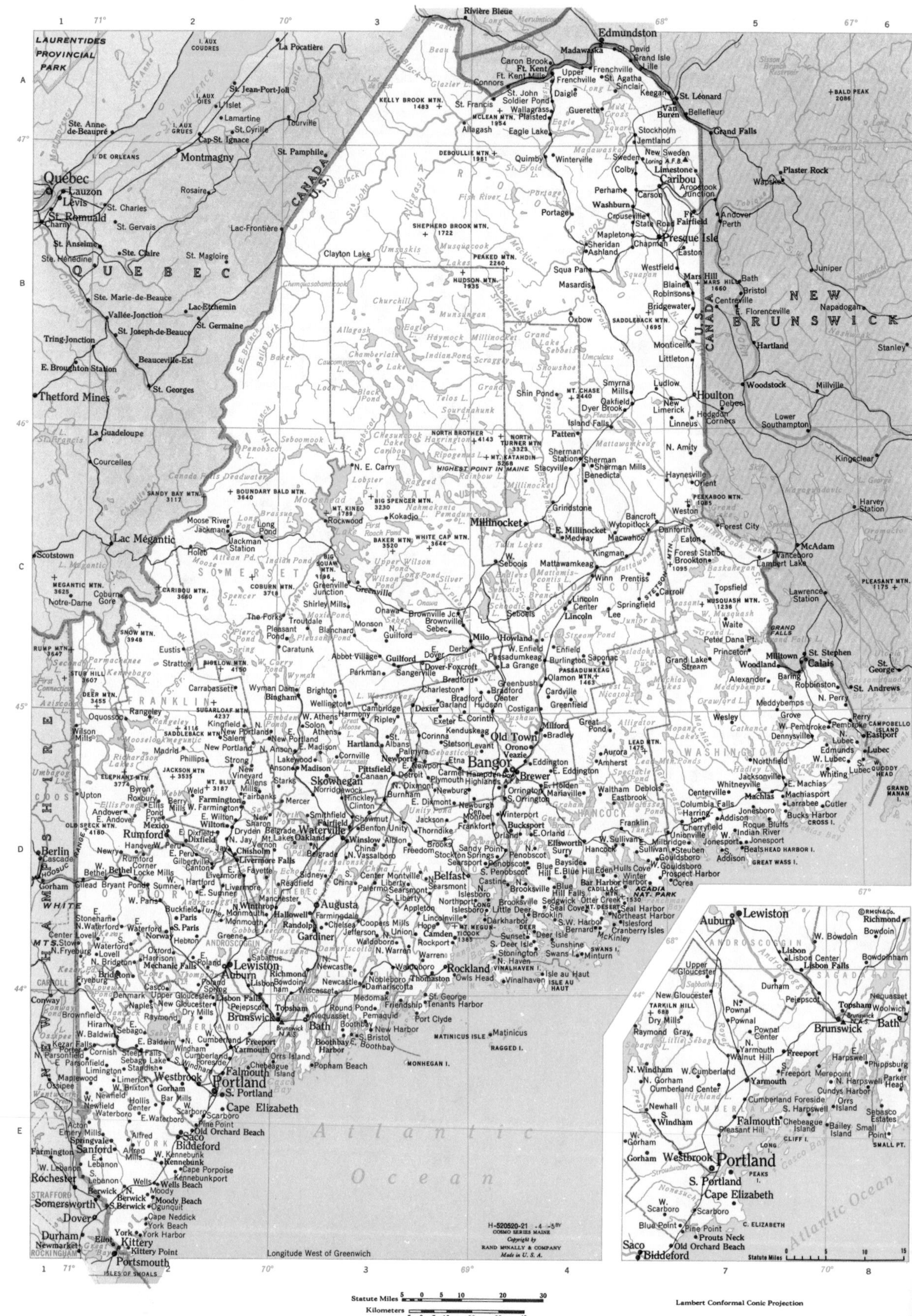
LAURENTIDES PROVINCIAL PARK
La Pocatière
St. Jean-Port-Joli
L'Islet
Ste. Anne-de-Beaupré
Montmagny
Cap-St. Ignace
St. Pamphile
I. DE ORLEANS
Québec
Lauzon
Levis
St. Charles
St. Romuald
St. Gervais
Lac-Frontière
St. Anselme
Ste. Claire
St. Magloire
QUEBEC
Ste. Marie-de-Beauce
Lac-Etchemin
Vallée-Jonction
St. Germaine
St. Joseph-de-Beauce
Tring-Jonction
Beauceville-Est
E. Broughton Station
St. Georges
Thetford Mines
La Guadeloupe
Courcelles
Lac Mégantic
Scotstown
Notre-Dame
CANADA
U.S.
Rivière Bleue
Edmundston
Madawaska
St. David
Grand Isle
Lille
Caron Brook
Ft. Kent
Ft. Kent Mills
Upper Frenchville
Frenchville
St. Agatha
Sinclair
Connors
St. Francis
St. John
Soldier Pond
Wallagrass
Plaisted
Allagash
Eagle Lake
Daigle
Guerette
Keegan
Van Buren
St. Léonard
Bellefleur
Grand Falls
Stockholm
Jemtland
New Sweden
Loring A.F.B.
Limestone
Caribou
Colby
Perham
Washburn
Carson
Aroostook Junction
Crouseville
State Road
Fort Fairfield
Andover
Perth
Mapleton
Presque Isle
Sheridan
Ashland
Chapman
Easton
Quimby
Winterville
Portage
Clayton Lake
Plaster Rock
Juniper
Bath
Bristol
Florenceville
Centreville
Napadogan
NEW BRUNSWICK
Hartland
Stanley
Squa Pan
Masardis
Westfield
Mars Hill
Blaine
Robinsons
Bridgewater
Oxbow
Monticello
Littleton
Houlton
Woodstock
Millville
Smyrna Mills
Oakfield
Dyer Brook
Island Falls
Patten
Ludlow
New Limerick
Linneus
Hodgdon
Lower Southampton
Kingsclear
Shin Pond
Sherman Station
Sherman Mills
Benedicta
Stacyville
N. Amity
Haynesville
Orient
Weston
Bancroft
Wytopitlock
Danforth
Forest City
Harvey Station
Millinocket
E. Millinocket
Medway
Grindstone
Mattawamkeag
Kingman
Eaton
McAdam
Vanceboro
Lambert Lake
Forest Station
Brookton
Moose River
Jackman
Jackman Station
Long Pond
Rockwood
Kokadjo
Greenville
Greenville Junction
Shirley Mills
The Forks
Caratunk
Monson
Guilford
Dover-Foxcroft
Milo
Brownville Jc.
Brownville
Howland
Eustis
Stratton
Bingham
Wyman Dam
Carrabassett
Rangeley
Oquossoc
Kingfield
New Portland
Phillips
Madrid
Strong
Solon
Athens
Harmony
Cambridge
Ripley
Dexter
Garland
Charleston
Corinth
Kenduskeag
Old Town
Orono
Veazie
Bangor
Brewer
Hampden
Lincoln
Lincoln Center
Enfield
Passadumkeag
La Grange
Greenbush
Topsfield
Waite
Carroll
Springfield
Lee
Prentiss
Princeton
Calais
St. Stephen
St. Andrews
Woodland
Baileyville
Milltown
Robbinston
Perry
Eastport
Pembroke
Lubec
Campobello Island
Dennysville
Machias
Machiasport
Jonesport
Jonesboro
Cherryfield
Milbridge
Steuben
Gouldsboro
Columbia Falls
Harrington
Addison
Ellsworth
Bar Harbor
Blue Hill
Surry
Bucksport
Belfast
Searsport
Stockton Springs
Castine
Rockland
Camden
Thomaston
Waldoboro
Wiscasset
Damariscotta
Boothbay Harbor
Bath
Brunswick
Topsham
Freeport
Yarmouth
Falmouth
Portland
S. Portland
Westbrook
Gorham
Cape Elizabeth
Old Orchard Beach
Saco
Biddeford
Kennebunk
Kennebunkport
Wells
Sanford
Springvale
Ogunquit
York
Kittery
Portsmouth
Dover
Somersworth
Rochester
Durham
Newmarket
Berlin
Gorham
Rumford
Dixfield
Mexico
Farmington
Wilton
Jay
Livermore Falls
Lewiston
Auburn
Augusta
Hallowell
Gardiner
Waterville
Winslow
Oakland
Skowhegan
Norridgewock
Madison
Pittsfield
Newport
Unity
Norway
S. Paris
Mechanic Falls
Bridgton
Fryeburg
Conway
Atlantic Ocean
MATINICUS ISLE
MONHEGAN I.
RAGGED I.
ISLES OF SHOALS
Longitude West of Greenwich
H-520520-21 -4 -5
COSMO SERIES MAINE
Copyright by RAND McNALLY & COMPANY
Made in U. S. A.
Statute Miles 5 0 5 10 20 30
Kilometers 5 0 5 10 20 30 40
Lambert Conformal Conic Projection

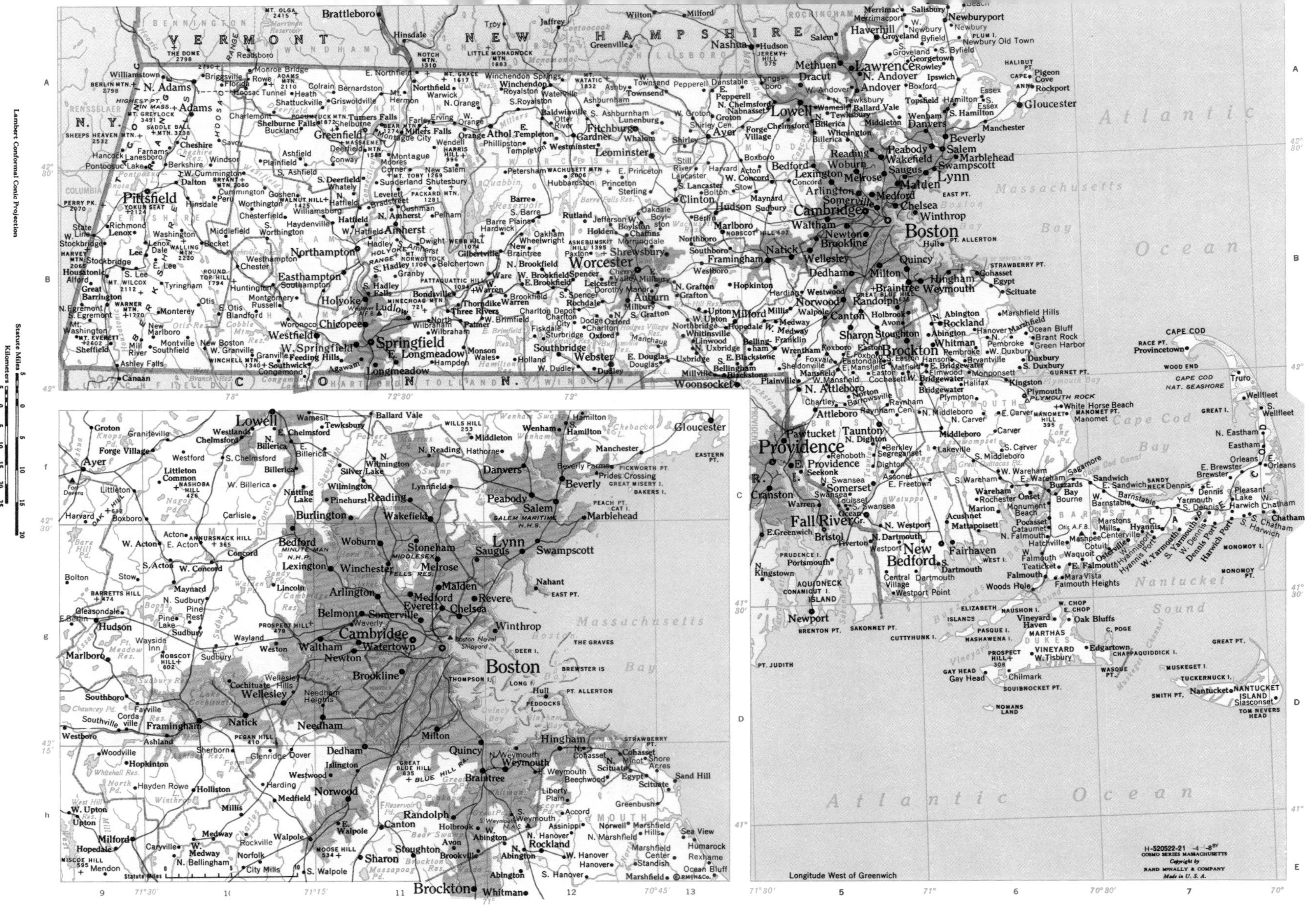
Lambert Conformal Conic Projection
Statute Miles 5 0 5 10 15 20
Kilometers 5 0 5 10 15 20 25
Longitude West of Greenwich
H-520522-21 -4- -8-BY
COSMO SERIES MASSACHUSETTS
Copyright by RAND McNALLY & COMPANY
Made in U. S. A.
VERMONT
NEW HAMPSHIRE
N. Y.
CONN.
R. I.
Atlantic Ocean
Massachusetts Bay
Cape Cod Bay
Nantucket Sound
CAPE COD
CAPE COD NAT. SEASHORE
Boston
Worcester
Springfield
Providence
Cambridge
Lowell
Lawrence
Brockton
New Bedford
Fall River
Pittsfield
Gloucester
Provincetown
Nantucket
Chatham

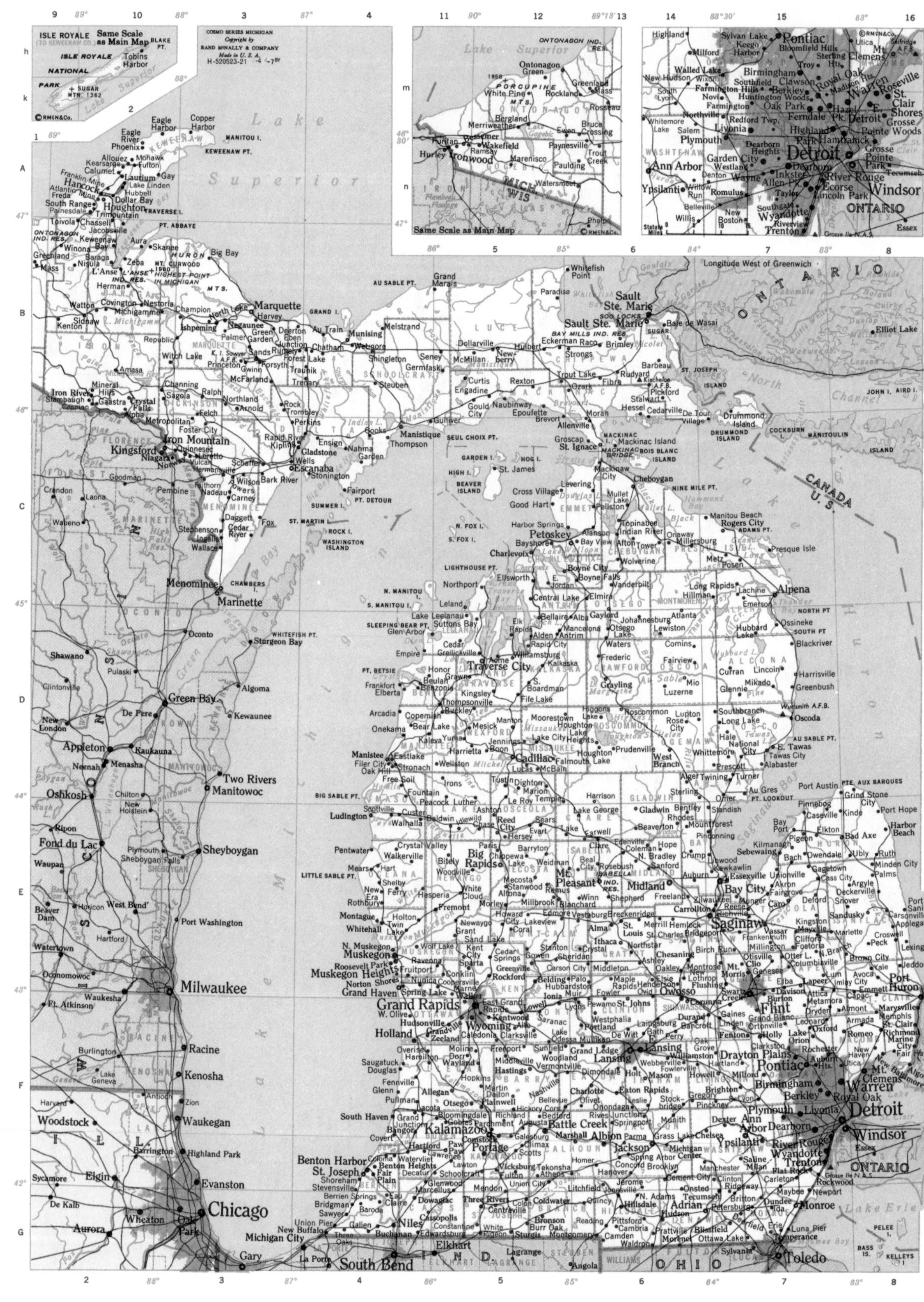

ISLE ROYALE (TO KEWEENAW CO.)
Same Scale as Main Map
ISLE ROYALE NATIONAL PARK
SUGAR MTN. 1362
COSMO SERIES MICHIGAN
Copyright by RAND McNALLY & COMPANY
Made in U. S. A.
H-520523-21
Lake Superior
ONTONAGON IND. RES.
PORCUPINE MTS.
Same Scale as Main Map
Longitude West of Greenwich
ONTARIO
CANADA
U.S.
Lake Huron
Lake Michigan
Lake Erie
Green Bay
Saginaw Bay
WISCONSIN
ILLINOIS
INDIANA
OHIO
Detroit
Windsor
Lansing
Grand Rapids
Flint
Saginaw
Kalamazoo
Marquette
Sault Ste. Marie
Traverse City
Milwaukee
Chicago
Toledo
South Bend
Statute Miles
Kilometers
Lambert Conformal Conic Projection

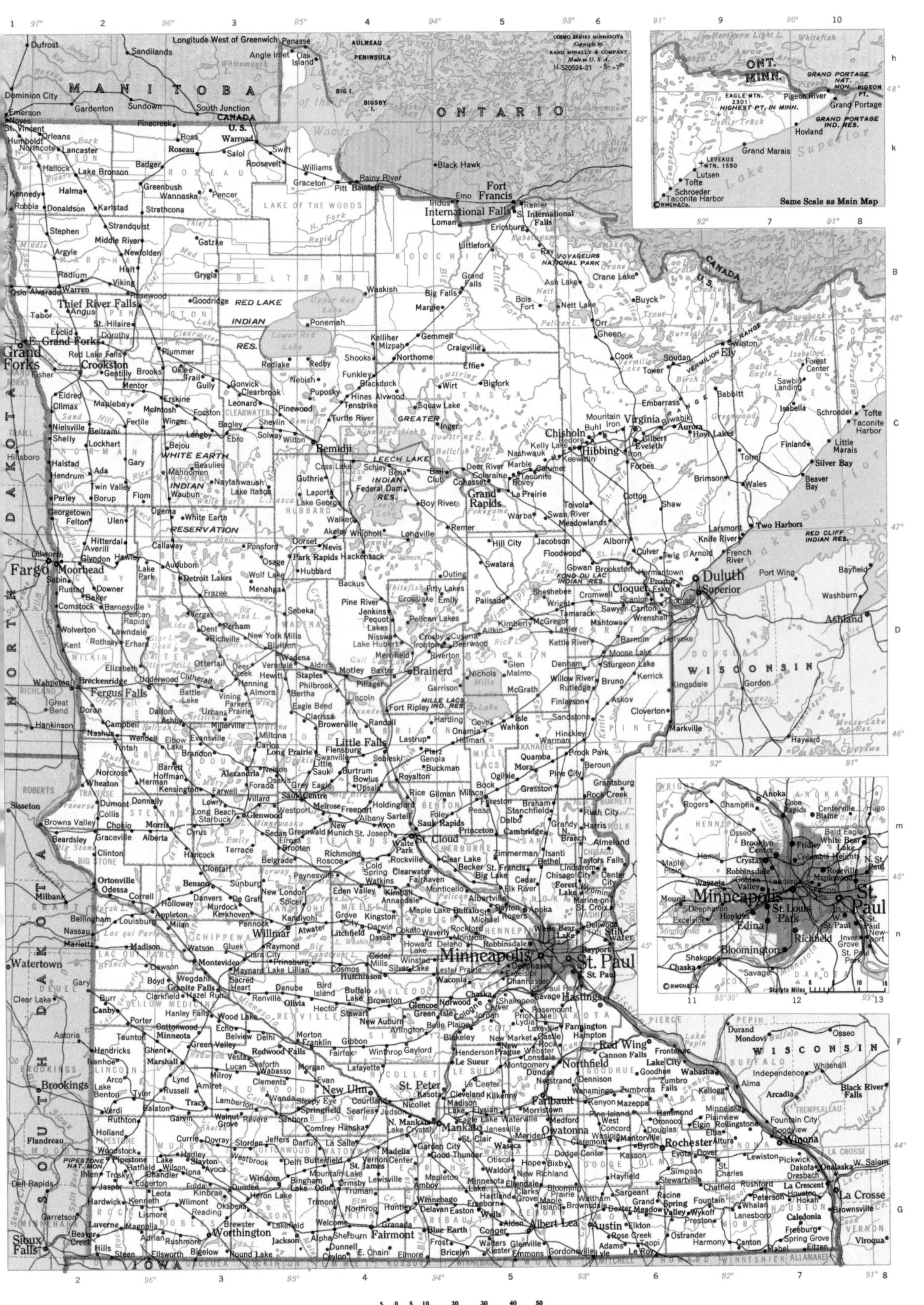

Longitude West of Greenwich
MANITOBA
ONTARIO
CANADA
U.S.
LAKE OF THE WOODS
RED LAKE INDIAN RES.
WHITE EARTH INDIAN RESERVATION
LEECH LAKE INDIAN RES.
VOYAGEURS NATIONAL PARK
NORTH DAKOTA
SOUTH DAKOTA
IOWA
WISCONSIN
Lake Superior
Minneapolis
St. Paul
Duluth
Superior
Rochester
St. Cloud
Fargo
Moorhead
Grand Forks
Sioux Falls
La Crosse
Mankato
Bemidji
Brainerd
Hibbing
Virginia
International Falls
Fort Francis
Winona
Austin
Albert Lea
EAGLE MTN. 2301 HIGHEST PT. IN MINN.
GRAND PORTAGE NAT. MON.
GRAND PORTAGE IND. RES.
Same Scale as Main Map
PIPESTONE NAT. MON.
Lambert Conformal Conic Projection
Statute Miles
Kilometers

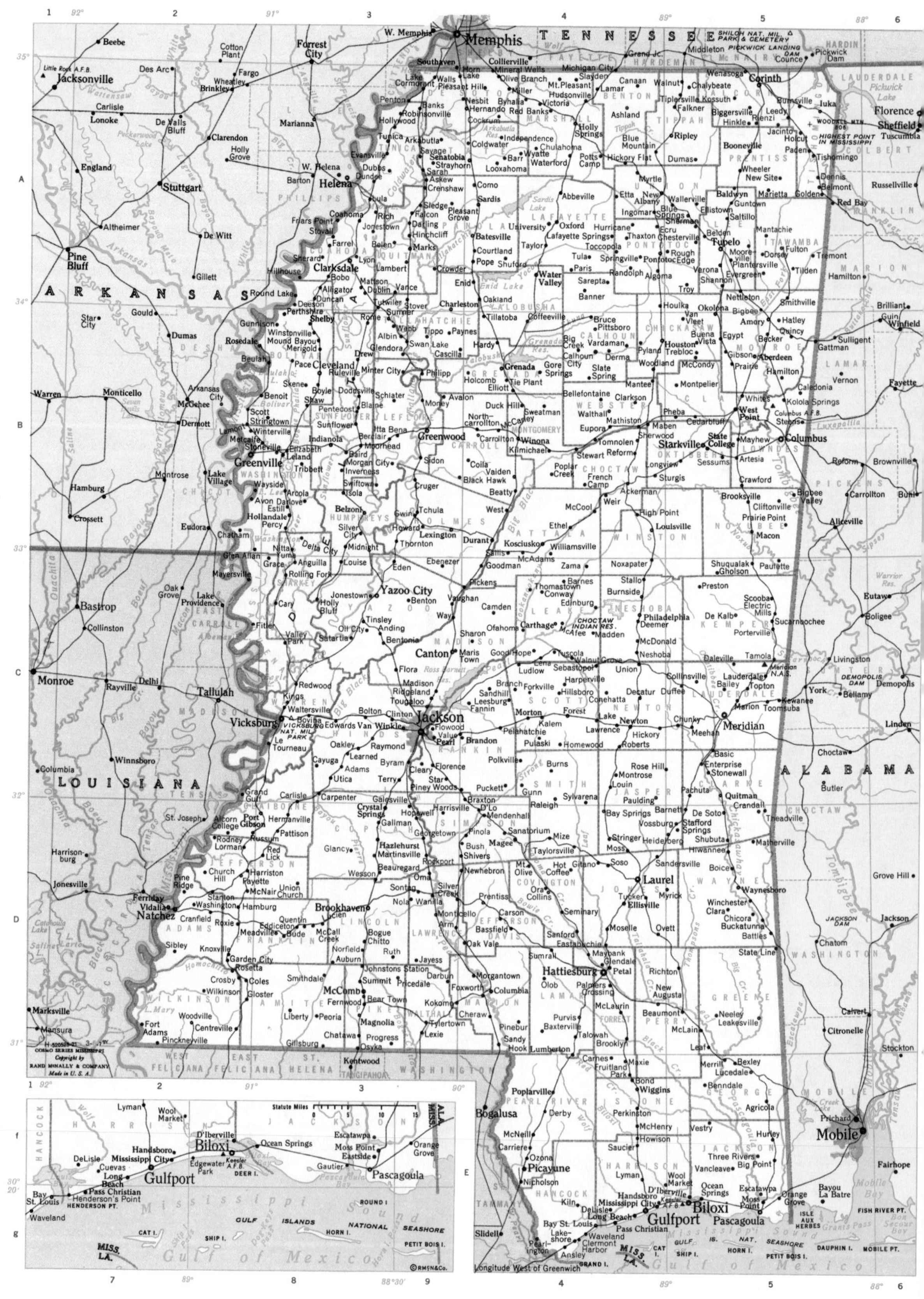

Statute Miles 5 0 5 10 20 30 40

Kilometers 5 0 5 15 25 35 45 55

Lambert Conformal Conic Projection

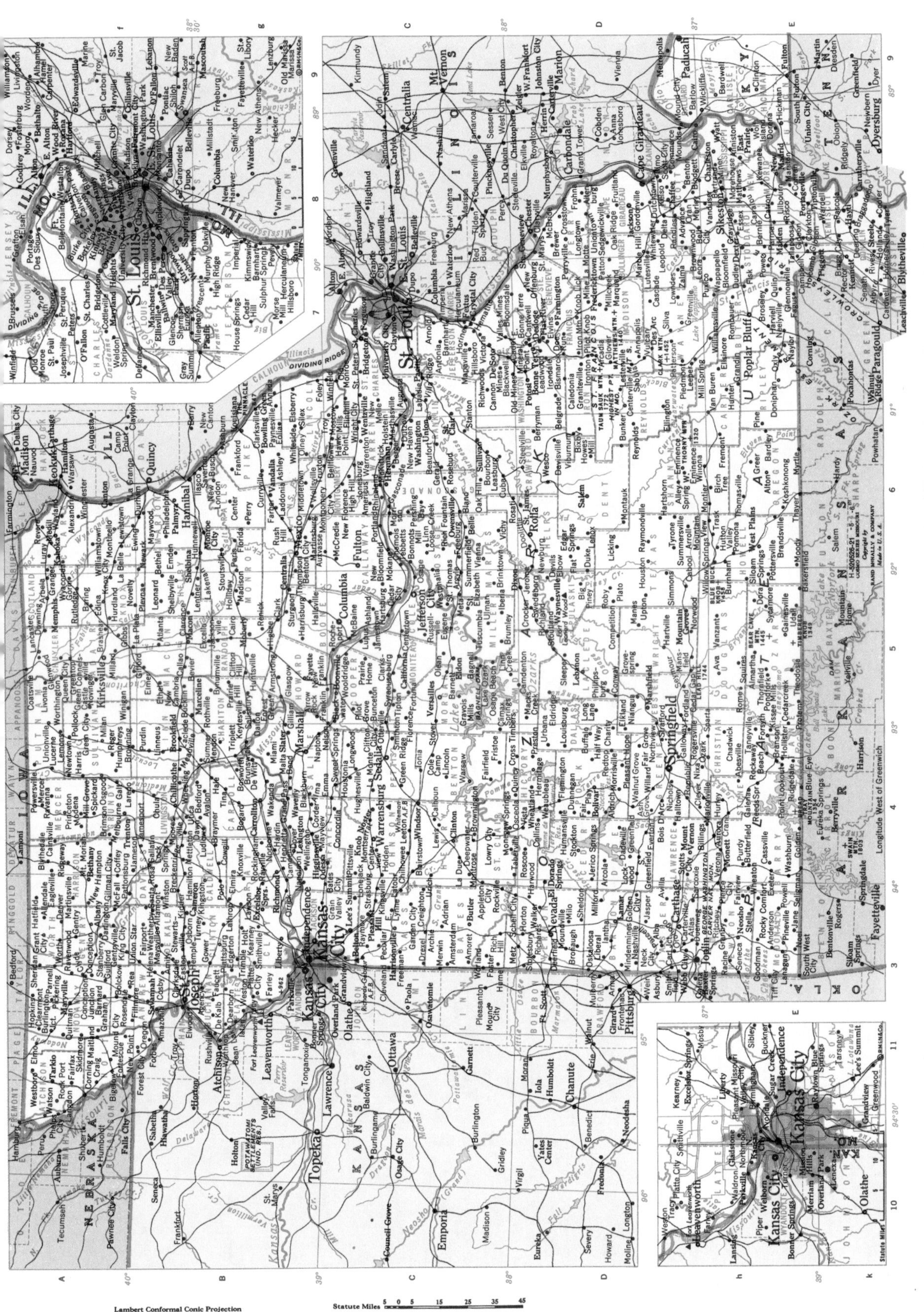
IOWA
ILLINOIS
KENTUCKY
TENNESSEE
ARKANSAS
OKLAHOMA
KANSAS
NEBRASKA
St. Louis
Kansas City
Springfield
Jefferson City
St. Joseph
Independence
Columbia
Longitude West of Greenwich
Copyright by RAND McNALLY & COMPANY
Made in U. S. A.
Lambert Conformal Conic Projection
Statute Miles 5 0 5 15 25 35 45
Kilometers 5 0 5 15 25 35 45 55 65

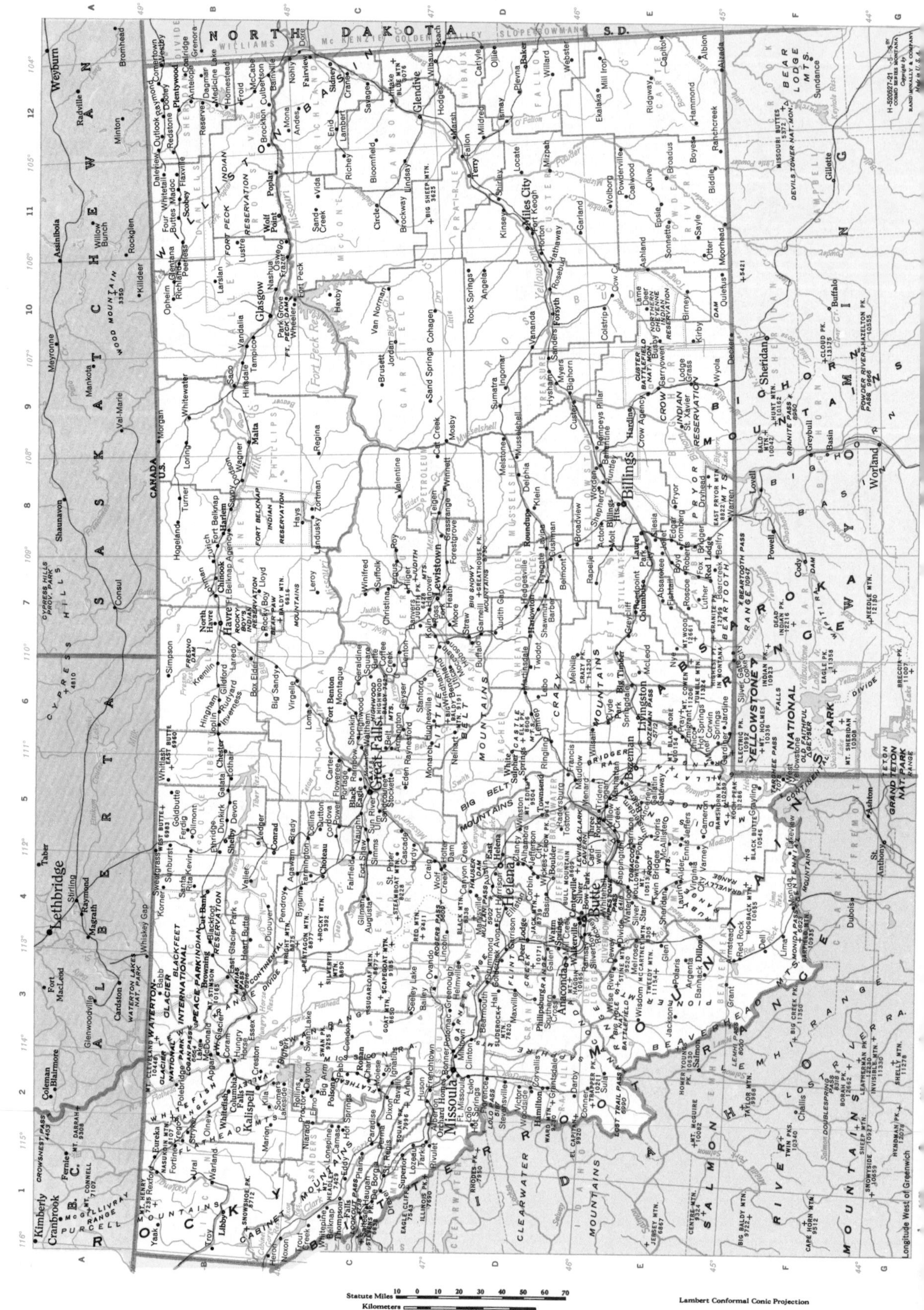

Statute Miles 10 0 10 20 30 40 50 60 70

Kilometers 10 0 10 30 50 70 90

Lambert Conformal Conic Projection

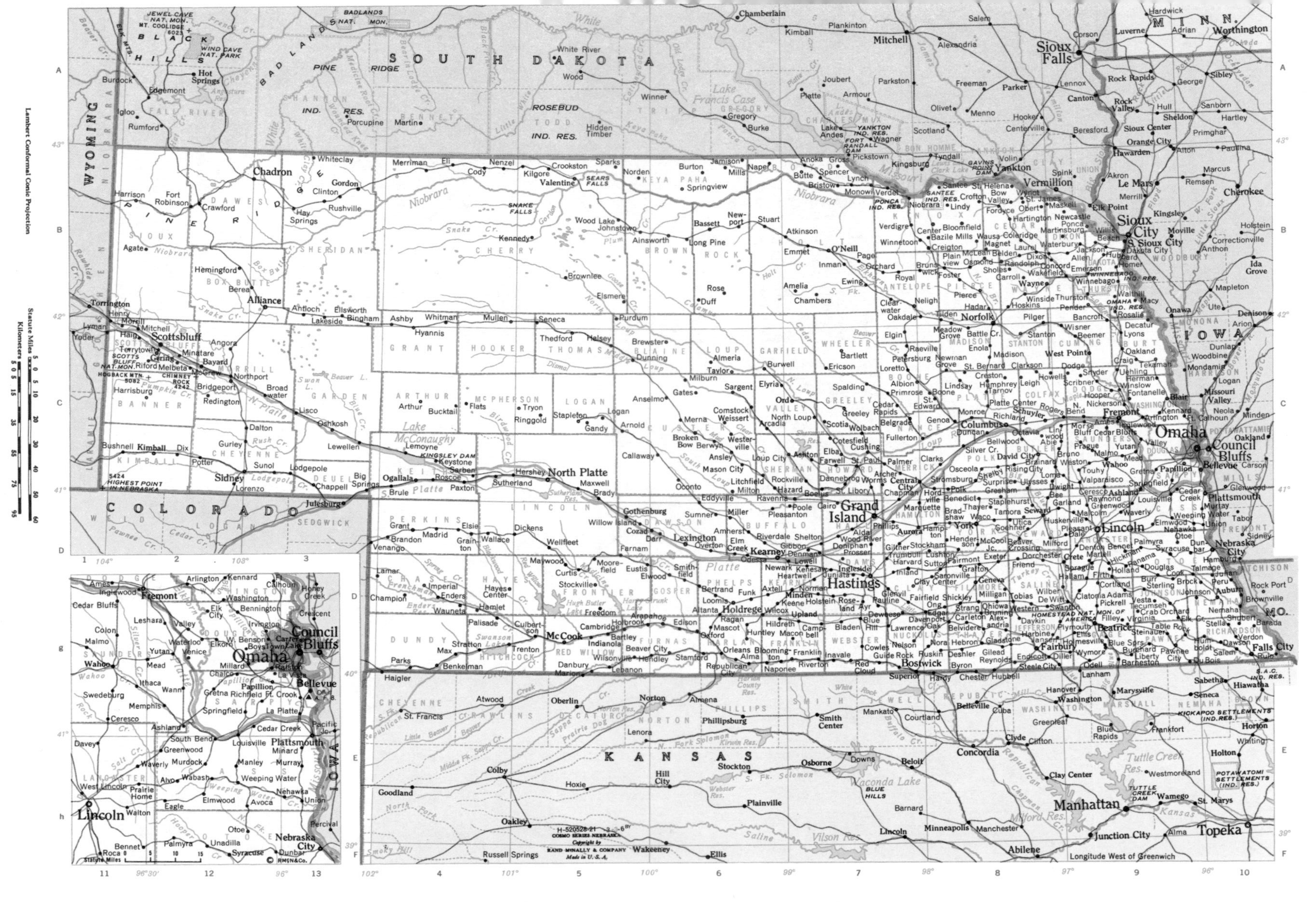
Lambert Conformal Conic Projection
Statute Miles 5 0 5 10 20 30 40 50 60
Kilometers 5 0 5 15 35 55 75 95
SOUTH DAKOTA
IOWA
KANSAS
COLORADO
WYOMING
MINN.
MO.
Longitude West of Greenwich
H-520528-21
COSMO SERIES NEBRASKA
Copyright by RAND McNALLY & COMPANY
Made in U.S.A.

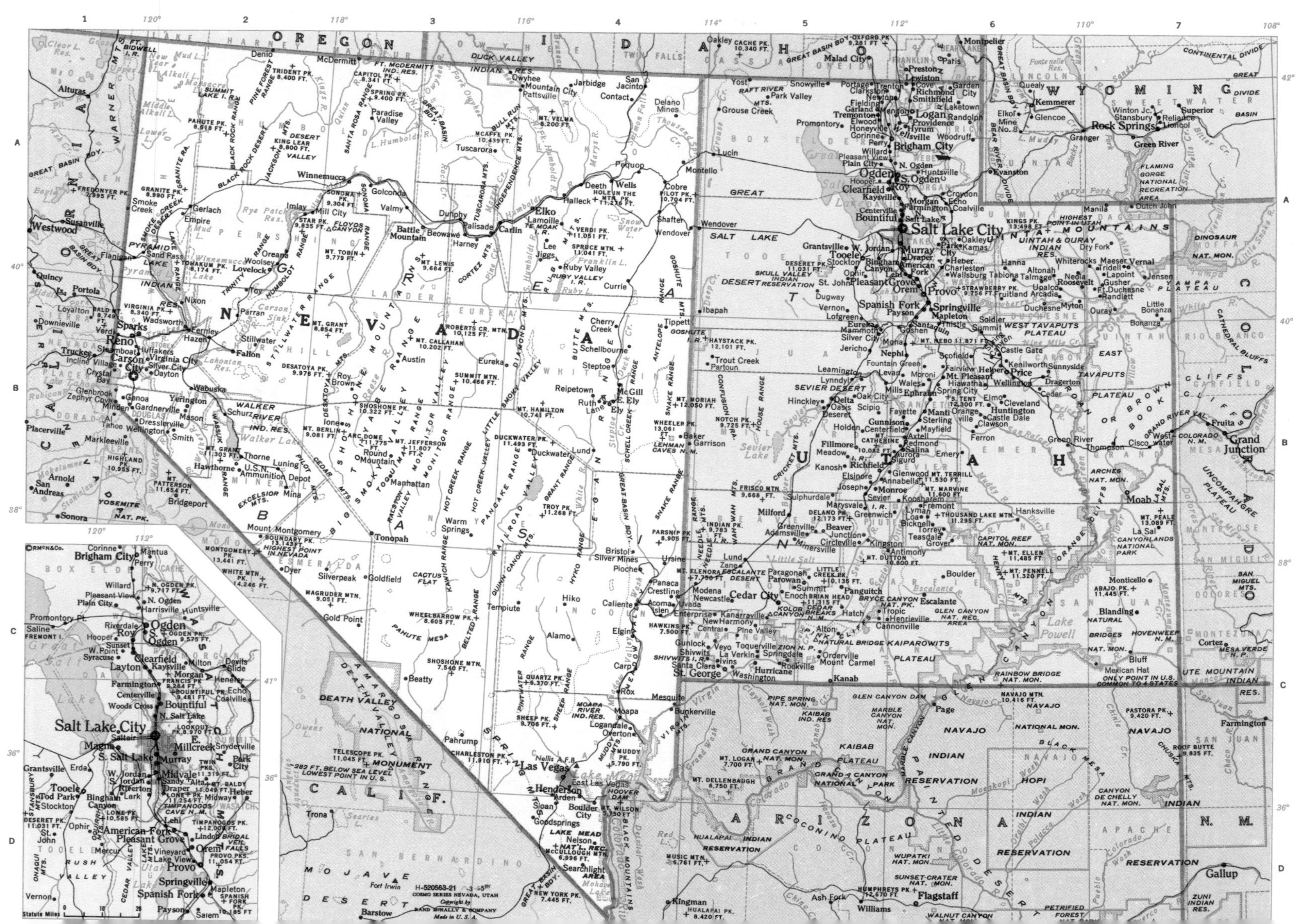

Statute Miles 5 0 5 10 20 30 40 50 60 70 80
Kilometers 5 0 10 20 40 60 80 100 120

Lambert Conformal Conic Projection

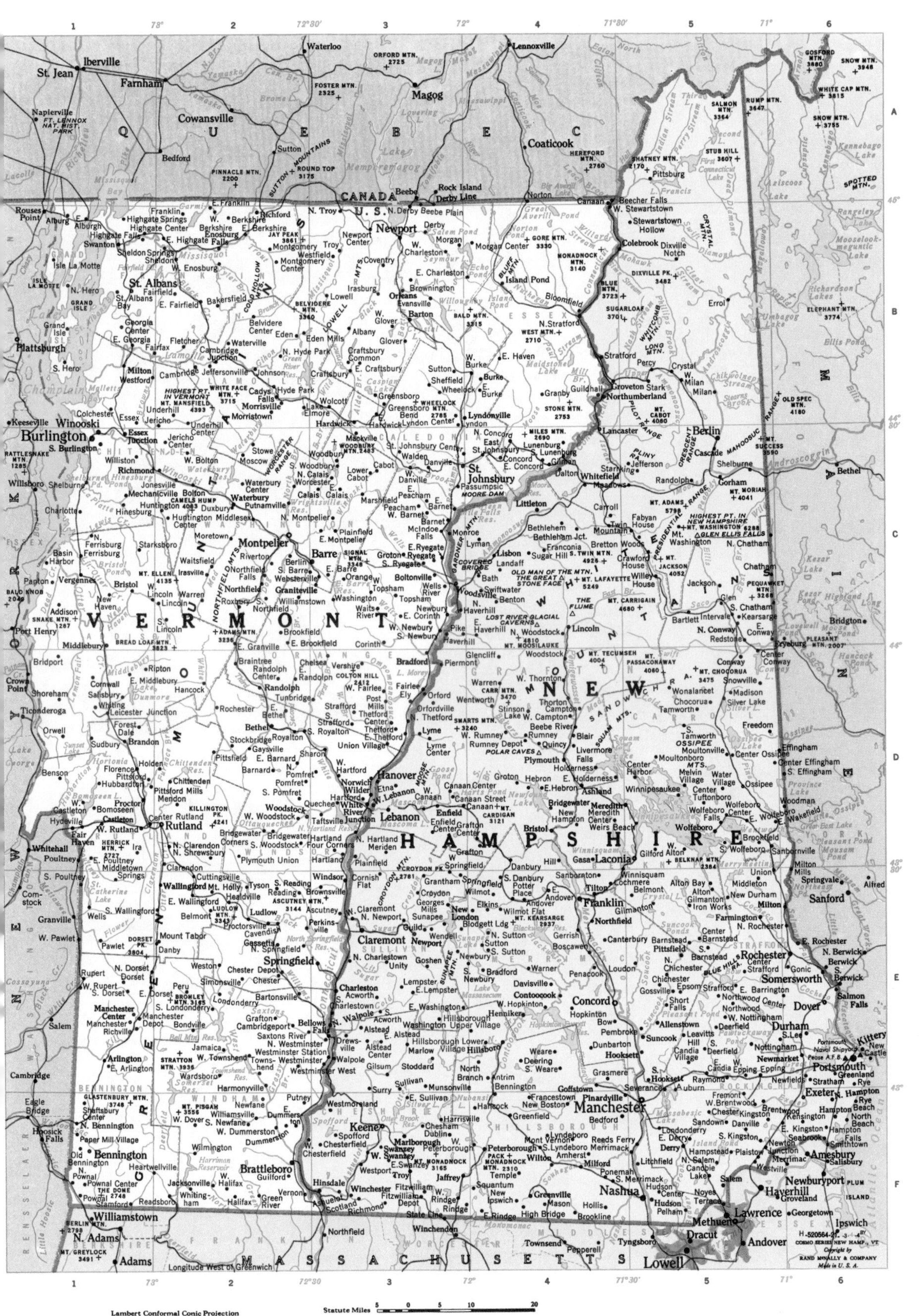
QUEBEC
CANADA
U.S.
VERMONT
NEW HAMPSHIRE
MAINE
NEW YORK
MASSACHUSETTS
Burlington
Montpelier
Barre
Rutland
St. Albans
Newport
St. Johnsbury
Bennington
Brattleboro
Springfield
White River Junction
Concord
Manchester
Nashua
Portsmouth
Keene
Laconia
Dover
Rochester
Berlin
Claremont
Lebanon
Hanover
Lawrence
Lowell
Haverhill
Sanford
Magog
Coaticook
Iberville
St. Jean
Farnham
Cowansville
Plattsburgh
Williamstown
Lambert Conformal Conic Projection
Statute Miles
Kilometers
Longitude West of Greenwich
RAND McNALLY & COMPANY
Made in U. S. A.

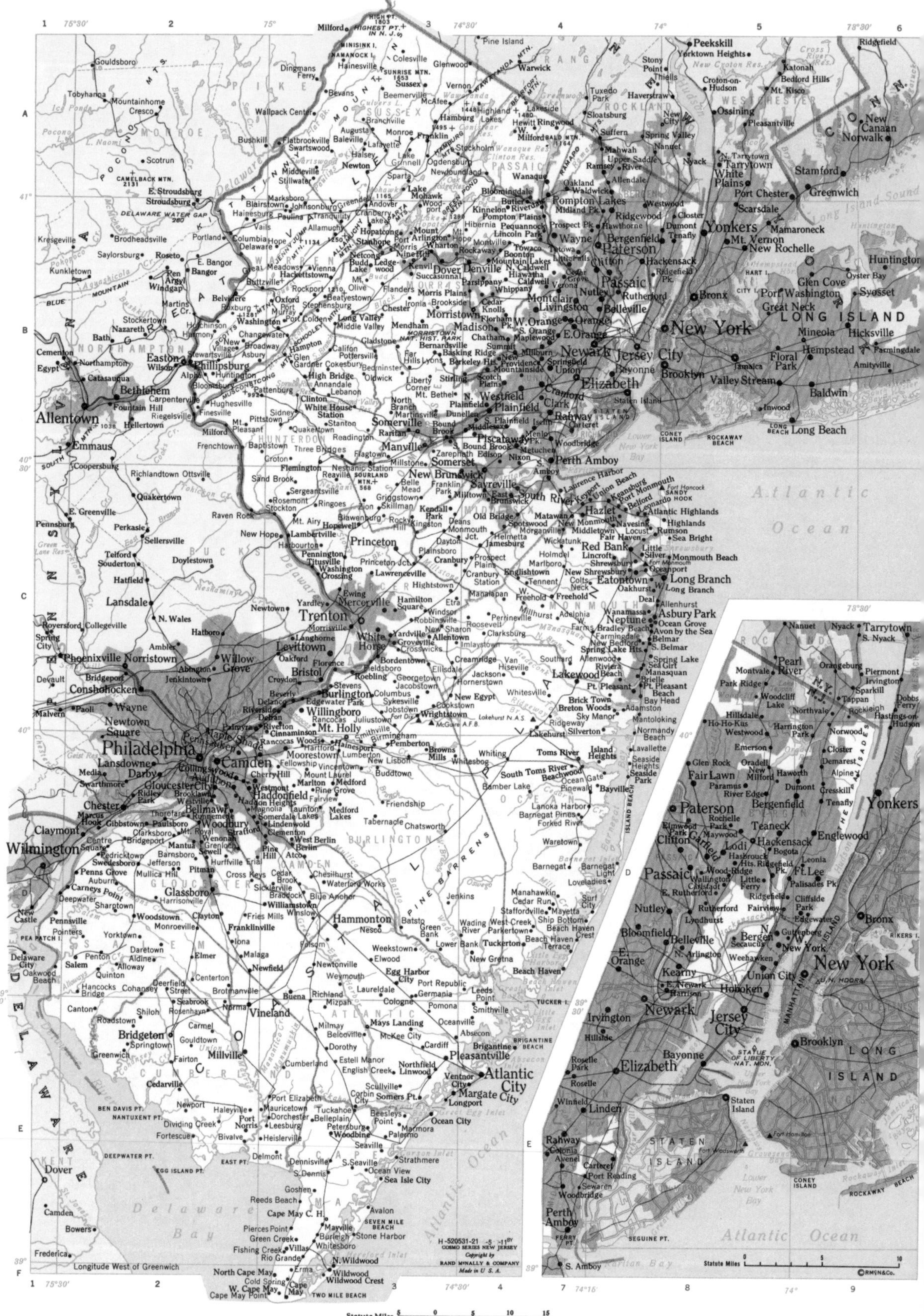
Milford
HIGHEST PT. IN N. J.
Pine Island
Peekskill
Yorktown Heights
Ridgefield
SUSSEX
PIKE
MONROE
ROCKLAND
WESTCHESTER
PASSAIC
WARREN
MORRIS
BERGEN
HUNTERDON
SOMERSET
MIDDLESEX
MONMOUTH
MERCER
BURLINGTON
OCEAN
CAMDEN
GLOUCESTER
SALEM
CUMBERLAND
ATLANTIC
CAPE MAY
BUCKS
NORTHAMPTON
DELAWARE
KENT
LONG ISLAND
KITTATINNY
GREAT VALLEY
PINE BARRENS
Stroudsburg
E. Stroudsburg
DELAWARE WATER GAP
Newton
Sparta
Dover
Morristown
Paterson
Passaic
Hackensack
Newark
Jersey City
Elizabeth
Bayonne
New York
Bronx
Brooklyn
Yonkers
Stamford
Greenwich
Norwalk
White Plains
New Rochelle
Mt. Vernon
Hempstead
Long Beach
Staten Island
Allentown
Bethlehem
Easton
Phillipsburg
Emmaus
Lansdale
Norristown
Conshohocken
Phoenixville
Philadelphia
Camden
Chester
Wilmington
Trenton
Princeton
New Brunswick
Somerville
Plainfield
Perth Amboy
Sayreville
South River
Red Bank
Long Branch
Asbury Park
Neptune
Lakewood
Toms River
Freehold
Levittown
Bristol
Burlington
Willingboro
Mt. Holly
Cherry Hill
Haddonfield
Woodbury
Glassboro
Hammonton
Vineland
Millville
Bridgeton
Atlantic City
Pleasantville
Ventnor City
Margate City
Ocean City
Sea Isle City
Cape May C. H.
Wildwood
N. Wildwood
Cape May
Dover
Atlantic Ocean
Delaware Bay
Long Island Sound
Lower New York Bay
Longitude West of Greenwich
H-520531-21 COSMO SERIES NEW JERSEY
Copyright by RAND McNALLY & COMPANY
Made in U. S. A.
Statute Miles
Kilometers
Lambert Conformal Conic Projection

Lambert Conformal Conic Projection

Statute Miles 5 0 5 10 20 30 40

Kilometers 5 0 5 15 25 35 45 55

Statute Miles 5 0 5 10 20 30 40

Kilometers 5 0 5 15 25 35 45 55

Lambert Conformal Conic Projection

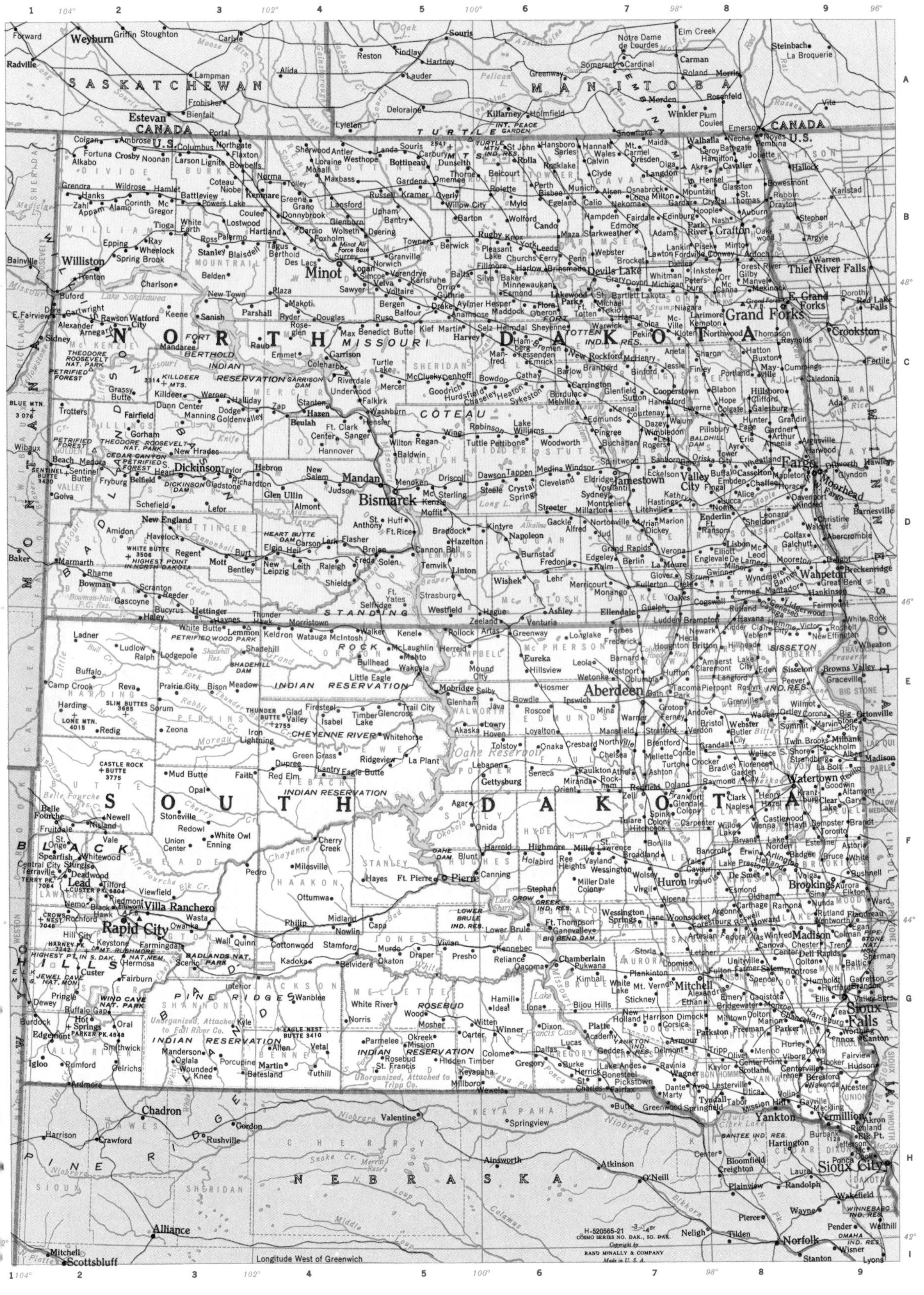

Lambert Conformal Conic Projection

Statute Miles 5 0 5 10 20 30 40 50 60

Kilometers 5 0 5 15 25 35 45 55 65 75

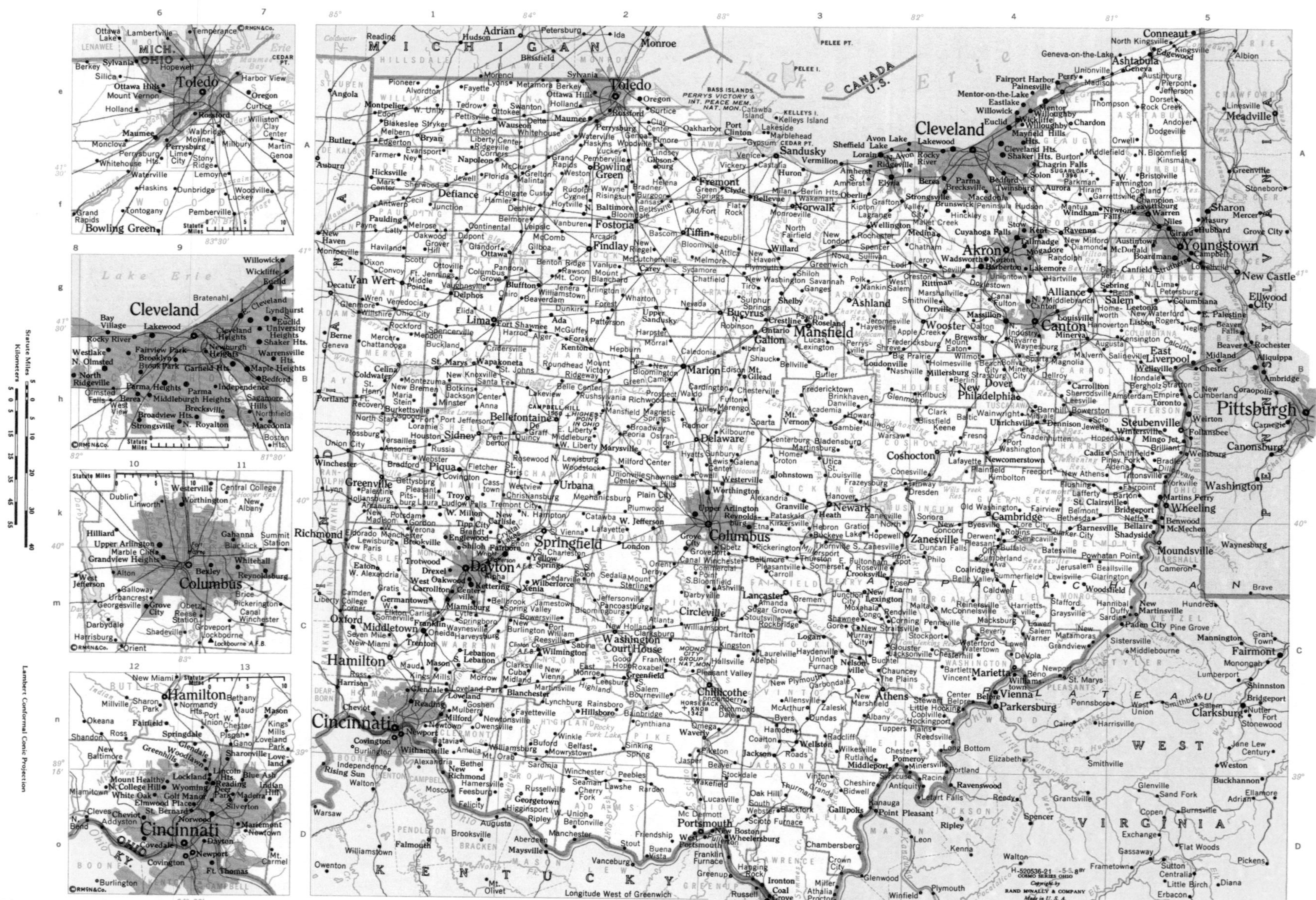

Statute Miles 5 0 5 10 20 30 40

Kilometers 5 0 5 15 25 35 45 55

Lambert Conformal Conic Projection

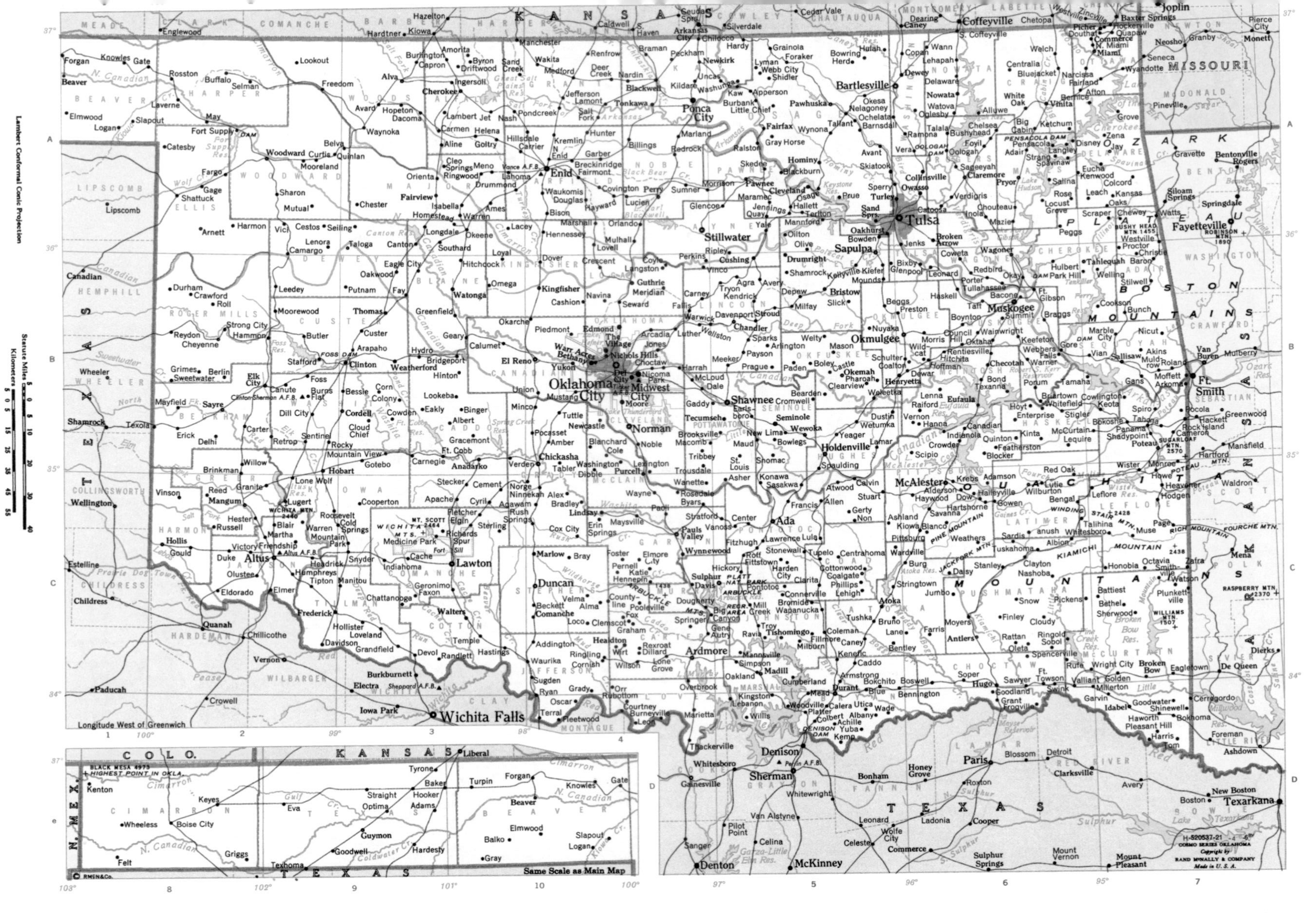

Oklahoma City
Tulsa
Wichita Falls
Lawton
Muskogee
Enid
Norman
Shawnee
Stillwater
Bartlesville
Ponca City
Ardmore
Ada
Duncan
McAlester
Okmulgee
Altus
Sapulpa
Fort Smith
Texarkana
Denison
Sherman
Paris
McKinney
Denton
Coffeyville
Joplin
Fayetteville
Chickasha
El Reno
Clinton
Guymon
Liberal
MISSOURI
KANSAS
TEXAS
Same Scale as Main Map
Longitude West of Greenwich
Lambert Conformal Conic Projection
Statute Miles
Kilometers

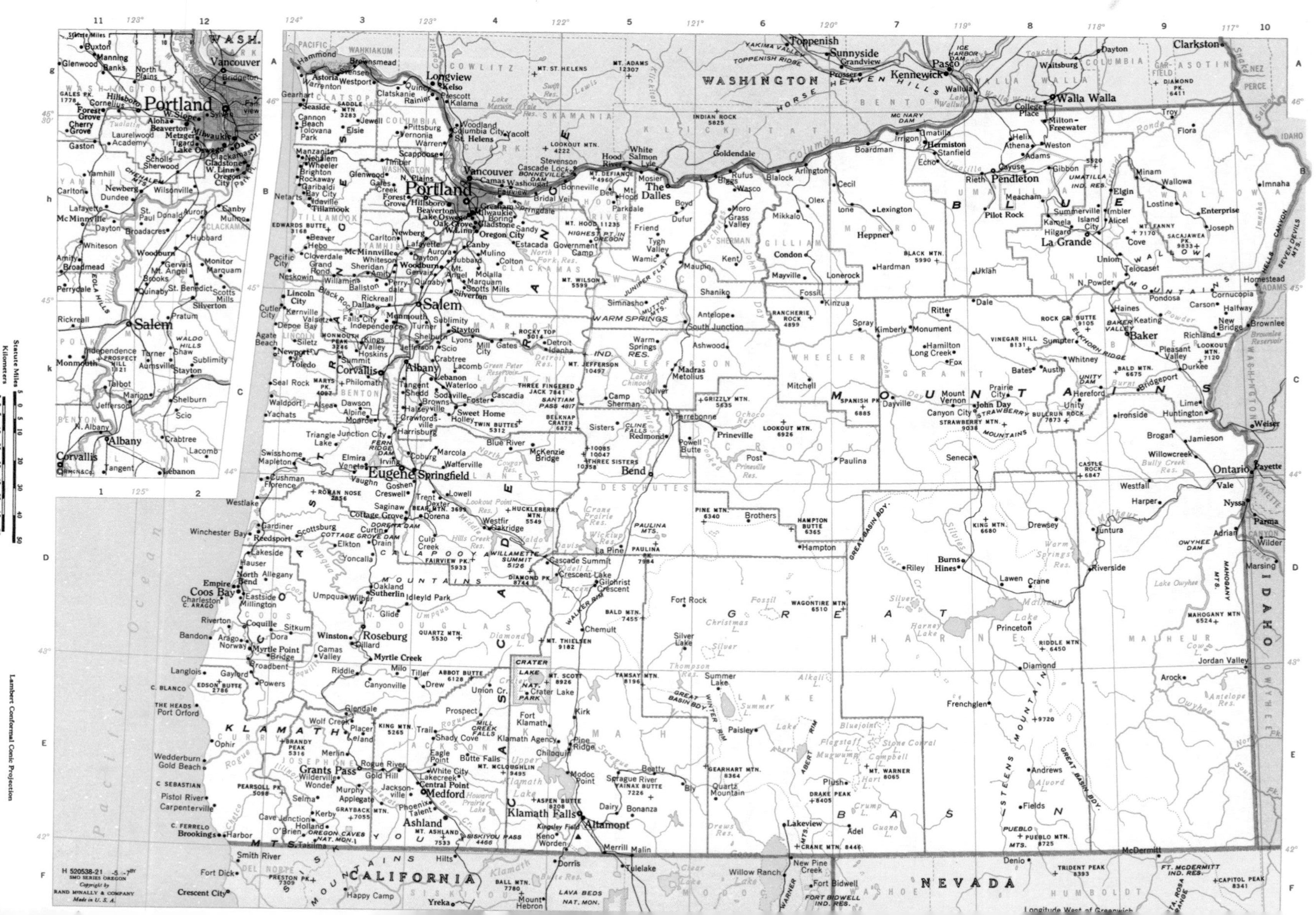

Statute Miles 5 0 5 10 20 30 40 50

Kilometers 5 0 5 15 25 35 45 55 65 75

Lambert Conformal Conic Projection

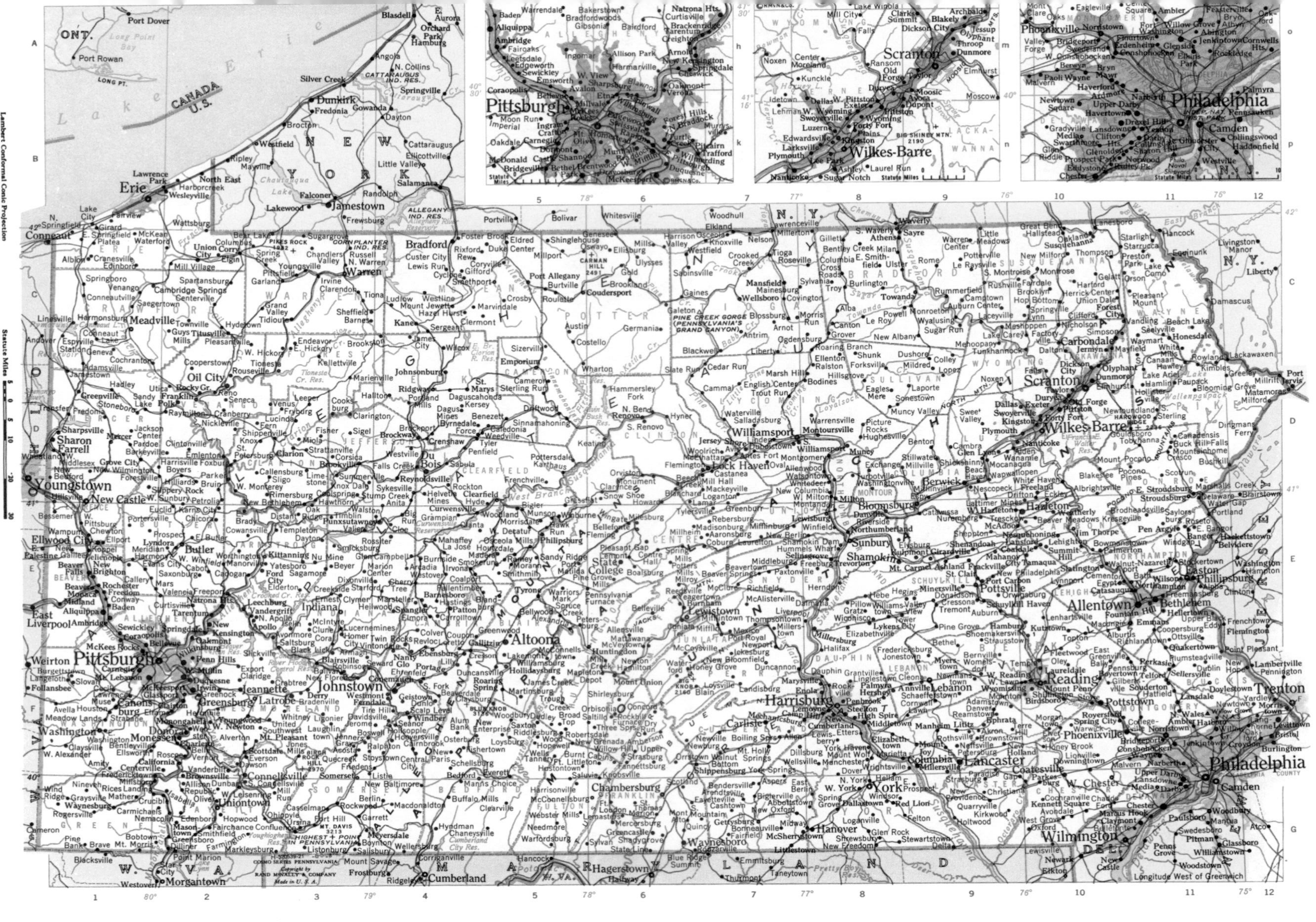
Pittsburgh
Scranton
Wilkes-Barre
Philadelphia
Erie
Harrisburg
Allentown
Lancaster
Altoona
Johnstown
Reading
Lambert Conformal Conic Projection
Statute Miles
Kilometers

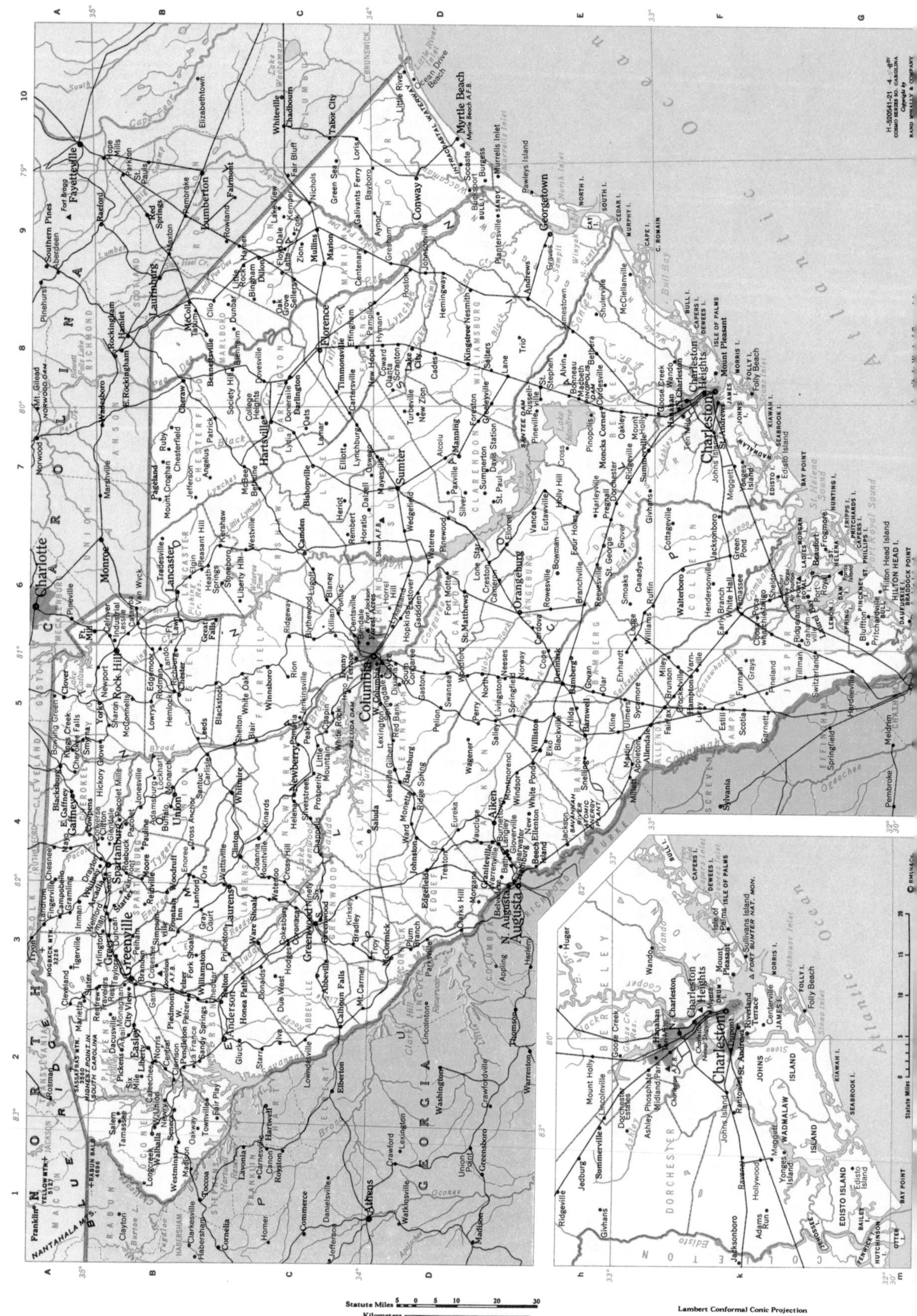

Statute Miles 5 0 5 10 20 30

Kilometers 5 0 5 15 25 35 45

Lambert Conformal Conic Projection

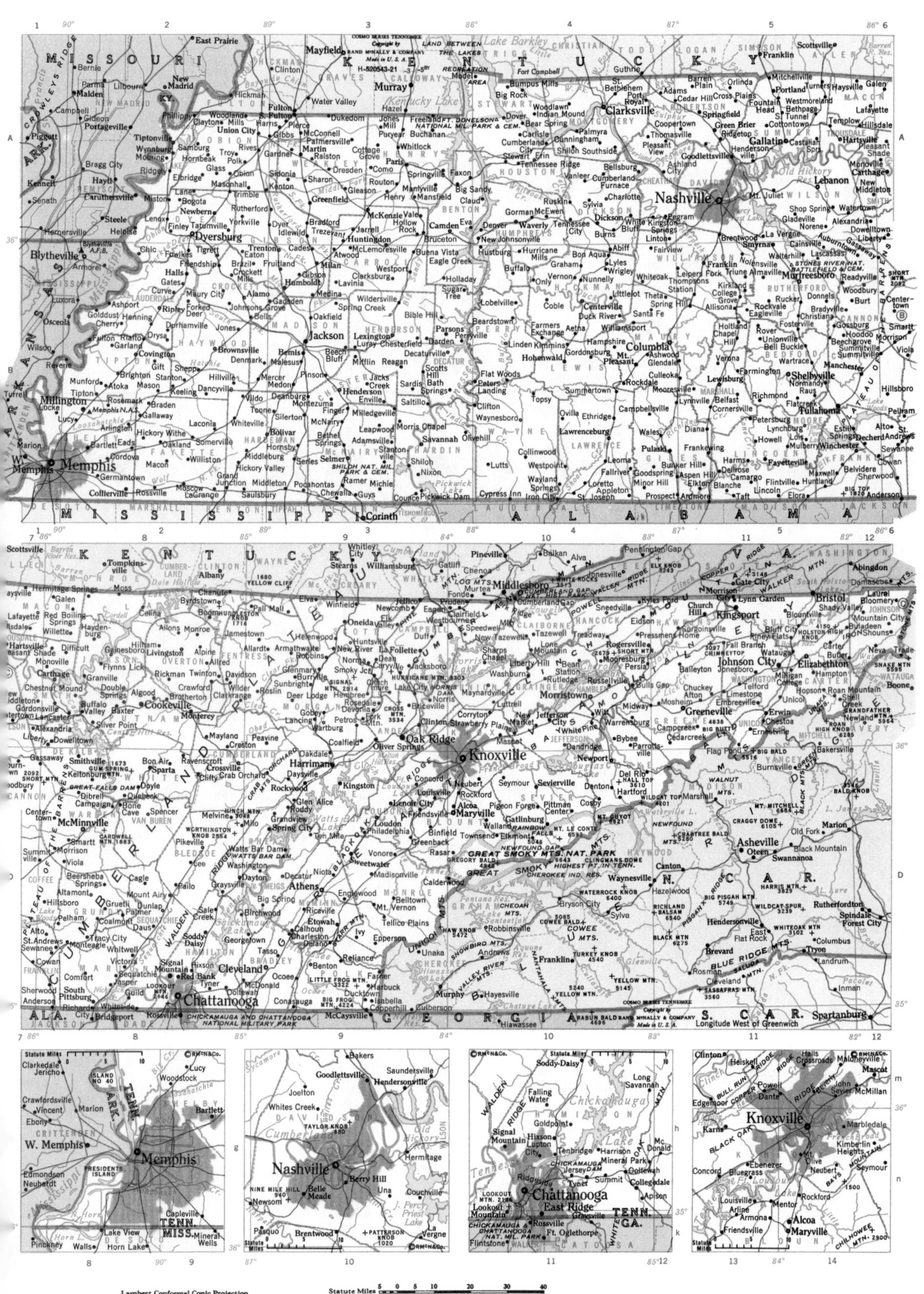

Lambert Conformal Conic Projection

Statute Miles 5 0 5 10 20 30 40

Kilometers 5 0 5 15 25 35 45 55

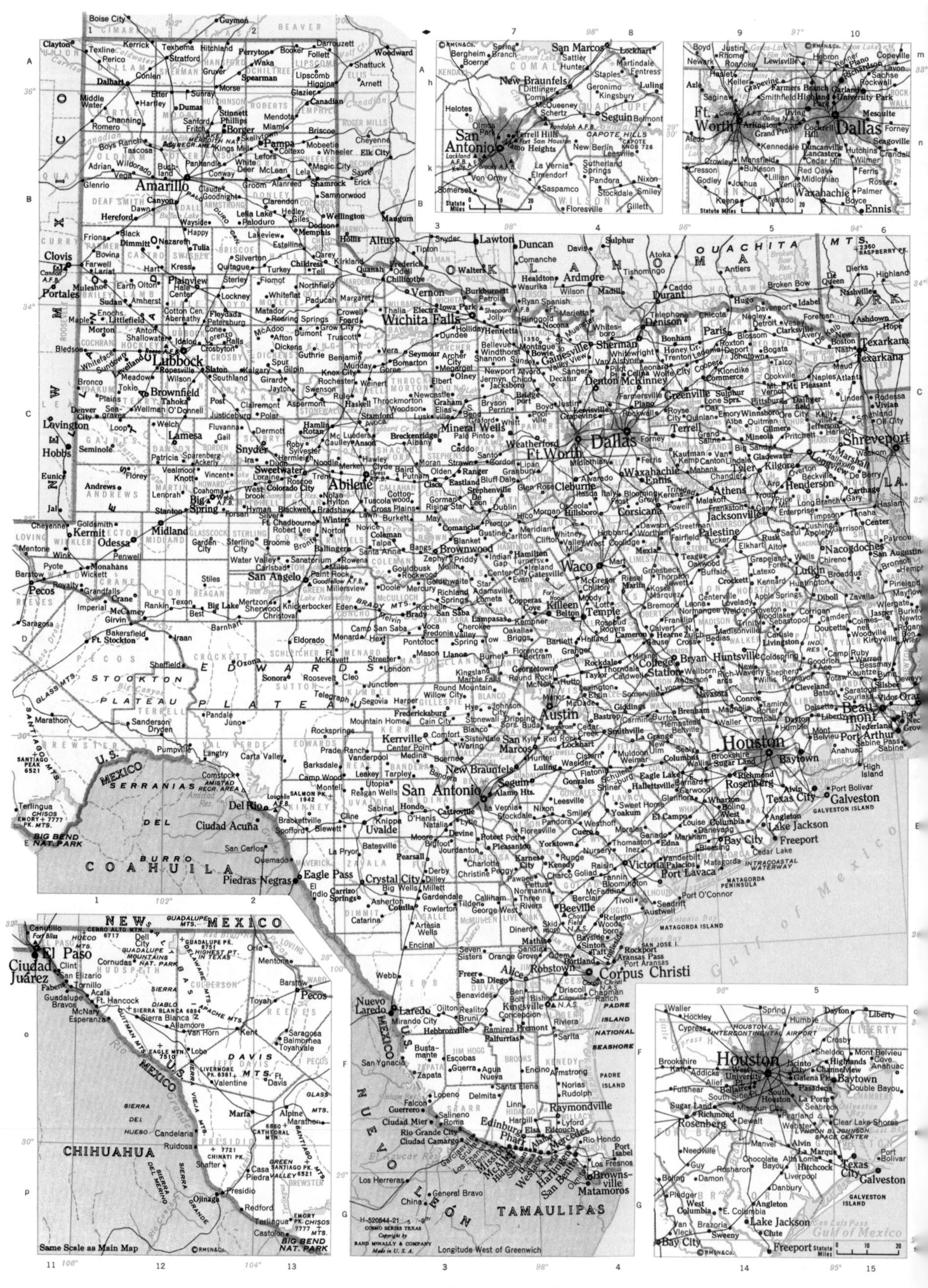
Amarillo
Lubbock
Dallas
Ft. Worth
Wichita Falls
Abilene
Midland
Odessa
San Angelo
Waco
Austin
San Antonio
Houston
Corpus Christi
Laredo
El Paso
Beaumont
Galveston
Texarkana
Shreveport
EDWARDS PLATEAU
STOCKTON PLATEAU
COAHUILA
CHIHUAHUA
TAMAULIPAS
NUEVO LEÓN
Gulf of Mexico
Same Scale as Main Map
H-520544-21
COSMO SERIES TEXAS
RAND McNALLY & COMPANY
Made in U. S. A.
Longitude West of Greenwich
Statute Miles
Kilometers
Lambert Conformal Conic Projection

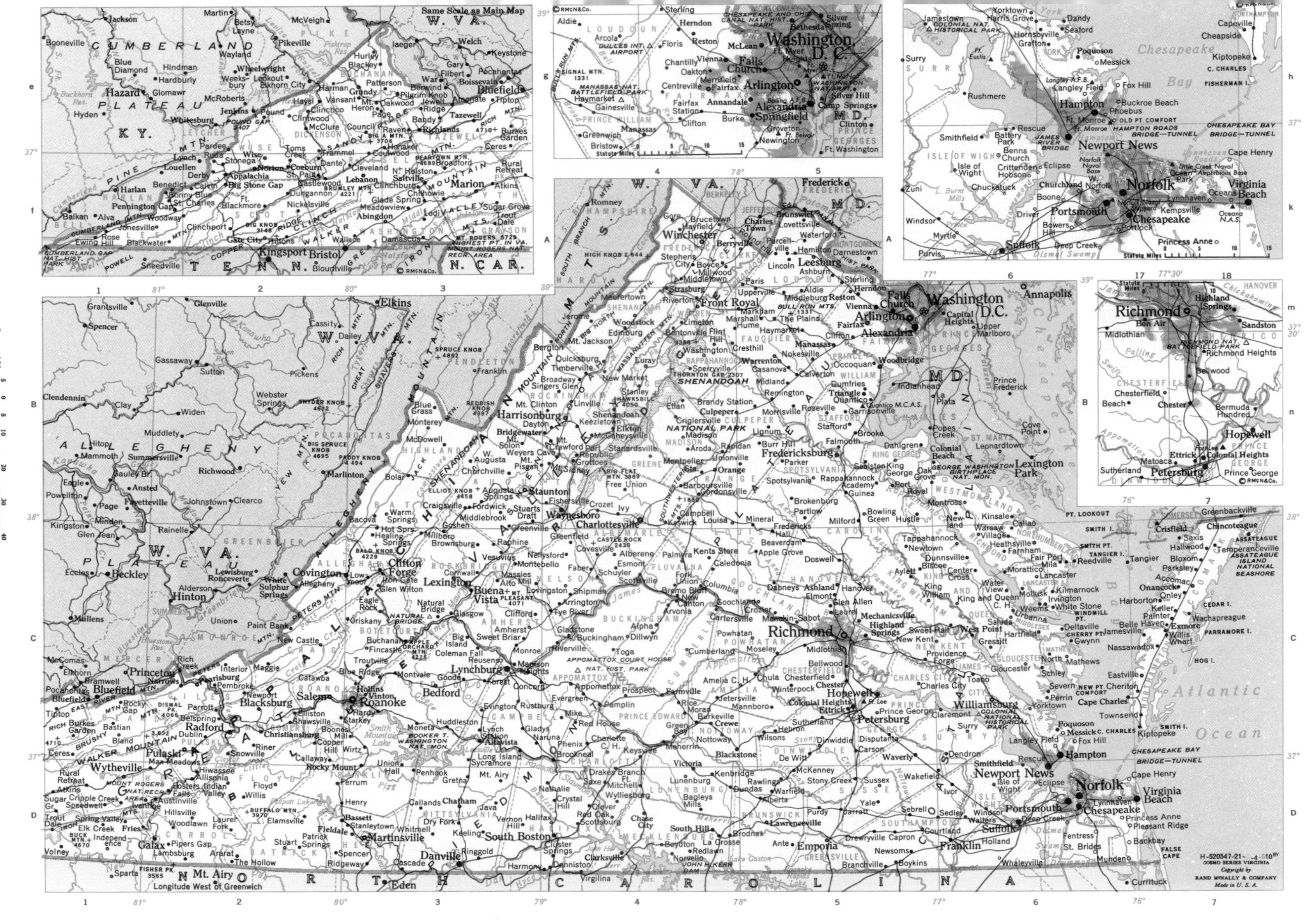

Lambert Conformal Conic Projection

Statute Miles 5 0 5 10 20 30 40

Kilometers 5 0 5 15 25 35 45 55

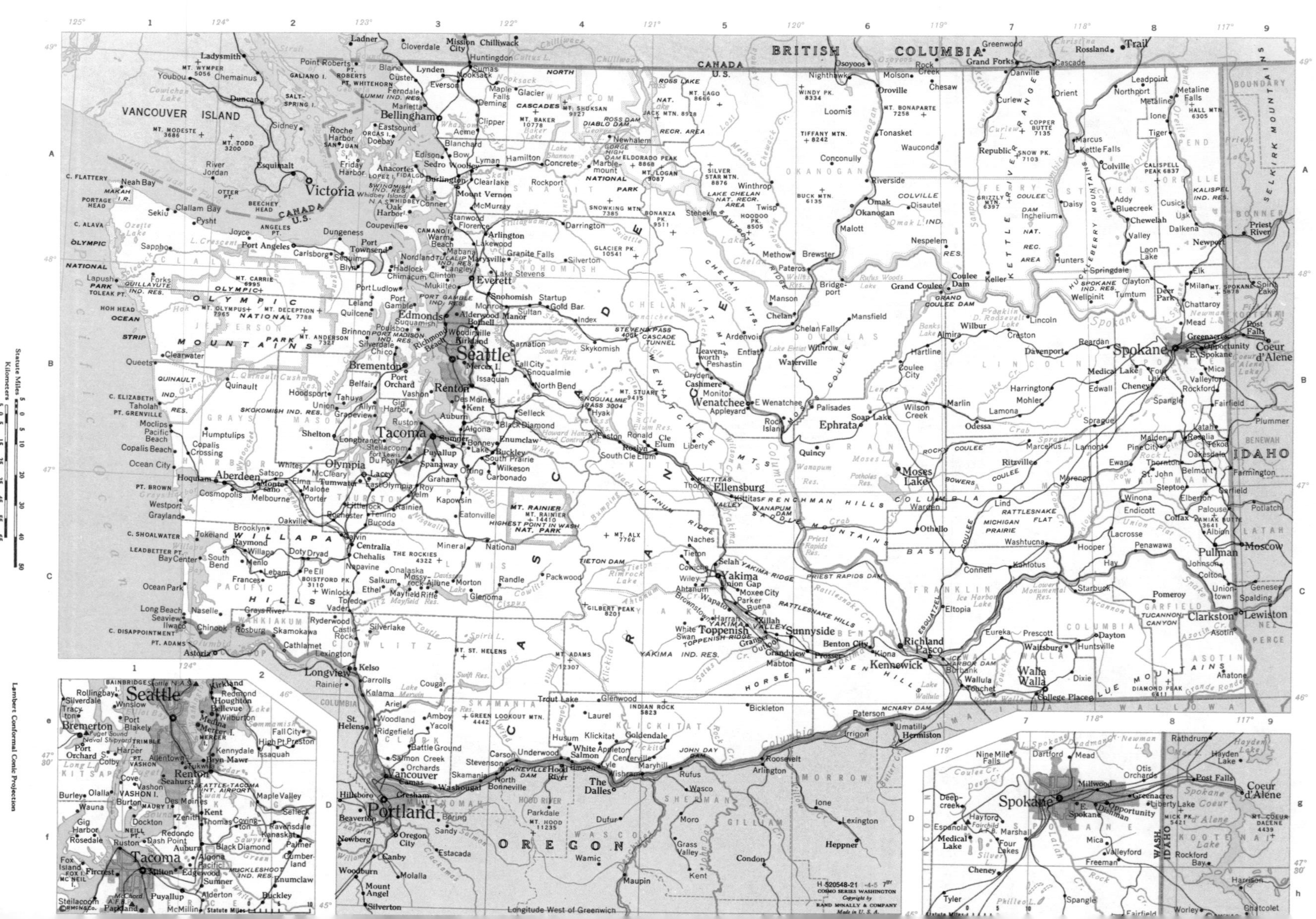

Statute Miles 5 0 5 10 20 30 40 50

Kilometers 5 0 5 15 25 35 45 55 65

Lambert Conformal Conic Projection

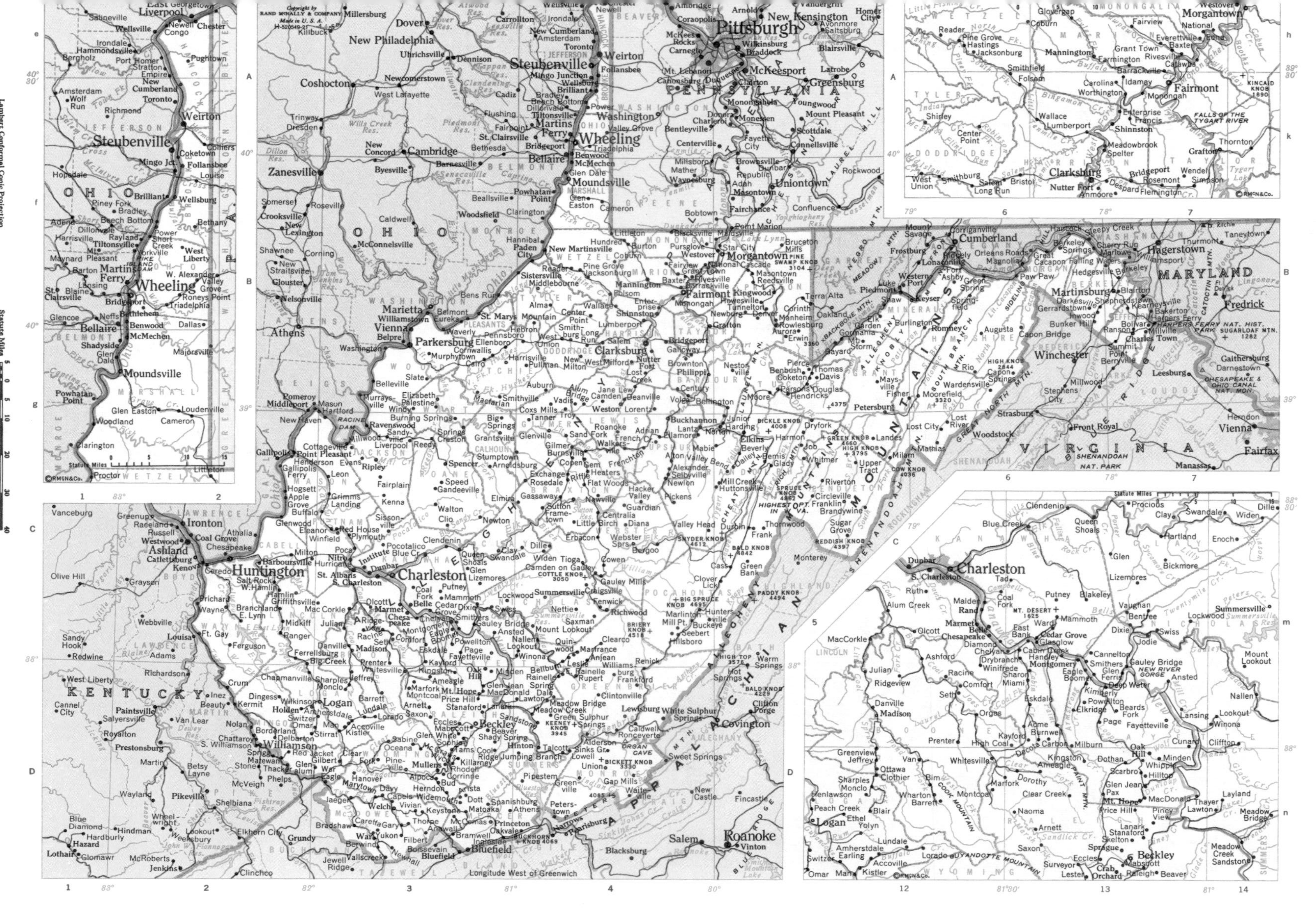
Pittsburgh
Wheeling
Steubenville
Weirton
Morgantown
Fairmont
Clarksburg
Parkersburg
Charleston
Huntington
Beckley
Bluefield
Cumberland
Hagerstown
Martinsburg
Winchester
Roanoke
MARYLAND
VIRGINIA
KENTUCKY
OHIO
PENNSYLVANIA
Longitude West of Greenwich
Lambert Conformal Conic Projection
Statute Miles 5 0 5 10 20 30 40
Kilometers 5 0 5 15 25 35 45 55

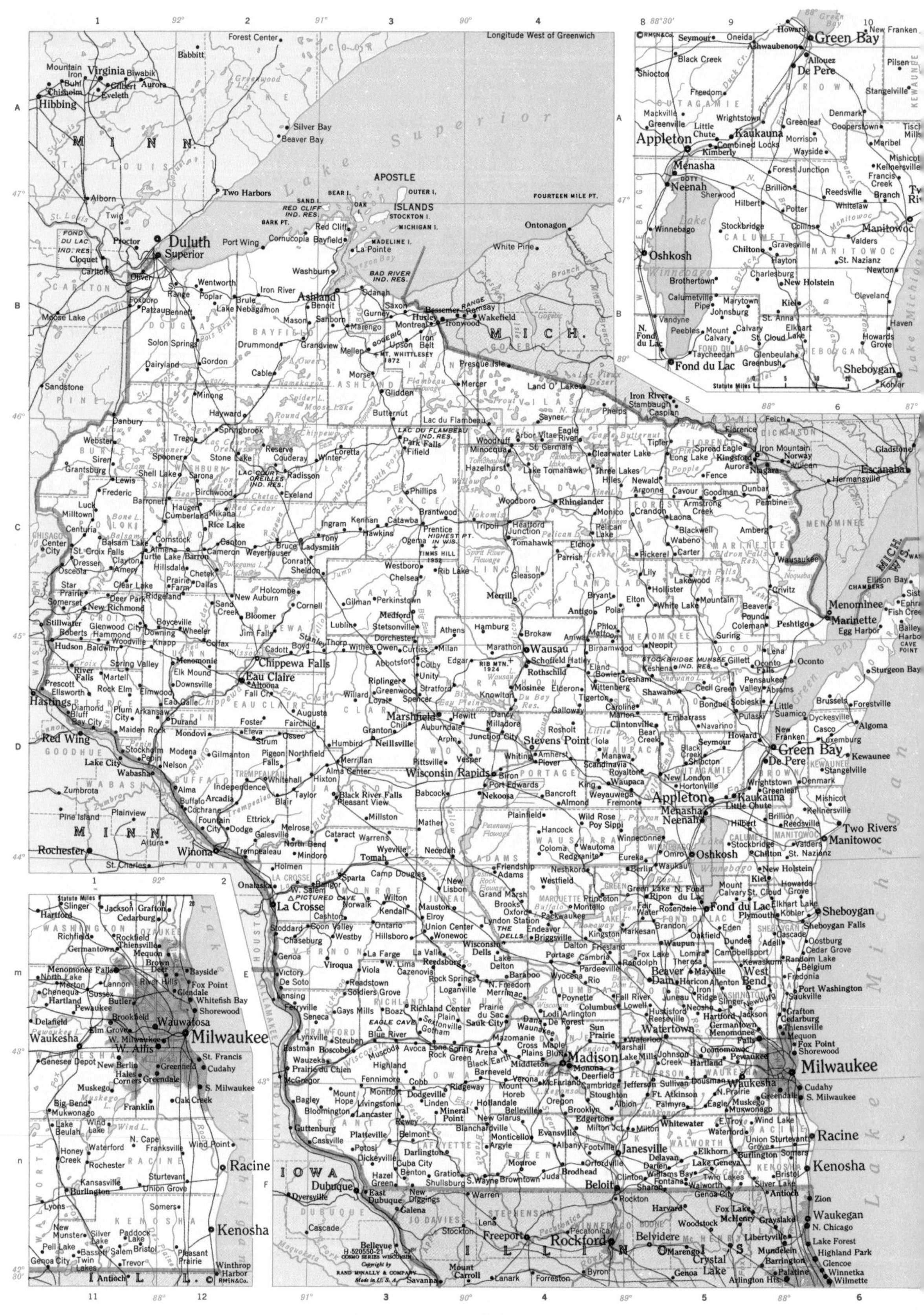
Longitude West of Greenwich
Lake Superior
APOSTLE ISLANDS
MINN.
MICH.
IOWA
ILLINOIS
Lake Michigan
Green Bay
Duluth
Superior
Ashland
Eau Claire
Chippewa Falls
Wausau
Stevens Point
Wisconsin Rapids
Marshfield
La Crosse
Madison
Milwaukee
Waukesha
Racine
Kenosha
Janesville
Beloit
Rockford
Sheboygan
Manitowoc
Two Rivers
Appleton
Oshkosh
Fond du Lac
Neenah
Menasha
De Pere
Green Bay
Dubuque
Winona
Rochester
Red Wing
Hastings
Marinette
Menominee
Escanaba
Rhinelander
Wauwatosa
W. Allis
Lambert Conformal Conic Projection
Statute Miles
Kilometers
Copyright by RAND McNALLY & COMPANY Made in U. S. A.

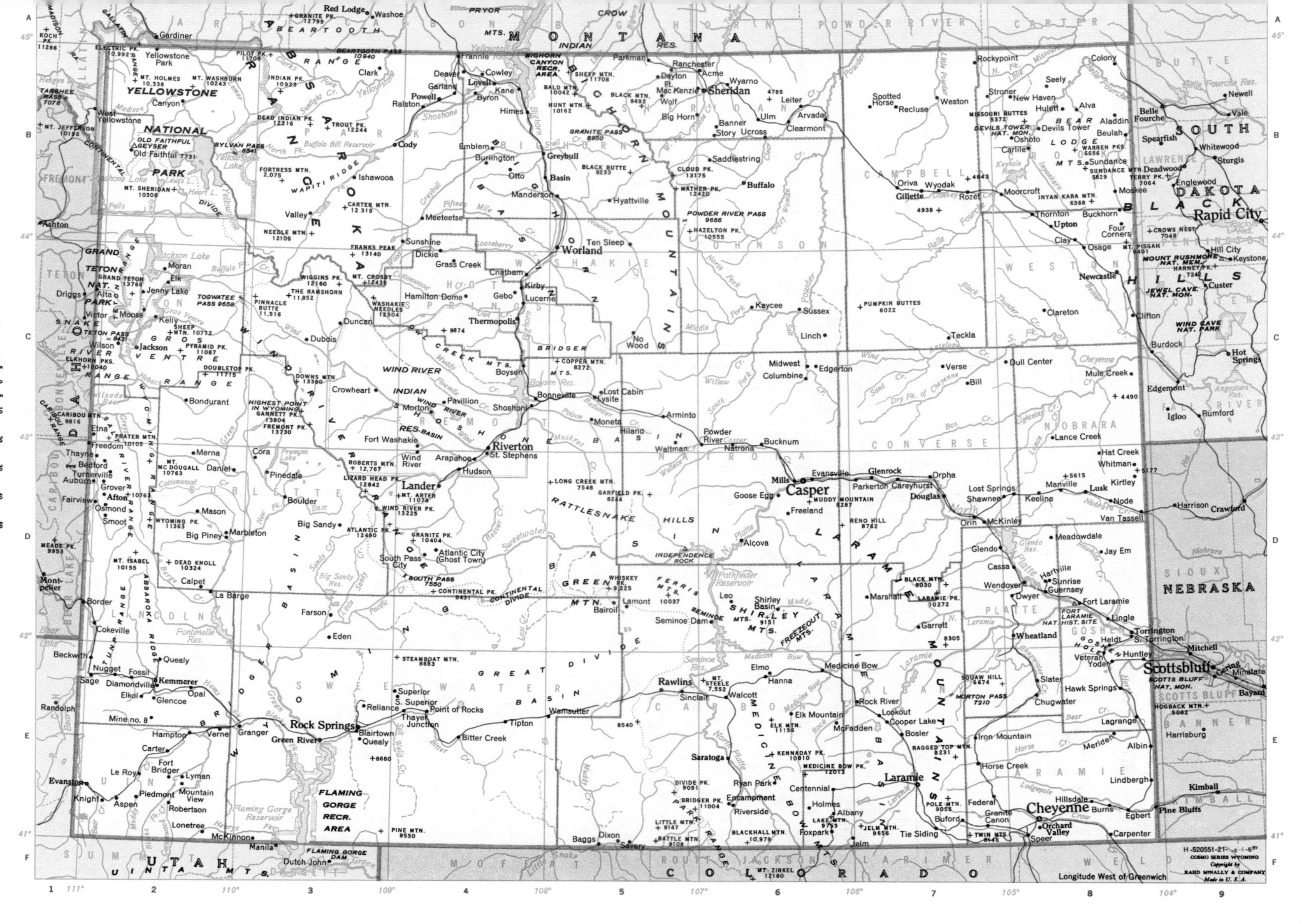
MONTANA
SOUTH DAKOTA
NEBRASKA
COLORADO
UTAH
IDAHO
YELLOWSTONE NATIONAL PARK
BIGHORN MOUNTAINS
LARAMIE MOUNTAINS
MEDICINE BOW MTS.
WIND RIVER RANGE
GREAT DIVIDE BASIN
RATTLESNAKE HILLS
FLAMING GORGE RECR. AREA
Cheyenne
Casper
Laramie
Rock Springs
Sheridan
Rawlins
Riverton
Lander
Gillette
Worland
Scottsbluff
Rapid City
Longitude West of Greenwich
H-520551-21
COSMO SERIES WYOMING
Copyright by RAND McNALLY & COMPANY
Made in U. S. A.
Lambert Conformal Conic Projection
Statute Miles 5 0 5 10 20 30 40 50
Kilometers 5 0 5 15 25 35 45 55 65 75

Historical Maps of the United States

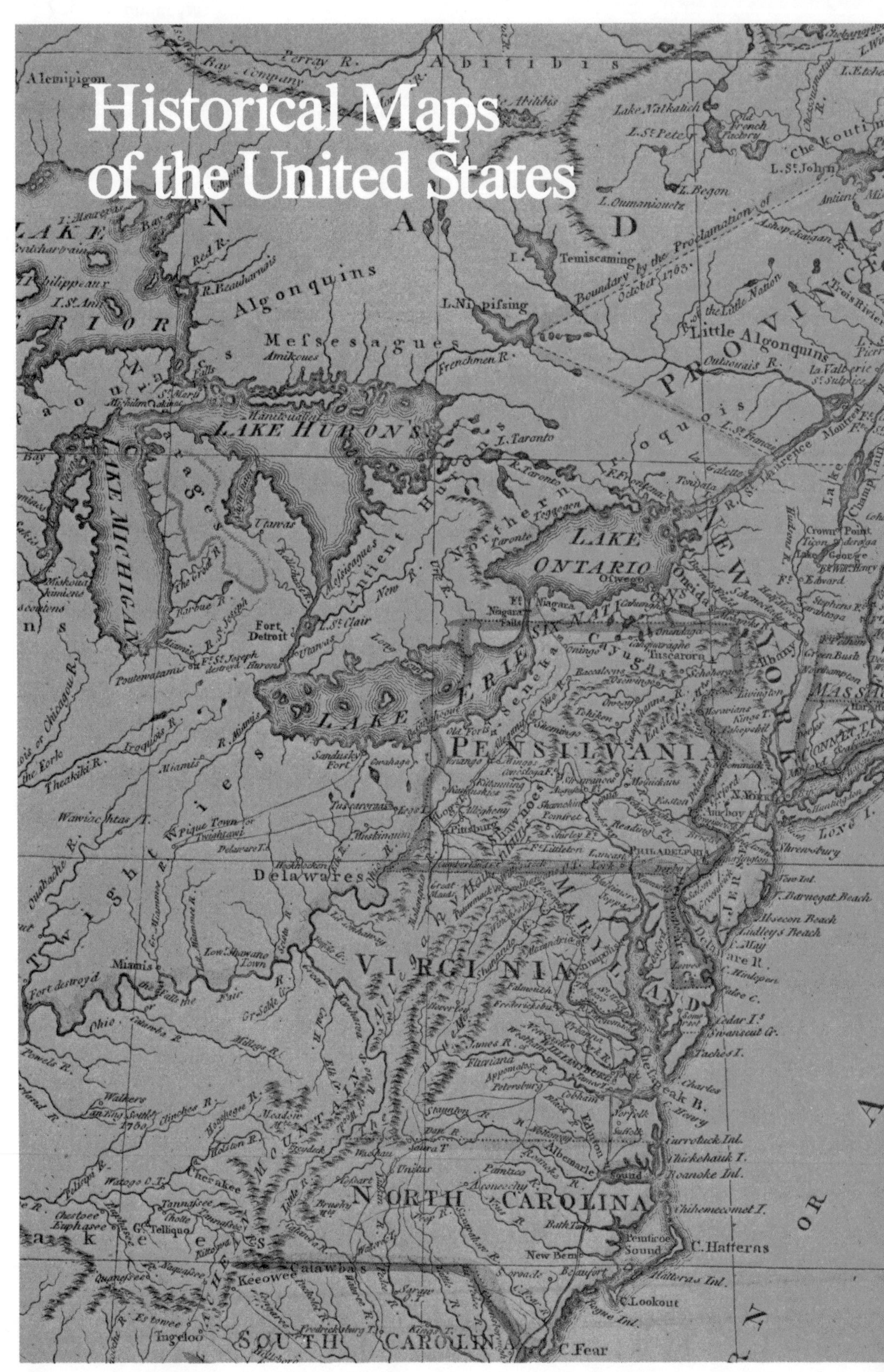

Introduction

The search for adventure, wealth, and freedom has inspired those coming to America since the discovery of the New World. This vast land offered settlers abundant natural resources and the opportunity to experiment with social, religious, and political ideals. Freed from traditional constraints, Americans created an economy and industry that outstripped the combined production of European countries.

But along with its progress, the nation has also had its problems. Minority groups have long struggled for equality. As far back as the early 1800's, some people felt commercial development meant neglecting the consequences of uncontrolled growth. And World War II's legacy of America's continued expansion left the country somewhat unprepared for future problems. The energy crisis and worldwide inflation and instability now challenge the United States on several fronts.

Yet Americans are a confident and energetic people. Perhaps the experience of taming a continent, creating a vast industry, and absorbing millions of immigrants may be adequate preparation for meeting today's problems. History has shown that this nation is never more resourceful than when faced with a challenge.

The maps that follow chronicle the remarkable development of the United States from a colony to a great nation. Covering eight historical periods from 1700 to 1970, the maps illustrate the country's foundation and expansion westward, its richly varied population, and its three major conflicts—the Revolutionary and Civil wars and World War II. Text accompanying the maps provides detailed information about each period.

The American Colonies, 1700 *page 190*

The fabulous wealth discovered by Spain in Central and South America touched off a race among nations to share in the riches of the New World. By the early 1600's, Spain, France, and Great Britain had each made their claim for territory.

Dreams of finding easy treasure faded, and France and England realized the commercial and military value of these lands. With the exception of several settlements, few people immigrated to the French regions. But America fired the imagination of the British.

The early British settlers of Jamestown and similar camps struggled against disease and starvation, and many died. Slowly, however, the settlements began to prosper as more immigrants arrived, bringing their varied religious, social, and political beliefs.

Provincetown, Plymouth, Philadelphia, and the Chesapeake settlements became thriving commercial centers by the late 1600's. Boston and New York prospered as port cities, and coastal towns benefited from a growing fishing industry. The climate and farmlands of Maryland, Virginia, and the Carolinas proved ideal for cash crops such as tobacco and cotton. As the transplanted European population increased, native American Indians were forced out of coastal areas and pushed west.

By 1700, the colonies were loosely organized into eleven provinces. The population, with its unusual social, political, and religious makeup, was already markedly different from any society in Europe.

Independence, 1775–1783 *page 191*

The Revolutionary War instilled in the American people a sense of their nation's special destiny. The war arose from conflicts between a fiercely independent colonial population and a British government determined to tighten its control over King George's colonies. Colonial resistance became armed rebellion, and the war began in 1775.

At Lexington, Concord, and Bunker Hill, the British unexpectedly suffered heavy losses in defeating the Yankee militia. By July 1776, Britain was mounting a full-scale military effort to end the rebellion. Though well equipped and trained, the British had to fight an angry population in wilderness terrain. The Americans, outnumbered and poorly equipped, were fighting for their own land.

The British sought to isolate New England and defeated George Washington's Continental Army at Long Island and New York. But by the end of 1776, Continental troops had captured Princeton and Trenton. The American victory at Saratoga in October 1777 dealt a final blow to Britain's northern strategy.

From 1778 onward, Britain concentrated on the South and the coast, but British commander Cornwallis could not secure the countryside. In October 1781 at Yorktown, Cornwallis surrendered his entire command.

The peace treaty of 1783 recognized American independence and more than doubled the size of the former territory. The Americans believed their nation was destined to lead the world toward liberty.

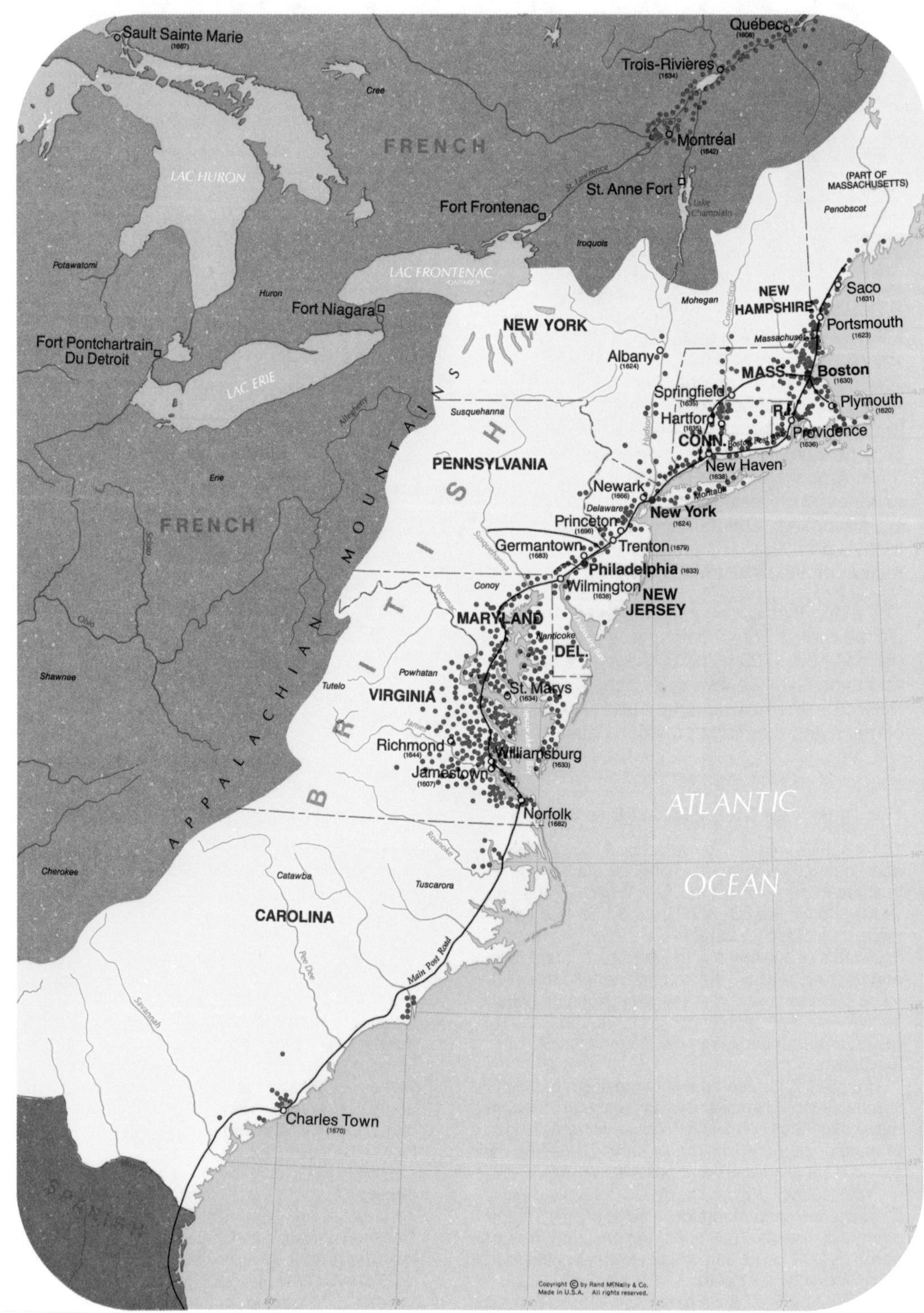

MAP LEGEND

- Settled area: each dot represents 500 rural population.
- ● More than 5,000 people
- ○ Less than 5,000 people
- *Huron* Indian Tribe
- (1634) Founding Date

SCALE

miles 0 50 100 150

kilometers 0 50 100 150 200

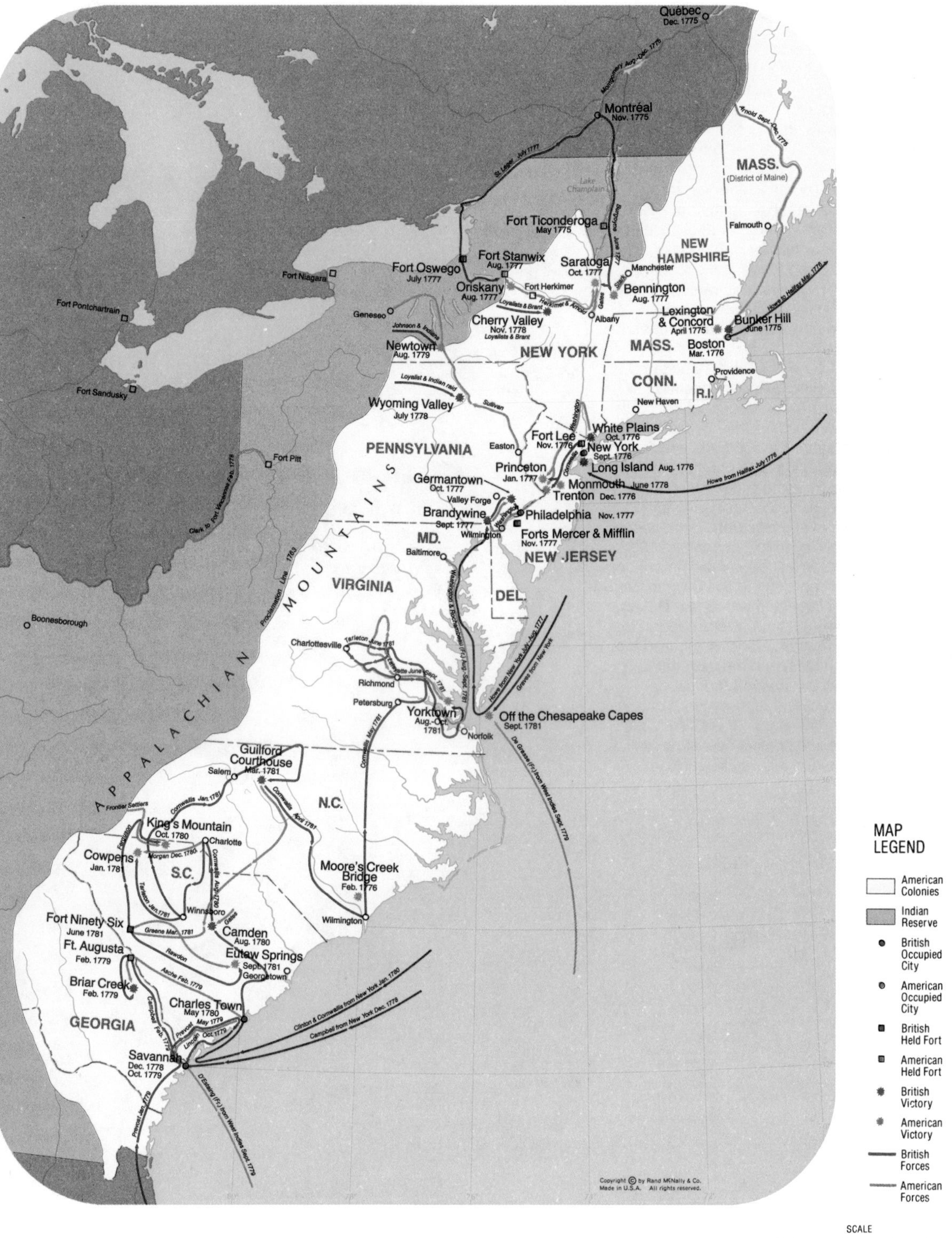
Québec
Dec. 1775
Montréal
Nov. 1775
MASS.
(District of Maine)
Falmouth
Fort Ticonderoga
May 1775
NEW HAMPSHIRE
Fort Stanwix
Aug. 1777
Saratoga
Oct. 1777
Manchester
Fort Oswego
July 1777
Fort Niagara
Fort Pontchartrain
Oriskany
Aug. 1777
Fort Herkimer
Bennington
Aug. 1777
Albany
Geneseo
Cherry Valley
Nov. 1778
Loyalists & Brant
Lexington & Concord
April 1775
Bunker Hill
June 1775
Newtown
Aug. 1779
NEW YORK
MASS.
Boston
Mar. 1776
Fort Sandusky
Providence
CONN.
R.I.
New Haven
Wyoming Valley
July 1778
White Plains
Oct. 1776
Fort Lee
Nov. 1776
New York
Sept. 1776
Long Island Aug. 1776
Fort Pitt
PENNSYLVANIA
Easton
Princeton
Jan. 1777
Germantown
Oct. 1777
Monmouth June 1778
Trenton Dec. 1776
Valley Forge
Brandywine
Sept. 1777
Philadelphia Nov. 1777
Forts Mercer & Mifflin
Nov. 1777
Wilmington
MD.
NEW JERSEY
Baltimore
VIRGINIA
DEL.
APPALACHIAN MOUNTAINS
Proclamation Line 1763
Boonesborough
Charlottesville
Richmond
Petersburg
Yorktown
Aug.-Oct. 1781
Norfolk
Off the Chesapeake Capes
Sept. 1781
Guilford Courthouse
Mar. 1781
Salem
N.C.
King's Mountain
Oct. 1780
Charlotte
Cowpens
Jan. 1781
S.C.
Moore's Creek Bridge
Feb. 1776
Winnsboro
Wilmington
Fort Ninety Six
June 1781
Camden
Aug. 1780
Ft. Augusta
Feb. 1779
Eutaw Springs
Sept. 1781
Georgetown
Briar Creek
Feb. 1779
Charles Town
May 1780
GEORGIA
Savannah
Dec. 1778
Oct. 1779
Copyright © by Rand McNally & Co.
Made in U.S.A. All rights reserved.
MAP LEGEND
American Colonies
Indian Reserve
British Occupied City
American Occupied City
British Held Fort
American Held Fort
British Victory
American Victory
British Forces
American Forces
SCALE
miles 0 50 100 150
kilometers 0 50 100 150 200

The rallying cry of "Manifest Destiny!" reflected the American belief that Providence had granted the United States exclusive right to settle North America. An expanding population, European immigrants, commercial development, and a growing transportation system all played a part in the first great westward migration.

In 1803, Thomas Jefferson made the bold step of purchasing the Louisiana Territory from France. In 1819, Spain ceded the remainder of Florida to the Republic. Soon roads, railroads, and canal and river systems carried settlers into the Mississippi Valley and parts of Texas and opened the lands to eastern markets.

As the Louisiana Territory became densely settled, pioneers pushed beyond the formal borders of the country. Wagon trains headed west over the Oregon, Santa Fe, Frémont, and California trails. Mexico, attempting to stop the flow of settlers into its lands, was soon at war with America, losing Texas in 1836 and its southwestern territories in 1848. The Gadsden Purchase of 1853 completed America's southernmost border. American claim to the Oregon Territory was jointly held with Great Britain, and in 1848 the land was divided at the forty-ninth parallel. Settlers poured into these territories, and native American Indians were forced off their lands.

In a little over half a century, America had fulfilled its Manifest Destiny. Only the deepening conflict over slavery seemed to dim the nation's brilliant future.

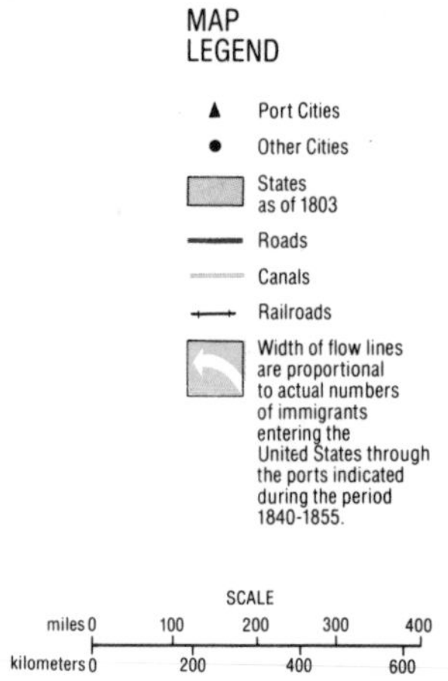

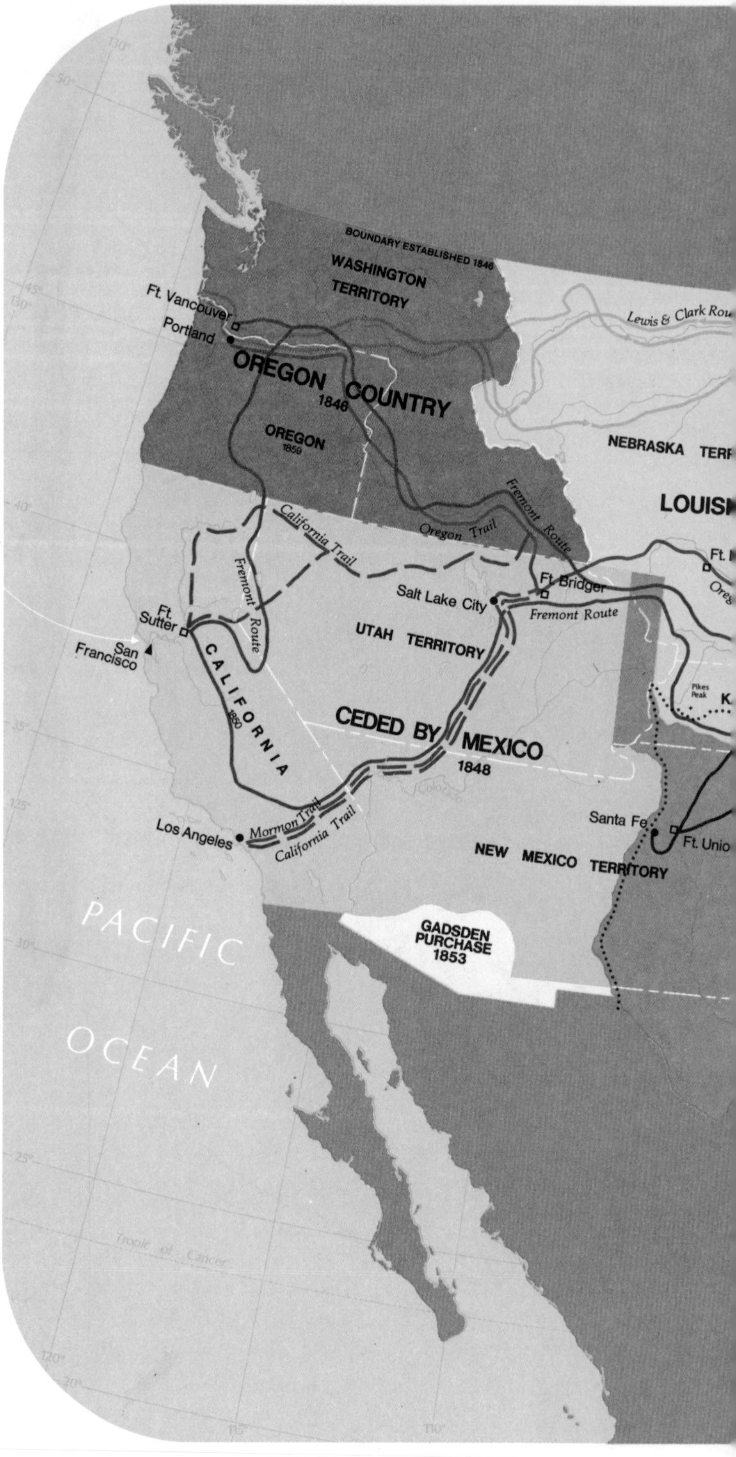

MAP LEGEND

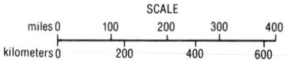

- ▲ Port Cities
- ● Other Cities
- States as of 1803
- Roads
- Canals
- Railroads
- Width of flow lines are proportional to actual numbers of immigrants entering the United States through the ports indicated during the period 1840-1855.

SCALE

miles 0 100 200 300 400

kilometers 0 200 400 600

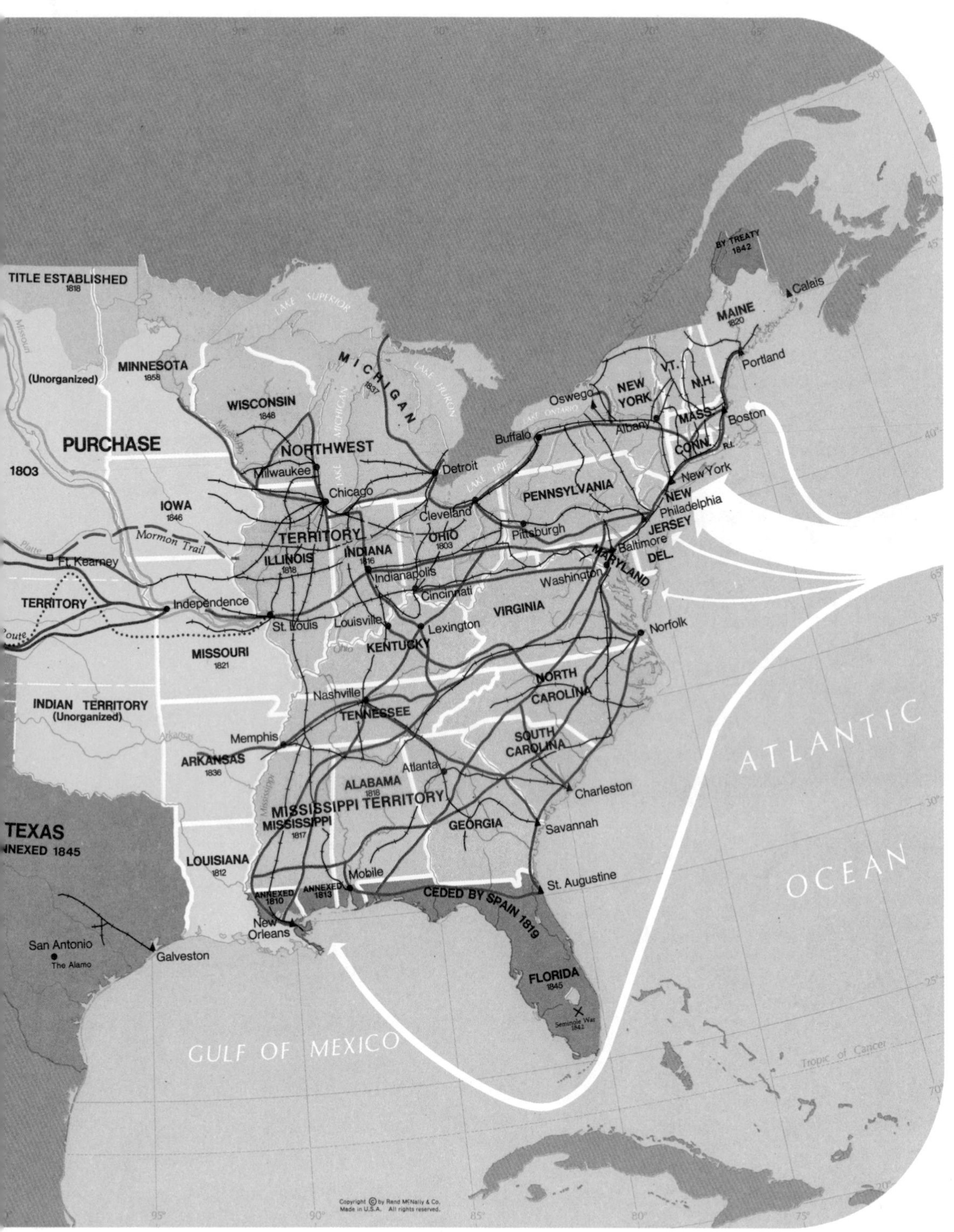
TITLE ESTABLISHED
1818
MINNESOTA
1858
(Unorganized)
PURCHASE
1803
WISCONSIN
1848
MICHIGAN
1837
NORTHWEST
TERRITORY
Lake Superior
Lake Michigan
Lake Huron
Lake Ontario
Lake Erie
Milwaukee
Chicago
Detroit
IOWA
1846
Mormon Trail
Platte
Ft. Kearney
TERRITORY
Independence
St. Louis
ILLINOIS
1818
INDIANA
1816
OHIO
1803
Cleveland
Indianapolis
Cincinnati
Louisville
Lexington
KENTUCKY
MISSOURI
1821
INDIAN TERRITORY
(Unorganized)
Nashville
TENNESSEE
Memphis
ARKANSAS
1836
Atlanta
ALABAMA
1818
MISSISSIPPI TERRITORY
MISSISSIPPI
1817
GEORGIA
LOUISIANA
1812
ANNEXED
1810
ANNEXED
1813
Mobile
New Orleans
CEDED BY SPAIN 1819
FLORIDA
1845
Seminole War
1842
TEXAS
NNEXED 1845
San Antonio
The Alamo
Galveston
GULF OF MEXICO
ATLANTIC
OCEAN
Tropic of Cancer
St. Augustine
Savannah
Charleston
SOUTH
CAROLINA
NORTH
CAROLINA
VIRGINIA
Norfolk
Washington
MARYLAND
Baltimore
DEL.
NEW
JERSEY
Philadelphia
New York
PENNSYLVANIA
Pittsburgh
Buffalo
Oswego
NEW
YORK
Albany
VT.
N.H.
MASS.
Boston
CONN.
R.I.
MAINE
1820
Portland
Calais
BY TREATY
1842
Copyright © by Rand McNally & Co.
Made in U.S.A. All rights reserved.

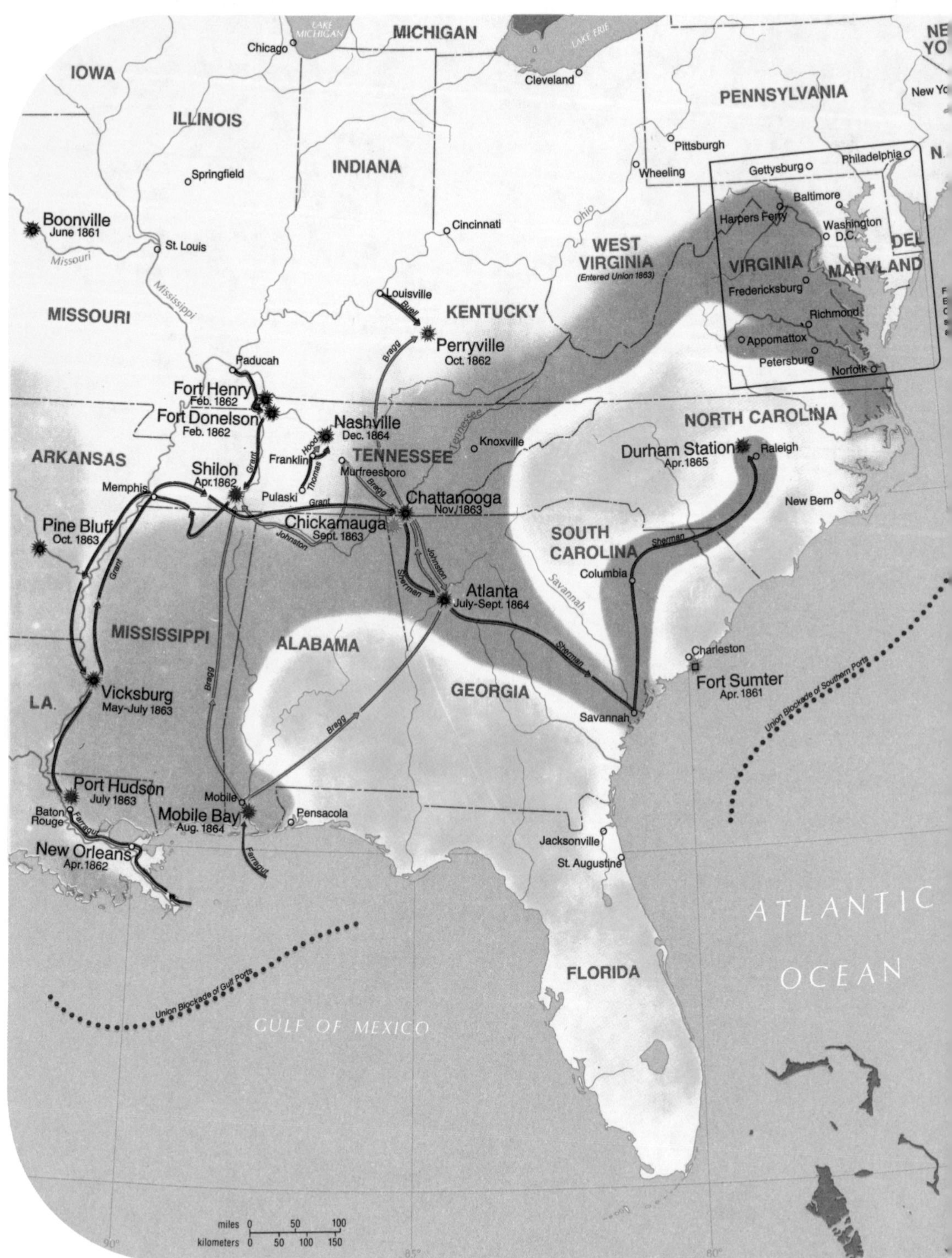
LAKE MICHIGAN
MICHIGAN
LAKE ERIE
Chicago
Cleveland
IOWA
PENNSYLVANIA
New York
ILLINOIS
Pittsburgh
Philadelphia
Gettysburg
Wheeling
INDIANA
Springfield
Baltimore
Harpers Ferry
Washington D.C.
Boonville
June 1861
Cincinnati
Ohio
St. Louis
WEST VIRGINIA
(Entered Union 1863)
DEL
Missouri
VIRGINIA
MARYLAND
Fredericksburg
Mississippi
Louisville
Buell
KENTUCKY
MISSOURI
Richmond
Appomattox
Bragg
Perryville
Oct. 1862
Petersburg
Paducah
Norfolk
Fort Henry
Feb. 1862
Fort Donelson
Feb. 1862
Nashville
Dec. 1864
Tennessee
NORTH CAROLINA
Knoxville
Hood
ARKANSAS
Franklin
Thomas
TENNESSEE
Durham Station
Apr. 1865
Raleigh
Shiloh
Apr. 1862
Grant
Murfreesboro
Memphis
Pulaski
Chattanooga
Nov. 1863
New Bern
Pine Bluff
Oct. 1863
Chickamauga
Sept. 1863
Johnston
SOUTH CAROLINA
Sherman
Columbia
Atlanta
July-Sept. 1864
Savannah
MISSISSIPPI
ALABAMA
Charleston
Fort Sumter
Apr. 1861
Vicksburg
May-July 1863
GEORGIA
LA.
Union Blockade of Southern Ports
Port Hudson
July 1863
Mobile
Baton Rouge
Farragut
Mobile Bay
Aug. 1864
Pensacola
New Orleans
Apr. 1862
Jacksonville
St. Augustine
ATLANTIC OCEAN
FLORIDA
Union Blockade of Gulf Ports
GULF OF MEXICO
miles 0 50 100
kilometers 0 50 100 150
90°
85°
80°

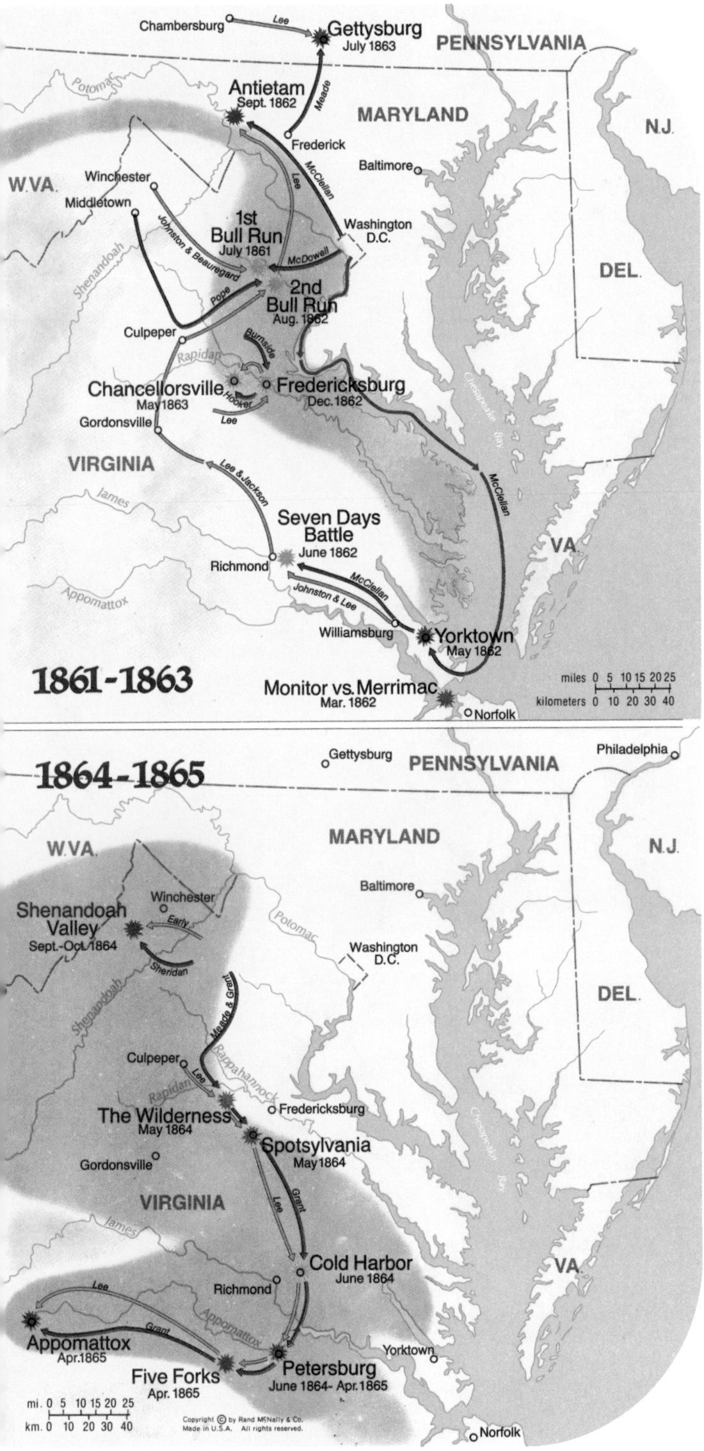

By the 1860 presidential election, compromise on the issue of slavery could no longer hold the nation together. While the North vehemently denounced slavery, the South passionately defended its way of life. After Abraham Lincoln was elected, the South seceded from the Union and chose Jefferson Davis to head a new government in Richmond. By April 1861, the United States and the Confederacy were at war.

The Battle of Bull Run in July was a decisive Confederate victory. In early 1862, the Union army, under George Brinton McClellen and Ulysses S. Grant, took the offensive, winning at Fort Henry, Fort Donelson, and Shiloh. McClellen's subsequent move against Richmond was stopped by Confederate forces under Robert E. Lee. The Confederacy launched an invasion of the North, reaching Antietam before being pushed back into Virginia. Attempting a second invasion in July 1863, Lee was defeated at Gettysburg. Grant captured Vicksburg and, joining William Tecumseh Sherman, commander of the Tennessee troops, drove the Confederate troops back into Georgia.

In May 1864, Grant and George Meade, commander of the Army of the Potomac, marched toward Richmond. Sherman marched to the sea, capturing Atlanta, Savannah, and Columbia before turning north to Raleigh. On April 9, 1865, Lee surrendered to Grant at Appomattox.

Slavery had been abolished, and the South's economy lay in ruins. But the conflict had awakened the industrial might of the North. If one way of life had been lost, another was rising to take its place.

MAP
LEGEND

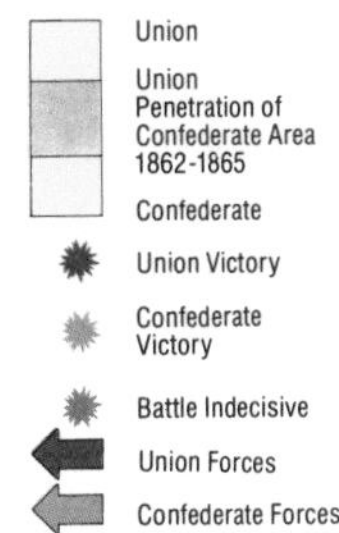

The final settlement of the West involved the greatest movement of people in the nation's history. In just thirty years, the "Great American Desert" was transformed into a mineral and agricultural empire.

The railroad boom opened the plains and mountain-desert regions to settlement. Between 1869 and 1884, four transcontinental railways were built; along with the overland stage, they linked the industrial East to the West. In a few years, the railroads were carrying cattle, grain, mail, payrolls, supplies and settlers into western territories.

The first settlers were miners. In the 1860's and 1870's, gold and silver strikes brought prospectors swarming into American Indian lands. War broke out with tribes in the North and the Southwest. Although the Indians won isolated battles, they could not prevail against the army's superior weapons. By 1887, the Indians and the buffalo were gone from the open range.

Ranchers and farmers followed in the miners' wake. From the mid-1860's to the late 1880's, a vast cattle empire dominated Texas, Wyoming, and Montana. But sheepherders soon challenged the ranchers, and farmers began fencing off grazing land and planting crops in the semiarid soil. In the end, windmills and barbed wire tamed the West as effectively as railroads and the Colt revolver.

By 1890, an almost continuous line of settlements stretched from the Midwest to the Pacific, and population in the territories had soared. The "frontier" had all but disappeared. Only the great waves of immigration in the early 1900's would compare with the extensive migration of this era.

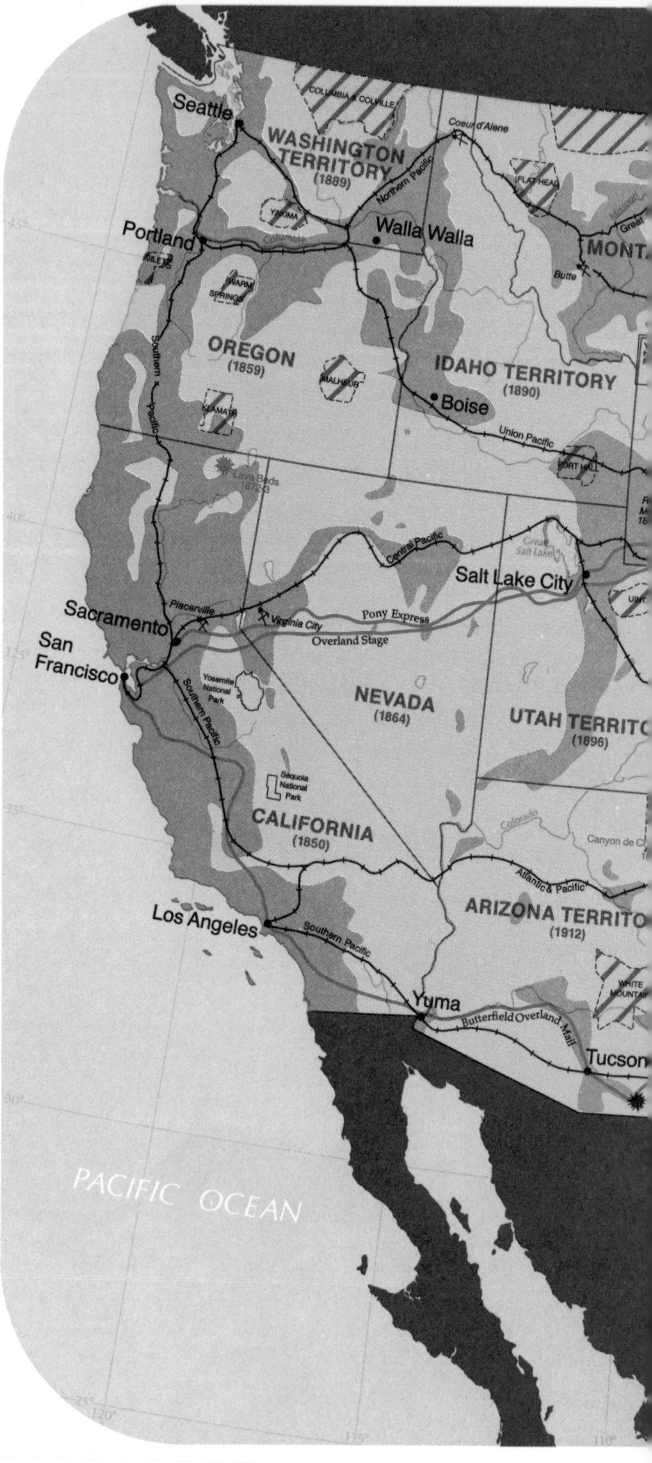

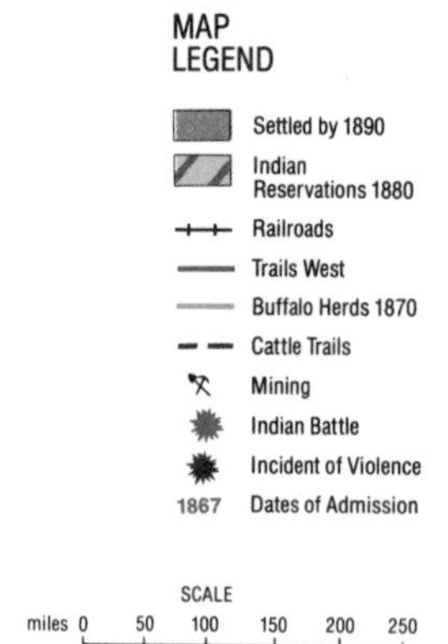

NORTH DAKOTA
(Part of Dakota Territory until 1889)
Bismarck
Northern Pacific
MINNESOTA
Great Northern
St. Paul
Minneapolis
End of James-Younger Gang Northfield September 7, 1876
SOUTH DAKOTA
(Part of Dakota Territory until 1889)
Deadwood
Younger Brothers Captured Madelia September 11, 1876
WISCONSIN
MICHIGAN
LAKE SUPERIOR
LAKE HURON
LAKE MICHIGAN
LAKE ERIE
Chicago
Cleveland
IOWA
OHIO
WYOMING TERRITORY
(1890)
NEBRASKA
(1867)
Des Moines
Laramie
Cheyenne
Ogallala
Union Pacific
James-Younger First Train Robbery July 21, 1873
Omaha
Pony Express
Overland Stage
ILLINOIS
INDIANA
Cincinnati
Denver
St. Joseph
Jesse James First Bank Robbery February 14, 1866
Leadville
COLORADO
(1876)
Salina
Abilene
St. Louis
James Brothers Train Robbery Oct. 3, 1879
Sedalia
KENTUCKY
KANSAS
(1861)
Sand Creek
MISSOURI
Wichita
Dodge City
Coffeyville
Butterfield Overland Mail
Illinois Central
TENNESSEE
Chattanooga
INDIAN TERRITORY
(OKLAHOMA 1907)
ARKANSAS
Adobe Walls 1874
Judge Parkers Federal Court
Santa Fe - Ft. Smith
GEORGIA
Billy the Kid Killed July 14, 1881
Lincoln County War 1875-1881
FORT STANTON
(1912)
Western Trail
Dallas
Fort Worth
ALABAMA
LOUISIANA
MISSISSIPPI
Mobile
FLORIDA
El Paso
Overland Mail
Pecos Trail
Butterfield
Lower Emigrant Trail
Southern Pacific
TEXAS
Chisholm Trail
Sedalia Trail
New Orleans
Houston
Judge Roy Bean
San Antonio
Rio Grande

For the first one hundred years of its history, the United States opened its doors to all nationalities. Millions journeyed to the American shores.

European immigrants arriving before and two decades after the Civil War came primarily from Ireland, England, Scandinavia, and Germany. The Irish tended to remain in the East. Others went to Oregon, then later to the northern plains states and Texas and California. Many were skilled farmers and artisans, blending into American life.

By the early 1900's, conditions in Europe led over eight million people to journey across the Atlantic. Most crowded into the cities' poorer sections, creating ethnic communities insulated from the language and customs of their new country. Yet these people answered the demand for labor and built the industrial might of the nation.

On the West Coast, the large number of Chinese and Japanese alarmed American workers. In 1882, the first in a series of immigration laws was passed, restricting the entry of Asians. Mexicans and Latin Americans often encountered the same resistance and hostility.

The South lacked heavy industry and available land, so immigrants favored the North and West. Also, restrictive immigration laws made it difficult for the foreign-born to settle in the South.

This constant stream of newcomers created a rich culture. Immigrants and their descendants have contributed immeasurably to the country's industry, science, and arts.

MAP
LEGEND

Immigrants

Foreign born whites and children of foreign or mixed parentage; by counties.

Source: U.S. Decennial Census, 1910

- Less Than 10%
- 10% To 25%
- 25% To 50%
- 50% To 75%
- 75% & Over

MONTANA 94,713 Total Foreign born population in 1910

SCALE

miles 0 100 200 300 400

kilometers 0 200 400 600

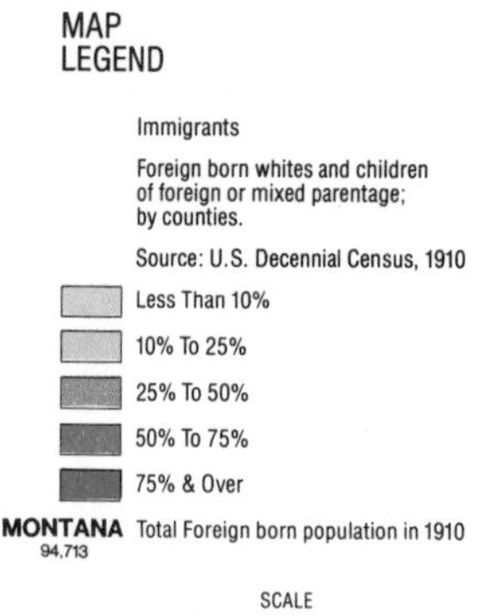

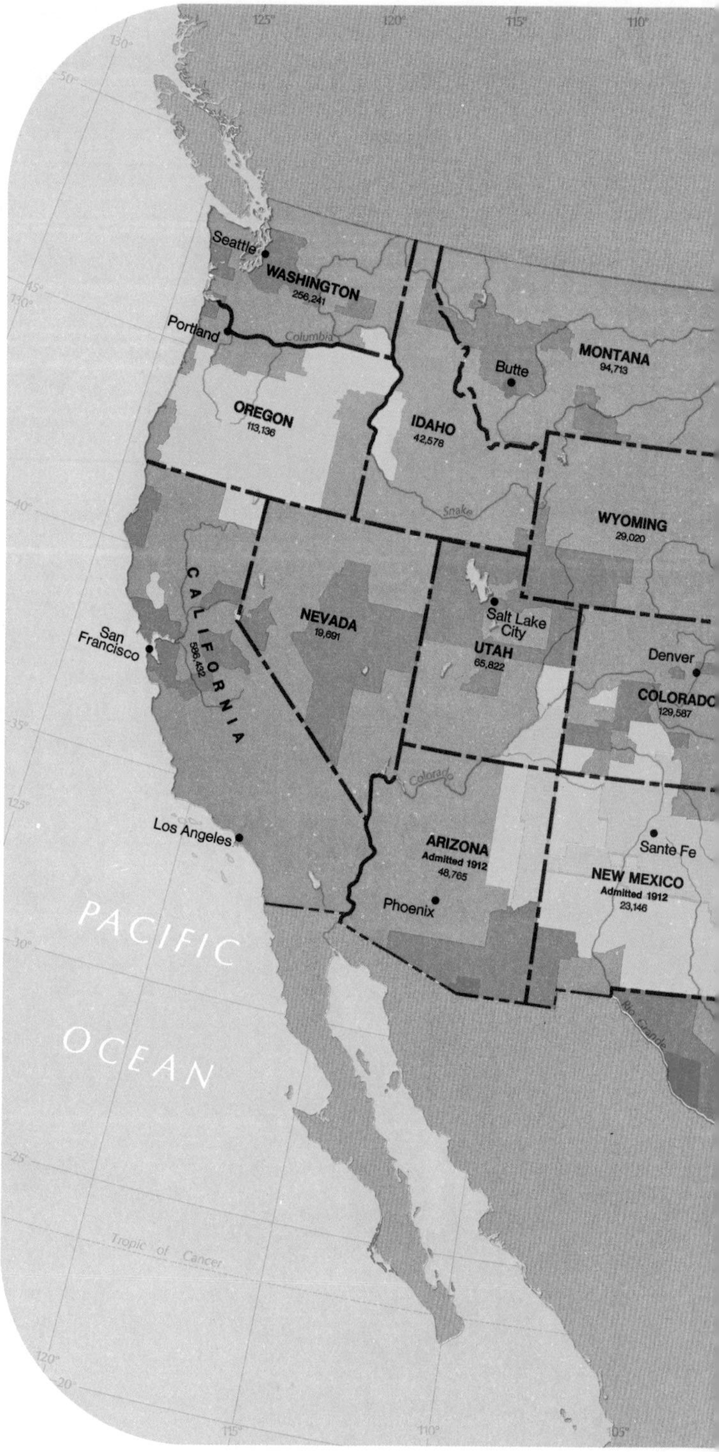

MINNESOTA
543,595
Minneapolis
WISCONSIN
512,865
Milwaukee
MICHIGAN
597,550
Detroit
IOWA
273,765
Chicago
ILLINOIS
1,205,314
INDIANA
159,663
OHIO
598,374
Cleveland
Cincinnati
Kansas City
St. Louis
KANSAS
135,450
MISSOURI
229,779
KENTUCKY
40,162
Nashville
TENNESSEE
18,607
OKLAHOMA
40,442
ARKANSAS
17,046
TEXAS
241,938
San Antonio
LOUISIANA
52,766
New Orleans
MISSISSIPPI
9,770
ALABAMA
19,286
Atlanta
GEORGIA
15,477
SOUTH CAROLINA
6,179
NORTH CAROLINA
6,092
Jacksonville
FLORIDA
40,633
WEST VIRGINIA
57,218
VIRGINIA
27,057
Washington D. C.
24,902
MARYLAND
104,944
Baltimore
DEL.
17,492
Philadelphia
Pittsburgh
PENNSYLVANIA
1,442,374
Newark
N.J.
New York
NEW YORK
2,748,011
Buffalo
CONN.
329,574
R.I.
179,141
MASS.
1,059,245
Boston
VT.
49,921
N.H.
96,667
MAINE
110,562
LAKE SUPERIOR
LAKE MICHIGAN
LAKE HURON
LAKE ERIE
LAKE ONTARIO
Missouri
Ohio
ATLANTIC OCEAN
GULF OF MEXICO
Tropic of Cancer

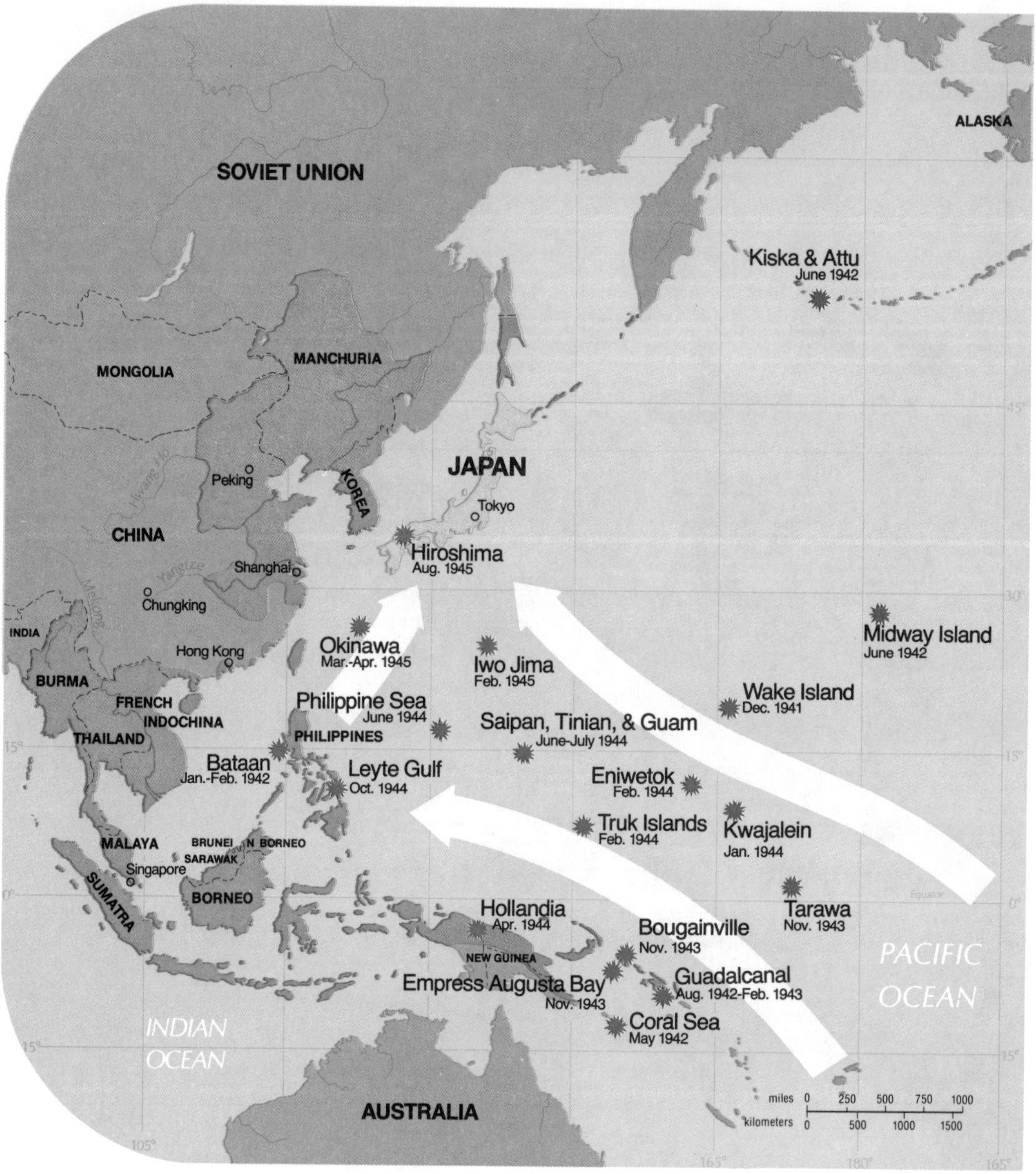

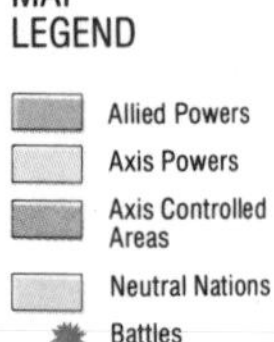

The United States entered World War II almost totally unprepared to fight on the two fronts of Europe and the Pacific. Yet its industrial capacity became a decisive factor in the Allied victory and eventually thrust America into a position of world leadership. Early in the war, however, the Axis powers seemed invincible.

By 1942, Germany had swept through most of Europe, isolated Great Britain, and launched an invasion of Russia. In North Africa, Rommel, commander of the German forces, threatened the vital Suez Canal. Russian leader Stalin desperately called for help to relieve his troops, but the Allies were not prepared to invade. Instead, in November 1942, Eisenhower, U.S. general and Allied Supreme Commander in North Africa, led an attack on Morocco and Algeria and by the next year had driven the Axis powers out of North Africa. Bolstered by American materiel, Soviet troops regained the offensive in the 1942–43 winter war and began forcing the Germans toward Berlin. The Allies landed at Normandy and southern France in June 1944. Caught between advancing Russian and Allied troops, Germany surrendered on May 7, 1945.

In the early months of the Pacific war, Japan had overrun Manchuria, Southeast Asia, Singapore, and Indonesia and had gained control of the seas. But by 1942, Allied forces had defeated the Japanese at the Coral Sea, Midway, and the Solomon Islands and in 1944 destroyed the remaining fleet at Leyte Gulf. MacArthur, commander of the U.S. forces in the Far East, liberated the Philippines in October of that year and with Nimitz, commander of the U.S. Pacific Fleet, launched an attack on Japan. Capturing one island after another, American forces were soon poised to invade the Japanese mainland. Instead, in early August 1945, the first atomic bombs were exploded over Hiroshima and Nagasaki. Japan surrendered on August 14.

The war profoundly changed the world. The United States and Russia now faced each other as rival superpowers over a divided Europe, and the power of the atom bomb haunted the world. It was hoped that the newly chartered United Nations would provide a forum for all nations to seek peaceful solutions to world problems and to begin building a lasting peace throughout the world.

Whenever opportunity has diminished in one region, Americans have moved to where jobs or land is more plentiful. Most recently, people have migrated to the West and South in search of opportunity.

Until the late 1950's, the industrial belt stretching from the Northeast to St. Louis continued to attract business and labor. Southern blacks and Appalachian whites migrated to the cities, while inner-city whites moved to the suburbs. By the late 1950's and early 1960's, many light industries were also leaving the inner city for the suburbs and the Sun Belt of the West and South. In addition, the aerospace and electronics industries drew a large work force to Florida, Texas, and California. Though the suburbs continued their growth, the inner-city areas of most northern cities began to lose population.

Changing American life-styles also contributed to the exodus to warmer climates. The ecology movement of the 1960's encouraged people to escape to less developed sections in the Southwest and Pacific states. More people looked to the Sun Belt as a place to retire.

By 1970, the search for a better life had created new communities and industrial areas in the South and West. Life-styles were changing, and there was a shift from heavy industry and manufacturing to light industry and service-oriented businesses. Cities in the industrial northern regions struggled to regain their vitality. As the shift in population continues, it remains to be seen what type of society will emerge from this latest American migration.

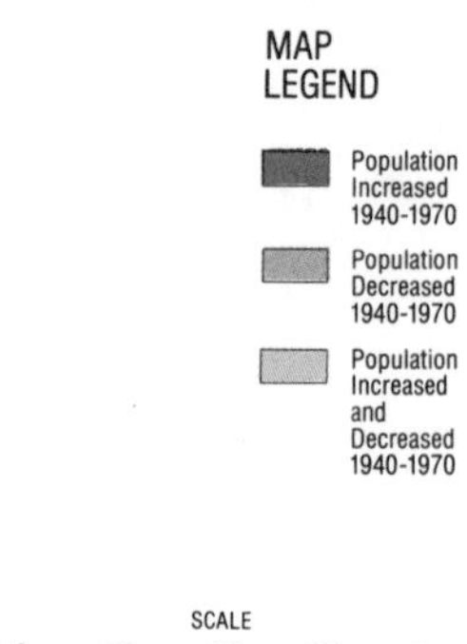

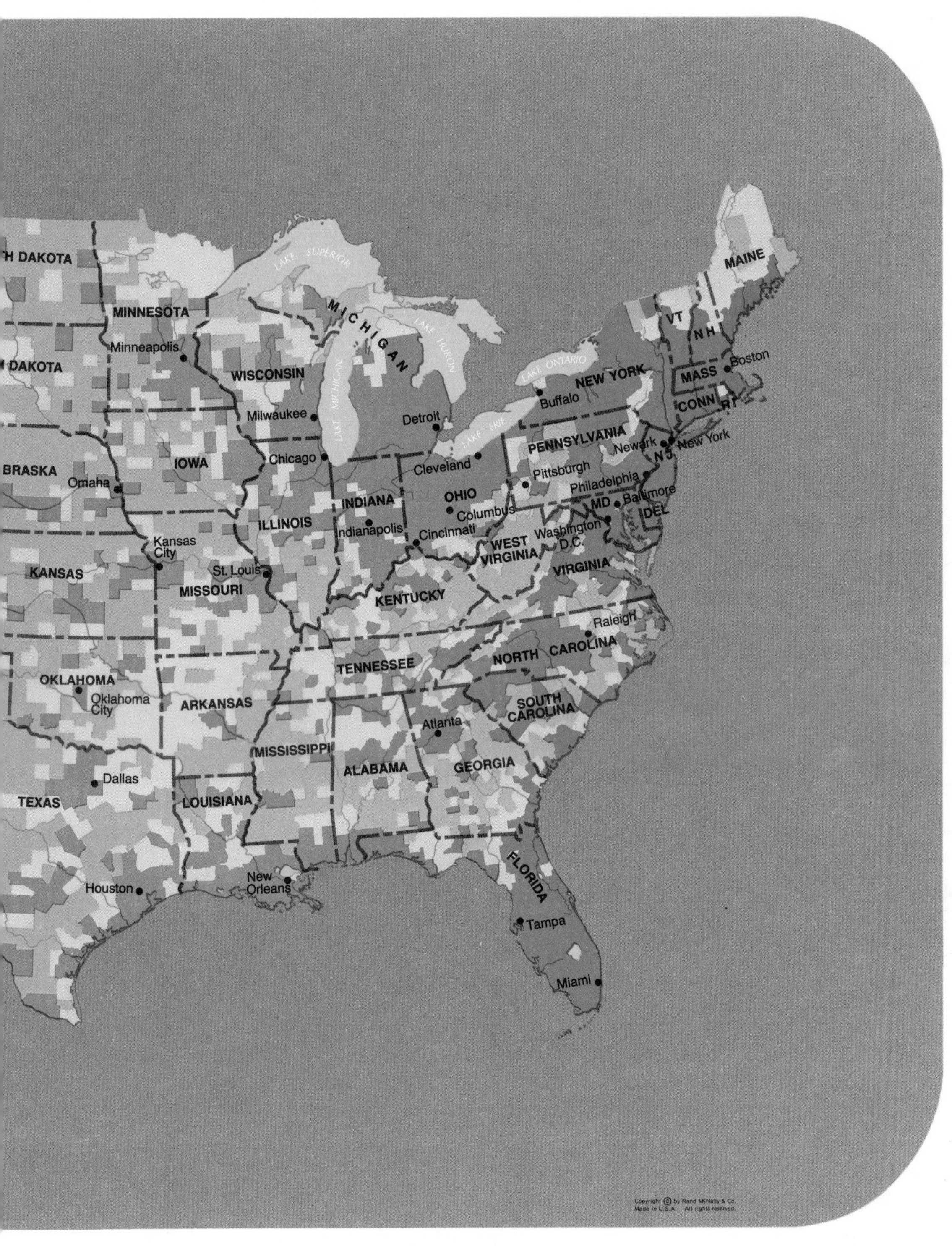
MINNESOTA
Minneapolis
WISCONSIN
Milwaukee
LAKE SUPERIOR
MICHIGAN
LAKE MICHIGAN
LAKE HURON
Detroit
LAKE ONTARIO
LAKE ERIE
MAINE
VT
NH
MASS
Boston
CONN
RI
NEW YORK
Buffalo
PENNSYLVANIA
Newark
NJ
New York
Pittsburgh
Philadelphia
MD
Baltimore
DEL
Washington D.C.
Cleveland
OHIO
Columbus
Cincinnati
INDIANA
Indianapolis
Chicago
IOWA
Omaha
ILLINOIS
Kansas City
KANSAS
St. Louis
MISSOURI
WEST VIRGINIA
VIRGINIA
KENTUCKY
Raleigh
NORTH CAROLINA
TENNESSEE
OKLAHOMA
Oklahoma City
ARKANSAS
SOUTH CAROLINA
Atlanta
MISSISSIPPI
ALABAMA
GEORGIA
Dallas
TEXAS
LOUISIANA
FLORIDA
Houston
New Orleans
Tampa
Miami

Travel Maps of the United States

Explanation of Map Symbols

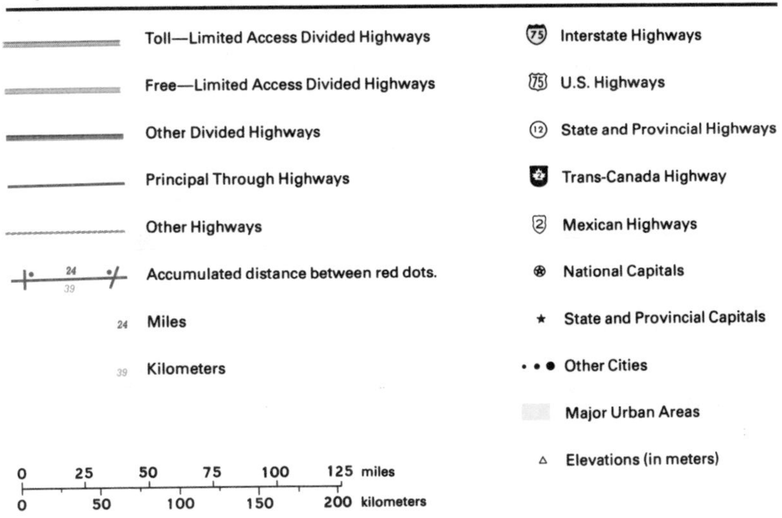

Scale 1:4,500,000 One inch equals approximately 72 miles.
One centimeter equals approximately 45 kilometers.

ALBERS CONICAL EQUAL AREA PROJECTION

Hawaii

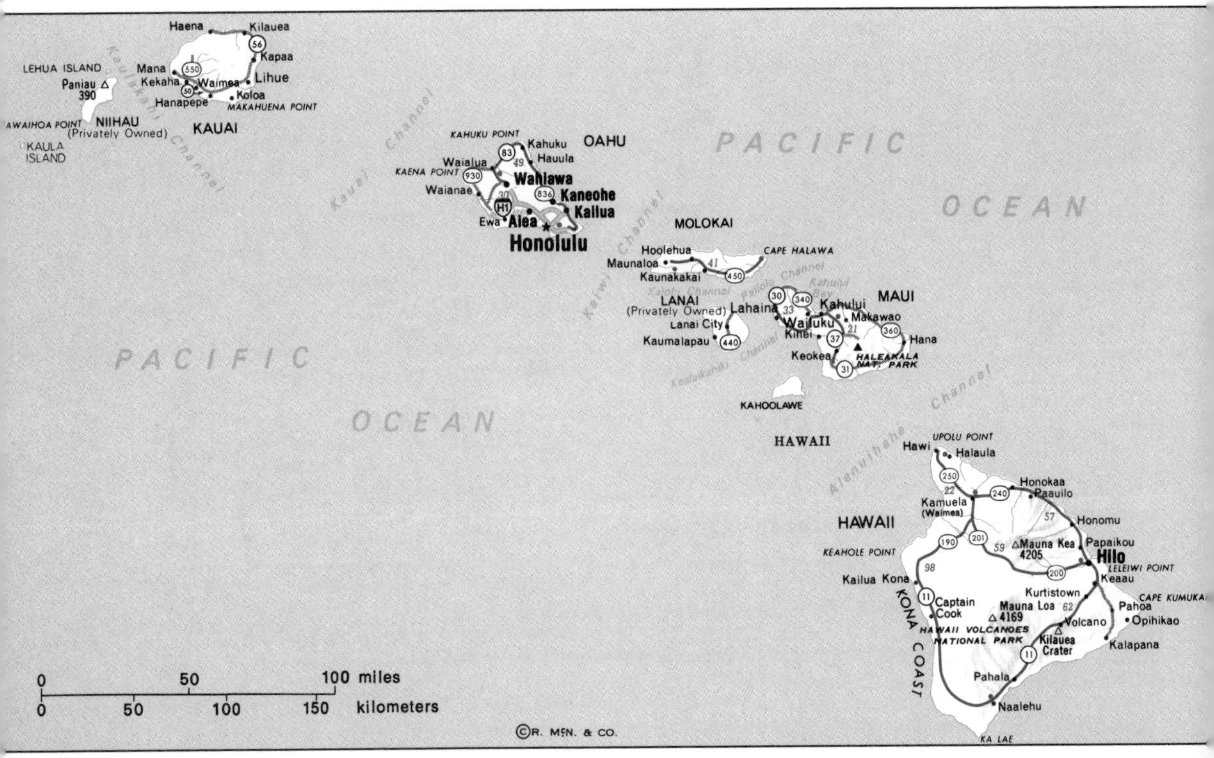

Haena
Kilauea
Kapaa
LEHUA ISLAND
Mana
Kekaha
Waimea
Lihue
Paniau 390
Hanapepe
Koloa
MAKAHUENA POINT
KAWAIHOA POINT
NIIHAU
(Privately Owned)
KAUAI
KAULA ISLAND
Kaulakahi Channel
Kauai Channel
KAHUKU POINT
Kahuku
OAHU
Hauula
Waialua
KAENA POINT
Wahiawa
Waianae
Kaneohe
Kailua
Ewa
Aiea
Honolulu
PACIFIC
OCEAN
MOLOKAI
Kaiwi Channel
Hoolehua
Maunaloa
Kaunakakai
CAPE HALAWA
Pailolo Channel
Kalohi Channel
Kahului Bay
LANAI
(Privately Owned)
Lanai City
Kaumalapau
Lahaina
Kahului
Wailuku
Kihei
Makawao
MAUI
Hana
Keokea
HALEAKALA NAT. PARK
Kealaikahiki Channel
KAHOOLAWE
Alenuihaha Channel
PACIFIC
OCEAN
HAWAII
UPOLU POINT
Hawi
Halaula
Honokaa
Paauilo
Kamuela (Waimea)
HAWAII
Honomu
Mauna Kea 4205
Papaikou
Hilo
KEAHOLE POINT
LELEIWI POINT
Keaau
Kailua Kona
Kurtistown
KONA COAST
Captain Cook
Mauna Loa 4169
CAPE KUMUKAHI
Pahoa
Opihikao
Volcano
HAWAII VOLCANOES NATIONAL PARK
Kilauea Crater
Kalapana
Pahala
Naalehu
KA LAE

0 50 100 miles
0 50 100 150 kilometers

Timmins
Foleyet
Wawa
Chapleau
Gogama
Kirkland Lake
Matachewan
Englehart
Virginiatown
Noranda
Rouyn
Malartic
Val-d'Or
Bourlamaque
Senneterre
Belcourt
New Liskeard
Haileybury
Cobalt
CAPE GARGANTUA
ONTARIO
MICHIGAN
Whitefish Point
Grand Marais
PICTURED ROCKS NATIONAL LAKESHORE
Munising
Sault Ste. Marie
Sault Ste. Marie
Raco
Newberry
Germfask
Rexton
Rudyard
Gould City
Manistique
Bruce Mines
Thessalon
Iron Bridge
Blind River
Spanish
Algoma Mills
Webbwood
Espanola
Levack
Chelmsford
Sudbury
Lively
Naughton
Coniston
Verner
Sturgeon Falls
North Bay
Témiscaming
Mattawa
QUEBEC
ONTARIO
Deep River
Chalk River
Petawawa
SEUL CHOIX POINT
Saint Ignace
Mackinac Island
Mackinaw City
Cheboygan
DRUMMOND ISLAND
COCKBURN ISLAND
MANITOULIN ISLAND
GREAT CLOCHE ISLAND
Little Current
Manitowaning
South Baymouth
Rutter
South River
Sundridge
Byng Inlet
HIGH ISLAND
HOG I.
POINT DETOUR
SUMMER ISLAND
BEAVER I.
Levering
SOUTH FOX ISLAND
NORTH MANITOU ISLAND
Petoskey
Charlevoix
Indian River
Wolverine
Onaway
Rogers City
FITZWILLIAM ISLAND
Georgian Bay
GEORGIAN BAY ISLANDS NAT. PARK
Parry Sound
PARRY ISLAND
MacTier
Huntsville
Killaloe Station
Whitney
Barrys Bay
Leland
East Jordan
Vanderbilt
Gaylord
Atlanta
Hillman
Alpena
Elk Rapids
Alba
BRUCE PENINSULA
CAPE CROKER
Bracebridge
Bancroft
Gravenhurst
Minden
Traverse City
Kalkaska
Grayling
Harrisville
CANADA
UNITED STATES
LAKE HURON
Wiarton
Midland
Orillia
Beulah
Thompsonville
Fife Lake
Roscommon
Rose City
West Branch
Oscoda
Owen Sound
Meaford
Thornbury
Southampton
Port Elgin
Collingwood
Stayner
Barrie
Lindsay
Beaverton
Lakefield
Peterborough
Marmora
Madoc
Norwood
Cadillac
Lake City
McBain
Houghton Lake
Whittemore
Tawas City
Oak Hill
Marion
Harrison
Kincardine
Hanover
Walkerton
Dundalk
Shelburne
Sutton
Custer
Baldwin
Evart
Scottville
Farwell
Clare
Sterling
Standish
POINTE AUX BARQUES
Port Austin
Caseville
Kinde
Port Hope
Mount Forest
Aurora
Cobourg
Trenton
Brighton
Big Rapids
Reed City
Barryton
Coleman
Sanford
Pinconning
Bay Port
Bad Axe
Whitby
Oshawa
Bowmanville
Port Hope
North York
Hesperia
White Cloud
Rosebush
Mount Pleasant
Midland
Essexville
Unionville
Goderich
Clinton
Seaforth
Elora
Georgetown
Brampton
Scarborough
TORONTO
Etobicoke
Mississauga
Newaygo
Howard City
Edmore
Freeland
Saginaw
Bay City
Alma
Bridgeport
Millington
Marlette
Port Sanilac
Lexington
Mitchell
Waterloo
Kitchener
Guelph
Stratford
Cambridge
Dundas
Oakville
Burlington
Hamilton
LAKE ONTARIO
Albion
Irondequoit
Webster
Rochester
Sparta
Fruitport
Marne
Rockford
Cedar Springs
Chesaning
Birch Run
Grand Bend
Tavistock
Saint Marys
Woodstock
Beachville
St. Catharines
Niagara Falls
Lockport
Niagara Falls
Tonawanda
Welland
Grand Rapids
Saint Johns
Owosso
Flint
Lapeer
Capac
Sarnia
London
Ingersoll
Brantford
Dunnville
Buffalo
Batavia
Bergen
Le Roy
Canandaigua
Ionia
Lyons
Portland
East Grand Rapids
Perry
Grand Blanc
Fenton
Port Huron
Wyoming
Mount Brydges
Dorchester
Delhi
Tillsonburg
Saint Clair
Cheektowaga
Lackawanna
Hamburg
East Aurora
Wayland
Hastings
Lansing
East Lansing
Williamston
Rochester
Pontiac
Charlotte
Birmingham
Royal Oak
Marine City
Wallaceburg
Bothwell
Dutton
West Lorne
St. Thomas
Angola
Silver Creek
Dunkirk
Fredonia
Springville
Arcade
Dansville
Otsego
Battle Creek
Olivet
Howell
Brighton
Leslie
Holt
Warren
Thamesville
Chatham
Ridgetown
LONG POINT
Kalamazoo
Portage
Marshall
Albion
Jackson
Ann Arbor
Ypsilanti
Livonia
Dearborn
DETROIT
Windsor
Tilbury
LAKE ERIE
North East
Westfield
Jamestown
Salamanca
Olean
Hornell
Wellsville
Corning
Three Rivers
Coldwater
Jonesville
Tecumseh
Adrian
Southgate
Leamington
POINTE AUX PINS
Erie
Girard
Lakewood
Frewsburg
ALLEGANY IND. RES.
NEW YORK
PENNSYLVANIA
Bradford
Smethport
Port Allegany
Sturgis
White Pigeon
Dundee
Monroe
POINT PELEE NAT. PARK
PELEE POINT
PELEE ISLAND
Ashtabula
Geneva
Corry
Warren
Elkhart
South Bend
Goshen
Kendallville
INDIANA
MICHIGAN
OHIO
Toledo
Maumee
Perrysburg
KELLEYS ISLAND
CLEVELAND
Euclid
Painesville
Mentor
Meadville
Titusville
Kane
Coudersport
Wellsboro
Auburn
Bryan
Napoleon
Bowling Green
Sandusky
Lorain
Elyria
Shaker Heights
Parma
Oil City
Franklin
Emporium
Ridgway
Renovo
Fort Wayne
Defiance
Fremont
Fostoria
Tiffin
Norwalk
Oberlin
Akron
Warren
Youngstown
Sharon
New Castle
Williamsport
Huntington
Decatur
Van Wert
Findlay
Willard
New London
Ashland
Kent
Ravenna
Stow
Clearfield
Lock Haven
Wabash
Peru
Delphos
Lima
Bucyrus
Mansfield
Wooster
Massillon
Canton
Alliance
Salem
East Liverpool
Ellwood City
Butler
Kittanning
Indiana
Punxsutawney
Bellefonte
State College
Marion
Celina
Wapakoneta
Kenton
Marion
Mount Gilead
Beaver Falls
Aliquippa
Tyrone
Altoona
Lewistown
Muncie
Saint Marys
Sidney
Bellefontaine
Delaware
Mount Vernon
Coshocton
Dover
New Philadelphia
PITTSBURGH
Steubenville
Weirton
Wilkinsburg
McKeesport
Johnstown
Huntingdon
Anderson
New Castle
Piqua
Urbana
Marysville
Newark
Cambridge
Washington
Greensburg
Carlisle
INDIANAPOLIS
Richmond
Dayton
Springfield
Columbus
Zanesville
Wheeling
Moundsville
Monessen
Uniontown
Chambersburg
Gettysburg
Kettering
Xenia
Middletown
Lancaster
Circleville
Logan
MOUND CITY GROUP NAT'L MON.
Chillicothe
Athens
Marietta
Parkersburg
Morgantown
Fairmont
Clarksburg
Cumberland
Hagerstown
Martinsburg
Hamilton
Wilmington
CINCINNATI
Covington
Newport
Portsmouth
Gallipolis
Point Pleasant
Buckhannon
Elkins
SPRUCE KNOB-SENECA ROCKS NATIONAL RECREATION AREA
Winchester
WASHINGTON
Arlington
MARYLAND
W. VIRGINIA

La Tuque
Québec
Ste.-Foy
Lauzon
Lévis
Montmagny
PARC NATIONAL DE LA MAURICIE
Grand' Mère
Shawinigan
Trois-Rivières
Plessisville
Victoriaville
Thetford Mines
Joliette
Sorel
Drummondville
Saint-Jérôme
Saint-Hyacinthe
Laval
MONTREAL
Richmond
Sherbrooke
Granby
Magog
Coaticook
Saint-Jean
Ottawa
Cornwall
Massena
Ogdensburg
Malone
Plattsburgh
Burlington
Saint Albans
Montpelier
Barre
Mount Mansfield 1339
Saranac Lake
Mount Marcy 1629
ADIRONDACK
MOUNTAINS
Watertown
Lake Placid
Glens Falls
Saratoga Springs
Rome
Utica
Syracuse
Schenectady
Troy
Albany
Amsterdam
Cortland
Oneonta
CATSKILL
MOUNTAINS
Kingston
Binghamton
Poughkeepsie
Newburgh
Middletown
Scranton
Rutland
Bennington
Brattleboro
North Adams
Pittsfield
Northampton
Holyoke
Springfield
Chicopee
Worcester
Fitchburg
Lowell
Lawrence
Haverhill
Gloucester
Salem
Lynn
Cambridge
BOSTON
Quincy
Brockton
Providence
Pawtucket
Woonsocket
Cranston
Warwick
Newport
Fall River
New Bedford
Plymouth
CAPE COD
CAPE COD NATIONAL SEASHORE
Hyannis
Falmouth
MARTHA'S VINEYARD
NANTUCKET ISLAND
BLOCK ISLAND
Hartford
New Britain
Bristol
Waterbury
Meriden
Middletown
Norwich
New London
Westerly
New Haven
Bridgeport
Danbury
Norwalk
Stamford
White Plains
Yonkers
NEW YORK
Paterson
Passaic
Newark
Jersey City
Elizabeth
Freeport
FIRE ISLAND NATIONAL SEASHORE
Montauk
Southampton
Riverhead
Allentown
Bethlehem
Easton
Reading
Trenton
Levittown
Norristown
PHILADELPHIA
Camden
Chester
Wilmington
Lancaster
Vineland
Atlantic City
Cape May
Dover
BALTIMORE
Rehoboth Beach
CAPE HENLOPEN
Asbury Park
Long Branch
Red Bank
Toms River
Lakewood
Keene
Manchester
Nashua
Concord
Claremont
Laconia
Rochester
Dover
Portsmouth
Portland
South Portland
Saco
Biddeford
Sanford
Lewiston
Auburn
Brunswick
Bath
Augusta
Waterville
Bangor
Orono
Brewer
Rockland
Camden
Belfast
ACADIA NATIONAL PARK
MATINICUS ISLAND
Ellsworth
Machias
Calais
Millinocket
Mount Katahdin 1606
Presque Isle
Caribou
Fredericton
Woodstock
Berlin
Mount Washington 1917
WHITE MTS.
GREEN MTS.
APPALACHIAN MTS.
ATLANTIC
OCEAN
©RAND McNALLY & CO

VIRGINIA
MARYLAND
NORTH CAROLINA
SOUTH CAROLINA
GEORGIA
ALABAMA
KENTUCKY
TENNESSEE
Virginia Beach
Norfolk
Chesapeake
Portsmouth
Suffolk
Newport News
Hampton
Richmond
Petersburg
Fredericksburg
Charlottesville
Lynchburg
Roanoke
Danville
Raleigh
Durham
Greensboro
Winston-Salem
Charlotte
Fayetteville
Wilmington
Columbia
Charleston
Savannah
Augusta
Macon
ATLANTA
Columbus
Montgomery
Chattanooga
Knoxville
Huntsville
Lexington
Louisville
Frankfort
Asheville
Greenville
Spartanburg
Myrtle Beach
Elizabeth City
ROANOKE ISLAND
CAPE HATTERAS
OCRACOKE ISLAND
CAPE LOOKOUT
CAPE FEAR
CAPE ROMAIN
HILTON HEAD ISLAND
FORT SUMTER NATIONAL MONUMENT

OCEAN
Jacksonville
Jacksonville Beach
St. Augustine
Daytona Beach
Ormond Beach
New Smyrna Beach
Titusville
Cape Canaveral
Merritt Island
Cocoa
Melbourne
Vero Beach
Fort Pierce
Stuart
Jupiter
West Palm Beach
Lake Worth
Delray Beach
Boca Raton
Deerfield Beach
Pompano Beach
Fort Lauderdale
Hollywood
MIAMI
Miami Beach
Coral Gables
Hialeah
Homestead
Florida City
Key Largo
KEYS
EVERGLADES NATIONAL PARK
BISCAYNE NATIONAL PARK
Naples
Fort Myers
Cape Coral
Punta Gorda
Port Charlotte
Venice
Sarasota
Bradenton
St. Petersburg
Clearwater
Tampa
Plant City
Lakeland
Winter Haven
Orlando
Kissimmee
Sanford
Winter Park
WALT DISNEY WORLD
Ocala
Gainesville
Lake City
Tallahassee
Panama City
Port Saint Joe
Apalachicola
Dothan
Thomasville
Valdosta
Waycross
Brunswick
Moultrie
Bainbridge
Marianna
Sebring
Lake Placid
Okeechobee
Clewiston
Belle Glade
Immokalee
Arcadia
GRAND BAHAMA
Freeport
West End
GREAT ABACO
LITTLE ABACO ISLAND
BIMINI ISLANDS
BERRY ISLANDS
ANDROS ISLAND
Nassau
NEW PROVIDENCE
ELEUTHERA
©RAND McNALLY & CO.

Amarillo
Bushland
Canyon
Claude
Groom
McLean
Shamrock
Sayre
Cordell
Bethany
Norman
Shawnee
Seminole
Okemah
Sallisaw
Hereford
Goodnight
Clarendon
Hedley
Memphis
Wellington
Hollis
Hobart
Gotebo
Carnegie
Anadarko
Verden
Chickasha
Purcell
Noble
Lexington
Wewoka
Calvin
Crowder
Eufaula
McAlester
Poteau
Red Oak
Wilburton
Hartshorne
Talihina
Dimmitt
Tulia
Happy
Kress
Silverton
Lakeview
Estelline
Childress
Carey
Altus
Blair
Duke
Snyder
Lawton
Fletcher
Duncan
Lindsay
Pauls Valley
Ada
Roff
Stonewall
Tupelo
Coalgate
Lehigh
Kiowa
Stringtown
Atoka
Clebit
Antlers
Wynnewood
Davis
Muleshoe
Plainview
Sudan
Amherst
Hale Center
Littlefield
Abernathy
Floydada
Kirkland
Quanah
Vernon
Frederick
Grandfield
Davidson
Randlett
Comanche
Ringling
Ardmore
Tishomingo
Madill
Caddo
Durant
Boswell
Hugo
Paducah
Crowell
Harrold
Electra
Wichita Falls
Waurika
Ryan
Terral
Marietta
OKLAHOMA
TEXAS
Lubbock
Shallowater
Levelland
Ropesville
Slaton
Southland
Rails
Dickens
Guthrie
Benjamin
Bomarton
Seymour
Henrietta
Bowie
Gainesville
Sherman
Denison
Bonham
Paris
Powderly
Detroit
Idabel
LLANO
ESTACADO
Brownfield
Tahoka
Post
Jayton
Clairemont
Swenson
Aspermont
Rule
Haskell
Munday
Throckmorton
Jacksboro
Bryson
Bridgeport
Decatur
Valley View
Sanger
Denton
McKinney
Commerce
Cooper
Sulphur Springs
Mount Pleasant
Daingerfield
Odonnell
Sagerton
Stamford
Woodson
Graham
Greenville
Winnsboro
Lone Star
Seminole
Lamesa
Gail
Snyder
Hermleigh
Sylvester
Anson
Breckenridge
Mineral Wells
Weatherford
Fort Worth
Halton City
Irving
Richardson
Garland
Mesquite
Terrell
Edgewood
Quitman
Mineola
Van
Longview
Ackerly
Colorado City
Roscoe
Sweetwater
Loraine
Westbrook
Coahoma
Big Spring
Abilene
Merkel
Clyde
Cisco
Ranger
Strawn
Eastland
Putnam
Grand Prairie
Arlington
DALLAS
Waxahachie
Alvarado
Cleburne
Kemp
Ennis
Athens
Tyler
Henderson
Kilgore
Andrews
Stanton
Midland
Odessa
Garden City
Sterling City
Blackwell
Tuscola
Lawn
Novice
Coleman
Talpa
Bangs
Brownwood
Comanche
Stephenville
Dublin
Hico
Glen Rose
Itasca
Corsicana
Richland
Frankston
Jacksonville
Neches
Mount Enterprise
Crane
Bronte
Rowena
Miles
Ballinger
Paint Rock
Carlsbad
San Angelo
Zephyr
Mullin
Goldthwaite
Hamilton
Clifton
Waco
West
Mexia
Teague
Fairfield
Palestine
Rusk
Alto
Douglass
Elkhart
Oakwood
Buffalo
Grapeland
Crockett
Lufkin
Diboll
Rankin
Texon
Big Lake
Mertzon
Barnhart
McCamey
Bakersfield
Iraan
Sheffield
Eden
Melvin
Brady
San Saba
Lometa
Gatesville
McGregor
Copperas Cove
Killeen
Belton
Temple
Troy
Marlin
Lampasas
Rogers
Calvert
Franklin
Hearne
Cameron
Austonio
EDWARDS
PLATEAU
STOCKTON
Ozona
Eldorado
Menard
Mason
Burnet
Briggs
Georgetown
Rockdale
Taylor
Thorndale
Milano
Bryan
College Station
Wellborn
Huntsville
New Waverly
Livingston
Goodrich
Shepherd
Sonora
Junction
Hutto
Manor
Austin
Johnson City
Fredericksburg
Harper
Somerville
Washington
Navasota
Willis
Conroe
Cleveland
Sanderson
Dryden
Langtry
Ingram
Kerrville
Blanco
Buda
Kyle
Bastrop
Paige
Giddings
Burton
Brenham
Hempstead
Prairie View
Porter
Smithville
Lockhart
San Marcos
New Braunfels
La Grange
Bellville
Columbus
Sealy
Wallis
HOUSTON
Bellaire
Jacinto City
Pasadena
Baytown
Channelview
Comstock
AMISTAD NAT'L RECR. AREA
BALCONES ESCARPMENT
Leakey
Castle Hills
Alamo Heights
Luling
Waelder
Flatonia
Weimar
Eagle Lake
Rosenberg
Del Rio
Ciudad Acuña
Brackettville
Sabinal
Knippa
Hondo
D'Hanis
Castroville
Lytle
Terrell Hills
San Antonio
Seguin
Gonzales
Hallettsville
Garwood
El Campo
Wharton
West Columbia
Alvin
Texas City
Galveston
Lake Jackson
Freeport
SERRANÍAS DEL BURRO
Uvalde
Devine
Sapanco
Floresville
Westhoff
Cuero
Quemado
La Pryor
Batesville
Pearsall
Leming
Poth
Pleasanton
Karnes City
Edna
Inez
Bay City
Piedras Negras
Eagle Pass
Crystal City
Dilley
Kenedy
Pettus
Goliad
Victoria
Point Comfort
Palacios
Port Lavaca
MATAGORDA PENINSULA
Nava
Río Bravo
Carrizo Springs
Asherton
Catarina
Fowlerton
Cotulla
Tilden
Three Rivers
Calliham
George West
Beeville
Refugio
Tivoli
Nueva Rosita
Sabinas
COAHUILA
TEXAS
Encinal
Mathis
Sinton
Taft
Odem
Fulton
Rockport
Aransas Pass
Freer
San Diego
Robstown
Corpus Christi
Benavides
Ben Bolt
Alice
Nuevo Laredo
Laredo
Oilton
Kingsville
Primero de Mayo
NUEVO LEON
Hebbronville
Premont
Riviera
PADRE ISLAND NATIONAL SEASHORE
San Buenaventura
Villa Frontera
Monclova
San Ygnacio
Zapata
Falfurrias
Sarita
Encino
Armstrong
La Palmita
PADRE ISLAND
Sabinas Hidalgo
Ciudad Mier
Los Guerras
Rio Grande City
Edinburg
Raymondville
Mission
Sebastian
Harlingen
McAllen
Pharr
Weslaco
San Benito
Cerralvo
Reynosa
Mercedes
Port Isabel
Hidalgo
Salinas Victoria
Brownsville
San Nicolás de los Garzas
Matamoros
Monterrey
Guadalupe
General Bravo

GULF OF MEXICO

SOUTH DAKOTA
NEBRASKA
WYOMING
COLORADO
KANSAS
OKLAHOMA
TEXAS
NEW MEXICO
IOWA
MISSOURI
AGATE FOSSIL BEDS NATIONAL MONUMENT
SCOTTS BLUFF NAT'L MON.
SAND HILLS
BLUE HILLS UPLAND
SANTEE INDIAN RESERVATION
WINNEBAGO INDIAN RESERVATION
OMAHA INDIAN RESERVATION
POTAWATOMIE INDIAN RESERVATION
OSAGE INDIAN RESERVATION
ROSEBUD INDIAN RESERVATION
YANKTON IND. RES.
LAKE MEREDITH NAT'L RECR. AREA
Oglala
Pine Ridge
Martin
Mission
Colome
Gregory
Burke
Lake Andes
Armour
Freeman
Olivet
Tripp
Canton
Rock Valley
Orange City
Hull
Hartley
Spencer
Chadron
Gordon
Merriman
Cody
Valentine
Springview
Bonesteel
Fairfax
Pickstown
Wagner
Avon
Tyndall
Tabor
Yankton
Vermillion
Springfield
Harrison
Crawford
Hay Springs
Wood Lake
Ainsworth
Bassett
Stuart
Atkinson
O'Neill
Niobrara
Verdigre
Lynch
Spencer
Wynot
Jefferson
Le Mars
Elk Point
Sioux City
South Sioux City
Cherokee
Hemingford
Alliance
Mullen
Hyannis
Thedford
Orchard
Ewing
Osmond
Plainview
Laurel
Randolph
Homer
Winnebago
Onawa
Scottsbluff
Morrill
Bridgeport
Broadwater
Arthur
Brewster
Dunning
Taylor
Burwell
Ericson
Anselmo
Sargent
Clearwater
Neligh
Oakdale
Tilden
Norfolk
Battle Creek
Pilger
Wisner
Bartlett
Madison
Beemer
Lyons
Oakland
Kimball
Dix
Potter
Sidney
Lodgepole
Chappell
Oshkosh
Lewellen
Ogallala
Brule
Paxton
Sutherland
Hershey
North Platte
Stapleton
Broken Bow
Ansley
Ashton
Greeley
Cedar Rapids
Albion
Humphrey
Scribner
Hooper
Blair
Platte Center
Columbus
Schuyler
North Bend
Kennard
Fremont
Arlington
Omaha
Council Bluffs
Bellevue
Missouri Valley
Julesburg
Big Springs
Sedgwick
Crook
Iliff
Sterling
Fleming
Haxtun
Holyoke
Grant
Wallace
Maxwell
Brady
Gothenburg
Cozad
Lexington
Litchfield
Ravenna
Grand Island
Cairo
Saint Paul
Central City
Silver Creek
Clarks
Osceola
Stromsburg
Shelby
Brainard
Wahoo
Weston
Ashland
Greenwood
Waverly
Plattsmouth
Aurora
Hampton
York
Seward
Utica
Lincoln
Brush
Fort Morgan
Akron
Otis
Yuma
Imperial
Wauneta
Palisade
Maywood
Eustis
Elwood
Kearney
Elm Creek
Gibbon
Axtell
Minden
Juniata
Harvard
Hastings
Sutton
Fairmont
Geneva
Bradshaw
Milford
Dorchester
Cortland
Nebraska City
Sidney
Hamburg
Stratton
Benkelman
Haigler
Trenton
Culbertson
McCook
Cambridge
Indianola
Arapahoe
Holbrook
Oxford
Holdrege
Beaver City
Danbury
Franklin
Riverton
Red Cloud
Superior
Deshler
Hebron
Chester
Fairbury
Beatrice
Tecumseh
Johnson
Auburn
Blue Springs
Pawnee City
Falls City
Rock Port
Tarkio
Craig
Bird City
Saint Francis
Atwood
Herndon
McDonald
Oberlin
Norton
Almena
Smith Center
Lebanon
Mankato
Jewell
Belleville
Hanover
Marysville
Seneca
Sabetha
Hiawatha
Cope
Phillipsburg
Washington
Waterville
Blue Rapids
Concordia
Arriba
Flagler
Seibert
Burlington
Kanorado
Brewster
Colby
Rexford
Selden
Jennings
Stockton
Alton
Osborne
Beloit
Clay Center
Horton
Stratton
Goodland
Hill City
Morland
Plainville
Riley
Wamego
Leavenworth
Hugo
Oakley
Grainfield
Quinter
Winona
Weskan
Sharon Springs
Cheyenne Wells
Kit Carson
Wakeeney
Ellis
Hays
Victoria
Russell
Lincoln
Bennington
Junction City
Manhattan
Topeka
Lawrence
Perry
Abilene
Solomon
Salina
Dorrance
Ellsworth
Kanopolis
Lindsborg
Tribune
Scott City
Ness City
Rush Center
Hoisington
Great Bend
Holyrood
Chase
Ellinwood
McPherson
Lyons
Canton
Herington
Council Grove
Strong City
Emporia
Osage City
Ottawa
Wellsville
Garnett
Hartford
Burlington
Lamar
Hasty
Las Animas
La Junta
Granada
Holly
Syracuse
Deerfield
Lakin
Garden City
Burdett
Jetmore
Larned
Garfield
Nickerson
Hesston
Hutchinson
Newton
Peabody
Florence
Kinsley
Spearville
Macksville
Stafford
Sylvia
Cimarron
Dodge City
Wichita
El Dorado
Augusta
Eureka
Yates Center
Iola
Chanute
Springfield
Pritchett
Kim
Walsh
Johnson
Ulysses
Satanta
Sublette
Montezuma
Mullinville
Bucklin
Haviland
Greensburg
Pratt
Kingman
Rolling Hills
Mulvane
Toronto
Altoona
Neodesha
Fowler
Minneola
Meade
Plains
Coldwater
Protection
Medicine Lodge
Ashland
Attica
Harper
Anthony
Wellington
Belle Plaine
Winfield
Moline
Grenola
Cedar Vale
Independence
Coffeyville
Parsons
Campo
Hugoton
Rolla
Elkhart
Liberal
Boise City
Keyes
Tyrone
Hooker
Forgan
Gate
Buffalo
Alva
Hardtner
Kiowa
Arkansas City
Newkirk
Braman
Cherokee
Lamont
Ponca City
Bartlesville
Nowata
Guymon
Goodwell
Clayton
Texline
Stratford
Texhoma
Perryton
Fort Supply
Woodward
Waynoka
Pondcreek
Enid
Perry
Pawnee
Hominy
Cleveland
Chelsea
Dalhart
Waka
Spearman
Higgins
Arnett
Vici
Seiling
Chester
Fairview
Meno
Hennessey
Stillwater
Tulsa
Sapulpa
Owasso
Catoosa
Hartley
Dumas
Canadian
Glazier
Canton
Watonga
Dover
Guthrie
Perkins
Kellyville
Haskell
Wagoner
Channing
Stinnett
Borger
Miami
Kingfisher
Okarche
Luther
Chandler
Depew
Nara Visa
Masterson
Boys Ranch
Pampa
Cheyenne
Hammon
Thomas
Geary
The Village
Okmulgee
Muskogee
Logan
White Deer
Panhandle
Wheeler
Elk City
Clinton
Weatherford
El Reno
Oklahoma City
Midwest City
Bethany
Henryetta
Checotah
Adrian
Vega
Amarillo
Bushland
Groom
McLean
Shamrock
Sayre
Cordell
Minco
Norman
Shawnee
Seminole
Okemah
Eufaula
Claude
Goodnight
Canyon
Hereford
Clarendon
Hedley
Wellington
Hobart
Gotebo
Carnegie
Anadarko
Verden
Chickasha
Noble
Lexington
Wewoka
Purcell
Calvin
Crowder
McAlester
Happy
Friona
Bovina
Dimmitt
Tulia
Memphis
Hollis
Blair
Lone Wolf
Fletcher
Lindsay
Pauls Valley
Ada
Stonewall
Hartshorne
Farwell
Muleshoe
Lakeview
Estelline
Duke
Altus
Snyder
Lawton
Duncan
Wynnewood
Davis
Roff
Tupelo
Coalgate
Lehigh
Kiowa
Stringtown
Atoka
Kress
Silverton
Plainview
Childress
Kirkland
Quanah
Vernon
Frederick
Grandfield
Davidson
Randlett
Comanche
Ringling
Tishomingo
Antlers
Sudan
Amherst
Littlefield
Hale Center
Floydada
Paducah
Crowell
Harrold
Electra
Wichita Falls
Waurika
Ryan
Ardmore
Madill
Caddo
Durant
Boswell
Hugo
Abernathy
Cone
Levelland
Shallowater
Burkburnett
Terral
Henrietta
Marietta
Denison
Powderly
H.E. BAILEY TPK.
CIMARRON TPK.
TURNER TPK.
MUSKOGEE TPK.
INDIAN NATION TPK.
WILL ROGERS
KANSAS TURNPIKE
RAND McNALLY & CO.

MILWAUKEE
Madison
Janesville
Beloit
WISCONSIN
ILLINOIS
Rockford
Waukegan
Evanston
CHICAGO
Gary
Hammond
Joliet
Aurora
Elgin
Dubuque
Waterloo
Cedar Falls
Cedar Rapids
Iowa City
Davenport
Rock Island
Moline
Des Moines
Ottumwa
Burlington
Keokuk
IOWA
Galesburg
Peoria
Bloomington
Champaign
Urbana
Danville
Decatur
Springfield
Quincy
Hannibal
South Bend
Fort Wayne
INDIANA
MICHIGAN
Kalamazoo
Lafayette
Kokomo
Muncie
Anderson
INDIANAPOLIS
Terre Haute
Bloomington
Evansville
Louisville
ST. LOUIS
East St. Louis
Belleville
Columbia
Jefferson City
Sedalia
Rolla
Cape Girardeau
Carbondale
Paducah
Cairo
Owensboro
Bowling Green
Hopkinsville
Clarksville
Nashville
Murfreesboro
Jackson
Memphis
TENNESSEE
MISSISSIPPI
ALABAMA
MISSOURI
ARKANSAS
Springfield
OZARK PLATEAU
SALEM UPLAND
OZARK ESCARPMENT
CROWLEYS RIDGE
BOSTON MOUNTAINS
Jonesboro
Blytheville
Little Rock
North Little Rock
Pine Bluff
Hot Springs National Park
Fort Smith
Tupelo
Huntsville
Decatur
Florence
Birmingham
Clarksdale
Greenwood
Cleveland

Regina
Weyburn
Estevan
Assiniboia
Brandon
Portage-la-Prairie
Minnedosa
Virden
MANITOBA
NORTH DAKOTA
CANADA
UNITED STATES
TURTLE MOUNTAIN INDIAN RESERVATION
FORT PECK INDIAN RESERVATION
WILLISTON
Williston
Minot
Bottineau
Rugby
Devils Lake
Grafton
SOURIS PLAIN
FORT BERTHOLD INDIAN RESERVATION
FORT TOTTEN INDIAN RESERVATION
THEODORE ROOSEVELT NAT'L PARK
COTEAU DU MISSOURI
BASIN
BAD LANDS
Glendive
Miles City
Dickinson
Mandan
Bismarck
Jamestown
Valley City
Fargo
MONTANA
NORTH DAKOTA
SOUTH DAKOTA
STANDING ROCK INDIAN RESERVATION
CHEYENNE RIVER INDIAN RESERVATION
Lemmon
Mobridge
Aberdeen
Watertown
Huron
Pierre
Fort Pierre
CROW CREEK INDIAN RESERVATION
Belle Fourche
Spearfish
Sturgis
Lead
DEVILS TOWER NAT'L MON.
Gillette
BLACK HILLS
Rapid City
Harney Peak
MOUNT RUSHMORE NAT'L MEM.
Custer
Hot Springs
WIND CAVE NAT'L PARK
BADLANDS NAT'L PARK
BADLANDS
PINE RIDGE INDIAN RESERVATION
ROSEBUD INDIAN RESERVATION
YANKTON IND. RES.
Chamberlain
Mitchell
Sioux Falls
Yankton
Winner
WYOMING
NEBRASKA
SOUTH DAKOTA
Chadron
Valentine
AGATE FOSSIL BEDS NATIONAL MONUMENT
SANTEE INDIAN RESERVATION
WINNEBAGO RES.
LARAMIE MOUNTAINS
Douglas
Torrington
Scottsbluff
SCOTTS BLUFF NAT'L MON.
SAND HILLS
Alliance
O'Neill
Norfolk
Columbus
Laramie
Cheyenne
Sidney
Ogallala
North Platte
Grand Island
Kearney
COLORADO
Fort Collins
©RAND McNALLY & CO.

CANADA
UNITED STATES
ONTARIO
MINNESOTA
WISCONSIN
MICHIGAN
IOWA
ILLINOIS
LAKE SUPERIOR
LAKE MICHIGAN
ISLE ROYALE
ISLE ROYALE NATIONAL PARK
VOYAGEURS NAT'L PARK
GRAND PORTAGE NAT'L MON.
APOSTLE ISLANDS NATIONAL LAKESHORE
EFFIGY MOUNDS NAT'L MON.
KEWEENAW PENINSULA
MESABI RANGE
SUPERIOR UPLAND
HURON MOUNTAINS
DOOR PENINSULA
RED LAKE INDIAN RESERVATION
NETT LAKE INDIAN RESERVATION
LEECH LAKE INDIAN RESERVATION
FOND DU LAC INDIAN RESERVATION
BAD RIVER INDIAN RESERVATION
LAC DU FLAMBEAU INDIAN RES.
LAC COURTE OREILLES INDIAN RES.
L'ANSE INDIAN RESERVATION
STOCKBRIDGE MUNSEE INDIAN RESERVATION
Kenora
Dryden
Sioux Lookout
Thunder Bay
Nipigon
Marathon
International Falls
Fort Frances
Bemidji
Hibbings
Virginia
Ely
Duluth
Superior
Two Harbors
Grand Marais
Brainerd
St. Cloud
MINNEAPOLIS
St. Paul
Bloomington
Mankato
Rochester
Winona
Austin
Albert Lea
Worthington
Marquette
Escanaba
Iron Mountain
Houghton
Hancock
Ashland
Ironwood
Eau Claire
Wausau
La Crosse
Green Bay
Appleton
Oshkosh
Fond du Lac
Sheboygan
Manitowoc
Madison
MILWAUKEE
Racine
Kenosha
Janesville
Beloit
Rockford
Waukegan
CHICAGO
Joliet
Aurora
Elgin
Dubuque
Waterloo
Cedar Rapids
Iowa City
Davenport
Rock Island
Moline
Des Moines
Ames
Fort Dodge
Council Bluffs
Ottumwa
Burlington
Fort Madison
Galesburg
Peoria
Bloomington
Kankakee

ROCKY MOUNTAINS
COLORADO PLATEAU
WYOMING BASIN
LARAMIE MOUNTAINS
WYOMING RANGES
WASATCH RANGE
UINTA MOUNTAINS
FRONT RANGE
SANGRE DE CRISTO MTS.
SAN JUAN MOUNTAINS
SAN LUIS VALLEY
BOOK CLIFFS
ROAN PLATEAU
YAMPA PLATEAU
SAND HILLS
GREAT SALT LAKE DESERT
PLAIN
IDAHO
UTAH
WYOMING
COLORADO
NEBRASKA
KANSAS
NEW MEXICO
ARIZONA
OKLAHOMA
DENVER
Colorado Springs
Pueblo
Boulder
Fort Collins
Greeley
Cheyenne
Laramie
Casper
Rock Springs
Rawlins
Salt Lake City
Ogden
Provo
Orem
Logan
Grand Junction
Durango
Farmington
Trinidad
Scottsbluff
Pocatello
Sterling
Lakewood
Aurora
Longmont
Glenwood Springs
Leadville
Moab
Green River
Pikes Peak 4300
Mount Elbert 4399
Kings Peak 4123
Blanca Peak 4378
Uncompahgre Peak 4361
ROCKY MOUNTAIN NAT'L PARK
ARCHES NAT'L PARK
CANYONLANDS NATIONAL PARK
CAPITOL REEF NATIONAL PARK
BRYCE CANYON NAT'L PARK
ZION NAT'L PARK
MESA VERDE NAT'L PARK
GREAT SAND DUNES NAT'L MON.
BLACK CANYON OF THE GUNNISON NAT'L MON.
DINOSAUR NAT'L MON.
COLORADO NAT'L MON.
FLAMING GORGE NATIONAL RECREATION AREA
GLEN CANYON NATIONAL RECREATION AREA
UINTAH AND OURAY INDIAN RESERVATION
SOUTHERN UTE INDIAN RESERVATION
UTE MOUNTAIN INDIAN RESERVATION
NAVAJO INDIAN RESERVATION

Conversion of Meters to Feet
1 Meter = 3.28 Feet
Meters 6000 4000 3000 2000 1000 500 200 0
Feet 19685 13124 9843 6562 3281 1640 656 0
NEW MEXICO
ARIZONA
TEXAS
UNITED STATES
MEXICO
CHIHUAHUA
SONORA
SIERRA MADRE OCCID
LLANO ESTACADO
PECOS PLAINS
DIABLO PLATEAU
MOGOLLON RIM
NAVAJO INDIAN RESERVATION
SAN CARLOS INDIAN RESERVATION
FORT APACHE INDIAN RESERVATION
PAPAGO INDIAN RESERVATION
MESCALERO INDIAN RESERVATION
WHITE SANDS NATIONAL MONUMENT
CARLSBAD CAVERNS NAT'L PARK
GUADALUPE MOUNTAINS NATIONAL PARK
BIG BEND NAT'L PARK
PETRIFIED FOREST NAT'L PARK
GILA CLIFF DWELLINGS NAT'L MON.
CHIRICAHUA NAT'L MON.
ORGAN PIPE CACTUS NATIONAL MONUMENT
SAN ANDRES MTS.
TULAROSA VALLEY
JORNADO DEL MUERTO
BLACK RANGE
Santa Fe
Albuquerque
Amarillo
Las Vegas
Roswell
Alamogordo
Las Cruces
El Paso
Ciudad Juárez
Carlsbad
Hobbs
Clovis
Tucumcari
Gallup
Flagstaff
Phoenix
Tucson
Prescott
Nogales
Douglas
Agua Prieta
Cananea
Ojinaga
Pecos
©RAND McNALLY & CO.

Lincoln City
Dallas
Salem
Woodburn
Maupin
WARM SPRINGS INDIAN RESERVATION
DESCHUTES-UMATILLA PLATEAU
Ukiah
La Grande
Enterprise
Riggins
SALMON RIVER MOUNTAINS
Salmon
Baker
BEAVERHEAD MOUNTAINS
RANGE
LEMHI RANGE
Leadore
Newport
Toledo
Albany
Corvallis
Jefferson
Mill City
Detroit
Warm Springs
Mount Jefferson 3199
Madras
OCHOCO MTS.
Mitchell
Spray
Long Creek
BLUE MOU
Rock Creek Butte 2775
Baker
North Powder
Sacajawea Peak 2997
New Meadows
McCall
Diamond Peak 3718
Challis
Waldport
Lebanon
Monroe
Halsey
Sweet Home
Junction City
Santiam Pass 1468
JOHN DAY FOSSIL BEDS NATIONAL MONUMENT
John Day
Prairie City
Midvale
Huntington
Weiser
Payette
Clayton
Diamond Peak 3718
Borah Peak 3859
LOST RIVER RANGE
McKenzie Bridge
Sisters
Three Sisters 3074
Redmond
Prineville
Strawberry Mountain 2755
Seneca
Florence
Eugene
Springfield
Creswell
Lowell
Bend
Cottage Grove
Reedsport
Gardiner
OREGON DUNES NATIONAL RECREATION AREA
North Bend
Coos Bay
Oakridge
La Pine
Crescent
Chemult
GREAT SANDY DESERT
HARNEY BASIN
Burns
Crane
Vale
Ontario
Nyssa
Caldwell
Nampa
Marsing
Boise
Lowman
Idaho City
SAWTOOTH NATIONAL RECREATION AREA
Ketchum
Hailey
Sun Valley
Moore
Arco
Butte City
Atomic City
CRATERS OF THE MOON NAT'L MON.
Oakland
Roseburg
Bandon
Langlois
Myrtle Creek
Riddle
Canyonville
Port Orford
Mount Thielsen 2799
Mount Scott 2721
CRATER LAKE NAT'L PARK
Fort Klamath
Chiloquin
Gold Beach
Grants Pass
Rogue River
Medford
Ashland
OREGON CAVES NAT'L MON.
Kerby
O'Brien
Brookings
Smith River
Crescent City
Klamath Falls
Altamont
Bly
Paisley
Drake Peak 2562
Lakeview
Adel
New Pine Creek
Mount Bidwell 2527
COLUMBIA PLATEAU
SNAKE RIVER PLAIN
Jordan Valley
Mountain Home
King Hill
Glenns Ferry
Bruneau
Shoshone
Gooding
Wendell
Jerome
Richfield
Buhl
Twin Falls
Hazelton
Rupert
Burley
American Falls
Pocatello
OREGON
CALIFORNIA
OREGON
NEVADA
IDAHO
NEVADA
IDAHO
UTAH
IDAHO
OREGON
Merrill
Tulelake
LAVA BEDS NAT'L MON.
KLAMATH MOUNTAINS
Happy Camp
Yreka
Klamath
REDWOOD NAT'L PARK
Orick
Orleans
HOOPA VALLEY INDIAN RESERVATION
Hoopa
McKinleyville
Arcata
Eureka
Salyer
Weed
Mount Shasta 4317
Mount Shasta
Dunsmuir
Alturas
Canby
Cedarville
WARNER MOUNTAINS
Eagle Peak 3015
McDermitt
Duffer Peak 2864
BLACK ROCK DESERT
Granite Peak 2966
DUCK VALLEY INDIAN RESERVATION
Owyhee
Mountain City
Matterhorn 3304
GREAT SALT LAKE DESERT
Adin
Bieber
Fall River Mills
Burney
Lewiston
Fortuna
Rio Dell
CAPE MENDOCINO
Project City
Shasta
Redding
Anderson
Lassen Peak 3187
LASSEN VOLCANIC NAT'L PARK
Susanville
Granite Peak 2760
GREAT BASIN
Winnemucca
Golconda
Battle Mountain
Carlin
Elko
Wells
Montello
Wendover
Deseret Peak 3362
SKULL VALLEY INDIAN RESERVATION
Miranda
Garberville
Leggett
Laytonville
Fort Bragg
Willits
Mendocino
SACRAMENTO VALLEY
Red Bluff
Gerber
Corning
Orland
Chico
Paradise
Willows
Princeton
Oroville
Chester
Westwood
Greenville
Quincy
Portola
PYRAMID LAKE INDIAN RESERVATION
Imlay
Mount Tobin 2979
Lovelock
Beowawe
Ruby Dome 3471
RUBY MOUNTAINS
Spruce Mountain 3128
Nixon
Sparks
Reno
Fernley
Fallon
Truckee
Tahoe City
Meeks Bay
South Lake Tahoe
Carson City
Gardnerville
WALKER RIVER INDIAN RESERVATION
Austin
SHOSHONE MOUNTAINS
TOIYABE RANGE
VALLEY
Eureka
Mount Hamilton 3275
Currant Mountain 3509
Mount Jefferson 3642
EGAN RANGE
McGill
Ely
LEHMAN CAVES NAT'L MON.
Wheeler Peak 3982
GOSHUTE INDIAN RESERVATION
Hinkley
Ukiah
Redwood Valley
Maxwell
Talmage
Lucerne
Lakeport
Arbuckle
Yuba City
Marysville
Point Arena
Cloverdale
Healdsburg
Woodland
Auburn
Folsom
Placerville
Carmichael
Santa Rosa
COAST RANGES
CASCADE RANGE
SIERRA
CALIFORNIA
NEVADA
NEVADA
UTAH

PACIFIC OCEAN
NEVADA
CALIFORNIA
ARIZONA
SONORA
BAJA CALIFORNIA NORTE
MEXICO
U.S.
COAST RANGES
SIERRA NEVADA
SAN JOAQUIN VALLEY
DIABLO RANGE
SANTA LUCIA RANGE
TEMBLOR RANGE
SAN RAFAEL MOUNTAINS
SAN GABRIEL MOUNTAINS
SAN BERNARDINO MTS
MOJAVE DESERT
SONORA DESERT
DEATH VALLEY
AMARGOSA RANGE
DEATH VALLEY NATIONAL MONUMENT
JOSHUA TREE NAT'L MON.
IMPERIAL VALLEY
CHOCOLATE MTS
DESIERTO DE ALTAR
SIERRA DE JUÁREZ
CHANNEL ISLANDS
SANTA CRUZ ISLAND
SANTA ROSA ISLAND
SAN MIGUEL ISLAND
SANTA CATALINA ISLAND
SAN CLEMENTE ISLAND
SAN NICOLAS ISLAND
LAKE MEAD NATIONAL RECREATIONAL AREA
GRAND CANYON
COCONINO PLATEAU
HUALAPAI INDIAN RESERVATION
FORT MOHAVE INDIAN RESERVATION
COLORADO RIVER INDIAN RESERVATION
FORT YUMA INDIAN RESERVATION
TULE RIVER INDIAN RESERVATION
KINGS CANYON NATIONAL PARK
SEQUOIA NATIONAL PARK
DEVILS POSTPILE NAT'L MON.
PINNACLES NAT'L MON.
Las Vegas
North Las Vegas
Henderson
Boulder City
Kingman
Needles
Lake Havasu City
Parker
Blythe
Yuma
San Luis Rio Colorado
Mexicali
Calexico
El Centro
Brawley
Indio
Palm Springs
San Bernardino
Riverside
LOS ANGELES
Pasadena
Long Beach
Santa Ana
Anaheim
San Clemente
Oceanside
Escondido
SAN DIEGO
Tijuana
Ensenada
Barstow
Victorville
Lancaster
Palmdale
Mojave
Bakersfield
Visalia
Fresno
Madera
Merced
Modesto
Los Banos
Salinas
Monterey
San Jose
Santa Cruz
San Luis Obispo
Santa Maria
Lompoc
Santa Barbara
Ventura
Oxnard
Bishop
Mount Whitney 4418
Telescope Peak 3368
Charleston Peak 3633
Mount Trumbull 2447
Castle Dome Peak 1155
©RAND McNALLY & CO.

COAST MOUNTAINS
PACIFIC RANGES
Mount Waddington 3994
Mount Tatlow 3066
Good Hope Mountain 3235
Monmouth Mountain 3194
Mount Gilbert 3109
Gold Bridge
Seton Portage
D' Arcy
Pemberton
Lillooet
Cache Creek
Clinton
Forest Grove
Blue River
Clearwater
Avola
Little Fort
Chinook Cove
McLure
Ashcroft
Kamloops
Chase
Monte Creek
Sicamous
Canoe
Salmon Arm
Enderby
Armstrong
Vernon
Kelowna
Okanagan Centre
Peachland
Summerland
Penticton
Okanagan Falls
Hedley
Princeton
Merritt
Nicola
Spences Bridge
Lytton
Skihist Mountain 2944
North Bend
Spuzzum
Hope
Agassiz
Chilliwack
Garibaldi
Mount Garibaldi 2678
Brackendale
Squamish
Mount Breakenridge 2402
MONASHEE MOUNTAINS
SELKIRK MOUNTAINS
Mount Columbia 3747
Mount Forbes
Mount Freshfield 3340
Mount Sir Sandford 3522
GLACIER NATIONAL PARK
MOUNT REVELSTOKE NATIONAL PARK
YOHO NATIONAL PARK
Golden
Mount Dawson 3390
Revelstoke
Beaton
Radium Hot Springs
PURCELL MTS.
ROCKY
Nakusp
Burton
Fauquier
Slocan
Silverton
Riondel
Nelson
Ymir
Castlegar
Kinnaird
Rossland
Trail
Sirdar
Wynndel
Creston
Kelsey Bay
Rock Bay
Brem River
QUADRA ISLAND
REDONDA ISLANDS
Bloedel
Campbell River
Powell River
Stillwater
Courtenay
Irvines Landing
Fanny Bay
Sechelt
VANCOUVER ISLAND RANGES
Tofino
Port Alberni
Kildonan
PACIFIC RIM NATIONAL PARK
Bamfield
Nanaimo
North Vancouver
VANCOUVER
Port Coquitlam
New Westminster
Ladysmith
White Rock
Honeymoon Bay
Duncan
Port Renfrew
Sidney
Esquimalt
Victoria
BRITISH COLUMBIA
WASHINGTON
IDAHO
OREGON
Osoyoos
Grand Forks
Cascade
Oroville
Orient
Tonasket
Ferndale
Bellingham
SAN JUAN ISLANDS
CAPE FLATTERY
MAKAH INDIAN RESERVATION
Neah Bay
Oak Harbor
Port Angeles
Sequim
Port Townsend
Forks
Mount Olympus 2428
OLYMPIC NATIONAL PARK
Quilcene
QUINAULT INDIAN RESERVATION
Burlington
Mount Vernon
Concrete
Newhalem
ROSS LAKE NAT'L RECR. AREA
NORTH CASCADES NAT'L PARK
LAKE CHELAN NAT'L RECR. AREA
Twisp
Omak
Okanogan
COLVILLE INDIAN RESERVATION
COULEE DAM NAT'L RECR. AREA
Brewster
Bridgeport
Chelan
Grand Coulee
Kettle Falls
Colville
Chewelah
Marysville
Everett
Edmonds
Poulsbo
Sultan
SEATTLE
Bremerton
Bellevue
Renton
Kent
Auburn
Tacoma
Puyallup
Enumclaw
Olympia
Tumwater
Hoquiam
Aberdeen
Parkland
Mount Rainier 4392
MOUNT RAINIER NATIONAL PARK
CASCADE RANGE
Leavenworth
Cashmere
Wenatchee
Cle Elum
Ellensburg
Kittitas
Quincy
Waterville
Almira
Wilbur
Coulee City
Davenport
Reardan
Spokane
SPOKANE INDIAN RESERVATION
Deer Park
Mount Spokane 1792
Coeur d'Alene
Opportunity
Kellogg
COEUR D'ALENE INDIAN RES.
Plummer
Saint Maries
Bonners Ferry
Naples
Cusick
Usk
Sandpoint
Newport
Priest River
Clark Fork
Odessa
Ritzville
Moses Lake
Sprague
Othello
Washtucna
Connell
Lacrosse
Colfax
Pullman
Moscow
Potlatch
Bovill
Raymond
South Bend
Centralia
Chehalis
Morton
Yakima
CAPE DISAPPOINTMENT
Astoria
Longview
Kelso
Castle Rock
Seaside
Clatskanie
Kalama
Cannon Beach
Saint Helens
Wapato
Toppenish
Granger
Sunnyside
YAKIMA INDIAN RESERVATION
Grandview
Prosser
Richland
Pasco
Kennewick
Walla Walla
Dayton
Lewiston
Craigmont
NEZ PERCE INDIAN RESERVATION
Kooskia
Garibaldi
Tillamook
Minnehaha
Vancouver
PORTLAND
Beaverton
Milwaukie
Carson
Goldendale
Hood River
The Dalles
Wasco
Umatilla
Hermiston
Weston
Pendleton
UMATILLA INDIAN RESERVATION
Pilot Rock
BLUE MOUNTAINS
Elgin
Enterprise
La Grande
Newberg
McMinnville
Oregon City
Mount Hood 3426
Tygh Valley
Maupin
Grass Valley
Heppner
Lincoln City
Dallas
Woodburn
Salem
WARM SPRINGS INDIAN RESERVATION
DESCHUTES-UMATILLA PLATEAU
Ukiah
Sacajawea Peak 2997
Riggins
Newport
Toledo
Albany
Corvallis
Jefferson
Mill City
Detroit
Warm Springs
Mount Jefferson 3199
Madras
Spray
North Powder
Rock Creek Butte 2775
Baker
New Meadows
McCall
Waldport
Lebanon
Halsey
Monroe
Sweet Home
Santiam Pass 1468
OCHOCO MTS.
Mitchell
Long Creek
JOHN DAY FOSSIL BEDS NATIONAL MONUMENT
John Day
Prairie City
Junction City
McKenzie Bridge
Sisters
Three Sisters 3074
Redmond
Prineville
Eugene
Springfield
Florence
Creswell
Lowell
Bend
Strawberry Mountain 2755
Seneca
Huntington
Midvale
Weiser
Reedsport
Gardiner
OREGON DUNES NATIONAL RECREATION AREA
Cottage Grove
Oakridge
North Bend
Coos Bay
Oakland
La Pine
GREAT SANDY DESERT
Burns
Crane
Vale
Ontario
Nyssa
Payette
Caldwell
Nampa
Boise
Marsing
Bandon
Roseburg
Crescent
Chemult
Langlois
Riddle
Myrtle Creek
Canyonville
Mount Thielsen 2799
Port Orford
Mount Scott 2721
CRATER LAKE NAT'L PARK
HARNEY BASIN
Gold Beach
Grants Pass
Rogue River
Fort Klamath
Chiloquin
Mountain Home
Jordan Valley
Paisley
Medford
Kerby
O'Brien
Brookings
Ashland
Klamath Falls
Bly
Bruneau
©RAND McNALLY & CO.

Red Deer
Stettler
Provost
Macklin
Saskatoon
Castor
Innisfail
Big Valley
Bowden
Olds
Huxley
Craigmyle
Hanna
Munson
Drumheller
Youngstown
Chinook
Cereal
Oyen
Sibbald
Alsask
Flaxcombe
Kindersley
Rosetown
Zealandia
Brock
Hanley
Kenaston
Watrous
Lanigan
Jansen
Bladworth
Davidson
Imperial
Craik
Holdfast
Last Mountain Lake
Chamberlain
Silton
Bethune
Tuxford
Irricana
Balzac
Cochrane
Calgary
Midnapore
Okotoks
Carseland
Bassano
Wardlow
Bindloss
Empress
Kyle
Cabri
Brooks
Tilley
Herbert
Morse
Mortlach
Caron
Moose Jaw
Swift Current
Stavely
Claresholm
Granum
Vauxhall
Redcliff
Medicine Hat
Irvine
Walsh
Maple Creek
Piapot
Gull Lake
Ardill
Wilcox
Coleman
Fort Macleod
Coaldale
Taber
Burdett
Lethbridge
Stirling
Magrath
Foremost
Bellevue
Cowley
Mount Darrah 2755
Cardston
Warner
Cypress L.
Ravenscrag
Eastend
Shaunavon
Admiral
Ponteix
Meyronne
Lafleche
Cadillac
Aneroid
Assiniboia
Ogema
Scout Lake
Lisieux
Val-Marie
Masefield
Morgan
WATERTON-GLACIER
ALBERTA
Coutts
CANADA
UNITED STATES
SASKATCHEWAN
MONTANA
Sunburst
Kevin
BLACKFEET INDIAN RESERVATION
INTERNATIONAL
Logan Pass 2031
PEACE PARK
Browning
Cut Bank
Shelby
Joplin
Chester
Gildford
Rudyard
North Havre
Havre
Chinook
Harlem
Dodson
Malta
Loring
Opheim
Scobey
Flaxville
Plentywood
FORT PECK INDIAN RESERVATION
Saco
Hinsdale
Glasgow
Nashua
Wolf Point
Brockton
Poplar
Medicine Lake
Whitefish
Columbia Falls
Coram
East Glacier Park
Kalispell
Somers
Lakeside
Flathead Lake
Conrad
Box Elder
ROCKY BOYS INDIAN RESERVATION
Big Sandy
Baldy Mountain 2108
FORT BELKNAP INDIAN RESERVATION
Fort Peck
Fort Peck Lake
Brady
Dutton
Choteau
Fort Benton
Swan Peak 2821
Rocky Mountain 2863
Polson
Ronan
FLATHEAD INDIAN RESERVATION
LEWIS RANGE
Fairfield
Black Eagle
Great Falls
Ulm
Sandcoulee
Belt
Cascade
Missouri
Richey
Circle
Jordan
Arlee
Alberton
Red Mountain 2868
Geyser
Stanford
Hobson
Lewistown
Grassrange
Winnett
Moore
Neihart
Big Baldy Mountain 2797
LITTLE BELT MOUNTAINS
Wolf Creek
Lincoln
Missoula
Bonner
Drummond
Avon
Helena
East Helena
White Sulphur Springs
Judith Gap
Melstone
Ingomar
Musselshell
Roundup
Klein
Harlowton
Lavina
Ryegate
Martinsdale
Mount Edith 2897
Terry
Fallon
Kinsey
Miles City
Rosebud
Forsyth
Sliderock Mountain 2384
Victor
Hamilton
Philipsburg
Deer Lodge
Anaconda
Butte
Basin
Crow Peak 2869
Boulder
Townsend
Bull Mountain 2624
Three Forks
Manhattan
Belgrade
Bozeman
Livingston
Wilsall
Clyde Park
Big Timber
Worden
Ballantine
Huntley
Billings
Laurel
Columbus
Custer
Hardin
Darby
Whitehall
Twin Bridges
Wisdom
Gibbonsville
BITTERROOT RANGE
ROCKY MOUNTAINS
Ennis
Virginia City
Dillon
MADISON RANGE
ABSAROKA RANGE
Granite Peak 3901
Red Lodge
Joliet
Park City
Fromberg
Bridger
Roberts
CROW INDIAN RESERVATION
CUSTER BATTLEFIELD NAT'L MON.
Crow Agency
Lodge Grass
BIGHORN CANYON NAT'L RECR. AREA
Busby
Ashland
NORTHERN CHEYENNE INDIAN RESERVATION
Broadus
Biddle
Salmon
Baker
BEAVERHEAD MOUNTAINS
LEMHI RANGE
Leadore
Challis
Gardiner
Yellowstone National Park
Mount Holmes 3150
YELLOWSTONE NATIONAL PARK
West Yellowstone
Lima
Trout Peak 3732
Pahaska
Cody
Powell
Lovell
Cowley
WYOMING
Ranchester
Dayton
Sheridan
Clearmont
BIGHORN MOUNTAINS
Greybull
Cloud Peak 4016
Buffalo
Gillette
Manderson
BIG HORN BASIN
Meeteetse
Worland
Ten Sleep
Spencer
Island Park
Dubois
Mount Sheridan 3142
Carter Mountain 3724
Diamond Peak 3718
Borah Peak 3859
LOST RIVER RANGE
Ashton
Saint Anthony
Rexburg
GRAND TETON NAT'L PARK
Hamilton Dome
Thermopolis
Pumpkin Buttes 1836
Kaycee
Sun Valley
Hailey
Moore
Arco
Butte City
Atomic City
Idaho Falls
Rigby
Ririe
Ucon
Grand Teton 4196
Victor
Elk
Jackson
Dubois
WIND RIVER INDIAN RESERVATION
Midwest
CRATERS OF THE MOON NAT'L MON.
Shelley
Palisades
IDAHO
WYOMING
Gannett Peak 4202
Shoshoni
Blackfoot
FORT HALL INDIAN RESERVATION
Richfield
PLAIN
Pocatello
American Falls
Jerome
Bancroft
Soda Springs
Etna
Afton
Pinedale
Fort Washakie
Lander
Riverton
Casper
Mountain View
Evansville
Douglas

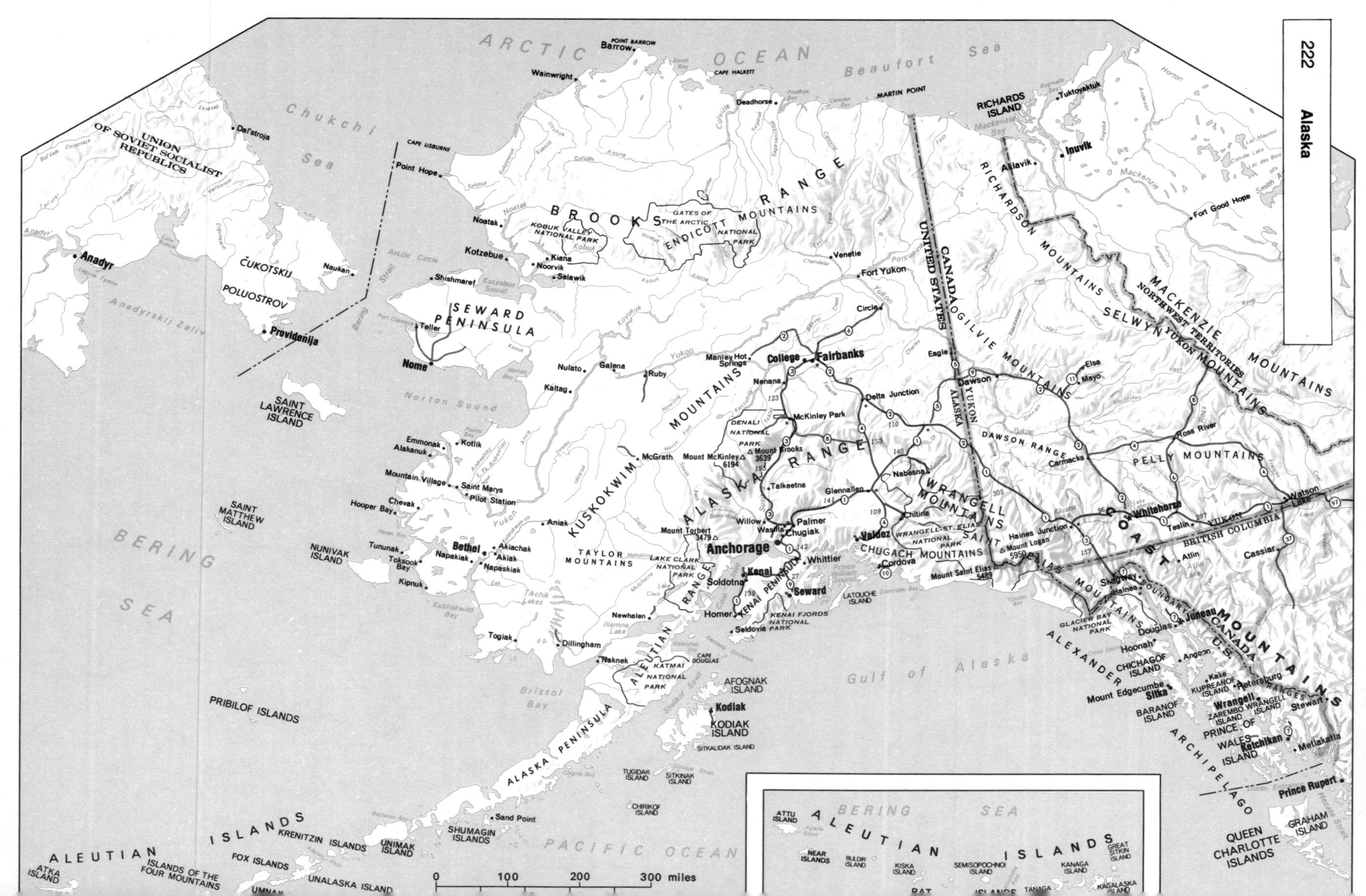
ARCTIC OCEAN
Beaufort Sea
Chukchi Sea
BERING SEA
Gulf of Alaska
PACIFIC OCEAN
Norton Sound
Bristol Bay
CANADA
UNITED STATES
YUKON
ALASKA
NORTHWEST TERRITORIES
BRITISH COLUMBIA
U.S.
UNION OF SOVIET SOCIALIST REPUBLICS
ČUKOTSKIJ POLUOSTROV
BROOKS RANGE
ENDICOTT MOUNTAINS
GATES OF THE ARCTIC NATIONAL PARK
KOBUK VALLEY NATIONAL PARK
ALASKA RANGE
DENALI NATIONAL PARK
KUSKOKWIM MOUNTAINS
TAYLOR MOUNTAINS
ALEUTIAN RANGE
KATMAI NATIONAL PARK
LAKE CLARK NATIONAL PARK
KENAI FJORDS NATIONAL PARK
KENAI PENINSULA
CHUGACH MOUNTAINS
WRANGELL MOUNTAINS
WRANGELL-ST. ELIAS NATIONAL PARK
SAINT ELIAS MOUNTAINS
GLACIER BAY NATIONAL PARK
COAST MOUNTAINS
MACKENZIE MOUNTAINS
SELWYN MOUNTAINS
RICHARDSON MOUNTAINS
OGILVIE MOUNTAINS
DAWSON RANGE
PELLY MOUNTAINS
ALEXANDER ARCHIPELAGO
SEWARD PENINSULA
ALASKA PENINSULA
ALEUTIAN ISLANDS
SAINT LAWRENCE ISLAND
SAINT MATTHEW ISLAND
NUNIVAK ISLAND
PRIBILOF ISLANDS
KODIAK ISLAND
AFOGNAK ISLAND
SHUMAGIN ISLANDS
UNIMAK ISLAND
UNALASKA ISLAND
FOX ISLANDS
ISLANDS OF THE FOUR MOUNTAINS
ATKA ISLAND
KRENITZIN ISLANDS
RICHARDS ISLAND
QUEEN CHARLOTTE ISLANDS
GRAHAM ISLAND
BARANOF ISLAND
CHICHAGOF ISLAND
PRINCE OF WALES ISLAND
ATTU ISLAND
KISKA ISLAND
NEAR ISLANDS
POINT BARROW
CAPE LISBURNE
CAPE HALKETT
MARTIN POINT
Barrow
Wainwright
Point Hope
Kotzebue
Nome
Teller
Shishmaref
Noatak
Kiana
Noorvik
Selawik
Nulato
Kaltag
Galena
Ruby
McGrath
Manley Hot Springs
Fairbanks
College
Nenana
Circle
Fort Yukon
Venetie
Deadhorse
Eagle
Delta Junction
McKinley Park
Talkeetna
Glennallen
Valdez
Cordova
Whittier
Seward
Anchorage
Palmer
Wasilla
Chugiak
Willow
Kenai
Soldotna
Homer
Seldovia
Kodiak
Naknek
Dillingham
Togiak
Bethel
Aniak
Akiak
Akiachak
Napaskiak
Napakiak
Kipnuk
Toksook Bay
Tununak
Hooper Bay
Chevak
Mountain Village
Saint Marys
Pilot Station
Emmonak
Alakanuk
Kotlik
Newhalen
Sand Point
Juneau
Sitka
Ketchikan
Wrangell
Petersburg
Haines
Skagway
Douglas
Hoonah
Angoon
Kake
Metlakatla
Prince Rupert
Stewart
Whitehorse
Dawson
Mayo
Elsa
Carmacks
Haines Junction
Teslin
Atlin
Cassiar
Watson Lake
Ross River
Inuvik
Aklavik
Tuktoyaktuk
Fort Good Hope
Mount McKinley 6194
Mount Brooks 3639
Mount Torbert 3479
Mount Logan 5950
Mount Saint Elias 5489
Providenija
Anadyr
Dal'stroja
Naukan
Mount Edgecumbe
0 100 200 300 miles

United States Mileage Chart

83-7501

	Atlanta, Ga.	Boston, Mass.	Cheyenne, Wyo.	Chicago, Ill.	Cincinnati, Ohio	Cleveland, Ohio	Dallas, Texas	Denver, Colo.	Des Moines, Iowa	Detroit, Mich.	Houston, Texas	Indianapolis, Ind.	Kansas City, Mo.	Los Angeles, Calif.	Louisville, Ky.	Memphis, Tenn.	Milwaukee, Wis.	Minneapolis, Minn.	New Orleans, La.	New York, N.Y.	Omaha, Nebr.	Philadelphia, Pa.	Pittsburgh, Pa.	Portland, Oreg.	St. Louis, Mo.	Salt Lake City, Utah	San Francisco, Calif.	Seattle, Wash.	Toledo, Ohio	Tulsa, Okla.	Washington, D.C.	Wichita, Kans.
Albuquerque, N. Mex.	1381	2172	517	1281	1372	1560	638	417	977	1525	834	1266	782	807	1301	1010	1319	1190	1134	1979	858	1899	1619	1371	1038	604	1115	1440	1469	645	1824	593
Amarillo, Texas	1097	1897	511	1043	1096	1285	358	423	742	1269	596	991	547	1091	1019	726	1084	975	850	1704	643	1624	1344	1655	756	888	1399	1724	1210	361	1549	350
Atlanta, Ga.		1037	1442	674	440	672	795	1398	870	699	789	493	798	2182	382	371	761	1068	479	841	986	741	687	2601	541	1878	2496	2618	640	772	608	903
Austin, Texas	919	1911	994	1110	1083	1327	193	906	877	1315	164	1037	682	1374	982	615	1184	1129	517	1715	837	1615	1367	2069	823	1302	1748	2138	1256	450	1482	548
Baltimore, Md.	645	392	1608	668	497	343	1356	1621	981	503	1412	563	1048	2636	598	904	755	1073	1115	196	1113	96	218	2751	798	2044	2796	2681	444	1194	37	1244
Birmingham, Ala.	150	1165	1347	642	465	709	645	1286	787	724	639	475	697	2032	364	246	728	1006	342	969	898	869	741	2505	465	1781	2366	2535	665	647	736	778
Bismarck, N. Dak.	1495	1794	572	831	1118	1166	1141	671	670	1097	1384	1012	777	1617	1123	1228	758	427	1583	1633	581	1569	1283	1265	979	916	1604	1195	1063	958	1502	776
Boise, Idaho	2174	2639	732	1683	1906	2011	1582	811	1359	1942	1778	1800	1382	849	1893	1832	1692	1405	2078	2478	1227	2410	2122	432	1633	340	658	501	1908	1486	2343	1312
Boston, Mass.	1037		1907	963	840	628	1748	1949	1280	695	1804	906	1391	2979	941	1296	1050	1368	1507	206	1412	296	561	3046	1141	2343	3095	2976	739	1537	429	1587
Buffalo, N. Y.	859	446	1466	522	431	187	1346	1508	839	253	1460	481	966	2554	532	899	609	927	1217	372	971	353	216	2605	716	1902	2654	2535	298	1112	356	1162
Charleston, S. Car.	289	929	1722	877	603	730	1072	1678	1150	842	1054	696	1078	2459	591	660	964	1282	720	733	1266	633	666	2881	821	2158	2785	2890	783	1061	500	1192
Cheyenne, Wyo.	1442	1907		954	1174	1279	869	100	627	1211	1107	1068	650	1137	1161	1101	987	788	1361	1746	495	1678	1390	1159	901	436	1188	1228	1176	765	1611	583
Chicago, Ill.	674	963	954		287	335	917	996	327	266	1067	181	499	2054	292	530	87	405	912	802	459	738	452	2083	289	1390	2142	2013	232	683	671	696
Cincinnati, Ohio	440	840	1174	287		244	920	1164	571	259	1029	106	591	2179	101	468	374	692	786	647	693	567	287	2333	340	1610	2362	2300	200	736	481	787
Cleveland, Ohio	672	628	1279	335	244		1159	1321	652	170	1273	294	779	2367	345	712	422	740	1030	473	784	413	129	2418	529	1715	2467	2348	111	925	346	975
Columbus, Ohio	533	735	1235	308	108	139	1028	1229	618	192	1137	171	656	2244	209	576	395	713	894	542	750	462	182	2391	406	1671	2423	2321	133	802	387	852
Dallas, Texas	795	1748	869	917	920	1159		781	684	1143	243	865	489	1387	819	452	991	936	496	1552	644	1452	1204	2009	630	1242	1753	2078	1084	257	1319	365
Denver, Colo.	1398	1949	100	996	1164	1321	781		669	1253	1019	1058	600	1059	1120	1040	1029	841	1273	1771	537	1691	1411	1238	857	504	1235	1307	1218	681	1616	509
Des Moines, Iowa	870	1280	627	327	571	652	684	669		584	905	465	195	1727	566	599	361	252	978	1119	132	1051	763	1786	333	1063	1815	1749	255	443	984	392
Detroit, Mich.	699	695	1211	266	259	170	1143	1253	584		1265	278	743	2311	360	713	353	671	1045	637	716	573	287	2349	513	1647	2399	2279	59	909	506	940
Duluth, Minn.	1139	1428	918	465	752	800	1086	994	402	707	1307	646	597	2016	757	943	392	153	1331	1267	510	1203	917	1705	662	1315	2044	1635	697	845	1136	794
El Paso, Texas	1415	2316	754	1430	1515	1704	620	654	1126	1674	748	1410	931	790	1438	1072	1468	1339	1098	2123	1007	2043	1763	1635	1175	868	1164	1704	1618	780	1939	742
Flagstaff, Ariz.	1704	2495	757	1604	1695	1883	961	657	1300	1848	1157	1589	1105	484	1624	1333	1642	1481	1457	2302	1171	2222	1942	1241	1361	511	792	1347	1792	968	2147	916
Fort Wayne, Ind.	593	825	1093	156	153	197	983	1135	466	160	1105	118	586	2175	216	553	243	561	901	662	598	585	297	2239	353	1529	2281	2169	101	749	518	783
Fort Worth, Texas	826	1779	845	941	951	1183	31	757	708	1167	262	889	513	1356	850	483	1015	960	527	1583	655	1483	1235	1978	654	1211	1722	2047	1108	279	1350	359
Harrisburg, Pa.	700	373	1579	639	468	314	1383	1592	952	474	1439	534	1019	2607	569	931	726	1044	1142	180	1084	102	189	2722	769	2015	2767	2652	415	1165	107	1215
Helena, Mont.	2030	2388	685	1425	1712	1760	1554	781	1161	1691	1792	1606	1251	1190	1717	1702	1352	1020	2033	2227	1050	2163	1877	658	1493	477	1098	588	1657	1416	2096	1234
Houston, Texas	789	1804	1107	1067	1029	1273	243	1019	905	1265		987	710	1538	928	561	1142	1157	356	1608	865	1508	1313	2205	779	1438	1912	2274	1206	478	1375	608
Indianapolis, Ind.	493	906	1068	181	106	294	865	1058	465	278	987		485	2073	111	435	268	586	796	713	587	633	353	2227	235	1504	2256	2194	219	631	558	681
Jackson, Miss.	391	1406	1257	742	655	899	404	1169	809	914	406	646	644	1791	554	212	824	1036	178	1210	845	1110	939	2401	495	1646	2157	2470	855	527	977	708
Jacksonville, Fla.	306	1155	1748	980	746	915	990	1704	1176	1003	889	799	1104	2377	688	674	1067	1374	555	959	1292	859	851	2907	847	2184	2743	2924	944	1075	726	1206
Kansas City, Mo.	798	1391	650	499	591	779	489	600	195	743	710	485		1589	520	451	537	447	806	1198	201	1118	838	1809	257	1086	1835	1839	687	248	1043	197
Knoxville, Tenn.	193	911	1372	527	253	485	837	1328	800	512	893	346	728	2202	241	385	614	932	596	715	916	615	511	2531	471	1808	2510	2540	453	786	482	871
Las Vegas, Nev.	1964	2725	855	1772	1941	2097	1221	777	1445	2029	1417	1835	1365	282	1884	1593	1805	1607	1717	2548	1313	2468	2188	981	1621	433	564	1152	1994	1228	2393	1176
Lexington, Ky.	362	896	1233	352	78	317	861	1192	636	337	970	171	592	2180	72	409	439	757	727	703	758	623	343	2392	335	1669	2421	2365	278	731	514	782
Little Rock, Ark.	509	1434	1035	640	606	850	314	947	561	838	427	560	389	1687	505	138	715	813	418	1238	590	1138	890	2179	352	1438	1995	2228	779	271	1005	453
Los Angeles, Calif.	2182	2979	1137	2054	2179	2367	1387	1059	1727	2311	1538	2073	1589		2108	1817	2087	1889	1883	2786	1595	2706	2426	959	1845	715	379	1131	2276	1452	2631	1400
Louisville, Ky.	382	941	1161	292	101	345	819	1120	566	360	928	111	520	2108		367	379	697	685	748	687	668	388	2320	263	1597	2349	2305	301	659	582	710
Mackinaw City, Mich.	935	*916	1291	387	495	439	1281	1341	673	284	1427	460	864	2392	562	880	368	508	1247	906	805	842	556	2128	651	1691	2443	2058	328	1047	775	1061
Madison, Wis.	812	1103	912	140	427	475	968	954	286	406	1137	321	483	2012	432	622	77	272	1006	942	418	878	592	1950	358	1348	2100	1880	372	727	811	676
Memphis, Tenn.	371	1296	1101	530	468	712	452	1040	599	713	561	435	451	1817	367		612	826	390	1100	652	1000	752	2259	285	1535	2125	2290	654	401	867	532
Miami, Fla.	655	1504	2097	1329	1095	1264	1300	2037	1525	1352	1190	1148	1448	2687	1037	997	1416	1723	856	1308	1641	1208	1200	3256	1196	2532	3053	3273	1293	1398	1075	1529
Milwaukee, Wis.	761	1050	987	87	374	422	991	1029	361	353	1142	268	537	2087	379	612		332	994	889	493	825	539	2010	363	1423	2175	1940	319	757	758	734
Minneapolis, Minn.	1068	1368	788	405	692	740	936	841	252	671	1157	586	447	1889	697	826	332		1214	1207	357	1143	857	1678	552	1186	1940	1608	637	695	1076	644
Mobile, Ala.	335	1372	1443	851	706	950	590	1355	954	965	478	716	812	1977	605	363	933	1173	144	1176	1013	1076	982	2587	632	1832	2343	2651	906	713	943	893
Montreal, Que.	1181	318	1773	828	805	561	1705	1815	1146	562	1827	840	1305	2873	906	1273	915	1163	1591	378	1278	449	583	2755	1075	2209	2961	2685	621	1471	579	1502
Nashville, Tenn.	242	1088	1200	446	269	513	660	1156	628	528	769	279	556	2025	168	208	532	826	517	892	744	792	553	2359	299	1636	2333	2376	469	609	659	699
New Orleans, La.	479	1507	1361	912	786	1030	496	1273	978	1045	356	796	806	1883	685	390	994	1214		1311	1007	1211	1070	2505	673	1738	2249	2574	986	647	1078	816
New York, N. Y.	841	206	1746	802	647	473	1552	1771	1119	637	1608	713	1198	2786	748	1100	889	1207	1311		1251	100	368	2885	948	2182	2934	2815	578	1344	233	1394
Norfolk, Va.	540	558	1764	831	604	508	1329	1758	1141	666	1328	700	1162	2694	642	877	918	1236	1019	362	1273	263	384	2914	905	2200	2952	2844	607	1278	188	1352
Oklahoma City, Okla.	839	1641	697	787	840	1029	206	609	544	1013	449	735	349	1349	763	468	861	796	668	1448	455	1368	1088	1841	500	1100	1657	1910	954	105	1293	159
Omaha, Nebr.	986	1412	495	459	693	784	644	537	132	716	865	587	201	1595	687	652	493	357	1007	1251		1183	895	1654	449	931	1683	1638	681	387	1116	298
Orlando, Fla.	435	1294	1876	1109	875	1054	1078	1815	1305	1134	968	928	1226	2465	817	775	1196	1503	634	1098	1421	998	990	3034	976	2310	2831	3053	1075	1176	865	1307
Philadelphia, Pa.	741	296	1678	738	567	413	1452	1691	1051	573	1508	633	1118	2706	668	1000	825	1143	1211	100	1183		288	2821	868	2114	2866	2751	514	1264	133	1314
Phoenix, Ariz.	1793	2604	892	1713	1804	1992	998	792	1409	1957	1149	1698	1214	389	1733	1442	1751	1616	1494	2411	1290	2331	2051	1266	1470	648	763	1437	1901	1077	2256	1025
Pierre, S. Dak.	1361	1726	434	763	1050	1098	943	518	492	1029	1186	944	592	1524	1055	1043	690	394	1394	1565	391	1501	1215	1353	824	823	1575	1283	995	760	1434	578
Pittsburgh, Pa.	687	561	1390	452	287	129	1204	1411	763	287	1313	353	838	2426	388	752	539	857	1070	368	895	288		2535	588	1826	2578	2465	228	984	221	1034
Portland, Me.	1139	106	1986	1042	942	707	1850	2028	1359	775	1906	1001	1486	3074	1043	1398	1129	1447	1609	308	1491	398	663	3125	1236	2422	3174	3055	818	1632	531	1682
Portland, Ore.	2601	3046	1159	2083	2333	2418	2009	1238	1786	2349	2205	2227	1809	959	2320	2259	2010	1678	2505	2885	1654	2821	2535		2060	767	636	172	2315	1913	2754	1739
Raleigh, N. Car.	372	685	1695	784	534	561	1166	1661	1092	683	1160	631	1061	2545	541	728	871	1189	851	489	1214	389	445	2854	804	2131	2853	2797	624	635	256	1215
Rapid City, S. Dak.	1487	1859	295	896	1177	1231	1050	394	618	1162	1288	1071	708	1363	1182	1159	840	565	1507	1698	507	1634	1348	1204	950	662	1414	1134	1128	873	1567	691
Reno, Nev.	2374	2866	959	1913	2133	2238	1668	1011	1586	2170	1864	2027	1609	469	2120	2003	1946	1711	2164	2705	1454	2637	2349	538	1860	523	229	710	2135	1640	2570	1471
Richmond, Va.	510	535	1674	748	514	425	1266	1668	1058	583	1298	610	1072	2631	552	814	835	1153	989	339	1190	239	301	2831	815	2110	2862	2761	524	1211	106	1262
St. Louis, Mo.	541	1141	901	289	340	529	630	857	333	513	779	235	257	1845	263	285	363	552	673	948	449	868	588	2060		1337	2089	2081	454	396	793	447
Salt Lake City, Utah	1878	2343	436	1390	1610	1715	1242	504	1063	1647	1438	1504	1086	715	1597	1535	1423	1186	1738	2182	931	2114	1826	767	1337		752	836	1612	1172	2047	1003
San Antonio, Texas	983	1988	1027	1187	1160	1404	270	939	954	1392	197	1114	759	1363	1059	692	1261	1206	550	1792	914	1692	1444	2086	900	1319	1737	2155	1333	527	1559	625
San Diego, Calif.	2126	2955	1186	2064	2155	2343	1331	1108	1760	2308	1482	2049	1565	125	2084	1783	2102	1938	1827	2762	1641	2682	2402	1084	1821	764	504	1256	2252	1428	2607	1376
San Francisco, Calif.	2496	3095	1188	2142	2362	2467	1753	1235	1815	2399	1912	2256	1835	379	2349	2125	2175	1940	2249	2934	1683	2866	2578	636	2089	752		808	2364	1760	2799	1695
Seattle, Wash.	2618	2976	1228	2013	2300	2348	2078	1307	1749	2279	2274	2194	1839	1131	2305	2290	1940	1608	2574	2815	1638	2751	2465	172	2081	836	808		2245	1982	2684	1808
Spokane, Wash.	2340	2698	995	1735	2022	2070	1864	1089	1471	2001	2102	1916	1561	1205	2027	2012	1662	1330	2343	2537	1360	2473	2187	348	1803	712	882	278	1967	1726	2406	1544
Springfield, Ill.	592	1099	888	189	299	473	728	865	291	433	879	193	310	1899	275	370	263	480	758	906	412	826	546	2047	100	1324	2076	2039	377	494	751	507
Springfield, Mo.	652	1353	820	499	552	741	419	759	342	725	629	447	170	1636	475	281	573	594	636	1160	371	1080	800	1978	212	1254	1944	2009	666	185	1005	251
Toledo, Ohio	640	739	1176	232	200	111	1084	1218	255	59	1206	219	687	2276	301	654	319	637	986	578	681	514	228	2315	454	1612	2364	2245		850	447	884
Topeka, Kans.	863	1456	595	562	656	844	480	535	549	806	701	550	65	1531	585	508	598	508	863	1263	165	1183	903	1751	322	1028	1770	1802	750	223	1108	139
Tulsa, Okla.	772	1537	765	683	736	925	257	681	443	909	478	631	248	1452	659	401	757	695	647	1344	387	1264	984	1913	396	1172	1760	1982	850		1189	182
Washington, D. C.	608	429	1611	671	481	346	1319	1616	984	506	1375	558	1043	2631	582	867	758	1076	1078	233	1116	133	221	2754	793	2047	2799	2684	447	1189		1239
Wichita, Kans.	903	1587	583	696	787	975	365	509	392	940	608	681	197	1400	710	532	734	644	816	1394	298	1314	1034	1739	447	1003	1695	1808	884	182	1239	

Tables, Charts, and Facts

Gazetteer of the World

Note: In this Gazetteer, population figures for countries are recent estimates based on UN statistics except where otherwise stated. Populations of cities and towns are also the latest estimates or census figures. Adult literacy rates are generally for 1975, average life expectancies for 1978 and per capita GNPs (in US$) for 1979.

AFGHANISTAN, a landlocked republic in south-eastern Asia. The land is mostly mountainous: major ranges include the Hindu Kush and the Pamirs. The north is arid. Rainfall generally averages 300 mm (12 in). Temperatures vary from 49°C (120°F) in the south in summer to −26°C (−15°F) in winter in the mountains. Some 79 per cent of the workforce are farmers, mainly in the subsistence sector. Only 10 per cent of the land is cultivable, mostly in irrigated valleys. Many people are nomads: sheep are the most numerous animals. Natural gas is exported, but mining and manufacturing are small-scale. Afghanistan, once part of the Persian Empire, was conquered by Alexander the Great in 331 BC. Islam was introduced in the 8th century. Modern Afghanistan was founded in 1747 by an Afghan chief, Ahmad Shah. His dynasty continued until 1973 when a republic was declared. In 1979 Soviet troops invaded Afghanistan and a long war began against Muslim rebel forces opposed to the pro-Soviet government.

Area: 647,497 km^2 (250,014 sq mi); **Population:** 16,024,000; **Capital:** Kabul (pop 749,000); **Other cities:** Kandahar (209,000), Herat (157,000); **Highest point:** 7620 m (25,000 ft) in the Hindu Kush; **Official languages:** Pushtu, Dari (Persian); **Religion:** Islam; **Adult literacy rate:** 12 per cent; **Average life expectancy at birth:** 42 years; **Unit of currency:** Afghani; **Main exports:** cotton, natural gas, fruit, karakul skins; **Per capital GNP:** US$170.

ALBANIA, the smallest European communist nation, borders the Adriatic Sea. The climate on the dry coast is Mediterranean in type. The land is mostly mountainous. Farmland covers 17 per cent of Albania, with fertile basins in the wetter uplands where the rainfall averages 1800 mm (71 in). Maquis and oak and pine forest cover 44 per cent of the land and pasture another 25 per cent. Farming is collectivized and 62 per cent of the workforce is employed on farms. But mining and manufacturing are the leading industries. Ottoman Turks introduced Islam in the 15th century. Albania became independent in 1912 and a kingdom in 1928. After World War II a communist republic was set up In 1961 Albania broke with the USSR and became allied to China, which helped it to industrialize. Albania officially became an 'atheist state' in 1967. The special relationship with China ended in 1977, since when Albania has followed an independent course.

Area: 28,748 km^2 (11,100 sq mi); **Population:** 2,873,000; **Capital:** Tiranë (pop 198,000); **Other cities:** Shkodër (62,500), Durres (61,000); **Highest point:** Mt Korah, 2762 m (9063 ft); **Official language:** Albanian; **Religion:** formerly mainly Islam (all mosques and churches were closed in 1967); **Average life expectancy at birth:** 69 years; **Unit of currency:** Lek; **Main exports:** metal ores and metals (including chrome, copper, nickel), oil, bitumen, tobacco, fruit, vegetables; **Per capita GNP:** US$840.

ALGERIA, a large republic bordering the Mediterranean Sea in North Africa. The Sahara, which covers 85 per cent of the nation, yields oil and natural gas and oil accounts for 90 per cent of the exports. Between 1960 and 1980 the urban population increased from 30 per cent to 61 per cent. Of the workforce, agriculture now employs only 30 per cent, industry 25 per cent and services 45 per cent. Most people live in the northern Atlas mountain region and the fertile coastal plains. Barley, fruit, grapes, olives, vegetables and wheat are grown. Livestock are raised in the uplands. Islam and the Arabic language were introduced in the 7th century, but Berber languages survived in some areas. France ruled Algeria from 1848, but the Arab FLN (National Liberation Front) spear-headed a guerrilla war from 1954. In 1962 Algeria became independent: most of the 1 million French settlers left. Algeria became a one-party state, ruled by the FLN. An army junta took power in 1965, but the 1976 Constitution restored elections.

Area: 2,381,741 km^2 (919,646 sq mi); **Population:** 20,042,000; **Capital:** Algiers (pop 1,503,700); **Other cities:** Oran (485,000), Constantine (350,000), Annaba (313,000); **Highest point:** Mt Tahat, 2918 m (9573 ft); **Official language:** Arabic; **Religion:** Islam; **Adult literacy rate:** 37 per cent; **Average life expectancy at birth:** 56 years; **Unit of currency:** Dinar; **Main exports:** oil and oil products, natural gas, wine, fruit, vegetables; **Per capita GNP:** US$1580.

ANDORRA, a tiny, mountainous co-principality in the Pyrenees between France and Spain, Sovereignty is technically exercised by the 'co-princes', the Spanish Bishop of Urgel and the French President, but an elected, 28-member General Council effectively rules the state. Tourism is the main industry: over 6 million people visited Andorra in 1978. Tobacco is the chief cash crop.

Area: 453 km² (175 sq mi); **Population:** 32,700 (1980); **Capital:** Andorra la Vella (pop 12,000); **Official language:** Catalan; **Units of currency:** French franc, Spanish peseta.

ANGOLA, a republic in west-central Africa, including the small enclave of Cabinda. Behind the narrow coastal plain are plateaux. The altitude affects the climate which is generally warmest and wettest in the north. Savanna covers much of the country, with forests in the south and north-east. Most people speak Bantu languages. The main groups are the Ovimbundu, the Mbundu and the Kongo. Tribalism has divided the nationalist movement in Angola. About 60 per cent of the people are farmers, mostly at subsistence level. The main food crops are cassava and maize. Mining is becoming increasingly important. The Portuguese explored Angola's coasts in the 1480s and later engaged in the slave trade there. In 1961 nationalists began a war against the Portuguese. Angola achieved independence in 1975. In the power struggle at the time of independence, the socialist MPLA, supported by the Mbundu and by *mestiços*, emerged triumphant. But the southern Ovimbundu UNITA continued to resist into the 1980s, with assistance from South Africa.

Area: 1,246,700 km² (481,380 sq mi); **Population:** 7,414,000; **Capital:** Luanda (pop 481,000); **Other towns:** Huambo (62,000), Lobito (59,000); **Highest point:** Mt Moco, 2620 m (8596 ft); **Official language:** Portuguese; **Religion:** traditional religions, Christianity; **Adult literacy rate:** 20 per cent; **Average life expectancy at birth:** 41 years; **Unit of currency:** Kwanza; **Main exports:** oil, coffee, diamonds, iron ore, cotton, fish meal, sisal; **Per capita GNP:** US$440.

ANGUILLA, a low-lying coral island, about 110 km (68 mi) north-west of St Kitts, in the Leeward Islands. Its main products are lobsters and salt, but light industry and tourism have been developing recently. Anguilla has superb beaches and temperatures range between 24°C and 29°C (75°–84°F) all the year round. Anguilla became part of St Kitts-Nevis-Anguilla, a British Associated State, in 1967. But the Anguillans objected to rule from St Kitts and Britain appointed a Commissioner to handle the island's affairs. In 1976 Anguilla was granted a separate Constitution and formal separation from St Kitts-Nevis was achieved in 1980.

Area: 90 km² (35 sq mi); **Population:** 6500 (1977); **Status:** British colony.

ANTIGUA, including the smaller and also low-lying islands of Barbuda and the uninhabited Redonda in the Leeward Islands, became an independent nation in the Commonwealth in 1981. The British monarch is its Head of State. Antigua exports cotton and rum, but tourism is the most important industry in this dry, sunny country. Discovered by Christopher Columbus in 1493, Antigua was named after a church in Seville, Spain. British settlers colonized the islands in 1632 and they were declared a British possession in 1667. Antigua became a British Associated State in 1967. Most Antiguans are descendants of African slaves, but some are of European or Middle Eastern origin.

Area: 442 km² (171 sq mi); **Population:** 77,000; **Capital:** St John's (23,500).

ARGENTINA, South America's second largest nation after Brazil, extends north-south through more than 32° of latitude. As a result the climate varies considerably. There are four main regions. The tropical, largely forested north is comparatively little developed. The west is arid, except around 'oases' where such towns as Mendoza and Tucumán have grown up, rising in the far west to the Andes Mountains. Here, on the border with Chile is Mt Aconcagua, the highest mountain in the western hemisphere. Southern Argentina, called Patagonia, consists of sparsely populated, wind-swept and semi-arid plateaux. In the far south is half of the barren and cold archipelago, Tierra del Fuego, whose southern tip is only about 960 km (600 mi) from Antarctica. The fourth and most densely populated region is the central *pampas* (or plains) which cover nearly 25 per cent of the country. The soils of the pampas are fertile and the climate is mild, with an average annual temperature range of 9°–23°C (48°–73°F) and an average annual rainfall of 510–760 mm (20–30 in). The *pampas* lie to the north-west and south of Buenos Aires, the elegant capital city. About 90 per cent of the population is of European descent, another 8 per cent being *mestizos* of mixed white and Indian origin, and 2 per cent pure Indians. Argentina is one of the world's leading food producers. Dairy products, hides, maize, meat, oats, vegetable oils, wheat and wool are major products. About 11 per cent of the country is cultivated and pastureland

Argentinian cowboys who work on the pampas (grasslands) are called gauchos. Pasture covers more than two-fifths of Argentina and supports vast herds of cattle and sheep.

covers another 41 per cent. In 1979 Argentina had 60 million cattle and 35 million sheep. In recent years, mining (for coal and oil) and manufacturing have become important. In the late 1970s, they accounted for 45 per cent of the GDP (manufacturing making up 37 per cent), while agriculture contributed only 13 per cent. The other 42 per cent came from service industries. The cities are growing quickly. The proportion of people in urban areas increased from 74 per cent in 1960 to 82 per cent in 1980. The Spanish explorer Juan de Solás was the first European to see the Rio de la Plata estuary, into which the Paraguay and Uruguay rivers flow, in 1516. The first permanent Spanish settlers arrived in 1535 and the city of Buenos Aires was founded one year later, although it was not permanently settled until 1580. Spanish rule continued until Buenos Aires declared itself independent in May 1810, followed by the provinces in 1816. Civil disorder ensued until a federal Constitution was adopted in 1853. In recent years Argentina has been disturbed by political and economic turmoil. Between 1946 and 1981, the Republic of Argentina had 14 presidents, seven of whom were deposed. Kidnappings, political murders, high unemployment and inflation (averaging 120 per cent per year between 1970 and 1978) have created instability, aggravating the problems.

Area: 2,766,889 km^2 (1,068,360 sq mi); **Population:** 27,796,000; **Capital:** Buenos Aires (pop with suburbs, 9,677,000); **Other cities:** Rosario (798,000), Córdoba (798,000), La Plata (408,000); **Highest point:** Mt Aconcagua, 6960 m (22,835 ft); **Official language:** Spanish; **Religion:** mainly Roman Catholicism, **Adult literacy rate:** 94 per cent; **Average life expectancy at birth:** 71 years; **Unit of currency:** Peso; **Main exports:** vegetable products, food, drink and tobacco, animals and animal products, textiles and leather, machinery and transport equipment; **Per capita GNP:** US$2280.

AUSTRALIA, the world's sixth largest country, has a low average population density of 2 people per sq km (5 per sq mi), because large tracts are desert or semi-desert. Some 89 per cent of the population is urban (1980), with more than 50 per cent of the people concentrated in the four largest cities. The western part of Australia is a vast plateau, averaging 300 m (984 ft) above sea level, although occasional mountain ranges rise above this level. The central plains extend from the Gulf of Carpentaria in the north to the Great Australian Bight in the south. These plains include the Great Artesian Basin, comprising western Queensland, the south-east of the Northern Territory, the north-east of South Australia and the northern part of New South Wales. Here artesian wells tap ground water that originally fell as rain on the Great Dividing Range in the east, and which has seeped through aquifers beneath the plains. The Lake Eyre basin in the south-west of the Great Artesian Basin, is usually dry and covered by salt. It is an internal drainage basin. The highest peak in the Great Dividing Range, an uplifted block of land, is Mt Kosciusko, in that part of the Range called the Australian Alps. The Range continues in the island state of Tasmania in the south-east, which is separated from the mainland by the shallow Bass Strait. In the north-east is the Great Barrier Reef, the world's longest reef, 2027 km (1260 mi) long. Australia's chief rivers are the Murray, 2575 km (1600 mi) long, and its tributaries, including the Darling, 2740 km (1703 mi) long, in the south-east. The climate varies according to the latitude. The north is tropical with summer monsoon rains. In the south, winters are cooler and rains are

Sydney is Australia's largest conurbation and chief seaport. This view looking north shows the expressway leading to Harbour Bridge and, beyond the bridge, North Sydney.

brought by the prevailing westerlies. However, about two-thirds of Australia is too dry for farming. The tropical region in the north contains tropical forest and savanna and tropical crops, such as sugar-cane, flourish in Queensland. Deserts cover most of Western Australia, the southern part of Northern Territory, much of South Australia and the eastern parts of New South Wales. The mid-latitude grasslands are west of the Great Dividing Range in south-central Queensland and central New South Wales. The coastlands of New South Wales and south-eastern Victoria form a warm temperate zone, where eucalypt forests grow. The south-western part of Western Australia and parts of South Australia and western Victoria have a Mediterranean climate, with much scrub woodland vegetation. The cool temperate climate of Tasmania supports forests of beech and eucalypts. Australia has a wide range of animals, including kangaroos, koalas, platypuses and wallabies. Birds include the flightless emu and cassowary and the lyre bird. The first people in Australia were probably the Tasmanian Aborigines who were driven into Tasmania by the Australian Aborigines who arrived from Asia about 16,000 years ago. The Tasmanian Aborigines became extinct in 1876 and contact with Europeans caused the Australian Aborigines to decline in numbers. Today there are about 100,000 Australian Aborigines, but many are of mixed ancestry. Most Australians are of British origin, although the proportion of citizens of British origin has decreased to about 80 per cent. This is because many recent settlers have come from other parts of Europe. In 1978 industry accounted for 32 per cent of the GDP (manufacturing alone made up 19 per cent), agriculture for 5 per cent and services for 63 per cent. Australia has vast mineral reserves and is a major world producer of bauxite, iron ore and lead. Other metal ores, coal and oil are also mined, together with thorium and uranium. The Eastern Highlands contain many minerals, but the most spectacular finds since 1950 have been in Western Australia. The main product of the country is wool; Australia had 136 million sheep in 1980. New South Wales is the chief wool state, followed by Western Australia. There are also 26 million cattle and beef and dairy products are of great importance. Queensland is the chief cattle state. Only about 2 per cent of the land is cultivated, but yields are high and crops are varied because of the wide climatic range. But despite its importance, only 6 per cent of the workforce is employed in agriculture. Manufacturing industries are mostly in the towns and cities. The main steel centres are Newcastle, Wollongong and Whyalla. Dutch navigators landed in northern and eastern Australia in the early 17th century and in 1642 the Dutch explorer Abel Tasman discovered Tasmania without ever sighting the mainland. But the Dutch were not attracted by the arid coasts and their hostile inhabitants, the Aborigines. In 1770, however, the British Captain James Cook explored the fertile eastern coast and, in 1788, a British convict settlement was established on the present site of Sydney. In 1793 the first free settlers arrived. Gold rushes in the 1850s and 1890s accelerated immigration. In 1901 the Australian states united to form the Commonwealth of Australia and Parliament was moved to Canberra in Australian Capital Territory in 1927. Since 1945 immigrants to Australia have included people from central Europe, Greece, Italy, the Netherlands, Poland, Turkey and Yugoslavia, as well as Britons. In recent years, Australia's ties with Britain have been weakened by Britain's membership of the EEC and also by a new orientation of Australian foreign policy towards south-eastern Asia and the United States. But Australia, now one of the world's most prosperous nations, remains a member of the Commonwealth and the British monarch, represented by a Governor-General, is Head of State.

Area: 7,686,849 km^2 (2,968,071 sq mi); **Population:** 15,066,000; **Capital:** Canberra (pop 241,000); **Other cities:** Sydney (3,193,000), Melbourne (2,740,000), Brisbane (1,015,000), Adelaide (933,000), Perth (884,000), Newcastle (380,000), Wollongong (224,000), Hobart (168,000), Gold Coast (143,000), Geelong (141,000); **Highest point:** Mt Kosciusko, 2228 m (7310 ft), in the Australian Alps; **Official language:** English; **Religion:** mainly Anglicanism and Roman Catholicism; **Adult literacy rate:** 100 per cent; **Average life expectancy at birth:** 73 years; **Unit of currency:** Dollar; **Main exports:** metals and metal ores; cereals, meat, coal and coke, textiles, sugar and honey, iron and steel, **Per capita GNP:** US$9100.

AUSTRIA, a federal republic in central Europe. The Alps cover about 75 per cent of the land and tourism is a major industry, especially winter sports. The Danube river valley in the north is the chief farming region. Livestock are also important: the uplands contain much summer pasture. Forests occupy about 40 per cent of the land. Industry

STATES AND TERRITORIES OF AUSTRALIA

State or territory	Area (sq km)	Area (sq mi)	Population (1979)	Capital
Australian Capital Territory	2,432	939	227,200	Canberra
New South Wales	801,428	309,450	5,111,600	Sydney
Northern Territory	1,347,519	520,308	117,700	Darwin
Queensland	1,727,522	667,036	2,213,900	Brisbane
South Australia	984,377	380,091	1,297,200	Adelaide
Tasmania	68,322	26,385	420,100	Hobart
Victoria	227,618	87,889	3,874,500	Melbourne
Western Australia	2,527,621	975,973	1,257,000	Perth

accounted for 42 per cent of the GDP in 1978 (agriculture supplied 5 per cent). Iron ore and lignite are mined, forming the basis of the iron and steel industry. Vienna is the main manufacturing and cultural centre; 54 per cent of the people lived in urban areas in 1980. Austria, part of the Holy Roman Empire, became a possession of the Hapsburg family in 1282. From 1438 this family supplied all but one of the Holy Roman Emperors. After the Empire ended (1806), the Hapsburg ruler became Emperor of Austria. From 1867 Austria became part of the dual monarchy of Austria-Hungary, which collapsed in 1918 ending Hapsburg power. In 1938 Germany annexed Austria. In 1945 Austria was partitioned between the Allies, but it became a neutral federal republic in 1955.

Area: 83,849 km^2 (32,376 sq mi); **Population:** 7,526,000; **Capital:** Vienna (pop 1,615,000); **Other cities:** Graz (248,000), Linz (203,000), Salzburg (129,000), Innsbruck (115,000); **Highest point:** Gross Glockner, 3797 m (12,457 ft); **Official language:** German; **Religion:** Roman Catholicism (88 per cent); **Adult literacy rate:** 99 per cent; **Average life expectancy at birth:** 72 years; **Unit of currency:** Schilling; **Main exports:** iron and steel, machinery, timber and wood products, chemicals, textiles and craft items; **Per capita GNP:** US$8620.

BAHAMAS, a group of 14 large and about 700 small islands with a mild climate, to the south-east of Florida. Tourism is the main industry and 1.8 million tourists, many from the USA, visited the islands in 1979. Christopher Columbus discovered the islands in 1492: the island of San Salvador was probably his first landing place. The Bahamas became a British colony in 1717. Full independence within the Commonwealth was achieved in 1973. About 85 per cent of the people are descendants of African Negroes (former slaves).

Area: 13,935 km^2 (5381 sq mi); **Population:** 257,000; **Capital:** Nassau (pop 130,000); **Official language:** English; **Unit of currency:** Bahamian dollar; **Per capita GNP:** US$2780.

BAHRAIN, a densely populated island nation in the Persian Gulf. The capital Manama is on the largest island, also called Bahrain. This hot, arid country is an important oil producer and revenue from oil sales has been used to provide free education, health and other services. The Arabs occupied Bahrain in the 7th century. British influence began in the early 19th century and, in 1861, it became a British protectorate. It became a fully independent sheikhdom in 1971.

Area: 622 km^2 (240 sq mi); **Population:** 467,000; **Capital:** Manama (pop 114,000); **Official language:** Arabic; **Unit of currency:** Dinar; **Per capita GNP:** US$5640.

BANGLADESH, a densely populated country in Asia, is one of the world's poorest. It has a tropical monsoon climate, with hot, dry winters and hot, wet summers. It is mostly flat, largely occupying the fertile deltas of the Ganges, Brahmaputra and other rivers. The rivers are the main transport arteries but they often flood causing disease and starvation. Coastal floods are also caused when cyclones in the Bay of Bengal drive the sea inland. About 71 per cent of the mainly Muslim Bengali population is engaged in agriculture, which accounts for 57 per cent of the GDP (13 per cent comes from industry). In 1980 only 11 per cent of the population was urban. Formerly part of British India, Bangladesh became the province of East Pakistan in 1947. A bitter, 9-month war between East and West Pakistan in 1971 ended with the secession of East Pakistan which became the People's Republic of Bangladesh.

Area: 143,998 km^2 (55,601 sq mi); **Population:** 94,472,000; **Capital:** Dacca (pop 2,000,000); **Other cities:** Khulna (437,000), Chittagong (417,000); **Highest point:** Mt Keokradong, 1230 m (4035 ft); **Official language:** Bengali; **Religion:** Islam (80 per cent), Hinduism (10 per cent), Buddhism, Christianity; **Adult literacy rate:** 26 per cent; **Average life expectancy at birth:** 47 years; **Unit of currency:** Taka; **Main exports:** jute, hides and skins, leather, tea; **Per capita GNP:** US$100.

BARBADOS, the most easterly island in the West Indies. It is mostly flat, with a mild climate: annual temperatures average 25°–28°C (77°–82°F). More than 90 per cent of the people are descendants of African slaves, the rest being white or of mixed origin. Sugar and sugar products (molasses and rum) are the main products but tourism is now the chief industry; there were 371,000 visitors in 1979. British colonization dates back to 1628. Full independence within the Commonwealth was achieved in 1966.

Area: 431 km^2 (166 sq mi); **Population:** 257,000; **Capital:** Bridgetown (pop with suburbs 88,000); **Official language:** English; **Unit of currency:** Dollar; **Per capita GNP:** US$2400.

BELGIUM, a densely populated, prosperous industrial nation in western Europe. Two-thirds of the land is flat, but the largely forested Ardennes rise in the south-east. The navigable Meuse and Scheldt rivers drain the fertile central plains. Antwerp, near the mouth of the Scheldt, is the main port. The 66-km (41-mi) coastline contains several resorts and fishing ports. The climate is mild and average temperatures in Brussels range between 3°C (37°F) and 17°C (63°F). The rainfall averages 720 mm (28 in) on the coast and 1200 mm (47 in) in the Ardennes. Three languages are spoken: Flemish (a Dutch dialect) in the north; French by the Walloons in the south; and German by a small group in the south-east. Conflict between Flemish- and French-speakers has led to rioting and complaints about discrimination. The population is highly urbanized: 72 per cent lived in urban areas in 1980. The lowlands are intensely cultivated. Most farms are small and only 3 per cent of the workforce is engaged solely in agriculture (which accounts for 2 per cent of the GDP): many farmers have jobs in industry, which employs 43 per cent of the workforce and contributes 37 per cent of the GDP. The main crops are cereals, notably wheat, flax, potatoes and sugar beet. There are 2.9 million cattle and 5 million pigs. Coal is mined in the north-eastern Campine (Kempen) region, which has become a major industrial area. The older industrial areas are in the south, in the Sambre-Meuse valley. This zone is based on coalfields which extend from Mons to Liège, but extraction of the coal has become expensive and the region has declined in consequence. Antwerp is a major industrial centre, some industries being based on imported oil, as is Brussels whose varied industries produce luxury goods and many other items. Textiles are important, particularly in Flanders; the main centre is Ghent. Belgium was divided into small counties in the Middle Ages. It came under the Austrian Hapsburgs in 1477 and the Spanish Hapsburgs in 1506. After a spell of independence (1598–1621), it came successively under Spain, Austria, France and the Netherlands. It declared its independence from the Netherlands in 1830. Germany occupied Belgium in both World Wars. After World War II, Belgium recovered quickly through economic co-operation with the Netherlands and Luxembourg in the Benelux customs union. It joined the European Coal and Steel Community in 1953 and was a founder-member of the EEC in 1957. Brussels is headquarters of the EEC Commission and Council of Ministers. The Kingdom of Belgium is a constitutional, representative and hereditary monarchy, with an elected Senate and Chamber of Deputies.

Area: 30,513 km^2 (11,782 sq mi); **Population:** 9,941,000; **Capital:** Brussels (pop 1,009,000); **Other cities:** Ghent (242,000), Charleroi (222,000), Liège (220,000), Antwerp (194,000), Bruges (118,000), Namur (101,000); **Highest point:** Botrange Mt, 694 m (2277 ft); **Official languages:** Dutch, French, German; **Religions:** Roman Catholicism, Protestantism; **Adult literacy rate:** 99 per cent; **Average life expectancy at birth:** 72 years; **Unit of currency:** Belgian franc; **Main exports:** engineering products, textiles, chemicals, glass, food, diamonds; **Per capita GNP:** US$10,890.

BELIZE, which faces the Caribbean Sea in Central America, is flat in the north, with uplands in the south. Forests flourish and sugar-cane is the chief cash crop in this hot, wet nation. More than 50 per cent of the people are Creoles; most of the others are of Mayan Indian, black Carib or European descent. Britain's contacts with Belize date back to the early 17th century. Belize was first declared a British colony in 1862, although neighbouring Guatemala has claimed it since 1821. The continuing dispute with Guatemala delayed full independence for Belize until 1981.

Area: 22,965 km^2 (8867 sq mi); **Population:** 135,000; **Capital:** Belmopan (pop 4000); **Official language:** English; **Unit of currency:** Dollar; **Per capita GNP:** US$1030.

BENIN, a People's Republic on the Gulf of Guinea in West Africa. Behind the sandy coast are low plateaux, with the highest land in the north-west. The formerly forested south has an equatorial climate but winters are dry in the tropical northern savanna. The black African population is divided into 50 groups, the largest being the Fon, Adja, Bariba and Yoruba. Agriculture employs 46 per cent of the workforce and accounts for 31 per cent of the GDP (13 per cent comes from industry). The chief food crops are maize and millet and the chief cash crop is palm kernels and oil. Oil was discovered offshore in the late 1970s. Benin (known as Dahomey until 1975) was ruled by France from the 1890s to 1960. Between 1960 and 1972 there were 6 coups. In 1977 there was an unsuccessful attempt by mercenaries to overthrow the government.

Area: 112,622 km^2 (43,486 sq mi); **Population:** 3,734,000; **Capital:** Porto Novo (pop 104,000); **Other cities:** Cotonou (178,000); **Official language:** French; **Religions:** traditional religions (65 per cent), Christianity (17 per cent), Islam (15 per cent); **Adult literacy rate:** 11 per cent; **Average life expectancy at birth:** 46 years; **Unit of currency:** Franc CFA; **Main exports:** palm kernels and oil, cotton, groundnuts; **Per capita GNP:** US$250.

This market is in La Paz, Bolivia's seat of government. La Paz stands in a valley in the Andes range and is the world's highest large city.

BERMUDA, a British island colony in the North Atlantic, about 920 km (572 miles) from Cape Hatteras in the USA. Of the 150 islands, 20 are uninhabited. The climate is mild: annual temperatures average 21°C (70°F). About 60 per cent of the people are black. Tourism accounts for 41 per cent of the GDP: many of the 600,000 tourists come from the USA. Farming and fishing are important locally. Bermuda was named after its discoverer, the Spaniard Juan Bermúdez, in 1503. Britain took the islands in 1684 and internal self-government was granted in 1968.

Area: 53 km^2 (20 sq mi); **Population:** 62,000; **Capital:** Hamilton (pop 3000); **Per capita GNP:** US$9260 (1978).

BHUTAN, a mountainous landlocked kingdom between China and India. Most people, who are of Tibetan or Hindu Nepalese origin, live in fertile valleys where the climate is warm and wet. Agriculture, mostly at subsistence level, employed 93 per cent of the workforce in 1978; only 4 per cent lived in towns. Some rice, fruit and timber are exported.

American Indians hunt fish in the Xingu River in the Amazon basin of Brazil. Economic development is now threatening the survival of the Indians.

Most manufactures and fuels must be imported. Contact with the West began in 1774. The present ruling dynasty was founded in 1907, but an elected National Assembly can now dismiss the king. India assumed responsibility for Bhutan's foreign affairs in 1949.

Area: 47,000 km^2 (18,148 sq mi); **Population:** 1,352,000; **Capital:** Thimphu; **Official language:** Dzongkha; **Religion:** Buddhism; **Adult literacy rate:** 5 per cent; **Average life expectancy at birth:** 41 years; **Unit of currency:** Ngultrum; **Per capita GNP:** US$80.

BOLIVIA, a landlocked republic in South America. The Andes mountains in the south-west contain a central plateau, the Altiplano, where most Bolivians live. It has a cool climate, contrasting with the hot Amazon rain forests in the north-east. Lake Titicaca, the world's highest navigable lake, is on the border with Peru. More than 50 per cent of the people are American Indians, a third are *mestizos* and the rest of European origin. Agriculture employs 51 per cent of the people, but mining is the most valuable industry. Bolivia is the world's 2nd largest tin producer and antimony, copper, lead, oil and natural gas, silver and wolfram are also mined. Spain ruled Bolivia from 1532 to 1825 when Simón Bolívar's army liberated the country (then Upper Peru). Oil discoveries have recently offered hope for Bolivia, South America's poorest nation.

Area: 1,098,581 km^2 (424,188 sq mi); **Population:** 5,897,000; **Capital:** La Paz (seat of government, pop 655,000), Sucre (legal capital, 63,000); **Other cities:** Santa Cruz (256,000), Cochabamba (204,000); **Highest point:** Mt Tocopuri, 6755 m (22,162 ft); **Official language:** Spanish; **Religion:** Roman Catholicism; **Adult literacy rate:** 63 per cent; **Average life expectancy at birth:** 52 years; **Unit of currency:** Peso; **Main exports:** tin, oil, natural gas, cotton; **Per capita GNP:** US$550.

BOTSWANA, a thinly populated, landlocked republic in southern Africa. Most of the country is a plateau between 600 and 1200 m (1969–3937 ft) high. Average temperatures range between 27°C (81°F) and 32°C (90°F). The rainfall is less than 250 mm (10 in) in the south-west, but 760 mm (30 in) in the north. The Kalahari, a semi-desert, covers 84 per cent of the country and only a few nomadic Bushmen live there. Most people belong to the Bantu-speaking Tswana group, including the Bamangwato and Bangwaketse. They live mostly in the east around the Botswanan section of the Cape Town-Bulawayo railway. Minerals now dominate the economy: diamonds and copper-nickel matte made up 57 per cent of the exports in 1978. Most people work in agriculture. Arable land covers only 2 per cent of the country, but cattle farming is important – there were 3.3 million cattle in 1979. Botswana (formerly called Bechuanaland) became a British protectorate in 1885. It became fully independent within the Commonwealth in 1966.

Area: 600,372 km^2 (231,818 sq mi); **Population:** 820,000; **Capital:** Gaborone (pop 54,000); **Official language:** English; **Religions:** Christianity, traditional beliefs; **Adult literacy rate:** 20 per cent; **Average life expectancy at birth:** 46 years; **Unit of currency:** Pula; **Main exports:** diamonds, meat and meat products, copper, nickel; **Per capita GNP:** US$720.

BRAZIL, the world's 5th largest nation, occupies nearly half of South America. In the north, the equatorial Amazon basin covers more than 5.3 million km^2 (2 million sq mi). It contains the world's largest rain forest (*selvas*), which are now being reduced as economic development proceeds. The Amazon river, 6437 km (4000 mi) long, is the world's second longest, with a greater volume than any other. It is navigable into Peru. South of the *selvas* is a huge tropical grassland, plateau region, the *campos*. This region is still little developed despite the inauguration in its heart of the new capital of Brasilia in 1960. The north-east around Recife and Salvador has a forested coastal plain, but the inland plateaux are dry: long droughts cause much hardship to an already impoverished population. The central coastal region is the most densely populated and includes the great industrial cities of São Paulo and Rio de Janeiro. Inland are fertile plateaux and pleasant, mineral-rich highlands. The plateaux near São Paulo are Brazil's main coffee-producing region. The southern region around Porto Alegre has a temperate climate: pastoral farming is important. About 75 per cent of Brazil's population is of Portuguese or other

European origin. There are many people of mixed European/Indian/Negro descent, perhaps 200,000 pure Indians and some blacks: colour prejudice is almost absent. The population is increasing quickly (2.9 per cent per year in 1970–78). There is also a rapid shift of population from rural to urban areas. The urban population increased from 46 per cent in 1960 to 65 per cent in 1980 and slums now surround many cities. Agriculture still provides work for two-fifths of the people, although its contribution to the GDP is only 11 per cent. Brazil leads the world in producing bananas and coffee, and it is among the top world producers of beef, veal, cocoa, cotton, maize, sugar-cane, soya beans and tobacco. Industry accounts for 37 per cent of the GDP. Brazil is the leading producer in Latin America of cars, merchant ships, steel and cement. It has huge reserves of minerals, many of which are unexploited. Such minerals as asbestos, chrome ore, industrial diamonds, iron ore, quartz crystal and manganese are exported. In 1500 the Portuguese explorer Pedro Alvares Cabral claimed Brazil for Portugal. At that time an estimated 1.3 million Indians lived in the country. However, many were killed by Europeans and others died (and are still dying in the *selvas*) of European diseases to which they lack resistance. African slaves were introduced to work European estates. Brazil declared itself an independent empire in 1822 but it became a republic in 1889, one year after slavery was abolished. Since 1964 Brazil has been ruled by military regimes which have sought to modernize the economy, although in doing so they have been accused of infringing civil liberties.

Area: 8,511,965 km^2 (3,286,668 sq mi); **Population:** 133,882,000; **Capital:** Brasilia (pop 979,000); **Other cities:** São Paulo (8,408,000), Rio de Janeiro (5,395,000), Belo Horizonte (1,857,000), Salvador (1,446,000), Recife (1,184,000), Fortaleza (1,256,000), Pôrto Alegre (1,184,000), Nova Iguacu (1,130,000); **Highest point:** Pico da Bandeira, 2890 m (9482 ft); **Official language:** Portuguese; **Religion:** Roman Catholicism (91 per cent); **Adult literacy rate:** 76 per cent; **Average life expectancy at birth:** 62 years; **Unit of currency:** Cruzeiro; **Main exports:** coffee, machinery, soya beans, vehicles, cocoa; **Per capita GNP:** US$1690.

BRUNEI, a small Sultanate in north-western Borneo. Behind the narrow coastal plain, the interior is rugged and forested. The climate is tropical. Some 68 per cent of the people are of Malay origin and 25 per cent are Chinese. Oil is the main product. Natural gas, rubber and timber are also exported. Brunei ruled all of Borneo and nearby islands in the early 16th century, after which it gradually declined. It was a British protectorate between 1888 and 1971, although Britain still retains responsibility for Brunei's foreign affairs. A treaty of 1979 stated that Brunei would become fully independent at the end of 1983.

Area: 5765 km^2 (2226 sq mi); **Population:** 248,000; **Capital:** Bandar Seri Begawan (pop 58,000); **Official language:** Malay; **Unit of currency:** Brunei dollar; **Per capita GNP:** US$10,680.

BULGARIA, a Communist People's Republic facing the Black Sea in south-eastern Europe. The climate is transitional between Mediterranean and continental, the latter prevailing in the north and in the mountains. The mountains include the Balkans in the north and the higher Rhodope Mts in the south. The capital Sofia is in a fertile mountain basin. The River Danube plain is in the north, but the central plains are the main farming region, producing fruit, mulberry leaves, attar of rose, sugar beet, tobacco and wine. Agriculture accounted for 18 per cent of the GDP in 1978 (employing 40 per cent of the workforce). 64 per cent of the GDP came from industry: lignite, copper, iron ore and oil are mined and manufactures include cement, iron and steel goods and textiles. COMECON countries account for 80 per cent of Bulgaria's trade. Tourism is increasing. The Turks ruled Bulgaria from 1396. Bulgaria became an independent principality in 1878, East Rumelia (southern Bulgaria) being added in 1885. Bulgaria became an independent kingdom in 1908. After World War II, in which Bulgaria was allied with Germany, a Soviet-type republic was established.

Area: 110,912 km^2 (42,826 sq mi); **Population:** 8,999,000; **Capital:** Sofia (pop 1,032,000); **Other cities:** Plovdiv (333,000), Varna (279,000); **Highest point:** Musalla Mt, 2925 m (9596 ft); **Official language:** Bulgarian; **Religion:** Eastern Orthodox Church (27 per cent), Islam (7 per cent); **Average life expectancy at birth:** 72 years; **Unit of currency:** Lev; **Main exports:** machinery, metals and metal ores, food, tobacco, textiles; **Per capita GNP:** US$3690.

BURMA, a Socialist Republic in south-eastern Asia. The north, east and west are mountainous, but the southern valleys of the Irrawaddy and Sittang rivers are fertile. The Irrawaddy delta is one of the world's great rice-growing areas. The climate is tropical. The average temperature in the delta is 27°C (81°F) and the average annual rainfall is 2500 mm (98 in). Central Burma is much drier. Two-thirds of the people are Tibeto-Burmese and there are many small groups of isolated hill peoples. In 1978 agriculture employed 53 per cent of the workforce and accounted for 46 per cent of the GDP. Forests cover half the country and teak is a major product. Many minerals, including oil and natural gas, are mined. Manufacturing is mostly small-scale and concentrated in urban areas where 27 per cent of the people live. Britain took Burma between 1823 and 1855, making it a province of India. It became independent in 1948. Revolts by communists and hill tribesmen led to the setting up of military regimes in 1958 and again in 1962. The Union of Burma is now a one-party state.

Area: 676,552 km^2 (261,232 sq mi); **Population:** 35,211,000; **Capital:** Rangoon (pop 3,662,000); **Other cities:** Mandalay (417,000); **Highest point:** 5881 m (19,295 ft); **Official language:** Burmese; **Religion:** Buddhism; **Adult literacy rate:** 67 per cent; **Average life expectancy at birth:** 53 years; **Unit of currency:** Kyat; **Main exports:** teak, oil cake, jute, rubber, minerals; **Per capita GNP:** US$160.

BURUNDI, a small, densely populated, landlocked republic in east-central Africa. Part of Lake Tanganyika is in the Rift Valley in the west, with highlands and high plateaux in the east. The altitude moderates the equatorial climate. The highlands are grassy, but woodlands flourish on the warmer plateaux. There are a few pygmies, but the main ethnic groups are the Bantu-speaking Hutu (85 per cent) and the Hamitic Tutsi (13 per cent). Agriculture employs 85 per cent of the people, accounting for 56 per cent of the GDP. The pastoralist Tutsi entered the area from the north in the 17th century. They founded a feudal society under their *mwami* (king), making the Hutu serfs. Germany occupied Burundi and Rwanda (then Ruanda-Urundi) in 1890, but Belgium took the area in World War I. Burundi became an independent monarchy in 1962, but a republic was set up in 1966. Hutu attempts to overthrow the Tutsi government have all failed, leading to the deaths of thousands of Hutu.

Area: 27,834 km^2 (10,747 sq mi): **Population:** 4,293,000; **Capital:** Bujumbura (pop 157,000); **Official languages:** French, Kirundi; **Religions:** Roman Catholicism (60 per cent), Protestantism (7 per cent), traditional beliefs; **Adult literacy rate:** 25 per cent; **Average life expectancy at birth:** 45 years; **Unit of currency:** Burundi franc; **Main exports:** coffee (about 90 per cent); **Per capita GNP:** US$180.

CAMEROON, a republic in west-central Africa, bordering the Gulf of Guinea. Behind narrow coastal plains are plateaux that slope down in the north to the Lake Chad basin. The main uplands are on the western border: the highest peak is the volcanic Mt Cameroon on the coast. The equatorial south is forested; the tropical centre contains wooded savanna; the drier north has open grassland. Most people are black, speaking one of about 200 Bantu or Sudanic languages. Agriculture employs 82 per cent of the people. Mining (for bauxite and oil) is becoming important, but manufacturing is on a small scale. Portuguese explorers reached the coast in 1472. Germany made Cameroon a colony in 1884 but, after World War I, it was partitioned between Britain and France. French Cameroon became independent in 1960 and was joined in a federal republic in 1961 by part of British Cameroon – the other part joined Nigeria. A unitary state was established in 1972.

Area: 475,442 km^2 (183,579 sq mi); **Population:** 8,804,000; **Capital:** Yaoundé (pop 314,000); **Other cities:** Douala (458,000); **Highest point:** Mt Cameroon, 4070 m (13,353 ft); **Official languages:** English, French; **Religions:** Christianity (52 per cent), Islam (18 per cent), traditional beliefs; **Adult literacy rate:** 19 per cent; **Average life expectancy at birth:** 46 years; **Unit of currency:** Franc CFA; **Main exports:** coffee, cocoa, timber; **Per capita GNP:** US$560.

CANADA, the world's 2nd largest nation after the USSR, but it has only 2.5 persons per sq km (6 per sq mi). There are 7 main regions. The *Appalachian region* in the north-east is an extension of the Appalachian region in the USA. The *St Lawrence and Lower Great Lakes* region is Canada's most densely populated. The *Canadian Shield* is a vast region of ancient rocks, mineral deposits, and innumerable lakes and rivers. The *Hudson Bay* Lowland is a plain between the Canadian Shield and Hudson Bay. The *Western Interior Plains* are between the Canadian Shield and the *Western Mountains*, which include the Canadian Rockies and the Coast Range. In the far north are the bleak *Arctic Islands*. Canada has extremely cold winters, especially north of the Arctic Circle. Southern Canada has warm, moist summers. Rainfall varies from 2500 mm (98 in) per year in parts of the west to 300-500 mm (12–20 in) on the central prairies to 760 mm (30 in) in the south-east. Forests cover 35 per cent of Canada. There are also vast grasslands and tundra regions. The origins of the people are as follows: British (45 per cent), French (29 per cent), German (6 per cent), Italian (3 per cent) and Ukrainian (3 per cent). Most of the rest come from other parts of Europe. American Indians and Eskimos number 289,000 and 17,500 respectively. Canada has two official languages, English and French. Quebec is the main French-speaking province. In a referendum there in 1980, 40.5 per cent

The Niagara Falls are on the border between Canada and the United States between Lake Erie and Lake Ontario. The Falls are one of North America's finest natural wonders. Goat Island divides the Falls into the 56-metre (184-ft) high American Falls and the 54-metre (177-ft) high Canadian Falls. Much hydroelectricity is generated at the Falls.

COUNTRIES OF THE WORLD

PROVINCES AND TERRITORIES OF CANADA

Province or territory	Area (sq km)	Area (sq mi)	Population (1980)	Capital
Alberta	661,187	255,300	2,009,000	Edmonton
British Columbia	948,599	366,276	2,567,000	Victoria
Manitoba	650,089	251,014	1,030,000	Winnipeg
New Brunswick	73,437	28,356	701,000	Fredericton
Newfoundland	404,518	156,194	574,000	St John's
Northwest Territory	3,379,693	1,304,978	43,000	Yellowknife
Nova Scotia	55,491	21,426	847,000	Halifax
Ontario	1,068,586	412,606	8,500,000	Toronto
Prince Edward Is.	5,657	2,184	123,000	Charlottetown
Quebec	1,540,685	594,894	6,299,000	Quebec
Saskatchewan	651,902	251,795	957,100	Regina
Yukon Territory	536,326	207,088	22,000	Whitehorse

of the people voted for and 59.5 per cent against 'separatism'. Canada is a prosperous country. Only 7.2 per cent of the land is cultivated, but Canada is one of the world's leading producers of barley, fruits, oats, wheat, rye and timber. Livestock ranching and dairy farming are also important. But agriculture contributes only 4 per cent of the GDP as opposed to 31 per cent from industry. Canada is among the top six world producers of asbestos, copper, gold, iron ore, lead, molybdenum, natural gas, nickel, potash, silver, uranium and zinc. But more important than mining is manufacturing. The chief industrial area is the St Lawrence and Lower Great Lakes region. Much traffic is carried along the St Lawrence Seaway, the world's longest artificial seaway at 304 km (189 mi). Canada's first people, the Indians, entered North America from Asia around 20,000 years ago. The Eskimos were later arrivals. Vikings sailed down Canada's coasts in about AD 1000, but the first definite European landfall was made in 1497. Quebec was founded by Samuel de Champlain in 1604, but intense rivalry soon developed between the French and British. Between 1689 and 1763, the British conquered the French settlements. In 1867 the Dominion of Canada, comprising Quebec, Ontario, Nova Scotia and New Brunswick, was established. Canada is now a federation of 10 self-governing provinces and 2 territories. The federal parliament consists of a Senate and a House of Commons.

Area: 9,976,139 km^2 (3,852,019 sq mi); **Population:** 24,620,000; **Capital:** Ottawa (pop with suburbs 693,000); **Other cities:** Toronto (2,803,000), Montreal (2,802,000), Vancouver (1,166,000), Winnipeg (578,000), Edmonton (554,000), Quebec (542,000), Hamilton (529,000), Calgary (470,000); **Highest point:** Mt Logan, 6050 m (19,849 ft); **Official languages:** English, French; **Religions:** Roman Catholicism (46 per cent), Protestantism (42 per cent); **Adult literacy rate:** 98 per cent; **Average life expectancy at birth:** 74 years; **Unit of currency:** Dollar; **Main exports:** motor cars and vehicle parts, newsprint and wood pulp, oil and natural gas, wheat, industrial machinery, iron ore; **Per capita GNP:** US$9650.

CAPE VERDE, an island republic about 500 km (311 mi) west of Senegal in West Africa. The 10 large islands and 5 islets are of volcanic origin. The climate is tropical, but the rainfall is very unreliable. Most people are of mixed Portuguese and African origin; 28 per cent are classed as 'pure' Africans. Most people are subsistence farmers, but severe droughts in the 1970s forced many people to emigrate and the government has had to provide work for destitute farmers. Portugal claimed the islands in 1460. From 1836 to 1879, Cape Verde was ruled with Portuguese Guinea (now Guinea-Bissau) and close ties between the two territories continued. In 1963–74, Cape Verdeans fought alongside Guineans against the Portuguese in Portuguese Guinea. Independence for Cape Verde was achieved in 1975.

Area: 4033 km^2 (1557 sq mi); **Population:** 324,000; **Capital:** Praia (pop 21,000); **Highest point:** Pico do Cano, 2829 m (9281 ft); **Official language:** Portuguese; **Religions:** Roman Catholicism (97 per cent), Protestantism (3 per cent), a few animists; **Adult literacy rate:** 28 per cent; **Average life expectancy at birth:** 50 years; **Unit of currency:** Escudo; **Main exports:** fish and lobsters, salt, sugar, bananas; **Per capita GNP:** US$270.

CAYMAN ISLANDS, a British island group in the West Indies. These tropical islands export turtle shells, turtle meat and fish, but tourism is more important. The people are of European, African or mixed origin. Columbus discovered in the islands in 1503. Britons settled there in the 17th century.

Area: 259 km^2 (100 sq mi); **Population:** 11,000; **Capital:** George Town (pop 4000).

CENTRAL AFRICAN REPUBLIC, a landlocked nation, consists largely of plateaux between 600 and 900 m (1969–2953 ft). Temperatures average 26°C (79°F) all the year. The south has an average annual rainfall of 2030 mm (80 in); the far north gets 510 mm (20 in). The south is forested, but wooded savanna covers most of the land. Wildlife is abundant. Most people speak Sudanese languages. Agriculture employs 89 per cent of the workforce, contributing 36 per cent of the GDP. Diamonds are mined and large uranium deposits have been found, but manufacturing is on a small scale. The country became part of French Equatorial Africa in the 1880s. It became independent in 1960. From 1965 it was ruled by Jean-Bédel Bokassa who, in 1977, made himself 'emperor'. The country was then named the Central African Empire. Bokassa was overthrown in 1979 and the nation again became a republic.

Area: 622,984 km^2 (240,549 sq mi); **Population:** 2,086,000; **Capital:** Bangui (pop 302,000); **Official language:** French; **Religions:** Roman Catholicism (46 per cent), Protestantism (36 per cent), traditional beliefs; **Adult literacy rate:** 8 per cent (1973); **Average life expectancy at birth:** 46 years; **Unit of currency:** Franc CFA; **Main exports:** coffee, diamonds, timber, cotton; **Per capita GNP:** US$290.

CHAD, a landlocked nation in north-central Africa. Lake Chad, the remains of an inland sea, is in the west. Southern Chad is savanna-covered, but sandy deserts and bare rocky uplands, notably the high Tibesti massif, are in the north. About 100 languages are spoken in Chad. In the south, where most of the population lives, most people are Negroid. Muslim Arabs and Berbers live in the north. Cultural divisions have caused much civil conflict and periodic war since the mid-1960s. In 1980 Libyan troops intervened in Chad but they were replaced in 1981 by an OAU force. Agriculture employs 86 per cent of the workers in this poor nation. Cotton is the chief crop. Chad became a French colony in 1897 and an independent republic in 1960.

Area: 1,284,000 km^2 (495,782 sq mi); **Population:** 4,714,000; **Capital:** N'Djamena (pop 242,000); **Highest point:** Emi Koussi, 3415 m (11,204 ft); **Official language:** French; **Religions:** Islam (45 per cent), Christianity (5 per cent); traditional beliefs (50 per cent); **Adult literacy rate:** 15 per cent; **Average life expectancy at birth:** 43 years; **Unit of currency:** Franc CFA; **Main exports:** cotton (66 per cent), meat and cattle, fish; **Per capita GNP:** US$110.

CHILE, a narrow country stretching through 38° of latitude in South America. Its greatest width is about 400 km (249 miles). From west to east, there are generally three regions; coastal uplands, central lowland basins and valleys, and the high Andes. In the glaciated south, the coastal uplands are islands, the central lowlands becoming arms of the sea. Chile's climate changes north-south. The north is hot and arid, including the rainless Atacama Desert with its large mineral reserves. Central Chile, where most Chileans live, has hot summers and mild moist winters. The forested south with its beautiful fiords is cool: heavy rain falls in all seasons. Cape Horn, South America's stormy tip, is in the far south. People of mixed European and Indian origin make up 68 per cent of the population, Europeans 30 per cent, and Araucanian Indians 2 per cent. Agriculture provides work for 20 per cent of the people, accounting for 18 per cent of the GDP. Farmland covers 15 per cent of Chile, pasture 27 per cent and forests 29 per cent. The main farm products are barley, fruit, maize, wheat and wine. Industry accounts for 29 per cent of the GDP (with 20 per cent from manufacturing). Minerals include copper, which makes up 48 per cent of the exports, iron ore, nitrates and oil. Manufacturing industries are powered mainly by hydro-electricity. Chile was a Spanish colony for about 300 years before becoming independent in 1818. It gained its mineral-rich northern provinces in a war with Peru and Bolivia in 1879–83. In 1970 a Marxist government led by Salvador Allende was elected to office, but it was overthrown in 1973 by the armed forces. The military government of General Augusto Pinochet revived the flagging economy, but was accused of violating civil liberties.

Area: 756,945 km^2 (292,274 sq mi); **Population:** 11,478,000; **Capital:** Santiago (pop with suburbs 3,692,000); **Other cities:** Valparaiso (611,000), Concepción (513,000); **Highest point:** Ojos de Salado, 6885 m (22,590 ft); **Official language:** Spanish; **Religion:** Roman Catholicism (90 per cent); **Adult literacy rate:** 88 per cent; **Average life expectancy at birth:** 67 years; **Unit of currency:** Peso; **Main exports:** copper, paper and wood pulp, timber, iron ore, nitrates; **Per capita GNP:** US$1690.

CHINA, the world's 3rd largest country, contains about 20 per cent of the world's population. The land is extremely varied. In the north-east is the basin of the Hwang Ho, one of the world's longest rivers at 4345 km (2700 mi) long. It cuts through a loess plateau which has coloured its waters yellow. The lower course of the Hwang Ho crosses the North China Plain. To the north lie the central plain and eastern highlands of Manchuria. To the south, beyond the Tsin Ling Mountains lies the Yangtze Kiang basin of Central China. The Yangtze is Asia's longest river, 5470 km (3400 mi) in length. China's third important river basin is that of the Si Kiang in the south-east, south of the South China Highlands. Outer or Western China contains the high and vast Tibetan plateau which rises in the south to the Himalayan range, crowned by Mt Everest. In the far west are other ranges including the lofty Pamirs and Tien Shan. North-eastern China contains some large deserts, including the vast Tarim and Dzungaria basins. The Gobi desert straddles the frontier between Inner Mongolia (in China) and Mongolia. The climate varies from north to south. North-eastern China has bitterly cold winters and warm summers. The average annual rainfall is between 635 and 760 mm (25–30 in). Central China has milder winters and more rainfall – about 1000–1500 mm (39–59 in) per year, while south-eastern China has a subtropical monsoon climate and many places get more than 2030 mm (80 in) of rain per year. The north-eastern deserts have less than 100 mm (4 in). About 94 per cent of the population are Han, or true, Chinese. But there are also large national minorities, including Manchus, Mongols, Tibetans and Uighurs, who maintain their own cultures. The population is densest in the fertile river basins and along the coasts of eastern China. Some 25 per cent of the population lives in urban areas. The rural population has been encouraged to live in communes, which are groups of villages where up to 20,000 people work together, share the produce and get wages that are geared to production. Some 62 per cent of the workforce is engaged in agriculture. China leads the world in millet, rice and tobacco production. It is among the top three

COUNTRIES OF THE WORLD

Left and below: A vase of the Chinese Ch'ing dynasty (1644–1911) and a ginger jar of the Ming dynasty (1368–1644). Right: A jade Han-dynasty monster (206 BC–AD 220).

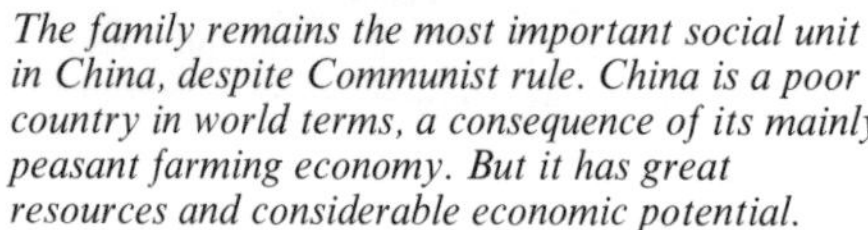

The family remains the most important social unit in China, despite Communist rule. China is a poor country in world terms, a consequence of its mainly peasant farming economy. But it has great resources and considerable economic potential.

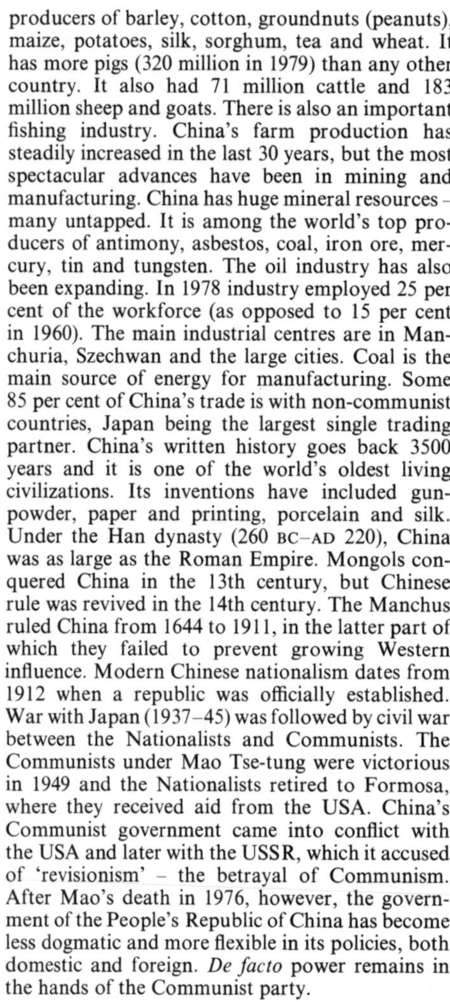

producers of barley, cotton, groundnuts (peanuts), maize, potatoes, silk, sorghum, tea and wheat. It has more pigs (320 million in 1979) than any other country. It also had 71 million cattle and 183 million sheep and goats. There is also an important fishing industry. China's farm production has steadily increased in the last 30 years, but the most spectacular advances have been in mining and manufacturing. China has huge mineral resources – many untapped. It is among the world's top producers of antimony, asbestos, coal, iron ore, mercury, tin and tungsten. The oil industry has also been expanding. In 1978 industry employed 25 per cent of the workforce (as opposed to 15 per cent in 1960). The main industrial centres are in Manchuria, Szechwan and the large cities. Coal is the main source of energy for manufacturing. Some 85 per cent of China's trade is with non-communist countries, Japan being the largest single trading partner. China's written history goes back 3500 years and it is one of the world's oldest living civilizations. Its inventions have included gunpowder, paper and printing, porcelain and silk. Under the Han dynasty (260 BC–AD 220), China was as large as the Roman Empire. Mongols conquered China in the 13th century, but Chinese rule was revived in the 14th century. The Manchus ruled China from 1644 to 1911, in the latter part of which they failed to prevent growing Western influence. Modern Chinese nationalism dates from 1912 when a republic was officially established. War with Japan (1937–45) was followed by civil war between the Nationalists and Communists. The Communists under Mao Tse-tung were victorious in 1949 and the Nationalists retired to Formosa, where they received aid from the USA. China's Communist government came into conflict with the USA and later with the USSR, which it accused of 'revisionism' – the betrayal of Communism. After Mao's death in 1976, however, the government of the People's Republic of China has become less dogmatic and more flexible in its policies, both domestic and foreign. *De facto* power remains in the hands of the Communist party.

Area: 9,596,961 km^2 (3,705,610 sq km); **Population:** 1,012,358,000; **Capital:** Peking (or Beijing, pop 8,706,000); **Other cities:** Shanghai (11,320,000), Tientsin (7,390,000), Chungking (6,200,000), Canton (5,000,000), Shenyang (4,400,000), Lüta (4,200,000), Wuhan (3,500,000), Nanking (2,400,000), Harbin (2,100,000); **Highest point:** Mt Everest, 8848 m (29,028 ft); **Official language:** Chinese; **Religions:** Confucianism, Taoism, Buddhism, Islam, Christianity; **Average life expectancy at birth:** 70 years; **Unit of currency:** Renminbi or Yuan; **Main exports:** industrial products (including petroleum, chemicals, machinery, equipment), agricultural products; **Per capita GNP:** US$230 (1978).

CHRISTMAS ISLAND, an Australian territory in the Indian Ocean populated by Chinese, Malays and Europeans. The only industry is phosphate mining. It came under the Governor of the Straits Settlement in 1889 and was incorporated with Singapore in 1900. Australia took over in 1958.

Area: 135 km^2 (52 sq mi); **Population:** 3200; **Status:** Australian external territory.

COCOS (KEELING) ISLANDS, an Australian territory in the Indian Ocean comprising 27 coral islands that export copra. Britain annexed them in 1857 and they came under the Governor of the Straits Settlement in 1886. They were placed under Australian rule in 1955.

Area: 14 km^2 ($5\frac{1}{2}$ sq mi); **Population:** 500; **Status:** Australian external territory.

COLOMBIA, a republic in north-eastern South America, contains three ranges of the Andes whose high, fertile valleys contain most of the people. In eastern Colombia, *llanos* grasslands merge into the forests of the upper Amazon and Orinoco basins. The coastal lowlands are hot and wet, with average temperatures of 26°–28°C (79°–82°F) and about 2540 mm (100 in) of rain. The highlands are cooler and less rainy. The *llanos* have dry winters but wet summers. More than two-thirds of the people are of mixed Indian and European origin; most others are of pure Indian, European or Negroid descent. Agriculture accounts for 31 per cent of the GDP. The chief export, coffee, is grown in the highlands. Industry accounts for 27 per cent of the GDP and 70 per cent of the people now live in urban areas. Spaniards opened up the region in the early 16th century. Spanish rule was overthrown in 1819. Greater Colombia then included Venezuela, Ecuador and parts of Panama. Venezuela and Ecuador soon split off and Panama broke away in 1903. A civil war in 1948–53 led to a military seizure of power but, after 1957, democracy was restored.

Area: 1,138,914 km^2 (439,761 sq mi); **Population:** 27,966,000; **Capital:** Bogotá (pop 3,831,000); **Other cities:** Medellin (1,442,000), Cali (1,255,000); **Highest point:** Pico Cristobal Colón, 5775 m (18,947 ft); **Official language:** Spanish; **Religion:** Roman Catholicism; **Adult literacy rate:** 81 per cent; **Average life expectancy at birth:** 62 years; **Unit of currency:** Peso; **Main exports:** coffee, emeralds, meat, sugar, petroleum, fuel oils, hides and skins; **Per capita GNP:** US$1010.

COMOROS, an island Federal and Islamic Republic at the northern end of the Mozambique Channel. Geographically, there are 4 islands: Njazidja, Nzwani, Mahoré (or Mayotte) and Mwali. The republic contains three of them, but Mayotte is a French territory. The islands are mountainous: Mt Kartala, 2361 m (7746 ft), is an active volcano. The population is mixed, including elements from Africa, Asia and Europe. These tropical islands have few resources and most people are subsistence farmers. They came under French protection in 1886–1909 and became a colony in 1912. In 1946 they became a French overseas department. The people voted for independence in 1974, except in Mayotte where a majority opposed it. In 1975 the Chamber of Deputies voted for immediate independence, which France recognized on January 1, 1976. But Mayotte (a French colony since 1843) became a *collectivité particulière*, a status part-way between a French Overseas Territory and an Overseas Department.

Area: 2171 km^2 (838 sq mi); **Population:** 448,000; **Capital:** Moroni; **Official languages:** Arabic, French; **Religions:** mainly Islam, Roman Catholicism (4 per cent); **Average life expectancy at birth:** 42; **Unit of currency:** Franc CFA; **Main exports:** vanilla, vegetable oils, cloves, copra, coffee, cocoa; **Per capita GNP:** US$210.

CONGO, a People's Republic in equatorial Africa. Behind a narrow coastal plain is an upland region; the north is a swampy plain drained by the Congo (Zaire) and Oubangui rivers. High temperatures and heavy rainfall, except on the coast, have encouraged the growth of rain forests and woodland savanna. Most people speak Bantu languages (including Kongo, Téké, Mbochi), but 12,000 pygmies live in central Congo. Less than 2 per cent of Congo is cultivated, but agriculture employs 35 per cent of the workforce, accounting for 13 per cent of the GDP. Industry accounts for 33 per cent; oil extraction and processing industries are especially important. 37 per cent of the population lives in urban areas. Discovered in 1482, Congo later became a slave trade centre. French rule was established in the 1880s; Congo later became part of French Equatorial Africa. Full independence was achieved in 1960. Military governments have ruled the country since 1968.

Area: 342,000 km^2 (132,054 sq mi); **Population:** 1,613,000; **Capital:** Brazzaville (pop 301,000); **Other towns:** Pointe-Noire (147,000); **Official language:** French; **Religions:** traditional beliefs (50 per cent); Christianity (48 per cent), Islam (2 per cent); **Adult literacy rate:** 50 per cent; **Average life expectancy at birth:** 46 years; **Unit of currency:** Franc CFA; **Main exports:** oil, timber, potash, fertilizers, coffee, cocoa; **Per capita GNP:** US$630.

COOK ISLANDS, a self-governing territory of New Zealand in the South Pacific. Of the 15 islands, 9 are atolls and 6 volcanic. Most people are Polynesians. Exports include fruits and copra. The islands became a British protectorate in 1888 and part of New Zealand in 1901.

Area: 234 km^2 (90 sq mi); **Population:** 18,000; **Capital:** Avarua; **Official language:** English.

COSTA RICA, a Central American republic with coastlines on the Caribbean Sea and the Pacific Ocean. Inland it is mountainous with volcanic peaks. Fertile plateaux lie between the mountains. About 70 per cent of the people live in the largest of these, the Central Plateau. The tropical climate is modified by the relief. More than 80 per cent of the population is of European origin. There are 1200 Indians and a few thousand blacks, but most non-whites are of mixed European and Indian origin. Agriculture employs 29 per cent of the people, accounting for 22 per cent of the GDP; industry accounts for 27 per cent and services 51 per cent. The main cash crop is coffee. Costa Rica is one of the more prosperous nations of Central America. Spain ruled the country from around 1530 to 1821. Dictatorships and revolutions marred its early years of independence, but it has enjoyed democracy since 1919.

Area: 50,700 km^2 (19,576 sq miles); **Population:** 2,329,000; **Capital:** San José (pop 250,000); **Highest point:** Chirripo, 3820 m (12,861 ft); **Official language:** Spanish; **Religion:** Roman Catholicism; **Adult literacy rate:** 90 per cent; **Average life expectancy at birth:** 70 years; **Unit of currency:** Colón; **Main exports:** manufactures, coffee, bananas; **Per capita GNP:** US$1810.

CUBA, the largest nation in the West Indies. Small islands, reefs and mangrove swamps skirt much of the coast. More than half of the land is flat and fertile. Forested mountain ranges occupy about 25 per cent of the land, the rest being gently undulating country. The climate is tropical, with average temperatures of 22°–28°C (72°–82°F). The rainfall averages 1270 mm (50 in) per year. About 75 per cent of the people are descendants of Spaniards, the rest being blacks or mulattos. Some 65 per cent of the population lives in urban areas. Agriculture employs 25 per cent of the workforce, industry 31 per cent and service industries 44 per cent. About 34 per cent of Cuba is cultivated, most being government-owned. Sugar and its by-products, molasses and rum, are the main products. Minerals, tobacco, bananas and fish are also exported. Columbus discovered Cuba in 1492 and Spain ruled it between 1511 and 1898 (except when Britain occupied it in 1762–63). US influence was strong in the 20th century until Communist guerrillas led by Dr Fidel Castro seized power in 1959. Cuba became an ally of the USSR and, in the late 1970s and early 1980s, Cuban troops aided left-wing regimes in Africa.

Area: 114,524 km^2 (44,220 sq mi); **Population:** 10,346,000; **Capital:** Havana (pop 1,735,000); **Official language:** Spanish; **Religions:** Roman Catholicism, Protestantism; **Adult literacy rate:** 96 per cent; **Average life expectancy at birth:** 72 years; **Unit of currency:** Peso; **Main exports:** sugar (80 per cent); **Per capita GNP:** US$1410.

CYPRUS, an island republic in the north-eastern Mediterranean Sea. There are fertile coastal plains and a broad central plain (the Mesaoria). The Kyrenia and Karpass mountains are in the north and the Troödos mountains in the south. The climate is typically Mediterranean. Greek Cypriots form 80 per cent of the population, Turkish Cypriots 18 per cent and Armenian, Maronite and other minorities also live there. Communal conflict characterizes social life; most people feel themselves to be Greeks or Turks rather than Cypriots. About 60 per cent of the land is cultivated; one-third of the work-force is employed in farming. Agriculture supplies about half of the exports and minerals (notably copper) about 30 per cent. Britain rented Cyprus from the Ottoman Empire in 1878 but it annexed it in 1914 and proclaimed it a colony in 1927. A fierce guerrilla war preceded independence in 1960. The independence Constitution, providing for power-sharing between the communities, proved unworkable. In 1974 Turkish forces occupied the north. The island was partitioned, the northern 40 per cent being proclaimed the 'Turkish Cypriot Federated State'.

Area: 9251 km^2 (3572 sq mi); **Population:** 665,000; **Capital:** Nicosia (pop 121,000); **Other cities:** Limassol (102,000); **Highest point:** Mt Olympus, 1951 m (6401 ft); **Official languages:** Greek, Turkish; **Religions:** Eastern Orthodox Christianity, Islam; **Average life expectancy at birth:** 71 years; **Unit of currency:** Pound; **Main exports:** fruit and vegetables, manufactures (including wine), minerals; **Per capita GNP:** US$2940.

CZECHOSLOVAKIA, a landlocked Communist republic in eastern Europe. The saucer-shaped Bohemian plateau, bounded by mountains, is in the east. It is drained by the upper Elbe (the Vltava) on which Prague stands. Moravia, in the centre, is largely lowland, with rivers draining to the Danube. Slovakia, in the east, is mainly upland, with some plains in the south. The climate is continental. Average temperatures range between −7°C and 20°C (20°–68°F). The rainfall is between 500 and 1000 mm (20–39 in) per year. The people include the Czechs (65 per cent of the population), in Bohemia and Moravia, the Slovaks (30 per cent) and various minorities. Industry, which is nationalized, accounts for 72 per cent of the GDP: 63 per cent of the population lives in urban areas. The country is rich in coal and lignite and has many metal ores, although metals are imported. Farmland covers 55 per cent of the country. Crops include barley, hops, rye, sugar beet and wheat. The republic was created in 1918. Germany occupied Czechoslovakia in 1939. After World War II, in 1948, the Communists gained control. Demands for more freedom in 1968 led to an invasion by Soviet troops.

Area: 127,869 km^2 (49,373 sq mi); **Population:** 15,556,000; **Capital:** Prague (pop 1,189,000); **Other cities:** Brno (369,000); Bratislava (368,000); **Highest point:** 2655 m (8737 ft); **Official languages:** Czech, Slovak; **Religions:** Roman Catholicism, Protestantism; **Average life expectancy at birth:** 70 years; **Unit of currency:** Koruna; **Main exports:** machinery, industrial consumer goods, raw materials and fuels; **Per capita GNP:** US$5290.

DENMARK, the smallest but most densely populated nation in northern Europe. It consists of the low-lying Jutland peninsula and about 500 islands, the largest of which, Sjaelland, contains Copenhagen. Moraine covers much of the land, but two-thirds is fertile farmland or pasture. Animal products (bacon, butter, cheese, eggs) are particularly important as is sea fishing. But only 8 per cent of the workforce is engaged in agriculture, forestry and fishing. The leading sector of the economy is manufacturing. Products include superb silverware, furniture, processed food, chemicals, engineering goods, machinery and ships. Denmark formed a union with Norway and Sweden in the late 14th century. Sweden became independent in 1523 and Denmark ceded Norway to Sweden in 1814. Neutral in World War I, Denmark was occupied by Germany in World War II. After the war, it helped to set up the Nordic Council. It joined the EEC in 1973. The Faeroe Islands and Greenland are parts of Denmark.

Area: 43,069 km^2 (16,630 sq mi), not including Greenland; **Population:** 5,175,000; **Capital:** Copenhagen (pop 654,000); **Other cities:** Aarhus (245,000), Odense (169,000), Aalborg (154,000); **Highest point:** 173 m (568 ft); **Official language:** Danish; **Religion:** Lutheran Church; **Adult literacy rate:** 99 per cent; **Average life expectancy at birth:** 74 years; **Unit of currency:** Krone; **Main exports:** machinery and equipment, live animals and meat, dairy products and eggs, metals and metal manufactures; **Per capita GNP:** US$11,900.

DJIBOUTI, a small republic on the Red Sea in north-eastern Africa. The land is mostly hot desert. The people include the Somali-speaking Issas (40 per cent), the nomadic Afars (or Danakils, 33 per cent), both of whom are Muslims, and some

Europeans, Arabs and other foreigners. Stock raising is the main occupation. It became a French colony in 1881, called French Somaliland. In 1967 it was renamed the Territory of the Afars and Issas. It became independent as Djibouti in 1977.

Area: 22,000 km^2 (8495 sq mi); **Population:** 371,000; **Capital:** Djibouti (pop 150,000); **Official language:** French; **Main exports:** hides and skins, cattle; **Per capita GNP:** US$420.

DOMINICA, a volcanic island in the Windward Islands in the eastern Caribbean Sea. Its wet tropical climate supports dense forests. Most people are blacks or of mixed origin. There is a small Carib community, mostly of mixed origin. Agriculture and tourism are the main industries. Columbus discovered Dominica in 1493. It became a British colony in 1805 and a British Associated State in 1967. The Commonwealth of Dominica became an independent republic in 1978.

Area: 751 km^2 (290 sq mi); **Population:** 82,000; **Capital:** Roseau (pop 17,000); **Main exports:** bananas, citrus fruits; **Per capita GNP:** US$410.

DOMINICAN REPUBLIC, a nation occupying the eastern half of Hispaniola, an island in the West Indies. The land is mountainous and the climate tropical, with average temperatures of more than 20°C (68°F) and an average annual rainfall of 1000 mm (39 in). Rain forests are widespread, but the valleys are fertile. More than 70 per cent of the population is of mixed black and white descent, 15 per cent are white and 10 per cent are black. Agriculture employs 57 per cent of the workforce, contributing 21 per cent of the GDP (1978). Sugar is the chief export. Industry accounts for 35 per cent of the GDP: some bauxite, nickel, gold and silver are mined and there is some light industry. Tourism is increasingly important. Columbus discovered Hispaniola in 1492. Spain lost the area to France in 1795 but ruled it again in 1809–21. From 1822 to 1844 Haitians occupied the area. The Dominican Republic was founded in 1844, but its history has been marred by violence. From 1930–61 the country was a dictatorship. Elections were held in 1962, but a military coup in 1963 led to civil war in 1965 when US forces intervened. Since then the country has had elected governments.

Area: 48,734 km^2 (18,817 sq mi); **Population:** 5,776,000; **Capital:** Santo Domingo (pop 818,000); **Highest point:** Pico Duarte, 3124 m (10,249 ft); **Official language:** Spanish; **Religion:** Roman Catholicism; **Adult literacy rate:** 67 per cent; **Average life expectancy at birth:** 60 years; **Unit of currency:** Peso; **Main exports:** sugar, coffee; **Per capita GNP:** US$990.

ECUADOR, a republic on the Equator in north-western South America. It includes the 15 Galápagos Islands, about 970 km (603 mi) to the west. The Pacific coastlands have an average annual temperature of 27°C (81°F). The Andes ranges are much cooler; Quito at 2850 m (9350 ft) has an average temperature of 13°C (55°F). The hot Amazon basin occupies eastern Ecuador. The annual rainfall varies between 1020 and 1520 mm (40–60 in). More than half the people are Indians. There are also people of European, African and mixed descent. Agriculture employs 46 per cent of the people, contributing 21 per cent of the GDP. Industry accounts for 35 per cent, oil being the leading product. The Incas ruled the area from about 1470 until Spaniards conquered it in 1533. Independence was achieved in 1822 and Ecuador became a separate republic in 1830. Weak governments, armed rebellions and military coups have marred much of Ecuador's recent history. In 1979, however, elections were held and civilian rule was restored.

Area: 283,561 km^2 (109,489 sq mi); not including land disputed with Peru; **Population:** 8,893,000; **Capital:** Quito (pop 560,000); **Other cities:** Guayaquil (823,000); **Highest point:** Mt Chimborazo, 6272 m (20,577 ft); **Official language:** Spanish; **Religion:** Roman Catholicism; **Adult literacy rate:** 74 per cent; **Average life expectancy at birth:** 60 years; **Unit of currency:** Sucre; **Main exports:** oil, bananas, cocoa, coffee; **Per capita GNP:** US$1050.

EGYPT, an Arab Republic in north-eastern Africa. The fertile, irrigated Nile valley contains 99 per cent of the population, although it covers less than 4 per cent of the country. The Nile flows about 1200 km (746 mi) through Egypt. Near the Mediterranean Sea it divides into two branches, the Dumyat (Damietta) and Rashid (Rosetta), which enclose the triangular delta. The rest of Egypt is desert. The western (Libyan) desert contains several large oases and depressions, notably the Qattara depression, which is 133 m (436 ft) below sea level. The eastern, or Arabian, desert rises to highlands that border the Red Sea. But the highest peak, Jabal Katrinah, is in the Sinai peninsula, east of the Suez Canal. This international waterway, opened in 1869, is 173 km (107 mi) long, linking the Mediterranean and Red seas. Average temperatures in Egypt vary between 27°C and 32°C (81°–90°F) in summer and 13°–21°C (55°–70°F) in winter. The average annual rainfall is about 200 mm (8 in) in the far north and barely 25 mm (1 in) in the south. Most Egyptians are Arabs, but there are Berber, Nubian and Sudanese minorities. Egypt is a poor country, although it is the 2nd most industrialized in Africa. About 45 per cent of the population lives in urban areas and industry contributes 30 per cent of the GDP. Energy comes mainly from hydro-electric stations, especially at the Aswan High Dam. Manufactures include cement, chemicals, plastics, steel, sugar and textiles. Some phosphates, iron ore and oil are mined. Agriculture accounts for 29 per cent of the GDP, employing 51 per cent of the workforce. The chief export is cotton, but most farmers are peasants (*fellahin*) who practise subsistence farming. Tourism is important: over 1 million foreigners visited Egypt in 1979. Ancient Egypt's pyramids and other monuments are special attractions. Ancient Egypt's history is divided into 30 dynasties. The first began in 3100 BC, when Upper and Lower Egypt were united. It reached its peak under King Thutmose III (1490–36 BC). From 525 BC Egypt was mostly under foreign rule. In 30 BC it became part of the Roman empire and, in AD 395, it was the centre of

COUNTRIES OF THE WORLD

The pyramids of Egypt testify to the glories of one of the world's most important early civilizations. Today more than a million people visit Egypt every year to see the pyramids and other magnificent remains of ancient Egypt. The money they spend is a major source of foreign exchange. The camel of North Africa and South-West Asia is a leading work animal and a means of transport across the burning hot, arid wastes that fully justifies the animal's popular name, 'the ship of the desert'.

the Coptic Christian Church. Arabs occupied Egypt in 639–642, introducing Islam and Arabic. In 1517 Egypt became part of the Ottoman empire, but it came under French rule in 1798–1801. In 1881 Britain occupied Egypt and made it a protectorate in 1914. In 1922 Egypt gained a degree of independence, becoming a monarchy. In 1948–49 Egypt fought alongside other Arabs against the creation of the state of Israel. Egypt became a republic in 1953 and, in 1956, nationalized the Suez Canal. Anglo-French and Israeli forces invaded Egypt, but they withdrew under UN and US pressure. Short Egyptian-Israeli wars occurred in 1967 and 1973. President Anwar as-Sadat initiated peace talks with Israel in 1977 and a Peace Treaty (opposed by most Arab nations) was signed in 1979. Sadat was assassinated in 1981.

Area: 1,001,449 km^2 (386,683 sq mi); **Population:** 43,611,000; **Capital:** Cairo (pop 5,715,000); **Other cities:** Alexandria (2,259,000), Giza (854,000); **Highest point:** Jabal Katrinah, 2637 m (8652 ft); **Official language:** Arabic; **Religions:** Islam (91 per cent), Coptic Christianity; **Adult literacy rate:** 44 per cent; **Average life expectancy at birth:** 54 years; **Unit of currency:** Egyptian pound; **Main exports:** cotton and cotton textiles, rice, fruit, vegetables; **Per capita GNP:** US$460.

EL SALVADOR, a densely populated republic in Central America, with a 270 km (168 mi) long coastline on the Pacific Ocean. The country is mountainous and the altitude modifies the tropical climate. San Salvador has an average temperature range of 24°–26°C (75°–79°F) and about 1800 mm (71 in) of rain per year. About 90 per cent of the population is of mixed European and Indian descent. Agriculture employs 52 per cent of the workforce, accounting for 29 per cent of the GDP; the main crops being coffee and cotton. Industry (mostly manufacturing) contributes 21 per cent of the GDP. Spain conquered the area in 1526. Independence from Spain was achieved in 1821 and El Salvador became an independent republic in 1841. The country has suffered from political instability. A military coup occurred in 1979 and a bitter war began between the US-backed government and left-wing guerrillas.

Area: 21,041 km^2 (8124 sq mi); **Population:** 4,820,000; **Capital:** San Salvador (pop 682,000); **Highest point:** Mt Santa Ana, 2385 m (7825 ft); **Official language:** Spanish; **Religion:** Roman Catholicism; **Adult literacy rate:** 62 per cent; **Average life expectancy at birth:** 63 years; **Unit of currency:** Colón; **Main exports:** coffee, cotton; **Per capita GNP:** US$670.

EQUATORIAL GUINEA, a republic in west-central Africa, comprises Río Muni on the mainland and the islands of Bioko (formerly Fernando Póo) and Pagalu. The islands are volcanic; Río Muni contains hills and plateaux. The climate is equatorial. The Bantu Fang form the majority in Río Muni. Fang, Bubi (the original inhabitants) and Fernandinos (descendants of liberated slaves) live on the islands. Most people are farmers: coffee is the main crop. Spain took the territory in the 1840s. Independence was achieved in 1968. The first President Francisco Macías Nguema ruled with much brutality until he was deposed in 1979.

Area: 28,051 km^2 (10,831 sq mi); **Population:** 378,000; **Capital:** Malabo (pop 37,000); **Highest point:** Pico de Santa Isabel, 3007 m (9865 ft); **Official language:** Spanish; **Religions:** Roman Catholicism (88 per cent), traditional religions (8 per cent); **Average life expectancy at birth:** 43 years; **Unit of currency:** Ekuele; **Main exports:** cocoa, coffee, timber; **Per capita GNP:** US$330 (1976).

ETHIOPIA, a republic in north-eastern Africa. The highlands are divided into two blocks by the deep Rift Valley. Lowlands occur in the east near the Red Sea coast. The main river, the Blue Nile, flows from Lake Tana in the north. The lowlands are hot and arid, contrasting with the cooler, moister uplands. About 100 languages are spoken: most belong to the Cushitic, Semitic or Nilotic families. Cushites include the nomadic Galla, the largest single ethnic group. The Amhara, who form the ruling class, speak a Semitic language while Nilotic languages are spoken by Negroid people in the east. Agriculture employs 81 per cent of the population. It accounts for 54 per cent of the GDP. Coffee makes up about 75 per cent of the exports.

Finland is a tranquil, beautiful land of forests and lakes. The lakes occupy ice-scoured rock basins or depressions dammed by moraine deposited during the Pleistocene Ice Age. Forestry is a major industry. Paper, pulp and other timber products account for 40 per cent of Finland's export earnings. But heavy industry has increased greatly in recent years and, in consequence, the proportion of Finns who live in urban areas increased from 38 per cent in 1960 to 62 per cent in 1980.

Ethiopia is the home of an ancient monarchy which embraced Christianity in the 4th century AD. It never became a colony, although it was occupied by Italy in 1935–41. The monarchy was abolished in 1974 and the country was ruled by a left-wing military group. Aided by the USSR, government forces fought against secessionist forces in Eritrea in the east and against Somali-speaking people in the Ogaden in the south-east.

Area: 1,221,900 km^2 (471,804 sq mi); **Population:** 34,244,000; **Capital:** Addis Ababa (pop 1,104,000); **Other cities:** Asmara (353,000); **Highest point:** Ras Dashan, 4620 m (15,157 ft); **Official language:** Amharic; **Religions:** Orthodox (Coptic) Christianity (46 per cent), Islam (34 per cent), traditional beliefs (14 per cent); **Adult literacy rate:** 10 per cent; **Average life expectancy at birth:** 39 years; **Unit of currency:** Ethiopian dollar; **Main exports:** coffee, hides and skins, pulses; **Per capita GNP:** US$130.

FALKLAND ISLANDS, a British colony in the South Atlantic, about 480 km (298 mi) east of the Strait of Magellan. There are 200 islands but only two are sizeable. Sheep farming is the main occupation. France founded a settlement in 1764 followed by Britain in 1765. Spain took over in 1770. From the early 19th century, independent Argentina claimed the islands which became a British Crown Colony in 1832. In 1982 Argentine forces occupied the islands and Britain sent a task force to recover the territory.

Area: 12,173 km^2 (4700 sq mi); **Population:** 1776 (1979).

FIJI, a nation in the south-central Pacific. Two mountainous, volcanic islands, Viti Levu and Vanua Levu, make up 87 per cent of the total area, although there are 320 other small islands. About 48 per cent of the people are Indians (mainly Hindus); 44 per cent are Melanesians; there are also Europeans, Chinese and other Pacific islanders. Agriculture is the main activity and tourism is important. Discovered in 1643, the islands became a British colony in 1874 and an independent nation within the Commonwealth in 1970.

Area: 18,274 km^2 (7056 sq mi); **Population:** 656,000; **Capital:** Suva (pop 64,000); **Main exports:** sugar, coconut oil; **Per capita GNP:** US$1690.

FINLAND, a republic in north-eastern Europe. It contains 55,000 or so lakes that fill hollows created during the Ice Age; water covers 9 per cent of the country. Much of Lapland in the north is within the Arctic Circle. Winters are long and severe, but the short summers are warm. Forests cover more than four-fifths of the country and timber has been the mainstay of the economy. About 62 per cent of the people live in urban areas and industry contributes 35 per cent of the GDP, as opposed to 8 per cent from agriculture, which is mostly confined to the far south. In the past Sweden and Russia have struggled for control of the Baltic Sea region. Russia occupied Finland in 1809 but Finland declared itself independent in 1917, becoming a republic in 1919. In 1939 the USSR declared war on Finland and Finland lost one-third of its territory. It allied itself to Germany but lost more land to the USSR after World War II. Finland signed peace treaties with the USSR in 1948, 1955 and 1970.

Area: 337,009 km^2 (130,127 sq mi); **Population:** 4,829,000; **Capital:** Helsinki (pop with suburbs, 893,000); **Other cities:** Tampere (243,000), Turku (240,000); **Highest point:** 1328 m (4357 ft); **Official languages:** Finnish, Swedish; **Religion:** Lutheran National Church (90 per cent); **Adult literacy rate:** 100 per cent; **Average life expectancy at birth:** 72 years; **Unit of currency:** Markka; **Main exports:** paper and paperboard, machinery and transport equipment, wood and wood pulp; **Per capita GNP:** US$8260.

FRANCE, the 2nd largest nation in Europe after the USSR. Mountain ranges (the French Alps which contain France's highest peak, Mont Blanc, and the lower Jura Mts) form the south-eastern border. The Vosges Mts are in the north-east, overlooking the Rhine rift valley and the scenic Massif Central, which rises to 1886 m (6188 ft), is in south-central France. This latter region contains the headwaters of the Dordogne, Garonne,

COUNTRIES OF THE WORLD

Top left: France contains many magnificent medieval churches, including the 12th-13th-century cathedral at Chartres. Top right: Vineyards are a common sight in France, which leads the world in producing top-quality wine. Above: Superb châteaux adorn many rural areas in France.

Loire and Seine rivers. The north-west peninsula, including Brittany, is lower but also scenic, with a superb indented coastline. The Paris basin is a saucer-shaped depression enclosed by rings of hills with outward facing scarps. The Aquitaine basin in the south-west is a low plain, partly fringed by coastal sand dunes. It extends to the high Pyrenees along the border with Spain. The Rhône-Saône valley, in the south-east between the Massif Central and the south-eastern mountains, ends in the marshy Camargue. The climate varies from the moist, temperate north to the Mediterranean coastlands, with their hot, dry summers and mild, moist winters. The climate also changes from west to east. The west has a maritime temperate climate moderated by the North Atlantic Drift, but to the east it becomes increasingly continental, with colder winters especially in upland regions. Rain falls all the year round except for the Mediterranean region. Several minority languages are spoken: Breton, a Celtic tongue, in Brittany; Basque in the western Pyrenees; Catalan in the eastern Pyrenees; Provençal in the south-east; and German in the north-east. Foreign-born people, including Portuguese, Algerians, Spaniards and Italians, make up about 6½ per cent of the population. Some 78 per cent of the population lives in urban areas; industry and services accounted for 37 per cent and 51 per cent of the GDP respectively in 1978. The chief mineral resource is iron ore, notably in Lorraine. Some coal, oil and natural gas are mined, but France imports much coal from West Germany. Energy also comes from hydro-electric stations and the River Rance tidal power station in Brittany. There is a wide range of manufacturing industries. Paris is known especially for its luxury and fashion products; Lyons is known for textiles; Marseilles and Bordeaux are major industrial ports; and Lille, on the north-western coalfield, is centre of a large industrial region. Farming is also important. In 1978 it contributed 5 per cent of the GDP (as against 10 per cent in 1960), employing 9 per cent of the workforce (22 per cent in 1960). Despite this trend away from the land, the proportion of farm workers in France is three times that in West Germany and the UK. The leading farming regions are the Paris basin, the Loire valley, the Aquitaine basin and the Rhône-Saône valley. Arable land covers 32 per cent of the country, pasture 24 per cent, vineyards 2 per cent, and forests 26 per cent. Agricultural yields per hectare tend to be low, because a high proportion of the farms are small and unmechanized, but France is a leading producer of wheat, barley, oats, flax and sugar beet. Livestock, including dairy cattle, are extremely important; in 1979 there were 23.5 million cattle, 11.5 million sheep and 11.7 million pigs. France is famous for its quality wines and cheeses, which are associated with particular regions. The fishing industry employs 28,000 fishermen. The tourist industry, a major source of foreign earnings, employs about half a million people. West Germany is France's leading trading partner; the EEC as a whole accounts for more than half of France's trade. The Romans conquered France (then called Gaul) in the 50s BC and imposed on it a common language and government. Roman rule declined because of attacks by Germanic tribes. In AD 486 the Frankish realm (as France was called) became independent under a Christian king, Clovis. Charlemagne, who became king in 768, extended the Frankish realm and, in 800, he was crowned Emperor of the West by the Pope. In 843, however, his empire was divided into three, with France coming under Charles the Bald. France contracted in size and, after the Norman invasion of Britain

Boules, *or bowls, is a popular game in France. It can be played on any piece of land and does not require carefully prepared lawns.*

in 1066, large areas came under English rule. Following the French victory by Joan of Arc at Orléans in 1429, English rule in France was finally ended in 1453. A powerful monarchy was established, but in 1792 the 1st Republic was set up, a consequence of the French Revolution of 1789. In 1799 Napoleon Bonaparte took power. After a period of brilliant military exploits, which took him as far as Moscow, he was finally defeated in 1815. The monarchy was restored until 1848 when the short-lived 2nd Republic was established by a revolution. In 1852 Napoleon's nephew Napoleon III became monarch. The 3rd Republic began in 1875. In the 20th century France suffered greatly during World Wars I and II. In 1946 a new Constitution established the 4th Republic. But economic recovery was delayed by costly colonial wars and political instability, although France sponsored the successful European Coal and Steel Community (founded in 1952) and was a founder member of the EEC in 1957. In 1958 Charles de Gaulle was elected President. He introduced a new Constitution, extending the President's powers and establishing the 5th Republic. Under stable right-wing governments, France made rapid economic progress. In 1981 the French socialist leader François Mitterrand was elected President and his Socialist Party gained majorities in parliament, which consists of two houses: the 305-member Senate and the 491-member National Assembly.

Area: 547,026 km² (211,219 sq mi); **Population:** 54,414,000; **Capital:** Paris (pop with suburbs, 8,550,000); **Other cities:** Lyons (1,171,000), Marseilles (1,071,000), Lille (936,000), Bordeaux (612,000), Toulouse (510,000), Nantes (454,000), Nice (438,000); **Highest point:** Mt Blanc, 4810 m (15,781 ft); **Official language:** French; **Religions:** Roman Catholicism, Islam (about 2 million people in 1978); Protestantism (about 750,000 people); **Adult literacy rate:** 99 per cent; **Average life expectancy at birth:** 73 years; **Unit of currency:** Franc; **Main exports:** cars, chemical products, iron and steel, textiles and leather goods, electrical equipment, wine, cereals; **Per capita GNP:** US$9940.

FRENCH GUIANA, a French Overseas Department on the Atlantic Ocean in north-eastern South America. Most of the land is low-lying with uplands in the south. Average temperatures are between 29°C and 32°C (84°–90°F) all the year round. Cayenne has an average annual rainfall of 3560 mm (140 in); parts of the interior are even rainier. Dense forest covers 88 per cent of the land. Most people are Creoles; pure Indians make up 11 per cent of the population. Cultivated land covers only 6000 ha. Bananas, maize, manioc and rice are the main crops. Shrimp fishing is important, but the main prospect is the bauxite deposits that have been discovered recently. The territory came under French control by the mid-17th century. The French set up convict settlements – Devil's Island was the best known. These were all closed by 1945 and Guiana became a department of France in 1946.

Area: 91,000 km² (35,137 sq mi); **Population:** 76,000; **Capital:** Cayenne (pop 36,000); **Per capita GNP:** US$2580.

FRENCH POLYNESIA, a French Overseas Territory in the eastern Pacific Ocean. There are about 130 tropical islands scattered across 4 million km² (1.5 million sq mi). The island groups are: the *Windward Islands*, including Tahiti and Moorea, capital Papeete; the *Leeward Islands* which, with the Windward Is, are often called the Society Islands, main town Uturoa; the *Tuamotu Archipelago*, comprising 78 atolls; the *Gambier Islands*, chief town Rikitea; the *Austral* (*Tubuai*) *Islands*, chief town Mataura; and the *Marquesas Islands*. Tourism is the main industry and copra the leading product. The islands have been French protectorates since 1843. They were given the status of an Overseas Territory in 1958.

Area 4000 km² (1544 sq mi); **Population:** 166,000; **Capital:** Papeete; **Per capita GNP:** US$6350.

GABON, a republic on the equator in west-central Africa. Behind the coastal plain are plateaux and mountains. Most of Gabon is in the River Ogooué drainage basin. Average annual temperatures are between 26°C and 28°C (79°–82°F). The average annual rainfall varies from 1500 mm (59 in) in the south-west to 4000 mm (157 in) in the north-west. Rain forests cover 75 per cent of the land. About 40 languages are spoken: the Bantu-speaking Fang form the largest ethnic group; a few pygmies form the smallest. About 70 per cent of the population is engaged in agriculture, the chief cash crops being cocoa, coffee, palm oil and bananas. But the main wealth of Gabon, which has the 2nd highest per capita GNP in Africa, comes from oil and natural gas, manganese and uranium. France established a settlement on the coast in 1843 and founded Libreville for free slaves in 1849. Gabon became a French colony in the 1880s and an independent republic in 1980. Many people visit Gabon to see the Nobel prize winner Dr Schweitzer's mission hospital at Lambaréné, which was founded in 1910.

Area: 267,667 km² (103,352 sq mi); **Population:** 667,000; **Capital:** Libreville (pop 251,000); **Highest point:** Mt Iboundji, 1580 m (5184 ft); **Official language:** French; **Religions:** Roman Catholicism (60 per cent), Protestantism and local Christian sects (29 per cent), traditional beliefs (10 per cent), Islam (1 per cent); **Adult literacy rate:** 30 per cent; **Unit of currency:** Franc CFA; **Main exports:** oil, manganese, uranium and thorium, timber; **Per capita GNP:** US$3280.

GAMBIA, in West Africa, is the smallest nation in mainland Africa. It is a narrow strip of land bordering the Gambia River, being entirely enclosed by Senegal except along its short Atlantic coast. The climate is tropical, with an average annual temperature of 27°C (81°F) and an average annual rainfall of 750–1140 mm (30–45 in). Wooded savanna covers much of the land. The largest of the 5 main ethnic groups are the Mandingo and the Fulbe (or Fulani). About 85 per cent of the population is engaged in agriculture, which accounts for 60 per cent of the GDP. The only major cash crop is groundnuts; they usually make up over 90 per cent of the exports. Tourism is expanding rapidly. Gambia became a British colony in 1888. Full independence was achieved in 1965 and Gambia became a republic in 1970. Attempts to merge Gambia and Senegal failed until 1981 when Senegalese troops helped to put down a coup in Gambia. Following the coup, Gambia and Senegal set up a confederation called Senegambia, which came into effect in 1982, although both countries retained their sovereignty.

Area: 11,295 km² (4361 sq mi); **Population:** 642,000; **Capital:** Banjul (pop 39,000); **Official language:** English; **Religions:** Islam (80 per cent), Christianity, traditional beliefs; **Adult literacy rate:** 35 per cent; **Average life expectancy at birth:** 41 years; **Unit of currency:** Dalasi; **Main exports:** groundnuts, groundnut products; **Per capita GNP:** US$260.

GERMANY, EAST, officially the German Democratic Republic. The Baltic sea coast is fringed by sand bars and lagoons. The north is part of the North European Plain, which is largely covered by moraine, including hills of boulder clay, between which there are many lakes and marshes, and vast areas of glacial sands, many of which are heathlands. Soil fertility is generally low. The south, which is more fertile, contains low plateaux and mountains, including the Harz Mountains and the Thüringer Wald in the south-west and the Erzgebirge in the south-east. The main rivers are the Elbe which flows into West Germany, and the Oder-Neisse rivers which form the frontier with Poland. Most river valleys run from south-east to north-west. They are wide and shallow, having been formed by melt waters from receding glaciers at the end of the Ice Age. The climate is continental, with an average annual range of −1°C (30°F) in winter to 19°C (66°F) in summer. Rainfall varies between 530 and 640 mm (21–25 in). About 77 per cent of the population lives in urban areas, industry and services accounting for 69 per cent and 21 per cent of the GDP respectively in 1978. East Germany is the world's top producer of lignite and has large deposits of potash. It also mines copper, iron ore, nickel, tin and uranium, but many metals are imported. Before World War II, East Germany's economy was primarily agricultural. After 1945 the USSR encouraged the setting up of manufacturing industries and East Germany is now one of the world's top 10 industrial powers. Most factories are government-owned. About one-third of the output comes from engineering industries. Consumer goods, precision and optical goods, chemicals, textiles and plastics are all important. The main industrial centres are the Dresden, Erfurt, Gera, Halle, Karl-Marx-Stadt and Leipzig districts in the south and the area around Berlin. Agriculture accounted for 10 per cent of the GDP in 1978, employing 10 per cent of the workforce. Arable land covers 44 per cent of the area, pasture 11 per cent and forests 27 per cent. The north contains large state and collective farms (once privately owned), but the most fertile land is in the centre and south. Barley, oats, potatoes, rye, sugar beet and wheat are leading crops. In 1979 there were 5.6 million cattle, 12.1 million pigs and 2 million

Leipzig, East Germany's second largest city, is a major industrial, commercial and cultural centre. It is about 150 km (93 miles) south-south-west of Berlin. Leipzig is also known for its industrial fairs, and its old buildings and cultural life have recently been attracting many tourists.

Above: The Brandenburg Gate stands in East Berlin, just behind the wall that separates the capital of Communist East Germany from West Berlin. Above right: The Rhine valley in West Germany is a vital artery of trade. Much of the valley is adorned by castles and pretty villages.

sheep. In 1945 Germany was partitioned and East Germany, including East Berlin, corresponds to the former Soviet Occupation Zone. After World War II, the country's population was swollen by German-speaking refugees from Poland and Czechoslovakia. Discontent with the Soviet-controlled Communist government, which led to riots in East Berlin in 1953, caused many refugees and East Germans to migrate to West Germany. By 1961, after nearly 3 million people had emigrated, the government built the Berlin Wall. In 1972 tensions were eased when a treaty was signed establishing diplomatic relations between West and East Germany. This led to the admission of both Germanies to the UN in 1973. Effective power in East Germany is vested in the Socialist Unity Party.

Area: 108,178 km^2 (41,770 sq mi); **Population:** 16,748,000; **Capital:** East Berlin (pop 1,134,000); **Other cities:** Leipzig (564,000), Dresden (515,000), Karl-Marx-Stadt (315,000), Magdeburg (284,000); **Highest point:** Brocken, 1142 m (3747 ft); **Official language:** German; **Religion:** Protestantism, Roman Catholicism; **Average life expectancy at birth:** 72 years; **Unit of currency:** Mark; **Main exports:** engineering goods, precision instruments, optical equipment, chemicals; **Per capita GNP:** US$6430.

GERMANY, WEST, officially the Federal Republic of Germany. The coasts on the Baltic and North seas are fringed by sandy islands and dunes. The northern plains, drained by the Elbe, Weser and Ems rivers, are largely covered by moraine deposited during the Ice Age. Generally infertile, the natural vegetation is moorland and heath, as on the Lüneburg Heath, but large areas have been cleared for farming. Central Germany contains hills, plateaux and low block mountains. The northern foothills are a fertile loess belt, but the leading region is the industrial Ruhr valley, with its rich coalfield. South-western Germany, the chief farm region, includes *horsts* (block mountains) that border the Rhine rift valley, which extends more than 300 km (186 mi) from Basle to Bingen. The horsts include the Black Forest and the Odenwald. The south-east is an upland zone which includes the scenic Bavarian Alps in the far south, where the highest peak, the Zugspitze, is situated. The Danube, which rises in the Black Forest, is Europe's 2nd longest river after the Volga in the USSR. It drains much of the south-east. Average annual temperatures range from 0°C to 16°C (32°–61°F) in the north. The centre and south have slightly warmer summers (the Rhine rift valley is the warmest place) and colder winters; for instance, Munich in the south-east has average annual temperatures between −2°C and 18°C (28°–64°F). Rainfall varies between 510 and 1020 mm (20–40 in) per year. West Germany's population was reduced by about 7 million in World War II but it now has half as many people again as it had in 1939. This was not the consequence of natural population increase (which averaged 0.1 per cent per year in 1970–78) but rather of immigration. After World War II millions of refugees from East Germany and eastern Europe flooded in; nearly 25 per cent of West Germans today are former refugees. Also in recent years, many immigrants, or 'guest workers', from Turkey, Yugoslavia, Italy and other places have found jobs in the country: there were 1.9 million such workers in West Germany in 1979. West Germany is a highly industrialized nation, having achieved an 'economic miracle' since 1945. In 1978 industry accounted for 48 per cent of the GDP, agriculture 3 per cent, and services 49 per cent. In 1980 85 per cent of the people lived in urban areas. The largest city, West Berlin, is an enclave in East Germany. Hamburg and Bremen are the chief seaports, but the river port of Duisburg, at the confluence of the Ruhr and Rhine, has a greater annual tonnage of shipping than Hamburg. The ships ply to Rotterdam in the Netherlands which handles a substantial part of German trade. West Germany is the world's 8th largest coal-producer (the main coalfields being the Ruhr, Aachen and Saar), the 3rd largest producer of lignite and it also produces some iron ore, potash, salt, metal ores and oil. Lignite is used in the chemical industry, as is imported petroleum which has enabled industrial development in such cities as Munich and Nuremberg, far from any coalfield. Chemical and iron and steel industries underpin the economy. Other major industries include electrical engineering, machinery, textiles and vehicles. Agriculture employed only 4 per cent of the workforce in 1978 (as opposed to 14 per cent in 1960). But farming remains important, although food is imported. Arable land covers 29.3 per cent of the country, pasture 19.3 per cent, and orchards and vineyards 0.9 per cent. The main crops in the north are potatoes and rye. In the central uplands and south-west, crops include fruits, grapes (for wine), hops, tobacco, sugar beet and wheat. The south-east is mainly pastoral. In 1979 there were 15 million cattle: dairy products are especially important. The EEC accounts for nearly half of the external trade. Between the 4th and 6th centuries AD, German tribes conquered the western provinces of the Roman Empire. The Frankish ruler Charlemagne, who became Emperor of the West in 800, united German tribes into a *Reich* (empire) but it divided into a loose federation of principalities in the 9th century. In the 12th century, German territory was extended to Prussia but, by the 15th century, the country was again disunited. Martin Luther launched the Reformation in 1517, splitting Germany along religious lines. In 1618 religious conflict sparked off the 30 Years' War which ravaged Germany. At the end of the war, however, the combined electorate of Brandenburg and the Duchy of Prussia emerged as a strong Protestant state: its ruler Frederick took the title 'King of Prussia' in 1701. Prussia became a major European state and its troops played a major part in the defeat of Napoleon at Waterloo in 1815. In the following Congress of Vienna, Prussian territory was extended. German nationalism developed and in the 1860s Prince Otto von Bismarck placed Prussia at the head of the movement for German unity. Following victory in the Franco-Prussian War (1870–71), a 2nd Reich was set up with the Prussian king becoming *Kaiser* (emperor). After World War I, a republic was established. Adolf Hitler became Chancellor in 1933 inaugurating the 3rd Reich. In 1945 Germany was divided into 4 military zones, governed by the Americans, British, French and Russians. Berlin was also partitioned into 4 zones. By 1948 the American, British and French zones had amalgamated. But the Russians kept control of their zone and East Berlin. In 1949 West Germany became a federal republic and East Germany a people's democracy. A treaty between the two Germanies (1972) lessened tension and paved the way for their entry into the UN.

Area: 248,577 km² (95,981 sq mi); **Population:** 61,392,000; **Capital:** Bonn (pop 286,000); **Other cities:** West Berlin (1,902,000); Hamburg (1,653,000), Munich (1,300,000), Cologne (976,000), Essen (653,000), Frankfurt am Main (628,000), Dortmund (610,000), Düsseldorf (595,000), Stuttgart (582,000), Duisburg (559,000), Bremen (556,000), Hanover (536,000); **Highest point:** Zugspitze, 2968 m (9738 ft); **Official language:** German; **Religions:** Protestantism (49 per cent), Roman Catholicism (45 per cent); **Adult literacy rate:** 99 per cent; **Average life expectancy at birth:** 72 years; **Unit of currency:** Mark; **Main exports:** finished and semi-finished manufactures, chemicals, coke, consumer products; **Per capita GNP:** US$11,730.

GHANA, a republic in West Africa. It is mostly low-lying and contains the man-made Lake Volta, area, 8482 km² (3275 sq mi). The most fertile region is in the hilly south-west. The only highlands are in the south-east. The average annual temperature is 26°C (79°F) in the south and 28°C (82°F) in the north. The south-west has more than 2000 mm (79 in) of rain per year, the south-east has 730 mm (29 in), and the north 1080 mm (43 in). The people are Negroid: about 100 languages and dialects are spoken. Agriculture employs 54 per cent of the workforce, contributing 38 per cent of the GDP. The main crop and export is cocoa. Bauxite, diamonds, gold and manganese are mined, but manufacturing is small-scale. Portuguese mariners reached Ghana in 1471. The coast became a British colony in 1875 but the Ashanti prevented colonization of the interior until 1901. Independence was achieved in 1957 and Ghana became a republic in 1960. From 1966 to 1979 military and civilian regimes alternated. A new Constitution in 1979 led to the election of a civilian government, but this was overthrown in December 1981.

Area: 238,537 km² (92,105 sq mi); **Population:** 12,413,000; **Capital:** Accra (pop with suburbs, 738,000); **Highest point:** Mt Afadjato, 885 m (2904 ft); **Official language:** English; **Religions:** Christianity, traditional beliefs, Islam; **Adult literacy rate:** 30 per cent; **Average life expectancy at birth:** 48 years; **Unit of currency:** Cedi; **Main exports:** cocoa, timber, gold; **Per capita GNP:** US$400.

GIBRALTAR, a British fortress occupying a rocky peninsula in southern Spain. The climate is Mediterranean in type. Most people are of British, Genoese, Portuguese, Maltese or Spanish descent. English and Spanish are spoken. There is no agriculture or mining. Most people work in the ship repair depot, the NATO bases or in tourism. Gibraltar became a British colony in 1713. Spain has demanded its return but nearly all Gibraltarians voted in 1967 to retain the British connection.

Area: 6½ km² (2½ sq mi); **Population:** 31,000; **GNP per capita:** US$4320.

GREECE, a republic in south-eastern Europe. It contains the southern part of the mountainous and deeply indented Balkan peninsula and many islands. The southern Peloponnesus is linked to the north by the narrow Isthmus of Corinth. The 6.4 km (4 mi) long Corinth Canal cuts through the Isthmus, connecting the Gulf of Corinth to the Saronic Gulf. The northern part of the peninsula contains the Pindus Mts and Greece's highest peak, Mt Olympus. It also includes the Plain of Thessaly, the largest lowland apart from the coastal plains of Macedonia and Thrace in the north-east. Islands make up 20 per cent of the area of Greece. The Cyclades are 220 islands east of the Peloponnesus in the Aegean Sea. The South Sporades (or Dodecanese), including Rhodes, are Aegean islands nearer to Turkey than Greece. The North Sporades are north-east of Euboea. The Ionian Islands, including Corfu, lie off the west coast. In the south, the largest island, Crete, covers 8331 km² (3217 sq mi). The climate is Mediterranean, with hot, arid summers and mild, moist winters, but winters are severe in the mountains. Until recently most Greeks lived in tiny farming communities. But today 62 per cent of the population lives in urban areas, as opposed to 43 per cent in 1960. Industry now accounts for 31 per cent of the GDP compared with 17 per cent from agriculture. Mining is not important but Greece has many processing industries and manufactures are now the leading exports. Only one-third of the land is cultivable. Citrus fruits, grapes, olives, tobacco and wheat are major crops. In 1979 there were 8 million sheep, 4 million goats and nearly 1 million cattle. In 1978 5 million tourists visited Greece, providing much foreign exchange. The merchant navy, one of the world's largest, is another money-earner. Thousands of Greeks emigrate every year, finding work especially in Australia, West Germany and the US. Crete was the centre of the first Greek civilization (the Minoan) between about 3000 and 1400 BC. On the mainland, the Mycenean period (1580–1100 BC) ended when Dorians invaded the peninsula from the north. In about 750 BC the Greeks began to colonize the Mediterranean and trade brought wealth to Greece. Athens reached its peak in 461–431 BC but, in 338 BC, Macedonia became the dominant power. In 334–331 BC Alexander the Great conquered South-west Asia. In 146 BC Greece became a Roman province and, in AD 365, it became part of the East Roman (Byzantine) Empire, which collapsed when the Turks took Constantinople (Istanbul) in 1453. The Greeks rebelled against Turkey in the 1820s and became an independent monarchy in 1830. After World War II, when Greece was occupied by Germany, a civil war raged between communist and nationalist forces until 1949. From 1967 Greece was a military dictatorship. This regime collapsed in 1974 when it failed to stop the Turkish invasion of northern Cyprus. Democracy was restored and Greece became a republic. Greece joined the EEC in 1981.

Area: 131,944 km² (50,947 sq mi); **Population:** 9,665,000; **Capital:** Athens (pop with suburbs, 2,540,000); **Other cities:** Salonika (346,000); **Highest point:** Mt Olympus, 2917 m (9570 ft); **Official language:** Greek; **Religion:** Eastern Orthodox Christianity (98 per cent). **Adult literacy rate:** 88 per cent (1972 est); **Average life expectancy at birth:** 73 years, **Unit of currency:** Drachma; **Main exports:** manufactured goods, food and live animals, raw materials, beverages and tobacco, chemicals; **Per capita GNP:** US$3890.

GREENLAND, a self-governing Danish county. It is the world's largest island and contains the world's 2nd largest ice sheet: only 341,700 km² (131,938 sq mi), or 16 per cent of the land, is ice-free. The main industry is fishing. Vikings founded a colony in Greenland in about AD 960 but it disappeared about 500 years later. Greenland became a Danish colony in 1721 and a Danish county in 1953. A 21-member parliament was elected in 1979.

Area: 2,175,600 km² (840,050 sq mi); **Population:** 50,000; **Capital:** Godthaab (pop 9000); **Per capita GNP:** US$7990.

GRENADA, a West Indian nation, the southernmost in the Windward Islands. The land is mountainous and largely forested. Temperatures remain around 27°C (81°F) throughout the year. Descendants of African slaves form the largest ethnic group. Most of the rest are of mixed black and European descent. The main exports are cocoa, nutmegs and bananas. Tourism is becoming important. Columbus discovered the island in 1498. In 1674–1763 it was a French colony. Thereafter, except for a period of French rule in 1779–83, it was ruled by Britain. It became a British Associated State in 1967 and a fully independent monarchy in the Commonwealth in 1974.

The skyline of Athens, capital of Greece, is dominated by the Acropolis, a rocky hill on which the ruins of the Parthenon and other ancient temples testify to 'the glory that was Greece'.

Greenland is thinly populated and ice sheets cover more than four-fifths of its area. Fishing is the leading industry and tiny fishing villages are scattered along its fiord-strewn coasts.

COUNTRIES OF THE WORLD

Area: 344 km² (133 sq mi); **Population:** 113,000; **Capital:** St George's (pop 30,000); **Official language:** English; **Per capita GNP:** US$630.

GUADELOUPE, a French Overseas Department in the Lesser Antilles. There are two main islands, Basse-Terre (or Guadeloupe) and Grande-Terre, and five small ones. Mt Soufriére, a volcano on Basse-Terre, is 1467 m (4813 ft) high. Temperatures exceed 24°C (75°F) for most of the time and the rainfall is more than 2000 mm (79 in) per year. Most people are of mixed African, Asian and French descent. Bananas and sugar are the main crops. Columbus discovered the islands in 1493. France colonized them in 1635 but had to fight off British attacks and put down a slave revolt in 1703. Slavery was abolished in 1848. Guadeloupe became a French Overseas Department in 1946.

Area: 1779 km² (687 sq mi); **Population:** 332,000; **Capital:** Basse-Terre (pop 15,000); **Per capita GNP:** US$3260.

GUAM, an 'unincorporated territory' of the United States in the Marianas Archipelago in the North Pacific Ocean. There are volcanic mountains in the south of the island and coral reefs in the north. The climate is tropical and crops include bananas, cassava, citrus fruits, coconuts, maize, sugar-cane, sweet potatoes and taro. Fishing is important and tourism is developing. Many people are Chamorros, of mixed Indonesian and Spanish descent. Spain ceded Guam to the US in 1898. The island was occupied by Japan in 1941–44. Full US citizenship for Guam's people was conferred in 1950.

Area: 549 km² (212 sq mi); **Population:** 99,000; **Capital:** Agaña; **Per capita GNP:** US$7830.

GUATEMALA, a Central American republic. Coastal lowlands face the Pacific Ocean in the south-west; a central highland region with 27 volcanoes, some active, is in the earthquake-prone centre; a low forested plain covers the north; and there is a short Caribbean coastline. The altitude modifies the climate. The capital, at about 1500 m (4291 ft), has average temperatures between 16°C and 20°C (61°–68°F) and 1320 mm (52 in) of rain per year. The lowlands are hotter and generally wetter. More than 50 per cent of the people are Indians; most of the rest are mixed European and Indian origin. In 1978 57 per cent of the people were farmers, mainly in the highlands. Coffee is the main crop. Mining is becoming important, especially for nickel. Spain conquered the area in the 1520s. Guatemala became independent in 1821 but attempts to form a Central American Federation failed and Guatemala became an independent republic in 1839. Dictatorships and violence have marred its modern history. In the 1970s Guatemala came into conflict with Britain over its claims on Belize, which was a British territory until 1981.

Area: 108,889 km² (42,045 sq mi); **Population:** 7,436,000; **Capital:** Guatemala City (pop 1,500,000); **Highest point:** Tajumulco, 4220 m (13,845 ft); **Official language:** Spanish; **Religion:** Roman Catholicism; **Adult literacy rate:** 47 per cent; **Average life expectancy at birth:** 57 years; **Unit of currency:** Quetzal; **Main exports:** coffee, cotton, bananas, beef; **Per capita GNP:** US$1020.

GUINEA, a West African republic. Behind the Atlantic coastal plain is the Fouta Djallon plateau, where the Gambia, Niger and Senegal rivers rise. The north-east contains the Upper Niger plains, while the south-east is mountainous, rising to Mt Nimba on the border. Guinea has a tropical monsoon climate and savanna covers most areas. Most people are Negroes and a large number of tribal languages are spoken. In 1978 82 per cent of the population was engaged in agriculture, which accounted for 32 per cent of the GDP. Industry accounted for 41 per cent of the GDP in 1978. The leading industry is bauxite mining: Guinea is the world's 2nd largest producer. France annexed part of Guinea in 1849 and gradually extended its rule. In 1958 the people of Guinea voted for independence. France withdrew its personnel and equipment rapidly and chaos was prevented only with Ghanaian and Soviet aid. Guinea adopted socialist policies and a one-party system of government. Despite attempted coups, Guinea's first president, Sékou Touré, survived into the 1980s. But most people remain poor.

Area: 245,957 km² (94,970 sq mi); **Population:** 5,741,000; **Capital:** Conakry (pop 526,000); **Highest point:** Mt Nimba, 1752 m (5748 ft); **Official language:** French; **Religions:** Islam (70 per cent), traditional beliefs, Christianity; **Adult literacy rate:** 10 per cent (1970); **Average life expectancy at birth:** 43 years; **Unit of currency:** Syli; **Main exports:** bauxite and aluminium, palm kernels, pineapples, coffee; **Per capita GNP:** US$270.

GUINEA-BISSAU, a West African republic. The land is mostly low-lying, with a broad coastal plain and flat offshore islands. It has a tropical monsoon climate. Most people are Negroes belonging to various tribal groups. There is a small mestiço (mulatto) community of Guinean and Cape Verdean descent. It has played an important part in the government. Most people are subsistence farmers, although arable land covers only 12 per cent of the country. The main food crop is rice; the main cash crop is groundnuts. There is no mining and little manufacturing. Portuguese explorers first sighted the coast in 1446. In 1836–79 Portugal ruled the country jointly with the Cape Verde Islands, establishing close ties that were to continue. A long guerrilla war began in 1963, led by Guineans and Cape Verdeans. Guinea-Bissau became independent in 1974, followed by Cape Verde in 1975, although no fighting had occurred on the islands. Guinea-Bissau became a one-party socialist state. A military coup in 1980 caused a deterioration in relations with Cape Verde, with which Guinea-Bissau had hoped to amalgamate.

Area: 36,125 km² (13,949 sq mi); **Population:** 817,000; **Capital:** Bissau (pop 109,000); **Official language:** Portuguese; **Religions:** Islam, traditional beliefs, Christianity; **Adult literacy rate:** 25 per cent; **Average life expectancy at birth:** 39

years; **Unit of currency:** Escudo; **Main exports:** groundnuts, fish; **Per capita GNP:** US$170.

GUYANA, a republic in north-eastern South America. Behind the flat, cultivated coastal zone, which is about 48 km (30 mi) wide, the land rises to a hilly upland and then to the Guiana Highlands in the east and south. Forest covers 83 per cent of the land with grassland in the highest mountain areas. The main river is the Essequibo. The climate is tropical and the rainfall varies between 2290 mm (90 in) on the coast to 1470 mm (58 in) inland. Most people live in the coastal zone: 51 per cent are of Asian origin; 33 per cent are descendants of African slaves; about 10 per cent are of mixed origin; and 5 per cent are Indians who live mostly in the forested interior. Antagonism between the two main groups has been reflected in political life. Bauxite is the main resource and diamonds and gold are also mined. The chief cash crop is sugar and the main food crop is rice. The Dutch and British struggled for ascendancy in the 17th and 18th centuries. The territory was finally ceded to Britain in 1814. Independence was achieved in 1966. The 1980 Constitution provided for a 53-member National Assembly.

Area: 214,969 km^2 (83,005 sq mi); **Population:** 887,000; **Capital:** Georgetown (pop with suburbs, 183,000); **Highest point:** Mt Roraima, 2810 m (9219 ft); **Official language:** English; **Religions:** Christianity (over 50 per cent), Hinduism (33 per cent), Islam (10 per cent); **Unit of currency:** Guyanese dollar; **Main exports:** bauxite and alumina, sugar and byproducts, rice, timber; **Per capita GNP:** US$570.

HAITI, a republic in the western part of the West Indian island of Hispaniola. The interior consists of wooded mountains: the Massif du Nord, the Massif de la Selle (in the south-east), and the Massif de la Hotte (in the south-west), Most people live on the fertile plains which make up about one-fifth of the country. About 95 per cent of the population is of black African descent. The mulattoes who form 5 per cent make up a social elite. Most people are subsistence farmers. The chief cash crops are coffee and sugar. Haiti is the poorest nation in Latin America. Columbus discovered Hispaniola in 1492 and Spain became established in the east (now the Dominican Republic), while France took the west in 1697. Independence was proclaimed in 1804 after a successful slave revolt in the 1790s. Haiti had a disturbed history in 1843–1915 when 16 of its 20 rulers were either deposed or assassinated. The US occupied Haiti from 1915 to 1934. In 1957 François Duvalier became president, assuming dictatorial powers and maintaining his authority through voodoo and his *Tontons macoutes* (police). He died in 1971 and was succeeded by his son, Jean-Claude Duvalier.

Area: 27,750 km^2 (10,715 sq mi); **Population:** 5,220,000; **Capital:** Port-au-Prince (pop 507,000); **Highest point:** Pic La Selle, 2680 m (8793 ft); **Official language:** French; **Religions:** Roman Catholicism, Protestantism; **Adult literacy rate:** 23 per cent; **Average life expectancy at birth:** 51 years; **Unit of currency:** Gourde; **Main exports:** coffee, manufactures; **Per capita GNP:** US$260.

HONDURAS, a wedge-shaped Central American republic. It has a 720 km (447 mi) coastline on the Caribbean Sea and an outlet to the Pacific Ocean through the Gulf of Fonseca. Behind the hot and humid Caribbean coastal plain, there are mountains and high plateaux with a healthy climate. Most Hondurans are of mixed European and Indian origin. About 8 per cent are pure Indians and 2 per cent are Negroes. Honduras is Central America's poorest nation. In 1978 64 per cent of the people were engaged in agriculture, which accounted for 32 per cent of the GDP. Bananas and coffee are the main cash crops. Forests cover 45 per cent of the country and timber is exported. Some lead, zinc and silver are also exported and there are many, mostly small, manufacturing and processing industries. Spain ruled Honduras between 1525 and 1821. It became part of a Central American Federation but it withdrew in 1838. Independent Honduras suffered from autocratic rulers, internal violence and disputes with neighbouring countries. In recent years, military regimes have alternated with elected civilian governments.

Area: 112,088 km^2 (43,280 sq mi); **Population:** 3,941,000; **Capital:** Tegucigalpa (pop 445,000); **Highest point:** Cerros de Celaque, 2865 m (9400 ft); **Official language:** Spanish; **Religion:** Roman Catholicism; **Adult literacy rate:** 57 per cent; **Average life expectancy at birth:** 57 years; **Unit of currency:** Lempira; **Main exports:** bananas, coffee, meat, timber; **Per capita GNP:** US$530.

HONG KONG, a British colony on the south-eastern coast of China, consisting of 236 islands and an area on the mainland. Most of the land is rocky and hilly. The climate is tropical with heavy monsoon rains in May–September. Most people are Chinese; some are refugees from Communist China. There is little farmland in this densely populated colony (90 per cent of the population lives in urban areas) and much food is imported although every possible piece of land is farmed. Fishing is also important (many people live on boats), but the economy is based on manufacturing and entrepôt trade. A great variety of light manufactures are exported to Western nations, bringing much wealth to Hong Kong. Hong Kong Island was ceded to Britain in 1842. Kowloon peninsula and Stonecutters Island were added in 1860 and the New Territories, comprising numerous islands and an area on the mainland, were obtained from China in 1898.

Area: 1045 km^2 (403 sq mi); **Population:** 4,957,000; **Capital:** Victoria (pop 767,000); **Adult literacy rate:** 90 per cent; **Average life expectancy at birth:** 72 years; **Unit of currency:** Hong Kong dollar; **Main exports:** a wide range of light manufactures; **Per capita GNP:** US$4000.

HUNGARY, a landlocked People's Republic in eastern Europe. It is mostly low-lying and drained by the Danube and the Tisza, its tributary. The

COUNTRIES OF THE WORLD

Iceland is dotted with volcanoes, geysers and hot springs, barren lava fields, ice caps and valley glaciers. There are more than 100 volcanoes, including clusters of craters like those in the picture, and about one out of every four volcanoes has erupted in historic times. The reason for all this volcanic activity is that Iceland straddles the northern part of the mid-Atlantic ridge, along which new coastal rock is being formed. This addition of this rock is slowly widening the Atlantic Ocean and Iceland itself.

fertile, hilly Little Alföld is in the north-west. It is separated from the Great Alföld, or Hungarian Plain (56 per cent of the country), by a limestone ridge, the Bakony Forest. Low mountains north-east of Budapest are renowned for their wine. Winters are cold and summers hot. The rainfall averages 635 mm (25 in) on the plains, and 790 mm (31 in) on the uplands. Hungarians, or Magyars, are of Finno-Ugric and Turkic descent, mixed with local peoples. In 1980 64 per cent of the population lived in urban areas. Industry, which has developed rapidly in the last 30 years, accounted for 59 per cent of the GDP in 1978. Bauxite, coal and some other minerals are produced, but many raw materials must be imported. More than 50 per cent of the factories, all of which are nationalized, are in or around Budapest. Farming employs 18 per cent of the workforce and accounts for 15 per cent of the GDP. Arable land, orchards and vineyards cover 53 per cent of the land, pasture 14 per cent and forests 17 per cent. Maize and wheat are the main crops. There are about 2 million cattle, 2.8 million sheep, 8 million pigs and 63 million poultry. Hungary and Austria jointly controlled the Austro-Hungarian Empire from 1867 until it broke up in 1918. In World War II Hungary supported Germany but when it tried to negotiate a separate armistice, it was invaded by German troops. Soviet forces occupied Hungary in 1945 and a communist government was in power by 1948. In 1956 Russian troops put down an anti-Stalinist uprising. Since then, anti-Soviet feeling has been suppressed.

Area: 93,030 km^2 (35,921 sq mi); **Population:** 10,850,000; **Capital:** Budapest (pop 2,093,000); **Highest point:** Mt Kékes, 1015 m (3330 ft); **Official language:** Magyar (Hungarian); **Religions:** Roman Catholicism (50 per cent), Protestantism; **Adult literacy rate:** 98 per cent; **Average life expectancy at birth:** 70 years; **Unit of currency:** Forint; **Main exports:** transport equipment, electrical goods, bauxite and aluminium, food, pharmaceuticals, wine; **Per capita GNP**: US$3850.

ICELAND, an island republic in the North Atlantic Ocean. Large snowfields, glaciers, volcanoes, hot springs (which are used to heat homes in Reykjavik) and a deeply indented coastline are features of this rugged island. The warm North Atlantic Drift keeps the southern coats ice-free in winter. Summers are cool. Less than 1 per cent of the land is cultivated; the main crops are hay, potatoes and turnips. Iceland has about 57,000 cattle and 797,000 sheep, but fishing is the main industry. Norewegian Vikings colonized Iceland in AD 874. In 1262 it was united with Norway and, in 1380, it came under Denmark. Independence was achieved in 1918 although it stayed under the nominal rule of the Danish monarch. It became a republic in 1944. Between 1958 and 1976 it was involved in various fishing disputes. In 1963 it acquired a new volcanic island, Surtsey, which appeared from the sea near Iceland.

Area: 103,000 km^2 (39,771 sq mi); **Population:** 234,000; **Capital:** Reykjavik (pop 84,000); **Highest point:** Oraefajökull, 2119 m (6952 ft); **Official language:** Icelandic; **Religion:** Evangelical Lutheran; **Unit of currency:** Krona; **Main exports:** fish and whale products; **Per capita GNP:** US$10,490.

INDIA, the world's 7th largest nation, but the 2nd largest in terms of population. The Himalayan mountains in the north include India's highest peak, Nanda Devi. In the north-west Kashmir contains parts of the Karakoram and Hindu Kush ranges. The Indus, Ganges and Brahmaputra rivers rise in the Himalayas and reach the sea via broad alluvial plains. The fertile northern plains of India are densely populated. To the south, the Vindhya range borders the Deccan, a huge, triangular-shaped plateau. It is bounded by two other ranges: the Western Ghats and the lower Eastern Ghats. The main rivers, the Cauvery, Krishna and Godavari, flow from west to east into the Bay of Bengal. The climate and vegetation vary greatly. The highest mountains have an Arctic climate; the Thar desert borders Pakistan; Cherrapunji in the north-east holds the world rainfall record for one year – 26,461 mm (1041.7 in) were recorded in 1860–61; and the Deccan lies in the tropics. Most of India has three seasons: winter in October-February when it is cool and dry; the hot season in March–June when temperatures reach 49°C (120°F) in the northern plains; and the rainy season, June–September, when monsoon winds are drawn into

The river Ganges which drains the northern alluvial plains of India is regarded as sacred by Hindus, who make up just over four-fifths of India's population. Pilgrims visit the holy city of Varanasi on the Ganges to bathe in the water, regarding this as a form of spiritual cleansing. Religion plays a vital part in Indian life, as shown by the Hindu prohibition on the slaughter of cattle. Non-violence, as advocated by Mahatma Gandhi in the struggle for independence, and respect for life, are basic Hindu principles.

eastern India from the south-west. Hundreds of languages are spoken in India, but the government recognizes only 15 national languages: Assamese, Bengali, Gujerati, Hindi, Kannada, Kashmiri, Malayalam, Marathi, Oriya, Punjabi, Sanskrit, Sindhi, Tamil, Telegu and Urdu. India is a mainly poor agricultural nation; only 22½ per cent of the population lived in urban areas in 1980. In 1978 agriculture employed 74 per cent of the workforce and accounted for 40 per cent of the GDP (industry for 26 per cent and services 34 per cent). India is the world's top producer of groundnuts, hemp (fibre), sugar-cane and tea; the 2nd leading producer of millet, rice and sorghum; the 3rd largest producer of coconuts, copra and tobacco; and the 4th producer of cotton and wheat. It has more cattle (182 million) than any other nation, but Hinduism forbids their slaughter. India has various minerals, including bauxite, coal, iron ore and manganese. Manufacturing has expanded greatly since 1947; the chief products are textiles, but there is also much heavy industry. Most Indians are descendants of the original Dravidians and the Aryans who invaded India in about 1500 BC. India gave birth to several religions, including Hinduism, Buddhism, Jainism and Sikhism. The Muslim Mughal Empire was founded in 1526, but it declined in the 17th century. The British East India Company became the dominant European trading group in India in 1757 and, in 1858, Britain took over the rule of India. Independence was achieved in 1947 when British India was partitioned into the mainly Hindu India and the Muslim Pakistan. A war in Kashmir ended in 1949 with its partition. India became a republic in 1950. It has been ruled by the Congress party which has controlled the bicameral parliament except in 1977–80.

Area: 3,287,590 km² (1,269,415 sq mi); **Population:** 698,632,000; **Capital:** Delhi (pop 3,647,000); **Other cities:** Calcutta (7,031,000); Bombay (5,971,000), Madras (3,170,000), Hyderabad (1,796,000), Ahmadabad (or Ahmedabad, 1,742,000), Bangalore (1,654,000), Kanpur (1,275,000), Pune (1,135,000); **Highest point:** Nanda Devi, 7817 m (25,646 ft); **Official languages:** Hindi, English; **Religions:** Hinduism (82.7 per cent), Islam (11.2 per cent), Christianity (2.6 per cent), Sikhism (1.9 per cent), Buddhism (0.7 per cent), Jainism (0.5 per cent); **Adult literacy rate:** 36 per cent; **Average life expectancy at birth:** 51 years: **Unit of currency:** Rupee; **Main exports:** textiles, jute, tea; **Per capita GNP:** US$190.

INDONESIA, an island republic in South-East Asia. The largest regions are Kalimantan (part of Borneo), Sumatra, West Irian (part of New Guinea), Sulawesi (Celebes) and Java, the most densely populated island. There are many mountain ranges and more active volcanoes than in any other country: 77 have erupted in recent times. The climate is equatorial, hot and wet all the year round. Rain forests cover large areas. Most people are of Malay origin, mixed with Melanesians and Australasians, and at least 70 languages are spoken. In 1980 20 per cent of the population lived in urban areas. Agriculture employs 60 per cent of the workforce, accounting for 31 per cent of the GDP (33 per cent came from industry and 36 per cent from services). Rice is the main food. Coffee, copra, palm oil and kernels, rubber, tea and tobacco are major cash crops. Forestry is important. Indonesia is the leading oil producer in the Far East. Manufacturing is important, including shipbuilding, textiles, cement and chemicals. Indonesian princes adopted Islam in the 16th century as a political weapon against the Portuguese traders. It gradually replaced Hinduism. Dutch influence began in the late 16th century and the territory became Dutch in 1799. The Republic of Indonesia was formed in 1949. In 1957 army officers revolted because of communist influence in the government: a civil war continued until 1961. The formation of Malaysia in 1963 led to fighting between the two nations in 1964. A communist attempt to overthrow the government failed in 1965. Military leaders seized power in 1966, outlawing the Communist Party and ending confrontation with Malaysia. East (formerly Portuguese) Timor was incorporated into Indonesia in 1976.

Area: 2,027,087 km² (782,705 sq mi); **Population:** 146,527,000; **Capital:** Djakarta (pop 6,506,000); **Other cities:** Surabaya (1,762,000), Bandung (1,265,000), Semarang (916,000); **Highest point:** Djaja Peak (Mt Carstensz), 5030 m (16,503 ft); **Official language:** Bahasa Indonesian; **Religions:**

COUNTRIES OF THE WORLD

Islam (80 per cent), Christianity, Hinduism, Buddhism; **Adult literacy rate:** 62 per cent; **Average life expectancy at birth:** 47 years; **Unit of currency:** Rupiah; **Main exports:** oil (73 per cent), coffee, rubber, palm products, tin, tea, tobacco; **Per capita GNP:** US$380.

IRAN, a republic in south-western Asia. Around a barren plateau, which contains the Dasht e Kavir (Great Salt Desert) and the Dasht e Lut (Great Sand Desert), are mountains: the highest are the northern Elburz Mts; the Zagros Mts in the west and south; and several ranges in the east. The only fertile areas are near the Caspian Sea and in mountain foothills. The central plateau is arid and hot, but the Zagros Mts can be bitterly cold. Rainfall in the Caspian Sea region is about 2000 mm (79 in) per year; the south-east is arid. About 90 per cent of the people are Shia Muslims. Ethnically, two-thirds of the people are Persian in type and one-fourth are Turki. There are some Arabs and Sunni Muslim Kurds live in the north. In 1980 50 per cent of the population lived in urban areas. Industry, mainly oil and gas production, accounted for 54 per cent of the GDP in 1978, as opposed to 9 per cent from agriculture, although 40 per cent of the people were farmers. Cereals, fruit, cotton and tobacco are grown. Income from oil has been used to develop heavy industries and improve social services. Ancient Persia was a powerful empire between 550 and 330 BC. The country was Islamized in AD 641. Later it was invaded by Turks and Mongols. In the 19th century Britain and France competed for influence. In 1925 the Pahlavi family took power. In 1979 the Shah, Mohammad Reza Pahlavi, left Iran after much rioting. A religious leader, Ayatollah Khomeini, exiled since 1964, returned and Iran became an Islamic Republic. War broke out between Iran and Iraq in 1980, continuing into 1982.

Area: 1,648,000 km^2 (636,331 sq mi); **Population:** 40,288,000; **Capital:** Tehran (pop 4,496,000); **Other cities:** Esfahan (672,000), Mashhad (670,000), Tabriz (599,000); **Highest point:** Mt Damavand, 5604 m (18,386 ft); **Official language:** Persian (Farsi); **Religion:** Islam; **Adult literacy rate:** 50 per cent; **Average life expectancy at birth:** 52 years; **Unit of currency:** Rial; **Main exports:** oil, natural gas, cotton; **Per capita GNP:** US$2160 (1977).

IRAQ, a republic in south-western Asia. It contains Mesopotamia, the valleys of the Tigris and Euphrates rivers where the ancient civilizations of Babylonia and Assyria arose. There are swamps in the south where the two rivers join, deserts in the west and mountains in the north-east. Summers are hot and winters cool. The rainfall is generally 250 mm (10 in), but more falls on the uplands. More than half of the people are Shia Muslims. In 1978 72 per cent of the people lived in urban areas, as compared with 43 per cent in 1960. Oil production dominates the economy. The main crops are dates, cereals, pulses and cotton. In 1979 Iran had 11.6 million sheep, 3.6 million goats and 2.7 million cattle. Manufacturing is expanding but, in 1980, the Israelis destroyed a nuclear reactor near Baghdad in a lightning raid. Iraq was Islamized in AD 637 and, in 1638, it became part of the Ottoman Empire. British forces occupied Iraq in World War I and stayed until it became an independent monarchy in 1932. Since the 1950s oil production has provided income for developing social services. In 1958, however, the monarchy was overthrown and the army established a republic. Fighting with the Sunni Muslim Kurds in the north broke out in the 1960s. The Kurds wanted a Kurdish state, joining Kurdish territory in Iran, Turkey and the USSR, but they failed. A peace agreement was signed in 1974. War with Iran broke out in 1980 and continued into 1982.

Area: 434,924 km^2 (167,934 sq mi); **Population:** 13,977,000; **Capital:** Baghdad (pop 3,206,000); **Other cities:** Basrah (334,000), Mosul (293,000); **Official language:** Arabic; **Religion:** Islam; **Average life expectancy at birth:** 55 years; **Unit of currency:** Iraqui dinar; **Main exports:** oil, iron ore, copper; **Per capita GNP:** US$2410.

IRELAND, REPUBLIC OF, occupies 80 per cent of the island of Ireland. It contains 26 counties, divided into 4 provinces: Connacht, Leinster, Munster and Ulster. But the 6 north-eastern counties of Ulster constitute Northern Ireland, which is part of the United Kingdom. Central Ireland is a moraine-covered lowland, containing areas of peat bog and some rich farmland. A broken rim of uplands surrounds the plain. The highest peak, Carrantuohill, is in scenic County Kerry in the south-west. The River Shannon, 386 km (240 mi) long, is the longest river in the British Isles. Along its course are several lakes, including Lough Ree and Lough Derg. Ireland has mild, wet winters and cool, wet summers. The average annual temperature range is around 5°–15°C (41°–59°F). The uplands have an average annual rainfall of 1020 to 1520 mm (40–60 in) and the lowlands about 760 mm (30 in). Most people are of Celtic or mixed Celtic and English descent. About 20 per cent speak Irish, but English is used in daily life. In 1980 58 per cent of the population lived in urban areas. In 1978 20 per cent were employed in agriculture, 37 per cent in industry and 43 per cent in services. But farming forms the basis of the economy. Arable land and pasture cover two-thirds of the land. Major crops are barley, hay, oats, potatoes, sugar beet and wheat. In 1979 there were 7.1 million cattle, 3.4 million sheep and 1.1 million pigs. There are many processing industries. The only large-scale manufacturing industries are in Dublin and Cork: most of the minerals and raw materials needed are imported. Fishing employs about 9000 men. Tourism is important: nearly 10 million people visited Ireland in 1979. Celts from France and Spain settled in Ireland in the early 4th century BC. Christianity was introduced by St Patrick in AD 432. Vikings arrived in about 795, but most of them were driven out in the 11th century. The Normans invaded Ireland in the 12th century and the island came under English rule. Much of Ireland's subsequent history was concerned with a struggle against English rule and, from the 1530s, the preservation of Roman Catholicism. In 1801 the Act of Union created the

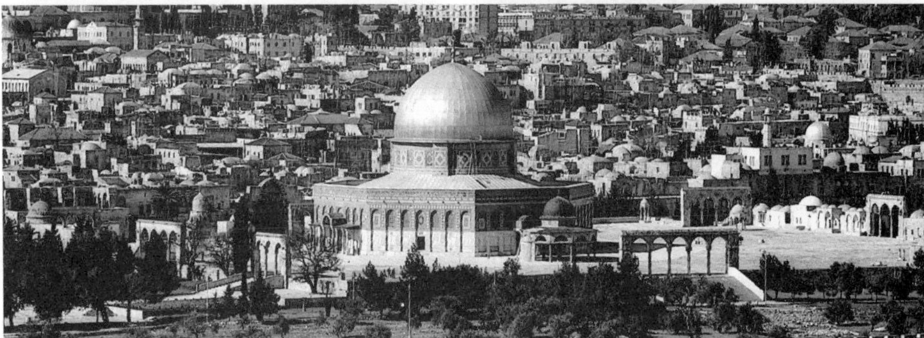

Top left: Iran is an Islamic nation as exemplified by this mosque at Isfahan. Top right: Rural Ireland has great charm. Above: The Dome of the Rock in Jerusalem contains a rock on which Abraham supposedly prepared to sacrifice Isaac.

United Kingdom of Great Britain and Ireland. A potato famine in the 1840s, caused by a blight, led to the deaths of more than a million Irish people; another million emigrated. In 1916 there was an uprising in Dublin (the Easter Rebellion) which was put down. In 1919–21 the Irish fought for independence, finally achieving dominion status as the Irish Free State. Northern Ireland remained part of the UK. Ireland became a republic in 1949 and it joined the EEC in 1973. The unification of Ireland remains a central political issue.

Area: 70,283 km^2 (27,138 sq mi); **Population:** 3,366,000; **Capital:** Dublin (pop 545,000); **Other cities:** Cork (139,000), Limerick (61,000); **Highest point:** Carrantuohill, 1042 m (3419 ft); **Official languages:** Irish, English; **Religion:** mainly Roman Catholicism; **Adult literacy rate:** 98 per cent; **Average life expectancy at birth:** 73 years; **Unit of currency:** Pound; **Main exports:** dairy products, meat and meat products, beer, whiskey; **Per capita GNP:** US$4230.

ISRAEL, a Middle Eastern republic created in 1948. The Galilee highlands containing Mt Meron are in the north. To the east is an extension of the East African Rift Valley, enclosing the Sea of Galilee (Lake Tiberias), the River Jordan and, in the south, the Dead Sea whose shoreline is 393 m (1289 ft) below sea level, the world's lowest point on land. South of the Galilee Highlands are fertile plains and hilly regions. The Negev in the far south is desert. The coast has a Mediterranean climate; the rainfall decreases inland and to the south. More than 80 per cent of the people are Jews: the rest are Arabs. In 1980 89 per cent of the population lived in urban areas. In 1978 agriculture accounted for 7 per cent of the GDP, industry 37 per cent and services 57 per cent. Israel makes most industrial products and diamond finishing is the most valuable industry. Farming is efficient because of extensive irrigation and co-operative and collective farming methods. Cereals, citrus fruits, cotton, olives, tobacco and vegetables are important. About 1.1 million tourists visited Israel in 1979. Israel did not exist as a state for about 2500 years before 1948. Some Jews have always lived in Palestine, but most Israelis are descendants of settlers since the 1880s or recent immigrants. Britain ruled Palestine from 1917 but withdrew in 1948 when Israelis fought against their Arab neighbours, holding most of Palestine. In short Arab-Israeli wars in 1956, 1967 and 1973, Israel gained Arab territory. But in 1979 Israel and Egypt signed a peace treaty which led to a gradual return of the Sinai to Egypt.

Area: 20,770 km^2 (8020 sq mi); **Population:** 4,093,000; **Capital:** Jerusalem (pop 398,000); **Other cities:** Tel-Aviv/Jaffa (336,000), Haifa (229,000); **Highest point:** Mt Meron, 1208 m (3963 ft); **Official languages:** Hebrew, Arabic; **Religions:** Judaism, Islam; **Adult literacy rate:** 88 per cent; **Average life expectancy at birth:** 72 years; **Unit of currency:** Shekel; **Main exports:** cut diamonds, chemical and oil products, beverages and tobacco, citrus fruits; **Per capita GNP:** US$4170.

COUNTRIES OF THE WORLD

Many of Italy's cities are museums of history and architecture. Left: The Forum at Rome recalls the days when the city was the capital of the western world. Above: Superb medieval buildings in Venice can be viewed from gondolas. Right: Exquisite churches, palaces and magnificent art galleries are among the many attractions of Florence.

ITALY, a republic in southern Europe. It consists largely of a 1220 km (758 mi) long peninsula projecting like a boot between the Adriatic Sea to the east and the Ligurian and Tyrrhenian seas to the west. The scenic Alps, Italy's highest region, form a broad arc in the north. They overlook the North Italian plain which consists mainly of the River Po drainage basin. This is Italy's most densely populated region. The Po is Italy's longest river – it is about 650 km (404 mi) long. The Apennine Mts occupy much of peninsular Italy. Their highest point is Monte Corno, 2914 m (9560 ft) high, north-east of Rome. Within the Apennines are many fertile valleys and basins, and there are some rich coastal plains. Most rivers are short. The most important are the Arno on which Florence stands and the Tiber which flows through Rome. In the south-west are a series of volcanoes: Vesuvius, 1277 m (4190 ft) is near the port of Naples; Stromboli and Vulcano in the Lipari Islands; and Etna, Europe's highest volcano, reaches 3363 m (11,033 ft) in Sicily. Sicily is the largest of Italy's 70 or so islands, covering 25,708 km^2 (9926 sq mi). Southern Italy is subject to earthquakes: it lies near a subduction zone in the Earth's crust. Italy's second largest island is Sardinia to the west. This rugged island covers 24,090 km^2 (9302 sq mi). Southern Italy has hot, dry summers and mild winters. Winter rainfall is highest in the mountains and it increases northwards. Winters are colder in the more continental North Italian plain, where temperatures in January average between 1°C and 3°C (34°–37°F). The Alps are cold and snowy. In 1980 69 per cent of the population lived in urban areas. In 1978 industry accounted for 42 per cent of the GDP, agriculture for 7 per cent and services for 51 per cent. Oil and natural gas are extracted in the North Italian plain and in Sicily, but oil and coal have to be imported. Hydro-electric projects are numerous and 32 per cent of Italy's total electricity supply came from hydro-electric plants in 1977. Generally, Italy lacks minerals and metal ores are major imports. Leading industrial products include textiles, especially silk, engineering goods, including transport equipment and motor vehicles (Alfa-Romeo, Fiat and Maserati are internationally known names), office and household equipment, chemicals and iron and steel. There are also many craft industries. The chief industrial region is the triangular area formed by Turin, Milan and Genoa. Farmland covers about two-thirds of the land, but agriculture now employs only 13 per cent of the workforce, as opposed to 31 per cent in 1960. Forests cover 21 per cent of the land, but timber is imported. Major crops include barley, citrus and other fruits, grapes (for wine-making), maize, olives, sugar beet, tobacco, vegetables and wheat. In 1979 there were 8.6 million cattle, 9.8 million pigs and 10 million sheep and goats. Italy is a major milk producer and its cheeses, such as Gorgonzola, are famous. In the 1970s Italy's main trading partners were West Germany, France, the United States and the UK. Adverse trade balances were partly covered by income from the huge tourist industry: Italy received 48.7 million foreign visitors in 1979. Tourist attractions include sunny beaches, historic sites, like the Forum in Rome and the lost city of Pompeii, the Vatican City State, and magnificent medieval cities, such as Florence and Venice, with their superb art galleries and churches. The most prosperous parts of Italy are in the north; this is reflected in the migration of poor farmers from the south to the north or abroad. The Roman empire developed around 500 BC and lasted until the 5th century AD. In the Middle Ages, Italy was divided into small rival states, although these made an enormous contribution to the Renaissance in

the 14th–16th centuries. After a long struggle for unity which began in 1848, Italy became a united kingdom in 1861 under King Victor Emmanuel II of Sardinia, although the Papal territories were not added until 1870. Italy entered World War I on the side of the Allies. In 1922 Benito Mussolini and his Fascist party took power. In 1935 Italian forces invaded Ethiopia and Italy entered World War II in 1940 on Germany's side. Italy surrendered in 1943 and declared war on Germany. In 1946 the monarchy was abolished and Italy became a republic. It was a founder member of NATO in 1949 and of the EEC in 1958. The economy expanded rapidly and attempts were made through the EEC to increase job opportunities for people in the relatively impoverished south. However, a succession of weak coalition governments, unemployment, high inflation (averaging 14 per cent per year in 1970–78), strikes and terrorist violence and assassinations have marred progress in recent years. Italy has a bicameral parliament, with an elected, 600-member Chamber of Deputies and a Senate elected on a regional basis. Members of both houses serve 5-year terms.

Area: 301,225 km² (116,310 sq mi); **Population:** 58,085,000; **Capital:** Rome (pop 3,700,000); **Other cities:** Milan (4,000,000), Naples (1,250,000), Turin (1,000,000), Genoa (850,000), Palermo (694,000), Bologna (487,000), Florence (465,000); **Highest point:** Mt Rosa, 4634 m (15,203 ft); **Official language:** Italian; **Religion:** Roman Catholicism; **Adult literacy rate:** 98 per cent; **Average life expectancy at birth:** 73 years; **Unit of currency:** Lira; **Main exports:** machinery, motor vehicles, iron and steel, textiles, footwear, plastics, fruit and vegetables; **Per capita GNP:** US$5240.

IVORY COAST, a republic in West Africa with a 550 km (342 mi) coastline on the Gulf of Guinea. Behind the broad coastal lowlands are high plains between 150 and 450 m (492–1476 ft). The main highlands are in the north-west: the highest peak, Mt Nimba, is on the Ivory Coast-Liberia-Guinea border. The south has an equatorial climate. The north is often scorched by the north-easterly Harmattan, a wind from the Sahara that may raise temperatures to 38°C (100°F). There is some forest in the south but savanna is the main type of vegetation. About 60 languages and dialects are spoken by the Negroid peoples. Ivory Coast is prosperous by African standards, but prosperity is confined mostly to the south-east. In 1978 agriculture employed 81 per cent of the workforce and accounted for 21 per cent of the GDP: 23 per cent came from industry and 56 per cent from services. Ivory Coast leads the world in cocoa production and is the 4th largest coffee producer. There is some mining, but the processing and consumer goods industries in Abidjan make a larger contribution to the economy. Ivory Coast became a French colony in 1893, although French influence dates back to the 17th century. Independence was achieved in 1960, since when Ivory Coast has pursued private enterprise economic policies, proving to be one of the most stable nations in Africa.

Area: 322,463 km² (124,510 sq mi); **Population:** 9,564,000; **Capital:** Abidjan (pop 686,000); **Highest point:** Mt Nimba, 1752 m (5748 ft); **Official language:** French; **Religions:** traditional beliefs (56 per cent), Islam (24 per cent), Roman Catholicism (20 per cent); **Adult literacy rate:** 20 per cent; **Average life expectancy at birth:** 46 years; **Unit of currency:** Franc CFA; **Main exports:** coffee, cocoa, timber, petroleum products; **Per capita GNP:** US$1060.

JAMAICA, a West Indian island nation. The land is mainly mountainous, with spectacular scenery. The coast has a tropical climate, with average temperatures of 27°–30°C (81°–86°F), although there are pleasant ocean breezes. The altitude lowers temperatures inland. The Blue Mountains have an average annual rainfall of 5000 mm (197 in). The coasts are drier: Kingston has about 760 mm (30 in) per year. More than 75 per cent of the people are black, 14 per cent are of mixed black and white origin, and there are minorities of Asians, Afro-Asians and whites. In 1980 50 per cent of the population lived in urban areas where manufacturing is growing. Jamaica is the world's 3rd largest producer of bauxite, the main export. Agriculture employs 28 per cent of the people: bananas and sugar are the main products. Tourism is a major industry and more than 500,000 visitors went to Jamaica in 1978. Discovered by Columbus in 1494, Jamaica was ruled by Spain until 1655 when the English captured it. Full independence in the Commonwealth was achieved in 1962. The Head of State is the British monarch who is represented by a Governor-General.

Area: 10,991 km² (4244 sq mi); **Population:** 2,297,000; **Capital:** Kingston (pop 635,000); **Highest point:** Blue Mt Peak, 2256 m (7402 ft); **Official language:** English; **Religion:** Christianity, (Rastafarian minority); **Adult literacy rate:** 86 per cent; **Average life expectancy at birth:** 70 years; **Unit of currency:** Dollar; **Main exports:** alumina and bauxite, sugar; **Per capita GNP:** US$1240.

COUNTRIES OF THE WORLD

Left: Express trains reflect Japan's outstanding technological progress in recent times, while the volcano Mount Fuji reminds us that Japan lies on a particularly unstable part of the Earth's crust. Religion plays a major part in life in Japan and Mount Fuji is a sacred mountain. Above: The Kinkakuji Temple is in Tokyo. Shintoism and Buddhism are Japan's chief religions. Right: This mosque is in Nairobi, capital of Kenya.

JAPAN, an island nation in the Far East that is separated from the Asian mainland by the Sea of Japan. There are 4 large islands (Honshu, Hokkaido, Kyushu and Shikoku) and about 3000 small ones, including the Ryukyu island chain that stretches towards Taiwan. The islands are largely mountainous, the most rugged region being the Japanese Alps on Honshu, including the highest peak Fujiyama, a dormant volcano south-west of Tokyo which last erupted in 1707. Japan contains more than 160 volcanoes; 54 are active. Earthquakes are common; about 1500 occur every year, but most cause little damage. The world's most destructive earthquake occurred in the Kwanto plain in 1923 when 575,000 buildings in Tokyo and Yokohama were destroyed and 143,000 lives were lost. Volcanic and seismic activity are caused because Japan lies above a subduction zone where the Pacific plate is being forced beneath the Eurasian plate. Earthquakes originating offshore trigger off tsunamis, destructive waves that strike the coasts with great force. Along the deeply indented coasts are some small coastal plains that are alluvial deltas formed by the short rivers that cascade from the mountains. The longest river, the Shinano on Honshu, is only 480 km (298 mi) long. Japan has a monsoon climate, with plentiful rain. The heaviest rains fall in June–July and September–October and typhoons are common. Temperatures are affected by the warm Kuro Siwa ocean current which comes from the south and the cold Oyashio current that chills the coasts of western Hokkaido and northern Honshu. Average January temperatures are −6°C (21°F) in Hokkaido and 7°C (45°F) in southern Kyushu. Average July temperatures are 20°C (68°F) in the north and 28°C (82°F) in the south. Most people are Mongoloid descendants of people who came from mainland Asia and Pacific islands. But one of the earliest peoples is Caucasoid. These are the bushy-haired Ainu, 15,000 of whom live in Hokkaido. Japan is Asia's most prosperous and industrialized nation. In 1980 78 per cent of the population lived in urban areas, compared with 62 per cent in 1960. In 1978 industry employed 39 per cent of the workforce, services 48 per cent and agriculture 13 per cent. Contributions to the GDP were industry 40 per cent, services 55 per cent and agriculture 5 per cent. Some minerals, including coal and copper, are mined, but the amounts are generally too small for the needs of manufacturers. Hence, many materials, including iron ore and oil, must be imported. Japan has a wide range of light and heavy industry. It is the world's 3rd largest producer of electrical energy, after the US and the USSR. In 1977 hydroelectricity made up 14 per cent of the total and nuclear power 6 per cent. Japan leads the world in producing many items, including motor cycles, merchant ships and television sets. Only the US makes more motor vehicles and Hong Kong more radios. Japan's main industrial regions are in the coastal lowlands between Tokyo and northern Kyushu. Most of Japan is too mountainous for farming; forests cover nearly 70 per cent of the land. Arable land makes up less than 15 per cent of Japan, but yields are high and farming intensive. Rice is the chief food and is grown on nearly 50 per cent of the farmland. Other major crops are barley, fruits, soya beans and wheat. Cattle number about 4.1 million and pigs 9.5 million: goats and sheep are unimportant because of the lack of pasture. About 50 per cent of Japan's protein comes from its large fishing and whaling industry. Seaweed is also harvested for food. But food is imported: it made up 13 per cent of the imports in 1979. According to tradition, Japan's monarchy dates back to 660 BC. Buddhism was introduced in AD 552. Emperors ruled Japan until a new warrior class, the *shoguns* ('great generals'), emerged in the 12th century. In 1192 the first shogun took power, ruling in the name of the emperor. Shogun rule continued until Emperor Meiji regained power in 1868. European contacts began when Portuguese navigators reached Japan in 1542. But in 1637 Japan expelled all Europeans, except for the Dutch, from Japan and outlawed Christianity. Isolationism continued until, in 1854, the American Commander Perry, with a fleet of warships, forced Japan to

agree a treaty with the US. This was followed by treaties with other western powers. Japan's imperialist ambitions began in the 1880s. In 1894–95 it fought a war with China and in 1904–05 it defeated Russia in a dispute over Russia's claims on Korea. In 1931 it occupied Manchuria and, in 1937, started a war with China. In 1941 Japan attacked US bases at Pearl Harbor, but defeat in World War II came when the US dropped atomic bombs on Hiroshima and Nagasaki in 1945. The US occupied Japan until 1952. In the 1960s and 1970s Japan became one of the world's great industrial powers. The 1947 Constitution made Japan a constitutional monarchy. The Emperor is Head of State. Power is vested in the Diet, which consists of an elected 511-member House of Representatives and a 252-member House of Chancellors.

Area: 372,313 km^2 (143,759 sq mi); **Population:** 120,055,000; **Capital:** Tokyo (pop 11,695,000); **Other cities:** Yokohama (2,786,000), Osaka (2,682,000), Nagoya (2,079,000), Kyoto (1,468,000), Sapporo (1,397,000), Kobe (1,372,000), Kitakyushu (1,068,000), Kawasaki (1,050,000); **Highest point:** Fujiyama, 3776 m (12,388 ft); **Official language:** Japanese; **Religions:** mainly Shintoism and Buddhism; **Adult literacy rate:** 99 per cent; **Average life expectancy at birth:** 76 years; **Unit of currency:** Yen; **Main exports:** chemicals, electronic goods, machinery and transport equipment, optical equipment, ships, textiles; **Per capita GNP:** US$8800.

JORDAN, a kingdom in south-western Asia. The fertile western uplands (the West Bank, occupied by Israel) overlook the rift valley which contains the River Jordan and the Dead Sea whose shoreline is 393 m (1289 ft) below sea level, the world's lowest point on land. The valley continues south to the Gulf of Aqabah, Jordan's only outlet to the sea. The east consists mainly of barren uplands: the highest point is Jebel Ram, 1754 m (5755 ft) high in the south. About 87 per cent of Jordan is desert. Some highland regions are cooler and have an average annual rainfall of 520 mm (20 in). Most people are Arabs and 56 per cent lived in urban areas in 1980. In 1978 agriculture employed 27 per cent of the population, industry 39 per cent and services 34 per cent; they contributed 11 per cent, 29 per cent and 60 per cent respectively to the GDP. Fruit and vegetables are grown and there are about 1.25 million sheep and goats. The main export is phosphates. British forces occupied what is now Israel and Jordan in World War I. Transjordan became a separate country in 1923 and full independence was achieved in 1946. In 1948 Jordan was involved in the Arab-Israeli war and, in 1949, it adopted its present name, the Hashemite Kingdom of Jordan. In 1967 Israel occupied the West Bank, Jordan's most fertile region. In 1970–71 civil war broke out when Jordan tried to expel militant refugees belonging to the Palestinian Liberation Organization. In 1975, however, King Hussein gave up his claim to the West Bank and passed responsibility for it to the PLO.

Area: 97,740 km^2 (37,740 sq mi); **Population:** 3,403,000; **Capital:** Amman (pop 750,000); **Official language:** Arabic; **Religion:** Islam; **Adult literacy rate:** 70 per cent; **Average life expectancy at birth:** 56 years; **Unit of currency:** Jordanian dinar; **Main exports:** phosphates, fruit and vegetables; **Per capita GNP:** US$1180.

KAMPUCHEA, officially Democratic Kampuchea, is a South-East Asian nation formerly called Cambodia and, briefly, the Khmer Republic. Much of the land is low-lying, in the drainage basin of the lower Mekong River; hills surround the plain. Kampuchea has a tropical monsoon climate and dense forests cover nearly 50 per cent of the land. Khmers make up 90 per cent of the population. There are Chinese and Vietnamese minorities. The economy is based on agriculture. Rice occupied much of the cultivated land (15 per cent of the total), but reliable data has not been available since the capital Phnom Penh fell to communist forces (the Khmer Rouge) in 1975. In 1978 Vietnamese forces invaded the country but resistance was reported to be continuing into the 1980s. The impressive Khmer empire flourished in the area between 800 and 1450. The country was a French colony in 1863–1954. In the 1970s the country became involved in the Vietnamese War when North Vietnamese took supplies for South Vietnamese guerrillas through Kampuchea.

Area: 181,035 km^2 (69,902, sq mi); **Population:** 8,559,000 (1978 est); **Capital:** Phnom Penh (formerly 2.5 million); **Official language:** Khmer; **Religion:** Buddhism; **Unit of currency:** Riel; **Main exports:** rice, rubber; in the 1970s the economy came to a virtual standstill.

KENYA, an East African republic. Behind the narrow coastal plain is a large grassy or savanna-covered plateau broken by volcanic mountains, including the highest peak, Mt Kenya. The East African Rift Valley in Kenya contains lakes Nakuru, Naivasha and Turkana. Part of Lake Victoria is in the south-east. The altitude moderates the equatorial climate, but only 15 per cent of Kenya has a reliable 760 mm (30 in) of rain per year. There are about 40 language groups: the largest are the Kikuyu and Luo. In 1978 agriculture employed 79 per cent of the workforce, industry 8 per cent and services 13 per cent: their contributions to the GDP were 41 per cent, 19 per cent and 40 per cent respectively. The chief cash crops are coffee and tea. In 1979 there were 10.5 million cattle, 4 million sheep and 4.5 million goats. Mining

COUNTRIES OF THE WORLD

Beirut, capital of Lebanon, is the country's chief seaport and educational centre. It was devastated by fighting in summer 1982 between Israeli forces and the Palestinian Liberation Movement.

is not important but manufacturing is growing rapidly. In 1979 350,000 tourists visited Kenya enjoying the wildlife, scenery and beaches. Kenya's coast became a British protectorate in 1895 and Kenya was declared a British colony in 1920. Independence was achieved in 1963 and republican status was adopted in 1964. Since then Kenya has enjoyed stable government.

Area: 582,646 km² (224,973 sq mi); **Population:** 16,922,000; **Capital:** Nairobi (pop 700,000); **Other cities:** Mombasa (340,000); **Highest point:** Mt Kenya, 5199 m (17,057 ft); **Official languages:** English, Swahili; **Religions:** traditional beliefs, Islam, Christianity (25 per cent); **Adult literacy rate:** 40 per cent; **Average life expectancy at birth:** 53 years; **Unit of currency:** Kenya shilling; **Main exports:** coffee, petroleum products, tea, cement, hides, meat; **Per capita GNP:** US$380.

KIRIBATI, an island republic in the Central Pacific. It includes Ocean (Banaba) Island, the 16 Gilbert Islands, 8 of the 11 Line Islands (the rest are uninhabited US dependencies), and the 8 Phoenix Islands. The climate is hot and generally wet. Most people are Micronesians. Copra is the only export. The Gilbert and Ellice Islands became a British protectorate in 1892. Banaba was added in 1900, the Line Islands in 1919, and the Phoenix Islands in 1937. The Ellice Islands became a separate country, Tuvalu, in 1975. Kiribati (pronounced *Kiribas*) became fully independent in 1979.

Area: 684 km² (264 sq mi); **Population:** 60,000; **Capital:** Tarawa; **Per capita GNP:** US$670.

KOREA, NORTH, officially the Democratic People's Republic of Korea. The northern part of a peninsula, North Korea is mostly mountainous, the population being concentrated in coastal plains in the east. The average annual temperature range is between −7°C (19°F) and 21°C (70°F) and the annual rainfall is between 580 and 1140 mm (23–45 in). The people are Mongoloid. Only 16 per cent of the land is cultivable, but in 1978 agriculture employed 49 per cent of the workforce, industry 32 per cent and services 19 per cent. Rice is the main crop in irrigated areas: maize, millet and wheat grow in drier places. There are many minerals – coal, copper, iron ore, lead, manganese, nickel, tungsten and zinc. There are many light and heavy industries. Korea was partitioned in 1945. The USSR occupied the north above latitude 38°N; the US controlled the south. The occupying powers withdrew in 1949. War between North and South (aided by other powers) raged between 1950–53, the cease-fire line being the present border. Talks on reunification in 1980 failed. See **Korea, South** for earlier history.

Area: 120,538 km² (46,543 sq mi); **Population:** 18,908,000; **Capital:** Pyongyang (pop 1,500,000); **Highest point:** Paektu-San, 2744 m (9003 ft); **Official language:** Korean; **Religion:** Buddhism; **Average life expectancy at birth:** 63 years; **Unit of currency:** Won; **Main exports:** iron ore, pig iron, other metal ores; **Per capital GNP:** US$1130.

KOREA, SOUTH, a republic in the Far East. The land is mostly mountainous with many islands in the west. Average annual temperatures vary from −3°C (27°F) to 24°C (75°F), although winters are warmer in the far south. Winters are dry. The average annual rainfall is between 1140 and 1400 mm (45–55 in). Forests cover 70 per cent of the land. Since partition, industry has overtaken agriculture in importance in South Korea. It accounted for 36 per cent of the GDP in 1978 (as opposed to 19 per cent in 1960). Agriculture accounted for 24 per cent (40 per cent in 1960) and services 40 per cent. Tungsten is the chief mineral; small deposits of many other minerals occur. The chief manufactures are light consumer goods, but chemical and heavy industries are growing. The chief crops are rice and other grains and tobacco. Livestock raising and fishing are also important. Korea became a united kingdom in the 7th century AD. It was occupied by Mongols between the 13th and 14th centuries and it was conquered by China in 1627. It became isolated until Japan forced it to open some ports to trade in 1876. In 1895 Japan defeated China in Korea and in 1905 it prevented Russia from taking it. Korea became a Japanese colony in 1910. In 1945 it was divided between the USSR and the US but their forces withdrew in 1949. In the Korean War (1950–53) the UN supported the South and Communist China the North. In the 1960s and 1970s the army has played an important part in the government of South Korea and attempts at reunification have failed.

Area: 98,484 km² (38,027 sq mi); **Population:** 39,546,000; **Capital:** Seoul (pop 8,367,000); **Other cities:** Pusan (3,160,000), Taegu (1,607,000), Inchon (1,084,000); **Highest point:** Halla-San, 1950 m (6398 ft); **Official language:** Korean; **Religions:** Buddhism, Confucianism, Christianity; **Adult literacy rate:** 93 per cent; **Average life expectancy at birth:** 63 years; **Unit of currency:** Won; **Main exports:** textiles, manufactures, chemicals; **Per capita GNP:** US$1500.

KUWAIT, a small Emirate at the head of the Persian Gulf. This low-lying, desert nation has erratic rainfall between 10 mm (0.4 in) per year and 380 mm (15 in). The average summer temperature is 24°C (75°F) but it occasionally soars to 52°C (126°F). Winters are cooler. Most people are Arabs. Kuwait has the world's highest per capita GNP, because of its oil production, which began in 1946. It is now one of the world's 10 top producers and revenue from oil sales finances one of the world's most elaborate welfare states. In 1899 Kuwait accepted British protection for certain rights. Kuwait became independent in 1914, but Britain remained responsible for Kuwait's foreign policy until 1961, when Kuwait became fully independent.

Area: 17,818 km² (6880 sq mi); **Population:** 1,516,000; **Capital:** Kuwait (pop 400,000); **Official language:** Arabic; **Religion:** Islam; **Adult literacy rate:** 60 per cent; **Average life expectancy at birth:** 69 years; **Unit of currency:** Kuwait dinar; **Main export:** oil; **Per capita GNP:** US$17,270.

LAOS, a poor, landlocked People's Democratic Republic in South-East Asia. Forested mountains and plateaux cover much of the country: most people live in the Mekong River plains. Laos has a tropical monsoon climate, with most rain in May–September. The average annual rainfall is 1020–2030 mm (40–80 in) in the north and 3800 mm (150 in) in southern uplands. The Lao-Lum (or Valley Lao, a Thai people, make up 56 per cent of the population; the Lao-Theung, consisting of many groups of animist tribes in the uplands, make up 34 per cent; and the Lao-Soung, including the Meo and Yao who are shifting agriculturalists, make up 9 per cent. Among the minorities, the Chinese and Vietnamese are important in business. In 1978 75 per cent of the people were employed in agriculture, which accounted for 60 per cent of the GDP, as opposed to 14 per cent from industry and 26 per cent from services. Rice is the main food crop; timber and coffee are the main exports. Tin is the only important mineral. A united kingdom was established in what is now Laos and northern Thailand in the 14th century. But Thailand and Laos were often in conflict. Laos became a French protectorate in 1893. Full independence as a kingdom was achieved in 1954. From 1953 there was a long struggle between the Royal Lao government and the pro-communist Pathet Lao (the Lao Patriotic Front's armed force). A coalition government was established in 1973, but the Pathet Lao took over in 1975. The King abdicated.

Area: 236,800 km² (91,434 sq mi); **Population:** 3,611,000 **Capital:** Vientiane (pop 90,000); **Highest point:** Phu Bia, 2820 m (9252 ft); **Official language:** Lao; **Religions:** Buddhism, animism; **Average life expectancy at birth:** 42 years; **Unit of currency:** Kip; **Main exports:** timber, coffee; **Per capita GNP:** US$90 (1978).

LEBANON, a Middle Eastern republic. Behind the narrow coastal plain are the western Lebanon Mts, an interior plateau containing the fertile Bekaa valley, and the Anti-Lebanon Mts in the east. The climate is Mediterranean in type. Most people are Arabs but only 60 per cent of the population is Muslim: the rest are Christians. Lebanon has long been a financial and commercial centre and, in normal times, it has a major tourist industry. Hence, services are the leading sector of the economy, followed by industry and agriculture. Consumer goods are manufactured and cereals and fruit are the main farm products; 38 per cent of the land is cultivated. Lebanon was the centre of the ancient Phoenician empire. It came under the Romans in 64 BC and under Ottoman rule from 1517. France became involved from the 1860s in order to protect the Maronite (Christian) community which was under attack from the Druses, a sect founded in the 11th century AD. France ruled Lebanon from 1918 to 1946 when it became a fully independent republic. Lebanon was involved in the Arab-Israeli War in 1948; in 1969 and 1973 Lebanese forces clashed with Palestinian refugees; and in 1975–76 civil war broke out between Muslim and Christian forces. In 1978 Israel invaded southern Lebanon to destroy Palestinian bases but largely withdrew when a UN force arrived. There was more fighting in 1982. Lebanon's Constitution is carefully designed to balance Muslim and Christian representation.

Area: 10,400 km² (4016 sq mi); **Population:** 3,325,000; **Capital:** Beirut (pop 702,000); **Highest point:** Qurnet es Sauda, 3083 m (10,115 ft); **Official language:** Arabic; **Religions:** Islam, Christianity; **Average life expectancy at birth:** 65 years; **Unit of currency:** Lebanese pound; **Main exports:** jewellery, precious metals/stones, textiles; **Per capita GNP:** US$1070 (1974).

LESOTHO, a landlocked kingdom enclosed by South Africa. It was formerly called Basutoland. Mostly mountainous, it includes the high Drakensberg range, but most people live in the western lowlands and the southern Orange River valley. The climate is continental, with warm, moist summers and cold, dry winters. The people, called Basotho, speak Sesotho and English. In 1978 agriculture employed 87 per cent of the people. It accounted for 36 per cent of the GDP, with 15 per cent from industry and 49 per cent from services. Arable land covers 12 per cent of the land and pasture 82 per cent. The chief food crops are cereals and vegetables. The main exports are wool, mohair and alluvial diamonds. In 1979 there were 1.3 million sheep, 730,000 goats and 550,000 cattle. Tourism is increasing, mainly from South Africa. The nation was founded in the 1820s by Moshoeshoe I who united refugees from tribal wars in South Africa. The country became a British protectorate in 1884 and an independent kingdom in 1966, although it remained heavily dependent economically on South Africa. In the early 1980s a clandestine Lesotho Liberation Movement carried out a number of bombings in Maseru and other places.

Area: 30,355 km^2 (11,721 sq mi); **Population:** 1,406,000; **Capital:** Maseru (pop 60,000); **Highest point:** Thabana Ntlenyana, 3482 m (11,424 ft); **Official languages:** English, Sesotho; **Religion:** Christianity (80 per cent); **Adult literacy rate:** 55 per cent; **Average life expectancy at birth:** 50 years; **Unit of currency:** Loti; **Main exports:** wool, mohair, diamonds; **Per capita GNP:** US$340.

LIBERIA, a republic in West Africa. Behind the coastal plain, with its mangrove swamps and savanna country, are forested plateaux and grassy highlands. Average annual temperatures are between 21°C (70°F) and 26°C (79°F). The average rainfall on the coast is about 2540–4060 mm (100–160 in) per year; inland areas have 1780 mm (70 in). There are 16 main language groups. The 50,000 or so Americo-Liberians, descendants of freed slaves, have been important in ruling Liberia. In 1978 71 per cent of the workforce was employed in agriculture, which accounted for 35 per cent of the GDP. Industry accounted for 28 per cent and services for 37 per cent. Since 1973 iron ore has been the main product, having overtaken rubber. The main food crops are cassava and rice. Liberia has a large merchant navy: many foreign ships register in Liberia because of the low fees. In 1822 the American Colonization Society founded Monrovia for freed slaves. In 1847 Liberia became an independent republic, with a Constitution much like that of the US, but US influence remained strong. In 1980 there was a military coup led by Master-Sergeant Samuel Doe who led a military junta.

Area: 111,369 km^2 (43,002 sq mi); **Population:** 1,992,000; **Capital:** Monrovia (pop 220,000); **Highest point:** Mt Nimba, 1752 m (5748 ft); **Official language:** English; **Religion:** mainly Christianity; **Adult literacy rate:** 30 per cent; **Average life expectancy at birth:** 48 years; **Unit of currency:** Liberian dollar; **Main exports:** iron ore and concentrates, timber, rubber; **Per capita GNP:** US$490.

LIBYA, officially the Socialist People's Libyan Arab Jamahiriyah. (*Jamahiriyah* means 'state of the masses'.) About 95 per cent of Libya is desert or semidesert. The land rises towards the south. Most people live in the north-eastern and north-western coastal plains. Average annual temperatures on the coast range between 12°C–27°C (54°F–81°F). The world's highest shade temperature, 57.7°C (136.4°F) was recorded in 1922 at Al'Aziziyah, south of Tripoli. The rainfall averages 200–610 mm (8–24 in) per year in the north-east and 330 mm (13 in) in the north-west. Most people are of Arab or Berber origin. Industry, mainly oil production, dominates the economy, providing 71 per cent of the GDP in 1978, compared with 2 per cent from agriculture and 27 per cent from services. The main food crops are cereals, dates, olives and vegetables. There were 4.8 million sheep and 2.1 million goats in 1979. The Turks controlled Libya from 1551 to 1911, when Italy occupied Tripoli. Italy lost Libya in World War II. Libya was divided between Britain and France until it became an independent kingdom in 1951. Col Mu'ammar Gaddafi led a military coup in 1969, deposing the king and setting up a republic. In 1977 Libya became a Jamahiriyah, which was a form of direct democracy. With its great wealth, Libya has become involved in the affairs of many other countries. For example, it has opposed Egypt's peace initiative with Israel and it intervened in the Chad civil war between 1980 and 1981.

Area: 1,759,540 km^2 (679,399 sq mi); **Population:** 3,224,000; **Capital:** Tripoli (pop 837,000); **Other cities:** Benghazi (372,000); **Highest point:** Mt Bette, 2286 m (7500 ft); **Official language:** Arabic; **Religion:** Islam; **Adult literacy rate:** 50 per cent; **Average life expectancy at birth:** 55 years; **Unit of currency:** Libyan dinar; **Main export:** oil; **Per capita GNP:** US$8210 (the highest in Africa).

LIECHTENSTEIN, a small principality between Austria and Switzerland, with which it has close links. For example, it uses Swiss currency and is united with Switzerland in a customs union. The Rhine and Ill river plains are in the north, with mountains in the south. Most people are Roman Catholic. Farming, including the cultivation of cereals, fruits and vines and cattle rearing, was the most valuable activity, when light industry overtook it. The sale of postage stamps and tourism are also important. Liechtenstein was founded in 1719. It was part of the German Confederation from 1815, but it has been independent since 1866 and neutral since 1868. It is a constitutional monarchy with a unicameral parliament of 15 elected members.

Area: 157 km^2 (61 sq mi); **Population:** 26,000; **Capital:** Vaduz (pop 5000); **Official language:** German; **Per capita GNP:** US$8000 (1974).

LUXEMBOURG, a Grand Duchy between Belgium, France and West Germany. The north is part of the Ardennes plateau, with fertile lowlands in the south. The climate is mild and moist. Most people are Roman Catholics. Iron ore is the chief resource and there are large iron and steel works. About 52 per cent of the land is farmed: barley, oats, potatoes, sugar beet and wheat are major crops. Luxembourg became a Grand Duchy in 1354. The Spanish and then the Austrian Hapsburgs ruled it from 1482 to 1795, when France annexed it. In 1815 it became part of the Netherlands. In 1830 much of the Grand Duchy went to Belgium, but in 1839 the remaining eastern part (modern Luxembourg) achieved autonomy, although it was ruled by Dutch kings until 1890 when it broke away from the Netherlands. Germany occupied the country in World Wars I and II. In 1944 Belgium, the Netherlands and Luxembourg formed the Benelux Customs Union. Luxembourg was a founder member of NATO in 1949 and of the EEC in 1957. It is a constitutional monarchy with an elected Chamber of Deputies.

Area: 2586 km² (999 sq mi); **Population:** 360,000; **Capital:** Luxembourg (pop 80,000); **Official languages:** French, Luxemburgish; **Unit of currency:** Franc; **Per capita GNP:** US$12,280.

MACAO, or Macau, a small Portuguese territory on the south-eastern coast of China. It is densely populated. Most people are Chinese: less than 3 per cent are Portuguese. Little land is available for farming. There is a small fishing industry and manufacturing is important, especially textiles. Transit trade with China and tourism are other sources of income. Macao has been Portuguese since 1557. It became the chief European trading centre in China, but it declined after the British established Hong Kong in 1842.

Area: 16 km² (6 sq mi); **Population:** 330,000; **Capital:** Macao (pop 157,000); **Unit of currency:** Pataca; **Per capita GNP:** US$1750.

MADAGASCAR, an island republic separated from the African mainland by the 400 km (249 mi) wide Mozambique Channel. It was called the Malagasy Republic in 1960–75. A plateau 900–1500 m (2953–4921 ft) high covers about 66 per cent of the country; volcanic peaks, such as the Massif du Tsaratanana, rise above it. The coastal plain in the east is narrow, with broader lowlands in the west. The forested east coast is hot and humid. The grassy and savanna-covered plateau is cool, with an average annual temperature range of 14°–21°C (57°–70°F): the rainfall is between 1010 and 2030 mm (40–80 in) per year. The north-west is wet but the south-western lowlands are semi-desert. The people are of Indonesian and African origin: the largest of the main 18 groups is the Merina. In 1978 agriculture employed 86 per cent of the workforce, contributing 38 per cent of the GDP; industry accounted for 19 per cent and services 43 per cent. Only 5 per cent of the land is arable, 60 per cent is pasture and 21 per cent forest. Rice is the main food and coffee, cloves and vanilla are the main cash crops. There is little mining but there are many small processing industries and oil refining is important. Portuguese mariners discovered the island in 1500. France made it a protectorate in 1885. By 1896 the French had annexed the entire island and abolished the Merina monarchy. Independence was achieved in 1960. From 1972 the army has played a major part in government.

Area: 587,041 km² (226,670 sq mi); **Population:** 9,167,000; **Capital:** Antananarivo (pop 400,000); **Highest point:** Massif du Tsaratanana, 2876 m (9436 ft); **Official languages:** French, Malagasy; **Religions:** traditional beliefs (57 per cent), Christianity (40 per cent), Islam (3 per cent); **Adult literacy rate:** 50 per cent; **Average life expectancy at birth:** 46 years; **Unit of currency:** Franc Malgache; **Main exports:** coffee, cloves, vanilla; **Per capita GNP:** US$290.

MALAWI, a landlocked republic in southern Africa. It includes part of Lake Malawi (Nyasa) in the East African Rift Valley. The River Shire flows from the lake into the Zambezi in Mozambique. There are scenic highlands west of Lake Malawi, but the highest peak Mt Mlanje is east of the River Shire. An inland drainage basin around Lake Chilwa is in the south-east. The lowlands are hot and humid. The rainfall averages 760–1020 mm (30–40 in) per year. The highlands are wetter and cool. The people speak a number of Bantu languages. Agriculture employed 43 per cent of the workforce in 1978, accounting for 43 per cent of the GDP; industry contributed 19 per cent and services 38 per cent. Maize is the chief food crop. Tobacco accounted for 49 per cent of the exports and tea for 24 per cent in 1977. Arable land covers 19 per cent of the country, pasture 16 per cent, forests 20 per cent and water 21 per cent. The territory became the British Central African Protectorate in 1891: it was renamed Nyasaland in 1907. It became independent as Malawi in 1964 and adopted republican status in 1966. A one-party state, it has enjoyed stable government under its president-for-life, Dr Hastings Kamuzu Banda.

Area: 118,484 km² (45,749 sq mi); **Population:** 6,376,000; **Capital:** Lilongwe (pop 103,000); **Other cities:** Blantyre-Limbe (229,000); **Highest point:** Mt Mlanje, 3000 m (9843 ft); **Official languages:** English, Chichewa; **Religions:** traditional beliefs, Christianity (20 per cent); **Adult literacy rate:** 25 per cent; **Average life expectancy at birth:** 46 years; **Unit of currency:** Kwacha; **Main exports:** tobacco, tea, sugar, groundnuts; **Per capita GNP:** US$200.

MALAYSIA, a South-East Asian monarchy. It contains the southern Malay peninsula and Sabah and Sarawak in northern Borneo. Forested mountains cover large areas. The most important lowlands are in the Malay peninsula. The climate is tropical, with average annual temperatures of 21°–32°C (70°–90°F) and the average rainfall is about 2500 mm (98 in). The Malay peninsula contains 84 per cent of the population. In the country as a whole, 47 per cent are Malays, 34 per cent are Chinese, 9 per cent are Indians and Pakistanis, 5 per cent are Dayaks, 5 per cent belong to other tribes in Borneo, and 2 per cent belong to other groups. In 1978 agriculture employed 50 per cent of the workforce, but industry accounted for 32 per cent of the GDP, as opposed to 25 per cent from agriculture and 43 per cent from services. Tin is the main mineral. Some oil is also produced and manufacturing is increasing. The main cash crops are rubber and palm oil; rice is the main food crop. Timber is also important. Portuguese traders reached Malacca in 1509 but the Dutch took over in 1641. The British East India Company became established in Penang in 1786 and, in 1826, Penang, Malacca and Singapore became the British Straits Settlement. Britain took over its government in 1867. In 1888 North Borneo (Sabah) and Sarawak became British protectorates. Malaysia was created in 1963 when Malaya, Singapore, Sabah and Sarawak joined in a federation, although this led to fighting with Indonesia. However, Singapore seconded from the federation in 1965. Malaysia's Constitution provides that the 9 Rulers of the Malay states elect one of their number every 5 years to be *Yang di-Pertuan Agong* (Supreme Head of the Federation).

COUNTRIES OF THE WORLD

Area: 329,749 km² (127,324 sq mi); **Population:** 14,777,000; **Capital:** Kuala Lumpur (pop 770,000); **Highest point:** Mt Kinabalu, 4102 m (13,458 ft); **Official language:** Malay; **Religions:** mainly Islam, also Buddhism, Hinduism, Christianity; **Adult literacy rate:** 60 per cent; **Average life expectancy at birth:** 67 years; **Unit of currency:** Malaysian dollar; **Main exports:** rubber, tin, timber, palm oil; **Per capita GNP:** US$1320.

MALDIVES, an island republic about 650 km (404 mi) south-west of Sri Lanka. It includes about 2000 coral islands. Fishing is the main industry. Coconuts, millet and fruits are grown. The Maldives came under British protection in 1887. Full independence was achieved in 1965. The Maldives became a republic in 1968.

Area: 298 km² (115 sq mi); **Population:** 167,000; **Capital:** Malé (pop 30,000); **Official language:** Divehi; **Religion:** Islam; **Unit of currency:** Rupee; **Per capita GNP:** US$200.

MALI, a landlocked republic in north-western Africa. Plains cover most of Mali, with uplands in the north-east and south. The River Niger flows in a broad arc through southern Mali. Two-fifths of the river's total length of 4000 km (2486 mi) is in Mali. Average annual temperatures are 24°–35°C (75°–95°F). Bamako has about 1120 mm (44 in) of rain per year: the north is desert. There are people of Arab and Berber origin, such as Tuaregs, and some of mixed Caucasoid/Negroid origin, such as the Fulbe (Fulani). But more than 80 per cent of the population is Negroid. Agriculture employed 88 per cent of the workforce in 1978, accounting for 37 per cent of the GDP, as opposed to industry 18 per cent and services 45 per cent. Cultivated land covers only 8 per cent of this poor country. The chief cash crop is cotton. In 1979 Mali had 4.5 million cattle, 6.1 million sheep and 5.8 million goats. Mali was part of several medieval empires: Ancient Ghana, Mali and Songhai. In 1880 France made the area (then called French Sudan) a protectorate. Full independence was achieved in 1960. The army ruled from 1968 but elections were held in 1979. Mali is a one-party state.

Area: 1,240,000 km² (478,793 sq mi); **Population:** 6,966,000; **Capital:** Bamako (pop 404,000); **Official language:** French; **Religions:** Islam (65 per cent), traditional beliefs (30 per cent), Christianity (5 per cent); **Adult literacy rate:** 10 per cent; **Average life expectancy at birth:** 42 years; **Unit of currency:** Mali franc; **Main exports:** cotton and cotton products, groundnuts, live animals; **Per capita GNP:** US$140.

MALTA, a Mediterranean island republic, south of Sicily. It includes Malta, 246 km² (95 sq mi), Gozo, 67 km² (26 sq mi), Comino, 3 km² (1 sq mi) and two islets. The climate is Mediterranean in type. Most people are of Arab, Italian and English descent. Cultivable land covers 39 per cent of the country but only 6 per cent of the workforce is engaged in agriculture and fishing, as opposed to 28 per cent in manufacturing. In 1979 Malta received 618,000 tourists. Malta was held by the Phoenicians, Greeks, Carthaginians, Romans, Byzantines and Arabs until 1091 when it was joined to Sicily. From 1530 it was ruled by the Knights of St John. Napoleon's forces took it in 1798 but Britain aided the Maltese to drive out the French. In 1814 Malta became a British colony. It became fully independent in 1964 and a republic in 1974.

Area: 316 km² (122 sq mi); **Population:** 340,000; **Capital:** Valletta (pop 14,000); **Official languages:** Maltese, English; **Religion:** Roman Catholicism; **Unit of currency:** Maltese pound; **Main exports:** manufactures, machinery and transport equipment, food; **Per capita GNP:** US$2640.

MARTINIQUE, a French Overseas Department in the Lesser Antilles, between Dominica and St Lucia. It is a mountainous, volcanic island, with a warm, humid climate. The people are of African, Asian and French origin. The main activity is farming, but light manufacturing is developing. Discovered by Columbus in 1493, the island has been French for most of the time since 1635. It became a French Overseas Department in 1946.

Area: 1102 km² (426 sq mi); **Population:** 326,000; **Capital:** Fort-de-France (pop 99,000); **Highest point:** Mt Pelée, 1463 m (4800 ft); **Exports:** sugar, bananas, rum; **Per capita GNP:** US$4680.

MAURITANIA, an Islamic Republic in north-western Africa. Low plateaux cover most of the country which lies largely in the Sahara. But the fertile River Senegal plains are in the south-west. Average annual temperatures are between 25°C and 32°C (77°–90°F) and there are large diurnal variations in the Sahara. The average rainfall is 660 mm (26 inches) per year in the savanna-covered south. The north has little rainfall. About 80 per cent of the population is of Arab and Berber origin. The others are Negroid. Agriculture, particularly livestock rearing, employed 86 per cent of the workforce in 1978, accounting for 26 per cent of the GDP, as opposed to industry and services 37 per cent each. In 1979 Mauritania had 8.4 million sheep and goats and 1.6 million cattle. Sea fishing is important but the chief resource is iron ore: Mauritania is Africa's 3rd largest producer. Copper is also mined. France ruled Mauritania from 1903 to 1960. In 1976 Mauritania acquired one-third of neighbouring Western (formerly Spanish) Sahara. After prolonged resistance by Saharan guerrillas and an internal military coup in 1978, Mauritania withdrew from Western Sahara in 1979.

Area: 1,030,700 km² (397,977 sq mi); **Population:** 1,721,000; **Capital:** Nouakchott (pop 135,000); **Official language:** Arabic, French; **Religion:** Islam; **Adult literacy rate:** 17 per cent; **Average life expectancy at birth:** 42 years; **Unit of currency:** Ouguiya; **Main exports:** iron ore, fish, copper; **Per capita GNP:** US$320.

MAURITIUS, an island nation east of Madagascar in the Indian Ocean. It includes the mountainous, volcanic island of Mauritius and Rodrigues, 104 km² (40 sq mi) in area, which is about 560 km (348 mi) to the east. The climate is warm and humid, but it is modified by the altitude. The people are of Asian Hindu descent (53 per cent), Asian Muslim descent (17 per cent), and European, mixed and African descent (28 per cent). Sugar and its by-products form the basis of the economy. Tourism is increasing: foreign visitors numbered 128,000 in 1979. Britain captured Mauritius from France in 1810. It achieved independence in the Commonwealth in 1968 as a constitutional monarchy: the British monarch, represented by a Governor-General, is Head of State.

Area: 2045 km^2 (790 sq mi); **Population:** 973,000; **Capital:** Port Louis (pop 146,000); **Official language:** English; **Religions:** Hinduism, Christianity, Islam, Buddhism; **Unit of currency:** Rupee; **Main exports:** sugar, clothing; **Per capita GNP:** US$1040.

MEXICO, a republic in North America. It is largely mountainous, with high plateaux and volcanic peaks. The lowlands are in the Yucatán peninsula and along the Pacific and Gulf of Mexico coasts. The chief mountain ranges are the Sierra Madre Occidental and the Sierra Madre Oriental which enclose the central plateaux. These are dotted with lakes and volcanoes: one, Citlaltépetl, is Mexico's highest peak. The 760 km (472 mile) long peninsula, Lower or Baja California, is mostly separated from the rest of Mexico by the Gulf of California. It is a rugged, arid region. Mexico straddles the Tropic of Cancer, but there are 3 main climatic regions determined by the altitude: the tropical *tierra caliente*, below 1000 m (3281 ft); the mild *tierra templada*, between 1000 and 2500 m (3281–8202 ft), in which Mexico City is situated; and the *tierra fria* above 2500 m (8202 ft) with its cold winters. Rainfall in central Mexico averages 400–800 mm (16–31 in), but the north-west is arid. People of mixed European and Indian origin form 55 per cent of the population; Indians 29 per cent and Europeans 15 per cent. In 1978 agriculture employed 39 per cent of the people, industry 26 per cent and services 35 per cent. Contributions to the GDP were agriculture 11 per cent, industry 37 per cent and services 52 per cent. Crops vary according to the altitude. They include coffee, cotton, maize, sisal and sugar. In 1979 Mexico had 29.9 million cattle, 7.8 million sheep, 8.1 million goats and 12.6 million pigs. Mining is important. Mexico is a major oil producer. Coal, copper, gold, iron ore, lead, manganese, mercury, silver, zinc and other minerals are mined. Manufacturing includes light and heavy industry: textiles and steel are leading manufactures. Aztec and other Indian ruins are tourist attractions: 3.7 million tourists visited Mexico in 1978. Spain ruled Mexico from 1521 to 1821. The country became a republic in 1824. Instability, wars and dictatorships marred Mexico's progress. From 1917, however, Mexico has made social and economic progress. Membership of the Latin American Free Trade Association since 1961 has helped to reduce Mexico's dependency on the United States.

Area: 1,972,547 km^2 (761,646 sq mi); **Population:** 74,539,000; **Capital:** Mexico City (pop 9,618,000); **Other cities:** Guadalajara (1,725,000), Monterrey (1,132,000); **Highest point:** Citlaltépetl, 5760 m (18,898 ft); **Official language:** Spanish; **Religion:** mainly Roman Catholicism; **Adult literacy rate:** 76 per cent; **Average life expectancy at birth:** 65 years; **Unit of currency:** Peso; **Main exports:** manufactures, oil, coffee, sugar, cotton; **Per capita GNP:** US$1590.

MONACO, a tiny principality on the Mediterranean Sea in south-eastern France. There are 4 districts: Monaco-Ville, the capital; la Condamine, a resort area; Monte-Carlo, a luxury resort with a famous casino; and Fontvieille. French currency is used. From 1297 Monaco belonged to the Genoese Grimaldi family. It became fully independent in 1861 and joined a customs union with France in 1865. In 1963 it ceased to be a tax haven for French citizens. Monaco is a constitutional monarchy with an elected National Council and Communal Council.

Area: 190 ha (467 acres); **Population:** 25,000; **Capital:** Monaco; **Official language:** French.

Below: An Aztec mask. The Aztecs ruled Mexico from the 13th to the early 16th centuries, but they were crushed by Spanish conquistadores. Below right: Acapulco, a major resort on the Pacific coast of Mexico, attracts many foreign tourists.

COUNTRIES OF THE WORLD

MONGOLIA, a landlocked People's Republic in northern Asia. A featureless plateau covers much of Mongolia, with mountains in the west and the Gobi desert, which covers one-third of the country, in the south. The main rivers are the Selenga, which flows into Lake Baykal, and the Kerulen, a tributary of the Amur River. The climate is severe. Temperatures average about 15°C (59°F) in July, but they plummet to −34°C (−29°F) in January. The average annual rainfall ranges from 500 mm (20 in) in the north to 130 mm (5 in) in the Gobi desert. The land is thinly populated. In 1978 agriculture employed 56 per cent of the people, industry 21 per cent and services 23 per cent. Most people were formerly nomadic herdsmen and in 1979 there were 14 million sheep, 4.7 million goats, 2.5 million cattle and 2 million horses. But all farmland is now organized in large state or collective farms: these farms own 80 per cent of the animals. Some oil, coal and other minerals are produced, but manufacturing is small-scale. The Mongol Empire became important in the 13th century under Genghis Khan. Mongolia became a Chinese province in 1691 but it became an independent Buddhist kingdom in 1912. In 1924 the communist Mongolian People's Republic was set up and religion was suppressed in the 1930s. Mongolia has been a member of COMECON since 1962.

Area: 1,565,000 km² (604,283 sq mi); **Population:** 1,772,000; **Capital:** Ulan Bator (pop 400,000); **Official language:** Mongol; **Religion:** formerly Tibetan Buddhist Lamaism; **Average life expectancy at birth:** 63 years; **Unit of currency:** Tugrik; **Main exports:** cattle and horses, wool and hair, grains, hides, furs; **Per capita GNP:** US$780.

Mongolia's economy was traditionally based on nomadic herding and most people lived in tents called ger *or* yurts. *These portable homes were made of felt which was stretched over a wooden frame. In recent years, an increasing number of Mongolians have adopted a more settled life.*

MONTSERRAT, a British colony in the Leeward Islands of the West Indies. It is volcanic and largely mountainous: earthquakes are common. Agriculture is the main industry: hot peppers, tomatoes and manufactures are exported. In 1979 14,400 tourists visited Montserrat. Columbus discovered the island in 1493. Irish settlers colonized it in 1632. It came under the British Crown in 1783.

Area: 98 km² (38 sq mi); **Population:** 12,000; **Chief town:** Plymouth (pop 3000); **Per capita GNP:** US$920 (1978).

MOROCCO, a monarchy in north-eastern Africa. The folded Atlas ranges cover much of the country: the highest point is Djebel Toubkal in the High Atlas range. The Anti-Atlas in the south is an uplifted rim of the African plateau. The fertile Rharb-Sebou lowlands and the Moulouya valley are in the north. Low plateaux border the narrow coastal plain in central Morocco. Tangier has an average annual temperature range of 11°–29°C (52°–84°F), but the south is cooler because of the cold Canaries current offshore. The average annual rainfall is about 760 mm (30 in) in some uplands, but the south and east merge into the Sahara. Most people are Arabs. About 30 per cent are Berbers and there is a small European minority. In 1978 agriculture employed 53 per cent of the workforce, but contributed only 14 per cent to the GDP, as opposed to 36 per cent from industry. Barley, citrus fruits, grapes and wheat are important crops. There are 13 million sheep, 3.6 million cattle and 5.6 million goats. Forestry and fishing are also important, but the main resource is phosphates. Iron ore, lead, manganese, oil, zinc and other minerals are mined. France ruled most of Morocco from 1912, although Spain held the north. Morocco became an independent kingdom in 1956, but Spain retained garrisons at Ceuta and Melilla. In 1976 Morocco and Mauritania partitioned the barren but phosphate-rich Western (formerly Spanish) Sahara. But guerrilla forces resisted the Moroccan and Mauritanian troops. In 1979 Mauritania withdrew and Morocco took the entire territory. The war continued into the 1980s.

Area: 446,550 km² (172,423 sq mi), not including Western Sahara; **Population:** 21,280,000; **Capital:** Rabat (pop 368,000); **Other cities:** Casablanca (1,506,000), Marrakesh (333,000), Fès (325,000); **Highest point:** Mt Toubkal, 4165 m (13,665 ft); **Official language:** Arabic; **Religion:** Islam; **Adult literacy rate:** 28 per cent; **Average life expectancy at birth:** 55 years; **Unit of currency:** Dirham; **Main exports:** phosphates, citrus fruits, fish; **Per capita GNP:** US$740.

MOZAMBIQUE, a People's Republic in south-eastern Africa. Coastal plains cover 44 per cent of the land, plateaux and hills 43 per cent and uplands 13 per cent. The main rivers are the Rovuma, Zambezi and Limpopo. Lake Nyasa (Malawi) is shared with Malawi and Tanzania. There is also a man-made lake behind the Cabora Bassa Dam on the Zambezi. The centre and north have a tropical climate. The far south is subtropical. The rainfall is generally low: Maputo has 760 mm (30 in) per year. There are 12 major Bantu-speaking tribes and more than 30 minor ones. Agriculture employed 67 per cent of the people in this poor nation in 1978, accounting for 45 per cent of the GDP; industry contributed 16 per cent. Arable land covers 4 per cent of the land and pasture 56 per cent. Leading crops are cashew nuts, copra, cotton,

This Berber family lives north of the Atlas mountains in Morocco. Berbers were the original inhabitants of north-western Africa, but they rapidly embraced Islam during the Arab conquest of North Africa between the 7th and the 12th centuries, although they retained their own language. Today some Berbers are nomadic herdsmen; others are sedentary farmers or skilled craftsmen. About three out of every ten Moroccans are Berbers.

groundnuts, maize, rice, sisal, sugar-cane and tobacco. Disease-carrying tsetse flies restrict livestock-rearing. Some coal is mined and the towns contain some industries. Portugal became established in Mozambique in the early 16th century. A guerrilla war (1964–74) preceded independence in 1975. The Constitution of 1978 vests power in the sole political party, FRELIMO, and declares socialism to be the national objective.

Area: 783,030 km² (302,346 sq mi); **Population:** 10,987,000; **Capital:** Maputo (pop 355,000); **Official language:** Portuguese; **Religions:** mainly traditional beliefs, Christianity (21 per cent), Islam (12 per cent); **Adult literacy rate:** 15 per cent (1975); **Average life expectancy at birth:** 46 years; **Unit of currency:** Metical; **Main exports:** cashew nuts, textiles, tea, cotton, sugar; **Per capita GNP:** US$250.

NAMIBIA, a South African-ruled country whose status is disputed. It is called South West Africa by South Africa. Behind the coastal plain (the Namib desert) is the central plateau. The Kalahari, a semi-desert, is in the east. The north is tropical and the south sub-tropical. More than 66 per cent of Namibia has less than 400 mm (16 in) of rain per year. The Namib is almost rainless: the northern interior is the wettest place. The people include Europeans (12 per cent), people of mixed origin (6 per cent), Khoisan and related peoples, including Nama (Hottentots) and Bushmen (16 per cent) and Bantu-speaking people who make up the rest of the population. Mining contributes 33 per cent of the GDP. Diamonds, lead, tin, zinc and uranium are exported. Agriculture contributes 13 per cent: the main activity is pastoralism. Fishing contributes 3 per cent and manufacturing 7 per cent. Britain annexed Walvis Bay in 1878 and later transferred it to South Africa. Germany took the rest of the country in 1884. South Africa occupied it in World War I. In 1920 the League of Nations mandated South Africa to rule the country. But in 1946 it refused to accept the trusteeship status that replaced the old mandate. The UN and South Africa have since been in dispute, despite many attempts to achieve a settlement. A guerrilla war, begun in 1966, continued into the 1980s.

Area: 824,292 km² (318,278 sq mi); **Population:** 1,066,000; **Capital:** Windhoek (pop 76,000); **Highest point:** 2483 m (8146 ft); **Official languages:** Afrikaans, English; **Religions:** Christianity, traditional beliefs (17 per cent), **Adult literacy rate:** 12 per cent (1971); **Unit of currency:** Rand; **Main exports:** diamonds and other minerals, fish products, livestock, karakul pelts; **Per capita GNP:** US$1220.

NAURU, an island republic close to the equator in the western Pacific Ocean. A raised atoll, it contains rich phosphate deposits on which the economy is based. 50 per cent of the people are Polynesians, 27 per cent are other Pacific islanders, 16 per cent are Chinese and 7 per cent are Europeans. Discovered in 1798, Nauru was annexed by Germany in 1888. Australia occupied it in 1914 and the League of Nations mandated Britain to rule it in 1920. Full independence, with a special relationship with the Commonwealth, was achieved in 1968.

Area: 21 km² (8 sq mi); **Population:** 7250; **Capital:** Nauru; **Main export:** phosphates.

NEPAL, a landlocked monarchy between China and India. It includes some of the world's highest peaks in the Himalayas, including Mt Everest on the Chinese border. Two-thirds of Nepal is mountainous. There are temperate valleys and warm plains near the Indian border. The people are of Tibetan or Indian descent, including the warlike Gurkhas. In 1978 93 per cent of the people worked in agriculture, which accounted for 62 per cent of the GDP. Hydro-electricity and manufacturing are developing. The monarchs were figureheads between 1846 and 1951, but their power was restored in 1951. The monarch assumed absolute power in 1960, but a National Parliament was elected in 1981.

Area: 140,797 km² (54,365 sq mi); **Population:** 14,932,000; **Capital:** Katmandu (pop 195,000); **Highest point:** Mt Everest, 8848 m (29,028 ft); **Official language:** Nepáli; **Religion:** Hinduism (90 per cent); **Adult literacy rate:** 19 per cent; **Life expectancy at birth:** 43 years; **Unit of currency:** Rupee; **Main exports:** grains, timber, cattle, hides, resins, medicinal herbs; **Per capita GNP:** US$130.

NETHERLANDS, a prosperous monarchy, is one of the Low Countries. It is at the western edge of the North European Plain. About 40 per cent of the country is below sea-level at high tide: the sea is held back by dykes which enclose polders (reclaimed areas). The most recent polders are in

Amsterdam, capital of the Netherlands, is built around a network of concentric and radial canals. The city contains about 400 bridges.

The Maoris of New Zealand are a Polynesian people known for their skill in wood, stone and bone carving. Images of human figures are called tikis.

the IJsselmeer (Zuider Zee) and the Delta region in the south-west. Polders make up more than 25 per cent of the land. The centre of the country consists of the flood plains of the Rhine and Maas (Meuse) rivers, and their branches (the IJssel, Lek and Waal). The Schelde river enters the sea in the south-west. The coastal region contains many islands, deep estuaries, marshes, sand dunes and polders. The highest land is in the south-east (Limburg). The annual temperature range is 2°–20°C (36°–68°F) and the average annual rainfall is about 760 mm (30 in). With about 350 people per sq km (908 per sq mi), the Netherlands is one of the world's most densely populated nations: 76 per cent lived in urban areas in 1980. In 1978 agriculture employed 6 per cent of the workforce, industry 45 per cent and services 49 per cent; they accounted for 4 per cent, 34 per cent and 62 per cent respectively of the GDP. Nearly 70 per cent of the land is farmed. Most farms are small but the yields are among the world's highest. Livestock are important: in 1980 there were 5.2 million cattle, 10.1 million pigs and 81.2 million poultry. Butter, cheese and eggs are major products. Leading crops include flowers and bulbs, potatoes, sugar beet and wheat. There is little mining apart from the extraction of natural gas and oil: in 1979 the Netherlands was the world's 4th largest natural gas producer and Western Europe's 5th oil producer. The chief manufacturing region is the Randstadt, a ring of cities around the polders of the west-centre: Rotterdam with its port Europoort, The Hague, Haarlem, Amsterdam and Utrecht. Eindhoven is another industrial centre. Petroleum products, ships, radio and television sets, textiles, and china and earthenware goods are major products. The country has been largely independent since the late 16th century. In the 17th century it built up a large overseas empire. France invaded the Netherlands in 1795 but it became a constitutional monarchy in 1815. In 1830 Belgium broke away followed by Luxembourg in 1890. Neutral in World War I, the Netherlands was occupied by Germany in 1940. After the war its economy thrived within the Benelux Customs Union. It joined NATO in 1949, the European Coal and Steel Community in 1953, and the EEC in 1957. Its last 2 monarchs, Queen Wilhelmina and Queen Juliana, both abdicated in favour of their daughters. Queen Beatrix became Head of State in 1980. Parliament consists of a First, or Upper, Chamber with 75 members elected by the provincial legislatures, and a Second Chamber of 150 directly elected deputies.

Area: 40,844 km² (15,771 sq mi); **Population:** 14,324,000; **Capital:** Amsterdam (pop with suburbs, 1,015,000); **Other cities:** Rotterdam (1,018,000), The Hague (675,000), Utrecht (482,000), Eindhoven (369,000); **Highest point:** 332 m (1056 ft); **Official language:** Dutch; **Religions:** Roman Catholicism, Protestantism; **Adult literacy rate:** 99 per cent; **Average life expectancy at birth:** 74 years; **Unit of currency:** Florin (Guilder); **Main exports:** chemicals, petroleum products, machinery and engineering products, food, textiles; **Per capital GNP:** US$10,240.

NETHERLANDS ANTILLES, two groups of Dutch islands in the Caribbean Sea. Curaçao, Aruba and Bonaire are near the Venezuelan coast. St Maarten, St Eustatius and Saba are in the northern Leeward Islands, east of Puerto Rico. The refining of oil from Venezuela is the main industry. The islands became Dutch in the 17th century and were called Curaçao until 1949. They achieved full autonomy in internal affairs in 1954.

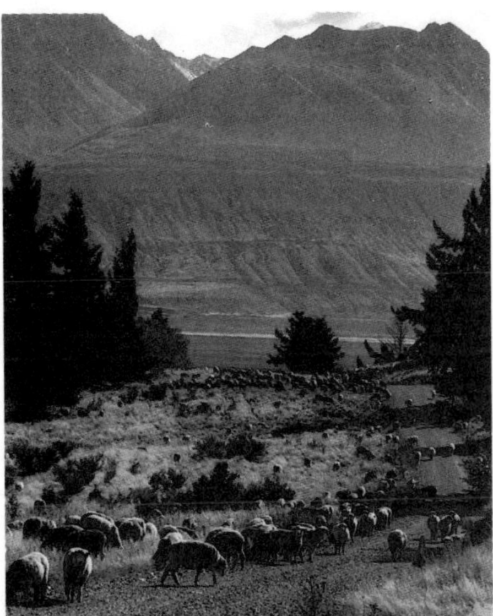

Sheep graze on Braemar Station at the foot of the Southern Alps on South Island, New Zealand. Lamb and wool are among the chief products.

Area: 961 km² (371 sq mi); **Population:** 273,000; **Capital:** Willemstad on Curaçao (pop 155,000); **Per capita GNP:** US$3540.

NEW CALEDONIA, a French Overseas Territory in the south-western Pacific, including New Caledonia and various small island dependencies, such as the Loyalty Islands. This tropical, mountainous country has a mainly Melanesian and European population. It possesses large reserves of nickel, chrome ore, iron ore and manganese, together with deposits of many other minerals. Only 6 per cent of the land is cultivable. Coffee, coconuts and meat are the main products. New Caledonia was discovered by Captain James Cook in 1774. It became a French colony in 1853 and an Overseas Territory in 1958.

Area: 19,058 km² (7359 sq mi); **Population:** 171,000; **Capital:** Nouméa (pop 74,000); **Per capita GNP:** US$5620.

NEW ZEALAND, a member nation of the Commonwealth in the south-western Pacific Ocean. It contains North Island, 114,681 km² (44,281 sq mi), South Island, 150,452 km² (58,093 sq mi), Stewart Island, 1735 km² (670 sq mi), the Chatham Islands, 963 km² (372 sq mi) and some smaller islands. North Island, where most people live, contains fertile plains, a volcanic central plateau, and fold mountain ranges in the east. Active volcanoes include Ngauruhoe, 2291 m (7516 ft), Ruapehu, 2796 m (9173 ft) and Tongariro, 1968 m (6457 ft). Lake Taupo in the centre is in a crater of an extinct volcano. North of the lake, hot springs are utilized to produce electricity. The eastern fold mountains continue in South Island as the Southern Alps, which reach their highest point in Mt Cook. Glaciers flow down high valleys and the south-western coast is glaciated with scenic fiords. Important lowlands include the Canterbury Plains in the east and the Otago plateau in the south-east. New Zealand has a cool, temperate climate. The average annual temperature range at Dunedin is 6°–14°C (43°–57°F), while at Auckland it is 11°–19°C (52°–66°F). Heavy rain falls in the Southern Alps but the Canterbury plains get only about 600 mm (24 in). North Island has between 1000–2000 mm (39–79 in) per year. About 91 per cent of the population is of European, mostly British, origin; 8 per cent are Maoris and 1 per cent other Pacific peoples. In 1978 agriculture employed 10 per cent of the workforce, accounting for 10 per cent of the GDP; industry employed 35 per cent and contributed 31 per cent of the GDP. Farming is efficient and yields high. In 1979 there were 8.5 million cattle and 78 million sheep. Wool, beef, lamb, mutton and dairy products are the leading exports. Arable farming is less important than pastoralism, but cereals, fruits, tobacco and vegetables are all important. New Zealand has a few minerals, including some coal and ironsands. Nearly 70 per cent of the electricity, however, is generated by hydro-electric stations. Most older manufacturing industries process farm products, but New Zealand now has a variety of light and heavy industry. Tourism is growing: there were 339,000 tourists in 1979–80. Maoris probably settled in New Zealand in the 14th century. The Dutch navigator Abel Tasman reached New Zealand in 1642 but his discovery was kept a secret. Captain James Cook rediscovered it in 1769. Wars between early British settlers and the Maoris occurred between 1845 and 1870, reducing the Maori population to 42,000: they numbered 270,000 in 1976. New Zealand became an independent dominion in 1907. Its parliament consists of a House of Representatives which, in 1978, had 92 members elected for 3-year terms. The British monarch, represented by a Governor-General, is Head of State.

Area: 268,676 km² (103,742 sq mi); **Population:** 3,400,000; **Capital:** Wellington (pop 350,000); **Other cities:** Auckland (806,000), Christchurch (327,000), Hamilton (158,000), Dunedin (120,000); **Highest point:** Mt Cook, 3764 m (12,349 ft); **Official language:** English; **Religion:** Christianity; **Adult literacy rate:** 99 per cent; **Average life expectancy at birth:** 73 years; **Unit of currency:** New Zealand dollar; **Main exports:** meat, wool, dairy products, hides, aluminium; **Per capita GNP:** US$5940.

NICARAGUA, a Central American republic. Forested plains border the Caribbean Sea. In the centre is a highland region with some active volcanoes. It is broadest and highest in the north. The Pacific coastlands contain two huge lakes, Managua and Nicaragua. The country has a hot and humid climate. About 80 per cent of the people are of mixed white and Indian origin, 10 per cent are blacks and 4 per cent are pure Indians. Agriculture employed 44 per cent of the workforce in 1978, contributing 23 per cent of the GDP (26 per cent came from industry). Coffee, cotton and meat are major products. Gold, silver and copper are mined and manufacturing is expanding rapidly. Spain conquered Nicaragua in the early 16th century. Independence was achieved in 1821, but the country came under Mexico in 1822 and in 1823–38 it was part of the Central American Federation. A new Constitution was adopted in 1974, providing for a bicameral parliament. But in 1979 the left-wing Sandinist National Liberation Front overthrew the government. A Junta of National Reconstruction was formed to rule the country.

Area: 130,000 km² (50,196 sq mi); **Population:** 2,851,000; **Capital:** Managua (pop 553,000); **Highest point:** Cordillera Isabella, 2438 m (7999 ft); **Official language:** Spanish; **Religion:** Roman Catholicism; **Adult literacy rate:** 57 per cent; **Average life expectancy at birth:** 55 years; **Unit of currency:** Córdoba; **Main exports:** coffee, cotton, meat, chemical products; **Per capita GNP:** US$660.

NIGER, a poor landlocked republic in north-central Africa. The highest peaks are in the Aïr massif in the north; plateaux and plains cover most of Niger. The only river is the Niger in the south-west. The north is mostly in the hot Sahara, although there is some pasture in the Aïr massif. The far south has about 560 mm (22 in) of rain per year. Nomadic Tuaregs live in the Sahara, but most of the people are black Africans who live in the south. In 1978 agriculture employed 91 per cent of the workforce, accounting for 43 per cent of the GDP. Live animals, animal products, groundnuts and vegetables are important products. Niger also has large uranium deposits. France occupied Niger in 1897–1900. Full independence was achieved in 1960. In 1974 a military group seized power and a Supreme Military Council was appointed to rule the country.

Area: 1,267,000 km² (489,218 sq mi); **Population:** 5,600,000; **Capital:** Niamey (pop 225,000); **Official language:** French; **Religions:** Islam (85 per cent), traditional beliefs (14.5 per cent), Christianity; **Adult literacy rate:** 8 per cent; **Average life expectancy at birth:** 42 years; **Unit of currency:** Franc CFA; **Main exports:** uranium concentrates, live animals, vegetables, groundnuts; **Per capita GNP:** US$240.

NIGERIA, a Federal Republic in West Africa. Most of the country is drained by the Niger and Benue rivers. North of these rivers are the high plains of Hausaland and higher plateaux. The land descends to the Sokoto plains in the north-west and the Lake Chad internal drainage basin in the north-east. South and west of the Niger River are hilly uplands bordered by a broad coastal plain which extends to the huge, swampy Niger delta. In the south-east the land rises to mountains on the Cameroon border. The climate is equatorial. Temperatures average 27°C (81°F) throughout the year. In the south Lagos has an average annual rainfall of 1780 mm (70 in) while the north has 250–1000 mm (10–39 in). Forest is the typical vegetation in the south with savanna in the north and semi-desert in the Chad basin. About 250

languages and dialects are spoken in Nigeria, Africa's most populous nation. The largest groups are the Muslim Hausa and Fulani in the north, the Ibo in the south-east and the Yoruba in the south-west. Agriculture employed 56 per cent of the population in 1978 but accounted for only 34 per cent of the GDP, as opposed to 43 per cent from industry. Tropical crops remain important, but oil has dominated the economy in recent years, accounting for more than 90 per cent of the exports. Revenue from oil sales is being used to diversify the economy and to improve the infrastructure, including the building of a new federal capital at Abuja in central Nigeria, which is due to be completed in the mid-1980s. Southern Nigeria was a centre of the slave trade from the 15th century. Britain abolished the slave trade in 1807 and, in 1861, annexed Lagos to stop the slave trade there. Between 1885 and 1903 Britain extended its control over Nigeria. Full independence was achieved in 1960 and Nigeria became a republic in 1963. From 1966–79 military regimes ruled Nigeria. In 1967–70 a civil war occurred when the people of the south-east tried to secede and set up a new nation, Biafra. Nigeria has sought to reduce tensions caused by cultural diversity by extending powers to the states, which number 19. Civilian rule was restored in 1979 under a Constitution that provides for a federal parliament consisting of a 96-member Senate and a 449-member House of Representatives, and an elected Governor and a State House of Assembly for each of the states.

Area: 923,768 km² (356,688 sq mi); **Population:** 88,847,000; **Capital:** Lagos (pop 1,061,000), but Abuja is scheduled to become capital in the mid-1980s; **Other cities:** Ibadan (847,000), Ogbomosho (432,000), Kano (399,000), Oshogbo (282,000), Ilorin (282,000); **Highest point:** about 2130 m (6988 ft) on Cameroon border; **Official language:** English; **Religions:** Islam, Christianity, traditional beliefs; **Average life expectancy at birth:** 48 years; **Unit of currency:** Naira; **Main exports:** oil, cocoa, palm kernels, tin, rubber; **Per capita GNP:** US$670.

NIUE ISLAND, a self-governing territory of New Zealand in the Cook Is in the South Pacific. These coral islands export copra and fruit. Britain annexed the island in 1899; New Zealand took over in 1901. It has been self-governing since 1974.

Opposite: Most people in northern Nigeria, including the Hausa and Fulani, are Muslims and mosques are common sights. Christianity and traditional religions are more important in southern Nigeria. Above: Norway's many fiords provide shelter for small fishing villages.

Area: 259 km² (100 sq mi); **Population:** 3954 (1976); **Chief town:** Alofi.

NORFOLK ISLAND, an Australian territory in the south-western Pacific. The climate of this volcanic island is pleasant: tourism is important. The island was an Australian penal colony in the 19th century. Most of the islanders are descendants of the *Bounty* mutineers.

Area: 36 km² (14 sq mi); **Population:** 2180 (1979); **Chief town:** Kingstown.

NORWAY, a monarchy in the western part of the mountainous Scandinavian peninsula. The Kjölen mountains form much of the border with Sweden. In the south there is an extensive region of high plateaux and mountains, including the highest peak, Galdhöppigen. The only large lowlands are in the south-east. The climate is mild, especially in winter, when the western coasts are warmed by the North Atlantic Drift. Even at North Cape, Norway's and Europe's most northerly point, the sea never freezes. Norway is thinly populated. In 1978 agriculture, forestry and fishing employed 8 per cent of the workforce and contributed 5 per cent of the GDP as opposed to 36 per cent from industry. Only 2 per cent of the land is cultivated and food must be imported. Coniferous forests cover 26 per cent of the land and the pulp and paper industry is important. Fishing is an important activity for people who live in the fiords or on the 50,000 or so islands. Bergen is the chief fishing port. Norway has rich oil reserves in the North Sea: it is Western Europe's 2nd largest oil producer. Iron ore, copper, lead and zinc are also mined and a high proportion of Norway's exports come from the electro-metallurgical, electro-chemical and paper industries. Hydro-electric power stations provide electricity for most purposes. Norway's large merchant shipping fleet is another major source of income. Between 1380 and 1814 Norway was united with Denmark under Danish rule. After a brief period of independence, Norway entered into a union with Sweden. This union was dissolved in 1905 and the Norwegians elected their own monarch, Haakon VII. After World War II, when it was occupied by Germany, Norway has made much economic progress and it now enjoys one of the world's highest standards of living. It rejected EEC membership in 1971. Norway is a constitutional monarchy with an elected *Storting* (parliament).

Area: 324,219 km² (125,188 sq mi); **Population:** 4,138,000; **Capital:** Oslo (pop 455,000); **Other cities:** Bergen (209,000), Trondheim (135,000); **Highest point:** Galdhöppigen, 2472 m (8110 ft); **Official language:** Norwegian; **Religion:** Evangelical Lutheran Church; **Adult literacy rate:** 99 per cent; **Average life expectancy at birth:** 75 years; **Unit of currency:** Krone; **Main exports:** machinery and transport equipment, metals and metal products, oil, animal products, paper; **Per capita GNP:** US$10,710.

OMAN, a Sultanate in the south-eastern corner of the Arabian peninsula. Behind the fertile northern coast (the Batinah north-west of Muscat) is a barren upland that merges into an arid interior plateau. The only other fertile region is in the far south (Dhufar). Temperatures at Muscat vary between 21°C and 43°C (70°–109°F). The average annual rainfall is only 10 mm (0.4 inches). Arabs make up 90 per cent of the population. There are also some Indians, Iranians, Negroes and Pakistanis. Most people are farmers or fishermen, but the oil industry dominates the economy. Oil production began in 1967 and it is now the leading export, although dates, dried fish, limes and other fruits, tobacco and vegetables are also exported. Muscat was a major Indian Ocean trading centre from early times. Portugal controlled it in 1508–1648. The present royal family was founded in 1741. Britain established a special relationship with the area in 1891. Oman is now an independent, absolute monarchy, but it retains ties with Britain, which helped to suppress left-wing guerrilla activity in the south in 1964–75.

Area: 212,457 km² (82,035 sq mi); **Population:** 950,000; **Capital:** Muscat (pop 7000); **Highest point:** Jabal Akhdar, 3047 m (9997 ft); **Official language:** Arabic; **Religion:** Islam; **Adult literacy rate:** 20 per cent; **Unit of currency:** Rial Omani; **Main exports:** oil, dates, limes, tobacco, frankincense; **Per capita GNP:** US$2970.

PACIFIC ISLANDS, TRUST TERRITORY OF, Micronesian islands governed by the United States since 1946. It includes the Mariana Is (excluding Guam), the Caroline Is and the Marshall Is. Tourism, fishing and farming are the main activities. From the late 1970s the US established Constitutions and set up local governments with the aim of creating a new status, either full independence or a continuing free association.

Area: 1779 km² (687 sq mi); **Population:** 149,000; **Capital:** Saipan; **Official language:** English; **Per capita GNP:** US$1340.

COUNTRIES OF THE WORLD

PAKISTAN, an Islamic Republic in southern Asia. The land is mountainous in the north where the Hindu Kush and Himalayas rise. Central and southern Pakistan contain fertile plains drained and irrigated by the River Indus and its tributaries (the Beas, Chenab, Jhelum, Ravi and Sutlej). The south-west includes the arid Baluchistan plateau and the Thar desert is in the south-east. Winters are cold in the mountainous north and cold north-easterly winds chill the northern plains in November–February. For example, the average January temperature in Lahore is 12°C (54°F) as compared with 18°C (64°F) in Karachi. In the hot season, March–May, the average temperature in Karachi rises to 29°C (84°F) but the northern plains are even hotter. It is cooler in the monsoon season, June–October, but the rainfall brought by the south-westerly winds is generally low. Karachi has an average annual rainfall of only 130 mm (5 in) although the north-east has 630–760 mm (25–30 in). Modern Pakistanis are descendants of the many peoples who have invaded the area. Several languages are spoken, including Urdu, Punjabi, Sindhi, Pashto and Baluchi. In 1980 72 per cent of the population of this extremely poor country lived in rural areas. Agriculture is the main activity, accounting for 32 per cent of the GDP as opposed to 24 per cent from industry in 1978. Leading crops are rice, winter wheat, cotton, maize and sugar-cane. Hydro-electricity is important and Pakistan has large reserves of natural gas. Textiles, cement, sugar and fertilizers are leading manufactures. The Indus valley was the home of early civilizations dating back to 2500 BC. Islam was introduced in the 8th century AD. From 1526 the area came under the Mughal Empire, but this began to decline in the 17th century. By the 19th century, Britain was the dominant power and Pakistan became part of British India. At independence in 1947, however, the predominantly Muslim Pakistan broke away from India, although fighting for the disputed province of Kashmir continued until 1949. Newly-independent Pakistan consisted of two parts: West Pakistan, now Pakistan itself, and East Pakistan which became Bangladesh after a civil war in 1971. Pakistan withdrew from the Commonwealth in 1972, and armed forces took over the government in 1977.

Area: 803,943 km² (310,421 sq mi); **Population:** 85,558,000; **Capital:** Islamabad (pop 235,000); **Other cities:** Karachi (3,499,000), Lahore (2,165,000), Faisalbad (822,000), Rawalpindi (615,000); **Official language:** Urdu; **Religions:** Islam (88 per cent), Hinduism (11 per cent), Christianity, Buddhism; **Adult literacy rate:** 21 per cent; **Average life expectancy at birth:** 52 years; **Unit of currency:** Rupee; **Main exports:** cotton and cotton goods, rice, carpets and rugs, leather; **Per capita GNP:** US$270.

PANAMA, a narrow Central American republic linking North and South America. Behind the Pacific and Caribbean coastal plains the interior is mountainous, the highest peak being Mt Chiriqui in the west. Panama's greatest width is only about 190 km (118 mi). It is at its narrowest at the point where the 81.6 km (50.7 mi) long Panama Canal is situated. The United States governed the Panama Canal Zone, a strip of land along the Canal, until 1979 when it reverted to Panama, although the US retained control over the Canal itself until 1999. Panama has a tropical climate, with an average annual rainfall of 3300 mm (130 in) on the Caribbean coast and 1500 mm (59 in) on the Pacific coast. More than 75 per cent of the people are of mixed white and Indian descent and in 1980 54 per cent of the population lived in urban areas. Only 18.5

per cent of the land is cultivated, although agriculture employed 35 per cent of the workforce in 1978, compared with 18 per cent in industry and 47 per cent in services. Bananas, rice and sugar-cane are major crops and there are copper reserves. But Panama's chief resource is the Canal. Panama became independent from Spain in 1819 as part of Colombia. It became a separate nation in 1914.

Area: 75,650 km² (29,210 sq mi); **Population:** 2,012,000; **Capital:** Panamá (pop 467,000); **Highest point:** Mt Chiriqui, 3374 m (11,070 ft); **Official language:** Spanish; **Religions:** Roman Catholicism (95 per cent); **Adult literacy rate:** 78 per cent; **Average life expectancy at birth:** 70 years; **Unit of currency:** Balboa; **Main exports:** petroleum products, bananas, sugar, shrimps; **Per capita GNP:** US$1350.

PAPUA NEW GUINEA, a nation in the south-western Pacific Ocean. It consists of the eastern part of New Guinea, the Bismarck Archipelago, including Manus Is, New Britain and New Ireland; Bougainville and Buka in the northern Solomon Is; the D'Entrecasteaux Is; the Louisiade Archipelago and the Trobriand Is; and about 600 smaller islands. New Guinea contains forested mountain ranges and broad, swampy river valleys. There are 40 active volcanoes in the north: this volcanic zone extends eastwards through the islands. The climate is hot and humid, but the uplands are cooler, Port Moresby has an average annual rainfall of 1200 mm (47 in). About 700 languages are spoken by the various tribal groups, a few of which have never come into contact with Western civilization. Tribal warfare still occurs. Agriculture employed 82 per cent of the people in 1978, accounting for 33 per cent of the GDP as opposed to 26 per cent from industry. The main resource, copper, is mined on Bougainville. Coffee, cocoa, copra, timber and fish are other major products. The Dutch took western New Guinea in 1828. Germany took the north-east in 1884 and Britain took the south-east, transferring it to Australia in 1906. Australia occupied German New Guinea in 1914 and ruled it with the south-east, called Papua. The combined territory was named Papua New Guinea in 1971 and it achieved full independence as a monarchy in the Commonwealth in 1975.

Area: 461,691 km² (178,270 sq mi); **Population:** 3,221,000; **Capital:** Port Moresby (pop 122,000); **Highest point:** Mt Wilhelm, 4694 m (15,400 ft); **Official language:** English; **Religions:** Protestantism (61 per cent), Roman Catholicism (31 per cent), tribal beliefs; **Adult literacy rate:** 32 per cent; **Average life expectancy at birth:** 50 years; **Unit of currency:** Kina; **Main exports:** copper ore and concentrates, coffee, cocoa, copra; **Per capita GNP:** US$650.

PARAGUAY, a landlocked republic in South America. Its main river, the Paraguay, divides it into the Chaco, a thinly populated, flat region of marsh and scrubland in the west, and a fertile plain and hills, rising to the Parana plateau, in the east. The climate is subtropical. About 75 per cent of the people are of mixed Indian and white descent, 21 per cent are of European origin, and 3 per cent are pure Indians. Agriculture employed 50 per cent of the workforce in 1978 and accounted for 32 per cent of the GDP, as compared with 24 per cent from industry. Cotton and soya beans are major crops. Forestry is also important: the bark of the quebracho tree is used to make tannin. Yerba maté, the plant from which a green tea is made, grows wild. In 1979 Paraguay had 5.2 million cattle. Mining is unimportant and most manufacturing is involved in processing farm products. Paraguay declared its independence in 1811. Wars against its neighbours in 1865–70 and in 1932–35 have marred its progress. A military coup in 1954 brought Gen Alfredo Stroessner to power. He introduced the 1967 Constitution which provides for a bicameral parliament (a Senate and Chamber of Deputies).

Area: 406,752 km² (157,056 sq mi); **Population:** 3,254,000; **Capital:** Asunción (pop 463,000); **Official language:** Spanish; **Religion:** mainly Roman Catholicism; **Adult literacy rate:** 81 per cent; **Average life expectancy at birth:** 63 years; **Unit of currency:** Guarani; **Main exports:** cotton, soya beans, timber; **Per capita GNP:** US$1060.

Opposite: Rawalpindi is Pakistan's fourth largest city. It is a commercial and industrial centre. Above left: Asunción, Paraguay's capital, was founded on the Paraguay River by Spanish pioneers in 1537. Above: Inca ruins in the Peruvian Andes. The Incas were conquered by Spanish conquistadores in the early 16th century.

PERU, a republic in western South America. Behind the narrow, arid coastal plain are high Andean ranges. These mountains, which reach their highest peak at Mt Huascarán, contain the headwaters of the Amazon River, notably the Maranon and Ucayali. Lake Titicaca, the world's highest navigable lake, straddles the border with Bolivia. It has a total area of 8290 km² (3201 sq mi). Eastern Peru is in the low Amazon basin. The climate is tropical, but the highlands are cooler. People of mixed Indian and white origin and a roughly equal number of pure Indians make up the bulk of the population. There are also some people of European and Negroid origin. In 1978 39 per cent of the people worked in agriculture, which accounted for 21 per cent of the GDP (23 per cent came from industry). Sugar, cotton, coffee and wool are important: in 1979 there were 14.5 million sheep and 4.2 million cattle. Fishing is usually a major industry but catches in the late 1970s were reduced because of overfishing and abnormal conditions. Peru produces oil and a variety of minerals, which provide its main wealth. These include copper, lead, zinc, silver and iron ore. Manufacturing industries are mostly based in Lima. Spain conquered the Incas in 1531–33 and ruled Peru until it declared its independence in 1821. Military governments have governed for long periods, but democratic rule was restored in 1980. The 1980 Constitution provided for a bicameral parliament, with a Senate and a Chamber of Deputies.

Area: 1,285,216 km² (496,252 sq mi); **Population:** 18,786,000; **Capital:** Lima (pop 3,158,000); **Other cities:** Arequipa (305,000); **Highest point:** Mt Huascarán, 6768 m (22,205 ft); **Official languages:** Spanish, Quechua; **Religion:** Roman Catholicism; **Adult literacy rate:** 72 per cent; **Average life expectancy at birth:** 56 years; **Unit of currency:** Gold sol; **Main exports:** minerals and metals, fish and fish-meal, oil; **Per capita GNP:** US$730.

PHILIPPINES, a South-East Asian republic consisting of more than 7000 islands. The largest, Luzon, 104,682 km² (40,420 sq mi), and Mindanao, 94,625 km² (36,537 sq mi), together make up two-thirds of the land area. The large islands are volcanic and mountainous, but many islands are small coral outcrops. The country has a tropical monsoon climate. The plains are hot and humid: the uplands are cooler. Manila has an average annual rainfall of 2080 mm (82 in). Most Filipinos are of Malay-Polynesian origin. There are also some people of Pygmy, European and mixed descent. The Philippines is Asia's only predominantly Christian country. Agriculture employed 48 per cent of the workforce in 1978, but it accounted for only 27 per cent of the GDP, as opposed to industry 35 per cent and services 38 per cent. Rice and maize are the main food crops. Coconut products and sugar-cane are major cash crops. Copper is the leading mineral. Textiles, footwear, chemicals, beverages and food are leading manufactures. Nearly a million tourists visited the country in 1979. Spain ruled the Philippines from 1565 to 1898, when the archipelago was ceded to the United States. Independence was achieved in 1946. Communist guerrillas and political rivalries caused instability and martial law was declared in 1972.

Area: 300,000 km² (115,837 sq mi); **Population:** 50,697,000; **Capital:** Manila (pop 1,626,000); **Other cities:** Quezon City (1,166,000), Davao (611,000); **Highest point:** Mt Apo, 2954 m (9692 ft); **Official language:** Philipino; **Religions:** Roman Catholicism (85 per cent), Islam (4 per cent); **Adult literacy rate:** 87 per cent; **Average life expectancy at birth:** 60 years; **Unit of currency:** Peso; **Main exports:** coconut oil, copper concentrates, timber; **Per capita GNP:** US$600.

PITCAIRN ISLAND, a British possession in the South Pacific Ocean (latitude 25°05′S, 130°05′W). Fruit and vegetables are grown, but postage stamps are the island's main source of revenue. Discovered in 1767, it received its first inhabitants, 9 *Bounty* mutineers and 18 Tahitians, in 1790. In 1856 the entire population (then 194) moved to Norfolk Island, but 43 returned in 1859–64. Britain took responsibility for the island in 1898.

Area: 5 km² (2 sq mi); **Population:** 63 (1981).

POLAND, a People's Republic in eastern Europe. Behind the lagoon-fringed Baltic coast is a broad plain, the northern part of which is mostly covered by infertile glacial deposits and forest. The central lowlands, in which Warsaw, Poznan and Łódź are situated, are more fertile. A low plateau in the south rises to the Sudeten Mts in the south-west and the Carpathians in the south-east. The plateau contains much fertile land and the major industrial region built around the Upper Silesian coalfield, major industrial centres being Katowice, Krakow and Wroclaw. The south is drained by the Oder and Vistula river systems. The climate becomes more continental from west to east, where the average annual temperature range is −5°–18°C (23°–64°F). Summers become warmer from north to south. Warsaw has an average annual rainfall of 560 mm (22 in): the south is wetter. In 1978 33 per cent of the population was employed in agriculture and 39 per cent in industry, as compared with 48 per cent and 29 per cent respectively in 1960. Farmland covers 60 per cent of Poland: unusually for a Communist country, 75 per cent is privately owned. Cereals, potatoes and sugar beet are major crops. In 1979 Poland had 13 million cattle, 21 million pigs, 85 million poultry and 4.2 million sheep. Poland is the world's 4th largest coal producer and it has large reserves of copper, lignite, lead, nickel, salt, sulphur and zinc. But much iron ore for the large steel industry is imported. With its massive, government-owned light and heavy industries, Poland is now one of the world's 15 top industrial nations. Poland's frontiers have changed several times in the last 200 years. In the late 18th century it disappeared from the map. Nominal independence was restored in 1807, but it was partitioned between Austria, Prussia and Russia in 1815. Poland was proclaimed an independent republic in 1918 but, in 1939, it was divided between Germany and the USSR. It again became independent in 1945, losing land to the USSR but gaining some from Germany. A Communist government was set up, but its attempts to nationalize farmland and discourage religious worship have failed. Dissatisfaction with the pro-Soviet government was expressed in strikes and riots in 1970, 1976 and again in 1980, when a strike committee demanded the right to form independent trade unions. A national confederation of unions (Solidarity) was formed, but its leaders were arrested in December 1981 when a military government took power.

Area: 312,677 km² (120,732 sq mi); **Population:** 36,300,000; **Capital:** Warsaw (pop 1,572,000); **Other cities:** Łódź (832,000), Krakow (705,000), Wroclaw (608,000), Poznan (544,000); **Highest point:** Rysy Peak in the High Tatra, 2503 m (8212 ft); **Official language:** Polish; **Religion:** Roman Catholicism (93 per cent); **Adult literacy rate:** 98 per cent; **Average life expectancy at birth:** 71 years: **Unit of currency:** Zloty; **Main exports:** coal, lignite, coke, iron and steel goods, ships, transport equipment, textiles, food; **Per capita GNP:** US$3830.

PORTUGAL, a republic in the Iberian peninsula. Much of the land is an extension of the Spanish meseta: there are plateaux and continuations of the central Sierras of Spain. Lowlands border the coast. Portugal has hot, dry summers and mild, moist winters, but the rainfall decreases and temperatures increase from north to south. Lisbon has an average annual temperature range of 10°–21°C (50°–70°F) and 760 mm (30 in) of rain per year. Portugal has a lower per capita GNP than any other country in Western Europe. In 1978 agriculture, forestry and fishing employed 27 per cent of the workforce. It accounted for 13 per cent of the GDP, as opposed to 46 per cent from industry and 41 per cent from services. Cereals are the main crops. About 12 per cent of the land is devoted to vineyards and olive groves. Forests cover one-third of Portugal, which leads the world in cork production. About 37,000 people worked in fishing in 1979: sardines and cod form the bulk of the catch. Portugal produces some minerals, including coal, copper and some iron ore. Manufacturing, including iron and steel, chemicals and textiles, has increased rapidly in recent years. About 3 million tourists visited Portugal in 1977. Portugal's modern frontiers were established in the 13th century and Spain recognized Portugal as an independent kingdom in 1385. In the 15th century Portugal initiated the Age of Exploration and built up a large overseas empire. Portuguese power began to decline in the 16th century. Brazil was lost in 1822. In 1910 the monarchy was abolished and a republic proclaimed. Between the 1930s and early 1970s Portugal had an autocratic government. A coup in 1974 led to the restoration of democracy and to independence to Angola, Cape Verde, Guinea-Bissau and Mozambique in Africa.

Below left: Gdansk, formerly Danzig, is a Baltic seaport and industrial centre in Poland. Strikes and riots in the city in the 1970s and 1980s were linked with a workers' movement to establish free trade unions in Communist Poland. Below: The Madeira Islands are a volcanic archipelago in the Atlantic Ocean west of Morocco. These Portuguese islands produce wine and attract many tourists.

Area: 92,082 km² (35,555 sq mi); **Population:** 10,390,000; **Capital:** Lisbon (pop with suburbs, 1,034,000); **Other cities:** Porto (693,000); **Highest point:** Malhao, 1991 m (6532 ft); **Official language:** Portuguese; **Religion:** Roman Catholicism; **Adult literacy rate:** 70 per cent; **Average life expectancy at birth:** 69 years; **Unit of currency:** Escudo; **Main exports:** timber and wood products, textiles, machinery, wine, chemicals, sardines; **Per capita GNP:** US$2160.

PUERTO RICO, a United States self-governing Commonwealth in the Caribbean Sea. The land is mostly rugged and scenic. The climate is tropical. Most people are of African and European descent. Over-population has caused substantial emigration to the US. Sugar cane is the chief product, but light industry and tourism are important. Columbus discovered the island in 1493 and it became a Spanish possession. It was ceded to the US in 1898. It has most of the powers of an American state, but its citizens cannot vote in US elections.

Area: 8897 km² (3435 sq mi); **Population:** 3,666,000; **Capital:** San Juan (pop 433,000); **Official languages:** Spanish, English; **Main exports:** sugar, rum, tobacco; **Per capita GNP:** US$2970.

QATAR, an Arab Emirate occupying a peninsula in the Persian Gulf. This hot, arid and mostly desert nation has little agriculture, although fruits and vegetables are grown. Oil, which was discovered in the 1930s, dominates the economy. Much oil revenue has been used to finance an elaborate welfare state. Qatar signed a treaty of friendship with Britain in 1916, but it became fully independent in 1971 when Britain withdrew from the Gulf.

Area: 11,000 km² (4247 sq mi); **Population:** 294,000; **Capital:** Doha (pop 130,000); **Official language:** Arabic; **Religion:** Islam; **Unit of currency:** Qatar Riyal; **Main export:** oil; **Per capita GNP:** US$16,590.

RÉUNION, a French Overseas Department about 780 km (485 mi) east of Madagascar. It contains 9 dormant and 1 active volcanoes. The island has a tropical climate and sugar cane is the chief product. The people are descendants of African slaves, French settlers, Malays, Indians and other South-East Asians. France annexed Réunion in the 1640s. It became an Overseas Department in 1946.

Area: 2510 km² (969 sq mi); **Population:** 546,000; **Capital:** St Denis (pop 104,000); **Highest point:** 3069 m (10,069 ft); **Religion:** Roman Catholicism; **Main exports:** sugar, molasses and rum; **Per capita GNP:** US$4180.

COUNTRIES OF THE WORLD

Attractive villages are a feature of the Romanian countryside. In 1980, 52 per cent of the population of Romania lived in rural areas, as compared with 66 per cent in 1960. Although the rural population has declined, it is still substantially greater than in most eastern European countries. Industry is currently expanding and so the population drift from the countryside to the cities will probably continue.

ROMANIA, a Socialist Republic on the Black Sea. Transylvania forms the heart of Romania. It includes a central plateau surrounded by the Bihor Mts to the west, the Carpathians to the east and the Transylvanian Alps to the south, where the country's highest peak is situated. In the far west are fertile plains. Other plains lie in the east and south. They are drained by the River Danube and its tributaries. A limestone plateau (Dobrogea) borders the Black Sea coast. The climate is continental. The average rainfall varies from 400 mm (16 in) in the east to 1400 mm (55 in) in the mountains. The people are descendants of several peoples, including the Romanized Dacian tribes of the Danube valley and Slavs. The Romanian language is based on Latin and contains many Slav words. In 1978 agriculture employed 50 per cent of the workforce, industry 31 per cent and services 19 per cent. Farmland covers 63 per cent of the country; most is government-owned. Cereals, potatoes, oilseeds and sugar beet are major crops and, in 1979, Romania had 6.5 million cattle, 10.9 million pigs and 15.8 million sheep. There are rich mineral resources, including oil and natural gas, coal, lignite, copper, chromite, gold, iron ore, manganese and zinc. The manufacturing sector has expanded greatly since the 1960s. In 1861 Moldavia and Walachia united to form the monarchy of Romania, which gradually extended its frontiers. In World War II it supported Germany at first but joined the Allies in 1944. In 1947 King Michael abdicated and a Communist government took control. In the 1970s, however, Romania pursued foreign policies that were increasingly independent of the USSR.

Area: 237,500 km² (91,704 sq mi); **Population:** 22,653,000; **Capital:** Bucharest (pop with suburbs, 1,960,000); **Highest point:** Moldoreanu, 2543 m (8343 ft); **Official language:** Romanian; **Religion:** Romanian Orthodox Church (80 per cent); **Adult literacy rate:** 98 per cent; **Average life expectancy at birth:** 70 years; **Unit of currency:** Leu; **Main exports:** machinery, ores and metals, oil and natural gas, food, chemicals; **Per capita GNP:** US$1900.

RWANDA, a small, poor, landlocked republic in east-central Africa. The East African Rift Valley in the west contains part of Lake Kivu. It is bordered by highlands that descend in a series of plateaux to the River Kagera in the east. The equatorial climate is modified by the altitude. Bantu-speaking Hutu form 90 per cent of the population. There are also Nilo-Hamitic Tutsi and Pygmy, European and Asian minorities. Agriculture employed 91 per cent of the workforce in 1978, accounting for 46 per cent of the GDP (22 per cent came from industry and 32 per cent from services). The main cash crop is coffee. Cassiterite is mined and there are various small-scale manufacturing industries. Rwanda and Burundi were once part of German East Africa, but Belgium occupied them in 1916 and ruled them as Ruanda-Urundi. A Hutu peasants' revolt in 1959 caused the deaths of many Tutsi, who formed the ruling class. The Tutsi monarchy was abolished and Rwanda became an independent republic controlled by the Hutu in 1962. Communal conflict caused instability in the 1960s and 1970s.

Area: 26,338 km² (10,170 sq mi); **Population:** 5,067,000; **Capital:** Kigali (pop 118,000); **Highest point:** 4507 m (14,787 ft); **Official languages:** Kinyarwanda, French; **Religions:** traditional beliefs (about 50 per cent), Christianity; **Adult literacy rate:** 23 per cent; **Average life expectancy at birth:** 46 years; **Unit of currency:** Rwanda franc; **Main exports:** coffee, tin, tea; **Per capita GNP:** US$210.

ST HELENA, a British island territory in the South Atlantic, about 1930 km (1199 mi) west of Angola. It is a mountainous, volcanic island. There is some farming and fishing, but no mining or industry. St Helena became a British colony in 1833. In 1922 the volcanic island of Ascension, 1130 km (702 mi) to the north-west, was made a dependency of St Helena, as were the 4 islands of Tristan da Cunha in 1938. Ascension Island covers 88 km² (34 sq mi) and has a population of 991 (1979). Tristan da Cunha has an area of 98 km² (38 sq miles) and 320 people (1979).

Area: 122 km² (47 sq mi); **Population:** 5200 (1979); **Chief town:** Jamestown (pop 1500).

ST KITTS-NEVIS, a British Associated State in the Leeward Is in the West Indies. The islands are of volcanic origin and export sugar and molasses. From 1623 they came under alternate French and British rule, but they were ceded to Britain in 1783. In 1967 St Kitts (or Christopher)-Nevis-

Left: Castries is the capital of St Lucia, a beautiful island in the West Indies. Although small, Castries is becoming a tourist centre.

Anguilla became an Associated State in the Commonwealth. Because Anguilla objected to rule from St Kitts, Britain appointed a Commissioner to handle its affairs. Anguilla was formally separated from St Kitts-Nevis in 1980.

Area: 262 km² (101 sq mi); **Population:** 51,000; **Chief town:** Basseterre (pop 14,700); **Per capita GNP:** US$780.

ST LUCIA, a picturesque island nation in the Windward Is in the West Indies. Volcanic in origin, it has a tropical climate and bananas, cocoa, coconut oil and copra, and textiles are exported. Tourism is developing; there were 107,000 visitors in 1978. The island was contested between Britain and France from 1605, but it was ceded to Britain in 1814. Self-government was achieved in 1967 and full independence within the Commonwealth was gained in 1979.

Area: 616 km² (238 sq mi); **Population:** 130,000; **Capital:** Castries (pop 45,000).

ST PIERRE AND MIQUELON, a French Overseas Department consisting of 8 islands off the southern coast of Newfoundland, Canada. These rocky islands have a temperate, moist climate. The people are descendants of French immigrants, who have maintained their French culture. Fishing and fish processing are the main activities. The islands have been French almost continuously since 1660.

Area: 242 km² (93 sq mi); **Population:** 6000; **Capital:** St Pierre.

ST VINCENT AND THE GRENADINES, a West Indian nation in the Windward Is, consisting of the island of St Vincent, 345 km² (133 sq mi), and the small islands that make up the Northern Grenadines. St Vincent is a volcanic island with a tropical climate. Most people are blacks or of mixed origin. Farming is the main activity, but tourism is expanding. France and Britain alternately held St Vincent until it finally became British in 1805. It became a British Associated State in 1969 and a fully independent member of the Commonwealth in 1979.

Area: 388 km² (150 sq mi); **Population:** 113,000; **Capital:** Kingstown (pop 23,000); **Main export:** bananas; **Per capita GNP:** US$490.

SAMOA, AMERICAN, a group of 8 islands in the South Pacific, about 1050 km (652 mi) north-east of Fiji. The largest island, Tutuila, contains the capital Pago Pago. This mountainous island has heavy rainfall: the climate throughout is tropical. Most people are Polynesians. The chief exports are fish products, copra and handicrafts. The first recorded European landfall was in 1722. In 1899 a treaty between the US, Britain and Germany assigned the eastern Samoan islands to the US and the western islands (now Western Samoa) to Germany. A popularly elected Samoan Governor was inaugurated in 1978.

Area: 197 km² (76 sq mi); **Population:** 35,000; **Capital:** Pago Pago; **Per capita GNP:** US$8030.

SAMOA, WESTERN, a Pacific island nation about 720 km (447 mi) north-east of Fiji. The largest islands are Savai'i, 1714 km² (662 sq mi), and Upolu, 1118 km² (432 sq mi), where the capital Apia is situated. There are also two small islands, Manono and Apolima, and several uninhabited islets. The islands are volcanic in origin and have a tropical climate. The people are Polynesians and Christianity is the main religion. The chief products are bananas, cocoa and coconuts. Germany ruled the islands before World War I and New Zealand was in control in 1920–61. Western Samoa became a fully independent monarchy on January 1, 1962. HH Malietoa Tanumafili II became Head of State in 1963 and Western Samoa became a member of the Commonwealth in 1970.

Area: 2842 km² (1097 sq mi); **Population:** 164,000; **Capital:** Apia (pop 32,000).

SAN MARINO, the world's smallest independent republic. It is landlocked and situated in central Italy, south of Rimini. Its capital is on the slopes of Mt Titano, a 743 m (2438 ft) high spur of the Apennines. Most people are farmers, but tourism is the main industry. Building stone, textiles and wine are exported. Founded in the 4th century AD, San Marino joined a customs union with Italy in 1862.

Area: 61 km² (24 sq mi); **Population:** 21,000; **Capital:** San Marino (pop 4000).

SÃO TOMÉ AND PRINCIPE, an island republic in the Gulf of Guinea. It includes the volcanic island of São Tomé, 854 km² (330 sq mi) in area, Principe to the north, and some smaller islands. The people are descendants of slaves from the mainland and Europeans. Agriculture is the main activity. Portuguese mariners discovered the then uninhabited islands in 1471. From 1522 they were governed as a province of Portugal until full independence was achieved in 1975.

Area: 964 km² (372 sq mi); **Population:** 110,000; **Capital:** São Tomé (pop 17,000); **Highest point:**

2024 m (6640 ft); **Official language:** Portuguese; **Religion:** Roman Catholicism; **Unit of currency:** Dobra; **Main exports:** cocoa, copra, palm kernels; **Per capita GNP:** US$450.

SAUDI ARABIA, a kingdom occupying much of the Arabian peninsula. Behind the narrow, Red Sea coastal plain is a highland zone, including the Hejaz in the north and the Asir highlands in the south. East of these highlands are plateaux that slope gently towards the Persian Gulf coastal plain. The plateaux, which cover 90 per cent of the country, include the Nafud Desert in the north and the Rub'al-Khali (the 'Empty Quarter') in the south. The lowlands are hot, but the altitude modifies temperatures. The rainfall varies between 380 mm (15 in) in the Asir highlands to 80 mm (3 in) at Riyadh: virtually no rain falls in the Rub'al-Khali. Most Saudis are Muslim Arabs and Mecca, the birthplace of the Prophet Muhammad, and Medina are the two holiest places of Islam. In 1978 agriculture employed 62 per cent of the workforce, but it accounted for only 1 per cent of the GDP, while industry accounted for 76 per cent (of which only 5 per cent came from manufacturing). The economy is dominated by oil which was discovered in 1938. In 1980 only the USSR and US produced more oil than Saudi Arabia. The country was under the nominal rule of the Ottoman Turks in 1517–1916, when they were driven out. In 1927 the Sultan of Nejd, Abd Al-Aziz Ibn Saud, founded modern Saudi Arabia and became its king. The king now rules with a cabinet, but remains the focus of power. In recent years revenue from oil has been used to develop welfare services, industries, transport facilities and water conservation and land reclamation projects.

Area: 2,149,690 km² (830,045 sq mi); **Population:** 9,418,000; **Capital:** Riyadh (pop 669,000); **Other cities:** Jidda (561,000); Mecca (367,000), Medina (198,000); **Highest point:** around 3048 m (10,000 ft) in the Asir range; **Official language:** Arabic; **Religion:** Islam; **Average life expectancy at birth:** 53 years; **Unit of currency:** Riyal; **Main export:** oil; **Per capita GNP:** US$7370.

SENEGAL, a West African republic. It is mostly low-lying and covered by savanna. There is a low plateau in the south-east. Senegal is drained by the Senegal, Saloum, Gambia and Casamance rivers. The climate on the coast is pleasant but the interior is hot. The rainfall increases from the arid north to the south. Dakar has an average annual rainfall of 580 mm (23 in) while the far south-west has 1630 mm (64 in). Most people are Negroid. Agriculture employed 77 per cent of the workforce in 1978 but accounted for only 26 per cent of the GDP as opposed to 25 per cent from industry. Groundnuts and groundnut products dominate the economy. There were 2.8 million cattle and 2.9 million sheep and goats in 1979. Dakar is West Africa's most industrialized city. Tourism is growing: there were 198,000 tourists in 1979. French contacts date back to the early 17th century, but France did not colonize all of Senegal until 1887. In 1959 Senegal became part of the Federation of Mali, but it became a separate, fully independent republic in 1960. In 1981 Senegalese troops helped to put down an uprising in Gambia, which is an enclave within Senegal. Soon afterwards Senegal and Gambia set up a confederation called Senegambia. This came into being in February 1982, although both nations retained their sovereignty.

Area: 196,192 km² (75,754 sq mi); **Population:** 5,967,000; **Capital:** Dakar (pop 800,000); **Official language:** French; **Religions:** Islam (90 per cent), traditional beliefs (5 per cent), Christianity (5 per cent); **Adult literacy rate:** 10 per cent; **Average life expectancy at birth:** 42 years; **Unit of currency:** Franc CFA; **Main exports:** groundnuts and groundnut products, fish, phosphate of lime; **Per capita GNP:** US$430.

SEYCHELLES, an Indian Ocean island republic north-east of Madagascar. There are about 90 islands. The rugged Mahé, or Granitic, islands make up 80 per cent of the area: the rest are flat coral islands. The largest island, Mahé, 144 km² (56 sq mi), contains the capital Victoria. The climate is tropical. Most people are Creoles, of mixed French and African origin. There are also some Chinese, Europeans and Indians. Tourism and agriculture are the main activities. French settlers arrived in the 1770s. Britain ruled the islands from 1810 until independence in the Commonwealth was achieved in 1976. A successful coup took place in 1977, but a mercenary invasion in 1981 was defeated.

Area: 280 km² (108 sq mi); **Population:** 70,000; **Capital:** Victoria (pop 23,000); **Official languages:** English, French; **Religion:** Roman Catholicism (90 per cent); **Unit of currency:** Rupee; **Main exports:** copra, cinnamon, fish; **Per capita GNP:** US$1400.

SIERRA LEONE, a West African republic. Behind the broad coastal plain are interior plateaux and mountains. The climate is tropical. Freetown has an average annual rainfall of 3360 mm (132 in): the wettest months are July–September. Most people are black Africans: there are 18 main groups. A Creole minority is composed of descendants of freed slaves brought to Freetown 200 years ago. In 1978 agriculture employed 67 per cent of the workforce and accounted for 39 per cent of the GDP, as compared with industry 22 per cent. Rice is the main food crop and coffee, cocoa and palm kernels are the chief cash crops. But diamonds and bauxite made up 67 per cent of the exports in 1978. Forestry and fishing are expanding, as is manufacturing, and tourism is being developed. In 1787 Britain founded Freetown as a settlement for freed slaves. In 1808 the Sierra Leone peninsula was made a colony and the interior was declared a protectorate in 1898. Full independence was achieved in 1961. Sierra Leone became a republic in 1971: it is now a one-party state with an elected House of Representatives.

Area: 71,740 km² (27,700 sq mi); **Population:** 3,643,000; **Capital:** Freetown (pop 274,000); **Highest point:** 1948 m (6391 ft); **Official language:** English; **Religions:** mainly traditional beliefs,

Islam (20 per cent), Christianity; **Adult literacy rate:** 15 per cent; **Average life expectancy at birth:** 46 years; **Unit of currency:** Leone; **Main exports:** diamonds, coffee, cocoa, bauxite; **Per capita GNP:** US$250.

SINGAPORE, a prosperous island republic off the southern tip of the Malay peninsula. A causeway links Singapore Island to the mainland. There are also many islets that make up 8 per cent of the country. The climate is hot and humid. Temperatures stay around 25°–27°C (77°–81°F) throughout the year and the average annual rainfall is 2440 mm (96 in). The main groups of people are Chinese (76 per cent), Malays (15 per cent) and Indians (7 per cent). Agriculture employed only 2 per cent of the people in 1978 and accounted for 2 per cent of the GDP. Industry contributed 35 per cent and services 63 per cent. Manufacturing is extremely important. The many products include ships, petrochemicals, steel and textiles. The port of Singapore is one of the world's largest and Singapore is a major financial centre. Britain took over the island in 1824. It was part of Malaysia from 1963 but it became a separate republic in 1965.

Area: 581 km^2 (224 sq mi); **Population:** 2,476,000; **Capital:** Singapore; **Highest point:** 177 m (581 ft); **Official languages:** Malay, Chinese, Tamil, English; **Religions:** Buddhism, Confucianism and Taoism (among the Chinese), Islam (the Malays), Hinduism (Indians), Christianity; **Adult literacy rate:** 75 per cent; **Average life expectancy at birth:** 70 years; **Unit of currency:** Singapore dollar; **Main exports:** petroleum products, electronic products, rubber, machinery; **Per capita GNP:** US$3820.

SOLOMON ISLANDS, an island nation in the Commonwealth in the south-western Pacific. It lies to the east of New Guinea and Papua New Guinea includes the two most northern islands, Bougainville and Buka. The largest of the Solomon Islands is Guadalcanal which, like the other large islands in the group, is volcanic and mountainous. The climate is equatorial. Most people are Melanesians. Agriculture, forestry and fishing are the main activities: copra, timber and palm-oil are major exports. The Solomons became a British protectorate in 1893–99. Full independence was achieved in 1978. The British monarch, represented by a Governor-General, is the official Head of State.

Area: 28,446 km^2 (10,984 sq mi); **Population:** 242,000; **Capital:** Honiara on Guadalcanal (pop 15,000); **Unit of currency:** Solomon Islands dollar; **Per capita GNP:** US$430 (1978).

SOMALI REPUBLIC, in the Horn of Africa, faces the Gulf of Aden in the north and the Indian Ocean to the east. Behind the narrow northern coastal plain are highlands containing Somalia's highest peaks. The south consists of plateaux and plains. It contains the only permanent rivers: the Wabi Shebele and the Juba. Rainfall increases from the north, where less than 250 mm (10 in) falls per year, to the south. Mogadishu has 400 mm (16 in). Temperatures are high throughout the year. The main types of vegetation are semi-desert and savanna. Most people speak a Cushitic language, Somali, which is also used in parts of Djibouti, Ethiopia and Kenya. In 1978 agriculture employed 82 per cent of the people and accounted for 60 per cent of the GDP (industry contributed 11 per cent). Most people are nomadic pastoralists: there were 16 million goats, 10 million sheep, 5.4 million camels and 3.8 million cattle in 1979. Animals, meat and hides and skins account for about 70 per cent of the exports. The main arable areas are in the southern river valleys. The north became a British protectorate in 1884, while Italy took the south in 1905. The two territories merged and became an independent republic in 1960. The army took control in 1969 and, in 1977–78 it supported Somali-speaking secessionists in the Ethiopian Ogaden who wanted to join a Greater Somalia. Sporadic fighting continued in the Ogaden and hundreds of thousands of refugees flooded into Somalia. A People's Assembly was elected in 1979 but a state of emergency was declared in 1980.

Area: 637,657 km^2 (246,214 sq mi); **Population:** 4,125,000; **Capital:** Mogadishu (pop 400,000); **Highest point:** Erigavo, 2406 m (7894 ft); **Official language:** Somali; **Religion:** Islam; **Adult literacy rate:** 60 per cent; **Average life expectancy at birth:** 43 years; **Unit of currency:** Somali shilling; **Main exports:** live animals, fruit, hides and skins; **Per capita GNP:** US$130 (1978).

SOUTH AFRICA, a republic since 1961. The interior is a vast, saucer-shaped plateau, with an uptilted rim, the highest section being the Drakensberg range in the south-east. The Orange and Limpopo rivers drain much of the plateau. Around the plateau, the land descends in steps to the sea. In southern Cape province two such steps are the Great and Little Karoo; these are plateaux bounded by mountain ranges. Most of South Africa has a subtropical climate, modified by the altitude. About 90 per cent of the land has an average annual rainfall of less than 760 mm (30 in) and about 50 per cent is arid. The population includes black Africans (70.2 per cent), people of European origin (17.5 per cent), Coloureds of mixed descent (9.4 per cent) and Asians (2.9 per cent). The whites, who are mostly Afrikaans or English speakers, control the country. Since 1948 a policy of separate development has been pursued, whereby each ethnic group is supposed to develop separately. Hence, 10 African tribal Homelands have been set up for the main black groups, including the Zulu, Xhosa, Tswana, Sepedi (North Sotho) and Seshoeshoe (South Sotho). Agriculture employed 30 per cent of the workforce in 1978, industry 29 per cent and services 41 per cent. Their respective contributions to the GDP were 8 per cent, 45 per cent and 47 per cent. Manufacturing is especially important in the southern Transvaal and around the main ports: Cape Town, Durban and Port Elizabeth. South Africa produces most of the non-Communist world's gold and many other minerals, including asbestos, coal, diamonds, copper, iron ore, manganese, tin, uranium and zinc. Arable land covers 5 per cent of the country and pasture about 80 per cent: there were 13.2 million cattle and 31.5

COUNTRIES OF THE WORLD

PROVINCES OF SOUTH AFRICA

Province	Area sq km	Area sq mi	Population 1970	Seat of government
Cape of Good Hope	721,001	278,395	6,732,000	Cape Town
Natal	86,967	33,580	4,237,000	Pietermaritzburg
Transvaal	283,917	109,627	8,718,000	Pretoria
Orange Free State	129,152	49,869	1,716,000	Bloemfontein

million sheep in 1979. The chief food crop is maize, but a wide variety of cash crops is produced. Forestry, fishing and tourism are also important. The Portuguese Bartholomeu Dias rounded the Cape in 1488. The Dutch made the first settlement at the Cape in 1652. Gradually, European farmers spread inland where they clashed with Bantu-speaking peoples. In 1795–1803 and again in 1806, Britain occupied the Cape which became a British colony in 1814. The Dutch (called the Boers or Afrikaaners) resented British rule and many moved eastwards and north-eastwards to escape it. Anglo-Dutch rivalry finally led to wars in 1880–81 and 1899–1902. In 1910 the country was united in the Union of South Africa. In World War I, South Africa occupied Namibia (see Namibia). Since 1948 the racial policies involved in separate development have been increasingly criticized by the rest of the world. In 1961 South Africa became a republic and left the Commonwealth. In the 1970s and early 1980s four African Homelands (Transkei, Bophuthatswana, Venda and Ciskei) were declared independent, but the UN refused to accept that they had the status of independent sovereign states.

Area: 1,221,037 km² (471,471 sq mi); **Population:** 30,844,000; **Capitals:** Cape Town (seat of legislature, pop 1,097,000), Pretoria (seat of government, 562,000); **Other cities:** Johannesburg (1,433,000), Durban (843,000), Port Elizabeth (469,000); **Highest point:** Mont aux Sources, 3299 m (10,823 ft); **Official languages:** Afrikaans, English; **Religion:** mainly Christianity; **Average life expectancy at birth:** 60 years; **Unit of currency:** Rand; **Main exports:** minerals (including gold and diamonds), mineral products, metals and metal products, food, vegetable products, textiles, machinery, wool; **Per capita GNP:** US$1720.

SPAIN, a kingdom in the Iberian peninsula. Most of Spain is a plateau, or *Meseta*, between 610 and 910 m (2001–2986 ft) which is broken by several mountain ranges, including the Sierra de Gredos and the Sierra de Guadarrama near the capital Madrid, which itself is about 655 m (2149 ft) above sea level. The fold ranges of the Pyrenees and the Cantabrian Mts are in the north, while the Sierra Nevada in the south contains Muhacen, Spain's highest peak. The coastal plains vary in width. Some, like those around Alicante and Valencia, are fertile. Four major rivers. the Duero, Tagus, Guadiana and Guadalquivir, rise in the Meseta and discharge into the Atlantic. The Ebro River rises in the Cantabrian Mts and flows into the Mediterranean. The Balearic Islands (notably Majorca, Minorca and Ibiza) form a province in the Mediterranean. The volcanic Canary Islands, about 100 km (62 mi) off southern Morocco, consists of 2 provinces: Las Palmas de Gran Canaria and Santa

HOMELANDS OF SOUTH AFRICA

The Homelands, with the main peoples in them, are as follows: Basotho-Qwaqwa (South Sotho); Bophuthatswana (Tswana, independent 1977); Ciskei (Xhosa, independent 1981); Gazankulu (Shangaan); Kwazulu (Zulu); Lebowa (Pedi); Ndebele (Ndebele); Swazi (Swazi); Transkei (Xhosa, independent 1976); Venda (Venda, independent 1979).

Cruz de Tenerife. The northern Atlantic coast region has mild wet winters and cool summers, with an average annual temperature range of 9°–21°C (48°–70°F), as compared with 5°–26°C (41°–79°F) on the Meseta and 10°–27°C (50–81°F) on the southern and eastern Mediterranean coasts. The average annual rainfall varies from 1230 mm (48 in) at Bilbao in the north to 440 mm (17 in) at Madrid and 600 mm (24 in) at Málaga in the south. The Spanish language is Castilian. Basque is spoken in the north in the provinces bordering the Bay of Biscay and also in south-western France. Catalan is spoken in the north-east and Galician in the north-west. Separatist movements have developed in these regions and, in 1980, regional governments were established for the Basques and Catalans. In 1981 a similar government was set up in Galicia. In 1980 74 per cent of Spain's people lived in urban areas, as compared with 57 per cent in 1960. This change reflected a fall in the relative importance of agriculture in the economy. In 1978 industry employed 43 per cent of the population, services 39 per cent and agriculture 18 per cent; their respective contributions to the GDP were 38 per cent, 53 per cent and 9 per cent. Important minerals include coal, iron ore, copper, lead and zinc. In 1978 hydro-electric and nuclear power stations supplied 43 per cent and 7 per cent respectively of Spain's electrical energy. The leading manufacturing centres are Madrid and the Mediterranean port of Barcelona. Textiles are the leading manufactures, but Spain has a wide range of light and heavy industry. In 1979 38.9 million tourists visited Spain; tourism is a major source of foreign exchange. Crops vary according to the climate; irrigation is practised in many arid areas. Barley, citrus fruits, grapes (for wine), olives, potatoes, wheat and vegetables are leading crops. Spain is Europe's 3rd largest wine producer. Spain had 4.65 million cattle (mostly in the wetter north), 14.5 million sheep, 2.3 million goats and 9.9 million pigs in 1979. The fishing fleet contained more than 17,000 vessels in 1978. The Phoenicians, Carthaginians and Romans colonized Spain in early times. From about AD 400, Germanic tribes, first Vandals and later Visigoths, occupied Spain. The Moorish invasion began in 711. A Christian revival was mounted in the 11th century and, by 1276, the

Cape Peninsula extends south of Cape Town in South Africa. It was at Cape Town that the first European settlement in southern Africa was founded in 1652, as a provisioning centre for Dutch ships plying between Europe and Asia.

Moors had been driven back to the southern state of Granada, where the superb Alhambra testifies to their architectural genius. Granada finally fell to Christian armies in 1492. In the early 15th century, Castile had become the dominant kingdom in Spain and its union with Aragon in 1479 began the process that finally united the entire country. From the late 15th century, Spain became a world power, colonizing most of South America, parts of North America and Africa, and the Philippines in Asia. However, a gradual decline began in the late 16th century. The great Spanish Armada was destroyed in 1588 and Spanish sea power was finally crushed in the Battle of Trafalgar in 1805. France occupied Spain in 1808–13 and in the 1810s and 1820s most Spanish American colonies declared their independence. By the early 20th century, Spain was a poor agricultural nation. In 1931 Spain was declared a republic but a civil war in 1936–39 ended in defeat for the republicans. General Francisco Franco became dictator and Head of State, although Spain was technically a monarchy. When Franco died in 1975, Prince Don Juan Carlos de Borbón became king. Democracy was restored and a new Constitution was promulgated in 1978. An unsuccessful army coup took place in February 1981. Spain has a bicameral parliament, or *Cortes*, consisting of a 350-member Chamber of Deputies and a 248-member Senate.

Area: 504,782 km² (194,908 sq mi); **Population:** 38,671,000; **Capital:** Madrid (pop 3,146,000); **Other cities:** Barcelona (1,750,000), Valencia (648,000), Seville (546,000), Zaragoza (470,000); **Highest point:** Mulhacén, 3478 m (11,411 ft); **Official language:** Spanish; **Religion:** Roman Catholicism; **Average life expectancy at birth:** 73 years; **Unit of currency:** Peseta; **Main exports:** manufactures, textiles, chemical products, footwear and leather goods, food, wine, fruit, fish, olive oil, vegetables; **Per capita GNP:** US$4340.

SRI LANKA, called Ceylon until 1972, is a South Asian republic and member of the Commonwealth. It is mostly low-lying; the central highlands which cover less than 20 per cent of the land reach their highest peak in Pidurutalagala. The climate is tropical and the capital Colombo has an average annual temperature of 27°C (81°F) throughout the year. The average annual rainfall varies from 1000 mm (39 in) in the north and east to 2000 mm (79 in) or more in the south and west. In 1981 74 per cent of the people were Sinhalese, 18 per cent were Tamils and 7 per cent were Moors. There are Burgher (European) and Malay minorities. In 1978 agriculture employed 54 per cent of the people, industry 15 per cent and services 31 per cent. About 36 per cent of Sri Lanka is cultivated. Rice is the main food. Tea, rubber and coconuts are the main cash crops. There were 1.6 million cattle in 1979. Gemstones and graphite are mined and there is a variety of manufacturing industries. The Sinhalese, from northern India, conquered the island in the 6th century BC, pushing the Veddas into the interior. Tamils arrived in the 11th century AD and Arabs (Moors) in the 12th and 13th centuries. Portugal ruled the island in 1505–1655, being replaced by the Dutch. Britain took over in 1796. Full independence was achieved in 1948. In 1960 Mrs Sirimavo Bandaranaike became prime minister, the first woman ever to hold this rank. Sri Lanka became a republic in 1972 and in 1978 it adopted the title the Democratic Socialist Republic of Sri Lanka.

Area: 65,610 km² (25,334 sq mi); **Population:** 15,398,000; **Capital:** Colombo (pop 624,000); **Highest point:** Pidurutalagala, 2527 m (8291 ft); **Official language:** Sinhala; **Religions:** Buddhism (67 per cent), Hinduism (18 per cent), Christianity (8 per cent), Islam (7 per cent); **Adult literacy rate:** 78 per cent; **Average life expectancy at birth:** 69 years; **Unit of currency:** Rupee; **Main exports:** tea, rubber, industrial products, coconut products; **Per capita GNP:** US$230.

SUDAN, Africa's largest nation. The land is mostly flat. It includes much of the Upper Nile basin. Highlands border the Red Sea plains in the north-east, the Darfur highlands are in the west, but the highest peak, Kinyeti, is in the far south. The average annual temperature is about 21°C (70°F) but the central lowlands are hotter and the uplands cooler. The average annual rainfall varies from 50 mm (2 in) in the north to 1520 mm (60 in) in the far south. Much of Sudan is desert but large areas of *sudd* (masses of floating plants) occur in the Nile region south of latitude 10°N. In the north most people are Muslim Arabs, Hamites and Negroes. Negroid peoples predominate in the south: there is a cultural rift between the northerners and the animist and Christian southerners. In 1978 agriculture employed 79 per cent of the people, accounting for 43 per cent of the GDP, as opposed to industry 12 per cent and services 45 per cent. Cotton and cotton goods dominate the exports. Pastoral farming is also important: there were 17.3 million cattle, 17.2 million sheep and 12.2 million goats in 1979. Britain and Egypt ruled Sudan jointly as a condominium from 1899. Full independence was achieved in 1956. A North-South civil war (1964–72) ended when the government granted regional autonomy to the southern provinces but executive power is vested in the President and legislative power in the 304-member People's Assembly.

Area: 2,505,813 km² (967,553 sq mi); **Population:** 19,373,000; **Capital:** Khartoum (pop 1,000,000); **Other cities:** Omdurman (299,000); **Highest point:** Mt Kinyeti, 3187 m (10,456 ft); **Official language:** Arabic; **Religions:** Islam, traditional beliefs, Christianity; **Adult literacy rate:** 20 per cent; **Average life expectancy at birth:** 46 years; **Unit of currency:** Sudanese pound; **Main exports:** cotton, groundnuts, sesame, gum arabic; **Per capita GNP:** US$370.

SURINAM, a republic in north-eastern South America, formerly called Dutch Guiana. Behind the 25–80 km (16–50 mi) wide marshy coastal plain are savanna-covered hills that rise to forested highlands. The climate is tropical and the rainfall plentiful. About 35 per cent of the people are Creoles of mixed African and European origin, 35 per cent are Indians, 15 per cent are Javanese, 9 per cent are 'Bush Negroes' (descendants of runaway slaves), 2 per cent are Chinese and 2 per cent are pure Indians. Farming is confined to the coastal plain. Fruit, rice and sugar cane are major crops. Forestry is also important, but the most valuable resource is bauxite. Britain founded a colony in Surinam in 1650 but ceded the territory to the Dutch in 1667. The Dutch ruled it for most of the time until full independence was achieved in 1975.

Area: 163,265 km² (63,040 sq mi); **Population:** 404,000; **Capital:** Paramaribo (pop 152,000); **Official languages:** Dutch, English; **Religions:** Hinduism (29 per cent), Islam (19 per cent), Roman Catholicism (18 per cent), other Christians (14 per cent); **Unit of currency:** Guilder; **Main exports:** bauxite and aluminium, rice, citrus fruits; **Per capita GNP:** US$2360.

SWAZILAND, a landlocked kingdom in southern Africa between South Africa and Mozambique. There are 4 regions aligned north-south. The western High Veld, between 900 and 1830 m (2953–6004 ft), covers 30 per cent of Swaziland. The Middle Veld, mostly 400–850 m (1312–2789 ft) high, covers 28 per cent, and the Low Veld, 150–300 m (492–984 ft) above sea level, covers another 33 per cent. The fourth region, the Lebombo plateau in the east, reaches about 820 m (2690 ft). The average annual rainfall decreases from 1900 mm (75 in) in parts of the High Veld to 500 mm (20 in) in the east. Temperatures are modified by the altitude. Most Swazis live in rural areas. The main crops are citrus fruits, cotton, maize, pineapples, rice, sorghum, sugar cane and tobacco. In 1979 there were 650,000 cattle, 265,000 goats and 33,000 sheep. Asbestos and coal are mined and there are various factories in the towns. Tourism and remittances from Swazis working abroad are sources of foreign exchange. Swaziland came under the Transvaal Republic in 1894 but Britain ruled it after the Anglo-Boer War (1899–1902). Full independence in the Commonwealth was achieved in 1968. In 1973 the king (or Ngwenyama) took supreme power. Elections were held in 1978 but the king retained many powers.

Area: 17,363 km² (6704 sq mi); **Population:** 581,000; **Capital:** Mbabane (pop 22,000); **Official language:** English; **Religions:** Christianity (60 per cent), traditional beliefs (40 per cent); **Unit of currency:** Lilangeni; **Main exports:** sugar, wood pulp, asbestos, fruit; **Per capita GNP:** US$650.

SWEDEN, a Scandinavian monarchy. Norrland, north of latitude 61° North, contains vast coniferous forests and many streams and lakes in the glaciated valleys. Mountains run along the border with Norway; the highest peak Kebnekaise is in the north-west. But a plateau covers most of Norrland. In the far north of this thinly-populated region is part of Lapland, where some Lapps still follow their traditional nomadic way of life. South of Norrland, between Göteborg and Stockholm, is the Central Lake region, where lakes Vänern and Vättern are situated. This region has a milder climate than Norrland. South of the Lake region are the infertile southern uplands, but Scania in the far south is the most fertile region. Most of Sweden has long, cold winters and short, warm summers. Rainfall averages 500 mm (20 in) per year in the east and south-east. More than 2000 mm (79 in) falls on the western mountains. In 1980 87 per cent of the population lived in urban areas and Sweden is one of the world's most prosperous nations. In 1978 industry employed 37 per cent of the workforce, services 58 per cent and agriculture 5 per cent, their contributions to the GDP being 33 per cent, 63 per cent and 4 per cent. Sweden has little coal but hydro-electric and nuclear power stations produce 59 per cent and 22 per cent respectively of Sweden's electric energy. There are major reserves of metal ores, notably iron ore at Kiruna, Gällivare and Grängesberg. Steel and steel products are the chief manufactures. Forests cover 57 per cent of Sweden and timber and wood pulp are major exports. Only 8 per cent of the land is cultivated: cereals, potatoes, sugar beet and cattle fodder are grown. In 1979 Sweden had 1.9 million cattle and 2.7 million pigs. In the 9th–11th centuries. Swedish Vikings went eastwards and southwards, plundering, trading and colonizing. Sweden was united with Denmark and Norway in 1397. It broke away in 1523, becoming a major power in the 17th century. In 1809 Sweden lost Finland to Russia but, after Napoleon's defeat in 1814, it gained Norway, which became independent in 1905. Sweden was neutral in World Wars I and II. It is a constitutional monarchy, with a unicameral parliament (*Riksdag*) with 349 members elected to 3-year terms.

Area: 449,964 km² (173,742 sq mi); **Population:** 8,347,000; **Capital:** Stockholm (pop 654,000); **Other cities:** Göteborg (437,000), Malmö (237,000); **Highest point:** Mt Kebnekaise, 2117 m (6946 ft); **Official language:** Swedish; **Religion:** Evangelical Lutheran Church; **Adult literacy rate:** 99 per cent; **Average life expectancy at birth:** 75 years; **Unit of currency:** Krona; **Main exports:** machinery and transport equipment, metals and metal goods, timber and timber products; **Per capita GNP:** US$11,920.

Stockholm, Sweden's capital, is a pleasant, largely modern city. It is called the 'Venice of the North', because part of the city stands on a group of islands in the Baltic Sea.

SWITZERLAND, a landlocked federal republic. The Jura Mts run from the north-east to south-west along the border with France. These mountains are separated from the spectacularly scenic Alps, which make up 60 per cent of Switzerland, by the central plateau (*Mittelland*). This plateau contains 75 per cent of the population. It has many lakes between Lake Geneva in the south-west and Lake Constance in the north-east. Switzerland contains the headwaters of the Inn, Rhine, Rhône and Ticino rivers. The average annual temperature range on the plateau is 0°–19°C (32°–66°F). Basle has an average annual rainfall of 840 mm (33 in). The mountains are colder and wetter, although much of the precipitation falls as snow. Switzerland is a multilingual nation. In 1970 65 per cent of the population spoke German, 18 per cent French, 12 per cent Italian and 1 per cent Romansch (which is related to Latin). In 1978 agriculture employed 6 per cent of the workforce and industry and services 47 per cent each. Dairy farming is the main agricultural activity: there were 2 million cattle in 1979. Cereals, potatoes, sugar beet and fruits are grown and wine is produced. Switzerland is highly industrialized. Its superb precision instruments made it famous, but chemicals, processed foods, glassware, machinery, metal products and textiles are all important today. Tourism is a major source of foreign exchange. In 1291 the people of Schwyz, Unterwalden and Uri formed a league to win their independence from Hapsburg rule. This league gradually grew into a loose alliance of independent cantons, whose existence was recognized formally in 1648. France conquered the area in 1798 but, in 1815, the Congress of Vienna guaranteed Switzerland neutrality. In 1848 a new Constitution was adopted by the 22 cantons; it was revised in 1874 to give more power to the federal government. In 1979 a 23rd canton, Jura, was created. Each canton has its own government. There is a bicameral federal parliament, comprising a 46-member *Ständerat* (Council of States) and a 200-member *Nationalrat* (National Council).

Area: 41,288 km² (15,942 sq mi); **Population:** 6,350,000; **Capital:** Bern (pop with suburbs, 282,000); **Other cities:** Zürich (707,000), Basle (364,000); **Highest point:** Mt Rosa, 4634 m (15,203 ft); **Official languages:** French, German, Italian; **Religions:** Roman Catholicism (49 per cent), Protestantism (48 per cent); **Adult literacy rate:** 99 per cent; **Average life expectancy at birth:** 74 years: **Unit of currency:** Franc; **Main exports:** machinery, pharmaceutical goods, watches, processed foods; **Per capita GNP:** US$14,240.

The canton of Valais in southern Switzerland contains fertile valleys and pleasant villages, overlooked by Alpine mountains that rise in altitude towards the Italian border.

SYRIA, an Arab republic in south-western Asia. Behind the coastal plain, with its Mediterranean climate, is a low mountain range that overlooks the fertile River Orontes valley. The River Euphrates drains the inland plains in the north. The highest peaks are in the Anti-Lebanon range in the south-west. To the east, the land slopes down to the hot Syrian desert. The rainfall decreases from west to east: about 60 per cent of Syria has less than 250 mm (10 in) of rain a year. About 90 per cent of the people are Arabs, 6 per cent are Kurds and there is a Palestinian minority. In 1978 agriculture employed 49 per cent of the people, industry 22 per cent and services 29 per cent. But their respective contributions to the GDP were 20 per cent, 28 per cent and 52 per cent. Cotton is the leading crop. Oil is produced and manufacturing is increasing. Tourism is important in peaceful times. The Euphrates valley was the home of early civilizations and the Syrian coast was part of Phoenicia. But, for most of its history, Syria has been under foreign rule. Islam was introduced in AD 636. After World War I, France ruled the area, but Syria was fully independent by 1946. Syria has participated in the Arab-Israeli wars which have sapped its resources. Power is concentrated in the army, although the 1973 Constitution declares Syria to be 'a democratic, popular Socialist state'.

Area: 185,180 km² (71,502 sq mi); **Population:** 9,227,000; **Capital:** Damascus (pop 1,042,000); **Other cities:** Halab (1,523,000), Homs (629,000); **Highest point:** Jabal ash Sheikh (Mt Hermon), 2814 m (9232 ft); **Official language:** Arabic; **Religion:** Islam; **Adult literacy rate:** 53 per cent; **Average life expectancy at birth:** 57 years; **Unit of currency:** Syrian pound; **Main exports:** cotton, oil, cereals, live animals; **Per capita GNP:** US$1070.

TAIWAN, an island republic (formerly called Formosa) off the coast of China. It is largely mountainous, with fertile plains in the west. The climate is tropical. Nearly all the people are Chinese. Rice, sugar cane, sweet potatoes and tea are major crops, but agriculture accounts for only 10 per cent of the GDP as compared with industry 48 per cent. Taiwan produces coal, some oil and natural gas, and various metals. But manufactures dominate the exports. Taiwan became Chinese in the 1680s. Japan ruled it between 1895–1945. When the Communists took over China in 1949, their Nationalist opponents led by Gen Chiang Kai-shek, set up a government on Taiwan. The economy expanded rapidly with US aid. Taiwan represented China in the UN until 1971, when Communist China was admitted.

Area: 35,961 km² (13,885 sq mi); **Population:** 17,100,000 (1978); **Capital:** Taipei (pop 3,050,000); **Other cities:** Kaohsiung (1,115,000); **Highest point:** Yu Shan, 3997 m (13,114 ft); **Official language:** Chinese; **Religions:** Confucianism, Buddhism, Taoism, Christianity; **Adult literacy rate:** 82 per cent; **Average life expectancy at birth:** 72 years; **Unit of currency:** Dollar; **Main exports:** textiles, electrical machinery, food, other machinery, plastics; **Per capita GNP:** US$1400 (1978).

TANZANIA, a United Republic in East Africa, consisting of mainland Tanganyika and the coral islands of Zanzibar and Pemba. Most of Tanganyika is a plateau between 900 and 1500 m (2953–4921 ft) high. The plateau is broken by arms of the East African Rift Valley: the western arm encloses lakes Nyasa (Malawi) and Tanganyika; the eastern arm contains smaller salt lakes. Lake Victoria in the north-west occupies a shallow depression and is not in the Rift Valley. There are mountains in the north and south. Mt Kilimanjaro is Africa's highest peak. The climate is equatorial, but modified by the altitude. The rainfall around Lake Victoria averages 1100 mm (43 in) a year; the central plateau is drier and droughts are common. Savanna vegetation is the most common. The wildlife is rich and national parks cover 3 per cent of the land: tourism is expanding. The people are divided into 120 tribal groups. About 94 per cent of the people speak Bantu languages. Others speak Cushitic and Khoisan tongues. In 1978 agriculture employed 83 per cent of the people and accounted for 51 per cent of the GDP, as opposed to 13 per cent from industry. Major crops are coffee, cotton, cashew nuts and sisal. Diamonds are mined, but manufacturing is small-scale. In 1890 Tanganyika became a German territory, while Zanzibar (including Pemba) became a British protectorate. Britain occupied Tanganyika in World War I and ruled it until 1961 when it became an independent member of the Commonwealth. It became a republic in 1962. Zanzibar became independent in 1963 but, following a coup, it joined with Tanganyika in 1964, adopting the official title of the United Republic of Tanzania in October. But by 1981, Zanzibar was still not fully integrated into the union. Tanzania is a one-party state and it pursues socialist policies, concentrating on rural development.

Area: 945,087 km² (364,920 sq mi); **Population:** 19,388,000; **Capital:** Dar es Salaam (pop 757,000), but Dodoma is scheduled to become capital by the mid-1980s; **Highest point:** Mt Kilimanjaro, 5895 m (19,341 ft); **Official languages:** English, Swahili; **Religions:** Christianity (40 per cent), Islam (30 per cent), traditional beliefs (30 per cent); **Adult literacy rate:** 66 per cent; **Average life expectancy at birth:** 51 years; **Unit of currency:** Tanzanian shilling; **Main exports:** coffee, cloves, sisal, cotton, diamonds, cashew nuts; **Per capita GNP:** US$270.

THAILAND, a South-East Asian kingdom, called Siam until 1939. The fertile Chao Phraya river basin, the main farming region, is bordered by mountains in the east, west and north, where the highest peak, Inthanon, is situated. North-eastern Thailand, a plateau drained by the Mekong River, is infertile. The climate is tropical. Much of Thailand has an average annual rainfall of 1500 mm (59 in), but the north-eastern plateau has less than 250 mm (10 in). About 85 per cent of the people are Thais. There is a sizeable Chinese community, tribesmen in remote areas (Karen, Khmu, Mao and Yao), Malays and Indians. In 1978 agriculture employed 77 per cent of the people. It accounted for 27 per cent of the GDP, the same as industry. The main products are rice, rubber and tin. Manufacturing is increasing. The Thai state was founded in the 14th century. Its area was reduced in the 19th century but it remained independent. It was an absolute monarchy until 1932. In World War II it supported Japan. A military dictatorship ruled in 1947–51 and later it suffered from instability and frequent coups. Elections were held in 1979 under a new, democratic Constitution. A coup attempt was put down in 1981.

Area: 514,000 km² (198,467 sq mi); **Population:** 49,414,000; **Capital:** Bangkok (pop 4,871,000); **Highest point:** Inthanon Peak, 2595 m (8514 ft); **Official language:** Thai; **Religions:** Buddhism (94 per cent), Islam (4 per cent); **Adult literacy rate:** 84 per cent; **Average life expectancy at birth:** 61 years; **Unit of currency:** Baht; **Main exports:** rice, rubber, tapioca products, tin, maize; **Per capita GNP:** US$590.

TOGO, a West African republic. The Togo-Atacora Mts in the centre separate a low plateau in the north from the fertile southern plains. The climate is tropical, with an average temperature of 27°C (81°F) throughout the year. Lomé has an average annual rainfall of 740 mm (29 in). The rainfall increases inland to 1780 mm (70 in) in the mountains. There are about 30 tribal groups among the Negroid population. Farming is the main activity: cocoa and coffee are the leading crops. Phosphates made up 39 per cent of the exports in 1978, but manufacturing is small-scale. Togo was a German protectorate from 1884. It was invaded by British and French troops in World War I and partitioned between them. In 1957 the western (British) section joined Ghana. French Togo became a fully independent republic in 1960. Col Etienne Eyadéma took power in a coup in 1967. He was the sole candidate in an election in 1979 and remained the effective ruler of Togo.

Area: 56,000 km² (21,623 sq mi); **Population:** 2,693,000; **Capital:** Lomé (pop 229,000); **Highest point:** 1026 m (3366 ft); **Official language:** French; **Religions:** traditional beliefs (60 per cent), Christianity (25 per cent), Islam (7 per cent); **Adult literacy rate:** 18 per cent; **Average life expectancy at birth:** 46 years; **Unit of currency:** Franc CFA; **Main exports:** phosphates, cocoa, coffee; **Per capita GNP:** US$340.

TONGA, or the Friendly Islands, an island kingdom in the South Pacific. The 169 islands and islets are divided into 3 groups: Vava'u in the north; Ha'apai in the centre; and Tongatapu in the south, where Nuku'alofa is situated. There are both coral and volcanic islands. The climate is pleasant. Most people are Polynesians. Coconuts and bananas are leading products. Tonga was united under King George Tupou I in 1845. The islands were a British protectorate from 1900. Full independence within the Commonwealth was achieved in 1970.

Area: 699 km² (270 sq mi); **Population:** 99,000; **Capital:** Nuku'alofa (pop 18,000); **Unit of currency:** Pa'anga; **Per capita GNP:** US$460.

TRINIDAD AND TOBAGO, a West Indian republic close to South America. Trinidad covers 94 per cent of the country. Both islands are hilly and have a tropical climate. The people include Negroes (45 per cent), East Indians (35 per cent), people of mixed origin (17 per cent), Europeans (2 per cent) and Chinese (1 per cent). Oil is the main product. Citrus fruits, cocoa, coffee and sugar cane are grown. Columbus discovered the islands in 1498. They were both British by 1802. Full independence within the Commonwealth was achieved in 1962 and republican status was adopted in 1976.

Area: 5130 km² (1981 sq mi); **Population:** 1,193,000; **Capital:** Port-of-Spain (pop 63,000); **Official language:** English; **Unit of currency:** Dollar; **Main exports:** petroleum products, chemicals, food; **Per capita GNP:** US$3390.

TUNISIA, a North African republic. An extension of the Atlas Mts is in the north, surrounded by plains. A depression containing salt lakes, the Chott el-Djerid, is in the centre. Saharan plateaux are in the south. Tunis has an average annual temperature range of 10°–27°C (50°–81°F) and 460 mm (18 in) of rain a year. It becomes drier from north to south. Most people are Arabs or Berbers. In 1978 agriculture employed 45 per cent of the workforce, accounting for 18 per cent of the GDP as compared with 30 per cent from industry. Major crops are cereals, olives, grapes (for wine), fruit and vegetables. Fishing is important. Mining for oil, phosphates and metal ores has increased in recent years; manufacturing is also growing. Tourism is important: there were a million tourists in 1977. Carthage was founded (near present-day Tunis) in 814 BC, but Rome destroyed it in 146 BC. The Arabs conquered Tunisia in AD 647. France made Tunisia a protectorate in 1883. Full independence as a monarchy was achieved in 1956 and a republic was proclaimed in 1957. The first President, Habib Bourguiba, was elected President-for-life in 1974.

Area: 163,610 km² (63,174 sq mi); **Population:** 6,625,000; **Capital:** Tunis (pop 505,000); **Highest point:** Djebel Chambi, 1544 m (5066 ft); **Official language:** Arabic; **Religion:** Islam; **Adult literacy rate:** 55 per cent; **Average life expectancy at birth:** 57 years; **Unit of currency:** Dinar; **Main exports:** oil, olive oil, phosphates; **Per capita GNP:** US$1120.

TURKEY, a republic partly in Europe and partly in Asia. European Turkey, area 23,623 km² (9121 sq mi), lies west of the Dardanelles, the Sea of Marmara and the Bosporus. These waterways link the Mediterranean and Black seas. European Turkey is a fertile, low-lying region. Asian Turkey (Anatolia) has fertile coastal plains, with a Mediterranean climate. Central Anatolia, a mainly flat plateau, is arid with less than 250 mm (10 in) of rain per year. About 90 per cent of the people speak Turkish; Kurds make up 7 per cent of the population. In 1978 agriculture employed 60 per cent of the people and industry 14 per cent; their respective contributions to the GDP were 27 per cent and 28 per cent. Nearly 31 per cent of Turkey is cultivated. Major crops include barley, cotton, grapes (for wine), fruits, nuts, raisins, sugar beet and wheat. In 1979 Turkey had 14.9 million cattle, 43.9 million sheep (only the USSR, Australia, China and New Zealand had more), and 18.4 million goats. Turkey produces coal and lignite, chromium and some iron ore, copper and oil. Manufactures include iron and steel, petroleum products, paper, cement, chemicals, textiles and machinery. Tourism is important: there were more than 1.75 million tourists in 1978. From AD 330 Istanbul (then Constantinople) was capital of the Byzantine Empire. The Seljuk Turks invaded the area in the 11th century. The Ottoman Turks arrived in the late 13th century and, in 1453, they took Constantinople.

COUNTRIES OF THE WORLD

Right: Vast tracts of fertile land, particularly in the south-west, have made the USSR one of the world's great farming nations. This collective farm in the Caucasus region produces tobacco.

The Ottoman Empire gradually spread through south-eastern Europe, south-western Asia and northern Africa. It began its slow decline in the late 16th century and collapsed in World War I. In 1923 Mustafa Kemal (called Atatürk) made Turkey a republic and began to modernize it. Conflict with Greece continues and, in 1974, Turkey occupied northern Cyprus.

Area: 780,576 km² (301,399 sq mi); **Population:** 47,663,000; **Capital:** Ankara (pop 1,236,000); **Other cities:** Istanbul (2,132,000), Izmir (521,000); **Highest point:** Mt Ararat, 5165 m (16,946 ft); **Official language:** Turkish; **Religion:** Islam (98 per cent); **Adult literacy rate:** 60 per cent; **Average life expectancy at birth:** 61 years; **Unit of currency:** Turkish lira; **Main exports:** cotton, nuts, fruit, tobacco; **Per capita GNP:** US$1330.

TURKS AND CAICOS ISLANDS, a British colony in the south-eastern Bahamas. Only 6 of the 30 or so small islands are inhabited. The largest is Grand Caicos, but the seat of government is on Grand Turk. Most people are descendants of African slaves. Fishing is the main industry. The islands became British in 1670 and from 1848 to 1962 they were dependencies of Jamaica.

Area: 430 km² (166 sq mi); **Population:** 7200; **Seat of government:** Cockburn Town.

TUVALU, an independent member of the Commonwealth (formerly the Ellice Is) north of Fiji in the South Pacific. The islands are coral atolls. The people are Polynesians. Coconuts and copra are major products. The Gilbert and Ellice Is became a British protectorate in 1892. The Ellice Is broke away from the Micronesian Gilbert Is (now Kiribati) in 1975 to become Tovalu. Full independence was achieved in 1978.

Area: 8 km² (3 sq mi); **Population:** 7349; **Capital:** Funafuti (pop 2000).

UGANDA, a landlocked republic in equatorial Africa. Part of Africa's largest lake, Victoria, is in the south-east; the marshy Lake Kyoga is in the centre; and lakes Edward and Mobutu Sese Seko are in the Rift Valley in the west. The high Ruwenzori borders the Rift Valley. Most of Uganda is a plateau between 1100–1400 m (3609–4593 ft). Temperatures in the south-east are around 21°–24°C (70°–75°F) throughout the year. The average annual rainfall is between 760 and 1520 mm (30–60 in). Uganda has about 40 tribal groups. Two-thirds of the people, including the largest single group, the Baganda, speak Bantu languages. Some Nilotic languages are also spoken. In 1978 agriculture employed 83 per cent of the workforce, accounting for 57 per cent of the GDP. Coffee, cotton, tea and hides and skins are important and copper is mined. Manufacturing is developing. Britain took over Uganda between 1894 and 1914. Full independence was achieved in 1962 and Uganda became a republic in 1967. Gen Idi Amin ruled as a military dictator in 1971–79. After his overthrow by Ugandan and Tanzanian forces, political conditions remained unstable despite elections being held in 1980.

Area: 236,036 km² (91,139 sq mi); **Population:** 13,983,000; **Capital:** Kampala (pop 332,000); **Highest point:** Ruwenzori range on Zaire border, 5119 m (16,795 ft); **Official language:** English; **Religions:** Roman Catholicism (33 per cent), Protestantism (30 per cent), Islam (6 per cent), traditional beliefs; **Average life expectancy at birth:** 53 years; **Unit of currency:** Ugandan shilling; **Main exports:** coffee, cotton, tea, copper; **Per capita GNP:** US$290.

UNION OF SOVIET SOCIALIST REPUBLICS, the USSR, is the world's largest nation. The European part, west of the Ural Mts, covers 5,571,000 km² (2,151,092 sq mi) – 25 per cent of the country – but it contains 75 per cent of the population. Much of the land is flat, including the fertile Ukraine, but there are many hilly areas. Major rivers are the Dnepr and Don which flow into the Black Sea, and the Volga which empties into the Caspian Sea. The Caspian Sea, at 438,695 km² (169,390 sq mi) is the world's largest lake, while the Volga, at 3690 km (2293 mi), is Europe's longest river. The highest point in the Urals is only 1894 m (6214 ft) but the Caucasus in the south contain Mt Elbruz, which, at 5633 m (18,481 ft), is Europe's highest. East of the Urals is the West Siberian Plain, drained by the

Top: The Trans-Siberian Railway links the USSR's capital Moscow to Vladivostok on the Pacific. Above: The Church of St Basil in Moscow.

REPUBLICS OF THE USSR	Population 1980	Capital
Armenia	3,000,000	Yerevan
Azerbaijan	6,100,000	Baku
Belorussia	9,600,000	Minsk
Estonia	1,500,000	Tallinn
Georgia	5,000,000	Tbilisi
Kazakhstan	14,900,000	Alma-Ata
Kirgizia	3,600,000	Frunze
Latvia	2,500,000	Riga
Lithuania	3,400,000	Vilnius
Moldavia	4,000,000	Kishinev
Russian SFRS	138,400,000	Moscow
Tadzhikistan	3,900,000	Dushanbe
Turkmenistan	2,800,000	Ashkhabad
Ukraine	50,000,000	Kiev
Uzbekistan	15,800,000	Tashkent

River Ob. Between the Yenisey and Lena rivers is the Central Siberian plateau, which is mostly between 500 and 1500 m (1640–4921 ft). In the far east are a series of mountain ranges. The south-east, which is drained by the Amur River, contains Lake Baykal, the world's deepest lake. South of the West Siberian plain is the Kazakh plateau, several mountain ranges, including the Pamir, Altai and Tien Shan, and in the west the plains around the Aral Sea. The climate varies from the Arctic north to the warm Mediterranean climates along the Black and Caspian sea coasts. Inland areas have a continental climate. Moscow's average July temperature of 21°C (70°F) is nearly 30°C (54°F) higher than the average January temperature. The north-west and the Caucasus region are the wettest places. There are deserts east of the Caspian Sea (the Kara Kum and the Kyzyl Kum). About 60 languages are spoken in the USSR. In 1979 the largest groups were Russians (52.2 per cent), Ukrainians (16 per cent), Uzbeks (4.8 per cent), Belorussians (3.6 per cent), Kazakhs (2.5 per cent), Tatars (2.4 per cent), Azerbaijanians (2.1 per cent), Armenians (1.6 per cent), Georgians (1.4 per cent), Moldavians (1.1 per cent), Tadzhiks (1.1 per cent), Lithuanians (1.1 per cent) and Turkmenians (0.8 per cent). The USSR is divided into 15 republics. The largest, the Russian Soviet Federal Socialist Republic (RSFSR) covers 76 per cent of the country. In 1978 agriculture employed 17 per cent of the people, industry 47 per cent and services 36 per cent; their respective contributions to the GDP were 17 per cent, 62 per cent and 21 per cent. Arable land covers 10 per cent and pasture 17 per cent of the land. Crops vary with the climate. In 1979 the USSR led the world in producing apples, barley, coniferous wood, milk, mutton, lamb and goat's meat, oats, potatoes, rye, sugar beet and wheat. In 1980 there were 115 million cattle, 73.7 million pigs and 143 million sheep. Forests cover about one-third of the USSR. Most of the land and all industry are government-owned, but most farm workers have a private plot. The USSR has vast mineral resources. It leads the world in asbestos, coal, oil, iron ore, lead, manganese, mercury, nickel, potash and silver production. But manufacturing is the chief economic sector. The main industrial areas are: the Moscow region, the Ukraine; the Urals; Transcaucasia; and the area around Leningrad. Only the US produces more electrical energy than the USSR, and the USSR is the world's top steel producer. In the 10th–12th centuries, Kiev was the capital of the Russians but Kiev fell to Mongol invaders in the 13th century. Moscow then became the chief principality and by 1480 it had ended Mongol domination. In 1613 the Romanov dynasty was established. It lasted until 1917. Peter the Great westernized Russia in the early 18th century and extended its boundaries. By 1812, when Napoleon was defeated on Russian soil, Russia was a great European power. It was allied with Britain and France in World War I but Nicholas II, the last of the Romanovs, was forced to abdicate in 1917. The November 1917 Revolution led by Vladimir Lenin ousted a moderate government. The Bolsheviks

COUNTRIES OF THE WORLD

THE UNITED KINGDOM

	Area sq km	Area sq mi	Population (1981)	Capital	Population of capital
England	130,363	50,336	46,221,000	London	6,696,008
Wales	20,763	8,017	2,790,000	Cardiff	273,856
Scotland	78,772	30,416	5,116,000	Edinburgh	436,271
Northern Ireland	14,148	5,463	1,543,000[a]	Belfast	362,000[d]
Isle of Man	588	227	62,000[b]	Douglas	20,000
Channel Islands	195	75	131,000[c]	–	–

a 1979 est; b 1976 est; c estimates vary between islands; d 1971

took over and successfully overcame their enemies in 1918–22. From 1924, under Joseph Stalin, all opposition was ruthlessly suppressed. The economy was rebuilt with special emphasis on industrialization. The German invasion of 1941 caused much devastation and an estimated 20 million deaths. After the war, the USSR brought eastern Europe under its control and relations with the West deteriorated. Relations improved after Stalin's death in 1953, although relations with China then deteriorated. Soviet technology has made it one of the world's super-powers. It was the first, in 1961, to put a man into space.

Area: 22,402,200 km² (8,650,010 sq mi); **Population:** 270,376,000; **Capital:** Moscow (pop 8,099,000); **Other cities:** Leningrad (4,638,000), Kiev (2,192,000), Tashkent (1,816,000), Kharkhov (1,464,000), Gorki (1,358,000), Novosibirsk (1,328,000), Minsk (1,295,000), Kuibyshev (1,226,000), Sverdlovsk (1,225,000), Dnepropetrovsk (1,083,000), Tbilisi (1,080,000), Odessa (1,057,000), Chelyabinsk (1,042,000), Yerevan (1,036,000), Donetsk (1,032,000), Baku (1,030,000), Omsk (1,028,000), Perm (1,008,000), Kazan (1,002,000); **Highest point:** Communism Peak, 7495 m (24,590 ft); **Official language:** Russian; **Religions:** Christianity, Islam, Judaism, but all religions have been discouraged since 1917; **Adult literacy rate:** 99 per cent; **Average life expectancy at birth:** 70 years; **Unit of currency:** Rouble; **Main exports:** engineering products, transport equipment, oil and mineral ores, cotton, paper; **Per capita GNP:** US$4110.

UNITED ARAB EMIRATES, an oil-rich federation of 7 Emirates (formerly the Trucial States), with coastlines on the Persian Gulf and the Gulf of Oman. The Emirates are Abu Dhabi, Ajman, Dubai, Fujairah, Ras al Khaimah, Sharjah and Umm al Qaiwain. The main resource of this flat, hot, desert nation is oil. About 70 per cent of the people are Arabs. The rest are Iranians or other Asians. The states entered into treaties with Britain from 1820. Britain withdrew in 1971 and ended its responsibility for the states' defence and foreign relations. The states then joined in an independent federation. The 7 rulers form a Supreme Council, which appoints the Council of Ministers.

Area: 83,600 km² (32,280 sq mi); **Population:** 1,040,000; **Capital:** Abu Dhabi; **Unit of currency:** Dirham; **Main exports:** oil and natural gas; **Per capita GNP:** US$15,590.

UNITED KINGDOM OF GREAT BRITAIN AND NORTHERN IRELAND (Great Britain consists of England, Scotland and Wales.) The Channel Islands (Jersey, Guernsey and Guernsey's dependencies: Alderney, Brechou, Great Sark, Herm, Jethou, Lihou and Little Sark) and the Isle of Man in the Irish Sea are dependencies of the British Crown, but they are largely self-governing. *Scotland* has 3 main land regions. The highlands are divided by Glen More into the rugged north-western highlands and the Grampians, which include Ben Nevis. The main island groups are the Orkney and Shetland Islands to the north and the Hebrides to the west. The central lowlands are the most densely populated region, with coalfields, the leading cities and much farmland. Scotland's southern uplands are a mainly farming region. Northern *England* contains the Cumbrian Mts (or the Lake District), where England's highest peak, Scafell Pike, 978 m (3209 ft), is situated, and the Pennines which run north-south. Coalfields near the edge of the Pennines have stimulated the growth of major industrial regions. England's other highland region includes Exmoor and Dartmoor in the south-west. Lowland England contains many fertile plains crossed by ranges of low hills, such as the Cotswolds, Chilterns and the North and South Downs in the south-east. *Wales* is a mainly highland country, rising to Snowdon, 1085 m (3560 ft). South Wales contains a large coalfield on which a major industrial region has been built. *Northern Ireland* contains uplands and plains. In the east Lough Neagh, the UK's largest lake, covers 396 km² (153 sq mi). The UK's longest rivers are the Severn and the Thames, on which the capital London stands. The UK has a moist, temperate climate, moderated by the warm North Atlantic Drift (Gulf Stream). Average temperatures seldom exceed 18°C (64°F) in summer or fall below 3°C (37°F) in winter. The highlands are wet, with about 2030 mm (80 in) of rain a year in places. The rainfall decreases to the east, where it averages 760 mm (30 in) per year. The UK is highly urbanized: 91 per cent of the population lived in urban areas in 1980. In 1978 agriculture employed only 2 per cent of the population, industry 43 per cent and services 55 per cent; their respective contributions to the GDP were 2 per cent, 36 per cent and 62 per cent. Farming is highly efficient but food is imported. Generally, livestock farming is most important in the wetter west. In 1979 there were 13.5 million cattle, 29.9 million sheep and 7.8 million pigs. Arable farming is most important in the drier east. Major crops are cereals, potatoes, sugar beet and vegetables. Fishing is

This aerial view of London shows that this great city, the capital of the UK, is a mixture of the old and new. One of its principal landmarks is Big Ben which is part of the Houses of Parliament in Westminster. Winding through the city is the river Thames, London's outlet to the sea.

ENGLISH COUNTIES

Metropolitan counties	Population 1981 census	Administrative HQ
Greater London	6,696,008	–
Greater Manchester	2,594,778	–
Merseyside	1,513,070	Liverpool
South Yorkshire	1,301,813	Sheffield
Tyne and Wear	1,143,245	South Shields
West Midlands	2,644,634	Wolverhampton
West Yorkshire	2,037,510	Wakefield
Other counties		
Avon	909,408	Bristol
Bedfordshire	504,986	Bedford
Berkshire	675,153	Reading
Buckinghamshire	565,992	Aylesbury
Cambridgeshire	575,177	Cambridge
Cheshire	926,293	Chester
Cleveland	565,775	Middlesborough
Cornwall and the Isles of Scilly	430,506	Truro
Cumbria	483,427	Carlisle
Derbyshire	906,929	Matlock
Devon	952,000	Exeter
Dorset	591,990	Dorchester
Durham	604,728	Durham
East Sussex	652,568	Lewes
Essex	1,469,065	Chelmsford
Gloucestershire	499,351	Gloucester
Hampshire	1,456,367	Winchester
Hereford & Worcester	630,218	Worcester
Hertfordshire	954,535	Hertford
Humberside	847,666	Kingston upon Hull
Isle of Wight	118,192	Newport
Kent	1,463,055	Maidstone
Lancashire	1,372,118	Preston
Leicestershire	842,577	Leicester
Lincolnshire	547,560	Lincoln
Norfolk	693,490	Norwich
Northamptonshire	527,532	Northampton
Northumberland	299,905	Newcastle upon Tyne
North Yorkshire	666,610	Northallerton
Nottinghamshire	982,631	Nottingham
Oxfordshire	515,079	Oxford
Shropshire	375,610	Shrewsbury
Somerset	424,988	Taunton
Staffordshire	1,012,320	Stafford
Suffolk	596,354	Ipswich
Surrey	999,393	Kingston upon Thames
Warwickshire	473,620	Warwick
West Sussex	658,562	Chichester
Wiltshire	518,167	Trowbridge

WELSH COUNTIES

	Population 1981 census	Administrative HQ
Clwyd	390,173	Mold
Dyfed	329,977	Carmarthen
Gwent	439,684	Cwmbran
Gwynedd	230,468	Caernarvon
Mid-Glamorgan	537,866	Cardiff
Powys	110,467	Llandrindod
South Glamorgan	384,633	Cardiff
West Glamorgan	367,194	Swansea

SCOTTISH REGIONS

	Population 1981 census	Administrative HQ
Borders	99,248	Newton St Boswalls
Central	273,078	Stirling
Dumfries & Galloway	145,078	Dumfries
Fife	326,480	Glenrothes
Grampian	470,596	Aberdeen
Highland	200,030	Inverness
Lothian	735,892	Edinburgh
Strathclyde	2,397,827	Glasgow
Tayside	391,529	Dundee
Island Authorities		
Orkney	18,906	Kirkwall
Shetland	27,716	Lerwick
Western Isles	31,766	Stornaway

COUNTIES OF NORTHERN IRELAND

	Population 1971 census	Administrative HQ
Antrim	356,000	Belfast
Armagh	134,000	Armagh
Belfast CB	362,000	–
Down	312,000	Downpatrick
Fermanagh	50,000	Enniskillen
Londonderry	131,000	Londonderry
Londonderry CB	52,000	–
Tyrone	139,000	Omagh

important: there were nearly 7000 fishing vessels in 1979. The UK's industrial economy was originally based on its abundant coal and iron ore resources. Coal-mining, however, has declined, although the economy has recently been boosted by the discovery of oil and natural gas in the North Sea. Manufactures are extremely varied. Invisible earnings from banking, insurance, tourism and other services make a vital contribution to the economy. The UK's early history is one of successive invasions by various peoples, including Iberians, Celts, Romans, Angles, Saxons, Jutes, Norsemen, Danes and Normans (1066). Resistance to Norman rule continued in Wales, which was conquered in 1282 and united with England. In 1603 James VI of Scotland became James I of England. But the Act of Union giving England and Scotland a common parliament was not passed until 1707. In 1801 Ireland became part of the United Kingdom of Great Britain and Ireland. In the 18th century the UK began to build a great empire, although it lost its 13 American colonies in 1783. In the late 18th century, the UK was the first nation to change from an agricultural to an industrial society. Wealth from trade and industry made the UK one of the world's greatest nations in the 19th century. It played a major role in World War I, but this sapped its resources. After the war, southern Ireland broke away to become the Irish Free State (see Ireland). World War II proved an even greater drain on the UK's economy than World War I, and financial problems have marked its post-war history. However, the UK transformed its empire into the Commonwealth, which has given it a voice in world affairs. Many people from the non-white Commonwealth have settled in the UK, making up an estimated 3 per cent of the population in 1975. The UK joined the EEC in 1973, but it suffered from the world recession in the early 1980s. Its many problems included high inflation, increasing competition for its manufactures in world markets, and violent conflict in Northern Ireland.

Area: 244,046 km² (94,232 sq mi), not including the Isle of Man and the Channel Islands; **Population:** 55,670,000; **Capital:** London (pop 6,696,000); **Other cities** (prelim 1981 census): Birmingham (920,389), Glasgow (763,162), Liverpool (510,306), Sheffield (477,142), Manchester (449,168), Leeds (448,528), Edinburgh (436,271), Bristol (387,977), Belfast (362,000 in 1971), Coventry (314,124), Bradford (280,691), Leicester (279,791), Cardiff (273,856), Nottingham (271,080), Kingston upon Hull (268,302), Wolverhampton (252,447), Stoke-on-Trent (252,351); **Highest point:** Ben Nevis, 1347 m (4419 ft); **Official language:** English; **Religion:** mainly Christianity; **Adult literacy rate:** 99 per cent; **Average life expectancy at birth:** 73 years; **Unit of currency:** Pound sterling; **Main exports:** electrical and engineering products, transport equipment, textiles, chemicals and plastics, ceramics; **Per capita GNP:** US$6340 (Channel Is, US$5240 and Is of Man US$3890).

UNITED STATES OF AMERICA, a federal republic and the world's 4th largest nation. The bulk of the US lies between Canada and Mexico. The 49th state, Alaska, is in north-western North America, while the 50th state, Hawaii, is in the North Pacific Ocean, about 3870 km (2404 mi) south-west of San Francisco. (Both Alaska and Hawaii became states in 1959.) The main part of the US contains 5 land regions. The *eastern coastal plains* are broadest around the Gulf of Mexico. The Atlantic coastal plains are broadest in the south and narrowest in New England. The Atlantic coast is deeply indented and contains several natural harbours. West of the Atlantic seaboard are the *Appalachian Mts.* This complex region which runs roughly from Newfoundland (Canada) in the north-east to Alabama in the south-west contains many ridges, plateaux and deep valleys. The *central (interior) lowlands* stretch westwards from the Appalachians. In the north are the five Great Lakes: Lake Superior, which covers 82,409 km² (31,820 sq mi), is the world's largest freshwater lake. To the south, the central plains are drained by the Mississippi River and its tributaries, notably the Missouri and Ohio. To the west are the higher Great Plains, mostly between 450 and 1800 m (1476–5906 ft). Beyond these plains the land rises to the *western highlands*, which include the folded Rocky Mountains, the Sierra Nevada range and the Cascade range, which includes the volcano Mt St Helens which erupted in 1980. The Colorado

San Francisco, California's third largest city after Los Angeles and San Diego, is a largely modern city. It was rebuilt after it was devastated by the 1906 earthquake and the ensuing fires. A seaport with a fine harbour, San Francisco is a colourful, cosmopolitan city; its Chinatown district is the largest Chinese settlement outside Asia. California has a larger population than any other state in the United States and its thriving mixed economy is more substantial than those of many nations that are members of the United Nations.

US STATES

State	Capital	Area sq km	Area sq mi	Population (1980)	State Bird/State Flower
Alabama	Montgomery	133,667	51,612	3,890,061	Yellowhammer/Camellia
Alaska	Juneau	1,518,800	586,444	400,481	Willow ptarmigan/Forget-me-not
Arizona	Phoenix	295,023	113,915	2,717,866	Cactus wren/Saguaro
Arkansas	Little Rock	137,539	53,107	2,285,513	Mockingbird/Apple blossom
California	Sacramento	411,013	158,702	23,668,562	California valley quail/Golden poppy
Colorado	Denver	269,998	104,253	2,888,834	Lark bunting/Rocky Mountain columbine
Connecticut	Hartford	12,973	5,009	3,107,576	Robin/Mountain laurel
Delaware	Dover	5,328	2,057	595,225	Blue hen chicken/Peach blossom
Florida	Tallahassee	151,670	58,563	9,739,992	Mockingbird/Orange blossom
Georgia	Atlanta	152,488	58,879	5,464,265	Brown thrasher/Cherokee rose
Hawaii	Honolulu	16,705	6,450	965,000	Hawaiian goose/Hibiscus
Idaho	Boise	216,412	83,562	943,935	Mountain bluebird/Syringa
Illinois	Springfield	146,075	56,403	11,418,461	Cardinal/Native violet
Indiana	Indianapolis	93,993	36,293	5,490,179	Cardinal/Peony
Iowa	Des Moines	145,790	56,293	2,913,387	Eastern goldfinch/Wild rose
Kansas	Topeka	213,063	82,269	2,363,208	Western meadow lark/Sunflower
Kentucky	Frankfort	104,623	40,397	3,661,433	Kentucky cardinal/Goldenrod
Louisiana	Baton Rouge	125,674	48,526	4,203,972	Brown pelican/Magnolia
Maine	Augusta	86,026	33,217	1,124,660	Chickadee/White pine cone and tassel
Maryland	Annapolis	27,394	10,577	4,216,446	Baltimore oriole/Black-eyed Susan
Massachusetts	Boston	21,386	8,258	5,737,037	Chickadee/Mayflower
Michigan	Lansing	150,779	58,219	9,258,344	Robin/Apple blossom
Minnesota	St Paul	217,735	84,073	4,077,148	Common loon/Pink and white lady's-slipper
Mississippi	Jackson	123,584	47,719	2,520,638	Mockingbird/Magnolia
Missouri	Jefferson City	180,486	69,690	4,917,444	Bluebird/Hawthorn
Montana	Helena	381,086	147,146	786,690	Western meadow lark/Bitterroot
Nebraska	Lincoln	200,017	77,231	1,570,006	Western meadow lark/Goldenrod
Nevada	Carson City	286,297	110,546	799,184	Mountain bluebird/Sagebrush
New Hampshire	Concord	24,097	9,304	920,610	Purple finch/Purple lilac
New Jersey	Trenton	20,295	7,836	7,364,158	Eastern goldfinch/Purple violet
New Mexico	Santa Fe	315,113	121,672	1,299,968	Roadrunner/Yucca
New York	Albany	128,401	49,579	17,557,288	Bluebird/Rose
North Carolina	Raleigh	136,197	52,589	5,874,429	Cardinal/Flowering dogwood
North Dakota	Bismarck	183,022	70,669	652,695	Western meadow lark/Wild prairie rose
Ohio	Columbus	106,765	41,224	10,797,419	Cardinal/Scarlet carnation
Oklahoma	Oklahoma City	181,089	69.923	3,025,266	Scissor-tailed flycatcher/Mistletoe
Oregon	Salem	251,180	96,986	2,632,663	Western meadow lark/Oregon grape
Pennsylvania	Harrisburg	117,412	45,336	11,866,728	Ruffed grouse/Mountain laurel
Rhode Island	Providence	3,144	1,214	947,154	Rhode Island Red/Violet
South Carolina	Columbia	80,432	31,057	3,119,208	Carolina wren/Carolina jessamine
South Dakota	Pierre	199,551	77,051	690,178	Ring-necked pheasant/Pasqueflower
Tennessee	Nashville	109,411	42,246	4,590,750	Mockingbird/Iris
Texas	Austin	692,402	267,353	14,228,383	Mockingbird/Bluebonnet
Utah	Salt Lake City	219,931	84,920	1,461,037	Sea gull/Sego lily
Vermont	Montpelier	24,887	9,609	511,456	Hermit thrush/Red clover
Virginia	Richmond	105,716	40,819	5,346,279	Cardinal/Flowering dogwood
Washington	Olympia	176,617	68,196	4,130,163	Willow goldfinch/Coast rhododendron
West Virginia	Charlestown	62,629	24,183	1,949,644	Cardinal/Rhododendron
Wisconsin	Madison	145,438	56,157	4,705,335	Robin/Wood violet
Wyoming	Cheyenne	253,596	97,919	470,816	Meadow lark/Indian paintbrush

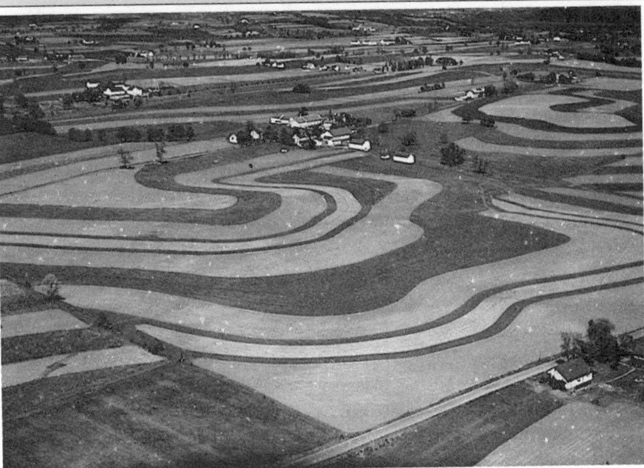

Much of Pennsylvania, a state in the north-eastern United States, lies in the Appalachian mountain region. The Appalachians, which extend from Newfoundland to Alabama, are a far older and more eroded range than the Rockies in the west. Hence, they have much gentler slopes and contain extensive farming regions. However, because of the slopes, soil erosion is always a danger in this moist region and contour ploughing is one of the ways of combatting this threat. Pennsylvania was one of the original 13 states of the USA.

COUNTRIES OF THE WORLD

River in the south-west has carved the Grand Canyon, which is more than 349 km (217 mi) long and 1675 m (5495 ft) deep in places. The *Pacific slope* contains fertile valleys and coastal ranges. One feature is the 960 km (597 mi) long San Andreas Fault in California. Movements along the fault cause earthquakes. Alaska also has much earthquake and volcanic activity and the Alaska range contains North America's highest peak, Mt McKinley. Hawaii consists of a string of volcanic and coral islands. The climate varies greatly from Arctic conditions in Alaska to deserts in the south-west, including Death Valley, the US's lowest point at 86 m (282 ft) below sea level, and a humid, subtropical climate in the south-east. California has a pleasant Mediterranean climate, but much of the interior has a continental climate, with hot summers, cold winters and a relatively low annual rainfall. The first inhabitants, American Indians, entered North America about 20,000 years ago. In 1970 they numbered 790,000. In 1980 about 83 per cent of the population was of European descent and 12 per cent were blacks, the descendants of slaves. Other races, including American Indians, Chinese, Japanese, Filipino and Mexican Americans, made up the other 5 per cent. Nearly 47 per cent of the land is farmed but only 2 per cent of the workforce was engaged in agriculture in 1978, as opposed to 33 per cent in industry and 65 per cent in services. Farming is highly efficient and the US is among the world's top producers of cotton, fruits, maize, oats, soya beans, sugar beet, tobacco, timber, wheat and livestock. In 1979 there were 110.9 million cattle, 59.9 million pigs and 12.2 million sheep. In 1979 agriculture accounted for 3 per cent of the GDP, industry 34 per cent and services 63 per cent. The US is one of the world's top producers of copper, iron ore, oil and natural gas, lead, phosphates, sulphur and uranium. The US is the world's most industrialized nation, accounting for about half of the world's industrial goods. Its technology was exemplified by its feat of landing men on the Moon in 1969. The first European to land in North America was probably Leif Ericson, a Viking, in about AD 986. The continent was rediscovered in 1497 by John Cabot. The first Europeans to settle in large numbers were the English, who founded a settlement in Virginia in 1607. By 1760 there were 13 colonies between Georgia and Massachusetts. The American War of Independence (1775–83) ended British rule. Under the 1787 Constitution, George Washington was elected the first President in 1789. In 1803 Louisiana was purchased from France and Florida was bought from Spain in 1809. The US-Mexican War of 1846–48 ended with the acquisition of much of the south-west: the US-Mexico border was fixed in 1853–54. The Civil War (1861–65) ended the threat of the secession of the South and slavery was abolished. Industrialization and the opening up of the West caused the economy to expand in the late 19th century. The US intervened in World War I in 1917. Between the wars there was a severe economic depression, but the New Deal policy of the 32nd President Franklin D Roosevelt helped it to recover. Roosevelt led the US into World War II in 1941 after the Japanese attack on Pearl Harbor in Hawaii. After World War II, the US accepted its role as a super-power, becoming involved in wars in Korea (1950–53) and Vietnam (1964–73) aimed at halting the spread of communism in Asia. Internally, the US has been troubled by ethnic conflict and assassinations of leading figures.

Spanish cultural influences are evident throughout Uruguay where more than 90 per cent of the people are of European descent. This Roman Catholic church is in Soriano, in south-western Uruguay.

Area: 9,363,123 km² (3,615,319 sq mi); **Population:** 226,504,825 (1980 census); **Capital:** Washington DC (pop of District of Columbia, 637,651, pop of city, 635,185); **Other cities:** New York City (7,015,608), Chicago (2,969,570), Los Angeles (2,950,010), Philadelphia (1,680,235), Houston (1,544,992), Detroit (1,192,222), Dallas (901,450), San Diego (870,006), Baltimore (783,320), San Antonio (783,296), Phoenix (781,443), Indianapolis (695,040), Honolulu (681,004), San Francisco (674,063), Memphis (644,838), Milwaukee (632,989), San Jose (625,763), Cleveland (572,532), Boston (562,118), Columbus (561,943), New Orleans (556,913), Jacksonville (541,269); **Highest point:** Mt McKinley (Alaska), 6194 m (20,322 ft); **Official language:** English; **Religions:** in 1978, 54.7 per cent of church members were Protestants, 37.2 per cent were Roman Catholics, and 4.3 per cent were Jews; **Adult literacy rate:** 99 per cent; **Average life expectancy at birth:** 73 years; **Unit of currency:** Dollar; **Main exports:** machinery, vehicles, grains, aircraft and parts, chemicals, coal, soya beans, textiles, cotton, iron and steel goods; **Per capita GNP:** US$10,820.

UPPER VOLTA, a poor, remote and landlocked West African republic. Low plateaux cover most of the country. The east is in the River Niger basin; the centre and west are drained by the Black, Red and White Volta rivers. Upper Volta has a hot, tropical climate. The main rainy season is July–October and the average annual rainfall varies between 500 mm (20 in) in the north to 1140 mm (45 in) in the south-west. But droughts are common. Most people are Negroes: the Mossi (48 per cent) are the largest single group. In 1978 83 per cent of the population was engaged in agriculture, which accounted for 38 per cent of the GDP, with 20 per

Caracas, capital and by far the largest city of Venezuela, has grown rapidly in recent years, much of the development having been financed by revenue from the country's massive oil sales.

cent from industry and 42 per cent from services. Pastoralism is important: there were 2.7 million cattle, 1.8 million sheep and 2.7 million goats in 1979. Cotton and other cash crops are grown in the south and south-west. There are few minerals. Food, textiles and metal products are the main manufactures. Remittances from migrant workers and revenue from transit trade play a major part in the economy. France subdued the country by 1896. Full independence was achieved in 1960. Military coups occurred in 1966, 1974 and 1980, when power was vested in a Military Committee for National Recovery and Progress.

Area: 274,200 km² (105,875 sq mi); **Population:** 5,917,000; **Capital:** Ouagadougou (pop 173,000); **Official language:** French; **Religions:** traditional beliefs, Islam (30 per cent), Roman Catholicism (9 per cent); **Adult literacy rate:** 5 per cent; **Average life expectancy at birth:** 42 years; **Unit of currency:** Franc CFA; **Main exports:** cotton, livestock, karité nuts and oil, groundnuts; **Per capita GNP:** US$180.

URUGUAY, a South American republic facing the Atlantic Ocean. It is mostly low-lying, with hills in the north. The River Negro, a tributary of the Uruguay on the western border, drains the central region. The average annual temperature range is 10°–23°C (50°–73°F), while the annual rainfall averages 1000 mm (39 in) in the south and 1260 (50 in) in the north. More than 90 per cent of the population are of European descent. Most others are of mixed European and Indian descent. In 1979 agriculture employed 12 per cent of the workforce, industry 33 per cent and services 55 per cent. About 89 per cent of the land is farmed; 90 per cent of this is pasture. In 1979 Uruguay had 10 million cattle and 18.7 million sheep; livestock products are the chief exports. Crops include fruits, maize, rice, sugar and wheat. There are processing, oil refining, light engineering, transport, chemical and textile industries. Europeans first landed in Uruguay in 1515. Spain founded Montevideo in 1726 to stem Portugese influence in the area. The Portuguese were driven out in the late 18th century. Brazil annexed Uruguay in 1820, but Uruguay joined with Argentina in 1825 to fight Brazil. Uruguay finally became an independent nation in 1828. In 1903 José Batlle y Ordóñez became president and introduced many reforms, including extensive welfare services. Economic problems and the activities of the Tupamaros (an urban guerrilla movement) have caused political instability and army intervention in government in recent years.

Area: 176,215 km² (68,041 sq mi); **Population:** 2,934,000; **Capital:** Montevideo (pop 1,230,000); **Official language:** Spanish; **Religion:** Roman Catholicism; **Adult literacy rate:** 94 per cent; **Average life expectancy at birth:** 71 years; **Unit of currency:** Peso; **Main exports:** meat, wool, hides and skins; **Per capita GNP:** US$2090.

VANUATU, an island republic in the south-western Pacific Ocean, formerly called the New Hebrides. There are about 80 islands, which are mountainous and volcanic. The climate is tropical and the rainfall is generally abundant. Most people are Melanesians. Copra and fish are exported. Tourism is growing: there were 30,450 tourists in 1979. A Spanish explorer discovered the islands in 1606. Britain and France jointly ruled the islands as a condominium from 1906 until independence in 1980.

Area: 14,763 km² (5700 sq mi); **Population:** 113,000; **Capital:** Vila (pop 14,000); **Per capita GNP:** US$590.

VATICAN CITY STATE, the world's smallest independent state. It is in north-western Rome, on a hill on the right bank of the River Tiber. It contains the government of the Roman Catholic Church, headed by the Pope, and the magnificent St Peter's Basilica. It has been the residence of the Pope since the 5th century and was formerly centre of the Papal States in central Italy. In 1870 Victor Emmanuel II took Rome, making it capital of the newly united kingdom which included the Papal States. The Pope refused to recognize the new government. But, in 1929, the Italian government and Pope Pius IX signed the Lateran Treaty, which officially recognized the independence of the Vatican City State.

Area: 44 ha (108.7 acres); **Population:** 1000.

VENEZUELA, an oil-rich republic in northern South America. The hot Maracaibo lowlands surround Lake Maracaibo, a freshwater lake open to the sea, beneath which are large oil deposits. Overlooking the lowlands are the Venezuelan highlands, extensions of the Andes. The central plain is drained by the River Orinoco, one of the world's longest at 2560 km (1591 mi). This plain is covered by *llanos* (savanna). The south-eastern Guiana Highlands are thinly populated. They contain the world's highest waterfall, Angel Falls, with a drop of 979 m (3212 ft). The equatorial climate is modified by the altitude. About 70 per cent of the people are *mestizos* (of mixed white and Indian origin), 18 per cent are mulattos or blacks, 10 per cent are whites and 2 per cent are Indians. In 1978 agriculture employed 20 per cent of the people, industry 27 per cent and services 53 per cent. Their respective contributions to the GDP were 6 per cent, 46 per cent and 48 per cent. The chief resource is oil: Venezuela was the world's 5th largest producer in 1980. Other minerals, including bauxite, gold and iron ore, are now being exploited and manufacturing has been expanding quickly. Coffee, cocoa, maize and sugar cane are major crops; livestock are reared in the central plains. Spain ruled the area from the 16th century. Simón Bolívar liberated Venezuela from Spain in 1821, but it became part of Grand Colombia until 1830. Violence and dictatorships have marked much of its history. But democratic governments have ruled since 1958. The elected National Congress consists of a Senate and a Chamber of Deputies.

Area: 912,050 km² (352,164 sq mi); **Population:** 15,920,000; **Capital:** Caracas (pop 3,508,000); **Other cities:** Maracaibo (652,000); **Highest point:** Pico Bolívar, in Sierra Nevada de Mérida, 5007 m (16,427 ft); **Official language:** Spanish; **Religion:** Roman Catholicism; **Adult literacy rate:** 82 per cent; **Average life expectancy at birth:** 66 years; **Unit of currency:** Bolívar; **Main exports:** oil, iron ore, coffee, cocoa; **Per capita GNP:** US$3130.

VIETNAM, a Socialist Republic in South-East Asia. The northern Red River delta is ringed by hills and mountains, including Fan Si Pan, the nation's highest peak. In central Vietnam, a narrow coastal plain is backed by the Annamite range. In the far south is the huge delta of the Mekong River, one of the world's longest at 4184 km (2600 mi). Temperatures are around 26°C (79°F) throughout the year in the south, but temperatures average 17°C (63°F) in January–February in the north. The rainfall is generally abundant. About 84 per cent of the people are Vietnamese (Kinh). There are also Khmers, Thais and various remote tribal groups. In 1978 agriculture employed 73 per cent of the population, industry 8 per cent and services 19 per cent. Rice, maize, sugar cane, sweet potatoes and cotton are major crops. In 1979 there were 1.6 million cattle and 9.3 million pigs. Fishing is also important. The north is rich in minerals, including coal, lignite, bauxite, chromite, iron ore, manganese and titanium. Manufacturing has been steadily increasing. In the past the north was often under Chinese rule, while the south came under the Khmers. By 1802, Vietnam was united and independent. Between the 1860s and 1880s, France took over Vietnam which, with Laos and Cambodia (Kampuchea), became French Indochina. Japan occupied the area in World War II. In 1946 war began between the French and the nationalist Viet Minh. France withdrew in 1954 and Vietnam was partitioned into the Communist North and the non-Communist South. From 1959 Communist Viet Cong guerrillas fought against the government of South Vietnam, which was aided by the US. American forces withdrew in 1973 and South Vietnam fell to the North in 1975. Vietnam was united as a Socialist Republic with close relations with the USSR in 1976. Vietnamese troops attacked Kampuchea in December 1978 in support of a group friendly to the USSR. This group formed a government in 1979 although resistance to it continued into the 1980s. China attacked North Vietnam in 1979 but soon withdrew its forces.

Area: 329,556 km² (127,249 sq mi); **Population:** 51,742,000 (1978); **Capital:** Hanoi (pop 2,000,000); **Other cities:** Ho Chi Minh City (3,500,000); **Highest point:** Fan Si Pan, 3143 m (10,312 ft); **Official language:** Vietnamese; **Religions:** Buddhism, Taoism, Christianity; **Adult literacy rate:** 87 per cent; **Average life expectancy at birth:** 62 years; **Unit of currency:** Dong; **Main exports:** coal, farm produce, fish; **Per capita GNP:** US$170 (1978).

VIRGIN ISLANDS (British), a territory in the West Indies east of Puerto Rico. There are 36 main islands: 16 are inhabited. The climate is tropical. Most people are Negroes. The chief products are fish, fruit, livestock and vegetables, but tourism is the basis of the economy. British settlers became established on the islands in 1666.

Areas: 153 km² (59 sq mi); **Population:** 11,500; **Capital:** Road Town (pop 3500).

VIRGIN ISLANDS (US), an archipelago east of Puerto Rico. It includes 3 sizeable islands, St Thomas, St Croix and St John, and about 50 islets. The climate is tropical. About 90 per cent of the people are descendants of African slaves. Most others are Europeans. Tourism is the main industry: there were 1.2 million visitors in 1979. The US bought the islands from Denmark in 1917. The islanders were made US citizens in 1927, but the islands remain an 'unincorporated territory'.

Area: 344 km² (133 sq mi); **Population:** 119,000; **Capital:** Charlotte Amalie (pop 15,000); **Per capita GNP:** US$5580.

WALLIS AND FUTUNA ISLANDS, a French Overseas Territory in the south-western Pacific, about 400 km (249 mi) west of Samoa. The Wallis group contains Uvea on which the capital Mata-Utu is situated. The people are Polynesians. Bananas, copra, taro roots and yams are grown. The Wallis Islands became French in 1842 and the entire group became a French protectorate in 1887. The islands became an Overseas Territory of France in 1961.

Area: 200 km² (77 sq mi); **Population:** 9000; **Capital:** Mata-Utu (pop 6000).

WESTERN SAHARA, a North African territory facing the Atlantic Ocean. It was called Spanish Sahara until 1976. Behind the coastal plains are low plateaux dissected by watercourses formed when the region had a moist climate. Today, however, the climate is hot and arid, with generally less than 50 mm (2 in) of rain per year. There is little farming: most people are nomadic pastoralists. Fishing is important, but the chief resource is a huge deposit of phosphates at Bu Craa in the north, discovered in 1963. Spain ruled Western Sahara from 1884.

Beef Island and Guana Island are in the British Virgin Islands, the easternmost group in the Greater Antilles. Beef Island contains the chief airport. A bridge links Beef Island to Tortola, the largest of the islands where more than four-fifths of the territory's population lives.

In the 1970s the nationalist Popular Front for the Liberation of Saharan Territories (POLISARIO) demanded independence. In 1975, after consultation with community leaders and local chiefs, Spain agreed to withdraw and divide the territory between Morocco and Mauritania. In early 1976 Morocco took the northern two-thirds and Mauritania occupied the south. However, POLISARIO, with support from Algeria, proclaimed their country independent as the Sahrawi Arab Democratic Republic and launched a guerrilla war. Mauritania withdrew from the south in 1979 and Morocco moved in. In 1981 the Organization of African Unity sought to persuade Morocco to hold a referendum in Western Sahara on its future.

Area: 266,000 km² (102,709 sq mi); **Population:** 76,000 (1970); **Capital:** formerly El Aiun.

YEMEN ARAB REPUBLIC, in the south-western Arabian peninsula. The Red Sea coastal plain, called the *Tihama*, is 30–80 km (19–50 mi) wide. Behind it the land is mountainous, rising to 3760 m (12,336 ft), Arabia's highest point, west of San'a. The coastal plain is hot and arid, with an average annual rainfall of 130 mm (5 in). The highlands have around 510 mm (20 in) and contain Arabia's best farmland. Most people are Arabs; 90 per cent live in rural areas. In 1978 agriculture employed 76 per cent of the people, as compared with industry 11 per cent and services 13 per cent. Their respective contributions to the GDP were 35 per cent, 14 per cent and 51 per cent. Cereals, coffee, cotton, fruits and vegetables are grown and hides and skins are important products. In 1979 there were 7.8 million goats, 3.7 million sheep and nearly 1 million cattle. Some salt is mined and manufacturing is expanding, with aid from Arab and other nations. Yemen was part of the Ottoman Empire in 1849–1918. In 1962 the monarch (*Imam*) was overthrown and a republic proclaimed. A People's Constituent Assembly was established in 1978 as the legislative body, replacing the military Command Council.

Area: 195,000 km² (75,294 sq mi); **Population:** 6,142,000; **Capital:** San'a (pop 448,000); **Highest point:** Hadur Shu'ayb, 3760 m (12,336 ft); **Official language:** Arabic; **Religion:** Islam; **Adult literacy rate:** 13 per cent; **Average life expectancy at birth:** 39 years; **Unit of currency:** Riyal; **Main exports:** cotton, coffee, hides and skins; **Per capita GNP:** US$420.

YEMEN PEOPLE'S DEMOCRATIC REPUBLIC, in the southern Arabian peninsula, was formerly the Federation of South Arabia, including Aden. Behind the narrow coastal plain are mountains, a fertile valley (the Hadhramawt) and large deserts in the east. The average annual temperature range in Aden is 24°–32°C (75°–90°F) and the rainfall averages 130 mm (5 in) a year. But parts of the Hadhramawt have 760 mm (30 in). Most people are Arabs and 37 per cent live in urban areas. In 1978 agriculture employed 60 per cent of the people, industry 21 per cent and services 19 per cent. The chief crops are cereals; cotton is the main cash crop. In 1979 there were 1.3 million goats and nearly 1 million sheep. Fishing is also important. Aden has an oil refinery and oil products, made from imported oil, are exported. Transit trade is generally important. British influence in the area began in 1802 and Aden was annxed in 1839. It became a major strategic and trading centre after the opening of the Suez Canal in 1869. Nationalist unrest preceded independence in 1967. The rulers of the 17 Sultanates which made up the Federation of South Arabia were deposed by the Marxist National Liberation Front, which made the country a People's Republic.

Area: 332,968 km² (128,567 sq mi); **Population:** 1,905,000; **Capital:** Aden (pop 264,000); **Highest point:** 2469 m (8100 ft); **Official language:** Arabic; **Religion:** Islam; **Adult literacy rate:** 27 per cent; **Average life expectancy at birth:** 44 years; **Unit of currency:** Dinar; **Main exports:** cotton, fish, refined oil; **Per capita GNP:** US$500.

COUNTRIES OF THE WORLD

YUGOSLAVIA, a Socialist Federal Republic on the Adriatic Sea. Large areas are mountainous; the mountains are extensions of the Alpine system. They are narrowest in the north, but the entire south is mountainous. The limestone Dinaric Alps display typical karst scenery. The mountains on the coast have been submerged, such that former ridges now form long, narrow islands parallel to the coast and former valleys are harbours. To the north and east is hill country descending to the interior plains drained by the Danube river system. The coastal climate is typically Mediterranean, but the interior plains, the main farming region, have a continental climate. Belgrade has an average annual temperature range of −2°C to 22°C (28°–72°F). Its average annual rainfall is 610 mm (24 in). Most people are South Slavs: the Serbs and Croats are the two largest groups; the Slovenes live in the north; and the Montenegrins and Macedonians live in the south. Various non-Slav minorities live mainly in the east and south. The division of Yugoslavia into 6 republics reflects its cultural diversity. In 1978 agriculture employed 33 per cent of the workforce, industry 32 per cent and services 35 per cent. They contributed 16 per cent, 45 per cent and 39 per cent to the GDP respectively. Cereals, cotton, fruits, olives, sugar beet, sunflower seeds and tobacco are grown. In 1980 there were 7.3 million sheep, 7.5 million pigs and 5.4 million cattle. Forestry is important. Yugoslavia has many mineral resources and manufacturing has steadily expanded since 1945. Between 1459 and the mid-19th century, Turkey ruled most of the area, but before World War I, some parts, including Serbia, were independent, while other parts were in Austria-Hungary. The murder of Archduke Franz Ferdinand of Austria-Hungary by a Bosnian-Serb sparked off World War I. Yugoslavia was founded as a union of South Slavs in 1918, although the name Yugoslavia was not adopted until 1929. Germany invaded Yugoslavia in World War II. After the war, the monarchy was abolished and a socialist republic was established by the partisan leader Josip Broz (Tito). In 1948 Yugoslavia and the USSR severed relations. Yugoslavia then pursued an independent policy, After President Tito died in 1980, a collective presidency was established.

Area: 255,804 km² (98,772 sq mi); **Population:** 22,745,000; **Capital:** Belgrade (pop with suburbs, 1,209,000); **Other cities:** Zagreb (668,000); **Highest point:** Triglav, 2863 m (9393 ft); **Official languages:** Serbo-Croat, Slovene, Macedonian; **Religions** (1953): Orthodox (41 per cent), Roman Catholicism (32 per cent), Islam (12 per cent), Protestantism (1 per cent); **Adult literacy rate:** 85 per cent; **Average life expectancy at birth:** 69 years; **Unit of currency:** Dinar; **Main exports:** machinery, electrical goods and transport equipment, other manufactures, chemicals; **Per capita GNP:** US$2430.

ZAIRE, a republic in west-central Africa, is the continent's 2nd largest nation. Most of the country lies in the drainage basin of the River Zaire (formerly Congo), which is one of the world's longest at 4828 km (3000 mi). There are highlands and plateaux in the south and east along the Rift Valley where Zaire's border passes through lakes Tanganyika, Kivu, Edward and Mobutu Sese Seko (formerly Albert). The climate is equatorial with an average annual rainfall of 1250–2030 mm (49–80 in). There is rain forest in the centre and savanna in the north and south. About 200 language and ethnic groups live in Zaire. About two-thirds of the people speak Bantu languages: Hamitic, Nilotic, Sudanic and pygmy languages are also spoken. In 1978 agriculture employed 76 per cent of the people, accounting for 27 per cent of the GDP; 20 per cent came from industry and 53 per cent from services. The chief cash crops are coffee, cotton, palm products and rubber. Fishing is important but livestock can be reared only in areas free from the disease-carrying tsetse fly. Minerals made up 74 per cent of the exports in 1976–78. The main mining region is Shaba, where copper (the most valuable export), cobalt, manganese, silver, uranium and zinc are mined. Some oil is produced and diamonds are mined in the Kasai provinces. Hydroelectricity is being developed and manufacturing is growing especially around Kinshasa and Lubumbashi. The Portuguese reached the area in 1482 and slavery was practised along the coast. Henry Morton Stanley explored the Zaire River in 1874–77 and the country became the personal property of King Leopold of Belgium in 1884. Because of ill-treatment of local people by concessionaires, Belgium took over the country in 1908 as the Belgian Congo. Full independence in 1960 was followed by civil war, including a secessionist struggle in Shaba. In 1965 the army under Mobutu Sese Seko took power. Stability was restored although rebel forces had to be driven out of Shaba in 1977 and in 1978.

Area: 2,345,409 km² (905,617 sq mi); **Population:** 29,826,000; **Capital:** Kinshasa (pop 2,444,000); **Other cities:** Kananga (704,000), Lubumbashi (451,000); **Highest point:** Ruwenzori range on the Ugandan border, 5119 m (16,795 ft); **Official language:** French; **Religions:** traditional beliefs (59 per cent), Roman Catholicism (36 per cent), Protestantism (4 per cent), Islam (0.5 per cent); **Adult literacy rate:** 15 per cent; **Average life expectancy at birth:** 46 years; **Unit of currency:** Zaire; **Main exports:** copper, cobalt, coffee, diamonds, oil, cassiterite; **Per capita GNP:** US$260.

ZAMBIA, a landlocked republic in south-central Africa, called Northern Rhodesia until 1964. It consists mostly of a plateau, 900–1520 m (2953–

4987 ft). In the south and east, the Zambezi and Luangwa rivers occupy downfaulted troughs that are part of the East African Rift Valley system. The Zambezi has been dammed to form Lake Kariba, which Zambia shares with Zimbabwe. Kariba's hydro-electric plants have given Zambia an abundance of electrical energy. Parts of lakes Mweru and Tanganyika are in Zambia, as is the entire Lake Bangweulu. The main upland region is the Muchinga Mts in the north-east; they rise to more than 2100 m (6890 ft). The tropical climate is modified by the altitude. The rainfall varies between 1300 mm (51 in) in the north to 500 mm (20 in) in the south. Wildlife is abundant in the savanna, which covers most of Zambia. Six major Bantu languages and 66 dialects are spoken. In 1978 agriculture employed 68 per cent of the workforce (mostly at subsistence level), but it accounted for only 17 per cent of the GDP, compared with 39 per cent from industry and 44 per cent from services. The chief resource is copper, which accounts for 90 per cent of the exports. Cobalt, lead and zinc are also exported as are maize and tobacco, the main cash crop. There are processing and metal industries in the towns. The British South Africa Company entered the area in 1889 and, in 1911, it became the British protectorate of Northern Rhodesia. Full independence as the Republic of Zambia was achieved in 1964. Zambia became a one-party state in 1972.

Opposite: The Yugoslav market town of Mostar is on the river Neretva, which flows to the Adriatic Sea. It is the centre of a wine- and fruit-producing region. Its 16th-century Turkish bridge possibly stands on Roman foundations. Left: The man-made Lake Kariba is on the Zimbabwe-Zambia border. These countries share the electricity generated at the Kariba Dam.

Area: 752,614 km² (290,602 sq mi); **Population:** 5,992,000; **Capital:** Lusaka (pop 559,000); **Official language:** English; **Religions:** mostly Christianity; **Adult literacy rate:** 39 per cent; **Average life expectancy at birth:** 48 years; **Unit of currency:** Kwacha; **Main exports:** copper, zinc, cobalt, lead, tobacco; **Per capita GNP:** US$510.

ZIMBABWE, a landlocked republic in southern Africa, formerly called Rhodesia. The north is in a deep trough through which the River Zambezi flows. Lake Kariba, a man-made lake on the Zambezi, is shared with Zambia, as is the electricity produced at Kariba dam. Central Zimbabwe (the high veld) is between 1220 and 1530 m (4003–5020 ft), but the land rises to 2595 m (8514 ft) on the Mozambique border. The southern low veld is drained by the River Limpopo. These lowlands are less than 910 m (2986 ft) in height. The high veld has a pleasant climate with an average annual temperature of 20°C (68°F). The lowlands are much hotter. The high veld has an average annual rainfall of 700–900 mm (28–35 in), the eastern highlands getting 1520 mm (60 in). But the low veld is arid with 410 mm (16 in) per year. About 96 per cent of the people are black Africans who speak Bantu languages. The largest groups are the Ndebele in the south and the Shona in the north. Most other people are of European descent. There were 244,000 Europeans in mid-1979, but some emigration has occurred since then. Asians and Coloureds numbered 35,000 in 1979. In 1978 agriculture employed 60 per cent of the workforce. In 1977 it accounted for 20 per cent of the GDP, compared with 35 per cent from industry and 45 per cent from services. European farming is efficient but African farming is mostly at subsistence level. Tobacco, sugar cane, tea and fruits are the leading cash crops. In 1979 there were 5 million cattle. Asbestos, chrome, coal and gold are mined. Manufacturing is important in the towns. Political conditions have retarded the development of Zimbabwe's great tourist potential. Cecil Rhodes obtained mining rights in the area in the 1880s. Between 1898 and 1923, Southern Rhodesia (as Zimbabwe was then called) was ruled by a British High Commissioner based in South Africa. In 1923 it became a self-governing British colony. Its white government passed a law in 1930 reserving 47.6 per cent of the land for European settlement. This created long-term resentment among black Africans. In 1963 the white leaders asked for independence, which Britain did not grant because the whites were not prepared to give up their dominant status, a condition demanded by African nationalists. In 1965 Rhodesia declared its independence unilaterally. Britain declared this act illegal and imposed economic sanctions through the UN. A guerrilla war began in the early 1970s. Britain negotiated an independence Constitution in 1979 and independence, with a majority black government led by Prime Minister Robert Mugabe, was achieved in 1980.

Area: 390,580 km² (150,812 sq mi); **Population:** 7,878,000; **Capital:** Harare (pop 616,000); **Other cities:** Bulawayo (357,000); **Highest point:** Mt Inyangani, 2595 m (8514 ft); **Official language:** English; **Religions:** traditional beliefs, Christianity; **Average life expectancy at birth:** 54 years; **Unit of currency:** Dollar; **Main exports:** tobacco, asbestos, gold, cotton, steel, meat, ferrochrome, copper, maize; **Per capita GNP:** US$470.

Largest Metropolitan Areas of the World

This table lists the major metropolitan areas of the world according to their estimated population on January 1, 1981. For convenience in reference, the areas are grouped by major region, and the number of areas in each region and size group is given.

There are 27 areas with more than 5,000,000 population each; these are listed in rank order of estimated population, with the world rank given in parentheses following the name. For example, New York's 1981 rank is second. Below the 5,000,000 level, the metropolitan areas are listed alphabetically within region, not in order of size.

For ease of comparison, each metropolitan area has been defined by Rand McNally & Company according to consistent rules. A metropolitan area includes a central city, neighboring communities linked to it by continuous built-up areas, and more distant communities if the bulk of their population is supported by commuters to the central city. Some metropolitan areas have more than one central city, for example Tōkyō–Yokohama or San Francisco–Oakland–San Jose.

POPULATION CLASSIFICATION	UNITED STATES and CANADA	LATIN AMERICA	EUROPE (excl. U.S.S.R.)	U.S.S.R.	ASIA	AFRICA–OCEANIA
Over 15,000,000 (4)	New York, U.S. (2)	Mexico City, Mex. (4)			Tōkyō–Yokohama, Jap. (1) Ōsaka–Kōbe–Kyōto, Jap. (3)	
10,000,000–15,000,000 (6)		São Paulo, Braz. (5) Buenos Aires, Arg. (10)	London, Eng. (8)	Moscow (6)	Seoul, Kor. (7) Calcutta, India (9)	
5,000,000–10,000,000 (17)	Los Angeles, U.S. (11) Chicago, U.S. (17) Philadelphia–Trenton–Wilmington, U.S. (26)	Rio de Janeiro, Braz. (12)	Paris, Fr. (13) Essen–Dortmund–Duisburg (The Ruhr), Ger., Fed. Rep. of (27)	Leningrad (23)	Bombay, India (14) Shanghai, China (16) Manila, Phil. (18) Jakarta, Indon. (19) Delhi–New Delhi, India (20) Peking, China (21) Tehrān, Iran (22) Bangkok, Thai. (24) Karāchi, Pak. (25)	Cairo, Eg. (15)
3,000,000–5,000,000 (31)	Boston, U.S. Detroit, U.S.–Windsor, Can. San Francisco–Oakland–San Jose, U.S. Washington, U.S.	Bogotá, Col. Caracas, Ven. Lima, Peru Santiago, Chile	Athens, Greece Barcelona, Sp. Berlin, Ger. İstanbul, Tur. Madrid, Sp. Milan, It. Rome, It.		Baghdād, Iraq Chungking, China Dacca, Bngl. Lahore, Pak. Madras, India Mukden, China Nagoya, Jap. Pusan, Kor. Rangoon, Bur. Taipei, Taiwan Tientsin, China Victoria, Hong Kong Wuhan, China	Alexandria, Eg. Johannesburg, S. Afr. Sydney, Austl.

2,000,000–3,000,000 (45)	Cleveland, U.S. Dallas– Fort Worth, U.S. Houston, U.S. Miami–Fort Lauderdale, U.S. Montréal, Can. Pittsburgh, U.S. St. Louis, U.S. San Diego, U.S.– Tijuana, Mex. Seattle– Tacoma, U.S. Toronto, Can.	Guadalajara, Mex. Havana, Cuba Medellín, Col. Monterrey, Mex. Porto Alegre, Braz. Recife, Braz.	Brussels, Bel. Bucharest, Rom. Budapest, Hung. Hamburg, Ger., Fed. Rep. of Katowice–Bytom– Gliwice, Pol. Lisbon, Port. Manchester, Eng. Naples, It. Warsaw, Pol.	Kiev Tashkent	Ankara, Tur. Bangalore, India Canton, China Chengtu, China Harbin, China Ho Chi Minh City (Saigon), Viet. Hyderābād, India Sian, China Singapore, Singapore	Casablanca, Mor. Kinshasa, Zaire Lagos, Nig. Melbourne, Austl.
1,500,000–2,000,000 (35)	Atlanta, U.S. Baltimore, U.S. Minneapolis– St. Paul, U.S. Phoenix, U.S.	Salvador, Braz. San Juan, P.R.	Amsterdam, Neth. Cologne, Ger., Fed. Rep. of Copenhagen, Den. Frankfurt am Main, Ger., Fed. Rep. of Glasgow, Scot. Leeds–Bradford, Eng. Liverpool, Eng. Munich, Ger., Fed. Rep. of Stuttgart, Ger., Fed. Rep. of Turin, It. Vienna, Aus.	Baku Gorki Kharkov	Bandung, Indon. Chittagong, Bngl. Colombo, Sri Lanka Damascus, Syria Fukuoka, Jap. Hanoi, Viet. Hiroshima–Kure, Jap. Kanpur, India Kaohsiung, Taiwan Kitakyūshū– Shimonoseki, Jap. Nanking, China Pune, India Surabaya, Indon. Taegu, Kor.	Cape Town, S. Afr.
1,000,000–1,500,000 (86)	Buffalo–Niagara Falls, U.S.–St. Catharines– Niagara Falls, Can. Cincinnati, U.S. Denver, U.S. El Paso, U.S.–Ciudad Juárez, Mex. Hartford–New Britain, U.S. Indianapolis, U.S. Kansas City, U.S. Milwaukee, U.S. New Orleans, U.S. Portland, U.S. San Antonio, U.S. Vancouver, Can.	Barranquilla, Col. Brasília, Braz. Cali, Col. Córdoba, Arg. Curitiba, Braz. Fortaleza, Braz. Guatemala, Guat. Guayaquil, Ec. Montevideo, Ur. Rosario, Arg. Santo Domingo, Dom. Rep.	Antwerp, Bel. Belgrade, Yugo. Bilbao, Sp. Dublin, Ire. Düsseldorf, Ger., Fed. Rep. of Hannover, Ger., Fed. Rep. of Lille, Fr. Łódź, Pol. Lyon, Fr. Mannheim, Ger., Fed. Rep. of Marseille, Fr. Newcastle– Sunderland, Eng. Nürnberg, Ger., Fed. Rep. of Porto, Port. Prague, Czech. Rotterdam, Neth. Sofia, Bul. Stockholm, Swe. Valencia, Sp.	Chelyabinsk Dnepropetrovsk Kazan Kuybyshev Minsk Novosibirsk Odessa Omsk Perm Rostov-na-Donu Saratov Sverdlovsk Tbilisi Ufa Volgograd Yerevan	Anshan, China Beirut, Leb. Chengchou, China Dairen, China Faisalabad (Lyallpur), Pak. Fushun, China Hsinking, China İzmir, Tur. Kuala Lumpur, Mala. Kunming, China Kuwait, Kuw. Lanchou, China Lucknow, India Nāgpur, India Pyŏngyang, Kor. Rāwalpindi– Islāmābād, Pak. Sapporo, Jap. Shihchiachuang, China Taiyuan, China Tel Aviv–Yafo, Isr. Tsinan, China Tsingtao, China	Abidjan, I.C. Addis Ababa, Eth. Brisbane, Austl. Durban, S. Afr. Khartoum, Sud. Tunis, Tun.
Total by Region **(224)**	**34**	**28**	**50**	**24**	**72**	**16**

Geographical Features of the World

The Earth: Land and Water

	Total Area km²	Total Area *sq mi*	Area of Land km²	Area of Land *sq mi*	%	Area of Oceans and Seas km²	Area of Oceans and Seas *sq mi*	%
Earth	510,100,000	*197,000,000*	149,400,000	*57,700,000*	29.3	360,700,000	*139,300,000*	70.7
N. Hemisphere	255,050,000	*98,500,000*	106,045,650	*40,950,000*	41.6	149,004,350	*57,550,000*	58.4
S. Hemisphere	255,050,000	*98,500,000*	43,354,350	*16,750,000*	17.0	211,695,650	*81,750,000*	83.0

The Continents

Continent	Area km² *sq mi*	Population Estimate (1/1/82)	Population per km² *sq mi*	Mean Elevation m/*ft* *	Highest Elevation m/*ft*	Lowest Elevation m/*ft* (below sea level)	Highest Recorded Temperature °C/ *°F*	Lowest Recorded Temperature °C/ *°F*
Europe	9,932,000 *3,835,000*	666,400,000	67 *174*	340 *1,000*	Mt. Elbrus, U.S.S.R. 5,642/ *18,510*	Caspian Sea, U.S.S.R.-Iran −28/ *−92*	Sevilla, Spain 50°/ *122°*	Ust-Ščugor, U.S.S.R. −55°/ *−67°*
Asia	44,798,000 *17,297,000*	2,724,900,000	61 *158*	960 *3,150*	Mt. Everest, China-Nepal 8,848/ *29,028*	Dead Sea, Israel-Jordan −396/ *−1,299*	Tirat Ẕevi, Israel 54°/ *129°*	Ojmjakon, Verkhoyansk U.S.S.R.; −68°/ *−90°*
Africa	30,323,000 *11,708,000*	490,300,000	16 *42*	750 *2,450*	Kilimanjaro, Tanzania 5,895/ *19,340*	Lac Assal, Djibouti −155/ *−509*	Al 'Azīzīyah, Libya 58°/ *136°*	Ifrane, Morocco −24°/ *−11°*
North America	24,360,000 *9,406,000*	379,400,000	16 *40*	720 *2,350*	Mt. McKinley, United States 6,194/ *20,320*	Death Valley, United States −86/ *−282*	Death Valley, United States 57°/ *134°*	Northice, Greenland −66°/ *−87°*
South America	17,828,000 *6,883,000*	247,800,000	14 *36*	590 *1,940*	Aconcagua, Argentina 6,959/ *22,831*	Salinas Chicas, Argentina −42/ *−138*	Rivadavia, Argentina 49°/ *120°*	Sarmiento, Argentina −33°/ *−27°*
Oceania, incl. Australia	8,513,000 *3,287,000*	23,200,000	3 *7*	....	Mt. Wilhelm, Papua N. Gui. 4,509/ *14,793*	Lake Eyre, Australia −16/ *−52*	Cloncurry, Australia 53°/ *128°*	Charlotte Pass, Australia −22°/ *−8°*
Australia	7,686,850 *2,967,909*	14,910,000	2 *5*	340 *1,100*	Mt. Kosciusko, Australia 2,228/ *7,310*	Lake Eyre, Australia −16/ *−52*	Cloncurry, Australia 53°/ *128°*	Charlotte Pass, Australia −22°/ *−8°*
Antarctica	14,000,000 *5,405,000*	....	... ...	2,600 *8,550*	Vinson Massif 5,140/ *16,864*	unknown	Esperanza 14°/ *58°*	Vostok −90°/ *−127°*
World	149,754,000 *57,821,000*	4,532,000,000	30 *78*	840 *2,750*	Mt. Everest, China-Nepal 8,848/ *29,028*	Dead Sea, Israel-Jordan −396/ *−1,299*	Al 'Azīzīyah, Libya 58°/ *136°*	Vostok −90°/ *−127°*

All temperatures are rounded to the nearest degree. * Elevations in feet are converted from metric equivalents and rounded.

Principal Mountains

Mountain	Country	Height M	Height *Ft*
Europe			
Elbrus, Mount	U.S.S.R.	5,642	*18,510*
Dykh-Tau	U.S.S.R.	5,203	*17,070*
Blanc, Mont	△France-△Italy	4,807	*15,771*
Rosa, Monte	Italy-△Switzerland	4,633	*15,200*
Matterhorn	Italy-Switzerland	4,476	*14,685*
Jungfrau	Switzerland	4,166	*13,668*
Grossglockner	△Austria	3,797	*12,457*
Teide, Pico de	△Spain (Canary Is.)	3,707	*12,162*
Mulhacén	Spain	3,482	*11,424*
Aneto, Pico de	Spain	3,404	*11,168*
Etna, Mount	Italy	3,390	*11,122*
Corno Grande	Italy	2,914	*9,560*
Gerlachovka	△Czechoslovakia	2,663	*8,737*
Glittertinden	△Norway	2,472	*8,110*
Narodnaya	U.S.S.R.	1,885	*6,184*
Nevis, Ben	△United Kingdom	1,343	*4,406*
Snowdon	United Kingdom	1,085	*3,560*
Asia			
Everest, Mount	△China-△Nepal	8,848	*29,028*
K2 (Godwin Austen)	China-△Pakistan	8,611	*28,250*
Kānchenjunga	△India-Nepal	8,598	*28,208*
Dhaulagiri	Nepal	8,172	*26,810*
Annapurna	Nepal	8,078	*26,504*
Ulugh Muztagh	China	7,723	*25,338*
Tirich Mīr	Pakistan	7,690	*25,230*
Communism Peak (pik Kommunizma)	△U.S.S.R.	7,495	*24,590*
Pobeda Peak (pik Pobedy)	China-U.S.S.R.	7,439	*24,406*
Demavend, Mount (Qolleh-ye Damāvand)	△Iran	5,604	*18,386*
Ararat, Mount (Büyük Ağrı Dağı)	△Turkey	5,185	*17,011*
Jaya Peak	△Indonesia	5,030	*16,503*
Klyuchevskaya Sopka (vulkan Ključevskaja Sopka)	U.S.S.R.	4,750	*15,584*
Kinabalu, Gunong	△Malaysia	4,101	*13,455*
Hsinkao	△Taiwan	3,997	*13,113*
Kerinci, Gunong	Indonesia	3,800	*12,467*
Fuji-San	△Japan	3,776	*12,388*
Hadūr Shu'ayb	△Yemen	3,760	*12,336*
Sauda, Qurnet es	△Lebanon	3,088	*10,131*
Shām, Jabal ash	△Oman	3,035	*9,957*
Apo, Mount	△Philippines	2,954	*9,692*
Hermon, Mount	Lebanon-△Syria	2,814	*9,232*
Mayon, Mount	Philippines	2,462	*8,077*

Mountain	Country	Height M	Height *Ft*
Africa			
Kilimanjaro	△Tanzania	5,895	*19,34*
Kirinyaga (Mount Kenya)	△Kenya	5,199	*17,05*
Margherita Peak (Ruwenzori Range)	△Uganda-△Zaire	5,109	*16,76*
Ras Dashen	△Ethiopia	4,620	*15,15*
Toubkal, Jebel	△Morocco	4,165	*13,66*
Cameroun, Mont	△Cameroon	4,070	*13,35*
North America			
McKinley, Mount	△U.S.	6,194	*20,32*
Logan, Mount	△Canada	5,950	*19,52*
Citlaltépetl (Orizaba)	△Mexico	5,700	*18,70*
Popocatépetl, Volcán	Mexico	5,452	*17,88*
Whitney, Mount	U.S.	4,418	*14,49*
Elbert, Mount	U.S.	4,399	*14,43*
Rainier, Mount	U.S.	4,392	*14,41*
Shasta, Mount	U.S.	4,317	*14,16*
Pikes Peak	U.S.	4,301	*14,11*
Tajumulco, Volcán	△Guatemala	4,220	*13,84*
Kea, Mauna	U.S.	4,205	*13,79*
Grand Teton	U.S.	4,196	*13,76*
Waddington, Mount	Canada	3,994	*13,104*
Chirripó Grande	△Costa Rica	3,820	*12,53*
Hood, Mount	U.S.	3,426	*11,23*
Duarte, Pico	△Dominican Republic	3,175	*10,41*
Mitchell, Mount	U.S.	2,037	*6,684*
Clingmans Dome	U.S.	2,025	*6,64*
Washington, Mount	U.S.	1,917	*6,28*
South America			
Aconcagua, Cerro	△Argentina	6,959	*22,831*
Ojos del Salado, Nevado	Argentina-△Chile	6,885	*22,59*
Huascarán, Nevado	△Peru	6,768	*22,20*
Chimborazo, Volcán	△Ecuador	6,267	*20,561*
Cristóbal Colón, Pico	△Colombia	5,800	*19,02*
Bolívar, Pico	△Venezuela	5,002	*16,411*
Neblina, Pico da	△Brazil	3,014	*9,88*
Oceania			
Wilhelm, Mount	△Papua New Guinea	4,509	*14,79*
Cook, Mount	△New Zealand	3,764	*12,34*
Kosciusko, Mount	△Australia	2,228	*7,31*
Antarctica			
Vinson Massif	△Antarctica	5,140	*16,864*
Jackson, Mount	Antarctica	4,190	*13,747*

△ Highest mountain in country.

Oceans, Seas, and Gulfs

Name	Area km²	Area sq mi	Greatest Depth m	Greatest Depth ft
Pacific Ocean	165,200,000	*63,800,000*	11,022	*36,161*
Atlantic Ocean	82,400,000	*31,800,000*	9,220	*30,249*
Indian Ocean	74,900,000	*28,900,000*	7,450	*24,442*
Arctic Ocean	14,000,000	*5,400,000*	5,450	*17,881*
Arabian Sea	3,863,000	*1,492,000*	5,800	*19,029*
South China Sea	3,447,000	*1,331,000*	5,560	*18,241*
Caribbean Sea	2,754,000	*1,063,000*	7,680	*25,197*
Mediterranean Sea	2,505,000	*967,000*	5,020	*16,470*
Bering Sea	2,270,000	*876,000*	4,191	*13,750*
Bengal, Bay of	2,172,000	*839,000*	5,258	*17,251*
Okhotsk, Sea of	1,580,000	*610,000*	3,372	*11,063*
Norwegian Sea	1,547,000	*597,000*	4,020	*13,189*
Mexico, Gulf of	1,544,000	*596,000*	4,380	*14,370*
Hudson Bay	1,230,000	*475,000*	259	*850*
Greenland Sea	1,205,000	*465,000*	4,846	*15,899*

Waterfalls

Waterfall	Country	River	Height m	Height ft
Angel	Venezuela	Churún	972	*3,189*
Tugela	South Africa	Tugela	948	*3,110*
Yosemite	United States	Yosemite Creek	739	*2,425*
Sutherland	New Zealand	Arthur	579	*1,900*
Gavarnie	France	Gave de Pau	421	*1,381*
Lofoi	Zaire	Lofoi	384	*1,260*
Krimml	Austria	Krimml	381	*1,250*
Takakkaw	Canada	Yoho	380	*1,248*
Staubbach	Switzerland	Staubbach	305	*1,001*
Mardalsfoss	Norway	. . .	297	*974*
Gersoppa	India	Sharavati	253	*830*
Kaieteur	Guyana	Potaro	247	*810*

Principal Rivers

River	Location	Length km	Length mi
Nile-Kagera	Africa	6,671	*4,145*
Yangtze (Chang Jiang)	China	6,300	*3,915*
Amazon-Ucayali	Brazil-Peru	6,280	*3,902*
Mississippi-Missouri-Red Rock	U.S.	6,019	*3,741*
Yellow (Huang He)	China	5,464	*3,395*
Ob-Irtysh	China-U.S.S.R.	5,410	*3,362*
Río de la Plata-Paraná	South America	4,700	*2,920*
Mekong	Asia	4,500	*2,796*
Paraná	South America	4,500	*2,796*
Amur	China-U.S.S.R.	4,416	*2,744*
Lena	U.S.S.R.	4,400	*2,734*
Mackenzie	Canada	4,241	*2,635*
Congo (Zaire)	Africa	4,200	*2,610*
Niger	Africa	4,160	*2,585*
Yenisey (Jenisej)	U.S.S.R.	4,092	*2,543*
Mississippi	U.S.	3,778	*2,348*
Missouri	U.S.	3,725	*2,315*
Ob	U.S.S.R.	3,680	*2,287*
Volga	U.S.S.R.	3,531	*2,194*
Murray-Darling	Australia	3,490	*2,169*
Madeira-Mamoré	Bolivia-Brazil	3,200	*1,988*
Purus	Brazil-Peru	3,200	*1,988*
Yukon	Canada-U.S.	3,185	*1,979*
Indus	Asia	3,180	*1,976*
Rio Grande	Mexico-U.S.	3,033	*1,885*
Syr Darya (Syrdarja)	U.S.S.R.	2,991	*1,859*
Brahmaputra	Asia	2,900	*1,802*
São Francisco	Brazil	2,900	*1,802*
Danube	Europe	2,860	*1,777*
Salween	Asia	2,849	*1,770*
Euphrates	Asia	2,760	*1,715*
Orinoco	Colombia-Venezuela	2,736	*1,700*
Darling	Australia	2,720	*1,690*
Ganges	Bangladesh-India	2,700	*1,678*
Saskatchewan	Canada	2,672	*1,660*
Zambezi	Africa	2,660	*1,653*
Tocantins	Brazil	2,640	*1,640*
Amu Darya (Amudarja)	Afghanistan-U.S.S.R.	2,600	*1,616*
Murray	Australia	2,589	*1,609*
Kolyma	U.S.S.R.	2,575	*1,600*
Paraguay	South America	2,549	*1,584*
Ural	U.S.S.R.	2,428	*1,509*
Arkansas	U.S.	2,333	*1,450*
Colorado	Mexico-U.S.	2,333	*1,450*
Irrawaddy	Burma	2,293	*1,425*
Dnepr	U.S.S.R.	2,201	*1,368*
Araguaia	Brazil	2,199	*1,367*
Kasai	Angola-Zaire	2,153	*1,338*
Tarim	China	2,137	*1,328*
Brazos	U.S.	2,106	*1,309*

Principal Islands

Island	Area km²	Area sq mi	Highest Point Name	Highest Point m	Highest Point ft
Greenland (Grønland)	2,175,600	*840,004*	Gunnbjørns Fjeld	3,700	*12,139*
New Guinea	785,000	*303,090*	Puncak Jaya	5,030	*16,503*
Borneo	746,545	*288,243*	Gunong Kinabalu	4,101	*13,455*
Madagascar	587,041	*226,658*	Maromokotro	2,876	*9,436*
Baffin	476,065	*183,810*	unnamed	2,147	*7,045*
Sumatra (Sumatera)	473,606	*182,860*	Kerinci	3,800	*12,467*
Great Britain	227,581	*87,870*	Ben Nevis	1,343	*4,406*
Honshū	227,414	*87,805*	Fuji	3,776	*12,388*
Ellesmere	212,687	*82,119*	Barbeau Peak	2,604	*8,543*
Victoria	212,198	*81,930*	unnamed	655	*2,150*
Celebes (Sulawesi)	189,216	*73,057*	Rantekombola	3,455	*11,335*
South Island	150,461	*58,093*	Cook	3,764	*12,349*
Java (Jawa)	132,187	*51,038*	Semeru	3,676	*12,060*
North Island	114,728	*44,297*	Ruapehu	2,797	*9,177*
Cuba	114,524	*44,218*	Pico Turquino	1,994	*6,542*
Newfoundland	112,299	*43,359*	Lewis Hills	814	*2,671*
Luzon	104,687	*40,420*	Pulog	2,930	*9,613*
Iceland (Ísland)	103,000	*39,769*	Hvannadalshnúkur	2,119	*6,952*
Mindanao	94,630	*36,537*	Apo	2,954	*9,692*
Ireland	84,403	*32,588*	Carrantuohill	1,041	*3,415*
Hokkaidō	78,073	*30,144*	Daisetzu-Zan	2,290	*7,513*
Sakhalin (Sahalin)	76,400	*29,498*	Lopatina	1,609	*5,279*
Hispaniola	76,192	*29,418*	Pico Duarte	3,175	*10,417*
Banks	70,028	*27,038*	Durham	747	*2,450*
Tasmania	68,332	*26,383*	Ossa	1,617	*5,305*
Sri Lanka (Ceylon)	65,000	*25,097*	Pidurutalagala	2,524	*8,281*
Devon	55,247	*21,331*	Treuter	1,887	*6,191*
Novaya Zemlya (N. part)	48,904	*18,882*	unnamed	1,547	*5,075*
Tierra del Fuego	48,174	*18,600*	Yogan	2,469	*8,100*
Kyūshū	41,997	*16,215*	Kuju-San	1,787	*5,863*

Major Lakes

Lake	Country	Area km²	Area sq mi	Depth m	Depth ft
Caspian Sea	Iran-U.S.S.R	371,000	*143,200*	1,025	*3,363*
Superior	Canada-U.S.	82,414	*31,820*	406	*1,333*
Victoria	Africa	68,100	*26,293*	80	*262*
Aral Sea (Aral'skoje more)	U.S.S.R.	66,500	*25,676*	68	*223*
Huron	Canada-U.S.	59,596	*23,010*	229	*750*
Michigan	U.S.	58,016	*22,400*	281	*923*
Tanganyika	Africa	32,893	*12,700*	1,436	*4,711*
Baikal (ozero Bajkal)	U.S.S.R.	31,500	*12,162*	1,620	*5,315*
Great Bear	Canada	31,328	*12,096*	413	*1,356*
Nyasa	Africa	30,800	*11,892*	678	*2,224*
Great Slave	Canada	28,570	*11,031*	559	*1,834*
Erie	Canada-U.S.	25,745	*9,940*	64	*210*
Winnipeg	Canada	24,390	*9,417*	18	*60*
Ontario	Canada-U.S.	19,529	*7,540*	244	*802*
Ladoga (Ladožskoje ozero)	U.S.S.R.	18,400	*7,104*	225	*738*
Balkhash (ozero Balhaš)	U.S.S.R.	18,200	*7,027*	26	*85*
Chad (Lac Tchad)	Africa	16,300	*6,293*	4	*13*
Onega (Onežskoje ozero)	U.S.S.R.	9,610	*3,710*	120	*393*
Eyre	Australia	9,583	*3,700*	1	*4*
Rudolf	Ethiopia-Kenya	8,600	*3,320*	61	*200*
Nicaragua	Nicaragua	8,430	*3,255*	43	*141*
Titicaca	Bolivia-Peru	8,300	*3,205*	272	*892*
Athabasca	Canada	7,936	*3,064*	124	*407*
Gairdner	Australia	7,700	*2,973*	☆	☆
Reindeer	Canada	6,651	*2,568*	219	*720*
Issyk-Kul	U.S.S.R.	6,280	*2,425*	702	*2,303*
Urmia (Daryācheh-ye Orūmīyeh)	Iran	5,800	*2,239*	15	*49*
Torrens	Australia	5,776	*2,230*	☆	☆
Vänern	Sweden	5,585	*2,156*	100	*328*
Winnipegosis	Canada	5,374	*2,075*	12	*38*

☆ Intermittently dry lake

Drainage Basins

Name	Continent	Area km²	Area sq mi
Amazon-Ucayali	South America	7,050,000	*2,722,000*
Congo (Zaire)	Africa	3,690,000	*1,425,000*
Mississippi-Missouri	North America	3,221,000	*1,243,700*
Río de la Plata-Paraná	South America	3,140,000	*1,212,000*
Ob	Asia	2,975,000	*1,149,000*
Nile	Africa	2,867,000	*1,107,000*
Yenisey (Jenisej)	Asia	2,580,000	*996,000*
Lena	Asia	2,490,000	*961,000*
Niger	Africa	2,092,000	*808,000*
Amur	Asia	1,855,000	*716,000*
Yangtze (Chang Jiang)	Asia	1,807,000	*698,000*
Mackenzie	North America	1,760,000	*680,000*
Saint Lawrence-Great Lakes	North America	1,463,000	*565,000*
Volga	Europe	1,360,000	*525,000*

Historical Population of the World

AREA	1650	1750	1800	1850	1900	1914	1920	1939	1950	1982*
Europe	*100,000,000*	*140,000,000*	*190,000,000*	265,000,000	400,000,000	470,000,000	453,000,000	526,000,000	530,000,000	666,400,00
Asia	*335,000,000*	*476,000,000*	*593,000,000*	*754,000,000*	*932,000,000*	*1,006,000,000*	*1,000,000,000*	*1,247,000,000*	*1,418,000,000*	2,724,900,00
Africa	*100,000,000*	*95,000,000*	*90,000,000*	*95,000,000*	*118,000,000*	*130,000,000*	*140,000,000*	170,000,000	199,000,000	490,300,00
North America	*5,000,000*	*5,000,000*	*13,000,000*	*39,000,000*	106,000,000	141,000,000	147,000,000	186,000,000	219,000,000	379,400,00
South America	*8,000,000*	*7,000,000*	*12,000,000*	*20,000,000*	38,000,000	55,000,000	61,000,000	90,000,000	111,000,000	247,800,00
Oceania, incl. Australia	*2,000,000*	*2,000,000*	*2,000,000*	*2,000,000*	6,000,000	8,000,000	9,000,000	11,000,000	13,000,000	23,200,00
Australia					4,000,000	5,000,000	6,000,000	7,000,000	8,000,000	14,910,00
World	*550,000,000*	*725,000,000*	*900,000,000*	*1,175,000,000*	*1,600,000,000*	*1,810,000,000*	*1,810,000,000*	*2,230,000,000*	*2,490,000,000*	*4,532,000,00*

* *Figures prior to 1982 are rounded to the nearest million.* *Figures in italics represent very rough estimates.*

Largest Countries: Population

	Country	Population 1/1/82
1.	China	995,000,000
2.	India	695,230,000
3.	U.S.S.R	268,740,000
4.	United States	231,160,000
5.	Indonesia	151,500,000
6.	Brazil	124,760,000
7.	Japan	118,650,000
8.	Pakistan	92,070,000
9.	Bangladesh	91,860,000
10.	Nigeria	80,765,000
11.	Mexico	70,515,000
12.	Germany, Fed. Rep.	61,680,000
13.	Italy	57,270,000
14.	United Kingdom	56,035,000
15.	Vietnam	55,455,000
16.	France	54,045,000
17.	Philippines	50,960,000
18.	Thailand	48,860,000
19.	Turkey	46,435,000
20.	Egypt	43,565,000
21.	Korea, South	40,755,000
22.	Iran	38,565,000
23.	Spain	37,865,000
24.	Poland	36,035,000
25.	Burma	35,710,000
26.	South Africa	30,495,000
27.	Ethiopia	30,370,000
28.	Zaire	29,060,000
29.	Argentina	28,420,000
30.	Colombia	28,185,000
31.	Canada	24,335,000
32.	Yugoslavia	22,635,000
33.	Romania	22,445,000
34.	Morocco	21,795,000
35.	Sudan	20,180,000
36.	Algeria	19,270,000
37.	Tanzania	19,115,000
38.	Korea, North	18,540,000
39.	Peru	18,510,000
40.	Taiwan	18,365,000
41.	Kenya	17,790,000
42.	German Dem. Rep.	16,750,000
43.	Sri Lanka	15,605,000
44.	Nepal	15,520,000
45.	Czechoslovakia	15,345,000

Largest Countries: Area

	Country	Area (km²)	(sq mi)
1.	U.S.S.R	22,274,900	8,600,383
2.	Canada	9,922,330	3,831,033
3.	China	9,560,939	3,691,500
4.	United States	9,528,318	3,678,896
5.	Brazil	8,511,965	3,286,487
6.	Australia	7,686,850	2,967,909
7.	India	3,203,975	1,237,061
8.	Argentina	2,766,889	1,068,301
9.	Sudan	2,505,813	967,500
10.	Algeria	2,381,741	919,595
11.	Zaire	2,345,409	905,567
12.	Greenland	2,175,600	840,004
13.	Saudi Arabia	2,149,690	830,000
14.	Mexico	1,972,547	761,604
15.	Indonesia	1,919,270	741,034
16.	Libya	1,759,540	679,362
17.	Iran	1,648,000	636,296
18.	Mongolia	1,565,000	604,250
19.	Peru	1,285,216	496,224
20.	Chad	1,284,000	495,755
21.	Niger	1,267,000	489,191
22.	Angola	1,246,700	481,353
23.	Mali	1,240,000	478,766
24.	Ethiopia	1,223,600	472,434
25.	South Africa	1,221,042	471,447
26.	Colombia	1,138,914	439,737
27.	Bolivia	1,098,581	424,164
28.	Mauritania	1,030,700	397,955
29.	Egypt	1,001,400	386,643
30.	Tanzania	945,087	364,900
31.	Nigeria	923,768	356,669
32.	Venezuela	912,050	352,144
33.	Pakistan	828,453	319,867
34.	Mozambique	783,030	302,329
35.	Turkey	779,452	300,948
36.	Chile	756,626	292,135
37.	Zambia	752,614	290,586
38.	Burma	676,577	261,228
39.	Afghanistan	647,497	250,000
40.	Somalia	637,657	246,200
41.	Central African Republic	622,984	240,535
42.	Botswana	600,372	231,805
43.	Madagascar	587,041	226,658
44.	Kenya	582,646	224,961
45.	France	547,026	211,208

Smallest Countries: Population

	Country	Population 1/1/82
1.	Vatican City	1,000
2.	Niue	3,000
3.	Anguilla	7,900
	Nauru	7,900
4.	Tuvalu	8,100
5.	Cook Islands	18,000
6.	San Marino	24,000
7.	Liechtenstein	27,000
	Monaco	27,000
8.	Andorra	40,000
9.	St. Kitts-Nevis	41,000
10.	Faeroe Islands	45,000
11.	Greenland	51,000
12.	Kiribati	59,000
13.	Isle of Man	66,000
14.	Seychelles	68,000
15.	Dominica	75,000
16.	Antigua	77,000
17.	Sao Tome and Principe	89,000
18.	Tonga	101,000
19.	Grenada	112,000
20.	Vanuatu	120,000
21.	Djibouti	124,000
	Saint Lucia	124,000
22.	St. Vincent	128,000
23.	Maldives	155,000
	Western Samoa	155,000
24.	Belize	160,000
25.	Iceland	230,000
26.	Bahamas	235,000
	Qatar	235,000
	Solomon Is.	235,000
27.	Brunei	245,000
28.	Barbados	260,000
	Netherlands Antilles	260,000
29.	Cape Verde	330,000
30.	Luxembourg	355,000
31.	Malta	360,000
32.	Suriname	365,000
33.	Equatorial Guinea	375,000
34.	Comoros	380,000
35.	Bahrain	400,000
36.	Gabon	560,000
37.	Swaziland	580,000
38.	Gambia	625,000

Smallest Countries: Area

	Country	Area (km²)	(sq mi)
1.	Vatican City	0.4	0
2.	Monaco	1.5	0
3.	Nauru	21	8
4.	Tuvalu	26	10
5.	San Marino	61	24
6.	Anguilla	88	34
7.	Liechtenstein	160	62
8.	Cook Islands	236	91
9.	Niue	263	102
10.	St. Kitts-Nevis	269	104
11.	Maldives	298	115
12.	Malta	316	122
13.	Grenada	344	133
14.	St. Vincent	389	150
15.	Barbados	430	166
16.	Antigua	440	170
17.	Seychelles	443	171
18.	Andorra	453	175
19.	Singapore	581	224
20.	Isle of Man	588	227
21.	Saint Lucia	616	238
22.	Bahrain	662	256
23.	Tonga	699	270
24.	Dominica	752	290
25.	Kiribati	754	291
26.	Sao Tome and Principe	964	372
27.	Netherlands Antilles	993	383
28.	Faeroe Islands	1,399	540
29.	Mauritius	2,045	790
30.	Comoros	2,171	838
31.	Luxembourg	2,586	999
32.	Western Samoa	2,842	1,097
33.	Cape Verde	4,033	1,557
34.	Trinidad and Tobago	5,128	1,980
35.	Brunei	5,765	2,226
36.	Puerto Rico	8,897	3,435
37.	Cyprus	9,251	3,572
38.	Lebanon	10,400	4,015
39.	Jamaica	10,991	4,244
40.	Qatar	11,000	4,247
41.	Gambia	11,295	4,361
42.	Bahamas	13,939	5,382
43.	Vanuatu	14,800	5,714
44.	Swaziland	17,364	6,704
45.	Kuwait	17,818	6,880

Highest Population Densities

	Country	Density per (km²)	(sq mi)
1.	Monaco	18,000	45,000
2.	Singapore	4,923	12,768
3.	Vatican City	2,500	5,000
4.	Malta	1,139	2,951
5.	Bangladesh	638	1,652
6.	Barbados	605	1,566
7.	Bahrain	604	1,563
8.	Maldives	520	1,348
9.	Taiwan	510	1,322
10.	Mauritius	482	1,247
11.	Korea, South	414	1,072
12.	San Marino	393	1,000
13.	Nauru	376	963
14.	Puerto Rico	368	952
15.	Netherlands	347	900
16.	St. Vincent	329	853
17.	Grenada	326	842
18.	Belgium	324	839
19.	Japan	319	825
20.	Lebanon	315	816
21.	Tuvalu	312	810
22.	Netherlands Antilles	262	679
23.	El Salvador	250	649
24.	Germany, Fed. Rep. of	248	642
25.	Sri Lanka	240	622
26.	United Kingdom	230	595
27.	Trinidad and Tobago	227	588
28.	India	217	562
29.	Jamaica	203	527
30.	Saint Lucia	201	521

Lowest Population Densities

	Country	Density per (km²)	(sq mi)
1.	Greenland	0.02	0.06
2.	Mongolia	1.1	2.9
3.	Botswana	1.5	3.8
4.	Mauritania	1.7	4.3
5.	Libya	1.8	4.6
6.	Australia	1.9	5.0
7.	Gabon	2.1	5.4
8.	Iceland	2.2	5.8
	Suriname	2.2	5.8
9.	Canada	2.5	6.4
10.	Chad	3.6	9.4
11.	Central African Republic	3.7	9.6
12.	Saudi Arabia	4.1	11
13.	Guyana	4.3	11
14.	Niger	4.4	11
	Oman	4.4	11
15.	Congo	4.7	12
16.	Bolivia	5.3	14
17.	Djibouti	5.4	14
18.	Mali	5.8	15
19.	Angola	5.9	15
20.	Yemen, P.D.R. of	6.2	16
21.	Papua New Guinea	6.7	17
22.	Belize	7.0	18
23.	Zambia	7.8	20
24.	Paraguay	7.9	20
	Solomon Islands	7.9	20
25.	Somalia	8.0	21
26.	Algeria	8.1	21
	Vanuatu	8.1	21

Air Distances Between World Cities

GIVEN IN STATUTE MILES

	Apia, Western Samoa	Azores Islands	Berlin, Germany	Bombay, India	Buenos Aires, Argentina	Calcutta, India	Cape Town, South Africa	Cape Verde Islands	Chicago, U. S. A.	Darwin, Australia	Denver, U. S. A.	Gibraltar	Hong Kong
Apia		9644	9743	8154	6931	7183	9064	10246	6557	3843	5653	10676	5591
Azores Islands	9644		2185	5967	5417	6549	5854	1499	3093	10209	3991	1249	7572
Berlin	9743	2185		3910	7376	4376	5977	3194	4402	8036	5077	1453	5500
Bombay	8154	5967	3910		9273	1041	5134	6297	8054	4503	8383	4814	2673
Buenos Aires	6931	5417	7376	9273		10242	4270	4208	5596	9127	5928	5963	11463
Calcutta	7183	6549	4376	1041	10242		6026	7148	7981	3744	8050	5521	1534
Cape Town	9064	5854	5977	5134	4270	6026		4509	8449	6947	9327	5076	7372
Cape Verde Islands	10246	1499	3194	6297	4208	7148	4509		4066	10664	4975	1762	8539
Chicago	6557	3093	4402	8054	5596	7981	8449	4066		9346	920	4258	7790
Darwin	3843	10209	8036	4503	9127	3744	6947	10664	9346		8557	9265	2642
Denver	5653	3991	5077	8383	5928	8050	9327	4975	920	8557		5122	7465
Gibraltar	10676	1249	1453	4814	5963	5521	5076	1762	4258	9265	5122		6828
Hong Kong	5591	7572	5500	2673	11463	1534	7372	8539	7790	2642	7465	6828	
Honolulu	2604	7180	7305	8020	7558	7037	11532	8311	4244	5355	3338	8075	5537
Istanbul	10175	2975	1078	2991	7568	3646	5219	3507	5476	7390	6154	1874	4980
Juneau	5415	4526	4560	6866	7759	6326	10330	5911	2305	7105	1831	5273	5634
London	9789	1527	574	4462	6918	4954	6005	2731	3950	8598	4688	1094	5981
Los Angeles	4828	4794	5782	8701	6118	8148	9969	5772	1745	7835	831	5936	7240
Manila	4993	8250	6128	3148	11042	2189	7525	9221	8128	1979	7661	7483	693
Melbourne	3113	12101	9919	6097	7234	5547	6412	10856	9668	1964	8759	10798	4607
Mexico City	5449	4385	6037	9722	4633	9495	8511	4857	1673	9081	1434	5629	8776
Moscow	9116	3165	996	3131	8375	3447	6294	3982	4984	7046	5485	2413	4439
New Orleans	6085	3524	5116	8865	4916	8803	8316	4194	833	9545	1082	4757	8480
New York	7242	2422	3961	7794	5297	7921	7801	3355	713	9959	1631	3627	8051
Nome	5438	4954	4342	5901	8848	5271	10107	6438	3314	6235	2925	5398	4547
Oslo	9247	2234	515	4130	7613	4459	6494	3444	4040	8022	4653	1791	5337
Panamá	6514	3778	5849	9742	3381	10114	7014	3734	2325	10352	2636	4926	10084
Paris	9990	1659	542	4359	6877	4889	5841	2666	4133	8575	4885	964	5956
Peking (Peiping)	5903	6565	4567	2964	11974	2024	8045	7763	6592	3728	6348	6009	1226
Port Said	10485	3391	1747	2659	7362	3506	4590	3672	6103	7159	6819	2179	4975
Quebec	7406	2240	3583	7371	5680	7481	7857	3355	878	9724	1752	3383	8650
Reykjavík	8678	1777	1479	5191	7099	5409	7111	3248	2954	8631	3596	2047	6031
Rio de Janeiro	8120	4428	6144	8257	1218	9376	3769	3040	5296	9960	5871	4775	10995
Rome	10475	2125	734	3843	6929	4496	5249	2772	4808	8190	5561	1034	5768
San Francisco	4786	4872	5657	8392	6474	7809	10241	5921	1858	7637	949	5936	6894
Seattle	5222	4501	5041	7741	6913	7224	10199	5714	1737	7619	1021	5462	6471
Shanghai	5399	7229	5215	3133	12197	2112	8059	8443	7053	3142	6698	6646	772
Singapore	5850	8326	6166	2429	9864	1791	6016	8700	9365	2075	9063	7231	1652
Tokyo	4656	7247	5538	4188	11400	3186	9071	8589	6303	3367	5795	6988	1796
Valparaíso	6267	5678	7795	10037	761	10993	4998	4649	5268	8961	5452	6408	11607
Washington, D. C.	7066	2667	4167	7988	5216	8088	7894	3486	597	9923	1494	3822	8148
Wellington	2062	11269	11265	7677	6260	7042	7019	10363	8349	3310	7516	12060	5853
Wien (Vienna)	10010	2291	328	3718	7368	4259	5671	3147	4694	7974	5383	1386	5429
Winnipeg	6283	3389	4286	7644	6297	7424	9054	4556	714	8684	798	4435	7096
Zanzibar	9892	5323	4309	2855	6421	3859	2346	4635	8358	6409	9221	4103	5414

Continued on following page

Honolulu, Hawaii, U. S. A.	Istanbul (Constantinople), Turkey	Juneau, Alaska, U. S. A.	London, United Kingdom	Los Angeles, U.S.A.	Manila, Philippines	Melbourne, Australia	Mexico City, Mexico	Moscow, Soviet Union	New Orleans, U. S. A.	New York, U. S. A.	Nome, Alaska, U. S. A.	Oslo, Norway	Panamá, Panama	Paris, France	Peking (Peiping), China	Port Said, Egypt
2604	10175	5415	9789	4828	4993	3113	5449	9116	6085	7242	5438	9247	6514	9990	5903	104
7180	2975	4526	1527	4794	8250	12101	4385	3165	3524	2422	4954	2234	3778	1659	6565	33
7305	1078	4560	574	5782	6128	9919	6037	996	5116	3961	4342	515	5849	542	4567	17
8020	2991	6866	4462	8701	3148	6097	9722	3131	8865	7794	5901	4130	9742	4359	2964	26
7558	7568	7759	6918	6118	11042	7234	4633	8375	4916	5297	8848	7613	3381	6877	11974	73
7037	3646	6326	4954	8148	2189	5547	9495	3447	8803	7921	5271	4459	10114	4889	2024	35
11532	5219	10330	6005	9969	7525	6412	8511	6294	8316	7801	10107	6494	7014	5841	8045	45
8311	3507	5911	2731	5772	9221	10856	4857	3982	4194	3355	6438	3444	3734	2666	7763	36
4244	5476	2305	3950	1745	8128	9668	1673	4984	833	713	3314	4040	2325	4133	6592	61
5355	7390	7105	8598	7835	1979	1964	9081	7046	9545	9959	6235	8022	10352	8575	3728	71
3338	6154	1831	4688	831	7661	8759	1434	5485	1082	1631	2925	4653	2636	4885	6348	68
8075	1874	5273	1094	5936	7483	10798	5629	2413	4757	3627	5398	1791	4926	964	6009	21
5537	4980	5634	5981	7240	693	4607	8776	4439	8480	8051	4547	5337	10084	5956	1226	49
	8104	2815	7226	2557	5296	5513	3781	7033	4207	4959	3004	6784	5245	7434	5067	87
8104		5498	1551	6843	5659	9088	7102	1088	6171	5009	5101	1518	6750	1401	4379	6
2815	5498		4418	1842	5869	8035	3219	4534	2905	2854	1094	4045	4460	4628	4522	62
7226	1551	4418		5439	6667	10501	5541	1549	4627	3459	4381	714	5278	213	5054	21
2557	6843	1842	5439		7269	7931	1542	6068	1673	2451	2876	5325	3001	5601	6250	75
5296	5659	5869	6667	7269		3941	8829	5130	8724	8493	4817	6016	10283	6673	1770	56
5513	9088	8035	10501	7931	3941		8422	8963	9275	10355	7558	9926	9022	10396	5667	86
3781	7102	3219	5541	1542	8829	8422		6688	934	2085	4309	5706	1495	5706	7733	76
7033	1088	4534	1549	6068	5130	8963	6688		5756	4662	4036	1016	6711	1541	3597	17
4207	6171	2905	4627	1673	8724	9275	934	5756		1171	3937	4795	1603	4788	7314	67
4959	5009	2854	3459	2451	8493	10355	2085	4662	1171		3769	3672	2231	3622	6823	55
3004	5101	1094	4381	2876	4817	7558	4309	4036	3937	3769		3836	5541	4574	3428	57
6784	1518	4045	714	5325	6016	9926	5706	1016	4795	3672	3836		5691	832	4360	22
5245	6750	4460	5278	3001	10283	9022	1495	6711	1603	2231	5541	5691		5382	8906	71
7434	1401	4628	213	5601	6673	10396	5706	1541	4788	3622	4574	832	5382		5101	19
5067	4379	4522	5054	6250	1770	5667	7733	3597	7314	6823	3428	4360	8906	5101		45
8738	693	6215	2154	7528	5619	8658	7671	1710	6756	5590	5745	2211	7146	1975	4584	
5000	4644	2660	3101	2579	8124	10497	2454	4242	1534	439	3489	3263	2659	3235	6423	52
6084	2558	3268	1171	4306	6651	10544	4622	2056	3711	2576	3366	1083	4706	1380	4903	32
8190	6395	7598	5772	6296	11254	8186	4770	7179	4796	4820	8586	6482	3294	5703	10768	62
8022	854	5247	887	6326	6457	9934	6353	1474	5439	4273	5082	1243	5903	682	5047	13
2392	6700	1525	5355	347	6963	7854	1885	5868	1926	2571	2547	5181	3322	5441	5902	73
2678	6063	899	4782	959	6641	8186	2337	5199	2101	2408	1976	4591	3651	4993	5396	67
4934	4959	4869	5710	6477	1152	5005	8039	4235	7720	7357	3784	5020	9324	5752	662	51
6710	5373	7235	6744	8767	1479	3761	10307	5238	10082	9630	6148	6246	11687	6671	2774	56
3850	5556	4011	5938	5470	1863	5089	7035	4650	6858	6735	2983	5221	8423	6033	1307	58
6793	8172	7271	7263	5527	10930	6998	4053	8792	4514	5094	8360	7914	2943	7251	11774	86
4829	5216	2834	3665	2300	8560	10173	1878	4883	966	205	3792	3870	2080	3828	6922	57
4708	10663	7475	11682	6714	5162	1595	6899	10279	7794	8946	7383	10974	7433	11791	6698	10
7626	783	4895	772	6108	6120	9792	6306	1044	5385	4224	4657	850	6026	644	4639	1
3806	5361	1597	3918	1525	7414	9319	2097	4687	1418	1281	2599	3854	2998	4118	5907	6
10869	3312	8795	4604	10021	5763	6802	9484	4270	8754	7698	8209	4803	8245	4396	5803	2

	Reykjavík, Iceland	Rio de Janeiro, Brazil	Rome, Italy	San Francisco, U. S. A.	Seattle, U. S. A.	Shanghai, China	Singapore, Singapore	Tokyo, Japan	Valparaíso, Chile	Washington, D. C., U. S. A.	Wellington, New Zealand	Wien (Vienna), Austria	Winnipeg, Canada	Zanzibar, Tanzania	
406	8678	8120	10475	4786	5222	5399	5850	4656	6267	7066	2062	10010	6283	9892	Apia
240	1777	4428	2125	4872	4501	7229	8326	7247	5678	2667	11269	2291	3389	5323	Azores Is.
583	1479	6114	734	5657	5041	5215	6166	5538	7795	4167	11265	328	4286	4309	Berlin
571	5191	8257	3843	8392	7741	3133	2429	4188	10037	7988	7677	3718	7644	2855	Bombay
580	7099	1218	6929	6474	6913	12197	9864	11400	761	5216	6260	7368	6297	6421	Buenos Aires
481	5409	9376	4496	7809	7224	2112	1791	3186	10993	8088	7042	4259	7424	3859	Calcutta
357	7111	3769	5249	10241	10199	8059	6016	9071	4998	7894	7019	5671	9054	2346	Cape Town
555	3248	3040	2772	5921	5714	8443	8700	8589	4649	3486	10363	3147	4556	4635	C. Verde Is.
578	2954	5296	4808	1858	1737	7053	9365	6303	5268	597	8349	4694	714	8358	Chicago
724	8631	9960	8190	7637	7619	3142	2075	3367	8961	9923	3310	7974	8684	6409	Darwin
752	3596	5871	5561	949	1021	6698	9063	5795	5452	1494	7516	5383	798	9221	Denver
383	2047	4775	1034	5936	5462	6646	7231	6988	6408	3822	12060	1386	4435	4103	Gibraltar
350	6031	10995	5768	6894	6471	772	1652	1796	11607	8148	5853	5429	7096	5414	Hong Kong
900	6084	8190	8022	2392	2678	4934	6710	3850	6793	4829	4708	7626	3806	10869	Honolulu
544	2558	6395	854	6700	6063	4959	5373	5556	8172	5216	10663	783	5361	3312	Istanbul
560	3268	7598	5247	1525	899	4869	7235	4011	7271	2834	7475	4895	1597	8795	Juneau
101	1171	5772	887	5355	4782	5710	6744	5938	7263	3665	11682	772	3918	4604	London
579	4306	6296	6326	347	959	6477	8767	5470	5527	2300	6714	6108	1525	10021	Los Angeles
124	6651	11254	6457	6963	6641	1152	1479	1863	10930	8560	5162	6120	7414	5763	Manila
497	10544	8186	9934	7854	8186	5005	3761	5089	6998	10173	1595	9792	9319	6802	Melbourne
454	4622	4770	6353	1885	2337	8039	10307	7035	4053	1878	6899	6306	2097	9484	Mexico City
242	2056	7179	1474	5868	5199	4235	5238	4650	8792	4883	10279	1044	4687	4270	Moscow
534	3711	4796	5439	1926	2101	7720	10082	6858	4514	966	7794	5385	1418	8754	New Orleans
439	2576	4820	4273	2571	2408	7357	9630	6735	5094	205	8946	4224	1281	7698	New York
489	3366	8586	5082	2547	1976	3784	6148	2983	8360	3792	7383	4657	2599	8209	Nome
263	1083	6482	1243	5181	4591	5020	6246	5221	7914	3870	10974	859	3854	4803	Oslo
559	4706	3294	5903	3322	3651	9324	11687	8423	2943	2080	7433	6026	2998	8245	Panamá
235	1380	5703	682	5441	4993	5752	6671	6033	7251	3828	11791	644	4118	4396	Paris
423	4903	10768	5047	5902	5396	662	2774	1307	11774	6922	6698	4639	5907	5803	Peking(Peiping)
250	3227	6244	1317	7394	6759	5132	5088	5842	8088	5796	10249	1429	6032	2729	Port Said
	2189	5125	3943	2642	2353	6981	9097	6417	5504	610	9228	3858	1199	7443	Quebec
189		6118	2044	4199	3614	5559	7160	5472	7225	2800	10724	1805	2804	5757	Reykjavík
125	6118		5684	6619	6891	11340	9774	11535	1855	4797	7349	6136	6010	5589	Rio de Jan.
943	2044	5684		6240	5659	5677	6232	6124	7420	4435	11524	463	4803	3712	Rome
542	4199	6619	6240		678	6132	8479	5131	5876	2442	6739	5988	1504	9958	San Francisco
353	3614	6891	5659	678		5703	8057	4777	6230	2329	7242	5376	1150	9359	Seattle
981	5559	11340	5677	6132	5703		2377	1094	11650	7442	6054	5270	6350	5971	Shanghai
997	7160	9774	6232	8479	8057	2377		3304	10226	9834	5292	6036	8685	4480	Singapore
417	5472	11535	6124	5131	4777	1094	3304		10635	6769	5760	5679	5575	7040	Tokyo
504	7225	1855	7420	5876	6230	11650	10226	10635		4977	5785	7783	5931	7184	Valparaíso
310	2800	4797	4435	2442	2329	7442	9834	6769	4977		8745	4429	1243	7884	Wash., D.C.
228	10724	7349	11524	6739	7242	6054	5292	5760	5785	8745		11278	8230	8122	Wellington
358	1805	6136	463	5988	5376	5270	6036	5679	7783	4429	11278		4604	3983	Wien
199	2804	6010	4803	1504	1150	6350	8685	5575	5931	1243	8230	4604		8416	Winnipeg
443	5757	5589	3712	9958	9359	5971	4480	7040	7184	7884	8122	3983	8416		Zanzibar

Facts About the United States

GEOGRAPHICAL FACTS

ELEVATION

The highest elevation in the United States is Mount McKinley, Alaska, 20,320 feet.

The lowest elevation in the United States is in Death Valley, California, 282 feet below sea level.

The average elevation of the United States is 2,500 feet.

EXTREMITIES

Direction	Location	Latitude	Longitude
North	Point Barrow, Alaska	71°23′N.	156°29′W.
South	Ka Lae (point) Hawaii	18°56′N.	155°41′W.
East	West Quoddy Head, Maine	44°49′N.	66°57′W.
West	Cape Wrangell, Alaska	52°55′N.	172°27′E.

The two places in the United States separated by the greatest distance are Kure Island, Hawaii, and Mangrove Point, Florida. These points are 5,848 miles apart.

LENGTH OF BOUNDARIES

The total length of the Canadian boundary of the United States is 5,525 miles.

The total length of the Mexican boundary of the United States is 1,933 miles.

The total length of the Atlantic coastline of the United States is 2,069 miles.

The total length of the Pacific and Arctic coastline of the United States is 8,683 miles.

The total length of the Gulf of Mexico coastline of the United States is 1,631 miles.

The total length of all coastlines and land boundaries of the United States is 19,841 miles.

The total length of the tidal shoreline and land boundaries of the United States is 96,091 miles.

GEOGRAPHIC CENTERS

The geographic center of the United States (including Alaska and Hawaii) is in Butte County, South Dakota at 44°58′N., 103°46′W.

The geographic center of North America is in North Dakota, a few miles west of Devils Lake, at 48°10′N., 100°10′W.

EXTREMES OF TEMPERATURE

The highest temperature ever recorded in the United States was 134°F., at Greenland Ranch, Death Valley, California, on July 10, 1913.

The lowest temperature ever recorded in the United States was —76°F., at Tanana, Alaska, in January, 1886.

PRECIPITATION

The average annual precipitation for the United States is approximately 29 inches.

Hawaii is the wettest state, with an average annual rainfall of 82.48 inches. Nevada, with an average annual rainfall of 8.81 inches, is the driest state.

The greatest local average annual rainfall in the United States is at Mt. Waialeale, Kauai, Hawaii, 460 inches.

Greatest 24-hour rainfall in the United States, 23.22 inches at New Smyrna, Florida, October 10–11, 1924.

Extreme minimum rainfall records in the United States include a total fall of only 3.93 inches at Bagdad, California, for a period of 5 years, 1909–13, and an annual average of 1.78 inches at Death Valley, California.

Heavy snowfall records include 76 inches at Silver Lake, Colorado, in 1 day; 42 inches at Angola, New York, in 2 days; 87 inches at Giant Forest, California, in 3 days; and 108 inches at Tahoe, California, in 4 days.

Greatest seasonal snowfall, 1,000.3 inches, more than 83 feet, at Paradise Ranger Station, Washington, during the winter of 1955–56.

HISTORICAL FACTS

TERRITORIAL ACQUISITIONS

Accession	Date	Area (sq. mi.)	Cost in Dollars
Original territory of the Thirteen States	1790	888,685	....
Purchase of Louisiana Territory, from France	1803	827,192	$11,250,000.00
By treaty with Spain: Florida	1819	58,560	$ 5,000,000.00
Other areas	1819	13,443	
Annexation of Texas	1845	390,144	....
Oregon Territory, by treaty with Great Britain	1846	285,580	....
Mexican Cession	1848	529,017	$15,000,000.00
Gadsden Purchase, from Mexico	1853	29,640	$10,000,000.00
Purchase of Alaska, from Russia	1867	586,412	7,200,000.00
Annexation of Hawaiian Islands	1898	6,450	....
Puerto Rico, by treaty with Spain	1899	3,435	....
Guam, by treaty with Spain	1899	212	....
American Samoa, by treaty with Great Britain and Germany	1900	76	....
Virgin Islands, by purchase from Denmark	1917	133	$25,000,000.00
Total		3,618,979	$73,450,000.00

Note: The Philippines, ceded by Spain in 1898 for $20,000,000.00, were a territorial possession of the United States from 1898 to 1946. On July 4, 1946 they became the independent republic of the Philippines.

Note. The Canal Zone, ceded by Panama in 1903 for $10,000,000.00, was a territory of the United States from 1903 to 1979. As a result of treaties signed in 1977, sovereignty over the Canal Zone reverted to Panama in 1979.

WESTWARD MOVEMENT OF CENTER OF POPULATION

Year	U.S. Population Total at Census	Approximate Location
1790	3,929,214	23 miles east of Baltimore, Md.
1800	5,308,483	18 miles west of Baltimore, Md.
1810	7,239,881	40 miles northwest of Washington, D.C.
1820	9,638,453	16 miles east of Moorefield, W. Va.
1830	12,866,020	19 miles southwest of Moorefield, W. Va.
1840	17,069,453	16 miles south of Clarksburg, W. Va.
1850	23,191,876	23 miles southeast of Parkersburg, W. Va.
1860	31,443,321	20 miles southeast of Chillicothe, Ohio
1870	39,818,449	48 miles northeast of Cincinnati, Ohio
1880	50,155,783	8 miles southwest of Cincinnati, Ohio
1890	62,947,714	20 miles east of Columbus, Ind.
1900	75,994,575	6 miles southeast of Columbus, Ind.
1910	91,972,266	Bloomington, Ind.
1920	105,710,620	8 miles southeast of Spencer, Ind.
1930	122,775,046	3 miles northeast of Linton, Ind.
1940	131,669,275	2 miles southeast of Carlisle, Ind.
1950	150,697,361	8 miles northwest of Olney, Ill.
1960	179,323,175	6 miles northwest of Centralia, Ill.
1970	204,816,296	5 miles southeast of Mascoutah, Ill.

State	Land Area (square miles)	Water Area* (square miles)	Total Area (square miles)	Area Rank (land area)	1980 Resident Population	1980 Population (per square mile†)	1970 Population	1960 Population	1950 Population	Population Rank 1980	Population Rank 1970	Population Rank 1960
Alabama	50,767	938	51,705	28	3,893,888	77	3,444,165	3,266,740	3,061,743	22	21	19
Alaska	570,835	20,171	591,006	1	401,851	0.7	302,173	226,167	128,643	50	50	50
Arizona	113,509	491	114,000	6	2,718,425	24	1,772,482	1,302,161	749,587	29	33	35
Arkansas	52,079	1,108	53,187	27	2,286,435	44	1,923,295	1,786,272	1,909,511	33	32	31
California	156,299	2,407	158,706	3	23,667,565	151	19,953,134	15,717,204	10,586,223	1	1	2
Colorado	103,595	496	104,091	8	2,889,735	28	2,207,259	1,753,947	1,325,089	28	30	33
Connecticut	4,871	147	5,018	48	3,107,576	638	3,032,217	2,535,234	2,007,280	25	24	25
Delaware	1,932	112	2,044	49	594,317	308	548,104	446,292	318,085	47	46	46
District of Columbia	63	6	69	. .	638,432	10,134	756,510	763,956	802,178	. .	. .	. .
Florida	54,153	4,511	58,664	26	9,746,342	180	6,789,443	4,951,560	2,771,305	7	9	10
Georgia	58,056	854	58,910	21	5,463,105	94	4,589,575	3,943,116	3,444,578	13	15	16
Hawaii	6,425	46	6,471	47	964,691	150	769,913	632,772	499,794	39	40	43
Idaho	82,412	1,153	83,565	11	944,038	11	713,008	667,191	588,637	41	42	42
Illinois	55,645	2,226	57,871	23	11,426,596	205	11,113,976	10,081,158	8,712,176	5	5	4
Indiana	35,932	482	36,414	38	5,490,260	153	5,193,669	4,662,498	3,934,224	12	11	11
Iowa	55,965	311	56,276	24	2,913,808	52	2,825,041	2,757,537	2,621,073	27	25	24
Kansas	81,778	500	82,278	13	2,364,236	29	2,249,071	2,178,611	1,905,299	32	28	28
Kentucky	39,669	740	40,409	37	3,660,257	92	3,219,311	3,038,156	2,944,806	23	23	22
Louisiana	44,521	3,231	47,752	33	4,206,312	94	3,643,180	3,257,022	2,683,516	19	20	20
Maine	30,995	2,270	33,265	39	1,125,027	36	993,663	969,265	913,774	38	38	36
Maryland	9,837	623	10,460	42	4,216,975	429	3,922,399	3,100,689	2,343,001	18	18	21
Massachusetts	7,824	460	8,284	45	5,737,037	733	5,689,170	5,148,578	4,690,514	11	10	9
Michigan	56,954	40,148	97,102	22	9,262,078	163	8,875,083	7,823,194	6,371,766	8	7	7
Minnesota	79,548	7,066	86,614	14	4,075,970	51	3,805,069	3,413,864	2,982,483	21	19	18
Mississippi	47,233	457	47,690	31	2,520,638	53	2,216,912	2,178,141	2,178,914	31	29	29
Missouri	68,945	753	69,698	18	4,916,759	71	4,677,399	4,319,813	3,954,653	15	13	13
Montana	145,389	1,657	147,046	4	786,690	5.4	694,409	674,767	591,024	44	43	41
Nebraska	76,644	712	77,356	15	1,569,825	20	1,483,791	1,411,330	1,325,510	35	35	34
Nevada	109,894	667	110,561	7	800,493	7.3	488,738	285,278	160,083	43	47	49
New Hampshire	8,993	285	9,278	44	920,610	102	737,681	606,921	533,242	42	41	45
New Jersey	7,468	319	7,787	46	7,364,823	986	7,168,164	6,066,782	4,835,329	9	8	8
New Mexico	121,336	257	121,593	5	1,302,981	11	1,016,000	951,023	681,187	37	37	37
New York	47,377	5,358	52,735	30	17,558,072	371	18,241,266	16,782,304	14,830,192	2	2	1
North Carolina	48,843	3,826	52,669	29	5,881,813	120	5,082,059	4,556,155	4,061,929	10	12	12
North Dakota	69,300	1,403	70,703	17	652,717	9.4	617,761	632,446	619,636	46	45	44
Ohio	41,004	3,783	44,787	35	10,797,624	263	10,652,017	9,706,397	7,946,627	6	6	5
Oklahoma	68,655	1,301	69,956	19	3,025,290	44	2,559,253	2,328,284	2,233,351	26	27	27
Oregon	96,185	888	97,073	10	2,633,149	27	2,091,385	1,768,687	1,521,341	30	31	32
Pennsylvania	44,888	1,155	46,043	32	11,863,895	264	11,793,909	11,319,366	10,498,012	4	3	3
Rhode Island	1,055	157	1,212	50	947,154	898	949,723	859,488	791,896	40	39	39
South Carolina	30,204	909	31,113	40	3,121,833	103	2,590,516	2,382,594	2,117,027	24	26	26
South Dakota	75,952	1,164	77,116	16	690,768	9.1	666,257	680,514	652,740	45	44	40
Tennessee	41,155	989	42,144	34	4,591,120	112	3,924,164	3,567,089	3,291,718	17	17	17
Texas	262,018	4,790	266,808	2	14,229,288	54	11,196,730	9,579,677	7,711,194	3	4	6
Utah	82,073	2,827	84,900	12	1,461,037	18	1,059,273	890,627	688,862	36	36	38
Vermont	9,273	341	9,614	43	511,456	55	444,732	389,881	377,747	48	48	47
Virginia	39,704	1,063	40,767	36	5,346,818	135	4,648,494	3,966,949	3,318,680	14	14	14
Washington	66,511	1,628	68,139	20	4,132,180	62	3,409,169	2,853,214	2,378,963	20	22	23
West Virginia	24,119	112	24,231	41	1,950,279	81	1,744,237	1,860,421	2,005,552	34	34	30
Wisconsin	54,426	11,789	66,215	25	4,705,521	86	4,417,933	3,951,777	3,434,575	16	16	15
Wyoming	96,990	820	97,810	9	469,557	4.8	332,416	330,066	290,529	49	49	48
United States	3,539,297	139,907	3,679,204	. .	226,547,346	64	203,235,298	179,323,175	151,325,798	. .	. .	. .

*Includes the United States area of the Great Lakes.
†Land area.

Populations of United States Colonies and States, 1650–1980

STATES	1650	1700	1750	1770	1790	1800	1820	1840
Alabama	......	......	......	......	......	......	127,901	590,756
Alaska	......	......	......	......	......	......	......	......
Arizona	......	......	......	......	......	......	......	......
Arkansas	......	......	......	......	......	......	14,273	97,574
California	......	......	......	......	......	......	......	......
Colorado	......	......	......	......	......	......	......	......
Connecticut	4,139	25,970	111,280	183,881	237,946	251,002	275,248	309,978
Delaware	185	2,470	28,704	35,496	59,096	64,273	72,749	78,085
District of Columbia	......	......	......	......	......	8,144	23,336	33,745
Florida	......	......	......	......	......	......	......	54,477
Georgia	......	......	5,200	23,375	82,548	162,686	340,989	691,392
Hawaii	......	......	......	......	......	......	......	......
Idaho	......	......	......	......	......	......	......	......
Illinois	......	......	......	......	......	......	55,211	476,183
Indiana	......	......	......	......	......	5,641	147,178	685,866
Iowa	......	......	......	......	......	......	......	43,112
Kansas	......	......	......	......	......	......	......	......
Kentucky	......	......	......	15,700	73,677	220,955	564,317	779,828
Louisiana	......	......	......	......	......	......	153,407	352,411
Maine[4]	......	......	......	31,257	96,540	151,719	298,335	501,793
Maryland	4,504	29,604	141,073	202,599	319,728	341,548	407,350	470,019
Massachusetts[4]	16,603	55,941	188,000	235,308	378,787	422,845	523,287	737,699
Michigan	......	......	......	......	......	......	8,896	212,267
Minnesota	......	......	......	......	......	......	......	......
Mississippi	......	......	......	......	......	8,850	75,448	375,651
Missouri	......	......	......	......	......	......	66,586	383,702
Montana	......	......	......	......	......	......	......	......
Nebraska	......	......	......	......	......	......	......	......
Nevada	......	......	......	......	......	......	......	......
New Hampshire	1,305	4,958	27,505	62,396	141,885	183,858	244,161	284,574
New Jersey	......	14,010	71,393	117,431	184,139	211,149	277,575	373,306
New Mexico	......	......	......	......	......	......	......	......
New York	4,116	19,107	76,696	162,920	340,120	589,051	1,372,812	2,428,921
North Carolina	......	10,720	72,984	197,200	393,751	478,103	638,829	753,419
North Dakota[3]	......	......	......	......	......	......	......	......
Ohio	......	......	......	......	......	45,365	581,434	1,519,467
Oklahoma[5]	......	......	......	......	......	......	......	......
Oregon	......	......	......	......	......	......	......	......
Pennsylvania	......	17,950	119,666	240,057	434,373	602,365	1,049,458	1,724,033
Rhode Island	785	5,894	33,226	58,196	68,825	69,122	83,059	108,830
South Carolina	......	5,704	64,000	124,244	249,073	345,591	502,741	594,398
South Dakota[3]	......	......	......	......	......	......	......	......
Tennessee	......	......	......	1,000	35,691	105,602	422,823	829,210
Texas	......	......	......	......	......	......	......	......
Utah	......	......	......	......	......	......	......	......
Vermont	......	......	......	10,000	85,425	154,465	235,981	291,948
Virginia[6]	18,731	58,560	231,033	447,016	691,737	807,557	938,261	1,025,227
Washington	......	......	......	......	......	......	......	......
West Virginia[6]	......	......	......	......	55,873	78,592	136,808	224,537
Wisconsin	......	......	......	......	......	......	......	30,945
Wyoming	......	......	......	......	......	......	......	......
Total[1]	50,368	250,888	1,170,760	2,148,076	3,929,214	5,308,483	9,638,453	17,069,453[2]

[1] All figures prior to 1890 exclude uncivilized Indians. Figures for 1650 through 1770 include only the British colonie that later became the United States. No areas are included prior to their annexation to the United States. How ever, many of the figures refer to territories prior to their admission as States. U.S. total includes Alaska from 1880 through 1970 and Hawaii from 1900 through 1970.

[2] U.S. total for 1840 includes 6,100 persons on public ships in service of the United States, not credited to any State

[3] South Dakota figure for 1860 represents entire Dakota Territory. North and South Dakota figures for 1880 ar for the parts of Dakota Territory which later constituted the respective States.

1860	1880	1900	1920	1940	1950	1960	1970	1980
964,201	1,262,505	1,828,697	2,348,174	2,832,961	3,061,743	3,266,740	3,444,165	3,893,888
......	33,426	63,592	55,036	72,524	128,643	226,167	302,173	401,851
......	40,440	122,931	334,162	499,261	749,587	1,302,161	1,772,482	2,718,425
435,450	802,525	1,311,564	1,752,204	1,949,387	1,909,511	1,786,272	1,923,295	2,286,435
379,994	864,694	1,485,053	3,426,861	6,907,387	10,586,223	15,717,204	19,953,134	23,667,565
34,277	194,327	539,700	939,629	1,123,296	1,325,089	1,753,947	2,207,259	2,889,735
460,147	622,700	908,420	1,380,631	1,709,242	2,007,280	2,535,234	3,032,217	3,107,576
112,216	146,608	184,735	223,003	266,505	318,085	446,292	548,104	594,317
75,080	177,624	278,718	437,571	663,091	802,178	763,956	756,510	638,432
140,424	269,493	528,542	968,470	1,897,414	2,771,305	4,951,560	6,789,443	9,746,342
057,286	1,542,180	2,216,331	2,895,832	3,123,723	3,444,578	3,943,116	4,589,575	5,463,105
......	......	154,001	255,881	422,770	499,794	632,772	769,913	964,691
......	32,610	161,772	431,866	524,873	588,637	667,191	713,008	944,038
711,951	3,077,871	4,821,550	6,485,280	7,897,241	8,712,176	10,081,158	11,113,976	11,426,596
350,428	1,978,301	2,516,462	2,930,390	3,427,796	3,934,224	4,662,498	5,193,669	5,490,260
674,913	1,624,615	2,231,853	2,404,021	2,538,268	2,621,073	2,757,537	2,825,041	2,913,808
107,206	996,096	1,470,495	1,769,257	1,801,028	1,905,299	2,178,611	2,249,071	2,364,236
155,684	1,648,690	2,147,174	2,416,630	2,845,627	2,944,806	3,038,156	3,219,311	3,660,257
708,002	939,946	1,381,625	1,798,509	2,363,880	2,683,516	3,257,022	3,643,180	4,206,312
628,279	648,936	694,466	768,014	847,226	913,774	969,265	993,663	1,125,027
687,049	934,943	1,188,044	1,449,661	1,821,244	2,343,001	3,100,689	3,922,399	4,216,975
231,066	1,783,085	2,805,346	3,852,356	4,316,721	4,690,514	5,148,578	5,689,170	5,737,037
749,113	1,636,937	2,420,982	3,668,412	5,256,106	6,371,766	7,823,194	8,875,083	9,262,078
172,023	780,773	1,751,394	2,387,125	2,792,300	2,982,483	3,413,864	3,805,069	4,075,970
791,305	1,131,597	1,551,270	1,790,618	2,183,796	2,178,914	2,178,141	2,216,912	2,520,638
182,012	2,168,380	3,106,665	3,404,055	3,784,664	3,954,653	4,319,813	4,677,399	4,916,759
......	39,159	243,329	548,889	559,456	591,024	674,767	694,409	786,690
28,841	452,402	1,066,300	1,296,372	1,315,834	1,325,510	1,411,330	1,483,791	1,569,825
6,857	62,266	42,335	77,407	110,247	160,083	285,278	488,738	800,493
326,073	346,991	411,588	443,083	491,524	533,242	606,921	737,681	920,610
672,035	1,131,116	1,883,669	3,155,900	4,160,165	4,835,329	6,066,782	7,168,164	7,364,823
93,516	119,565	195,310	360,350	531,818	681,187	951,023	1,016,000	1,302,981
880,735	5,082,871	7,268,894	10,385,227	13,479,142	14,830,192	16,782,304	18,241,266	17,558,072
992,622	1,399,750	1,893,810	2,559,123	3,571,623	4,061,929	4,556,155	5,082,059	5,881,813
......	36,909	319,146	646,872	641,935	619,636	632,446	617,761	652,717
339,511	3,198,062	4,157,545	5,759,394	6,907,612	7,946,627	9,706,397	10,652,017	10,797,624
......	......	790,391	2,028,283	2,336,434	2,233,351	2,328,284	2,559,253	3,025,290
52,465	174,768	413,536	783,389	1,089,684	1,521,341	1,768,687	2,091,385	2,633,149
,906,215	4,282,891	6,302,115	8,720,017	9,900,180	10,498,012	11,319,366	11,793,909	11,863,895
174,620	276,531	428,556	604,397	713,346	791,896	859,488	949,723	947,154
703,708	995,577	1,340,316	1,683,724	1,899,804	2,117,027	2,382,594	2,590,516	3,121,833
4,837	98,268	401,570	636,547	642,961	652,740	680,514	666,257	690,768
,109,801	1,542,359	2,020,616	2,337,885	2,915,841	3,291,718	3,567,089	3,924,164	4,591,120
604,215	1,591,749	3,048,710	4,663,228	6,414,824	7,711,194	9,579,677	11,196,730	14,229,288
40,273	143,963	276,749	449,396	550,310	688,862	890,627	1,059,273	1,461,037
315,098	332,286	343,641	352,428	359,231	377,747	389,881	444,732	511,456
,219,630	1,512,565	1,854,184	2,309,187	2,677,773	3,318,680	3,966,949	4,648,494	5,346,818
11,594	75,116	518,103	1,356,621	1,736,191	2,378,963	2,853,214	3,409,169	4,132,180
376,688	618,457	958,800	1,463,701	1,901,974	2,005,552	1,860,421	1,744,237	1,950,279
775,881	1,315,497	2,069,042	2,632,067	3,137,587	3,434,575	3,951,777	4,417,933	4,705,521
......	20,789	92,531	194,402	250,742	290,529	330,066	332,416	469,557
,443,321	50,189,209	76,212,168	106,021,537	132,164,569	151,325,798	179,323,175	203,235,298	226,547,346

[4] Maine figures for 1770 through 1800 are for that area of Massachusetts which became the State of Maine in 1820. Massachusetts figures exclude Maine from 1770 through 1800, but include it from 1650 through 1750. Massachusetts figure for 1650 also includes population of Plymouth (1,566), a separate colony until 1691.

[5] Oklahoma figure for 1900 includes population of Indian Territory (392,060).

[6] West Virginia figures for 1790 through 1860 are for that area of Virginia which became West Virginia in 1863. These figures are excluded from the figures for Virginia from 1790 through 1860.

General Information About U.S. States

STATE	CAPITAL	ENTERED UNION AS STATE: LARGEST CITY	Date of Entry	Rank of Entry	Greatest N-S Measurement (miles)	Greatest E-W Measurement (miles)
Alabama	Montgomery	Birmingham	Dec. 14, 1819	22	330	200
Alaska	Juneau	Anchorage	Jan. 3, 1959	49	1,332	2,250
Arizona	Phoenix	Phoenix	Feb. 14, 1912	48	390	335
Arkansas	Little Rock	Little Rock	June 15, 1836	25	240	275
California	Sacramento	Los Angeles	Sept. 9, 1850	31	800	375
Colorado	Denver	Denver	Aug. 1, 1876	38	270	380
Connecticut*	Hartford	Hartford	Jan. 9, 1788	5	75	90
Delaware*	Dover	Wilmington	Dec. 7, 1787	1	95	35
District of Columbia	Washington	Washington	March 3, 1791	..	15	15
Florida	Tallahassee	Jacksonville	March 3, 1845	27	460	400
Georgia*	Atlanta	Atlanta	Jan. 2, 1788	4	315	250
Hawaii	Honolulu	Honolulu	Aug. 21, 1959	50	...	1,600
Idaho	Boise	Boise	July 3, 1890	43	480	305
Illinois	Springfield	Chicago	Dec. 3, 1818	21	380	205
Indiana	Indianapolis	Indianapolis	Dec. 11, 1816	19	265	160
Iowa	Des Moines	Des Moines	Dec. 28, 1846	29	205	310
Kansas	Topeka	Wichita	Jan. 29, 1861	34	205	410
Kentucky	Frankfort	Louisville	June 1, 1792	15	175	350
Louisiana	Baton Rouge	New Orleans	April 30, 1812	18	275	300
Maine	Augusta	Portland	March 15, 1820	23	310	210
Maryland*	Annapolis	Baltimore	April 28, 1788	7	120	200
Massachusetts*	Boston	Boston	Feb. 6, 1788	6	110	190
Michigan	Lansing	Detroit	Jan. 26, 1837	26	400	310
Minnesota	St. Paul	Minneapolis	May 11, 1858	32	400	350
Mississippi	Jackson	Jackson	Dec. 10, 1817	20	340	180
Missouri	Jefferson City	St. Louis	Aug. 10, 1821	24	280	300
Montana	Helena	Billings	Nov. 8, 1889	41	315	570
Nebraska	Lincoln	Omaha	March 1, 1867	37	210	415
Nevada	Carson City	Las Vegas	Oct. 31, 1864	36	485	315
New Hampshire*	Concord	Manchester	June 21, 1788	9	185	90
New Jersey*	Trenton	Newark	Dec. 18, 1787	3	166	70
New Mexico	Santa Fe	Albuquerque	Jan. 6, 1912	47	390	350
New York*	Albany	New York	July 26, 1788	11	310	330
North Carolina*	Raleigh	Charlotte	Nov. 21, 1789	12	200	520
North Dakota	Bismarck	Fargo	Nov. 2, 1889	39	210	360
Ohio	Columbus	Cleveland	March 1, 1803	17	230	205
Oklahoma	Oklahoma City	Oklahoma City	Nov. 16, 1907	46	210	460
Oregon	Salem	Portland	Feb. 14, 1859	33	290	375
Pennsylvania*	Harrisburg	Philadelphia	Dec. 12, 1787	2	180	310
Rhode Island*	Providence	Providence	May 29, 1790	13	50	35
South Carolina*	Columbia	Columbia	May 23, 1788	8	215	285
South Dakota	Pierre	Sioux Falls	Nov. 2, 1889	40	240	360
Tennessee	Nashville	Memphis	June 1, 1796	16	120	430
Texas	Austin	Houston	Dec. 29, 1845	28	710	760
Utah	Salt Lake City	Salt Lake City	Jan. 4, 1896	45	345	275
Vermont	Montpelier	Burlington	March 4, 1791	14	155	90
Virginia*	Richmond	Norfolk	June 25, 1788	10	205	425
Washington	Olympia	Seattle	Nov. 11, 1889	42	230	340
West Virginia	Charleston	Huntington	June 20, 1863	35	200	225
Wisconsin	Madison	Milwaukee	May 29, 1848	30	300	290
Wyoming	Cheyenne	Cheyenne	July 10, 1890	44	275	365
United States	Washington, D.C.	New York	....	..	...	...

*One of the Thirteen Original States.

HIGHEST POINT		STATE FLOWER	STATE BIRD	STATE NICKNAME
Location	Altitude (feet)			
Cheaha Mountain	2,407	Camellia	Yellowhammer	Yellowhammer
Mt. McKinley	20,320	Forget-me-not	Willow Ptarmigan	Last Frontier
Humphreys Peak	12,633	Saguaro Cactus	Cactus Wren	Grand Canyon
Magazine Mtn.	2,753	Apple Blossom	Mockingbird	Land of Opportunity
Mt. Whitney	14,494	Golden Poppy	California Valley Quail	Golden
Mt. Elbert	14,433	Rocky Mountain Columbine	Lark Bunting	Centennial
S. slope of Mt. Frissell	2,380	Mountain Laurel	Robin	Constitution
Ebright Road, New Castle Co.	442	Peach Blossom	Blue Hen Chicken	First
Tenleytown	410	American Beauty Rose	Wood Thrush	....
N. boundary, Walton Co.	345	Orange Blossom	Mockingbird	Sunshine
Brasstown Bald (mtn.)	4,784	Cherokee Rose	Brown Thrasher	Peach
Mauna Kea	13,796	Red Hibiscus	Nene (Hawaiian Goose)	Aloha
Borah Peak	12,662	Syringa	Mountain Bluebird	Gem
Charles Mound	1,235	Violet	Cardinal	Prairie
Near Spartanburg	1,257	Peony	Cardinal	Hoosier
N. W. corner Osceola Co.	1,670	Wild Rose	Eastern Goldfinch	Hawkeye
Mt. Sunflower	4,039	Sunflower	Western Meadowlark	Sunflower
Black Mountain	4,145	Goldenrod	Kentucky Cardinal	Bluegrass
Driskill Mountain	535	Magnolia	Pelican	Pelican
Mt. Katahdin	5,268	White Pine	Chickadee	Pine Tree
Backbone Mountain	3,360	Black-eyed Susan	Baltimore Oriole	Old Free
Mt. Greylock	3,491	Mayflower	Chickadee	Old Bay
Mt. Curwood	1,980	Apple Blossom	Robin	Wolverine
Eagle Mtn.	2,301	Showy Lady's-slipper	Loon	Gopher
Woodall Mountain	806	Magnolia	Mockingbird	Magnolia
Taum Sauk Mountain	1,772	Hawthorne	Bluebird	Show Me
Granite Peak	12,799	Bitterroot	Western Meadowlark	Big Sky
S.W. corner Kimball Co.	5,426	Goldenrod	Western Meadowlark	Cornhusker
Boundary Peak	13,143	Shrub Sagebrush	Mountain Bluebird	Silver
Mt. Washington	6,288	Purple Lilac	Purple Finch	Granite
High Point	1,803	Purple Violet	Eastern Goldfinch	Garden
Wheeler Peak	13,161	Yucca	Roadrunner	Land of Enchantment
Mt. Marcy	5,344	Rose	Bluebird	Empire
Mt. Mitchell	6,684	Dogwood	Cardinal	Tar Heel
White Butte	3,506	Wild Prairie Rose	Western Meadowlark	Flickertail
Campbell Hill	1,550	Scarlet Carnation	Cardinal	Buckeye
Black Mesa	4,973	Mistletoe	Scissor-tailed Flycatcher	Sooner
Mt. Hood	11,239	Oregon Grape	Western Meadowlark	Beaver
Mt. Davis	3,213	Mountain Laurel	Ruffed Grouse	Keystone
Jerimoth Hill	812	Violet	Rhode Island Red	Little Rhody
Sassafras Mountain	3,560	Carolina Jessamine	Carolina Wren	Palmetto
Harney Peak	7,242	Pasque	Ringnecked Pheasant	Coyote
Clingmans Dome	6,643	Iris	Mockingbird	Volunteer
Guadalupe Peak	8,751	Bluebonnet	Mockingbird	Lone Star
Kings Peak	13,528	Sego Lily	Seagull	Beehive
Mt. Mansfield	4,393	Red Clover	Hermit Thrush	Green Mountain
Mt. Rogers	5,729	Flowering Dogwood	Cardinal	Old Dominion
Mt. Rainier	14,410	Rhododendron	Willow Goldfinch	Evergreen
Spruce Knob	4,862	Rhododendron	Cardinal	Mountain
Timms Hill	1,952	Violet	Robin	Badger
Gannett Peak	13,804	Indian Paint Brush	Meadowlark	Equality
Mt. McKinley, Alaska	20,320	....	Bald Eagle	....

State	Governor	U.S. Senators	Principal Mineral Products
Alabama	Forrest H. James, Jr. (D) 1979–83	Jeremiah Denton (R) 1981–87 Howell Heflin (D) 1979–85	coal, cement, petroleum, stone
Alaska	Jay S. Hammond (R) 1981–85	Frank H. Murkowski (R) 1981–87 Theodore F. Stevens (R) 1979–85	petroleum, coal, natural gas, sand and gravel
Arizona	Bruce Babbitt (D) 1979–83	Dennis DeConcini (D) 1977–83 Barry Goldwater (R) 1981–87	copper, sand and gravel, molybdenum, cement
Arkansas	Frank White (R) 1981–83	Dale L. Bumpers (D) 1981–87 David H. Pryor (D) 1979–85	petroleum, stone, bauxite, cement
California	Edmund G. Brown, Jr. (D) 1979–83	Alan Cranston (D) 1981–87 S. I. Hayakawa (R) 1977–83	petroleum, natural gas, sand and gravel, cement
Colorado	Richard D. Lamm (D) 1979–83	William L. Armstrong (R) 1979–85 Gary W. Hart (D) 1981–87	petroleum, molybdenum, coal, sand and gravel
Connecticut	William A. O'Neill (D) 1981–83	Christopher J. Dodd (D) 1981–87 Lowell P. Weicker, Jr. (R) 1977–83	stone, sand and gravel, feldspar, lime
Delaware	Pierre S. du Pont IV (R) 1981–85	Joseph R. Biden, Jr. (D) 1979–85 William V. Roth, Jr. (R) 1977–83	sand and gravel, stone, clays, gemstones
Florida	Robert Graham (D) 1979–83	Lawton Mainor Chiles, Jr. (D) 1977–83 Paula Hawkins (R) 1981–87	phosphate rock, stone, cement, clays
Georgia	George D. Busbee (D) 1979–83	Mack Mattingly (R) 1981–87 Sam Nunn (D) 1979–85	clays, stone, cement, sand and gravel
Hawaii	George R. Ariyoshi (D) 1981–85	Daniel K. Inouye (D) 1981–87 Spark M. Matsunaga (D) 1977–83	cement, stone, sand and gravel, pumice
Idaho	John V. Evans (D) 1979–83	James A. McClure (R) 1979–85 Steven D. Symms (R) 1981–87	silver, phosphate rock, lead, zinc
Illinois	James R. Thompson (R) 1979–83	Alan Dixon (D) 1981–87 Charles H. Percy (R) 1979–85	coal, petroleum, stone, sand and gravel
Indiana	Robert D. Orr (R) 1981–85	Richard G. Lugar (R) 1977–83 Dan Quayle (R) 1981–87	coal, cement, stone, petroleum
Iowa	Robert D. Ray (R) 1979–83	Charles E. Grassley (R) 1981–87 Roger W. Jepsen (R) 1979–85	cement, stone, sand and gravel, gypsum
Kansas	John Carlin (D) 1979–83	Robert J. Dole (R) 1981–87 Nancy Landon Kassebaum (R) 1978–85	petroleum, natural gas, liquids, helium
Kentucky	John Y. Brown, Jr. (D) 1979–83	Wendell H. Ford (D) 1981–87 Walter Huddleston (D) 1979–85	coal, petroleum, stone, natural gas
Louisiana	David C. Treen (R) 1980–84	J. Bennett Johnston, Jr. (D) 1979–85 Russell B. Long (D) 1981–87	petroleum, natural gas, natural gas liquids
Maine	Joseph E. Brennan (D) 1979–83	William S. Cohen (R) 1979–85 George Mitchell (D) 1981–87	cement, sand and gravel, stone, peat
Maryland	Harry R. Hughes (D) 1979–83	Charles McC. Mathias, Jr. (R) 1981–87 Paul S. Sarbanes (D) 1977–83	stone, cement, sand and gravel, coal
Massachusetts	Edward J. King (D) 1979–83	Edward M. Kennedy (D) 1977–83 Paul E. Tsongas (D) 1979–85	sand and gravel, stone, lime, clays
Michigan	William G. Milliken (R) 1979–83	Carl Levin (D) 1979–85 Donald W. Riegle, Jr. (D) 1977–83	iron ore, sand and gravel, bromine, cement
Minnesota	Albert H. Quie (IR) 1979–83	Rudy Boschwitz (R) 1978–85 David Durenberger (R) 1978–83	iron ore, sand and gravel, stone, cement
Mississippi	William Winter (D) 1980–84	Thad Cochran (R) 1978–85 John C. Stennis (D) 1977–83	petroleum, natural gas, sand and gravel, clays

Principal Agricultural Products	Principal Forest and Fishery Products	Principal Manufactures
poultry, cattle, eggs, dairy products	yellow pine, oak, gum, hickory; shrimp, oysters	steel, cotton, textiles, paper products, agricultural chemicals
dairy products, potatoes, eggs, cattle	western hemlock, spruce; salmon, crabs, halibut	lumber, wood products, canned and frozen food
cattle, cotton, lettuce, dairy products	ponderosa pine, Douglas fir, true firs	machinery, food and beverage products
soybeans, poultry, rice, cotton	yellow pine, oak, gum, hickory	food, paper, and wood products; lumber; electrical equipment
cattle, dairy products, tomatoes, eggs	Douglas fir, true firs, ponderosa pine, redwood; tuna, salmon, crabs, sole	aircraft, other transportation, communication, electrical equipment, food, beverage, machinery
cattle, dairy products, wheat, sugar beets	spruce, lodge pole pine, ponderosa pine, true firs	food, beverage, machinery, aircraft, electrical equipment
dairy products, eggs, tobacco, cattle	oak, hemlock, hickory; lobsters, oysters	machinery, electrical equipment, fabricated and primary metals
poultry, corn, dairy products, soybeans	yellow pine, oak, sweetgum	chemicals, food and beverage products, apparel
oranges, cattle, dairy products, tomatoes	yellow pine, cypress, gum, oak; shrimp, lobsters	food, beverage, and paper products; chemicals; paper; ordnance
poultry, poultry products, peanuts, cattle	yellow pine, oak, gum, cypress; shrimp	textiles; food, paper products; transportation equipment
sugarcane, pineapple, cattle, dairy products	sandalwood, ohia, lehua; tuna	food, food products, printed products
cattle, potatoes, wheat, dairy products	Douglas fir, true firs, ponderosa, lodgepole pine	food, beverage, and wood products; lumber; chemicals
corn, hogs, cattle, soybeans	oak, hickory	food, beverage, fabricated metal, machinery, and electrical products
hogs, corn, cattle, soybeans	oak, hickory, beech, maple	primary metals, transportation equipment, machinery, steel
cattle, hogs, corn, soybeans	oak, hickory	food and beverage products, machinery, electrical equipment
cattle, wheat, hogs, sorghum	oak, cottonwood, aspen	transportation equipment, and food, petroleum products, chemicals
tobacco, cattle, dairy products, hogs	oak, hickory, yellow poplar, yellow pine	electrical equipment, food products, machinery, chemicals
rice, cattle, soybeans, sugarcane	yellow pine, oak, gum, hickory; shrimp, menhaden	industrial chemicals; food, petroleum, paper products; paper
potatoes, poultry, poultry products, dairy products	spruce, balsam fir, beech, birch, maple; lobsters, ocean perch, herring, clams	paper, footwear; food, beverage, and wood products; lumber
poultry, dairy products, cattle, tobacco	oak, yellow pine, yellow poplar; oysters, crabs	food products, steel, chemicals, transportation equipment
dairy products, eggs, cranberries, tobacco	oak, hemlock; haddock, flounders, scallops	electrical equipment, machinery, fabricated metal products
cattle, dairy products, hogs, beans	oak, beech, birch, maple; chubs, whitefish	motor vehicles, machinery, fabricated metal products
cattle, dairy products, hogs, soybeans	cottonwood, aspen, spruce, balsam fir	machinery, food and beverage products, electrical equipment
cotton, cattle, soybeans, poultry	yellow pine, oak, gum; shrimp, menhaden, oysters	apparel; lumber, wood, and food products; chemicals

State	Governor	U.S. Senators	Principal Mineral Products
Missouri	Christopher S. Bond (R) 1981–85	John C. Danforth (R) 1977–83 Thomas F. Eagleton (D) 1981–87	stone, cement, lead, iron ore
Montana	Ted Schwinden (D) 1981–85	John Melcher (D) 1977–83 Max Baucus (D) 1978–85	petroleum, copper, sand and gravel, phosphate rock
Nebraska	Charles Thone (R) 1979–83	J. James Exon (D) 1979–85 Edward Zorinsky (D) 1977–83	petroleum, cement, sand and gravel, stone
Nevada	Robert List (R) 1979–83	Howard W. Cannon (D) 1977–83 Paul D. Laxalt (R) 1981–87	copper, gold, sand and gravel, diatomite
New Hampshire	Hugh J. Gallen (D) 1981–83	Gordon J. Humphrey (R) 1979–85 Warren Rudman (R) 1981–87	sand and gravel, stone, clays, feldspar
New Jersey	Thomas H. Kean (R) 1982–86	Bill Bradley (D) 1979–85 Harrison A. Williams, Jr. (D) 1977–83	sand and gravel, stone, zinc, magnesium compounds
New Mexico	Bruce King (D) 1979-83	Pete V. Domenici (R) 1979–85 Harrison H. Schmitt (R) 1977–83	petroleum, natural gas, potassium salts, uranium
New York	Hugh L. Carey (D) 1979-83	Alfonse M. D'Amato (R) 1981–87 Daniel P. Moynihan (D-L) 1977–83	cement, sand and gravel, salt, stone
North Carolina	James B. Hunt, Jr. (D) 1981–85	John P. East (R) 1981–87 Jesse A. Helms (R) 1979–85	stone, sand and gravel, cement, phosphate rock
North Dakota	Allen I. Olsen (R) 1981–85	Mark Andrews (R) 1981–87 Quentin N. Burdick (D) 1977–83	petroleum, sand and gravel, coal, natural gas
Ohio	James A. Rhodes (R) 1979–83	John H. Glenn, Jr. (D) 1981–87 Howard Metzenbaum (D) 1977–83	coal, stone, sand and gravel, cement
Oklahoma	George Nigh (D) 1979–83	David L. Boren (D) 1979–85 Don Nickles (R) 1981–87	petroleum, natural gas, natural gas liquids
Oregon	Victor Atiyeh (R) 1979–83	Mark O. Hatfield (R) 1979–85 Robert W. Packwood (R) 1981–87	sand and gravel, stone, cement, nickel
Pennsylvania	Richard L. Thornburgh (R) 1979–83	H. John Heinz III (R) 1977–83 Arlen Specter (R) 1981–87	coal, cement, stone, sand and gravel
Rhode Island	J. Joseph Garrahy (D) 1981–83	John H. Chafee (R) 1977–83 Claiborne Pell (D) 1979–85	sand and gravel, stone
South Carolina	Richard W. Kiley (D) 1979–83	Ernest F. Hollings (D) 1981–87 Strom Thurmond (R) 1979–85	cement, stone, clays, sand and gravel
South Dakota	William J. Janklow (R) 1979–83	James Abdnor (R) 1981–87 Larry Pressler (R) 1979–85	gold, sand and gravel, stone, cement
Tennessee	Lamar Alexander (R) 1979–83	Howard H. Baker, Jr. (R) 1979–85 James R. Sasser (D) 1977–83	stone, zinc, cement, coal
Texas	William P. Clements (R) 1979–83	Lloyd M. Bentsen (D) 1977–83 John G. Tower (R) 1979–85	petroleum, natural gas, natural gas liquids
Utah	Scott M. Matheson (D) 1981–85	E. J. Garn (R) 1981–87 Orrin G. Hatch (R) 1977–83	copper, petroleum, coal, molybdenum
Vermont	Richard A. Snelling (R) 1981–83	Patrick J. Leahy (D) 1981–87 Robert T. Stafford (R) 1977–83	stone, asbestos, sand and gravel, talc
Virginia	Charles S. Robb (D) 1982–86	Harry F. Byrd, Jr. (I) 1977–83 John W. Warner (R) 1979–85	coal, stone, cement, sand and gravel
Washington	John Spellman (R) 1981–85	Henry M. Jackson (D) 1977–83 Slade Gorton (R) 1981–87	sand and gravel, cement, stone, zinc
West Virginia	John D. Rockefeller IV (D) 1981–85	Robert C. Byrd (D) 1977–83 Jennings Randolph (D) 1979–85	coal, natural gas, natural gas liquids
Wisconsin	Lee S. Dreyfus (R) 1979–83	Robert W. Kasten, Jr. (R) 1981–87 William Proxmire (D) 1977–83	sand and gravel, stone, cement, zinc
Wyoming	Ed Herschler (D) 1979–83	Alan K. Simpson (R) 1979–85 Malcolm Wollop (R) 1977–83	petroleum, uranium, natural gas, sodium salts

Principal Agricultural Products	Principal Forest and Fishery Products	Principal Manufactures
cattle, hogs, soybeans, dairy products	oak, hickory, yellow pine, cottonwood	motor vehicles, transportation equipment, food products
cattle, wheat, barley, sugar beets	Douglas fir; lodgepole, ponderosa pine; larch	lumber; wood, food, petroleum, coal products; primary metals
cattle, hogs, corn, wheat	oak	food and beverage products, machinery, chemicals
cattle, dairy products, hay, alfalfa seed	ponderosa pine	chemicals, printed products, food and food products
dairy products, eggs, cattle, apples	whitepine, red pine, beech, birch, maple; lobsters	electrical equipment, leather products, machinery, paper
dairy products, eggs, tomatoes, asparagus	oak, yellow pine; clams, oysters, flounders	chemicals, electrical equipment, food products, machinery
cattle, cotton, dairy products, hay	ponderosa pine, Douglas fir, cottonwood, aspen	food, beverage, printed, and petroleum products
dairy products, cattle, eggs, apples	beech, birch, maple; clams, scallops, flounders	printed products, apparel, electrical equipment, machinery
tobacco, poultry dairy, and poultry products	yellow pine, oak, gum; shrimp, menhaden, crabs	textiles, cigarettes, furniture, electrical equipment
wheat, cattle, barley, dairy products	cottonwood, aspen	food and beverage products, machinery
dairy products, cattle, hogs, soybeans	oak, hickory, beech, birch, maple	machinery, steel, and other primary metals, transportation equipment
cattle, wheat, dairy products, peanuts	oak, yellow pine, hickory	machinery, food, and fabricated metal products, aircraft
cattle, dairy products, wheat, pears	Douglas fir, ponderosa pine; salmon, tuna	lumber; wood, food, and paper products; electrical equipment
dairy products, cattle, eggs, corn	oak, beech, birch, maple, hemlock	steel, electrical equipment, machinery, food products
dairy products, eggs, potatoes, cattle	oak; lobsters, scup, flounders, clams	textiles, primary metals, machinery, jewelry, silverware
tobacco, soybeans, eggs, cattle	yellow pine, gum, oak, cypress; shrimp, oysters	textiles, chemicals, apparel, paper, paper products
cattle, hogs, dairy products, corn	ponderosa pine, cottonwood, aspen	food and beverage products, machinery
cattle, dairy products, tobacco, soybeans	oak, hickory, yellow pine, yellow poplar	chemicals, food products, electrical equipment, apparel
cattle, sorghum, cotton, dairy products	yellow pine, oak, gum, hickory; shrimp, oysters	chemicals, petroleum products, aircraft and other transportation
cattle, dairy products, turkeys, sheep	lodgepole pine, spruce, cottonwood, aspen	primary metals, transportation equipment, food products
dairy products, cattle, eggs, apples	beech, birch, maple, spruce, balsam fir	machinery, paper, paper products, electrical equipment
dairy products, cattle, tobacco, eggs	oak, yellow pine, gum; oysters, crabs, menhaden	plastics and other chemicals, cigarettes, foods, textiles
wheat, cattle, apples, dairy products	Douglas fir, western hemlock, sitka, spruce; salmon, oysters, halibut	aircraft and other transportation equipment; food, wood, and paper products; lumber; paper
dairy products, cattle, apples, eggs	oak, hickory, yellow poplar	industrial chemicals, primary metals, glass products
dairy products, cattle, hogs, corn	oak, cottonwood, aspen, white and red pine; chubs	machinery; electrical equipment; food, beverage, paper products
cattle, sheep, sugar beets, wheat	lodgepole pine, ponderosa pine, spruce, Douglas fir	petroleum products, food and beverage products, lumber, wood products

Guide to Major United States Cities

The following city-by-city guide lists population, important phone numbers and addresses, hotels, restaurants, cultural and recreational facilities, and other information on major United States cities.

Symbols
*Population of an entire metropolitan area
C Census

Atlanta, Georgia

Population: (*1,950,600)
425,022 (1980C); Metro Rank: 17
Altitude: 1,050 feet
Average Temp.: Jan., 52°F., July, 85°F.
Telephone Area Number: 404
Time: 522-8550 **Weather:** 936-7768
Time Zone: Eastern
Selected Hotels:
Atlanta Biltmore,
817 W. Peachtree St. NE, 881-9500
Atlanta Hilton,
Courtland & Harris sts., 659-2000
Atlanta Marriott Hotel, Courtland St. at International Blvd., 659-6500
Colony Square,
14th & Peachtree sts., 892-6000
Hilton Inn (Atlanta Airport),
1031 Virginia Ave., 767-0281
Holiday Inn, 175 Piedmont Ave. NE, 659-2727
Holiday Inn—Airport,
1380 Virginia Ave., 762-8411
Howard Johnson's Airport,
1377 Virginia Ave., 762-5111
Hyatt Regency—Atlanta,
265 Peachtree Center, 577-1234
Marriott at Perimeter Center,
246 Perimeter Center Pkwy., 394-6500
Omni International/Atlanta Hotel,
One Omni International,
659-0000
Sheraton-Atlanta Hotel,
590 W. Peachtree St., 881-6000
Stone Mountain Inn,
U.S. 78, Stone Mountain Pk., 469-3311
Westin Peachtree Plaza Hotel,
Peachtree St. at International Blvd., 659-1400
Selected Restaurants:
The Abbey, 163 Ponce de Leon Ave., 876-8532
Ambassador, 3850 Roswell Rd., 265-7171
Anthony's, 3109 Piedmont Rd. NE, 262-7379
Boston Tea Party, 3820 Roswell Rd., 233-1776
Bugatti's, Omni International Hotel, 659-0000
Cafe de la Paix, 255 Courtland St., 659-2000
Herren's, 84 Luckie St. NW, 524-4709
Hugo's, 265 Peachtree St. NE, 577-1234
The Midnight Sun, 225 Peachtree St. NE, 577-5050
Jonathan's Top of the Mart, Merchandise Mart, 688-8650
Pano's and Paul's, 1232 W. Paces Ferry Rd. NW, 261-4739
Liquor Laws: Liquor may be purchased at liquor stores, beer and wine at grocery stores daily except Sunday.
Newspapers:
Atlanta Constitution, 526-5151
Atlanta Daily World, 659-1110
Atlanta Journal, 526-5151
Television Stations:
WAGA (CBS) Channel 5
WSB (ABC) Channel 2
WXIA (NBC) Channel 11
AM Radio Stations:
WBIE (CBS) 1080 Country & Western
WGST (MBS) 920 News
WRNG (ABC) 680 Talk
WSB (ABC) 750 Variety
FM Radio Stations:
WQXI 94.1 Top 40
WSB 98.5 Popular
Airline Service:
Hartsfield Atlanta International Airport: —Bahamasair, Braniff, Delta, Eastern, Frontier, KLM, Northwest Orient, Ozark, Piedmont, Republic, Sabena
Airport Transportation:
Eight miles to downtown Atlanta. Taxicab and limousine bus service.
Car Rental Agencies: Avis (530-2700), Budget (530-3000), Dollar (530-3100), Hertz (530-2900), National (530-2800)
Railroad Passenger Service: Georgia Railroad, Southern Railway
Trade Exhibition Facilities:
Atlanta Civic Center,
395 Piedmont Rd. NE, 523-6275
Atlanta Merchandise Mart,
240 Peachtree St. NW, 688-8994
Georgia World Congress Center,
International Blvd., 656-7600
The Omni, 100 Techwood Dr. NW, 681-2100
Professional Sports Facilities:
Atlanta-Fulton County Stadium,
521 Capitol Ave. SE, 522-1967
(Braves, baseball, 522-7630; Falcons, football)
The Omni, 100 Techwood Dr. NW, 681-2100 (Hawks, basketball)
Theaters and Concert Hall:
Academy Theatre,
581 Peachtree St. NE, 873-2518
Alliance Theater,
1280 Peachtree St. NE, 892-2414
Atlanta Civic Center,
395 Piedmont Ave. NE, 523-6275
Atlanta Memorial Arts Center,
1280 Peachtree St. NE
(Atlanta Symphony Orchestra), 892-3600
Fox Theater,
650 Peachtree St., 881-1977
Peachtree Playhouse,
1150 Peachtree St. NE, 892-4110
Museums:
Atlanta Historical Society (Swan House, Tullie Smith House, McElreath Hall, and Margaret Mitchell Memorial Library), 3101 Andrews Dr. NW
Emory Museum, Bishops Hall, Emory University
Georgia State Museum, State Capitol
Art Museums:
Fernbank Science Center,
156 Heaton Park Dr.
Toy Museum of Atlanta,
2800 Peachtree Rd. NE
High Museum of Art,
1280 Peachtree St. NE
Points of Interest:
Six Flags Over Georgia, Peachtree Center, Stone Mountain, Underground Atlanta, Atlanta State Farmers Market, Martin Luther King, Jr. Historic District
Information Sources:
Atlanta Convention & Visitors Bureau
Suite 200, 233 Peachtree St. NE
Atlanta, Georgia 30043
(404) 659-4270

Atlanta Chamber of Commerce
1300 N. Omni International
Atlanta, Georgia 30303
(404) 521-0845

Baltimore, Maryland

Population: (*1,883,100)
786,775 (1980C); Metro Rank: 18
Altitude: Sea level to 489 feet
Average Temp.: Jan., 37°F.; July, 79°F.
Telephone Area Number: 301
Time: 844-1212 **Weather:** 936-1212
Time Zone: Eastern
Selected Hotels:
Baltimore Hilton, 101 W. Fayette St., 752-1100

Cross keys Inn, 5100 Falls Rd., 532-6900
International Hotel, Airport, 761-7700
Harbor City Inn, 1701 Russell St., 837-2400
Hilltop Motor Inn, 1660 Whitehead Ct., 944-7400
Holiday Inn—Inner Harbor, Howard & Lombard sts., 685-3500
Hunt Valley Inn, Shawan Rd., 666-7000
Lord Baltimore Hotel, Baltimore & Hanover sts., 539-8400
Hyatt Regency Baltimore, 300 Light St., 528-1234
Sheraton-Johns Hopkins Inn, Broadway & Orleans St., 675-6800
Warren House Motor Inn, 407 Reisterstown Rd., 484-1800

Selected Restaurants:
Cafe des Artistes, 9 Hopkins Plaza, 539-1804
Chiapparelli's, 237 S. High St., 685-9822
Chesapeake, 1701 N. Charles St., 837-7711
Danny's, 1201 N. Charles St., 539-1393
Haussner's, 3244 Eastern Ave., 327-8365
Peerce's Downtown, 225 N. Liberty St., 727-0910
Phillip's Harborplace, Light St. Pavillion, 685-6600
The Prime Rib, 1101 N. Calvert St., 539-1804
Tio Pepe, 10 E. Franklin St., 539-4675

Liquor Laws: Liquor may be purchased from 6 A.M. to 2 A.M. daily.

Newspapers:
Baltimore News American, 752-1212
Baltimore Sun, 332-6000

Television Stations:
WBAL (NBC) Channel 11
WJZ (ABC) Channel 13
WMAR (CBS) Channel 2

AM Radio Stations:
WBAL (NBC) 1090 Popular
WFBR (CBS) 1300 Popular
WITH (ABC) 1230 Mood Music

FM Radio Stations:
WBMD 105.7 Country-Western
WLIF 101.9 Mood Music
WMAR 106.5 Popular
WXYV 104 Contemporary

Airline Service:
Baltimore-Washington International Airport—Allegheny Commuter, American, Delta, Eastern, Piedmont, TWA, United, USAIR, VIASA (Venezuela), World Airways

Airport Transportation:
Ten miles to downtown Baltimore. Taxicab and limousine bus service.

Car Rental Agencies: Airways (796-8250), Avis (761-1620), Budget (837-6955), Hertz (760-6500), National (761-8860)

Railroad Passenger Service: Amtrak

Trade Exhibition Facilities:
Civic Center, 201 W. Baltimore St., 837-0900
Convention Center, One W. Pratt St., 659-7000

Professional Sports Facilities:
Civic Center, 201 W. Baltimore St., 837-0900
Memorial Stadium, 33rd & Ellerslie aves., 235-4047 (Colts, football, 356-6800; Orioles, baseball, 243-9800)

Theaters:
Center Stage, 700 N. Calvert St., 685-3200
Morris Mechanic, 1 W. Baltimore St., 752-1407
Spotlighters, 817 St. Paul St., 752-1225

Museums:
B & O Railroad Museum, Pratt & Poppleton sts.
Lovely Lane Museum, St. Paul & 22nd sts.
Maryland Historical Society, 201 W. Monument St.
Streetcar Museum, 1901 Falls Rd.
Babe Ruth Birthplace Shrine & Museum, 216 Emory St.

Art Museums and Galleries:
Baltimore Museum of Art, Charles and 32nd sts.
Downtown Gallery, Charles & Redwood sts.
Gallery at the Mechanic, Hopkins Place
Maryland Institute, College of Art, 1300 W. Mount Royal Ave.
Peale Museum, 225 N. Holliday St.
Walters Art Gallery, Charles & Centre sts.

Points of Interest:
Fort McHenry National Monument, Star-Spangled Banner Flag House, Washington Monument, Mount Clare, U.S.F. *Constellation,* Carroll Mansion, Harborplace, Maryland Science Center and Planetarium, National Aquarium

Information Sources:
Baltimore Office of Promotion and Tourism, 110 W. Baltimore St.
Baltimore, Maryland 21201
(301) 752-8632

Greater Baltimore Committee
Mercantile Building
Suite 900, 2 Hopkins Plaza
Baltimore, Maryland 21201
(301) 727-2820

Boston, Massachusetts

Population: (*3,738,800) 562,994 (1980C); Metro Rank: 7
Altitude: Sea level to 330 feet
Average Temp.: Jan., 29°F.; July, 72°F.
Telephone Area Number: 617
Time: 637-1234 **Weather:** 936-1234
Time Zone: Eastern

Selected Hotels:
The Colonade Hotel, 120 Huntington Ave., 424-7000
Copley Plaza Hotel, Copley Square, 267-5300
Hilton Inn, Logan International Airport, 569-9300
Holiday Inn, 5 Blossom St., 742-7630
Howard Johnson "57" Motor Hotel, 200 Stuart St., 482-1800
Lenox Motor Hotel, 710 Boylston St., 536-5300
Parker House, 60 School St., 227-8600
Park Plaza Hotel, 64 Arlington St., at Park Sq., 426-2000
Ritz-Carlton Hotel, Arlington & Newbury sts., 536-5700
Sheraton-Boston Hotel, Prudential Center, 236-2000

Selected Restaurants:
Anthony's Pier 4, Northern Ave., 423-6363
Cafe Budapest., 90 Exeter St., 734-3388
Felicia's, 145A Richmond St., 523-9885
57 Restaurant, Park Plaza Hotel, 64 Arlington St., 423-5700
Jimmy's Harborside, 242 Northern Ave., 423-1000
Joseph's, 279 Dartmouth St., 536-4200
Locke-Ober, 3 Winter Pl., 542-1340
Maitre Jacques, Emerson Pl., 742-5480
Maison Robert, Old City Hall, 45 School St., 227-3370
Ritz Carlton, Arlington & Newbury sts., 536-5700
Top of the Hub, Prudential Tower, 536-1775
Zachary's, The Colonnade Hotel, 120 Huntington Ave., 261-2800

Liquor Laws: Drinks may be purchased in restaurants and hotels from 8 A.M. to 2 A.M. weekdays, Saturday until 1 A.M., Sunday from 1 P.M. to 2 A.M.

Newspapers:
Boston Globe, 929-2000
Boston Herald American, HA 6-3000
Christian Science Monitor, 262-2300

Television Stations:
WBZ (NBC) Channel 4
WCVB (ABC) Channel 5
WGBH (PBS) Channel 2
WLVI Channel 56
WNAC (CBS) Channel 7
WSBK Channel 38

AM Radio Stations:
WBZ 1030 News/Sports/Music
WCRB (ABC) 1330 Classical
WCOP (NBC) 1150 Country-Western
WEEI (CBS) 590 News
WEZE (ABC) 1260 Music
WHDH 850 Sports/Music

FM Radio Stations:
WBOS 92.9 Classical—*Stereo*
WBZ 106.7 Semi-classical
WCRB 102.5 Classical—*Stereo*
WHDH 94.5 Popular—*Stereo*

Airline Service:
Logan International Airport—Aer Lingus (Ireland), Air Canada, Alitalia (Italy), American, British Airways,

Delta, Eastern, Lufthansa (Germany), Northwest Orient, Pan American, Piedmont, Republic, Swissair, TAP (Portugal), TWA, United, USAIR

Airport Transportation:
Three miles to downtown Boston. Taxicab and limousine bus service.

Car Rental Agencies: Avis (262-3300), Budget (569-4000), Econo-Car (542-9800), Hertz (569-7272), National (569-6700)

Railroad Passenger Service: Amtrak

Trade Exhibition Facilities:
Commonwealth Pier Exhibition Hall, Northern Ave., near Pier 4, 542-8828
John B. Hynes Veterans Auditorium, 800 Boylston St., 262-8000
Northeast Trade Center, 100 Sylvan Rd., Woburn, 935-8090
Suffolk Downs, East Boston, 567-3900

Professional Sports Facilities:
Boston Garden, North Station, 227-3200 (Celtics, basketball; Bruins, hockey)
Fenway Park, 24 Yawkey Way, 267-8661 (Red Sox, baseball)

Theaters and Concert Halls:
Berklee Performance Center, 136 Massachusetts Ave., 266-1400
Boston Ballet Co., 553 Tremont St., 542-3945
Charles Playhouse Theatre, 76 Warrenton St., 426-6912
Colonial Theatre, 106 Boylston St., 426-9366
Shubert Theatre, 265 Tremont St., 426-4520
Symphony Hall, 251 Huntington Ave., 266-1492 (Boston Symphony and Pops Orchestras)
Wilbur Theatre, 246 Tremont St., 423-4008

Museums:
Blue Hills Trailside Museum, 1904 Canton Ave., Milton
Isabella Stewart Gardner, 2 Palace Rd.
Museum of Science and Charles Hayden Planetarium, Science Park
New England Aquarium, Central Wharf

Art Museums:
Fogg Art Museum, 33 Quincy St., Harvard University
Museum of Fine Arts, 465 Huntington Ave.

Points of Interest:
Boston National Historical Park, Freedom Trail, New City Hall, Harvard University, Massachusetts Institute of Technology

Information Sources:
Greater Boston Convention & Tourist Bureau, Inc.
900 Boylston St.
Boston, Massachusetts 02115
(617) 367-9275

Greater Boston Chamber of Commerce
125 High St.
Boston, Massachusetts 02110
(617) 426-1250

Buffalo, New York

Population: (*1,154,600) 357,870 (1980C); Metro Rank: 27
Altitude: 570 to 699 feet
Average Temp.: Jan., 26°F.; July, 71°F.
Telephone Area Number: 716
Time: 844-6161 **Weather:** 643-1234
Time Zone: Eastern

Selected Hotels:
Buffalo Hilton, Church and Terrace sts., 845-5100
Buffalo Marriott Inn, 1340 Millersport Hwy., 689-6800
The Executive Motor Inn, 4243 Genesee St., 634-2300
Holiday Inn Midtown, 620 Delaware Ave., 886-2121
Howard Johnson's, 475 Dingens St., 896-2800
Howard Johnson's, 6700 Transit Rd., Williamsville, 634-7500
Howard Johnson's Motor Lodge—Airport, 4217 Genesee St., Cheektowaga, 633-5500
Lord Amherst, 5000 Main St., 839-2000
Regency Motor Hotel, 4408 Milestrip Rd., 825-8100
Sheraton Inn-Buffalo East, 2040 Walden Ave., Cheektowaga, 681-2400
Statler Hotel, 107 Delaware Ave., 856-1000

Selected Restaurants:
Asa Ransom House, 10529 Main St., 759-2315
Davio, 899 Niagara Falls Blvd., 836-3366
Gepetto's, 3902 Maple Rd., 837-2950
Old Red Mill Inn, 8326 Main St., Williamsville, 633-7878
Park Lane Manor House, 33 Gates Circle, 885-3250
Plaza Suite, 1 M & T Plaza, 842-5555
Valentine's, 91 Niagara St., 856-8373

Liquor Laws: Liquor may be purchased six days a week from 8 A.M. to 4 A.M., on Sunday from noon.

Newspapers:
Buffalo Courier-Express, 847-5353
Buffalo Evening News, 856-3333

Television Stations:
WIVB (CBS) Channel 4
WGR (NBC) Channel 2
WKBW (ABC) Channel 7
WNED (PBS) Channel 17

AM Radio Stations:
WBEN (CBS) 930 Popular/News
WEBR (ABC) 970 Popular/News
WGR (NBC) 550 Popular/News
WKBW 1520 Popular/News

FM Radio Stations:
WADV 106.5 Music—*Stereo*
WBEN 102.5 Music/News
WBNY 96.1 Semi-classical—*Stereo*
WEBR 94.5 Music/News

Airline Service:
Greater Buffalo International Airport: American, Eastern, United, USAIR

Airport Transportation:
Nine miles to downtown Buffalo. Taxicab and limousine bus service.

Car Rental Agencies: Avis (632-1808), Hertz (632-4772), National (632-0203)

Railroad Passenger Service: Amtrak

Trade Exhibition Facilities:
Memorial Auditorium, 140 Main St., 856-4200
Buffalo Convention Center, Convention Center Plaza, 855-5555

Professional Sports Facilities:
Memorial Auditorium, 140 Main St., 856-4200 (Sabres, hockey)
Rich Stadium, Orchard Park (Buffalo Bills, football)

Theater and Concert Hall:
Kleinhans Music Hall, 370 Pennsylvania St., 885-5000 (Buffalo Philharmonic)
Studio Arena Theatre, 710 Main St., 856-8025

Museums:
Buffalo & Erie County Historical Museum, 25 Nottingham Ct.
Buffalo Museum of Science, Humboldt Park
Wilcox Mansion, 641 Delaware Ave.

Art Gallery:
Albright-Knox Art Gallery, 1285 Elmwood Ave.

Points of Interest:
Delaware Park, Buffalo Zoo, Observation Tower, Buffalo City Hall, National Shrine and Basilica of Our Lady of Victory, Botanical Gardens, Naval Park

Information Sources:
Buffalo Area Convention and Visitors Bureau
115 Delaware Ave.
Buffalo, New York 14202
(716) 849-6609

Buffalo Area Chamber of Commerce
107 Delaware Ave.
Buffalo, New York 14202
(716) 849-6677

Chicago, Illinois

Population: (*7,803,800) 3,005,072 (1980C); Metro Rank: 3
Altitude: 579 to 672 feet
Average Temp.: Jan., 27°F.; July, 75°F
Telephone Area Number: 312
Time: 976-1616 **Weather:** 976-1212
Time Zone: Central

Selected Hotels:
Ambassador East, 1301 N. State Pkwy., 787-7200
Ambassador West, 1300 N. State Pkwy., 787-7900
Chicago Marriott, 540 N. Michigan Ave., 836-0100
Chicago Marriott O'Hare, 8535 W. Higgins Rd., 693-4444
Conrad Hilton, 720 S. Michigan Ave., 922-4400
Drake Hotel, 140 E. Walton Place, SU 7-2200

Executive House, 71 E. Wacker Dr., 346-7100
Holiday Inn, 644 N. Lake Shore Dr., 943-9200; 350 N. Orleans St., 836-5000
Howard Johnson's O'Hare International, Mannheim & Irving Park rds., 671-6000
Hyatt Regency Chicago, 151 E. Wacker Dr., 565-1000
Hyatt Regency O'Hare, River Rd. & Kennedy Expwy., 696-1234
McCormick Inn, 23rd St. & Lake Shore Dr., 791-1900
O'Hare Hilton, O'Hare Airport, 686-8000
Palmer House, 17 E. Monroe St., RA 6-7500
Radisson Chicago Hotel, 505 N. Michigan Ave., 944-4100
Ritz-Carlton, 160 E. Pearson St., 266-1000
Sheraton Plaza, 160 E. Huron St., 787-2900
Tremont Hotel, 102 E. Chestnut St., 751-5000
The Westin, 909 N. Michigan Ave., 943-7200

Selected Restaurants:
Arnie's, 2619 N. Clark St., 266-4800
The Bakery, 2218 N. Lincoln Ave., 472-6942
Biggs, 1150 N. Dearborn St., 787-0900
Blackhawk, 139 N. Wabash Ave., 726-0100
Cape Cod Room, 140 E. Walton St., SU 7-2200
Chiam Restaurant, 2323 W. Wentworth St. (Chinatown), 225-6336
The Consort, The Westin, 909 N. Michigan Ave., 943-7200
Italian Village, 71 W. Monroe St., 332-7005
L'Epuisette, 21 W. Goethe, 944-2288
Le Perroquet, 70 E. Walton Pl., 944-7990
Maxim's de Paris, 1300 N. Astor St., 943-1111
The Ninety-Fifth, 875 N. Michigan Ave., 787-9596
Pump Room, 1300 N. State Pkwy., 266-0360

Liquor Laws: Bars are open Monday through Friday 7 A.M. to 2 A.M., Saturday from 7 A.M. to 3 A.M., Sunday from noon to 1 A.M., "special" license bars to 4 A.M.

Newspapers:
The Chicago Defender, 225-2400
Chicago Sun-Times, 321-3000
Chicago Tribune, 222-3232
Wall Street Journal, Midwest Edition, 648-7600

Television Stations:
WBBM (CBS) Channel 2
WGN Channel 9
WLS (ABC) Channel 7
WMAQ (NBC) Channel 5
WTTW (PBS) Channel 11

AM Radio Stations:
WBBM (CBS) 780 News
WGN 720 Popular/Talk
WLS (ABC) 890 Rock
WMAQ (NBC) 670 Popular

FM Radio Stations:
WBBM 96.3 Contemporary—*Stereo*
WFMT 98.7 Classical—*Stereo*
WNIB 97.1 Classical—*Stereo*

Airline Service:
O'Hare International Airport—Aer Lingus (Ireland), Air Canada, Air France, Air Jamaica, A.L.I.A. (Royal Jordanian Airlines), Alitalia, Allegheny Commuter, American, Braniff, British Airways, Continental, Delta, Eastern, Frontier, Icelandic, KLM (Royal Dutch Airlines), Lufthansa (Germany), Mexicana de Aviación, Northwest Orient, Ozark, Piedmont, Republic, Sabena, SAS (Scandinavian Airlines), Swissair, TWA, United, USAIR

Airline Service:
Midway Airport—Delta, Midway

Airport Transportation:
Nineteen miles from O'Hare to downtown Chicago; 10 miles from Midway to downtown. Taxicab and limousine bus service from each.

Airline Service:
Meigs Field. Lakefront downtown. Commuter air service.

Car Rental Agencies: Avis (694-2222), Budget (686-4950), Econo-Car (297-7740), Hertz (686-7272), National (686-7722)

Railroad Passenger Service: Amtrak, Rock Island Lines

Trade Exhibition Facilities:
Apparel Center, 350 N. Orleans St., 527-1466
McCormick Place, lakefront at 23rd St., 791-6000
Navy Pier, lakefront at Grand Ave., 744-4000
O'Hare International Trade & Exposition Center, Rosemont, 692-2220
Arlington Park Convention-Exposition Center, Euclid Ave. & Rohlwing Rd., Arlington Heights, 394-2000

Professional Sports Facilities:
Chicago Stadium, 1800 W. Madison St. (Black Hawks, hockey, 733-5300; Bulls, basketball, 733-5300)
Comiskey Park, 324 W. 35th St., 924-1000 (White Sox, baseball, 225-5769; Chicago Sting, soccer, 332-2292)
Rosemont Horizon, 6920 Mannheim Rd., Rosemont, 635-6600
Soldier Field, 425 E. 14th Blvd., 663-5408 (Bears, football, 663-5100)
Wrigley Field, 1060 W. Addison St., 281-5050 (Cubs, baseball)

Theaters and Concert Halls:
Arie Crown Theater, McCormick Place, 791-6000
Auditorium Theater, 70 E. Congress St., 922-2110
Blackstone, 60 E. Balbo St., 236-8240
Civic Opera House, 20 N. Wacker Dr., 346-0270 (Lyric Opera)
Drury Lane South, 2500 W. 94th Pl. 779-4000
Drury Lane Water Tower Place, 175 E. Chestnut St., 266-0500
Goodman Memorial Theatre, Monroe St. & Columbus Dr., 236-2337
Mill Run Theatre, junc. State 21 & 58, 298-2170
Orchestra Hall, 220 S. Michigan Ave., 427-7711 (Chicago Symphony Orchestra; summer concerts, Ravinia, 782-9696)
The Playhouse, McCormick Place, 791-6000
Shubert, 22 W. Monroe St., 236-8240

Museums:
Adler Planetarium, Roosevelt Rd. & Lake Shore Dr.
Chicago Historical Society, Clark St. at North Ave.
DuSable Museum of African-American History, 740 E. 56th Pl.
Field Museum, Roosevelt Rd. & Lake Shore Dr.,
Museum of Science and Industry, E. 57th St. & S. Lake Shore Dr.
Oriental Institute, 1155 E. 58th St.
Shedd Aquarium, lakefront at Roosevelt Rd.

Art Museums:
Art Institute of Chicago, Michigan Ave. at Adams St.
Museum of Contemporary Art, 237 E. Ontario St.
Renaissance Society at University of Chicago, 5845 S. Ellis Ave.
Spertus Museum of Judaica, 618 S. Michigan Ave.

Points of Interest:
John Hancock Center, Civic Center, Lake Shore Drive, Lincoln Park, Buckingham Fountain, North Michigan Avenue, Planetarium, Sears Tower

Information Sources:
Chicago Convention & Tourism Bureau
McCormick Place-on-the-Lake
Chicago, Illinois 60616
(312) 225-5000

Chicago Association of Commerce and Industry
130 S. Michigan Ave.
Chicago, Illinois 60603
(312) 786-0111

Cincinnati, Ohio

Population: (*1,476,600) 385,457 (1980C); Metro Rank: 21
Altitude: 433 to 960 feet
Average Temp.: Jan., 35°F.; July, 78°F.
Telephone Area Number: 513
Time: 721-1700 **Weather:** 936-4850
Time Zone: Eastern

Selected Hotels:
Carrousel Inn, 8001 Reading Rd., 821-5110
Drawbridge Inn, Buttermilk Pike, Ft. Mitchell, 341-2800

Holiday Inn—Downtown,
800 W. 8th St., 241-8660
Howard Johnson's North,
11440 Chester Rd., 771-3400
Marriott Inn, 11320 Chester Rd.,
772-1720
Pick-Americana Inn, at Airport, 371-1776
Stouffer's Cincinnati Towers,
141 W. 6th St., 352-2100
Terrace Hilton, 15 W. 6th St., 381-4000
Vernon Manor, 400 Oak St., 281-3300
The Westin, Fountain Square, 621-7700

Selected Restaurants:
Gourmet Room, Terrace Hilton,
15 W. 6th St., 381-4000
Grammer's, 1440 Walnut St., 721-6570
La Normandie Taverne & Chop House,
114 E. 6th St., 721-2260
Maisonette, 114 E. 6th St., 721-2260
Mecklenburg Gardens,
302 University Ave., 281-5353
Pigall's, 127 W. 4th St., 721-1345
Sky Chef's River Queen
(atop Greater Cincinnati
International Airport
Terminal), 371-5553

Liquor Laws: Liquor available seven days a week. May be purchased at state-owned stores Monday through Saturday.

Newspapers:
Cincinnati Enquirer, 721-2700
Cincinnati Post, 721-1111

Television Stations:
WCET (PBS) Channel 48
WCPO (CBS) Channel 9
WKRC (ABC) Channel 12
WLWT (NBC) Channel 5
WXIX (Metro-Media) Channel 19

AM Radio Stations:
WCIN (ABC) 1480 Soul/Top 40
WCKY (CBS) 1530 Newsradio
WKRC (ABC) 550 Popular/News
WLW (NBC) 700 Popular
WUBE (ABC) 1230 Country
WSAI 1360 Country

FM Radio Stations:
WAKW 93.3 Religious
WGUC 90.9
Classical/Drama/Educational
WRRM 98.5 Contemporary
WSAI 94.1 Country
WWEZ 92.5 Music

Airline Service:
Greater Cincinnati International Airport—American, Delta, Piedmont, Republic, TWA, United, USAIR

Airport Transportation:
Thirteen miles to downtown Cincinnati. Taxicab and limousine bus service

Car Rental Agencies: Avis (283-3764), Budget (283-3131), Hertz (283-3535), National (283-3655)

Railroad Passenger Service: Amtrak

Trade Exhibition Facility:
Cincinnati Convention Exposition Center, 525 Elm St., 352-3750

Professional Sports Facilities:
Riverfront Coliseum, 100 Broadway, 241-1818
Riverfront Stadium, 2nd & Elm sts. (Reds, baseball, 421-4510; Bengals, football, 621-3550)
Cincinnati Gardens, 2250 Seymour Ave., 731-8300

Theaters and Concert Hall:
Music Hall, 1243 Elm St., 621-1919 (Cincinnati Summer Opera, Symphony Orchestra, Ballet Company)
Playhouse-in-the-Park, Mt. Adams, 421-5440

Museums:
Fire Department Historical Museum, 329 E. 9th St.
John Hauck House, 812 Dayton St.
Museum of Natural History, 1720 Gilbert Ave.
Stowe House State Museum, 2950 Gilbert Ave.

Art Museums and Galleries:
Cincinnati Art Museum, Art Museum Dr. in Eden Park
Contemporary Arts Center, 115 E. 5th St.
Taft Museum, 316 Pike St.

Points of Interest:
Union Terminal Building, Carew Tower, Krohn Conservatory, Cincinnati Zoological Garden, University of Cincinnati Observatory, Kings' Island, College Football Hall of Fame

Information Sources:
Greater Cincinnati Convention and Visitors Bureau
200 W. Fifth St.
Cincinnati, Ohio 45202
(513) 621-2142

Greater Cincinnati Chamber of Commerce
120 W. Fifth St.
Cincinnati, Ohio 45202
(513) 579-3100

Cleveland, Ohio

Population: (*2,218,300) 573,822 (1980C); Metro Rank: 12
Altitude: 570 to 1,050 feet
Average Temp.: Jan., 29°F.; July, 74°F.
Telephone Area Number: 216
Time: 471-1212 **Weather:** 931-1212
Time Zone: Eastern

Selected Hotels:
Bond Court Hotel, 777 St. Clair Ave., 771-7600
Harley Hotel—East,
6051 Center Rd., 944-4300
Harley Hotel—West,
17000 Bagley Rd., 243-5200
Hilton Inn—South,
Int. 77 & Rockside Rd., 447-1300
Holiday Inn—Lakeside City Center,
Lakeside Ave. at E. 12th St., 241-5100
Hollenden House, E. 6th St., at Superior Ave., 621-0700
Marriott Inn—Airport, Int. 71 & 150th St., 252-5333
Marriott Inn—Cleveland—East, Int. 271 & Chagrin Blvd., 464-5950
Sheraton Inn—Airport,
5300 Riverside Dr., 267-1500
Stouffer's Inn on the Square,
24 Public Sq., 696-5600
Stouffer's Somerset Inn,
3550 Northfield Rd., 752-6500

Selected Restaurants:
Au Pere Jacques, 34105 Chagrin Blvd., Chagrin Falls, 831-8558
Don's Lighthouse Inn, 8905 Lake Ave., 961-6767
D'Poo's on the River,
1146 Old River Rd., 579-0828
Earth by April, 2151 Lee Rd., Cleveland Heights, 371-1438
Fagan's, 966 Old River Rd., 241-6116
French Connection, 24 Public Sq., 696-5600
Keg & Quarter, 1800 Euclid Ave., 861-5501
Pat Joyce's on the Green,
114 Chester Ave., 771-1010
Pier W (Stouffer's), 12700 Lake Ave., 228-2250
Sammy's Restaurant,
1400 W. 10th St., 523-5560
Steffon's, 29425 Chagrin Blvd., 464-2980
Theatrical Restaurant, 711 Vincent Ave., 241-6166
Top of the Town (Stouffer's),
100 Erieview Plaza, 771-1600
Yesterday's, 1407 Euclid Ave., 861-2241

Liquor Laws: Beer and wine may be purchased at privately owned stores. Liquor may be purchased at state-owned stores, open daily from 11 A.M. to 6 P.M., closed Sunday. Drinks are served at restaurants, bars, and hotels.

Newspapers:
Cleveland Plain Dealer, 523-4500
Cleveland Press, 623-1111

Television Stations:
WEWS (ABC) Channel 5
WJKW (CBS) Channel 8
WKYC (NBC) Channel 3
WVIZ (PBS) Channel 25
WUAB (UAB) Channel 43

AM Radio Stations:
WERE (NBC) 1300 Talk/News
WGAR 1220 Popular/News
WJW (CBS) 850 Popular Music/News
WWWE (NBC) 1100
Popular Music/News

FM Radio Stations:
WCLV 95.5 Concert Music
WMMS 101 Popular Music/News
WZAK 93.1 Nationality Station

Airline Service:
Hopkins International Airport—Air Canada, Allegheny Commuter, American, Delta, Eastern, Northwest Orient, Republic, TWA, United, USAIR

Airline Service:
Lakefront Airport—Wright

Airport Transportation:
Twelve miles from Hopkins to downtown Cleveland. Taxicab, train, and limousine bus service.

Car Rental Agencies: Avis (265-3700), Budget (267-2080), Dollar Rent-A-Car (267-3133), Econo-Car (228-4940), Hertz (696-6066), National (267-6811), Thrifty (267-8611)

Railroad Passenger Service: Amtrak

Trade Exhibition Facility:
Cleveland Convention Center, 1220 E. 6th St., 523-2200

Professional Sports Facilities:
Coliseum, 2923 Streetsboro Rd., Richfield (Cavaliers, basketball, 659-9100)
Cleveland Stadium, W. 3rd St. and Lakeside Ave. (Browns, football, 696-5555; Indians, baseball, 861-1200)
George Finnie Stadium, Baldwin-Wallace College (Cobras, soccer, 771-5425)

Theaters and Concert Halls:
Blossom Music Center, Cuyahoga Falls, Ohio (Cleveland Symphony Orchestra summer season, 231-7300)
Cleveland PlayHouse, 2040 E. 86th St., 795-7000
Convention Center, 1220 E. 6th St., 523-2200 (Metropolitan Opera)
Front Row Theatre, 6199 Wilson Mills Rd., 449-5000
Hanna Theater, 2067 E. 14th St., 621-5000
Karamu Performing Arts Theatre, 2355 E. 89th St., 795-3322
Lakewood Little Theatre, 17801 Detroit Ave., Lakewood, 521-2540
Severance Hall, 11001 Euclid Ave., 231-1111 (Cleveland Symphony Orchestra)

Museums:
Cleveland Health Museum, 8911 Euclid Ave.
Dunham Tavern Museum, 6709 Euclid Ave.
F. C. Crawford Auto-Aviation Museum, 10825 East Blvd.
Howard Dittrick Museum of Historical Medicine, 11000 Euclid Ave.
Museum of Natural History, 10600 East Blvd.
NASA Lewis Visitor Center, 21000 Brookpark Rd.
Western Reserve Historical Society, 10825 E. Blvd.

Art Museums:
Cleveland Museum of Art, 11150 East Blvd.
Temple Museum of Religious Art and Music, University Circle & Silver Park

Points of Interest:
Terminal Tower, Garden Center of Greater Cleveland, The Arcade, Sea World (Aurora) Cleveland Aquarium, Cleveland Zoo

Information Sources:
Cleveland Convention and Visitors Bureau
1301 E. 6th St.
Cleveland, Ohio 44114, (216) 621-4110
Greater Cleveland Growth Association
690 Union Commerce Building
East 9th & Euclid sts.
Cleveland, Ohio 44115 (216) 621-3300

Columbus, Ohio

Population: (*943,300) 564,871 (1980C); Metro Rank: 31
Altitude: 685 to 893 feet
Average Temp.: Jan., 31°F.; July, 76°F.
Telephone Area Number: 614
Time and Weather: 430-8211
Time Zone: Eastern

Selected Hotels:
Carrousel Inn of Columbus, 4900 Sinclair Rd., 846-0300
The Christopher Inn, 300 E. Broad St., 228-3541
Hilton Inn—North, 7007 N. High St., 436-0700
Hilton Inn—East, 4560 Truro Station Rd., 868-1380
Holiday Inn—Downtown, 175 E. Town St., 221-3281
Holiday Inn—Ohio State University, 328 W. Lane Ave., 294-4848
Howard Johnson's—South, Int. 71 & Stringtown Rd., Grove City, 871-0440
Hyatt Regency Columbus, 350 N. High St., 463-1234
Imperial House North, 900 Morse Rd., 885-8244
Marriott Inn, 2124 S. Hamilton Rd., 861-7220
Marriott Inn, North, 6660 Doubletree Ave., 885-1885
Sheraton-Columbus Hotel, 50 N. 3rd St., 228-6060
Stouffer's Dublin Hotel, 600 Metro Center North, Dublin, 764-2200
Stouffer's University Inn, 3025 Olentangy River Rd., 267-9291
University Hilton Inn, 3110 Olentangy River Rd., 267-7461

Selected Restaurants:
Clarmont Steak House, 684 S. High St., 443-1125
Engine House #5, 121 E. Thurman Ave., 443-4877
The Inner Circle, 16 W. Beck St., 221-8953
Jai Lai, 1421 Olentangy River Rd., 421-7337
J. Ross Brown's Whaling Station, 60 E. Wilson Bridge Rd., 436-9797
Kahiki, 3583 E. Broad St., 237-5425
L'Armagnac, 121 S. Sixth St., 221-4046
One Nation, One Nationwide Plaza, 221-0001
Water Works Restaurant, 225 N. Front St., 224-2444
Wine Cellar, 1777 E. Granville Rd., 885-0016

Liquor Laws: State Store System sells bottled goods. Drinks may be purchased weekdays 5:30 A.M. to 1 or 2:30 A.M.; Sunday, 1 P.M. to midnight in most hotel-motel precincts.

Newspapers:
Columbus Citizen-Journal, 461-5000
Columbus Dispatch, 461-5000

Television Stations:
WBNS (CBS) Channel 10
WCMH (NBC) Channel 4
WOSU (PBS) Channel 34
WTVN (ABC) Channel 6

AM Radio Stations:
WBNS (CBS) 1460 General
WMNI (MBS) 920 General
WTVN (ABC) 610 Popular

FM Radio Stations:
WBNS 97.1 Popular—*Stereo*
WMNI 99.7 General

Airline Service:
Port Columbus International Airport—Allegheny Commuter, American, Delta, Eastern, Piedmont, Republic, TWA, United, USAIR, Wright

Airport Transportation:
Eight miles to downtown Columbus. Taxicab and limousine bus service.

Car Rental Agencies: Avis (221-5888), Budget (228-1058), Hertz (221-3000), National (328-4567)

Railroad Passenger Service: Amtrak

Trade Exhibition Facility:
Veterans Memorial Building, 300 W. Broad St., 221-4341

Theaters and Concert Hall:
Columbus Symphony Orchestra, 200 E. Town St., 224-3291
Hughes Hall Theatre, Ohio State University, 422-2295
Kenley Summer Theater, Veterans Memorial Building, 224-4247
Merschon Auditorium, Ohio State University, E. 15th Ave. & N. High St., 433-2251
Ohio Theatre, 39 E. State St., 469-0939

Museum:
Ohio Historical Society, Ohio State Fairgrounds
Center of Science and Industry, 280 E. Broad St.
Ohio Railway Museum, 990 Proprietors Rd.

Art Gallery:
Columbus Museum of Art, 480 E. Broad St.

Points of Interest:
State Capitol, Ohio Historical Center, Ohio State University, German Village, Battelle Planetarium

Information Sources:
Columbus Convention & Visitors Bureau
50 W. Broad St.
Columbus, Ohio 43215
(614) 221-1321

Columbus Area Chamber of Commerce
Columbus, Ohio 43215
50 W. Broad St.
(614) 221-6623

Dallas, Texas

Population: (*2,811,800)
(Includes Fort Worth)
904,078 (1980C); Metro Rank: 9
Altitude: 450 to 750 feet
Average Temp.: Jan., 44°F:; July, 86°F.
Telephone Area Number: 214
Time: 844-6611 **Weather:** 336-4416
Time Zone: Central
Selected Hotels:
Adolphus Hotel,
1321 Commerce St., 742-8200
Dallas Hilton Hotel,
1914 Commerce St., 747-2011
Dunfey's Dallas Hotel,
3800 W. Northwest Hwy., 357-9561
Executive Inn,
3232 W. Mockingbird St., 357-5601
Fairmont Hotel, Ross & Akard sts.,
748-5454
Hilton Inn,
5600 N. Central Expwy., 827-4100
Holiday Inn—Downtown,
Elm & Griffin sts., 748-9951
Howard Johnson's Motor Lodge,
3111 Stemmons Frwy., 637-0060
Hyatt Regency Dallas,
300 Reunion Blvd., 651-1234
Le Baron Hotel, 1055 Regal Row,
634-8550
Lowe's Anatole Dallas,
2201 Stemmons Frwy., 748-1200
Marriott Market Center,
2101 Stemmons Frwy., 748-8551
Plaza of the Americas Hotel,
703 N. Pearl St., 747-7222
Sheraton-Dallas Hotel,
Southland Center, 748-6211
Selected Restaurants:
Anatares, Top of the Dome,
Hyatt Regency, 300 Reunion Blvd.,
741-3663
Cafe Royale,
Plaza of the Americas Hotel, 747-7222
Chateaubriand, 2515 McKinney St.,
741-1223
La Vieille Varsovie, 2610 Maple Ave.,
528-0032
Marcel's, 5721 W. Lovers Lane, 358-2103
Mr. Peppe, 5617 W. Lovers Lane,
352-5976
The Pyramid Room, Fairmont Hotel,
748-5454
Liquor Laws: Liquor is available in public bars and restaurants.
Newspapers:
Dallas Morning News, 745-8383
Dallas Times Herald, 744-6111
Wall Street Journal, Southwest Edition,
631-7250
Television Stations:
KDFW (CBS) Channel 4
KERA (PBS) Channel 13
KTVT Channel 11
KXAS (NBC) Channel 5
WFAA (ABC) Channel 8
AM Radio Stations:
KAAM 1310 Middle-of-the-Road
KLIF 1190 Popular
KRLD (CBS) 1080 News/Music/Sports
KVIL 1150 Contemporary
WFAA (ABC) 570 Popular/News
FM Radio Stations:
KAFM 92.5 Middle-of-the-Road
KNUS 98.7 Rock
KVIL 103.7 Contemporary
KWXI 97.1 Semi-classical
WRR 101.1 Classical
Airline Service:
Dallas-Ft. Worth Airport—Air Canada, Air Florida, Air Jamaica, American, Braniff, British Caledonia, Delta, Eastern, Frontier, Lufthansa, Mexicana de Aviación, Ozark, Piedmont, Texas International, Thai Airways, USAIR, Western
Airport Transportation:
Seventeen miles from Dallas-Ft. Worth Airport to downtown Dallas. Taxicab and limousine bus service.
Car Rental Agencies:
Avis (335-3211), Budget (574-3300), Dollar Rent-a-Car (357-8422), Econo-Car (256-4551), Hertz (574-2000), National (335-1030)
Railroad Passenger Service: Amtrak
Trade Exhibition Facilities:
Dallas Convention Center,
717 S. Akard St., 658-7000
State Fair Park, Dallas Fair Park,
823-9931
Dallas Market Center,
2100 Stemmons Frwy., 651-6100
Professional Sports Facilities:
Arlington Stadium, Int. 20, 265-3331
(Texas Rangers, baseball, 273-5100)
Reunion Arena, 777 Sports St.
(Dallas Mavericks, basketball, 988-0117)
State Fair Coliseum, State Fair Park
(Black Hawks, hockey, 823-6362)
Texas Stadium, State 183 & 114
(Cowboys, football, 369-3211;
Tornado, soccer, 750-0900)
Theaters and Concert Hall:
Bob Hope Theatre,
Southern Methodist University,
692-2573
Country Dinner Playhouse, Abrams Rd.
at LBJ Frwy., 231-9457
Dallas Repertory Theater,
NorthPark Mall, 369-8966
Dallas Theater Center,
3636 Turtle Creek St., 526-8857
Granny's Dinner Playhouse,
12205 Coil Rd., 239-0153
Kalita Humphreys Theater,
3636 Turtle Creek St., 526-0107
Margo Jones Theatre,
Southern Methodist University, 692-2573
Music Hall, State Fair Park,
2nd & Parry Aves. (Dallas Symphony Orchestra, Civic Opera)
New Arts Theatre Company,
301 N. Market St. at Ross Ave., 761-9064
Theatre Three, 2800 Routh St., 748-5191
Museums:
Age of Steam Railroads Museum,
7226 Wentwood Dr., Fair Park
Dallas Health and Science Museum and Planetarium, 1st & Forest aves.,
Fair Park
Dallas Museum of Natural History,
2nd & Grand aves., Fair Park
Art Museums:
Dallas Museum of Fine Arts, 2nd
& Parry aves., Fair Park
Owen Fine Arts, Southern Methodist University
Points of Interest:
Dallas Aquarium, The Dallas Zoo,
John F. Kennedy Plaza,
John F. Kennedy Museum,
Old City Park, Six Flags Over Texas,
Dallas Market Center Complex,
White Rock Lake, Dallas
Garden Center, Southwestern Historical
Wax Museum, Texas Sports Hall of
Fame, Thanksgiving Square,
Dallas Underground, Dallas City Hall
Information Sources:
Dallas Convention & Visitors Bureau
1507 Pacific Ave.
Dallas, Texas 75201
(214) 651-1020
Dallas Visitor Information Centers
400 S. Houston St., 747-2355
Plaza of the Americas, 655-1359

Dallas Chamber of Commerce
Information Department
1507 Pacific Ave.
Dallas, Texas 75201
(214) 651-1020

Denver, Colorado

Population: (*1,414,200)
491,396 (1980C); Metro Rank: 22
Altitude: 5,130 to 5,470 feet
Average Temp.: Jan., 31°F.; July, 74°F.
Telephone Area Number: 303
Time: 639-1311 **Weather:** 639-1515
Time Zone: Mountain
Selected Hotels:
The Brown Palace Hotel,
17th St. & Tremont Pl., 825-3111
Denver Hilton Hotel, 16th St. &
Court Pl., 893-3333
Denver Marriott,
6363 E. Hampden Ave., 758-7000
Fairmont Hotel, 1750 Welton St.,
527-4727
Four Winds Motor Hotel,
4600 W. Colfax Ave., 893-0600
Hampshire House, 1000 Grant St.,
292-1200
Holiday Inn—Downtown,
1450 Glenarm Pl., 573-1450
Radisson Denver Hotel, 1790 Grant St.,
292-1500

Stapleton Plaza, 3333 Quebec St., 525-1315

Selected Restaurants:
The Broker, 17th & Champa sts., 893-5065
Colorado Mine Co., 4490 E. Virginia Ave., 321-6555
Emerson St. East, 900 E. Colfax Ave., 832-1349
Lafitte Restaurant, 1400 Larimer St., 222-5811
Normandy French Restaurant, 1515 Madison St., 321-3311
Northwoods Inn, 6115 S. Santa Fe Dr., 794-2112
Quorum Restaurant, Colfax Ave. & Grant St., 861-8686
Stouffer's Top of the Rockies, 1616 Glenarm Pl., 825-3321

Liquor Laws: Beer (3.2%) establishments are open 5 A.M. to midnight year-round. Beer, wine, and liquors are sold 7 A.M. to 2 A.M. weekdays, 8 A.M. to midnight Sundays.

Newspapers:
Denver Post, 820-1010
Denver Rocky Mountain News, 892-5000

Television Stations:
KBTV (ABC) Channel 9
KMGH (CBS) Channel 7
KOA (NBC) Channel 4
KRMA (PBS) Channel 6
KWGN Channel 2

AM Radio Stations:
KLZ (CBS) 560 General
KOA (NBC) 850 General
KTLK 1280 General

FM Radio Stations:
KHOW 95.7 Music/News
KLZ 106.7
KOA 103.5 Music/News
KOSI 101.1 Music/News
KVOD 99.5 Classical

Airline Service:
Stapleton International Airport—Air Midwest, American, Aspen Airways, Braniff, Continental, Delta, Eastern, Frontier, Mexicana de Aviación, Ozark, Republic, Texas International, TWA, United, Western

Airport Transportation:
Seven miles to downtown Denver. Bus, taxicab, and limousine bus service.

Car Rental Agencies: Avis (398-3725), Budget (399-0444), Hertz (398-3683), National (388-1677)

Railroad Passenger Service: Amtrak, Denver & Rio Grande Western

Trade Exhibition Facilities:
Denver Convention Complex, 1323 Champa St., 575-2638
Denver Merchandise Mart, 451 E. 58th Ave., 292-1050

Professional Sports Facilities:
Denver Arena, 1323 Champa St., 297-2511 (wrestling)
McNichols Sports Arena, 1635 Clay St., 297-3217 (Nuggets, basketball)
Mile High Stadium, W. 19th & Eliot sts. (Broncos, football, 433-7466; Bears, baseball, 433-8645)

Theaters and Concert Hall:
Auditorium Theatre, 14th & Curtis sts., 297-2600
Denver Center for the Performing Arts, 13th & Curtis sts., 893-4000 (Boettcher Concert Hall, Denver Symphony Orchestra, 292-1584; opera), Helen G. Bonfils Theatre Complex, 893-4200
Bonfils Theatre, E. Colfax Ave. at Elizabeth St., 322-7725
The Changing Scene, 1527½ Champa St., 893-5775
Country Dinner Playhouse, 6875 S. Clinton Dr., 771-1410
Gaslight Theatre, 4201 Hooker St., 455-6077
Germinal Stage Denver, 1820 Market St., 572-0944
Heritage Square Opera House, Heritage Square, 279-7881

Museums:
Buffalo Bill Museum, Lookout Mountain, I-70
Children's Museum, 931 Bannock St.
Colorado Heritage Center, 1300 Broadway
Denver Museum of Natural History, Montview & Colorado Blvd.
Forney Transportation Museum, 1416 Platte St.
Wax Museum, 919 Bannock St.

Art Museum and Gallery:
Carson Gallery of Western American Art, 730 17th St.
Denver Art Museum, 100 W. 14th Pkwy.

Points of Interest:
Celebrity Sports Center, U.S. Mint, Denver Botanic Gardens, State Capitol, Red Rocks Park, Elitch's Gardens, Larimer Square

Information Sources:
Denver & Colorado Convention and Visitors Bureau
225 W. Colfax Ave.
Denver, Colorado 80202
(303) 892-1112

Denver Chamber of Commerce
1301 Welton St.
Denver, Colorado 20204
(303) 534-3211

Detroit, Michigan

Population: (*4,399,000) 1,203,339 (1980C); Metro Rank: 6
Altitude: 573 to 672 feet
Average Temp.: Jan., 26°F.; July, 73°F.
Telephone Area Number: 313
Time: 472-1212 **Weather:** 932-1212
Time Zone: Eastern

Selected Hotels:
Book Cadillac Hotel 1114 Washington Blvd., 256-8000
Hilton Airport Inn, 31500 Wick, 292-3400
Holiday Inn—Airport, 31200 Industrial Expwy., 728-2800
Hotel Pontchartrain, 2 Washington Blvd., 965-0200
Hotel St. Regis, 3071 W. Grand Blvd., 873-3000
Howard Johnson's, Michigan Ave. & Washington Blvd., 965-1050
Hyatt Regency Dearborn, Fairlane Town Center, 593-1234
Northfield Hilton Inn, 5500 Crooks Rd. at Int. 75, Troy, 879-1216
Troy Hilton Inn, 1455 Stephenson Hwy., Troy, 583-9000
Westin, Renaissance Center, 568-8000

Selected Restaurants:
Baker's Keyboard Lounge, 20510 Livernois at 8 mile, 864-1200
Caucus Club, 150 W. Congress St., 965-4970
Charley's Raw Bar & Seafood, Hotel Pontchartrain, 2 Washington Blvd., 965-0200
Jim's Garage, 300 W. Larned St., 961-5175
Joe Muer's, 2000 Gratiot Ave., WO 2-1088
La Place, Hotel St. Regis, 3071 W. Grand Blvd., 873-3000
Little Harry's, 2681 E. Jefferson Ave., 259-2636
London Chop House, 155 W. Congress St., 962-0278
Mario's, 4222 2nd Ave., TE 3-9425
Pontchartrain Wine Cellar, 234 W. Larned St., WO 3-1785
Schweizer's Since 1862, 260 Schweizer Place, 568-1862
Victor Lim's, 48 W. Adams St., 961-0063

Liquor Laws: Liquor may be purchased daily until 2 A.M., Sunday after 12 noon.

Newspapers:
Detroit Free Press, 222-6400
The Detroit News, 222-2000

Television Stations:
CBET (Canadian) Channel 9
WDIV (NBC) Channel 4
WJBK (CBS) Channel 2
WKBD (Educational) Channel 50
WTVS (PBS) Channel 56
WXON Channel 20
WXYZ (ABC) Channel 7

AM Radio Stations:
WJR (NBC) 760 Talk/News/Music
WWJ (CBS) 950 Talk/News/Music
WXYZ (ABC) 1270 News/Talk

FM Radio Stations:
WABX 99.5 Rock/Talk—part *Stereo*
WDET 101.9 Classical/Talk/Jazz
WJR 96.3 Music
WQRS 105.1 Classical/Talk/Jazz
WRIF 101.1 Rock/Talk—part Stereo

Airline Service:
Detroit Metropolitan Airport—American, Braniff, British Airways, Delta, Eastern, Frontier, Northwest

Orient, Ozark, Pan American, Republic, Sabena, TWA, United, USAIR
Airline Service:
Detroit City Airport—Wright
Airport Transportation:
Twenty-three miles from Metropolitan Airport to downtown Detroit. Taxicab and limousine bus service.
Car Rental Agencies: Americar (326-4300), Avis (964-0494), Budget (326-6800), Hertz (644-2748), National (941-5030)
Railroad Passenger Service: Amtrak
Trade Exhibition Facilities:
Cobo Hall, 1 Washington Blvd., 224-1010
Detroit Light Guard Armory, 4400 E. 8 Mile Rd., 366-8900
Masonic Temple, 500 Temple St., 832-7100
State Fairgrounds, 19600 Woodward Ave., 368-1000
Professional Sports Facilities:
Joe Louis Arena, 600 Civic Center Dr., (Red Wings, hockey, 962-2000)
Tiger Stadium, Trumbull & Michigan aves. (Tigers, baseball, 962-4000)
Pontiac Silverdome, 1200 Featherstone Rd. (Lions, football, 857-8000; Pistons, basketball, 338-4667)
Theaters and Concert Halls:
Art Institute Auditorium, 5200 Woodward Ave., 833-7900
Attic Theater, 525 E. Lafayette St.
Bonstelle Theater, 3424 Woodward Ave., 577-2960
Fisher Theater, W. Grand Blvd. & 2nd Ave., 872-1000
Ford Auditorium, 20 Auditorium Dr. (Detroit Symphony Orchestra, 962-5524
Hilberry Classic Theatre, 4743 Cass Ave., 577-2962
Music Hall Center for the Performing Arts, 350 Madison Ave., 963-7680
Orchestra Hall, Parsons St. at Woodward St., 833-3700
Museums:
The Children's Museum, 67 E. Kirby St.
Detroit Historical Museum, 5401 Woodward Ave.
Detroit Science Center, 5020 John R St.
Dossin Great Lakes Museum, Strand Drive, Belle Isle
Greenfield Village and Henry Ford Museum, Dearborn
Art Museum:
Detroit Institute of Arts, 5200 Woodward Ave.
Points of Interest:
International Institute, Belle Isle, Civic Center, Greenfield Village, Detroit Zoo, Bob-Lo Island, Children's Zoo, Eastern Market, Historic Fort Wayne, Renaissance Center
Information Sources:
Metropolitan Detroit Convention & Visitors Bureau
Suite 1950, 100 Renaissance Center
Detroit, Michigan 48243
(313) 259-4333

Detroit Visitor Information Center
2 E. Jefferson Ave.,
Detroit, Michigan 48226
(313) 963-0879

Greater Detroit Chamber of Commerce
150 Michigan Ave.
Detroit, Michigan 48226
(313) 964-4000

Hartford, Connecticut

Population: (*1,055,700) 136,392 (1980C); Metro Rank: 29
Altitude: 10 to 290 feet
Average Temp.: Jan., 28°F.; July, 74° F.
Telephone Area Number: 203
Time Zone: Eastern **Time:** 524-8123
Selected Hotels:
Holiday Inn of East Hartford, 363 Roberts St., 528-9611
Holiday Inn of Hartford, 50 Morgan St., 549-2400
Hotel Sonesta, 5 Constitution Plaza, 278-2000
Howard Johnson Conference Center, Int. 91 & Center St., Windsor Locks, 623-9811
Park View Hilton, 1 Hilton Plaza, 249-5611
Ramada Inn of East Hartford, 100 East River Dr., 528-9703
Sheraton-Hartford, Trumbull St. at Civic Center Plaza, 728-5151
Sheraton Tobacco Valley Inn, Bloomfield Ave., Windsor, 688-5221
Selected Restaurants:
Carbone's Ristorante, 588 Franklin Ave., 249-9646
Chuck's Steak House, One Civic Center Plaza, 524-0337
Club 60, 60 Washington St., 527-6060
Frank's Restaurant, 159 Asylum St., 527-9291
Honiss' Oyster House Co., 44 State St., 522-4177
Last National Bank, 750 Main St., 246-5387
Rib Room, 5 Constitution Plaza, 278-2000
Rising Sun, One Civic Center Plaza, 527-2609
Signature Restaurant, One Civic Center Plaza, 249-1629
The Brownstone, 124 Asylum St., 525-1171
36 Lewis St., 36 Lewis St., 247-2300
Liquor Laws: Liquor may be purchased at restaurants and lounges, Monday through Thursday, 9 A.M. to 1 A.M.; Friday and Saturday, 9 A.M. to 2 A.M.; Sunday, noon to 11 P.M.; package stores, 8 A.M. to 8 P.M. daily.
Newspaper:
Hartford Courant, 249-6411
Television Stations:
CPTV (PBS) Channel 24
WFSB (CBS) Channel 3
WHCT Channel 18
WTNH (ABC) Channel 8
WVIT (NBC) Channel 30
AM Radio Stations:
WCCC (ABC) 1300 Popular/News
WDRC 1360 Rock
WKND 1480 Rock/Soul
WRCH 910 Mood/Semi-classical
WTIC (NBC) 1080 News/Popular
FM Radio Stations:
WDRC 102.9 Popular/News—*Stereo*
WKSS 96 Music
WRCH 100.5 Semi-classical—*Stereo*
WRTC 89.3 Hard Rock/Jazz
WTIC 96.5 Popular/News
Airline Service:
Bradley International Airport—Allegheny Commuter, American, Bar Harbor, Braniff, Delta, Eastern, Pan American, Texas International, TWA, United, USAIR
Airport Transportation:
Seventeen miles to downtown Hartford. Taxicab and limousine bus service.
Car Rental Agencies: Avis (246-5649), Budget (249-5225), Hertz (278-1100), National (522-2111), American International (236-5938), Thrifty (623-8214)
Railroad Passenger Service: Amtrak
Trade Exhibition Facilities:
Hartford Armory, 130 Broad St., 566-4210
Hartford Civic Center, One Civic Center Plaza, 728-6789
West Hartford Armory, 836 Farmington Ave., 523-7246
Theaters and Concert Halls:
Avery Theater, 25 Atheneum Square, 247-3695
Bushnell Memorial Hall, 166 Capitol Ave. (Hartford Symphony Orchestra, 278-1450; Hartford Ballet, 525-9396; Connecticut Opera Assoc., 527-0713)
Goodspeed Opera House, East Haddam St., 873-8668
Hartford Stage Co., 50 Church St., 525-5601
Hartford Civic Center, One Civic Center Plaza, 566-6000
Museums:
Children's Museum, 950 Trout Brook Dr., West Hartford
Connecticut Historical Society, 1 Elizabeth St.
Old State House, 800 Main St.
Art Museum and Gallery:
Wadsworth Atheneum, 600 Main St.
Points of Interest:
Nook Farm (Mark Twain and Harriet Beecher Stowe houses), Constitution Plaza, Elizabeth Park, Connecticut State Library and Capitol, Old Newgate Prison, Center Church and Burying Ground, Butler-McCook Homestead, Bradley Air Museum,

Mystic Seaport

Information Sources:

Greater Hartford Convention & Visitors Bureau, Inc.
One Civic Center Plaza
Hartford, Connecticut 06103
(203) 728-6789

Greater Hartford Chamber of Commerce
250 Constitution Plaza
Hartford, Connecticut 06103
(203) 525-4451

Honolulu, Hawaii

Population: (*762,900)
365,048 (1980C); Metro Rank: 39
Altitude: Sea level to 951 feet
Average Temp.: Jan., 72°F.; July, 78°F.
Telephone Area Number: 808
Time: 543-3211 **Weather:** 847-0234
Time Zone: Hawaiian (Two hours earlier than Pacific standard time)

Selected Hotels:

Halekulani, 2199 Kalia Rd., 923-2311
Hawaiian Regent, 2552 Kalakaua Ave., 922-6611
Hilton Hawaiian Village, 2005 Kalia Rd., 949-4321
Hyatt Regency Waikiki, 2424 Kalakana Ave., 922-9292
Ilikai, 1777 Ala Moana Ave., 949-3811
Kahala Hilton, 5000 Kahala Ave., 734-2211
Moana Hotel, 2365 Kalakaua Ave., 923-3111
Outrigger, 2335 Kalakaua Ave., 923-0711
Princess Kaiulani, 120 Kaiulani Ave., 922-5811
Queen Kapiolani, 150 Kapahulu Ave., 922-1941
Royal Hawaiian, 2259 Kalakaua Ave., 923-7311
Surfrider, 2353 Kalakaua Ave., 922-3111

Selected Restaurants:

Canlis, 2100 Kalakaua Ave., 923-2324
Cavalier, 1630 Kapiolani Blvd., 949-4134
Chez Michel, 2126 B Kalakaua Ave., 923-0626
Furusato, 134 Kapahulu Ave., 923-8878; 2500 Kalakaua Ave., 922-5502
Golden Dragon Room (Chinese), 2005 Kalia Rd., 949-4321
Maile Room, 5000 Kahala Ave., 734-2211
Michel's, 2895 Kalakaua Ave., 923-6552
Prince Kuhio's, Ala Moana Center, 946-2102
The Third Floor, Hawaiian Regent Hotel, 2552 Kalakaua Ave., 922-6611
The Willows, 901 Hausten St., 946-4808

Liquor Laws: Package goods available seven days a week. Bar service, 10 A.M. to 2 A.M., depending on license.

Newspapers:

Honolulu Advertiser, 525-8000
Honolulu Star-Bulletin, 525-8000

Television Stations:

KGMB (CBS) Channels 9 and 3
KHET (Public) Channels 10 and 11
KHON (NBC) Channel 2
KIKU Channel 13
KITV (ABC) Channel 4

AM Radio Stations:

KCCN 1420 Hawaiian Music
KGMB 590 Popular
KGU (NBC) 760 News
KHVH (CBS) 990 News
KPOI 1380 Rock

FM Radio Stations:

KAIM 95.5 Classical—*Stereo*
KGMQ 93.1 Rock—*Stereo*
KHSS 97.5 Popular—*Stereo*
KUMU 94.7 Popular—*Stereo*

Airline Service:

Honolulu International Airport—Air New Zealand, Aloha Airlines, American, Braniff, Canadian Pacific Air, China, Continental, Hawaiian, Japan, Korean, Northwest Orient, Pan American, Philippine, QANTAS (Australia), United, Western

Inter-Island Commuter Air Taxi Service:

Air Hawaii, Air Molokai, Ananda Air, Brandt, Oahu-Kauai, Royal Hawaiian Air Service

Airport Transportation:

Nine miles to Waikiki.
Taxicab and limousine bus service.

Car Rental Agencies:

Avis (847-9311), Budget (922-5533), Hertz (841-8011), National (922-3331)

Railroad Passenger Service: None

Trade Exhibition Facility:

Blaisdell Center, 777 Ward Ave., 536-7331

Theaters and Concert Hall:

Community Theater, Ruger Theater Bldg., 734-0274
Blaisdell Center Concert Hall, 777 Ward Ave., 536-7331 (Honolulu Symphony Orchestra and Opera Theater, 537-6171)
Manoa Valley Theatre, 2833 E. Manoa Rd., 988-6131 (Hawaii Performing Arts Company)

Museums:

Bishop Museum and Planetarium, 1355 Kalihi St.
Iolani Palace, King & Richards sts.
Mission Houses Museum, 553 S. King St.
Queen Emma Summer Palace, 2913 Pali Hwy.

Art Galleries:

Honolulu Academy of Arts, 900 S. Beretania St.
Tennent Art Foundation Gallery, 203 Prospect St.

Points of Interest:

Foster Botanic Gardens, Paradise Park, Pearl Harbor, Kawaiahao Church, Punchbowl—National Memorial Cemetery, Nuuanu Pali Lookout

Information Sources:

Hawaii Visitors Bureau
Administrative Offices
P. O. Box 8527
(Walk-in office, 2270 Kalakaua Ave.)
Honolulu, Hawaii 96815
(808) 923-1811

Hawaii Chamber of Commerce
735 Bishop St.
Honolulu, Hawaii 96813
(808) 531-4111

Houston, Texas

Population: (*2,689,200)
1,594,086 (1980C); Metro Rank: 10
Altitude: Sea level to 50 feet
Average Temp.: Jan., 59°F.; July, 82°F
Telephone Area Number: 713
Time: 844-7171 **Weather:** 228-8703
Time Zone: Central

Selected Hotels:

The Grand, 2525 W. Loop South, 961-3000
Guest Quarters Hotel, 2929 S. Post Oak Rd., 877-8100
Holiday Inn—Downtown, 801 Calhoun St., 659-2222
Hotel Meridien, 400 Dallas St., 759-0202
Holiday Inn—Medical Center, 8701 S. Main St., 797-1110
Hyatt Regency Houston, 1200 Louisiana St., 654-1234
Inn on the Park—Four Seasons Hotel, 4 Riverway Dr., 871-8181
Lamar Hotel, Main St. at Lamar Ave., 658-8511
Marriott Inn—West Loop, 1750 W. Loop S, 960-0111
Shamrock Hilton, Main St. at Holcombe Blvd., 668-9211
Sheraton Houston Hotel, 777 Polk Ave., 651-9041
Stouffer's Greenway Plaza Hotel, Southwest Frwy. at Edloe, 629-1200
The Warwick, 5701 Main St., 526-1991
Westin Galleria, 5060 W. Alabama St., 960-8100
Westin Oaks, 5011 Westheimer Rd., 623-4300
The Whitehall, 1700 Smith St., 659-5000

Selected Restaurants:

Brennan's, Smith & Stuart sts., 522-9711
The Brownstone, 2736 Virginia St., 528-2844
Che, 5020 Montrose Blvd., 524-9071
Courtlandts, 611 Stuart St., 526-3247
The Great Caruso, 10001 Westheimer Rd., 780-4900
Look's Sir-Loin Inn, 9810 Main St., 666-4181
Maxim's, 802 Lamar St., 658-9595
The Rivoli, 5636 Richmond Ave., 789-1900
Tony's, 1801 S. Post Oak Rd., 622-6778
Vargo's, 2401 Fondren Rd., 782-3888

Liquor Laws: Most bars and some restaurants sell liquor by the drink. Others sell only beer, wine, or champagne.
Newspapers:
Houston Chronicle, 220-7171
Houston Post, 621-7000
Television Stations:
KHOU (CBS) Channel 11
KPRC (NBC) Channel 2
KTRK (ABC) Channel 13
AM Radio Stations:
KODA (MBS) 1010 Varied
KPRC (NBC) 950 Popular
KTRH (CBS) 740 Talk/News
KXYZ (ABC) 1320 Rock
FM Radio Stations:
KFMK 97.9 Rock—*Stereo*
KLEF 94.5 Classical—*Stereo*
KLYX 102 Soul—*Stereo*
KODA 99.1 Varied—*Stereo*
KQUE 102.9 Popular—*Stereo*
Airline Service:
Houston Intercontinental Airport—Aeromexico, Air Canada, Air France, Alia, American, Braniff, British Caledonian, Cayman, Continental, Delta, Eastern, KLM, (Royal Dutch Airlines), Pan American, Piedmont, Republic, TACA, Texas International, TWA, United, USAIR, VIASA
Airline Service:
William P. Hobby Airport—
Air Florida, Frontier, Ozark, Republic, Southwest
Airport Transportation:
Twenty miles from Intercontinental Airport to downtown Houston; 10 miles from Hobby Airport to downtown. Taxicab, limousine, coach bus, and helicopter service.
Car Rental Agencies: Avis (659-6537), Budget (449-0145), Hertz (443-0800), National (443-8850)
Railroad Passenger Service: Amtrak
Trade Exhibition Facilities:
Albert Thomas Convention & Exhibit Center, 612 Smith St., 222-3561
Astrodome, Astrohall & AstroArena, Int. 610 at Kirby Dr., 799-9500
Sam Houston Coliseum, Bagby St. at Walker Ave., 222-3267
Professional Sports Facilities:
Astrodome, Int. 610 at Kirby Dr., 799-9500 (Astros, baseball; Oilers, football)
The Summit, 10 Greenway Plaza (Rockets, basketball, 960-8731)
Theaters and Concert Hall:
Alley Theatre, 615 Texas Ave., 228-9341
Jones Hall for the Performing Arts, 615 Louisiana St., 222-3415 (Houston Symphony Orchestra, 224-4240; Society for the Performing Arts Houston Grand Opera, 227-1287; Houston Ballet, 225-0271)
Miller Outdoor Theatre, Hermann Park, 222-3576
Sam Houston Coliseum Music Hall, 810 Bagby St., 222-3561
The Tower Theatre,
1201 Westheimer Rd., 422-2452
Windmill Dinner Theatre,
390 Town & Country Blvd., 464-7655
Museums:
Bayou Bend Museum, 1 Westcott St.
Baker Planetarium, Hermann Park
Museum of Natural Science and Museum of Medical Science, Hermann Park
San Jacinto Museum of History, San Jacinto Battleground Park
Art Museums:
Contemporary Arts Museum, 5216 Montrose Blvd.
Museum of Fine Arts, 1001 Bissonnet St.
Rothko Chapel, 1409 Sul Ross St.
Points of Interest:
Astrodome and Astroworld, Lyndon B. Johnson Space Center, Port of Houston, Hermann Park, Civic Center, Texas Medical Center, Tranquility Park, Sam Houston Park, McAshan Botanical Gardens, San Jacinto Battleground, U.S.S. *Texas*, The Underground (downtown sidewalk)
Information Sources:
Greater Houston Convention and Visitors Council
1522 Main St.
Houston, Texas 77002
(713) 658-4200

Houston Chamber of Commerce
1100 Milam St.
Houston, Texas 77002
(713) 651-1313

Indianapolis, Indiana

Population: (*1,104,200) 700,807 (1980C); Metro Rank: 28
Altitude: 664 to 845 feet
Average Temp.: Jan., 29°F.; July, 76°F.
Telephone Area Number: 317
Time: 632-1511 **Weather:** 222-2362
Time Zone: Eastern
Selected Hotels:
Hilton at the Circle,
Meridian & Ohio sts., 635-2000
Hilton Inn—Airport, 2500 S. High School Rd., 244-3361
Holiday Inn—Airport, 2501 S. High School Rd., 244-6861
Holiday Inn—North,
Int. 465 at U.S. 421, 298-9790
Howard Johnson's—Downtown,
501 W. Washington St., 635-4443
Hyatt Regency Indianapolis,
Washington & Capital sts., 632-1234
Marriott, 7202 E. 21st St., 352-1231
Ramada Inn—East,
3525 N. Shadeland Ave., 547-5561
Sheraton Inn West, 2544 Executive Dr., 248-2481
Speedway, 4400 W. 16th St., 241-2392
Selected Restaurants:
Chanteclair Sur Le Toit, Holiday Inn—Airport, 2501 S. High School Rd., 244-7378
Harrison's, Hyatt Regency Indianapolis, Washington & Capital sts., 632-1234
Houlihan's Old Place,
6101 N. Keystone Ave., 257-4318
King Cole, 7 N. Meridian St., 638-5588
La Tour, One Indiana Square, 635-3535
Ramsgate Roof, 2820 N. Meridian, 924-1241
Liquor Laws: Liquor may be purchased by drink or bottle Monday through Saturday; by drink only Sunday. Liquor store hours 9 A.M. to 2 A.M.
Newspapers:
Indianapolis Business Journal, 259-8222
Indianapolis News, 633-1240
Indianapolis Star, 633-1240
Television Stations:
WFYI (PBS) Channel 20
WISH (CBS) Channel 8
WRTV (ABC) Channel 6
WTHR (NBC) Channel 13
AM Radio Stations:
WIBC 1070 Music/News
WIFE 1310 Music/Sports/News
WIRE 1430 Country/Sports/News
WNDE 1260 Music/News
Airline Service:
Indianapolis International Airport—American, Continental, Delta, Eastern, Northwest Orient, Ozark, TWA, USAIR
Airport Transportation:
Eight miles to downtown Indianapolis. Taxicab and limousine bus service.
Car Rental Agencies: American International (243-6336), Avis (635-6444), Budget (297-0353), Dollar Rent-a-Car (241-8206), Hertz (634-6464), National (873-5364)
Railroad Passenger Service: Amtrak
Trade Exhibition Facilities:
Coliseum, Indiana State Fairgrounds, 923-3431
Indiana Convention Center,
100 S. Capitol Ave., 632-4321
Manufacturers Building, Indiana State Fairgrounds, 923-3431
Market Square Arena, 300 E. Market St., 639-6444
Professional Sports Facilities:
Indianapolis Motor Speedway,
4790 W. 16th St., 241-2501
(auto racing—Indianapolis 500)
Market Square Arena, 300 E. Market St. (Pacers, basketball, 924-5191)
Theaters and Concert Hall:
Civic Theater of Indianapolis,
1200 W. 38th St., 923-4597
Clowes Memorial Hall, 4600 Sunset Ave., 924-6321 (Indianapolis Symphony Orchestra)
Hilton U. Brown,
49th St. & Boulevard Pl., 926-1581
Indiana Repertory Theatre,

140 W. Washington St., 635-5252
Murat Theater, 502 N. New Jersey St., 635-2433
Museums:
Children's Museum, 3010 N. Meridian St.
Indiana State Museum, 202 N. Alabama St.
Indianapolis Motor Speedway Museum, 4700 W. 16th St.
Museum of Indian Heritage, 6040 DeLong Rd.
Art Museum and Gallery:
Indianapolis Museum of Art, 1200 W. 38th St.
Oldfields (Lilly Pavilion of the Decorative Arts), 4200 N. Michigan Rd.
Points of Interest:
State Capitol, Soldiers and Sailors Monument, Garfield Park, World War Memorial Plaza, Benjamin Harrison & James Whitcomb Riley homes, Basketball Hall of Fame, Conner Prairie Settlement
Information Sources:
Indianapolis Convention and Visitors Bureau
100 S. Capitol Ave.
Indianapolis, Indiana 46225
(317) 635-9567

Indianapolis Chamber of Commerce
320 N. Meridian St.
Indianapolis, Indiana 46204
(317) 635-4747

Kansas City, Missouri

Population: (*1,254,600)
448,159 (1980C); Metro Rank: 24
Altitude: 722 to 1,105 feet
Average Temp.: Jan., 30°F.; July, 81°F.
Telephone Area Number: 816
Time: 844-1212 **Weather:** 384-6600
Time Zone: Central
Selected Hotels:
Alameda Plaza Hotel, Wornall Rd. & Ward Pkwy., 756-1500
Continental Hotel, 106 West 11th St., 421-6040
Hilton Airport Plaza Inn, 112th St. & Int. 29, 891-8900
Hilton Plaza Inn, 45th & Main sts., 753-7400
Holiday Inn—City Center, 13th & Wyandotte sts., 221-8800
Howard Johnson's Downtown, 6th & Main sts., 842-6090
Radisson Muehlebach, 12th St. & Baltimore Ave., 471-1400
Kansas City Marriott, K.C.I. Airport, 464-2200
Sheraton Royal, Int. 70 at the Truman Sports Complex, 737-0200
The Westin Crown Center Hotel, 1 Pershing Rd., 474-4400
Selected Restaurants:
The American Restaurant, 25th & Grand Sts., 471-8050
Buttonwood Tree Inn & Pub, 4800 Main St., 753-0500
Golden Ox, 1600 Genessee St., 842-2866
Hereford House, 2 E. 20th St., 842-1080
Jasper's Italian Restaurant, 405 W. 75th St., 363-3003
Kona Kai, Galleria and El Patio, 45th & Main sts., 753-7400
La Mediterranee, 4742 Pennsylvania St., 561-2916
Plaza III, 4749 Pennsylvania Ave., 753-0000
Mr. Putsch's, 210 W. 47th St., 561-2000
Ralph Gaines Colony Steak House, Union Station, 842-5007
Savoy Grill, 9th & Central sts., 842-3890
Stephenson's Apple Farm, U.S. 40 & Old Lee's Summit Rd., 373-5345
Trader Vic's, The Westin Crown Center Hotel, 1 Pershing Rd., 474-4000
Liquor Laws: Bars open to 1:30 A.M. weekdays; Sunday, restaurants only.
Newspaper:
Kansas City Star, 234-4141
Kansas City Times, 234-4141
Television Stations:
KBMA (Ind.) Channel 41
KCMO (CBS) Channel 5
KCPT (PBS) Channel 19
KMBC (ABC) Channel 9
WDAF (NBC) Channel 4
AM Radio Stations:
KBEA (NBC) 1480 Contemporary
KCMO (CBS) 810 News/Talk
KPRS (MBS) 1590 Jazz
WDAF (ABC) 610 Country
FM Radio Stations:
KBEY 104.3 Contemporary
KCEZ 94.9 Contemporary
Airline Service:
Kansas City International Airport—Air Midwest, Braniff, Continental, Delta, Frontier, Midway, Ozark, Republic, Texas International, TWA, United
Airport Transportation:
Eighteen miles to downtown Kansas City. Taxicab and limousine bus service.
Car Rental Agencies:
Avis (471-2421), Budget (243-5755), Hertz (421-0300), Holiday (648-0145), National (471-2755)
Railroad Passenger Service: Amtrak
Trade Exhibition Facilities:
American Royal Center, 19th & Genessee sts., 421-6460
Kansas City Convention Center, 13th & Wyandotte sts., 421-8000 (Municipal Auditorium, H. Roe Bartle Exhibition Hall)
Professional Sports Facilities:
Kemper Arena, 17th & Genessee St., 421-6460 (Kings, basketball, 421-3131)
Harry S. Truman Sports Complex, inter. Int. 435 & Int. 70 (Chiefs, football, 924-9400; Royals, baseball, 921-8000)
Theaters and Concert Halls:
Music Hall, Municipal Auditorium, 421-8000 (Kansas City Philharmonic, 842-9300)
Lyric Theatre, 9th & Central sts., 471-4933 (Lyric Opera, ballet)
Missouri Repertory Theatre, 4949 Cherry St., 276-2705
Starlight Theatre (musicals during summer), Swope Park, 471-5510
Tiffany's Attic & Waldo Astoria Dinner Playhouse, 5028 Main St., 561-9876
Museums:
Harry S. Truman Library and Museum, U.S. 24 at Delaware St., Independence
K. C. Museum of History and Science, 3218 Gladstone Blvd.
Liberty Memorial & Museum, 100 W. 26th St.
Art Museums and Gallery:
Kansas City Art Institute, 4415 Warwick Blvd.
Nelson Gallery and Atkins Museum, 4525 Oak St.
Points of Interest:
Swope Park and Zoo, Board of Trade, Stockyards, Observation Tower at City Hall, Trail Town, Jesse James Farm Home, Country Club Plaza, Crown Center, Westport Square, City Center Square, Truman Historical District in Independence
Information Sources:
Convention and Visitors Bureau of Greater Kansas City
City Center Square, 1100 Main St., Suite 2550
Kansas City, Missouri 64105
(816) 221-5242

Chamber of Commerce of Greater Kansas City
920 Main St.
Kansas City, Missouri 64105
(816) 221-2424

Los Angeles, California

Population: (*9,840,200)
2,966,763 (1980C); Metro Rank: 2
Altitude: Sea level to 5,074 feet
Average Temp.: Jan., 55°F.; July, 73°F.
Telephone Area Number: 213
Time: 853-1212 **Weather:** 554-1212
Time Zone: Pacific
Selected Hotels:
Airport Century Inn, 5547 W. Century Blvd., 649-4000
Ambassador Hotel, 3400 Wilshire Blvd., 387-7011
Biltmore Hotel, 515 S. Olive St., 624-1011
Century Plaza, 2025 Avenue of the Stars, 277-2000
Holiday Inn, 1755 N. Highland Ave., 462-7181
Hyatt House Hotel 6225 W. Century Blvd., 670-9000
Hyatt Regency Los Angeles, 711 S. Hope St., 683-1234

Los Angeles Hilton, 930 Wilshire Blvd., 629-4321
Los Angeles Marriott Hotel, 5855 W. Century Blvd., 641-5700
New Otani Hotel & Garden, 250 E. 1st St., 629-1200
Sheraton Airport Hotel, 9750 Airport Blvd., 645-4600
Sheraton-Universal, 3838 Lankershim Blvd., Universal City, 980-1212
Sheraton-West, 2961 Wilshire Blvd., 382-7171
The Westin Bonaventure, 5th & Figueroa sts., 624-1000
Wilshire Hyatt House, 3515 Wilshire Blvd., 381-7411

Selected Restaurants:
Bernard's, Biltmore Hotel, 624-0183
Casey's Bar & Grill, 613 S. Grand Ave., 629-2353
Francois, 555 S. Flower St., 680-2727
Lawry's Prime Rib, 55 N. La Cienega Blvd., 652-2827
L'Escoffier, 9876 Wilshire Blvd., 274-7777
The Lobster House, 4211 Admiralty Way, 823-5339
Perino's, 4101 Wilshire Blvd., 383-1221
Scandia, 9040 Sunset Strip, 278-3555
The Tower, 1150 S. Olive St., 746-1554
Yamato Restaurant, 2025 Ave. of the Stars, Century City, 277-1840

Liquor Laws: Legal hours of sale are from 6 A.M. to 2 A.M.

Newspapers:
Los Angeles Herald-Examiner, 748-1212
Los Angeles Times, 625-2345

Television Stations:
KABC (ABC) Channel 7
KCET (PBS) Channel 28
KNBC (NBC) Channel 4
KNXT (CBS) Channel 2

AM Radio Stations:
KABC (ABC) 790 Talk/News
KFI (NBC) 640 Music/Sports/News
KHJ 930 Rock
KMPC 710 Popular/Sports
KNX (CBS) 1070 News

FM Radio Stations:
KBCA 105.1 Jazz
KFAC 92.3 Classical—*Stereo*
KPFK 90.7 News/Talk/Classical/Rock/Folk—part *Stereo*
KRHM 102.7 Popular—*Stereo*

Airline Service:
Los Angeles International Airport—Aerolineas Argentina, Aeromexico, Air Canada, Air France, Air New Zealand, Air Panama, American, AVIANCA (Colombia), Braniff, British Airways, Canadian Pacific Air, China, Continental, Delta, Eastern, Empresa Ecuatoriana de Aviación (Ecuador), Japan, Korean, Lufthansa (Germany), Mexicana de Aviación, National, Northwest Orient, Pan American, SAS (Scandinavian Airlines), Texas International, TWA, United, UTA (Union de Transports Aeriens), VARIG (Brazil), Western

Airport Transportation:
Seventeen miles to downtown Los Angeles. Taxicab, limousine bus and city bus service.

Car Rental Agencies: Alamo (649-2242), Avis (646-5600), Budget (800-527-0700), Dollar (645-4500), Econo-Car (776-6184), Hertz (646-2851), National (670-4950)

Railroad Passenger Service: Amtrak

Trade Exhibition Facilities:
Great Western Exhibit Center, 2120 S. Eastern Ave., 723-3678
Pan Pacific Auditorium, 7600 Beverly Blvd., 938-4692
Los Angeles Convention Center, 1201 S. Figueroa St., 741-1151
Shrine Exposition Hall, 665 W. Jefferson Blvd., 748-5116

Professional Sports Facilities:
Dodger Stadium, 1000 Elysian Park Ave., 225-1411 (Dodgers, baseball)
Los Angeles Memorial Coliseum & Sports Arena, Exposition Park, 3911 S. Figueroa St., 747-7111
Anaheim Stadium, 2000 State College Blvd., Anaheim, 625-1123 (Angels, baseball; Rams, football)
The Forum, 3900 W. Manchester Blvd., Inglewood, 673-1300 (Kings, hockey; Lakers, basketball)

Theaters and Concert Hall:
Ivar Theatre, 1605 Ivar Ave., 464-7121
Los Angeles County Music Center (Dorothy Chandler Pavilion, Mark Taper Forum, Ahmanson Theatre), 135 N. Grand Ave., 972-7211 (Los Angeles Philharmonic and Southern California Symphony Orchestra in winter, Hollywood Bowl, summer; Los Angeles Civic Light Opera)
Shubert Theatre, 2020 Avenue of The Stars, 553-9000

Museums:
California Museum of Science and Industry, 700 State Dr., Exposition Park
Griffith Observatory and Planetarium, Griffith Park
La Brea Tar Pits & George C. Page Museum, 5801 Wilshire Blvd.
Los Angeles County Museum of Natural History, 900 Exposition Blvd.
Southwest Museum, 234 Museum Dr., Highland Park

Art Museums and Gallery:
Huntington Library, Art Gallery, and Botanical Gardens, 1151 Oxford Rd., San Marino
Los Angeles County Museum of Art, 5905 Wilshire Blvd.
Municipal Art Gallery, 4800 Hollywood Blvd.
J. Paul Getty Museum, 17985 Pacific Coast Hwy., Malibu

Points of Interest:
Disneyland, Farmers Market, Marineland of the Pacific, Universal Studios Tour, Los Angeles Zoo, Lion Country Safari, *Queen Mary*, Magic Mountain, Mann's Chinese Theatre, El Pueblo de Los Angeles State Historic Park

Information Sources:
Greater Los Angeles Visitors & Convention Bureau
505 S. Flower St.
Los Angeles, California 90071
(213) 488-9100

Los Angeles Chamber of Commerce
404 S. Bixel St.
Los Angeles, California 90054
(213) 629-0711

Louisville, Kentucky

Population: (*881,100) 298,451 (1980C); Metro Rank: 34
Altitude: 382 to 761 feet
Average Temp.: Jan., 35°F.; July, 78°F
Telephone Area Number: 502
Time: 585-5961 **Weather:** 363-9655
Time Zone: Eastern

Selected Hotels:
Breckinridge Inn, 2800 Breckinridge Lane, 456-5050
Executive Inn, Freedom Way at Phillips Lane, 367-6161
Executive West, Freedom Way at Phillips Lane, 367-2251
Galt House, 4th St. & River Rd., 589-5200
Holiday Inn—South, 3317 Fern Valley Rd., 964-3311
Howard Johnson's—Downtown, 100 E. Jefferson St., 582-2481
Hyatt Regency, 320 W. Jefferson St., 587-3434
Ramada Inn, 9700 Bluegrass Pkwy., 267-8201
Sheraton Inn-Louisville East, 9608 Blairwood Rd., 426-4500
Stouffer's Louisville Inn, 120 W. Broadway, 582-2241

Selected Restaurants:
Bauer's Since 1870, 3612 Brownsboro Rd., 895-5493
Captain's Quarters, 6222 Guthrie Beach Rd., 228-1651
Casa Grisanti, 1000 E. Liberty St., 584-4377
Cup and Stirrup, 120 W. Broadway, 582-2241
Empire Room, Freedom Way & Phillips Lane, 367-6161
The Fig Tree, 234 W. Broadway, 583-1522
Hasenour's, 1028 Barrett Ave., 451-5210
Kunz's The Dutchman, 526 River City Mall, 584-1158
Labms, 320 W. Jefferson St., 587-3434
New Orleans House, 412 W. Chestnut St., 583-7231
Normandy Inn, 644 W. Washington St., 585-2849
Top of the Tower, First National Tower, 101 S. Fifth St., 585-2233

Liquor Laws: Liquor is sold at bars, restaurants, and privately owned stores

Newspapers:
Louisville Courier-Journal, 582-4011
Louisville Times, 582-4011
Television Stations:
WAVE (NBC) Channel 3
WDRB Channel 41
WHAS (CBS) Channel 11
WKPC (PBS) Channel 15
WLKY (ABC) Channel 32
AM Radio Stations:
WAVE (NBC) 970
WHAS (CBS) 84
WTMT 620 Country-Western
WXVW (ABC) 1450 News/Sports/Music
FM Radio Stations:
WLRS 102 Adult—*Stereo*
WNNS 97.5 News
WSAC 105.5 Popular
Airline Service:
Standiford Field—Allegheny Commuter, American, Delta, Eastern, Ozark, Piedmont, TWA, USAIR
Airport Transportation:
Five miles to downtown Louisville.
Taxicab service.
Car Rental Agencies: Avis (368-5851), Budget (363-2648), Hertz (361-0181), National (361-2515), Thrifty (367-6461)
Trade Exhibition Facilities:
Bluegrass Convention Hall,
9700 Bluegrass Pkwy., 267-8201
Commonwealth Convention Center,
221 River City Mall, 583-8403
Kentucky Exposition Center, Freedom Way, 366-9592
Louisville Gardens, 525 W. Walnut St., 582-2601
Theaters and Concert Hall:
Actors Theatre of Louisville,
316-20 Main St., 584-1205
Beef & Boards, Simpsonville, 451-4900
Macauley Theatre, 315 W. Broadway, 589-2727 (Kentucky Opera, 584-4101; Louisville Orchestra)
Museums:
The American Saddle Horse Museum,
730 W. Main St.
Centennial Library, Southern Baptist Theological Seminary Campus
The Filson Club, 118 W. Breckinridge St.
Kentucky Derby Museum,
Churchill Downs, 700 Central Ave.
Kentucky Railroad Museum,
LaGrange Rd. & Dorsey Lane
Museum of Natural History & Science
727 W. Main St.
Art Museums and Galleries:
Allen R. Hite Art Institute,
University of Louisville
Art Center Association, 1622 Story Ave.
First National Bank, 5th & Main sts.
Frame House Gallery, 110 E. Market St.
J. B. Speed Art Museum, 2035 S. 3rd St.
The Thor Gallery, 734 S. 1st St.
Points of Interest:
Churchill Downs, American Printing House for the Blind, Locust Grove (Home of George Rogers Clark), Farmington, Excursion Boat Belle of Louisville, Belvedere-Plaza, River City Mall, Founders Square, Louisville Zoo, Bakery Square
Information Sources:
Louisville Convention & Visitors Bureau
226 W. Muhammad Ali Blvd.
Louisville, Kentucky 40202
(502) 584-2121
Louisville Tourist Information
Founders Square
5th & Walnut sts.
Louisville, Kentucky 40202
(502) 583-3377
Louisville Area Chamber of Commerce
300 W. Liberty St.
Louisville, Kentucky 40202
(502) 582-2421

Memphis, Tennessee

Population: (*843,200)
646,356 (1980C); Metro Rank: 36
Altitude: 195 to 335 feet
Average Temp.: Jan., 43°F.; July, 80° F.
Telephone Area Number: 901
Time: 526-5261 **Weather:** 345-6700
Time Zone: Central
Selected Hotels:
Admiral Benbow Inn, 1220 Union Ave., 725-0630
Admiral Benbow Inn—Airport,
2201 Winchester Rd., 398-6251
Coach and Four, 1318 Lamar Ave., 278-5000
Hilton Inn—Memphis Airport,
2240 Democrat Rd.,
332-1130
Holiday Inn—Overton Square,
1837 Union Ave., 278-4100
Holiday Inn, Rivermont,
200 W. Georgia St., 525-0121
Hyatt Regency Memphis at Ridgeway,
939 Ridge Lake Blvd., 761-1234
The Peabody Hotel,
159 Union Ave., 529-4000
Sheraton Convention Center Hotel,
300 N. Second St., 525-2511
Sheraton Inn—Airport,
2411 Winchester Rd., 332-2370
Selected Restaurants:
Anderton's Restaurant,
1901 Madison Ave., 726-4010
Cafe St. Clair, 717 N. White Station Rd., 685-5404
Chesterfield's, 4726 Poplar Ave., 761-1880
The Chez Philippe, The Peabody Hotel, 149 Union Ave., 529-4000
Four Flames, 1085 Poplar Ave., 526-3181
Grisanti's, 1489 Airways Blvd., 458-2648
Hugo's, Hyatt Regency,
939 Ridge Lake Blvd., 761-1234
Justine's, 919 Coward Pl., 527-3815
Paulette's, 210 Madison Ave., 726-5128
Sciara's Palazzino, 6155 Poplar Ave., 767-9541
Liquor Laws: You may buy drinks at the better hotels, motels, and restaurants. At others you may buy the setups, but must provide your own liquor.
Newspapers:
Memphis Commercial Appeal, 526-8811
Memphis Press-Scimitar, 526-2141
Television Stations:
WHBQ (ABC) Channel 13
WKNO (PBS) Channel 10
WMC (NBC) Channel 5
WPTY Channel 24
WRAG (CBS) Channel 3
AM Radio Stations:
WMC (NBC) 790 Country
WMPS 680 Contemporary
WREC (CBS) 600 Popular
FM Radio Stations:
KWAM 101.1 Country-Western—*Stereo*
WMC 99.7 Popular/Semi-classical—*Stereo*
WREC 102.7 Popular/Semi-classical—*Stereo*
Airline Service:
Memphis International Airport—American, Braniff, Delta, Frontier, Piedmont, Republic, United, USAIR
Airport Transportation:
Ten miles to downtown Memphis.
Taxicab and limousine bus service.
Car Rental Agencies: American International (345-2440), Avis (345-2847), Budget (345-9000), Holiday (794-8244), Hertz (345-5680), National (345-4700), Thrifty (345-0170)
Railroad Passenger Service: Amtrak
Trade Exhibition Facilities:
Cook Convention & Exhibition Center,
255 N. Main St., 523-2322
Holiday Hall, 200 W. Georgia Ave., 525-0121
Mid-South Coliseum,
Fairgrounds, 274-3982
Professional Sports Facilities:
Liberty Bowl Memorial Stadium,
Fairgrounds, 278-4747
Mid-South Coliseum, Fairgrounds, 274-7400
Theaters and Concert Hall:
Auditorium, 255 N. Main St.,
(Memphis Symphony Orchestra, 287-4262)
Memphis Children's Theatre,
Fairgrounds, 275-0835
Theatre Memphis, 630 Perkins St., 682-8323
Museums:
Chucalissa Indian Village and Museum,
1987 Indian Village Dr.
Memphis Pink Palace Museum,
232 Tilton Rd.
Art Museum and Gallery:
Brooks Memorial Art Gallery,
Overton Park
Memphis Academy of Arts,
Overton Park
Points of Interest:
Memphis Botanic Garden, Memphis Zoological Garden and Aquarium, Memphis Queen Excursion Boat on Mississippi River, Lakeland Amusement and Recreation Park, Beale Street, Graceland (Elvis Presley home), Libertyland

Information Source:
Convention & Visitors Bureau of Memphis, 12 S. Main St., Memphis, Tennessee 38103
(901) 526-1919
Memphis Area Chamber of Commerce
P.O. Box 224
Memphis, Tennessee 38101
(901) 523-2322

Miami, Florida

Population: (*2,689,200)
346,931 (1980C); Mentro Rank: 11
Altitude: Sea level to 30 feet
Average Temp.: Jan., 69°F.; July, 82°F.
Telephone Area Number: 305
Time: 324-8811 **Weather:** 661-5065
Time Zone: Eastern
Selected Hotels:
Columbus, 284 NE. 1st St., 373-4411
Dupont Plaza, 300 Biscayne Blvd. Way, 358-2541
Everglades, 244 Biscayne Blvd., 379-5461
Four Ambassadors,
801 S. Bayshore Dr., 377-1966
Holiday Inn—Civic Center,
1170 NW. 11th St., 324-0800
Howard Johnson's—Airport,
1980 Le Jeune Rd., 871-4370
Marriott Hotel & Racquet Club,
1201 NW. LeJeune Rd., 649-5000
Omni International,
1550 Biscayne Blvd., 374-0000
Ramada Inn (Airport),
3941 NW. 22nd St., 871-1700
Sheraton River House (Airport),
3900 NW. 21st St., 871-3800
Selected Restaurants:
Cafe Chauveron, 9561 E. Bay Harbor Dr., 866-8779
Casa Santino, 10999 Biscayne Blvd., 895-1440
Cye's Rivergate, 444 Brickell Ave., 358-9100
The Depot, 5830 S. Dixie Hwy., South Miami, 665-6261
El Baturro, 2322 NW. 7th St., 642-1413
Flamenco, 991 NE. 79th St., 751-8631
La Belle Epoque, 1045 95th St., Bay Harbor Island, 865-6011
Les Violins, 1751 Biscayne Blvd., 371-8668
Raimondo, 201 NW. 79th St., 757-9071
Rotisserie, Four Ambassadors,
801 S. Bayshore Dr., 377-1966
Liquor Laws: Drinks may be purchased weekdays until 1 A.M. at bars and 5 A.M. at night clubs. None sold Sunday.
Newspapers:
Miami Herald, 350-2111
Miami News, 350-2200
Television Stations:
WCIX Channel 6
WCKT (NBC) Channel 7
WPBT Channel 2
WPLG (ABC) Channel 10
WTVJ (CBS) Channel 4
WLTV Channel 33 (Spanish)
AM Radio Stations:
WGBS (ABC) 710 Music
WINZ 940 (CBS) News
WIOD (NBC) 610 Music/Talk
WKAT (CBS) 1360 Talk/Sports
WVCG 1080 Music
FM Radio Stations:
WAIA 97.3 General—*Stereo*
WLYF 101.5 Popular—*Stereo*
WMJX 96.3 Popular—*Stereo*
WTMI 93.1 Classical—*Stereo*
Airline Service:
Miami International Airport—Aerocondor (Colombia), Aerolineas Argentinas, Aeromexico, Aeroperu, Air Canada, Air France, Air Jamaica, Air Panama, ALM (Dutch Antillean Airlines), AVIANCA (Colombia), Aviateca (Guatemala), Bahamasair, Belize Airways, Braniff, British Airways, BWIA (British West Indian Airways), Cayman Airways, Continental, Delta, Dominicana Eastern, Empresa Ecuatoriana de Aviación (Ecudor), Iberia (Spain), LACSA (Costa Rica), LAN Chile, LANICA (Nicaragua), Lloyd Aereo Boliviano, Mexicana de Aviación, National, Northwest Orient, Pan American, Republic, TACA (El Salvador), TAN (Honduras), TWA, United, VARIG (Brazil), VIASA (Venezuela), Western
Airport Transportation:
Five miles to downtown Miami. Taxicab and limousine bus service.
Car Rental Agencies: Alamo (526-6510), Avis (331-1212), Budget (871-3053), Econo-Car (445-8787), Hertz (526-5645), National (526-5200)
Railroad Passenger Service: Amtrak
Trade Exhibition Facilities:
Dinner Key Exposition Hall,
Dinner Key, 579-6335
Miami Merchandise Mart,
Palmetto Expwy, 261-2900
Municipal Auditorium,
499 Biscayne Blvd., 579-6335
Professional Sports Facilities:
Orange Bowl, 1400 NW. 4th St., 579-6971 (Dolphins, football, 358-2444)
Theater and Concert Halls:
Coconut Grove Playhouse,
3500 Main Hwy., 442-4000
Dade County Auditorium for the Performing Arts, 2901 W. Flagler St., 642-9061 (Greater Miami Opera Guild)
Maurice Gusman Cultural Center
174 E. Flagler St., 358-3430 (Greater Miami Philharmonic)
Museums:
Historical Museum of Southern Florida, 3280 S. Miami Ave.
Museum of Science & Space Transit Planetarium, 3280 S. Miami Ave.
Vizcaya, 3251 S. Miami Ave.
Art Museum and Gallery:
Lowe Gallery, University of Miami, Coral Gables
Miami Museum of Modern Art,
381 NE. 20th St.
Points of Interest:
Coral Castle, Seaquarium, Greyhound Racing, Horse Racing, Jai-Alai, Japanese Garden, University of Miami, Parrot Jungle, Watson Island,
Information Sources:
Miami Office of Information & Visitors Bureau, 150 SE. 2nd Ave.
Miami, Florida 33131
(305) 579-6327

Greater Miami Chamber of Commerce
1200 Biscayne Blvd.
Miami, Florida 33132
(305) 374-1800

Milwaukee, Wisconsin

Population: (*1,358,600)
636,212 (1980C); Metro Rank: 23
Altitude: 579 to 799 feet
Average Temp.: Jan., 21°F.; July, 71°F.
Telephone Area Number: 414
Time: 844-1414 **Weather:** 936-1212
Time Zone: Central
Selected Hotels:
Holiday Inn—South,
6331 S. 13th St., 764-1500
Hyatt Regency Milwaukee,
333 W. Kilbourn Ave., 276-1234
Marc Plaza,
509 W. Wisconsin Ave., 271-7250
Pfister Hotel & Tower,
424 E. Wisconsin Ave., 273-8222
Ramada Inn,
633 W. Michigan St., 272-8410
Red Carpet Hotel—Airport,
4747 S. Howell Ave., 481-8000
Selected Restaurants:
Jean-Paul's Gourmet,
811 E. Wisconsin Ave., 271-5400
English Room, Pfister Hotel & Tower,
424 E. Wisconsin Ave., 273-8222
John Ernst Cafe,
600 E. Ogden Ave., 273-5918
Karl Ratzsch's, 320 E. Mason St., 276-2720
Le Bestro, 509 W. Wisconsin Ave., 271-7250
Mader's, 1037 N. 3rd St., 271-3377
Magic Pan Creperie,
770 N. Jefferson St., 289-9814
Liquor Laws: Alcoholic beverages may be purchased seven days a week.
Newspapers:
Milwaukee Journal, 224-2000
Milwaukee Sentinel, 224-2000
Television Stations:
WISN (ABC) Channel 12
WITI (CBS) Channel 6
WMVS (PBS) Channel 10
WTMJ (NBC) Channel 4
WVTV Channel 18
AM Radio Stations:
WEMP 1250 Country
WISN (ABC) 1130 General
WOKY 920 Rock
WTMJ (NBC) 620 Popular

FM Radio Stations:
WFMR 96.5 Classical—*Stereo*
WISN 97.3 Popular—*Stereo*
WKTI 94.5 Popular—*Stereo*
WNUW 99.1 Popular

Airline Service:
General Mitchell Airport—Delta, Eastern, Northwest Orient, Ozark, Republic, United

Airport Transportation:
Eight miles to downtown Milwaukee. Taxicab, bus, and limousine bus service.

Car Rental Agencies: Avis (744-2266), Budget (481-2409), Hertz (747-5200), United Leasing Services (476-9650)

Railroad Passenger Service: Amtrak
Trade Exhibition Facility:
MECCA (Milwaukee Exposition, Convention Center, Arena)
555 W. Kilbourn Ave., 271-4000

Professional Sports Facilities:
Milwaukee Arena, 500 W. Kilbourn Ave., 271-5421 (Bucks, basketball; Admirals, hockey)
Milwaukee County Stadium, 201 S. 46th St., 278-4380 (Brewers, baseball, 933-1818; Green Bay Packers, football, 342-2717)
State Fair Park, West Allis, 257-8800 (auto racing—USAC Championship)

Theaters and Concert Halls:
Melody Top Theatre, 7201 W. Good Hope Rd., 353-7700
Performing Arts Center (Milwaukee Repertory Theater, Uihlein Hall, Charles P. Vogel Recital Hall, Todd Wehr Theatre) 929 N. Water St., 273-7121 (Milwaukee Symphony Orchestra, Florentine Opera Co., Milwaukee Ballet Co., Repertory Theater)
Skylight Theatre, 813 N. Jefferson St. 271-8815
Sunset Playhouse, Inc., 800 Elm Grove Rd., 782-4430
Theatre East, 2844 N. Oakland Ave., 962-6611

Museums:
Experimental Aircraft Museum, 11311 W. Forest Home Ave.
Milwaukee County Historical Center, 910 N. 3rd St.
Milwaukee Public Museum, 800 W. Wells Ave.

Art Museum and Galleries:
Charles Allis Art Museum, 1801 N. Prospect Ave.
Milwaukee Art Museum, 750 N. Lincoln Memorial Dr.
Villa Terrace Decorative Arts Museum, 2220 N. Terrace Ave.

Points of Interest:
Milwaukee County Zoo, Church of the Annunciation, Mitchell Park Conservatory, St. Joan of Arc Chapel, Whitnall Park Botanical Gardens

Information Sources:
Greater Milwaukee Convention & Visitors Bureau
756 N. Milwaukee St.
Milwaukee, Wisconsin 53202
(414) 273-3950

Metropolitan Milwaukee Association of Commerce
756 N. Milwaukee St.
Milwaukee, Wisconsin 53202
(414) 273-3000

Minneapolis-St. Paul, Minnesota

Population: (*1,978,000) (Minneapolis) 370,951, (St. Paul) 270,230 (1980C); Metro Rank: 16
Altitude: 687 to 1,060 feet
Average Temp.: Jan., 15°F.; July, 74°F.
Telephone Area Number: 612
Time: 874-8700 **Weather:** 725-6090
Time Zone: Central

Selected Hotels: Minneapolis
Granada Royale Hometel, 2800 W. 80th St., 884-4811
Holiday Inn—Downtown, 1313 Nicollet Mall, 332-0371
Hyatt Regency, 1300 Nicollet Mall, 370-1234
L'Hotel Sofitel, 5600 W. 78th St., 853-1900
Marquette Inn, 710 Marquette Ave., 332-2351
Marriott Hotel, 1919 E. 78th St., 854-7441
Northstar Inn, 618 2nd Ave. S, 338-2288
Radisson—South, 7800 Normandale Blvd., 835-7800
Ramada Inn, 4200 W. 78th St., 831-4200
Sheraton Airport Inn, 2525 E. 78th St., 854-1771
Sheraton-Ritz, 315 Nicollet Mall, 336-5711

St. Paul
Capp Towers, 77 E. 9th St., 227-7331
Holiday Inn, 161 St. Anthony St., 227-8711
McGuire's—Arden Hills, 1201 W. County Rd. E, 636-4123
Radisson Plaza St. Paul, 411 Minnesota St., 291-8800
Ramada Inn, 1870 Old Hudson Rd., 735-2330

Selected Restaurants: Minneapolis
Camelot, 5300 W. 78th St., 835-2455
Charlie's Cafe Exceptionale, 701 4th Ave. S, 335-8851
Edgewater Inn, 2420 N.E. Marshall St., 781-3444
Flame Room, 45 S. 7th St., 333-2181
Lord Fletcher's of the Lake, 3746 Sunset Dr., 471-8513
Wine Cellar, 618 2nd Ave. S, 338-2288

St. Paul
Bali Hai, 2305 White Bear Ave., 777-5500
The Blue Horse, 1355 University Ave., 645-8101
Don the Beachcomber, 11 E. Kellogg Blvd., 222-4484
Hafner's, 1560 White Bear Ave., 774-9696

Liquor Laws: Liquor may be purchased from package stores Monday through Friday, 8 A.M. to 8 P.M.; Saturday, 8 A.M. to 10 P.M.; closed Sunday. Drinks may be purchased from restaurants Monday through Saturday, 8 A.M. to 1 A.M.; Sunday, 12 noon to midnight.

Newspapers:
Minneapolis Star, 372-4141
Minneapolis Tribune, 372-4141
St. Paul Dispatch, 222-5011
St. Paul Pioneer Press, 222-5011

Television Stations:
KMSP Channel 9
KSTP (ABC) Channel 5
KTCA (PBS) Channel 2
WCCO (CBS) Channel 4
WTCN (NBC) Channel 11

AM Radio Stations:
KDWB (ABC) 630 Rock
KSTP (NBC) 1500 Rock
WCCO (CBS) 830 Popular
WLOL (MBS) 1330 Country
WWTC 1280 News

FM Radio Stations:
KTCR 97.1 Country
WAYL 93.7 General—*Stereo*
WCAL 92.5 Classical
WLOL 99.5 General

Airline Service:
Minneapolis/St. Paul International Airport—American, Braniff, Eastern, Northwest Orient, Ozark, Republic, United, USAIR, Western

Airport Transportation:
About 8 miles to downtown Minneapolis and St. Paul. Taxicab, bus, and limousine bus service to Minneapolis and St. Paul.

Car Rental Agencies: Avis (726-1723), Budget (726-5622), Dollar Rent-a-Car (726-9494), Hertz (726-1600), National (830-2345)

Railroad Passenger Service: Amtrak
Trade Exhibition Facilities: Minneapolis
Auditorium and Convention Center, 1400 3rd Ave. S, 870-4436

St. Paul
Aldrich Arena, 1850 N. White Bear Ave., 777-1361
National Guard Armory, 600 Cedar St., 296-6249
St. Paul Civic Center & Auditorium, O'Shaughnessy Plaza, 224-7361
Wacouta Arena, 1040 Villaume St., 451-1727

Professional Sports Facilities:
Metropolitan Stadium, 8001 Cedar Ave., Bloomington (Twins, baseball, 375-1116; Vikings, football, 941-9060; Kicks, soccer, 831-5425)

Metropolitan Sports Center,
7901 Cedar Ave., Bloomington
(North Stars, hockey, 853-9310)
St. Paul Civic Center & Auditorium,
143 W. 4th St.

Theaters and Concert Halls: Minneapolis
Children's Theatre,
2400 3rd Ave. S, 874-0400
Cricket Theatre,
528 Hennepin Ave., 379-1411
Dudley Riggs' Brave New Workshop,
2605 Hennepin Ave. & 1430 Washington Ave. S, 377-2120
Guthrie Theater, 725 Vineland Pl., 377-2224
Orchestra Hall, 1111 Nicollet Ave., 371-5656 (Minnesota Orchestra)
Theatre in the Round, 245 Cedar Ave., 336-9123

St. Paul
I.A. O'Shaughnessy Auditorium,
2004 Randolph Ave., 690-6700 (St. Paul Chamber Orchestra)
Park Square Theatre, 400 Sibley St., 291-7005

Museums: Minneapolis
Bell Museum of Natural History,
University & 17th Ave. SE
Hennepin County Historical Society,
2303 3rd Ave. S
Science Museum & Planetarium,
300 Nicollet Mall

St. Paul
Gibbs Farm Museum,
2097 W. Larpenteur Ave.
Minnesota Historical Society,
690 Cedar St.
Musical Instrument Museum,
1124 Dionne St.
Round Tower of Fort Snelling, St. 55 & 5
Science Museum of Minnesota,
10th and Wabasha aves.

Art Museums and Galleries: Minneapolis
The American Swedish Institute,
2600 Park Ave. S
The Minneapolis Institute of Arts,
2400 3rd Ave. S
University Art Gallery, University of Minnesota
Walker Art Center, Vineland Pl.

St. Paul
Minnesota Museum of Art,
Permanent Collection Gallery,
305 St. Peter St.
Mount Zion Temple, 1300 Summit Ave.

Points of Interest: Minneapolis
IDS Tower, Minneapolis Grain Exchange, St. Anthony Falls, Minnehaha Falls and Park, Stone Arch Bridge

St. Paul
Como Park, Indian God of Peace, Minnesota State Capitol, Fort Snelling State Historical Area, Indian Mounds State Park, St. Paul Cathedral

Information Sources:
Minneapolis Convention &
Tourism Commission
15 S. 5th St.
Minneapolis, Minnesota 55402
(612) 348-4330 (Tourism)
(612) 348-4313 (Conventions)

Greater Minneapolis Chamber of Commerce
15 S. 5th St.
Minneapolis, Minnesota 55402
(612) 370-9132

St. Paul Convention & Visitors Bureau
St. Paul Area Chamber of Commerce
Osborn Building
St. Paul, Minnesota 55102
(612) 222-5561

New Orleans, Louisiana

Population: (*1,175,800)
557,482 (1980C); Metro Rank: 26
Altitude: −5 to 25 feet
Average Temp.: Jan., 55°F.; July, 82°F.
Telephone Area Number: 504
Time: 529-6111 **Weather:** 525-8831
Time Zone: Central

Selected Hotels:
Fairmount, 123 Baronne St., 527-4727
Hyatt Regency, 500 Poydras Plaza, 561-1234
The Monteleone, 214 Royal St., 523-3341
New Orleans Hilton, Poydras S. at the Mississippi River, 561-0500
New Orleans Marriott, 555 Canal St., 581-1000
Pontchartrain, 2031 St. Charles Ave., 524-0581
Royal Orleans, 621 St. Louis St., 529-5333
Royal Sonesta, 300 Bourbon St., 586-0300

Selected Restaurants:
Antoine's, 713 St. Louis St., 581-4422
The Bon Ton, 401 Magazine St., 524-3386
Brennan's, 417 Royal St., 525-9711
Broussard's, 819 Conti St., 581-3866
Caribbean Room, Pontchartrain Hotel, 2031 St. Charles Ave., 524-0581
Commander's Palace, Washington Ave. at Coliseum St., 899-8221
Corinne Dunbar's,
1617 St. Charles Ave., 525-2957
Galatoire's, 209 Bourbon St., 525-2021
Le Ruth's, 636 Franklin St., 362-4914
Jonathan, 714 N. Rampart St., 586-1930
Louis XVI French Restaurant,
829 Toulouse St., 581-7000
Masson's Restaurant Français,
7200 Pontchartrain Blvd., 283-2525
Rib Room, Royal Orleans,
621 St. Louis St., 529-5333
Sazerac Restaurant, Fairmont Hotel,
123 Baronne St., 529-7111
Winston's, New Orleans Hilton, Poydras St. at the Mississippi River, 561-0500

Liquor Laws: Bars serve drinks at all hours. Liquor may also be purchased in food, liquor, and drug stores.

Newspapers:
Times Picayune/States Item, 586-3560

Television Stations:
WDSU (NBC) Channel 6
WGNO Channel 26
WVUE (ABC) Channel 8
WWL (CBS) Channel 4
WYES (PBS) Channel 12

AM Radio Stations:
WGSO (ABC) 1280 Music/News/Sports
WNOE (ABC) 1060 Music/News/Sports
WTIX 690 Music/News
WWL (CBS) 870 Music
WYLD 940 Rhythm/Blues

FM Radio Stations:
WBYU 95.7 Popular
WNOE 101.1 Country/Popular—*Stereo*
WQUE 93.3 Popular—*Stereo*
WWL 101.9 Popular—*Stereo*
WWOM 98.5 Music—*Stereo*

Airline Service:
New Orleans International Airport—American, Aviateca (Guatemala), Braniff, British Airways, Continenal, Delta, Eastern, National, Northwest Orient, Pan American, Republic, Royale, SAHSA (Honduras), TACA (El Salvador), Texas International, United, USAIR

Airport Transportation:
Fifteen miles to downtown New Orleans. Taxicab and limousine bus service.

Car Rental Agencies: Avis (523-4317), Budget (525-9417), Econo-Car (522-2992) Hertz (568-1645), National (525-0416), Thrifty (729-5773)

Railroad Passenger Service: Amtrak, Southern Railway

Trade Exhibition Facilities:
Louisiana Superdome, Int. 10 & Poydras St., 587-3663
Rivergate, Canal St., 529-2861

Professional Sports Facilities:
Louisiana Superdome, Int. 10 & Poydras St. (Saints, football, 523-4174)

Theaters and Concert Halls:
Contemporay Arts Center, 900 Camp St.
Municipal Auditorium, 1201 St. Peter St. (New Orleans Opera Guild, 525-7672
New Orleans Theatre for the Performing Arts, 801 N. Rampart St. (New Orleans Philharmonic Symphony Orchestra, 524-0404)
Saenger Performing Arts Center,
143 N. Rampart St.

Museums:
Cabildo, Jackson Square, 751 Chartres St.
Louisiana Maritime Museum, I. T. Bldg.
Louisiana Wildlife and Fisheries Museum, 400 Royal St.
Musée Conti Wax Museum, 917 Conti St.
New Orleans Museum of Art, City Park

Points of Interest:
French Quarter, Pontchartrain Beach Amusement Park, International Trade Mart, French Market, Cafe du Monde, (New Orleans coffee), Garden District, Longue Vue Gardens, Audubon Park and Zoo

Information Sources:
New Orleans Tourist & Convention Commission
334 Royal St.
New Orleans, Louisiana 70130
(504) 566-5011
Chamber of Commerce of the New Orleans Area
310 Camp St.
New Orleans, Louisiana 70130
(504) 527-6900

New York, New York

Population: (*16,573,600) 7,071,030 (1980C); Metro Rank: 1
Altitude: Sea level to 410 feet
Average Temp.: Jan., 33°F.; July, 75°F.
Telephone Area Number: 212
Time: 936-1616 **Weather:** 976-1212
Time Zone: Eastern
Selected Hotels:
Carlyle, Madison Ave. at E. 76th St., 744-1600
Helmsley Palace, 455 Madison Ave., 888-7000
Marriott's Essex House, 160 Central Park S, 247-0300
New York Hilton, 6th Ave. bet. W. 53rd & W. 54th sts., 586-7000
Pierre, 5th Ave. at E. 61st St., 838-8000
Plaza, 5th Ave. at W. 59th St., 759-3000
Regency, Park Ave. at 61st St., 759-4100
Sherry-Netherland, 781 5th Ave., 355-2800
St. Regis-Sheraton, 5th Ave. at 55th St., 753-4500
United Nations Plaza, 1 U.N. Plaza, 355-3400
Waldorf-Astoria, 301 Park Ave., 355-3000
Selected Restaurants:
Box Tree, 242 E. 50th St., 758-8320
Casa Brazil, 406 E. 85th St., 288-5284
Chez Pascal, 151 E. 82nd St., 249-1334
The Coach House, 110 Waverly Pl., 777-0303
The Four Seasons, 99 E. 52nd St., 754-9494
La Caravelle, 33 W. 55th St., 586-4252
La Cote Basque, 5 E. 55th St., 688-6525
Le Chantilly, 106 E. 57th St., 751-2931
Le Perigord Park, 575 Park Ave., 752-0050
Lutèce, 249 E. 50th St., 752-2225
Quo Vadis, 26 E. 63rd St., 838-0590
"21" Club, 21 W. 52nd St., 582-7200
Liquor Laws: You may buy drinks at restaurants, bars, and cocktail lounges each weekday until 4 A.M., Sunday from 12 noon to 3 A.M.
Newspapers:
Journal of Commerce, 425-1616
New York Daily News, 949-1234
New York Post, 349-5000
New York Times, 556-1234
Wall Street Journal, 285-5000
Women's Wear Daily, 741-4000
Television Stations:
WABC (ABC) Channel 7
WCBS (CBS) Channel 2
WNBC (NBC) Channel 4
WNET (PBS) Channel 13
WNEW Channel 5
WOR Channel 9
WPIX Channel 11
AM Radio Stations:
WABC (ABC) 770 General/Music
WCBS (CBS) 880 News
WHN (MBS) 1050 Country & Western
WNBC (NBC) 660 General
WOR 710 Talk
FM Radio Stations:
WCBS 101.1 Music
WNEW 102.7 General
WQXR 96.3 Classical/Talk
Airline Service:
John F. Kennedy International Airport—Aer Lingus (Ireland), Aeroflot (U.S.S.R.), Aerolineas Argentinas, Aeromexico, Air Afrique (Ivory Coast), Air Canada, Air France, Air India, Air Jamaica, Air Panama, Alia (Jordan), Alitalia (Italy), Allegheny, American, AVIANCA (Colombia), Braniff, British Airways, BWIA (British West Indian Airways), Czechoslovak, Delta, Dominicana, Eastern, El Al (Israel), Empresa Ecuatoriana de Aviación (Ecuador), Finnair (Finland), Icelandic, Iberia (Spain), Japan, KLM (Royal Dutch Airlines), LAN (Chile), LOT (Poland), Lufthansa (Germany), National, Nigeria Airways, Northwest Orient, Olympic Airways (Greece), Pakistan, Pan American, Royal Air Maroc (Morocco), SABENA (Belgium), SAS (Scandinavian Airlines), South African Airways, Swisssair, TAP (Portugal), Tarom (Romania), TWA, United, VARIG (Brazil), VIASA (Venezuela), Yugoslav
Airport Transportation:
Fifteen miles to Manhattan. Taxicab; limousine bus service to and from East Side Airlines Terminal, JFK Express Subway/bus service from Manhattan to JFK Airport
Car Rental Agencies: Avis (656-5266), Hertz (656-7930), All City (689-0100)
Airline Service:
La Guardia Airport—Allegheny Commuter, American, Braniff, Delta, Eastern, Northwest Orient, Ozark, Piedmont, Republic, TWA, United, USAIR
Car Rental Agencies: Hertz (478-5300)
Airline Service:
Newark International Airport—American, Braniff, Delta, Eastern, Northwest Orient, Piedmont, TWA, United, USAIR
Airport Transportation:
Eight miles from LaGuardia Airport to Manhattan; 10 miles from Newark Airport to Manhattan. Taxicab; limousine bus service to and from East Side Airlines Terminal.
Car Rental Agencies: Avis (201-643-1025), Hertz (201-621-7200)
Railroad Passenger Service: Amtrak
Trade Exhibition Facilities:
Coliseum Exhibition Corp., Columbus Circle, 757-5000
Madison Square Garden, 7th & 8th aves. at 33rd St., 564-4400
Professional Sports Facilities:
Madison Square Garden, 7th & 8th aves. at 33rd St., 564-4400 (Knicks, basketball; Rangers, hockey)
Shea Stadium, Flushing, 672-3000 (Jets, football; Mets, baseball)
Yankee Stadium, Bronx, 293-4300 (Yankees, baseball)
Giants Stadium, Meadowlands, N.J. (201) 935-8111 (Cosmos, soccer; Giants, football)
Theaters (ticket brokers) **and Concert Halls:**
Accent on Theatre Parties, 1619 Broadway, 265-6240
Leblangs Theatre Tickets, 207 W. 45th St., 757-2300
Lenore Tobin Theatre, 234 W. 44th St., 564-5180
Theatre Service Americana, Inc., 7th Ave. & 52nd St., 581-6660
Lincoln Center for the Performing Arts, Broadway & 65th St., 765-5100 (American Ballet Theater, N.Y. Philharmonic, N.Y. City Ballet, N.Y. City Opera, Metropolitan Opera)
Museums:
American Museum of Natural History, Central Pk. W & 79th St.
American Museum and Hayden Planetarium, Central Pk. W & 81st St.
Pierpont Morgan Library, 29 E. 36th St.
Museum of the American Indian, Broadway & W. 155th St.
New York Historical Society, 170 Central Park W (77th St.)
Art Museums and Galleries:
Cooper-Hewitt Museum, 5th Ave. at 91st St.
Frick Collection, 1 E. 70th St.
Metropolitan Museum of Art, 5th Ave. at 81st St.
Museum of Modern Art, 11 W. 53rd St.
Solomon R. Guggenheim Museum, 89th St. & 5th Ave.
The Cloisters, Ft. Tryon Park, off Riverside Dr.
Whitney Museum of American Art, 75th St. & Madison Ave.
Points of Interest:
The United Nations, Lincoln Center, New York and American Stock Exchanges, Statue of Liberty, Times Square, Greenwich Village, Rockefeller Center, Empire State Building, Chinatown, Little Italy, Bronx Zoo, World Trade Center, South Street Seaport, Citicorp Center
Information Sources:
New York Convention and Visitors Bureau, Inc.
Two Columbus Circle
New York, New York 10019
(212) 397-8200

New York Chamber of Commerce
and Industry
65 Liberty Street
New York, New York 10005
(212) 766-1300

Philadelphia, Pennsylvania

Population: (*5,153,900)
1,688,200 (1980C); Metro Rank: 4
Altitude: Sea level to 441 feet
Average Temp.: Jan., 35°F.; July, 78°F.
Telephone Area Number: 215
Time: 846-1212 **Weather:** 937-1212
Time Zone: Eastern
Selected Hotels:
Barclay, 18th St. & Rittenhouse Sq., 545-0300
Bellevue Stratford, Broad & Walnut sts., 893-1776
Franklin Plaza, 2 Franklin Plaza, 448-2000
Hilton Hotel, 34th & Civic Center Blvd., 387-8333
Hilton Stadium Inn, 10th St. & Packer Ave., 755-9500
Holiday Inn, Center City, 561-7500
Holiday Inn Independence Mall, 4th & Arch sts., 923-8660
Hotel Latham, 17th & Walnut sts., 563-7474
Marriott, City Line Ave. & Monument Rd. at Schuylkill Expwy., 667-0200
Penn Center Inn, 20th & Market sts., 569-3000
Sheraton Airport Inn, 365-4150
University City Holiday Inn, 36th & Chestnut sts., 387-8000
Warwick, 1701 Locust St., 735-6000
Selected Restaurants:
Arthur's Steak House, 1512 Walnut St., 735-2590
Bookbinders, Old Original, 125 Walnut St., 925-7027
Bookbinder's Seafood House, 215 S. 15th St., 545-1137
Commissary Upstairs, 1710 Sansom St., 569-2240
Deja Vu, 1609 Pine St., 546-1190
Deux Cheminees, 251 Camac St., 985-0367
Hoffman House, 1214 Sansom St., 925-2772
In Season, 313 S. 13th St., 545-5115
Frankie Bradley's, Juniper & Chancellor sts., 545-4350
La Camargue, 1119 Walnut St., 922-3148
La Famaglia, 8 S. Front St., 922-2803
La Panatiere, 1602 Locust St., 546-5452
Le Bec Fin, 1312 Spruce St., 732-3000
Maureen's, 11 S. 12th St., 561-3542
Piccolo Padre, 303 S. 11th St., 925-8192
Liquor Laws: Package liquor stores close at 9 P.M. Licensed restaurants and bars serve drinks 7 A.M. to 2 A.M. weekdays, Sunday 1 to 2 A.M.
Newspapers:
Philadelphia Daily News, 854-2000
Philadelphia Inquirer, 854-2000
The Journal, 243-1400
Television Stations:
KYW (NBC) Channel 3
WCAU (CBS) Channel 10
WPVI (ABC) Channel 6
WHYY (PBS) Channel 12
AM Radio Stations:
KYW 1060 News
WCAU (CBS) 1210 News/Talk
WRCP (ABC) 1540 Country/News
WFLN (NBC) 900 Classical
FM Radio Stations:
WCAU 98.1 Popular
WMGK 102.9 Popular
WUHY 90.9 Public Radio
WWDB 96.5 Talk
Airline Service:
Philadelphia International Airport—Air Florida, Air Jamaica, Altair, Allegheny Commuter, American, Braniff, British Airways, Delta, Eastern, Lufthansa (Germany), Mexicana, National, Northwest Orient, Ozark, Piedmont, Republic, TWA, United, USAIR
Airport Transportation:
Eight miles to downtown Philadelphia. Taxicab and limousine bus service.
Car Rental Agencies: Airways (673-5868), Avis (492-1600), Hertz (963-9679), National (492-2750)
Railroad Passenger Service: Amtrak
Trade Exhibition Facility:
Civic Center, Civic Center Blvd. & 34th St., 823-7350 (Firebirds, hockey)
Professional Sports Facilities:
Franklin Field, 33rd St. below Walnut St., 386-0961
John F. Kennedy Stadium, Broad St. & Pattison Ave., 686-1776
Philadelphia Veterans Stadium, Broad St. & Pattison Ave., 463-1000 (Eagles, football, 463-5500; Phillies, baseball, 463-1000)
Spectrum, Broad St. & Pattison Ave., 463-4300 (76ers, basketball, 339-7676; Flyers, hockey, 755-9700)
Theaters and Concert Hall:
Academy of Music, Broad & Locust sts., 893-1930 (Philadelphia Orchestra; Philadelphia Opera Co.)
Annenberg Center for Communication Arts & Sciences, 3680 Walnut St., 243-6791
Forrest, 1114 Walnut St., 923-1515
Shubert Theater, 250 S. Broad St., 735-4768 (Pennsylvania Ballet, 978-1400)
Museums:
Academy of Natural Sciences, 19th St. & Franklin Pkwy.
Afro-American Historical & Cultural Museum, 7th & Arch sts.
American-Swedish Historical Museum, 1900 Pattison Ave.
Atwater Kent Museum of Philadelphia History, 15 S. 7th St.
Balch Institute, 18 S. 7th St.
Civic Center Museum, 34th St. & Civic Center Blvd.
Fireman's Hall Museum, 2nd & Quarry sts.
Franklin Institute Science Museum, 20th St. & Franklin Pkwy.
Mummers Museum, 2nd St. & Washington Ave.
Philadelphia Maritime Museum, 321 Chestnut St.
Perelman Antique Toy Museum, 270 S. 2nd St.
Art Museums and Galleries:
Ile-Ife Museum of Afro-American Culture, 2300 Germantown Ave.
Institute of Contemporary Art, University of Pennsylvania
Pennsylvania Academy of the Fine Arts, Broad & Cherry sts.
Philadelphia Art Alliance, 251 S. 18th St.
Philadelphia Museum of Art, 25th St. & Benjamin Franklin Pkwy.
Rodin Museum, 22nd St. & Franklin Pkwy.
University Museum, 33rd & Spruce sts.
Points of Interest:
Independence National Historical Park, Penn Mutual Observatory, Penn Center, Christ Church, Powel House, Betsy Ross House, Elfreth's Alley, Fairmount Park, U.S.S. *Olympia,* Philadelphia Zoo, U.S. Mint, Chinese Cultural Center, Penn's Landing, New Market, Italian Market
Information Sources:
Philadelphia Convention
& Visitors Bureau
1525 John F. Kennedy Blvd.
Philadelphia, Pennsylvania 19102
(215) 864-1976

Greater Philadelphia Chamber
of Commerce
1617 John F. Kennedy Blvd.
Philadelphia, Pennsylvania 19103
(215) 568-4040

Phoenix, Arizona

Population: (*1,483,500)
749,900 (1980C); Metro Rank: 20
Altitude: 1,086 to 1,160 feet
Average Temp.: Jan., 51°F.; July, 85.9°F.
Telephone Area Number: 602
Time and Weather: 258-7600
Time Zone: Mountain
Selected Hotels:
Arizona Biltmore, 24th St. & Missouri Ave., 955-6600
Doubletree Inn, 212 W. Osborn St., 248-0222
Granada Royale Hometel, 2333 E. Thomas Rd., 957-1910
Hyatt Regency, 122 N. 2nd St., 257-1110
The Pointe, 7677 N. 16th St., 997-2626
Ramada Inn, 3801 E. Van Buren St., 275-7878
Sheraton Airport Inn, 2901 E. Sky Harbor Blvd., 275-3634
Selected Restaurants:
Avanti's of Phoenix, 2726 E. Thomas Rd., 956-0900

Cork 'n Cleaver, 5101 N. 44th St., 274-3913
Golden Eagle, 201 N. Central Ave., 257-7700
Hungry Tiger, 102 W. Camelback Rd., 264-6636
Mancuso's, 4622 N. 7th Ave., 266-9594
Bobby McGee's, Scottsdale & McDowell Rds., Scottsdale, 947-5757
Navarre's, 52 E. Camelback Rd., 264-5355
North Bank, 40th St. & Camelback Rd., 956-7171
Victoria Station, 1720 E. Camelback Rd., 264-6076

Liquor Laws: You may buy liquor weekdays from 6 A.M. to 1 A.M.; Sunday from noon until 1 A.M.

Newspapers:
Phoenix Arizona Republic, 271-8000
Phoenix Gazette, 271-8000

Television Stations:
KOOL (CBS) Channel 10
KPHO Channel 5
KTAR (NBC) Channel 12
KTVK (ABC) Channel 3

AM Radio Stations:
KOOL (CBS) 960 Rock
KRUX (ABC) 1360 Rock
KTAR (NBC) 620 News

FM Radio Stations:
KMEO 96.9 Music—*Stereo*
KNIX 102.5 Popular—*Stereo*
KTAR 98.6 Popular/News

Airline Service:
Phoenix Sky Harbor International Airport—American, Continental, Delta, Eastern, Frontier, Northwest Orient, Pan American, Republic, TWA, United, USAIR

Airport Transportation:
Four miles to downtown Phoenix. Taxicab, bus, and limousine bus service.

Car Rental Agencies: Avis (273-3222), Budget (244-8121), Hertz (254-7051), National (275-4471)

Railroad Passenger Service: Amtrak

Trade Exhibition Facilities:
Arizona Veterans Memorial Coliseum & Exposition Center, 1826 W. McDowell Rd., 258-6711
Phoenix Civic Plaza, 225 E. Adams St., 262-6225

Professional Sports Facility:
Arizona Veterans Memorial Coliseum & Exposition Center, 1826 W. McDowell Rd., 258-6711 (Suns, basketball, 258-7111)

Theaters and Concert Hall:
Celebrity Theater, 440 N. 32nd St., 267-7501
Phoenix Civic Plaza, 225 E. Adams St., 262-6225 (Phoenix Symphony Orchestra)
Phoenix Little Theater, 25 E. Coronado Rd., 254-0688
Windmill Dinner Theater, 10345 N. Scottsdale Rd., Scottsdale, 948-6170

Museums:
Arizona History Room, 411 N. Central Ave.
Arizona Mineral Museum, Mineral Building, Fairgrounds
Arizona Museum, 1002 W. Van Buren St.
Heard Museum, 22 E. Monte Vista Rd.
Pueblo Grande Ruins Museum, 4619 E. Washington St.

Art Museum:
Phoenix Art Museum, 1625 N. Central Ave.

Points of Interest:
Japanese Flower Gardens, Pueblo Grande, Mystery Castle, Desert Botanical Garden, Hopi Indian Reservation, Phoenix Zoo, Big Surf

Information Sources:
Phoenix & Valley of the Sun Convention & Visitors Bureau
2701 E. Camelback Rd.
Phoenix, Arizona 85016
(602) 957-0070

Phoenix Chamber of Commerce
34 W. Monroe St.
Phoenix, Arizona 85004
(602) 254-5521

Pittsburgh, Pennsylvania

Population: (*2,165,100) 423,938 (1980C); Metro Rank: 14
Altitude: 710 to 1,370 feet
Average Temp.: Jan., 33°F.; July, 75°F.
Telephone Area Number: 412
Time: 391-9500 **Weather:** 936-1212
Time Zone: Eastern

Selected Hotels:
Carlton House, 550 Grant St., 471-6060
Hilton Airport Inn, Cliff Mine Rd., 262-3800
Holiday Inn—Airport, 1406 Beers School Rd., 771-6500
Howard Johnson's, 3401 Blvd. of the Allies, Oakland, 683-6100
Marriott, 101 Mariott Dr., Greentree, 922-8400
Pittsburgh Hilton, Gateway Center at Point State Park, 391-4600
Pittsburgh Hyatt at Chatham Center, opp. Civic Arena, 391-5000
Sheraton—Airport, 1160 Thorn Run Rd., 262-2400
William Penn, 530 William Penn Pl., 281-7100

Selected Restaurants:
Christopher's, 1411 Grandview Ave., Mt. Washington, 381-4500
Common Plea, 308 Ross St., 281-5140
De Foro's, 428 Forbes Ave., 391-8873
Hugo's Rotisserie, Hyatt at Chatham Center, 391-5000
Klein's Restaurant, 330 4th Ave., 566-8615
La Cite, 9999 Klummer St., Allison Park, 931-0661
La Plume, William Penn, 530 William Penn Pl., 281-7100
Le Mont, 1114 Grandview Ave., Mt. Washington, 431-3100
Louie Tambellini's, 160 Southern Ave., Mt. Washington, 481-1118
Park Schenley, 3955 Bigelow Blvd., Oakland Civic Center, 681-0800
Poli's, 2607 Murray Ave., Squirrel Hill, 521-6400
Rifle & Plow, Hilton Hotel, Gateway Center, 391-4600
Tin Angel, 1204 Grandview Ave., Mt. Washington, 381-1919
Top of the Triangle, U.S. Steel Bldg., downtown, 471-4100

Liquor Laws: Liquor may be purchased from 7 A.M. to 2 A.M. weekdays at restaurants, bars, etc. Drinks are sold only at restaurants and hotels on Sunday.

Newspapers:
Pittsburgh Post-Gazette, 263-1601
Pittsburgh Press, 263-1100

Television Stations:
KDKA (CBS) Channel 2
WIIC (NBC) Channel 11
WQED (PBS) Channel 13
WTAE (ABC) Channel 4

AM Radio Stations:
KDKA 1020 General
KQV (TBC) 1410 Talk/News
WAMO 860 Jazz/Gospel
WEEP (ABC) 1080 Country-Western
WEDO (CBS) 810
WTAE 1250 General

FM Radio Stations:
WAMO 106 Jazz/Rock—*Stereo*
WDVE 105 Popular Rock—*Stereo*
WLOA 97 Soft Rock—*Stereo*
WWSW 97 (CBS) Contemporary

Airline Service:
Greater Pittsburgh International Airport—Allegheny Commuter, American, Braniff, Eastern, Nordair (Canada), Northwest Orient, Piedmont, TWA, United, USAIR

Airport Transportation:
Seventeen miles to downtown Pittsburgh. Taxicab and limousine bus service.

Car Rental Agencies: Avis (262-5160), Budget (261-1500), Hertz (261-3883), National (262-2312), Thrifty (264-1775)

Railroad Passenger Service: Amtrak

Trade Exhibition Facilities:
Civic Arena & Exhibit Hall, Downtown, 391-4545
Greater Pittsburgh Merchandise Mart, Monroeville, 243-8716

Professional Sports Facilities:
Civic Arena, Downtown, 471-1312 (Penguins, hockey, 765-3939)
Three Rivers Stadium, Stadium Circle, (Pirates, baseball, 323-5000; Steelers, football, 323-1200)

Theaters and Concert Hall:
Heinz Hall for the Performing Arts, 600 Penn Ave., 281-8185 (Pittsburgh Symphony Orchestra, Pittsburgh Ballet, Pittsburgh Opera, Civic Light Opera,

Pittsburgh Dance Council)
Pittsburgh Playhouse, 222 Craft Ave., 621-4445
Pittsbugh Public Theatre/ Allegheny Community Theatre, Allegheny Square, 765-3400
Stanley Theatre, 107 Sixth St., 261-2800
Syria Mosque, Bigelow Blvd., Oakland, 621-8700

Museums:
Carnegie Museum of Natural History, 4400 Forbes Ave., opp. University of Pittsburgh
Depreciation Lands Museum, Pioneer Rd., Allison Park
Fort Pitt Museum, Point State Park
Historical Society of Western Pennsylvania, 4338 Bigelow Blvd., Oakland
Old Post Office Museum, Allegheny Square, Allegheny Center
Stephen Foster Memorial, Forbes Ave. at Bigelow Blvd., Oakland

Art Galleries:
Arts and Crafts Center, Fifth & Shady aves., Shadyside
The Clay Place, 5600 Walnut St.
The Frick Art Museum, 7727 Reynolds St.
King Center, 1251 N. Negley Ave., Highland Park
Pittsburgh Plan for Art, 407 S. Craig St., Oakland
Sarah Scaife Gallery, Carnegie Institute, 4400 Forbes Ave.

Points of Interest:
Buhl Planetarium, Carnegie Mellon University, Allegheny Observatory, Aviary, Fallingwater (Frank Lloyd Wright "house over a waterfall"), Phipps Conservatory, Heinz Hall, Pittsburgh Zoo, Kennywood Park, Hartwood, Duquesne Incline, Nationality Classrooms, University of Pittsburgh, Flag Plaza

Information Sources:
Pittsburgh Convention & Visitors Bureau, Inc.
200 Roosevelt Building
Pittsburgh, Pennsylvania 15222
(412) 281-7711
Greater Pittsburgh Chamber of Commerce
Chamber of Commerce Building
Pittsburgh, Pennsylvania 15222
(412) 392-4500

Portland, Oregon

Population: (*1,200,100) 366,383 (1980C); Metro Rank: 25
Altitude: Sea level to 1,073 feet
Average Temp.: Jan., 40°F.; July, 69°F.
Telephone Area Number: 503
Time: 229-1212 **Weather:** 255-6660
Time Zone: Pacific

Selected Hotels:
Best Western Flamingo, 9727 NE. Sandy Blvd., 255-1400
Cosmopolitan Airtel, 6221 NE. 82nd Ave., 255-6511
Holiday Inn—Airport, 82nd Ave. & Columbia Blvd., 256-5000
Portland Hilton, SW. 6th Ave. at Salmon St., 226-1611
Portland Marriott, Front Ave. & Clay St., 226-7600
Portland Motor Hotel, 1414 SW. 6th Ave., 221-1611
Red Lion Motor Inn—Jantzen Beach, 909 N. Hayden Island Dr., 283-4466
Red Lion Inn—Portland Center, 310 SW. Lincoln Ave., 221-0450
Sheraton Inn—Airport, 8235 N.E. Airport Way, 288-7171
Thunderbird Motor Inn—Coliseum, 1225 Thunderbird Way, 235-8311
Thunderbird Motor Inn—Jantzen Beach, 1401 N. Hayden Island Dr., 283-2111
The Westin Benson, SW. Broadway at Oak St., 228-9611

Selected Restaurants:
Bush Garden, SW. 9th Ave. & Morrison St., 226-7181
Couch Street Fish House, 3rd & Couch sts., 223-6173
Dan & Louis Oyster Bar, 208 SW. Ankeny St., 227-8038
Henry Ford's, 9589 SW. Barbur Blvd. 245-2434
Jade West, 122 SW. Harrison St., 226-1128
Jake's Famous Crawfish, 401 SW. 12th Ave., 226-1419
L'Omelette, 815 SW. Alder St., 248-9661
The London Grill, The Westin Benson, SW. Broadway at Oak St., 228-9611
Panorama Room, atop Portland Hilton, SW 6th Ave. at Salmon St., 228-7475
Ringside, 2165 W. Burnside St., 223-1513
Top of the Cosmo, 1030 N.E. Union Ave., 235-8433
Trader Vic's, SW. Broadway St. at Oak St., 228-9611

Liquor Laws: State liquor stores open noon to 8 P.M. daily except Sunday and holidays.

Newspapers:
Daily Journal of Commerce, 226-1311
The Oregonian, 226-2121
The Oregon Journal, 222-5511

Television Stations:
KATU (ABC) Channel 2
KGW (NBC) Channel 8
KOAP (PBS) Channel 10
KOIN (CBS) Channel 6
KPTV—Channel 12

AM Radio Stations:
KBPS (PBS) 1450
KGW (NBC) 620 Rock/Folk
KOIN (CBS) 970 Music
KPOK (MBS) 1330 Music/Talk
KWJJ (ABC) 1080 Country-Western
KXL 750 Music

FM Radio Stations:
KJIB 99.5 Popular/Classical—*Stereo*
KLIQ 92.3 Talk/Popular
KOAP 91.5 Educational
KOIN 101.1 Classical/Semi-classical
KXL 95.5 Popular—*Stereo*

Airline Service:
Portland International Airport—Air California, Alaska, American, Braniff, Continental, Delta, Eastern, Northwest Orient, Republic, United, Western, Wien Air Alaska

Airport Transportation:
Nine miles to downtown Portland. Taxicab and limousine bus service.

Car Rental Agencies: Avis (226-1456), Budget (222-9123), Hertz (224-7700), National (228-6637), Thrifty (254-6563)

Railroad Passenger Service: Amtrak

Trade Exhibition Facilities:
Memorial Coliseum, 1401 N. Wheeler Ave., 235-8771
Multnomah County Exposition Center, 2060 N. Marine Dr., 285-7756

Professional Sports Facilities:
Memorial Coliseum, 1401 N. Wheeler Ave., 235-8771 (Trail Blazers, basketball)
Civic Stadium, 1844 SW. Morrison St., (Timbers, soccer, 245-6404)

Theaters and Concert Hall:
Firehouse Theatre, 1436 SW. Montgomery St., 228-4737
Play Box Players, 4001 SW. Canyon Rd., 226-6501
Portland Civic Auditorium, 222 SW. Clay St., 248-4496 (Oregon Symphony Orchestra, 228-1353; Portland Opera, 224-1907)
Portland Civic Theatre, 1530 S.W. Yamhill St., 226-3048

Museums:
Children's Museum of Portland Park Bureau, 3037 SW. 2nd Ave.
Oregon Historical Society, 1230 SW. Park Ave.
Oregon Museum of Science and Industry, 4015 SW. Canyon Rd.
Western Forestry Center, 4020 SW. Canyon Rd.

Art Museum and Gallery:
Oregon Society of Artists, 2185 SW. Park Ave.
Portland Art Museum, 1219 SW. Park Ave.

Points of Interest:
Washington Park, Washington Park Zoo, Pittock Mansion, Sanctuary of Our Sorrowful Mother, International Rose Test Garden, American Rhododendron and Azalea Test Garden, Columbia River Highway, Mt. Hood

Information Source:
Greater Portland Convention & Visitors Association, Inc.
26 SW. Salmon St.
Portland, Oregon 97204
(503) 222-2223

St. Louis, Missouri

Population: (*2,216,100)
453,085 (1980C); Metro Rank: 13
Altitude: 385 to 614 feet
Average Temp.: Jan., 32°F.; July, 79°F.
Telephone Area Number: 314
Time: 321-2522 **Weather:** 946-7570
Time Zone: Central

Selected Hotels:
Breckenridge Inn,
1335 S. Lindbergh Blvd., 933-1100
Chase Park Plaza,
212 N. Kingshighway Blvd., 361-2500
Cheshire Inn & Lodge,
6300 Clayton Rd., 647-7300
Marriott Hotel at the Airport,
Int. 70 at Lambert Airport, 423-9700
Marriott's Pavilion, 1 S. Broadway,
421-1776
Sheraton—West Port Inn,
191 West Port Plaza, 878-1500
Hilton Inn,
10330 Natural Bridge Rd., 426-5500
Stouffer's Riverfront Towers,
200 S. 4th St., 241-9500

Selected Restaurants:
Anthony's, 10 S. Broadway, 231-2434
Cheshire Inn, 6306 Clayton Rd.,
647-7300
Crest House, 101 N. Broadway, 241-3700
Dominic's, 5101 Wilson Ave., 771-1632
Henry VIII, 4690 N. Lindbergh Blvd.,
731-4888
Kemoll's, 4201 N. Grand Blvd., 534-2705
Robert E. Lee, 100 S. Wharf St., 241-1282
Sea Chase, Chase Park Plaza,
212 N. Kingshighway Blvd., 361-2500
Stan Musial & Biggie's,
5130 Oakland Ave., 652-2626
Tenderloin Room, Chase-Park Plaza,
212 N. Kingshighway Blvd., 361-2500
Tony's, 826 N. Broadway St., 231-7007
Top of the Riverfront, 200 S. 4th St.,
241-9500
Top of the Sevens, 7777 Bonhomme
Ave., Clayton, 725-7777
Wade's A Gathering Place,
611 N. Lindbergh Blvd., 997-5151

Liquor Laws: Hours of sale are from 6:00 A.M. to 1:30 A.M. weekdays; Sundays, 1 P.M. to 12:00 A.M.

Newspapers:
St. Louis Globe Democrat, 342-1212
St. Louis Post Dispatch, 621-1111

Television Stations:
KETC (PBS) Channel 9
KMOX (CBS) Channel 4
KPLR Channel 11
KSD (NBC) Channel 5
KTVI (ABC) Channel 2

AM Radio Stations:
KMOX (CBS) 1120 News/Music
KSD (NBC) 550 General
WIL (ABC) 1430 Country-Western
WRTH 590 Music

FM Radio Stations:
KCFM 93.7 Popular—*Stereo*
KGRV 107.7 Rock—*Stereo*
KMOX 103.3 General—*Stereo*
WIL 92.3 Country-Western—*Stereo*

Airline Service:
Lambert International Airport—American, Braniff, British Caledonian, Delta, Eastern, Frontier, Northwest Orient, Ozark, Republic, Texas International, TWA, USAIR

Airport Transportation:
Fifteen miles to downtown St. Louis. Taxicab and limousine bus service.

Car Rental Agencies: Avis (426-7766), Budget (423-3000), Hertz (426-7555)

Railroad Passenger Service: Amtrak

Trade Exhibition Facilities:
Checkerdome, 5700 Oakland Ave.,
644-0900
Henry W. Kiel Auditorium,
1416 Market St., 241-1010
Cervantes Convention & Exhibition
Center, 801 Convention Plaza, 342-5000

Professional Sports Facilities:
Busch Memorial Stadium, (Cardinals, baseball, 421-3060; Cardinals, football, 421-1600)
Checkerdome, 5700 Oakland Ave.,
644-0900 (Blues, hockey)

Theaters and Concert Hall:
American Theatre, 416 N. 9th St.,
231-7000
Loretto-Hilton Repertory Theatre,
130 Edgar Rd., 968-4925
Municipal Opera Theater (summer),
Forest Park, 361-1900
Powell Symphony Hall, 718 N. Grand
Blvd., 533-2500 (St. Louis Symphony Orchestra)

Museums:
Missouri Historical Society, Forest Park
Museum of Science and Natural History,
Clayton Rd. & Big Bend Blvd.
Museum of Westward Expansion,
Gateway Arch
National Museum of Transport,
3015 Barretts Station Rd.

Art Museum and Gallery:
City Art Museum, Art Hill,
Forest Park
Craft Alliance Gallery,
6640 Delmar Blvd.

Points of Interest:
Gateway Arch, Six Flags Over Mid-America, McDonnell Planetarium, St. Louis Zoo, Grant's Farm, Missouri Botanical Garden, St. Louis Cathedral (old and new), River Excursion Boats, Museum Homes, Brewery Tours

Information Sources:
Convention & Visitors Bureau
of Greater St. Louis
1300 Convention Plaza
St. Louis, Missouri 63103
(314) 421-1023
St. Louis Regional Commerce &
Growth Association
10 Broadway
St. Louis, Missouri 63102
(314) 231-5555

San Antonio, Texas

Population: (*1,012,300)
785,410 (1980C); Metro Rank: 30
Altitude: 505 to 1,000 feet
Average Temp.: Jan., 51°F.; July, 84°F.
Telephone Area Number: 512
Time: 226-3232 **Weather:** 828-3384
Time Zone: Central

Selected Hotels:
Four Seasons—Plaza Nacional,
5555 S. Alamo St., 229-1000
Hilton Palacio del Rio, 200 S. Alamo St.,
222-2481
Holiday Inn Northwest,
6023 NW. Expwy., 732-5141
The Inn at Turtle Creek,
3830 Parkdale Dr., 696-5600
La Mansion del Norte, 37 NE. Loop
(Int. 410) Expwy., 341-3535
La Mansion de Rio, 112 College St.,
225-2581
Marriott Hotel, 711 E. River Walk,
224-4555
Ramada Inn Airport, 333 NW. Loop
(Int. 410) Expwy., 344-4581
St. Anthony, 300 E. Travis St., 227-4392

Selected Restaurants:
Casey's John Charles Restaurant,
16900 San Pedro Ave., 494-2051
Caso Rio, 430 E. Commerce St., 225-6718
Chez Ardid, 7701 Broadway, 824-6567
Crystal Baking Company, 1039 NE. Loop
(Int. 410) Expwy., 826-2371
Fig Tree, 515 Villita St., 224-1976
La Fonda, 2415 N. Main Ave., 733-0621
La Louisiane, 2632 Broadway, 225-7984
Las Canarias, La Mansion del Rio,
200 S. Alamo St., 225-4000
Little Rhein Steak House,
231 S. Alamo St., 225-2111
Luigi's, 6825 San Pedro Ave., 349-5251
Old San Francisco Steakhouse,
10223 Sahara Dr., 342-2321
Paesano's, 1715 McCullough Ave.,
226-9541

Liquor Laws: Liquor may be purchased in public bars and restaurants.

Newspapers:
San Antonio Express News, 225-7411
San Antonio Light, 226-4271

Television Stations:
KENS (CBS) Channel 5
KLRN (PBS) Channel 9
KSAT (ABC) Channel 12
KWEX Channel 41
KMOL (NBC) Channel 4

AM Radio Stations:
KBUC (ABC) 1310 Country-Western
KKYX 680 Country-Western
KMAC 630 Country-Western/General
KONO (ABC) Rock
KTSA 550 Contemporary/General
WOAI (CBS) Talk

FM Radio Stations:
KBUC 106.3 Country
KCOR 101.9 Continental-Latin—*Stereo*
KISS 99.5 Music/News/Sports
KITY 92.9 General

Airline Service:
San Antonio International Airport—American, Braniff, Continenatl, Delta, Eastern, Mexicana de Aviación, Southwest, Texas International, USAIR
Airport Transportation:
Eight miles to downtown San Antonio. Taxicab and limousine bus service.
Car Rental Agencies: Avis (826-6332), Budget (824-0547), Hertz (826-0651), National (824-7544)
Railroad Passenger Service: Amtrak
Trade Exhibition Facilities:
Convention Center, Market & S. Alamo sts., 299-8500
Villita Assembly Hall, Villita & Presa sts., 227-3211
Professional Sports Facility:
HemisFair Arena, Market & S. Alamo sts. (Spurs, basketball, 224-9578)
Theaters and Concert Hall:
San Antonio Little Theater, San Pedro Playhouse, 733-7258
Theater for the Performing Arts, Convention Center, 229-8500 (San Antonio Symphony Orchestra, 223-5591, Opera, and Ballet)
Museums:
Hertzberg Circus Collection, 210 W. Market St., Library Annex
Museum of Transportation, HemisFair Plaza
Witte Memorial Museum, Brackenridge Park
Art Galleries:
McNay Art Institute, 6000 N. New Braunfels Ave.
San Antonio Museum of Art, 200 W. Jones Ave.
Points of Interest:
Alamo and Mission Trail, HemisFair Plaza, La Villita, Paseo del Rio, Mexican Quarter, Mission Trail, Institute of Texan Cultures-HemisFair, Spanish Governor's Palace
Information Sources:
San Antonio Convention and Visitors Bureau
P.O. Box 2277
San Antonio, Texas 78298
(512) 223-9133

Visitor Information Center
321 Alamo Plaza
San Antonio, Texas 78205
(512) 226-2345

San Antonio Chamber of Commerce
602 E. Commerce St.
San Antonio, Texas 78205
(512) 229-2100

San Diego, California

Population: (*1,597,000) 875,504 (1980C); Metro Rank: 19
Altitude: Sea level to 823 feet
Average Temp.: Jan., 57°F.; July, 71°F.
Telephone Area Number: 714
Time: 853-1212 **Weather:** 289-1212
Time Zone: Pacific
Selected Hotels:
Executive Hotel, 1055 First Ave., 232-6141
Hanalei Hotel, 2270 Hotel Circle N, 297-1101
Holiday Inn—Embarcadero, Harbor Dr. at Ash St., 232-3861
Hotel del Coronado, 1500 Orange Ave., Coronado, 435-6611
Hyatt House Islandia, 1441 Quivira Rd., 224-3541
Mission Valley Inn, 875 Hotel Circle S, 298-8281
San Diego Hilton, 1775 E. Mission Bay Dr., 276-4010
Sheraton-Harbor Island Hotel, 1380 Harbor Island Dr., 291-2900
Sheraton Inn-Airport, 1590 Harbor Island Dr., 291-6400
Town and Country Hotel, 500 Hotel Circle N, 291-7131
Vacation Village Hotel, W. Vacation Isle, 274-4630
Westgate Plaza Hotel, 1055 2nd Ave., 232-5011
Selected Restaurants:
Anthony's Star of the Sea Room, Harbor Dr. & Ash St., 232-7408
Casina Valadier Restaurant, 445 Lamont St., 270-8650
Fontainebleau, Westgate Plaza Hotel, 1055 2nd Ave., 238-1818
La Maison des Pescadoux, 2265 Bacon St., 225-9579
Lubach's, Hawthorn at the Waterfront, 232-5129
Mister A's, 5th Ave. & Laurel St., 239-1377
Prince Wales Grill, Hotel del Coronado, Coronado, 435-6611
Thee Bungalow, 4996 W. Point Loma Blvd., 224-2884
Tom Ham's Lighthouse, 2150 Harbor Island Dr., 291-9110
Liquor Laws: Liquor may be purchased from 6 A.M. to 2 A.M. daily.
Newspapers:
San Diego Evening Tribune, 299-3131
San Diego Union, 299-3131
Television Stations:
KCST (NBC) Channel 39
KFMB (CBS) Channel 8
KGTV (ABC) Channel 10
KPBS (PBS) Channel 15
XETV Channel 6
AM Radio Stations:
KOGO (NBC) 600 Pop/Contemporary
KSON (ABC) 1240 Country-Western
KSPO (CBS) 760 Popular/Contemporary
1130 News/Talk Shows
FM Radio Stations:
KFSD 94.1 Classical
KITT 105.3 General
KLRO 94.9 Popular—*Stereo*
Airline Service:
International-Lindbergh Field Airport—American, Continental, Delta, Pan American, Republic, United, Western
Airport Transportation:
Three miles to downtown San Diego. Taxicab and bus service.
Car Rental Agencies: Alamo (297-0311), Avis (231-7171), Budget (297-3851), Hertz (231-7000), National (231-7100), Thrifty (239-2281)
Railroad Passenger Service: Amtrak
Trade Exhibition Facilities:
Convention & Performing Arts Center, 202 C St., 236-6500
San Diego Sports Arena, 3500 Sports Arena Blvd., 224-4171
Town & Country Convention Center, 500 Hotel Circle N, 291-7131
Professional Sports Facilities:
San Diego Stadium, 9449 Friars Rd., 283-5503 (Chargers, football, 280-2121; Padres, baseball, 283-4494; Sockers, soccer, 280-4625)
San Diego Sports Arena, 3500 Sports Arena Blvd., 224-4171 (Clippers, basketball, 226-8456; Hawks, hockey, Pacific Coast League)
Theaters and Concert Hall:
Actors Quarter Theater, 480 Elm St., 465-4509
Civic Theatre, Convention & Performing Arts Center 236-6510 (San Diego Symphony Orchestra, San Diego Opera, San Diego Ballet Company, California Ballet Company, Los Angeles Philharmonic)
Coronado Playhouse, Silver Strand, Coronado, 435-4856
Mission Playhouse, 3960 Mason St., 295-6453
Old Globe Theatre, Balboa Park, 239-2255
Spreckels Theatre, 121 Broadway St., 233-6541
Museums:
Hall of Champions, Balboa Park
Maritime Museum Ships, 1036 N. Harbor Dr.
Museum of Man, Balboa Park
Natural History Museum, Balboa Park
Reuben H. Fleet Space Theater & Science Center, Balboa Park
Seely Stable, Old Town
Serra Museum, Presidio Park
Villa Montezuma, 1925 K St.
Art Museums and Galleries:
Timken Art Gallery, Balboa Park
Kesler Art Gallery, 2521 San Diego Ave.
La Jolla Museum of Contemporary Art, 700 Prospect St., La Jolla
San Diego Museum of Art, Balboa Park
Spanish Village Arts & Crafts Center, Balboa Park
Thackery Gallery, 321 Robinson Ave.
Points of Interest:
Balboa Park, San Diego Zoo and Wild Animal Park, House of Pacific Relations, Palomar Observatory, Sea World, Cabrillo National Monument, Mission Bay

Aquatic Park, Mission San Diego de Alcalá, Old Town State Park, Seaport Village, Heritage Park, Presidio Park, Coronado, La Jolla, Anza-Borrego Desert State Park, Torrey Pines State Park, Silver Strand State Park
Information Sources:
San Diego Convention and Visitors Bureau
1200 Third Ave., Suite 824
San Diego, California 92101
(714) 232-3101
San Diego Chamber of Commerce
110 West C Street, Suite 1600
San Diego, California 92101
(714) 232-0124

San Francisco, California

Population: (*4,665,500) 678,974 (1980C); Metro Rank: 5
Altitude: Sea level to 934 feet
Average Temp.: Jan., 50°F.; July, 59°F.
Telephone Area Number: 415
Time: 767-8900 **Weather:** 936-1212
Time Zone: Pacific
Daily Events: 391-2000 (recorded)
Selected Hotels:
Fairmont, California & Mason sts., 772-5000
Four Seasons Hotel, Geary & Taylor sts., 775-4700
Holiday Inn—Union Square, Sutter & Powell sts., 398-8900
Hyatt on Union Square, Post & Stockton sts., 398-1234
Hyatt Regency San Francisco, Five Embarcadero Center, 788-1234
Mark Hopkins, 1 Nob Hill, 392-3434
San Francisco Hilton, 333 O'Farrell St., 771-1400
Sheraton-Palace, Market & New Montgomery sts., 392-8600
Sir Francis Drake, Powell & Sutter sts., 392-7755
Stanford Court, California & Powell sts., 989-3500
Westin Miyako, Post & Laguna sts., 922-3200
Westin St. Francis, Union Square, 397-7000
Selected Restaurants:
Alexis, 1001 California St., 885-6400
Amelio's, 1630 Powell St., 397-4339
Blue Fox, 659 Merchant St., 981-1177
Doros, 714 Montgomery St., 397-6822
Empress of China, 838 Grant Ave., 434-1345
Ernie's, 847 Montgomery St., 397-5969
Fleur de Lys, 777 Sutter St., 673-7779
Fournou's Ovens, Stanford Court Hotel, California & Powell sts., 989-1910
La Bourgogne, 330 Mason St., 362-7352
La Mirabelle, 1326 Powell St., 421-3374
Le Club, 1250 Jones St., 771-5400
Liquor Laws: Liquor may be purchased from 6 A.M. to 2 A.M. daily.
Newspapers:
San Francisco Chronicle, 777-1111
San Francisco Examiner, 777-2424
Wall Street Journal, Pacific Coast Edition, 433-3200
Television Stations:
KBHK Channel 44
KGO (ABC) Channel 7
KPIX (CBS) Channel 5
KQED (PBS) Channel 9
KRON (NBC) Channel 4
KTYU Channel 2
AM Radio Stations:
KCBS (CBS) 740 News
KGO (ABC) 810 Talk
KNBR (NBC) 680 Popular
KSAY (ABC & MBS) 1010 Country
FM Radio Stations:
KGO 103.7 Rock—*Stereo*
KKHI 95.7 Classical—*Stereo*
KNBR 99.7 Popular—*Stereo*
Airline Service:
San Francisco International Airport—Air California, Air Canada, Alaska, American, Braniff, British Airways, China, Continental, CP Air, Delta, Eastern, Japan, Lufthansa, Mexicana, Northwest Orient, Pan American, Philippine, PSA, QANTAS (Australia), Republic, Singapore, Transamerica, TWA, United, Western
Airport Transportation:
Fifteen miles to downtown San Francisco. Taxicab, bus, and limousine bus service.
Car Rental Agencies: Airways (673-5772), Alamo (348-8666), Avis (885-5011), Budget (776-3588), Econo-Car (885-6000), Hertz (771-2200), National (474-5300)
Railroad Passenger Service: Amtrak
Trade Exhibition Facilities:
Brooks Hall, Fulton & Hyde sts., 558-5065
Civic Auditorium, Grove & Larkin sts., 558-5065
Cow Palace, Geneva Ave. & Rio Verde St., 469-6000
George R. Moscone Convention Center, 4th & Howard sts.
Masonic Temple Building, 1111 California St., 776-4702
Professional Sport Facility:
Candlestick Park, Jamestown Ave. & Harney Way (Giants, baseball, 467-8000; 49ers, football, 468-2249)
Theaters and Concert Halls:
Alcazar Theatre, 650 Geary St., 775-7100
Curran, 445 Geary St., 673-4400
Davies Symphony Hall, Civic Center (San Francisco Symphony Orchestra, 431-5400)
Geary, 415 Geary St., 673-6440
Golden Gate, Golden Gate & Market sts., 775-8800
Opera House, Civic Center (Ballet, 621-3838; Opera, 431-1210)
Orpheum Theatre, 1192 Market St., 552-4002
Museums:
Cable Car Barn, Washington & Mason sts.
California Academy of Sciences, Golden Gate Park
Fort Point National Historic Site and Presidio Army Museum, Presidio of San Francisco
National Maritime Museum, foot of Polk St.
Old Mint, Fifth & Mission sts.
Hyde Street Pier, foot of Hyde St.
Wells Fargo Bank History Room, 420 Montgomery St.
Wine Museum of San Francisco, 633 Beach St.
Art Museums and Galleries:
Asian Art Museum, Golden Gate Park
California Palace of the Legion of Honor, Lincoln Park
M. H. de Young Memorial Museum, Golden Gate Park
San Francisco Museum of Modern Art, Veterans Bldg., McAllister St. at Van Ness Ave.
Points of Interest:
Golden Gate Bridge, Golden Gate Park, Chinatown, Fisherman's Wharf, Ghirardelli Square, The Cannery, Presidio of San Francisco, National Maritime Museum, Twin Peaks, Embarcadero, Telegraph Hill, Coit Tower, Alcatraz, Pier 39
Information Sources:
San Francisco Convention & Visitors Bureau
1390 Market Street
San Francisco, California 94102
(415) 626-5500
San Francisco Visitor Information Center (operated by Convention & Visitors Bureau)
Swig Pavilion, Hallidie Plaza
Powell & Market streets
San Francisco Chamber of Commerce
465 California Street
San Francisco, California 94104
(415) 392-4511

Seattle, Washington

Population: (*2,077,100) 493,846 (1980C); Metro Rank: 15
Altitude: Sea level to 520 feet
Average Temp.: Jan., 41°F.; July, 66°F.
Telephone Area Number: 206
Time: 844-1111 **Weather:** 662-1111
Time Zone: Pacific
Selected Hotels:
Doubletree Inn, 205 Strander Blvd., 246-8220
Holiday Inn—Airport, 17338 Pacific Hwy. S, 248-1000

Hyatt House, 17001 Pacific Hwy. S, 244-6000
Park Hilton, 6th Ave. and Seneca St., 464-1980
Red Lion Inn/Sea-Tac, 18740 Pacific Hwy. S, 246-8600
Seattle Downtown Hilton, 6th Ave. & University St., 624-0500
Seattle Marriott, 3201 S. 176th St., 241-2000
University Tower, 4507 Brooklyn Ave. NE, 634-2000
Westin Hotel—Seattle, 5th Ave. at Westlake Ave., 624-7400

Selected Restaurants:
Benihana of Tokyo, IBM Building, 682-4686
Brasserie Pittsbourg, 601 1st Ave., 623-4167
Canlis' Charcoal Broiler, 2576 Aurora Ave. N, 283-3313
Ivar's Indian Salmon House, 401 NE. Northlake Way, 632-0767
Mirabeau, Sea-First Bank Building, 624-4550
Space Needle, 4th Ave., North & Harrison sts., 682-5656
Rosellinis' Four-10, 4th Ave. & Wall St., 624-5464
Rosellinis' Other Place, 319 Union St. 623-7340

Liquor Laws: Liquor is sold by the drink in licensed bars and restaurants. Bars are open 11:30 A.M. to 2 A.M. weekdays; Sunday 12 P.M. to 12 A.M.

Newspapers:
Seattle Daily Journal of Commerce, 622-8272
Seattle Post-Intelligencer, 628-8000
Seattle Times, 464-2111

Television Stations:
KCTS (PBS) Channel 9
KING (NBC) Channel 5
KIRO (CBS) Channel 7
KOMO (ABC) Channel 4
KSTW Channel 11

AM Radio Stations:
KAYO 1150 Talk
KING (NBC) 1090 Popular
KOMO (ABC) 1000 Contemporary

FM Radio Stations:
KEZX 98.9 Instrumental—*Stereo*
KIXI 95.7 Romantic
KOL 94.1 Rock—*Stereo*

Airline Service:
Seattle/Tacoma International Airport—Alaska, American, Braniff, British Airways, Continental, Delta, Eastern, Finnair, Mexicana, Northwest Orient, Pacific Western, Pan American, Republic, SAS (Scandinavian Airlines), Thai Airways, TWA, United, Western, Wien Air Alaska

Airport Transportation:
Fourteen miles to downtown Seattle. Taxicab, limousine bus, Metro Transit, and Airporter service.

Car Rental Agencies: American International (682-8989), Avis (433-5231), Budget (244-4088), Dollar-A-Day (246-5400), Hertz (433-5262), National (433-5500), Thrifty (246-7565)

Railroad Passenger Service: Amtrak

Trade Exhibition Facilities:
Kingdome, 201 S. King St., 628-3663
Seattle Center, 305 Harrison St., 625-4227
Seattle Trade Center, 2601 Elliot Ave., 682-9222
Washington Plaza, 5th Ave. at Westlake Ave., 624-7400

Professional Sports Facilities:
Arena, Seattle Center, 625-4234 (Breakers, hockey)
Coliseum, Seattle Center, 625-4234
Kingdome, 201 S. King St., 344-5254 (Seahawks, football, 827-9766; Mariners, baseball, 628-3300; Sounders, soccer, 628-3620; Supersonics, basketball, 628-8448)

Theaters:
ACT Theatre, 100 W. Roy St., 285-5110
5th Avenue Theater, 1308 5th Ave., 625-1900
Opera House, Seattle Center, (Seattle Symphony Orchestra, Seattle Opera, Pacific Northwest Ballet, 447-4700)
Penthouse Theatre, University of Washington Campus, 543-5638
Seattle Repertory, 225 Mercer St., 447-4764

Museums:
Burke Memorial—Washington State Museum, 17th Ave. NE & NE. 45th St.
Hall of Fire Engines and Hall of Aviation, Seattle Center
Museum of History and Industry, 2161 E. Hamlin St.
Pacific Science Center, 200 2nd Ave. N
Wing Luke Memorial Museum, 414 8th Ave. S

Art Museums and Galleries:
Frye Art Museum, 704 Terry Ave.
Henry Art Gallery, University of Washington
Seattle Art Museum, 14th Ave. E & E. Prospect St. and at the Seattle Center

Points of Interest:
Seattle Center, Shilshole Bay Marina, Pike Place Market, Pioneer Square, Volunteer Park, Seward Park, University of Washington Arboretum, Klondike Gold Rush National Historical Park, International District, Seattle Aquarium, Waterfront Park, Freeway Park

Information Sources:
Seattle/King County Convention & Visitors Bureau
1815 7th Ave.
Seattle, Washington 98101
(206) 447-7273

Seattle Chamber of Commerce
215 Columbia St.
Seattle, Washington 98104
(206) 447-7200

Washington, D.C.

Population: (*3,220,700) 637,651 (1980C); Metro Rank: 8
Altitude: 1 to 410 feet
Average Temp.: Jan., 36°F.; July, 79°F.
Telephone Area Number: 202
Time: 844-2525 **Weather:** 936-1212
Time Zone: Eastern

Selected Hotels:
The Capital Hilton, 16th & K sts. NW, 393-1000
Fairfax Hotel, 2100 Massachusetts Ave. NW, 293-2100
Four Seasons Hotel, 2800 Pennsylvania Ave. NW, 342-0444
Georgetown Inn, 1310 Wisconsin Ave. NW, 333-8900
The Madison, 15th & M sts. NW, 785-1000
Hay–Adams Hotel, 800 16th St. NW, 638-2260
One Washington Circle Hotel, One Washington Circle NW, 872-1680
Loew's L'Enfant Plaza, 480 L'Enfant Plaza, SW, 484-1000
Sheraton–Carlton, 923 16th St. NW, 638-2626
Washington Hilton, 1919 Connecticut Ave. NW, 483-3000
The Watergate Hotel, 2650 Virginia Ave. NW, 965-2300

Selected Restaurants:
Aux Beau Champs, Four Seasons Hotel, 2800 Pennsylvania Ave., 342-0444
Cantina D'italia, 1214A 18th St., NW, 659-1830
Jockey Club Restaurant, Fairfax Hotel, 2100 Massachusetts Ave. NW, 659-8000
Le Bagatelle, 2000 K St. NW, 872-8677
Le Lion D'or, 1150 Connecticut Ave., 296-7972
Le Pavillon, 1850 K St. NW, 883-3846
Le Provencal, 1234 20th St. NW, 223-2420
Sans Souci, 726 17th St. NW, 298-7424
Trader Vic's, 16th & K sts. NW, 393-1000

Liquor Laws: Liquor is sold weekdays, 8 A.M. to 2 A.M.; Saturday, 8 A.M. to 2 A.M.; Sunday, noon to 2 A.M

Newspapers:
Washington Post, 223-6000

Television Stations:
WDCA Channel 20
WDVM (CBS) Channel 9
WETA (PBS) Channel 26
WJLA (ABC) Channel 7
WRC (NBC) Channel 4
WTTG Channel 5

AM Radio Stations:
WAVA 780 News
WGMS 570 Classical
WMAL (ABC) 630 General
WRC (NBC) 980 News
WTOP (CBS) 1500 News

FM Radio Stations:
WAMU 88.5 Educational
WASH 97.1 Popular/News—*Stereo*
WETA 90.9 Classical/Talk—*Stereo*
WGMS 103.5 Classical—*Stereo*

VMAL 107.3 General—*Stereo*
irline Service:
Vashington National Airport—
ir Florida, Allegheny Commuter,
merican, Braniff, Delta, Eastern,
Jorthwest Orient, Pan American,
iedmont, Republic, TWA, United,
JSAIR
irline Service:
)ulles International Airport—
eroflot (U.S.S.R.), Air France,
merican, Braniff, British Airways,
)elta, Eastern, Northwest Orient,
)zark, Pan American, Piedmont,
epublic, TWA, United
irport Transportation:
hree miles from Washington National
irport to downtown Washington, D.C.;
6 miles from Dulles International
o Washington, D.C.
Jational: Taxicab and bus service.
)ulles: Taxicab and bus service.
ar Rental Agencies: Avis (683-6700),
udget (628-2750), Econo-Car (638-6533),
Iertz (549-3404)
ailroad Passenger Service: Amtrak,
hessie System, Southern Railway
rade Exhibition Facilities:
). C. National Guard Armory,
001 E. Capitol St., LI 7-9077
aurel Exhibition Center, Laurel, Md.,
A 5-0400
Vashington Coliseum,
rd & M sts. NE, LI 7-5800

Professional Sports Facilities:
Capital Centre, Largo, Md., 350-3900
(Capitals, hockey; Bullets, basketball)
RFK Stadium, E. Capitol St. & 22nd
St., NE, 546-2222 (Redskins, football;
Diplomats, soccer)

Theaters and Concert Halls:
Arena Stage, 6th & Maine sts., 554-7890
Constitution Hall, 18th & D sts.,
ME 8-2661
Ford's Theatre, 511 10th St. NW,
347-6260
JFK Center for the Performing Arts,
Rock Creek Pkwy., 254-3600
(Ballet, National Symphony
Orchestra, Opera)
National Theatre, 1321 E St. NW,
466-8500
Warner Theater Music Hall,
501 13th St., NW, 842-8050

Museums:
Anacostia Neighborhood Museum,
2405 Martin Luther King Ave.
Dumbarton Oaks, 1703 32nd St. NW
Hirshhorn Museum and Sculpture
Garden, 8th St. & Independence
Ave. SW
National Museum of African Art,
316 A St., NE
National Museum of American History,
14th St. & Constitution Ave. NW
National Museum of Natural History,
10th St. & Constitution Ave. NW
National Air and Space Museum,
7th St. & Independence Ave. SW
Truxtun-Decatur Naval Museum,
1610 H St. NW
U.S. Navy Memorial Museum,
9th & M sts. SE

Art Galleries:
Corcoran Gallery of Art,
17th St. & New York Ave. NW
National Museum of American Art,
9th & G sts. NW
National Gallery of Art,
6th St. & Constitution Ave. NW
National Portrait Gallery,
8th & F sts. NW
Phillips Art Gallery, 1600 21st St. NW

Points of Interest:
The Capitol, Senate Office Buildings,
Smithsonian Institution,
Lincoln and Jefferson Memorials,
Mount Vernon, Washington
Monument, White House, The Mall,
National Zoological Park

Information Sources:
Washington Area Convention and
Visitors Association
15751 I St., NW
Washington, D.C. 20005
(202) 789-7000

Greater Washington Board of Trade
of Trade
1129 20th St., NW
Washington, D.C. 20036
(202) 857-5900

Populations of United States Cities, Towns, Counties, and States

This table lists alphabetically by state populations for approximately 20,000 places in the United States. Most populations are from the 1980 census. The populations given for unincorporated places, not available from the 1980 census, are Rand McNally estimates or 1970 census figures. These population figures are identified by a circle (○).

Populations followed by a triangle (▲) represent township or New England "town" populations. These "town" populations usually include a central village of the same name, as well as other nearby communities and surrounding rural areas.

If a place is within a metropolitan area, the name of the Ranally Metropolitan Area (RMA) is designated in an abbreviated form after the place-name. Each RMA includes one or more central cities, as well as socially and economically integrated surrounding areas. The central city for each RMA is identified by the use of CAPITAL LETTERS.

ALABAMA

1980 Census **3,893,888**

CITIES

Place	Population
Abbeville	3,155
Adamsville BIR	2,498
Addison	746
Akron	604
Alabaster BIR	7,079
Albertville	12,039
Aldrich	600 ○
Alexander City	13,807
Aliceville	3,207
Altoona	928
Andalusia	10,415
ANNISTON ANNI	29,523
Arab	5,967
Ardmore	1,096
Ariton	844
Ashford DOTH	2,165
Ashland	2,052
Ashville	1,489
Athens HNTS	14,558
Atmore	8,789
Attalla GAD	7,737
Auburn OP-AU	28,471
Autaugaville	843
Axis	600 ○
Babbie	553
Bay Minette	7,455
Bayou La Batre	2,005
Bayview BIR	830 ○
Beatrice	558
Bellamy	750 ○
Berry	916
Bessemer BIR	31,729
BIRMINGHAM BIR	286,799
Blountsville	1,509
Bluff Park BIR	12,000 ○
Boaz	7,151
Bon Secour	600 ○
Brantley	1,151
Brent	2,862
Brewton	6,680
Bridgeport	2,974
Brighton BIR	5,308
Brilliant	871
Brookside BIR	1,409
Brookwood	492
Brundidge	3,213
Butler	1,882
Cahaba Heights BIR	3,800 ○
Calera	2,035
Calvert	500 ○
Camden	2,406
Camp Hill	1,628
Carbon Hill	2,452
Carrollton	1,104
Carrville	820
Castleberry	847
Cedar Bluff	1,129
Center Point BIR	23,317
Centre	2,351
Centreville	2,504
Chatom	1,122
Chelsea	600 ○
Cherokee	1,589
Chickasaw MOB	7,402
Childersburg	5,084
Citronelle	2,841
Clanton	5,832
Clayhatchee	560
Clayton	1,589
Cleveland	487
Clio	1,224
Coaling	500 ○
Coden	500 ○
Coffeeville	448
Colbert Heights FLO-	500 ○
Collinsville	1,383
Columbia	881
Columbiana	2,655
Coosada MTGY	980
Cordova	3,123
Cottondale TUSC	2,300 ○
Cottonwood	1,352
Courtland	456
Creola	1,652
Crossville	1,222
Cuba	486
Cullman	13,084
Dadeville	3,263
Daleville	4,250
Daphne MOB	3,406
De Armanville ANNI	450 ○
DECATUR DEC	42,002
Demopolis	7,678
Dixiana BIR	600 ○
Docena BIR	1,140 ○
Dolomite BIR	2,400 ○
Dora BIR	2,327
DOTHAN DOTH	48,750
Double Springs	1,057
Dozier	494
East Brewton	3,012
Eclectic	1,124
Edgewater BIR	1,400 ○
Elba	4,355
Elberta	491
Enterprise	18,033
Eufaula	12,097
Eulaton ANNI	1,869
Eutaw	2,444
Evergreen	4,171
Fairfield BIR	13,242
Fairhope MOB	7,286
Falkville	1,310
Fayette	5,287
Flint City DEC	673
Flomaton	1,882
Florala	2,165
FLORENCE FLO-	37,029
Foley	4,003
Fort Deposit	1,519
Fort Payne	11,485
Frisco City	1,424
Fulton	606
Fultondale BIR	6,217
Fyffe	1,305
GADSDEN GAD	47,565
Gallant	550 ○
Garden City	655
Gardendale BIR	7,928
Geneva	4,866
Georgiana	1,993
Geraldine	911
Glencoe GAD	4,648
Goodwater	1,895
Gordo	2,112
Grand Bay PSCG	3,185
Grant	632
Graysville BIR	2,642
Greenhill	550 ○
Green Pond	500 ○
Greensboro	3,248
Greenville	7,807
Grove Hill	1,912
Guin	2,418
Gulf Shores	1,349
Guntersville	7,041
Gurley	735
Hackleburg	883
Haleyville	5,306
Hamilton	5,093
Hanceville	2,220
Harpersville	934
Hartford	2,647
Hartselle	8,858
Hayneville	592
Hazel Green	1,503
Headland	3,327
Heflin ANNI	3,014
Helena BIR	2,130
Hokes Bluff GAD	3,216
Holly Pond	493
Hollywood	1,110
Holt TUSC	4,300 ○
Homewood BIR	21,412
Hoover BIR	19,792
Hueytown BIR	13,478
Huguley	2,947
HUNTSVILLE HNTS	142,513
Hurtsboro	752
Irondale BIR	6,510
Irvington MOB	450 ○
Jackson	6,073
Jacksonville ANNI	9,735
Jasper	11,894
Jemison	1,828
Kennedy	604
Kent	500 ○
Ketona BIR	600 ○
Killen FLO-	747
Kimberly BIR	1,043
Kinsey DOTH	1,239
Kinston	604
Lafayette	3,647
Lanett	6,897
Leeds BIR	8,638
Leighton FLO-	1,218
Lexington	884
Lillian	600
Lincoln	2,081
Linden	2,773
Lineville	2,257
Lipscomb BIR	3,741
Lisman	638
Littleville FLO-	1,262
Livingston	3,187
Lockhart	547
Louisville	791
Loxley	804
Luverne	2,639
Lynn	554
McCalla BIR	500
McKenzie	605
Madison HNTS	4,057
Madison MTGY	500
Malvern	558
Maplesville	754
Margaret	757
Marion	4,467
Mentone	476
Meridianville HNTS	1,403
Midfield BIR	6,203
Midland City DOTH	1,903
Midway	593
Millbrook MTGY	3,101
Millport	1,287
Millry	956
MOBILE MOB	200,452
Monroeville	5,674
Montevallo	3,965
MONTGOMERY MTGY	177,857
Montrose MOB	1,200
Morris BIR	623
Moulton	3,197
Moundville	1,310
Mountain Brook BIR	19,718
Mount Olive BIR	1,900
Mount Vernon	1,038
Munford ANNI	600
Muscle Shoals FLO-	8,911
New Brockton	1,392
New Castle BIR	1,000
New Hope HNTS	1,546
New Market	550
Newton	1,540
Newville	814
Normal HNTS	5,000
Northport TUSC	14,291
Notasulga	876
Oakman	770
Odenville	724
Ohatchee	860
Oneonta	4,824
OPELIKA OP-AU	21,896
Opp	7,204
Owens Cross Roads HNTS	804
Oxford ANNI	8,939
Ozark	13,188

○ Rand McNally estimate
▲ Population of entire township or "town", including rural areas.
● Independent city. Population not included in county total.

Parrish . . . 1,583
Pelham BIR . . . 6,759
Pell City . . . 6,616
Perdido . . . 1,100 ○
Peterman . . . 500 ○
Peterson TUSC . . . 550 ○
Petersville FLO- . . . 2,000 ○
Phenix City COL . . . 26,928
Phil Campbell . . . 1,549
Piedmont . . . 5,544
Pinckard . . . 771
Pine Hill . . . 510
Pinson BIR . . . 1,600 ○
Pisgah . . . 699
Plantersville . . . 650 ○
Pleasant Grove BIR . . . 7,102
Point Clear MOB . . . 1,812
Prattville MTGY . . . 18,647
Prichard MOB . . . 39,541
Ragland . . . 1,860
Rainbow City GAD . . . 6,299
Rainsville . . . 3,907
Red Bay . . . 3,232
Red Level . . . 504
Reece City GAD . . . 718
Reform . . . 2,245
River Falls . . . 669
Riverside . . . 849
Roanoke . . . 5,896
Robertsdale . . . 2,306
Rockford . . . 494
Rogersville . . . 1,224
Russellville . . . 8,195
Rutledge . . . 496
St. Bernard . . . 600 ○
St. Elmo MOB . . . 450 ○
Samson . . . 2,402
Saraland MOB . . . 9,833
Satsuma MOB . . . 3,822
Sayreton BIR . . . 550 ○
Scottsboro . . . 14,758
Section . . . 821
Selma . . . 26,684
Semmes MOB . . . 1,200 ○
Sheffield FLO- . . . 11,903
Shelby . . . 600 ○
Silverhill . . . 624
Sipsey BIR . . . 678
Slocomb . . . 2,153
Smiths COL . . . 900 ○
Southside GAD . . . 5,141
Spanish Fort MOB . . . 3,415
Springville . . . 1,476
Spruce Pine . . . 600 ○
Stapleton . . . 900 ○
Steele . . . 795
Stevenson . . . 2,568
Sulligent . . . 2,130
Sumiton BIR . . . 2,815
Summerdale . . . 546
Sycamore . . . 900 ○
Sylacauga . . . 12,708
Sylvania . . . 1,156
Talladega . . . 19,128
Tallassee . . . 4,763
Tanner HNTS . . . 550 ○
Tarrant City BIR . . . 8,148
Theodore MOB . . . 6,392
Thomaston . . . 679
Thomasville . . . 4,387
Thorsby . . . 1,422
Tillmans Corner MOB . . . 5,000 ○
Town Creek . . . 1,201
Townley . . . 500 ○
Trinity DEC . . . 1,328
Troy . . . 12,945
Trussville BIR . . . 3,507
TUSCALOOSA TUSC . . . 75,211
Tuscumbia FLO- . . . 9,137
Tuskegee . . . 13,327
Underwood . . . 750 ○
Union Springs . . . 4,431
Uniontown . . . 2,112
Valhermoso Springs . . . 550 ○
Valley Head . . . 609
Vernon . . . 2,609
Vestavia Hills BIR . . . 15,722
Vincent . . . 1,652
Vinemont . . . 615
Wadley . . . 532
Walnut Grove . . . 510
Warrior BIR . . . 3,260
Weaver ANNI . . . 2,765
Webb DOTH . . . 448
Wedowee . . . 908
West Blocton . . . 1,147
Wetumpka MTGY . . . 4,341
Whatley . . . 450 ○
Wilmer MOB . . . 581
Wilsonville . . . 914
Wilton . . . 642
Winfield . . . 3,781
York . . . 3,392

COUNTIES

Autauga . . . 32,259
Baldwin . . . 78,556
Barbour . . . 24,756
Bibb . . . 15,723
Blount . . . 36,459
Bullock . . . 10,596
Butler . . . 21,680
Calhoun . . . 119,761
Chambers . . . 39,191
Cherokee . . . 18,760
Chilton . . . 30,612
Choctaw . . . 16,839
Clarke . . . 27,702
Clay . . . 13,703
Cleburne . . . 12,595
Coffee . . . 38,533
Colbert . . . 54,519
Conecuh . . . 15,884
Coosa . . . 11,377
Covington . . . 36,850
Crenshaw . . . 14,110
Cullman . . . 61,642
Dale . . . 47,821
Dallas . . . 53,981
De Kalb . . . 53,658
Elmore . . . 43,390
Escambia . . . 38,440
Etowah . . . 103,057
Fayette . . . 18,809
Franklin . . . 28,350
Geneva . . . 24,253
Greene . . . 11,021
Hale . . . 15,604
Henry . . . 15,302
Houston . . . 74,632
Jackson . . . 51,407
Jefferson . . . 671,324
Lamar . . . 16,453
Lauderdale . . . 80,546
Lawrence . . . 30,170
Lee . . . 76,283
Limestone . . . 46,005
Lowndes . . . 13,253
Macon . . . 26,829
Madison . . . 196,966
Marengo . . . 25,047
Marion . . . 30,041
Marshall . . . 65,622
Mobile . . . 364,980
Monroe . . . 22,651
Montgomery . . . 197,038
Morgan . . . 90,231
Perry . . . 15,012
Pickens . . . 21,481
Pike . . . 28,050
Randolph . . . 20,075
Russell . . . 47,356
St. Clair . . . 41,205
Shelby . . . 66,298
Sumter . . . 16,908
Talladega . . . 73,826
Tallapoosa . . . 38,676
Tuscaloosa . . . 137,541
Walker . . . 68,660
Washington . . . 16,821
Wilcox . . . 14,755
Winston . . . 21,953

ALASKA

1980 Census . . . 401,851

CITIES

Alakanuk . . . 522
ANCHORAGE ANCH . . . 174,431
Anderson . . . 517
Angoon . . . 465
Barrow . . . 2,207
Bethel . . . 3,576
Chevak . . . 466
College FRBK . . . 800 ○
Cordova . . . 1,879
Craig . . . 527
Delta Junction . . . 945
Dillingham . . . 1,563
Emmonak . . . 567
FAIRBANKS FRBK . . . 22,645
Fort Yukon . . . 619
Galena . . . 765
Gambell . . . 445
Glennallen . . . 511
Haines . . . 993
Homer . . . 2,209
Hoonah . . . 680
Hooper Bay . . . 627
Juneau . . . 19,528
Kake . . . 555
Kenai . . . 4,324
Ketchikan . . . 7,198
King Cove . . . 460
King Salmon . . . 545
Kodiak . . . 4,756
Kotzebue . . . 2,054
Kwethluk . . . 454
Metlakatla . . . 1,056
Mountain Village . . . 583
Nenana . . . 470
Nikishka . . . 1,109
Nome . . . 2,301
Noorvik . . . 492
Palmer ANCH . . . 2,141
Petersburg . . . 2,821
Point Hope . . . 464
St. Paul . . . 551
Sand Point . . . 625
Savoonga . . . 491
Seldovia . . . 479
Seward . . . 1,843
Sitka . . . 7,803
Skagway . . . 768
Soldotna . . . 2,320
Sterling . . . 919
Togiak . . . 470
Tok . . . 589
Unalakleet . . . 623
Unalaska . . . 1,322
Valdez . . . 3,079
Wasilla . . . 1,559
Wrangell . . . 2,184
Yakutat . . . 449

ARIZONA

1980 Census . . . 2,718,425

CITIES

Aguila . . . 600 ○
Ajo . . . 5,189
Alpine . . . 500 ○
Apache Junction PHOE . . . 9,935
Arizona Sunsites . . . 900 ○
Ash Fork . . . 600 ○
Avondale PHOE . . . 8,168
Bagdad . . . 2,331
Benson . . . 4,190
Bisbee . . . 7,154
Black Canyon City . . . 600 ○
Bouse . . . 450 ○
Bowie . . . 600 ○
Buckeye . . . 3,434
Bullhead City . . . 5,000 ○
Bylas . . . 1,175
Cameron . . . 500 ○
Camp Verde . . . 1,125
Casa Grande . . . 14,971
Casas Adobes TUC . . . 5,300 ○
Cashion PHOE . . . 3,014
Catalina Foothills TUC . . . 1,500 ○
Cave Creek . . . 1,589
Central Heights . . . 1,500 ○
Chandler PHOE . . . 29,673
Chandler Heights PHOE . . . 750 ○
Chinle . . . 2,815
Chino Valley . . . 2,858
Cibecue . . . 950 ○
Clarkdale . . . 1,512
Claypool . . . 2,362
Clifton . . . 4,245
Colorado City . . . 450 ○
Congress . . . 450 ○
Coolidge . . . 6,851
Cornville . . . 800 ○
Cottonwood . . . 4,550
Crane YUMA . . . 2,400 ○
Dennehotso . . . 500 ○
Douglas . . . 13,058
Dreamland Villa PHOE . . . 3,200 ○
Duncan . . . 603
Eagar . . . 2,791
Ehrenberg . . . 900 ○
El Mirage PHOE . . . 4,307
Eloy . . . 6,240
Flagstaff . . . 34,743
Florence . . . 3,391
Fort Defiance . . . 3,431
Fredonia . . . 1,040
Gadsden . . . 500 ○
Ganado . . . 1,200 ○
Gila Bend . . . 1,585
Gilbert PHOE . . . 5,717
Glendale PHOE . . . 97,172
Globe . . . 6,886
Goodyear PHOE . . . 2,747
Grand Canyon . . . 1,348
Greasewood . . . 450 ○
Green Valley TUC . . . 7,999
Guadalupe PHOE . . . 4,506
Hayden . . . 1,205
Heber . . . 600 ○
Holbrook . . . 5,785
Hotevilla . . . 700 ○
Houck . . . 600 ○
Huachuca City . . . 1,661
Indian Ridge Estates TUC . . . 2,300 ○
Joseph City . . . 900 ○
Kayenta . . . 3,343
Keams Canyon . . . 600 ○
Kearny . . . 2,646
Kingman . . . 9,257
Kykotsmovi Village . . . 600 ○
Lake Havasu City . . . 15,909
Lakeside . . . 1,333
Laveen PHOE . . . 600 ○
Litchfield Park PHOE . . . 3,657
Little Acres . . . 600 ○
Lukachukai . . . 1,049
McNary . . . 1,320
Mammoth . . . 1,906
Marana . . . 1,674
Maricopa . . . 900 ○
Mayer . . . 950 ○
Mesa PHOE . . . 152,453
Miami . . . 2,716
Moenkopi . . . 900 ○

○ Rand McNally estimate
▲ Population of entire township or "town", including rural areas.
● Independent city. Population not included in county total.

ARIZONA continued

City	Population
Mohave Valley	750 ○
Morenci	1,200 ○
Mountainaire	700 ○
Naco	800 ○
NOGALES NOGLS	15,683
Oracle	2,484
Page	4,907
Paradise Valley PHOE	11,085
Parker	2,542
Patagonia	980
Payson	5,068
Peach Springs	600 ○
Peoria PHOE	12,307
PHOENIX PHOE	789,704
Picacho	550 ○
Pima	1,599
Pine	500 ○
Pinetop	1,527
Plantsite	1,500 ○
Polacca	600 ○
Prescott	20,055
Quartzsite	600 ○
Riviera	4,500 ○
Sacaton	1,951
Safford	7,010
Sahuarita	600 ○
St. David	950 ○
St. Johns	3,368
Salome	600 ○
San Carlos	2,668
San Luis	1,946
San Manuel	5,443
Scottsdale PHOE	88,622
Sedona	5,368
Seligman	950 ○
Sells	1,864
Shonto	600 ○
Show Low	4,298
Sierra Vista	24,937
Silver Bell	600 ○
Snowflake	3,510
Somerton	5,761
South Tucson TUC	6,554
Springerville	1,452
Stanfield	900 ○
Stargo	1,038
Sun City PHOE	40,505
Superior	4,600
Surprise PHOE	3,723
Tacna	500 ○
Taylor	1,915
Tempe PHOE	106,743
Thatcher	3,374
Tolleson PHOE	4,433
Tombstone	1,632
Tuba City	5,045
TUCSON TUC	330,537
Twin Knolls PHOE	4,700 ○
Valencia	1,300 ○
Velda Rose Estates PHOE	2,250 ○
Wellton	911
Whiteriver	1,400 ○
Wickenburg	3,535
Willcox	3,243
Williams	2,266
Window Rock	2,230
Winkelman	1,060
Winslow	7,921
Wittmann	700 ○
Yarnell	950 ○
Youngtown PHOE	2,254
YUMA YUMA	42,481

COUNTIES

County	Population
Apache	52,108
Cochise	85,686
Coconino	75,008
Gila	37,080
Graham	22,862
Greenlee	11,406
La Paz	12,500
Maricopa	1,509,262
Mohave	55,865
Navajo	67,629
Pima	531,443
Pinal	90,918
Santa Cruz	20,459
Yavapai	68,145
Yuma	78,054

ARKANSAS

1980 Census **2,286,435**

CITIES

City	Population
Alma FTSM	2,755
Altheimer	1,231
Altus	441
Amity	859
Arkadelphia	10,005
Arkansas City	668
Ashdown	4,218
Ash Flat	524
Atkins	3,002
Augusta	3,496
Bald Knob	2,756
Barling FTSM	3,761
Batesville	8,263
Bay	1,605
Bearden	1,191
Beebe	3,599
Bella Vista	2,589
Belleville	571
Benton L.R.	17,717
Bentonville	8,756
Berryville	2,966
Biscoe	486
Black Rock	848
Blytheville	23,844
Bonanza	553
Bono	967
Booneville	3,718
Bradford	950
Bradley	790
Brinkley	4,909
Brookland	840
Bryant L.R.	2,682
Bull Shoals	1,312
Cabot L.R.	4,806
Calico Rock	1,046
Calion	638
Camden	15,356
Cammack Village L.R.	920
Caraway	1,165
Carlisle	2,567
Carthage	568
Cave City	1,634
Charleston	1,748
Cherokee Village	3,200 ○
Cherry Valley	729
Clarendon	2,361
Clarksville	5,237
Clinton	1,284
Coal Hill	859
Conway	20,375
Corning	3,650
Cotter	920
Cotton Plant	1,323
Crawfordsville	685
Crossett	6,706
Cushman	556
Danville	1,698
Dardanelle	3,621
Decatur	1,013
De Queen	4,594
Dermott	4,731
Des Arc	2,001
Desha	750 ○
De Valls Bluff	738
De Witt	3,928
Diaz	1,192
Dierks	1,249
Dover	948
Dumas	6,091
Dyer	608
Dyess	446
Earle	3,517
Elaine	991
El Dorado	25,270
Elkins	579
Elm Springs FAY-	781
Emerson	444
Emmet	475
England	3,081
Eudora	3,840
Eureka Springs	1,989
Farmington FAY-	1,283
FAYETTEVILLE FAY-	36,608
Flippin	1,072
Fordyce	5,175
Foreman	1,377
Forrest City	13,803
FORT SMITH FTSM	71,626
Garland City	660
Gassville	859
Gentry	1,468
Gillett	927
Gilmore	503
Glenwood	1,402
Gosnell	3,215
Gould	1,671
Grady	488
Gravette	1,218
Greenbrier	1,423
Green Forest	1,609
Greenland FAY-	622
Greenwood	3,317
Grubbs	546
Gurdon	2,707
Hackett	505
Hamburg	3,394
Hampton	1,627
Hardy	643
Harrisburg	1,921
Harrison	9,567
Hartford	613
Hartman	517
Haskell	1,074
Hazen	1,636
Heber Springs	4,589
Hector	449
Helena	9,598
Hensley L.R.	450 ○
Hickory Ridge	478
Holly Grove	754
Hope	10,290
Horatio	989
HOT SPRINGS NATIONAL PARK HTSPR	35,781
Hoxie	2,961
Hughes	1,919
Humnoke	442
Humphrey	872
Huntington	662
Huntsville	1,394
Huttig	976
Imboden	661
Jacksonville L.R.	27,589
Jasper	519
Johnson FAY-	519
Joiner	725
Jonesboro	31,530
Jones Mill	850 ○
Judsonia	2,025
Junction City	813
Keiser	962
Kensett	1,751
Knobel	503
Lake City	1,842
Lake Hamilton HTSPR	1,054
Lakeview	512
Lake Village	3,088
Lamar	708
Lavaca FTSM	1,092
Leachville	1,882
Leola	481
Lepanto	1,964
Leslie	501
Lewisville	1,476
Lexa	500 ○
Lincoln	1,422
LITTLE ROCK L.R.	158,461
Lockesburg	616
London	859
Lonoke	4,128
Lowell FAY-	1,078
Luxora	1,739
Mabelvale L.R.	550 ○
McAlmont L.R.	1,600 ○
McCrory	1,942
McGehee	5,671
McNeil	725
McRae	641
Madison	1,238
Magazine	799
Magnet Cove	500 ○
Magnolia	11,909
Malvern	10,163
Mammoth Spring	1,158
Mandeville	700 ○
Manila	2,553
Mansfield	1,000
Marianna	6,220
Marion MEM	2,996
Marked Tree	3,201
Marmaduke	1,168
Marshall	1,595
Marvell	1,724
Mayflower L.R.	1,381
Melbourne	1,619
Mena	5,154
Mineral Springs	936
Monette	1,165
Monticello	8,259
Montrose	641
Morrilton	7,355
Mountainburg	595
Mountain Home	8,066
Mountain Pine	1,068
Mountain View	2,147
Mount Ida	1,023
Mulberry	1,444
Murfreesboro	1,883
Nashville	4,554
Newark	1,128
Newport	8,339
Norman	539
Norphlet	756
North Crossett	3,513
North Little Rock L.R.	64,288
Ola	1,121
Oppelo	486
Osceola	8,881
Oxford	520
Ozark	3,597
Palestine	976
Pangburn	673
Pankey	450 ○
Paragould	15,248
Paris	3,991
Parkdale	471
Parkin	2,035
Patterson	567
Pea Ridge	1,488
Perryville	1,058
Piggott	3,762
PINE BLUFF PNBLF	56,636
Plainview	752
Plumerville	785
Pocahontas	5,995
Portia	480
Portland	701
Pottsville	564
Prairie Grove	1,708
Prescott	4,103
Quitman	556
Rector	2,336
Redfield	745
Reyno	521

○ Rand McNally estimate
▲ Population of entire township or "town", including rural areas.
● Independent city. Population not included in county total.

Place	Population
Rison	1,325
Rogers	17,429
Russellville	867
Salem	1,424
Searcy	13,612
Sheridan	3,042
Sherwood L.R.	10,406
Siloam Springs	7,940
Smackover	2,453
Sparkman	622
Springdale FAY-	23,458
Stamps	2,859
Star City	2,066
Stephens	1,366
Strong	785
Stuttgart	10,941
Subiaco	744
Sulphur Springs	496
Summit	506
Sweet Home L.R.	1,100 ○
Swifton	859
Sylvan Hills L.R.	2,900 ○
Taylor	657
TEXARKANA TEXR-	21,459
Thornton	711
Tontitown FAY-	615
Traskwood	459
Trumann	6,405
Tuckerman	2,078
Turrell	1,041
Tyronza	777
Van Buren FTSM	12,020
Vilonia	736
Waldo	1,685
Waldron	2,642
Walnut Ridge	4,152
Ward	981
Warren	7,646
Watson Chapel PNBLF	900 ○
Weiner	750
West Crossett	1,466
West Fork	1,526
West Helena	11,367
West Memphis MEM	28,138
Wheatley	523
White Hall PNBLF	2,214
Wickes	464
Wilmar	747
Wilmot	1,227
Wilson	1,115
Wilton	495
Woodson L.R.	600 ○
Wrightsville L.R.	1,400
Wynne	7,805
Yellville	1,044

COUNTIES

County	Population
Arkansas	24,175
Ashley	26,538
Baxter	27,409
Benton	78,115
Boone	26,067
Bradley	13,803
Calhoun	6,079
Carroll	16,203
Chicot	17,793
Clark	23,326
Clay	20,616
Cleburne	16,909
Cleveland	7,868
Columbia	26,644
Conway	19,505
Craighead	63,239
Crawford	36,892
Crittenden	49,499
Cross	20,434
Dallas	10,515
Desha	19,760
Drew	17,910
Faulkner	46,192
Franklin	14,705
Fulton	9,975
Garland	70,531
Grant	13,008
Greene	30,744
Hempstead	23,635
Hot Spring	26,819
Howard	13,459
Independence	30,147
Izard	10,768
Jackson	21,646
Jefferson	90,718
Johnson	17,423
Lafayette	10,213
Lawrence	18,447
Lee	15,539
Lincoln	13,369
Little River	13,952
Logan	20,144
Lonoke	34,518
Madison	11,373
Marion	11,334
Miller	37,766
Mississippi	59,517
Monroe	14,052
Montgomery	7,771
Nevada	11,097
Newton	7,756
Ouachita	30,541
Perry	7,266
Phillips	34,772
Pike	10,373
Poinsett	27,032
Polk	17,007
Pope	39,021
Prairie	10,140
Pulaski	340,613
Randolph	16,834
St. Francis	30,858
Saline	53,161
Scott	9,685
Searcy	8,847
Sebastian	95,172
Sevier	14,060
Sharp	14,607
Stone	9,022
Union	48,573
Van Buren	13,357
Washington	100,494
White	50,835
Woodruff	11,222
Yell	17,026

CALIFORNIA

1980
Census 23,667,565

CITIES

Place	Population
Acton	900 ○
Adelanto	2,164
Adin	575 ○
Agoura L.A.	600 ○
Ahwahnee	900 ○
Alameda SF-O-	63,852
Albany SF-O-	15,130
Alhambra L.A.	64,615
Alondra L.A.	12,096
Alpaugh	900 ○
Altadena L.A.	40,983
Alturas	3,025
Alum Rock SF-O-	16,890
Anaheim L.A.	219,494
Anderson REDD	7,381
Angels Camp	2,302
ANTIOCH ANT-P	42,683
Apple Valley	14,305
Aptos S.CRZ	7,039
Arbuckle	1,306
Arcade SAC	37,600 ○
Arcadia L.A.	45,994
Arcata EUR	12,850
Arden SAC	52,000 ○
Arnold	2,385
Arroyo Grande	11,290
Artesia L.A.	14,301
Arvin	6,863
Ashland SF-O-	13,893
Atascadero	16,232
Atherton SF-O-	7,797
Atwater MRCD-	17,530
Auberry	1,100 ○
Auburn SAC	7,540
Avalon L.A.	2,022
Avenal	4,137
Avila Beach	600 ○
Avocado Heights L.A.	11,721
Azusa L.A.	29,380
Baker	650 ○
BAKERSFIELD BAK	105,735
Baldwin Park L.A.	50,554
Banning	14,020
Barstow	17,690
Beaumont	6,818
Bell L.A.	25,450
Bellflower L.A.	53,441
Bell Gardens L.A.	34,117
Belmont SF-O-	24,505
Benicia SF-O-	15,376
Berkeley SF-O-	103,328
Beverly Hills L.A.	32,367
Bieber	600 ○
Big Bear City	3,500 ○
Big Creek	700 ○
Biggs	1,413
Big Pine	1,510
Big Sur	520 ○
Biolá	800 ○
Bishop	3,333
Bloomington SBDO-	12,781
Blue Lake	1,201
Blythe	6,805
Boonville	1,000 ○
Borrego Springs	1,405
Brawley	14,946
Brea L.A.	27,913
Brentwood ANT-P	4,434
Broderick SAC	9,900 ○
Buena Park L.A.	64,165
Burbank L.A.	84,625
Burlingame SF-O-	26,173
Burney	3,187
Buttonwillow	1,350
Byron	900 ○
Calabasas L.A.	900 ○
Calavo Gardens SDGO	6,100 ○
CALEXICO CLEX	14,412
Calipatria	2,636
Calistoga	3,879
Calwa FRES	6,640
Camarillo V-OX	37,797
Cambria	3,061
Cambrian Park SF-O-	4,000 ○
Camino	900 ○
Campbell SF-O-	26,910
Canby	450 ○
Capitola S.CRZ	9,095
Cardiff By The Sea SDGO	10,054
Carlotta	500 ○
Carlsbad OC-V	35,490
Carmel MTRY	4,707
Carmichael SAC	43,108
Carpinteria S.BAR	10,835
Carson L.A.	81,221
Caspar	550 ○
Castella	525 ○
Castle Park SDGO	6,300 ○
Castro Valley SF-O-	44,011
Castroville SLNS	4,396
Cathedral City	11,096
Cedarville	950 ○
Central Valley REDD	3,424
Ceres MOD	13,281
Cerritos L.A.	53,020
Cherryland SF-O-	9,425
Chester	1,756
CHICO CHICO	26,603
Chino L.A.	40,165
Chowchilla	5,122
Chula Vista SDGO	83,927
Citrus Heights SAC	85,911
City of Commerce L.A.	10,509
Claremont L.A.	30,950
Cloverdale	3,989
Clovis FRES	33,021
Coachella	9,129
Coalinga	6,593
Colfax	981
Colton SBDO-	15,201
Columbia	950 ○
Colusa	4,075
Comptche	555 ○
Compton L.A.	81,286
Concord SF-O-	103,255
Corcoran	6,454
Corning	4,745
Corona L.A.	37,791
Coronado SDGO	18,790
Corte Madera SF-O-	8,074
Costa Mesa L.A.	82,562
Cottonwood REDD	1,553
Coulterville	500 ○
Covelo	1,448
Covina L.A.	33,751
Crescent City	3,075
Crockett SF-O-	2,900 ○
Cucamonga L.A.	55,250
Cudahy L.A.	17,984
Culver City L.A.	38,139
Cupertino SF-O-	34,265
Cypress L.A.	40,391
Daggett	650 ○
Daly City SF-O-	78,519
Danville SF-O-	26,000
Davis	36,640
Del Aire L.A.	3,900 ○
Delano	16,491
Del Mar SDGO	5,017
Desert Hot Springs	5,941
Diamond Bar L.A.	28,045
Diamond Springs	2,287
Dinuba	9,907
Dixon	7,541
Dorris	836
Downey L.A.	82,602
Downieville	950 ○
Doyle	900 ○
Duarte L.A.	16,766
Dublin SF-O-	13,491
Dunsmuir	2,253
Durham CHICO	950 ○
Earlimart	4,578
East Los Angeles L.A.	110,017
East Palo Alto SF-O-	18,191
East Tustin L.A.	10,000 ○
El Cajon SDGO	73,892
El Centro	23,996
El Cerrito SF-O-	22,731
El Encanto Heights S.BAR	7,700 ○
Elk Grove SAC	10,959
El Monte L.A.	79,494
El Portal	850 ○
El Rio V-OX	5,674
El Segundo L.A.	13,752
El Sobrante SF-O-	10,535
Encinitas SDGO	10,796
Escalon	3,127
Escondido SDGO	64,355
Esparto	1,303
Etna	754
EUREKA EUR	24,153
Exeter VISL	5,606
Fairfax SF-O-	7,391

○ Rand McNally estimate
▲ Population of entire township or "town", including rural areas.
● Independent city. Population not included in county total.

CALIFORNIA continued

FAIRFIELD FRFL- . . . 58,099
Fair Oaks SAC . . . 22,602
Fallbrook OC-V . . . 14,041
Fall River Mills . . . 900 ○
Farmersville VISL . . . 5,544
Felton S.CRZ . . . 4,000 ○
Ferndale . . . 1,367
Fig Garden FRES . . . 9,000 ○
Fillmore . . . 9,602
Firebaugh . . . 3,740
Florence L.A. . . . 38,000 ○
Florin SAC . . . 16,523
Folsom SAC . . . 11,003
Fontana SBDO- . . . 37,107
Foothill Farms SAC . . . 13,700
Forest Knolls SF-O- . . . 2,000 ○
Fort Bragg . . . 5,019
Fort Jones . . . 544
Fortuna . . . 7,591
Foster City SF-O- . . . 23,287
Fountain Valley L.A. . . . 55,080
Fowler FRES . . . 2,496
Frazier Park . . . 1,444
Freedom S.CRZ . . . 6,416
Fremont SF-O- . . . 131,945
French Gulch . . . 600 ○
FRESNO FRES . . . 217,289
Friant . . . 500 ○
Fullerton L.A. . . . 102,034
Galt . . . 5,514
Garberville . . . 1,200 ○
Gardena L.A. . . . 45,165
Garden Grove L.A. . . . 123,307
Georgetown . . . 2,000 ○
Gerber . . . 950 ○
Geyserville . . . 950 ○
Gilroy . . . 21,641
Glen Avon SBDO- . . . 8,444
Glendale L.A. . . . 139,060
Glendora L.A. . . . 38,500
Goleta S.BAR . . . 28,100 ○
Gonzales . . . 2,891
Graham L.A. . . . 10,600 ○
Grand Terrace SBDO- . . . 8,498
Grass Valley . . . 6,697
Greenfield . . . 4,181
Greenville . . . 1,537
Grenada . . . 450 ○
Gridley . . . 3,982
Grossmont SDGO . . . 2,600 ○
Grover City . . . 8,827
Guadalupe . . . 3,629
Gualala . . . 700 ○
Gustine . . . 3,142
Hacienda Heights L.A. . . . 49,422
Half Moon Bay SF-O- . . . 7,282
Hamilton City . . . 1,337
Hanford . . . 20,958
Happy Camp . . . 1,110
Hawaiian Gardens L.A. . . . 10,548
Hawthorne L.A. . . . 56,447
Hayfork . . . 1,788
Hayward SF-O- . . . 94,342
Healdsburg . . . 7,217
Hemet . . . 22,454
Hercules SF-O- . . . 5,963
Hermosa Beach L.A. . . . 18,070
Hesperia . . . 13,540
Highland SBDO- . . . 10,400 ○
Hillcrest Center BAK . . . 30,000 ○
Hillsborough SF-O- . . . 10,372
Hinkley . . . 700 ○
Hollister . . . 11,488
Holtville . . . 4,399
Home Gardens L.A. . . . 5,783
Homewood . . . 500 ○
Hopland . . . 900 ○
Huntington Beach L.A. . . . 170,505
Huntington Park L.A. . . . 46,223
Imperial . . . 3,451
Imperial Beach SDGO . . . 22,689
Independence . . . 1,000 ○
Indio . . . 21,611
Inglewood L.A. . . . 94,245
Inverness . . . 1,400 ○
Inyokern . . . 900 ○
Ione . . . 2,207
Irvine L.A. . . . 62,134
Isla Vista S.BAR . . . 16,700 ○
Isleton . . . 914
Jackson . . . 2,331
Jacumba . . . 600 ○
Jamestown . . . 2,206
Jamul . . . 1,826
Janesville . . . 1,200 ○
Joshua Tree . . . 2,083
Julian . . . 1,320
June Lake . . . 900 ○
Kelseyville . . . 1,567
Kensington SF-O- . . . 5,342
Kernville . . . 1,660
Kettleman City . . . 1,051
King City . . . 5,495
Kingsburg . . . 5,115
Klamath . . . 850 ○
Klamath Glen . . . 600 ○
Knights Landing . . . 1,000 ○
La Canada Flintridge L.A. . . . 20,153
La Crescenta L.A. . . . 12,500 ○
Ladera Heights L.A. . . . 6,647
Lafayette SF-O- . . . 20,879
Laguna Beach L.A. . . . 17,901
Laguna Hills L.A. . . . 16,400 ○
La Habra L.A. . . . 45,232
Lake Arrowhead . . . 2,500 ○
Lake Elsinore L.A. . . . 5,982
Lake Hughes L.A. . . . 800 ○
Lakeport . . . 3,675
Lakeside SDGO . . . 23,921
Lakewood L.A. . . . 74,654
La Mesa SDGO . . . 50,308
La Mirada L.A. . . . 40,986
Lamont . . . 9,616
LANCASTER LANC . . . 48,027
La Palma L.A. . . . 15,399
La Puente L.A. . . . 30,882
Larkspur SF-O- . . . 11,064
Laton . . . 1,100
La Verne L.A. . . . 23,508
Lawndale L.A. . . . 23,460
Laytonville . . . 1,096
Lebec . . . 900 ○
Lee Vining . . . 900 ○
Leggett . . . 700 ○
Le Grand . . . 1,500 ○
Lemon Grove SDGO . . . 20,780
Lemoore . . . 8,832
Lennox L.A. . . . 18,445
Leucadia SDGO . . . 9,478
Liberty Acres L.A. . . . 4,600 ○
Lincoln . . . 4,132
Lincoln Acres SDGO . . . 1,800 ○
Lincoln Village STOC . . . 6,476
Linda MRYS- . . . 10,225
Lindsay . . . 6,924
Live Oak S.CRZ . . . 10,000 ○
Live Oak . . . 3,103
Livermore SF-O- . . . 48,349
Livingston . . . 5,326
Lodi STOC . . . 35,221
Loma Linda SBDO- . . . 10,694
Lomita L.A. . . . 18,807
LOMPOC LOMP . . . 26,267
Lone Pine . . . 1,684
Long Beach L.A. . . . 361,334
Los Alamitos L.A. . . . 11,529
Los Alamos . . . 950 ○
Los Altos SF-O- . . . 25,769
Los Altos Hills SF-O- . . . 7,421
LOS ANGELES L.A. . . . 2,966,850
Los Banos . . . 10,341
Los Gatos SF-O- . . . 26,906
Los Molinos . . . 1,241
Los Nietos L.A. . . . 7,100 ○
Lost Hills . . . 800 ○
Loyalton . . . 1,030
Lucerne . . . 1,767
Lucerne Valley . . . 1,300 ○
Lynwood L.A. . . . 48,548
McCloud . . . 1,656
McFarland . . . 5,151
McKinleyville EUR . . . 7,772
Madera . . . 21,732
Magalia . . . 950 ○
Malibu L.A. . . . 10,000 ○
Mammoth Lakes . . . 3,000 ○
Manhattan Beach L.A. . . . 31,542
Manteca STOC . . . 24,925
Maricopa . . . 946
Marina MTRY . . . 20,647
Marina Del Rey L.A. . . . 8,065
Mariposa . . . 1,150
Martinez SF-O- . . . 22,582
MARYSVILLE MRYS- . . . 9,898
Maxwell . . . 800 ○
Maywood L.A. . . . 21,810
Mecca . . . 1,698
Meiners Oaks V-OX . . . 5,600 ○
Mendocino . . . 1,008
Mendota . . . 5,038
Menlo Park SF-O- . . . 26,369
MERCED MRCD- . . . 36,499
Middletown . . . 2,000 ○
Millbrae SF-O- . . . 20,058
Mill Valley SF-O- . . . 12,967
Milpitas SF-O- . . . 37,820
Mira Loma SBDO- . . . 8,707
Mission Viejo L.A. . . . 50,666
MODESTO MOD. . . . 106,602
Mojave . . . 2,886
Mokelumne Hill . . . 950 ○
Monrovia L.A. . . . 30,531
Montague . . . 1,285
Montclair L.A. . . . 22,628
Montebello L.A. . . . 52,929
Montecito S.BAR . . . 9,300 ○
MONTEREY MTRY . . . 27,558
Monterey Park L.A. . . . 54,338
Montgomery Creek . . . 800 ○
Moraga SF-O- . . . 15,014
Morgan Hill SF-O- . . . 17,060
Morro Bay . . . 9,064
Mountain View SF-O- . . . 58,655
Mount Shasta . . . 2,837
Murphys . . . 1,183
Muscoy SBDO- . . . 6,188
Napa SF-O- . . . 50,879
National City SDGO . . . 48,772
Needles . . . 4,120
Nevada City . . . 2,431
Newark SF-O- . . . 32,126
Newberry Springs . . . 900 ○
Newhall L.A. . . . 12,029
Newman . . . 2,785
Newport Beach L.A. . . . 62,556
Niland . . . 1,042
Nipomo S.MAR . . . 5,247
Norco L.A. . . . 21,126
North Fair Oaks SF-O- . . . 10,294
North Fork . . . 950 ○
North Highlands SAC . . . 37,825
North Oaks L.A. . . . 5,800 ○
Norwalk L.A. . . . 85,286
Novato SF-O- . . . 43,916
Oakdale . . . 8,474
Oakland SF-O- . . . 339,337
OCEANSIDE OC-V . . . 76,698
Oildale BAK . . . 23,382
Ojai V-OX . . . 6,816
Olancha . . . 450 ○
Olivehurst MRYS- . . . 8,929
Ontario L.A. . . . 88,820
Opal Cliffs S.CRZ . . . 5,041
Orange L.A. . . . 91,450
Orangevale SAC . . . 20,585
Orcutt S.MAR . . . 1,500 ○
Orick . . . 600 ○
Orinda SF-O- . . . 16,825
Orland . . . 4,031
Orleans . . . 900 ○
Oro Grande . . . 900 ○
Oroville . . . 8,683
Otay SDGO . . . 6,400 ○
Oxnard V-OX . . . 108,195
Pacifica SF-O- . . . 36,866
Pacific Grove MTRY . . . 15,755
Palmdale LANC . . . 12,277
Palm Desert . . . 11,801
Palm Springs . . . 32,366
Palo Alto SF-O- . . . 55,225
Palos Verdes Estates L.A. . . . 14,376
Palo Verde . . . 600 ○
Paradise . . . 22,571
Paramount L.A. . . . 36,407
Parkway SAC . . . 12,000 ○
Parlier . . . 2,902
Pasadena L.A. . . . 118,072
Paso Robles . . . 9,163
Perris . . . 6,827
Pescadero . . . 500 ○
Petaluma SF-O- . . . 33,834
Pico Rivera L.A. . . . 53,387
Piedmont SF-O- . . . 10,498
Piedra . . . 500 ○
Pine Valley . . . 950 ○
Pinole SF-O- . . . 14,253
Pismo Beach . . . 5,364
Pittsburg ANT-P . . . 33,034
Pixley . . . 2,488
Placentia L.A. . . . 35,041
Placerville . . . 6,739
Pleasant Hill SF-O- . . . 25,124
Pleasanton SF-O- . . . 35,160
Pomona L.A. . . . 92,742
Porterville . . . 19,707
Port Hueneme V-OX . . . 17,803
Portola . . . 1,885
Potter Valley . . . 1,500 ○
Poway SDGO . . . 33,439
Princeton . . . 540 ○
Quincy . . . 2,700 ○
Ramona SDGO . . . 8,173
Rancho Cordova SAC . . . 42,881
Rancho Mirage . . . 6,281
Rancho Palos Verdes L.A. . . . 36,577
Rancho Rinconado SF-O- . . . 5,100 ○
Rancho Santa Fe SDGO . . . 4,014

○ Rand McNally estimate
▲ Population of entire township or "town", including rural areas.
● Independent city. Population not included in county total.

Place	Population
Red Bluff	9,490
REDDING REDD	41,995
Redlands SBDO-	43,619
Redondo Beach L.A.	57,102
Redwood City SF-O-	54,951
Redwood Valley	1,300 ○
Reedley	11,071
Rialto SBDO-	37,474
Richmond SF-O-	74,676
Ridgecrest	15,929
Rio Dell	2,687
Rio Linda SAC	7,359
Rio Vista	3,142
Ripley	500 ○
Riverbank MOD	5,695
Riverdale	1,866
Riverside SBDO-	170,591
Rocklin SAC	7,344
Rodeo SF-O-	8,286
Rohnert Park SF-O-	22,965
Rolling Hills Estates L.A.	7,701
Rosamond	2,869
Roseland S.ROS	7,915
Rosemead L.A.	42,604
Roseville SAC	24,347
Rossmoor L.A.	10,457
Rowland Heights L.A.	28,252
Rubidoux SBDO-	13,200 ○
SACRAMENTO SAC	275,741
St. Helena	4,898
SALINAS SLNS	80,479
Salyer	950 ○
Samoa EUR	850 ○
San Andreas	1,912
San Anselmo SF-O-	12,067
San Ardo	450 ○
SAN BERNARDINO SBDO-	118,794
San Bruno SF-O-	35,417
San Carlos SF-O-	24,710
San Clemente L.A.	27,325
SAN DIEGO SDGO	875,538
San Dimas L.A.	24,014
San Fernando L.A.	17,731
SAN FRANCISCO SF-O-	678,974
San Gabriel L.A.	30,072
Sanger FRES	12,542
San Jacinto	7,098
San Jose SF-O-	629,546
San Juan Capistrano L.A.	18,959
San Leandro SF-O-	63,952
San Lorenzo SF-O-	20,545
San Luis Obispo	34,252
San Marcos SDGO	17,479
San Marino L.A.	13,307
San Mateo SF-O-	77,640
San Miguel	800 ○
San Pablo SF-O-	19,750
San Rafael SF-O-	44,700
Santa Ana L.A.	204,023
SANTA BARBARA S.BAR	74,414
Santa Clara SF-O-	87,700
SANTA CRUZ S.CRZ	41,483
Santa Fe Springs L.A.	14,520
Santa Margarita	1,200 ○
SANTA MARIA S.MAR	39,685
Santa Monica L.A.	88,314
Santa Paula V-OX	20,552
SANTA ROSA S.ROS	83,320
Santa Ynez	3,335
Santee SDGO	40,298
Saratoga SF-O-	29,261
Saugus L.A.	16,283
Sausalito SF-O-	7,338
Scotia	1,200 ○
Scotts Valley S.CRZ	6,891
Seal Beach L.A.	25,975
Seaside MTRY	36,567
Sebastopol S.ROS	5,595
Seeley	1,058
Selma	10,942
Shafter	7,010
Shandon	800 ○
Sierra City	800 ○
Sierra Madre L.A.	10,837
Signal Hill L.A.	5,734
Simi Valley L.A.	77,500
Smith River	1,000 ○
Solana Beach SDGO	13,047
Soledad	5,928
Sonoma SF-O-	6,054
Sonora	3,247
Soquel S.CRZ	6,212
South Dos Palos	850 ○
South El Monte L.A.	16,623
South Gate L.A.	66,784
South Lake Tahoe	20,681
South Modesto MOD	12,492
South Pasadena L.A.	22,681
South San Francisco SF-O-	49,393
South San Gabriel L.A.	5,421
South San Jose Hills L.A.	16,049
South Whittier L.A.	43,815
Spring Valley SDGO	40,191
Stanford SF-O-	11,045
Stanton L.A.	23,723
STOCKTON STOC	149,779
Stratford	850 ○
Strathmore	1,221 ○
Suisun City FRFL-	11,087
Sun City	6,500 ○
Sunnymead SBDO-	11,554
Sunnyvale SF-O-	106,618
Sunol	750 ○
Susanville	6,520
Sutter Creek	1,705
Taft	5,316
Tahoe City	1,300 ○
Tara Hills SF-O-	6,000 ○
Tarpey FRES	4,000 ○
Tehachapi	4,126
Temecula	1,783
Temple City L.A.	28,972
Thousand Oaks L.A.	77,072
Tiburon SF-O-	6,685
Tipton	1,185
Torrance L.A.	129,881
Tracy	18,428
Tranquillity	950 ○
Trinity Center	650 ○
Trona	1,400 ○
Truckee	2,389
Tulare	22,526
Tulelake	783
Tuolumne	1,708
Turlock	26,287
Tustin L.A.	32,317
Twentynine Palms	7,465
Ukiah	12,035
Union City SF-O-	39,406
Upland L.A.	47,647
Vacaville FRFL-	43,367
Valinda L.A.	18,700
Vallejo SF-O-	80,303
VENTURA V-OX	74,393
Victorville	14,220
View Park L.A.	5,900 ○
Villa Park L.A.	7,137
VISALIA VISL	49,729
Vista OC-V	35,834
Walnut L.A.	12,478
Walnut Creek SF-O-	53,643
Walnut Park L.A.	11,811
Wasco	9,613
Watsonville	23,663
Weaverville	2,787
Weed	2,879
Weott	450 ○
West Athens L.A.	8,531
West Carson L.A.	17,997
West Covina L.A.	80,291
West Hollywood L.A.	35,703
Westminster L.A.	71,133
West Modesto MOD	6,135 ○
Westmont L.A.	27,916
Westmorland	1,590
West Pittsburg ANT-P	6,000 ○
West Point	1,500 ○
West Puente Valley L.A.	20,445
West Sacramento SAC	10,875
West Whittier L.A.	13,800 ○
Westwood	2,081
Wheatland	1,474
Whittier L.A.	69,717
Williams	1,655
Willits	4,008
Willow Brook L.A.	30,845
Willows	4,777
Windsor Hills L.A.	6,200 ○
Winters	2,652
Woodlake	4,343
Woodland	30,235
Woodside SF-O-	5,291
Wrightwood	2,511
Yermo	1,092
Yorba Linda L.A.	28,254
Yosemite National Park	1,073
Yreka	5,916
Yuba City MRYS-	18,736
Yucaipa SBDO-	20,000 ○

COUNTIES

County	Population
Alameda	1,105,379
Alpine	1,097
Amador	19,314
Butte	143,851
Calaveras	20,710
Colusa	12,791
Contra Costa	656,380
Del Norte	18,217
El Dorado	85,812
Fresno	514,229
Glenn	21,350
Humboldt	108,514
Imperial	92,110
Inyo	17,895
Kern	403,089
Kings	73,738
Lake	36,366
Lassen	21,661
Los Angeles	7,477,503
Madera	63,116
Marin	222,592
Mariposa	11,108
Mendocino	66,738
Merced	134,558
Modoc	8,610
Mono	8,577
Monterey	290,444
Napa	99,199
Nevada	51,645
Orange	1,932,709
Placer	117,247
Plumas	17,340
Riverside	663,199
Sacramento	783,381
San Benito	25,005
San Bernardino	895,016
San Diego	1,861,846
San Francisco	678,974
San Joaquin	347,342
San Luis Obispo	155,435
San Mateo	587,329
Santa Barbara	298,694
Santa Clara	1,295,071
Santa Cruz	188,141
Shasta	115,715
Sierra	3,073
Siskiyou	39,732
Solano	235,203
Sonoma	299,681
Stanislaus	265,900
Sutter	52,246
Tehama	38,888
Trinity	11,858
Tulare	245,738
Tuolumne	33,928
Ventura	529,174
Yolo	113,374
Yuba	49,733

COLORADO

1980 Census 2,889,735

CITIES

Place	Population
Adams City DEN	2,200 ○
Aguilar	624
Akron	1,716
Alamosa	6,830
Alamosa East	1,175
Antonito	1,103
Applewood DEN	7,200 ○
Arvada DEN	84,576
Aspen	3,678
Ault	1,056
Aurora DEN	158,588
Avondale	800 ○
Basalt	529
Bayfield	724
Bennett	942
Berthoud	2,362
Beulah	500 ○
Black Forest CSPG	3,372
Blende PUEB	1,500 ○
BOULDER BOUL	76,685
Bow Mar DEN	930
Breckenridge	818
Brighton DEN	12,773
Broadmoor CSPG	1,900 ○
Brookridge DEN	1,200 ○
Broomfield DEN	20,730
Brush	4,082
Buena Vista	2,075
Burlington	3,107
Byers	1,100 ○
Calhan	541
Canon City	13,037
Carbondale	2,084
Cascade CSPG	600 ○
Castle Rock	3,921
Cedaredge	1,184
Center	1,630

○ Rand McNally estimate
▲ Population of entire township or "town", including rural areas.
● Independent city. Population not included in county total.

COLORADO continued

Cherry Hills Village DEN ... 5,127
Cheyenne Canon CSPG ... 1,100 ○
Cheyenne Wells ... 950
Clifton GDJC ... 5,223
Colorado City ... 950 ○
COLORADO SPRINGS CSPG ... 214,821
Commerce City DEN ... 16,234
Cortez ... 7,095
Craig ... 8,133
Creede ... 610
Crested Butte ... 959
Cripple Creek ... 655
Dacono ... 2,321
Deer Trail ... 463
Del Norte ... 1,709
Delta ... 3,931
DENVER DEN ... 492,365
Dolores ... 802
Dove Creek ... 826
Dupont DEN ... 2,000 ○
Durango ... 11,649
Eads ... 878
Eagle ... 950
Eaton ... 1,932
Edgewater DEN ... 4,766
Eldorado Springs ... 500 ○
Elizabeth ... 789
El Jebel ... 900 ○
Englewood DEN ... 30,021
Erie ... 1,254
Estes Park ... 2,703
Evans GRLY ... 5,063
Evergreen DEN ... 6,376
Federal Heights DEN ... 7,846
Firestone ... 1,204
Flagler ... 550
Florence ... 2,987
FORT COLLINS FTCL ... 65,092
Fort Lupton DEN ... 4,251
Fort Morgan ... 8,768
Fountain CSPG ... 8,324
Fowler ... 1,227
Fraser ... 470
Frederick ... 855
Frisco ... 1,221
Fruita ... 2,810
Georgetown ... 830
Gilcrest ... 1,025
Glendale DEN ... 2,496
Glenwood Springs ... 4,637
Golden DEN ... 12,237
Granada ... 557
Granby ... 963
GRAND JUNCTION GDJC ... 27,956
GREELEY GRLY ... 53,006
Green Mountain Falls CSPG ... 607
Greenwood Village DEN ... 5,729
Gunnison ... 5,785
Gypsum ... 743
Haxtun ... 1,014
Hayden ... 1,720
Holly ... 969
Holyoke ... 2,092
Hotchkiss ... 849
Hudson ... 698
Hugo ... 776
Idaho Springs ... 2,077
Ignacio ... 667
Indian Hills DEN ... 900 ○
Ivywild CSPG ... 4,000 ○
Johnstown ... 1,535
Julesburg ... 1,528
Keenesburg ... 541
Kersey ... 913
Kremmling ... 1,296
Lafayette DEN ... 8,985
La Jara ... 858
La Junta ... 8,338
Lakewood DEN ... 113,808
Lamar ... 7,713
Laporte FTCL ... 900 ○
La Salle GRLY ... 1,929
Las Animas ... 2,818
La Veta ... 611
Leadville ... 3,879
Limon ... 1,805
Lincoln Park ... 3,426
Littleton DEN ... 28,631
Log Lane Village ... 709
Longmont ... 42,942
Louisville BOUL ... 5,593
Loveland ... 30,244
Lyons ... 1,137
Manassa ... 945
Mancos ... 870
Manitou Springs CSPG ... 4,475
Manzanola ... 459
Meeker ... 2,356
Milliken ... 1,506
Minturn ... 1,060
Monte Vista ... 3,902
Montrose ... 8,722
Monument CSPG ... 690
Morrison DEN ... 478
Mountain View DEN ... 584
Mountain View FTCL ... 1,693 ○
Naturita ... 819
Nederland ... 1,212
New Castle ... 563
Niwot BOUL ... 500 ○
Northglenn DEN ... 29,847
North La Junta ... 1,076
Norwood ... 478
Nucla ... 1,027
Oak Creek ... 929
Olathe ... 1,262
Orchard City ... 1,914
Orchard Mesa GDJC ... 4,876
Ordway ... 1,135
Otis ... 534
Ouray ... 684
Pagosa Springs ... 1,331
Palisade ... 1,551
Palmer Lake CSPG ... 1,130
Paonia ... 1,425
Perl-Mack DEN ... 6,002
Pierce ... 878
Platteville ... 1,662
Pleasant View DEN ... 4,500 ○
PUEBLO PUEB ... 101,686
Rangely ... 2,113
Rifle ... 3,215
Rocky Ford ... 4,804
Saguache ... 656
Salida ... 4,870
Sanford ... 687
San Luis ... 842
Security CSPG ... 11,000 ○
Sheridan DEN ... 5,377
Sherrelwood DEN ... 11,450 ○
Silt ... 923
Silverton ... 794
Simla ... 494
Skyway CSPG ... 3,600 ○
Southglenn DEN ... 3,800 ○
Southwood DEN ... 2,600 ○
Springfield ... 1,657
Steamboat Springs ... 5,098
Sterling ... 11,385
Stratton ... 705
Stratton Meadows CSPG ... 6,223 ○
Swink ... 668
Telluride ... 1,047
Thornton DEN ... 40,343
Trinidad ... 9,663
Uravan ... 800 ○
USAF Academy CSPG ... 8,000 ○
Vail ... 2,261
Walden ... 947
Walsenburg ... 3,945
Walsh ... 884
Wellington ... 1,215
Western Hills DEN ... 6,000 ○
Westminster DEN ... 50,211
Wheat Ridge DEN ... 30,293
Widefield CSPG ... 7,500 ○
Wiggins ... 531
Windsor ... 4,277
Winter Park ... 480
Woodland Acres ... 800 ○
Woodland Park ... 2,634
Wray ... 2,131
Yampa ... 472
Yuma ... 2,824

COUNTIES

Adams ... 245,944
Alamosa ... 11,799
Arapahoe ... 293,621
Archuleta ... 3,664
Baca ... 5,419
Bent ... 5,945
Boulder ... 189,625
Chaffee ... 13,227
Cheyenne ... 2,153
Clear Creek ... 7,308
Conejos ... 7,794
Costilla ... 3,071
Crowley ... 2,988
Custer ... 1,528
Delta ... 21,225
Denver ... 492,365
Dolores ... 1,658
Douglas ... 25,153
Eagle ... 13,320
Elbert ... 6,850
El Paso ... 309,424
Fremont ... 28,676
Garfield ... 22,514
Gilpin ... 2,441
Grand ... 7,475
Gunnison ... 10,689
Hinsdale ... 408
Huerfano ... 6,440
Jackson ... 1,863
Jefferson ... 371,753
Kiowa ... 1,936
Kit Carson ... 7,599
Lake ... 8,830
La Plata ... 27,195
Larimer ... 149,184
Las Animas ... 14,897
Lincoln ... 4,663
Logan ... 19,800
Mesa ... 81,530
Mineral ... 804
Moffat ... 13,133
Montezuma ... 16,510
Montrose ... 24,352
Morgan ... 22,513
Otero ... 22,567
Ouray ... 1,925
Park ... 5,333
Phillips ... 4,542
Pitkin ... 10,338
Prowers ... 13,070
Pueblo ... 125,972
Rio Blanco ... 6,255
Rio Grande ... 10,511
Routt ... 13,404
Saguache ... 3,935
San Juan ... 833
San Miguel ... 3,192
Sedgwick ... 3,266
Summit ... 8,848
Teller ... 8,034
Washington ... 5,304
Weld ... 123,438
Yuma ... 9,682

CONNECTICUT

1980 Census ... 3,107,576

CITIES

Abington ... 500 ○
Addison H-NB ... 1,100 ○
Ansonia BRDG ... 19,039
Attawaugan ... 450 ○
Avon H-NB 11,201▲ ... 1,434
Bakersville H-NB ... 450 ○
Ballouville ... 500 ○
Baltic N.LON- ... 1,500 ○
Bantam TORR ... 860
Beacon Falls WATB 3,995▲ ... 1,500 ○
Bel Aire Estates N.LON- ... 900 ○
Berlin H-NB 15,121▲ ... 2,000 ○
Bethany N.HAV- 4,330▲ ... 890 ○
Bethel DANB ... 8,755
Bethlehem WATB 2,573▲ ... 1,762
Black Point Beach Club N.LON- ... 500 ○
Bloomfield H-NB 18,608▲ ... 7,400 ○
Blue Hills H-NB ... 6,600 ○
Branford N.HAV- 23,363▲ ... 5,438
Branford Hills N.HAV- ... 2,200 ○
Branford Point N.HAV- ... 700 ○
BRIDGEPORT BRDG ... 142,546
Bristol H-NB ... 57,370
Broad Brook H-NB ... 1,548 ○
Brookfield DANB 12,872▲ ... 1,000 ○
Brookfield Center DANB ... 900 ○
Brooklyn 5,691▲ ... 900 ○
Canaan ... 1,160
Candlewood Isle DANB ... 750 ○
Candlewood Shores DANB ... 1,950 ○
Cannondale N.Y. ... 1,300 ○
Canton H-NB 7,635▲ ... 1,680
Centerbrook ... 900 ○
Central Village ... 1,200 ○
Cheshire N.HAV- 21,788▲ ... 5,722
Chester 3,068▲ ... 1,388
Clinton N.HAV- ... 11,195
Colchester H-NB 7,761▲ ... 3,190
Collinsville H-NB ... 2,555
Coventry H-NB 8,895▲ ... 3,769
Cromwell H-NB ... 10,100 ○
Crystal Lake H-NB ... 500 ○
DANBURY DANB ... 60,470
Danielson ... 4,553
Darien N.Y. ... 18,892
Dayville ... 1,100 ○
Deep River 3,994▲ ... 2,495
Derby BRDG ... 12,346
Durham H-NB 5,143▲ ... 2,641
Eagleville H-NB ... 450 ○
East Berlin H-NB ... 900 ○
East Brooklyn ... 1,251
East Canaan ... 800 ○
Eastford 1,028▲ ... 500 ○
East Granby H-NB 4,102▲ ... 500 ○

○ Rand McNally estimate
▲ Population of entire township or "town", including rural areas.
● Independent city. Population not included in county total.

East Haddam 5,621▲ .... 600 ○
East Hampton H-NB 8,572▲ 2,152
East Hartford H-NB 52,563
East Hartland .... 700 ○
East Haven N.HAV- 25,028
East Lyme N.LON- 13,870▲ .... 700 ○
East River N.HAV- ... 1,800 ○
East Windsor H-NB .... 1,850 ○
Ellington H-NB 9,711▲ ..... 1,000 ○
Enfield H-NB 42,695▲ 8,151
Essex 5,078▲ 2,501
Fairfield BRDG ..... 54,849 ○
Fall Mountain Lake H-NB .... 730 ○
Falls Village .... 500 ○
Farmington H-NB 16,407▲ .... 2,000 ○
Field Crest Estates N.LON- .... 1,200 ○
Fitchville N.LON- ...... 600 ○
Gales Ferry N.LON- 1,191
Georgetown N.Y. 1,834
Giants Neck N.LON- .... 1,150 ○
Glastonbury H-NB 24,327▲ 7,049
Goshen 1,706▲ ...... 450 ○
Granby H-NB 7,956▲ 1,192
Green Manorville H-NB .... 3,250 ○
Greenwich N.Y. 59,578
Grosvenor Dale .... 700 ○
Groton N.LON- 41,062▲ . 10,086
Groton Long Point N.LON- .... 800 ○
Guilford N.HAV- 17,375▲ .. 2,555
Haddam H-NB 6,383▲ ...... 600 ○
Hadlyme .... 450 ○
Hamden N.HAV- 51,071
HARTFORD H-NB 136,392
Harwinton TORR 4,889▲ 3,293
Hazardville H-NB 5,436
Hebron H-NB 5,453▲ ...... 500 ○
Heritage Village WATB .... 5,200 ○
Higganum H-NB 1,660
Hitchcock Lake WATB .... 1,600 ○
Honeypot Glen N.HAV- .... 900 ○
Huckleberry Hill H-NB .... 700 ○
Indian Neck N.HAV- .... 2,200 ○
Ivoryton .... 950 ○
Jewett City N.LON- .. 3,294
Kensington H-NB 7,502
Kent 2,505▲ .... 500 ○
Lake Beseck H-NB .... 500 ○
Lakeside WATB ...... 900 ○
Lakeville .... 1,200 ○
Leffingwell N.LON- .... 450 ○
Litchfield TORR 7,605▲ 1,489
Lords Point N.LON- .... 460 ○
Lyme N.LON- .... 500 ○
Madison N.HAV- 14,031▲ .. 2,069
Manchester H-NB ... 49,761
Mansfield Center H-NB 1,043
Marion H-NB .... 800 ○
Marlborough H-NB 4,746▲ 1,039
Meriden N.HAV- 57,118
Middlebury WATB 5,995▲ .... 3,900 ○
Middlefield H-NB 3,796▲ ...... 600 ○
Middle Haddam H-NB .... 500 ○
Middletown H-NB ... 39,040
Milford BRDG 49,101
Milldale H-NB ...... 1,100 ○
Monroe BRDG 14,010▲ ..... 760 ○
Monroe Center BRDG .... 6,950 ○
Montville N.LON- 16,455▲ .. 1,711
Moodus H-NB 1,179
Moosup 3,308
Mystic N.LON- 2,333
Naugatuck WATB ... 26,456
Nautilus Park N.LON- .... 6,500 ○
New Britain H-NB ... 73,840
New Canaan N.Y. ... 17,931
New Fairfield DANB 11,260▲ ... 2,150 ○
New Hartford H-NB 4,884▲ 1,310
NEW HAVEN N.HAV- 126,109
Newington H-NB 28,841
NEW LONDON N.LON- 28,842
New Milford DANB 19,420▲ ... 5,186
New Preston 1,209
Newtown DANB 19,107▲ ... 2,022
Niantic N.LON- 3,151
Noank N.LON- 1,406
Norfolk 2,156▲ ..... 1,500 ○
North Branford N.HAV- 11,554▲ .. 5,200 ○
Northfield TORR ...... 600 ○
Northford N.HAV- .... 2,800 ○
North Grosvenor Dale .. 1,856
North Haven N.HAV- 22,080
North Windham H-NB .... 750 ○
Norwalk N.Y. 77,767
Norwich N.LON- 38,074
Oakville WATB 8,737
Old Mystic N.LON- .... 500 ○
Old Saybrook 9,287▲ 1,857
Oneco .... 500 ○
Orange N.HAV- 13,237
Oxford BRDG 6,634▲ ..... 900 ○
Pawcatuck N.LON- ... 5,216
Pequabuck H-NB .... 1,400 ○
Pine Bridge WATB .... 870 ○
Pine Orchard N.HAV- .... 1,500 ○
Plainfield 12,774▲ ... 2,799
Plainville H-NB 16,401
Plantsville H-NB ..... 5,700 ○
Pleasure Beach N.LON- 1,356
Plymouth WATB 10,732▲ ... 1,000 ○
Pomfret 2,775▲ ...... 500 ○
Poquonock H-NB ..... 900 ○
Poquonock Bridge N.LON- 2,549
Portland H-NB 8,383
Prospect WATB 6,807
Putnam 8,580▲ 6,855
Quaker Hill N.LON- 2,052
Quinebaug 1,088
Redding N.Y. 7,272▲ .... 800 ○
Ridgefield N.Y. 20,120▲ 6,066
Rockfall H-NB .... 500 ○
Rocky Hill H-NB 14,559
Rogers .... 500 ○
Salisbury 3,896▲ ..... 900 ○
Sandy Hook DANB .... 950 ○
Saybrook Manor 1,140
Seymour BRDG 13,434
Sharon 2,623▲ .... 900 ○
Shelton BRDG 31,314
Sherwood Manor H-NB 6,303
Short Beach N.HAV- .... 1,200 ○
Simsbury H-NB 21,161▲ 5,488
Somers H-NB 8,473▲ 1,643
Somersville H-NB ..... 750 ○
Southbury WATB 14,156▲ ..... 900 ○
South Glastonbury H-NB .... 1,600 ○
Southington H-NB 36,879▲ ... 17,400 ○
South Windham H-NB 1,399
South Windsor H-NB 17,198▲ ... 10,200 ○
Southwood Acres H-NB 9,779
South Woodstock 1,319
Stafford H-NB 9,268▲ ...... 500 ○
Stafford Springs H-NB 3,392
Staffordville H-NB ..... 600 ○
Stamford N.Y. 102,453
Stevenson BRDG ..... 450 ○
Stonington N.LON- 16,220▲ .. 1,228
Stony Creek N.HAV- ... 700 ○
Storrs H-NB 11,394
Stratford BRDG 50,541
Suffield H-NB 9,294▲ 1,122
Tariffville H-NB 1,324
Terryville H-NB 5,234
Thomaston WATB 6,276▲ .... 3,500 ○
Thompson 8,141▲ .... 500 ○
Tolland H-NB 9,694▲ ...... 500 ○
TORRINGTON TORR 30,987
Trumbull BRDG 32,989
Uncasville N.LON- ... 1,597
Unionville H-NB ..... 4,900 ○
Vernon H-NB 27,974
Wallingford N.HAV- .... 37,274 ○
Washington 3,657▲ ... 600 ○
Washington Depot ...... 600 ○
WATERBURY WATB 103,266
Waterford N.LON- 17,843▲ .. 2,736
Watertown WATB 19,489▲ ... 6,000 ○
Wauregan .... 900 ○
Weatogue H-NB 2,249
Wequetequock N.LON- .... 800 ○
Westbrook 5,216▲ ... 2,035
West Goshen .... 600 ○
West Granby H-NB .... 600 ○
West Hartford H-NB 61,301
West Haven N.HAV- 53,184
West Mystic N.LON- 3,364
Weston N.Y. 8,284▲ ...... 1,200 ○
Westport N.Y. 25,290
West Simsbury H-NB .. 2,140
West Stafford H-NB .... 450 ○
West Suffield H-NB .... 500 ○
Wethersfield H-NB 26,013
Whitacres H-NB ..... 2,500 ○
Willimantic H-NB ... 14,652
Wilton N.Y. 15,351▲ ..... 6,500 ○
Windham H-NB 21,062▲ ..... 700 ○
Windsor H-NB 25,204▲ ... 17,517
Windsor Locks H-NB 12,190
Winsted 8,092
Wolcott WATB 13,008▲ ... 5,500 ○
Woodbridge N.HAV- .... 7,600 ○
Woodbury WATB 6,942▲ 1,290
Woodmont BRDG 1,797

COUNTIES

Fairfield 807,143
Hartford 807,766
Litchfield 156,769
Middlesex 129,017
New Haven 761,337
New London 238,409
Tolland 114,823
Windham 92,312

DELAWARE

1980 Census 594,317

CITIES

Arden PHIL- 516
Bear PHIL- .... 950 ○
Bellefonte PHIL- 1,279
Belvidere PHIL- ..... 1,100 ○
Birchwood Park PHIL- .... 1,500 ○
Blades 664
Briar Park DOVR ..... 600 ○
Bridgeville 1,238
Brookside PHIL- 15,255
Camden DOVR 1,757
Canterbury DOVR ..... 500 ○
Capitol Park DOVR .... 900 ○
Carrcroft PHIL- .... 800 ○
Castle Hills PHIL- .... 1,950 ○
Chalfonte PHIL- ..... 2,200 ○
Chelsea Estates PHIL- .... 1,500 ○
Chestnut Hill Estates PHIL- .... 2,000 ○
Christiana PHIL- ...... 500 ○
Clarksville .... 450 ○
Claymont PHIL- 10,022
Clayton DOVR 1,216
Cleland Heights PHIL- .... 1,500 ○
Collins Park PHIL- ... 2,850 ○
Delaware City PHIL- 1,858
Delmar SLSB 948
Dewey Beach .... 1,500 ○
DOVER DOVR 23,507
Dunleith PHIL- ...... 2,700 ○
Du Ross Heights PHIL- .... 600 ○
Edgemoor PHIL- 7,397
Elsmere PHIL- 6,493
Fairfax PHIL- .... 2,850 ○
Felton DOVR 547
Frankford 828
Frederica DOVR 864

○ Rand McNally estimate
▲ Population of entire township or "town", including rural areas.
● Independent city. Population not included in county total.

DELAWARE continued

Garfield Park PHIL- 1,000 ○
Georgetown 1,710
Graylyn Crest PHIL- 5,000 ○
Greenwood 578
Gwinhurst PHIL- 1,400 ○
Harmony Hills PHIL- 1,350 ○
Harrington 2,405
Hockessin PHIL- 950 ○
Holloway Terrace PHIL- 1,000 ○
Jefferson Farms PHIL- 2,400 ○
Kent Acres 900 ○
Laurel 3,052
Leedom Estates PHIL- 1,300 ○
Lewes 2,197
Lincoln 500 ○
Manor Park Apartments PHIL- 800 ○
Marshallton PHIL- 3,950 ○
Meadowood PHIL- 2,260 ○
Middletown 2,946
Midway 500 ○
Milford 5,366
Millsboro 1,233
Milton 1,359
Minquadale PHIL- 1,700 ○
Newark PHIL- 25,247
New Castle PHIL- 4,907
Newkirk Estates PHIL- 600 ○
Newport PHIL- 1,167
Ocean View 495
Penn Acres PHIL- 1,950 ○
Penny Hill PHIL- 700 ○
Rambleton Acres PHIL- 1,500 ○
Rehoboth Beach 1,730
Rodney Village DOVR 1,100 ○
St. Georges PHIL- 500 ○
Seaford 5,256
Selbyville 1,251
Silview PHIL- 1,650 ○
Smyrna DOVR 4,750
Stanton PHIL- 5,495
Stratford PHIL- 2,100 ○
Swanwyck Estates PHIL- 1,700 ○
Talleyville PHIL- 6,880
Todd Estates PHIL- 2,050 ○
Willow Run PHIL- 1,950 ○
Wilmington PHIL- 70,195
Wilmington Manor PHIL- 2,000 ○
Wilmington Manor Gardens PHIL- 1,600 ○
Windy Hills PHIL- 1,300 ○
Wyoming DOVR 960
Yorklyn PHIL- 600 ○

COUNTIES

Kent 98,219
New Castle 398,115
Sussex 97,983

DISTRICT OF COLUMBIA

1980 Census 638,432

CITIES

WASHINGTON WASH 638,432

FLORIDA

1980 Census 9,746,342

CITIES

Alachua 3,561
Alford 548
Altamonte Springs ORL 22,028
Altha 478
Altoona 1,300 ○
Alva 1,200 ○
Anna Maria SAR-B 1,537
Anthony 1,200 ○
Apalachicola 2,565
Apopka ORL 6,019
Arcadia 6,002
Archer 1,230
Astor 950 ○
Atlantic Beach JAX 7,847
Atlantis WPB 1,325
Auburndale WNHV 6,501
Avon Park 8,026
Azalea Park ORL 8,301
Babson Park 950 ○
Bagdad 1,479
Baker 600 ○
Baldwin JAX 1,526
Balm 600 ○
Bartow 14,780
Baskin ST.PET- 800 ○
Bayou George PNCY 1,500 ○
Bayshore Gardens SAR-B 14,945
Bee Ridge SAR-B 3,313
Bellair JAX 5,200 ○
Belle Glade 16,535
Belle Isle ORL 2,848
Belleview 1,913
Biscayne Gardens MIA- 13,000 ○
Biscayne Park MIA- 3,088
Blountstown 2,632
Boca Grande 1,200 ○
Boca Raton MIA- 49,505
Bokeelia 900 ○
Bonifay 2,534
Bonita Springs 3,400 ○
Bostwick 500 ○
Bowling Green 2,310
Boynton Beach 35,624
Bradenton SAR-B 30,170
Bradley 1,108
Brandon TAM 29,100 ○
Branford 622
Bratt 550 ○
Brent PENS 4,100 ○
Bristol 1,044
Broadview Park MIA- 6,022
Bronson 853
Brooksville 5,582
Browardale MIA- 7,409
Brownsville MIA- 18,058
Bryant 500 ○
Buena Vista 3,000 ○
Bunche Park MIA- 4,000 ○
Bunnell 1,816
Bushnell 983
Callahan 869
Callaway PNCY 7,154
Campbell 2,941
Canal Point 950 ○
Candler 500 ○
Cantonment PENS 3,200 ○
Cape Canaveral COCO 5,733
Cape Coral 32,103
Captiva 1,200 ○
Carol City MIA- 47,349
Carrabelle 1,304
Carver Ranch Estates MIA- 5,600 ○
Caryville 633
Casselberry ORL 15,247
Cedar Key 700
Center Hill 751
Century 1,805
Charlotte Harbor 2,084
Chattahoochee 5,332
Chiefland 1,986
Chipley 3,330
Christmas 1,200 ○
Citra 1,500 ○
City Of Sunrise MIA- 39,681
Clair-Mel City TAM 7,000 ○
Clearwater ST.PET- 85,528
Clermont 5,461
Clewiston 5,219
COCOA COCO 16,096
Cocoa Beach COCO 10,926
Cocoa West COCO 6,432
Coconut Creek MIA- 6,288
Coleman 1,022
Conway ORL 16,000 ○
Cooper City MIA- 10,140
Copeland 700 ○
Coral Gables MIA- 43,241
Cortez SAR-B 1,450 ○
Cottondale 1,056
Crawfordville 1,110
Crescent City SAR-B 1,722
Cresthaven MIA- 2,400 ○
Crestview 7,617
Cross City 2,154
Crystal Beach ST.PET- 1,450 ○
Crystal Lake LKLD 6,827
Crystal River 2,778
Crystal Springs 800 ○
Cutler Ridge MIA- 20,886
Cypress Quarters 1,479
Dade City 4,923
Dania MIA- 11,811
Davenport 1,509
Davie MIA- 20,877
DAYTONA BEACH D.BCH 54,176
De Bary 4,980
Deerfield Beach MIA- 39,193
De Funiak Springs 5,563
De Land 15,354
De Leon Springs 1,669
Delray Beach 34,325
Deltona 4,868 ○
Destin FTWL 3,672
Doctors Inlet JAX 600 ○
Dover TAM 2,354
Dundee 2,227
Dunedin ST.PET- 30,203
Dunnellon 1,427
East Naples 9,000 ○
East Palatka 1,613
Eastpoint 1,246
Edgewater 6,726
Ellenton SAR-B 1,561
Eloise WNHV 1,408
El Portal MIA- 2,055
Elwood Park 500 ○
Englewood 9,633
Ensley PENS 3,850 ○
Estero 950 ○
Eustis 9,453
Fairbanks 500 ○
Fairview Shores ORL 6,100 ○
Fellsmere 1,161
Fernandina Beach 7,224
Flagler Beach 2,208
Florahome 600 ○
Floral City 1,181
Florida City MIA- 6,174
Fort Lauderdale MIA- 153,279
Fort Meade 5,546
FORT MYERS FTMY 36,638
Fort Myers Beach 5,753
Fort Ogden 900 ○
FORT PIERCE FTPI 33,802
FORT WALTON BEACH FTWL 20,829
Fountain 500 ○
Freeport 669
Frostproof 2,995
Fruitland Park 2,259
Fruitville SAR-B 3,070
GAINESVILLE GAIN 81,371
Gibsonton TAM 3,700 ○
Gifford 6,240
Glen Saint Mary 462
Glenwood 950 ○
Golden Beach MIA- 612
Gonzalez PENS 6,084
Goodland 1,000 ○
Goulds MIA- 7,078
Graceville 2,918
Grand Ridge 591
Grant 900 ○
Greenacres City WPB 8,843
Green Cove Springs 4,154
Greensboro 562
Greenville 1,096
Greenwood 577
Gretna 1,448
Grove City 1,932
Groveland 1,992
Gulf Breeze PENS 5,478
Gulf Gate Estates SAR-B 9,248
Gulfport ST.PET- 11,180
Haines City 10,799
Hallandale MIA- 36,517
Hampton 466
Harlem 2,669
Hastings 636
Havana 2,782
Hawthorne 1,303
Hedges 900 ○
Hernando 1,653
Hialeah MIA- 145,254
High Springs 2,491
Hilliard 1,869
Hobe Sound 6,822
Holden Heights ORL 8,000 ○
Holiday 15,400 ○
Holly Hill D.BCH 9,953
Hollywood MIA- 121,323
Holt 780 ○
Homeland 500 ○
Homestead MIA- 20,668
Homosassa 1,426
Hosford 700 ○
Hudson 5,799
Immokalee 11,038
Indian Harbour Beach MELB 5,967
Indian Rocks Beach ST.PET- 3,717
Indiantown 3,383
Intercession City 950 ○
Interlachen 848
Inverness 4,095
Inwood WNHV 6,668
Islamorada 1,441
JACKSONVILLE JAX 540,920
Jacksonville Beach JAX 15,462
Jasmine Estates 3,500 ○
Jasper 2,093
Jay 633

○ Rand McNally estimate
▲ Population of entire township or "town", including rural areas.
● Independent city. Population not included in county total.

Jennings . . . 749
Jensen Beach . . . 6,639
Jerome . . . 675 ○
Jupiter WPB . . . 9,868
Kathleen LKLD . . . 1,866
Kenansville . . . 700 ○
Kendall MIA- . . . 51,000 ○
Key Largo . . . 7,447
Keystone Heights . . . 1,056
Key West . . . 24,382
Kissimmee . . . 15,487
La Belle . . . 2,287
Lacoochee . . . 1,720
Lady Lake . . . 1,193
Lagrange TITUS . . . 460 ○
Lake Alfred WNHV . . . 3,134
Lake Butler . . . 1,830
Lake City . . . 9,257
Lake Forest MIA- . . . 5,400 ○
Lake Helen . . . 2,047
LAKELAND LKLD . . . 47,406
Lake Magdalene TAM . . . 13,331
Lake Mary . . . 2,853
Lake Park WPB . . . 6,909
Lake Placid . . . 963
Lake Wales . . . 8,466
Lake Worth WPB . . . 27,048
Lanark Village . . . 650 ○
Lantana WPB . . . 8,048
Largo ST.PET- . . . 58,977
Lauderdale Lakes MIA- . . . 25,426
Lauderhill MIA- . . . 37,271
Laurel . . . 1,500 ○
Laurel Hill . . . 610
Lawtey . . . 692
Lealman ST.PET- . . . 19,873
Leesburg . . . 13,191
Lehigh Acres . . . 9,604
Leisure City MIA- . . . 17,905
Leto TAM . . . 9,003
Lighthouse Point MIA- . . . 11,488
Live Oak . . . 6,732
Lockhart ORL . . . 10,571
Longboat Key SAR-B . . . 4,843
Longwood ORL . . . 10,029
Lorida . . . 620 ○
Loughman . . . 800 ○
Lutz TAM . . . 5,555
Lynne . . . 500 ○
Lynn Haven PNCY . . . 6,239
Macclenny . . . 3,851
Madison . . . 3,487
Maitland ORL . . . 8,763
Malabar MELB . . . 1,118
Malone . . . 897
Marathon . . . 7,568
Marco . . . 4,679
Margate MIA- . . . 35,900
Marianna . . . 7,006
Masaryktown . . . 800 ○
Mayo . . . 891
MELBOURNE MELB . . . 46,536
Melbourne Beach MELB . . . 2,713
Melrose . . . 1,700 ○
Melrose Park MIA- . . . 5,672
Memphis SAR-B . . . 5,501
Merritt Island COCO . . . 30,708
MIAMI MIA- . . . 346,865
Miami Beach MIA- . . . 96,298
Miami Shores MIA- . . . 9,244
Miami Springs MIA- . . . 12,350
Micanopy . . . 737
Micco . . . 3,585
Middleburg . . . 2,500 ○
Midway . . . 450 ○
Milligan . . . 500 ○
Milton . . . 7,206
Mims TITUS . . . 7,583

Miramar MIA- . . . 32,813
Molino . . . 1,456
Monticello . . . 2,994
Moore Haven . . . 1,250
Mount Dora . . . 5,883
Mulberry . . . 2,932
Myrtle Grove PENS . . . 14,238
Naples . . . 17,581
Naranja MIA- . . . 5,000 ○
Neptune Beach JAX . . . 5,248
Newberry . . . 1,826
New Port Richey . . . 11,196
New Smyrna Beach . . 13,557
Niceville FTWL . . . 8,543
Nocatee . . . 1,300 ○
Nokomis . . . 3,108
Norland MIA- . . . 19,471
North Andrews Gardens MIA- . . . 8,967
North Fort Myers FTMY . . . 17,200 ○
North Lauderdale MIA- . . . 18,653
North Miami MIA- . . . 42,566
North Miami Beach MIA- . . . 36,553
North Naples . . . 7,950
North Palm Beach WPB . . . 11,344
North Port . . . 6,205
Oak Hill . . . 938
Oakland . . . 658
Oakland Park MIA- . . . 23,035
Ocala . . . 37,170
Ocean City FTWL . . . 5,582
Ocoee ORL . . . 7,803
Odessa . . . 950 ○
Okeechobee . . . 4,225
Oklawaha . . . 1,200 ○
Oldsmar TAM . . . 2,608
Old Town . . . 550 ○
Olustee . . . 450 ○
Olympia Heights MIA- . . . 33,112
Oneco SAR-B . . . 6,417
Opa-Locka MIA- . . . 14,460
Orange City . . . 2,795
Orange Lake . . . 950 ○
Orange Park JAX . . . 8,766
ORLANDO ORL . . . 128,291
Ormond Beach D.BCH . . . 21,378
Osprey SAR-B . . . 1,660
Osteen . . . 900 ○
Ozona ST.PET- . . . 1,200 ○
Pace . . . 5,006
Pahokee . . . 6,346
Paisley . . . 600 ○
Palatka . . . 10,175
Palm Bay MELB . . . 18,560
Palm Beach WPB . . . 9,729
Palm Beach Gardens WPB . . . 14,407
Palmetto SAR-B . . . 8,637
Palm Harbor ST.PET- . . . 5,215
Palm Springs WPB . . . 8,166
Panacea . . . 950 ○
PANAMA CITY PNCY . . . 33,346
Panama City Beach PNCY . . . 2,148
Parker PNCY . . . 4,298
Parrish . . . 950 ○
Paxton . . . 659
Pembroke Pines MIA- . . . 35,776
Penney Farms . . . 630
PENSACOLA PENS . . . 57,619
Perrine MIA- . . . 16,129
Perry . . . 8,254
Pierson . . . 1,085
Pine Castle ORL . . . 9,992

Pine Hills ORL . . . 26,000 ○
Pinellas Park ST.PET- . . . 32,811
Pinewood MIA- . . . 7,900 ○
Placida . . . 700 ○
Plantation MIA- . . . 48,653
Plant City . . . 17,064
Plymouth . . . 2,700 ○
Polk City . . . 576
Pomona Park . . . 791
Pompano Beach MIA- . . . 52,618
Pompano Beach Highlands MIA- . . . 9,000 ○
Ponce de Leon . . . 454
Ponte Vedra Beach JAX . . . 1,700 ○
Port Charlotte . . . 25,770
Port Orange D.BCH . . . 18,756
Port Richey . . . 2,165
Port Salerno . . . 4,511
Port St. Joe . . . 4,027
Port St. Lucie FTPI . . . 14,690
Princeton MIA- . . . 5,300 ○
Punta Gorda . . . 6,797
Quincy . . . 8,591
Reddick . . . 657
Richmond Heights MIA- . . . 8,577
Rio . . . 1,205
Riverview TAM . . . 3,200 ○
Riviera Beach WPB . . . 26,489
Rockledge COCO . . . 11,877
Rocky Creek TAM . . . 7,800 ○
Roseland . . . 1,607
Rubonia SAR-B . . . 550 ○
Ruskin . . . 5,117
Safety Harbor ST.PET- . . . 6,461
St. Augustine . . . 11,985
St. Cloud . . . 7,840
St. James City . . . 1,298
St. Leo . . . 917
St. Lucie FTPI . . . 593
ST. PETERSBURG ST.PET- . . . 238,647
St. Petersburg Beach ST.PET- . . . 9,354
Salt Springs . . . 1,500 ○
Samoset SAR-B . . . 5,747
San Antonio . . . 529
Sanford . . . 23,176
Sanibel . . . 3,363
San Mateo . . . 950 ○
Santa Rosa Beach . . . 950 ○
SARASOTA SAR-B . . . 48,868
Satellite Beach MELB . . . 9,163
Satsuma . . . 950 ○
Sebastian . . . 2,831
Sebring . . . 8,736
Seminole Park ST.PET- . . . 8,000 ○
Seville . . . 800 ○
Sharpes COCO . . . 1,250 ○
Silver Springs . . . 1,082
Sneads . . . 1,690
Solana . . . 1,408
Sopchoppy . . . 444
Sorrento . . . 950 ○
South Bay . . . 3,886
South Daytona D.BCH . . . 11,252
South Miami MIA- . . . 10,944
South Miami Heights MIA- . . . 18,000 ○
South Patrick Shores MELB . . . 9,816
Southport PNCY . . . 1,992
South Venice . . . 8,075
Sparr . . . 1,100 ○
Springfield PNCY . . . 7,220

Spring Hill . . . 6,468
Starke . . . 5,306
Steinhatchee . . . 800 ○
Stuart . . . 9,467
Summerfield . . . 550 ○
Sun City . . . 700 ○
Sunnyland SAR-B . . . 650 ○
Sunnyside . . . 600 ○
Surfside MIA- . . . 3,763
Sweetwater Creek TAM . . . 18,000 ○
Switzerland . . . 2,400 ○
TALLAHASSEE TALL . . . 81,548
Tamarac MIA- . . . 29,376
TAMPA TAM . . . 271,523
Tarpon Springs . . . 13,251
Tavares . . . 4,103
Tavernier . . . 1,834
Temple Terrace TAM . . . 11,097
Thonotosassa TAM . . . 1,500 ○
Tice FTMY . . . 6,645
TITUSVILLE TITUS . . . 31,910
Treasure Island ST.PET- . . . 6,316
Trenton . . . 1,131
Trilby . . . 950 ○
Uleta MIA- . . . 10,000 ○
Umatilla . . . 1,872
Valparaiso FTWL . . . 6,142
Venice . . . 12,153
Vernon . . . 885
Vero Beach . . . 16,176
Wabasso . . . 2,157
Waldo . . . 993
Warrington PENS . . . 15,792
Watertown . . . 600 ○
Wauchula . . . 2,986
Webster . . . 856
Weirsdale . . . 1,500 ○
Welaka . . . 492
Westchester MIA- . . . 20,000 ○
Westgate WPB . . . 2,100 ○
West Melbourne MELB . . . 5,078
West Miami MIA- . . . 6,076
WEST PALM BEACH WPB . . . 63,305
West Pensacola PENS . . . 24,371
Westwood Lakes MIA- . . . 11,478
Wewahitchka . . . 1,742
White City . . . 725 ○
White City FTPI . . . 4,110
White Springs . . . 781
Whitfield Estates SAR-B . . . 3,000 ○
Wildwood . . . 2,665
Williston . . . 2,240
Wilton Manors MIA- . . . 12,742
Wimauma . . . 1,477
Winston LKLD . . . 5,500 ○
Winter Beach . . . 700 ○
Winter Garden . . . 6,789
WINTER HAVEN WNHV . . . 21,119
Winter Park ORL . . . 22,339
Winter Springs ORL . . . 10,475
Woodville . . . 1,768
Yalaha . . . 950 ○
Yankeetown . . . 600
Zephyrhills . . . 5,742
Zolfo Springs . . . 1,495

COUNTIES

Alachua . . . 151,348
Baker . . . 15,289
Bay . . . 97,740
Bradford . . . 20,023

○ Rand McNally estimate
▲ Population of entire township or "town", including rural areas.
● Independent city. Population not included in county total.

FLORIDA continued

Brevard 272,959
Broward 1,018,200
Calhoun 9,294
Charlotte 58,460
Citrus 54,703
Clay 67,052
Collier 85,971
Columbia 35,399
Dade 1,625,781
De Soto 19,039
Dixie 7,751
Duval 571,003
Escambia 233,794
Flagler 10,913
Franklin 7,661
Gadsden 41,565
Gilchrist 5,767
Glades 5,992
Gulf 10,658
Hamilton 8,761
Hardee 19,379
Hendry 18,599
Hernando 44,469
Highlands 47,526
Hillsborough 646,960
Holmes 14,723
Indian River 59,896
Jackson 39,154
Jefferson 10,703
Lafayette 4,035
Lake 104,870
Lee 205,266
Leon 148,655
Levy 19,870
Liberty 4,260
Madison 14,894
Manatee 148,442
Marion 122,488
Martin 64,014
Monroe 63,188
Nassau 32,894
Okaloosa 109,920
Okeechobee 20,264
Orange 471,016
Osceola 49,287
Palm Beach 576,863
Pasco 193,661
Pinellas 728,531
Polk 321,652
Putnam 50,549
St. Johns 51,303
St. Lucie 87,182
Santa Rosa 55,988
Sarasota 202,251
Seminole 179,752
Sumter 24,272
Suwannee 22,287
Taylor 16,532
Union 10,166
Volusia 258,762
Wakulla 10,887
Walton 21,300
Washington 14,509

GEORGIA

1980
Census 5,463,105

CITIES

Abbeville 985
Acworth ATL 3,648
Adairsville 1,739
Adel 5,592
Adrian 756
Ailey 579
Alamo 993
Alapaha 771
ALBANY ALB 74,550
Allenhurst 606
Alma 3,819
Alpharetta ATL 3,128
Alto 618
Americus 16,120
Aragon 855
Arlington 1,572
Ashburn 4,766
ATHENS ATH 42,549
ATLANTA ATL 425,022
Attapulgus 623
Auburn ATL 692
AUGUSTA AUG 47,532
Austell ATL 3,939
Avondale Estates ATL 1,313
Baconton 763
Bainbridge 10,553
Baldwin 1,080
Ball Ground 640
Barnesville 4,887
Baxley 3,586
Belvedere Park ATL 17,766
Berlin 538
Bibb City COL 667
Blackshear 3,222
Blairsville 530
Blakely 5,880
Bloomingdale SAV 1,855
Blue Ridge 1,376
Bogart ATH 819
Boston 1,424
Bowdon 1,743
Bowman 890
Bremen 3,966
Bronwood 524
Brooklet 1,035
Broxton 1,117
BRUNSWICK BRUNS 17,605
Buchanan 1,019
Buena Vista 1,544
Buford ATL 6,578
Butler 1,959
Byromville 567
Byron MAC- 1,661
Cairo 8,777
Calhoun 5,563
Camilla 5,414
Canon 704
Canton 3,601
Carnesville 465
Carrollton 14,078
Cartersville 9,247
Cataula 500 ○
Cave Spring 883
Cedartown 8,619
Chamblee ATL 7,137
Chatsworth 2,493
Chickamauga CHTN 2,232
Chicopee 900 ○
Clarkdale ATL 550 ○
Clarkesville 1,348
Clarkston ATL 4,539
Claxton 2,694
Clayton 1,838
Cleveland 1,578
Cobbtown 494
Cochran 5,121
Colbert ATH 498
College Park ATL 24,632
Collins 639
Colquitt 2,065
COLUMBUS COL 169,441
Comer 930
Commerce 4,092
Conyers ATL 6,567
Coolidge 736
Cordele 11,184
Cornelia 3,203
Covington ATL 10,586
Crawfordville 594
Cumming ATL 2,094
Cusseta COL 1,218
Cuthbert 4,340
Dacula ATL 1,577
Dahlonega 2,844
Dallas ATL 2,508
Dalton 20,939
Danville 529
Darien 1,731
Dawson 5,699
Dearing 539
Decatur ATL 18,404
Demorest 1,130
Dexter 527
Dock Junction BRUNS 6,189
Doerun 1,062
Donalsonville 3,320
Doraville ATL 7,414
Douglas 10,980
Douglasville ATL 7,641
Dublin 16,083
Duluth ATL 2,956
Dunaire ATL 5,400 ○
Dunwoody ATL 5,100 ○
East Ellijay 469
Eastman 5,330
East Newnan 1,495
East Point ATL 37,486
Eatonton 4,833
Eden SAV 450 ○
Edison 1,128
Elberta MAC- 500 ○
Elberton 5,686
Eldorado 1,000 ○
Elizabeth ATL 1,700 ○
Ellaville 1,684
Ellenwood ATL 500 ○
Ellijay 1,507
Emerson ATL 1,110
Enigma 574
Evans AUG 800 ○
Experiment 3,000 ○
Fairburn ATL 3,466
Fairmount 842
Fair Oaks ATL 8,486
Fargo 600 ○
Fayetteville ATL 2,715
Fitzgerald 10,187
Flovilla 458
Flowery Branch ATL 755
Folkston 2,243
Forest Park ATL 18,782
Forsyth 4,624
Fort Gaines 1,260
Fort Oglethorpe CHTN 5,443
Fort Valley 9,000
Franklin 711
Gainesville 15,280
Garden City SAV 6,895
Georgetown 935
Gibson 730
Glennville 4,144
Glenwood 824
Gordon 2,768
Gracewood AUG 500 ○
Grantville 1,110
Gray MAC- 2,145
Grayson ATL 464
Greensboro 2,985
Greenville 1,213
Gresham Park ATL 6,232
Griffin 20,728
Grovetown AUG 3,384
Guyton 749
Haddock 700 ○
Hagan 880
Hahira 1,534
Hamilton 506
Hampton ATL 2,059
Hapeville ATL 6,166
Hardwick 6,000 ○
Harlem AUG 1,485
Harrison 456
Hartwell 4,855
Hawkinsville 4,372
Hazlehurst 4,249
Helena 1,390
Hephzibah 1,452
Hiawassee 491
Hilltonia 515
Hinesville 11,309
Hiram ATL 1,030
Hoboken 514
Hogansville 3,362
Holly Springs ATL 687
Homeland 683
Homer 734
Homerville 3,112
Hoschton 490
Ideal 619
Irwinton 841
Jackson 4,133
Jasper 1,556
Jefferson 1,820
Jeffersonville 1,473
Jesup 9,418
Jonesboro ATL 4,132
Kennesaw ATL 5,095
Kingsland 2,008
Kingston 733
La Fayette 6,517
La Grange 24,204
Lakeland 2,647
Lake Park VALD 448
Là Vista ATL 5,200 ○
Lavonia 2,024
Lawrenceville ATL 8,928
Leary 783
Leesburg 1,301
Lenox 965
Leslie 470
Lilburn ATL 3,765
Lincoln Park 1,755
Lincolnton 1,406
Lindale ROME 2,958
Lithia Springs ATL 9,145
Lithonia ATL 2,637
Lizella MAC- 600 ○
Locust Grove ATL 1,479
Loganville ATL 1,841
Louisville 2,823
Ludowici 1,286
Lula 857
Lumber City 1,426
Lumpkin 1,335
Luthersville 597
Lyerly 482
Lyons 4,203
Mableton ATL 20,200 ○
McCaysville 1,219
McDonough ATL 2,778
MACON MAC- 116,896
McRae 3,409
Madison 2,954
Manchester 4,796
Marietta ATL 30,829
Marshallville 1,540
Maysville 619
Meigs 1,231
Menlo 611
Metter 3,531
Midville 670
Milan 1,115
Milledgeville 12,176
Millen 3,988
Milstead ATL 1,157 ○
Monroe 8,854
Montezuma 4,830
Monticello 2,382
Morrow ATL 3,791
Morven 471
Moultrie 15,708
Mountain City 701
Mount Airy 670
Mount Berry ROME 500 ○
Mount Vernon 1,737
Mount Zion 445
Nahunta 951
Nashville 4,831
Nelson 562
New Holland 800 ○
Newnan 11,449
Newton 711
Nicholls 1,114
Norcross ATL 3,317
Norman Park 757
North Atlanta ATL 22,800 ○

○ Rand McNally estimate
▲ Population of entire township or "town", including rural areas.
● Independent city. Population not included in county total.

North Druid Hills ATL 8,700 ○
Oakdale ATL 800 ○
Oakwood 723
Ochlocknee 627
Ocilla 3,436
Oglethorpe 1,305
Omega 996
Oxford ATL 1,750
Palmetto ATL 2,086
Panthersville ATL 11,366
Patterson 763
Pavo 830
Peach Orchard AUG 14,000 ○
Peachtree City 6,429
Pearson 1,827
Pelham 4,306
Pembroke 1,400
Pendley Hills ATL 5,800 ○
Perry MAC- 9,453
Pine Lake ATL 901
Pine Mountain 984
Pineview 564
Plains 651
Pooler SAV 2,543
Portal 694
Porterdale ATL 1,451
Port Wentworth SAV 3,947
Poulan 818
Powder Springs ATL 3,381
Quitman 5,188
Raoul 1,400 ○
Ray City 658
Red Oak ATL 1,200 ○
Reidsville 2,296
Remerton VALD 443
Reynolds 1,298
Rhine 590
Richland 1,802
Richmond Hill 1,177
Rincon SAV 1,988
Ringgold CHTN 1,882
Riverdale ATL 7,121
Roberta 859
Rochelle 1,626
Rockmart 3,645
ROME ROME 29,654
Rossville CHTN 3,851
Roswell ATL 23,337
Royston 2,404
Rutledge 694
St. Marys 3,596
St. Simons Island BRUNS 6,566
Sandersville 6,137
Sandy Springs ATL 20,300 ○
Sardis 1,180
Sargent 700 ○
SAVANNAH SAV 141,390
Scottdale ATL 8,770
Screven 872
Senoia 900
Shannon ROME 2,040
Shellman 1,254
Siloam 446
Smithville 867
Smyrna ATL 20,312
Snellville ATL 8,514
Social Circle 2,591
Soperton 2,981
South Decatur ATL 24,000 ○
Sparks 1,353
Sparta 1,745
Springfield 1,075
Statenville 650 ○
Statesboro 14,866
Statham 1,101
Stillmore 527
Stockbridge ATL 2,103
Stone Mountain ATL 4,867
Sugar Hill ATL 2,473
Summerville 4,878
Suwanee ATL 1,026
Swainsboro 7,602
Sycamore 474
Sylvania 3,352
Sylvester 5,860
Talbotton 1,140
Tallapoosa 2,647
Tate 900 ○
Temple 1,520
Tennille 1,709
Thomaston 9,682
Thomasville 18,463
Thomson 7,001
Thunderbolt SAV 2,165
Tifton 13,749
Tignall 733
Toccoa 9,104
Toomsboro 673
Trenton CHTN 1,636
Trion 1,732
Tucker ATL 18,200 ○
Tunnel Hill 936
Twin City 1,402
Tybee Island SAV 2,240
Ty Ty 618
Unadilla 1,566
Union City ATL 4,780
Union Point 1,750
Uvalda 646
VALDOSTA VALD 37,596
Vidalia 10,393
Vienna 2,886
Villa Rica ATL 3,420
Waco 471
Wadley 2,438
Waleska 450
Walthourville 905
Warner Robins MAC- 39,893
Warrenton 2,172
Warwick 488
Washington 4,662
Watkinsville ATH 1,240
Waverly Hall 913
Waycross 19,371
Waynesboro 5,760
West Point 4,294
Whigham 507
White 501
Whitesburg 775
Willacoochee 1,166
Winder 6,705
Windsor Forest SAV 7,288 ○
Winterville ATH 621
Woodbine 910
Woodbury 1,738
Woodland 664
Woodstock ATL 2,699
Woodville 455
Wrens 2,415
Wrightsville 2,526
Young Harris 687
Zebulon 995

COUNTIES

Appling 15,565
Atkinson 6,141
Bacon 9,379
Baker 3,808
Baldwin 34,686
Banks 8,702
Barrow 21,354
Bartow 40,760
Ben Hill 16,000
Berrien 13,525
Bibb 150,256
Bleckley 10,767
Brantley 8,701
Brooks 15,255
Bryan 10,175
Bulloch 35,785
Burke 19,349
Butts 13,665
Calhoun 5,717
Camden 13,371
Candler 7,518
Carroll 56,346
Catoosa 36,991
Charlton 7,343
Chatham 202,226
Chattahoochee 21,732
Chattooga 21,856
Cherokee 51,699
Clarke 74,498
Clay 3,553
Clayton 150,357
Clinch 6,660
Cobb 297,718
Coffee 26,894
Colquitt 35,376
Columbia 40,118
Cook 13,490
Coweta 39,268
Crawford 7,684
Crisp 19,489
Dade 12,318
Dawson 4,774
Decatur 25,495
De Kalb 483,024
Dodge 16,955
Dooly 10,826
Dougherty 100,718
Douglas 54,573
Early 13,158
Echols 2,297
Effingham 18,327
Elbert 18,758
Emanuel 20,795
Evans 8,428
Fannin 14,748
Fayette 29,043
Floyd 79,800
Forsyth 27,958
Franklin 15,185
Fulton 589,904
Gilmer 11,110
Glascock 2,382
Glynn 54,981
Gordon 30,070
Grady 19,845
Greene 11,391
Gwinnett 166,903
Habersham 25,020
Hall 75,649
Hancock 9,466
Haralson 18,422
Harris 15,464
Hart 18,585
Heard 6,520
Henry 36,309
Houston 77,605
Irwin 8,988
Jackson 25,343
Jasper 7,553
Jeff Davis 11,473
Jefferson 18,403
Jenkins 8,841
Johnson 8,660
Jones 16,579
Lamar 12,215
Lanier 5,654
Laurens 36,990
Lee 11,684
Liberty 37,583
Lincoln 6,716
Long 4,524
Lowndes 67,972
Lumpkin 10,762
McDuffie 18,546
McIntosh 8,046
Macon 14,003
Madison 17,747
Marion 5,297
Meriwether 21,229
Miller 7,038
Mitchell 21,114
Monroe 14,610
Montgomery 7,011
Morgan 11,572
Murray 19,685
Muscogee 170,108
Newton 34,489
Oconee 12,427
Oglethorpe 8,929
Paulding 26,110
Peach 19,151
Pickens 11,652
Pierce 11,897
Pike 8,937
Polk 32,386
Pulaski 8,950
Putnam 10,295
Quitman 2,357
Rabun 10,466
Randolph 9,599
Richmond 181,629
Rockdale 36,747
Schley 3,433
Screven 14,043
Seminole 9,057
Spalding 47,899
Stephens 21,763
Stewart 5,896
Sumter 29,360
Talbot 6,536
Taliaferro 2,032
Tattnall 18,134
Taylor 7,902
Telfair 11,445
Terrell 12,017
Thomas 38,098
Tift 32,862
Toombs 22,592
Towns 5,638
Treutlen 6,087
Troup 50,003
Turner 9,510
Twiggs 9,354
Union 9,390
Upson 25,998
Walker 56,470
Walton 31,211
Ware 37,180
Warren 6,583
Washington 18,842
Wayne 20,750
Webster 2,341
Wheeler 5,155
White 10,120
Whitfield 65,789
Wilcox 7,682
Wilkes 10,951
Wilkinson 10,368
Worth 18,064

HAWAII

1980 Census 964,691

CITIES

Aiea HON 15,200 ○
Anahola 915
Captain Cook 2,008
Crestview HON 1,000 ○
Eleele 580
Ewa HON 2,637
Ewa Beach HON 14,369
Foster Village HON 3,700 ○
Haiku 619
Halawa Heights HON 7,000 ○
Haleiwa HON 2,412
Haliimaile 741
Hana 643
Hanalei 483
Hanamaulu 3,227
Hanapepe 1,417

○ Rand McNally estimate
▲ Population of entire township or "town", including rural areas.
● Independent city. Population not included in county total.

HAWAII continued

Hauula HON 2,997
Hawi 795
HILO HILO 35,269
Holualoa 1,243
Honaunau 600 ○
Honokaa 1,936
HONOLULU HON 365,048
Honomu HILO 559
Honouliuli HON 600 ○
Kaaawa HON 959
Kahaluu HON 2,925
Kahuku HON 935
Kahului 12,978
Kailua HON 35,812
Kailua Kona 4,751
Kainaliu 512
Kalaheo 2,500
Kaneohe HON 29,919
Kapaa 4,467
Kapaau 612
Kaumakani 888
Kaunakakai 2,231
Keaau 775
Kealakekua 1,033
Kealia 700 ○
Kekaha 3,260
Keokea 900 ○
Kihei 5,644
Kilauea 895
Koloa 1,457
Kualapuu 502
Kula 1,300 ○
Kunia HON 550 ○
Kurtistown 1,200 ○
Lahaina 6,095
Laie HON 4,643
Lanai City 2,092
Laupahoehoe 500
Lawai 950 ○
Lihue 4,000
Lower Paia 1,500
Maili HON 5,026
Makaha HON 6,582
Makakilo City HON 7,691
Makaweli 700 ○
Maunaloa 633
Maunawili HON 2,200 ○
Mililani Town HON 21,365
Mountain View 540
Naalehu 1,168
Nanakuli HON 8,185
Paauilo 755
Pacific Palisades HON 9,500 ○
Pahala 1,619
Pahoa 923
Paia 1,000 ○
Papaikou HILO 1,567
Pauwela 468
Pearl City HON 33,000 ○
Pepeekeo HILO 1,800 ○
Poipu 685
Puhi 991
Pukalani 3,950
Puunene 572
Sunset Beach HON 800 ○
Volcano 900 ○
Wahiawa HON 16,911
Waialua HON 4,051
Waianae HON 5,000 ○
Waikapu 698
Wailua 1,587
Wailuku 10,260
Waimalu HON 3,600 ○
Waimanalo HON 3,562
Waimanalo Beach HON 4,161
Waimea HON 600 ○
Waimea 1,569
Waipahu HON 29,139
Waipio Acres HON 4,091
Whitmore Village HON 2,318

COUNTIES

Hawaii 92,053
Honolulu 762,565
Kalawao 144
Kauai 39,082
Maui 70,847

IDAHO

1980 Census 944,038

CITIES

Aberdeen 1,528
American Falls 3,626
Ammon IDFL 4,669
Arco 1,241
Ashton 1,219
Bancroft 505
Bellevue 1,016
Blackfoot 10,065
BOISE BOIS 102,160
Bonners Ferry 1,906
Buhl 3,629
Burley 8,761
Caldwell 17,699
Carey 600 ○
Cascade 945
Challis 758
Chubbuck POC 7,052
Clark Fork 449
Coeur d'Alene 20,054
Cottonwood 941
Council 917
Craigmont 617
Dalton Gardens 1,795
Deary 539
Downey 645
Driggs 727
Eagle BOIS 2,620
Elk City 670 ○
Emmett 4,605
Fernwood 680 ○
Filer 1,645
Firth 460
Fort Hall 900 ○
Fruitland 2,559
Garden City BOIS 4,571
Genesee 791
Georgetown 544
Glenns Ferry 1,374
Gooding 2,949
Grace 1,216
Grangeville 3,666
Hagerman 602
Hailey 2,109
Hansen 1,078
Hayden 2,586
Hazelton 496
Heyburn 2,889
Homedale 2,078
Horseshoe Bend 700
IDAHO FALLS IDFL 39,590
Inkom 830
Iona IDFL 1,072
Jerome 6,891
Juliaetta 522
Kamiah 1,478
Kellogg 3,417
Ketchum 2,200
Kimberly 2,307
Kingston 1,000 ○
Kooskia 784
Kuna 1,767
Lapwai 1,043
Lava Hot Springs 467
LEWISTON LEW 27,986
Lewisville 502
Lincoln IDFL 700 ○
McCall 2,188
McCammon 770
Mackay 541
Malad City 1,915
Marsing 786
Menan 605
Meridian BOIS 6,658
Middleton 1,901
Montpelier 3,107
Moscow 16,513
Mountain Home 7,540
Mullan 1,269
Nampa 25,112
New Meadows 576
New Plymouth 1,186
Nezperce 517
Oakley 663
Orofino 3,711
Osburn 2,220
Paris 707
Parma 1,820
Paul 940
Payette 5,448
Pierce 1,060
Plummer 634
POCATELLO POC 46,340
Post Falls SPOK 5,736
Potlatch 819
Preston 3,759
Priest River 1,639
Rathdrum 1,369
Rexburg 11,559
Rigby 2,624
Riggins 527
Ririe 555
Roberts 466
Rupert 5,476
St. Anthony 3,212
St. Maries 2,794
Salmon 3,308
Samuels 650 ○
Sandpoint 4,460
Shelley IDFL 3,300
Shoshone 1,242
Silverton 750 ○
Smelterville 776
Soda Springs 4,051
Spirit Lake 834
Star 600 ○
Sugar City 1,022
Sun Valley 545
Teton 559
Troy 820
Twin Falls 26,209
Ucon IDFL 833
Wallace 1,736
Weippe 828
Weiser 4,771
Wendell 1,974
Wilder 1,260

COUNTIES

Ada 173,036
Adams 3,347
Bannock 65,421
Bear Lake 6,931
Benewah 8,292
Bingham 36,489
Blaine 9,841
Boise 2,999
Bonner 24,163
Bonneville 65,980
Boundary 7,289
Butte 3,342
Camas 818
Canyon 83,756
Caribou 8,695
Cassia 19,427
Clark 798
Clearwater 10,390
Custer 3,385
Elmore 21,565
Franklin 8,895
Fremont 10,813
Gem 11,972
Gooding 11,874
Idaho 14,769
Jefferson 15,304
Jerome 14,840
Kootenai 59,770
Latah 28,749
Lemhi 7,460
Lewis 4,118
Lincoln 3,436
Madison 19,480
Minidoka 19,718
Nez Perce 33,220
Oneida 3,258
Owyhee 8,272
Payette 15,825
Power 6,844
Shoshone 19,226
Teton 2,897
Twin Falls 52,927
Valley 5,604
Washington 8,803

ILLINOIS

1980 Census 11,426,596

CITIES

Abingdon 4,210
Addison CHI 29,826
Albion 2,285
Aledo 3,881
Alexis 1,076
Algonquin CHI 5,834
Alsip CHI 17,134
Altamont 2,389
Alton ST.L 34,171
Amboy 2,377
Anna 5,408
Annawan 908
Antioch CHI 4,419
Arcola 2,714
Argenta DEC 994
Arlington Heights CHI 66,116
Aroma Park KANK 673
Arthur 2,122
Ashland 1,351
Ashton 1,140
Assumption 1,283
Astoria 1,370
Athens 1,371
Atkinson 1,138
Atlanta 1,807
Atwood 1,464
Auburn 3,616
Augusta 764
Aurora CHI 81,293
Ava 811
Avon 1,019
Barrington CHI 9,029
Barry 1,487
Bartlett CHI 13,254
Bartonville PEOR 6,137
Batavia CHI 12,574
Beardstown 6,338
Beckemeyer 1,119
Beecher 2,024
Belleville ST.L 41,580
Bellwood CHI 19,811
Belvidere RKFD 15,176
Bement 1,770
Benld 1,638
Bensenville CHI 16,124
Benton 7,778
Berkeley CHI 5,467
Berwyn CHI 46,849
Bethalto ST.L 8,630
Bethany 1,550
Blandinsville 886
Bloomingdale CHI 12,659
BLOOMINGTON BLMNG 44,189
Blue Island CHI 21,855
Blue Mound 1,338
Bolingbrook CHI 37,261
Boulder Hill CHI 9,333

○ Rand McNally estimate
▲ Population of entire township or "town", including rural areas.
● Independent city. Population not included in county total.

Bourbonnais KANK 13,280
Bradford 924
Bradley KANK 11,008
Braidwood 3,429
Breese 3,516
Bridgeport 2,281
Bridgeview CHI 14,155
Brighton ST.L. 2,364
Brimfield 890
Broadview CHI 8,618
Brookfield CHI 19,395
Brookport PAD 1,128
Brownstown 708
Buda 668
Buffalo Grove CHI 22,230
Bunker Hill 1,700
Burbank CHI 28,462
Bushnell 3,811
Byron 2,035
Cahokia ST.L 18,904
Cairo 5,931
Calumet City CHI . . . 39,697
Calumet Park CHI . . . 8,788
Cambridge 2,217
Camp Point 1,285
Canton 14,626
Carbondale 26,414
Carlinville 5,439
Carlyle 3,388
Carmi 6,264
Carol Stream CHI . . . 15,472
Carpentersville CHI 23,272
Carrier Mills 2,268
Carrollton 2,816
Carterville 3,445
Carthage 2,978
Cary CHI 6,640
Casey 3,026
Catlin DANV 2,226
Central City 1,505
Centralia 15,126
Centreville ST.L 9,747
Cerro Gordo 1,553
CHAMPAIGN CH-U 58,133
Chandlerville 842
Charleston 19,355
Chatham SPRG 5,597
Chatsworth 1,187
Chebanse KANK 1,191
Chenoa 1,847
Cherry 541
Cherry Valley RKFD . . . 946
Chester 8,401
CHICAGO CHI . . . 3,005,072
Chicago Heights CHI 37,026
Chicago Ridge CHI 13,473
Chillicothe PEOR 6,176
Chrisman 1,413
Christopher 3,086
Cicero CHI 61,232
Cissna Park 825
Clarendon Hills CHI 6,870
Clay City 1,038
Clayton 889
Clifton 1,390
Clinton 8,014
Coal City 3,028
Cobden 1,210
Colchester 1,729
Colfax 920
Collinsville ST.L 19,613
Columbia ST.L 4,269
Coulterville 1,118
Country Club Hills CHI 14,676
Countryside CHI 6,538
Creal Springs 845
Crest Hill CHI 9,252
Crestwood CHI 10,852
Crete CHI 5,417
Creve Coeur PEOR 6,851
Crossville 944
Crystal Lake CHI . . . 18,590
Crystal Lawns CHI . . . 2,800 ○
Cuba 1,648
Dallas City 1,408
Danvers 921
DANVILLE DANV . . . 38,985
Darien CHI 14,536
DECATUR DEC 94,081
Deerfield CHI 17,430
DE KALB DKLB 33,099
Delavan 1,973
Depue 1,873
De Soto 1,589
Des Plaines CHI 53,568
Divernon 1,081
Dixon 15,701
Dolton CHI 24,766
Dongola 886
Downers Grove CHI 42,572
Dundee CHI 3,551
Du Quoin 6,594
Durand 1,073
Dwight 4,146
Earlville 1,382
East Alton ST.L 7,096
East Chicago Heights CHI 5,347
East Dubuque DUB 2,194
East Galesburg GLSB 928
East Moline D-RI-M 20,907
East Peoria PEOR 22,385
East St. Louis ST.L 55,200
Edinburg 1,231
Edwardsville ST.L . . . 12,480
Effingham 11,270
Elburn CHI 1,224
Eldorado 5,198
Elgin CHI 63,981
Elizabeth 772
Elizabethtown 478
Elk Grove Village CHI 28,907
Elkville 973
Elmhurst CHI 44,276
Elmwood 2,117
Elmwood Park CHI 24,016
El Paso 2,676
Enfield 890
Equality 831
Erie 1,725
Eureka PEOR 4,306
Evanston CHI 73,706
Evansville 863
Evergreen Park CHI 22,260
Fairbury 3,544
Fairfield 5,954
Fairmont CHI . . . . 2,600 ○
Fairview Heights ST.L 12,414
Farina 594
Farmer City 2,252
Farmington 3,118
Findlay 868
Fisher 1,572
Flanagan 978
Flat Rock 493
Flora 5,379
Flossmoor CHI 8,423
Forest Park CHI 15,177
Forrest 1,246
Forreston 1,384
Fox Lake CHI 6,831
Fox River Grove CHI 2,515
Frankfort CHI 4,357
Franklin Grove 965
Franklin Park CHI . . . 17,507
Freeburg ST.L 2,989
Freeport 26,266
Fulton CLNT 3,936
Galatia 1,042
Galena 3,876
GALESBURG GLSB 35,305
Galva 3,185
Gardner 1,322
Geneseo D-RI-M 6,373
Geneva CHI 9,881
Genoa 3,276
Georgetown DANV . . . 4,220
Gibson City 3,498
Gillespie 3,740
Gilman 1,913
Girard 2,246
Glasford PEOR 1,201
Glen Carbon ST.L . . . 5,197
Glencoe CHI 9,200
Glendale Heights CHI 23,163
Glen Ellyn CHI 23,717
Glenview CHI 32,060
Glenwood CHI 10,538
Godfrey ST.L . . . . 2,600 ○
Golconda 960
Grafton 1,024
Grand Tower 748
Granite City ST.L . . . 36,815
Grant Park 1,038
Granville 1,537
Grayslake CHI 5,260
Grayville 2,313
Greenfield 1,090
Greenup 1,655
Greenview 830
Greenville 5,271
Gridley 1,246
Griggsville 1,301
Gurnee CHI 7,179
Hamilton 3,509
Hampshire 1,735
Hanna City PEOR . . . 1,361
Hanover 1,069
Hanover Park CHI 28,719
Hardin 1,107
Harrisburg 10,410
Harristown DEC 1,456
Hartford ST.L 1,887
Harvard 5,126
Harvey CHI 35,810
Harwood Heights CHI 8,228
Havana 4,277
Hazel Crest CHI 13,973
Hebron 786
Henry 2,740
Herrin 10,708
Heyworth 1,598
Hickory Hills CHI . . . 13,778
Highland 7,122
Highland Park CHI 30,611
Highwood CHI 5,452
Hillsboro 4,408
Hillside CHI 8,279
Hinckley 1,447
Hinsdale CHI 16,726
Hoffman Estates CHI 37,272
Homer 1,279
Hometown CHI 5,324
Homewood CHI 19,724
Hoopeston 6,411
Hopedale 913
Huntley CHI 1,646
Hurst 938
Hutsonville 705
Illiopolis 1,118
Ipava 661
Itasca CHI 7,129
Jacksonville 20,284
Jerseyville 7,506
Johnston City 3,873
Joliet CHI 77,956
Jonesboro 1,842
Joppa 535
Justice CHI 10,552
KANKAKEE KANK 30,141
Kansas 791
Karnak 646
Keithsburg 936
Kenilworth CHI 2,708
Ken Rock RKFD . . . . . 5,945 ○
Kewanee 14,508
Kincaid 1,591
Kinmundy 945
Kirkland 1,155
Kirkwood 1,008
Knoxville GLSB 3,432
Lacon 2,135
Ladd 1,337
La Grange CHI 15,445
La Grange Highlands CHI . . . . 7,100 ○
La Grange Park CHI 13,359
La Harpe 1,471
Lake Bluff CHI 4,434
Lake Forest CHI 15,245
Lake In The Hills CHI 5,651
Lake Zurich CHI 8,225
La Moille 734
Lanark 1,483
Lansing CHI 29,039
La Salle 10,347
Lawrenceville 5,652
Lebanon ST.L 3,245
Lemont CHI 5,640
Lena 2,295
Le Roy 2,870
Lewistown 2,758
Lexington 1,806
Libertyville CHI 16,520
Lincoln 16,327
Lincolnwood CHI . . . 11,921
Lindenhurst CHI 6,220
Lisle CHI 13,625
Litchfield 7,204
Livingston 949
Lockport CHI 9,170
Lombard CHI 36,897
London Mills 587
Louisville 1,166
Loves Park RKFD . . . 13,192
Lovington 1,313
Lyons CHI 9,925
McHenry CHI 11,949
Mackinaw 1,354
McLean 836
McLeansboro 2,960
Macomb 19,863
Macon DEC 1,300
Madison ST.L 5,915
Mahomet CH-U 1,986
Manito 1,869
Mansfield 921
Manteno 3,155
Marengo 4,361
Marine 957
Marion 14,031
Marissa 2,568
Markham CHI 15,172
Maroa 1,760
Marseilles 4,766
Marshall 3,655
Martinsville 1,298
Mascoutah ST.L 4,962
Mason City 2,719
Matteson CHI 10,223
Mattoon 19,055
Maywood CHI 27,998
Mazon 828
Melrose Park CHI . . . 20,735
Mendon 979
Mendota 7,134
Meredosia 1,272
Metamora PEOR 2,482
Metropolis 7,171

○ Rand McNally estimate
▲ Population of entire township or "town", including rural areas.
● Independent city. Population not included in county total.

ILLINOIS continued

Midlothian CHI . . . 14,274
Milan D-RI-M . . . 6,264
Milford . . . 1,716
Milledgeville . . . 1,209
Millstadt ST.L . . . 2,736
Minier . . . 1,261
Minonk . . . 2,039
Mokena CHI . . . 4,578
Moline D-RI-M . . . 46,278
Momence . . . 3,297
Monmouth . . . 10,706
Montgomery CHI . . . 3,369
Monticello . . . 4,753
Mooseheart CHI . . . 600 ○
Morris . . . 8,833
Morrison . . . 4,605
Morrisonville . . . 1,208
Morton PEOR . . . 14,178
Morton Grove CHI . . . 23,747
Mound City . . . 1,102
Mounds . . . 1,669
Mount Carmel . . . 8,908
Mount Carroll . . . 1,936
Mount Morris . . . 2,989
Mount Olive . . . 2,357
Mount Prospect CHI . . . 52,634
Mount Pulaski . . . 1,783
Mount Sterling . . . 2,186
Mount Vernon . . . 17,193
Moweaqua . . . 1,922
Mulberry Grove . . . 707
Mundelein CHI . . . 17,053
Murphysboro . . . 9,866
Naperville CHI . . . 42,601
Nashville . . . 3,186
Nauvoo . . . 1,133
Neoga . . . 1,736
New Athens . . . 1,937
New Baden ST.L . . . 2,476
New Berlin . . . 834
New Boston . . . 731
New Haven . . . 559
New Lenox CHI . . . 5,792
Newman . . . 1,079
Newton . . . 3,186
New Windsor . . . 863
Niles CHI . . . 30,363
Noble . . . 832
Nokomis . . . 2,656
Normal BLMNG . . . 35,672
Norridge CHI . . . 16,483
Norris City . . . 1,515
North Aurora CHI . . . 5,205
Northbrook CHI . . . 30,778
North Chicago CHI . . . 38,774
Northfield CHI . . . 5,807
Northlake CHI . . . 12,166
North Park RKFD . . . 15,806
North Riverside CHI . . . 6,764
Oak Brook CHI . . . 6,641
Oak Forest CHI . . . 26,096
Oakland . . . 1,035
Oak Lawn CHI . . . 60,590
Oak Park CHI . . . 54,887
Oakwood DANV . . . 1,627
Oblong . . . 1,840
Odell . . . 1,083
Odin . . . 1,285
O'Fallon ST.L . . . 12,241
Oglesby . . . 3,979
Okawville . . . 1,337
Olive Branch . . . 550 ○
Olney . . . 9,026
Onarga . . . 1,269
Oneida . . . 765
Oquawka . . . 1,533
Oreana DEC . . . 999
Oregon . . . 3,559
Orient . . . 480
Orion D-RI-M . . . 2,013
Orland Park CHI . . . 23,045
Oswego CHI . . . 3,021
Ottawa . . . 18,166
Palatine CHI . . . 32,166
Palestine . . . 1,718
Palmyra . . . 864
Palos Heights CHI . . . 11,096
Palos Hills CHI . . . 16,654
Palos Park CHI . . . 3,150
Pana . . . 6,040
Paris . . . 9,885
Park Forest CHI . . . 26,222
Park Forest South CHI . . . 6,245
Park Ridge CHI . . . 38,704
Patoka . . . 662
Pawnee . . . 2,577
Paw Paw . . . 839
Paxton . . . 4,258
Pecatonica . . . 1,732
Pekin PEOR . . . 33,967
PEORIA PEOR . . . 124,160
Peoria Heights PEOR . . . 7,453
Peotone . . . 2,832
Percy . . . 1,053
Peru . . . 10,886
Petersburg . . . 2,419
Phoenix CHI . . . 2,850
Pinckneyville . . . 3,319
Piper City . . . 905
Pittsfield . . . 4,170
Plainfield CHI . . . 3,767
Plano CHI . . . 4,875
Pleasant Hill . . . 1,112
Pleasant Plains . . . 688
Plymouth . . . 649
Pocahontas . . . 866
Polo . . . 2,643
Pontiac . . . 11,227
Port Byron D-RI-M . . . 1,289
Posen CHI . . . 4,642
Prairie Du Rocher . . . 701
Princeton . . . 7,342
Princeville . . . 1,712
Prophetstown . . . 2,141
Prospect Heights CHI . . . 11,808
QUINCY QUIN . . . 42,554
Ramsey . . . 1,058
Rankin . . . 727
RANTOUL RNTL . . . 20,161
Raymond . . . 957
Red Bud . . . 2,850
Richmond CHI . . . 1,068
Richton Park CHI . . . 9,403
Ridge Farm DANV . . . 1,096
Ridgway . . . 1,245
Riverdale CHI . . . 13,233
River Forest CHI . . . 12,392
River Grove CHI . . . 10,368
Riverside CHI . . . 9,236
Roanoke . . . 2,001
Robbins CHI . . . 8,853
Robinson . . . 7,285
Rochelle . . . 8,982
Rockdale CHI . . . 1,913
Rock Falls . . . 10,633
Rockford RKFD . . . 139,712
Rock Island D-RI-M . . . 46,928
Rockton BLOIT . . . 2,313
Rolling Meadows CHI . . . 20,167
Romeoville CHI . . . 15,519
Roodhouse . . . 2,364
Roselle CHI . . . 16,948
Roseville . . . 1,254
Rosewood Heights ST.L . . . 5,085
Rosiclare . . . 1,441
Rossville . . . 1,363
Round Lake Beach CHI . . . 12,921
Royalton . . . 1,320
Rushville . . . 3,348
St. Anne KANK . . . 1,421
St. Charles CHI . . . 17,492
St. David . . . 786
St. Elmo . . . 1,611
St. Francisville . . . 1,040
St. Joseph CH-U . . . 1,900
Salem . . . 7,813
Sandoval . . . 1,734
Sandwich CHI . . . 5,244
San Jose . . . 784
Sauk Village CHI . . . 10,906
Savanna . . . 4,529
Saybrook . . . 882
Schaumburg CHI . . . 53,305
Schiller Park CHI . . . 11,458
Schram City . . . 708
Seneca . . . 2,098
Sesser . . . 2,238
Shabbona . . . 851
Shannon . . . 938
Shawneetown . . . 1,841
Sheffield . . . 1,130
Shelbyville . . . 5,259
Sheldon . . . 1,215
Silvis D-RI-M . . . 7,130
Skokie CHI . . . 60,278
Somonauk . . . 1,344
South Beloit BLOIT . . . 4,088
South Chicago Heights CHI . . . 3,932
South Elgin CHI . . . 5,970
South Holland CHI . . . 24,977
South Jacksonville . . . 3,382
South Pekin PEOR . . . 1,243
South Streator . . . 2,334
South Wilmington . . . 747
Sparta . . . 4,957
SPRINGFIELD SPRG . . . 100,054
Spring Valley . . . 5,822
Staunton . . . 4,744
Steeleville . . . 2,240
Steger CHI . . . 9,269
Sterling . . . 16,281
Stewardson . . . 745
Stickney CHI . . . 5,893
Stockton . . . 1,872
Stonington . . . 1,184
Streamwood CHI . . . 23,456
Streator . . . 14,795
Stronghurst . . . 865
Sullivan . . . 4,526
Summit CHI . . . 10,110
Sumner . . . 1,238
Swansea ST.L . . . 5,347
Sycamore DKLB . . . 9,219
Tampico . . . 966
Taylorville . . . 11,386
Teutopolis . . . 1,414
Tilden . . . 1,025
Tilton DANV . . . 2,405
Tinley Park CHI . . . 26,171
Tiskilwa . . . 990
Toledo . . . 1,284
Tolono CH-U . . . 2,434
Toluca . . . 1,471
Tonica . . . 695
Toulon . . . 1,390
Tower Hill . . . 715
Tremont PEOR . . . 2,096
Trenton ST.L . . . 2,504
Troy ST.L . . . 3,772
Tuscola . . . 3,839
Urbana CH-U . . . 35,978
Utica . . . 1,067
Valmeyer . . . 898
Vandalia . . . 5,338
Venice ST.L . . . 3,480
Vermont . . . 885
Vernon Hills CHI . . . 9,827
Vienna . . . 1,420
Villa Grove . . . 2,707
Villa Park CHI . . . 23,185
Viola . . . 1,144
Virden . . . 3,899
Virginia . . . 1,825
Walnut . . . 1,513
Wamac . . . 1,665
Warren . . . 1,595
Warrenville CHI . . . 7,519
Warsaw . . . 1,842
Washburn . . . 1,206
Washington PEOR . . . 10,364
Washington Park ST.L . . . 8,223
Waterloo ST.L . . . 4,646
Waterman . . . 943
Watseka . . . 5,543
Wauconda CHI . . . 5,688
Waukegan CHI . . . 67,653
Waverly . . . 1,537
Wayne City . . . 1,132
Westchester CHI . . . 17,730
West Chicago CHI . . . 12,550
West City . . . 886
Westdale CHI . . . 10,300 ○
West End RKFD . . . 7,554 ○
Western Springs CHI . . . 12,876
West Frankfort . . . 9,437
Westmont CHI . . . 16,718
West Peoria PEOR . . . 5,219
West Salem . . . 1,145
Westville DANV . . . 3,573
Wheaton CHI . . . 43,043
Wheeling CHI . . . 23,266
White Hall . . . 2,935
Williamsville . . . 996
Willow Springs CHI . . . 4,147
Wilmette CHI . . . 28,229
Wilmington . . . 4,424
Winchester . . . 1,716
Windsor . . . 1,228
Winnebago RKFD . . . 1,644
Winnetka CHI . . . 12,772
Winthrop Harbor CHI . . . 5,431
Witt . . . 1,205
Wood Dale CHI . . . 11,251
Woodhull . . . 901
Woodridge CHI . . . 22,561
Wood River ST.L . . . 12,446
Woodstock . . . 11,725
Worden . . . 953
Worth CHI . . . 11,592
Wyanet . . . 1,069
Wyoming . . . 1,614
Yates City . . . 860
Yorkville CHI . . . 3,422
Zeigler . . . 1,858
Zion CHI . . . 17,861

COUNTIES

Adams . . . 71,622
Alexander . . . 12,264
Bond . . . 16,224
Boone . . . 28,630
Brown . . . 5,411
Bureau . . . 39,114
Calhoun . . . 5,867
Carroll . . . 18,779
Cass . . . 15,084
Champaign . . . 168,392
Christian . . . 36,446
Clark . . . 16,913
Clay . . . 15,283
Clinton . . . 32,617
Coles . . . 52,260
Cook . . . 5,253,655
Crawford . . . 20,818
Cumberland . . . 11,062
De Kalb . . . 74,624
De Witt . . . 18,108
Douglas . . . 19,774
Du Page . . . 658,829
Edgar . . . 21,725
Edwards . . . 7,961
Effingham . . . 30,944
Fayette . . . 22,167
Ford . . . 15,265

○ Rand McNally estimate
▲ Population of entire township or "town", including rural areas.
● Independent city. Population not included in county total.

Franklin 43,201
Fulton 43,687
Gallatin 7,590
Greene 16,661
Grundy 30,582
Hamilton 9,172
Hancock 23,877
Hardin 5,383
Henderson 9,114
Henry 57,968
Iroquois 32,976
Jackson 61,649
Jasper 11,318
Jefferson 36,558
Jersey 20,538
Jo Daviess 23,520
Johnson 9,624
Kane 278,405
Kankakee 102,926
Kendall 37,202
Knox 61,607
Lake 440,372
La Salle 112,033
Lawrence 17,807
Lee 36,328
Livingston 41,381
Logan 31,802
McDonough 37,467
McHenry 147,897
McLean 119,149
Macon 131,375
Macoupin 49,384
Madison 247,661
Marion 43,523
Marshall 14,479
Mason 19,492
Massac 14,990
Menard 11,700
Mercer 19,286
Monroe 20,117
Montgomery 31,686
Morgan 37,502
Moultrie 14,546
Ogle 46,338
Peoria 200,466
Perry 21,714
Piatt 16,581
Pike 18,896
Pope 4,404
Pulaski 8,840
Putnam 6,085
Randolph 35,652
Richland 17,587
Rock Island 165,968
St. Clair 267,531
Saline 28,448
Sangamon 176,070
Schuyler 8,365
Scott 6,142
Shelby 23,923
Stark 7,389
Stephenson 49,536
Tazewell 132,078
Union 17,765
Vermilion 95,222
Wabash 13,713
Warren 21,943
Washington 15,472
Wayne 18,059
White 17,864
Whiteside 65,970
Will 324,460
Williamson 56,538
Winnebago 250,884
Woodford 33,320

INDIANA

1980
Census 5,490,260

CITIES

Advance 559
Akron 1,045
Albany MUN 2,625
Albion 1,637
Alexandria AND 6,028
Amboy 450
Amo 444
ANDERSON AND . . . 64,695
Andrews 1,243
Angola 5,486
Arcadia IND 1,801
Ardmore S.B.- . . . . . . 3,400 ○
Argos 1,547
Arlington . . . . 500 ○
Ashley 841
Atlanta IND 657
Attica 3,841
Auburn FTWA 8,122
Aurora CIN- 3,816
Austin 4,857
Avilla 1,272
Bainbridge 644
Bargersville IND 1,647
Bass Lake . . . . 1,500 ○
Batesville 4,152
Battle Ground LAF 812
Bedford 14,410
Beech Grove IND . . . 13,196
Berne 3,300
Beverly Shores CHI 864
Bicknell 4,713
Birdseye 533
Black Oak CHI . . . . . 10,000 ○
Blanford T.H. . . . . 700 ○
Bloomfield 2,705
BLOOMINGTON BLMNG 52,044
Bluffton 8,705
Boonville EV 6,300
Boswell 810
Bourbon 1,522
Brazil T.H. 7,852
Bremen 3,565
Bristol S.B.- 1,203
Brook 926
Brooklyn IND 889
Brookston 1,701
Brookville 2,874
Brownsburg IND 6,242
Brownstown 2,704
Butler 2,509
Cambridge City 2,407
Camden 618
Campbellsburg 695
Cannelton 2,373
Carlisle 717
Carmel IND 18,272
Carthage 886
Cayuga 1,258
Cedar Lake CHI 8,754
Centerville RICH 2,284
Chalmers 554
Chandler EV 3,043
Charlestown LOU 5,596
Chesterfield AND 2,701
Chesterton IND . . . . 900 ○
Chesterton CHI 8,531
Chrisney 537
Churubusco 1,638
Cicero IND 2,557
Clarks Hill 653
Clarksville LOU 15,164
Clay City 883
Claypool 464
Clayton IND 703
Clinton T.H. 5,267
Cloverdale 1,357
Coalmont . . . . 450 ○
Coatesville 474
Colfax 823
Collegeville 1,059
Columbia City 5,091
COLUMBUS COL . . . 30,614
Connersville 17,023
Converse 1,279
Corydon 2,724
Covington 2,883
Crawfordsville 13,325
Cromwell 458
Crothersville 1,747
Crown Point CHI . . . 16,455
Culver 1,601
Cynthiana 874
Dale 1,693
Dana 803
Danville IND 4,220
Darlington 811
Dayton LAF 781
Decatur 8,649
Delphi 3,042
Demotte CHI 2,559
Denver 589
Dillsboro CIN- 1,038
Dublin 979
Dubois . . . . 550 ○
Dugger 1,118
Dunkirk 3,180
Dunlap S.B.- . . . . 2,500 ○
Dyer CHI 9,555
Earl Park 469
East Chicago CHI . . . 39,786
Eaton MUN 1,804
Edgewood AND 2,215
Edinburgh COL 4,856
Edwardsport 459
Elberfeld 640
Elizabethtown COL 603
Elkhart S.B.- 41,305
Ellettsville BLMNG . . . 3,328
Elnora 756
Elwood AND 10,867
English 633
Etna Green 522
EVANSVILLE EV 130,496
Fairland IND . . . . 900 ○
Fairmount MRN 3,286
Fairview Park T.H. . . . 1,545
Farmersburg 1,240
Farmland MUN 1,560
Ferdinand 2,192
Fillmore . . . . 550 ○
Fishers IND 2,008
Flora 2,303
Floyds Knobs LOU . . . . 500 ○
Fontanet T.H. . . . . 450 ○
Fort Branch 2,504
Fortville IND 2,787
FORT WAYNE FTWA 172,028
Fountain City RICH 839
Fowler 2,319
Francesville 944
Francisco 612
Frankfort 15,168
Franklin IND 11,563
Frankton AND 2,080
Freelandville . . . . 680 ○
Freetown . . . . 600 ○
Fremont 1,180
French Lick 2,265
Galveston KOK 1,822
Garrett FTWA 4,751
Gary CHI 151,953
Gas City MRN 6,370
Gaston MUN 1,150
Geneva 1,430
Georgetown LOU 1,494
Goodland 1,200
Goshen S.B.- 19,665
Gosport 729
Grabill FTWA 658
Grandview 670
Greencastle 8,403
Greendale CIN- 3,795
Greenfield IND 11,299
Greensburg 9,254
Greentown KOK 2,265
Greenville LOU 537
Greenwood IND 19,327
Griffith CHI 17,026
Hagerstown 1,950
Hamilton 587
Hamlet 738
Hammond CHI 93,714
Hanna . . . . 500 ○
Hanover 4,054
Harlan FTWA . . . . 1,000 ○
Harmony T.H. 613
Hartford City 7,622
Hatfield . . . . 600 ○
Haubstadt EV 1,389
Hebron CHI 2,696
Heltonville . . . . 500 ○
Henryville LOU 1,132
Highland CHI 25,935
Hillsboro 561
Hoagland FTWA . . . . . . 650 ○
Hobart CHI 22,987
Holland 683
Holton 487
Home Corner MRN . . . . 500 ○
Homecroft IND 831
Home Place IND . . . . 2,000 ○
Hope COL 2,185
Howe . . . . 500 ○
Hudson 447
Hudson Lake 1,347
Huntertown FTWA . . . 1,265
Huntingburg 5,376
Huntington 16,202
Hymera 1,054
Idaville . . . . 625 ○
INDIANAPOLIS IND 700,807
Indian Heights KOK 4,277
Ingalls AND 909
Ireland . . . . 450 ○
Jamestown 924
Jasonville 2,497
Jasper 9,097
Jeffersonville LOU 21,220
Jonesboro MRN 2,279
Kendallville 7,299
Kennard 441
Kentland 1,936
Kewanna 711
Kingman 566
Kirklin 662
Knightstown 2,325
Knightsville T.H. 763
Knox 3,674
KOKOMO KOK 47,808
Koontz Lake 1,436
Kouts 1,619
La Crosse 713
Ladoga 1,151
LAFAYETTE LAF . . . 43,011
La Fontaine 946
Lagrange 2,164
Lagro 549
Lake Station CHI . . . 14,294
Laketon . . . . 500 ○
Lake Village . . . . 650 ○
Lakeville S.B.- 629
Lanesville LOU 570
Lapaz 651
Lapel AND 1,881
La Porte 21,796
Laurel 819
Lawrence IND 25,591
Lawrenceburg CIN- 4,403
Lebanon IND 11,456
Leesburg 629
Leo FTWA . . . . 800 ○
Lewisville 577
Liberty 1,844
Ligonier 3,134
Linden 700
Linton 6,315
Lizton 456
Logansport 17,731
Long Beach MICH . . . 2,262
Loogootee 3,100
Lowell CHI 5,827
Lynn 1,250
Lynnville 566
Lyons 782
Madison 12,472
Marengo 892
MARION MRN 35,874

○ Rand McNally estimate
▲ Population of entire township or "town", including rural areas.
● Independent city. Population not included in county total.

INDIANA continued

Markle 975
Martinsville IND 11,311
Matthews MRN 745
Mecca 482
Medaryville 731
Medora 853
Memphis LOU 500 ○
Mentone 973
Merrillville CHI 27,677
Mexico 850 ○
MICHIGAN CITY MICH 36,850
Michigantown 453
Middlebury S.B.- 1,665
Middletown AND 2,978
Milan 1,566
Milford 1,153
Millersburg S.B.- 809
Milltown 1,006
Milroy 900 ○
Mishawaka S.B.- 40,201
Mitchell 4,641
Monon 1,540
Monroe 739
Monroe City 569
Monroeville 1,372
Monrovia IND 450 ○
Montezuma 1,352
Monticello 5,162
Montpelier 1,995
Mooreland 479
Moores Hill 566
Mooresville IND 5,349
Morgantown 897
Morocco 1,348
Morristown 989
Mount Vernon 7,656
Mulberry 1,225
MUNCIE MUN 77,216
Munster CHI 20,671
Nappanee 4,694
Nashville 705
New Albany LOU 37,103
Newburgh EV 2,906
New Carlisle 1,439
New Castle 20,056
New Goshen T.H. 500 ○
New Harmony 945
New Haven FTWA 6,714
New Market 608
New Palestine IND 749
New Paris S.B.- 1,062
Newport 704
New Washington 600 ○
New Whiteland IND 4,502
Noblesville IND 12,056
North Judson 1,653
North Liberty 1,211
North Manchester 5,998
North Salem 581
North Terre Haute T.H. 1,500 ○
North Vernon 5,768
North Webster 709
Oakland City 3,301
Oaktown 776
Odon 1,463
Oldenburg 770
Oolitic 1,495
Orestes AND 539
Orleans 2,161
Osceola S.B.- 1,990
Osgood 1,554
Ossian FTWA 1,945
Otterbein 1,118
Otwell 500 ○
Owensville 1,261
Oxford 1,327
Palmyra LOU 692
Paoli 3,637
Paragon 538
Parker City MUN 1,414
Patoka 832
Pekin 1,125

Pendleton AND 2,130
Pennville 805
Perrysville 532
Peru 13,764
Petersburg 2,987
Pierceton 1,086
Pittsboro IND 891
Plainfield IND 9,191
Plainville 556
Pleasant Lake 500 ○
Plymouth 7,693
Portage CHI 27,409
Porter CHI 2,988
Portland 7,074
Poseyville 1,247
Princes Lakes 937
Princeton 8,976
Redkey 1,537
Remington 1,268
Rensselaer 4,944
Reynolds 632
Richland 550 ○
RICHMOND RICH 41,349
Ridgeville 933
Rising Sun 2,478
Riverhaven FTWA 700 ○
Roachdale 958
Roann 548
Roanoke 891
Rochester 5,050
Rockport 2,590
Rockville 2,785
Rocky Ripple IND 778
Rome City 1,319
Rosedale T.H. 744
Roseland S.B.- 832
Rossville 1,148
Royal Center 908
Royerton MUN 650 ○
Rushville 6,113
Russiaville KOK 973
St. Bernice 900 ○
St. Joe FTWA 546
St. John CHI 3,974
St. Mary-of-the-Woods T.H. 650 ○
St. Marys S.B.- 1,700 ○
St. Meinrad 500 ○
St. Paul 976
Salem 5,290
Sandborn 576
Santa Claus 514
Schererville CHI 13,209
Scottsburg 5,068
Seelyville T.H. 1,374
Sellersburg LOU 3,211
Selma MUN 1,056
Seymour 15,050
Sharpsville KOK 617
Shelburn 1,259
Shelby CHI 700 ○
Shelbyville IND 14,989
Sheridan IND 2,200
Shipshewana 466
Shirley AND 919
Shoals 967
Silver Lake 576
SOUTH BEND S.B.- 109,727
South Haven CHI 6,679
South Milford 500 ○
Southport IND 2,266
South Whitley 1,575
Speed LOU 650 ○
Speedway IND 12,641
Spencer BLMNG 2,732
Spiceland 940
Spring Grove RICH 469
Star City 500 ○
Staunton T.H. 607
Stockwell 500 ○
Stroh 450 ○
Sullivan 4,774
Summitville AND 1,085
Sunman 924
Swayzee 1,127

Sweetser MRN 944
Syracuse 2,579
Taylorsville COL 1,247
Tell City 8,704
TERRE HAUTE T.H. 61,125
Thorntown 1,468
Tipton 5,004
Topeka 876
Trafalgar 466
Trail Creek MICH 2,581
Tri-Lakes 1,356
Troy 550
Underwood LOU 500 ○
Union City 3,908
Union Mills 550 ○
Upland MRN 3,335
Utica LOU 501
Vallonia 500 ○
Valparaiso CHI 22,247
Van Buren 935
Veedersburg 2,261
Versailles 1,560
Vevay 1,343
Vincennes 20,857
Wabash 12,985
Wakarusa S.B.- 1,281
Waldron IND 800 ○
Walkerton 2,051
Wallen FTWA 1,200 ○
Walton KOK 1,202
Wanatah 879
Warren 1,254
Warren Park IND 1,803
Warsaw 10,647
Washington 11,325
Waterloo 1,951
Waveland 559
Waynetown 915
West Baden Springs 796
West College Corner 614
Westfield IND 2,783
West Lafayette LAF 21,247
West Lebanon 946
Westpoint 500 ○
Westport 1,450
West Terre Haute T.H. 2,806
Westville 2,887
Wheatfield 755
Wheatland 532
Wheeler CHI 600 ○
Whitestown IND 497
Whiting CHI 5,630
Wilkinson AND 493
Williamsport 1,747
Winamac 2,370
Winchester 5,659
Windfall 911
Winona Lake 2,827
Winslow 1,017
Wolcott 923
Wolcottville 890
Wolflake 450 ○
Woodburn FTWA 1,002
Worthington 1,574
Yorktown MUN 3,945
Zanesville 550 ○
Zionsville IND 3,948

COUNTIES

Adams 29,619
Allen 294,335
Bartholomew 65,088
Benton 10,218
Blackford 15,570
Boone 36,446
Brown 12,377
Carroll 19,722
Cass 40,936
Clark 88,838
Clay 24,862
Clinton 31,545
Crawford 9,820
Daviess 27,836
Dearborn 34,291
Decatur 23,841
De Kalb 33,606
Delaware 128,587
Dubois 34,238
Elkhart 137,330
Fayette 28,272
Floyd 61,205
Fountain 19,033
Franklin 19,612
Fulton 19,335
Gibson 33,156
Grant 80,934
Greene 30,416
Hamilton 82,027
Hancock 43,939
Harrison 27,276
Hendricks 69,804
Henry 53,336
Howard 86,896
Huntington 35,596
Jackson 36,523
Jasper 26,138
Jay 23,239
Jefferson 30,419
Jennings 22,854
Johnson 77,240
Knox 41,838
Kosciusko 59,555
Lagrange 25,550
Lake 522,965
La Porte 108,632
Lawrence 42,472
Madison 139,336
Marion 765,233
Marshall 39,155
Martin 11,001
Miami 39,820
Monroe 98,785
Montgomery 35,501
Morgan 51,999
Newton 14,844
Noble 35,443
Ohio 5,114
Orange 18,677
Owen 15,841
Parke 16,372
Perry 19,346
Pike 13,465
Porter 119,816
Posey 26,414
Pulaski 13,258
Putnam 29,163
Randolph 29,997
Ripley 24,398
Rush 19,604
St. Joseph 241,617
Scott 20,422
Shelby 39,887
Spencer 19,361
Starke 21,997
Steuben 24,694
Sullivan 21,107
Switzerland 7,153
Tippecanoe 121,702
Tipton 16,819
Union 6,860
Vanderburgh 167,515
Vermillion 18,229
Vigo 112,385
Wabash 36,640
Warren 8,976
Warrick 41,474
Washington 21,932
Wayne 76,058
Wells 25,401
White 23,867
Whitley 26,215

IOWA

1980
Census 2,913,808

○ Rand McNally estimate
▲ Population of entire township or "town", including rural areas.
● Independent city. Population not included in county total.

CITIES

Ackley 1,900
Adair 883
Adel 2,846
Afton 985
Agency OTUM 657
Ainsworth 547
Akron 1,517
Albert City 818
Albia 4,184
Albion 739
Alden 953
Algona 6,289
Allerton 670
Allison 1,132
Alta 1,720
Alton 986
Altoona DES 5,764
Amana 600 ○
AMES AMES 45,775
Anamosa 4,958
Anita 1,153
Ankeny DES 15,429
Anthon 687
Aplington 1,027
Arcadia 454
Arlington 498
Armstrong 1,153
Arnolds Park 1,051
Ashton 441
Atlantic 7,789
Audubon 2,841
Aurelia 1,143
Avoca 1,650
Avon Lake DES 600 ○
Badger 653
Bancroft 1,082
Batavia 525
Battle Creek 919
Baxter 951
Bayard 637
Beacon 530
Bedford 1,692
Belle Plaine 2,903
Bellevue 2,450
Belmond 2,505
Bennett 458
Bettendorf D-RI-M 27,381
Blairstown 695
Bloomfield 2,849
Blue Grass D-RI-M 1,377
Bonaparte 489
Bondurant DES 1,283
Boone 12,602
Boyden 708
Breda 502
Brighton 804
Britt 2,185
Brooklyn 1,509
Buffalo D-RI-M 1,569
Buffalo Center 1,233
BURLINGTON BUR 29,529
Burt 689
Bussey 579
Calamus 452
Callender 446
Calmar 1,053
Camanche CLNT 4,725
Cambridge 732
Capitol Heights DES 815 ○
Carlisle DES 3,073
Carroll 9,705
Carson 716
Carter Lake OMA- 3,438
Cascade 1,912
Casey 473
Cedar Falls WATL 36,322
CEDAR RAPIDS CEDR 110,243
Center Point 1,591
Centerville 6,558
Central City 1,067
Chariton 4,987
Charles City 8,778
Charlotte 442
Charter Oak 615
Cherokee 7,004
Churdan 540
Cincinnati 598
Clarence 1,001
Clarinda 5,458
Clarion 3,060
Clarksville 1,424
Clear Lake MSCY 7,458
Clermont 602
CLINTON CLNT 32,828
Clive DES 6,064
Coggon 639
Colesburg 463
Colfax 2,234
Collins 451
Colo 808
Columbus Junction 1,429
Conrad 1,133
Coon Rapids 1,448
Coralville IACY 7,687
Corning 1,939
Correctionville 935
Corwith 480
Corydon 1,818
Council Bluffs OMA- 56,449
Crescent 547
Cresco 3,860
Creston 8,429
Dakota City 1,072
Dallas 451
Dallas Center 1,360
Danbury 492
Danville BUR 994
DAVENPORT D-RI-M 103,264
Dayton 941
Decorah 7,991
Delhi 511
Delmar 633
Delta 482
Denison 6,675
Denver WATL 1,647
DES MOINES DES 191,003
De Soto 1,035
De Witt 4,512
Dexter 678
Dike 987
Donnellson 972
Doon 537
Dow City 616
Dows 771
DUBUQUE DUB 62,321
Dumont 815
Duncombe 504
Dunkerton 718
Dunlap 1,374
Durant 1,583
Dyersville 3,825
Dysart 1,355
Eagle Grove 4,324
Earlham 1,140
Earling 520
Earlville 844
Early 670
Eddyville 1,116
Edgewood 900
Eldon 1,255
Eldora 3,063
Eldridge D-RI-M 3,279
Elgin 702
Elkader 1,688
Elk Horn 746
Elliott 493
Ellsworth 480
Elma 714
Emerson 502
Emmetsburg 4,621
Epworth 1,380
Essex 1,001
Estherville 7,518
Evansdale WATL 4,798
Everly 796
Exira 978
Fairbank 980
Fairfax CEDR 683
Fairfield 9,428
Farley 1,287
Farmington 869
Farnhamville 461
Farragut 603
Fayette 1,515
Fonda 863
Fontanelle 805
Forest City 4,270
FORT DODGE FTDO 29,423
Fort Madison 13,520
Fredericksburg 1,075
Fremont 730
Fruitland 461
Garnavillo 723
Garner 2,908
Garwin 626
George 1,241
Gilbert AMES 805
Gilbertville WATL 740
Gilman 642
Gilmore City 626
Gladbrook 970
Glenwood 5,280
Glidden 1,076
Goldfield 789
Gowrie 1,089
Graettinger 923
Grand Junction 970
Grand Mound 674
Grandview 473
Granger 619
Greene 1,332
Greenfield 2,243
Greenfield Plaza DES 2,100 ○
Grimes DES 1,973
Grinnell 8,868
Griswold 1,176
Grundy Center 2,880
Guthrie Center 1,713
Guttenberg 2,428
Hamburg 1,597
Hampton 4,630
Harlan 5,357
Hartford 761
Hartley 1,700
Hawarden 2,722
Hawkeye 512
Hazleton 877
Hedrick 847
Hiawatha CEDR 4,825
Hills 547
Hinton 659
Holstein 1,477
Hopkinton 774
Hospers 655
Hubbard 852
Hudson WATL 2,267
Hull 1,714
Humboldt 4,794
Humeston 671
Huxley AMES 1,884
Ida Grove 2,285
Independence 6,392
Indianola DES 10,843
Inwood 755
IOWA CITY IACY 50,508
Iowa Falls 6,174
Ireton 588
Janesville WATL 840
Jefferson 4,854
Jesup 2,343
Jewell 1,145
Johnston DES 2,617
Kalona 1,862
Kanawha 756
Kellogg 654
Keokuk 13,536
Keosauqua 1,003
Keota 1,034
Keystone 618
Kingsley 1,209
Klemme 620
Knoxville 8,143
Lake City 2,006
Lake Mills 2,281
Lake Park 1,123
Lakeside 589
Lake View 1,291
Lakewood DES 900 ○
Lamoni 2,705
Lamont 554
Lansing 1,181
La Porte City WATL 2,324
Larchwood 701
Latimer 441
Laurens 1,606
Lawler 534
Lawton 447
Le Claire D-RI-M 2,899
Le Grand 921
Lehigh 654
Le Mars 8,276
Lenox 1,338
Leon 2,094
Letts 473
Lewis 497
Lime Springs 476
Lisbon CEDR 1,458
Little Rock 490
Livermore 490
Logan 1,540
Lohrville 521
Lone Tree 1,014
Long Grove 596
Lost Nation 524
Lovilia 637
Lovington DES 850 ○
Lowden 717
McGregor 945
Madrid 2,281
Malvern 1,244
Manchester 4,942
Manilla 1,020
Manly 1,496
Manning 1,609
Manson 1,924
Mapleton 1,495
Maquoketa 6,313
Marathon 442
Marcus 1,206
Marengo 2,308
Marion CEDR 19,474
Marquette 528
Marshalltown 26,938
MASON CITY MSCY 30,144
Massena 518
Maxwell 783
Maynard 561
Mechanicsville 1,166
Mediapolis 1,685
Melbourne 732
Melcher 953
Merrill 737
Middletown BUR 487
Milford 2,076
Milo 778
Milton 567
Missouri Valley 3,107
Mitchellville DES 1,530
Monona 1,530
Monroe 1,875
Montezuma 1,485
Monticello 3,641
Montrose 1,038
Moravia 706
Morning Sun 959
Moulton 762
Mount Ayr 1,938
Mount Pleasant 7,322
Mount Vernon CEDR 3,325
Moville 1,273
Murray 703
Muscatine 23,467
Mystic 665

○ Rand McNally estimate
▲ Population of entire township or "town", including rural areas.
● Independent city. Population not included in county total.

IOWA continued

Nashua . . . 1,846
Neola . . . 839
Nevada AMES . . . 5,912
New Albin . . . 609
Newell . . . 913
Newhall . . . 899
New Hampton . . . 3,940
New Hartford . . . 764
New London . . . 2,043
New Market . . . 554
New Sharon . . . 1,225
Newton . . . 15,292
New Virginia . . . 512
Nora Springs . . . 1,572
North Cedar WATL . . . 1,950 ○
North English . . . 990
North Liberty IACY . . . 2,046
Northwood . . . 2,193
Norwalk DES . . . 2,676
Norway . . . 633
Norwoodville DES . . . 1,400 ○
Oakland . . . 1,552
Oakville . . . 470
Ocheyedan . . . 599
Odebolt . . . 1,299
Oelwein . . . 7,564
Ogden . . . 1,953
Okoboji . . . 559
Olin . . . 735
Onawa . . . 3,283
Orange City . . . 4,588
Orleans . . . 546
Osage . . . 3,718
Osceola . . . 3,750
Oskaloosa . . . 10,989
Ossian . . . 829
Otho FTDO . . . 692
OTTUMWA
OTUM . . . 27,381
Oxford . . . 676
Oxford Junction . . . 600
Pacific Junction . . . 511
Palo CEDR . . . 529
Panora . . . 1,211
Parkersburg . . . 1,968
Paullina . . . 1,224
Pella . . . 8,349
Perry . . . 7,053
Peterson . . . 470
Plainfield . . . 469
Pleasant Hill DES . . . 3,493
Pleasant Valley
D-RI-M . . . 750 ○
Pleasantville . . . 1,531
Plymouth . . . 463
Pocahontas . . . 2,352
Polk City DES . . . 1,658
Pomeroy . . . 895
Postville . . . 1,475
Prairie City . . . 1,278
Preston . . . 1,120
Primghar . . . 1,050
Princeton . . . 965
Quasqueton . . . 599
Radcliffe . . . 593
Readlyn . . . 858
Redfield . . . 959
Red Oak . . . 6,810
Reinbeck . . . 1,808
Remsen . . . 1,592
Riceville . . . 919
Richland . . . 600
Ringsted . . . 557
Riverdale D-RI-M . . . 462
Riverside . . . 826
Robins CEDR . . . 726
Rockford . . . 1,012
Rock Rapids . . . 2,693
Rock Valley . . . 2,706
Rockwell . . . 1,039
Rockwell City . . . 2,276
Roland . . . 1,005
Rolfe . . . 796
Royal . . . 522
Rudd . . . 460
Russell . . . 593
Ruthven . . . 769
Sabula . . . 824
Sac City . . . 3,000
St. Ansgar . . . 1,100
St. Charles . . . 507
Salem . . . 463
Sanborn . . . 1,398
Saydel DES . . . 4,200 ○
Saylorville DES . . . 780 ○
Schleswig . . . 868
Scranton . . . 748
Sergeant Bluff
SXCY . . . 2,416
Seymour . . . 1,036
Sheffield . . . 1,224
Shelby . . . 665
Sheldon . . . 5,003
Shell Rock . . . 1,478
Shellsburg . . . 771
Shenandoah . . . 6,274
Sibley . . . 3,051
Sidney . . . 1,308
Sigourney . . . 2,330
Sioux Center . . . 4,588
SIOUX CITY
SXCY . . . 82,003
Sioux Rapids . . . 897
Slater AMES . . . 1,312
Sloan . . . 978
Solon CEDR . . . 969
Spencer . . . 11,726
Spirit Lake . . . 3,976
Springville . . . 1,165
Stacyville . . . 538
Stanhope . . . 492
Stanton . . . 747
Stanwood . . . 705
State Center . . . 1,292
Storm Lake . . . 8,814
Story City . . . 2,762
Stratford . . . 806
Strawberry Point . . . 1,463
Stuart . . . 1,650
Sully . . . 828
Sumner . . . 2,335
Sutherland . . . 897
Swea City . . . 813
Swisher CEDR . . . 654
Tabor . . . 1,088
Tama . . . 2,968
Thompson . . . 668
Thornton . . . 442
Tipton . . . 3,055
Titonka . . . 607
Toledo . . . 2,445
Traer . . . 1,703
Treynor . . . 981
Tripoli . . . 1,280
Underwood . . . 448
Union . . . 515
University Heights
IACY . . . 1,069
University Park . . . 645
Urbana . . . 574
Urbandale DES . . . 17,869
Ute . . . 479
Vail . . . 490
Van Horne . . . 682
Van Meter . . . 747
Ventura MSCY . . . 614
Victor . . . 1,046
Villisca . . . 1,434
Vinton . . . 5,040
Walcott D-RI-M . . . 1,425
Walker . . . 733
Wall Lake . . . 892
Walnut . . . 897
Wapello . . . 2,011
Washburn WATL . . . 1,400 ○
Washington . . . 6,584
WATERLOO
WATL . . . 75,985
Waukee DES . . . 2,227
Waukon . . . 3,983
Waverly . . . 8,444
Wayland . . . 720
Webster City . . . 8,572
Wellman . . . 1,125
Wellsburg . . . 761
Wesley . . . 598
West Bend . . . 941
West Branch IACY . . . 1,867
West Burlington
BUR . . . 3,371
West Des Moines
DES . . . 21,894
West Liberty . . . 2,723
West Point . . . 1,133
West Union . . . 2,783
What Cheer . . . 803
Wheatland . . . 840
Whiting . . . 734
Whittemore . . . 647
Williamsburg . . . 2,033
Wilton . . . 2,502
Windsor Heights
DES . . . 5,474
Winfield . . . 1,042
Winterset . . . 4,021
Winthrop . . . 767
Woodbine . . . 1,463
Woodward . . . 1,212
Wyoming . . . 702
Zearing . . . 630

COUNTIES

Adair . . . 9,509
Adams . . . 5,731
Allamakee . . . 15,108
Appanoose . . . 15,511
Audubon . . . 8,559
Benton . . . 23,649
Black Hawk . . . 137,961
Boone . . . 26,184
Bremer . . . 24,820
Buchanan . . . 22,900
Buena Vista . . . 20,774
Butler . . . 17,668
Calhoun . . . 13,542
Carroll . . . 22,951
Cass . . . 16,932
Cedar . . . 18,635
Cerro Gordo . . . 48,458
Cherokee . . . 16,238
Chickasaw . . . 15,437
Clarke . . . 8,612
Clay . . . 19,576
Clayton . . . 21,098
Clinton . . . 57,122
Crawford . . . 18,935
Dallas . . . 29,513
Davis . . . 9,104
Decatur . . . 9,794
Delaware . . . 18,933
Des Moines . . . 46,203
Dickinson . . . 15,629
Dubuque . . . 93,745
Emmet . . . 13,336
Fayette . . . 25,488
Floyd . . . 19,597
Franklin . . . 13,036
Fremont . . . 9,401
Greene . . . 12,119
Grundy . . . 14,366
Guthrie . . . 11,983
Hamilton . . . 17,862
Hancock . . . 13,833
Hardin . . . 21,776
Harrison . . . 16,348
Henry . . . 18,890
Howard . . . 11,114
Humboldt . . . 12,246
Ida . . . 8,908
Iowa . . . 15,429
Jackson . . . 22,503
Jasper . . . 36,425
Jefferson . . . 16,316
Johnson . . . 81,717
Jones . . . 20,401
Keokuk . . . 12,921
Kossuth . . . 21,891
Lee . . . 43,106
Linn . . . 169,775
Louisa . . . 12,055
Lucas . . . 10,313
Lyon . . . 12,896
Madison . . . 12,597
Mahaska . . . 22,867
Marion . . . 29,669
Marshall . . . 41,652
Mills . . . 13,406
Mitchell . . . 12,329
Monona . . . 11,692
Monroe . . . 9,209
Montgomery . . . 13,413
Muscatine . . . 40,436
O'Brien . . . 16,972
Osceola . . . 8,371
Page . . . 19,063
Palo Alto . . . 12,721
Plymouth . . . 24,743
Pocahontas . . . 11,369
Polk . . . 303,170
Pottawattamie . . . 86,561
Poweshiek . . . 19,306
Ringgold . . . 6,112
Sac . . . 14,118
Scott . . . 160,022
Shelby . . . 15,043
Sioux . . . 30,813
Story . . . 72,326
Tama . . . 19,533
Taylor . . . 8,353
Union . . . 13,858
Van Buren . . . 8,626
Wapello . . . 40,241
Warren . . . 34,878
Washington . . . 20,141
Wayne . . . 8,199
Webster . . . 45,953
Winnebago . . . 13,010
Winneshiek . . . 21,876
Woodbury . . . 100,884
Worth . . . 9,075
Wright . . . 16,319

KANSAS

1980
Census . . . 2,364,236

CITIES

Abilene . . . 6,572
Alma . . . 925
Almena . . . 517
Altamont . . . 1,054
Altoona . . . 564
Americus . . . 915
Andale . . . 538
Andover WICH . . . 2,801
Anthony . . . 2,661
Arcadia . . . 460
Argonia . . . 587
Arkansas City . . . 13,201
Arlington . . . 631
Arma . . . 1,676
Ashland . . . 1,096
Atchison . . . 11,407
Attica . . . 730
Atwood . . . 1,665
Auburn . . . 890
Augusta WICH . . . 6,968
Axtell . . . 470
Baldwin City . . . 2,829
Basehor K.C. . . . 1,483
Baxter Springs . . . 4,730
Bel Aire WICH . . . 2,395
Belle Plaine WICH . . . 1,706
Belleville . . . 2,805
Beloit . . . 4,367
Bennington . . . 579
Benton . . . 609
Bird City . . . 546
Blue Rapids . . . 1,280
Bonner Springs
K.C. . . . 6,266

○ Rand McNally estimate
▲ Population of entire township or "town", including rural areas.
● Independent city. Population not included in county total.

Place	Population
Bucklin	786
Buhler	1,188
Burden	518
Burlingame	1,239
Burlington	2,901
Burrton	976
Caldwell	1,401
Callahan WICH	900 ○
Caney	2,284
Canton	926
Carbondale TOP	1,518
Cawker City	640
Cedar Vale	848
Centralia	486
Chanute	10,506
Chapman	1,255
Chase	753
Cheney	1,404
Cherokee	775
Cherryvale	2,769
Chetopa	1,751
Cimarron	1,491
Claflin	764
Clay Center	4,948
Clearwater	1,684
Clifton	695
Clyde	909
Coffeyville	15,185
Colby	5,544
Coldwater	989
Colony	474
Columbus	3,426
Colwich WICH	935
Concordia	6,847
Conway Springs	1,313
Cottonwood Falls	954
Council Grove	2,381
Cunningham	540
Dearing	475
Deerfield	538
Delphos	570
Derby WICH	9,786
De Soto	2,061
Dighton	1,390
Dodge City	18,001
Douglass	1,450
Downs	1,324
Eastborough WICH	854
Easton	460
Edgerton	1,214
Edna	537
Edwardsville K.C.	3,364
Effingham	634
El Dorado	10,510
Elkhart	2,243
Ellinwood	2,508
Ellis	2,062
Ellsworth	2,465
Elwood ST.JO	1,275
Emporia	25,287
Enterprise	839
Erie	1,415
Eskridge	603
Eudora	2,934
Eureka	3,425
Fairway K.C.	4,619
Florence	729
Fort Scott	8,893
Fowler	592
Frankfort	1,038
Fredonia	3,047
Frontenac	2,586
Galena JOP	3,587
Galva	651
Garden City	18,256
Garden Plain	775
Gardner K.C.	2,392
Garnett	3,310
Gas	543
Geneseo	496
Girard	2,888
Glasco	710
Glen Elder	491
Goddard WICH	1,427
Goodland	5,708
Great Bend	16,608
Greenleaf	462
Greensburg	1,885
Halstead	1,994
Hanover	802
Harper	1,823
Hartford	551
Haven	1,125
Haviland	770
Hays	16,301
Haysville WICH	8,006
Herington	2,930
Hesston	3,013
Hiawatha	3,702
Highland	954
Hill City	2,028
Hillsboro	2,717
Hoisington	3,678
Holcomb	816
Holton	3,132
Holyrood	567
Hope	468
Horton	2,130
Howard	965
Hoxie	1,462
Hoyt	536
Hugoton	3,165
Humboldt	2,230
HUTCHINSON HUCH	40,284
Independence	10,598
Inman	947
Iola	6,938
Jamestown	440
Jetmore	862
Jewell	589
Johnson	1,244
Junction City	19,305
Kanopolis	729
KANSAS CITY K.C.	161,148
Kensington	681
Kingman	3,563
Kinsley	2,074
Kiowa	1,409
La Crosse	1,618
La Cygne	1,025
La Harpe	687
Lakin	1,823
Lansing LEAV	5,307
Larned	4,811
LAWRENCE LAWR	52,738
LEAVENWORTH LEAV	33,656
Leawood K.C.	13,360
Lebanon	440
Lebo	966
Lecompton	576
Lenexa K.C.	18,639
Lenora	444
Leon	667
Leoti	1,869
Le Roy	701
Lewis	551
Liberal	14,911
Lincoln	1,599
Lindsborg	3,155
Linn	483
Little River	529
Logan	720
Louisburg	1,744
Lucas	524
Lyndon	1,132
Lyons	4,134
McCune	528
Macksville	546
McLouth	700
McPherson	11,753
Madison	1,099
Maize WICH	1,294
Manhattan	32,644
Mankato	1,205
Marion	1,951
Marquette	639
Marysville	3,670
Meade	1,777
Medicine Lodge	2,384
Melvern	481
Meriden TOP	707
Merriam K.C.	10,794
Midland Park WICH	1,350 ○
Milford	465
Miltonvale	588
Minneapolis	2,075
Minneola	712
Mission K.C.	8,643
Mission Hills K.C.	3,904
Moline	553
Montezuma	730
Moran	643
Mound City	755
Moundridge	1,453
Mount Hope	791
Mulberry	647
Mulvane WICH	4,254
Natoma	515
Neodesha	3,414
Ness City	1,769
Newton	16,332
Nickerson	1,292
Norton	3,400
Nortonville	692
Norwich	476
Oaklawn WICH	4,200 ○
Oakley	2,343
Oberlin	2,387
Ogden	1,804
Olathe K.C.	37,258
Olpe	477
Onaga	752
Osage City	2,667
Osawatomie	4,459
Osborne	2,120
Oskaloosa	1,092
Oswego	2,218
Ottawa	11,016
Overbrook	930
Overland Park K.C.	81,784
Oxford	1,125
Ozawkie	472
Paola	4,557
Park City WICH	4,056
Parsons	12,898
Peabody	1,474
Perry	907
Phillipsburg	3,229
Piper K.C.	730 ○
Pittsburg	18,770
Plains	1,044
Plainville	2,458
Pleasanton	1,303
Pomona	868
Potwin	563
Prairie Village K.C.	24,657
Pratt	6,885
Pretty Prairie	655
Protection	684
Quinter	951
Ransom	448
Richmond	510
Riley	779
Riverton JOP	550 ○
Roeland Park K.C.	7,962
Rose Hill WICH	1,557
Rossville	1,045
Russell	5,427
Sabetha	2,286
St. Francis	1,610
St. John	1,501
St. Marys	1,598
St. Paul	746
SALINA SLN	41,843
Satanta	1,117
Scammon	501
Scandia	480
Scott City	4,154
Scranton	664
Sedan	1,579
Sedgwick	1,471
Seneca	2,389
Severy	447
Sharon Springs	982
Shawnee K.C.	29,653
Silver Lake TOP	1,350
Smith Center	2,240
Solomon	1,018
South Hutchinson HUCH	2,226
Spearville	693
Spring Hill	2,005
Stafford	1,425
Sterling	2,312
Stockton	1,825
Strong City	675
Sublette	1,293
Sunset Park WICH	1,050 ○
Syracuse	1,654
Thayer	517
Tonganoxie	1,864
TOPEKA TOP	115,266
Toronto	466
Towanda	1,332
Tribune	955
Troy	1,240
Turon	481
Udall	891
Ulysses	4,653
Valley Center WICH	3,300
Valley Falls	1,189
Victoria	1,328
WaKeeney	2,388
Wakefield	803
Wamego	3,159
Washington	1,488
Waterville	694
Wathena ST.JO	1,418
Waverly	671
Weir	705
Wellington	8,212
Wellsville	1,612
Westmoreland	598
Westwood K.C.	1,783
White City	534
Whitewater	751
WICHITA WICH	279,835
Wilson	978
Winchester	570
Winfield	10,736
Yates Center	1,998

COUNTIES

County	Population
Allen	15,654
Anderson	8,749
Atchison	18,397
Barber	6,548
Barton	31,343
Bourbon	15,969
Brown	11,955
Butler	44,782
Chase	3,309
Chautauqua	5,016
Cherokee	22,304
Cheyenne	3,678
Clark	2,599
Clay	9,802
Cloud	12,494
Coffey	9,370
Comanche	2,554
Cowley	36,824
Crawford	37,916
Decatur	4,509
Dickinson	20,175
Doniphan	9,268
Douglas	67,640
Edwards	4,271
Elk	3,918
Ellis	26,098
Ellsworth	6,640
Finney	23,825
Ford	24,315
Franklin	22,062
Geary	29,852
Gove	3,726
Graham	3,995
Grant	6,977
Gray	5,138

○ Rand McNally estimate
▲ Population of entire township or "town", including rural areas.
● Independent city. Population not included in county total.

KANSAS continued

Place	Population
Greeley	1,845
Greenwood	8,764
Hamilton	2,514
Harper	7,778
Harvey	30,531
Haskell	3,814
Hodgeman	2,269
Jackson	11,644
Jefferson	15,207
Jewell	5,241
Johnson	270,269
Kearny	3,435
Kingman	8,960
Kiowa	4,046
Labette	25,682
Lane	2,472
Leavenworth	54,809
Lincoln	4,145
Linn	8,234
Logan	3,478
Lyon	35,108
McPherson	26,855
Marion	13,522
Marshall	12,787
Meade	4,788
Miami	21,618
Mitchell	8,117
Montgomery	42,281
Morris	6,419
Morton	3,454
Nemaha	11,211
Neosho	18,967
Ness	4,498
Norton	6,689
Osage	15,319
Osborne	5,959
Ottawa	5,971
Pawnee	8,065
Phillips	7,406
Pottawatomie	14,782
Pratt	10,275
Rawlins	4,105
Reno	64,983
Republic	7,569
Rice	11,900
Riley	63,505
Rooks	7,006
Rush	4,516
Russell	8,868
Saline	48,905
Scott	5,782
Sedgwick	367,088
Seward	17,071
Shawnee	154,916
Sheridan	3,544
Sherman	7,759
Smith	5,947
Stafford	5,694
Stanton	2,339
Stevens	4,736
Sumner	24,928
Thomas	8,451
Trego	4,165
Wabaunsee	6,867
Wallace	2,045
Washington	8,543
Wichita	3,041
Wilson	12,128
Woodson	4,600
Wyandotte	172,335

KENTUCKY

1980
Census 3,660,257

CITIES

Place	Population
Adairville	1,105
Albany	2,083
Alexandria CIN-	4,735
Anchorage LOU	1,726
Arjay	650 ○
Arlington	511
Artemus	500 ○
Ashland HNTG-	27,064
Auburn	1,467
Augusta	1,455
Auxier	900 ○
Barbourville	3,333
Bardstown	6,155
Bardwell	988
Barlow	746
Beattyville	1,068
Beauty	450 ○
Beaver Dam	3,185
Bedford	835
Belfry	900 ○
Bellevue CIN-	7,678
Benham	936
Benton	3,700
Berea	8,226
Betsy Layne	900 ○
Bloomfield	954
BOWLING GREEN BOWLG	40,450
Brandenburg	1,831
Brodhead	686
Brooks LOU	1,344
Brooksville	680
Brownsville	674
Buechel LOU	6,709
Bulan	440 ○
Burgin	1,008
Burkesville	2,051
Burlington CIN-	550 ○
Burnside	775
Butler	663
Cadiz	1,661
Calhoun	1,080
Calvert City PAD	2,388
Campbellsburg	714
Campbellsville	8,715
Campton	486
Caneyville	642
Cannonsburg	600 ○
Carlisle	1,757
Carrollton	3,967
Catlettsburg HNTG-	3,005
Cave City	2,098
Cawood	800 ○
Cecilia	500 ○
Centertown	462
Central City	5,214
Clarkson	666
Clay	1,356
Clay City	1,276
Clearfield	1,250
Clinton	1,720
Cloverport	1,585
Cold Spring CIN-	2,117
Columbia	3,710
Combs	700 ○
Corbin	8,075
Corydon	874
Covington CIN-	49,563
Crab Orchard	843
Crescent Springs CIN-	1,951
Crestwood LOU	531
Crittenden	597
Crofton	823
Cromona	700 ○
Cumberland	3,712
Cynthiana	5,881
Danville	12,942
Dayton CIN-	6,979
Dixon	533
Dorton	600 ○
Drakesboro	798
Drift	600 ○
Dry Ridge	1,250
Earlington	2,011
East Bernstadt	700 ○
Eddyville	1,949
Edgewood CIN-	7,230
Edmonton	1,401
Elizabethtown	15,380
Elkhorn City	1,446
Elkton	1,815
Elsmere CIN-	7,203
Eminence	2,260
Erlanger CIN-	14,433
Evarts	1,234
Fairdale LOU	7,315
Falmouth	2,482
Ferguson	1,009
Fern Creek LOU	16,866
Flat Lick	700 ○
Flatwoods HNTG-	8,354
Flemingsburg	2,835
Florence CIN-	15,586
Fordsville	561
Fort Mitchell CIN-	7,297
Fort Thomas CIN-	16,012
Fort Wright CIN-	4,481
Fourmile	500 ○
Frankfort	25,973
Franklin	7,738
Fredonia	535
Frenchburg	550
Fullerton PTSM	500 ○
Fulton	3,137
Gamaliel	456
Garrison	650 ○
Georgetown LEX	10,972
Glasgow	12,958
Grahn	500 ○
Grapevine	900 ○
Gray	750 ○
Grayson HNTG-	3,423
Greensburg	2,377
Greenup HNTG-	1,386
Greenville	4,631
Guthrie	1,361
Hanson	485
Hardin	545
Hardinsburg	2,211
Harlan	3,024
Harrodsburg	7,265
Hartford	2,512
Hawesville	1,036
Hazard	5,371
Hazel	465
Hebron CIN-	500 ○
Heidrick	600 ○
Henderson EV	24,834
Hickman	2,894
Highview LOU	13,286
Hillview LOU	5,196
Hima	700 ○
Hindman	876
Hitchins	700 ○
Hodgenville	2,531
HOPKINSVILLE HPKNV	27,318
Horse Cave	2,045
Hyden	488
Independence CIN-	7,998
Irvine	2,889
Irvington	1,409
Island	532
Jackson	2,651
Jamestown	1,441
Jeffersontown LOU	15,795
Jeffersonville	1,528
Jenkins	3,271
Junction City	2,045
Kenvir	950 ○
Kitts	500 ○
Kuttawa	560
La Center	1,044
La Grange	2,971
Lakeside Park CIN-	3,038
Lancaster	3,365
Langley	600 ○
Lawrenceburg	5,167
Lebanon	6,590
Lebanon Junction	1,581
Leitchfield	4,533
Lejunior	600 ○
Lewisburg	972
Lewisport	1,832
LEXINGTON LEX	204,165
Liberty	2,206
Livermore	1,672
London	4,002
Lone Oak PAD	443
Long View	650 ○
Lookout	550 ○
Loretto	954
Lothair	600 ○
Louisa	1,832
LOUISVILLE LOU	298,840
Lovely	700 ○
Loyall	1,210
Ludlow CIN-	4,959
Lynch	1,614
Lyndon LOU	1,553
McHenry	582
McKee	759
McRoberts	1,106
McVeigh	800 ○
Madisonville	16,979
Magnolia	450 ○
Manchester	1,838
Maple Mount	500 ○
Marion	3,392
Marshes Siding	500 ○
Martin	827
Maryville LOU	6,000 ○
Mayfield	10,705
Maysville	7,983
Melbourne CIN-	628
Melvin	700 ○
Middlesboro	12,251
Midway LEX	1,445
Millersburg	987
Milton	718
Monticello	5,677
Morehead	7,789
Morganfield	3,781
Morgantown	2,000
Mortons Gap	1,201
Mount Sterling	5,820
Mount Vernon	2,334
Mount Washington LOU	3,997
Muldraugh	1,752
Munfordville	1,783
Murray	14,248
Nazareth	700 ○
New Castle	832
New Haven	926
Newport CIN-	21,587
Nicholasville LEX	10,319
North Corbin	1,000 ○
North Middletown	637
Nortonville	1,336
Oak Grove	2,088
Okolona LOU	20,039
Olive Hill	2,539
Oneida	600 ○
OWENSBORO OWNS	54,450
Owenton	1,341
Owingsville	1,419
PADUCAH PAD	29,315
Paintsville	3,815
Paris	7,935
Park City	614
Park Hills CIN-	3,500
Pembroke	636
Perryville	841
Pewee Valley LOU	982
Phelps	1,120 ○
Pikeville	4,756
Pine Knot	1,389
Pineville	2,599
Pittsburg	620 ○
Pleasure Ridge Park LOU	27,332
Pleasureville	837
Prestonsburg	4,011
Princeton	7,073
Prospect LOU	1,981
Providence	4,434

○ Rand McNally estimate
▲ Population of entire township or "town", including rural areas.
● Independent city. Population not included in county total.

Raceland HNTG- 1,970
Radcliff 14,519
Ravenna 793
Revelo 550 ○
Richmond 21,705
Rineyville 450 ○
Robards 500 ○
Rockport 511
Russell HNTG- 3,824
Russell Springs 1,831
Russellville 7,520
Sacramento 538
St. Matthews LOU 13,519
Salem 833
Salyersville 1,352
Sandy Hook 627
Science Hill 655
Scottsville 4,278
Sebree 1,516
Shelbiana 500 ○
Shelby City 700 ○
Shelbyville 5,329
Shepherdsville LOU 4,454
Shively LOU 16,819
Silver Grove CIN- 1,260
Simpsonville 642
Smithland 512
Smiths Grove 767
Somerset 10,649
Southgate CIN- 2,833
South Portsmouth PTSM 550 ○
South Williamson 1,016
Spottsville 500 ○
Springfield 3,179
Staffordsville 700 ○
Stamping Ground 562
Stanford 2,764
Stanton 2,691
Stearns 1,557
Sturgis 2,293
Summersville 450 ○
Symsonia 550 ○
Tateville 725 ○
Taylor Mill CIN- 4,509
Taylorsville 801
Thealka 500 ○
Toler 500 ○
Tollesboro 808
Tompkinsville 4,366
Trenton 465
Union CIN- 601
Uniontown 1,169
Upton 731
Valley Station LOU 20,000 ○
Vanceburg 1,939
Van Lear 2,035
Veachland 700 ○
Verda 1,132
Versailles LEX 6,427
Vicco 456
Vine Grove 3,583
Walton CIN- 1,651
Warfield 450
Warsaw 1,328
Washington 624
Wayland 601
Weeksbury 700 ○
West Liberty 1,381
West Point 1,339
West Van Lear 900 ○
Wheelwright 865
White Plains 859
Whitesburg 1,525
Whitesville 788
Whitley City 1,683
Wickliffe 1,034
Williamsburg 5,560
Williamstown 2,502
Wilmore LEX 3,787
Winchester 15,216
Wingo 606
Woodbine 500 ○
Woodlawn PAD 1,200 ○
Worthington HNTG- 1,948

COUNTIES

Adair 15,233
Allen 14,128
Anderson 12,567
Ballard 8,798
Barren 34,009
Bath 10,025
Bell 34,330
Boone 45,842
Bourbon 19,405
Boyd 55,513
Boyle 25,066
Bracken 7,738
Breathitt 17,004
Breckinridge 16,861
Bullitt 43,346
Butler 11,064
Caldwell 13,473
Calloway 30,031
Campbell 83,317
Carlisle 5,487
Carroll 9,270
Carter 25,060
Casey 14,818
Christian 66,878
Clark 28,322
Clay 22,752
Clinton 9,321
Crittenden 9,207
Cumberland 7,289
Daviess 85,949
Edmonson 9,962
Elliott 6,908
Estill 14,495
Fayette 204,165
Fleming 12,323
Floyd 48,764
Franklin 41,830
Fulton 8,971
Gallatin 4,842
Garrard 10,853
Grant 13,308
Graves 34,049
Grayson 20,854
Green 11,043
Greenup 39,132
Hancock 7,742
Hardin 88,917
Harlan 41,889
Harrison 15,166
Hart 15,402
Henderson 40,849
Henry 12,740
Hickman 6,065
Hopkins 46,174
Jackson 11,996
Jefferson 684,565
Jessamine 26,065
Johnson 24,432
Kenton 137,058
Knott 17,940
Knox 30,239
Larue 11,922
Laurel 38,982
Lawrence 14,121
Lee 7,754
Leslie 14,882
Letcher 30,687
Lewis 14,545
Lincoln 19,053
Livingston 9,219
Logan 24,138
Lyon 6,490
McCracken 61,310
McCreary 15,634
McLean 10,090
Madison 53,352
Magoffin 13,515
Marion 17,910
Marshall 25,637
Martin 13,925
Mason 17,765
Meade 22,854
Menifee 5,117
Mercer 19,011
Metcalfe 9,484
Monroe 12,353
Montgomery 20,046
Morgan 12,103
Muhlenberg 32,238
Nelson 27,584
Nicholas 7,157
Ohio 21,765
Oldham 27,795
Owen 8,924
Owsley 5,709
Pendleton 10,989
Perry 33,763
Pike 81,123
Powell 11,101
Pulaski 45,803
Robertson 2,265
Rockcastle 13,973
Rowan 19,049
Russell 13,708
Scott 21,813
Shelby 23,328
Simpson 14,673
Spencer 5,929
Taylor 21,178
Todd 11,874
Trigg 9,384
Trimble 6,253
Union 17,821
Warren 71,828
Washington 10,764
Wayne 17,022
Webster 14,832
Whitley 33,396
Wolfe 6,698
Woodford 17,778

LOUISIANA

1980 Census 4,206,312

CITIES

Abbeville 12,391
Abita Springs N.O. 1,072
Addis B.R. 1,320
Albany 857
ALEXANDRIA ALEX 51,565
Ama N.O. 875 ○
Amelia MRGCY 3,617
Amite 4,301
Anacoco 820
Anandale ALEX 2,000 ○
Arabi N.O. 10,248
Arcadia 3,403
Arlington B.R. 850 ○
Arnaudville 1,679
Avery Island 575 ○
Avondale N.O. 6,699
Baker B.R. 12,865
Baldwin 2,644
Ball ALEX 3,405
Barataria 1,123
Basile 2,635
Bastrop 15,527
BATON ROUGE B.R. 219,419
Bawcomville MONR 2,500 ○
Bayou Cane HOMA 15,723
Bayou Goula 800 ○
Belle Chasse N.O. 5,412
Belle Rose 700 ○
Benton 1,864
Bernice 1,956
Berwick 4,466
Blanchard SHRE 1,128
Bogalusa 16,976
Bonfouca N.O. 480 ○
Bonita 503
Boothville 600 ○
Bossier City SHRE 50,817
Bourg HOMA 2,073
Boutte 1,200 ○
Boyce 1,198
Breaux Bridge LAF 5,922
Bridge City N.O. 2,500 ○
Broussard LAF 2,923
Brownfields B.R. 1,800 ○
Brownsville MONR 3,000 ○
Brusly B.R. 1,762
Bunkie 5,364
Buras 2,600 ○
Cameron 1,736
Campti 1,069
Carencro LAF 3,712
Carville 1,037
Centerville 500 ○
Chalmette N.O. 33,847
Charenton 950 ○
Chatham 714
Chauvin 3,338
Cheneyville 865
Choudrant 809
Church Point 4,599
Claiborne MONR 2,000 ○
Clarence 612
Clarks 931
Clayton 1,204
Clinton 1,919
Colfax 1,680
Columbia 687
Converse 449
Cooper Road SHRE 10,000 ○
Cottonport 1,911
Cotton Valley 1,445
Coushatta 2,084
Covington N.O. 7,892
Crowley 16,036
Crown Point 950 ○
Cullen 1,869
Cut Off 5,049
Delcambre 2,216
Delhi 3,290
Denham Springs B.R. 8,563
De Quincy 3,966
De Ridder 11,057
Des Allemands 2,920
Destrehan N.O. 2,382
Dodson 469
Donaldsonville 7,901
Doyline 801
Dry Prong 526
Dubach 1,161
Duson LAF 1,253
Elizabeth 454
Elton 1,450
Empire 630 ○
Epps 672
Erath 2,133
Erwinville 475 ○
Estherwood 691
Eunice 12,479
Farmerville 3,768
Fenton 491
Ferriday 4,472
Florien 964
Fordoche 676
Forest Glen 600 ○
Forest Hill 494
Forest Park MONR 1,500 ○
Fountain Place B.R. 9,200 ○
Franklin 9,584
Franklinton 4,119
French Settlement 761
Galliano 5,159
Garyville 2,856
Gibsland 1,354
Gilbert 800
Glenmora 1,479
Golden Meadow 2,282
Goldonna 526
Gonzales B.R. 7,287

○ Rand McNally estimate
▲ Population of entire township or "town", including rural areas.
● Independent city. Population not included in county total.

LOUISIANA continued

Good Pine 900 ○
Grambling 4,226
Gramercy 3,211
Grand Caillou 1,400 ○
Grand Coteau LAF 1,165
Grand Ecore 450 ○
Grand Isle 1,982
Gray 4,000 ○
Grayson 564
Greensburg 662
Greenwood SHRE 1,043
Gretna N.O. 20,615
Grosse Tete 749
Gueydan 1,695
Hackberry 800 ○
Hahnville N.O. 2,947
Hammond 15,043
Harahan N.O. 11,384
Harrisonburg 610
Harvey N.O. 15,000 ○
Haughton SHRE 1,510
Hayes 830 ○
Haynesville 3,454
Henderson 1,560
Hessmer 743
Hineston 500 ○
Hodge 708
Homer 4,307
Hornbeck 470
Hosston 480
HOUMA HOMA 32,602
Independence 1,684
Inniswold B.R. 1,800 ○
Iota 1,326
Iowa 2,437
Jackson 3,133
Jeanerette 6,511
Jefferson N.O. 15,550
Jena 4,375
Jennings 12,401
Jonesboro 5,061
Jonesville 2,828
Joyce 900 ○
Junction City 727
Kaplan 5,016
Kennedy Heights N.O. 2,000 ○
Kenner N.O. 66,382
Kentwood 2,667
Killian 611
Killona 600 ○
Kinder 2,603
Kraemer 500 ○
Krotz Springs 1,374
Lacombe N.O. 5,146
LAFAYETTE LAF 81,961
Lafayette Southwest LAF 5,500 ○
Lafitte 1,312
Lafourche 600 ○
Lagonda MRGCY 5,805
Lake Arthur 3,615
LAKE CHARLES LKCH 75,226
Lake Providence 6,361
La Place 16,112
Larose 5,234
Lawtell 1,014
Lecompte 1,661
Leesville 9,054
Leonville 1,143
Libuse ALEX 700 ○
Live Oak Manor N.O. 1,500 ○
Livingston 1,260
Livonia 980
Lockport 2,424
Logansport 1,565
Loreauville 860
Lucy 450 ○
Luling N.O. 4,006
Lutcher 4,730
Madisonville N.O. 799
Mamou 3,194
Mandeville N.O. 6,076
Mangham 867
Mansfield 6,485
Mansura 2,074
Many 3,988
Maringouin 1,291
Marion 989
Marksville 5,113
Marrero N.O. 36,548
Martin 584
Mathews 900 ○
Maurice LAF 478
Melville 1,764
Meraux N.O. 4,100 ○
Mermentau 771
Mer Rouge 802
Merryville 1,286
Metairie N.O. 164,160
Mimosa Park N.O. 3,737
Minden 15,084
MONROE MONR 57,597
Montegut 800 ○
Montgomery 843
Montz 500 ○
Mooringsport SHRE 911
Moreauville 853
MORGAN CITY MRGCY 16,114
Morganza 846
Morrow 460 ○
Morse 835
Moss Bluff LKCH 7,004
Napoleonville 829
Natalbany 700 ○
Natchitoches 16,664
Newellton 1,726
NEW IBERIA NWIB 32,766
Newllano 2,213
NEW ORLEANS N.O. 557,927
New Roads 3,924
New Sarpy N.O. 2,249
Norco N.O. 4,416
North Merrydale B.R. 3,500 ○
Oakdale 7,155
Oak Grove 2,214
Oberlin 1,764
Oil City 1,323
Olla 1,603
Opelousas 18,903
Paincourtville 2,004
Paradis 800 ○
Parks 545
Patterson MRGCY 4,693
Paulina 980 ○
Pearl River N.O. 1,693
Pierre Part 3,153
Pine Prairie 734
Pineville ALEX 12,034
Pitkin 750 ○
Plain Dealing 1,213
Plaquemine 7,521
Pointe a la Hache 600 ○
Ponchatoula 5,469
Port Allen B.R. 6,114
Port Barre 2,625
Port Sulphur 3,318
Port Vincent B.R. 450
Provencal 695
Raceland 6,302
Rayne 9,066
Rayville 4,610
Reddell 550 ○
Red Oaks B.R. 2,000 ○
Reserve 7,288
Ringgold 1,655
River Ridge N.O. 17,146
Roanoke 600 ○
Roseland 1,346
Rosepine 953
Ruston 20,585
St. Bernard 720 ○
St. Francisville 1,471
St. Joseph 1,687
St. Martinville 7,965
St. Rose N.O. 2,800 ○
Samtown ALEX 4,125 ○
Sarepta 831
Schriever 500 ○
Scotlandville B.R. 15,113
Scott LAF 2,239
Seymourville 2,891
SHREVEPORT SHRE 205,820
Sicily Island 691
Siegle MONR 1,400 ○
Simmesport 2,293
Simpson 534
Simsboro 553
Slaughter B.R. 729
Slidell N.O. 26,718
Sorrento 1,197
South Mansfield 1,463
Springhill 6,516
Starks 780 ○
Sterlington MONR 1,400
Stonewall 1,175
Sulphur LKCH 19,709
Sunset LAF 2,300
Swartz MONR 450 ○
Tallulah 11,634
Tangipahoa 493
Thibodaux 15,810
Tickfaw 571
Tioga ALEX 1,200 ○
Triumph 1,600 ○
Trout 500 ○
Tullos 776
Union 600 ○
Urania 849
Vacherie 2,169
Vidalia NCHZ 5,936
Vienna 519
Ville Platte 9,201
Vinton 3,631
Violet N.O. 6,000 ○
Vivian 4,146
Walker B.R. 2,957
Washington 1,266
Waterproof 1,339
Welcome 450 ○
Welsh 3,515
Westlake LKCH 5,246
West Monroe MONR 14,993
Westwego N.O. 12,663
White Castle 2,160
Willow Glen 500 ○
Wilson 656
Winnfield 7,311
Winnsboro 5,921
Wisner 1,424
Youngsville LAF 1,053
Zachary B.R. 7,297
Zwolle 2,602

PARISHES

Acadia 56,427
Allen 21,390
Ascension 50,068
Assumption 22,084
Avoyelles 41,393
Beauregard 29,692
Bienville 16,387
Bossier 80,721
Caddo 252,358
Calcasieu 167,223
Caldwell 10,761
Cameron 9,336
Catahoula 12,287
Claiborne 17,095
Concordia 22,981
De Soto 25,727
East Baton Rouge 366,191
East Carroll 11,772
East Feliciana 19,015
Evangeline 33,343
Franklin 24,141
Grant 16,703
Iberia 63,752
Iberville 32,159
Jackson 17,321
Jefferson 454,592
Jefferson Davis 32,168
Lafayette 150,017
Lafourche 82,483
La Salle 17,004
Lincoln 39,763
Livingston 58,806
Madison 15,975
Morehouse 34,803
Natchitoches 39,863
Orleans 557,927
Ouachita 139,241
Plaquemines 26,049
Pointe Coupee 24,045
Rapides 135,282
Red River 10,433
Richland 22,187
Sabine 25,280
St. Bernard 64,097
St. Charles 37,259
St. Helena 9,827
St. James 21,495
St. John the Baptist 31,924
St. Landry 84,128
St. Martin 40,214
St. Mary 64,253
St. Tammany 110,869
Tangipahoa 80,698
Tensas 8,525
Terrebonne 94,393
Union 21,167
Vermilion 48,458
Vernon 53,475
Washington 44,207
Webster 43,631
West Baton Rouge 19,086
West Carroll 12,922
West Feliciana 12,186
Winn 17,253

MAINE

1980
Census 1,125,027

CITIES

Alfred 1,890▲ 500 ○
Andover 470 ○
Anson 2,226▲ 900 ○
Ashland 1,865▲ 800 ○
Auburn LEW- 23,128
AUGUSTA AUG 21,819
Bailey Island BR-BA 650 ○
BANGOR BANG 31,643
Bar Harbor 4,124▲ 2,685
Bar Mills POR 825 ○
Bath BR-BA 10,246
Belfast 6,243
Berwick DOV- 4,149▲ 2,378
Bethel 2,340▲ 1,225 ○
Biddeford POR 19,638
Bingham 1,184▲ 1,074
Blaine 922▲ 620 ○
Blue Hill 700 ○
Boothbay 2,308▲ 450 ○
Boothbay Harbor 2,207
Bradley BANG 1,149▲ 625 ○
Brewer BANG 9,017
Bridgton 3,528▲ 1,639
Brownville Junction 775 ○
BRUNSWICK BR-BA 10,990
Bucksport 4,345▲ 2,853
Calais 4,262
Camden 4,584▲ 3,743
Canton 500 ○

○ Rand McNally estimate
▲ Population of entire township or "town", including rural areas.
● Independent city. Population not included in county total.

Cape Elizabeth POR 7,838
Cape Porpoise 500○
Caribou 9,916
Castine 1,304▲ 550○
Chisholm 1,796
Clinton 2,696▲ 1,305
Corinna 1,887▲ 950○
Cornish 600○
Cumberland Center POR 2,015
Cumberland Foreside POR 1,000○
Damariscotta 1,493▲ 950○
Danforth 500○
Dexter 4,286▲ 3,118
Dixfield 2,389▲ 1,725
Dover-Foxcroft 4,323▲ 2,974
Dryden 500○
Eagle Lake 600○
East Hampden BANG 950○
East Holden 570○
East Millinocket 2,361
Eastport 1,982
East Wilton 500○
Eliot PTSM 4,948▲ 2,450○
Ellsworth 5,179
Fairfield WATRVL 6,113▲ 3,169
Falmouth POR 6,853
Farmingdale AUG 2,535▲ 2,014
Farmington 6,730▲ 3,583
Fort Fairfield 4,376▲ 2,282
Fort Kent 4,826▲ 2,375
Freeport POR 5,863▲ 1,906
Frenchville 1,450▲ 615○
Friendship 585○
Fryeburg 2,715▲ 1,644
Gardiner AUG 6,485
Gorham POR 10,101▲ 4,052
Grand Isle 460○
Gray POR 4,344▲ 900○
Greenville 1,839▲ 1,640
Greenville Junction 600○
Guilford 1,793▲ 1,235
Hallowell AUG 2,502
Hampden BANG 5,250▲ 2,300○
Hampden Highlands BANG 1,540○
Harrison 1,667▲ 465○
Hartland 1,669▲ 1,041
Houlton 6,766▲ 5,730
Howland 1,602
Island Falls 981▲ 650○
Jackman 1,003▲ 800○
Jay 5,080▲ 500○
Jonesport 1,512▲ 1,050
Kennebunk 6,621▲ 3,294
Kennebunkport 2,952▲ 1,685
Kezar Falls 900○
Kingfield 1,083▲ 700○
Kittery PTSM 9,314▲ 5,465
Kittery Point PTSM 1,260
LEWISTON LEW- 40,481
Limestone 8,719▲ 1,334
Lincoln 5,066▲ 3,524
Lisbon LEW- 8,769▲ 1,200○
Lisbon Center LEW- 625○
Lisbon Falls LEW- 4,370
Littleton 1,009▲ 600○
Livermore Falls 3,572▲ 2,441
Lubec 2,045▲ 990○
Machias 2,458▲ 1,277
Madawaska 5,282▲ 4,165
Madison 4,367▲ 2,788
Manchester AUG 1,949▲ 600○
Mapleton 1,895▲ 500○
Mars Hill 1,892▲ 1,500○
Mattawamkeag 1,000▲ 750○
Mechanic Falls LEW- 2,616
Medway 1,871▲ 525○
Mexico 3,698▲ 3,207
Milbridge 1,306▲ 465○
Milford BANG 2,160▲ 1,688
Millinocket 7,567
Milo 2,624▲ 2,255
Monmouth LEW- 2,888▲ 500○
Monson 500○
Moody 515○
Newcastle 1,227▲ 490○
New Harbor 450○
Newport 2,755▲ 1,748
Norridgewock 2,552▲ 1,318
North Anson 600○
North Berwick 2,878▲ 1,436
North Bridgton 500○
Northeast Harbor 550○
North Vassalboro WATRVL 850○
North Windham POR 5,492
Norway 4,042▲ 2,653
Oakfield 847▲ 500○
Oakland WATRVL 5,162▲ 3,387
Ogunquit 1,492
Old Orchard Beach POR 6,291
Old Town BANG 8,422
Orono BANG 10,578
Orrs Island BR-BA 500○
Oxford 3,143▲ 625○
Patten 1,368▲ 1,057
Phillips 1,092▲ 700○
Pine Point POR 700○
Pittsfield 4,125▲ 3,117
Portage 450○
Port Clyde 500○
PORTLAND POR 61,572
Presque Isle 11,172
Princeton 994▲ 800○
Randolph AUG 1,834
Rangeley 1,023▲ 700○
Raymond POR 2,251▲ 500○
Richmond 2,627▲ 1,578
Rockland 7,919
Rockport 2,749▲ 1,000○
Rumford 8,240▲ 6,256
Sabattus LEW- 3,081▲ 1,234
Saco POR 12,921
Sanford 18,020▲ 10,268
Sangerville 1,219▲ 550○
Scarborough POR 11,347▲ 2,280
Searsport 2,309▲ 1,348
Sebago Lake POR 600○
Sherman Mills 450○
Skowhegan 8,098▲ 6,517
South Berwick DOV- 4,046▲ 2,120
South Bristol 600○
South Paris 2,128
South Portland POR 22,712
Southwest Harbor 1,855▲ 1,052
South Windham POR 1,350○
Springvale 2,940
Stonington 1,273▲ 700○
Strong 1,506▲ 700○
Thomaston 2,900▲ 2,348
Topsham BR-BA 6,431▲ 4,657
Union 1,569▲ 500○
Unity 1,431▲ 445○
Van Buren 3,557▲ 3,282
Veazie BANG 1,610
Vinalhaven 1,211▲ 900○
Waldoboro 3,985▲ 1,195
Washburn 2,028▲ 1,221
Waterboro 2,943▲ 500○
WATERVILLE WATRVL 17,779
Wells 6,719▲ 850○
Westbrook POR 14,976
West Cumberland POR 800○
West Enfield 440○
West Paris 1,390▲ 500○
West Scarborough POR 700○
Wilton 4,382▲ 2,262
Windham Center POR 500○
Winslow WATRVL 8,057▲ 5,903
Winter Harbor 1,120▲ 900○
Winterport BANG 2,675▲ 1,126
Winthrop AUG 5,889▲ 3,264
Wiscasset 2,832▲ 1,350○
Woodland 1,363
Woolwich BR-BA 2,156▲ 500○
Yarmouth POR 6,585▲ 2,981
York PTSM 8,465▲ 3,130○
York Beach PTSM 860○
York Harbor PTSM 1,400○

COUNTIES

Androscoggin 99,657
Aroostook 91,331
Cumberland 215,789
Franklin 27,447
Hancock 41,781
Kennebec 109,889
Knox 32,941
Lincoln 25,691
Oxford 48,968
Penobscot 137,015
Piscataquis 17,634
Sagadahoc 28,795
Somerset 45,046
Waldo 28,414
Washington 34,963
York 139,666

MARYLAND

1980 Census 4,216,975

CITIES

Aberdeen 11,533
Abingdon BAL 450○
ANNAPOLIS ANPLS 31,740
Annapolis Junction BAL 600○
Ardmore WASH 900○
Arundel Village BAL 5,300○
Ashton WASH 1,010○
Aspen Hill WASH 9,800○
Avenel WASH 5,600○
BALTIMORE● BAL 786,775
Baltimore Highlands BAL 6,750○
Barton CUMB 617
Bay Ridge ANPLS 1,989
Bel Air BAL 7,814
Belcamp BAL 650○
Beltsville WASH 12,760
Benedict 700○
Berlin 2,162
Bethesda WASH 62,736
Birchwood City WASH 8,000○
Bladensburg WASH 7,691
Boonsboro 1,908
Boulevard Heights WASH 1,700○
Bowie WASH 33,695
Braddock Heights 4,223
Bradshaw BAL 800○
Brandywine WASH 1,319
Brentwood WASH 2,988
Brooklandville BAL 500○
Brooklyn Park BAL 2,800○
Broomes Island 450○
Brunswick 4,572
Bryans Road WASH 3,739
Cabin John WASH 1,500○
Calverton WASH 7,649
Cambridge 11,703
Camp Springs WASH 2,500○
Capitol Heights WASH 3,271
Cardiff BAL 450○
Cavetown HAG- 1,533
Cecilton 508
Centreville 2,018
Charlestown PHIL- 720
Charlotte Hall 1,000○
Chase BAL 700○
Cheltenham WASH 500○
Chesapeake Beach WASH 1,408
Chesapeake City 899
Chester 600○
Chestertown 3,300
Cheverly WASH 5,751
Chillum WASH 14,900○
Churchton WASH 800○
Clarksburg WASH 600○
Clear Spring 477
Clinton WASH 16,438
Cockeysville BAL 17,013
College Park WASH 23,614
Colmar Manor WASH 1,286
Coltons Point 500○
Corriganville CUMB 1,020
Cresaptown CUMB 4,645
Crisfield 2,924
Crofton WASH 12,009
CUMBERLAND CUMB 25,933
Damascus WASH 4,129
Darlington BAL 500○
Dayton BAL 700○
Deale WASH 3,008
Deal Island 500○
Deer Park 486
Delmar 1,232
Denton 1,927
Derwood WASH 550○
District Heights-Forestville WASH 6,799
Dorsey BAL 1,186
Dublin BAL 500○
Dundalk BAL 71,293

○ Rand McNally estimate
▲ Population of entire township or "town", including rural areas.
● Independent city. Population not included in county total.

MARYLAND continued

Easton 7,536
Eckhart Mines CUMB 1,333
Edgemere BAL . . . . . . 7,800 ○
Edgewater WASH . . . . . 800 ○
Edgewood BAL 19,455
Edmondson Heights BAL . . . . 5,000 ○
Elk Ridge BAL . . . . . . 2,100 ○
Elkton PHIL- 6,468
Ellerslie CUMB . . . . . . 1,150 ○
Ellicott City BAL . . . . . 4,000 ○
Emmitsburg 1,552
Essex BAL 39,614
Fairmount Heights WASH 1,616
Federalsburg 1,952
Ferndale BAL . . . . 2,600 ○
Fishing Creek . . . . 650 ○
Forest Hill BAL . . . . 550 ○
Forestville WASH . . . 16,401
Fort Howard BAL . . . . 1,050 ○
Fort Washington Forest WASH . . . . 1,800 ○
Frederick 28,086
Friendsville 511
Frostburg CUMB 7,715
Fruitland SLSB 2,694
Fulton WASH . . . . 600 ○
Funkstown HAG- 1,103
Gaithersburg WASH 26,424
Galesville WASH . . . . . . 600 ○
Gambrills ANPLS . . . . . 650 ○
Garrett Park WASH 1,178
Garrison BAL . . . . 750 ○
Germantown WASH 9,721
Glen Burnie BAL . . . 30,000 ○
Glyndon BAL . . . . 1,100 ○
Grantsville 498
Grasonville 1,910
Greenbelt WASH . . . 17,332
Greensboro 1,253
HAGERSTOWN HAG- 34,132
Halethorpe BAL 20,163
Halfway HAG- 8,659
Hampstead BAL 1,293
Hancock 1,887
Harmans . . . . 600 ○
Havre de Grace 8,763
Hebron 714
Hereford BAL . . . . 600 ○
Hillcrest Heights . . . . . 24,900 ○
Hillcrest Heights WASH 17,021
Hughesville 1,208
Hurlock 1,690
Hyattsville WASH . . . 12,709
Indian Head WASH 1,381
Jarrettsville BAL 1,485
Jessup BAL 4,288
Joppa BAL 11,348
Keedysville HAG- 476
Kensington WASH . . . 1,822
Kettering WASH 6,972
Kingstown 1,192
Kingsville BAL 2,824
Lake Shore BAL . . . . . 2,100 ○
Langley Park WASH . . . . 11,100 ○
Lanham WASH . . . . . 7,300 ○
Lansdowne BAL . . . . 10,000 ○
La Plata WASH 2,484
Laurel WASH 12,103
La Vale CUMB . . . . . . 5,500 ○
Lawsonia 1,687
Leonardtown 1,448
Lexington Park 10,361
Libertytown . . . . 500 ○
Linthicum Heights BAL 7,457
Loch Lynn Heights 503
Lonaconing CUMB . . . 1,420
Londontowne WASH . . . . 3,500 ○
Long Bar Harbor . . . . 700 ○
Long Beach . . . . 900 ○
Lutherville-Timonium BAL 16,871
Lynne Acres BAL . . . . 7,700 ○
McAlpine BAL . . . . . . 2,500 ○
Manchester BAL 1,830
Marbury 1,189
Margate BAL . . . . 4,800 ○
Marion Station . . . . 500 ○
Marley BAL . . . . 4,800 ○
Maryland City WASH . . . . 6,250 ○
Maugansville HAG- . . . 1,707
Mayo WASH . . . . 1,500 ○
Middle River BAL . . . 26,756
Middletown 1,748
Midland CUMB 601
Millington 546
Montgomery Village WASH . . . . 16,600 ○
Mountain Lake Park . . . 1,597
Mount Airy BAL 2,450
Mount Rainier WASH 7,361
Mount Savage CUMB 1,640
New Carrollton WASH 12,632
New Windsor 799
North Beach WASH 1,504
North East PHIL- 1,469
Oakland 1,994
Ocean City 4,946
Odenton BAL . . . . 7,500 ○
Olney WASH . . . . . . 10,000 ○
Owings Mills BAL 9,526
Oxford 754
Oxon Hill WASH . . . . . 8,100 ○
Palmer Park WASH 7,986
Paramount HAG- 1,878
Parkville BAL 35,159
Parsonsburg SLSB . . . . 500 ○
Pasadena BAL . . . . . . 3,900 ○
Perry Hall BAL 13,455
Perryman BAL 1,819
Perry Point . . . . 500 ○
Pikesville BAL . . . . . 20,000 ○
Piney Point . . . . 900 ○
Pittsville 519
Pocomoke City 3,558
Poolesville 3,428
Port Deposit 664
Potomac WASH . . . . 22,800 ○
Potomac Heights WASH 2,456
Preston 498
Prince Frederick 1,805
Princess Anne 1,499
Pumphrey BAL . . . . . . 3,300 ○
Queenstown 491
Randallstown BAL . . . . 20,500 ○
Randolph Hills WASH . . . . 500 ○
Reisterstown BAL . . . 19,385
Ridgely 933
Rising Sun 1,160
Riverdale WASH 4,748
Riviera Beach BAL . . . 5,600 ○
Rockdale BAL . . . . . . 4,200 ○
Rock Hall 1,511
Rockville WASH 43,811
Rosedale BAL 19,956
St. Marys City . . . . 900 ○
St. Michaels 1,301
SALISBURY SLSB 16,429
Savage BAL . . . . 2,000 ○
Seabrook WASH . . . . 7,100 ○
Seat Pleasant WASH 5,217
Secretary 487
Severn BAL 20,147
Severna Park BAL 21,253
Shady Side WASH . . . 2,877
Sharpsburg HAG- 721
Sharptown 654
Silver Hill WASH . . . . 2,400 ○
Silver Spring WASH . . . . 64,100 ○
Smithsburg HAG- 833
Snow Hill 2,192
Solomons . . . . 500 ○
South Laurel WASH . . . . 8,500 ○
Spencerville WASH . . . . 1,100 ○
Stevensville . . . . 450 ○
Sudlersville 443
Suitland WASH . . . . 24,800 ○
Sykesville BAL 1,712
Takoma Park WASH 16,231
Taneytown 2,618
Thurmont 2,934
Tilghman . . . . 900 ○
Town Creek Manor . . . . . 900 ○
Towson BAL 51,083
Trappe 739
Union Bridge 927
Upper Marlboro WASH 828
Waldorf WASH 9,782
Walkersville 2,212
Westernport 2,706
West Friendship BAL . . . 500 ○
Westminster BAL 8,808
Westover . . . . 525 ○
Wheaton WASH . . . . 48,600 ○
White Plains WASH 5,167
Willards 540
Williamsport HAG- . . . 2,153
Woodlawn BAL . . . . . 8,000 ○
Woodmoor BAL . . . . . 7,600 ○
Woodsboro 506
Woodstock BAL . . . . . . 700 ○

COUNTIES

Allegany 80,548
Anne Arundel 370,775
Baltimore 655,615
Calvert 34,638
Caroline 23,143
Carroll 96,356
Cecil 60,430
Charles 72,751
Dorchester 30,623
Frederick 114,792
Garrett 26,498
Harford 145,930
Howard 118,572
Kent 16,695
Montgomery 579,053
Prince Georges 665,071
Queen Annes 25,508
St. Marys 59,895
Somerset 19,188
Talbot 25,604
Washington 113,086
Wicomico 64,540
Worcester 30,889

MASSACHUSETTS

1980
Census 5,737,037

CITIES

Abington BOS 13,517
Acton BOS 17,544▲ 2,500
Acushnet N.BED 8,704▲ 6,400
Adams PTSF 10,381
Agawam SPRG- 26,271▲ . . 10,300
Amesbury BOS 13,971
AMHERST AMH 17,773
Andover BOS 26,370▲ 8,445
Arlington BOS 48,219
Ashburnham FTCH- 4,075▲ 1,150
Ashby FTCH- 2,311▲ 600
Ashfield 1,458▲ 600
Ashland BOS 9,165
Assinippi BOS 1,400
Assonet F.R. 900
Athol 10,634
Attleboro PROV- 34,196
Auburn WORC 14,845
Avon BOS 5,026
Ayer 6,993
Baldwinville 1,709
Ballardvale BOS 1,300
Barnstable 30,898▲ 2,033
Barre 4,102▲ 1,136
Barre Plains 550
Becket 1,339▲ 500
Bedford BOS 13,067
Belchertown SPRG- 8,339▲ 2,531
Bellingham BOS 14,300
Belmont BOS 26,100
Berkshire PTSF 500
Berlin BOS 2,215▲ . . . 550 ○
Bernardston 1,750▲ . . . 700
Beverly BOS 37,655
Billerica BOS 36,727▲ 6,400
Blackstone PROV- 6,570▲ . . . . 5,100 ○
Blandford 1,038▲ 800
Bolton BOS 2,530▲ . . . . 500 ○
Bondsville SPRG- 1,906
BOSTON BOS 562,994
Bourne 13,874▲ 800
Boxborough BOS 3,126▲ 500
Boxford BOS 5,374▲ 1,841
Boylston WORC 3,470▲ . . . . . 950 ○
Braintree BOS 36,337
Brant Rock BOS . . . . . 1,500 ○
Brewster 5,226▲ 1,744
Bridgewater BOS 17,202▲ 6,781
Brimfield SPRG- . . . . . . 500 ○
Brockton BOS 95,172
Brookfield WORC 2,397▲ 1,037
Brookline BOS 55,062
Brooks Place BOS 500
Brookville BOS . . . . 950 ○
Bryantville BOS 1,500
Burlington BOS 23,486
Buzzards Bay 3,375
Byfield BOS . . . . 950 ○
Cambridge BOS 95,322
Canton BOS 18,182
Carlisle BOS 3,306▲ 600
Carver BOS 6,988▲ . . . . 650 ○
Cataumet . . . . 800 ○
Centerville 3,640
Chaffin WORC . . . . . . 3,700 ○
Charlemont 1,149▲ . . . 500 ○

○ Rand McNally estimate
▲ Population of entire township or "town", including rural areas.
● Independent city. Population not included in county total.

Charlton City WORC ... 1,100 ○
Chartley PROV- ... 600 ○
Chatham 6,071▲ ... 1,922
Chelmsford BOS ... 31,174
Chelsea BOS ... 25,431
Cherry Valley WORC ... 1,400 ○
Cheshire PTSF 3,124▲ ... 1,100 ○
Chester 1,123▲ ... 750 ○
Chesterfield 1,000▲ ... 550 ○
Chicopee SPRG- ... 55,112
Clinton ... 12,771
Cohasset BOS 7,174▲ ... 5,300 ○
Concord BOS 16,293▲ ... 6,400 ○
Conway 1,213▲ ... 600 ○
Cordaville BOS ... 1,384
Cotuit ... 1,300 ○
Dalton PTSF ... 6,797
Danvers BOS ... 24,100
Dedham BOS ... 25,298
Deerfield 4,517▲ ... 550 ○
Dennis 12,360▲ ... 900 ○
Dennis Port ... 2,570
Dighton TAUN 5,352▲ ... 900 ○
Dorothy Pond WORC ... 1,900 ○
Dover BOS 4,703▲ ... 2,051
Dracut BOS ... 21,249
Dudley WORC 8,717▲ ... 3,700 ○
Dunstable BOS 1,671▲ ... 900 ○
Duxbury BOS 11,807▲ ... 1,685
East Acton BOS ... 1,200 ○
East Billerica BOS ... 2,900 ○
East Brewster ... 700 ○
East Bridgewater BOS 9,945▲ ... 3,300 ○
East Brookfield WORC 1,955▲ ... 1,443
East Dennis ... 800 ○
East Douglas WORC ... 1,683
East Falmouth ... 5,181
East Foxboro BOS ... 500 ○
East Freetown N.BED ... 500 ○
Eastham 3,472▲ ... 1,100 ○
Easthampton SPRG- ... 15,580
East Longmeadow SPRG- ... 12,905
East Mansfield BOS ... 500 ○
East Millbury WORC ... 1,000 ○
Eastondale BOS ... 900 ○
East Orleans ... 1,200 ○
East Pepperell BOS ... 2,212
East Sudbury BOS ... 1,500 ○
East Templeton ... 980 ○
East Walpole BOS ... 4,900 ○
East Wareham ... 1,000 ○
Edgartown 2,204▲ ... 1,138
Egypt BOS ... 1,100 ○
Elmwood BOS ... 750 ○
Essex BOS 2,998▲ ... 1,490
Everett BOS ... 37,195
Fairhaven N.BED ... 15,759
FALL RIVER F.R. ... 92,574
Falmouth 23,640▲ ... 4,200 ○
Fayville BOS ... 1,000 ○
Feeding Hills SPRG- ... 8,500 ○
Fiskdale ... 1,859
FITCHBURG FTCH- ... 39,580
Forge Village BOS ... 1,400 ○
Foxboro BOS ... 5,697
Foxvale BOS ... 500 ○
Framingham BOS ... 65,113
Franklin BOS ... 18,217
Gardner ... 17,900
Georgetown BOS 5,687▲ ... 2,600 ○
Gilbertville ... 1,029
Gloucester BOS ... 27,768
Grafton WORC 11,238▲ ... 2,000 ○
Granby SPRG- 5,380▲ ... 1,302
Graniteville BOS ... 1,000 ○
Gray Gables ... 500 ○
Great Barrington 7,405▲ ... 3,150
Greenfield ... 14,198
Green Harbor BOS ... 2,000 ○
Groton 6,154▲ ... 1,264
Groveland BOS ... 4,300 ○
Hadley AMH 4,125▲ ... 890 ○
Halifax BOS 5,513▲ ... 900 ○
Hamilton BOS 6,960▲ ... 1,000 ○
Hampden SPRG- 4,745▲ ... 700 ○
Hanover BOS 11,358▲ ... 2,500 ○
Hanover Center BOS ... 1,000 ○
Hanson BOS 8,617▲ ... 2,120
Hardwick 2,272▲ ... 500 ○
Harvard 12,170▲ ... 900 ○
Harwich 8,971▲ ... 1,000 ○
Harwich Port ... 1,900 ○
Harwood BOS ... 900 ○
Hatfield NHAMP 3,045▲ ... 1,251
Haverhill BOS ... 46,865
Haydenville NHAMP ... 900 ○
Hingham BOS 20,339▲ ... 12,800 ○
Hinsdale PTSF 1,707▲ ... 950 ○
Holbrook BOS ... 11,140
Holden WORC 13,336▲ ... 3,900 ○
Holliston BOS ... 12,622
Holyoke SPRG- ... 44,678
Hopedale BOS ... 3,905
Hopkinton BOS 7,114▲ ... 2,542
Housatonic ... 1,314
Hubbardston 1,797▲ ... 500 ○
Hudson BOS ... 14,156
Hull BOS ... 9,714
Huntington 1,804▲ ... 950 ○
Hyannis ... 8,000 ○
Hyannis Port ... 1,150 ○
Indian Mound Beach ... 800 ○
Ipswich BOS 11,158▲ ... 4,548
Island Creek BOS ... 450 ○
Islington BOS ... 5,100 ○
Jefferson WORC ... 800 ○
Kingston BOS 7,362▲ ... 4,405
Lakeville BOS 5,931▲ ... 1,948
Lancaster 6,334▲ ... 900 ○
Lanesboro PTSF ... 950 ○
Lawrence BOS ... 63,175
Lee PTSF 6,247▲ ... 2,140
Leicester WORC 9,446▲ ... 3,400 ○
Lenox PTSF 6,523▲ ... 2,668
Lenox Dale PTSF ... 600 ○
Leominster FTCH- ... 34,508
Lexington BOS ... 29,479
Lincoln BOS 7,098▲ . 3,300 ○
Linwood WORC ... 1,100 ○
Littleton BOS 6,970▲ ... 3,109
Longmeadow SPRG- ... 16,301
Lowell BOS ... 92,418
Ludlow SPRG- ... 18,150
Lunenburg FTCH- 8,405▲ ... 1,789
Lynn BOS ... 78,471
Lynnfield BOS ... 11,267
Malden BOS ... 53,386
Manchaug WORC ... 1,000 ○
Manchester BOS ... 5,424
Manomet BOS ... 950 ○
Mansfield BOS 13,453▲ ... 6,786
Marblehead BOS ... 20,126
Marion N.BED 3,932▲ ... 1,438
Marlborough BOS ... 30,617
Marshfield BOS 20,916▲ ... 4,421
Marshfield Hills BOS ... 2,308
Marstons Mills ... 600 ○
Mashpee 3,700▲ ... 500 ○
Matfield BOS ... 700 ○
Mattapoisett N.BED 5,597▲ ... 3,159
Maynard BOS ... 9,590
Medfield BOS 10,220▲ ... 6,108
Medford BOS ... 58,076
Medway BOS 8,447▲ ... 4,300 ○
Melrose BOS ... 30,055
Mendon BOS 3,108▲ ... 900 ○
Merrimac BOS 4,451▲ ... 2,300 ○
Merrimacport BOS ... 450 ○
Methuen BOS ... 36,701
Middleboro BOS ... 7,012
Middleton BOS ... 4,135
Milford BOS ... 23,390
Millbury WORC 11,808▲ ... 5,700 ○
Millers Falls ... 1,101
Millis BOS 6,908▲ ... 3,777
Millville PROV- ... 1,764
Milton BOS ... 25,860
Minot BOS ... 800 ○
Monponsett BOS ... 600 ○
Monson SPRG- 7,315▲ ... 2,167
Montague 8,011▲ ... 900 ○
Monterey 818▲ ... 500 ○
Monument Beach ... 1,500 ○
Morningdale WORC ... 1,150 ○
Mount Hermon ... 600 ○
Nabnasset BOS ... 4,800 ○
Nahant BOS ... 3,947
Nantucket 5,087▲ ... 3,229
Natick BOS ... 29,461
Needham BOS ... 27,901
NEW BEDFORD N.BED ... 98,478
New Braintree 671▲ ... 600 ○
Newbury BOS 4,529▲ ... 900 ○
Newburyport BOS ... 15,900
Newton BOS ... 83,622
Norfolk BOS 6,363▲ ... 450 ○
North Abington BOS ... 4,700 ○
North Acton BOS ... 900 ○
North Adams ... 18,063
North Amherst AMH ... 5,616
NORTHAMPTON NHAMP ... 29,286
North Andover BOS ... 20,129
North Attleboro PROV- ... 21,095
North Billerica BOS ... 6,700 ○
Northborough WORC 10,568▲ ... 5,670
Northbridge WORC 12,246▲ ... 3,321 ○
North Brookfield WORC 4,150▲ ... 2,543
North Carver BOS ... 700 ○
North Cohasset BOS ... 900 ○
North Dartmouth N.BED ... 6,000 ○
North Dighton TAUN ... 1,174
North Eastham ... 1,318
North Easton BOS ... 6,100 ○
North Falmouth ... 1,800 ○
Northfield 2,386▲ ... 1,182
North Grafton WORC ... 3,400 ○
North Hanover BOS ... 900 ○
North Hatfield NHAMP ... 450 ○
North Marshfield BOS ... 450 ○
North Oxford WORC ... 1,550 ○
North Pembroke BOS ... 2,215
North Reading BOS ... 11,455
North Scituate BOS ... 4,100 ○
North Sudbury BOS ... 1,700 ○
North Swansea F.R. ... 950 ○
North Tewksbury BOS ... 1,400 ○
North Truro ... 700 ○
North Uxbridge WORC ... 1,400 ○
North Wilmington BOS ... 4,200 ○
Norton PROV- 12,690▲ ... 2,035
Norwell BOS 9,182▲ ... 800 ○
Norwood BOS ... 29,711
Nutting Lake BOS ... 2,400 ○
Oak Bluffs ... 1,984 ○
Oakdale WORC ... 600 ○
Ocean Bluff BOS ... 2,500 ○
Ocean Grove F.R. ... 4,000 ○
Ocean Heights ... 500 ○
Oldham Village BOS ... 900 ○
Onset BOS ... 1,493
Orange 6,844▲ ... 3,942
Orleans 5,306▲ ... 1,811
Osterville ... 1,799
Otis 963▲ ... 500 ○
Otter River ... 600 ○
Oxford WORC 11,680▲ ... 6,369
Palmer SPRG- 11,389▲ ... 3,854
Paxton WORC 3,762▲ ... 1,800 ○
Peabody BOS ... 45,976
Pelham AMH 1,112▲ ... 500 ○
Pembroke BOS 13,487▲ ... 1,800 ○
Pepperell BOS 8,061▲ ... 2,076
Petersham 1,024▲ ... 550 ○
Pigeon Cove BOS ... 1,700 ○
Pinehurst BOS ... 6,588
Pine Lake BOS ... 800 ○
Pine Rest BOS ... 900 ○
PITTSFIELD PTSF ... 51,974
Plainville PROV- ... 4,953 ○
Plymouth BOS 35,913▲ ... 7,232
Pocasset ... 2,000 ○

○ Rand McNally estimate
▲ Population of entire township or "town", including rural areas.
● Independent city. Population not included in county total.

MASSACHUSETTS continued

Point Independence BOS ... 700 ○
Princeton WORC 2,425▲ ... 600 ○
Provincetown ... 3,536
Quincy BOS ... 84,743
Randolph BOS ... 28,218
Raynham TAUN 9,085▲ ... 2,124
Raynham Center TAUN ... 3,776
Reading BOS ... 22,678
Revere BOS ... 42,423
Rexhame BOS ... 550 ○
River Pines BOS ... 3,700 ○
Rochdale WORC ... 1,105
Rochester N.BED 3,205▲ ... 450 ○
Rock BOS ... 500 ○
Rockland BOS ... 15,695
Rockport BOS 6,345▲ ... 4,600 ○
Rowley BOS 3,867▲ ... 1,321
Russell SPRG- 1,570▲ ... 650 ○
Rutland WORC 4,334▲ ... 2,312
Sagamore ... 1,152
Sagamore Beach ... 800 ○
Salem BOS ... 38,220
Salisbury BOS 5,973▲ ... 3,265
Sand Hill BOS ... 1,750 ○
Sandwich 8,727▲ ... 1,784
Saugus BOS ... 24,746
Scituate BOS 17,317▲ ... 5,351
Seekonk PROV- ... 12,269
Sharon BOS ... 13,601
Sheffield 2,743▲ ... 1,100 ○
Shelburne Falls ... 2,046
Sherborn BOS 4,049▲ ... 950 ○
Shirley 5,124▲ ... 1,630
Shore Acres BOS ... 1,200 ○
Shrewsbury WORC ... 22,674
Silver Lake BOS ... 3,400 ○
Somerset F.R. ... 18,813
Somerville BOS ... 77,372
South Acton BOS ... 4,600 ○
South Amherst AMH ... 4,861
Southampton SPRG- 4,137▲ ... 500 ○
South Ashburnham FTCH- ... 1,123
South Barre ... 600 ○
Southborough BOS 6,193▲ ... 1,600 ○
Southbridge ... 16,665
South Carver BOS ... 600 ○
South Chatham ... 950 ○
South Dartmouth N.BED ... 7,000 ○
South Deerfield ... 1,926
South Dennis ... 1,500 ○
South Duxbury BOS ... 2,985
South Easton BOS ... 1,400 ○
South Egremont ... 600 ○
South Grafton WORC ... 3,000 ○
South Hadley SPRG- 16,399▲ ... 8,900 ○
South Hadley Falls SPRG- ... 5,600 ○
South Hamilton BOS ... 2,900 ○
South Hanover BOS ... 950 ○
South Harwich ... 900 ○
South Hingham BOS ... 5,200 ○
South Lancaster ... 2,329
South Lee PTSF ... 500 ○
South Swansea F.R. ... 1,700 ○
South Walpole BOS ... 1,600 ○
South Wellfleet ... 600 ○
Southwick SPRG- 7,382▲ ... 1,400 ○
South Yarmouth ... 7,525
Spencer WORC 10,774▲ ... 6,350
SPRINGFIELD SPRG- ... 152,319
Sterling WORC 5,440▲ ... 1,200 ○
Stockbridge PTSF 2,328▲ ... 1,109
Stoneham BOS ... 21,424
Stoughton BOS ... 26,710
Stow BOS 5,144▲ ... 1,100 ○
Sturbridge 5,976▲ ... 1,891
Sudbury BOS 14,027▲ ... 2,200 ○
Sudbury Center BOS ... 2,900 ○
Sunderland AMH 2,929▲ ... 600 ○
Sutton WORC 5,855▲ ... 500 ○
Swampscott BOS ... 13,837
Swansea F.R. 15,461▲ ... 750 ○
TAUNTON TAUN ... 45,001
Teaticket ... 2,000 ○
Templeton 6,070▲ ... 900 ○
Tewksbury BOS 24,635▲ ... 11,500 ○
Thorndike SPRG- ... 1,000 ○
Three Rivers SPRG- ... 3,322
Topsfield BOS 5,709▲ ... 2,647
Touisset F.R. ... 1,300 ○
Townsend FTCH- 7,201▲ ... 1,266
Truro 1,486▲ ... 500 ○
Turners Falls ... 4,711
Upton BOS 3,886▲ ... 1,500 ○
Uxbridge WORC 8,374▲ ... 3,500 ○
Vineyard Haven ... 1,704
Wakefield BOS ... 24,895
Wales 1,177▲ ... 500 ○
Walpole BOS 18,859▲ ... 5,274
Waltham BOS ... 58,200
Wamesit BOS ... 2,700 ○
Ware 8,953▲ ... 6,806
Wareham 18,457▲ ... 2,493
Warren SPRG- 3,777▲ ... 1,548
Watertown BOS ... 34,384
Wayland BOS 12,170▲ ... 5,500 ○
Webster WORC ... 14,480
Wellesley BOS ... 27,209
Wellfleet 2,209▲ ... 950 ○
Wenham BOS ... 3,897
West Abington BOS ... 2,000 ○
West Acton BOS ... 5,800 ○
West Andover BOS ... 3,700 ○
West Barnstable ... 500 ○
West Billerica BOS ... 2,000 ○
Westborough WORC ... 13,619
West Boylston WORC 6,204▲ ... 3,500 ○
West Bridgewater BOS 6,359▲ ... 2,100 ○
West Brookfield 3,026▲ ... 1,423
West Chatham ... 1,398
West Concord BOS ... 5,331
West Dennis ... 2,030
West Falmouth ... 1,200 ○
Westfield SPRG- ... 36,465
Westford BOS 13,434▲ ... 1,000 ○
West Groton ... 950 ○
West Hanover BOS ... 1,600 ○
West Hyannisport ... 1,200 ○
West Mansfield BOS ... 500 ○
West Medway BOS ... 2,269 ○
Westminster FTCH- 5,139▲ ... 950 ○
West Newbury BOS 2,861▲ ... 950 ○
Weston BOS ... 11,169
West Pelham AMH ... 450 ○
Westport F.R. 13,763▲ ... 1,850 ○
Westport Point F.R. ... 450 ○
West Springfield SPRG- ... 27,042
West Stockbridge PTSF 1,280▲ ... 800 ○
West Townsend FTCH- ... 700 ○
West Upton BOS ... 1,000 ○
West Wareham ... 1,837
West Warren SPRG- ... 1,200 ○
Westwood BOS 13,212▲ ... 6,500 ○
West Yarmouth BOS ... 3,882
Weymouth BOS ... 55,601
Whalom FTCH- ... 1,400 ○
Whately 1,341▲ ... 450 ○
White Horse Beach BOS ... 800 ○
White Island Shores ... 950 ○
Whitinsville WORC ... 5,379
Whitman BOS ... 13,534
Wilbraham SPRG- 12,053▲ ... 3,379
Williamsburg NHAMP 2,237▲ ... 950 ○
Williamstown 8,741▲ ... 4,798
Wilmington BOS ... 17,471
Winchendon 7,019▲ ... 4,030
Winchester BOS ... 20,701
Winthrop BOS ... 19,294
Woburn BOS ... 36,626
Woods Hole ... 1,080
WORCESTER WORC ... 161,799
Wrentham BOS 7,580▲ ... 1,400 ○
Yarmouth 18,449▲ ... 900 ○
Yarmouth Port ... 2,490

COUNTIES

Barnstable ... 147,925
Berkshire ... 145,110
Bristol ... 474,641
Dukes ... 8,942
Essex ... 633,632
Franklin ... 64,317
Hampden ... 443,018
Hampshire ... 138,813
Middlesex ... 1,367,034
Nantucket ... 5,087
Norfolk ... 606,587
Plymouth ... 405,437
Suffolk ... 650,142
Worcester ... 646,352

MICHIGAN

1980
Census ... 9,262,078

CITIES

Adrian ... 21,186
Akron ... 538
Alanson ... 508
Albion ... 11,059
Algonac DET ... 4,412
Allegan ... 4,576
Allen Park DET ... 34,196
Alma ... 9,652
Almont DET ... 1,857
Alpena ... 12,214
Amasa ... 600 ○
Ann Arbor DET ... 107,966
Armada DET ... 1,392
Ashley ... 570
Athens ... 960
Atlanta ... 650 ○
Auburn BC-M ... 1,921
Auburn Heights DET ... 4,000 ○
Au Gres ... 768
Augusta BTLCK ... 913
Bad Axe ... 3,184
Baldwin ... 674
Bancroft FLN ... 618
Bangor ... 2,001
Bangor Township BC-M ... 17,494
Baraga ... 1,055
Baroda BNTH- ... 627
Barron Lake S.B.- ... 1,600 ○
Bath LANS ... 600 ○
BATTLE CREEK BTLCK ... 35,724
BAY CITY BC-M ... 41,593
Bay Port ... 800 ○
Beaverton ... 1,025
Beecher FLN ... 17,178
Belding ... 5,634
Bellaire ... 1,063
Belleville DET ... 3,366
Bellevue ... 1,289
BENTON HARBOR BNTH- ... 14,707
Benton Heights BNTH- ... 6,787
Benzonia ... 466
Bergland ... 700 ○
Berkley DET ... 18,637
Berrien Springs S.B.- ... 2,042
Bertrand S.B.- ... 5,000 ○
Bessemer ... 2,553
Beulah ... 454
Beverly Hills DET ... 11,598
Big Rapids ... 14,361
Birch Run FLN ... 1,196
Birmingham DET ... 21,689
Blissfield ... 3,107
Bloomfield Hills DET ... 3,985
Bloomingdale ... 537
Boyne City ... 3,348
Breckenridge ... 1,495
Bridgeport SAG ... 3,500 ○
Bridgman BNTH- ... 2,235
Brighton DET ... 4,268
Brimley ... 500 ○
Britton ... 693
Bronson ... 2,271
Brooklyn JAC ... 1,110
Brown City ... 1,163
Buchanan S.B.- ... 5,142
Burr Oak ... 853
Burton FLN ... 29,976
Cadillac ... 10,199
Caledonia GDR ... 722
Calumet ... 1,013
Canton DET ... 5,000 ○
Capac ... 1,377

○ Rand McNally estimate
▲ Population of entire township or "town", including rural areas.
● Independent city. Population not included in county total.

Carleton DET 2,786
Caro 4,317
Carrollton SAG 7,482
Carson City 1,229
Carsonville 622
Caseville 851
Caspian 1,038
Cass City 2,258
Cassopolis S.B.- 1,933
Cedar Springs GDR 2,615
Cement City JAC 539
Center Line DET 9,293
Central Lake 895
Centreville 1,202
Champion 500 ○
Charlevoix 3,296
Charlotte 8,251
Chassell 700 ○
Cheboygan 5,106
Chelsea DET 3,816
Chesaning FLN 2,656
Clare 3,300
Clarkston DET 968
Clawson DET 15,103
Climax BTLCK 619
Clinton 2,342
Clio FLN 2,669
Coldwater 9,461
Coleman 1,429
Coloma BNTH- 1,833
Colon 1,190
Columbiaville FLN 953
Comstock KZOO 5,310 ○
Concord 900
Constantine 1,680
Coopersville 2,889
Corunna 3,206
Covert 600 ○
Crystal 600 ○
Crystal Falls 1,965
Cutlerville GDR 8,256
Davison FLN 6,087
Dearborn DET 90,660
Dearborn Heights DET 67,706
Decatur 1,915
Deckerville 887
Deerfield 957
De Tour Village 466
DETROIT DET 1,203,339
De Witt LANS 3,165
Dexter DET 1,524
Dimondale LANS 1,008
Dollar Bay 900 ○
Dorr GDR 500 ○
Douglas 948
Dowagiac 6,307
Drayton Plains DET 18,000 ○
Drummond Island 500 ○
Dryden 650
Dundee 2,575
Durand FLN 4,241
East Detroit DET 38,280
East Grand Rapids GDR 10,914
East Jordan 2,185
Eastlake 514
East Lansing LANS 51,392
East Tawas 2,584
Eastwood KZOO 7,186
Eaton Rapids 4,510
Eau Claire S.B.- 573
Eben Junction 450 ○
Ecorse DET 14,447
Edmore 1,176
Edwardsburg S.B.- 1,135
Elberta 556
Elk Rapids 1,504
Elkton 953
Elsie 1,022
Engadine 500 ○
Erie TOL 700 ○
Escanaba 14,355
Essexville BC-M 4,378
Evart 1,945
Ewen 500 ○
Fairgrove 691
Fair Haven DET 900 ○
Fair Plain BNTH- 8,289
Fairview 500 ○
Farmington DET 11,022
Farmington Hills DET 58,056
Farwell 804
Fennville 934
Fenton FLN 8,098
Ferndale DET 26,227
Flat Rock DET 6,853
FLINT FLN 159,611
Flushing FLN 8,624
Fowler 1,021
Fowlerville 2,289
Frankenmuth SAG 3,753
Frankfort 1,603
Fraser DET 14,560
Frederic 500 ○
Freeland BC-M 1,364
Freeport 479
Fremont 3,672
Fruitport MUS 1,143
Fulton 750 ○
Gaines FLN 440
Galesburg KZOO 1,822
Galien 692
Garden City DET 35,640
Gaylord 3,011
Genesee FLN 950 ○
Gladstone 4,533
Gladwin 2,479
Gobles 816
Grand Blanc FLN 6,848
Grand Haven MUS 11,763
Grand Ledge LANS 6,920
GRAND RAPIDS GDR 181,843
Grandville GDR 12,412
Grant 683
Grass Lake 900 ○
Grayling 1,792
Greenville 8,019
Greilickville 1,000 ○
Grosse Ile DET 9,320
Grosse Pointe DET 5,901
Grosse Pointe Park DET 13,639
Grosse Pointe Woods DET 18,886
Gwinn 1,408
Hamilton 800 ○
Hamtramck DET 21,300
Hancock 5,122
Hanover JAC 490
Harbor Beach 2,000
Harbor Springs 1,567
Harper Woods DET 16,361
Harrison 1,700
Harrisville 559
Hart 1,888
Hartford BNTH- 2,493
Hartland DET 450 ○
Harvey 1,341
Haslett LANS 7,025
Hastings 6,418
Hazel Park DET 20,914
Hemlock BC-M 1,362
Hermansville 700 ○
Hesperia 876
Higgins Lake 500 ○
Highland DET 1,000 ○
Highland Park DET 27,909
Hillsdale 7,432
HOLLAND HLND 26,281
Holly FLN 4,874
Holt LANS 10,097
Homer 1,791
Hopkins 536
Houghton 7,512
Houghton Lake 1,500 ○
Houghton Lake Heights 2,449
Howard City 1,118
Howell DET 6,976
Hubbell 1,278
Hudson 2,545
Hudsonville GDR 4,844
Huntington Woods DET 6,937
Ida TOL 1,000 ○
Imlay City 2,495
Inkster DET 35,190
Ionia 5,920
Iron Mountain 8,341
Iron River 2,426
Ironwood 7,741
Ishpeming 7,538
Ithaca 2,950
JACKSON JAC 39,739
Jenison GDR 16,330
Jonesville 2,172
KALAMAZOO KZOO 79,722
Kaleva 445
Kalkaska 1,654
Keego Harbor DET 3,083
Kent City 860
Kentwood GDR 30,438
Kinde 600
Kingsford 5,290
Kingsley 664
Laingsburg 1,145
Lake City 843
Lake Linden 1,181
Lake Odessa 2,171
Lake Orion DET 2,907
Lakeview BTLCK 13,345
Lakeview 1,139
Lambertville TOL 6,341
L'Anse 2,500
LANSING LANS 130,414
Lapeer FLN 6,198
Laurium 2,678
Lawrence 903
Lawton 1,558
Leland 600 ○
Leslie 2,110
Lewiston 600 ○
Lexington 765
Lincoln Park DET 45,105
Linden FLN 2,174
Litchfield 1,353
Livonia DET 104,814
Lowell GDR 3,707
Ludington 8,937
Luna Pier TOL 1,443
Luzerne 500 ○
Lyons 708
McBain 519
Mackinac Island 479
Mackinaw City 820
Madison Heights DET 35,375
Mancelona 1,432
Manchester 1,686
Manistee 7,566
Manistique 3,962
Manton 1,212
Maple Rapids 683
Marcellus 1,134
Marenisco 600 ○
Marine City 4,414
Marion 816
Marlette 1,761
Marne 500 ○
Marquette 23,288
Marshall 7,201
Martin 447
Marysville PTHU 7,345
Mason LANS 6,019
Maybee 490
Mayville 958
Melvindale DET 12,322
Memphis 1,171
Mendon 951
Menominee 10,099
Merrill BC-M 851
Metamora 552
Michigan Center JAC 5,244
Middleton 500 ○
Middleville GDR 1,797
Midland BC-M 37,250
Milan DET 4,182
Milford DET 5,041
Millington FLN 1,237
Mio 1,500 ○
Mohawk 950 ○
Moline GDR 800 ○
MONROE MONR 23,531
Montague MUS 2,332
Montrose FLN 1,706
Morenci 2,110
Morley 507
Mount Clemens DET 18,806
Mount Morris FLN 3,246
Mount Pleasant 23,746
Muir 698
Mulliken 550
Munising 3,083
MUSKEGON MUS 40,823
Muskegon Heights MUS 14,611
Nashville 1,628
Negaunee 5,189
Newaygo 1,271
New Baltimore DET 5,439
Newberry 2,120
New Boston DET 1,200
New Buffalo MICH 2,821
New Era 534
New Haven DET 1,871
New Hudson DET 800 ○
New Lothrop 646
Newport DET 900 ○
Niles S.B.- 13,115
North Adams 565
North Branch 896
North Lake 500 ○
North Muskegon MUS 4,024
Northport 611
Northville DET 5,698
Norton Shores MUS 22,025
Norway 2,919
Novi DET 22,525
Oak Hill 1,000 ○
Oak Park DET 31,537
Okemos LANS 8,882
Olivet 1,604
Onaway 1,084
Onekama 582
Onsted 670
Ontonagon 2,182
Ortonville DET 1,190
Oscoda 2,431
Otisville FLN 682
Otsego KZOO 3,802
Otter Lake FLN 456
Ovid 1,712
Owosso 16,455
Oxford DET 2,746
Painesdale 650 ○
Palmer 900 ○
Parchment KZOO 1,817
Parma JAC 873
Paw Paw 3,211
Peck 606
Pellston 565
Pentwater 1,165
Perry LANS 2,051
Petersburg 1,222
Petoskey 6,097
Pewamo 488
Pickford 500 ○
Pigeon 1,247
Pinckney DET 1,390
Pinconning BC-M 1,430

○ Rand McNally estimate
▲ Population of entire township or "town", including rural areas.
● Independent city. Population not included in county total.

MICHIGAN continued

Plainfield Heights GDR 5,000 ○
Plainwell KZOO 3,751
Plymouth DET 9,986
Pontiac DET 76,715
Portage KZOO 38,157
Port Austin 839
PORT HURON PTHU 33,981
Portland 3,963
Port Sanilac 598
Powers 490
Pullman 500 ○
Quincy 1,569
Quinnesec 900 ○
Ramsay 1,068 ○
Rapid River 700 ○
Ravenna 951
Reading 1,203
Redford DET 58,441
Reed City 2,221
Reese 1,645
Remus 450 ○
Republic 1,000 ○
Richland KZOO 486
Richmond DET 3,536
River Rouge DET 12,912
Riverview DET 14,569
Rives Junction JAC 450 ○
Rochester DET 7,203
Rock 475 ○
Rockford GDR 3,324
Rockwood DET 3,346
Rogers City 3,923
Romeo DET 3,509
Romulus DET 24,857
Roosevelt Park MUS 4,015
Roscommon 834
Rose City 661
Roseville DET 54,311
Rothbury 522
Royal Oak DET 70,893
Rudyard 900 ○
SAGINAW SAG 77,508
St. Charles SAG 2,276
St. Clair 4,780
St. Clair Shores DET 76,210
St. Ignace 2,632
St. Johns 7,376
St. Joseph BNTH- 9,622
St. Louis 4,107
Saline DET 6,483
Sandusky 2,216
Sanford BC-M 864
Saranac 1,421
Saugatuck 1,079
SAULT STE. MARIE SOO 14,448
Sawyer 550 ○
Schoolcraft KZOO 1,359
Scottville 1,241
Sebewaing 2,046
Shelby 1,624
Shepherd 1,534
Shoreham BNTH- 742
Southfield DET 75,568
Southgate DET 32,058
South Haven 5,943
South Lyon DET 5,214
South Range 861
Sparta GDR 3,373
Springfield BTLCK 5,917
Spring Lake MUS 2,731
Springport 675
Stambaugh 1,442
Standish 1,264
Stanton 1,315
Stephenson 967
Sterling 457
Sterling Heights DET 108,999
Stevensville BNTH- 1,268
Stockbridge 1,213
Sturgis 9,468
Sunfield 591
Suttons Bay 504
Swartz Creek FLN 5,013
Tawas City 1,967
Taylor DET 77,568
Tecumseh 7,320
Tekonsha 755
Temperance TOL 3,500 ○
Three Oaks 1,774
Three Rivers 7,015
Tower 500 ○
Traverse City 15,516
Trenton DET 22,762
Troy DET 67,102
Ubly 862
Union City 1,667
Union Lake DET 12,000 ○
Union Pier 1,039
Unionville 578
Utica DET 5,282
Vanderbilt 525
Vandercook Lake JAC 4,975
Vassar 2,727
Vermontville 832
Vicksburg KZOO 2,224
Vulcan 600 ○
Wakefield 2,591
Waldron 570
Walker GDR 15,088
Walled Lake DET 4,748
Warren DET 161,134
Waterford DET 64,250
Watersmeet 700 ○
Watervliet BNTH- 1,867
Waverly LANS 6,700 ○
Wayland 2,023
Wayne DET 21,159
Webberville 1,535
Weidman 450 ○
West Branch 1,785
Westland DET 84,603
Westphalia 896
West Willow DET 5,400 ○
Westwood KZOO 8,519
White Cloud 1,101
Whitehall MUS 2,856
White Pigeon 1,478
White Pine 1,142
Whitmore Lake DET 2,920
Williamston LANS 2,981
Willow Run DET 6,400 ○
Winn 450 ○
Wixom DET 6,705
Wolf Lake MUS 3,876
Woodhaven DET 10,902
Wyandotte DET 34,006
Wyoming GDR 59,616
Yale 1,814
Ypsilanti DET 24,031
Zeeland HLND 4,764
Zilwaukee SAG 2,201

COUNTIES

Alcona 9,740
Alger 9,225
Allegan 81,555
Alpena 32,315
Antrim 16,194
Arenac 14,706
Baraga 8,484
Barry 45,781
Bay 119,881
Benzie 11,205
Berrien 171,276
Branch 40,188
Calhoun 141,557
Cass 49,499
Charlevoix 19,907
Cheboygan 20,649
Chippewa 29,029
Clare 23,822
Clinton 55,893
Crawford 9,465
Delta 38,947
Dickinson 25,341
Eaton 88,337
Emmet 22,992
Genesee 450,449
Gladwin 19,957
Gogebic 19,686
Grand Traverse 54,899
Gratiot 40,448
Hillsdale 42,071
Houghton 37,872
Huron 36,459
Ingham 275,520
Ionia 51,815
Iosco 28,349
Iron 13,635
Isabella 54,110
Jackson 151,495
Kalamazoo 212,378
Kalkaska 10,952
Kent 444,506
Keweenaw 1,963
Lake 7,711
Lapeer 70,038
Leelanau 14,007
Lenawee 89,948
Livingston 100,289
Luce 6,659
Mackinac 10,178
Macomb 694,600
Manistee 23,019
Marquette 74,101
Mason 26,365
Mecosta 36,961
Menominee 26,201
Midland 73,578
Missaukee 10,009
Monroe 134,659
Montcalm 47,555
Montmorency 7,492
Muskegon 157,589
Newaygo 34,917
Oakland 1,011,793
Oceana 22,002
Ogemaw 16,436
Ontonagon 9,861
Osceola 18,928
Oscoda 6,858
Otsego 14,993
Ottawa 157,174
Presque Isle 14,267
Roscommon 16,374
Saginaw 228,059
St. Clair 138,802
St. Joseph 56,083
Sanilac 40,789
Schoolcraft 8,575
Shiawassee 71,140
Tuscola 56,961
Van Buren 66,814
Washtenaw 264,748
Wayne 2,337,891
Wexford 25,102

MINNESOTA

1980 Census 4,075,970

CITIES

Ada 1,971
Adams 797
Adrian 1,336
Aitkin 1,770
Akeley 486
Albany 1,569
Albert Lea 19,200
Albertville MPLS- 564
Alden 687
Alexandria 7,608
Amboy 606
Andover MPLS- 9,387
Annandale 1,568
Anoka MPLS- 15,634
Appleton 1,842
Apple Valley MPLS- 21,818
Arden Hills MPLS- 8,012
Argyle 741
Arlington 1,779
Arnold DUL- 1,350
Ashby 486
Atwater 1,128
Aurora 2,670
Austin 23,020
Avon 804
Bagley 1,321
Balaton 752
Barnesville 2,207
Barnum 464
Battle Lake 708
Baudette 1,170
Baxter 2,625
Bayport MPLS- 2,932
Becker 601
Belgrade 805
Belle Plaine 2,754
Bemidji 10,949
Benson 3,656
Bertha 510
Big Falls 490
Bigfork 457
Big Lake MPLS- 2,210
Bird Island 1,372
Biwabik 1,428
Blackduck 653
Blaine MPLS- 28,558
Blooming Prairie 1,969
Bloomington MPLS- 81,831
Blue Earth 4,132
Bovey 813
Braham 1,015
Brainerd 11,489
Brandon 473
Breckenridge 3,909
Brewster 559
Bricelyn 487
Brooklyn Center MPLS- 31,230
Brooklyn Park MPLS- 43,332
Brooten 647
Browerville 693
Brownsdale 691
Browns Valley 887
Brownton 697
Buffalo MPLS- 4,560
Buffalo Lake 782
Buhl 1,284
Burnsville MPLS- 35,674
Butterfield 634
Byron ROCH 1,715
Caledonia 2,691
Calumet 469
Cambridge 3,287
Canby 2,143
Cannon Falls 2,653
Carlton 862
Carver MPLS- 642
Cass Lake 1,001
Center City MPLS- 458
Ceylon 543
Champlin MPLS- 9,006
Chanhassen MPLS- 6,359
Chaska MPLS- 8,346
Chatfield 2,055
Chisago City MPLS- 1,634
Chisholm 5,930
Chokio 559
Circle Pines MPLS- 3,321
Clara City 1,574
Claremont 591
Clarissa 663
Clarkfield 1,171
Clarks Grove 620
Clearbrook 579

○ Rand McNally estimate
▲ Population of entire township or "town", including rural areas.
● Independent city. Population not included in county total.

Cleveland 699
Clinton 622
Cloquet 11,142
Cohasset 600 ○
Cokato 2,056
Cold Spring 2,294
Coleraine 1,116
Cologne 545
Columbia Heights MPLS- 20,029
Comfrey 548
Cook 800
Coon Rapids MPLS- 35,826
Corcoran MPLS- 4,252
Cosmos 571
Cottage Grove MPLS- 18,994
Cottonwood 924
Crookston 8,628
Crosby 2,218
Crosslake 1,064
Crystal MPLS- 25,543
Danube 590
Dassel 1,066
Dawson 1,901
Dayton MPLS- 4,070
Deer River 907
Deerwood 580
Delano MPLS- 2,480
Detroit Lakes 7,106
Dilworth FAR- 2,585
Dodge Center 1,816
DULUTH DUL- 92,811
Eagan MPLS- 20,700
Eagle Bend 593
Eagle Lake MNKT 1,470
East Bethel MPLS- 6,626
East Grand Forks GDFK 8,537
Eden Prairie MPLS- 16,263
Eden Valley 763
Edgerton 1,123
Edina MPLS- 46,073
Elbow Lake 1,358
Elgin 667
Elk River MPLS- 6,785
Ellendale 555
Ellsworth 629
Elmore 882
Ely 4,820
Elysian 454
Emmons 465
Erskine 585
Esko 500 ○
Evansville 571
Eveleth 5,042
Eyota 1,244
Fairfax 1,405
Fairmont 11,506
Falcon Heights MPLS- 5,291
Faribault 16,241
Farmington MPLS- 4,370
Fergus Falls 12,519
Fertile 869
Fisher 453
Floodwood 648
Foley 1,606
Forest Lake MPLS- 4,596
Fosston 1,599
Franklin 512
Frazee 1,284
Freeport 563
Fridley MPLS- 30,228
Fulda 1,308
Gaylord 1,933
Gibbon 787
Gilbert 2,721
Glencoe 4,396
Glenville 851
Glenwood 2,523
Glyndon 882
Golden Valley MPLS- 22,775

Goodhue 657
Good Thunder 560
Goodview 2,567
Graceville 780
Grand Marais 1,289
Grand Meadow 965
Grand Rapids 7,934
Granite Falls 3,451
Greenbush 817
Grove City 596
Hallock 1,405
Halstad 690
Ham Lake MPLS- 7,832
Hancock 877
Harmony 1,133
Harris 678
Hastings MPLS- 12,827
Hawley 1,634
Hayfield 1,243
Hector 1,252
Henderson 739
Hendricks 737
Henning 832
Herman 600
Hermantown DUL- 6,759
Heron Lake 783
Hibbing 21,193
Hill City 533
Hills 598
Hinckley 963
Hoffman 631
Hokah 686
Holdingford 635
Hopkins MPLS- 15,336
Houston 1,057
Howard Lake 1,240
Hoyt Lakes 3,186
Hugo MPLS- 3,771
Hutchinson 9,244
International Falls 5,611
Inver Grove Heights MPLS- 17,171
Ironton 537
Isanti 858
Isle 573
Ivanhoe 761
Jackson 3,797
Janesville 1,897
Jasper 731
Jordan MPLS- 2,663
Kandiyohi 447
Karlstad 934
Kasota 739
Kasson 2,827
Keewatin 1,443
Kellogg 440
Kelly Lake 900 ○
Kenyon 1,529
Kerkhoven 761
Kiester 670
Kimball 651
La Crescent LACRO 3,674
Lafayette 507
Lake Benton 869
Lake City 4,505
Lake Crystal MNKT 2,078
Lake Elmo MPLS- 5,296
Lakefield 1,845
Lake Park 716
Lakeville MPLS- 14,790
Lamberton 1,032
Lanesboro 923
La Prairie 536
Le Center 1,967
Le Roy 930
Lester Prairie 1,229
Le Sueur 3,763
Lewiston 1,226
Lindstrom MPLS- 1,972
Lino Lakes MPLS- 4,966
Litchfield 5,904
Little Canada MPLS- 7,102
Little Falls 7,250
Littlefork 918

Long Prairie 2,859
Lonsdale 1,160
Luverne 4,568
Lyle 576
Mabel 861
McGregor 447
McIntosh 681
Madelia 2,130
Madison 2,212
Madison Lake 592
Mahnomen 1,283
MANKATO MNKT 28,651
Mantorville 705
Maple Grove MPLS- 20,525
Maple Lake 1,132
Mapleton 1,516
Maplewood MPLS- 26,990
Marble 757
Marine On St. Croix 543
Marshall 11,161
Mazeppa 680
Medford 775
Melrose 2,409
Menahga 980
Mendota Heights MPLS- 7,288
Milaca 2,104
MINNEAPOLIS MPLS- 370,951
Minneota 1,470
Minnesota Lake 744
Minnetonka MPLS- 38,683
Montevideo 5,845
Montgomery 2,349
Monticello 2,830
Moorhead FAR- 29,998
Moose Lake 1,408
Mora 2,890
Morgan 975
Morris 5,367
Morristown 639
Morton 549
Motley 444
Mound MPLS- 9,280
Mounds View MPLS- 12,593
Mountain Iron 4,134
Mountain Lake 2,277
Nashwauk 1,419
New Brighton MPLS- 23,269
New Hope MPLS- 23,087
New London 812
Newport MPLS- 3,323
New Prague 2,952
New Richland 1,263
New Ulm 13,755
New York Mills 972
Nicollet 709
North Branch 1,597
Northfield 12,562
North Mankato MNKT 9,145
North St. Paul MPLS- 11,921
Norwood 1,219
Oakdale MPLS- 12,123
Oklee 536
Olivia 2,802
Onamia 691
Orono MPLS- 6,845
Oronoco ROCH 574
Ortonville 2,550
Osakis 1,355
Osseo MPLS- 2,974
Owatonna 18,632
Parkers Prairie 917
Park Rapids 2,976
Paynesville 2,140
Pelican Rapids 1,867
Pequot Lakes 681
Perham 2,086
Pierz 1,018
Pike Lake DUL- 1,004

Pine City 2,489
Pine Island 1,986
Pine River 881
Pipestone 4,887
Plainview 2,416
Plymouth MPLS- 31,615
Preston 1,478
Princeton 3,146
Prinsburg 557
Prior Lake MPLS- 7,284
Proctor DUL- 3,180
Ramsey MPLS- 10,093
Randall 527
Raymond 723
Redlake 600 ○
Red Lake Falls 1,732
Red Wing 13,736
Redwood Falls 5,210
Renville 1,493
Rice 499
Richfield MPLS- 37,851
Richmond 867
Robbinsdale MPLS- 14,422
ROCHESTER ROCH 57,890
Rockford MPLS- 2,408
Rockville 597
Rogers MPLS- 652
Rollingstone 528
Roseau 2,272
Rosemount MPLS- 5,083
Roseville MPLS- 35,820
Rothsay 476
Round Lake 480
Royalton 660
Rush City 1,198
Rushford 1,478
Sabin 446
Sacred Heart 666
St. Charles 2,184
St. Clair 655
ST. CLOUD ST.CLD 42,566
St. Francis 1,184
St. James 4,346
St. Joseph ST.CLD 2,994
St. Louis Park MPLS- 42,931
St. Michael MPLS- 1,519
St. Paul MPLS- 270,230
St. Peter 9,056
Sanborn 518
Sandstone 1,594
Sartell ST.CLD 3,427
Sauk Centre 3,709
Sauk Rapids ST.CLD 5,793
Scanlon 1,050
Sebeka 774
Shakopee MPLS- 9,941
Sherburn 1,275
Shoreview MPLS- 17,300
Shorewood MPLS- 4,646
Silver Bay 2,917
Silver Lake 698
Slayton 2,420
Sleepy Eye 3,581
Soudan 950 ○
South International Falls 2,806
South St. Paul MPLS- 21,235
Spicer 909
Springfield 2,303
Spring Grove 1,275
Spring Valley 2,616
Staples 2,887
Starbuck 1,224
Stephen 898
Stewart 616
Stewartville ROCH 3,925
Stillwater MPLS- 12,290
Taylors Falls 623
Thief River Falls 9,105
Tower 640
Tracy 2,478
Trimont 805

○ Rand McNally estimate
▲ Population of entire township or "town", including rural areas.
● Independent city. Population not included in county total.

MINNESOTA continued

Place	Population
Truman	1,392
Twin Valley	907
Two Harbors	4,039
Tyler	1,353
Ulen	514
Vadnais Heights MPLS-	5,111
Verndale	504
Virginia	11,056
Wabasha	2,372
Wabasso	745
Waconia MPLS-	2,638
Wadena	4,699
Waite Park ST.CLD	3,496
Walker	970
Walnut Grove	753
Wanamingo	717
Warren	2,105
Warroad	1,216
Waseca	8,219
Waterville	1,717
Watkins	757
Waverly	470
Welcome	855
Wells	2,777
Westbrook	978
West Concord	762
West St. Paul MPLS-	18,527
Wheaton	1,969
White Bear Lake MPLS-	22,538
Willmar	15,895
Windom	4,666
Winnebago	1,869
Winona	25,075
Winsted	1,522
Winthrop	1,376
Woodbury MPLS-	10,297
Worthington	10,243
Wykoff	482
Wyoming MPLS-	1,559
Zimmerman	1,074
Zumbrota	2,129

COUNTIES

County	Population
Aitkin	13,404
Anoka	195,998
Becker	29,336
Beltrami	30,982
Benton	25,187
Big Stone	7,716
Blue Earth	52,314
Brown	28,645
Carlton	29,936
Carver	37,046
Cass	21,050
Chippewa	14,941
Chisago	25,717
Clay	49,327
Clearwater	8,761
Cook	4,092
Cottonwood	14,854
Crow Wing	41,722
Dakota	194,279
Dodge	14,773
Douglas	27,839
Faribault	19,714
Fillmore	21,930
Freeborn	36,329
Goodhue	38,749
Grant	7,171
Hennepin	941,411
Houston	18,382
Hubbard	14,098
Isanti	23,600
Itasca	43,069
Jackson	13,690
Kanabec	12,161
Kandiyohi	36,763
Kittson	6,672
Koochiching	17,571
Lac qui Parle	10,592
Lake	13,043
Lake of the Woods	3,764
Le Sueur	23,434
Lincoln	8,207
Lyon	25,207
McLeod	29,657
Mahnomen	5,535
Marshall	13,027
Martin	24,687
Meeker	20,594
Mille Lacs	18,430
Morrison	29,311
Mower	40,390
Murray	11,507
Nicollet	26,929
Nobles	21,840
Norman	9,379
Olmsted	92,006
Otter Tail	51,937
Pennington	15,258
Pine	19,871
Pipestone	11,690
Polk	34,844
Pope	11,657
Ramsey	459,784
Red Lake	5,471
Redwood	19,341
Renville	20,401
Rice	46,087
Rock	10,703
Roseau	12,574
St. Louis	222,229
Scott	43,784
Sherburne	29,908
Sibley	15,448
Stearns	108,161
Steele	30,328
Stevens	11,322
Swift	12,920
Todd	24,991
Traverse	5,542
Wabasha	19,335
Wadena	14,192
Waseca	18,448
Washington	113,571
Watonwan	12,361
Wilkin	8,454
Winona	46,256
Wright	58,681
Yellow Medicine	13,653

MISSISSIPPI

1980
Census 2,520,638

CITIES

City	Population
Abbeville	448
Aberdeen	7,184
Ackerman	1,598
Amory	7,307
Anguilla	950
Arcola	588
Artesia	526
Ashland	532
Baldwyn	3,427
Batesville	4,692
Bay Saint Louis	7,891
Bay Springs	1,884
Bear Town	1,277
Beaumont	1,112
Belmont	1,420
Belzoni	2,982
Benoit	499
Bentonia	518
Bigpoint	900 ○
Biloxi GUL-B	49,311
Blue Mountain	867
Bogue Chitto	600 ○
Bolton	664
Booneville	6,199
Brandon JAC	9,626
Brookhaven	10,800
Brooklyn	800 ○
Brooksville	1,038
Bruce	2,208
Buckatunna	700 ○
Bude	1,092
Burnsville	889
Byhalia	757
Caledonia	497
Calhoun City	2,033
Canton	11,116
Carriere	500 ○
Carthage	3,453
Cary	470
Charleston	2,878
Clarksdale	21,137
Cleveland	14,524
Clinton JAC	14,660
Coffeeville	1,129
Coldwater	1,505
Collins	2,131
Columbia	7,733
COLUMBUS COL	27,383
Como	1,378
Corinth	13,839
Crawford	495
Crenshaw	1,019
Crowder	789
Cruger	540
Crystal Springs	4,902
Decatur	1,148
De Kalb	1,159
De Lisle GUL-B	600 ○
Derma	793
D'Iberville GUL-B	9,000 ○
D'Lo	463
Drew	2,528
Duck Hill	706
Duncan	501
Durant	2,889
Ecru	687
Edwards	1,515
Elliott	1,200 ○
Ellisville LAUR	4,652
Enterprise	607
Escatawpa PSCG	5,367
Ethel	486
Eupora	2,048
Fayette	2,033
Fernwood	600 ○
Flora	1,507
Florence JAC	1,111
Flowood JAC	943
Forest	5,229
Foxworth	1,000 ○
Friars Point	1,400
Fulton	3,238
Gautier PSCG	8,917
Glen Allan	600 ○
Glendale HATT	1,329
Gloster	1,726
Goodman	1,285
GREENVILLE GRNV	40,613
Greenwood	20,115
Grenada	12,641
GULFPORT GUL-B	39,676
Gunnison	708
Hamilton	500 ○
Harriston	450 ○
Hatley	497
HATTIESBURG HATT	40,829
Hazlehurst	4,437
Heidelberg	1,098
Henderson's Point GUL-B	1,114
Hernando MEM	2,969
Hickory	670
Hickory Flat	458
Hollandale	4,336
Holly Springs	7,285
Horn Lake MEM	4,326
Houlka	710
Houston	3,747
Hurley	600 ○
Indianola	8,221
Inverness	1,034
Isola	834
Itta Bena	2,904
Iuka	2,846
JACKSON JAC	202,895
Jonestown	1,231
Kilmichael	906
Kiln	650 ○
Kings VICK	1,165
Kosciusko	7,415
Lake	524
Lakeshore	800 ○
Lambert	1,624
Lauderdale	750 ○
LAUREL LAUR	21,897
Leakesville	1,120
Leland	6,667
Lexington	2,628
Liberty	669
Long Beach GUL-B	7,967
Lorman	650 ○
Louisville	7,323
Lucedale	2,429
Lumberton	2,217
Maben	855
McComb	12,331
McLain	688
McNeill	500 ○
Macon	2,396
Madison JAC	2,241
Magee	3,497
Magnolia	2,461
Mantachie	732
Marion MRID	771
Marks	2,260
Mathiston	632
Meadville	575
Mendenhall	2,533
MERIDIAN MRID	46,577
Merigold	574
Metcalfe GRNV	952
Mississippi State	4,600 ○
Monticello	1,834
Moorhead	2,358
Morgantown NCHZ	3,445
Morton	3,303
Moselle	500 ○
Moss Point PSCG	18,998
Mound Bayou	2,917
Mount Olive	993
NATCHEZ NCHZ	22,015
Nettleton	1,911
New Albany	7,072
New Augusta	589
Newhebron	470
Newton	3,708
North Carrollton	859
North Gulfport GUL-B	6,660
North Tunica	1,026
Noxapater	516
Oakland	540
Ocean Springs GUL-B	14,504
Okolona	3,409
Olive Branch MEM	2,067
Orange Grove GUL-B	2,700 ○
Osyka	581
Oxford	9,882
Pace	519
PASCAGOULA PSCG	29,318
Pass Christian GUL-B	5,014
Pearl JAC	18,580
Pearlington	600 ○
Pelahatchie	1,445
Perkinston	650 ○
Petal HATT	8,476
Philadelphia	6,434
Picayune	10,361
Pickens	1,386
Plantersville	920
Pontotoc	4,723
Poplarville	2,562

○ Rand McNally estimate
▲ Population of entire township or "town", including rural areas.
● Independent city. Population not included in county total.

Port Gibson 2,371
Potts Camp 525
Prentiss 1,465
Purvis 2,256
Quitman 2,632
Raleigh 998
Raymond JAC 1,967
Richton 1,205
Ridgeland JAC 5,461
Ripley 4,271
Rolling Fork 2,590
Rosedale 2,793
Roxie 591
Ruleville 3,332
Saltillo 1,271
Sanatorium 700 ○
Sandersville LAUR 800
Scooba 511
Senatobia 5,013
Shannon 680
Shaw 2,461
Shelby 2,540
Sherman 499
Shubuta 626
Shuqualak 554
Sidon 450
Sledge 699
Smithville 866
Southaven MEM 16,441
Star 500 ○
Starkville 15,169
State Line 484
Stonewall 1,345
Summit 1,753
Sumner 452
Sumrall 1,197
Sunflower 1,027
Taylorsville 1,387
Tchula 1,931
Terry JAC 655
Thomastown 500 ○
Tie Plant 450 ○
Tunica 1,361
Tupelo 23,905
Tutwiler 1,174
Tylertown 1,976
Union 1,931
Utica 865
Vaiden 924
Vancleave 1,330
Vardaman 1,009
Verona 2,497
VICKSBURG VICK 25,434
Victoria 950 ○
Walnut 513
Washington 900 ○
Water Valley 4,147
Waveland 4,186
Waynesboro 5,349
Webb 782
Weir 553
Wesson 1,313
West Point 8,811
Wheeler 600 ○
Wiggins 3,205
Winona 6,177
Winstonville 486
Woodville 1,512
Woolmarket GUL-B 670 ○
Yazoo City 12,092

COUNTIES

Adams 38,035
Alcorn 33,036
Amite 13,369
Attala 19,865
Benton 8,153
Bolivar 45,965
Calhoun 15,664
Carroll 9,776
Chickasaw 17,853
Choctaw 8,996
Claiborne 12,279
Clarke 16,945
Clay 21,082
Coahoma 36,918
Copiah 26,503
Covington 15,927
De Soto 53,930
Forrest 66,018
Franklin 8,208
George 15,297
Greene 9,827
Grenada 21,043
Hancock 24,537
Harrison 157,665
Hinds 250,998
Holmes 22,970
Humphreys 13,931
Issaquena 2,513
Itawamba 20,518
Jackson 118,015
Jasper 17,265
Jefferson 9,181
Jefferson Davis 13,846
Jones 61,912
Kemper 10,148
Lafayette 31,030
Lamar 23,821
Lauderdale 77,285
Lawrence 12,518
Leake 18,790
Lee 57,061
Leflore 41,525
Lincoln 30,174
Lowndes 57,304
Madison 41,613
Marion 25,708
Marshall 29,296
Monroe 36,404
Montgomery 13,366
Neshoba 23,789
Newton 19,944
Noxubee 13,212
Oktibbeha 36,018
Panola 28,164
Pearl River 33,795
Perry 9,864
Pike 36,173
Pontotoc 20,918
Prentiss 24,025
Quitman 12,636
Rankin 69,427
Scott 24,556
Sharkey 7,964
Simpson 23,441
Smith 15,077
Stone 9,716
Sunflower 34,844
Tallahatchie 17,157
Tate 20,119
Tippah 18,739
Tishomingo 18,434
Tunica 9,652
Union 21,741
Walthall 13,761
Warren 51,627
Washington 72,344
Wayne 19,135
Webster 10,300
Wilkinson 10,021
Winston 19,474
Yalobusha 13,139
Yazoo 27,349

MISSOURI

1980 Census 4,916,759

CITIES

Adrian 1,484
Advance 1,054
Affton ST.L 23,181
Alba 474
Albany 2,152
Allenton ST.L 500 ○
Alma 445
Alton 721
Anderson 1,237
Antonia ST.L 500 ○
Appleton City 1,257
Arcadia 683
Archie 753
Arnold ST.L 19,141
Ash Grove 1,157
Ashland 1,021
Atlanta 441
Aurora 6,437
Auxvasse 858
Ava 2,761
Avondale K.C. 612
Ballwin ST.L 12,656
Barnhart ST.L 800 ○
Bell City 539
Belle 1,233
Bellefontaine Neighbors ST.L 12,082
Bel-Nor ST.L 2,047
Belton K.C. 12,708
Benton 674
Berkeley ST.L 15,922
Bernie 1,975
Bertrand 688
Bethany 3,095
Billings 911
Birch Tree 622
Bismarck 1,625
Black Jack ST.L 5,293
Bland 662
Bloomfield 1,795
Blue Springs K.C. 25,927
Bolivar 5,919
Bonne Terre 3,797
Boonville 6,959
Bourbon 1,259
Bowling Green 3,022
Braggadocio 450 ○
Branson 2,550
Braymer 986
Breckenridge 523
Breckenridge Hills ST.L 5,666
Brentwood ST.L 8,209
Bridgeton ST.L 18,445
Brookfield 5,555
Brunswick 1,272
Bucklin 713
Buckner K.C. 2,848
Buffalo 2,217
Bunker 673
Burke City ST.L 2,600 ○
Burlington Junction 657
Butler 4,107
Cabool 2,090
Cainsville 496
California 3,381
Calverton Park ST.L 1,717
Camdenton 2,303
Cameron 4,519
Campbell 2,134
Canton 2,435
CAPE GIRARDEAU CPGIR 34,361
Cardwell 831
Carl Junction JOP 3,937
Carrollton 4,700
Carterville JOP 1,973
Carthage 11,104
Caruthersville 7,958
Cassville 2,091
Castle Point ST.L 6,500 ○
Cedar Hill ST.L 1,512
Center 669
Centralia 3,537
Chaffee 3,241
Chamois 546
Charleston 5,230
Chillicothe 9,089
Clarence 1,147
Clarksville 585
Clarkton 1,228
Clayton ST.L 14,273
Cleveland 485
Clever 551
Clinton 8,366
Cole Camp 1,022
COLUMBIA COL 62,061
Concord ST.L 20,896
Concordia 2,129
Conway 601
Cooter 479
Corder 483
Crane 1,185
Crestwood ST.L 12,815
Creve Coeur ST.L 11,757
Crocker 979
Crystal City ST.L 3,618
Cuba 2,120
Dearborn 547
Deepwater 475
Dellwood ST.L 6,200
Delta 524
Desloge 3,581
De Soto ST.L 5,993
Des Peres ST.L 8,254
Dexter 7,043
Dixon 1,402
Doe Run 900 ○
Doniphan 1,921
Doolittle 701
Downing 462
Drexel 908
Duenweg JOP 703
East Prairie 3,713
Edgerton 584
Edina 1,520
Eldon 4,342
El Dorado Springs 3,868
Ellington 1,215
Ellisville ST.L 6,233
Elsberry 1,272
Elvins 1,548
Eminence 614
Essex 545
Eureka ST.L 3,862
Excelsior Springs K.C. 10,424
Exeter 588
Fairfax 835
Fair Grove 863
Farber 503
Farmington 8,270
Fayette 2,983
Ferguson ST.L 24,740
Festus ST.L 7,574
Fisk 450
Flat River 4,443
Florissant ST.L 55,372
Fordland 569
Forsyth 1,010
Frankford 443
Fredericktown 4,036
Freeburg 554
Freeman 485
Fulton 11,046
Gainesville 707
Gallatin 2,063
Garden City 1,021
Gerald 921
Gideon 1,240
Gladstone K.C. 24,990
Glasgow 1,336
Glasgow Village ST.L 7,200 ○
Glencoe ST.L 500 ○
Glendale ST.L 6,035
Golden City 900
Goodman 1,030
Gower 1,276
Grain Valley K.C. 1,327
Granby 1,908
Grandview K.C. 24,502
Grant City 1,068
Gray Summit ST.L 500 ○
Green City 719
Greenfield 1,394
Green Ridge 488
Greenwood K.C. 1,315
Hale 529

○ Rand McNally estimate
▲ Population of entire township or "town", including rural areas.
● Independent city. Population not included in county total.

MISSOURI continued

Place	Population
Hallsville	624
Hamilton	1,582
Hannibal	18,811
Hardin	688
Harrisonville K.C.	6,372
Hartville	576
Hayti	3,964
Hayti Heights	1,023
Hazelwood ST.L	12,935
Herculaneum ST.L	2,293
Hermann	2,695
Higbee	817
Higginsville	4,595
High Ridge ST.L	900 ○
Hillsboro ST.L	1,508
Holcomb	632
Holden	2,195
Hollister	1,439
Hopkins	634
Horine ST.L	850 ○
Hornersville	704
Houston	2,157
Howardville	536
Humansville	907
Iberia	852
Illmo CPGIR	1,368
Imperial ST.L	950 ○
Independence K.C.	111,806
Ironton	1,743
Jackson CPGIR	7,827
Jamesport	651
Jasper	1,012
JEFFERSON CITY JFCY	33,619
Jennings ST.L	17,026
Jonesburg	614
JOPLIN JOP	39,023
Kahoka	2,101
KANSAS CITY K.C.	448,159
Kearney	1,433
Kelso CPGIR	455
Kennett	10,145
Keytesville	689
King City	1,063
Kinloch ST.L	4,455
Kirksville	17,167
Kirkwood ST.L	27,987
Knob Noster	2,040
La Belle	845
Laclede	445
Laddonia	726
Ladue ST.L	9,376
La Grange	1,217
Lamar	4,053
La Monte	1,054
Lanagan	440
Lancaster	855
La Plata	1,423
Lathrop	1,732
Lawson	1,688
Leadwood	1,371
Lebanon	9,507
Lees Summit K.C.	28,741
Leeton	604
Lemay ST.L	35,424
Lewistown	502
Lexington	5,063
Liberal	701
Liberty K.C.	16,251
Licking	1,272
Lilbourn	1,463
Lincoln	819
Linn	1,211
Lockwood	971
Louisiana	4,261
Lowry City	676
Lutesville	865
Macon	5,680
Madison	656
Malden	6,096
Manchester ST.L	6,191
Mansfield	1,423
Maplewood ST.L	10,960
Marble Hill	601
Marceline	2,938
Marionville	1,920
Marshall	12,781
Marshfield	3,871
Marston	742
Marthasville	543
Maryland Heights ST.L	5,676
Maryville	9,558
Matthews	547
Maysville	1,187
Mehlville ST.L	22,900 ○
Memphis	2,105
Mercer	442
Mexico	12,276
Milan	1,947
Miner	1,182
Moberly	13,418
Monett	6,148
Monroe City	2,557
Montgomery City	2,101
Montrose	498
Morehouse	1,220
Morley	745
Moscow Mills	484
Mound City	1,447
Mountain Grove	3,974
Mountain View	1,664
Mount Vernon	3,341
Murphy ST.L	8,121
Naylor	602
Neelyville	474
Neosho	9,493
Nevada	9,044
New Bloomfield	519
Newburg	743
New Florence	731
New Franklin	1,228
New Haven	1,581
New London	1,161
New Madrid	3,204
Nixa SPRG	2,662
Noel	1,161
Norborne	931
Normandy ST.L	5,174
North Kansas City K.C.	4,507
Northmoor K.C.	506
Northwoods ST.L	5,831
Novinger	626
Oakville ST.L	1,100 ○
Odessa	3,088
O'Fallon ST.L	8,677
Olivette ST.L	7,985
Oran	1,266
Oregon	901
Oronogo JOP	525
Orrick	922
Osage Beach	1,992
Osceola	841
Otterville	472
Overland ST.L	19,620
Owensville	2,241
Ozark SPRG	2,980
Pacific ST.L	4,410
Palmyra	3,469
Paris	1,598
Parkville K.C.	1,997
Parma	1,081
Pattonsburg	502
Peculiar K.C.	1,571
Perry	836
Perryville	7,343
Pevely ST.L	2,732
Piedmont	2,359
Pierce City	1,391
Pilot Grove	745
Pilot Knob	722
Pine Lawn ST.L	6,662
Pineville	504
Platte City K.C.	2,114
Plattsburg	2,095
Pleasant Hill K.C.	3,301
Pleasant Valley K.C.	1,545
Point Lookout	900 ○
Polo	583
Poplar Bluff	17,139
Portage Des Sioux	488
Portageville	3,470
Potosi	2,528
Princeton	1,264
Purdy	928
Puxico	833
Queen City	783
Qulin	545
Raymore K.C.	3,154
Raytown K.C.	31,759
Reeds Spring	461
Republic SPRG	4,485
Rich Hill	1,471
Richland	1,922
Richmond	5,499
Richmond Heights ST.L	11,516
Ridgeway	516
Risco	446
Rock Hill ST.L	5,702
Rock Port	1,511
Rogersville SPRG	741
Rolla	13,303
Russellville	667
St. Ann ST.L	15,523
St. Charles ST.L	37,379
St. Clair	3,485
Ste. Genevieve	3,485
Ste. Genevieve	4,481
St. James	3,328
St. Johns ST.L	7,854
ST. JOSEPH ST.JO	76,691
ST. LOUIS ● ST.L	453,085
St. Mary	565
St. Paul ST.L	607
St. Peters ST.L	15,700
Salem	4,454
Salisbury	1,975
Sappington ST.L	11,388
Sarcoxie	1,381
Savannah ST.JO	4,184
Scott City CPGIR	4,630
Sedalia	20,927
Seligman	508
Senath	1,728
Seneca	1,853
Seymour	1,535
Shelbina	2,169
Shelbyville	645
Sheldon	491
Shrewsbury ST.L	5,077
Sikeston	17,431
Slater	2,492
Smithton	559
Smithville K.C.	1,873
South Shore	450 ○
South West City	516
Spanish Lake ST.L	20,632
Sparta	743
SPRINGFIELD SPRG	133,116
Stanberry	1,387
Steele	2,419
Steelville	1,470
Stewartsville	832
Stockton	1,432
Stover	1,041
Strafford SPRG	1,121
Sturgeon	901
Sugar Creek K.C.	4,305
Sullivan	5,461
Summersville	551
Sweet Springs	1,694
Taos	759
Tarkio	2,375
Thayer	2,211
Tipton	2,155
Trenton	6,811
Troy	2,624
Union ST.L	5,506
Unionville	2,178
University City ST.L	42,738
Urich	509
Valley Park ST.L	3,232
Van Buren	850
Vandalia	3,170
Verona	592
Versailles	2,406
Viburnum	836
Vienna	514
Walnut Grove	504
Warrensburg	13,807
Warrenton	3,219
Warsaw	1,494
Washington	9,251
Waverly	941
Wayland	498
Waynesville	2,879
Weaubleau	464
Webb City JOP	7,309
Webster Groves ST.L	23,097
Wedgewood ST.L	5,700 ○
Wellington	780
Wellsville	1,546
Wentzville ST.L	3,193
West Alton ST.L	500 ○
Weston	1,440
West Plains	7,741
Wheaton	548
Willard SPRG	1,799
Willow Springs	2,215
Windsor	3,058
Winfield	592
Winona	1,050
Wright City	1,179
Wyatt	441

COUNTIES

County	Population
Adair	24,870
Andrew	13,980
Atchison	8,605
Audrain	26,458
Barry	24,408
Barton	11,292
Bates	15,873
Benton	12,183
Bollinger	10,301
Boone	100,376
Buchanan	87,888
Butler	37,693
Caldwell	8,660
Callaway	32,252
Camden	20,017
Cape Girardeau	58,837
Carroll	12,131
Carter	5,428
Cass	51,029
Cedar	11,894
Chariton	10,489
Christian	22,402
Clark	8,493
Clay	136,488
Clinton	15,916
Cole	56,663
Cooper	14,643
Crawford	18,300
Dade	7,383
Dallas	12,096
Daviess	8,905
De Kalb	8,222
Dent	14,517
Douglas	11,594
Dunklin	36,324
Franklin	71,233
Gasconade	13,181
Gentry	7,887
Greene	185,302
Grundy	11,959
Harrison	9,890
Henry	19,672
Hickory	6,367
Holt	6,882
Howard	10,008
Howell	28,807

○ Rand McNally estimate
▲ Population of entire township or "town", including rural areas.
● Independent city. Population not included in county total.

- Iron 11,084
- Jackson 629,266
- Jasper 86,958
- Jefferson 146,183
- Johnson 39,059
- Knox 5,508
- Laclede 24,323
- Lafayette 29,925
- Lawrence 28,973
- Lewis 10,901
- Lincoln 22,193
- Linn 15,495
- Livingston 15,739
- McDonald 14,917
- Macon 16,313
- Madison 10,725
- Maries 7,551
- Marion 28,638
- Mercer 4,685
- Miller 18,532
- Mississippi 15,726
- Moniteau 12,068
- Monroe 9,716
- Montgomery 11,537
- Morgan 13,807
- New Madrid 22,945
- Newton 40,555
- Nodaway 21,996
- Oregon 10,238
- Osage 12,014
- Ozark 7,961
- Pemiscot 24,987
- Perry 16,784
- Pettis 36,378
- Phelps 33,633
- Pike 17,568
- Platte 46,341
- Polk 18,822
- Pulaski 42,011
- Putnam 6,092
- Ralls 8,984
- Randolph 25,460
- Ray 21,378
- Reynolds 7,230
- Ripley 12,458
- St. Charles 144,107
- St. Clair 8,622
- Ste. Genevieve 15,180
- St. Francois 42,600
- St. Louis 973,896
- Saline 24,919
- Schuyler 4,979
- Scotland 5,415
- Scott 39,647
- Shannon 7,885
- Shelby 7,826
- Stoddard 29,009
- Stone 15,587
- Sullivan 7,434
- Taney 20,467
- Texas 21,070
- Vernon 19,806
- Warren 14,900
- Washington 17,983
- Wayne 11,277
- Webster 20,414
- Worth 3,008
- Wright 16,188

MONTANA

1980 Census 786,690

CITIES

- Absarokee 750 ○
- Anaconda 12,518
- Augusta 450 ○
- Baker 2,354
- Belgrade 2,336
- Belt 825
- Bigfork 1,080
- Big Sandy 835
- Big Timber 1,690
- BILLINGS BIL 66,824
- Billings Heights BIL 8,480
- Black Eagle GTFA 1,100 ○
- Boulder 1,441
- Bozeman 21,645
- Bridger 724
- Broadus 712
- Browning 1,226
- BUTTE BUT 37,205
- Cascade 773
- Chester 963
- Chinook 1,660
- Choteau 1,798
- Circle 931
- Colstrip 1,476
- Columbia Falls 3,112
- Columbus 1,439
- Conrad 3,074
- Crow Agency 750 ○
- Culbertson 887
- Cut Bank 3,688
- Darby 581
- Deer Lodge 4,023
- Dillon 3,976
- East Glacier Park 500 ○
- East Helena 1,647
- Ekalaka 620
- Ennis 660
- Eureka 1,119
- Fairfield 650
- Fairview 1,366
- Forsyth 2,553
- Fort Belknap Agency 500 ○
- Fort Benton 1,693
- Fort Peck 600 ○
- Fromberg 469
- Gardiner 600 ○
- Glasgow 4,455
- Glendive 5,978
- GREAT FALLS GTFA 56,725
- Hamilton 2,661
- Hardin 3,300
- Harlem 1,023
- Harlowton 1,181
- Havre 10,891
- Havre North 1,230
- Helena 23,938
- Hot Springs 601
- Hungry Horse 900 ○
- Hysham 449
- Joliet 580
- Jordan 485
- Kalispell 10,648
- Lakeside 500 ○
- Lame Deer 600 ○
- Laurel BIL 5,481
- Lewistown 7,104
- Libby 2,748
- Lincoln 500 ○
- Livingston 6,994
- Lockwood BIL 1,600 ○
- Lodge Grass 771
- Lolo 2,418
- Malta 2,367
- Manhattan 988
- Martin City 500 ○
- Miles City 9,602
- MISSOULA MSLA 33,388
- Nashua 495
- Orchard Homes MSLA 4,000 ○
- Philipsburg 1,138
- Plains 1,116
- Plentywood 2,476
- Polson 2,798
- Poplar 995
- Red Lodge 1,896
- Ronan 1,530
- Roundup 2,119
- Rudyard 600 ○
- St. Ignatius 877
- St. Regis 600 ○
- Scobey 1,382
- Seeley Lake 800 ○
- Shelby 3,142
- Sheridan 646
- Sidney 5,726
- Somers 800 ○
- Stanford 595
- Stevensville 1,207
- Sunburst 476
- Superior 1,054
- Terry 929
- Thompson Falls 1,478
- Three Forks 1,247
- Townsend 1,587
- Troy 1,088
- Valier 640
- Vaughn 2,270
- Victor 450 ○
- Walkerville BUT 887
- West Yellowstone 735
- Whitefish 3,703
- Whitehall 1,030
- White Sulphur Springs 1,302
- Wibaux 782
- Wolf Point 3,074

COUNTIES

- Beaverhead 8,186
- Big Horn 11,096
- Blaine 6,999
- Broadwater 3,267
- Carbon 8,099
- Carter 1,799
- Cascade 80,696
- Chouteau 6,092
- Custer 13,109
- Daniels 2,835
- Dawson 11,805
- Deer Lodge 12,518
- Fallon 3,763
- Fergus 13,076
- Flathead 51,966
- Gallatin 42,865
- Garfield 1,656
- Glacier 10,628
- Golden Valley 1,026
- Granite 2,700
- Hill 17,985
- Jefferson 7,029
- Judith Basin 2,646
- Lake 19,056
- Lewis and Clark 43,039
- Liberty 2,329
- Lincoln 17,752
- McCone 2,702
- Madison 5,448
- Meagher 2,154
- Mineral 3,675
- Missoula 76,016
- Musselshell 4,428
- Park 12,869
- Petroleum 655
- Phillips 5,367
- Pondera 6,731
- Powder River 2,520
- Powell 6,958
- Prairie 1,836
- Ravalli 22,493
- Richland 12,243
- Roosevelt 10,467
- Rosebud 9,899
- Sanders 8,675
- Sheridan 5,414
- Silver Bow 38,092
- Stillwater 5,598
- Sweet Grass 3,216
- Teton 6,491
- Toole 5,559
- Treasure 981
- Valley 10,250
- Wheatland 2,359
- Wibaux 1,476
- Yellowstone 108,035
- Yellowstone National Park 66

NEBRASKA

1980 Census 1,569,825

CITIES

- Ainsworth 2,256
- Air Park West LINC 3,100 ○
- Albion 1,997
- Alda GDIS 601
- Alliance 9,920
- Alma 1,369
- Ansley 644
- Arapahoe 1,107
- Arlington 1,117
- Arnold 813
- Ashland 2,274
- Atkinson 1,521
- Auburn 3,482
- Aurora 3,717
- Axtell 602
- Bancroft 552
- Bassett 1,009
- Battle Creek 948
- Bayard 1,435
- Beatrice 12,891
- Beaver City 775
- Beaver Crossing 458
- Beemer 853
- Bellevue OMA- 21,813
- Benkelman 1,235
- Bennet 523
- Bennington OMA- 631
- Bertrand 775
- Big Springs 505
- Blair 6,418
- Bloomfield 1,393
- Blue Hill 883
- Blue Springs 521
- Boys Town OMA- 622
- Bridgeport 1,668
- Broken Bow 3,979
- Burwell 1,383
- Butte 529
- Cairo 737
- Callaway 579
- Cambridge 1,206
- Campbell 441
- Cedar Bluffs 632
- Cedar Rapids 447
- Central City 3,083
- Ceresco 836
- Chadron 5,933
- Chappell 1,095
- Clarks 445
- Clarkson 817
- Clay Center 962
- Coleridge 673
- Columbus 17,328
- Cozad 4,453
- Crawford 1,315
- Creighton 1,341
- Crete 4,872
- Crofton 948
- Crown Point OMA- 700 ○
- Culbertson 767
- Curtis 1,014
- Dakota City SXCY 1,440
- Davenport 445
- David City 2,514
- Debolt OMA- 800 ○
- Decatur 723
- Deshler 997
- De Witt 642
- Dodge 815
- Doniphan 696
- Dorchester 611
- Eagle 832
- Edgar 705
- Elgin 807
- Elkhorn OMA- 1,344
- Elm Creek 862
- Elmwood 598
- Elwood 716

○ Rand McNally estimate
▲ Population of entire township or "town", including rural areas.
● Independent city. Population not included in county total.

NEBRASKA continued

Name	Population
Emerson	874
Eustis	460
Ewing	520
Exeter	807
Fairbury	4,885
Fairfield	543
Fairmont	767
Falls City	5,374
Fort Calhoun	641
Franklin	1,167
Fremont	23,979
Friend	1,079
Fullerton	1,506
Geneva	2,400
Genoa	1,090
Gering	7,760
Gibbon	1,531
Gordon	2,167
Gothenburg	3,479
GRAND ISLAND GDIS	33,180
Grant	1,270
Greeley	597
Greenwood	587
Gretna OMA-	1,609
Hartington	1,730
Harvard	1,217
Hastings	23,045
Hay Springs	794
Hebron	1,906
Hemingford	1,023
Henderson	1,072
Hershey	633
Hickman	687
Holdrege	5,624
Homer	564
Hooper	932
Howells	677
Humboldt	1,176
Humphrey	799
Imperial	1,941
Indianola	856
Irvington OMA-	500 ○
Juniata	703
Kearney	21,158
Kenesaw	854
Kimball	3,120
Laurel	1,031
La Vista OMA-	9,588
Leigh	509
Lexington	7,040
LINCOLN LINC.	171,932
Long Pine	521
Loomis	447
Louisville	1,022
Loup City	1,368
Lyman	551
Lyons	1,214
McCook	8,404
Macy	500 ○
Madison	1,950
Mead	506
Milford	2,108
Minatare	969
Minden	2,939
Mitchell	1,956
Morrill	1,097
Mullen	720
Murray	465
Nebraska City	7,127
Neligh	1,893
Nelson	733
Newman Grove	930
Norfolk	19,449
North Bend	1,368
North Oaks OMA-	600 ○
North Omaha OMA-	1,100 ○
North Platte	24,509
Oakland	1,393
Ogallala	5,638
OMAHA OMA-	313,911
O'Neill	4,049
Orchard	482
Ord	2,658
Orleans	527
Osceola	975
Oshkosh	1,057
Osmond	871
Overton	633
Oxford	1,109
Palmer	487
Palmyra	512
Papillion OMA-	6,399
Pawnee City	1,156
Paxton	568
Pender	1,318
Peru	998
Pierce	1,535
Plainview	1,483
Plattsmouth OMA-	6,295
Plymouth	506
Polk	440
Ponca	1,057
Ralston OMA-	5,143
Randolph	1,106
Ravenna	1,296
Red Cloud	1,300
Roanoke OMA-	900 ○
Rushville	1,217
St. Edward	891
St. Paul	2,094
Sargent	828
Schuyler	4,151
Scottsbluff	14,156
Scribner	1,011
Seward	5,713
Shelby	724
Shelton	1,046
Sidney	6,010
Silver Creek	496
South Sioux City SXCY	9,339
Spalding	645
Spencer	596
Springfield	782
Stanton	1,603
Sterling	526
Still Meadow OMA-	950 ○
Stratton	499
Stromsburg	1,290
Stuart	641
Sunnyslope OMA-	770 ○
Superior	2,502
Sutherland	1,238
Sutton	1,416
Syracuse	1,638
Tecumseh	1,926
Tekamah	1,886
Terrytown	727
Tilden	1,012
Trenton	796
Utica	689
Valentine	2,829
Valley	1,716
Valparaiso	484
Verdigre	617
Wahoo	3,555
Wakefield	1,125
Walthill	847
Waterloo OMA-	450
Wauneta	746
Wausa	647
Waverly LINC.	1,726
Wayne	5,240
Weeping Water	1,109
West Point	3,609
Wilber	1,624
Winnebago	902
Wisner	1,335
Wood River	1,334
Wymore	1,841
York	7,723
Yutan	631

COUNTIES

Name	Population
Adams	30,656
Antelope	8,675
Arthur	513
Banner	918
Blaine	867
Boone	7,391
Box Butte	13,696
Boyd	3,331
Brown	4,377
Buffalo	34,797
Burt	8,813
Butler	9,330
Cass	20,297
Cedar	11,375
Chase	4,758
Cherry	6,758
Cheyenne	10,057
Clay	8,106
Colfax	9,890
Cuming	11,664
Custer	13,877
Dakota	16,573
Dawes	9,609
Dawson	22,304
Deuel	2,462
Dixon	7,137
Dodge	35,847
Douglas	397,038
Dundy	2,861
Fillmore	7,920
Franklin	4,377
Frontier	3,647
Furnas	6,486
Gage	24,456
Garden	2,802
Garfield	2,363
Gosper	2,140
Grant	877
Greeley	3,462
Hall	47,690
Hamilton	9,301
Harlan	4,292
Hayes	1,356
Hitchcock	4,079
Holt	13,552
Hooker	990
Howard	6,773
Jefferson	9,817
Johnson	5,285
Kearney	7,053
Keith	9,364
Keya Paha	1,301
Kimball	4,882
Knox	11,457
Lancaster	192,884
Lincoln	36,455
Logan	983
Loup	859
McPherson	593
Madison	31,382
Merrick	8,945
Morrill	6,085
Nance	4,740
Nemaha	8,367
Nuckolls	6,726
Otoe	15,183
Pawnee	3,937
Perkins	3,637
Phelps	9,769
Pierce	8,481
Platte	28,852
Polk	6,320
Red Willow	12,615
Richardson	11,315
Rock	2,383
Saline	13,131
Sarpy	86,015
Saunders	18,716
Scotts Bluff	38,344
Seward	15,789
Sheridan	7,544
Sherman	4,226
Sioux	1,845
Stanton	6,549
Thayer	7,582
Thomas	973
Thurston	7,186
Valley	5,633
Washington	15,508
Wayne	9,858
Webster	4,858
Wheeler	1,060
York	14,798

NEVADA

1980 Census 800,493

CITIES

Name	Population
Babbitt	1,800 ○
Battle Mountain	2,749
Beatty	900 ○
Boulder City	9,590
Caliente	982
Carlin	1,232
Carson City ●	32,022
Crystal Bay	1,200 ○
East Las Vegas LASV	6,449
Elko	8,758
Ely	4,882
Eureka	500 ○
Fallon	4,262
Fernley	1,200 ○
Gabbs	811
Gardnerville	2,800 ○
Hawthorne	3,741
Henderson LASV	24,363
Indian Springs	900 ○
Jackpot	500 ○
LAS VEGAS LASV	164,674
Lemmon Valley RENO	2,000 ○
Lovelock	1,680
McGill	1,419
Mesquite	700 ○
Minden	1,300 ○
New Washoe City	2,543
North Las Vegas LASV	42,739
Overton	1,111
Owyhee	700 ○
Pahrump	1,000 ○
Panaca	550 ○
Paradise LASV	45,000 ○
Pioche	700 ○
RENO RENO	100,756
Ruth	735 ○
Skyland	500 ○
Sparks RENO	40,780
Stateline	1,500 ○
Sunrise Manor LASV	44,155
Sun Valley RENO	8,822
Tonopah	1,952
Topaz Ranch Estates	500 ○
Verdi RENO	800 ○
Virginia City	600 ○
Weed Heights	650 ○
Wells	1,218
Winchester LASV	19,728
Winnemucca	4,140
Yerington	2,021
Zephyr Cove	1,300 ○

COUNTIES

Name	Population
Churchill	13,917
Clark	463,087
Douglas	19,421
Elko	17,269
Esmeralda	777
Eureka	1,198
Humboldt	9,434
Lander	4,076
Lincoln	3,732
Lyon	13,594
Mineral	6,217
Nye	9,048
Pershing	3,408
Storey	1,503
Washoe	193,623
White Pine	8,167

○ Rand McNally estimate
▲ Population of entire township or "town", including rural areas.
● Independent city. Population not included in county total.

NEW HAMPSHIRE

1980
Census 920,610

CITIES

Alstead 1,461▲ ...... 500 ○
Alton 2,440▲ .... 900 ○
Alton Bay .... 900 ○
Amherst NSHUA 8,243▲ .... 750 ○
Antrim 2,208▲ 1,142
Ashland 1,807▲ 1,479
Atkinson BOS 4,397▲ .... 900 ○
Bartlett 1,566▲ .... 700 ○
Bedford MNCH 9,481▲ .... 1,300 ○
Belmont 4,026▲ ...... 900 ○
Bennington 890▲ ..... 500 ○
Berlin 13,084
Bethlehem 1,784▲ .... 700 ○
Bow CONC 4,015▲ ..... 500 ○
Bradford 1,115▲ ...... 450 ○
Bristol 2,198▲ 1,258
Campton 1,694▲ ...... 600 ○
Canaan 2,456▲ ...... 600 ○
Canobie Lake BOS .... 800 ○
Center Harbor 808▲ ... 500 ○
Center Ossipee .... 500 ○
Charlestown 4,417▲ 1,294
Chester BOS 2,006▲ .... 500 ○
Claremont 14,557
Colebrook 2,459▲ ... 1,131
CONCORD CONC 30,400
Contoocook CONC... 1,499
Conway 7,158▲ 1,781
Danville BOS 1,318▲ .... 500 ○
Derry BOS 18,875▲ 12,248
DOVER DOV- 22,377
Dublin 1,303▲ .... 600 ○
Durham 10,652▲ 8,448
East Derry BOS ...... 600 ○
East Hampstead BOS .... 900 ○
Enfield 3,175▲ 1,581
Epping 3,460▲ 1,384
Exeter 11,024▲ 8,947
Farmington DOV- 4,630▲ 3,284
Fitzwilliam 1,795▲ .... 600 ○
Franconia 743▲ ...... 600 ○
Franklin 7,901
Fremont 1,333▲ ...... 450 ○
Gilmanton 1,941▲ .... 600 ○
Gilsum 652▲ .... 500 ○
Goffstown MNCH 11,315▲ ... 2,500 ○
Gorham 3,322▲ 2,180
Greenfield 972▲ ...... 500 ○
Greenland PTSM 2,129▲ ...... 600 ○
Greenville NSHUA 1,988▲ ... 1,447
Groveton 1,389
Hampstead BOS 3,785▲ .... 500 ○
Hampton PTSM 10,493▲ ... 6,779
Hampton Beach .... 900 ○
Hampton Falls PTSM 1,372▲ ...... 500 ○
Hanover 9,119▲ 6,861
Henniker 3,246▲ 1,538
Hillsboro 1,797
Hinsdale 3,631▲ 1,546
Hooksett MNCH 7,303▲ 1,868
Hudson NSHUA 14,022▲ .. 6,248
Jaffrey 4,349▲ 2,684
Keene 21,449
Kingston BOS 4,111▲ .... 900 ○
Laconia 15,575
Lancaster 3,401▲ ... 2,134
Lebanon 11,134
Lincoln 1,313▲ .... 950 ○
Lisbon 1,517▲ 1,151
Little Boars Head PTSM .... 500 ○
Littleton 5,558▲ 4,480
Londonderry MNCH 13,598▲ .... 950 ○
MANCHESTER MNCH 90,936
Marlborough 1,846▲ 1,184
Meredith 4,646▲ 1,202
Merrimack NSHUA 15,406▲ .. 1,200 ○
Milford NSHUA 8,685▲ ... 6,269
Millville Lake BOS ..... 600 ○
Milton DOV- 2,438▲ ..... 1,000 ○
NASHUA NSHUA... 67,865
New Castle PTSM..... 975 ○
Newfields PTSM 817▲ .... 700 ○
New Ipswich FTCH- 2,433▲ ..... 500 ○
New London 2,935▲ 1,335
Newmarket PTSM 4,290▲ 3,749
Newport 6,229▲ 4,388
Newton BOS 3,068▲ .... 450 ○
Newton Junction BOS .... 450 ○
North Branch .... 800 ○
North Conway 2,104
Northfield 3,051▲ ... 1,340 ○
North Hampton PTSM 3,425▲ .... 1,000 ○
North Salem BOS ..... 600 ○
North Stratford .... 650 ○
North Swanzey .... 950 ○
North Walpole .... 950 ○
North Woodstock .... 600 ○
Pelham BOS 8,090▲ .... 500 ○
Peterborough 4,895▲ .... 2,100 ○
Pinardville MNCH .... 4,500 ○
Pittsfield CONC 2,889▲ 1,584
Plaistow BOS 5,609▲ ..... 1,800 ○
Plymouth 5,094▲ 3,628
PORTSMOUTH PTSM 26,254
Raymond MNCH 5,453▲ 1,192
Rochester DOV- 21,560
Rollinsford DOV- 2,319▲ 1,173
Rye PTSM 4,508▲ ... 800 ○
Rye Beach PTSM ..... 600 ○
Salem BOS 24,124▲ .... 11,500 ○
Sanbornville .... 800 ○
Seabrook BOS 5,917▲ .... 700 ○
Somersworth DOV- 10,350
South Hooksett MNCH .... 1,200 ○
Stratham PTSM 2,507▲ ...... 500 ○
Sunapee 2,312▲ ..... 900 ○
Suncook CONC 4,698
Swanzey Center .... 700 ○
Tilton 3,387▲ ...... 1,230 ○
Troy 2,131▲ 1,318
Walpole 3,188▲ ...... 700 ○
Warner 1,963▲ ...... 700 ○
Warren 650▲ .... 450 ○
West Chesterfield ...... 450 ○
West Peterborough ..... 500 ○
Westport .... 450 ○
West Swanzey 1,022
Westville BOS .... 700 ○
Whitefield 1,681▲ ... 1,005
Wilton NSHUA 1,310
Winchester 3,465▲ 1,732
Winnisquam .... 600 ○
Wolfeboro 3,968▲ ... 1,800 ○
Wolfeboro Falls .... 500 ○
Woodsville 1,195

COUNTIES

Belknap 42,884
Carroll 27,931
Cheshire 62,116
Coos 35,147
Grafton 65,806
Hillsborough 276,608
Merrimack 98,302
Rockingham 190,345
Strafford 85,408
Sullivan 36,063

NEW JERSEY

1980
Census 7,364,823

CITIES

Absecon ATCY 6,859
Adamston N.Y....... 1,300 ○
Allendale N.Y. 5,901
Allenhurst N.Y. 912
Allentown PHIL- 1,962
Allenwood N.Y. .... 500 ○
Alloway 1,370
Alpha AL-B-E 2,644
Alpine N.Y. 1,549
Andover N.Y. 892
Annandale N.Y. 1,040
Arrowhead Village N.Y. .... 3,100 ○
Asbury Park N.Y. ... 17,015
Atco PHIL- .... 2,100 ○
ATLANTIC CITY ATCY 40,199
Atlantic Highlands N.Y. 4,950
Audubon PHIL- 9,533
Avalon 2,162
Avenel N.Y. .... 11,500 ○
Avon by the Sea N.Y. 2,337
Barnegat 1,012
Barnegat Light 619
Barrington PHIL- 7,418
Basking Ridge N.Y. .... 4,800 ○
Bay Head N.Y. 1,340
Bayonne N.Y. 65,047
Bayville N.Y. .... 900 ○
Beach Haven 1,714
Beachwood N.Y. 7,687
Bedminster N.Y. ...... 500 ○
Belford N.Y. .... 6,000 ○
Belle Mead .... 600 ○
Belleville N.Y. 35,367
Bellmawr PHIL- 13,721
Belmar N.Y. 6,771
Belvidere 2,475
Bergenfield N.Y. 25,568
Berkeley Heights N.Y. 12,549
Berlin PHIL- 5,786
Bernardsville N.Y. ... 6,715
Beverly PHIL- 2,919
Blackwood PHIL- 5,219
Blairstown .... 700 ○
Bloomfield N.Y. ... 47,792
Bloomingdale N.Y. ... 7,867
Bloomsbury 864
Blue Anchor PHIL- .... 500 ○
Bogota N.Y. 8,344
Boonton N.Y. 8,620
Bordentown PHIL- ... 4,441
Bossert Estates PHIL- .... 2,800 ○
Bound Brook N.Y. ... 9,710
Bradley Beach N.Y. 4,772
Branchville 870
Breton Woods N.Y... 1,300 ○
Brick N.Y. .... 3,200 ○
Bridgeport PHIL- ...... 900 ○
BRIDGETON BRDGT 18,795
Bridgewater N.Y. .... 5,800 ○
Brielle N.Y. 4,068
Brigantine ATCY 8,318
Broadway .... 450 ○
Brooklawn PHIL- 2,133
Brookwood N.Y. ..... 4,000 ○
Browns Mills 10,568
Budd Lake N.Y. 6,523
Buena VINL- 3,642
Burleigh .... 600 ○
Burlington PHIL- ... 10,246
Butler N.Y. 7,616
Caldwell N.Y. 7,624
Califon N.Y. 1,023
Camden PHIL- 84,910
Cape May 4,853
Cape May Court House 3,597
Carlstadt N.Y. 6,166
Carmel VINL- .... 500 ○
Carneys Point PHIL- 7,574
Carteret N.Y. 20,598
Cedar Brook PHIL- .... 500 ○
Cedar Grove N.Y.... 12,600
Cedar Knolls N.Y.... 3,000 ○
Cedar Run .... 450 ○
Cedarville .... 990 ○
Centre City PHIL- .... 2,500 ○
Chatham N.Y. 8,537
Cherry Hill PHIL- ... 68,785
Chesilhurst PHIL- 1,590
Chester N.Y. 1,433
Cinnaminson PHIL- 16,072
Clark N.Y. 16,699
Clarksboro PHIL- ..... 800 ○
Clayton PHIL- 6,013
Clementon PHIL- 5,764
Cliffside Park N.Y. 21,464
Cliffwood Beach N.Y. .... 6,300 ○
Clifton N.Y. 74,388
Clinton N.Y. 1,910
Closter N.Y. 8,164
Cold Spring .... 850 ○
Collingswood PHIL- 15,838
Cologne ATCY .... 500 ○
Colonia N.Y. .... 20,900 ○
Colts Neck N.Y. ...... 500 ○
Columbus PHIL- ...... 700 ○
Cranberry Lake N.Y.... 600 ○
Cranbury N.Y. 1,255
Cranford N.Y. 24,573
Cresskill N.Y. 7,609
Crestwood Village N.Y. 7,965

○ Rand McNally estimate
▲ Population of entire township or "town", including rural areas.
● Independent city. Population not included in county total.

NEW JERSEY continued

Crosswicks PHIL- ..... 550 ○
Dayton N.Y. ..... 900 ○
Deal N.Y. 1,952
Deans N.Y. ..... 600 ○
Deepwater PHIL- ..... 650 ○
Delanco PHIL- 3,730
Delran PHIL- 10,065
Demarest N.Y. 4,963
Denville N.Y. 14,045
Dividing Creek ..... 500 ○
Dorchester ..... 500 ○
Dorothy ..... 600 ○
Dover N.Y. 14,681
Dumont N.Y. 18,334
Dunellen N.Y. 6,593
East Brunswick N.Y. 37,711
East Hanover N.Y. 9,319
East Newark N.Y. 1,923
East Orange N.Y. 77,690
East Rutherford N.Y. 7,849
East Windsor N.Y. ..... 15,000 ○
Eatontown N.Y. 12,703
Edgewater N.Y. 4,628
Edgewater Park PHIL- 9,273
Edison N.Y. 70,193
Egg Harbor City ATCY 4,618
Elizabeth N.Y. 106,201
Elmer PHIL- 1,569
Elmwood Park N.Y. 18,377
Elwood ..... 900 ○
Emerson N.Y. 7,793
Englewood N.Y. 23,701
Englewood Cliffs N.Y. 5,698
Englishtown N.Y. 976
Erial PHIL- ..... 900 ○
Erma ..... 1,200 ○
Essex Fells N.Y. 2,363
Estell Manor 848
Ewing Township PHIL- 34,842
Fairfield N.Y. 7,987
Fair Haven N.Y. 5,679
Fair Lawn N.Y. 32,229
Fairton BRDGT 1,107
Fairview N.Y. 10,519
Fanwood N.Y. 7,767
Far Hills N.Y. 677
Farmingdale N.Y. 1,348
Fellowship PHIL- ..... 1,900 ○
Fieldsboro PHIL- 597
Flagtown N.Y. ..... 800 ○
Flanders N.Y. ..... 6,000 ○
Flemington N.Y. 4,132
Florence PHIL- ..... 5,000 ○
Florham Park N.Y. 9,359
Folsom 1,892
Fords N.Y. ..... 12,600 ○
Forked River ..... 1,422 ○
Fort Lee N.Y. 32,449
Franklin N.Y. 4,486
Franklin Lakes N.Y. 8,769
Franklinville PHIL- ..... 900 ○
Freehold N.Y. 10,020
Frenchtown 1,573
Garfield N.Y. 26,803
Garwood N.Y. 4,752
Gibbstown PHIL- ..... 5,676 ○
Gladstone N.Y. 2,038
Glassboro PHIL- 14,574
Glendola N.Y. ..... 2,300 ○
Glendora PHIL- 5,632
Glen Gardner N.Y. 834
Glen Ridge N.Y. ..... 7,855 ○
Glen Rock N.Y. 11,497
Gloucester City PHIL- 13,121
Green Brook N.Y. ..... 4,500 ○
Green Creek ..... 500 ○
Groveville PHIL- ..... 1,200 ○
Guttenberg N.Y. 7,340
Hackensack N.Y. 36,039
Hackettstown N.Y. 8,850
Haddonfield PHIL- 12,337
Haddon Heights PHIL- 8,361
Hainesport PHIL- ..... 900 ○
Haledon N.Y. 6,607
Hamburg N.Y. 1,832
Hamilton Square PHIL- ..... 10,000 ○
Hammonton 12,298
Hampton N.Y. 1,614
Hancocks Bridge ..... 600 ○
Harrington Park N.Y. 4,532
Harrison N.Y. 12,242
Hasbrouck Heights N.Y. 12,166
Haworth N.Y. 3,509
Hawthorne N.Y. 18,200
Hazlet N.Y. 23,013
Heislerville ..... 600 ○
Helmetta N.Y. 955
High Bridge N.Y. 3,435
Highland Lakes N.Y. 2,888
Highland Park N.Y. 13,396
Highlands N.Y. 5,187
Hightstown N.Y. 4,581
Hillsdale N.Y. 10,495
Hillside N.Y. 21,440
Hoboken N.Y. 42,460
Ho Ho Kus N.Y. 4,129
Holmdel N.Y. ..... 800 ○
Hopatcong N.Y. 15,531
Hope N.Y. ..... 450 ○
Hopelawn N.Y. ..... 12,600 ○
Hopewell PHIL- 2,001
Huntington AL-B-E ..... 700 ○
Ironia N.Y. ..... 900 ○
Irvington N.Y. 61,493
Iselin N.Y. ..... 16,500 ○
Island Heights N.Y. 1,575
Jackson N.Y. ..... 600 ○
Jamesburg N.Y. 4,114
Jersey City N.Y. 223,532
Keansburg N.Y. 10,613
Kearny N.Y. 35,735
Kendall Park N.Y. 7,419
Kenilworth N.Y. 8,221
Kenvil N.Y. ..... 3,000 ○
Keyport N.Y. 7,413
Kingston ..... 900 ○
Kinnelon N.Y. 7,770
Lake Hiawatha N.Y. ..... 14,000 ○
Lakehurst N.Y. 2,908
Lake Telemark N.Y. 1,216
Lakewood N.Y. 22,863
Lambertville PHIL- 4,044
Lanoka Harbor ..... 700 ○
Laurence Harbor N.Y. ..... 5,000 ○
Lavallette N.Y. 2,072
Lawnside PHIL- 3,042
Lawrenceville PHIL- ..... 1,800 ○
Lebanon N.Y. 820
Ledgewood N.Y. ..... 1,100 ○
Leesburg ..... 700 ○
Leonardo N.Y. ..... 3,600 ○
Leonia N.Y. 8,027
Liberty Corner N.Y. ..... 800 ○
Lincoln Park N.Y. 8,806
Lincroft N.Y. ..... 4,100 ○
Linden N.Y. 37,836
Lindenwold PHIL- 18,196
Linwood ATCY 6,144
Little Falls N.Y. 11,496
Little Ferry N.Y. 9,399
Little Silver N.Y. 5,548
Livingston N.Y. 28,040
Locust N.Y. ..... 700 ○
Lodi N.Y. 23,956
Long Branch N.Y. 29,819
Longport ATCY 1,249
Long Valley N.Y. 1,682
Lumberton PHIL- ..... 700 ○
Lyndhurst N.Y. 20,326
McAfee N.Y. ..... 500 ○
McKee City ..... 600 ○
Madison N.Y. 15,357
Magnolia PHIL- 4,881
Mahwah N.Y. ..... 7,500 ○
Malaga VINL- ..... 950 ○
Manahawkin 1,467
Manasquan N.Y. 5,354
Mantua PHIL- ..... 1,900 ○
Manville N.Y. 11,278
Maple Shade PHIL- 20,525
Maplewood N.Y. 22,950
Margate City ATCY 9,179
Marlboro N.Y. ..... 5,700 ○
Marlton PHIL- 9,411
Marmora ..... 500 ○
Matawan N.Y. 8,837
Mauricetown ..... 500 ○
Mays Landing 2,054
Maywood N.Y. 9,895
Medford PHIL- ..... 1,448 ○
Medford Lakes PHIL- 4,958
Mendham N.Y. 4,899
Mercerville PHIL- ..... 15,500 ○
Merchantville PHIL- 3,972
Metuchen N.Y. 13,762
Middlesex N.Y. 13,480
Middletown N.Y. 61,615
Midland Park N.Y. 7,381
Milford 1,368
Millburn N.Y. 19,543
Millstone N.Y. 530
Milltown N.Y. 7,136
Millville VINL- 24,815
Mine Hill N.Y. ..... 3,250 ○
Mizpah ..... 600 ○
Monmouth Beach N.Y. 3,318
Monmouth Junction N.Y. 2,579
Montclair N.Y. 38,321
Montvale N.Y. 7,318
Montville N.Y. ..... 2,700 ○
Moonachie N.Y. 2,706
Moorestown PHIL- 15,596
Morganville N.Y. ..... 900 ○
Morris Plains N.Y. 5,305
Morristown N.Y. 16,614
Mountain Lakes N.Y. 4,153
Mountainside N.Y. 7,118
Mount Arlington N.Y. 4,251
Mount Ephraim PHIL- 4,863
Mount Freedom N.Y. ..... 1,621 ○
Mount Holly PHIL- 10,818
Mullica Hill PHIL- 1,050
National Park PHIL- 3,552
Navesink N.Y. ..... 1,500 ○
Neptune City N.Y. 5,276
Neptune Township N.Y. 28,366
Netcong N.Y. 3,557
Newark N.Y. 329,248
New Brunswick N.Y. 41,442
New Egypt 2,111
Newfield VINL- 1,563
Newfoundland N.Y. ..... 900 ○
New Gretna ..... 550 ○
New Milford N.Y. 16,876
New Providence N.Y. 12,426
Newton N.Y. 7,748
Newtonville VINL- ..... 500 ○
Norma VINL- ..... 800 ○
North Arlington N.Y. 16,587
North Bergen N.Y. 47,019
North Brunswick N.Y. 22,220
North Caldwell N.Y. ..... 5,832 ○
North Cape May 4,029
Northfield ATCY 7,795
North Haledon N.Y. 8,177
North Plainfield N.Y. 19,108
Northvale N.Y. 5,046
North Wildwood 4,714
Norwood N.Y. 4,413
Nutley N.Y. 28,998
Oakhurst N.Y. ..... 4,600 ○
Oakland N.Y. 13,443
Oaklyn PHIL- 4,223
Oak Valley PHIL- ..... 7,000 ○
Ocean City ATCY 13,949
Ocean Gate N.Y. 1,385
Ocean Grove N.Y. ..... 4,200 ○
Oceanport N.Y. 5,888
Oceanville ATCY ..... 600 ○
Ogdensburg N.Y. 2,737
Old Bridge N.Y. ..... 12,500 ○
Old Tappan N.Y. 4,168
Oldwick N.Y. ..... 450 ○
Oradell N.Y. 8,658
Orange N.Y. 31,136
Oxford 1,587
Palisades Park N.Y. 13,732
Palmyra PHIL- 7,085
Paramus N.Y. 26,474
Parkertown ..... 500 ○
Park Ridge N.Y. 8,515
Parsippany N.Y. ..... 8,000 ○
Passaic N.Y. 52,463
Paterson N.Y. 137,970
Paulsboro PHIL- 6,944
Pedricktown PHIL- ..... 900 ○
Pemberton 1,198
Pennington PHIL- 2,109
Pennsauken PHIL- 33,775
Penns Grove PHIL- 5,760
Pennsville PHIL- 12,467
Pequannock N.Y. 13,776
Perth Amboy N.Y. 38,951
Phillipsburg AL-B-E 16,647
Pine Hill PHIL- 8,684
Pinehurst ATCY ..... 1,500 ○
Pinewald N.Y. ..... 900 ○
Piscataway N.Y. 42,223
Pitman PHIL- 9,744
Plainfield N.Y. 45,555
Plainsboro N.Y. ..... 800 ○
Pleasantville ATCY 13,435
Point Pleasant N.Y. 17,747
Point Pleasant Beach N.Y. 5,415
Pomona ATCY 2,358
Pompton Lakes N.Y. 10,660
Port Elizabeth ..... 500 ○
Port Monmouth N.Y. ..... 3,600 ○
Port Morris N.Y. ..... 600 ○
Port Norris 1,730
Port Reading N.Y. ..... 4,300 ○
Port Republic ATCY 837
Princeton 12,035

○ Rand McNally estimate
▲ Population of entire township or "town", including rural areas.
● Independent city. Population not included in county total.

Princeton Junction N.Y. 2,419
Prospect Park N.Y. . . . 5,142
Quinton PHIL- . . . . 500 ○
Rahway N.Y. 26,723
Ramblewood
PHIL- 6,475
Ramsey N.Y. 12,899
Rancocas PHIL- . . . . . . 600 ○
Rancocas Woods
PHIL- . . . . 1,400 ○
Raritan N.Y. 6,128
Red Bank N.Y. 12,031
Richland VINL- . . . . 800 ○
Ridgefield N.Y. 10,294
Ridgefield Park
N.Y. 12,738
Ridgewood N.Y. 25,208
Ringoes PHIL- . . . . 650 ○
Ringwood N.Y. 12,625
Rio Grande 2,016
Riverdale N.Y. 2,530
River Edge N.Y. 11,111
Riverside PHIL- 7,941
Riverton PHIL- 3,068
River Vale N.Y. 9,489
Riviera Beach N.Y. . . . 2,000 ○
Robbinsville PHIL- . . . . . 550 ○
Rochelle Park N.Y. . . . 5,603
Rockaway N.Y. 6,852
Rocky Hill 717
Roebling PHIL- . . . . . . 3,600 ○
Roosevelt 835
Roseland N.Y. 5,330
Roselle N.Y. 20,641
Roselle Park N.Y. . . . 13,377
Rosenhayn VINL- . . . . . 750 ○
Rumson N.Y. 7,623
Runnemede PHIL- . . . 9,461
Rutherford N.Y. 19,068
Saddle Brook
N.Y. 14,084
Saddle River N.Y. 2,763
Salem PHIL- 6,959
Sayreville N.Y. 29,969
Scotch Plains
N.Y. 20,774
Sea Bright N.Y. 1,812
Seabrook BRDGT . . . 1,411
Sea Girt N.Y. 2,650
Sea Isle City 2,644
Seaside Heights
N.Y. 1,802
Seaside Park N.Y. . . . 1,795
Secaucus N.Y. 13,719
Sewaren N.Y. . . . . 2,300 ○
Sewell PHIL- . . . . 1,900 ○
Shiloh BRDGT 604
Ship Bottom 1,427
Shore Acres N.Y. . . . . 1,300 ○
Shrewsbury N.Y. 2,962
Sicklerville PHIL- . . . . . . 850 ○
Silverton N.Y. 7,236
Slackwood PHIL- . . . . 8,100 ○
Somerdale PHIL- 5,900
Somerset N.Y. 21,731
Somers Point
ATCY 10,330
Somerville N.Y. 11,973
South Amboy N.Y. . . . 8,322
South Belmar N.Y. . . . 1,566
South Bound Brook
N.Y. 4,331
South Hackensack
N.Y. 2,229
South Orange
N.Y. 15,864
South Plainfield
N.Y. 20,521
South River N.Y. . . . 14,361
South Toms River
N.Y. 3,954
Sparta N.Y. 8,498
Spotswood N.Y. 7,840
Springfield N.Y. 13,955
Spring Lake N.Y. 4,215
Spring Lake Heights
N.Y. 5,424

Stanhope N.Y. 3,638
Stewartsville AL-B-E . . . 900 ○
Stirling N.Y. . . . . 2,000 ○
Stockholm N.Y. . . . . 600 ○
Stockton PHIL- 643
Stone Harbor 1,187
Stratford PHIL- 8,005
Strathmore N.Y. . . . . . 7,674 ○
Succasunna N.Y. . . . . 9,000 ○
Summit N.Y. 21,071
Surf City 1,571
Sussex 2,418
Sutton Park N.Y. . . . . 2,500 ○
Swedesboro PHIL- . . . 2,031
Teaneck N.Y. 39,007
Tenafly N.Y. 13,552
Thorofare PHIL- . . . . . 1,400 ○
Three Bridges N.Y. . . . . 650 ○
Tinton Falls N.Y. 7,740
Titusville PHIL- . . . . 900 ○
Toms River N.Y. 7,465
Totowa N.Y. 11,448
Towaco N.Y. . . . . 1,400 ○
Trenton PHIL- 92,124
Tuckahoe . . . . 650 ○
Tuckerton 2,472
Twin Rivers N.Y. 7,742
Union N.Y. 50,184
Union Beach N.Y. 6,354
Union City N.Y. 55,593
Upper Greenwood Lake
N.Y. 2,734
Upper Saddle River
N.Y. 7,958
Vail Homes N.Y. . . . . . . 995 ○
Ventnor City
ATCY 11,704
Vernon N.Y. . . . . 900 ○
Verona N.Y. 14,166
Villas 5,909
Vincentown PHIL- . . . . . 800 ○
VINELAND VINL- . . . 53,753
Waldwick N.Y. 10,802
Wallington N.Y. 10,741
Wanaque N.Y. 10,025
Waretown 1,175
Washington 6,429
Washington Crossing
PHIL- . . . . 500 ○
Washington Township
N.Y. 9,550
Watchung N.Y. 5,290
Waterford Works
PHIL- . . . . 600 ○
Wayne N.Y. 46,474
Weehawken N.Y. . . . 13,168
Wenonah PHIL- 2,303
West Berlin PHIL- . . . . 3,300 ○
West Caldwell
N.Y. 11,407
West Cape May 1,091
West Creek . . . . 500 ○
Westfield N.Y. 30,447
West Long Branch
N.Y. 7,380
West Milford N.Y. . . . . 1,600 ○
Westmont PHIL- . . . . . 5,700 ○
West New York
N.Y. 39,194
West Orange
N.Y. . . . . 39,400 ○
West Paterson
N.Y. 11,293
Westville PHIL- 4,786
Westwood N.Y. 10,714
Wharton N.Y. 5,485
White Horse
PHIL- 10,098
White House Station
N.Y. . . . . 1,019 ○
White Meadow Lake
N.Y. 8,429
Whitesboro . . . . 900 ○
Whiting . . . . 700 ○
Whitman Square
PHIL- . . . . 2,600 ○
Wildwood 4,913

Wildwood Crest 4,149
Williamstown
PHIL- 5,768
Willingboro PHIL- . . . 39,912
Winfield N.Y. 1,785
Winslow PHIL- . . . . 500 ○
Woodbine 2,809
Woodbridge N.Y. . . . 16,400 ○
Woodbury PHIL- 10,353
Woodcliff Lake
N.Y. 5,644
Woodlynne PHIL- 2,578
Woodport N.Y. . . . . 500 ○
Wood-Ridge N.Y. 7,929
Woodstown PHIL- . . . 3,250
Wrightstown 3,031
Wyckoff N.Y. 15,500
Yardville PHIL- . . . . . . 8,400 ○

COUNTIES

Atlantic 194,119
Bergen 845,385
Burlington 362,542
Camden 471,650
Cape May 82,266
Cumberland 132,866
Essex 851,116
Gloucester 199,917
Hudson 556,972
Hunterdon 87,361
Mercer 307,863
Middlesex 595,893
Monmouth 503,173
Morris 407,630
Ocean 346,038
Passaic 447,585
Salem 64,676
Somerset 203,129
Sussex 116,119
Union 504,094
Warren 84,429

NEW MEXICO

1980
Census 1,302,981

CITIES

Adobe Acres
ALBU . . . . 3,400 ○
Agua Fria S.FE . . . . 850 ○
Alameda ALBU . . . . . 7,800 ○
Alamogordo 24,024
ALBUQUERQUE
ALBU 331,767
Alcalde . . . . 800 ○
Anthony ELP 3,285
Arenas Valley . . . . 500 ○
Armijo ALBU . . . . . . 18,900 ○
Arroyo Seco . . . . 500 ○
Artesia 10,385
Aztec 5,512
Bayard 3,036
Belen ALBU 5,617
Bernalillo ALBU 3,012
Black Rock . . . . 500 ○
Bloomfield 4,881
Capitan 762
Carlsbad 25,496
Carrizozo 1,222
Cedar Crest . . . . 900 ○
Central 1,968
Chama 1,090
Chamisal . . . . 600 ○
Chimayo 1,993
Church Rock . . . . 500 ○
Cimarron 888
Clayton 2,968
Cloudcroft 521
CLOVIS CLOV 31,194

Cordova . . . . 600 ○
Crownpoint 1,134
Cuba 609
Deming 9,964
Dexter 882
Dulce 1,648
Edgewood . . . . 600 ○
El Prado . . . . 700 ○
Espanola 6,803
Estancia 830
Eunice 2,970
Fairacres LSCR . . . . . . 600 ○
Farmington 31,222
Five Points ALBU . . . . 5,500 ○
Flora Vista . . . . 500 ○
Fort Sumner 1,421
Fort Wingate . . . . 900 ○
Fruitland . . . . 700 ○
Gallup 18,167
Grants 11,439
Hagerman 936
Hanover . . . . 500 ○
Happy Valley . . . . 630 ○
Hatch 1,028
High Rolls Mountain Park 650 ○
Hobbs 29,153
Hurley 1,616
Isleta ALBU 1,246
Jal 2,675
Jemez Pueblo 1,503
Kirtland 2,358
Laguna . . . . 800 ○
La Luz 1,194
La Mesa . . . . 900 ○
LAS CRUCES
LSCR 45,086
Las Vegas 14,322
Logan 735
Lordsburg 3,195
Los Alamos 11,039
Los Lunas ALBU 3,525
Los Padillas ALBU . . . 2,500 ○
Los Ranchos de
Albuquerque
ALBU 2,702
Los Trujillos . . . . 500 ○
Loving 1,355
Lovington 9,727
Magdalena 1,022
Melrose 649
Mescalero 1,259
Mesilla LSCR 2,029
Mexican Springs . . . . 500 ○
Milan 3,747
Mora . . . . 900 ○
Moriarty 1,276
Mountainair 1,170
Mountain View
ALBU . . . . 1,900 ○
New Laguna . . . . 600 ○
Ojo Caliente . . . . 500 ○
Organ . . . . 500 ○
Pajarito ALBU . . . . . . 2,000 ○
Paradise Hills
ALBU 5,096
Pecos 885
Penasco . . . . 900 ○
Placitas . . . . 450 ○
Pojoaque Valley . . . . 900 ○
Portales 9,940
Pueblo of Acoma . . . . 500 ○
Questa 1,202
Ramah . . . . 600 ○
Ranchoes de Taos 1,411
Raton 8,225
Rio Rancho ALBU . . . 9,989
ROSWELL RSWL . . . 39,676
Ruidoso 4,260
Ruidoso Downs 949
San Antonio . . . . 500 ○
San Juan Pueblo . . . . 600 ○
San Rafael . . . . 560 ○
Santa Clara Pueblo . . . . . 450 ○
Santa Cruz . . . . 600 ○
SANTA FE S.FE 48,953
Santa Rosa 2,469
Santo Domingo Pueblo . 2,082

○ Rand McNally estimate
▲ Population of entire township or "town", including rural areas.
● Independent city. Population not included in county total.

NEW MEXICO continued

Shiprock 7,237
Silver City 9,887
Socorro 7,173
Springer 1,657
Sunland Park ELP 3,377
Taos 3,369
Taos Pueblo 1,030 ○
Tatum 896
Tesuque S.FE 1,014
Texico 958
Thoreau 1,099
Tierra Amarilla 800 ○
Tohatchi 1,011
Truth or Consequences 5,219
Tucumcari 6,765
Tularosa 2,536
Tyrone 950 ○
University Park LSCR 4,383
Vaughn 737
Waterflow 500 ○
Zuni 5,551

COUNTIES

Bernalillo 419,700
Catron 2,720
Chaves 51,103
Cibola 30,102
Colfax 13,667
Curry 42,019
De Baca 2,454
Dona Ana 96,340
Eddy 47,855
Grant 26,204
Guadalupe 4,496
Harding 1,090
Hidalgo 6,049
Lea 55,993
Lincoln 10,997
Los Alamos 17,599
Luna 15,585
McKinley 56,536
Mora 4,205
Otero 44,665
Quay 10,577
Rio Arriba 29,282
Roosevelt 15,695
Sandoval 34,799
San Juan 81,433
San Miguel 22,751
Santa Fe 75,360
Sierra 8,454
Socorro 12,566
Taos 19,456
Torrance 7,491
Union 4,725
Valencia 31,013

NEW YORK

1980
Census 17,558,072

CITIES

Accord 500 ○
Adams 1,701
Adams Center 1,519
Addison 2,028
Afton 982
Akron 2,971
ALBANY A-S-T 101,727
Albertson N.Y. 5,561
Albion ROCH 4,897
Alden BUF- 2,488
Alexandria Bay 1,265
Alfred 4,967
Allegany 2,078
Almond 568
Altamont A-S-T 1,292
Amenia 1,183
Amherst BUF- 66,100 ○
Amityville N.Y. 9,076
Amsterdam A-S-T 21,872
Andover 1,120
Angelica 982
Angola BUF- 2,292
Antwerp 749
Apalachin BING 1,227
Aquebogue 1,800 ○
Arcade 2,052
Ardsley N.Y. 4,183
Arkport 811
Arkville 600 ○
Arlington POK 11,305
Armonk N.Y. 2,238
Athens 1,738
Atlanta 750 ○
Attica 2,659
AUBURN AUB 32,548
Aurora 926
Au Sable Forks 2,100 ○
Averill Park A-S-T 1,337
Avoca 1,144
Avon ROCH 3,006
Babylon N.Y. 12,388
Bainbridge 1,603
Baldwin N.Y. 31,630
Baldwinsville SYR 6,446
Ballston Spa A-S-T 4,711
Balmville NWBG 2,919
Barker 535
Barryville 600 ○
Batavia 16,703
Bath 6,042
Bayberry SYR 6,500 ○
Bayport N.Y. 9,282
Bay Shore N.Y. 33,200 ○
Bayville N.Y. 7,034
Beacon POK 12,937
Bedford Hills N.Y. 3,200 ○
Belfast 900 ○
Bellmore N.Y. 18,106
Bellport N.Y. 2,809
Belmont 1,024
Bemus Point JMST 444
Bergen ROCH 976
Bethpage N.Y. 16,840
Big Flats ELM- 2,892
BINGHAMTON BING 55,860
Black River WATN 1,384
Blasdell BUF- 3,288
Blauvelt N.Y. 5,426 ○
Bloomingdale 608
Bohemia N.Y. 9,308
Bolivar 1,345
Bolton Landing 1,500 ○
Boonville 2,344
Brant Lake 700 ○
Brentwood N.Y. 48,800 ○
Brewster N.Y. 1,650
Briarcliff Manor N.Y. 7,115
Bridgehampton 1,941
Brighton ROCH 35,776
Broadalbin A-S-T 1,415
Brockport ROCH 9,776
Brocton 1,416
Bronxville N.Y. 6,267
Brookfield 600 ○
Brookville N.Y. 3,290
Brownville WATN 1,099
BUFFALO BUF- 357,870
Burnt Hills A-S-T 2,000 ○
Cairo 1,281
Caledonia ROCH 2,188
Callicoon 500 ○
Cambridge 1,820
Camden 2,667
Canajoharie 2,412
Canandaigua 10,419
Canaseraga 700
Canastota 4,773
Candor 917
Canisteo 2,679
Canton 7,055
Cape Vincent 785
Carle Place N.Y. 5,470
Carthage 3,643
Cassadaga 821
Castile 1,135
Castleton on Hudson A-S-T 1,627
Cato SYR 475
Catskill 4,718
Cattaraugus 1,200
Cayuga Heights ITH 3,170
Cazenovia SYR 2,599
Cedarhurst N.Y. 6,162
Celoron JMST 1,405
Centereach N.Y. 30,136
Center Moriches N.Y. 5,703
Central Bridge 500 ○
Central Islip N.Y. 26,000 ○
Central Square SYR 1,418
Central Valley N.Y. 1,705
Chadwicks UT-R 1,500 ○
Champlain 1,410
Chappaqua N.Y. 5,100 ○
Chateaugay 869
Chatham A-S-T 2,001
Chaumont 620
Chazy 800 ○
Cheektowaga BUF- 92,145
Chenango Bridge BING 2,600 ○
Chenango Forks BING 500 ○
Cherry Creek 677
Cherry Valley 684
Chester N.Y. 1,910
Chestertown 750 ○
Chili Center ROCH 5,300 ○
Chittenango SYR 4,290
Churchville ROCH 1,399
Cincinnatus 500 ○
Clayton 1,816
Cleveland SYR 855
Clifton Knolls A-S-T 4,200 ○
Clifton Springs 2,039
Clinton UT-R 2,107
Clyde 2,491
Clymer 500 ○
Cobleskill 5,272
Cohocton 902
Cohoes A-S-T 18,144
Cold Spring Harbor N.Y. 5,336
Colonie A-S-T 8,869
Colton 450 ○
Commack N.Y. 34,719
Congers N.Y. 7,123
Conklin BING 1,900 ○
Constantia SYR 1,254
Cooperstown 2,342
Copake 700 ○
Copenhagen 656
Copiague N.Y. 20,132
Coram N.Y. 24,752
Corfu BUF- 689
Corinth 2,702
Corning ELM- 12,953
Cornwall On Hudson NWBG 3,164
Cortland 20,138
Coxsackie 2,786
Croghan 703
Croton-on-Hudson N.Y. 6,889
Crown Point 900 ○
Cuba 1,739
Cutchogue 1,400 ○
Dalton 500 ○
Dannemora 3,770
Dansville 4,979
Deer Park N.Y. 30,394
Delanson A-S-T 448
Delevan 1,113
Delhi 3,374
Delmar A-S-T 8,423
Depew BUF- 19,819
Deposit 1,897
Derby BUF- 1,200 ○
De Ruyter 542
De Witt SYR 9,024
Dexter WATN 1,053
Dix Hills N.Y. 10,500 ○
Dobbs Ferry N.Y. 10,053
Downsville 950 ○
Dryden ITH 1,761
Dundee 1,556
Dunkirk 15,310
Earlville 985
East Aurora BUF- 6,803
Eastchester N.Y. 20,305
East Glenville A-S-T 6,537
East Half Hollow Hills N.Y. 9,000 ○
East Hampton 1,886
East Hills N.Y. 7,160
East Islip N.Y. 13,852
East Marion 1,500 ○
East Meadow N.Y. 39,317
East Northport N.Y. 20,187
East Patchogue N.Y. 18,139
Eastport N.Y. 2,000 ○
East Randolph 655
East Rochester ROCH 7,596
East Rockaway N.Y. 10,917
East Vestal BING 5,300 ○
Eden BUF- 3,000
Edmeston 600 ○
Edwards 561
Elba 750
Elizabethtown 650 ○
Ellenville 4,405
Ellicottville 713
ELMIRA ELM- 35,327
Elmira Heights ELM- 4,279
Elmont N.Y. 27,592
Elsmere A-S-T 5,500 ○
Elwood N.Y. 11,847
Endicott BING 14,457
Endwell BING 13,745
Etna ITH 500 ○
Evans Mills 651
Fair Haven 976
Fairmount SYR 8,400 ○
Fairport ROCH 5,970
Fairview POK 5,852
Falconer JMST 2,778
Farmingdale N.Y. 7,946
Farmingville N.Y. 13,398
Fillmore 563
Fishkill POK 1,555
Floral Park N.Y. 16,805
Florida MIDD 1,947
Flower Hill N.Y. 4,558
Fonda A-S-T 1,006
Forestville 804
Fort Ann GLFLS 509
Fort Covington 1,200 ○
Fort Edward GLFLS 3,561
Fort Plain 2,555
Frankfort UT-R 2,995
Franklin 440
Franklin Square N.Y. 29,051
Franklinville 1,887
Fredonia 11,126
Freeport N.Y. 38,272
Freeville ITH 449
Frewsburg JMST 1,908
Friendship 1,461
Fulton SYR 13,312
Galeville SYR 5,600 ○
Gang Mills ELM- 2,300
Garden City N.Y. 22,927

○ Rand McNally estimate
▲ Population of entire township or "town", including rural areas.
● Independent city. Population not included in county total.

Garden City Park N.Y. 7,712
Garrison N.Y. 650 ○
Gasport LOCK 1,339
Gates ROCH 29,756
Geneseo 6,746
Geneva 15,133
Ghent 600 ○
Gilbertsville 455
Glasco KNGST 1,179
Glen Cove N.Y. 24,618
Glenham POK 2,832
Glen Head N.Y. 6,800 ○
GLENS FALLS GLFLS 15,897
Gloversville 17,836
Gorham 800 ○
Goshen MIDD 4,874
Gouverneur 4,285
Gowanda 2,713
Grand Gorge 800 ○
Granville 2,696
Great Neck N.Y. 5,604
Great Neck Estates N.Y. 2,936
Greece ROCH 63,700 ○
Greene 1,747
Green Island A-S-T 2,696
Greenlawn N.Y. 13,869
Greenport 2,273
Greenville N.Y. 8,706
Greenwich 1,955
Greenwood 450 ○
Greenwood Lake N.Y. 2,809
Groton 2,313
Hadley 850 ○
Haines Falls 700 ○
Half Hollow Hills N.Y. 7,800 ○
Hamburg BUF- 10,582
Hamilton 3,725
Hammondsport 1,065
Hampton Bays 6,000 ○
Hannibal SYR 680
Harrison N.Y. 23,046
Harrisville 937
Hartsdale N.Y. 10,216
Hartwick 600 ○
Hastings-on-Hudson N.Y. 8,573
Hauppauge N.Y. 20,960
Haverstraw N.Y. 8,800
Hawthorne N.Y. 5,010
Hemlock ROCH 500 ○
Hempstead N.Y. 40,404
Henrietta ROCH 1,200 ○
Herkimer UT-R 8,383
Hermon 490
Heuvelton 777
Hewlett N.Y. 6,986
Hicksville N.Y. 43,245
Highland POK 3,967
Highland Falls 4,187
Hillcrest N.Y. 5,733
Hilton ROCH 4,151
Hobart 473
Holbrook N.Y. 24,342
Holland BUF- 1,347
Holland Patent UT-R 534
Holley ROCH 1,882
Homer 3,635
Honeoye Falls ROCH 2,410
Hoosick Falls 3,609
Hopewell Junction POK 1,754
Hornell 10,234
Horseheads ELM- 7,348
Houghton 1,604
Hudson 7,986
Hudson Falls GLFLS 7,419
Huntington N.Y. 19,569
Huntington Bay N.Y. 1,783
Huntington Station N.Y. 28,769
Hurley KNGST 4,905
Hurleyville 500 ○
Hyde Park POK 2,550
Ilion UT-R 9,450
Indian Lake 450 ○
Interlaken 685
Inwood N.Y. 8,228
Irondequoit ROCH 57,648
Irvington N.Y. 5,774
Island Park N.Y. 4,847
Islip N.Y. 13,438
Islip Terrace N.Y. 5,588
ITHACA ITH 28,732
JAMESTOWN JMST 35,775
Jasper 450 ○
Jay 500 ○
Jeffersonville 554
Jericho N.Y. 12,739
Johnson City BING 17,126
Johnstown 9,360
Jordan SYR 1,371
Keene 450 ○
Keeseville 2,025
Kenmore BUF- 18,474
Kennedy JMST 500 ○
Kerhonkson 1,646
Kinderhook A-S-T 1,377
Kings Point N.Y. 5,234
KINGSTON KNGST 24,481
Lackawanna BUF- 22,701
Lacona 582
LaFargeville 500 ○
Lake Delta UT-R 2,400 ○
Lake Erie Beach BUF- 4,625
Lake George 1,047
Lake Grove N.Y. 9,692
Lake Katrine KNGST 2,011
Lake Luzerne 1,150 ○
Lake Placid 2,490
Lake Ronkonkoma N.Y. 9,600 ○
Lake View BUF- 4,600 ○
Lakeville ROCH 950 ○
Lakewood JMST 3,941
Lancaster BUF- 13,056
Larchmont N.Y. 6,308
Larchmont North N.Y. 11,500 ○
Latham A-S-T 11,182
Lawrence N.Y. 6,175
Leicester 462
Leonardsville 500 ○
Le Roy 4,900
Levittown N.Y. 57,045
Lewiston BUF- 3,326
Liberty 4,293
Lima ROCH 2,025
Limestone 466
Lindenhurst N.Y. 26,919
Little Falls 6,156
Little Valley 1,203
Livingston Manor 1,436
Livonia ROCH 1,238
Lloyd Harbor N.Y. 3,405
Locke 500 ○
LOCKPORT LOCK 24,844
Locust Grove N.Y. 9,670
Long Beach N.Y. 34,073
Long Lake 500 ○
Loudonville A-S-T 11,480
Lowville 3,364
Lyndonville 916
Lyon Mountain 950 ○
Lyons 4,160
Lyons Falls 755
Macedon ROCH 1,400
McGraw 1,188
Machias 850 ○
Madrid 800 ○
Mahopac N.Y. 7,681
Maine BING 700 ○
Malone 7,668
Malverne N.Y. 9,262
Mamaroneck N.Y. 17,616
Manchester ROCH 1,698
Manhasset N.Y. 8,485
Manlius SYR 5,241
Manorhaven N.Y. 5,384
Marathon 1,046
Margaretville 755
Marion ROCH 1,080
Marlboro NWBG 2,275
Massapequa N.Y. 24,454
Massapequa Park N.Y. 19,779
Massena 12,851
Mastic N.Y. 10,413
Mastic Beach N.Y. 8,318
Mattituck N.Y. 3,923
Mattydale SYR 7,511
Mayfield 944
Mayville 1,626
Mechanicville A-S-T 5,500
Medford N.Y. 20,418
Medina 6,392
Melville N.Y. 8,139
Menands A-S-T 4,012
Merrick N.Y. 24,478
Mexico SYR 1,621
Middleburgh 1,358
Middle Granville 600 ○
Middleport LOCK 1,995
MIDDLETOWN MIDD 21,454
Middleville 647
Milford 514
Millbrook POK 1,343
Millerton 1,013
Mineola N.Y. 20,757
Minetto 1,629
Mineville 1,000 ○
Mohawk UT-R 2,956
Monroe N.Y. 5,996
Monsey N.Y. 12,380
Montauk 2,828
Montgomery NWBG 2,316
Monticello 6,306
Montour Falls ELM- 1,791
Mooers 549
Moravia 1,582
Moriah 500 ○
Morris 681
Morrisonville 1,721
Morristown 461
Morrisville 2,707
Mountain Dale 1,200 ○
Mount Kisco N.Y. 8,025
Mount Morris 3,039
Mount Upton 500 ○
Mount Vernon N.Y. 66,713
Munnsville 499
Nanuet N.Y. 12,578
Napanoch 1,260
Naples 1,225
Narrowsburg 700 ○
Nassau A-S-T 1,285
Nassau Shores N.Y. 5,600 ○
Natural Bridge 650 ○
Nedrow SYR 3,000 ○
Nesconset N.Y. 10,706
Newark 10,017
Newark Valley BING 1,190
New Baltimore 700 ○
New Berlin 1,392
NEWBURGH NWBG 23,438
New Cassel N.Y. 9,635
New City N.Y. 35,869
Newcomb 800 ○
Newfane LOCK 3,120
New Hyde Park N.Y. 9,801
New Lebanon 800 ○
New Paltz 4,938
Newport UT-R 746
New Rochelle N.Y. 70,794
Newton Falls 560 ○
New Windsor NWBG 7,812
New Woodstock SYR 450 ○
NEW YORK N.Y. 7,071,639
Niagara Falls BUF- 71,384
Nichols BING 613
Niskayuna A-S-T 17,471
Norfolk 1,599
North Amityville N.Y. 13,140
North Babylon N.Y. 19,019
North Bellmore N.Y. 20,360
North Collins BUF- 1,496
North Creek 850 ○
Northeast Henrietta ROCH 12,000 ○
North Great River N.Y. 11,416
North Lindenhurst N.Y. 11,511
North Massapequa N.Y. 21,385
North Merrick N.Y. 12,848
North New Hyde Park N.Y. 15,114
North Norwich 500 ○
North Patchogue N.Y. 7,126
Northport N.Y. 7,651
North Rose 700 ○
North Syracuse SYR 7,970
North Tarrytown N.Y. 7,994
North Tonawanda BUF- 35,760
North Valley Stream N.Y. 14,530
Northville 1,304
North Wantagh N.Y. 12,677
Norwich 8,082
Norwood 1,902
Nunda 1,169
Nyack N.Y. 6,428
Oakdale N.Y. 8,090
Oakfield 1,791
Oceanside N.Y. 33,639
Odessa ELM- 613
Ogdensburg 12,375
Olcott LOCK 1,571
Old Bethpage N.Y. 6,215
Old Forge 1,061
Old Village N.Y. 9,168
Olean 18,207
Oneida 10,810
Oneonta 14,933
Ontario ROCH 750 ○
Orchard Park BUF- 3,671
Orient 1,500 ○
Oriskany UT-R 1,680
Oriskany Falls UT-R 802
Ossining N.Y. 20,196
Oswego 19,793
Otego 1,089
Ovid 666
Owego BING 4,364
Oxford 1,765
Oyster Bay N.Y. 6,497
Painted Post ELM- 2,196
Palmyra ROCH 3,729

○ Rand McNally estimate
▲ Population of entire township or "town", including rural areas.
● Independent city. Population not included in county total.

NEW YORK continued

Panama 511
Parish SYR 535
Parksville 500 ○
Patchogue N.Y. 11,291
Patterson N.Y. 950 ○
Pavilion 550 ○
Pawling POK 1,996
Pearl River N.Y. 15,893
Peconic 1,056
Peekskill N.Y. 18,236
Pelham N.Y. 6,848
Pelham Manor N.Y. 6,130
Penfield ROCH 9,600 ○
Penn Yan 5,242
Perry 4,198
Peru 1,716
Petersburg 500 ○
Phelps 2,004
Philadelphia 855
Philmont 1,539
Phoenicia 700 ○
Phoenix SYR 2,357
Pine Bush NWBG 1,255
Pine Island MIDD 950 ○
Plainview N.Y. 28,037
Plattsburgh 21,057
Pleasant Valley POK 1,255
Pleasantville N.Y. 6,749
Poland UT-R 553
Port Byron AUB 1,400
Port Chester N.Y. 23,565
Port Dickinson BING 1,974
Port Ewen KNGST 2,813
Port Henry 1,450
Port Jefferson N.Y. 6,731
Port Jefferson Station N.Y. 8,500 ○
Port Jervis 8,699
Portland 600 ○
Port Leyden 740
Portville 1,136
Port Washington N.Y. 14,521
Potsdam 10,635
Pottersville 600 ○
POUGHKEEPSIE POK 29,757
Prattsburg 750 ○
Prattsville 500 ○
Pulaski 2,415
Randolph 1,398
Ransomville BUF- 1,401
Ravena A-S-T 3,091
Raymondville 600 ○
Red Creek 645
Red Hook 1,692
Redwood 600 ○
Remsen UT-R 621
Rensselaer A-S-T 9,047
Rhinebeck POK 2,542
Richburg 494
Richfield Springs 1,561
Richmondville 792
Ridgemont ROCH 16,177
Ripley 1,205
Riverhead 6,339
ROCHESTER ROCH 241,741
Rockville Centre N.Y. 25,412
Roessleville A-S-T 11,685
Rome UT-R 43,826
Ronkonkoma N.Y. 20,200 ○
Roosevelt N.Y. 14,109
Roslyn Heights N.Y. 6,546
Rotterdam A-S-T 22,933
Round Lake A-S-T 791
Rouses Point 2,266
Roxbury 700 ○
Rushford 500 ○
Rushville 548
Rye N.Y. 15,083
Sackets Harbor 1,017
Sag Harbor 2,581
St. James N.Y. 12,122
St. Johnsville 1,974
St. Regis Falls 950 ○
Salamanca 6,890
Salem 959
Sandy Creek 765
San Remo N.Y. 9,000 ○
Saranac Lake 5,578
Saratoga Springs A-S-T 23,906
Saugerties KNGST 3,882
Savannah 640 ○
Savona ELM- 932
Sayville N.Y. 12,013
Scarsdale N.Y. 17,650
Schaghticoke A-S-T 677
Schenectady A-S-T 67,972
Schenevus 625
Schoharie 1,016
Schroon Lake 1,000 ○
Schuylerville 1,256
Scotia A-S-T 7,280
Scottsville ROCH 1,789
Sea Cliff N.Y. 5,364
Seaford N.Y. 16,117
Selden N.Y. 17,259
Seneca Falls 7,466
Shandaken 500 ○
Shelter Island 1,115
Sherburne 1,561
Sherman 775
Sherrill 2,830
Shirley N.Y. 18,082
Shortsville ROCH 1,669
Sidney 4,861
Sidney Center 600 ○
Silver Creek BUF- 3,088
Silver Springs 801
Sinclairville 772
Skaneateles SYR 2,789
Sloan BUF- 4,529
Sloatsburg N.Y. 3,154
Smithtown N.Y. 23,700 ○
Sodus ROCH 1,790
Sodus Point ROCH 1,334
Solvay SYR 7,140
Sound Beach N.Y. 8,071
Southampton 4,000
South Bethlehem A-S-T 500 ○
South Corning ELM- 1,195
South Dayton 661
South Fallsburg 2,196
South Farmingdale N.Y. 16,439
South Glens Falls GLFLS 3,714
South Huntington N.Y. 18,854
South New Berlin 450 ○
South Nyack N.Y. 3,602
Southold 2,030
South Otselic 450 ○
Southport ELM- 8,329
South Stony Brook N.Y. 9,100 ○
South Valley Stream N.Y. 5,462
South Westbury N.Y. 9,732
Spencer 863
Spencerport ROCH 3,424
Springs 3,197
Spring Valley N.Y. 20,537
Springville 4,285
Springwater 500 ○
Staatsburg POK 950 ○
Stamford 1,240
Stillwater A-S-T 1,572
Stony Brook N.Y. 7,100 ○
Stony Creek 450 ○
Stony Point N.Y. 8,686
Stottville 1,160
Suffern N.Y. 10,794
Sylvan Beach UT-R 1,243
Syosset N.Y. 9,818
SYRACUSE SYR 170,105
Tappan N.Y. 8,267
Tarrytown N.Y. 10,648
Terryville N.Y. 7,200 ○
Theresa 827
Thornwood N.Y. 1,300 ○
Three Mile Bay 600 ○
Ticonderoga 2,938
Tillson KNGST 1,529
Tivoli KNGST 711
Tomkins Cove N.Y. 700 ○
Tonawanda BUF- 18,693
Town of Tonawanda BUF- 72,795
Troy A-S-T 56,638
Trumansburg ITH 1,722
Tuckahoe N.Y. 6,076
Tully SYR 1,049
Tupper Lake 4,478
Unadilla 1,367
Uniondale N.Y. 20,016
Union Springs AUB 1,201
University Gardens N.Y. 5,400 ○
UTICA UT-R 75,632
Valatie A-S-T 1,492
Valhalla N.Y. 8,000 ○
Valley Cottage N.Y. 8,214
Valley Stream N.Y. 35,769
Van Etten 559
Vestal BING 6,000 ○
Vestal Center BING 900 ○
Victor ROCH 2,370
Waddington 980
Wading River 2,500 ○
Walden NWBG 5,659
Wallkill NWBG 2,064
Walton 3,329
Wampsville 569
Wantagh N.Y. 19,817
Wappingers Falls POK 5,110
Warrensburg 2,834
Warsaw 3,619
Warwick N.Y. 4,320
Waterford A-S-T 2,405
Waterloo 5,303
WATERTOWN WATN 27,861
Waterville UT-R 1,672
Watervliet A-S-T 11,354
Watkins Glen ELM- 2,440
Waverly 4,738
Wayland 1,846
Webster ROCH 5,499
Weedsport SYR 1,952
Wellsburg ELM- 647
Wellsville 5,769
West Amityville N.Y. 6,623
West Babylon N.Y. 41,699
West Bay Shore N.Y. 5,118
Westbury N.Y. 13,871
West Carthage 1,824
West Chazy 700 ○
West Elmira ELM- 5,485
Westfield 3,446
West Haverstraw N.Y. 9,181
West Hempstead N.Y. 18,536
West Huntington N.Y. 3,500 ○
West Islip N.Y. 23,000 ○
Westmere A-S-T 6,884
West Point 8,105
Westport 613
West Sayville N.Y. 8,185
West Seneca BUF- 51,210
Westvale SYR 6,169
West Webster ROCH 10,600 ○
West Winfield 979
Whitehall 3,241
White Plains N.Y. 46,999
Whitesboro UT-R 4,460
Whitesville 600 ○
Whitney Point BING 1,093
Willard 1,339
Williamson ROCH 1,768
Williamsville BUF- 6,017
Williston Park N.Y. 8,216
Willsboro 950 ○
Wilmington 500 ○
Wilson LOCK 1,259
Winthrop 550 ○
Witherbee 920 ○
Wolcott 1,496
Woodbourne 1,155 ○
Woodmere N.Y. 17,205
Woodstock KNGST 2,280
Worcester 950 ○
Wyandanch N.Y. 13,215
Wyoming 507
Yonkers N.Y. 195,351
Yorkshire 1,236
Yorktown N.Y. 7,100 ○
Yorktown Heights N.Y. 6,000 ○
Yorkville UT-R 3,115
Youngstown BUF- 2,191

COUNTIES

Albany 285,909
Allegany 51,742
Bronx 1,168,972
Broome 213,648
Cattaraugus 85,697
Cayuga 79,894
Chautauqua 146,925
Chemung 97,656
Chenango 49,344
Clinton 80,750
Columbia 59,487
Cortland 48,820
Delaware 46,824
Dutchess 245,055
Erie 1,015,472
Essex 36,176
Franklin 44,929
Fulton 55,153
Genesee 59,400
Greene 40,861
Hamilton 5,034
Herkimer 66,714
Jefferson 88,151
Kings 2,230,936
Lewis 25,035
Livingston 57,006
Madison 65,150
Monroe 702,238
Montgomery 53,439
Nassau 1,321,582
New York 1,428,285
Niagara 227,354
Oneida 253,466
Onondaga 463,920
Ontario 88,909
Orange 259,603
Orleans 38,496
Oswego 113,901
Otsego 59,075
Putnam 77,193

○ Rand McNally estimate
▲ Population of entire township or "town", including rural areas.
● Independent city. Population not included in county total.

Queens 1,891,325
Rensselaer 151,966
Richmond 352,121
Rockland 259,530
St. Lawrence 114,254
Saratoga 153,759
Schenectady 149,946
Schoharie 29,710
Schuyler 17,686
Seneca 33,733
Steuben 99,217
Suffolk 1,284,231
Sullivan 65,155
Tioga 49,812
Tompkins 87,085
Ulster 158,158
Warren 54,854
Washington 54,795
Wayne 84,581
Westchester 866,599
Wyoming 39,895
Yates 21,459

NORTH CAROLINA

1980
Census 5,881,813

CITIES

Aberdeen 1,945
Ahoskie 4,887
Albemarle 15,110
Alexander Mills 643
Alliance 616
Andrews 1,621
Angier RAL 1,709
Ansonville 794
Apex RAL 2,847
Arapahoe 467
Archdale GRNS- 5,326
Arden ASHE 500 ○
Arlington 872
Asheboro 15,252
ASHEVILLE ASHE 53,583
Atlantic 900 ○
Aulander 1,214
Aurora 698
Ayden 4,361
Badin 1,514
Bailey 685
Balfour 1,772
Banner Elk 1,087
Barker Heights 1,267
Barnardsville 500 ○
Battleboro RKYMT 632
Bayboro 759
Beaufort 3,826
Belfast GLDS 950 ○
Belhaven 2,430
Belmont CHRLT 4,607
Benson 2,792
Bessemer City GAST 4,787
Bethel 1,825
Beulaville 1,060
Biltmore Forest ASHE 1,499
Biscoe 1,334
Black Creek 523
Black Mountain 4,083
Bladenboro 1,428
Blowing Rock 1,337
Boger City 2,252
Boiling Springs 2,381
Bolton 563
Bonnie Doone FAY 5,950
Boone 10,191
Boonville 1,028
Brevard 5,323
Bridgeton 461
Broadway 908
Brookford HICK 467
Bryson City 1,556
Buies Creek 1,939
Bunn 505
Bunnlevel 500 ○
Burgaw 1,738
BURLINGTON BUR 37,266
Burnsville 1,452
Butner 4,240
Buxton 700 ○
Calypso 689
Candor 868
Canton 4,631
Caroleen 1,000 ○
Carolina Beach WILM 2,000
Carrboro DUR- 7,336
Carthage 925
Cary RAL 21,763
Cashiers 533
Castle Hayne WILM 1,087
Catawba 509
Chadbourn 1,975
Chapel Hill DUR- 32,421
CHARLOTTE CHRLT 314,447
Cherokee 600 ○
Cherryville 4,844
China Grove KANN- 2,081
Chocowinity 644
Claremont 880
Clarkton 664
Clayton RAL 4,091
Clemmons WNS 7,401
Cleveland 595
Cliffside 600 ○
Clinton 7,552
Clyde 1,008
Coats 1,385
Cofield 465
Columbia 758
Columbus 727
Concord KANN- 16,942
Conover 4,245
Conway 678
Cooleemee 1,448
Cordova 1,200 ○
Cornelius CHRLT 1,460
Cove City 500
Cramerton GAST 1,869
Creedmoor 1,641
Cricket 2,307
Cross Mill 1,200 ○
Crouse 900 ○
Cullowhee 2,000 ○
Cumberland FAY 900 ○
Dallas GAST 3,340
Dana 500 ○
Davidson CHRLT 3,241
Davis 500 ○
Delco 550 ○
Denton 949
Dobson 1,222
Dover 600
Drexel 1,392
Dublin 477
Dunn 8,962
DURHAM DUR- 100,538
East Bend 602
East Flat Rock 3,365
East Laurinburg 536
East Rockingham 5,190
East Spencer SLSB 2,150
Eden 15,672
Edenton 5,357
Efland 600 ○
Elizabeth City 14,004
Elizabethtown 3,551
Elkin 2,858
Elk Park 535
Ellenboro 560
Ellerbe 1,415
Elm City 1,561
Elon College BUR 2,873
Enfield 2,995
Engelhard 600 ○
Enka ASHE 5,567
Erwin 2,828
Fair Bluff 1,095
Fair Grove GRNS- 1,500 ○
Fairmont 2,658
Faison 636
Faith SLSB 552
Fallston 614
Farmville 4,707
FAYETTEVILLE FAY 59,507
Flat Rock 1,200 ○
Fletcher 700 ○
Forest City 7,688
Four Oaks 1,049
Franklin 2,640
Franklinton 1,394
Franklinville 607
Fremont GLDS 1,736
Fuquay-Varina RAL 3,110
Garland 885
Garner RAL 10,073
Garysburg 1,434
Gaston 883
GASTONIA GAST 47,333
Gibson 533
Gibsonville BUR 2,865
Glen Alpine 645
Glen Raven BUR 2,755
Glenville 500 ○
GOLDSBORO GLDS 31,871
Graham BUR 8,674
Grandy 600 ○
Granite Falls HICK 2,580
Granite Quarry SLSB 1,294
Grantsboro 550 ○
GREENSBORO GRNS- 155,642
Greenville 35,740
Grifton 2,179
Grimesland 453
Grover 597
Hallsboro 500 ○
Hamilton 638
Hamlet 4,720
Hampstead 700 ○
Harkers Island 1,901
Harmony 470
Hatteras 700 ○
Havelock 17,718
Haw River BUR 1,858
Hays 900 ○
Hazelwood 1,811
Henderson 13,522
Hendersonville 6,862
Henrietta 1,412
Hertford 1,941
HICKORY HICK 20,757
Hiddenite 800 ○
Highlands 653
High Point GRNS- 63,808
High Shoals GAST 586
Hillsborough 3,019
Hobgood 483
Hobucken 450 ○
Holly Ridge 465
Holly Springs RAL 688
Hookerton 460
Hope Mills FAY 5,412
Hot Springs 678
Hudson 2,888
Indian Trail CHRLT 811
Jackson 720
JACKSONVILLE JAX 18,237
James City 700 ○
Jamestown GRNS- 2,148
Jamesville 604
Jefferson 1,086
Jonesville 1,752
KANNAPOLIS KANN- 34,564
Kenansville 931
Kenly 1,433
Kernersville WNS 6,802
King WNS 5,000 ○
Kings Mountain GAST 9,080
Kinston 25,234
Kitty Hawk 849
Knightdale RAL 985
Lafayette FAY 4,100 ○
La Grange 3,147
Lake Waccamaw 1,133
Landis KANN- 2,092
Laurel Hill 2,314
Laurinburg 11,480
Lawndale 469
Lenoir 13,748
Lewiston Woodville 671
Lexington 15,711
Liberty 1,997
Lilesville 588
Lillington 1,948
Lincolnton 4,879
Littleton 820
LOCUST 1,590
Longview HICK 3,587
Louisburg 3,238
Lowell GAST 2,917
Lowland 600 ○
Lucama 1,070
Lumberton 18,241
Macclesfield 504
McGrady 500 ○
Madison 2,806
Magnolia 592
Maiden 2,574
Manteo 902
Maple Hill 550 ○
Marble 700 ○
Marion 3,684
Marshall 809
Marshallberg 600 ○
Mars Hill 2,126
Marshville 2,011
Matthews CHRLT 1,648
Maury 450 ○
Maxton 2,711
Mayodan 2,627
Maysville 877
Mebane BUR 2,782
Middlesex 837
Midland 600 ○
Mint Hill CHRLT 7,915
Misenheimer 1,250 ○
Mocksville 2,637
Moncure 600 ○
Monroe CHRLT 12,639
Montreat 741
Mooresville 8,575
Morehead City 4,359
Morganton 13,763
Morven 765
Mount Airy 6,862
Mount Gilead 1,423
Mount Holly CHRLT 4,530
Mount Olive HICK 4,876
Mount Pleasant KANN- 1,210
Moyock 700 ○
Mulberry 1,210
Murfreesboro 3,007
Murphy 2,070
Nags Head 1,020
Nashville RKYMT 3,033
New Bern 14,557
Newland 722
New London 454
Newport 1,883
Newton 7,624
Newton Grove 564
Norlina 901
North Belmont CHRLT 5,000 ○
North Wilkesboro 3,260

○ Rand McNally estimate
▲ Population of entire township or "town", including rural areas.
● Independent city. Population not included in county total.

NORTH CAROLINA continued

Norwood 1,818
Oakboro 587
Oak City 475
Oak Ridge GRNS- 950 ○
Ocracoke 600 ○
Old Fort 752
Olivia 500 ○
Oriental 536
Oteen ASHE 2,200 ○
Oxford 7,603
Parkton 564
Parkwood DUR- 3,420
Parmele 484
Paw Creek CHRLT 1,700 ○
Peachland 506
Pembroke 2,698
Pikeville 662
Pilot Mountain 1,090
Pinebluff 935
Pine Hall 500 ○
Pinehurst 1,746
Pine Level 953
Pinetops 1,465
Pineville CHRLT 1,525
Pink Hill 644
Pinnacle 600 ○
Pisgah Forest 1,899
Pittsboro 1,332
Pleasant Garden GRNS- 1,991
Plymouth 4,571
Polkton 762
Princeton 1,034
Princeville 1,508
Raeford 3,630
RALEIGH RAL 150,255
Ramseur 1,162
Randleman 2,156
Red Springs 3,607
Reidsville 12,492
Rhodhiss HICK 727
Richlands 825
Rich Square 1,057
Ridgecrest 500 ○
Roanoke Rapids 14,702
Robbins 1,256
Robbinsville 1,370
Robersonville 1,981
Rockingham 8,300
Rockwell SLSB 1,339
Rockwell Park CHRLT 2,600 ○
ROCKY MOUNT RKYMT 41,283
Rocky Point 600 ○
Ronda 457
Roper 795
Roseboro 1,227
Rose Hill 1,508
Rosman 512
Rougemont 500 ○
Rowland 1,841
Roxboro 7,532
Royal Pines ASHE 2,041 ○
Ruffin 600 ○
Rural Hall WNS 1,336
Rutherfordton 3,434
St. Pauls 1,639
Salemburg 742
Salisbury SLSB 22,677
Salter Path 600 ○
Saluda 607
Sanford 14,773
Saxapahaw 500 ○
Scotland Neck 2,834
Seaboard 687
Selma 4,762
Shallotte 680
Sharpsburg RKYMT 997
Shelby 15,310
Siler City 4,446
Skyland ASHE 2,200 ○
Smithfield 7,288
Sneads Ferry 600 ○
Snow Hill 1,374
Southern Pines 8,620
South Gastonia GAST 2,000 ○
South Mills 800 ○
Southmont 700 ○
Southport 2,824
Sparta 1,687
Spencer SLSB 2,938
Spindale 4,246
Spring Hope 1,254
Spring Lake FAY 6,273
Spruce Pine 2,282
Stanley CHRLT 2,341
Stanleyville WNS 5,039
Stantonsburg 920
Star 816
State Road 800 ○
Statesville 18,622
Stedman 723
Stokesdale GRNS- 1,070
Stoneville 1,054
Stony Point 1,150
Summerfield GRNS- 1,680
Sunbury 500 ○
Swannanoa ASHE 5,586
Swanquarter 450 ○
Swansboro 976
Swepsonville 900 ○
Sylva 1,699
Tabor City 2,710
Tarboro 8,634
Taylorsville 1,103
Thomasville GRNS- 14,144
Toast 2,339
Troutman 1,360
Troy 2,702
Tryon 1,796
Tuxedo 950 ○
Valdese 3,364
Vanceboro 833
Vander FAY 1,671
Vass 828
Verona JAX 600 ○
Wade FAY 474
Wadesboro 4,206
Wagram 617
Wake Forest RAL 3,780
Walkertown WNS 2,100 ○
Wallace 2,903
Walnut 550 ○
Walnut Cove 1,147
Wanchese 1,105
Warrenton 908
Warsaw 2,910
Washington 8,418
Waxhaw 1,208
Waynesville 6,765
Weaverville ASHE 1,495
Weeksville 450 ○
Weldon 1,844
Wendell 2,222
West Concord KANN- 3,200 ○
West End 900 ○
Westfield 600 ○
West Jefferson 822
West Marion 1,596
Whitakers 924
Whiteville 5,565
Whitsett BUR 500 ○
Whittier 500 ○
Wilkesboro 2,335
Williamston 6,159
WILMINGTON WILM 44,000
Wilson 34,424
Wilsons Mills 580 ○
Windsor 2,126
Winfall 634
Wingate CHRLT 2,615
WINSTON-SALEM WNS 131,885
Winterville 2,052
Winton 825
Wise 500 ○
Woodland 861
Wrightsville Beach WILM 2,910
Yadkinville 2,216
Yanceyville 1,511
Youngsville 486
Zebulon 2,055

COUNTIES

Alamance 99,319
Alexander 24,999
Alleghany 9,587
Anson 25,649
Ashe 22,325
Avery 14,409
Beaufort 40,355
Bertie 21,024
Bladen 30,491
Brunswick 35,777
Buncombe 160,934
Burke 72,504
Cabarrus 85,895
Caldwell 67,746
Camden 5,829
Carteret 41,092
Caswell 20,705
Catawba 105,208
Chatham 33,415
Cherokee 18,933
Chowan 12,558
Clay 6,619
Cleveland 83,435
Columbus 51,037
Craven 71,043
Cumberland 247,160
Currituck 11,089
Dare 13,377
Davidson 113,162
Davie 24,599
Duplin 40,952
Durham 152,785
Edgecombe 55,988
Forsyth 243,683
Franklin 30,055
Gaston 162,568
Gates 8,875
Graham 7,217
Granville 34,043
Greene 16,117
Guilford 317,154
Halifax 55,286
Harnett 59,570
Haywood 46,495
Henderson 58,580
Hertford 23,368
Hoke 20,383
Hyde 5,873
Iredell 82,538
Jackson 25,811
Johnston 70,599
Jones 9,705
Lee 36,718
Lenoir 59,819
Lincoln 42,372
McDowell 35,135
Macon 20,178
Madison 16,827
Martin 25,948
Mecklenburg 404,270
Mitchell 14,428
Montgomery 22,469
Moore 50,505
Nash 67,153
New Hanover 103,471
Northampton 22,584
Onslow 112,784
Orange 77,055
Pamlico 10,398
Pasquotank 28,462
Pender 22,262
Perquimans 9,486
Person 29,164
Pitt 90,146
Polk 12,984
Randolph 91,728
Richmond 45,481
Robeson 101,610
Rockingham 83,426
Rowan 99,186
Rutherford 53,787
Sampson 49,687
Scotland 32,273
Stanly 48,517
Stokes 33,086
Surry 59,449
Swain 10,283
Transylvania 23,417
Tyrrell 3,975
Union 70,380
Vance 36,748
Wake 301,327
Warren 16,232
Washington 14,801
Watauga 31,666
Wayne 97,054
Wilkes 58,657
Wilson 63,132
Yadkin 28,439
Yancey 14,934

NORTH DAKOTA

1980 Census 652,717

CITIES

Arthur 445
Ashley 1,192
Beach 1,381
Belcourt 1,803
Belfield 1,274
Berthold 485
Beulah 2,908
BISMARCK BIS- 44,485
Bottineau 2,829
Bowbells 587
Bowman 2,071
Burlington MNOT 762
Cando 1,496
Carrington 2,641
Carson 469
Casselton 1,661
Cavalier 1,505
Center 900
Cooperstown 1,308
Crosby 1,469
Devils Lake 7,442
Dickinson 15,924
Drake 479
Drayton 1,082
Dunseith 625
Edgeley 843
Elgin 930
Ellendale 1,967
Emerado 596
Enderlin 1,151
Fairmount 480
FARGO FAR- 61,383
Fessenden 761
Finley 718
Forman 629
Fort Totten 750 ○
Fort Yates 771
Gackle 456
Garrison 1,830
Glenburn 454
Glen Ullin 1,125
Grafton 5,293
GRAND FORKS GDFK 43,765
Gwinner 725
Hankinson 1,158
Harvey 2,527
Hatton 787
Hazen 2,365
Hebron 1,078
Hettinger 1,739
Hillsboro 1,600
Horace 494
Jamestown 16,280

○ Rand McNally estimate
▲ Population of entire township or "town", including rural areas.
● Independent city. Population not included in county total.

Place	Population
Kenmare	1,456
Killdeer	790
Kindred	568
Kulm	570
Lakota	963
La Moure	1,077
Langdon	2,335
Larimore	1,524
Leeds	678
Lidgerwood	971
Linton	1,561
Lisbon	2,283
McClusky	658
McVille	626
Maddock	677
Mandan BIS-	15,513
Mayville	2,255
Medina	521
Michigan	502
Milnor	716
Minnewaukan	461
MINOT MNOT	32,843
Minto	592
Mohall	1,049
Mott	1,315
Napoleon	1,103
Neche	471
New England	825
New Rockford	1,791
New Salem	1,081
New Town	1,335
Northwood	1,240
Oakes	2,112
Park River	1,844
Parshall	1,059
Pembina	673
Portland	627
Powers Lake	466
Ray	766
Richardton	699
Riverdale	500 ○
Rolette	667
Rolla	1,538
Rugby	3,335
St. Thomas	528
Stanley	1,631
Stanton	623
Steele	796
Strasburg	623
Surrey MNOT	999
Thompson	785
Tioga	1,597
Towner	867
Turtle Lake	802
Underwood	1,329
Valley City	7,774
Velva	1,101
Wahpeton	9,064
Walhalla	1,429
Washburn	1,767
Watford City	2,119
West Fargo FAR-	10,099
Westhope	741
Williston	13,336
Wilton	950
Wishek	1,345
Wyndmere	550
Zap	511

COUNTIES

County	Population
Adams	3,584
Barnes	13,960
Benson	7,944
Billings	1,138
Bottineau	9,239
Bowman	4,229
Burke	3,822
Burleigh	54,811
Cass	88,247
Cavalier	7,636
Dickey	7,207
Divide	3,494
Dunn	4,627
Eddy	3,554
Emmons	5,877
Foster	4,611
Golden Valley	2,391
Grand Forks	66,100
Grant	4,274
Griggs	3,714
Hettinger	4,275
Kidder	3,833
La Moure	6,473
Logan	3,493
McHenry	7,858
McIntosh	4,800
McKenzie	7,132
McLean	12,383
Mercer	9,404
Morton	25,177
Mountrail	7,679
Nelson	5,233
Oliver	2,495
Pembina	10,399
Pierce	6,166
Ramsey	13,048
Ransom	6,698
Renville	3,608
Richland	19,207
Rolette	12,177
Sargent	5,512
Sheridan	2,819
Sioux	3,620
Slope	1,157
Stark	23,697
Steele	3,106
Stutsman	24,154
Towner	4,052
Traill	9,624
Walsh	15,371
Ward	58,392
Wells	6,979
Williams	22,237

OHIO

1980 Census 10,797,624

CITIES

City	Population
Aberdeen	1,566
Ada	5,669
Addyston CIN-	1,195
Adelphi	472
Adena	1,062
AKRON AKR	237,177
Albany	905
Alexandria	489
Alger	992
ALLIANCE ALLI	24,315
Amanda	720
Amelia CIN-	1,108
Amherst CLEV	10,638
Amsterdam	783
Andover	1,205
Anna	1,038
Ansonia	1,267
Antwerp	1,765
Apple Creek	741
Arcadia	580
Arcanum	2,002
Archbold	3,318
Arlington	1,187
Ashland	20,326
Ashley	1,057
ASHTABULA ASHT	23,449
Ashville COL	2,046
Athens	19,743
Attica	865
Aurora CLEV	8,177
Austinburg	600 ○
Austintown YNGS-	33,636
Avon CLEV	7,241
Avondale DAY-	5,000 ○
Avon Lake CLEV	13,222
Bainbridge	1,042
Baltic	563
Baltimore	2,689
Barberton AKR	29,751
Barnesville	4,633
Barton WHL	1,039
Bascom	550 ○
Batavia CIN-	1,896
Bay Village CLEV	17,846
Beach City	1,083
Beachwood CLEV	9,983
Beallsville	601
Beavercreek DAY-	31,589
Beaverdam	492
Bedford CLEV	15,056
Bedford Heights CLEV	13,214
Bellaire WHL	8,241
Bellbrook DAY-	5,174
Belle Center	930
Bellefontaine	11,888
Bellevue	8,187
Bellville MANS	1,714
Belmont	714
Beloit ALLI	1,093
Belpre PRKB	7,193
Berea CLEV	19,567
Bergholz	914
Berlin Heights CLEV	756
Bethel CIN-	2,231
Bethesda	1,429
Bettsville	752
Beverly	1,471
Bexley COL	13,405
Blacklick Estates COL	11,223
Blanchester	3,202
Bloomdale	744
Bloomingburg	869
Bloomville	1,019
Blue Ash CIN-	9,506
Bluffton	3,310
Boardman YNGS-	39,161
Bolivar CAN-	989
Boston Heights CLEV	781
Botkins	1,372
Bowerston	487
Bowling Green	25,728
Bradford	2,166
Bradner	1,175
Bratenahl CLEV	1,485
Brecksville CLEV	10,132
Bremen	1,432
Brentwood CIN-	5,508
Brewster	2,321
Bridgeport WHL	2,642
Bridgetown CIN-	11,460
Brilliant STU-	1,751
Bristolville YNGS-	500 ○
Broadview Heights CLEV	10,920
Brooklyn CLEV	12,342
Brook Park CLEV	26,195
Brookville DAY-	4,322
Brunswick CLEV	28,104
Bryan	7,879
Buchtel	585
Buckeye Lake NWRK	2,521
Bucyrus	13,433
Buffalo	800 ○
Burton CLEV	1,401
Butler MANS	991
Byesville	2,572
Cadiz	4,058
Cairo	596
Calcutta E.LIV-	1,121
Caldwell	1,935
Caledonia MRN	759
Cambridge	13,573
Camden	1,971
Campbell YNGS-	11,619
Canal Fulton AKR	3,481
Canal Winchester COL	2,749
Canfield YNGS-	5,535
CANTON CAN-	93,077
Cardington	1,665
Carey	3,674
Carroll COL	641
Carrollton	3,065
Castalia SNDSK	973
Cedarville	2,799
Celina	9,137
Centerburg	1,275
Centerville DAY-	18,886
Chagrin Falls CLEV	4,335
Champion YNGS-	5,270 ○
Chardon CLEV	4,434
Chauncey	1,050
Chesapeake HNTG-	1,370
Cheviot CIN-	9,888
Chillicothe	23,420
Christiansburg	593
Churchill YNGS-	7,700 ○
CINCINNATI CIN-	385,457
Circleville	11,700
Clarington	558
Clarksburg	483
Clarksville	525
CLEVELAND CLEV	573,822
Cleveland Heights CLEV	56,438
Clyde	5,489
Coal Grove HNTG-	2,602
Coalton	639
Coldwater	4,220
Columbiana	4,987
COLUMBUS COL	565,032
Columbus Grove	2,313
Conesville	451
Conneaut	13,835
Continental	1,179
Convoy	1,140
Coolville	649
Corning	789
Cortland YNGS-	5,011
Coshocton	13,405
Covedale CIN-	6,530 ○
Covington	2,610
Crestline	5,406
Creston	1,828
Cridersville LIMA	1,843
Crooksville	2,766
Croton	444
Crown City	513
Cumberland	461
Curtice TOL	800 ○
Cuyahoga Falls AKR	43,890
Cygnet	646
Dalton CAN-	1,357
Danville	1,127
DAYTON DAY-	193,444
Deerfield	450 ○
Deer Park CIN-	6,745
Defiance	16,810
De Graff	1,358
Delaware	18,780
Delhi Hills CIN-	7,650 ○
Delphos	7,314
Delta TOL	2,831
Dennison	3,398
Deshler	1,870
Dillonvale WHL	912
Dover	11,782
Doylestown AKR	2,493
Dresden	1,646
Drexel DAY-	2,250 ○
Duncan Falls ZAN	1,200 ○
Dunkirk	954
East Cleveland CLEV	36,957
East Fultonham	650 ○
Eastlake CLEV	22,104
East Liberty	480 ○
EAST LIVERPOOL E.LIV-	16,687
East Palestine	5,306
East Sparta CAN-	868

○ Rand McNally estimate
▲ Population of entire township or "town", including rural areas.
● Independent city. Population not included in county total.

OHIO continued

Eaton DAY- 6,839
Edgerton 1,813
Edgewood ASHT 3,099
Edison 504
Edon 947
Eldorado. 509
Elida LIMA. 1,349
Elmore. 1,271
Elmwood Place
CIN- 2,840
Elyria CLEV 57,538
Empire STU- 484
Englewood DAY- . . . 11,329
Euclid CLEV. 59,999
Fairborn DAY- 29,702
Fairfield CIN- 30,777
Fairlawn AKR 6,100
Fairpoint . . . . 600 ○
Fairport Harbor
CLEV 3,357
Fairview Park
CLEV 19,311
Fayette 1,222
Fayetteville 478
Felicity 929
FINDLAY FIND. 35,594
Fletcher 498
Flushing. 1,266
Forest 1,633
Forest Park CIN- . . . 18,675
Fort Jennings 538
Fort Loramie 977
Fort McKinley
DAY- 11,536
Fort Recovery 1,370
Fort Shawnee
LIMA 4,541
Fostoria 15,743
Frankfort 1,008
Franklin MIDD 10,711
Frazeysburg. 1,025
Fredericksburg 511
Fredericktown. 2,299
Freeport 525
Fremont 17,834
Friendship. . . . . 600 ○
Gahanna COL 18,001
Galion 12,391
Gallipolis 5,576
Gambier. 2,056
Garfield Heights
CLEV 34,938
Garrettsville 1,769
Geneva 6,655
Genoa TOL 2,213
Georgetown 3,467
Germantown DAY- . . . 5,015
Gettysburg 545
Gibsonburg 2,479
Girard YNGS- 12,517
Glandorf 746
Glendale CIN- 2,368
Glouster. 2,211
Gnadenhutten 1,320
Golf Manor CIN- 4,317
Grafton CLEV 2,231
Grand Rapids 962
Grandview Heights
COL 7,420
Granville NWRK 3,851
Gratis 809
Green Camp 475
Greenfield 5,150
Greenhills CIN- 4,927
Green Springs 1,568
Greenville. 12,999
Greenwich 1,458
Groesbeck CIN- 9,594
Grove City COL 16,816
Groveport COL. 3,286
Grover Hill 486
Hamden. 1,010
Hamersville CIN- 688
Hamilton CIN- 63,189
Hamler 625
Hannibal . . . . 650 ○
Hanover NWRK 926
Hanoverton 490
Harrison CIN- 5,855
Harrod LIMA 506
Hartville CAN- 1,772
Haskins 568
Haydenville . . . . 500 ○
Hayesville 518
Heath NWRK 6,969
Hebron NWRK 2,035
Hicksville 3,929
Highland Heights
CLEV 5,739
Hilliard COL 8,008
Hillsboro 6,356
Hiram 1,360
Holgate 1,315
Holland TOL 1,048
Homewood CIN- . . . . . 2,550 ○
Hopedale 857
Howard. . . . . 450 ○
Hubbard YNGS- 9,245
Huber Heights
DAY- 35,480
Huber South DAY- . . . 4,800 ○
Hudson CLEV 4,615
Huron SNDSK 7,123
Independence
CLEV 6,607
Irondale E.LIV- 535
Ironton HNTG- 14,290
Jackson 6,675
Jackson Center 1,310
Jacksonville 651
Jamestown. 1,702
Jefferson 2,952
Jeffersonville 1,252
Jeromesville 582
Jewett 972
Johnstown 3,158
Junction City 754
Kent AKR. 26,164
Kenton. 8,605
Kenwood CIN- 9,928
Kettering DAY- 61,186
Killbuck. 937
Kings Mills CIN- . . . . . . 500 ○
Kingston 1,208
Kingsville ASHT 1,243
Kinsman . . . . 800 ○
Kirtland CLEV 5,969
Lafferty . . . . 600 ○
Lagrange CLEV 1,258
Lakemore AKR. 2,744
Lakeside . . . . 950 ○
Lakeview 1,089
Lakewood CLEV. . . . 61,963
LANCASTER
LANC 34,953
La Rue 861
Laura DAY- 501
Laurelville 591
Leavittsburg
YNGS- . . . . 2,220 ○
Lebanon DAY- 9,636
Leesburg 1,019
Leetonia. 2,121
Leipsic. 2,171
Lewisburg 1,450
Lexington MANS 3,823
Liberty Center 1,111
LIMA LIMA. 47,381
Lincoln Heights
CIN- 5,259
Lincoln Village
COL 10,548
Lindsey. 571
Linworth COL . . . . 650 ○
Lisbon 3,159
Lockland CIN- 4,292
Lodi CLEV. 2,942
Logan 6,557
London 6,958
Lorain CLEV 75,416
Lore City. 443
Loudonville. 2,945
Louisville CAN- 7,996
Loveland CIN- 9,106
Loveland Park
CIN- 1,653
Lowell. 729
Lowellville YNGS- 1,558
Lucas MANS 753
Lucasville PTSM 3,349
Luckey TOL 895
Lynchburg 1,205
Lyndhurst CLEV 18,092
Lyons 596
McArthur 1,912
McClure 694
McComb 1,608
McConnelsville 2,018
McDermott PTSM . . . . . 550 ○
Macedonia CLEV 6,571
McGuffey 646
Madeira CIN- 9,341
Madison CLEV 2,291
Magnolia. 986
Malta 956
Malvern 1,032
Manchester 2,313
MANSFIELD
MANS. 53,927
Mantua CLEV 1,041
Maple Heights
CLEV 29,735
Marble Cliff COL 630
Marblehead. 679
Mariemont CIN- 3,295
MARIETTA
MRIET 16,467
MARION MRN 37,040
Marshallville AKR 788
Martins Ferry WHL . . . 9,331
Martinsville 539
Marysville. 7,414
Mason CIN- 8,692
Massillon CAN- 30,557
Masury SHAR 1,836
Mauds CIN- . . . . 600 ○
Maumee TOL. 15,747
Mayfield Heights
CLEV 21,550
Mechanicsburg. 1,792
Medina CLEV. 15,268
Mendon 749
Mentor CLEV 42,065
Mentor-on-the-Lake
CLEV 7,919
Metamora 556
Miamisburg DAY- . . . 15,304
Miamitown CIN- . . . . . . 650 ○
Middleburg Heights
CLEV 16,218
Middlefield CLEV 1,997
Middle Point 709
Middleport 2,971
MIDDLETOWN
MIDD 43,719
Midvale. 654
Milan SNDSK. 1,569
Milford CIN- 5,232
Milford Center 764
Millbury TOL 955
Millersburg 3,247
Millersport. 844
Mineral City 884
Minerva 4,549
Mingo Junction
STU- 4,834
Mogadore AKR 4,190
Monfort Heights
CIN- 9,745
Monroe MIDD 4,256
Monroeville 1,329
Montgomery CIN- . . . 10,088
Montpelier 4,431
Moraine DAY- 5,325
Morral. 454
Morrow CIN- 1,254
Mount Blanchard 492
Mount Carmel CIN- . . . . 900 ○
Mount Gilead 2,911
Mount Healthy
CIN- 7,562
Mount Orab CIN- 1,573
Mount Sterling
COL 1,623
Mount Vernon. 14,323
Mount Victory 667
Mowrystown 475
Mulberry CIN- . . . . 800 ○
Murray City 579
Napoleon 8,614
Navarre CAN- 1,343
Neffs WHL 1,106
Negley . . . . 900 ○
Nevada. 945
NEWARK NWRK . . . 41,200
New Athens 440
New Boston PTSM. . . 3,188
New Bremen 2,393
Newburgh Heights
CLEV 2,678
New Carlisle DAY- . . . 6,498
Newcomerstown. 3,986
New Concord 1,860
New Holland 783
New Knoxville 760
New Lexington 5,179
New London. 2,449
New Madison 1,008
New Matamoras 1,172
New Miami CIN- 2,980
New Paris RICH. 1,709
New Philadelphia 16,883
Newport . . . . 950 ○
New Richmond
CIN- 2,769
New Straitsville 937
Newton Falls
YNGS- 4,960
Newtown CIN- 1,817
New Vienna 1,133
New Washington 1,213
New Waterford 1,314
Niles YNGS- 23,088
North Baltimore 3,127
North Bend CIN- 546
North Bloomfield . . . . 500 ○
Northbrook CIN- 8,357
North Canton
CAN- 14,228
North College Hill
CIN- 11,114
North Fairfield 525
Northfield CLEV 3,913
North Industry
CAN- . . . . 3,250 ○
North Kingsville
ASHT 2,939
North Lewisburg 1,072
North Lima YNGS- . . . . 900 ○
North Olmsted
CLEV 36,486
Northridge DAY- 5,559
Northridge DAY- 9,720
North Ridgeville
CLEV 21,522
North Royalton
CLEV 17,671
Northwood TOL 5,495
Norton AKR 12,242
Norwalk 14,358
Norwood CIN- 26,342
Oak Harbor 2,678
Oak Hill 1,713
Oakwood CLEV 3,786
Oakwood DAY- 9,372
Oakwood 886
Oberlin CLEV. 8,660
Obetz COL 3,095
Ohio City 881
Olmsted Falls
CLEV 5,868
Oneida MIDD. . . . . . . 1,650 ○
Ontario MANS 4,123
Oregon TOL. 18,675
Orrville. 7,511
Orwell 1,067

○ Rand McNally estimate
▲ Population of entire township or "town", including rural areas.
● Independent city. Population not included in county total.

Place	Population
Ottawa	3,874
Ottawa Hills TOL	4,065
Ottoville	833
Owensville CIN-	858
Oxford	17,655
Page Manor DAY-	9,300 ○
Painesville CLEV	16,391
Pandora	977
Park Layne DAY-	5,372
Parkman CLEV	600 ○
Parma CLEV	92,548
Parma Heights CLEV	23,112
Pataskala COL	2,284
Paulding	2,754
Payne	1,399
Peebles	1,790
Pemberville	1,321
Peninsula CLEV	604
Pepper Pike CLEV	6,177
Perry CLEV	961
Perry Heights CAN-	9,206
Perrysburg TOL	10,215
Perrysville MANS	836
Petersburg YNGS-	950 ○
Pettisville	500 ○
Philo ZAN	799
Pickerington COL	3,917
Piketon	1,726
Piney Fork	500 ○
Pioneer	1,133
Piqua	20,480
Pitsburg	460
Plain City	2,102
Pleasant City	481
Pleasant Hill	1,051
Pleasantville LANC	780
Plymouth	1,939
Pomeroy	2,728
Portage Lakes AKR	11,310
Port Clinton	7,223
Port Jefferson	482
PORTSMOUTH PTSM	25,943
Port Washington	622
Powhatan Point	2,181
Proctorville HNTG-	975
Prospect	1,159
Quaker City	698
Quincy	633
Racine	908
Randolph AKR	800 ○
Ravenna AKR	11,987
Rawson	477
Reading CIN-	12,843
Redbird CLEV	1,600 ○
Reedurban CAN-	6,650 ○
Republic	656
Reynoldsburg COL	20,661
Richmond Dale	650 ○
Richmond Heights CLEV	10,095
Richwood	2,181
Ridgeville Corners	600 ○
Ripley	2,174
Risingsun	698
Rittman	6,063
Rockbridge	450 ○
Rock Creek	652
Rockford	1,245
Rocky River CLEV	21,084
Rootstown AKR	650 ○
Roseland MANS	3,000 ○
Roseville	1,915
Rossford TOL	5,978
Rudolph	600 ○
Rushsylvania	610
Russellville	445
Rutland	635
Sabina	2,799
Sagamore Hills CLEV	4,700 ○
St. Bernard CIN-	5,396
St. Clairsville WHL	5,452
St. Henry	1,596
St. Marys	8,414
St. Paris	1,742
Salem	12,869
Salineville	1,629
SANDUSKY SNDSK	31,360
Sardinia	826
Sardis	500 ○
Scio	1,003
Seaman	1,039
Sebring ALLI	5,078
Senecaville	458
Seven Hills CLEV	13,650
Seven Mile CIN-	841
Seville	1,568
Shadyside WHL	4,315
Shaker Heights CLEV	32,487
Sharonville CIN-	10,108
Shawnee	924
Sheffield Lake CLEV	10,484
Shelby	9,646
Sherwood	915
Shiloh DAY-	4,700 ○
Shiloh	857
Shreve	1,608
Sidney	17,657
Silverton CIN-	6,172
Smithfield STU-	1,308
Smithville	1,467
Solon CLEV	14,341
Somerset	1,432
South Charleston	1,682
South Euclid CLEV	25,713
South Lebanon CIN-	2,700
South Vienna	464
South Webster	886
South Zanesville ZAN	1,739
Spencer	764
Spencerville	2,184
Springboro DAY-	4,962
Springdale CIN-	10,111
Springfield DAY-	72,563
Spring Valley	541
STEUBENVILLE STU-	26,400
Stockport	558
Stony Ridge TOL	450 ○
Stoutsville	537
Stow AKR	25,303
Strasburg	2,091
Streetsboro CLEV	9,055
Strongsville CLEV	28,577
Struthers YNGS-	13,624
Stryker	1,423
Summit Station COL	500 ○
Sunbury COL	2,101
Swanton TOL	3,424
Sycamore	1,059
Sylvania TOL	15,527
Syracuse	946
Tallmadge AKR	15,269
The Plains	2,044
The Village of Indian Hill CIN-	5,521
Thornville	838
Thurston	527
Tiffin	19,549
Tiltonsville WHL	1,750
Tipp City DAY-	5,595
TOLEDO TOL	354,635
Toronto STU-	6,934
Trenton MIDD	6,401
Trinway	500 ○
Trotwood DAY-	7,802
Troy	19,086
Twinsburg CLEV	7,632
Uhrichsville	6,130
Union DAY-	5,219
Union City	1,716
Uniontown AKR	1,450 ○
Unionville	500 ○
University Heights CLEV	15,401
Upper Arlington COL	35,648
Upper Sandusky	5,967
Urbana	10,762
Urbancrest COL	880
Utica	2,238
Vandalia DAY-	13,161
Van Wert	11,035
Vermilion CLEV	11,012
Verona DAY-	571
Versailles	2,384
Wadsworth AKR	15,166
Wakeman CLEV	906
Walbridge TOL	2,900
Wapakoneta LIMA	8,402
Warren YNGS-	56,629
Warrensville Heights CLEV	16,565
Warsaw	765
Washington Court House	12,682
Waterford	480 ○
Waterville TOL	3,884
Wauseon	6,173
Waverly	4,603
Wayne	894
Waynesburg	1,160
Waynesville DAY-	1,796
Wellington	4,146
Wellston	6,016
Wellsville E.LIV-	5,095
West Alexandria DAY-	1,313
West Carrollton DAY-	13,148
Westerville COL	23,414
West Farmington	563
Westfield Center CLEV	791
West Jefferson COL	4,448
West Lafayette	2,225
Westlake CLEV	19,483
West Liberty	1,653
West Manchester	448
West Mansfield	716
West Milton DAY-	4,119
Weston	1,708
West Portsmouth PTSM	4,095
West Salem	1,357
West Union	2,791
West Unity	1,639
Wheelersburg PTSM	4,796
Whitehall COL	21,299
Whitehouse TOL	2,137
White Oak CIN-	9,563
Wickliffe CLEV	16,790
Wickliffe YNGS-	8,800 ○
Wilberforce DAY-	2,512
Willard	5,720
Williamsburg CIN-	1,952
Williamsport	792
Willoughby CLEV	19,329
Willoughby Hills CLEV	8,612
Willowick CLEV	17,834
Wilmington	10,431
Winchester	1,080
Windham YNGS-	3,721
Wintersville STU-	4,724
Woodbourne DAY-	6,000 ○
Woodlawn CIN-	2,715
Woodsfield	3,145
Woodville	2,050
Wooster	19,289
Worthington COL	15,016
Wyoming CIN-	8,282
Xenia DAY-	24,653
Yellow Springs DAY-	4,077
Yorkville WHL	1,447
YOUNGSTOWN YNGS-	115,436
ZANESVILLE ZAN	28,655

COUNTIES

County	Population
Adams	24,328
Allen	112,241
Ashland	46,178
Ashtabula	104,215
Athens	56,399
Auglaize	42,554
Belmont	82,569
Brown	31,920
Butler	258,787
Carroll	25,598
Champaign	33,649
Clark	150,236
Clermont	128,483
Clinton	34,603
Columbiana	113,572
Coshocton	36,024
Crawford	50,075
Cuyahoga	1,498,400
Darke	55,096
Defiance	39,987
Delaware	53,840
Erie	79,655
Fairfield	93,678
Fayette	27,467
Franklin	869,126
Fulton	37,751
Gallia	30,098
Geauga	74,474
Greene	129,769
Guernsey	42,024
Hamilton	873,224
Hancock	64,581
Hardin	32,719
Harrison	18,152
Henry	28,383
Highland	33,477
Hocking	24,304
Holmes	29,416
Huron	54,608
Jackson	30,592
Jefferson	91,564
Knox	46,304
Lake	212,801
Lawrence	63,849
Licking	120,981
Logan	39,155
Lorain	274,909
Lucas	471,741
Madison	33,004
Mahoning	289,487
Marion	67,974
Medina	113,150
Meigs	23,641
Mercer	38,334
Miami	90,381
Monroe	17,382
Montgomery	571,697
Morgan	14,241
Morrow	26,480
Muskingum	83,340
Noble	11,310
Ottawa	40,076
Paulding	21,302
Perry	31,032
Pickaway	43,662
Pike	22,802
Portage	135,856
Preble	38,223
Putnam	32,991
Richland	131,205
Ross	65,004
Sandusky	63,267
Scioto	84,545
Seneca	61,901
Shelby	43,089
Stark	378,823
Summit	524,472
Trumbull	241,863
Tuscarawas	84,614

○ Rand McNally estimate
▲ Population of entire township or "town", including rural areas.
● Independent city. Population not included in county total.

OHIO continued

County	Population
Union	29,536
Van Wert	30,458
Vinton	11,584
Warren	99,276
Washington	64,266
Wayne	97,408
Williams	36,369
Wood	107,372
Wyandot	22,651

OKLAHOMA

1980 Census 3,025,290

CITIES

City	Population
Achille	480
Ada	15,902
Adair	508
Afton	1,174
Alex	769
Allen	998
Altus	23,101
Alva	6,416
Anadarko	6,378
Antlers	2,989
Apache	1,560
Arapaho	851
Ardmore	23,689
Arkoma FTSM	2,175
Arnett	714
Asher	659
Atoka	3,409
Avant	461
Barnsdall	1,501
Bartlesville	34,568
Beaver	1,939
Beggs	1,428
Bethany O.C.	22,130
Bethel Acres	2,314
Billings	632
Binger	791
Bixby TUL	6,969
Blackwell	8,400
Blair	1,092
Blanchard O.C.	1,688
Boise City	1,761
Bokchito	628
Bokoshe	556
Boswell	702
Bowlegs	522
Boynton	518
Bray	591
Bristow	4,702
Broken Arrow TUL	35,761
Broken Bow	3,965
Buffalo	1,381
Burns Flat	2,431
Byng	833
Cache	1,661
Caddo	923
Calera	1,390
Calumet	469
Canton	854
Canute	676
Carmen	516
Carnegie	2,016
Carney	622
Cashion	547
Catoosa TUL	1,561
Cement	884
Chandler	2,926
Checotah	3,454
Chelsea	1,754
Cherokee	2,105
Cheyenne	1,207
Chickasha	15,828
Chilocco	500 ○
Choctaw O.C.	7,520
Chouteau	1,559
Claremore TUL	12,085
Clayton	833
Cleo Springs	514
Cleveland	2,972
Clinton	8,796
Coalgate	2,001
Colbert	1,122
Colcord	530
Collinsville TUL	3,556
Comanche	1,937
Commerce	2,556
Cookson	500 ○
Copan	960
Cordell	3,301
Corn	542
Countyline	500 ○
Covington	715
Coweta TUL	4,554
Cowlington	546
Crescent	1,651
Cushing	7,720
Custer City	530
Cyril	1,220
Davenport	974
Davidson	501
Davis	2,782
Delaware	544
Del City O.C.	28,523
Depew	682
Dewar	1,048
Dewey	3,545
Dickson	996
Dill City	649
Disney	464
Dover	570
Drummond	482
Drumright	3,162
Duke	484
Duncan	22,517
Durant	11,972
Dustin	498
Eagletown	500 ○
Eakly	452
Edmond O.C.	34,637
Eldorado	688
Elgin	1,003
Elk City	9,579
Elmore City	582
El Reno	15,486
ENID ENID	50,363
Erick	1,375
Eufaula	3,159
Fairfax	1,949
Fairland	1,073
Fairview	3,370
Fittstown	500 ○
Fletcher	1,074
Forgan	611
Fort Cobb	760
Fort Gibson MSKOG	2,477
Fort Supply	559
Fort Towson	789
Frederick	6,153
Gage	667
Garber	1,215
Geary	1,700
Geronimo	726
Glencoe	490
Glenpool TUL	2,706
Goldsby O.C.	603
Goodwell	1,186
Gore	445
Gotebo	457
Gracemont	503
Grandfield	1,445
Granite	1,617
Grove	3,378
Guthrie	10,312
Guymon	8,492
Haileyville	832
Hammon	866
Harrah O.C.	2,897
Hartshorne	2,380
Haskell	1,953
Healdton	3,769
Heavener	2,776
Helena	710
Hennessey	2,287
Henryetta	6,432
Hinton	1,432
Hobart	4,735
Holdenville	5,469
Hollis	2,958
Hominy	3,130
Hooker	1,788
Howe	562
Hugo	7,172
Hulbert	633
Hydro	938
Idabel	7,622
Inola	1,550
Jay	2,100
Jenks TUL	5,876
Jones O.C.	2,270
Kansas	491
Kellyville	960
Keota	661
Keyes	557
Kiefer TUL	912
Kingfisher	4,245
Kingston	1,171
Kiowa	866
Konawa	1,711
Krebs	1,754
Lahoma	537
Lake Station TUL	800 ○
Lamont	571
Langley	582
Langston	443
Laverne	1,563
LAWTON LAWT	80,054
Leedey	499
Lexington	1,731
Lindsay	3,454
Locust Grove	1,179
Lone Grove	3,369
Lone Wolf	613
Luther O.C.	1,159
McAlester	17,255
McCurtain	549
McLoud O.C.	4,061
Madill	3,173
Mangum	3,833
Mannford	1,610
Mannsville	568
Marietta	2,494
Marlow	5,017
Maud	1,444
Maysville	1,396
Medford	1,419
Meeker	1,032
Miami	14,237
Midwest City O.C.	49,559
Minco	1,489
Moore O.C.	35,063
Mooreland	1,383
Morris	1,288
Morrison	671
Mounds TUL	1,086
Mountain Park	557
Mountain View	1,189
Muldrow	2,538
MUSKOGEE MSKOG	40,011
Mustang O.C.	7,496
Newcastle O.C.	3,076
Newkirk	2,413
Nichols Hills O.C.	4,171
Nicoma Park O.C.	2,588
Noble O.C.	3,497
Norman O.C.	68,020
North Enid ENID	992
North Miami	544
Nowata	4,270
Oakhurst TUL	2,000 ○
Oakland	485
Oaks	591
Ochelata	480
Oilton	1,244
Okarche	1,064
Okay MSKOG	554
Okeene	1,601
Okemah	3,381
OKLAHOMA CITY O.C.	403,136
Okmulgee	16,263
Olustee	721
Oologah	798
Owasso TUL	6,149
Paden	448
Panama	1,425
Paoli	573
Pauls Valley	5,664
Pawhuska	4,771
Pawnee	1,688
Perkins	1,762
Perry	5,796
Picher	2,180
Piedmont O.C.	2,016
Pocola	3,268
Ponca City	26,238
Pond Creek	949
Porter	642
Porum	668
Poteau	7,089
Prague	2,208
Prue	554
Pryor	8,483
Purcell	4,638
Quapaw	1,097
Quinton	1,228
Ralston	495
Ramona	567
Randlett	461
Ravia	487
Red Oak	676
Ringling	1,561
Ripley	451
Roff	729
Roland	1,472
Rush Springs	1,451
Ryan	1,083
Salina	1,115
Sallisaw	6,403
Sand Springs TUL	13,121
Sapulpa TUL	15,853
Savanna	828
Sayre	3,177
Seiling	1,103
Seminole	8,590
Sentinel	1,016
Shattuck	1,759
Shawnee	26,506
Shidler	708
Skiatook TUL	3,596
Snyder	1,848
Soper	465
South Coffeyville	873
Sparks	772
Spavinaw	623
Sperry TUL	1,276
Spiro	2,221
Springer	679
Sterling	702
Stigler	2,630
Stillwater	38,268
Stilwell	2,369
Stonewall	672
Stratford	1,459
Stringtown	1,047
Stroud	3,148
Sulphur	5,516
Taft MSKOG	489
Tahlequah	9,708
Talihina	1,387
Taloga	446
Tecumseh	5,123
Temple	1,339
Terral	604
Texhoma	785
The Village O.C.	11,049
Thomas	1,515
Tipton	1,475
Tishomingo	3,212
Tonkawa	3,524
TULSA TUL	360,919
Tupelo	542
Turley TUL	6,336
Tuttle	3,051
Tyrone	928
Union City	558

○ Rand McNally estimate
▲ Population of entire township or "town", including rural areas.
● Independent city. Population not included in county total.

Valliant . . . 927
Velma . . . 831
Verden . . . 625
Vian . . . 1,521
Vici . . . 845
Vinita . . . 6,740
Wagoner . . . 6,191
Wakita . . . 526
Walters . . . 2,778
Wanette . . . 473
Wapanucka . . . 472
Warner . . . 1,310
Warr Acres O.C. . . . 9,940
Washington . . . 477
Watonga . . . 4,139
Waukomis . . . 1,551
Waurika . . . 2,258
Wayne . . . 621
Waynoka . . . 1,377
Weatherford . . . 9,640
Webbers Falls . . . 461
Welch . . . 697
Weleetka . . . 1,195
Wellston . . . 802
Westville . . . 1,049
Wetumka . . . 1,725
Wewoka . . . 5,480
Wilburton . . . 2,996
Wilson . . . 1,585
Wister . . . 982
Woodward . . . 13,610
Wright City . . . 1,168
Wynnewood . . . 2,615
Wynona . . . 780
Yale . . . 1,652
Yukon O.C. . . . 17,112

COUNTIES

Adair . . . 18,575
Alfalfa . . . 7,077
Atoka . . . 12,748
Beaver . . . 6,806
Beckham . . . 19,243
Blaine . . . 13,443
Bryan . . . 30,535
Caddo . . . 30,905
Canadian . . . 56,452
Carter . . . 43,610
Cherokee . . . 30,684
Choctaw . . . 17,203
Cimarron . . . 3,648
Cleveland . . . 133,173
Coal . . . 6,041
Comanche . . . 112,456
Cotton . . . 7,338
Craig . . . 15,014
Creek . . . 59,016
Custer . . . 25,995
Delaware . . . 23,946
Dewey . . . 5,922
Ellis . . . 5,596
Garfield . . . 62,820
Garvin . . . 27,856
Grady . . . 39,490
Grant . . . 6,518
Greer . . . 7,028
Harmon . . . 4,519
Harper . . . 4,715
Haskell . . . 11,010
Hughes . . . 14,338
Jackson . . . 30,356
Jefferson . . . 8,183
Johnston . . . 10,356
Kay . . . 49,852
Kingfisher . . . 14,187
Kiowa . . . 12,711
Latimer . . . 9,840
Le Flore . . . 40,698
Lincoln . . . 26,601
Logan . . . 26,881
Love . . . 7,469
McClain . . . 20,291
McCurtain . . . 36,151
McIntosh . . . 15,562
Major . . . 8,772
Marshall . . . 10,550
Mayes . . . 32,261
Murray . . . 12,147
Muskogee . . . 66,939
Noble . . . 11,573
Nowata . . . 11,486
Okfuskee . . . 11,125
Oklahoma . . . 568,933
Okmulgee . . . 39,169
Osage . . . 39,327
Ottawa . . . 32,870
Pawnee . . . 15,310
Payne . . . 62,435
Pittsburg . . . 40,524
Pontotoc . . . 32,598
Pottawatomie . . . 55,239
Pushmataha . . . 11,773
Roger Mills . . . 4,799
Rogers . . . 46,436
Seminole . . . 27,473
Sequoyah . . . 30,749
Stephens . . . 43,419
Texas . . . 17,727
Tillman . . . 12,398
Tulsa . . . 470,593
Wagoner . . . 41,801
Washington . . . 48,113
Washita . . . 13,798
Woods . . . 10,923
Woodward . . . 21,172

OREGON

1980 Census . . . 2,633,149

CITIES

Albany . . . 26,678
Aloha POR . . . 10,000 ○
Altamont . . . 19,805
Amity . . . 1,092
Applegate . . . 800 ○
Arlington . . . 521
Ashland . . . 14,943
Astoria . . . 9,998
Athena . . . 965
Aumsville SAL . . . 1,432
Aurora POR . . . 523
Baker . . . 9,471
Bandon . . . 2,311
Banks POR . . . 489
Barview . . . 1,462
Bay City . . . 986
Beaverton POR . . . 30,582
Bend . . . 17,263
Bly . . . 750 ○
Boardman . . . 1,261
Boring POR . . . 500 ○
Brookings . . . 3,384
Brownsville . . . 1,261
Bunker Hill . . . 1,555
Burns . . . 3,579
Canby POR . . . 7,659
Cannon Beach . . . 1,187
Canyon City . . . 639
Canyonville . . . 1,288
Carlton . . . 1,302
Cascade Locks . . . 838
Cave Junction . . . 1,023
Cedar Hills POR . . . 8,000 ○
Central Point MEDF . . . 6,357
Charleston . . . 700 ○
Chenoweth . . . 2,820
Chiloquin . . . 778
Clackamas POR . . . 3,250 ○
Clatskanie . . . 1,648
Coburg EUG . . . 699
Columbia City POR . . . 678
Condon . . . 783
Coos Bay . . . 14,424
Coquille . . . 4,481
Cornelius POR . . . 4,462
CORVALLIS CORV . . . 40,960
Cottage Grove . . . 7,148
Cove . . . 451
Crescent . . . 700 ○
Creswell . . . 1,770
Culver . . . 514
Dallas . . . 8,530
Dayton . . . 1,409
Depoe Bay . . . 723
Dillard . . . 1,000 ○
Drain . . . 1,148
Dufur . . . 560
Dundee POR . . . 1,223
Eagle Point MEDF . . . 2,764
Eastside . . . 1,601
Echo . . . 624
Elgin . . . 1,701
Elmira EUG . . . 500 ○
Enterprise . . . 2,003
Errol Heights POR . . . 7,800 ○
Estacada . . . 1,419
EUGENE EUG . . . 105,624
Fairview POR . . . 1,749
Falcon Heights . . . 1,389 ○
Falls City . . . 804
Florence . . . 4,411
Forest Grove POR . . . 11,499
Fossil . . . 535
Foster . . . 600 ○
Four Corners SAL . . . 11,331
Garden Home POR . . . 5,500 ○
Gardiner . . . 600 ○
Garibaldi . . . 999
Gaston . . . 471
Gates . . . 455
Gearhart . . . 967
Gervais SAL . . . 799
Gilbert POR . . . 4,000 ○
Gilchrist . . . 600 ○
Gladstone POR . . . 9,500
Glendale . . . 712
Glenwood EUG . . . 1,600 ○
Glide . . . 900 ○
Gold Beach . . . 1,515
Gold Hill . . . 904
Grand Ronde . . . 550 ○
Grants Pass . . . 15,032
Green . . . 3,897
Gresham POR . . . 33,005
Halsey . . . 693
Hammond . . . 516
Happy Valley POR . . . 1,499
Harbor . . . 2,856
Harrisburg EUG . . . 1,881
Hauser . . . 630 ○
Hayesville SAL . . . 9,213
Heppner . . . 1,498
Hermiston . . . 9,408
Hillsboro POR . . . 27,664
Hines . . . 1,632
Hood River . . . 4,329
Hubbard POR . . . 1,640
Huntington . . . 539
Independence SAL . . . 4,024
Irrigon . . . 700
Island City . . . 477
Jacksonville MEDF . . . 2,030
Jefferson . . . 1,702
Jennings Lodge POR . . . 3,000 ○
John Day . . . 2,012
Jordan Valley . . . 473
Joseph . . . 999
Junction City EUG . . . 3,320
Keizer SAL . . . 18,592
Keno . . . 900 ○
Kerby . . . 550 ○
Klamath Falls . . . 16,661
Lafayette . . . 1,215
La Grande . . . 11,354
Lake Oswego POR . . . 22,527
Lakeside . . . 1,453
Lakeview . . . 2,770
La Pine . . . 900 ○
Lebanon . . . 10,413
Lincoln City . . . 5,469
Lowell EUG . . . 661
Lyons . . . 877
McMinnville . . . 14,080
McNulty POR . . . 1,805
Madras . . . 2,235
Malin . . . 539
Manzanita . . . 443
Mapleton . . . 900 ○
Marcola . . . 500 ○
Marlene Village POR . . . 1,500 ○
Maupin . . . 495
May Park . . . 1,466 ○
Maywood Park POR . . . 1,083
MEDFORD MEDF . . . 39,603
Merlin . . . 500 ○
Merrill . . . 809
Metolius . . . 451
Metzger POR . . . 5,544
Midway POR . . . 19,000 ○
Mill City . . . 1,565
Milton-Freewater . . . 5,086
Milwaukie POR . . . 17,931
Molalla . . . 2,992
Monmouth SAL . . . 5,594
Mount Angel . . . 2,876
Mount Vernon . . . 569
Myrtle Creek . . . 3,365
Myrtle Point . . . 2,859
Newberg POR . . . 10,394
Newport . . . 7,519
North Albany . . . 4,499
North Bend . . . 9,779
North Plains POR . . . 715
Nyssa . . . 2,862
Oak Grove POR . . . 11,640
Oakland . . . 886
Oakridge . . . 3,729
Odell . . . 600 ○
Ontario . . . 8,814
Oregon City POR . . . 14,673
Pacific City . . . 1,500 ○
Parkrose POR . . . 21,108
Pendleton . . . 14,521
Philomath CORV . . . 2,673
Phoenix MEDF . . . 2,309
Pilot Rock . . . 1,630
PORTLAND POR . . . 366,383
Port Orford . . . 1,061
Powell Butte . . . 600 ○
Powellhurst POR . . . 9,000 ○
Powers . . . 819
Prairie City . . . 1,106
Prineville . . . 5,276
Prospect . . . 1,200 ○
Rainier LNGV . . . 1,655
Raleigh Hills POR . . . 6,517
Redmond . . . 6,452
Reedsport . . . 4,984
Riddle . . . 1,265
River Road EUG . . . 10,370
Rockaway . . . 906
Rockwood POR . . . 11,000 ○
Rogue River . . . 1,308
Roseburg . . . 16,644
Russellville POR . . . 6,500 ○
St. Helens POR . . . 7,064
SALEM SAL . . . 89,233
Sandy POR . . . 2,905
Santa Clara EUG . . . 14,288
Scappoose POR . . . 3,213
Scio . . . 579
Seal Rock . . . 800 ○
Seaside . . . 5,193
Shady Cove . . . 1,097
Sheridan . . . 2,249
Sherwood POR . . . 2,386
Siletz . . . 1,001
Silverton . . . 5,168
Sisters . . . 696
South Medford MEDF . . . 2,898

○ Rand McNally estimate
▲ Population of entire township or "town", including rural areas.
● Independent city. Population not included in county total.

OREGON continued

Springfield EUG 41,621
Stanfield 1,568
Stayton 4,396
Sublimity 1,077
Sutherlin 4,560
Svensen . . . . 650 ○
Sweet Home 6,921
Talent MEDF 2,577
Tangent 478
Terrebonne . . . . 900 ○
The Dalles 10,820
Tigard POR 14,286
Tillamook 3,981
Toledo 3,151
Tri-City 3,439
Troutdale POR 5,908
Tualatin POR 7,483
Tumalo . . . . 500 ○
Turner SAL 1,116
Tygh Valley . . . . 500 ○
Umatilla 3,199
Union 2,062
Vale 1,558
Veneta EUG 2,449
Vernonia 1,785
Waldport 1,274
Wallowa 847
Warm Springs . . . . 500 ○
Warren POR . . . . 800 ○
Warrenton 2,493
Welches . . . . 500 ○
Wemme . . . . 500 ○
West Haven POR . . . . 3,400 ○
West Linn POR 12,956
Weston 719
Westport . . . . 500 ○
West Slope POR 5,364
White City MEDF 5,445
Willamina 1,749
Wilsonville POR 2,920
Winchester Bay . . . . 900 ○
Winston 3,359
Wolf Creek . . . . 600 ○
Woodburn SAL 11,196
Yachats 482
Yamhill 690
Yoncalla 805

COUNTIES

Baker 16,134
Benton 68,211
Clackamas 241,911
Clatsop 32,489
Columbia 35,646
Coos 64,047
Crook 13,091
Curry 16,992
Deschutes 62,142
Douglas 93,748
Gilliam 2,057
Grant 8,210
Harney 8,314
Hood River 15,835
Jackson 132,456
Jefferson 11,599
Josephine 58,855
Klamath 59,117
Lake 7,532
Lane 275,226
Lincoln 35,264
Linn 89,495
Malheur 26,896
Marion 204,692
Morrow 7,519
Multnomah 562,640
Polk 45,203
Sherman 2,172
Tillamook 21,164
Umatilla 58,861
Union 23,921
Wallowa 7,273
Wasco 21,732
Washington 245,860
Wheeler 1,513
Yamhill 55,332

PENNSYLVANIA

1980
Census 11,863,895

CITIES

Abington PHIL- . . . . 7,900 ○
Adamstown 1,119
Akron 3,471
Albion 1,818
Alburtis AL-B-E 1,428
Alden SCR- . . . . 800 ○
Aliquippa PGH 17,094
ALLENTOWN AL-B-E 103,758
Allison . . . . 1,040 ○
Allison Park PGH . . . . 5,600 ○
ALTOONA ALT 57,078
Ambler PHIL- 6,628
Ambridge PGH 9,575
Annville LEB 4,493
Apollo PGH 2,212
Archbald SCR- 6,295
Ardmore PHIL- . . . . 13,600 ○
Arnold PGH 6,853
Ashland 4,235
Ashley SCR- 3,512
Aspinwall PGH 3,284
Aston PHIL- . . . . 6,900 ○
Athens 3,622
Auburn 999
Austin 740
Avalon PGH 6,240
Avella STU- . . . . 950 ○
Avis WMSPT 1,718
Avoca SCR- 3,536
Avondale PHIL- 891
Avonmore 1,234
Baden PGH 5,318
Bairdford PGH . . . . 950 ○
Bala-Cynwyd PHIL- . . . . 8,600 ○
Baldwin PGH 24,712
Bally 1,051
Bangor 5,006
Barnesboro 2,741
Bath AL-B-E 1,953
Beaver PGH 5,441
Beaverdale JNST . . . . 1,000 ○
Beaver Falls PGH 12,525
Beaver Meadows HAZ 1,078
Bedford 3,326
Bellefonte STCOL 6,300
Belle Vernon PGH 1,489
Belleville 1,689
Bellevue PGH 10,128
Bellwood ALT 2,114
Bensalem 52,399
Bentleyville WASH 2,525
Benton 981
Berlin 1,999
Bernville READ 798
Berwick 11,850
Berwyn PHIL- . . . . 9,300 ○
Bessemer 1,293
Bethel Park PGH 34,755
Bethlehem AL-B-E 70,419
Biglerville 991
Big Run 822
Birdsboro 3,481
Black Lick 1,313
Blairsville 4,166
Blakely SCR- 7,438
Blandburg . . . . 775 ○
Blawnox PGH 1,653
Bloomsburg 11,717
Blossburg 1,757
Blue Ridge Summit . . . . 800 ○
Bobtown 1,008
Boiling Springs HRBG 2,323
Bolivar 706
Boothwyn PHIL- . . . . 7,100 ○
Boswell JNST 1,480
Boyertown PTSTN 3,979
Brackenridge PGH 4,297
Braddock PGH 5,634
Bradenville PGH . . . . 1,200 ○
Bradford 11,211
Brentwood PGH 11,861
Briarcliff PHIL- . . . . 9,300 ○
Bridgeville PGH 6,154
Bristol PHIL- 10,867
Brookhaven PHIL- 7,912
Brookville 4,568
Broomall PHIL- 23,642
Brownsville 4,043
Bryn Mawr PHIL- . . . . 9,500 ○
Burgettstown PGH 1,867
Burnham 2,457
BUTLER BUTL 17,026
Cadogan 459
Cairnbrook . . . . 800 ○
California 5,703
Cambridge Springs 2,102
Camp Hill HRBG 8,422
Canadensis . . . . 800 ○
Canonsburg PGH 10,459
Canton 1,959
Carbondale 11,255
Carlisle 18,314
Carmichaels 630
Carnegie PGH 10,099
Carnot PGH . . . . 5,600 ○
Castanea 1,148
Castle Shannon PGH 10,164
Catasauqua AL-B-E 6,711
Catawissa 1,568
Cecil . . . . 900 ○
Cementon AL-B-E . . . . 1,200 ○
Centerville 4,207
Central City JNST 1,496
Centre Hall STCOL 1,233
Chambersburg 16,174
Charleroi PGH 5,717
Cheltenham PHIL- . . . . 7,700 ○
Chester PHIL- 45,794
Chester Township PHIL- 5,687
Cheswick PGH 2,336
Chicora BUTL 1,192
Christiana COAT 1,183
Clairton PGH 12,188
Clarendon 776
Claridge PGH . . . . 600 ○
Clarion 6,198
Clarks Summit SCR- 5,272
Claysburg ALT 1,346
Claysville WASH 1,029
Clearfield 7,580
Cleona LEB 2,003
Clifton Heights PHIL- 7,320
Clymer 1,761
Coaldale 2,762
Coalport 739
COATESVILLE COAT 10,698
Cochranton 1,240
Collegeville PHIL- 3,406
Collingdale PHIL- 9,539
Colonial Park HRBG . . . . 10,000 ○
Columbia 10,466
Colver 1,165
Conemaugh JNST 2,128
Confluence 968
Conneautville 971
Connellsville 10,319
Conshohocken PHIL- 8,475
Conway PGH 2,747
Coopersburg AL-B-E 2,595
Coplay AL-B-E 3,130
Coral . . . . 700 ○
Coraopolis PGH 7,308
Cornwall LEB 2,653
Corry 7,149
Coudersport 2,791
Crabtree PGH . . . . 1,021 ○
Crafton PGH 7,623
Creighton PGH 1,658
Cresson 2,184
Cressona PTSVL 1,810
Croydon PHIL- . . . . 10,000 ○
Crucible . . . . 800 ○
Curtisville PGH 1,404
Curwensville 3,116
Dallas SCR- 2,679
Dallastown YORK 3,949
Dalton SCR- 1,383
Danville 5,239
Darby PHIL- 11,513
Dauphin HRBG 901
Dawson 661
Dayton 648
Delta 692
Denver 2,018
Derry LTROB 3,072
Devon PHIL- . . . . 6,700 ○
Dickson City SCR- 6,699
Dillsburg HRBG 1,733
Distant . . . . 575 ○
Dixonville . . . . 900 ○
Donald Son . . . . 465 ○
Donora PGH 7,524
Dormont PGH 11,275
Dover YORK 1,910
Downingtown COAT 7,650
Doylestown PHIL- 8,717
Drexel Hill PHIL- . . . . 29,600 ○
Drifton HAZ . . . . 600 ○
Du Bois 9,290
Duboistown WMSPT 1,218
Duke Center . . . . 900 ○
Dunbar 1,369
Duncannon HRBG 1,645
Duncansville ALT 1,355
Dunlo JNST . . . . 950 ○
Dunmore SCR- 16,781
Dupont SCR- 3,460
Duquesne PGH 10,094
Duryea SCR- 5,415
Dushore 692
East Bangor 955
East Berlin YORK 1,054
East Brady 1,153
East Greenville 2,456
East Norriton PHIL- 12,711
Easton AL-B-E 26,027
East Petersburg LANC 3,600
East Pittsburgh PGH 2,493
East Stroudsburg 8,039
East Washington WASH 2,241
Ebensburg 4,096
Economy PGH 9,538
Eddystone PGH 2,555
Edenborn . . . . 500 ○
Edgewood PGH 4,382
Edgeworth PGH 1,738
Edinboro 6,324
Edwardsville SCR- 5,729
Eldred 965
Elizabethtown HRBG 8,233
Elizabethville 1,531
Elkins Park PHIL- . . . . 14,000 ○
Elkland 1,974
Ellport PGH 1,290
Ellsworth PGH 1,228
Ellwood City PGH 9,998
Elmhurst 953

○ Rand McNally estimate
▲ Population of entire township or "town", including rural areas.
● Independent city. Population not included in county total.

Elmora ... 950 ○
Elrama ... 800 ○
Elysburg ... 1,477
Emmaus AL-B-E ... 11,001
Emporium ... 2,837
Emsworth PGH ... 3,074
Enola HRBG ... 3,600 ○
Ephrata ... 11,095
Erdenheim PHIL- ... 3,300 ○
ERIE ERIE ... 119,123
Ernest ... 584
Espy ... 1,571
Etna PGH ... 4,534
Evans City BUTL ... 2,299
Everett ... 1,828
Everson ... 1,032
Exeter SCR- ... 5,493
Export PGH ... 1,143
Factoryville SCR- ... 924
Fairchance UNTN ... 2,106
Fairless Hills PHIL- ... 12,500 ○
Fairoaks PGH ... 1,854
Fairview ERIE ... 1,855
Falls Creek ... 1,208
Farrell SHAR ... 8,645
Fayetteville ... 3,202
Feasterville PHIL- ... 6,900 ○
Ferndale JNST ... 2,204
Fleetwood ... 3,422
Flemington ... 1,416
Flourtown PHIL- ... 5,200 ○
Folcroft PHIL- ... 8,231
Folsom PHIL- ... 7,600 ○
Ford City ... 3,923
Forest City ... 1,924
Forest Hills PGH ... 8,198
Fort Washington PHIL- ... 4,500 ○
Forty Fort SCR- ... 5,590
Fountain Hill AL-B-E ... 4,805
Fox Chapel PGH ... 5,049
Frackville ... 5,308
Franklin OILC-F ... 8,146
Franklin Park PGH ... 6,135
Fredericktown ... 1,052
Freedom PGH ... 2,272
Freeland HAZ ... 4,285
Freemansburg AL-B-E ... 1,879
Freeport PGH ... 2,381
Galeton ... 1,462
Gallitzin ALT ... 2,315
Gap ... 1,000 ○
Garrett ... 563
Geistown JNST ... 3,304
Gettysburg ... 7,194
Girard ERIE ... 2,615
Girardville ... 2,268
Glassport PGH ... 6,242
Glen Lyon SCR- ... 2,352
Glenolden PHIL- ... 7,633
Glen Rock YORK ... 1,662
Glenshaw PGH ... 14,000 ○
Glenside PHIL- ... 17,400 ○
Grampian ... 464
Grassflat ... 750 ○
Great Bend BING ... 740
Greencastle HAG- ... 3,679
Greensburg PGH ... 17,558
Green Tree PGH ... 5,722
Greenville ... 7,730
Grove City ... 8,162
Halifax HRBG ... 909
Hallstead BING ... 1,280
Hamburg ... 4,011
HANOVER HANV ... 14,890
Harmony PGH ... 1,334
HARRISBURG HRBG ... 53,264
Harrisville ... 1,033
Hastings ... 1,574
Hatboro PHIL- ... 7,579
Hatfield PHIL- ... 2,533
Haverford PHIL- ... 5,800 ○
Havertown PHIL- ... 36,000 ○
Hawk Run ... 750 ○
Hawley ... 1,181
Hawthorn ... 547
HAZLETON HAZ ... 27,318
Hegins ... 900 ○
Heilwood ... 700 ○
Hellam YORK ... 1,428
Hellertown AL-B-E ... 6,025
Herminie PGH ... 1,100 ○
Hermitage SHAR ... 16,365
Herndon ... 483
Hershey HRBG ... 9,000 ○
Highspire HRBG ... 2,959
Hillsville ... 915 ○
Hollidaysburg ALT ... 5,892
Homer City ... 2,248
Homestead PGH ... 5,092
Honesdale ... 5,128
Honey Brook COAT ... 1,164
Hooversville JNST ... 863
Hopwood UNTN ... 2,190
Horsham PHIL- ... 6,000 ○
Houston PGH ... 1,568
Houtzdale ... 1,222
Howard ... 838
Hughesville ... 2,174
Hummels Wharf ... 750 ○
Huntingdon ... 7,042
Huntingdon Valley PHIL- ... 10,400 ○
Hyndman ... 1,106
Imperial PGH ... 2,500 ○
Indiana ... 16,051
Ingram PGH ... 4,346
Irvona ... 644
Irwin PGH ... 4,995
Isabella ... 700 ○
James City ... 450 ○
Jamestown ... 854
Jeannette PGH ... 13,106
Jefferson PGH ... 8,643
Jenkintown PHIL- ... 4,942
Jenners ... 800 ○
Jermyn SCR- ... 2,411
Jerome JNST ... 1,196
Jersey Shore WMSPT ... 4,631
Jessup SCR- ... 4,974
Jim Thorpe AL-B-E ... 5,263
Johnsonburg ... 3,938
JOHNSTOWN JNST ... 35,496
Jonestown LEB ... 814
Juniata Terrace ... 631
Kane ... 4,916
Kenmawr PGH ... 5,100 ○
Kennett Square PHIL- ... 4,715
Kersey ... 600 ○
King of Prussia PHIL- ... 18,200 ○
Kingston SCR- ... 15,681
Kittanning ... 5,432
Knox ... 1,364
Knoxville ... 650
Koppel PGH ... 1,146
Kulpmont ... 3,675
Kutztown ... 4,040
Lafayette Hill PHIL- ... 6,600 ○
Lake City ERIE ... 2,384
Lakemont ALT ... 1,500 ○
LANCASTER LANC ... 54,725
Lanesboro BING ... 465
Langeloth ... 950 ○
Langhorne PHIL- ... 1,697
Lansdale PHIL- ... 16,526
Lansdowne PHIL- ... 11,891
Lansford ... 4,466
Larksville SCR- ... 4,410
Latrobe LTROB ... 10,799
Lattimer Mines ... 650 ○
Laureldale READ ... 4,047
Laurel Run SCR- ... 725
Lawrence PGH ... 970 ○
LEBANON LEB ... 25,711
Leechburg PGH ... 2,682
Leetsdale PGH ... 1,604
Lehighton AL-B-E ... 5,826
Levittown PHIL- ... 78,600 ○
Lewisburg ... 5,407
Lewis Run ... 677
Lewistown ... 9,830
Ligonier ... 1,917
Lilly ... 1,462
Linesville ... 1,198
Lititz LANC ... 7,590
Littlestown HANV ... 2,870
Liverpool ... 809
Lock Haven ... 9,617
Loretto ... 1,395
Lower Burrell PGH ... 13,200
Lucernemines ... 1,380 ○
Ludlow ... 800 ○
Luzerne SCR- ... 3,703
Lykens ... 2,181
Lyndora BUTL ... 1,900 ○
McAdoo HAZ ... 2,940
McCandless PGH ... 26,250
McClure ... 1,024
McConnellsburg ... 1,178
McKeesport PGH ... 31,012
McKees Rocks PGH ... 8,742
McSherrystown HANV ... 2,764
Macungie AL-B-E ... 1,899
Madera ... 900 ○
Mahaffey ... 513
Mahanoy City ... 6,167
Manchester YORK ... 2,027
Manheim ... 5,015
Mansfield ... 3,322
Mapleton Depot ... 591
Marcus Hook PHIL- ... 2,638
Marienville ... 900 ○
Marietta ... 2,740
Mars PGH ... 1,803
Martinsburg ... 2,231
Marysville HRBG ... 2,452
Masontown ... 4,909
Matamoras ... 2,111
Mather ... 860 ○
Mayfield SCR- ... 1,812
Meadow Lands PGH ... 1,200 ○
Meadville ... 15,544
Mechanicsburg HRBG ... 9,487
Media PHIL- ... 6,119
Mercer SHAR ... 2,532
Mercersburg ... 1,617
Merion Station PHIL- ... 7,400 ○
Meyersdale ... 2,581
Middleburg ... 1,357
Middletown HRBG ... 10,122
Midland E.LIV- ... 4,310
Midway PGH ... 1,187
Mifflin ... 648
Mifflinburg ... 3,151
Mifflintown ... 783
Mifflinville ... 1,341
Mildred ... 800 ○
Milesburg STCOL ... 1,309
Milford ... 1,143
Millcreek ERIE ... 44,303
Millersburg ... 2,770
Millerstown ... 550
Millersville LANC ... 7,668
Mill Hall ... 1,744
Millheim ... 800
Millsboro ... 900 ○
Millvale PGH ... 4,772
Millville ... 975
Milroy ... 1,594
Milton ... 6,730
Minersville PTSVL ... 5,635
Mocanaqua ... 990 ○
Mohnton READ ... 2,156
Monaca PGH ... 7,661
Monessen PGH ... 11,928
Monongahela PGH ... 5,950
Monroeville PGH ... 30,977
Mont Alto HAG- ... 1,592
Mont Clare PHIL- ... 950 ○
Montgomery ... 1,653
Montoursville WMSPT ... 5,403
Montrose ... 1,980
Moon Run PGH ... 700 ○
Moosic SCR- ... 6,068
Morrisdale ... 600 ○
Morrisville PHIL- ... 9,845
Moscow SCR- ... 1,536
Mount Carmel ... 8,190
Mount Holly Springs ... 2,068
Mount Jewett ... 1,053
Mount Joy ... 5,680
Mount Lebanon PGH ... 34,414
Mount Pleasant ... 5,354
Mount Pocono ... 1,237
Mount Union ... 3,101
Mount Wolf YORK ... 1,517
Muncy ... 2,700
Munhall PGH ... 14,535
Murrysville PGH ... 16,036
Muse PGH ... 1,000 ○
Myerstown LEB ... 3,131
Nanticoke SCR- ... 13,044
Nanty Glo JNST ... 3,936
Narberth PHIL- ... 4,496
Natrona Heights PGH ... 13,252
Nazareth AL-B-E ... 5,443
Neffsville LANC ... 1,300 ○
Nemacolin ... 1,235
Nescopeck ... 1,768
Nesquehoning ... 3,346
New Bethlehem ... 1,441
New Bloomfield HRBG ... 1,109
New Brighton PGH ... 7,364
NEW CASTLE NWCS ... 33,621
New Cumberland HRBG ... 8,051
New Florence JNST ... 855
New Freedom ... 2,205
New Holland ... 4,147
New Hope ... 1,473
New Kensington PGH ... 17,660
Newmanstown ... 1,417
New Milford ... 1,040
New Oxford HANV ... 1,921
New Philadelphia PTSVL ... 1,341
Newport HRBG ... 1,600
Newtown Square PHIL- ... 11,775
Newville ... 1,370
New Wilmington ... 2,774
Nicholson ... 945
Norristown PHIL- ... 34,684
Northampton AL-B-E ... 8,240
North Apollo PGH ... 1,487
North Bend ... 700 ○
North Braddock PGH ... 8,711
North East ERIE ... 4,568
Northumberland ... 3,636
North Versailles PGH ... 13,294
North Wales PHIL- ... 3,391
North Warren ... 1,360
North York YORK ... 1,755
Norwood PHIL- ... 6,647
Noxen ... 800 ○
Nuremberg ... 800 ○
Oakdale PGH ... 1,955
Oakland BING ... 734
Oakmont PGH ... 7,039
Ohioville E.LIV- ... 4,217

○ Rand McNally estimate
▲ Population of entire township or "town", including rural areas.
● Independent city. Population not included in county total.

PENNSYLVANIA continued

OIL CITY OILC-F ... 13,881
Old Forge SCR- ... 9,304
Oliver UNTN ... 1,500 ○
Olyphant SCR- ... 5,204
Oreland PHIL- ... 9,000 ○
Orwigsburg PTSVL ... 2,700
Osceola Mills ... 1,466
Oxford ... 3,633
Palmerton AL-B-E ... 5,455
Palmyra HRBG ... 7,228
Paoli PHIL- ... 6,100 ○
Parker ... 808
Parkesburg COAT ... 2,578
Patton ... 2,441
Pen Argyl ... 3,388
Penbrook HRBG ... 3,006
Penn Hills PGH ... 57,632
Pennsburg ... 2,339
Penn Valley PHIL- ... 6,100 ○
Perkasie PHIL- ... 5,241
Perrysville PGH ... 5,300 ○
PHILADELPHIA PHIL- ... 1,688,210
Philipsburg ... 3,533
Phoenixville PHIL- ... 14,165
Pilgrim Gardens PHIL- ... 8,400 ○
Pine Grove ... 2,244
Pitcairn PGH ... 4,175
PITTSBURGH PGH ... 423,959
Pittston SCR- ... 9,930
Plains SCR- ... 5,455
Pleasant Gap STCOL ... 1,859
Pleasant Hills PGH ... 9,374
Pleasantville ... 1,099
Plum PGH ... 25,390
Plymouth SCR- ... 7,605
Plymouth Meeting PHIL- ... 6,000 ○
Plymouth Valley PHIL- ... 8,200 ○
Point Marion MORG ... 1,642
Polk OILC-F ... 1,884
Portage JNST ... 3,510
Port Allegany ... 2,593
Port Royal ... 835
Port Vue PGH ... 5,316
POTTSTOWN PTSTN ... 22,729
POTTSVILLE PTSVL ... 18,195
Prospect Park PHIL- ... 6,593
Punxsutawney ... 7,479
Quakertown ... 8,867
Quarryville ... 1,558
Rankin PGH ... 2,892
READING READ ... 78,686
Reamstown ... 1,308
Red Lion YORK ... 5,824
Reedsville ... 950 ○
Renovo ... 1,812
Republic UNTN ... 1,500 ○
Revloc ... 800 ○
Reynoldsville ... 3,016
Ridgway ... 5,604
Ridley Park PHIL- ... 7,889
Rimersburg ... 1,096
Roaring Spring ALT ... 2,962
Robertsdale ... 550 ○
Robinson ... 660 ○
Rochester PGH ... 4,759
Rockledge PHIL- ... 2,538
Rockwood ... 1,058
Roscoe PGH ... 1,123
Roseto ... 1,484
Roslyn PHIL- ... 13,400 ○
Rossiter ... 750 ○
Rothsville LANC ... 1,263
Roulette ... 1,100 ○
Rouseville OILC-F ... 734
Royersford PHIL- ... 4,243
Russell ... 800 ○
Saegertown ... 942
Sagamore ... 850 ○
St. Clair PTSVL ... 4,037
St. Marys ... 6,417
Salisbury ... 817
Saltsburg ... 964
Sandy Lake ... 779
Saxton ... 814
Sayre ... 6,951
Scalp Level JNST ... 1,186
Schaefferstown ... 800 ○
Schuylkill Haven PTSVL ... 5,977
Scottdale ... 5,833
Scott Township PGH ... 20,413
SCRANTON SCR- ... 88,117
Selinsgrove ... 5,227
Sellersville PHIL- ... 3,143
Sewickley PGH ... 4,778
Shamokin ... 10,357
Shamokin Dam ... 1,622
SHARON SHAR ... 19,057
Sharon Hill PHIL- ... 6,221
Sharpsburg PGH ... 4,351
Sharpsville SHAR ... 5,375
Sheffield ... 1,564
Shenandoah ... 7,589
Sheppton ... 650 ○
Shickshinny ... 1,192
Shillington READ ... 5,601
Shinglehouse ... 1,310
Shippensburg ... 5,261
Shoemakersville READ ... 1,391
Shrewsbury ... 2,688
Simpson ... 2,200 ○
Slatington AL-B-E ... 4,277
Slickville PGH ... 1,178
Sligo ... 798
Slippery Rock ... 3,047
Slovan ... 900 ○
Smethport ... 1,797
Smithfield ... 1,084
Somerset ... 6,474
Souderton PHIL- ... 6,657
Southampton PHIL- ... 9,500 ○
South Connellsville ... 2,296
South Fork JNST ... 1,401
South Renovo ... 663
South Waverly ... 1,176
South Williamsport WMSPT ... 6,581
Spangler ... 2,399
Spring City PHIL- ... 3,389
Springdale PGH ... 4,418
Springfield PHIL- ... 25,326
Spring Garden Township YORK ... 11,127
Spring Grove YORK ... 1,832
STATE COLLEGE STCOL ... 36,130
Steelton HRBG ... 6,484
Stewartstown ... 1,072
Stockertown AL-B-E ... 661
Stoneboro ... 1,177
Stowe PTSTN ... 3,860
Stowe Township PGH ... 9,202
Strabane PGH ... 1,900 ○
Strasburg LANC ... 1,999
Strattanville ... 555
Stroudsburg ... 5,148
Sugarcreek OILC-F ... 5,954
Sugar Notch SCR- ... 1,191
Summerville ... 830
Summit Hill ... 3,418
Sunbury ... 12,292
Susquehanna BING ... 1,994
Swarthmore PHIL- ... 5,950
Swissvale PGH ... 11,345
Swoyerville SCR- ... 5,795
Sykesville ... 1,537
Tamaqua ... 8,843
Tarentum PGH ... 6,419
Taylor SCR- ... 7,246
Telford PHIL- ... 3,507
Temple READ ... 1,486
Templeton ... 700 ○
Terre Hill ... 1,217
Throop SCR- ... 4,166
Tidioute ... 844
Titusville ... 6,884
Tobyhanna ... 700 ○
Topton AL-B-E ... 1,818
Towanda ... 3,526
Tower City ... 1,667
Trafford PGH ... 3,662
Tremont ... 1,796
Tresckow HAZ ... 1,128
Trevorton ... 2,192
Trevose PHIL- ... 7,000 ○
Troy ... 1,381
Tunkhannock ... 2,144
Turtle Creek PGH ... 6,959
Twin Rocks ... 700 ○
Tyrone ... 6,346
Union City ... 3,623
UNIONTOWN UNTN ... 14,510
United PGH ... 950 ○
Upper Darby PHIL- ... 50,200 ○
Upper St. Clair PGH ... 19,023
Valley Forge ... 950 ○
Valley View ... 1,722
Vanderbilt ... 689
Vandergrift PGH ... 6,823
Verona PGH ... 3,179
Villanova PHIL- ... 6,600 ○
Vintondale JNST ... 697
Walnutport AL-B-E ... 2,007
Wampum PGH ... 851
Wanamie SCR- ... 600 ○
Warminster PHIL- ... 35,543
Warren ... 12,146
Warrendale PGH ... 800 ○
WASHINGTON WASH ... 18,363
Waterford ERIE ... 1,568
Watsontown ... 2,366
Waymart ... 1,248
Wayne PHIL- ... 8,900 ○
Waynesboro HAG- ... 9,726
Waynesburg ... 4,482
Weatherly HAZ ... 2,891
Webster PGH ... 800 ○
Wellsboro ... 3,805
Wesleyville ERIE ... 3,998
Westbrook Park PHIL- ... 5,700 ○
West Chester PHIL- ... 17,435
West Decatur ... 600 ○
West Fairview HRBG ... 1,426
Westfield ... 1,268
West Grove PHIL- ... 1,820
West Hazleton HAZ ... 4,871
West Lawn READ ... 1,686
West Leisenring ... 700 ○
West Middlesex SHAR ... 1,064
West Mifflin PGH ... 26,552
West Milton ... 775 ○
Westmont JNST ... 6,113
West Newton PGH ... 3,387
West Norriton PHIL- ... 14,034
West Pittsburg ... 950 ○
West Pittston SCR- ... 5,980
West Reading READ ... 4,507
West View PGH ... 7,648
West Wyoming SCR- ... 3,288
West York YORK ... 4,526
Whitehall PGH ... 15,143
Whitehall AL-B-E ... 8,055
White Haven ... 1,921
White Oak PGH ... 9,480
Whitney LTROB ... 500 ○
Wiconisco ... 1,321
Wilcox ... 900 ○
Wilkes-Barre SCR- ... 51,551
Wilkinsburg PGH ... 23,669
Williamsburg ... 1,400
WILLIAMSPORT WMSPT ... 33,401
Williamstown ... 1,664
Willow Grove PHIL- ... 21,300 ○
Wilmerding PGH ... 2,421
Wilson AL-B-E ... 7,564
Winburne ... 650 ○
Windber JNST ... 5,585
Windgap ... 2,651
Windsor YORK ... 1,205
Womelsdorf ... 1,827
Wood ... 500 ○
Woodland ... 600 ○
Woodlyn PHIL- ... 6,000 ○
Worthington ... 760
Wrightsville LANC ... 2,365
Wyalusing ... 716
Wyncote PHIL- ... 5,300 ○
Wyndmoor PHIL- ... 5,800 ○
Wynnewood PHIL- ... 7,700 ○
Wyoming SCR- ... 3,655
Wyomissing READ ... 6,551
Yardley PHIL- ... 2,533
Yatesboro ... 700 ○
Yeadon PHIL- ... 11,727
Yeagertown ... 1,305
YORK YORK ... 44,619
York Haven YORK ... 746
Youngsville ... 2,006
Youngwood PGH ... 3,749
Zelienople PGH ... 3,502

COUNTIES

Adams ... 68,292
Allegheny ... 1,450,085
Armstrong ... 77,768
Beaver ... 204,441
Bedford ... 46,784
Berks ... 312,509
Blair ... 136,621
Bradford ... 62,919
Bucks ... 479,211
Butler ... 147,912
Cambria ... 183,263
Cameron ... 6,674
Carbon ... 53,285
Centre ... 112,760
Chester ... 316,660
Clarion ... 43,362
Clearfield ... 83,578
Clinton ... 38,971
Columbia ... 61,967
Crawford ... 88,869
Cumberland ... 178,541
Dauphin ... 232,317
Delaware ... 555,007
Elk ... 38,338
Erie ... 279,780
Fayette ... 159,417
Forest ... 5,072
Franklin ... 113,629
Fulton ... 12,842
Greene ... 40,476
Huntingdon ... 42,253
Indiana ... 92,281
Jefferson ... 48,303
Juniata ... 19,188

○ Rand McNally estimate
▲ Population of entire township or "town", including rural areas.
● Independent city. Population not included in county total.

Lackawanna 227,908
Lancaster 362,346
Lawrence 107,150
Lebanon 108,582
Lehigh 272,349
Luzerne 343,079
Lycoming 118,416
McKean 50,635
Mercer 128,299
Mifflin 46,908
Monroe 69,409
Montgomery 643,621
Montour 16,675
Northampton 225,418
Northumberland 100,381
Perry 35,718
Philadelphia 1,688,210
Pike 18,271
Potter 17,726
Schuylkill 160,630
Snyder 33,584
Somerset 81,243
Sullivan 6,349
Susquehanna 37,876
Tioga 40,973
Union 32,870
Venango 64,444
Warren 47,449
Washington 217,074
Wayne 35,237
Westmoreland 392,294
Wyoming 26,433
York 312,963

RHODE ISLAND

1980
Census 947,154

CITIES

Albion PROV- . . . . . . 1,200 ○
Allenton PROV- . . . . . . 600 ○
Anthony PROV- . . . . . 4,500 ○
Arnold Mills PROV- . . . . 600 ○
Ashaway N.LON- 1,747
Ashton PROV- . . . . 875 ○
Barrington PROV- . . . 16,174
Berkeley PROV- . . . . . . 930 ○
Block Island . . . . 620 ○
Bradford N.LON- 1,354
Bristol PROV- 20,128
Carolina . . . . 500 ○
Central Falls
PROV- 16,995
Charlestown
4,800▲ . . . . 1,200 ○
Chepachet PROV- . . . . 900 ○
Coventry
PROV- 27,065▲ . . . 8,000 ○
Cranston PROV- . . . 71,992
Cumberland Hill
PROV- 5,421
Davisville PROV- . . . . . 550 ○
Diamond Hill
PROV- . . . . 1,150 ○
East Greenwich
PROV- 10,211
East Providence
PROV- 50,980
Esmond PROV- . . . . . 3,500 ○
Forestdale PROV- . . . . . 450 ○
Glendale PROV- . . . . . . 600 ○
Greenville PROV- 7,576
Harmony PROV- . . . . . . 800 ○
Harris PROV- . . . . 1,000 ○
Harrisville PROV- 1,224
Hope PROV- . . . . 490 ○
Hope Valley 1,414
Island Park NWPT . . . 1,000 ○
Jamestown NWPT . . . 4,040
Johnston PROV- . . . 24,907
Kingston 5,479
La Fayette PROV- . . . . . 680 ○
Lonsdale PROV- . . . . 4,100 ○
Manville PROV- . . . . . 3,100 ○
Mapleville PROV- . . . . . 900 ○
Middletown NWPT . . . 3,350 ○
Mount View PROV- . . . . 560 ○
Narragansett
PROV- 12,088▲ . . . 3,342
NEWPORT
NWPT 29,259
North Kingstown
PROV- 21,938▲ . . . 3,100 ○
North Providence
PROV- 29,188
Oakland PROV- . . . . . . 500 ○
Pascoag PROV- 3,807
Pawtucket PROV- . . . 71,204
Peace Dale . . . . 3,100 ○
Portsmouth
NWPT 14,257▲ . . . 4,300 ○
PROVIDENCE
PROV- 156,804
Quidnessett
PROV- . . . . 3,300 ○
Quidnick PROV- . . . . . 2,300 ○
Saylesville PROV- . . . 3,200 ○
Shannock . . . . 600 ○
Slatersville PROV- . . . 2,000 ○
South Hopkinton
N.LON- . . . . 500 ○
Tiverton
F.R. 13,526▲ 7,653
Union Village
PROV- . . . . 2,400 ○
Valley Falls
PROV- 10,892
Wakefield . . . . 3,400 ○
Warren PROV- 10,640
Warwick PROV- 87,123
Watch Hill N.LON- . . . . . 500 ○
West Barrington
PROV- . . . . 3,700 ○
Westerly
N.LON- 18,580▲ . 14,093
West Kingston . . . . 700 ○
West Warwick
PROV- 27,026
Woonsocket
PROV- 45,914
Wyoming . . . . 600 ○
Yorktown Manor
PROV- . . . . 2,500 ○

COUNTIES

Bristol 46,942
Kent 154,163
Newport 81,383
Providence 571,349
Washington 93,317

SOUTH CAROLINA

1980
Census 3,121,833

CITIES

Abbeville 5,833
Adams Run . . . . 600 ○
Aiken 14,978
Alcolu . . . . 600 ○
Allendale 4,400
ANDERSON AND. . . 27,965
Andrews 3,129
Arcadia SPRT 2,088
Arlington SPRT . . . . 600 ○
Aynor 643
Baldwin . . . . 700 ○
Bamberg 3,672
Barnwell 5,572
Batesburg 4,023
Bath AUG 2,242
Beaufort 8,634
Beech Island AUG . . . 1,300 ○
Belton 5,312
Belvedere AUG 6,859
Bennettsville 8,774
Berea GRNV . . . . 7,500 ○
Bethune 481
Bishopville 3,429
Blacksburg 1,873
Blackville 2,840
Bluffton 541
Bowling Green . . . . 850 ○
Bowman 1,137
Branchville 1,769
Brandon GRNV . . . . . 2,170 ○
Brentwood CHAS . . . . 2,000 ○
Brooklyn . . . . 1,800 ○
Brunson 590
Bucksport 1,125
Buffalo 1,641
Calhoun Falls 2,491
Camden 7,462
Cameron 536
Campobello SPRT 472
Carlisle 503
Cateechee . . . . 500 ○
Cayce COL 11,701
Central 1,914
CHARLESTON
CHAS 69,510
Cheraw 5,654
Chesnee 1,069
Chester 6,820
Chesterfield 1,432
City View GRNV 1,662
Clearwater AUG 3,967
Clemson 8,118
Clifton SPRT . . . . 800 ○
Clinton 8,596
Clio 1,031
Clover 3,451
COLUMBIA
COL 100,385
Conestee GRNV . . . . . . 540 ○
Converse SPRT 1,173
Conway 10,240
Cowpens SPRT 2,023
Cross Hill 604
Darlington 7,989
Denmark 4,434
Denny Terrace
COL . . . . 1,885 ○
Dentsville COL . . . . . . 5,000 ○
Dillon 7,060
Doneraile 1,276
Drayton SPRT 1,443
Due West 1,366
Duncan SPRT 1,259
Easley GRNV 14,264
East Gaffney 4,092
Eastover 899
Edgefield 2,713
Elgin . . . . 900 ○
Elliott . . . . 500 ○
Elloree 909
Enoree 1,107
Estill 2,308
Eureka 1,627
Eutawville 615
Fairfax 2,154
FLORENCE FLO . . . 29,176
Folly Beach CHAS . . . 1,478
Forest Acres COL . . . 6,071
Fort Lawn 471
Fort Mill 4,162
Fountain Inn
GRNV 4,226
Gaffney 13,453
Gantt GRNV . . . . 1,600 ○
Gaston COL 960
Georgetown 10,144
Glendale SPRT 1,049
Gloverville 2,619
Gluck AND . . . . 650 ○
Goose Creek
CHAS 17,811
Graniteville 1,158
Gray Court 988
Great Falls 2,601
Greeleyville 593
GREENVILLE
GRNV 58,242
Greenwood 21,613
Greer GRNV 10,525
Hampton 3,143
Hanahan CHAS 13,224
Hardeeville 1,250
Harleyville 606
Hartsville 7,631
Heath Springs 979
Hemingway 853
Hilton Head Island . . . 11,344
Holly Hill 1,785
Hollywood CHAS 729
Honea Path 4,114
Hopkins COL . . . . 1,600 ○
Inman SPRT 1,554
Irmo COL 3,957
Isle of Palms
CHAS 3,421
Iva 1,369
Jackson 1,771
Jacksonboro . . . . 450 ○
James Island
CHAS 24,124
Jefferson 651
Jenkinsville . . . . 500 ○
Joanna 1,839
Johnsonville 1,421
Johnston 2,624
Jonesville 1,201
Kershaw 1,993
Kingstree 4,147
Ladson CHAS 13,246
La France AND . . . . 800 ○
Lake City 6,731
Lake View 939
Lamar 1,333
Lancaster 9,703
Lando . . . . 850 ○
Landrum 2,141
Lane 554
Langley AUG 1,714
Latta 1,804
Laurel Bay 5,238
Laurens 10,587
Leesville 2,296
Leslie RKHL 1,102
Lexington COL 2,131
Liberty 3,167
Lincolnville CHAS 808
Little River . . . . 500 ○
Little Rock . . . . 450 ○
Loris 2,193
Lugoff 2,939
Lyman SPRT 1,067
Lynchburg 534
McBee 774
McColl 2,677
McCormick 1,725
Manning 4,746
Marietta GRNV . . . . 900 ○
Marion 7,700
Mauldin GRNV 8,143
Mayesville SUMT 663
Mayo SPRT . . . . 900 ○
Midland Park
CHAS . . . . 1,300 ○
Monarch Mills 2,353
Moncks Corner 3,699
Montmorenci . . . . 900 ○
Mount Pleasant
CHAS 14,209
Mullins 6,068
Murrells Inlet 2,410
Myrtle Beach 18,446
Neeses 557
Newberry 9,866
New Ellenton 2,628
Nichols 606
Ninety Six 2,249
Norris 903
North 1,304
North Augusta
AUG 13,593
North Charleston
CHAS 62,534
North Myrtle Beach 3,960
Norway 518

○ Rand McNally estimate
▲ Population of entire township or "town", including rural areas.
● Independent city. Population not included in county total.

SOUTH CAROLINA continued

Olanta 699
Orangeburg 14,933
Pacolet 1,556
Pacolet Mills 1,051
Pageland 2,720
Pamplico 1,213
Pawleys Island 2,200 ○
Pelham 450 ○
Pendleton AND 3,154
Pickens GRNV 3,199
Piedmont GRNV 2,992
Pinewood 689
Pinopolis 500 ○
Port Royal 2,977
Prosperity 803
Ravenel CHAS 1,655
Reidville GRNV 460 ○
Ridgeland 1,143
Ridge Spring 969
Ridgeville 603
ROCK HILL RKHL 35,344
Roebuck SPRT 1,083
St. Andrews CHAS 9,908
St. Andrews COL 20,245
St. George 2,134
St. Matthews 2,496
St. Stephen 1,850
Salley 584
Saluda 2,752
Sandy Springs AND 1,100 ○
Saxon SPRT 1,200 ○
Scranton 861
Seneca 7,436
Shannontown SUMT 7,900 ○
Simpsonville GRNV 9,037
Six Mile 470
Slater GRNV 1,000 ○
Socastee 1,082
Society Hill 848
South Congaree COL 2,113
SPARTANBURG SPRT 43,826
Springdale COL 2,985
Springfield 604
Startex SPRT 1,006
Sullivans Island CHAS 1,867
Summerton 1,173
Summerville CHAS 6,706
SUMTER SUMT 24,890
Surfside Beach 2,522
Swansea 888
Taylors GRNV 12,100 ○
Timmonsville 2,112
Travelers Rest GRNV 3,017
Troy 705
Turbeville 549
Union 10,523
Valencia Heights COL 5,328
Varnville 1,948
Vaucluse 450 ○
Wagener 903
Walhalla 3,977
Walterboro 6,209
Wando Woods CHAS 5,253
Ware Shoals 2,370
Warrenville 1,029
Watts Mills 1,324
Waylyn CHAS 2,400 ○
Welcome GRNV 6,922
Wellford SPRT 2,143
West Columbia COL 10,409
Westminster 3,114
West Pelzer 944
Whitmire 2,038
Whitney SPRT 1,800 ○
Williamston 4,310
Williston 3,173
Windy Hill FLO 1,622
Winnsboro 2,919
Winnsboro Mills 1,890
Woodfield COL 5,560 ○
Woodruff 5,171
Yemassee 789
York RKHL 6,412

COUNTIES

Abbeville 22,627
Aiken 105,625
Allendale 10,700
Anderson 133,235
Bamberg 18,118
Barnwell 19,868
Beaufort 65,364
Berkeley 94,727
Calhoun 12,206
Charleston 276,974
Cherokee 40,983
Chester 30,148
Chesterfield 38,161
Clarendon 27,464
Colleton 31,776
Darlington 62,717
Dillon 31,083
Dorchester 58,761
Edgefield 17,528
Fairfield 20,700
Florence 110,163
Georgetown 42,461
Greenville 287,913
Greenwood 57,847
Hampton 18,159
Horry 101,419
Jasper 14,504
Kershaw 39,015
Lancaster 53,361
Laurens 52,214
Lee 18,929
Lexington 140,353
McCormick 7,797
Marion 34,179
Marlboro 31,634
Newberry 31,242
Oconee 48,611
Orangeburg 82,276
Pickens 79,292
Richland 269,735
Saluda 16,150
Spartanburg 201,861
Sumter 88,243
Union 30,764
Williamsburg 38,226
York 106,720

SOUTH DAKOTA

1980
Census 690,768

CITIES

Aberdeen 25,851
Alcester 885
Alexandria 588
Arlington 991
Armour 819
Aurora 507
Avon 576
Baltic 679
Belle Fourche 4,692
Beresford 1,865
Big Stone City 672
Bison 457
Black Hawk RAP 1,608
Bowdle 644
Box Elder RAP 3,186
Brandon SXFL 2,589
Bridgewater 653
Bristol 445
Britton 1,590
Brookings 14,951
Buffalo 453
Burke 859
Canistota 626
Canton 2,886
Castlewood 557
Centerville 892
Chamberlain 2,258
Clark 1,351
Clear Lake 1,310
Colman 501
Colton 757
Corsica 644
Crooks 594
Custer 1,830
Deadwood 2,035
De Smet 1,237
Dupree 562
Edgemont 1,468
Elk Point 1,661
Elkton 632
Estelline 719
Eureka 1,360
Faith 576
Faulkton 981
Flandreau 2,114
Fort Pierre 1,789
Freeman 1,462
Froehlich Addition SXFL 750 ○
Garretson 963
Gettysburg 1,623
Gregory 1,503
Groton 1,230
Harrisburg 558
Hartford 1,207
Hayward Addition SXFL 725 ○
Herreid 570
Highmore 1,055
Hill City 535
Hot Springs 4,742
Hoven 615
Howard 1,169
Humboldt 487
Huron 13,000
Ipswich 1,153
Irene 523
Jefferson 592
Kadoka 832
Kimball 752
Lake Andes 1,029
Lake Preston 789
Lead 4,330
Lemmon 1,871
Lennox 1,827
Leola 645
McCook Lake SXCY 600 ○
McLaughlin 754
Madison 6,210
Marion 830
Martin 1,018
Menno 793
Milbank 4,120
Miller 1,931
Mission 748
Mitchell 13,916
Mobridge 4,174
Murdo 723
Newell 638
New Underwood 517
North Eagle Butte 1,354
North Sioux City SXCY 1,992
Norton Acres SXFL 800 ○
Onida 851
Parker 999
Parkston 1,545
Philip 1,088
Pierre 11,973
Pine Ridge 3,059
Plankinton 644
Platte 1,334
Presho 760
RAPID CITY RAP 46,492
Redfield 3,027
Rosebud 600 ○
Rosholt 446
St. Francis 766
Salem 1,486
Scotland 1,022
Selby 884
SIOUX FALLS SXFL 81,343
Sisseton 2,789
Spearfish 5,251
Springfield 1,377
Sturgis 5,184
Tabor 460
Tea 729
Timber Lake 660
Tripp 804
Tyndall 1,253
Valley Springs 801
Vermillion 10,136
Viborg 812
Volga 1,221
Wagner 1,453
Wall 770
Watertown 15,649
Waubay 675
Webster 2,417
Webster Grove SXFL 540 ○
Wessington Springs 1,203
White 474
White River 561
Whitewood 821
Wilmot 507
Winner 3,472
Woonsocket 799
Yankton 12,011

COUNTIES

Aurora 3,628
Beadle 19,195
Bennett 3,044
Bon Homme 8,059
Brookings 24,332
Brown 36,962
Brule 5,245
Buffalo 1,795
Butte 8,372
Campbell 2,243
Charles Mix 9,680
Clark 4,894
Clay 13,689
Codington 20,885
Corson 5,196
Custer 6,000
Davison 17,820
Day 8,133
Deuel 5,289
Dewey 5,366
Douglas 4,181
Edmunds 5,159
Fall River 8,439
Faulk 3,327
Grant 9,013
Gregory 6,015
Haakon 2,794
Hamlin 5,261
Hand 4,948
Hanson 3,415
Harding 1,700
Hughes 14,220
Hutchinson 9,350
Hyde 2,069
Jackson 3,437
Jerauld 2,929
Jones 1,463
Kingsbury 6,679
Lake 10,724
Lawrence 18,339
Lincoln 13,942
Lyman 3,864
McCook 6,444
McPherson 4,027
Marshall 5,404
Meade 20,717
Mellette 2,249
Miner 3,739

○ Rand McNally estimate
▲ Population of entire township or "town", including rural areas.
● Independent city. Population not included in county total.

Minnehaha 109,435
Moody 6,692
Pennington 70,361
Perkins 4,700
Potter 3,674
Roberts 10,911
Sanborn 3,213
Shannon 11,323
Spink 9,201
Stanley 2,533
Sully 1,990
Todd 7,328
Tripp 7,268
Turner 9,255
Union 10,938
Walworth 7,011
Yankton 18,952
Ziebach 2,308

TENNESSEE

1980
Census 4,591,120

CITIES

Adams 600
Adamsville 1,453
Alamo 2,615
Alcoa KNOX- 6,870
Alexandria 689
Algood 2,406
Allardt 654
Altamont 679
Ardmore 835
Ashland City NASH 2,329
Athens 12,080
Atoka MEM 691
Atwood 1,143
Bartlett MEM 17,170
Baxter 1,411
Beersheba Springs 643
Bell Buckle 450
Bells 1,571
Bemis JAC 1,883 ○
Benton 1,115
Bethel Springs 873
Big Sandy 650
Blaine 1,147
Bloomingdale KNGSP 9,000 ○
Blountville KNGSP 2,554
Bluff City BRIS- 1,121
Bolivar 6,597
Bradford 1,146
Brentwood NASH 9,431
Briceville KNOX- 800 ○
Brighton 976
BRISTOL BRIS- 23,986
Brownsville 9,307
Bruceton 1,579
Bulls Gap 821
Burns 777
Byrdstown 884
Calhoun 590
Camden 3,279
Campaign 500 ○
Carson Spring 600 ○
Carthage 2,672
Caryville 2,039
Cedar Bluff KNOX- 1,200 ○
Celina 1,580
Centerville 2,824
Chapel Hill 861
Charleston 756
Charlotte 788
CHATTANOOGA CHTN 169,558
Church Hill KNGSP 4,110
CLARKSVILLE CLRKV 54,777
Cleveland 26,415
Clifton 773
Clinton KNOX- 5,245
Coalmont 625
Collierville MEM 7,839
Collinwood 1,064
Colonial Heights KNGSP 6,744
Columbia 26,571
Cookeville 20,535
Cornersville 722
Counce 600 ○
Covington 6,065
Cowan 1,790
Crab Orchard 1,065
Cross Plains 655
Crossville 6,394
Dandridge 1,383
Dayton 5,913
Decatur 1,069
Decaturville 1,004
Decherd 2,233
Dickson 7,040
Dover 1,197
Dresden 2,256
Ducktown 583
Dunlap 3,681
Dyer 2,419
Dyersburg 15,856
Eagleville 444
East Ridge CHTN 21,236
Elizabethton JNSC- 12,431
Elkton 540
Englewood 1,840
Erin 1,614
Erwin 4,739
Estill Springs 1,324
Ethridge 548
Etowah 3,758
Fairview NASH 3,648
Fall Branch KNGSP 1,340
Fayetteville 7,559
Finley 1,014
Franklin NASH 12,407
Friendship 763
Friendsville KNOX- 694
Gadsden 683
Gainesboro 1,119
Gallatin 17,191
Gallaway 804
Gates 729
Gatlinburg 3,210
Germantown MEM 21,482
Gibson 458
Gleason 1,335
Goodlettsville NASH 8,327
Gordonsville 893
Graysville 1,380
Greenback 546
Greenbrier NASH 3,180
Greeneville 14,097
Greenfield 2,109
Grimsley 600 ○
Halls 2,444
Hampton JNSC- 2,236
Harriman 8,303
Hartsville 2,674
Henderson 4,449
Hendersonville NASH 26,561
Henning 638
Hohenwald 3,922
Hollow Rock 955
Hornbeak 452
Humboldt 10,209
Huntingdon 3,962
Huntland 983
Huntsville 519
Iron City 482
Jacksboro 1,722
JACKSON JAC 49,131
Jamestown 2,364
Jasper 2,633
Jefferson City 5,612
Jellico 2,798
JOHNSON CITY JNSC- 39,753
Jonesboro JNSC- 2,829
Kenton 1,551
KINGSPORT KNGSP 32,027
Kingston KNOX- 4,441
Kingston Springs 1,017
KNOXVILLE KNOX- 175,045
Lafayette 3,808
La Follette 8,198
Lake City KNOX- 2,335
Lake Tansi 500 ○
La Vergne NASH 5,495
Lawrenceburg 10,184
Lebanon 11,872
Lenoir City KNOX- 5,446
Lewisburg 8,760
Lexington 5,934
Linden 1,087
Livingston 3,372
Lobelville 993
Loretto 1,612
Loudon 3,943
Luttrell 962
Lynchburg 668
Lynn Garden KNGSP 7,213
McEwen 1,352
McKenzie 5,405
McMinnville 10,683
Madisonville 2,884
Manchester 7,250
Martin 8,898
Maryville KNOX- 17,480
Mascot KNOX- 2,203
Mason 471
Maury City 989
Maynardville 924
Medina 687
MEMPHIS MEM 646,174
Michie 530
Middleton 596
Milan 8,083
Millington MEM 20,236
Minor Hill 564
Monteagle 1,126
Monterey 2,610
Morgantown 600 ○
Morrison 587
Morrison City KNGSP 2,032
Morristown 19,683
Moscow 499
Mosheim 1,539
Mountain City 2,125
Mount Juliet NASH 2,879
Mount Pleasant 3,375
Munford MEM 2,336
Murfreesboro 32,845
NASHVILLE NASH 455,651
Newbern 2,794
New Johnsonville 1,824
New Market 1,216
Newport 7,580
New Tazwell 1,677
Niota 765
Nolensville 500 ○
Norris KNOX- 1,374
Oakland 472
Oak Ridge KNOX- 27,662
Obion 1,282
Oliver Springs KNOX- 3,659
Oneida 3,717
Ooltewah CHTN 900 ○
Palmer 1,027
Paris 10,728
Parsons 2,422
Pegram NASH 1,081
Petersburg 681
Petros 1,286
Philadelphia 507
Pigeon Forge 1,822
Pikeville 2,085
Pittman Center 488
Portland 4,030
Pulaski 7,184
Puryear 624
Red Bank CHTN 13,299
Red Boiling Springs 1,173
Riceville 500 ○
Ridgely 1,932
Ripley 6,366
Roan Mountain 1,108
Robbins 450 ○
Rockford KNOX- 567
Rockwood 5,767
Rogersville 4,368
Russellville 1,069
Rutherford 1,378
Rutledge 1,058
St. Joseph 897
Sale Creek 900 ○
Samburg 465
Savannah 6,992
Scotts Hill 668
Selmer 3,979
Sevierville 4,556
Sewanee 2,298
Sharon 1,134
Shelbyville 13,530
Sherwood 450 ○
Signal Mountain CHTN 5,818
Smithville 3,839
Smyrna NASH 8,839
Sneedville 1,110
Soddy-Daisy CHTN 8,388
Somerville 2,264
South Fulton 2,735
South Pittsburg 3,636
Sparta 4,864
Spencer 1,126
Spring City 1,951
Springfield 10,814
Spring Hill 989
Stanton 540
Summitville 600 ○
Sunbright 500 ○
Surgoinsville 1,536
Sweetwater 4,725
Tazewell 2,090
Tellico Plains 698
Tennessee Ridge 1,325
Tiptonville 2,438
Tracy City 1,356
Trenton 4,601
Trezevant 921
Trimble 722
Troy 1,093
Tullahoma 15,800
Unicoi 600 ○
Union City 10,436
Vonore 528
Wartburg 761
Wartrace 540
Watertown 1,300
Waverly 4,405
Waynesboro 2,109
Westmoreland 1,754
Westover JAC 500 ○
White Bluff 2,055
White House 2,225
White Pine 1,900
Whiteville 1,270
Whitwell 1,783
Winchester 5,821
Woodbury 2,160

COUNTIES

Anderson 67,346
Bedford 27,916
Benton 14,901
Bledsoe 9,478
Blount 77,770
Bradley 67,547
Campbell 34,923

○ Rand McNally estimate
▲ Population of entire township or "town", including rural areas.
● Independent city. Population not included in county total.

TENNESSEE continued

Cannon	10,234
Carroll	28,285
Carter	50,205
Cheatham	21,616
Chester	12,727
Claiborne	24,595
Clay	7,676
Cocke	28,792
Coffee	38,311
Crockett	14,941
Cumberland	28,676
Davidson	477,811
Decatur	10,857
De Kalb	13,589
Dickson	30,037
Dyer	34,663
Fayette	25,305
Fentress	14,826
Franklin	31,983
Gibson	49,467
Giles	24,625
Grainger	16,751
Greene	54,422
Grundy	13,787
Hamblen	49,300
Hamilton	287,740
Hancock	6,887
Hardeman	23,873
Hardin	22,280
Hawkins	43,751
Haywood	20,318
Henderson	21,390
Henry	28,656
Hickman	15,151
Houston	6,871
Humphreys	15,957
Jackson	9,398
Jefferson	31,284
Johnson	13,745
Knox	319,694
Lake	7,455
Lauderdale	24,555
Lawrence	34,110
Lewis	9,700
Lincoln	26,483
Loudon	28,553
McMinn	41,878
McNairy	22,525
Macon	15,700
Madison	74,546
Marion	24,416
Marshall	19,698
Maury	51,095
Meigs	7,431
Monroe	28,700
Montgomery	83,342
Moore	4,510
Morgan	16,604
Obion	32,781
Overton	17,575
Perry	6,111
Pickett	4,358
Polk	13,602
Putnam	47,690
Rhea	24,235
Roane	48,425
Robertson	37,021
Rutherford	84,058
Scott	19,259
Sequatchie	8,605
Sevier	41,418
Shelby	777,113
Smith	14,935
Stewart	8,665
Sullivan	143,968
Sumner	85,790
Tipton	32,930
Trousdale	6,137
Unicoi	16,362
Union	11,707
Van Buren	4,728
Warren	32,653
Washington	88,755
Wayne	13,946
Weakley	32,896
White	19,567
Williamson	58,108
Wilson	56,064

TEXAS

1980 Census 14,229,288

CITIES

Abernathy	2,904
ABILENE ABIL	98,315
Addison D-FW	5,553
Alamo MCAL	5,831
Alamo Heights SANT	6,252
Albany	2,450
Alice	20,961
Allen D-FW	8,314
Alpine	5,465
Alto	1,203
Alvarado	2,701
Alvin HOU	16,515
AMARILLO AMA	149,230
Anahuac	1,840
Andrews	11,061
Angleton FREP-	13,929
Anson	2,831
Anthony ELP	2,640
Aransas Pass CRPX	7,173
Archer City	1,862
Arlington D-FW	160,113
Arp	939
Asherton	1,574
Aspermont	1,357
Athens	10,197
Atlanta	6,272
AUSTIN AUS	345,496
Azle D-FW	5,822
Baird	1,696
Balch Springs D-FW	13,746
Ballinger	4,207
Bartlett	1,567
Bastrop	3,789
Bay City	17,837
Baytown HOU	56,923
BEAUMONT B-PA-O	118,102
Bedford D-FW	20,821
Beeville	14,574
Bellaire HOU	14,950
Bellmead WACO	7,569
Bellville	2,860
Belton TMPL	10,660
Benavides	1,978
Benbrook D-FW	13,579
Big Lake	3,404
Big Spring	24,804
Big Wells	939
Bishop	3,706
Bloomington	1,884
Blossom	1,487
Boerne SANT	3,229
Boling	1,000 ○
Bonham	7,338
Borger	15,837
Bowie	5,610
Brackettville	1,676
Brady	5,969
Brazoria FREP-	3,025
Breckenridge	6,921
Bremond	1,025
Brenham	10,966
Bridge City B-PA-O	7,667
Bridgeport	3,737
Brookshire	2,175
Brownfield	10,387
BROWNSVILLE BRNS	84,997
Brownwood	19,396
BRYAN BRY	44,337
Burkburnett WIFL	10,668
Burleson D-FW	11,734
Burnet	3,410
Caldwell	2,953
Calvert	1,732
Cameron	5,721
Canadian	3,491
Canton	2,845
Canutillo ELP	2,000 ○
Canyon	10,724
Canyon Lake	6,000 ○
Carrizo Springs	6,886
Carrollton D-FW	40,595
Carthage	6,447
Castroville SANT	1,821
Cedar Hill D-FW	6,849
Celina	1,520
Center	5,827
Centerville	799
Channelview HOU	16,000 ○
Charlotte	1,443
Chico	890
Childress	5,817
Chillicothe	1,052
Chilton	500 ○
Cisco	4,517
Clarendon	2,220
Clarksville	4,917
Cleburne D-FW	19,218
Cleveland HOU	5,977
Clifton	3,063
Cloverleaf HOU	11,800 ○
Clute FREP-	9,577
Cockrell Hill D-FW	3,262
Coleman	5,960
College Station BRY	37,272
Colleyville D-FW	6,700
Colorado City	5,405
Columbus	3,923
Comanche	4,075
Comfort	950 ○
Commerce	8,136
Conroe HOU	18,034
Coolidge	810
Cooper	2,338
Copperas Cove KILL	19,469
CORPUS CHRISTI CRPX	231,999
Corrigan	1,770
Corsicana	21,712
Cotulla	3,912
Crandall	831
Crane	3,622
Crockett	7,405
Crosbyton	2,289
Cross Plains	1,240
Crowell	1,509
Crowley D-FW	5,852
Crystal City	8,334
Cuero	7,124
Daingerfield	3,030
Daisetta	1,177
Dalhart	6,854
DALLAS D-FW	904,078
Dawson	747
Dayton	4,908
Decatur	4,104
Deer Park HOU	22,648
De Kalb	2,217
De Leon	2,478
Del Rio SHRM-	30,034
Denison SHRM-	23,884
Denton D-FW	48,063
Denver City	4,704
De Soto D-FW	15,538
Devine SANT	3,756
Diboll LUFK	5,227
Dickinson GLV-	7,505
Dilley	2,579
Dimmitt	5,019
Donna	9,952
Dublin	2,723
Dumas	12,194
Duncanville D-FW	27,781
Eagle Lake	3,921
Eagle Pass	21,407
Eastland	3,747
Edcouch	3,092
Eden	1,294
EDINBURG EDIN	24,075
Edna	5,650
El Campo	10,462
Eldorado	2,061
Electra	3,755
Elgin	4,535
EL PASO ELP	425,259
Elsa	5,061
Encinal	704
Ennis	12,110
Euless D-FW	24,002
Everman D-FW	5,387
Fabens	3,500 ○
Fairfield	3,505
Falfurrias	6,103
Farmers Branch D-FW	24,863
Farmersville	2,360
Farwell	1,354
Ferris D-FW	2,228
Flatonia	1,070
Floresville	4,381
Floydada	4,193
Forest Hill D-FW	11,684
Forney D-FW	2,483
Fort Davis	850 ○
Fort Stockton	8,688
Fort Worth D-FW	385,164
Franklin	1,349
Frankston	1,255
Fredericksburg	6,412
FREEPORT FREP-	13,444
Freer	3,213
Friendswood HOU	10,719
Friona	3,809
Fritch	2,299
Gainesville	14,081
Galena Park HOU	9,879
GALVESTON GLV-	61,902
Garland D-FW	138,857
Gatesville	6,260
Georgetown	9,468
George West	2,627
Giddings	3,950
Gilmer	5,167
Gladewater LNGV	6,548
Glen Rose	2,075
Goldthwaite	1,783
Goliad	1,990
Gonzales	7,152
Gorman	1,258
Graham	9,170
Granbury	3,332
Grand Prairie D-FW	71,462
Grand Saline	2,709
Granger	1,236
Grapeland	1,634
Grapevine D-FW	11,801
Greater Richland Area D-FW	7,977
Greenville	22,161
Groesbeck	3,373
Groves B-PA-O	17,090
Groveton	1,262
Grulla	1,442
Hale Center	2,297
Hallettsville	2,865
Hallsville LNGV	1,556
Haltom City D-FW	29,014
Hamilton	3,189
Hamlin	3,248
Harker Heights KILL	7,345
HARLINGEN HRL	43,543
Haskell	3,782
Hearne	5,418

○ Rand McNally estimate
▲ Population of entire township or "town", including rural areas.
● Independent city. Population not included in county total.

Hebbronville 4,684
Hemphill 1,353
Hempstead 3,456
Henderson 11,473
Henrietta 3,149
Hereford 15,853
Hewitt WACO 5,247
Hico 1,375
Highland Park D-FW 8,909
Highlands HOU 6,467
Hillsboro 7,397
Hitchcock GLV- 6,655
Hondo 6,057
Honey Grove 1,973
HOUSTON HOU 1,595,138
Hubbard 1,676
Humble HOU 6,729
Huntington LUFK 1,672
Huntsville 23,936
Hurst D-FW 31,420
Idalou LUB 2,348
Ingleside CRPX 5,436
Iowa Park WIFL 6,184
Iraan 1,358
Irving D-FW 109,943
Italy 1,306
Itasca 1,600
Jacinto City HOU 8,953
Jacksboro 4,000
Jacksonville 12,264
Jasper 6,959
Jefferson 2,643
Johnson City 872
Jones Creek FREP- 2,634
Jourdanton 2,743
Junction 2,593
Karnes City 3,296
Katy 5,660
Kaufman 4,658
Keene D-FW 3,013
Keller D-FW 4,156
Kemp 1,035
Kenedy 4,356
Kennedale D-FW 2,594
Kerens 1,582
Kermit 8,015
Kerrville 15,276
Kilgore 11,006
KILLEEN KILL 46,296
Kingsville 28,808
Kirby SANT 6,435
Kirbyville 1,972
Klein HOU 9,000 ○
Knox City 1,546
Kountze 2,716
Kyle 2,093
Ladonia 761
La Feria HRL 3,495
La Grange 3,768
Lake Jackson FREP- 19,102
La Marque GLV- 15,372
Lamesa 11,790
Lampasas 6,165
Lancaster D-FW 14,807
La Porte HOU 17,053
LAREDO LAR 91,449
League City HOU 16,578
Leakey 468
Lefors 829
Leonard 1,421
Leon Valley SANT 9,088
Levelland 13,809
Lewisville D-FW 24,273
Liberty 7,945
Lindale 2,180
Linden 2,443
Littlefield 7,409
Little Mexico 600 ○
Live Oak SANT 8,183
Livingston 4,928
Llano 3,071
Lockhart 7,953
Lockney 2,334

Lometa 666
LONGVIEW LNGV 62,762
Loraine 929
Lott 865
LUBBOCK LUB 173,979
LUFKIN LUFK 28,562
Luling 5,039
Lyford 1,618
Lytle SANT 1,920
Mabank 1,443
MCALLEN MCAL 66,281
McCamey 2,436
McGregor 4,513
McKinney D-FW 16,256
McLean 1,160
Madisonville 3,660
Malakoff 2,082
Mansfield D-FW 8,102
Marble Falls 3,252
Marfa 2,466
Marlin 7,099
Marshall 24,921
Mart 2,324
Mason 2,153
Matador 1,052
Mathis 5,667
Memphis 3,352
Menard 1,697
Mercedes 11,851
Meridian 1,330
Merkel 2,493
Mesquite D-FW 67,053
Mexia 7,094
MIDLAND MIDL 70,525
Midlothian D-FW 3,219
Miles 720
Mineola 4,346
Mineral Wells 14,468
Mission MCAL 22,653
Missouri City HOU 24,533
Monahans 8,397
Mont Belvieu HOU 1,730
Moody 1,385
Morton 2,674
Mount Pleasant 11,003
Mount Vernon 2,025
Muleshoe 4,842
Munday 1,738
Nacogdoches 27,149
Naples 1,908
Natalia SANT 1,264
Navasota 5,971
Nederland B-PA-O 16,855
Needville 1,417
New Boston 4,628
New Braunfels 22,402
Newcastle 688
Newton 1,620
Nixon 2,008
Nocona 2,992
North Richland Hills D-FW 30,592
Oakwood 606
Odem 2,363
ODESSA ODES 90,027
O'Donnell 1,200
Olmos Park SANT 2,069
Olney 4,060
Olton 2,235
Orange B-PA-O 23,628
Orange Grove 1,212
Overton 2,430
Ozona 3,766
Paducah 2,216
Palacios 4,667
Palestine 15,948
Pampa 21,396
Panhandle 2,226
Paris 25,498
Pasadena HOU 112,560
Pearland HOU 13,248
Pearsall 7,383
Pecos 12,855
Perryton 7,991

Pharr MCAL 21,381
Phillips 1,729
Pilot Point 2,211
Pineland 1,111
Pittsburg 4,245
Plainview 22,187
Plano D-FW 72,331
Pleasanton 6,346
Port Arthur B-PA-O 61,251
Port Isabel 3,769
Portland CRPX 12,023
Port Lavaca 10,911
Port Neches B-PA-O 13,944
Post 3,961
Poteet 3,086
Prairie View 3,993
Premont 2,984
Presidio 1,603
Quanah 3,890
Queen City 1,748
Quitman 1,893
Ralls 2,422
Ranger 3,142
Raymondville 9,493
Refugio 3,898
Richardson D-FW 72,496
Richmond HOU 9,692
Rio Grande City 8,930
Rio Hondo 1,673
Rising Star 1,204
River Oaks D-FW 6,890
Robinson Plaza WACO 6,074
Robstown CRPX 12,100
Roby 814
Rockdale 5,611
Rockport 3,686
Rocksprings 1,317
Rockwall D-FW 5,939
Rogers 1,242
Roma 3,384
Roscoe 1,628
Rosebud 2,076
Rosenberg HOU 17,995
Rotan 2,284
Round Rock AUS 12,740
Rowlett D-FW 7,522
Royse City D-FW 1,566
Rule 1,015
Runge 1,244
Rusk 4,681
Sabinal 1,827
St. Jo 1,071
SAN ANGELO SANG 73,240
SAN ANTONIO SANT 786,023
San Augustine 2,930
San Benito HRL 17,988
Sanderson 1,241
San Diego 5,225
Sanger 2,574
San Isidro 700 ○
San Juan MCAL 7,608
San Marcos 23,420
San Pedro CRPX 5,294 ○
San Saba 2,847
Santa Anna 1,535
Schertz SANT 7,262
Schulenburg 2,469
Seabrook HOU 4,670
Seagoville D-FW 7,304
Seagraves 2,596
Sealy 3,875
Seguin 17,854
Seminole 6,080
Seymour 3,657
Shallowater LUB 1,932
Shamrock 2,834
SHERMAN SHRM- 30,413
Shiner 2,213
Silsbee 7,684
Sinton 6,044
Slaton LUB 6,804

Smithville 3,470
Snyder 12,705
Somerville 1,814
Sonora 3,856
Sour Lake 1,807
South Houston HOU 13,293
Southside Place HOU 1,366
Spearman 3,413
Spring HOU 3,000 ○
Spur 1,690
Stamford 4,542
Stanton 2,314
Stephenville 11,881
Sterling City 915
Stinnett 2,222
Stockdale 1,265
Stratford 1,917
Strawn 694
Sudan 1,091
Sugar Land HOU 8,826
Sulphur Springs 12,804
Sundown 1,511
Sunray 1,952
Sweeny 3,538
Sweetwater 12,242
Taft 3,686
Tahoka 3,262
Talco 751
Taylor 10,619
Teague 3,390
TEMPLE TMPL 42,354
Terrell D-FW 13,269
Terrell Hills SANT 4,644
TEXARKANA TEXR- 31,271
Texas City GLV- 41,403
The Colony D-FW 11,586
Thorndale 1,300
Thorntonville 717
Three Rivers 2,133
Throckmorton 1,174
Timpson 1,164
Trinidad 1,130
Trinity 2,620
Troup 1,911
Tulia 5,033
Turkey 644
TYLER TYL 70,508
Universal City SANT 10,720
University Park D-FW 22,254
Uvalde 14,178
Valley Mills 1,236
Van 1,881
Van Alstyne 1,860
Van Horn 2,772
Vernon 12,695
VICTORIA VICT 50,695
Vidor B-PA-O 11,834
WACO WACO 101,261
Waelder 942
Wallis 1,138
Watauga D-FW 10,284
Waxahachie D-FW 14,624
Weatherford D-FW 12,049
Weimar 2,128
Wellington 3,043
Weslaco 19,331
West 2,485
West Columbia FREP- 4,109
West University Place HOU 12,010
Wharton 9,033
Wheeler 1,584
Whitesboro 3,197
White Settlement D-FW 13,508
Whitewright 1,760
Whitney 1,631
WICHITA FALLS WIFL 94,201

○ Rand McNally estimate
▲ Population of entire township or "town", including rural areas.
● Independent city. Population not included in county total.

TEXAS continued

Willis	1,674
Windcrest SANT	5,332
Wink	1,182
Winnsboro	3,458
Winters	3,061
Wolfe City	1,594
Woodsboro	1,974
Woodville	2,821
Woodway WACO	7,091
Wortham	1,187
Yoakum	6,148
Yorktown	2,498
Zapata	3,831

COUNTIES

Anderson	38,381
Andrews	13,323
Angelina	64,172
Aransas	14,260
Archer	7,266
Armstrong	1,994
Atascosa	25,055
Austin	17,726
Bailey	8,168
Bandera	7,084
Bastrop	24,726
Baylor	4,919
Bee	26,030
Bell	157,820
Bexar	988,798
Blanco	4,681
Borden	859
Bosque	13,401
Bowie	75,301
Brazoria	169,587
Brazos	93,588
Brewster	7,573
Briscoe	2,579
Brooks	8,428
Brown	33,057
Burleson	12,313
Burnet	17,803
Caldwell	23,637
Calhoun	19,574
Callahan	10,992
Cameron	209,727
Camp	9,275
Carson	6,672
Cass	29,430
Castro	10,556
Chambers	18,538
Cherokee	38,127
Childress	6,950
Clay	9,582
Cochran	4,825
Coke	3,196
Coleman	10,439
Collin	144,576
Collingsworth	4,648
Colorado	18,823
Comal	36,446
Comanche	12,617
Concho	2,915
Cooke	27,656
Coryell	56,767
Cottle	2,947
Crane	4,600
Crockett	4,608
Crosby	8,859
Culberson	3,315
Dallam	6,531
Dallas	1,556,390
Dawson	16,184
Deaf Smith	21,165
Delta	4,839
Denton	143,126
De Witt	18,903
Dickens	3,539
Dimmit	11,367
Donley	4,075
Duval	12,517
Eastland	19,480
Ector	115,374
Edwards	2,033
Ellis	59,743
El Paso	479,899
Erath	22,560
Falls	17,946
Fannin	24,285
Fayette	18,832
Fisher	5,891
Floyd	9,834
Foard	2,158
Fort Bend	130,846
Franklin	6,893
Freestone	14,830
Frio	13,785
Gaines	13,150
Galveston	195,940
Garza	5,336
Gillespie	13,532
Glasscock	1,304
Goliad	5,193
Gonzales	16,949
Gray	26,386
Grayson	89,796
Gregg	99,495
Grimes	13,580
Guadalupe	46,708
Hale	37,592
Hall	5,594
Hamilton	8,297
Hansford	6,209
Hardeman	6,368
Hardin	40,721
Harris	2,409,547
Harrison	52,265
Hartley	3,987
Haskell	7,725
Hays	40,594
Hemphill	5,304
Henderson	42,606
Hidalgo	283,323
Hill	25,024
Hockley	23,230
Hood	17,714
Hopkins	25,247
Houston	22,299
Howard	33,142
Hudspeth	2,728
Hunt	55,248
Hutchinson	26,304
Irion	1,386
Jack	7,408
Jackson	13,352
Jasper	30,781
Jeff Davis	1,647
Jefferson	250,938
Jim Hogg	5,168
Jim Wells	36,498
Johnson	67,649
Jones	17,268
Karnes	13,593
Kaufman	39,029
Kendall	10,635
Kenedy	543
Kent	1,145
Kerr	28,780
Kimble	4,063
King	425
Kinney	2,279
Kleberg	33,358
Knox	5,329
Lamar	42,156
Lamb	18,669
Lampasas	12,005
La Salle	5,514
Lavaca	19,004
Lee	10,952
Leon	9,594
Liberty	47,088
Limestone	20,224
Lipscomb	3,766
Live Oak	9,606
Llano	10,144
Loving	91
Lubbock	211,651
Lynn	8,605
McCulloch	8,735
McLennan	170,755
McMullen	789
Madison	10,649
Marion	10,360
Martin	4,684
Mason	3,683
Matagorda	37,828
Maverick	31,398
Medina	23,164
Menard	2,346
Midland	82,636
Milam	22,732
Mills	4,477
Mitchell	9,088
Montague	17,410
Montgomery	128,487
Moore	16,575
Morris	14,629
Motley	1,950
Nacogdoches	46,786
Navarro	35,323
Newton	13,254
Nolan	17,359
Nueces	268,215
Ochiltree	9,588
Oldham	2,283
Orange	83,838
Palo Pinto	24,062
Panola	20,724
Parker	44,609
Parmer	11,038
Pecos	14,618
Polk	24,407
Potter	98,637
Presidio	5,188
Rains	4,839
Randall	75,062
Reagan	4,135
Real	2,469
Red River	16,101
Reeves	15,801
Refugio	9,289
Roberts	1,187
Robertson	14,653
Rockwall	14,528
Runnels	11,872
Rusk	41,382
Sabine	8,702
San Augustine	8,785
San Jacinto	11,434
San Patricio	58,013
San Saba	6,204
Schleicher	2,820
Scurry	18,192
Shackelford	3,915
Shelby	23,084
Sherman	3,174
Smith	128,366
Somervell	4,154
Starr	27,266
Stephens	9,926
Sterling	1,206
Stonewall	2,406
Sutton	5,130
Swisher	9,723
Tarrant	860,880
Taylor	110,932
Terrell	1,595
Terry	14,581
Throckmorton	2,053
Titus	21,442
Tom Green	84,784
Travis	419,573
Trinity	9,450
Tyler	16,223
Upshur	28,595
Upton	4,619
Uvalde	22,441
Val Verde	35,910
Van Zandt	31,426
Victoria	68,807
Walker	41,789
Waller	19,798
Ward	13,976
Washington	21,998
Webb	99,258
Wharton	40,242
Wheeler	7,137
Wichita	121,082
Wilbarger	15,931
Willacy	17,495
Williamson	76,507
Wilson	16,756
Winkler	9,944
Wise	26,575
Wood	24,697
Yoakum	8,299
Young	19,083
Zapata	6,628
Zavala	11,666

UTAH

1980
Census 1,461,037

CITIES

Alpine PRVO	2,649
American Fork PRVO	12,693
Annabella	463
Aurora	874
Ballard	558
Bear River City	540
Beaver	1,792
Belmont Heights	600 ○
Bennion S.L.C.	950 ○
Blanding	3,118
Bluffdale S.L.C.	1,300
Bountiful S.L.C.	32,877
Brigham City	15,596
Carbonville	500 ○
Castle Dale	1,910
Cedar City	10,972
Centerfield	653
Centerville S.L.C.	8,069
Circleville	445
Clarkston	562
Clearfield OGD	17,982
Cleveland	522
Clinton OGD	5,777
Coalville	1,031
Copperton	850 ○
Corinne	512
Cottonwood S.L.C.	11,554
Cottonwood Heights S.L.C.	18,000 ○
Delta	1,930
Draper S.L.C.	5,521
Duchesne	1,677
East Carbon	1,942
Eastwood Hills S.L.C.	1,200 ○
Elsinore	612
Elwood	481
Enoch	678
Enterprise	905
Ephraim	2,810
Escalante	652
Eureka	670
Fairview	916
Farmington S.L.C.	4,691
Ferron	1,718
Fillmore	2,083
Fountain Green	578
Fruit Heights OGD	2,728
Garland	1,405
Genola	630
Glenwood	447
Goshen	582
Granite	650 ○
Granite Park S.L.C.	5,554
Grantsville	4,419
Green River	1,048
Gunnison	1,255
Harrisville OGD	1,371
Heber City	4,362
Helper	2,724
Henefer	547
Herriman	600 ○
Highland PRVO	2,435

○ Rand McNally estimate
▲ Population of entire township or "town", including rural areas.
● Independent city. Population not included in county total.

Highlands ... 500 ○
Hildale ... 1,009
Hinckley ... 464
Holladay S.L.C. ... 22,189
Honeyville ... 915
Huntington ... 2,316
Huntsville ... 577
Hurricane ... 2,361
Hyde Park LOGN ... 1,495
Hyrum LOGN ... 3,952
Ivins ... 600
Kamas ... 1,064
Kanab ... 2,148
Kaysville OGD ... 9,811
Kearns S.L.C. ... 21,353
Lark ... 500 ○
La Verkin ... 1,174
Layton OGD ... 26,393
Lehi PRVO ... 6,848
Levan ... 453
Lewiston ... 1,438
Lindon PRVO ... 2,796
LOGAN LOGN ... 26,844
Maeser ... 2,216
Magna S.L.C. ... 13,138
Manti ... 2,080
Mantua ... 484
Mapleton PRVO ... 2,726
Mendon ... 663
Midvale S.L.C. ... 10,146
Midway ... 1,194
Milford ... 1,293
Millcreek S.L.C. ... 24,150
Millville LOGN ... 848
Minersville ... 552
Moab ... 5,333
Mona ... 536
Monroe ... 1,476
Monticello ... 1,929
Morgan ... 1,896
Moroni ... 1,086
Mount Olympus S.L.C. ... 6,068
Mount Pleasant ... 2,049
Murray S.L.C. ... 25,750
Myton ... 500
Naples ... 1,502
Neola ... 550 ○
Nephi ... 3,285
Newton ... 623
Nibley LOGN ... 1,036
North Logan LOGN ... 2,258
North Ogden OGD ... 9,309
North Salt Lake S.L.C. ... 5,548
Oakley ... 470
OGDEN OGD ... 64,407
Orangeville ... 1,309
Orem PRVO ... 52,399
Panguitch ... 1,343
Paradise ... 542
Park City ... 2,823
Park Terrace S.L.C. ... 850 ○
Parowan ... 1,836
Payson PRVO ... 8,246
Perry ... 1,084
Peruvian Park S.L.C. ... 600 ○
Plain City OGD ... 2,379
Pleasant Grove PRVO ... 10,833
Price ... 9,086
Providence LOGN ... 2,675
PROVO PRVO ... 74,108
Randolph ... 659
Redmond ... 619
Redwood S.L.C. ... 2,000 ○
Richfield ... 5,482
Richmond ... 1,705
Riverdale OGD ... 6,031
River Heights LOGN ... 1,211
Riverton S.L.C. ... 7,293
Roosevelt ... 3,842
Roy OGD ... 19,694
St. George ... 11,350
Salem PRVO ... 2,233
Salina ... 1,992
SALT LAKE CITY S.L.C. ... 163,697
Sandy S.L.C. ... 52,210
Santa Clara ... 1,091
Santaquin PRVO ... 2,175
Smithfield LOGN ... 4,993
South Jordan S.L.C. ... 7,492
South Ogden OGD ... 11,366
South Salt Lake S.L.C. ... 9,884
Spanish Fork PRVO ... 9,825
Spring City ... 671
Spring Glen ... 800 ○
Springville PRVO ... 12,101
Sunnyside ... 611
Sunset OGD ... 5,733
Syracuse OGD ... 3,702
Taylorsville S.L.C. ... 17,448
Tooele ... 14,335
Tremonton ... 3,464
Trenton ... 447
Union S.L.C. ... 3,100 ○
Val Verda S.L.C. ... 6,422
Vernal ... 6,600
Washington ... 3,092
Washington Terrace OGD ... 8,212
Wellington ... 1,406
Wellsville ... 1,952
Wendover ... 1,099
West Bountiful S.L.C. ... 3,556
West Jordan S.L.C. ... 27,192
West Point OGD ... 2,170
West Valley City S.L.C. ... 72,511
White City S.L.C. ... 7,188
Willard ... 1,241
Woods Cross S.L.C. ... 4,263

COUNTIES

Beaver ... 4,378
Box Elder ... 33,222
Cache ... 57,176
Carbon ... 22,179
Daggett ... 769
Davis ... 146,540
Duchesne ... 12,565
Emery ... 11,451
Garfield ... 3,673
Grand ... 8,241
Iron ... 17,349
Juab ... 5,530
Kane ... 4,024
Millard ... 8,970
Morgan ... 4,917
Piute ... 1,329
Rich ... 2,100
Salt Lake ... 619,066
San Juan ... 12,253
Sanpete ... 14,620
Sevier ... 14,727
Summit ... 10,198
Tooele ... 26,033
Uintah ... 20,506
Utah ... 218,106
Wasatch ... 8,523
Washington ... 26,065
Wayne ... 1,911
Weber ... 144,616

VERMONT

1980 Census ... 511,456

CITIES

Alburg 1,352▲ ... 496
Arlington 2,184▲ ... 800 ○
Barre MTPLR- ... 9,824
Barton 2,990▲ ... 1,062
Bellows Falls ... 3,456
Bennington 15,815▲ ... 9,349
Bethel 1,715▲ ... 1,016
Bomoseen RUTL ... 500 ○
Bradford 2,191▲ ... 831
Brandon 4,194▲ ... 1,925
Brattleboro ... 8,596
Bristol 3,293▲ ... 1,793
BURLINGTON BUR ... 37,712
Castleton RUTL 3,637▲ ... 600 ○
Center Rutland RUTL ... 475 ○
Chelsea 1,091▲ ... 500 ○
Chester 2,791▲ ... 500 ○
Chester Depot ... 500 ○
Danville 1,705▲ ... 450 ○
Derby 4,222▲ ... 598
Derby Line ... 874
Dorset 1,648▲ ... 550 ○
East Arlington ... 600 ○
East Barre MTPLR- ... 900 ○
East Middlebury ... 550 ○
East Montpelier 2,205▲ ... 600 ○
East Poultney ... 450 ○
Enosburg Falls ... 1,207
Essex BUR 14,392▲ ... 800 ○
Essex Junction BUR ... 7,033
Fair Haven ... 2,819
Forest Dale ... 500 ○
Gilman ... 550 ○
Graniteville MTPLR- ... 1,800 ○
Hardwick 2,613▲ ... 1,476
Hartford 7,963▲ ... 600 ○
Hartland 2,396▲ ... 500 ○
Hyde Park 2,021▲ ... 475
Hydeville RUTL ... 500 ○
Island Pond ... 1,216
Jeffersonville ... 491
Jericho BUR 3,575▲ ... 1,340
Johnson 2,581▲ ... 1,393
Ludlow 2,414▲ ... 1,352
Lyndonville ... 1,401
Manchester 3,261▲ ... 563
Manchester Center ... 1,719
Middlebury 7,574▲ ... 5,591
Milton BUR 6,829▲ ... 1,411
MONTPELIER MTPLR- ... 8,241
Morrisville ... 2,074
Newport ... 4,756
North Bennington ... 1,685
North Clarendon RUTL ... 500 ○
Northfield MTPLR- 5,435▲ ... 2,033
Northfield Falls MTPLR- ... 600 ○
North Springfield ... 750 ○
North Troy ... 717
Norwich 2,398▲ ... 1,000 ○
Orleans ... 983
Pittsford 2,590▲ ... 666
Plainfield MTPLR- 1,249▲ ... 599
Poultney 3,196▲ ... 1,554
Proctor RUTL ... 1,998
Putney 1,850▲ ... 1,100 ○
Quechee ... 500 ○
Randolph 4,689▲ ... 2,217
Richford 2,206▲ ... 1,471
Richmond BUR 3,159▲ ... 865
Riverton MTPLR- ... 500 ○
Rochester 1,054▲ ... 500 ○
RUTLAND RUTL ... 18,436
St. Albans ... 7,308
St. Johnsbury 7,938▲ ... 7,150
St. Johnsbury Center ... 450 ○
Saxtons River ... 593
Shaftsbury 3,001▲ ... 700 ○
South Barre MTPLR- ... 1,301
South Burlington BUR ... 10,679
South Royalton ... 700 ○
South Ryegate ... 450 ○
Springfield 10,190▲ ... 5,603
Stamford 773▲ ... 500 ○
Stowe 2,991▲ ... 531
Swanton 5,141▲ ... 2,520
Vergennes ... 2,273
Wallingford 1,893▲ ... 1,141
Warren 956▲ ... 500 ○
Waterbury 4,465▲ ... 1,892
Waterbury Center ... 500 ○
Websterville MTPLR- ... 600 ○
West Pawlet ... 500 ○
West Rutland RUTL ... 2,351
White River Junction ... 2,582
Wilder ... 1,461
Williamstown MTPLR- 2,284▲ ... 650 ○
Wilmington 1,808▲ ... 545 ○
Winooski BUR ... 6,318
Woodstock 3,214▲ ... 1,178

COUNTIES

Addison ... 29,406
Bennington ... 33,345
Caledonia ... 25,808
Chittenden ... 115,534
Essex ... 6,313
Franklin ... 34,788
Grand Isle ... 4,613
Lamoille ... 16,767
Orange ... 22,739
Orleans ... 23,440
Rutland ... 58,347
Washington ... 52,393
Windham ... 36,933
Windsor ... 51,030

VIRGINIA

1980 Census ... 5,346,818

CITIES

Abingdon ... 4,318
Accomac ... 522
Alexandria● WASH ... 103,217
Altavista ... 3,849
Amelia Court House ... 700 ○
Amherst LYNCH ... 1,135
Annalee Heights WASH ... 1,750 ○
Annandale WASH ... 49,524
Appalachia ... 2,418
Appomattox ... 1,345
Arlington WASH ... 152,599
Arvonia ... 700 ○
Ashland RICH ... 4,640
Atkins ... 500 ○
Austinville ... 800 ○

○ Rand McNally estimate
▲ Population of entire township or "town", including rural areas.
● Independent city. Population not included in county total.

VIRGINIA continued

Baileys Crossroads WASH . . . 12,564
Bassett MRTNV . . . 2,034
Bedford ● . . . 5,991
Belle Haven . . . 589
Belle View WASH . . . 3,500 ○
Bellwood RICH . . . 600 ○
Bensley RICH . . . 5,299
Berryville . . . 1,752
Big Stone Gap . . . 4,748
Blacksburg . . . 30,638
Blackstone . . . 3,624
Bland . . . 450 ○
Bluefield . . . 5,946
Blue Ridge ROAN . . . 1,200 ○
Boissevain . . . 900 ○
Bon Air RICH . . . 16,224
Bowling Green . . . 665
Boydton . . . 486
Boykins . . . 791
Bridgewater . . . 3,289
BRISTOL ● BRIS- . . . 19,042
Broadway . . . 1,234
Brodnax . . . 492
Brookfield WASH . . . 2,500 ○
Brookneal . . . 1,454
Broyhill Park WASH . . . 3,600 ○
Buchanan . . . 1,205
Bucknell Manor WASH . . . 2,350 ○
Buena Vista ● . . . 6,717
Burke WASH . . . 1,500 ○
Burkeville . . . 606
Callao . . . 450 ○
Cape Charles . . . 1,512
Cave Spring ROAN . . . 6,300 ○
Centreville WASH . . . 950 ○
Chantilly WASH . . . 950 ○
Chapel Square WASH . . . 2,000 ○
Charlotte Court House . . . 568
CHARLOTTESVILLE ● CHRLTV . . . 39,916
Chase City . . . 2,749
Chatham . . . 1,390
Cheriton . . . 695
Chesapeake ● NORF- . . . 114,486
Chester RICH . . . 11,728
Chilhowie . . . 1,269
Chincoteague . . . 1,607
Christiansburg . . . 10,345
Clarksville . . . 1,468
Clifton Forge ● . . . 5,046
Clinchco . . . 1,000 ○
Clintwood . . . 1,369
Cloverdale ROAN . . . 850 ○
Coeburn . . . 2,625
Collinsville MRTNV . . . 7,517
Colonial Beach . . . 2,474
Colonial Heights ● PET- . . . 16,509
Courtland . . . 976
Covington ● . . . 9,063
Craigsville . . . 845
Crewe . . . 2,325
Crozet . . . 2,553
Culpeper . . . 6,621
Dahlgren . . . 575 ○
Dale City WASH . . . 33,127
Damascus . . . 1,330
Dante . . . 1,200 ○
DANVILLE ● DANV . . . 45,642
Dayton . . . 1,017
Deltaville . . . 600 ○
Dillwyn . . . 637
Drakes Branch . . . 617
Dublin . . . 2,368
Dumfries WASH . . . 3,214
Dunn Loring Woods WASH . . . 2,800 ○
Edinburg . . . 752
Elkton . . . 1,520
Elliston . . . 750 ○
Emporia ● . . . 4,840
Engleside WASH . . . 21,400 ○
Ewing . . . 500 ○
Exmore . . . 1,300
Fairfax ● WASH . . . 19,390
Fairlawn . . . 2,000 ○
Falls Church ● WASH . . . 9,515
Falmouth . . . 970 ○
Farmville . . . 6,067
Ferrum . . . 500 ○
Ferry Farms . . . 1,300 ○
Fieldale MRTNV . . . 1,400 ○
Fishersville . . . 700 ○
Franklin ● . . . 7,308
Fredericksburg ● . . . 15,322
Fries . . . 758
Front Royal . . . 11,126
Gainesville WASH . . . 600 ○
Galax ● . . . 6,524
Gate City KNGSP . . . 2,494
Glade Spring . . . 1,722
Glasgow . . . 1,259
Glen Allen RICH . . . 1,100 ○
Glenwood DANV . . . 1,000 ○
Glenwood Farms RICH . . . 3,200 ○
Gloucester . . . 900 ○
Gloucester Point NN-H . . . 850 ○
Goochland . . . 450 ○
Gordonsville . . . 1,421
Grafton NN-H . . . 900 ○
Greenbriar WASH . . . 6,000 ○
Gretna . . . 1,255
Grindall Creek RICH . . . 1,900 ○
Grottoes . . . 1,369
Groveton WASH . . . 6,800 ○
Groveton Gardens WASH . . . 2,800 ○
Grundy . . . 1,699
Halifax . . . 772
Hamilton . . . 598
Hampton ● NN-H . . . 122,617
Harrisonburg ● . . . 19,671
Hayfield WASH . . . 2,200 ○
Herndon WASH . . . 11,449
Highland Springs RICH . . . 7,500 ○
Hillsville . . . 2,123
Hollins ROAN . . . 11,000 ○
Honaker . . . 1,475
Hopewell ● PET- . . . 23,397
Hurt . . . 1,481
Hybla Valley WASH . . . 15,533
Independence . . . 1,112
Iron Gate . . . 620
Irvington . . . 567
Ivanhoe . . . 600 ○
Jarratt . . . 614
Jefferson Manor WASH . . . 2,550 ○
Jefferson Village WASH . . . 2,800 ○
Jewell Ridge . . . 600 ○
Jonesville . . . 874
Kenbridge . . . 1,352
Keysville . . . 704
Kilmarnock . . . 945
Kings Park WASH . . . 4,450 ○
Kings Park West WASH . . . 5,000 ○
La Crosse . . . 734
Lake Barcroft WASH . . . 2,250 ○
Lake Ridge WASH . . . 6,500 ○
Lakeside RICH . . . 29,400 ○
Laurel RICH . . . 1,500 ○
Lawrenceville . . . 1,484
Lebanon . . . 3,206
Leesburg WASH . . . 8,357
Lexington ● . . . 7,292
Loch Lomond WASH . . . 2,300 ○
Louisa . . . 932
Lovettsville . . . 613
Lovingston . . . 550 ○
Lowmoor . . . 700 ○
Luray . . . 3,584
LYNCHBURG ● LYNCH . . . 66,743
McKenney . . . 473
McLean WASH . . . 22,000 ○
Madison Heights LYNCH . . . 3,500 ○
Manassas ● WASH . . . 15,438
Manassas Park ● WASH . . . 6,524
Mantua Hills WASH . . . 1,550 ○
Marion . . . 7,029
Marlboro RICH . . . 950 ○
Marshall . . . 600 ○
MARTINSVILLE ● MRTNV . . . 18,149
Mathews . . . 650 ○
Matoaca PET- . . . 2,000 ○
Max Meadows . . . 550 ○
Meadowview . . . 600 ○
Mechanicsville RICH . . . 9,269
Merrifield WASH . . . 2,100 ○
Middleburg . . . 619
Middletown . . . 841
Midlothian RICH . . . 1,000 ○
Milford . . . 500 ○
Montrose RICH . . . 2,200 ○
Montross . . . 456
Montvale . . . 450 ○
Monument Heights RICH . . . 3,100 ○
Mount Jackson . . . 1,419
Mount Sidney . . . 550 ○
Narrows . . . 2,516
Nassawadox . . . 630
New Market . . . 1,118
NEWPORT NEWS ● NN-H . . . 144,903
Nickelsville . . . 464
NORFOLK ● NORF- . . . 266,979
North Springfield WASH . . . 9,538
Norton ● . . . 4,757
Oakton WASH . . . 900 ○
Onancock . . . 1,461
Onley . . . 526
Orange . . . 2,631
Parksley . . . 979
Parrott . . . 525 ○
Pearisburg . . . 2,128
Pembroke . . . 1,302
Pennington Gap . . . 1,716
PETERSBURG ● PET- . . . 41,055
Pimmit Hills WASH . . . 7,200 ○
Pocahontas . . . 708
Poquoson ● NN-H . . . 8,726
Portsmouth ● NORF- . . . 104,577
Pound . . . 1,086
Pulaski . . . 10,106
Purcellville . . . 1,567
Quail Oaks RICH . . . 1,700 ○
Quantico WASH . . . 621
Radford ● . . . 13,225
Raven . . . 1,880 ○
Reedville . . . 500 ○
Reston WASH . . . 32,000 ○
Rich Creek . . . 746
Richlands . . . 5,796
RICHMOND ● RICH . . . 219,214
Ridgeway MRTNV . . . 858
Riverdale . . . 500 ○
ROANOKE ● ROAN . . . 100,220
Rocky Mount . . . 4,198
Rose Hill WASH . . . 5,700 ○
Rose Hill . . . 800 ○
Rural Retreat . . . 1,083
Rustburg LYNCH . . . 600 ○
St. Paul . . . 973
Salem ● ROAN . . . 23,958
Saltville . . . 2,376
Sandston RICH . . . 4,500 ○
Seaford NN-H . . . 1,700 ○
Shenandoah . . . 1,861
Smithfield NORF- . . . 3,718
South Boston ● . . . 7,093
South Hill . . . 4,347
Springfield WASH . . . 12,500 ○
Stafford WASH . . . 650 ○
Stanley . . . 1,204
Stanleytown MRTNV . . . 650 ○
Staunton ● . . . 21,857
Stephens City . . . 1,179
Sterling WASH . . . 12,000 ○
Stonega . . . 450 ○
Strasburg . . . 2,311
Stratford Landing WASH . . . 2,650 ○
Stuart . . . 1,131
Stuarts Draft . . . 950 ○
Suffolk ● NORF- . . . 47,621
Sugar Grove . . . 500 ○
Sugarland Run WASH . . . 4,500 ○
Sugar Loaf ROAN . . . 6,000 ○
Sweet Briar LYNCH . . . 900 ○
Tangier . . . 771
Tappahannock . . . 1,821
Tazewell . . . 4,468
Timberlake LYNCH . . . 2,700 ○
Timberville . . . 1,510
Toano . . . 750 ○
Trammel . . . 500 ○
Triangle WASH . . . 3,050 ○
Troutville ROAN . . . 496
Urbanna . . . 518
Vansant . . . 600 ○
Varina RICH . . . 2,000 ○
Victoria . . . 2,004
Vienna WASH . . . 15,469
Vinton ROAN . . . 8,027
Virginia Beach ● NORF- . . . 262,199
Wakefield . . . 1,355
Warrenton WASH . . . 3,907
Warsaw . . . 771
Waverly . . . 2,284
Waynesboro ● . . . 15,329
Waynewood WASH . . . 4,500 ○
Weber City KNGSP . . . 1,543
Westham RICH . . . 3,600 ○
West Point . . . 2,726
West Springfield WASH . . . 16,000 ○
Williamsburg ● . . . 9,870
Willston WASH . . . 2,500 ○
Winchester ● . . . 20,217
Windsor . . . 985
Wise . . . 3,894
Woodbridge WASH . . . 35,000 ○
Woodstock . . . 2,627
Wytheville . . . 7,135

COUNTIES

Accomack . . . 31,268
Albemarle . . . 55,783
Alleghany . . . 14,333
Amelia . . . 8,405
Amherst . . . 29,122
Appomattox . . . 11,971
Arlington . . . 152,599
Augusta . . . 53,732

○ Rand McNally estimate
▲ Population of entire township or "town", including rural areas.
● Independent city. Population not included in county total.

Bath 5,860
Bedford 34,927
Bland 6,349
Botetourt 23,270
Brunswick 15,632
Buchanan 37,989
Buckingham 11,751
Campbell 45,424
Caroline 17,904
Carroll 27,270
Charles City 6,692
Charlotte 12,266
Chesterfield 141,372
Clarke 9,965
Craig 3,948
Culpeper 22,620
Cumberland 7,881
Dickenson 19,806
Dinwiddie 22,602
Essex 8,864
Fairfax 596,901
Fauquier 35,889
Floyd 11,563
Fluvanna 10,244
Franklin 35,740
Frederick 34,150
Giles 17,810
Gloucester 20,107
Goochland 11,761
Grayson 16,579
Greene 7,625
Greensville 10,903
Halifax 30,599
Hanover 50,398
Henrico 180,735
Henry 57,654
Highland 2,937
Isle of Wight 21,603
James City 22,763
King and Queen 5,968
King George 10,543
King William 9,334
Lancaster 10,129
Lee 25,956
Loudoun 57,427
Louisa 17,825
Lunenburg 12,124
Madison 10,232
Mathews 7,995
Mecklenburg 29,444
Middlesex 7,719
Montgomery 63,516
Nelson 12,204
New Kent 8,781
Northampton 14,625
Northumberland 9,828
Nottoway 14,666
Orange 18,063
Page 19,401
Patrick 17,647
Pittsylvania 66,147
Powhatan 13,062
Prince Edward 16,456
Prince George 25,733
Prince William 144,703
Pulaski 35,229
Rappahannock 6,093
Richmond 6,952
Roanoke 72,945
Rockbridge 17,911
Rockingham 57,038
Russell 31,761
Scott 25,068
Shenandoah 27,559
Smyth 33,366
Southampton 18,731
Spotsylvania 34,435
Stafford 40,470
Surry 6,046
Sussex 10,874
Tazewell 50,511
Warren 21,200
Washington 46,487
Westmoreland 14,041
Wise 43,863
Wythe 25,522
York 35,463

WASHINGTON

1980
Census 4,132,180

CITIES

Aberdeen 18,739
Albion 631
Algona SEAT- 1,467
Allyn . . . . . 900 ○
Anacortes 9,013
Appleyard . . . . . 1,500 ○
Arlington SEAT- 3,282
Asotin LEW 943
Auburn SEAT- 26,417
Bainbridge Island
Winslow
SEAT- 2,196
Battle Ground
POR 2,774
Belfair . . . . . 450 ○
Bellevue SEAT- 73,903
BELLINGHAM
BELNG 45,794
Benton City 1,980
Bingen 644
Black Diamond
SEAT- 1,170
Blaine 2,363
Bonney Lake
SEAT- 5,328
Bothell SEAT- 7,943
BREMERTON
BREM 36,208
Brewster 1,337
Bridgeport 1,174
Brinnon . . . . . 600 ○
Bryn Mawr SEAT- . . . 2,100 ○
Buckley SEAT- 3,143
Bucoda 519
Buena . . . . . 800 ○
Burbank . . . . . 700 ○
Burien SEAT- 23,189
Burlington 3,894
Camas 5,681
Carbonado SEAT- 456
Carnation 913
Carson . . . . . 950 ○
Cashmere 2,240
Castle Rock 2,162
Cathlamet 635
Centralia 11,555
Central Park . . . . . 2,900 ○
Chehalis 6,100
Chelan 2,802
Cheney 7,630
Chewelah 1,888
Chico BREM . . . . . 750 ○
Chimacum . . . . . 600 ○
Chinook . . . . . 650 ○
Clallam Bay . . . . . 600 ○
Clarkston LEW 6,903
Clearlake . . . . . 900 ○
Cle Elum 1,773
Clinton SEAT- . . . . . 2,000 ○
Colfax 2,780
College Place 5,771
Colville 4,510
Concrete 592
Connell 1,981
Copalis Beach . . . . . 800 ○
Cosmopolis 1,575
Coulee City 510
Coulee Dam 1,412
Country Homes
SPOK . . . . . 3,850 ○
Coupeville 1,006
Custer . . . . . 500 ○
Darrington 1,064
Davenport 1,559
Dayton 2,565
Deer Park 2,140
Deming . . . . . 450 ○
Des Moines SEAT- . . . 7,378
Dishman SPOK 10,169

Du Pont SEAT- 559
Eastgate SEAT- 8,341
East Olympia OLYM . . . 700 ○
Eastsound . . . . . 900 ○
East Wenatchee 1,640
Eatonville 998
Edgewood SEAT- . . . . 1,800 ○
Edmonds SEAT- 27,679
Ellensburg 11,752
Elma 2,720
Entiat 445
Enumclaw SEAT- 5,427
Ephrata 5,359
Everett SEAT- 54,413
Everson 898
Fairfield 582
Fall City . . . . . 1,600 ○
Federal Way
SEAT- . . . . . 17,850 ○
Ferndale BELNG 3,855
Fircrest SEAT- 5,477
Fords Prairie . . . . . 2,000 ○
Forks 3,060
Friday Harbor 1,200
Fruitvale YAK . . . . . 3,600 ○
Garfield 599
Gig Harbor SEAT- . . . 2,429
Gold Bar 794
Goldendale 3,575
Grand Coulee 1,180
Grandview 5,615
Granger 1,812
Granite Falls SEAT- . . . 911
Grapeview . . . . . 500 ○
Grayland . . . . . 600 ○
Greenacres SPOK . . . 3,650 ○
Hadlock . . . . . 950 ○
Harrington 507
Hazel Dell POR . . . . . 6,000 ○
Hoodsport . . . . . 900 ○
Hoquiam 9,719
Ilwaco 604
Ione 594
Issaquah SEAT- 5,536
Kalama 1,216
Kelso LNGV 11,129
Kenmore SEAT- . . . . . 7,900 ○
Kennewick P-K-R . . . 34,397
Kennydale SEAT- . . . . 1,000 ○
Kent SEAT- 23,152
Kettle Falls 1,087
Kirkland SEAT- 18,779
Kittitas 782
Klickitat . . . . . 700 ○
Lacey OLYM 13,940
La Conner 633
Lake Stevens
SEAT- 1,660
Lakewood SEAT- . . . . . 500 ○
Lakewood Center
SEAT- 54,523
Langley SEAT- 650
La Push . . . . . 600 ○
Leavenworth 1,522
Lexington LNGV . . . . . 500 ○
Liberty Lake SPOK . . . . 900 ○
Lind 567
Long Beach 1,199
Longbranch SEAT- . . . . 900 ○
LONGVIEW
LNGV 31,052
Loon Lake . . . . . 650 ○
Lyle . . . . . 700 ○
Lynden 4,022
Lynnwood SEAT- . . . 22,641
Mabton 1,248
McCleary 1,419
Manson . . . . . 500 ○
Maple Valley . . . . . 900 ○
Marysville SEAT- 5,080
Mead SPOK . . . . . 1,400 ○
Medical Lake 3,600
Medina SEAT- 3,220
Mercer Island
SEAT- 21,522
Millwood SPOK 1,717
Milton SEAT- 3,162

Mineral . . . . . 500 ○
Moclips . . . . . 700 ○
Monroe SEAT- 2,869
Montesano 3,247
Morton 1,264
Moses Lake 10,629
Mossyrock 463
Mountlake Terrace
SEAT- 16,534
Mount Vernon 13,009
Moxee City 687
Mukilteo SEAT- 1,426
Naches 644
Napavine 611
Naselle . . . . . 900 ○
Neah Bay . . . . . 1,000 ○
Newport 1,665
Newport Hills
SEAT- . . . . . 6,000 ○
Nordland . . . . . 500 ○
North Bend 1,701
North City SEAT- . . . . 6,200 ○
Oakesdale 444
Oak Harbor 12,271
Oakville 537
Ocean City . . . . . 500 ○
Ocean Park . . . . . 1,500 ○
Odessa 1,009
Okanogan 2,302
Olalla BREM . . . . . 450 ○
OLYMPIA OLYM . . . 27,447
Omak 4,007
Onalaska . . . . . 560 ○
Opportunity
SPOK 21,241
Orchards POR 8,828
Oroville 1,483
Orting SEAT- 1,787
Othello 4,454
Otis Orchards
SPOK . . . . . 1,000 ○
Pacific SEAT- 2,261
Pacific Beach . . . . . 1,000 ○
Packwood . . . . . 1,150 ○
Palouse 1,005
Parker . . . . . 550 ○
Parkland SEAT- . . . . 22,300 ○
Parkwater SPOK . . . . 4,850 ○
PASCO P-K-R 18,425
Pateros 555
Pe Ell 617
Peshastin . . . . . 900 ○
Point Roberts . . . . . 750 ○
Pomeroy 1,716
Port Angeles 17,311
Port Ludlow . . . . . 500 ○
Port Orchard
BREM 4,787
Port Townsend 6,067
Poulsbo BREM 3,453
Preston SEAT- . . . . . 500 ○
Prosser 3,896
Pullman 23,579
Puyallup SEAT- 18,251
Quilcene . . . . . 950 ○
Quincy 3,525
Rainier 891
Randle . . . . . 600 ○
Ravensdale SEAT- . . . . 500 ○
Raymond 2,991
Reardan 498
Redmond SEAT- . . . 23,318
Redondo . . . . . 600 ○
Renton SEAT- 30,612
Republic 1,018
Richland P-K-R 33,578
Richmond Beach
SEAT- . . . . . 8,000 ○
Richmond Highlands
SEAT- 24,463
Ridgecrest SEAT- . . . . 7,000 ○
Ridgefield POR 1,062
Ritzville 1,800
Riverton Heights
SEAT- . . . . . 33,500 ○
Rochester . . . . . 900 ○
Rockford 442

○ Rand McNally estimate
▲ Population of entire township or "town", including rural areas.
● Independent city. Population not included in county total.

WASHINGTON continued

Rock Island 491
Rollingbay SEAT- 700 ○
Rosalia 572
Roslyn 938
Ruston SEAT- 612
St. John 529
Salmon Creek POR 1,950 ○
SEATTLE SEAT- 493,846
Seaview 500 ○
Sedro Woolley 6,110
Sekiu 600 ○
Selah YAK 4,500
Sequim 3,013
Shelton 7,629
Silverdale BREM 1,500 ○
Skyway SEAT- 12,500 ○
Snohomish SEAT- 5,294
Snoqualmie SEAT- 1,370
Soap Lake 1,196
South Bend 1,686
South Broadway YAK 3,620 ○
South Cle Elum 449
South Colby BREM 500 ○
Spanaway SEAT- 8,858
SPOKANE SPOK 171,300
Sprague 473
Stanwood SEAT- 1,646
Startup 450 ○
Steilacoom SEAT- 4,886
Stevenson 1,172
Sultan SEAT- 1,578
Sumas 712
Sumner SEAT- 4,936
Sunnyside 9,225
Suquamish BREM 1,500 ○
Tacoma SEAT- 158,501
Taholah 800 ○
Tekoa 854
Tenino 1,280
Tieton 528
Toledo 637
Tonasket 985
Toppenish 6,517
Town and Country SPOK 5,578
Tracyton BREM 1,600 ○
Trout Lake 550 ○
Tukwila SEAT- 3,578
Tumwater OLYM 6,705
Twisp 911
Union Gap YAK 3,184
University Place SEAT- 20,381
Vancouver POR 42,834
Waitsburg 1,035
Walla Walla 25,618
Wapato 3,307
Warden 1,479
Washougal 3,834
Waterville 908
Wenatchee 17,257
Westport 1,954
White Center SEAT- 19,700 ○
White Salmon 1,853
White Swan 600 ○
Wilbur 1,122
Winlock 1,052
Wishram 675 ○
Woodland 2,341
Yacolt 544
YAKIMA YAK 49,826
Yelm 1,294
Zillah 1,599

COUNTIES

Adams 13,267
Asotin 16,823
Benton 109,444
Chelan 45,061
Clallam 51,648
Clark 192,227
Columbia 4,057
Cowlitz 79,548
Douglas 22,144
Ferry 5,811
Franklin 35,025
Garfield 2,468
Grant 48,522
Grays Harbor 66,314
Island 44,048
Jefferson 15,965
King 1,269,749
Kitsap 147,152
Kittitas 24,877
Klickitat 15,822
Lewis 56,025
Lincoln 9,604
Mason 31,184
Okanogan 30,639
Pacific 17,237
Pend Oreille 8,580
Pierce 485,667
San Juan 7,838
Skagit 64,138
Skamania 7,919
Snohomish 337,720
Spokane 341,835
Stevens 28,979
Thurston 124,264
Wahkiakum 3,832
Walla Walla 47,435
Whatcom 106,701
Whitman 40,103
Yakima 172,508

WEST VIRGINIA

1980
Census 1,950,279

CITIES

Accoville 500 ○
Alderson 1,375
Alum Creek 500 ○
Amherstdale 800 ○
Anawalt 652
Ansted 1,952
Athens 1,147
Barboursville HNTG- 2,871
Barrackville FAIRM 1,815
Barrett 800 ○
Baxter FAIRM 500 ○
Bayard 540
Beaver BECK 1,400 ○
BECKLEY BECK 20,492
Beech Bottom STU- 507
Belington 2,038
Belle CHAS 1,621
Belmont 887
Benwood WHL 1,994
Berkeley Springs 789
Berwind 600 ○
Bethany STU- 1,336
Beverly 475
Blennerhassett PRKB 2,200 ○
Blue Creek 500 ○
Bluefield 16,060
Bluewell 1,000 ○
Bolivar 672
Boomer 1,100 ○
Bradley BECK 1,200 ○
Bradshaw 750
Bramwell 989
Brenton 800 ○
Bridgeport CLRKB 6,604
Brookhaven MORG 1,200 ○
Brownton 600 ○
Buckhannon 6,820
Buffalo 1,034
Bunker Hill 500 ○
Bunker Hill CHAS 800 ○
Burnsville 531
Cabin Creek 900 ○
Cameron 1,474
Cannelton 750 ○
Caretta 950 ○
Carolina 650 ○
Cedar Grove CHAS 1,479
Ceredo HNTG- 2,255
Chapmanville 1,164
CHARLESTON CHAS 63,968
Charles Town 2,857
Charlton Heights 600 ○
Charmco 800 ○
Chattaroy 1,200 ○
Chelyan CHAS 800 ○
Chesapeake CHAS 2,364
Chester E.LIV- 3,297
CLARKSBURG CLRKB 22,371
Clay 940
Clendenin CHAS 1,373
Clothier 600 ○
Coalwood 1,100 ○
Colliers STU- 600 ○
Corinne 500 ○
Cowen 723
Crab Orchard BECK 1,900 ○
Craigsville 900 ○
Cross Lanes CHAS 3,500 ○
Culloden CHAS 1,500 ○
Cunard 450 ○
Danville 727
Davis 979
Davy 882
Deep Water 500 ○
Delbarton 981
Dellslow 700 ○
Despard CLRKB 1,200 ○
Diamond 500 ○
Dixie 450 ○
Drybranch CHAS 700 ○
Dunbar CHAS 9,285
Dupont City CHAS 900 ○
East Bank CHAS 1,155
East Pea Ridge HNTG- 1,900 ○
East View CLRKB 1,222
Eccles BECK 1,162
Eckman 700 ○
Eleanor CHAS 1,282
Elizabeth 856
Elkhorn 700 ○
Elkins 8,536
Elkview CHAS 1,161
Enterprise 950 ○
Eskdale 500 ○
Fairlea 1,888
FAIRMONT FAIRM 23,863
Fairview 759
Farmington FAIRM 583
Fayetteville 2,366
Flemington CLRKB 452
Follansbee STU- 3,994
Fort Ashby CUMB 1,205
Fort Gay 886
Gary 2,233
Gassaway 1,225
Gauley Bridge 1,177
Gilbert 757
Glasgow CHAS 1,031
Glen Dale WHL 1,875
Glendale Heights WHL 700 ○
Glen Jean 500 ○
Glenville 2,155
Glen White 500 ○
Grafton 6,845
Grantsville 788
Grant Town FAIRM 987
Granville MORG 992
Great Cacapon 500 ○
Guthrie CHAS 800 ○
Hamlin 1,219
Handley CHAS 633
Harrisville 1,673
Hartford 556
Harvey 500 ○
Henderson 604
Henlawson 950 ○
Hico 700 ○
Hinton 4,622
Holden 2,036
Hooverson Heights STU- 1,500 ○
Hundred 485
HUNTINGTON HNTG- 63,684
Hurricane CHAS 3,751
Iaeger 833
Idamay 600 ○
Institute CHAS 1,500 ○
Jeffrey 900 ○
Jodie 450 ○
Julian 700 ○
Junior 591
Kearneysville 500 ○
Kenova HNTG- 4,454
Kermit 705
Keyser 6,569
Keystone 902
Kimball 871
Kimberly 800 ○
Kincaid 700 ○
Kingwood 2,877
Kistler 750 ○
Knollwood CHAS 700 ○
Lanark BECK 600 ○
Lansing 500 ○
Lester BECK 626
Lewisburg 3,065
Lilly Grove 1,700 ○
Logan 3,029
Longacre 450 ○
Lost Creek 604
Lumberport 939
Mabscott BECK 1,668
Mc Comas 800 ○
Mc Mechen WHL 2,402
Madison 3,228
Malden CHAS 950 ○
Mammoth CHAS 750 ○
Man 1,333
Mannington 3,036
Marlinton 1,352
Marlowe HAG- 700 ○
Marmet CHAS 2,196
Marrtown PRKB 900 ○
Martinsburg 13,063
Mason 1,432
Masontown 1,052
Matewan 822
Matoaka 613
Maxwell Acres WHL 1,000 ○
Maybeury 700 ○
Meadow Bridge 530
Meadowbrook CLRKB 500 ○
Miami 500 ○
Middlebourne 941
Mill Creek 801
Milton HNTG- 2,178
Minden 800 ○
Monongah FAIRM 1,132
Montgomery 3,104
Moorefield 2,257
MORGANTOWN MORG 27,605
Moundsville WHL 12,419
Mount Clare 900 ○
Mount Gay 1,650 ○
Mount Hope 1,849
Mullens 2,919
Naoma 600 ○
Nettie 600 ○
New Cumberland STU- 1,752

○ Rand McNally estimate
▲ Population of entire township or "town", including rural areas.
● Independent city. Population not included in county total.

Newell E.LIV- 2,032
New Haven 1,723
New Manchester STU- 600 ○
New Martinsville 7,109
Nitro CHAS 8,074
Nutter Fort CLRKB 2,078
Oak Hill 7,120
Oceana 2,143
Odd 550 ○
Omar 950 ○
Paden City 3,671
PARKERSBURG PRKB 39,967
Parsons 1,937
Paw Paw 644
Peach Creek 600 ○
Pennsboro 1,652
Petersburg 2,084
Peterstown 648
Philippi 3,194
Piedmont 1,491
Pineville 1,140
Piney View BECK 800 ○
Poca CHAS 1,142
Pocatalico CHAS 900 ○
Point Pleasant 5,682
Powellton 1,200 ○
Pratt CHAS 821
Princeton 7,493
Prosperity BECK 1,000 ○
Pursglove MORG 600 ○
Quinwood 460
Racine 650 ○
Rainelle 1,983
Raleigh BECK 900 ○
Rand CHAS 2,500 ○
Ranson 2,471
Ravenswood 4,126
Reader 700 ○
Red Jacket 1,000 ○
Reedsville 564
Rhodell 472
Richwood 3,568
Ridgeley CUMB 994
Ridgeview 500 ○
Ripley 3,464
Rivesville FAIRM 1,327
Roderfield 1,100 ○
Romney 2,094
Ronceverte 2,312
Rowlesburg 966
Rupert 1,276
St. Albans CHAS 12,402
St. Marys 2,219
Salem 2,706
Seth 650 ○
Shady Spring BECK 1,000 ○
Sharples 500 ○
Shepherdstown 1,791
Shinnston 3,059
Sissonville CHAS 500 ○
Sistersville 2,367
Smithers 1,482
Sophia BECK 1,216
South Charleston CHAS 15,968
Spelter 450 ○
Spencer 2,799
Sprague BECK 900 ○
Squire 900 ○
Stanaford BECK 1,000 ○
Star City MORG 1,464
Stollings 900 ○
Stonewood CLRKB 2,058
Summersville 2,972
Sutton 1,192
Switzer 1,000 ○
Tad CHAS 500 ○
Talcott 450 ○
Terra Alta 1,946
Thomas 747
Triadelphia WHL 1,461
Tunnelton 510
Tyler Heights CHAS 3,200 ○
Union 743
Valley Grove WHL 597
Vallscreek 900 ○
Van 500 ○
Verdunville 950 ○
Vienna PRKB 11,618
Wallace 900 ○
War 2,158
Wayne 1,495
Webster Springs 939
Weirton STU- 25,371
Welch 3,885
Wellsburg STU- 3,963
West Hamlin HNTG- 643
West Liberty WHL 744
Weston 6,250
Westover MORG 4,884
West Union 1,090
WHEELING WHL 43,070
White Sulphur Springs 3,371
Whitesville 689
Whitman 950 ○
Wilkinson 700 ○
Williamson 5,219
Williamstown MRIET 3,095
Winifrede CHAS 800 ○
Yukon 500 ○

COUNTIES

Barbour 16,639
Berkeley 46,775
Boone 30,447
Braxton 13,894
Brooke 31,117
Cabell 106,835
Calhoun 8,250
Clay 11,265
Doddridge 7,433
Fayette 57,863
Gilmer 8,334
Grant 10,210
Greenbrier 37,665
Hampshire 14,867
Hancock 41,053
Hardy 10,030
Harrison 77,710
Jackson 25,794
Jefferson 30,302
Kanawha 231,414
Lewis 18,813
Lincoln 23,675
Logan 50,679
McDowell 49,899
Marion 65,789
Marshall 41,608
Mason 27,045
Mercer 73,942
Mineral 27,234
Mingo 37,336
Monongalia 75,024
Monroe 12,873
Morgan 10,711
Nicholas 28,126
Ohio 61,389
Pendleton 7,910
Pleasants 8,236
Pocahontas 9,919
Preston 30,460
Putnam 38,181
Raleigh 86,821
Randolph 28,734
Ritchie 11,442
Roane 15,952
Summers 15,875
Taylor 16,584
Tucker 8,675
Tyler 11,320
Upshur 23,427
Wayne 46,021
Webster 12,245
Wetzel 21,874
Wirt 4,922
Wood 93,648
Wyoming 35,993

WISCONSIN

1980 Census 4,705,521

CITIES

Abbotsford 1,901
Adams 1,744
Adell 545
Albany 1,051
Algoma 3,656
Allenton 550 ○
Allouez GRBY 14,882
Alma 876
Alma Center 454
Almena 526
Almond 477
Altoona EAUC 4,393
Amery 2,404
Amherst 701
Antigo 8,653
APPLETON APP 58,913
Arcadia 2,109
Arena 451
Argyle 720
Arlington 440
Ashland 9,115
Ashwaubenon GRBY 14,486
Athens 988
Auburndale 641
Augusta 1,560
Avoca 505
Baldwin 1,620
Balsam Lake 749
Bangor 1,012
Baraboo 8,081
Barneveld 579
Barron 2,595
Bay City 543
Bayfield 778
Bayside MILW 4,724
Bear Creek 454
Beaver Dam 14,149
Belgium 892
Belleville 1,302
Belmont 826
BELOIT BLOIT 35,207
Beloit North BLOIT 5,457
Benton 983
Berlin 5,478
Big Bend MILW 1,345
Birnamwood 688
Biron 698
Black Creek 1,097
Black Earth 1,145
Black River Falls 3,434
Blair 1,142
Blanchardville 803
Bloomer 3,342
Bloomington 743
Bonduel 1,160
Boscobel 2,662
Boyceville 862
Boyd 660
Brandon 862
Brillion 2,907
Bristol CHI 500 ○
Brodhead 3,153
Brookfield MILW 34,035
Brooklyn 627
Brown Deer MILW 12,921
Bruce 905
Buffalo 894
Burlington 8,385
Butler MILW 2,059
Cadott 1,247
Cambria 680
Cambridge 844
Cameron 1,115
Campbellsport 1,740
Camp Douglas 589
Cascade 615
Casco 484
Cashton 827
Cassville 1,270
Cecil 445
Cedarburg MILW 9,005
Cedar Grove 1,420
Centuria 711
Chenequa MILW 532
Chetek 1,931
Chilton 2,965
Chippewa Falls EAUC 12,270
Clear Lake 899
Cleveland 1,270
Clinton BLOIT 1,751
Clintonville 4,567
Cochrane 512
Colby 1,496
Coleman 852
Colfax 1,149
Columbus 4,049
Combined Locks APP 2,573
Coon Valley 758
Cornell 1,583
Crandon 1,969
Crivitz 1,041
Cross Plains MAD 2,156
Cuba City 2,129
Cudahy MILW 19,547
Cumberland 1,983
Dallas 477
Dane 518
Darien 1,152
Darlington 2,300
Deerfield 1,466
De Forest MAD 3,367
Delafield MILW 4,083
Delavan 5,684
Delavan Lake 2,082
Denmark 1,475
De Pere GRBY 14,892
Dickeyville DUB 1,156
Dodgeville 3,458
Dorchester 613
Dousman MILW 1,153
Dresser 670
Durand 2,047
Eagle MILW 1,008
Eagle Lake 1,000 ○
Eagle River 1,326
East Troy MILW 2,385
EAU CLAIRE EAUC 51,509
Eden 534
Edgar 1,194
Edgerton JNSV 4,335
Elcho 450 ○
Eleva 593
Elkhart Lake 1,054
Elkhorn 4,605
Elk Mound 737
Ellsworth 2,143
Elm Grove MILW 6,735
Elmwood 885
Elroy 1,504
Embarrass 496
Ettrick 462
Evansville 2,835
Fairchild 577
Fall Creek 1,148
Fall River 850
Fennimore 2,212
Florence 575 ○
FOND DU LAC FDLC 35,863
Fontana 1,764
Footville 794
Forestville 455
Fort Atkinson 9,785
Fountain City 963
Fox Lake 1,373
Fox Point MILW 7,649
Francis Creek MNTW- 589
Franklin MILW 16,871
Frederic 1,039

○ Rand McNally estimate
▲ Population of entire township or "town", including rural areas.
● Independent city. Population not included in county total.

WISCONSIN continued

Fredonia MILW 1,437
Fremont 510
French Island LACRO . . . . 3,000 ○
Friendship 744
Galesville 1,239
Gays Mills 627
Genoa City CHI 1,202
Germantown MILW 10,729
Gillett 1,356
Glendale MILW 13,882
Glenwood City 950
Glidden . . . . 550 ○
Goodman . . . . 600 ○
Grafton MILW 8,381
Grantsburg 1,153
GREEN BAY GRBY 87,899
Greendale MILW . . . 16,928
Greenfield MILW . . . 31,467
Green Lake 1,208
Greenwood 1,124
Gresham 534
Hales Corners MILW 7,110
Hallie EAUC . . . . 1,223 ○
Hammond 991
Hartford 7,046
Hartland MILW 5,559
Hayward 1,698
Hazel Green 1,282
Hewitt 470
Highland 860
Hilbert 1,176
Hillsboro 1,263
Holmen LACRO 2,411
Horicon 3,584
Hortonville APP 2,016
Howard GRBY 8,240
Howards Grove-Millersville SHEB 1,838
Hudson MPLS- 5,434
Hurley 2,015
Hustisford 874
Independence 1,180
Iola 957
Iron Belt . . . . 520 ○
Iron Ridge 766
Iron River . . . . 650 ○
Jackson MILW 1,817
JANESVILLE JNSV 51,071
Jefferson 5,647
Johnson Creek 1,136
Juda . . . . 450 ○
Junction City 523
Juneau 2,045
Kaukauna APP 11,310
Kendall 486
KENOSHA CHI 77,685
Keshena . . . . 500 ○
Kewaskum 2,381
Kewaunee 2,801
Kiel 3,083
Kimberly APP 5,881
King . . . . 750 ○
Kohler SHEB 1,651
Lac du Flambeau . . . . . . 900 ○
LA CROSSE LACRO 48,347
Ladysmith 3,826
La Farge 746
Lake Butte des Morts OSH . . . . 1,111 ○
Lake Delton 1,158
Lake Geneva 5,612
Lake Mills 3,670
Lake Nebagamon 780
Lake Tomahawk . . . . 600 ○
Lake Wazeecha 2,176
Lake Wissota EAUC 1,788
Lancaster 4,076

Land O'Lakes . . . . 500 ○
Lannon MILW 987
Laona . . . . 700 ○
Lena 585
Little Chute APP 7,907
Livingston 642
Lodi 1,959
Lomira 1,446
Lone Rock 577
Loyal 1,252
Luck 997
Luxemburg 1,040
Lyons . . . . 540 ○
McFarland MAD 3,783
MADISON MAD . . . 170,616
Manawa 1,205
MANITOWOC MNTW- 32,547
Maple Bluff MAD 1,351
Marathon WAUS 1,552
Marinette 11,965
Marion 1,348
Markesan 1,446
Marshall 2,363
Marshfield 18,290
Mauston 3,284
Mayville 4,333
Mazomanie 1,248
Medford 4,035
Mellen 1,046
Melrose 507
Menasha APP 14,728
Menomonee Falls MILW 27,845
Menomonie 12,769
Mequon MILW 16,193
Mercer . . . . 1,250 ○
Merrill 9,578
Merrillan 587
Merton MILW 1,045
Middleton MAD 11,848
Milltown 732
Milton JNSV 4,092
MILWAUKEE MILW 636,236
Mineral Point 2,259
Minocqua . . . . 900 ○
Minong 557
Mishicot MNTW- 1,503
Mondovi 2,545
Monona MAD 8,809
Monroe 10,027
Montello 1,273
Montfort 616
Monticello 1,021
Montreal 887
Mosinee WAUS 3,015
Mount Calvary 585
Mount Horeb 3,251
Mukwonago MILW . . . 4,014
Muscoda 1,331
Muskego MILW 15,277
Necedah 773
Neenah APP 22,432
Neillsville 2,780
Nekoosa 2,519
Neopit 1,065
Neosho 575
New Auburn 466
New Berlin MILW . . . 30,529
Newburg 783
New Glarus 1,763
New Holstein 3,412
New Lisbon 1,390
New London 6,210
New Richmond 4,306
Niagara 2,079
North Fond du Lac FDLC 3,844
North Freedom 616
North Hudson MPLS- 2,218
North Lake MILW . . . . . 600 ○
North Prairie MILW 938
Norwalk 517
Oak Creek MILW . . . 16,932
Oakfield 990

Oconomowoc MILW 9,909
Oconto 4,505
Oconto Falls 2,500
Okauchee MILW . . . . 1,800 ○
Okauchee Lake MILW . . . . 1,400 ○
Omro OSH 2,763
Onalaska LACRO 9,249
Oostburg SHEB 1,647
Oregon MAD 3,876
Orfordville 1,143
Osceola 1,581
OSHKOSH OSH 49,620
Osseo 1,474
Owen 998
Paddock Lake CHI . . . 2,207
Palmyra 1,515
Pardeeville 1,594
Park Falls 3,192
Pell Lake CHI 1,826
Pembine . . . . 475 ○
Pepin 890
Peshtigo 2,807
Pewaukee MILW 4,637
Phelps . . . . 700 ○
Phillips 1,522
Pittsville 810
Plain 676
Plainfield 813
Platteville 9,580
Pleasant Prairie CHI . . . 500 ○
Pleasant View . . . . 700 ○
Plover 5,310
Plum City 505
Plymouth 6,027
Poplar 569
Portage 7,896
Port Edwards 2,077
Port Washington MILW 8,612
Potosi 736
Poynette 1,447
Poy Sippi . . . . 500 ○
Prairie du Chien 5,859
Prairie du Sac 2,145
Prentice 605
Prescott MPLS- 2,654
Princeton 1,479
Pulaski 1,875
RACINE RAC 85,725
Randolph 1,691
Random Lake 1,287
Redgranite 976
Reedsburg 5,038
Reedsville 1,134
Reeseville 649
Rhinelander 7,873
Rib Lake 945
Rice Lake 7,691
Richland Center 4,997
Ridgeway 503
Rio 785
Ripon 7,111
River Falls 9,019
River Hills MILW 1,642
Roberts 833
Rochester RAC 746
Rosendale 725
Rosholt 520
Rothschild WAUS 3,338
St. Cloud 560
St. Croix Falls 1,497
St Francis MILW 10,042
St. Nazianz 738
Salem CHI . . . . 1,000 ○
Sauk City 2,703
Saukville MILW 3,494
Schofield WAUS 2,226
Seymour 2,530
Sharon 1,280
Shawano 7,013
SHEBOYGAN SHEB 48,085
Sheboygan Falls SHEB 5,253
Shell Lake 1,135

Shiocton 805
Shorewood MILW . . . 14,327
Shorewood Hills MAD 1,837
Shullsburg 1,484
Silver Lake CHI 1,598
Siren 896
Sister Bay 564
Slinger MILW 1,612
Soldiers Grove 622
Solon Springs 590
Somerset 860
South Kenosha CHI . . . 875 ○
South Milwaukee MILW 21,069
South Wayne 495
Sparta 6,934
Spencer 1,754
Spooner 2,365
Spring Green 1,265
Spring Valley 982
Stanley 2,095
Stetsonville 487
Stevens Point 22,970
Stockbridge 567
Stoddard 762
Stoughton MAD 7,589
Stratford 1,385
Strum 944
Sturgeon Bay 8,847
Sturtevant RAC 4,130
Sun Prairie MAD . . . 12,931
Superior DUL- 29,571
Suring 581
Sussex MILW 3,482
Theresa 766
Thiensville MILW 3,341
Thorp 1,635
Three Lakes . . . . 600 ○
Tigerton 865
Tomah 7,204
Tomahawk 3,527
Trempealeau 956
Trevor CHI . . . . 500 ○
Turtle Lake 762
Twin Lakes CHI 3,474
Two Rivers MNTW- 13,354
Union Grove CHI 3,517
Valders MNTW- 984
Verona MAD 3,336
Vesper 554
Viola 696
Viroqua 3,716
Wabeno . . . . 700 ○
Walworth 1,607
Washburn 2,080
Waterford RAC 2,051
Waterloo 2,393
Watertown 18,113
Waukesha MILW . . . 50,365
Waunakee MAD 3,866
Waupaca 4,472
Waupun 8,132
WAUSAU WAUS . . . 32,426
Wausaukee 648
Wautoma 1,629
Wauwatosa MILW 51,308
Wauzeka 580
Webster 610
West Allis MILW 63,982
West Bend 21,484
Westby 1,797
Westfield 1,033
West Milwaukee MILW 3,535
Weston WAUS 8,775
West Salem LACRO 3,276
Weyauwega 1,549
Whitefish Bay MILW 14,930
Whitehall 1,530
Whitelaw MNTW- 649
Whitewater 11,520
Whiting 2,050

○ Rand McNally estimate
▲ Population of entire township or "town", including rural areas.
● Independent city. Population not included in county total.

Wild Rose . . . 741
Williams Bay . . . 1,763
Wilton . . . 465
Wind Lake MILW . . . 2,400 ○
Wind Point RAC . . . 1,695
Winneconne OSH . . . 1,935
Wisconsin Dells . . . 2,521
Wisconsin Rapids . . . 17,995
Withee . . . 509
Wittenberg . . . 997
Wonewoc . . . 842
Woodruff . . . 900 ○
Woodville . . . 725
Wrightstown APP . . . 1,169
Wyocena . . . 548

COUNTIES

Adams . . . 13,457
Ashland . . . 16,783
Barron . . . 38,730
Bayfield . . . 13,822
Brown . . . 175,280
Buffalo . . . 14,309
Burnett . . . 12,340
Calumet . . . 30,867
Chippewa . . . 52,127
Clark . . . 32,910
Columbia . . . 43,222
Crawford . . . 16,556
Dane . . . 323,545
Dodge . . . 75,064
Door . . . 25,029
Douglas . . . 44,421
Dunn . . . 34,314
Eau Claire . . . 78,805
Florence . . . 4,172
Fond du Lac . . . 88,964
Forest . . . 9,044
Grant . . . 51,736
Green . . . 30,012
Green Lake . . . 18,370
Iowa . . . 19,802
Iron . . . 6,730
Jackson . . . 16,831
Jefferson . . . 66,152
Juneau . . . 21,039
Kenosha . . . 123,137
Kewaunee . . . 19,539
La Crosse . . . 91,056
Lafayette . . . 17,412
Langlade . . . 19,978
Lincoln . . . 26,555
Manitowoc . . . 82,918
Marathon . . . 111,270
Marinette . . . 39,314
Marquette . . . 11,672
Menominee . . . 3,373
Milwaukee . . . 964,988
Monroe . . . 35,074
Oconto . . . 28,947
Oneida . . . 31,216
Outagamie . . . 128,730
Ozaukee . . . 66,981
Pepin . . . 7,477
Pierce . . . 31,149
Polk . . . 32,351
Portage . . . 57,420
Price . . . 15,788
Racine . . . 173,132
Richland . . . 17,476
Rock . . . 139,420
Rusk . . . 15,589
St. Croix . . . 43,262
Sauk . . . 43,469
Sawyer . . . 12,843
Shawano . . . 35,928
Sheboygan . . . 100,935
Taylor . . . 18,817
Trempealeau . . . 26,158
Vernon . . . 25,642
Vilas . . . 16,535
Walworth . . . 71,507
Washburn . . . 13,174
Washington . . . 84,848
Waukesha . . . 280,080
Waupaca . . . 42,831
Waushara . . . 18,526
Winnebago . . . 131,772
Wood . . . 72,799

WYOMING

1980
Census . . . 469,557

CITIES

Afton . . . 1,481
Basin . . . 1,349
Big Piney . . . 530
Buffalo . . . 3,799
Byron . . . 633
CASPER CASP . . . 51,016
CHEYENNE CHEY . . . 47,283
Cody . . . 6,790
Cokeville . . . 515
Cowley . . . 455
Dayton . . . 701
Diamondville . . . 1,000
Douglas . . . 6,030
Dubois . . . 1,067
Edgerton . . . 510
Encampment . . . 611
Evanston . . . 6,421
Evansville CASP . . . 2,335
Gillette . . . 12,134
Glenrock . . . 2,736
Green River . . . 12,807
Greybull . . . 2,277
Guernsey . . . 1,512
Hanna . . . 2,288
Hudson . . . 514
Jackson . . . 4,511
Kemmerer . . . 3,273
Lander . . . 7,867
Laramie . . . 24,410
Lingle . . . 475
Lovell . . . 2,447
Lusk . . . 1,650
Lyman . . . 2,284
Marbleton . . . 537
Medicine Bow . . . 953
Meeteetse . . . 512
Midwest . . . 638
Mills CASP . . . 2,139
Moorcroft . . . 1,014
Mountain View CASP . . . 1,500 ○
Mountain View . . . 628
Newcastle . . . 3,596
Orchard Valley CHEY . . . 800 ○
Paradise Valley CASP . . . 2,300 ○
Pine Bluffs . . . 1,077
Pinedale . . . 1,066
Powell . . . 5,310
Ranchester . . . 655
Rawlins . . . 11,547
Reliance . . . 500 ○
Riverton . . . 9,247
Rock Springs . . . 19,458
Saratoga . . . 2,410
Sheridan . . . 15,146
Shirley Basin . . . 450 ○
Shoshoni . . . 879
Sinclair . . . 586
South Laramie . . . 1,500 ○
South Superior . . . 586
Story . . . 700 ○
Sundance . . . 1,087
Thermopolis . . . 3,852
Torrington . . . 5,441
Upton . . . 1,193
Wamsutter . . . 681
West Laramie . . . 2,000 ○
Wheatland . . . 5,816
Worland . . . 6,391

COUNTIES

Albany . . . 29,062
Big Horn . . . 11,896
Campbell . . . 24,367
Carbon . . . 21,896
Converse . . . 14,069
Crook . . . 5,308
Fremont . . . 38,992
Goshen . . . 12,040
Hot Springs . . . 5,710
Johnson . . . 6,700
Laramie . . . 68,649
Lincoln . . . 12,177
Natrona . . . 71,856
Niobrara . . . 2,924
Park . . . 21,639
Platte . . . 11,975
Sheridan . . . 25,048
Sublette . . . 4,548
Sweetwater . . . 41,723
Teton . . . 9,355
Uinta . . . 13,021
Washakie . . . 9,496
Weston . . . 7,106

○ Rand McNally estimate
▲ Population of entire township or "town", including rural areas.
● Independent city. Population not included in county total.

Largest Metropolitan Areas of the United States

This table ranks the largest cities of the United States according to metropolitan area population. The Ranally Metropolitan Area (RMA) populations reflect Rand McNally's exclusive definition of metropolitan areas. Each RMA includes one or more central cities, as well as socially and economically integrated surrounding areas. The table also indicates central city populations and compares the latest available data to the previous census. Populations are rounded totals. 1980 populations reflect final census data.

Rank 1980	Metropolitan Area	RMA Abbrev.	Metro Area Population Census 4/1/80	Census 4/1/70	%Change 1970-80	City Population Census 4/1/80	%Change 1970-80
1	New York, NY-NJ-CT	N.Y.	16,573,600	17,326,300	−4.3	7,538,200	−10.5
	New York, NY					7,071,000	−10.4
	Newark, NJ					329,200	−13.8
	Paterson, NJ					138,000	−4.7
2	Los Angeles, CA	L.A.	9,840,200	8,716,600	12.9	2,966,800	5.5
3	Chicago, IL-IN-WI	CHI	7,803,800	7,676,200	1.7	3,005,100	−10.8
4	Philadelphia-, PA-NJ-DE-MD	PHIL-	5,153,900	5,285,400	−2.5	1,850,500	−13.3
	Philadelphia, PA					1,688,200	−13.4
	Trenton, NJ					92,100	−12.1
	Wilmington, DE					70,200	−12.7
5	San Francisco-Oakland-San Jose, CA	SF-O-	4,665,500	4,274,900	9.1	1,654,900	7.7
	San Francisco, CA					679,000	−5.1
	Oakland, CA					339,300	−6.2
	San Jose, CA					636,600	38.4
6	Detroit, MI-CAN.	DET	4,399,000	4,492,900	−2.1	1,310,600	−18.8
	Detroit, MI					1,203,300	−20.5
	Ann Arbor, MI					107,300	7.3
7	Boston, MA-NH	BOS	3,738,800	3,763,700	−.7	898,900	−8.1
	Boston, MA					563,000	−12.2
	Lowell, MA					92,400	−1.9
	Lawrence, MA					63,200	−5.5
	Haverhill, MA					46,900	1.7
	Brockton, MA					95,200	7.0
	Salem, MA					38,200	−5.9
8	Washington, DC-MD-VA	WASH	3,220,700	2,992,600	7.6	637,700	−15.7
9	Dallas-Fort Worth, TX	D-FW	2,811,800	2,263,200	24.2	1,289,200	4.1
	Dallas, TX					904,100	7.1
	Fort Worth, TX					385,100	−2.1
10	Houston, TX	HOU	2,689,200	1,871,100	43.7	1,594,100	29.2
11	Miami-Fort Lauderdale, FL	MIA-	2,689,100	1,914,400	40.5	500,200	5.4
	Miami, FL					346,900	3.6
	Fort Lauderdale, FL					153,300	9.8
12	Cleveland, OH	CLEV	2,218,300	2,360,600	−6.0	573,800	−23.6
13	St. Louis, MO-IL	ST. L	2,216,100	2,295,700	−3.5	453,100	−27.2
14	Pittsburgh, PA	PGH	2,165,100	2,302,600	−6.0	423,900	−18.5
15	Seattle-Tacoma, WA	SEAT-	2,077,100	1,823,500	13.9	706,700	−4.3
	Seattle, WA					493,800	−7.0
	Tacoma, WA					158,500	2.7
	Everett, WA					54,400	1.5
16	Minneapolis-St. Paul, MN-WI	MPLS-	1,978,000	1,869,100	5.8	641,300	−13.8
	Minneapolis, MN					371,000	−14.6
	St. Paul, MN					270,300	−12.8
17	Atlanta, GA	ATL	1,950,600	1,541,300	26.6	425,000	−14.1
18	Baltimore, MD	BAL	1,883,100	1,865,100	1.0	786,800	−13.1
19	San Diego, CA-MEX.	SDGO	1,597,000	1,206,800	32.3	875,500	25.5
20	Phoenix, AZ	PHOE	1,483,500	950,500	56.1	764,900	30.9
21	Cincinnati-, OH-KY-IN	CIN-	1,476,600	1,445,300	2.2	448,700	−13.9
	Cincinnati, OH					385,500	−15.0
	Hamilton, OH					63,200	−6.9
[illegible]	Denver, CO	DEN	[illegible]	[illegible]	[illegible]	[illegible]	[illegible]

Rank 1980	Metropolitan Area	RMA Abbrev.	Metro Area Population Census 4/1/80	Census 4/1/70	%Change 1970-80	City Population Census 4/1/80	%Change 1970-80
	Warren, OH					56,600	−10.9
60	Tuscon, AZ	TUC	495,200	324,800	52.5	330,500	25.7
61	Knoxville-, TN	KNOX-	490,000	419,400	16.8	228,300	5.4
	Knoxville, TN					183,100	4.9
	Maryville, TN					17,500	26.8
	Oak Ridge, TN					27,700	−2.1
62	Grand Rapids, MI	GDR	488,200	444,300	9.9	181,800	−8.0
63	Springfield-Holyoke, MA	SPRG-	485,800	498,300	−2.5	197,000	−7.9
	Springfield, MA					152,300	−7.1
	Holyoke, MA					44,700	−10.8
64	El Paso, TX-NM-MEX.	ELP	484,300	358,600	35.1	425,300	32.0
65	Charlotte, NC	CHRLT	479,200	416,800	15.0	314,400	30.2
66	Scranton Wilkes-Barre, PA	SCR-	467,400	478,300	−2.3	139,700	−13.6
	Scranton, PA					88,100	−14.2
	Wilkes-Barre, PA					51,600	−12.4
67	Albuquerque, NM	ALBU	445,400	327,400	36.0	331,800	35.7
68	Bridgeport, CT	BRDG	444,600	445,500	−.2	142,500	−8.9
69	Baton Rouge, LA	B.R.	441,800	337,400	30.9	219,500	32.3
70	Las Vegas, NV	LASV	441,600	261,900	68.6	164,700	30.9
71	South Bend-Elkhart, IN-MI	S.B.-	437,500	422,800	3.5	151,000	−10.5
	South Bend, IN					109,700	−12.7
	Elkhart, IN					41,300	−4.4
72	Austin, TX	AUS	422,700	292,800	44.4	345,500	36.3
73	Harrisburg, PA	HRBG	404,600	371,700	8.9	53,300	−21.7
74	West Palm Beach, FL	WPB	394,600	236,600	66.8	62,500	8.9
75	Little Rock, AR	L.R.	380,800	310,500	22.6	158,500	19.6
76	Fresno, CA	FRES	377,900	306,100	23.5	218,200	31.7
77	Greensboro-High Point, NC	GRNS-	371,100	334,100	11.1	219,700	6.0
	Greensboro, NC					155,600	8.0
	High Point, NC					64,100	1.4
78	Wichita, KS	WICH	367,400	350,400	4.9	279,300	1.0
79	Worcester, MA	WORC	361,200	358,100	.9	161,800	−8.4
80	Chattanooga, TN-GA	CHTN	360,000	317,300	13.5	169,600	41.5
81	Mobile, AL	MOB	353,500	305,900	15.6	200,500	5.5
82	Charleston, SC	CHAS	349,100	280,500	24.5	69,500	3.9
83	Columbia, SC	COL	345,000	286,000	20.6	99,300	−12.5
84	Beaumont-Port Arthur-Orange, TX	B-PA-O	339,400	315,600	7.5	202,900	1.8
	Beaumont, TX					118,100	.5
	Port Arthur, TX					61,200	6.6
	Orange, TX					23,600	−3.7
85	Greenville, SC	GRNV	329,400	266,900	23.4	58,200	−5.2
86	Lansing, MI	LANS	329,200	303,200	8.6	130,400	−.8
87	Davenport-Rock I.-Moline, IA-IL	D-RI-M	328,200	310,900	5.6	196,000	.6
	Davenport, IA					103,300	4.9
	Rock Island, IL					47,000	−6.4
	Moline, IL					45,700	−1.1
88	Des Moines, IA	DES	323,200	300,700	7.5	191,000	−5.2
89	Ventura-Oxnard, CA	V-OX	321,400	242,000	32.8	182,700	41.4
	Ventura, CA					74,500	28.4

24	Kansas City, MO-KS	K.C.	1,254,600	1,222,700	2.6	448,200	−9.8
25	Portland, OR-WA	POR	1,220,100	997,800	22.3	366,400	−3.6
26	New Orleans, LA	N.O.	1,175,800	1,042,000	12.8	557,500	−6.1
27	Buffalo-Niagara Falls, NY-CAN.	BUF-	1,154,600	1,265,200	−8.7	429,300	−21.7
	Buffalo, NY					357,900	−22.7
	Niagara Falls, NY					71,400	−16.6
28	Indianapolis, IN	IND	1,104,200	1,053,100	4.9	700,800	−6.2
29	Hartford-New Britain, CT	H-NB	1,055,700	1,039,100	1.6	210,200	−12.9
	Hartford, CT					136,400	−13.7
	New Britain, CT					73,800	−11.5
30	San Antonio, TX	SANT	1,012,300	846,600	19.6	785,400	20.1
31	Columbus, OH	COL	943,300	886,700	6.4	564,900	4.6
32	Dayton-Springfield, OH	DAY-	898,000	934,000	−3.9	276,200	−15.0
	Dayton, OH					203,600	−16.2
	Springfield, OH					72,600	−11.4
33	Providence-, RI-MA	PROV-	897,900	891,200	.8	273,900	−9.6
	Providence, RI					156,800	−12.5
	Pawtucket, RI					71,200	−7.5
	Woonsocket, RI					45,900	−1.9
34	Louisville, KY-IN	LOU	881,100	848,500	3.8	298,500	−17.5
35	Sacramento, CA	SAC	848,800	684,000	24.1	275,700	7.2
36	Memphis, TN-AR-MS	MEM	843,200	772,400	9.2	646,400	3.6
37	Rochester, NY	ROCH	809,500	805,400	.5	241,700	−18.1
38	Norfolk-Portsmouth, VA	NORF-	795,600	725,800	9.6	371,600	−11.3
	Norfolk, VA					267,000	−13.3
	Portsmouth, VA					104,600	−5.8
39	Honolulu, HI	HON	762,900	630,500	21.0	365,000	12.3
40	Oklahoma City, OK	O.C.	742,000	627,300	18.3	403,200	9.5
41	Albany-Schenectady-Troy, NY	A-S-T	740,300	727,000	1.8	226,300	−11.8
	Albany, NY					101,700	−12.2
	Schenectady, NY					68,000	−12.8
	Troy, NY					56,600	−10.0
42	San Bernardino-Riverside, CA	SBDO-	715,300	577,000	24.0	289,000	17.0
	San Bernardino, CA					118,100	10.5
	Riverside, CA					170,900	22.0
43	St. Petersburg-, FL	ST. PET-	699,800	509,300	37.4	322,400	20.2
	St. Petersburg, FL					236,900	9.6
	Clearwater, FL					85,500	64.1
44	Birmingham, AL	BIR	697,900	666,200	4.8	284,400	−5.5
45	Salt Lake City, UT	S.L.C.	686,200	503,700	36.2	163,000	−7.3
46	Jacksonville, FL	JAX	615,300	548,500	12.2	540,900	7.3
47	Akron, OH	AKR	614,100	635,300	−3.3	237,200	−13.9
48	Nashville, TN	NASH	608,400	520,100	17.0	455,700	7.0
49	Tampa, FL	TAM	573,100	442,700	29.5	271,500	−2.2
50	Toledo, OH-MI	TOL	571,200	566,600	.8	354,600	−7.4
51	Tulsa, OK	TUL	569,100	460,300	23.6	360,900	−9.2
52	Orlando, FL	ORL	568,300	367,400	54.7	128,400	29.7
53	Flint, MI	FLN	550,200	523,300	5.1	159,600	−17.4
54	Omaha-Council Bluffs, NE-IA	OMA-	548,400	525,500	4.4	368,100	−9.6
	Omaha, NE					311,700	−10.1
	Council Bluffs, IA					56,400	−6.5
55	Richmond, VA	RICH	548,100	494,500	10.8	219,200	−12.1
56	Syracuse, NY	SYR	546,200	546,900	−.1	170,100	−13.8
57	Allentown-Bethlehem-Easton, PA-NJ	AL-B-E	534,200	504,300	5.9	200,200	−5.6
	Allentown, PA					103,800	−5.6
	Bethlehem, PA					70,400	−3.2
	Easton, PA					26,000	−11.9
58	New Haven-Meriden, CT	N. HAV-	500,500	488,700	2.4	183,200	−5.4
	New Haven, CT					126,100	−8.4
	Meriden, CT					57,100	2.0
59	Youngstown-Warren, OH-PA	YNGS-	497,000	505,400	−1.7	172,000	−15.9
	Youngstown, OH					115,400	−18.1
91	Spokane, WA-ID	SPOK	316,200	263,800	19.9	171,300	.5
92	Newport News-Hampton, VA	NN-H	314,600	299,100	5.2	267,500	3.3
	Newport News, VA					144,900	4.8
	Hampton, VA					122,600	1.5
93	Canton-Massillon, OH	CAN-	311,200	311,100	.0	125,300	−12.1
	Canton, OH					94,700	−14.0
	Massillon, OH					30,600	−5.8
94	Fort Wayne, IN	FTWA	307,700	292,500	5.2	172,200	−3.4
95	Colorado Springs, CO	CSPG	303,500	230,600	31.6	215,200	58.8
96	Shreveport, LA-TX	SHRE	299,000	266,500	12.2	205,800	13.0
97	Jackson, MS	JAC	295,000	238,800	23.5	202,900	31.8
98	Stockton, CA	STOC	291,500	241,800	20.6	149,800	36.2
99	Madison, WI	MAD	287,300	259,600	10.7	170,600	−.7
100	Sarasota-Bradenton, FL	SAR-B	284,200	187,800	51.3	79,100	29.2
	Sarasota, FL					48,900	21.6
	Bradenton, FL					30,200	43.8
101	Raleigh, NC	RAL	282,800	216,900	30.4	149,800	22.0
102	Winston-Salem, NC	WNS	278,400	236,700	17.6	131,900	−1.3
103	Corpus Christi, TX	CRPX	277,100	243,800	13.7	232,000	13.4
104	Lexington, KY	LEX	262,900	217,900	20.7	204,200	88.9
105	Huntington-Ashland, WV-KY-OH	HNTG-	261,900	248,200	5.5	90,800	−12.3
	Huntington, WV					63,700	−14.3
	Ashland, KY					27,100	−7.2
106	Utica-Rome, NY	UT-R	259,900	281,800	−7.8	119,400	−15.6
	Utica, NY					75,600	−17.3
	Rome, NY					43,800	−12.6
107	Charleston, WV	CHAS	249,300	238,800	4.4	64,000	−10.5
108	Rockford, IL	RKFD	247,500	244,900	1.1	139,700	−5.2
109	New London-Norwich, CT-RI	N. LON-	244,600	237,600	2.9	66,900	−8.7
	New London, CT					28,800	−8.9
	Norwich, CT					38,100	−8.6
110	Binghamton, NY-PA	BING	240,500	248,600	−3.3	55,900	−12.8
111	Augusta, GA-SC	AUG	238,200	209,500	13.7	47,500	−20.7
112	Erie, PA	ERIE	237,300	228,100	4.0	119,100	−7.9
113	Fayetteville, NC	FAY	236,200	202,700	16.5	59,500	11.2
114	Macon-, GA	MAC-	235,900	209,700	12.5	156,800	.6
	Macon, GA					116,900	−4.5
	Warner Robins, GA					39,900	19.1
115	Columbus, GA-AL	COL	235,100	231,600	1.5	169,400	1.7
116	Bakersfield, CA	BAK	231,700	187,600	23.5	105,600	51.9
117	Poughkeepsie, NY	POK	231,200	205,300	12.6	29,800	−6.9
118	Evansville, IN-KY	EV	230,400	214,100	7.6	130,500	−6.0
119	Pensacola, FL	PENS	229,200	199,000	15.2	57,600	−3.2
120	Portland, ME	POR	225,200	203,500	10.7	61,600	−5.4
121	Kalamazoo, MI	KZOO	223,600	208,800	7.1	79,700	−6.9
122	Montgomery, AL	MTGY	223,600	183,400	21.9	178,200	33.6
123	Ogden, UT	OGD	221,700	175,500	26.3	64,400	−7.3
124	York, PA	YORK	220,000	199,100	10.5	44,600	−11.3
125	Eugene, OR	EUG	216,900	171,400	26.5	105,600	33.7
126	Provo, UT	PRVO	214,400	133,500	60.6	73,900	39.2
127	Oceanside-Vista, CA	OC-V	214,100	130,900	63.6	112,500	72.5
	Oceanside, CA					76,700	89.4
	Vista, CA					35,800	44.9
128	Waterbury, CT	WATB	213,900	204,100	4.8	103,300	−4.4
129	Reading, PA	READ	213,500	212,400	.5	78,700	−10.2
130	Roanoke, VA	ROAN	213,300	190,500	12.0	100,400	9.0
131	Savannah, GA	SAV	210,400	192,900	9.1	141,600	19.7
132	Lancaster, PA	LANC	209,700	189,200	10.8	54,700	−5.2
133	Huntsville, AL	HNTS	203,800	193,000	5.6	142,500	2.3
134	Durham-Chapel Hill, NC	DUR-	203,100	170,000	19.5	133,200	9.5
	Durham, NC					100,800	5.7
	Chapel Hill, NC					32,400	23.7

Colleges and Universities of the United States

NOTE: This list includes all accredited four-year colleges and universities with 200 or more students. The colleges and universities are arranged in alphabetical order, by State. The city or town in which the college or university is located, or is associated with, appears in italic type. The student enrollment for each school is the last item in each entry. These figures are based on Fall 1979 enrollment.

ALABAMA

Alabama A & M University, *Normal* 4,300
Alabama State University, *Montgomery* 4,100
Athens State College, *Athens* 1,200
Auburn University
  Auburn University, *Auburn* 18,300
  Auburn University at *Montgomery* 4,800
Birmingham Southern College, *Birmingham* 1,400
Huntingdon College, *Montgomery* 700
Jacksonville State University, *Jacksonville* 7,100
Judson College, *Marion* 350
Livingston University, *Livingston* 1,200
Miles College, *Fairfield* 1,100
Mobile College, *Mobile* 1,100
Oakwood College, *Huntsville* 1,300
Samford University, *Homewood* 4,100
Selma University, *Selma* 300
Southeastern Bible College, *Birmingham* 240
Spring Hill College, *Mobile* 900
Stillman College, *Tuscaloosa* 650
Talladega College, *Talladega* 700
Troy State University
  Troy State University, *Troy* 6,400
  Troy State University of Dothan-Fort Rucker, *Dothan* ..1,600
  Troy State University at *Montgomery* 2,600
Tuskegee Institute, *Tuskegee* 3,400
University of Alabama
  University of Alabama, The, *Tuscaloosa* 17,600
  University of Alabama in *Birmingham* 13,600
  University of Alabama in *Huntsville* 4,700
University of Montevallo, *Montevallo* 2,800
University of North Alabama, *Florence* 5,200
University of South Alabama, *Mobile* 7,300

ALASKA

Alaska Pacific University, *Anchorage* 270
University of Alaska
  University of Alaska, *Fairbanks* 3,500
  University of Alaska Anchorage Campus, *Anchorage* ...3,100
  University of Alaska, *Juneau* 350

ARIZONA

American Graduate School of International Management, *Glendale* 1,000
Arizona State University, *Tempe* 37,800
Devry Institute of Technology, *Phoenix* 2,600
Grand Canyon College, *Phoenix* 1,200
Northern Arizona University, *Flagstaff* 12,600
Southwestern Baptist Bible College, *Phoenix* 220
University of Arizona, *Tucson* 29,500
University of Phoenix, *Phoenix* 220

ARKANSAS

Arkansas Baptist College, *Little Rock* 350
Arkansas College, *Batesville* 500
Arkansas State University, *Jonesboro* 7,200
Arkansas Tech University, *Russellville* 3,000
Central Baptist College, *Conway* 220
College of the Ozarks, *Clarksville* 550
Harding University, *Searcy* 3,000
Henderson State University, *Arkadelphia* 3,000
Hendrix College, *Conway* 1,000
John Brown University, *Siloam Springs* 750
Ouachita Baptist University, *Arkadelphia* 1,600
Philander Smith College, *Little Rock* 600
Southern Arkansas University, *Magnolia* 1,900
University of Arkansas
  University of Arkansas, *Fayetteville* 16,600
  University of Arkansas at *Little Rock* 10,000
  University of Arkansas at *Monticello* 1,800
  University of Arkansas at *Pine Bluff* 2,900
  University of Arkansas Medical Sciences Campus, *Little Rock* 1,300
University of Central Arkansas, *Conway* 5,500

CALIFORNIA

Armstrong College, *Berkeley* 350
Art Center College of Design, *Pasadena* 1,400
Azusa Pacific College, *Azusa* 2,000
Bethany Bible College, *Santa Cruz* 600
Biola College, *La Mirada* 3,200
Brooks Institute, *Santa Barbara* 800
California Baptist College, *Riverside* 750
California College of Arts & Crafts, *Oakland* 1,100
California College of Podiatric Medicine, *San Francisco* 400
California Institute of the Arts, *Valencia* 750
California Institute of Technology, *Pasadena* 1,700
California Lutheran College, *Thousand Oaks* 2,500
California Maritime Academy, *Vallejo* 500
California School of Professional Psychology
  California School of Professional Psychology at *Berkeley* .. 300
  California School of Professional Psychology at *Los Angeles* 300
  California School of Professional Psychology at *San Diego*.230
California State University and Colleges
  California State College—*Bakersfield* 3,100
  California State College—*San Bernardino* 4,200
  California State College—Stanislaus, *Turlock* 3,700
  California Polytechnic State University—San Luis Obispo 16,000
  California State Polytechnic University—*Pomona* 15,400
  California State University—*Chico* 13,500
  California State University—*Fresno* 14,800
  California State University—*Fullerton* 23,100
  California State University—*Hayward* 11,300
  California State University—*Long Beach* 30,900
  California State University—*Los Angeles* 22,400
  California State University—*Sacramento* 21,200
  California State University—Dominguez Hills, *Carson* ..7,200
  California State University—Northridge, *Los Angeles*..28,000
  Humboldt State University, *Arcata* 7,500
  San Diego State University, *San Diego* 31,900
  San Francisco State University, *San Francisco* 23,800
  San Jose State University, *San Jose* 25,800
  Sonoma State University, *Rohhert Park* 5,500
California Western School of Law, *San Diego* 700
Chapman College, *Orange* 5,200
Christian Heritage College, *El Cajon* 400
Claremont University Center
  Claremont Men's College, *Claremont* 800
  Claremont Graduate School, *Claremont* 1,500
  Harvey Mudd College, *Claremont* 500
  Pitzer College, *Claremont* 800
  Pomona College, *Claremont* 1,300

Scripps College, *Claremont* 600
Cogswell College, *San Francisco* 450
Coleman College, *San Diego* 300
College of Notre Dame, *Belmont* 1,300
Dominican College of San Rafael, *San Rafael* 650
Fielding Institute, *Santa Barbara* 300
Fresno Pacific College, *Fresno* 750
Fuller Theological Seminary, *Pasadena* 2,400
Golden Gate Baptist Theological Seminary, *Mill Valley* 550
Golden Gate University, *San Francisco* 9,600
Graduate Theological Union, *Berkeley* 400
Heald Engineering College, *San Francisco* 750
Holy Names College, *Oakland* 600
Jesuit School of Theology, *Berkeley* 270
John F. Kennedy University, *Orinda* 1,000
L.I.F.E. Bible College, *Los Angeles* 450
Lincoln University, *San Francisco* 600
Loma Linda University, *Loma Linda* 2,800
Loma Linda University La Sierra Campus, *Riverside* . . . 2,400
Los Angeles Baptist College, *Newhall* 400
Los Angeles College of Chiropractic, *Glendale* 700
Loyola Marymount University, *Los Angeles* 6,100
Melodyland School of Theology, *Anaheim* 240
Menlo College, *Menlo Park* 700
Mills College, *Oakland* 1,000
Monterey Institute of International Studies, *Monterey* 450
Mount St. Mary's College, *Los Angeles* 1,100
National University, *San Diego* 4,600
Naval Postgraduate School, *Monterey* 1,300
New College of California, *San Francisco* 400
Northrop University, *Inglewood* 1,500
Occidental College, *Los Angeles* 1,700
Otis Art Institute of Parsons School of Design, *Los Angeles* 230
Pacific Christian College, *Fullerton* 600
Pacific Lutheran Theological Seminary, *Berkeley* 200
Pacific Oaks College, *Pasadena* 290
Pacific Union College, *Angwin* 2,100
Pepperdine University
Pepperdine University, *Los Angeles* 4,000
Pepperdine University, *Malibu* 3,100
Point Loma College, *San Diego* 1,800
Saint John's College, *Camarillo* 200
St. Mary's College of California, *Moraga* 2,500
San Fernando Valley College of Law, *Los Angeles* 300
San Francisco Art Institute, *San Francisco* 750
San Francisco Conservatory of Music, *San Francisco* 220
San Francisco Theological Seminary, *San Anselmo* 1,000
San Jose Bible College, *San Jose* 210
School of Theology at *Claremont* 220
Simpson College, *San Francisco* 290
Southern California College, *Costa Mesa* 700
Southern California College of Optometry, *Fullerton* 350
Southern California Institute of Architecture, *Santa Monica* 300
Southwestern University School of Law, *Los Angeles* 1,600
Stanford University, *Stanford* 13,300
United States International University, *San Diego* 2,900
University of California
University of California—*Berkeley* 30,400
University of California—*Davis* 18,000
University of California—*Irvine* 10,000
University of California—*Los Angeles* 33,000
University of California—*Riverside* 4,600
University of California—*San Diego* 11,200
University of California—*San Francisco* 3,800
University of California—*Santa Barbara* 14,800
University of California—*Santa Cruz* 6,100
University of California Hastings College of Law, *San Francisco* 1,500
University of La Verne, *La Verne* 3,900
University of the Pacific, *Stockton* 6,000
University of Redlands, *Redlands* 3,200
University of San Diego, *San Diego* 4,100
University of San Francisco, *San Francisco* 6,300
University of Santa Clara, *Santa Clara* 7,100
University of Southern California, *Los Angeles* 26,900
University of West Los Angeles, *Culver City* 800
West Coast Bible College, *Fresno* 210
West Coast University
West Coast University, *Los Angeles* 850
West Coast University Orange County Center, *Orange* . . . 550
Western State University College of Law
Western State University College of Law Orange County, *Fullerton* 1,700
Western State University College of Law of San Diego, *San Diego* 950
Westmont College, *Santa Barbara* 1,000
Whittier College, *Whittier* 1,600
Woodbury University, *Los Angeles* 1,400

COLORADO

Adams State College, *Alamosa* 2,500
Baptist Bible College of Denver, *Broomfield* 210
Colorado College, *Colorado Springs* 1,900
Colorado School of Mines, *Golden* 2,800
Colorado State University, *Fort Collins* 18,300
Colorado Technical College, *Colorado Springs* 450
Colorado Women's College, *Denver* 450
Conservative Baptist Theological Seminary, *Englewood* 400
Fort Lewis College, *Durango* 3,100
Iliff School of Theology, *Denver* 350
Loretto Heights College, *Denver* 850
Mesa College, *Grand Junction* 3,900
Metropolitan State College, *Denver* 12,100
Regis College, *Denver* 1,400
Rockmont College, *Lakewood* 280
United States Air Force Academy, *Colorado Springs* 4,600
University of Colorado
University of Colorado at *Boulder* 21,700
University of Colorado at *Colorado Springs* 4,700
University of Colorado at *Denver* 8,700
University of Colorado Health Sciences Center, *Denver* . . 1,400
University of Denver, *Denver* 8,000
University of Northern Colorado, *Greeley* 11,000
University of Southern Colorado, *Pueblo* 4,500
Western Bible College, *Morrison* 210
Western State College of Colorado, *Gunnison* 3,200

CONNECTICUT

Albertus Magnus College, *New Haven* 550
Board for State Academic Awards, *Hartford* 950
Bridgeport Engineering Institute, *Bridgeport* 650
Central Connecticut State College, *New Britain* 12,100
Connecticut College, *New London* 1,900
Eastern Connecticut State College, *Willimantic* 3,000
Fairfield University, *Fairfield* 4,700
Hartford Graduate Center, *Hartford* 1,300
Post College, *Waterbury* 1,100
Quinnipiac College, *Hamden* 3,800
Sacred Heart University, *Bridgeport* 3,500
St. Joseph College, *West Hartford* 1,300
Southern Connecticut State College, *New Haven* 11,700
Trinity College, *Hartford* 2,100
United States Coast Guard Academy, *New London* 850
University of Bridgeport, *Bridgeport* 7,000
University of Connecticut
University of Connecticut, *Storrs* 21,700
University of Connecticut Health Center, *Farmington* 350
University of Hartford, *West Hartford* 10,500
University of New Haven, *West Haven* 7,500
Wesleyan University, *Middletown* 2,800
Western Connecticut State College, *Danbury* 5,500
Yale University, *New Haven* 9,700

DELAWARE

Delaware State College, *Dover* 2,100
Goldey Beacom College, *Wilmington* 1,500
University of Delaware, *Newark* 19,000
Wesley College, *Dover* 1,300
Wilmington College, *New Castle* 750

DISTRICT OF COLUMBIA

American University, *Washington* 12,200
Catholic University of America, *Washington* 8,300
Corcoran School of Art, *Washington* 210
Gallaudet College, *Washington* 1,300
Georgetown University, *Washington* 11,800
George Washington University, *Washington* 23,100
Howard University, *Washington* 10,600
Mount Vernon College, *Washington* 600
Southeastern University, *Washington* 1,500
Strayer College, *Washington* 1,600
Trinity College, *Washington* 800
University of the District of Columbia, *Washington* 15,100
Washington International College, *Washington* 270
Wesley Theological Seminary, *Washington* 350

FLORIDA

Barry College, *Miami Shores* 2,000
Bethune Cookman College, *Daytona Beach* 1,700
Biscayne College, *Opa-Locka* 2,200
College of Boca Raton, *Boca Raton* 550
Eckerd College, *St. Petersburg* 1,000
Edward Waters College, *Jacksonville* 600
Embry-Riddle Aeronautical University, *Daytona Beach*...6,100
Flagler College, *St. Augustine* 800
Florida Institute of Technology, *Melbourne* 5,100
Florida Memorial College, *Opa-Locka* 750
Florida Southern College, *Lakeland* 2,500
Fort Lauderdale College, *Fort Lauderdale* 1,000
Jacksonville University, *Jacksonville* 2,400
Jones College
  Jones College, *Jacksonville* 1,200
  Jones College, *Orlando* 1,500
Miami Christian College, *Miami* 300
Nova University, *Davie* 5,200
Palm Beach Atlantic College, *West Palm Beach* 450
Ringling School of Art, *Sarasota* 450
Rollins College, *Winter Park* 4,400
Saint Leo College, *Saint Leo* 4,300
Southeastern College of the Assemblies of God, *Lakeland* ..1,200
State University of Florida
  Florida A. and M. University, *Tallahassee* 5,300
  Florida Atlantic University, *Boca Raton* 7,300
  Florida International University, *Sweetwater* 11,500
  Florida State University, *Tallahassee* 21,500
  University of Central Florida, *Orlando* 12,000
  University of Florida, *Gainesville* 32,600
  University of North Florida, *Jacksonville* 4,600
  University of South Florida, *Tampa* 23,500
  University of West Florida, *Pensacola* 5,200
Stetson University, *DeLand* 2,100
  Stetson University Law School, *St. Petersburg* 500
Tampa College, *Tampa* 1,400
University of Miami, *Coral Gables* 15,400
University of Tampa, *Tampa* 2,100
Warner Southern College, *Lake Wales* 250

GEORGIA

Agnes Scott College, *Decatur* 550
Albany State College, *Albany* 1,600
Armstrong State College, *Savannah* 2,900
Atlanta Christian College, *East Point* 210
Atlanta College of Art, *Atlanta* 270
Atlanta University, *Atlanta* 1,400
Augusta College, *Augusta* 3,700
Berry College, *Mount Berry* 1,500
Brenau College, *Gainesville* 1,300
Clark College, *Atlanta* 2,000
Columbia Theological Seminary, *Decatur* 350
Columbus College, *Columbus* 4,700
Covenant College, *Lookout Mountain, TN* 500
Emory University, *Atlanta* 8,000
Fort Valley State College, *Fort Valley* 1,800
Georgia College, *Milledgeville* 3,300
Georgia Institute of Technology
  Georgia Institute of Technology, *Atlanta* 11,200
  Southern Technical Institute, *Marietta* 2,400
Georgia Southern College, *Statesboro* 6,700
Georgia Southwestern College, *Americus* 2,100
Georgia State University, *Atlanta* 20,300
Interdenominational Theological Center, *Atlanta* 290
Kennesaw College, *Marietta* 4,100
La Grange College, *La Grange* 900
Life Chiropractic College, *Marietta* 1,200
Medical College of Georgia, *Augusta* 2,000
Mercer University
  Mercer University, *Macon* 2,800
  Mercer University in *Atlanta* 1,400
  Southern School of Pharmacy, *Atlanta* 350
Morehouse College, *Atlanta* 1,800
Morris Brown College, *Atlanta* 1,600
North Georgia College, *Dahlonega* 1,900
Oglethorpe University, *North Atlanta* 1,100
Paine College, *Augusta* 800
Piedmont College, *Demorest* 400
Savannah State College, *Savannah* 2,100
Shorter College, *Rome* 800
Spelman College, *Atlanta* 1,300
Tift College, *Forsyth* 750
Toccoa Falls College, *Toccoa Falls* 600
University of Georgia, Athens 22,900
Valdosta State College, *Valdosta* 4,900
Wesleyan College, *Macon* 500
West Georgia College, *Carrollton* 5,100

HAWAII

Brigham Young University Hawaii Campus, *Laie* 1,800
Chaminade University of Honolulu, *Honolulu* 2,300
Hawaii Loa College, *Kaneohe* 300
Hawaii Pacific College, *Honolulu* 1,500
University of Hawaii
  University of Hawaii Hilo at *Hilo* 3,100
  University of Hawaii at Manoa, *Honolulu* 20,700
  University of Hawaii West Oahu College, *Aiea* 260

IDAHO

Boise State University, *Boise* 10,700
College of Idaho, *Caldwell* 700
Idaho State University, *Pocatello* 6,500
Lewis-Clark State College, *Lewiston* 1,500
Northwestern Nazarene College, *Nampa* 1,300
University of Idaho, *Moscow* 8,700

ILLINOIS

American Conservatory of Music, *Chicago* 400
Augustana College, *Rock Island* 2,400
Aurora College, *Aurora* 1,000
Barat College, *Lake Forest* 700
Blackburn College, *Carlinville* 450
Bradley University, *Peoria* 5,300
Catholic Theological Union, *Chicago* 230
Chicago College of Osteopathic Medicine, *Chicago* 400
Chicago State University, *Chicago* 7,200
College of St. Francis, *Joliet* 3,200
Columbia College, *Chicago* 3,100
Concordia Teachers College, *River Forest* 1,100
De Lourdes College, *Des Plaines* 280
DePaul University, *Chicago* 12,900
Devry Institute of Technology, *Chicago* 2,900
Eastern Illinois University, *Charleston* 10,500
Elmhurst College, *Elmhurst* 3,300
Eureka College, *Eureka* 450
Garrett-Evangelical Theological Seminary, *Evanston* 300
George Williams College, *Downers Grove* 1,300
Governors State University, *Park Forest South* 4,400

Greenville College, *Greenville* .850
Illinois Benedictine College, *Lisle* 2,000
Illinois College, *Jacksonville* 750
Illinois College of Optometry, *Chicago* 600
Illinois College of Podiatric Medicine, *Chicago* 650
Illinois Institute of Technology, *Chicago* 7,100
Illinois State University, *Normal* 20,500
Illinois Wesleyan University, *Bloomington* 1,700
John Marshall Law School, *Chicago* 1,600
Judson College, *Elgin* 500
Keller Graduate School of Management, *Chicago* 1,000
Kendall College, *Evanston* 450
Knox College, *Galesburg* 1,000
Lake Forest College, *Lake Forest* 1,100
Lewis University, *Romeoville* 2,800
Lincoln Christian College, *Lincoln* 650
Loyola University of *Chicago* 14,900
Lutheran School of Theology at *Chicago* 250
MacMurray College, *Jacksonville* 700
McCormick Theological Seminary, *Chicago* 700
McKendree College, *Lebanon* 800
Midwest College of Engineering, *Lombard* 200
Millikin University, *Decatur* 1,500
Monmouth College, *Monmouth* 700
Moody Bible Institute, *Chicago* 1,400
Mundelein College, *Chicago* 1,500
National College of Chiropractic, *Lombard* 1,000
National College of Education
  National College of Education, *Evanston* 1,300
  National College of Education Urban Campus, *Chicago* 210
North Central College, *Naperville* 1,100
Northeastern Illinois University, *Chicago* 10,100
Northern Illinois University, *De Kalb* 25,300
North Park College & Theological Seminary, *Chicago* 1,400
Northwestern University, *Evanston* 10,500
  Northwestern University, *Chicago* 5,200
Olivet Nazarene College, *Bourbonnais* 1,900
Principia College, *Elsah* 850
Quincy College, *Quincy* 1,000
Rockford College, *Rockford* 1,200
Roosevelt University, *Chicago* 7,000
Rosary College, *River Forest* 1,500
Rush University, *Chicago* 1,000
St. Louis University-Parks College, *Cahokia* 950
St. Xavier College, *Chicago* 2,100
Sangamon State University, *Springfield* 3,500
School of The Art Institute of Chicago, *Chicago* 1,700
Southern Illinois University
  Southern Illinois University at *Carbondale* 22,700
  Southern Illinois University at *Edwardsville* 10,500
Spertus College of Judaica, *Chicago* 290
Trinity Christian College, *Palos Heights* 400
Trinity College, *Bannockburn* 750
Trinity Evangelical Divinity School, *Bannockburn* 700
University of Chicago, *Chicago* 9,200
University of Health Sciences-Chicago Medical School, *Chicago* 700
University of Illinois
  University of Illinois Chicago Circle, *Chicago* 20,300
  University of Illinois Medical Center at *Chicago* 4,900
  University of Illinois Urbana Campus, *Urbana* 34,400
Western Illinois University, *Macomb* 13,000
Wheaton College, *Wheaton* 2,500

INDIANA

Anderson College, *Anderson* 2,000
Ball State University, *Muncie* 17,600
Bethel College, *Mishawaka* 500
Butler University, *Indianapolis* 3,700
Calumet College, *Whiting* 1,500
Christian Theological Seminary, *Indianapolis* 300
Concordia Theological Seminary, *Fort Wayne* 550
DePauw University, *Greencastle* 2,400
Earlham College, *Richmond* 1,000
Fort Wayne Bible College, *Fort Wayne* 450
Franklin College of Indiana, *Franklin* 650
Goshen College, *Goshen* 1,300
Grace College, *Winona Lake* 1,200
Hanover College, *Hanover* 1,000
Huntington College, *Huntington* 550
Indiana Central University, *Indianapolis* 3,000
Indiana Institute of Technology, *Fort Wayne* 500
Indiana State University
  Indiana State University, *Terre Haute* 12,100
  Indiana State University Evansville Campus, *Evansville* 3,000
Indiana University
  Indiana University at *Bloomington* 31,800
  Indiana University at *Kokomo* 2,300
  Indiana University Northwest, *Gary* 4,100
  Indiana University at *South Bend* 5,800
  Indiana University Southeast, *New Albany* 4,100
Indiana University-Purdue University at *Fort Wayne* 9,200
Indiana University-Purdue University at *Indianapolis* 21,500
Manchester College, *North Manchester* 1,200
Marian College, *Indianapolis* 900
Marion College, *Marion* 1,100
Oakland City College, *Oakland City* 550
Purdue University
  Purdue University, *West Lafayette* 32,000
  Purdue University Calumet, *Hammond* 6,600
  Purdue University North Central Campus, *Westville* 2,000
Rose-Hulman Institute of Technology, *Terre Haute* 1,200
St. Francis College, *Fort Wayne* 1,400
St. Joseph's College, *Collegeville* 950
St. Mary's College, *Notre Dame* 1,700
St. Mary of the Woods College, *St. Mary-of-the Woods* 550
St. Meinrad College, *St. Meinrad* 210
Taylor University, *Upland* 1,600
Tri-State University, *Angola* 1,300
University of Evansville, *Evansville* 4,900
University of Notre Dame, *Notre Dame* 8,800
Valparaiso University, *Valparaiso* 4,500
Wabash College, *Crawfordsville* 800

IOWA

Briar Cliff College, *Sioux City* 1,200
Buena Vista College, *Storm Lake* 1,300
Central University of Iowa, *Pella* 1,500
Clarke College, *Dubuque* 650
Coe College, *Cedar Rapids* 1,300
College of Osteopathic Medicine & Surgery, *Des Moines* 550
Cornell College, *Mount Vernon* 900
Dordt College, *Sioux Center* 1,200
Drake University, *Des Moines* 6,500
Faith Baptist Bible College, *Ankeny* 550
Graceland College, *Lamoni* 1,300
Grand View College, *Des Moines* 1,100
Grinnell College, *Grinnell* 1,300
Iowa State University of Science & Technology, *Ames* 24,000
Iowa Wesleyan College, *Mount Pleasant* 750
Loras College, *Dubuque* 1,800
Luther College, *Decorah* 2,100
Maharishi International University, *Fairfield* 800
Marycrest College, *Davenport* 900
Morningside College, *Sioux City* 1,400
Mount Mercy College, *Cedar Rapids* 1,000
Mount Saint Clare College, *Clinton* 300
Northwestern College, *Orange City* 850
Palmer College of Chiropractic, *Davenport* 1,700
St. Ambrose College, *Davenport* 2,000
Simpson College, *Indianola* 850
University of Dubuque, *Dubuque* 1,000
University of Iowa, *Iowa City* 24,200
University of Northern Iowa, *Cedar Falls* 11,100
Upper Iowa University, *Fayette* 1,800
Vennard College, *University Park* 220
Wartburg College, *Waverly* 1,100
Wartburg Theological Seminary, *Dubuque* 270
Westmar College, *LeMars* 650
William Penn College, *Oskaloosa* 600

KANSAS

Baker University, *Baldwin City* 1,000

Benedictine College, *Atchison* 1,000
Bethany College, *Lindsborg* 850
Bethel College, *North Newton* 650
Emporia State University, *Emporia* 6,200
Fort Hays State University, *Hays* 5,600
Friends University, *Wichita* 900
Kansas Newman College, *Wichita* 650
Kansas State University of Agriculture & Applied Science,
Manhattan 18,600
Kansas Wesleyan, *Salina* 450
Manhattan Christian College, *Manhattan* 260
Marymount College of Kansas, *Salina* 800
McPherson College, *McPherson* 500
Mid-American Nazarene College, *Olathe* 1,300
Ottawa University, *Ottawa* 900
Pittsburg State University, *Pittsburg* 5,600
St. Mary College, *Leavenworth* 750
St. Mary of the Plains College, *Dodge City* 650
Southwestern College, *Winfield* 650
Sterling College, *Sterling* 500
Tabor College, *Hillsboro* 450
United States Army Command & General Staff College,
Fort Leavenworth 750
University of Kansas
University of Kansas, *Lawrence* 24,100
University of Kansas Medical Center, *Kansas City* 2,100
Washburn University of Topeka, *Topeka* 5,800
Wichita State University, *Wichita* 16,600

KENTUCKY

Alice Lloyd College, *Pippa Passes* 230
Asbury College, *Wilmore* 1,200
Asbury Theological Seminary, *Wilmore* 750
Bellarmine College, *Louisville* 2,100
Berea College, *Berea* 1,400
Brescia College, *Owensboro* 850
Campbellsville College, *Campbellsville* 650
Centre College of Kentucky, *Danville* 750
Cumberland College, *Williamsburg* 2,100
Eastern Kentucky University, *Richmond* 13,700
Georgetown College, *Georgetown* 1,200
Kentucky Christian College, *Grayson* 450
Kentucky State University, *Frankfort* 2,200
Kentucky Wesleyan College, *Owensboro* 900
Morehead State University, *Morehead* 7,100
Murray State University, *Murray* 7,800
Northern Kentucky University, *Highland Heights* 7,500
Pikeville College, *Pikeville* 600
Southern Baptist Theological Seminary, *Louisville* 2,000
Spalding College, *Louisville* 900
Thomas More College, *Crestview Hills* 1,300
Transylvania University, *Lexington* 800
Union College, *Barbourville* 900
University of Kentucky, *Lexington* 22,500
University of Louisville, *Louisville* 19,200
Western Kentucky University, *Bowling Green* 13,400

LOUISIANA

Centenary College of Louisiana, *Shreveport* 950
Dillard University, *New Orleans* 1,200
Grambling State University, *Grambling* 3,300
Louisiana College, *Pineville* 1,300
Louisiana State University
Louisiana State University and A. & M. College,
Baton Rouge 26,300
Louisiana State University Medical Center, *New Orleans* . 2,500
Louisiana State University, *Shreveport* 3,500
University of New Orleans, *New Orleans* 14,400
Louisiana Technological University, *Ruston* 9,300
Loyola University in *New Orleans* 4,500
McNeese State University, *Lake Charles* 5,100
New Orleans Baptist Theological Seminary, *New Orleans* .. 1,200
Nicholls State University, *Thibodaux* 6,500
Northeast Louisiana University, *Monroe* 9,200
Northwestern State University of Louisiana, *Natchitoches* . 6,100
Our Lady of Holy Cross College, *New Orleans* 750
St. Mary's Dominican College, *New Orleans* 700
Southeastern Louisiana University, *Hammond* 7,400
Southern University Agricultural & Mechanical College
Southern University A & M College, *Scotlandville* 8,100
Southern University in *New Orleans* 2,600
Tulane University of Louisiana, *New Orleans* 10,200
University of Southwestern Louisiana, *Lafayette* 13,300
Xavier University of Louisiana, *New Orleans* 1,900

MAINE

Bates College, *Lewiston* 1,500
Bowdoin College, *Brunswick* 1,400
Colby College, *Waterville* 1,700
Husson College, *Bangor* 1,300
Maine Maritime Academy, *Castine* 650
Nasson College, *Springvale* 600
Portland School of Art, *Portland* 230
St. Joseph's College, *North Windham* 450
Thomas College, *Waterville* 900
Unity College, *Unity* 650
University of Maine
University of Maine at *Farmington* 2,000
University of Maine at *Fort Kent* 600
University of Maine at *Machias* 750
University of Maine at *Orono* 11,600
University of Maine at *Presque Isle* 1,400
University of Southern Maine, *Portland* 8,000
University of New England, *Biddeford* 500
Westbrook College, *Portland* 950

MARYLAND

Bowie State College, *Bowie* 2,900
Capitol Institute of Technology, *Kensington* 700
College of Notre Dame of Maryland, *Baltimore* 1,100
Columbia Union College, *Takoma Park* 900
Coppin State College, *Baltimore* 2,800
Frostburg State College, *Frostburg* 3,600
Goucher College, *Towson* 1,000
Hood College, *Frederick* 1,800
Johns Hopkins University, *Baltimore* 9,500
Loyola College, *Baltimore* 5,200
Maryland Institute College of Art, *Baltimore* 950
Morgan State University, *Baltimore* 5,000
Mount St. Mary's College, *Emmitsburg* 1,700
Ner Israel Rabbinical College, *Baltimore* 260
Peabody Institute of John Hopkins University, *Baltimore* .. 450
St. John's College, *Annapolis* 400
St. Mary's College of Maryland, *St. Mary's City* 1,300
St. Mary's Seminary & University, *Baltimore* 300
Salisbury State College, *Salisbury* 4,400
Towson State University, *Towson* 15,300
United States Naval Academy, *Annapolis* 4,500
University of Baltimore, *Baltimore* 5,400
University of Maryland
University of Maryland Baltimore County Campus,
Catonsville 6,400
University of Maryland Baltimore Professional Schools,
Baltimore 4,800
University of Maryland College Park Campus,
College Park 37,200
University of Maryland-Eastern Shore, *Princess Anne* .. 1,100
University of Maryland University College,
College Park 11,700
Washington Bible College, *Lanham* 550
Washington College, *Chestertown* 800
Western Maryland College, *Westminster* 2,000

MASSACHUSETTS

American International College, *Springfield* 2,200

Amherst College, *Amherst* . . . 1,500
Andover Newton Theological School, *Newton* . . . 450
Anna Maria College, *Paxton* . . . 1,300
Assumption College, *Worcester* . . . 2,300
Atlantic Union College, *South Lancaster* . . . 600
Babson College, *Wellesley* . . . 3,000
Bentley College, *Waltham* . . . 6,400
Berklee College of Music, *Boston* . . . 2,600
Boston College, *Newton* . . . 14,000
Boston Conservatory of Music, *Boston* . . . 400
Boston University, *Boston* . . . 26,700
Bradford College, *Haverhill* . . . 350
Brandeis University, *Waltham* . . . 3,500
Central New England College of Technology, *Worcester* . . . 250
Clark University, *Worcester* . . . 3,200
College of the Holy Cross, *Worcester* . . . 2,500
College of our Lady of the Elms, *Chicopee* . . . 500
Curry College, *Milton* . . . 1,200
Eastern Nazarene College, *Quincy* . . . 800
Emerson College, *Boston* . . . 1,900
Emmanuel College, *Boston* . . . 1,100
Gordon College, *Wenham* . . . 1,000
Gordon-Conwell Theological Seminary, *South Hamilton* . . . 650
Hampshire College, *Amherst* . . . 1,300
Harvard University, *Cambridge* . . . 17,500
Lesley College, *Cambridge* . . . 2,600
Massachusetts College of Pharmacy and
  Allied Health Sciences, *Boston* . . . 1,300
Massachusetts Institute of Technology, *Cambridge* . . . 9,100
Massachusetts State College
  Boston State College, *Boston* . . . 9,500
  Bridgewater State College, *Bridgewater* . . . 7,300
  Fitchburg State College, *Fitchburg* . . . 5,700
  Framingham State College, *Framingham* . . . 6,100
  Massachusetts College of Art, *Boston* . . . 2,000
  Massachusetts Maritime Academy, *Buzzards Bay* . . . 900
  North Adams State College, *North Adams* . . . 3,000
  Salem State College, *Salem* . . . 8,100
  Westfield State College, *Westfield* . . . 4,200
  Worcester State College, *Worcester* . . . 5,300
Merrimack College, *North Andover* . . . 3,500
Mount Holyoke College, *South Hadley* . . . 2,000
New England College of Optometry, *Boston* . . . 350
New England Conservatory of Music, *Boston* . . . 850
New England School of Law, *Boston* . . . 950
Nichols College, *Dudley Hill* . . . 1,000
Northeastern University, *Boston* . . . 40,600
Pine Manor College, *Brookline* . . . 600
Radcliffe College, *Cambridge* . . . 2,300
Regis College, *Weston* . . . 1,200
School of the Museum of Fine Arts—*Boston* . . . 800
Simmons College, *Boston* . . . 2,800
Simon's Rock Early College, *Great Barrington* . . . 200
Smith College, *Northampton* . . . 3,000
Southeastern Massachusetts University, *North Dartmouth* . 7,400
Springfield College, *Springfield* . . . 2,700
Stonehill College, *North Easton* . . . 2,600
Suffolk University, *Boston* . . . 6,300
Tufts University, *Medford* . . . 5,500
  Tufts University, *Boston* . . . 1,300
University of Lowell, *Lowell* . . . 10,700
University of Massachusetts
  University of Massachusetts Amherst Campus,
    Amherst . . . 24,000
  University of Massachusetts Boston Campus, *Boston* . . . 8,100
  University of Massachusetts Medical School at *Worcester* . 400
Wellesley College, *Wellesley* . . . 2,200
Wentworth Institute of Technology, *Boston* . . . 2,600
Western New England College, *Springfield* . . . 5,200
Wheaton College, *Norton* . . . 1,200
Wheelock College, *Boston* . . . 950
Williams College, *Williamstown* . . . 2,000
Worcester Polytechnic Institute, *Worcester* . . . 3,400

MICHIGAN

Adrian College, *Adrian* . . . 950
Albion College, *Albion* . . . 1,800
Alma College, *Alma* . . . 1,200
Andrews University, *Berrien Springs* . . . 3,000
Aquinas College, *Grand Rapids* . . . 2,200
Calvin College, *Grand Rapids* . . . 4,000
Center for Creative Studies, *Detroit* . . . 1,000
Central Michigan University, *Mount Pleasant* . . . 17,600
Cleary College, *Ypsilanti* . . . 600
Concordia College, *Ann Arbor* . . . 550
Detroit Bible College, *Farmington Hills* . . . 400
Detroit College of Business Administration, *Dearborn* . . . 2,200
Detroit College of Law, *Detroit* . . . 800
Detroit Institute of Technology, *Detroit* . . . 850
Eastern Michigan University, *Ypsilanti* . . . 20,100
Ferris State College, *Big Rapids* . . . 10,600
General Motors Institute, *Flint* . . . 2,200
Grand Rapids Baptist College & Seminary, *Grand Rapids* . . 1,200
Grand Valley State College, *Allendale* . . . 7,100
Great Lakes Bible College, *Lansing* . . . 220
Hillsdale College, *Hillsdale* . . . 1,000
Hope College, *Holland* . . . 2,500
Kalamazoo College, *Kalamazoo* . . . 1,400
Kendall School of Design, *Grand Rapids* . . . 400
Lake Superior State College, *Sault Ste. Marie* . . . 2,300
Lawrence Institute of Technology, *Southfield* . . . 5,000
Madonna College, *Livonia* . . . 3,100
Marygrove College, *Detroit* . . . 950
Mercy College of Detroit, *Detroit* . . . 2,300
Michigan State University, *East Lansing* . . . 47,400
Michigan Technological University, *Houghton* . . . 7,700
Nazareth College, *Kalamazoo* . . . 500
Northern Michigan University, *Marquette* . . . 9,500
Northwood Institute, *Midland* . . . 1,800
Oakland University, *Rochester* . . . 11,700
Olivet College, *Olivet* . . . 650
Reformed Bible College, *Grand Rapids* . . . 210
Saginaw Valley State College, *Saginaw* . . . 3,800
Saint Mary's College, *Orchard Lake Village* . . . 210
Shaw College at *Detroit* . . . 600
Siena Heights College, *Adrian* . . . 1,200
Spring Arbor College, *Spring Arbor* . . . 1,000
Thomas M. Cooley Law School, *Lansing* . . . 1,100
University of Detroit, *Detroit* . . . 7,000
University of Michigan
  University of Michigan—*Ann Arbor* . . . 36,200
  University of Michigan—*Dearborn* . . . 6,400
  University of Michigan—*Flint* . . . 4,100
Walsh College of Accountancy and Business
  Administration, *Troy* . . . 1,600
Wayne State University, *Detroit* . . . 33,400
Western Michigan University, *Kalamazoo* . . . 22,800

MINNESOTA

Augsburg College, *Minneapolis* . . . 1,600
Bethany College and Seminary
  Bethel College, *St. Paul* . . . 2,000
  Bethel Theological Seminary, *St. Paul* . . . 450
Carleton College, *Northfield* . . . 1,700
College of St. Benedict, *St. Joseph* . . . 2,000
College of St. Catherine, *St. Paul* . . . 2,300
College of St. Scholastica, *Duluth* . . . 1,200
College of St. Teresa, *Winona* . . . 750
College of St. Thomas, *St. Paul* . . . 4,800
Concordia College at *Moorhead* . . . 2,600
Concordia College—St. Paul, *St. Paul* . . . 650
Dr. Martin Luther College, *New Ulm* . . . 850
Gustavus Adolphus College, *St. Peter* . . . 2,300
Hamline University, *St. Paul* . . . 1,700
Luther Theological Seminary, *St. Paul* . . . 600
Macalester College, *St. Paul* . . . 1,800
Minneapolis College of Art Design, *Minneapolis* . . . 650
North Central Bible College, *Minneapolis* . . . 600
Northwestern College, *Roseville* . . . 700
Northwestern College of Chiropractic, *St. Paul* . . . 400
Northwestern Lutheran Theological Seminary, *St. Paul* . . . 210
St. John's University, *Collegeville* . . . 2,000
St. Mary's College, *Winona* . . . 1,400
St. Olaf College, *Northfield* . . . 3,000

St. Paul Bible College, *St. Bonifacius* 650
State University of Minnesota
Bemidji State University, *Bemidji* 5,500
Mankato State University, *Mankato* 12,000
Metropolitan State University, *St. Paul* 2,000
Moorhead State University, *Moorhead* 6,100
St. Cloud State University, *St. Cloud* 11,000
Southwest State University, *Marshall* 2,100
Winona State University, *Winona* 5,100
United Theological Seminary, *New Brighton* 230
University of Minnesota
University of Minnesota at *Duluth* 9,100
University of Minnesota at *Morris* 1,600
University of Minnesota Mayo Graduate School of Medicine, *Rochester* 450
University of Minnesota of Minneapolis St. Paul, *Minneapolis* 63,700
Wm. Mitchell College of Law, *St. Paul* 1,100

MISSISSIPPI

Alcorn State University, *Lorman* 2,200
Belhaven College, *Jackson* 900
Blue Mountain College, *Blue Mountain* 400
Delta State University, *Cleveland* 3,200
Jackson State University, *Jackson* 7,800
Millsaps College, *Jackson* 900
Mississippi College, *Clinton* 3,100
Mississippi Industrial College, *Holly Springs* 230
Mississippi State University, *State College* 12,500
Mississippi University for Women, *Columbus* 2,300
Mississippi Valley State University, *Itta Bena* 2,700
Reformed Theological Seminary, *Jackson* 250
Rust College, *Holly Springs* 650
Tougaloo College, *Tougaloo* 900
University of Mississippi
University of Mississippi, *Oxford* 9,600
University of Mississippi Medical Center, *Jackson* 1,500
University of Southern Mississippi
University of Southern Mississippi, *Hattiesburg* 9,700
University of Southern Mississippi, *Natchez* 280
University of Southern Mississippi Gulf Park, *Long Beach* 1,200
William Carey College, *Hattiesburg* 1,800

MISSOURI

Assemblies of God Graduate School, *Springfield* 200
Avila College, *Kansas City* 2,000
Baptist Bible College, *Springfield* 2,000
Calvary Bible College, *Kansas City* 500
Central Bible College, *Springfield* 1,100
Central Methodist College, *Fayette* 650
Central Missouri State University, *Warrensburg* 9,900
Christ Seminary-Seminex, *St. Louis* 200
Cleveland Chiropractic College, *Kansas City* 240
Columbia College, *Columbia* 2,300
Concordia Seminary, *Clayton* 650
Culver-Stockton College, *Canton* 450
Drury College, *Springfield* 2,300
Eden Theological Seminary, *Webster Groves* 220
Evangel College, *Springfield* 1,600
Fontbonne College, *Clayton* 800
Hannibal-La Grange College, *Hannibal* 400
Harris Stowe State College, *St. Louis* 1,100
Kansas City Art Institute, *Kansas City* 600
Kirksville College of Osteopathic Medicine, *Kirksville* 500
Lincoln University, *Jefferson City* 2,400
Lindenwood Colleges, The, *St. Charles* 1,700
Logan College of Chiropractic, *Chesterfield* 550
Maryville College-St Louis, *St. Louis* 1,400
Midwestern Baptist Theological Seminary, *Kansas City* 400
Missouri Baptist College, *Creve Coeur* 450
Missouri Institute of Technology, *Kansas City* 950
Missouri Southern State College, *Joplin* 3,800
Missouri Valley College, *Marshall* 350
Missouri Western State College, *St. Joseph* 3,800
Nazarene Theological Seminary, *Kansas City* 450
Northeast Missouri State University, *Kirksville* 6,200
Northwest Missouri State University, *Maryville* 4,300
Park College, *Parkville* 5,500
Rockhurst College, *Kansas City* 3,700
St. Louis College of Pharmacy, *St. Louis* 700
St. Louis University, *St. Louis* 9,400
School of the Ozarks, *Point Lookout* 1,400
Southeast Missouri State University, *Cape Girardeau* 8,900
Southwest Baptist College, *Bolivar* 1,400
Southwest Missouri State University, *Springfield* 14,500
Stephens College, *Columbia* 1,500
Tarkio College, *Tarkio* 600
University of Health Sciences College of Osteopathic Medicine, *Kansas City* 600
University of Missouri
University of Missouri—*Columbia* 23,500
University of Missouri—*Kansas City* 10,800
University of Missouri—*Rolla* 6,100
University of Missouri—St. Louis, *Bellerive* 11,400
Washington University, *University City* 10,500
Webster College, *Webster Groves* 3,700
Westminster College, *Fulton* 600
William Jewell College, *Liberty* 1,700
William Woods College, *Fulton* 900

MONTANA

Big Sky Bible College, *Lewistown* 210
Carroll College, *Helena* 1,300
College of Great Falls, *Great Falls* 1,100
Montana University
Eastern Montana College, *Billings* 4,400
Montana College of Mineral Science & Technology, *Butte* 1,400
Montana State University, *Bozeman* 10,100
Northern Montana College, *Havre* 1,200
University of Montana, *Missoula* 8,700
Western Montana College, *Dillon* 800
Rocky Mountain College, *Billings* 500

NEBRASKA

Bellevue College, *Bellevue* 2,300
Chadron State College, *Chadron* 2,000
College of St. Mary, *Omaha* 600
Concordia Teachers College, *Seward* 1,200
Creighton University, *Omaha* 5,400
Dana College, *Blair* 500
Doane College, *Crete* 700
Grace College of the Bible, *Omaha* 450
Hastings College, *Hastings* 800
Kearney State College, *Kearney* 6,800
Midland Lutheran College, *Fremont* 800
Nebraska Wesleyan University, *Lincoln* 1,200
Peru State College, *Peru* 750
Union College, *Lincoln* 900
University of Nebraska
University of Nebraska—*Lincoln* 23,700
University of Nebraska at *Omaha* 14,700
University of Nebraska Medical Center, *Omaha* 2,500
Wayne State College, *Wayne* 2,400

NEVADA

Sierra Nevada College, *Incline Village* 270
University of Nevada
University of Nevada—Las Vegas, *Paradise* 9,200
University of Nevada—*Reno* 8,500

NEW HAMPSHIRE

Colby-Sawyer College, *New London* 650
Daniel Webster College, *Nashua* 700
Dartmouth College, *Hanover* 4,200
Franklin Pierce College, *Rindge* 900
Franklin Pierce Law Center, *Concord* 350
Nathaniel Hawthorne College, *Antrim* 550
New England College, *Henniker* 1,700
New Hampshire College, *Manchester* 4,200
Notre Dame College, *Manchester* 700
Rivier College, *Nashua* 1,700
St. Anselm College, *Pinardville* 1,900
University of New Hampshire
  University of New Hampshire, *Durham* 12,400
  University of New Hampshire, Keene State College, *Keene* 3,200
University of New Hampshire, Plymouth State College, *Plymouth* 3,200

NEW JERSEY

Beth Medrash Govoha, *Lakewood* 850
Bloomfield College, *Bloomfield* 2,300
Caldwell College, *Caldwell* 650
Centenary College, *Hackettstown* 800
College of Medicine and Dentistry of New Jersey at *Newark* 1,600
College of St. Elizabeth, *Convent Station* 800
Drew University, *Madison* 2,300
Fairleigh Dickinson University
  Fairleigh Dickinson University, *Madison* 5,000
  Fairleigh Dickinson University, *Rutherford* 5,200
  Fairleigh Dickinson University, *Teaneck* 8,700
Felician College, *Lodi* 750
Georgian Court College, *Lakewood* 1,300
Glassboro State College, *Glassboro* 10,500
Immaculate Conception Seminary, *Mahwah* 220
Jersey City State College, *Jersey City* 9,500
Kean College of New Jersey, *Union* 13,500
Monmouth College, *West Long Branch* 3,700
Montclair State College, *Montclair* 14,800
New Jersey Institute of Technology, *Newark* 5,900
Northeastern Bible College, *Essex Falls* 350
Princeton Theological Seminary, *Princeton* 850
Princeton University, *Princeton* 6,100
Rabbinical College of America, *Morristown* 220
Ramapo College of New Jersey, *Mahwah* 4,300
Rider College, *Lawrenceville* 5,600
Rutgers The State University of New Jersey
  Rutgers The State University of New Jersey Camden Campus, *Camden* 5,400
  Rutgers The State University of New Jersey Newark Campus, *Newark* 10,100
  Rutgers The State University of New Jersey New Brunswick Campus, *New Brunswick* 33,700
St. Peter's College, *Jersey City* 4,000
Seton Hall University, *South Orange* 9,400
  Seton Hall-School of Law, *Newark* 1,100
Stevens Institute of Technology, *Hoboken* 2,600
Stockton State College, *Pomona* 4,800
Thomas A. Edison College, *Trenton* 4,300
Trenton State College, *Ewing Township* 10,600
Upsala College, *East Orange* 1,800
Westminster Choir College, *Princeton* 450
William Paterson College, *Wayne* 12,600

NEW MEXICO

College of Santa Fe, *Santa Fe* 1,200
Eastern New Mexico University, *Portales* 3,800
New Mexico Highlands University, *Las Vegas* 2,200
New Mexico Institute of Mining & Technology, *Socorro* 1,200
New Mexico State University, *Las Cruces* 13,200
St. Johns College at *Santa Fe* 300
University of Albuquerque, *Albuquerque* 2,100
University of New Mexico, *Albuquerque* 22,100
Western New Mexico University, *Silver City* 1,600

NEW YORK

Adelphi University, *Garden City* 11,800
Albany College of Pharmacy, *Albany* 600
Albany Law School, *Albany* 700
Albany Medical College, *Albany* 600
Alfred University
  Alfred University, *Alfred* 1,400
  New York State College of Ceramics at Alfred University, *Alfred* 700
Bank Street College of Education, *New York* 550
Bard College, *Annandale-On-Hudson* 700
Beth Jacob Hebrew Teachers College, *New York* 350
Boricua College, *New York* 700
Brooklyn Law School, *New York* 1,100
Canisius College, *Buffalo* 4,000
Central Yeshiva Tomchei Tmimim Lubavitz, *New York* 350
City Universities of New York
  CUNY Bernard Baruch College, *New York* 14,700
  CUNY Brooklyn College, *New York* 18,100
  CUNY City College, *New York* 13,200
  CUNY College of Staten Island, *New York* 10,400
  CUNY Graduate School and University Center, *New York* 2,800
  CUNY Hunter College, *New York* 18,000
  CUNY John Jay College of Criminal Justice, *New York* 6,400
  CUNY Lehman College, *New York* 9,300
  CUNY Medgar Evers College, *New York* 3,000
  CUNY Queens College, *New York* 18,800
  CUNY York College, *New York* 3,800
  Sinai School of Medicine of CUNY, *New York* 450
Clarkson College of Technology, *Potsdam* 3,600
Colgate Rochester Divinity School—Bexley Hall—Crozer Theological Seminary, *Rochester* 210
Colgate University, *Hamilton* 2,400
College of Insurance, *New York* 1,900
College of Mount St. Vincent, *New York* 1,300
College of New Rochelle, *New Rochelle* 4,500
College of St. Rose, *Albany* 2,800
Columbia University
  Barnard College, *New York* 2,400
  Columbia University, *New York* 17,400
  Columbia University Teachers College, *New York* 4,900
Concordia College, *Bronxville* 450
Cooper Union, *New York* 900
Cornell University
  Cornell University Endowed Colleges, *Ithaca* 10,200
  Cornell University Medical Center, *New York* 550
  Cornell University Statutory Colleges, *Ithaca* 8,000
Daemen College, *Amherst* 1,400
Dominican College of Blauvelt, *Orangeburg* 1,200
Dowling College, *Oakdale* 2,300
D'Youville College, *Buffalo* 1,500
Elmira College, *Elmira* 2,700
Fashion Institute of Technology, *New York* 9,800
Fordham University, *New York* 14,600
Hamilton College, *Clinton* 1,600
Hartwick College, *Oneonta* 1,400
Hobart-Wm. Smith Colleges, *Geneva* 1,900
Hofstra University, *Hempstead* 11,200
Houghton College, *Houghton* 1,100
Iona College, *New Rochelle* 5,700
Ithaca College, *Ithaca* 4,800
Jewish Theological Seminary of America, *New York* 450
Juilliard School, The, *New York* 1,300
Kehilath Yakov Rabbinical Seminary, *New York* 210
Keuka College, *Keuka Park* 550
King's College, *Briarcliff Manor* 850
Le Moyne College, *De Witt* 1,900
Long Island University
  Long Island University Brooklyn Center, *New York* 8,900
  Long Island University CW Post Center, *Brookville* 12,900
  Long Island University Southampton Center, *Southampton* 1,400
Manhattan College, *New York* 4,900

Manhattan School of Music, *New York* 750
Manhattanville College, *Purchase* 1,300
Mannes College of Music, *New York* 400
Marist College, *Fairview* 2,200
Marymount College, *Tarrytown* 1,200
Marymount Manhattan College, *New York* 2,300
Medaille College, *Buffalo* 650
Mercy College, *Dobbs Ferry* 8,300
Mesivta Torah Vodaath Seminary, *New York* 550
Mirrer Yeshiva Central Institute, *New York* 350
Molloy College, *Rockville Centre* 1,500
Mount St. Mary College, *Newburgh* 1,100
Nazareth College of Rochester, *Rochester* 2,600
New School for Social Research, *New York* 3,500
New York Chiropractic College, *Glen Head* 750
New York College of Podiatric Medicine, *New York* 450
New York Institute of Technology
  New York Institute of Technology, *Old Westbury* 7,900
  New York Institute of Technology, *New York* 2,700
New York Law School, *New York* 1,300
New York Medical College, *Valhalla* 1,100
New York School of Interior Design, *New York* 800
New York Theological Seminary, *New York* 210
New York University, *New York* 32,500
Niagara University, *Niagara Falls* 3,900
Nyack College, *South Nyack* 750
Pace University
  Pace University-White Plains Campus, *White Plains* ..2,700
  Pace University New York Campus, *New York* 12,900
  Pace University Pleasantville-Briarcliff Campus, *Pleasantville* 5,200
Parsons School of Design, *New York* 2,200
Polytechnic Institute of New York, *New York* 4,700
Pratt Institute, *New York* 4,400
Rabbi Isaac Elchanan Theological Seminary, *New York* 210
Rabbinical Academy Mesivta Rabbi Chaim Berlin, *New York* 200
Rabbinical College Bobover Yeshiva B'nei Zion, *New York* 400
Rabbinical Seminary of Munkacs, *New York* 240
Rensselaer Polytechnic Institute, *Troy* 6,400
Roberts Wesleyan College, *North Chili* 650
Rochester Institute of Technology, *Rochester* 14,000
Russell Sage College, *Troy* 3,400
St. Bonaventure University, *Olean* 2,800
St. Francis College, *New York* 3,200
St. John Fisher College, *Rochester* 2,200
St. John's University, *New York* 17,800
Saint Joseph's College
  St. Joseph's College, *New York* 1,400
  Saint Joseph's College Suffolk Campus, *Patchoque* 450
St. Lawrence University, *Canton* 2,400
St. Thomas Aquinas College, *Sparkill* 1,400
Sarah Lawrence College, *Yonkers* 1,100
School of Visual Arts, *New York* 5,100
Siena College, *Loudonville* 3,000
Skidmore College, *Saratoga Springs* 2,400
State University of New York
  SUNY at *Albany* 15,400
  SUNY at *Binghamton* 10,600
  SUNY at *Buffalo* 21,800
  SUNY Health Science Center at *Buffalo* 2,900
  SUNY at Stony Brook, *South Stony Brook* 14,600
  SUNY Health Science Center at Stony Brook, *South Stony Brook* 1,400
  SUNY Downstate Medical Center, *New York* 1,400
  SUNY Upstate Medical Center, *Syracuse* 900
  SUNY College at *Brockport* 9,300
  SUNY College at *Buffalo* 10,900
  SUNY College at *Cortland* 5,900
  SUNY College at *Fredonia* 5,300
  SUNY College at *Geneseo* 5,600
  SUNY College at *New Paltz* 6,900
  SUNY College at *Old Westbury* 2,900
  SUNY College at *Oneonta* 6,200
  SUNY College at *Oswego* 7,600
  SUNY College at *Plattsburgh* 6,200
  SUNY College at *Potsdam* 4,700
  SUNY College at *Purchase* 3,200
  SUNY College of Environmental Sciences and Forestry, *Syracuse* 1,900
  SUNY College of Optometry, *New York* 250
  SUNY College of Technology at Utica-Rome, *Utica* 3,100
  SUNY Empire State College, *Saratoga Springs* 3,800
  SUNY Maritime College, *New York* 1,100
Syracuse University
  Syracuse University, *Syracuse* 20,200
  Utica College of Syracuse University, *Utica* 2,100
Touro College, *New York* 2,000
Union College, *Schenectady* 3,300
Union Theological Seminary, *New York* 300
United States Merchant Marine Academy, *Kings Point* ...1,100
United States Military Academy, *West Point* 4,300
United Talmudical Academy, *New York* 650
University of Rochester, *Rochester* 8,000
University of the State of New York Regents
  External Degree Program, *Albany* 16,400
Vassar College, *Arlington* 2,400
Wagner College, *New York* 2,500
Wells College, *Aurora* 550
Yeshiva University, *New York* 4,200

NORTH CAROLINA

Atlantic Christian College, *Wilson* 1,600
Barber-Scotia College, *Concord* 350
Belmont Abbey College, *Belmont* 800
Bennett College, *Greensboro* 600
Campbell College, *Buies Creek* 2,300
Catawba College, *Salisbury* 950
Davidson College, *Davidson* 1,400
Duke University, *Durham* 9,100
Elon College, *Elon College* 2,500
Gardner-Webb College, *Boiling Springs* 1,400
Greensboro College, *Greensboro* 700
Guilford College, *Greensboro* 1,700
High Point College, *High Point* 1,200
Johnson C. Smith University, *Charlotte* 1,400
Lenoir-Rhyne College, *Hickory* 1,400
Livingstone College, *Salisbury* 950
Mars Hill College, *Mars Hill* 2,000
Meredith College, *Raleigh* 1,500
Methodist College, *Fayetteville* 900
North Carolina Wesleyan College, *Rocky Mount* 850
Pfeiffer College, *Misenheimer* 850
Piedmont Bible College, *Winston-Salem* 450
Queens College, *Charlotte* 600
Sacred Heart College, *Belmont* 450
St. Andrew's Presbyterian College, *Laurinburg* 650
St. Augustine's College, *Raleigh* 1,800
Salem College, *Winston-Salem* 650
Shaw University, *Raleigh* 1,400
Southeastern Baptist Theological Seminary, *Wake Forest* ..1,200
University of North Carolina
  Appalachian State University, *Boone* 10,200
  East Carolina University, *Greenville* 13,200
  Elizabeth City State University, *Elizabeth City* 1,500
  Fayetteville State University, *Fayetteville* 2,300
  North Carolina Agricultural and Technical State University, *Greensboro* 5,500
  North Carolina Central University, *Durham* 4,900
  North Carolina School of the Arts, *Winston-Salem* 450
  North Carolina State University at *Raleigh* 19,600
  Pembroke State University, *Pembroke* 2,200
  University of North Carolina at *Asheville* 1,900
  University of North Carolina at *Chapel Hill* 21,100
  University of North Carolina at *Charlotte* 8,900
  University of North Carolina at *Greensboro* 9,900
  University of North Carolina at *Wilmington* 4,300
  Western Carolina University, *Cullowhee* 6,700
  Winston-Salem State University, *Winston-Salem* 2,200
Wake Forest University, *Winston-Salem* 4,800
Warren Wilson College, *Swannanoa* 500
Wingate College, *Wingate* 1,500

NORTH DAKOTA

Dickinson State College, *Dickinson* 1,100
Jamestown College, *Jamestown* 550
Mary College, *Bismarck* 900
Mayville State College, *Mayville* 650
Minot State College, *Minot* 2,300
North Dakota State University, *Fargo* 8,000
Northwest Bible College, *Minot* 210
Trinity Bible Institute, *Ellendale* 350
University of North Dakota, *Grand Forks* 9,700
Valley City State College, *Valley City* 1,100

OHIO

Air Force Institute of Technology, Wright Patterson, A.F.B., *Dayton* 650
Antioch University, *Yellow Springs* 4,200
Art Academy of Cincinnati, *Cincinnati* 210
Ashland College, *Ashland* 2,500
Baldwin-Wallace College, *Berea* 3,400
Bluffton College, *Bluffton* 650
Bowling Green State University, *Bowling Green* 16,900
Capital University, *Bexley* 2,600
Case Western Reserve University, *Cleveland* 7,900
Cedarville College, *Cedarville* 1,300
Central State University, *Wilberforce* 2,600
Cincinnati Bible Seminary, *Cincinnati* 600
Circleville Bible College, *Circleville* 230
Cleveland Institute of Art, *Cleveland* 800
Cleveland Institute of Music, *Cleveland* 300
Cleveland State University, *Cleveland* 17,400
College of Mount St. Joseph-on-the-Ohio, *Mount St. Joseph* 1,400
College of Steubenville, *Steubenville* 900
College of Wooster, *Wooster* 1,800
Columbus College of Art and Design, *Columbus* 1,000
Defiance College, *Defiance* 750
Denison University, *Granville* 2,100
Dyke College, *Cleveland* 1,400
Findlay College, *Findlay* 1,000
Franklin University, *Columbus* 4,700
Heidelberg College, *Tiffin* 850
Hiram College, *Hiram* 1,100
John Carroll University, *University Heights* 4,000
Kent State University, *Kent* 17,800
Kenyon College, *Gambier* 1,400
Lake Erie College, *Painesville* 1,100
Malone College, *Canton* 750
Marietta College, *Marietta* 1,500
Medical College of Ohio at *Toledo* 400
Methodist Theological School of Ohio, *Delaware* 260
Miami University, *Oxford* 13,400
Mount Union College, *Alliance* 1,100
Mount Vernon Nazarene College, *Mount Vernon* 1,000
Muskingum College, *New Concord* 900
Notre Dame College, *South Euclid* 600
Oberlin College, *Oberlin* 2,800
Ohio College of Podiatric Medicine, *Cleveland* 600
Ohio Dominican College, *Columbus* 850
Ohio Institute of Technology, *Columbus* 2,300
Ohio Northern University, *Ada* 2,700
Ohio State University, *Columbus* 53,300
Ohio University, *Athens* 14,200
Ohio Wesleyan University, *Delaware* 2,300
Otterbein College, *Westerville* 1,600
Rabbinical College of Telshe, *Wickliffe* 210
Rio Grande College, *Rio Grande* 1,100
Tiffin University, *Tiffin* 400
Trinity Lutheran Seminary, *Columbus* 280
Union for Experimenting Colleges and Universities, *Cincinnati* 650
United Theological Seminary, *Dayton* 300
University of Akron, *Akron* 23,400
University of Cincinnati, *Cincinnati* 39,100
University of Dayton, *Dayton* 10,300
University of Toledo, *Toledo* 18,200
Urbana College, *Urbana* 750
Ursuline College, *Cleveland Heights* 1,000
Walsh College, *Canton* 750
Wilberforce University, *Wilberforce* 1,100
Wilmington College, *Wilmington* 1,000
Wittenberg University, *Springfield* 2,600
Wright State University, *Fairborn* 14,100
Xavier University, *Cincinnati* 6,600
Youngstown State University, *Youngstown* 15,300

OKLAHOMA

Bartlesville Wesleyan College, *Bartlesville* 650
Bethany Nazarene College, *Bethany* 1,300
Cameron University, *Lawton* 4,700
Central State University, *Edmond* 11,400
East Central Oklahoma State University, *Ada* 3,900
Flaming Rainbow University, *Tahlequah* 350
Langston University, *Langston* 1,100
Northeastern Oklahoma State University, *Tahlequah* 5,800
Northwestern Oklahoma State University, *Alva* 2,000
Oklahoma Baptist University, *Shawnee* 1,500
Oklahoma Christian College, *Oklahoma City* 1,500
Oklahoma City Southwestern College, *Oklahoma City* 850
Oklahoma City University, *Oklahoma City* 2,600
Oklahoma College of Osteopathic Medicine and Surgery, *Tulsa* 240
Oklahoma Panhandle State University, *Goodwell* 1,300
Oklahoma State University, *Stillwater* 22,000
Oral Roberts University, *Tulsa* 3,900
Phillips University, *Enid* 1,300
Southeastern Oklahoma State University, *Durant* 4,200
Southwestern Oklahoma State University, *Weatherford* ... 4,500
University of Oklahoma
- University of Oklahoma, *Norman* 21,100
- University of Oklahoma Health Science Center, *Oklahoma City* 3,000

University of Science and Arts of Oklahoma, *Chickasha* .. 1,300
University of Tulsa, *Tulsa* 6,100

OREGON

Columbia Christian College, *Portland* 300
Concordia College, *Portland* 350
George Fox College, *Newberg* 800
Lewis & Clark College, *Portland* 3,100
Linfield College, *McMinnville* 1,100
Marylhurst Education Center, *Marylhurst* 550
Multnomah School of the Bible, *Portland* 750
Northwest Christian College, *Eugene* 290
Oregon State Higher Education
- Eastern Oregon State College, *La Grande* 1,600
- Oregon College of Education, *Monmouth* 3,200
- Oregon Institute of Technology, *Klamath Falls* 2,500
- Oregon State University, *Corvallis* 17,200
- Portland State University, *Portland* 16,800
- Southern Oregon State College, *Ashland* 4,400
- University of Oregon, *Eugene* 16,900
- University of Oregon Health Sciences Center, *Portland* .. 1,500

Pacific University, *Forest Grove* 1,100
Reed College, *Portland* 1,200
University of Portland, *Portland* 2,800
Warner Pacific College, *Portland* 400
Western Baptist College, *Salem* 400
Western Conservative Baptist Seminary, *Portland* 550
Western States Chiropractic College, *Portland* 450
Willamette University, *Salem* 1,800

PENNSYLVANIA

Albright College, *Reading* 1,700
Allegheny College, *Meadville* 1,900
Allentown College of St. Francis de Sales, *Center Valley* ... 700
Alliance College, *Cambridge Springs* 250
Alvernia College, *Reading* 750

American College, *Bryn Mawr* 700
Baptist Bible College of Pennsylvania, *Clarks Summit* 850
Beaver College, *Glenside* 1,900
Bloomsburg State College, *Bloomsburg* 6,500
Bryn Mawr College, *Bryn Mawr* 1,700
Bucknell University, *Lewisburg* 3,300
Cabrini College, *Radnor* 600
California State College, *California* 4,400
Carlow College, *Pittsburgh* 950
Carnegie-Mellon University, *Pittsburgh* 5,400
Cedar Crest College, *Allentown* 1,000
Chatham College, *Pittsburgh* 700
Chestnut Hill College, *Philadelphia* 900
Cheyney State College, *Cheyney* 2,500
Clarion State College, *Clarion* 4,800
College Misericordia, *Dallas* 1,000
Delaware Valley College of Science & Agriculture, *Doylestown* 1,700
Dickinson College, *Carlisle* 1,800
Dickinson School of Law, *Carlisle* 500
Drexel University, *Philadelphia* 11,200
Duquesne University, *Pittsburgh* 6,800
Eastern Baptist Theological Seminary, *Philadelphia* 260
Eastern College, *St. Davids* 700
East Stroudsburg State College, *East Stroudsburg* 3,900
Edinboro State College, *Edinboro* 5,600
Elizabethtown College, *Elizabethtown* 1,900
Franklin & Marshall College, *Lancaster* 3,000
Gannon University, *Erie* 3,700
Geneva College, *Beaver Falls* 1,400
Gettysburg College, *Gettysburg* 2,000
Grove City College, *Grove City* 2,200
Gwynedd-Mercy College, *Gwynedd Valley* 1,500
Hahnemann Medical College and Hospital, *Philadelphia* 1,800
Haverford College, *Haverford* 1,000
Holy Family College, *Philadelphia* 1,200
Immaculata College, *Immaculata* 1,400
Indiana University of Pennsylvania, *Indiana* 12,100
Juniata College, *Huntingdon* 1,300
King's College, *Wilkes-Barre* 2,100
Kutztown State College, *Kutztown* 5,200
Lafayette College, *Easton* 2,400
Lancaster Bible College, *Lancaster* 400
Lancaster Theological Seminary, *Lancaster* 240
La Roche College, *McCandless* 1,300
La Salle College, *Philadelphia* 6,600
Lebanon Valley College, *Annville* 1,300
Lehigh University, *Bethlehem* 6,200
Lincoln University, *Lincoln University* 1,300
Lock Haven State College, *Lock Haven* 2,400
Lutheran Theological Seminary at *Gettysburg* 240
Lutheran Theological Seminary at *Philadelphia* 220
Lycoming College, *Williamsport* 1,200
Mansfield State College, *Mansfield* 2,600
Marywood College, *Scranton* 3,100
Medical College of Pennsylvania, The, *Philadelphia* 550
Mercyhurst College, *Erie* 1,400
Messiah College, *Grantham* 1,200
Millersville State College, *Millersville* 6,200
Moore College of Art, *Philadelphia* 700
Moravian College, *Bethlehem* 1,800
Muhlenberg College, *Allentown* 2,100
Neumann College, *Aston* 700
Pennsylvania College of Optometry, *Philadelphia* 600
Pennsylvania College of Podiatric Medicine, *Philadelphia* 450
Pennsylvania State University
  Pennsylvania State University, *State College* 35,100
  Pennsylvania State University Behrend College, *Erie* 1,800
  Pennsylvania State University Capitol Campus, *Middletown* 2,500
  Pennsylvania State University Hershey Medical Center, *Hershey* 550
  Pennsylvania State University Radnor Center for Graduate Studies, *Radnor* 400
Philadelphia College of Art, *Philadelphia* 2,000
Philadelphia College of the Bible, *Langhorne* 550
Philadelphia College of Osteopathic Medicine, *Philadelphia* 800
Philadelphia College of the Performing Arts, *Philadelphia* 350
Philadelphia College of Pharmacy & Science, *Philadelphia* 1,200
Philadelphia College of Textiles & Science, *Philadelphia* 2,800
Pittsburgh Theological Seminary, *Pittsburgh* 300
Point Park College, *Pittsburgh* 2,100
Robert Morris College, *Coraopolis* 4,600
Rosemont College, *Rosemont* 600
St. Charles Borromeo Seminary, *Philadelphia* 600
St. Francis College, *Loretto* 1,800
St. Joseph's University, *Philadelphia* 5,500
St. Vincent College, *Latrobe* 900
Seton Hill College, *Greensburg* 900
Shippensburg State College, *Shippensburg* 5,900
Slippery Rock State College, *Slippery Rock* 5,700
Spring Garden College, *Philadelphia* 1,100
Susquehanna University, *Selinsgrove* 1,700
Swarthmore College, *Swarthmore* 1,300
Temple University, *Philadelphia* 33,600
Thiel College, *Greenville* 1,000
Thomas Jefferson University, *Philadelphia* 1,700
University Pennsylvania, *Philadelphia* 22,000
University of Pittsburgh
  University of Pittsburgh Bradford Campus, *Bradford* 850
  University of Pittsburgh, *Pittsburgh* 28,800
  University of Pittsburgh Johnstown Campus, *Johnstown* 3,000
University of Scranton, *Scranton* 4,400
Ursinus College, *Collegeville* 1,800
Valley Forge Christian College, *Phoenixville* 650
Villa Maria College, *Erie* 650
Villanova University, *Villanova* 9,800
Washington and Jefferson College, *Washington* 1,200
Waynesburg College, *Waynesburg* 850
West Chester State College, *West Chester* 8,600
Westminster College, *New Wilmington* 1,900
Westminister Theological Seminary, *Philadelphia* 350
Widener College of Widener University, *Chester* 4,300
Wilkes College, *Wilkes-Barre* 3,000
York College of Pennsylvania, *York* 3,600

RHODE ISLAND

Barrington College, *Barrington* 450
Brown University, *Providence* 6,800
Bryant College of Business Administration, *Smithfield* 5,600
Johnson and Wales College, *Providence* 4,600
Providence College, *Providence* 5,700
Rhode Island College, *Providence* 8,800
Rhode Island School of Design, *Providence* 1,600
Roger Williams College
  Roger Williams College, *Bristol* 2,300
  Roger Williams College Providence Branch, *Providence* 1,400
Salve Regina-The Newport College, *Newport* 1,700
University of Rhode Island, *Kingston* 10,600
  University of Rhode Island, *Providence* 3,100

SOUTH CAROLINA

Allen University, *Columbia* 280
Baptist College at *Charleston* 2,400
Benedict College, *Columbia* 1,600
Central Wesleyan College, *Central* 400
Citadel Military College of South Carolina, *Charleston* 3,300
Claflin College, *Orangeburg* 800
Clemson University, *Clemson* 11,600
Coker College, *Hartsville* 300
College of Charleston, *Charleston* 5,000
Columbia Bible College, *Columbia* 800
Columbia College, *Columbia* 1,100
Converse College, *Spartanburg* 1,000
Erskine College and Seminary, *Due West* 650
Francis Marion College, *Florence* 2,800
Furman University, *Greenville* 3,100
Lander College, *Greenwood* 1,700
Limestone College, *Gaffney* 1,200
Medical University of South Carolina, *Charleston* 2,100
Morris College, *Sumter* 750
Newberry College, *Newberry* 800
Presbyterian College, *Clinton* 900

South Carolina State College, *Orangeburg* 3,600
University of South Carolina
University of South Carolina at *Aiken* 1,700
University of South Carolina at *Columbia* 26,000
University of South Carolina at Coastal Carolina, *Conway* 2,100
University of South Carolina at *Spartanburg* 2,400
Voorhees College, *Denmark* 700
Winthrop College, *Rock Hill* 5,000
Wofford College, *Spartanburg* 1,100

SOUTH DAKOTA

Augustana College, *Sioux Falls* 2,200
Black Hills State College, *Spearfish* 3,000
Dakota State University, *Madison* 900
Dakota Wesleyan University, *Mitchell* 550
Huron College, *Huron* 300
Mount Marty College, *Yankton* 600
National College, *Rapid City* 2,400
Northern State College, *Aberdeen* 2,500
Sinte Gleska College, *Rosebud* 400
Sioux Falls College, *Sioux Falls* 750
South Dakota School of Mines & Technology, *Rapid City*. 2,200
South Dakota State University, *Brookings* 6,900
University of South Dakota
University of South Dakota, *Vermillion* 6,800
University of South Dakota at *Springfield* 850
Yankton College, *Yankton* 290

TENNESSEE

Belmont College, *Nashville* 1,500
Bethel College, *McKenzie* 400
Bristol College, *Bristol* 220
Bryan College, *Dayton* 650
Carson-Newman College, *Jefferson City* 1,600
Christian Brothers College, *Memphis* 1,300
David Libscomb College, *Nashville* 2,300
Fisk University, *Nashville* 1,100
Freed-Hardeman College, *Henderson* 1,500
Free Will Baptist Bible College, *Nashville* 550
Harding Graduate School of Religion, *Memphis* 250
Johnson Bible College, *Knoxville* 400
King College, *Bristol* 230
Knoxville College, *Knoxville* 700
Lambuth College, *Jackson* 700
Lane College, *Jackson* 700
Lee College, *Cleveland* 1,300
Le Moyne-Owen College, *Memphis* 1,000
Lincoln Memorial University, *Harrogate* 1,100
Maryville College, *Maryville* 650
Meharry Medical College, *Nashville* 1,100
Memphis Academy of the Arts, *Memphis* 220
Mid-America Baptist Theological Seminary, *Memphis* 250
Milligan College, *Milligan College* 750
Southern College of Optometry, *Memphis* 600
Southern Missionary College, *Collegedale* 2,000
Southwestern at Memphis, *Memphis* 1,000
State Universities & Colleges of Tennessee
Austin Peay State University, *Clarksville* 4,600
East Tennessee State University, *Johnson City* 10,300
Memphis State University, *Memphis* 21,200
Middle Tennessee State University, *Murfreesboro* 10,900
Tennessee State University, *Nashville* 8,400
Tennessee Technological University, *Cookeville* 7,800
Steed College, *Johnson City* 550
Tennessee Temple University, *Chattanooga* 3,700
Tennessee Wesleyan College, *Athens* 450
Trevecca Nazarene College, *Nashville* 1,000
Tusculum College, *Greenville* 400
Union University, *Jackson* 1,200
University of the South, *Sewanee* 1,100
University of Tennessee
University of Tennessee at *Chattanooga* 7,500
University of Tennessee at *Knoxville* 30,400
University of Tennessee at *Martin* 5,200
University of Tennessee
Center for the Health Sciences, *Memphis* 2,100
Vanderbilt University, *Nashville* 9,100

TEXAS

Abilene Christian University, *Abilene* 5,100
American Technological University, *Kileen* 800
Angelo State University, *San Angelo* 5,600
Austin College, *Sherman* 1,100
Baylor College of Dentistry, *Dallas* 550
Baylor College of Medicine, *Houston* 850
Baylor University, *Waco* 10,000
Bishop College, *Dallas* 950
Concordia Lutheran College, *Austin* 350
Dallas Baptist College, *Dallas* 1,000
Dallas Bible College, *Dallas* 220
Dallas Theological Seminary, *Dallas* 1,000
Devry Institute of Technology, *Dallas* 850
East Texas Baptist College, *Marshall* 900
East Texas State University, *Commerce* 8,800
Gulf Coast Bible College, *Houston* 350
Hardin-Simmons University, *Abilene* 1,800
Houston Baptist University, *Houston* 1,900
Howard Payne University, *Brownwood* 1,200
Huston-Tillotson College, *Austin* 650
Incarnate Word College, *San Antonio* 1,500
Jarvis Christian College, *Hawkins* 600
Lamar University, *Beaumont* 12,700
Le Tourneau College, *Longview* 950
Lubbock Christian College, *Lubbock* 1,200
McMurry College, *Abilene* 1,500
Midwestern State University, *Wichita Falls* 4,300
North Texas State University, *Denton* 17,200
Our Lady of the Lake University of *San Antonio* 1,700
Pan American University, *Edinburg* 9,400
Paul Quinn College, *Waco* 400
Rice University, *Houston* 3,500
St. Edward's University, *Austin* 2,200
St. Mary's University of *San Antonio* 3,400
Sam Houston State University, *Huntsville* 10,500
Southern Methodist University, *University Park* 8,900
South Texas College of Law, *Houston* 1,200
Southwestern Adventist College, *Keene* 750
Southwestern Assemblies of God College, *Waxahachie* 700
Southwestern Baptist Theological Seminary, *Fort Worth*. 3,600
Southwestern University, *Georgetown* 1,000
Southwest Texas State University, *San Marcos* 15,900
Stephen F. Austin State University, *Nacogdoches* 10,300
Sul Ross State University, *Alpine* 2,100
Texas A. and M. University
Prairie View A. & M. University, *Prairie View* 5,200
Tarleton State University, *Stephenville* 3,400
Texas A. & M. University, *College Station* 31,300
Texas A. & M. University at *Galveston* 650
Texas Chiropractic College, *Pasadena* 350
Texas Christian University, *Fort Worth* 6,300
Texas College, *Tyler* 450
Texas College of Osteopathic Medicine, *Fort Worth* 300
Texas Lutheran College, *Seguin* 1,400
Texas Southern University, *Houston* 8,500
Texas Technological University, *Lubbock* 23,100
Texas Wesleyan College, *Fort Worth* 1,600
Texas Woman's University, *Denton* 7,800
Trinity University, *San Antonio* 3,300
University of Dallas, *Irving* 2,400
University of Houston
University of Houston, *Houston* 28,400
University of Houston at Clear Lake City, *Houston* 5,400
University of Houston Downtown College, *Houston* 4,600
University of Houston Victoria Campus, *Victoria* 800
University of Mary Hardin-Baylor, *Belton* 1,100
University of St. Thomas, *Houston* 1,800
University of South Texas
Corpus Christi State University, *Corpus Christi* 2,700
Laredo State University, *Laredo* 750
Texas Agricultural & Industrial University, *Kingsville*. 5,400

University of Texas
- University of Texas at *Arlington* 19,100
- University of Texas at *Austin* 44,100
- University of Texas at Dallas, *Richardson* 5,900
- University of Texas at *El Paso* 15,800
- University of Texas Health Science Center at *Dallas* ... 1,400
- University of Texas Health Science Center at *Houston*. 2,500
- University of Texas Health Science Center at *San Antonio* 2,000
- University of Texas Medical Branch at *Galveston* 1,600
- University of Texas of the Permian Basin, *Odessa* 1,600
- University of Texas at *San Antonio* 9,500
- University of Texas at *Tyler* 2,000

Wayland Baptist College, *Plainview* 1,300
West Texas State University, *Canyon* 6,500
Wiley College, *Marshall* 600

UTAH

Brigham Young University, *Provo* 29,400
Utah Higher Education
- Southern Utah State College, *Cedar City* 2,000
- University of Utah, *Salt Lake City* 22,000
- Utah State University, *Logan* 9,300
- Weber State College, *Ogden* 9,700

Westminster College, *Salt Lake City* 1,200

VERMONT

Bennington College, *Bennington* 600
College of St. Joseph the Provider, *Rutland* 350
Goddard College, *Plainfield* 1,400
Green Mountain College, *Poultney* 500
Marlboro College, *Marlboro* 230
Middlebury College, *Middlebury* 1,900
Norwich University
- Norwich University Main Campus, *Northfield* 1,600
- Vermont College, *Montpelier* 500

St. Michael's College, *Winooski* 2,000
School for International Training, *Brattleboro* 750
Southern Vermont College, *Bennington* 400
Trinity College, *Burlington* 650
University of Vermont & State Agricultural College, *Burlington* 11,000
Vermont Law School, *South Royalton* 350
Vermont State College
- Castleton State College, *Castleton* 2,000
- Johnson State College, *Johnson* 1,000
- Lyndon State College, *Lyndonville* 1,100

VIRGINIA

Averett College, *Danville* 1,000
Bluefield College, *Bluefield* 400
Bridgewater College, *Bridgewater* 900
College of William and Mary
- Christopher Newport College, *Newport News* 3,900
- College of William & Mary, *Williamsburg* 6,400

Eastern Mennonite College and Seminary, *Park View* 1,100
Eastern Virginia Medical School of the Eastern Virginia Medical Authority, *Norfolk* 260
Emory & Henry College, *Emory* 800
Ferrum College, *Ferrum* 1,600
George Mason University, *Fairfax* 12,200
Hampden-Sydney College, *Hampden Sydney* 700
Hampton Institute, *Hampton* 3,200
Hollins College, *Hollins College* 950
James Madison University, *Harrisonburg* 9,000
Liberty Baptist College, *Lynchburg* 2,500
Longwood College, *Farmville* 2,500
Lynchburg College, *Lynchburg* 2,400
Mary Baldwin College, *Staunton* 800
Marymount College of Virginia, *Arlington* 950
Mary Washington College, *Fredericksburg* 2,500
Norfolk State University, *Norfolk* 6,800
Old Dominion University, *Norfolk* 18,000
Radford College, *Radford* 5,700
Randolph-Macon College, *Ashland* 950
Randolph-Macon Woman's College, *Lynchburg* 750
Roanoke College, *Salem* 1,400
St. Paul's College, *Lawrenceville* 600
Shenandoah College and Conservatory of Music, *Winchester* 800
Sweet Briar College, *Sweet Briar* 650
Union Theological Seminary in Virginia, *Richmond* 260
University of Richmond, *Richmond* 4,400
University of Virginia
- University of Virginia, *Charlottesville* 16,500
- University of Virginia Clinch Valley College, *Wise* 1,100

Virginia Commonwealth University, *Richmond* 19,200
Virginia Intermont College, *Bristol* 700
Virginia Military Institute, *Lexington* 1,300
Virginia Polytechnic Institute and State University, *Blacksburg* 22,500
Virginia State University, *Ettrick* 4,700
Virginia Union University, *Richmond* 1,200
Virginia Wesleyan College, *Norfolk* 800
Washington & Lee University, *Lexington* 1,700

WASHINGTON

Central Washington State College, *Ellensburg* 7,900
City College, *Seattle* 1,700
Cornish Institute, *Seattle* 400
Eastern Washington University, *Cheney* 7,700
Evergreen State College, *Olympia* 2,500
Fort Wright College of the Holy Names, *Spokane* 450
Gonzaga University, *Spokane* 3,500
Lutheran Bible Institute of Seattle, *Issaquah* 250
Northwest College of the Assemblies of God, *Kirkland* 800
Pacific Lutheran University, *Parkland* 3,400
St. Martin's College, *Lacey* 500
Seattle Pacific University, *Seattle* 2,500
Seattle University, *Seattle* 4,100
University of Puget Sound, *Tacoma* 3,900
University of Washington, *Seattle* 37,500
Walla Walla College, *College Place* 2,000
Washington State University, *Pullman* 17,000
Western Washington University, *Bellingham* 10,100
Whitman College, *Walla Walla* 1,100
Whitworth College, *Country Homes* 1,700

WEST VIRGINIA

Alderson Broaddus College, *Broaddus* 900
Appalachian Bible College, *Bradley* 230
Bethany College, *Bethany* 900
Bluefield State College, *Bluefield* 2,700
Concord College, *Athens* 2,100
Davis & Elkins College, *Elkins* 1,100
Fairmont State College, *Fairmont* 4,800
Glenville State College, *Glenville* 1,800
Marshall University, *Huntington* 11,500
Salem College, *Salem* 950
Shepherd College, *Shepherdstown* 2,900
University of Charleston, *Charleston* 1,900
West Liberty State College, *West Liberty* 2,600
West Virginia College of Graduate Studies, *Institute* 3,200
West Virginia Institute of Technology, *Montgomery* 3,100
West Virginia School of Osteopathic Medicine, *Lewisburg*.. 220
West Virginia State College, *Institute* 3,900
West Virginia University, *Morgantown* 21,300
West Virginia Wesleyan College, *Buckhannon* 1,700
Wheeling College, *Wheeling* 1,200

WISCONSIN

Alverno College, *Milwaukee* 1,300
Beloit College, *Beloit* 1,000

Cardinal Stritch College, *Glendale* 1,100
Carroll College, *Waukesha* 1,300
Carthage College, *Kenosha* 1,500
Concordia College, *Milwaukee* 350
Edgewood College, *Madison* 650
Lakeland College, *Howard's Grove* 600
Lawrence University, *Appleton* 1,100
Marian College of Fond du Lac, *Fond du Lac* 450
Marquette University, *Milwaukee* 11,200
Medical College of Wisconsin, *Milwaukee* 750
Milton College, *Milton* 750
Milwaukee Institute of Art and Design, *Milwaukee* 220
Milwaukee School of Engineering, *Milwaukee* 2,400
Mount Mary College, *Milwaukee* 1,100
Mount Senario College, *Ladysmith* 450
Northland College, *Ashland* 600
Northwestern College, *Watertown* 240
Ripon College, *Ripon* 900
St. Norbert College, *De Pere* 1,700
Silver Lake College, *Manitowoc* 300
University of Wisconsin
University of Wisconsin—*Eau Claire* 10,600
University of Wisconsin—*Green Bay* 3,800
University of Wisconsin—*La Crosse* 8,900
University of Wisconsin—*Madison* 40,200
University of Wisconsin—*Milwaukee* 25,100
University of Wisconsin—*Oshkosh* 10,300
University of Wisconsin—*Platteville* 4,800
University of Wisconsin—*River Falls* 5,100
University of Wisconsin—*Stevens Point* 8,900
University of Wisconsin—*Superior* 2,100
University of Wisconsin—*Whitewater* 9,700
University of Wisconsin—Parkside, *Kenosha* 5,300
University of Wisconsin—Stout, *Menomonie* 7,100
Viterbo College, *La Crosse* 1,100

WYOMING

University of Wyoming, *Laramie* 9,000

Major Military Installations of the United States

ALABAMA

Ft. McClellan .... Anniston
Ft. Rucker .... Ozark
Maxwell A.F.B. .... Montgomery
Mobile C.G.B. .... Mobile
Redstone Arsenal .... Huntsville

ALASKA

Adak N.S. .... Adak
Annette C.G.A.S. .... Annette
Eielson A.F.B. .... Fairbanks
Elmendorf A.F.G. .... Anchorage
Ft. Greely .... Big Delta
Ft. Jonathan Wainwright ...... Fairbanks
Ft. Richardson .... Anchorage
Ketchikan C.G.B. .... Ketchikan
Kodiak C.G.A.S. .... Kodiak
Shemya A.F.B. .... Anchorage

ARIZONA

Davis-Monthan A.F.B. .... Tucson
Ft. Huachuca .... Douglas
Luke A.F.B. .... Glendale
Williams A.F.B. .... Chandler
Yuma M.C.A.S. .... Yuma
Yuma Proving Ground .... Yuma

ARKANSAS

Blytheville A.F.B. .... Blytheville
Little Rock A.F.B. .... Jacksonville

CALIFORNIA

Alameda N.A.S. .... Alameda
Beale A.F.B. .... Marysville
Camp Pendleton M.C.B. ..... Oceanside
Castle A.F.B. .... Merced
China Lake Naval Weapons
Center .... Ridgecrest
Concord Naval Weapons
Station .... Concord
Coronado Naval
Amphibious Base .... Coronado
Edwards A.F.B. .... Edwards
El Toro M.C.A.S. .... Santa Ana
Ft. Ord .... Monterey
George A.F.B. .... Victorville
Lemoore N.A.S. .... Lemoore
Long Beach Naval
Shipyard .... Long Beach
McClellan A.F.B. .... Sacramento
March A.F.B. .... Riverside
Mare Island Naval
Shipyard .... Vallejo
Mather A.F.B. .... Sacramento
Miramar N.A.S. .... San Diego
Moffett Field N.A.S. ...... Mountain View
North Island N.A.S. .... San Diego
Norton A.F.B. .... San Bernardino
Oakland Army Base .... Oakland
Point Mugu, N.A.S. .... Oxnard
Presidio of
San Francisco .... San Francisco
San Diego N.B. .... San Diego
San Francisco C.G.A.S. .. San Francisco
Seal Beach Naval Weapons
Station .... Seal Beach
Terminal Island C.G.B. ...... San Pedro
Travis A.F.B. .... Fairfield
Twentynine Palms
M.C.B. .... Twentynine Palms
Vandenberg A.F.B. .... Lompoc

COLORADO

Ft. Carson .... Colorado Springs
Lowry A.F.B. .... Denver
Peterson A.F.B. .... Colorado Springs
Rocky Mountain Arsenal .... Denver
U.S. Air Force
Academy .... Colorado Springs

CONNECTICUT

New London Submarine Base .... Groton
U.S. Coast Guard
Academy .... New London

DELAWARE

Dover A.F.B. .... Dover

DISTRICT OF COLUMBIA

Bolling A.F.B. .... Washington, D.C.
Ft. McNair .... Washington, D.C.
Washington
Navy Yard .... Washington, D.C.

FLORIDA

Cecil Field N.A.S. .... Jacksonville
Eglin A.F.B. .... Valparaiso
Homestead A.F.B. .... Homestead
Jacksonville N.A.S. .... Orange Park
J. F. Kennedy
Space Center .... Orlando
Key West N.A.S. .... Key West
MacDill A.F.B. .... Tampa
Mayport N.S. .... Mayport
Miami C.G.A.S. .... Opa Locka
Miami Beach C.G.B. ...... Miami Beach
Orlando N.T.C. .... Orlando
Patrick A.F.B. .... Cocoa
Pensacola N.A.S. .... Penacola
St. Petersburg C.G.A.S. .. St. Petersburg
Tyndall A.F.B. .... Springfield
Whiting Field N.A.S. .... Milton

GEORGIA

Atlanta N.A.S. .... Marietta
Dobbins A.F.B. .... Marietta
Ft. Benning .... Columbus
Ft. Gordon .... Augusta
Ft. McPherson .... Atlanta
Ft. Stewart .... Hinesville
Moody A.F.B. .... Valdosta
Robins A.F.B. .... Warner Robins

HAWAII

Barbers Point N.A.S. .... Ewa Beach
Camp H. M. Smith
M.C.B. .... Halawa Heights
Ft. Shafter .... Honolulu
Hickam A.F.B. .... Honolulu
Kaneohe Bay M.C.A.S. .... Kailua
Pearl Harbor Nav. Res. .... Honolulu
Schofield Barracks .... Wahiawa
Wheeler A.F.B. .... Wahiawa

IDAHO

Mountain Home A.F.B. .. Mountain Home

ILLINOIS

Chanute A.F.B. .... Rantoul
Ft. Sheridan .... Highwood
Glenview N.A.S. .... Glenview
Great Lakes Naval Training
Center .... North Chicago
Joliet Army Ammunition
Plant .... Joliet
Rock Island Arsenal .... Rock Island
Scott A.F.B. .... Belleville

INDIANA

Ft. Benjamin Harrison ...... Indianapolis
Grissom A.F.B. .... Peru
Jefferson Proving Ground ...... Madison

KANSAS

Ft. Leavenworth .... Leavenworth
Ft. Riley .... Junction City
McConnell A.F.B. .... Wichita

KENTUCKY

Ft. Campbell .... Clarksville, Tenn.
Ft. Knox .... Louisville

LOUISIANA

Barksdale A.F.B. .... Shreveport
England A.F.B. .... Alexandria
Ft. Polk .... Leesville
New Orleans C.G.B. ...... New Orleans
New Orleans N.A.S. ...... New Orleans

MAINE

Brunswick N.A.S. .... Brunswick
Loring A.F.B. .... Limestone
Portsmouth Naval
Shipyard .... Portsmouth, N.H.
South Portland C.G.B. .... Portland
Southwest Harbor
C.G.B. .... Southwest Harbor

MARYLAND

Aberdeen Proving Ground .... Aberdeen
Andrews A.F.B. .... Camp Springs
Ft. Detrick .... Frederick
Ft. Meade .... Odenton
Ft. Ritchie .... Cascade
Patuxent River A.T.C. .... Patuxent River
U.S. Naval Academy .... Annapolis

MASSACHUSETTS

Ft. Devens .... Ayer
Hanscom A.F.B. .... Bedford
Natick Laboratories .... Natick
South Weymouth N.A.S. .... South Weymouth
Westover A.F.B. .... Chicopee
Woods Hole C.G.B. .... Woods Hole

MICHIGAN

Detroit C.G.B. .... Detroit
K. I. Sawyer A.F.B. .... Gwynn
Sault Ste. Marie C.G.B. . Sault Ste. Marie
Traverse City C.G.A.S. .... Traverse City
Wurtsmith A.F.B. .... Oscoda

MISSISSIPPI

Columbus A.F.B. .... Columbus
Keesler A.F.B. .... Biloxi
Meridian N.A.S. .... Meridian

MISSOURI

Ft. Leonard Wood .... Waynesville
Richards-Gebaur A.F.B. ...... Grandview
St. Louis C.G.B. .... St. Louis
Whiteman A.F.B. .... Knobnoster

MONTANA

Malmstrom A.F.B. .... Great Falls

NEBRASKA

Offutt A.F.B. .... Omaha

NEVADA

Nellis A.F.B. .... Las Vegas
Fallon N.A.S. .... Reno

NEW HAMPSHIRE

Pease A.F.B. .... Portsmouth

NEW JERSEY

Coast Guard Training Center . Cape May
Ft. Dix .... Wrightstown
Ft. Monmouth .... Oceanport
McGuire A.F.B. .... Wrightstown
Picatinny Arsenal .... Dover

NEW MEXICO

Cannon A.F.B. .... Clovis
Holloman A.F.B. .... Alamogordo
Kirtland A.F.B. .... Albuquerque
Sandia Base .... Albuquerque
White Sands Missile Range .... Las Cruces

NEW YORK

Buffalo C.G.B. .... Buffalo
Ft. Hamilton .... New York
Griffiss A.F.B. .... Rome
Plattsburgh A.F.B. .... Plattsburgh
U.S. Military Academy ...... West Point
Watervliet Arsenal .... Vatervliet

NORTH CAROLINA

Camp Lejeune M.C.B. ...... Jacksonville
Cherry Point M.C.A.S. .... Havelock
Elizabeth City C.G.A.S. ... Elizabeth City
Ft. Bragg .... Fayetteville
Ft. Macon C.G.B. .... Atlantic Beach
New River M.C.A.S. .... Jacksonville
Pope A.F.B. .... Springlake
Seymour Johnson A.F.B. ..... Goldsboro

NORTH DAKOTA

Grand Forks A.F.B. .... Grand Forks
Minot A.F.B. .... Minot

OHIO

Rickenbacker A.F.B. .... Columbus
Wright-Patterson A.F.B. .... Dayton

OKLAHOMA

Altus A.F.B. .... Altus
Ft. Sill .... Lawton
Tinker A.F.B. .... Oklahoma City
Vance A.F.B. .... Enid

OREGON

Astoria C.G.B. .... Astoria

PENNSYLVANIA

Carlisle Barracks .... Carlisle
Frankford Arsenal .... Philadelphia
Warminster Naval Air Development Center ...... Warminster
Philadelphia Naval Shipyard .... Philadelphia
Willow Grove N.A.S. ...... Willow Grove

SOUTH CAROLINA

Beaufort M.C.A.S. .... Beaufort
Charleston A.F.B. .... Charleston
Charleston C.G.B. .... Charleston
Charleston Naval Shipyard ... Charleston
Charleston Naval Weapons Station .... Charleston
Ft. Jackson .... Columbia
Myrtle Beach A.F.B. .... Myrtle Beach
Parris Island Marine Corps Recruit Depot .... Beaufort
Shaw A.F.B. .... Sumter

SOUTH DAKOTA

Ellsworth A.F.B. .... Box Elders

TENNESSEE

Memphis N.A.S. .... Millington

TEXAS

Bergstrom A.F.B. .... Austin
Brooks A.F.B. .... San Antonio
Carswell A.F.B. .... Fort Worth
Chase Field N.A.S. .... Beeville
Corpus Christi N.A.S. .... Corpus Christi
Dallas N.A.S. .... Dallas
Dyess A.F.B. .... Abilene
Ft. Bliss .... El Paso
Ft. Hood .... Killeen
Ft. Sam Houston .... San Antonio
Galveston C.G.B. .... Galveston
Goodfellow A.F.B. .... San Angelo
Kelly A.F.B. .... San Antonio
Kingsville N.A.S. .... Kingsville
Lackland A.F.B. .... San Antonio
Laughlin A.F.B. .... Del Rio
Lyndon B. Johnson Space Center .... Houston
Randolph A.F.B. .... Universal City
Reese A.F.B. .... Lubbock
Sheppard A.F.B. .... Wichita Falls

UTAH

Dugway Proving Ground .... Dugway
Hill A.F.B. .... Ogden

VIRGINIA

Ft. Belvoir .... Alexandria
Ft. Eustis .... Newport News
Ft. Lee .... Petersburg
Ft. Monroe .... Hampton
Ft. Myer .... Arlington
Langley A.F.B. .... Hampton
Little Creek Naval Amphibious Base .... Norfolk
Norfolk N.A.S. .... Norfolk
Norfolk Naval Base .... Norfolk
Norfolk Naval Shipyard ...... Portsmouth
Oceana N.A.S. .... Virginia Beach
Quantico M.C.A.S. .... Quantico
Yorktown Naval Weapons Station .... Yorktown

WASHINGTON

Fairchild A.F.B. .... Spokane
Ft. Lewis .... Tacoma
McChord A.F.B. .... Tacoma
Port Angeles C.G.A.S. .... Port Angeles
Puget Sound Naval Shipyard .... Bremerton
Whidbey Island N.A.S. ...... Oak Harbor

WISCONSIN

Milwaukee C.G.B. .... Milwaukee

WYOMING

Francis E. Warren A.F.B. ..... Cheyenne

Railroad Distances Between United States Cities

	Albuquerque, N. Mex.	Amarillo, Tex.	Atlanta, Ga.	Baltimore, Md.	Billings, Mont.	Birmingham, Ala.	Boston, Mass.	Buffalo, N.Y.	Butte, Mont.	Cheyenne, Wyo.	Chicago, Ill.	Cincinnati, Ohio	Cleveland, Ohio	Columbia, S.C.	Dallas, Tex.	Denver, Colo.	Des Moines, Iowa	Detroit, Mich.	Duluth, Minn.	El Paso, Tex.	Fargo, N. Dak.
Albuquerque, N. Mex.		374	1554	2102	1133	1388	2356	1862	1369	583	1338	1528	1678	1801	723	477	1108	1610	1515	253	1605
Amarillo, Tex.	374		1181	1728	1121	1014	2028	1534	1357	571	1010	1154	1339	1434	370	465	780	1282	1191	444	1281
Atlanta, Ga.	1554	1181		676	1921	167	1091	934	2157	1532	734	490	750	254	825	1526	952	748	1202	1471	1372
Baltimore, Md.	2102	1728	676		2085	799	416	395	2305	1791	796	582	459	515	1448	1822	1154	624	1265	2095	1435
Billings, Mont.	1133	1121	1921	2085		1788	2296	1802	236	550	1278	1559	1618	2142	1491	656	1041	1550	899	1386	640
Birmingham, Ala.	1388	1014	167	799	1788		1215	925	2024	1399	651	481	741	420	658	1373	819	739	1119	1304	1289
Boston, Mass.	2356	2028	1091	416	2296	1215		494	2526	2013	1018	938	678	930	1864	2044	1376	746	1486	2414	1656
Buffalo, N.Y.	1862	1534	934	395	1802	925	494		2032	1519	524	444	184	910	1418	1550	882	252	992	1920	1162
Butte, Mont.	1369	1357	2157	2305	236	2024	2526	2032		786	1514	1795	1854	2378	1727	892	1377	1780	1135	1622	876
Cheyenne, Wyo.	583	571	1532	1791	550	1399	2013	1519	786		995	1259	1335	1753	941	106	652	1267	1007	836	1097
Chicago, Ill.	1338	1010	734	796	1278	651	1018	524	1514	995		281	340	867	968	1026	358	272	468	1396	638
Cincinnati, Ohio	1528	1154	490	582	1559	481	938	444	1795	1259	281		260	586	975	1252	639	258	749	1561	919
Cleveland, Ohio	1678	1339	750	459	1618	741	678	184	1854	1335	340	260		846	1234	1366	698	164	808	1736	978
Columbia, S.C.	1801	1434	254	515	2142	420	930	910	2378	1753	867	586	846		1078	1747	1173	844	1335	1724	1513
Dallas, Tex.	723	370	825	1448	1491	658	1864	1418	1727	941	968	975	1234	1078		835	738	1200	1149	646	1239
Denver, Colo.	477	465	1526	1822	656	1373	2044	1550	892	106	1026	1252	1366	1747	835		683	1298	1038	730	1128
Des Moines, Iowa	1108	780	952	1154	1041	819	1376	882	1377	652	358	639	698	1173	738	683		630	411	1166	501
Detroit, Mich.	1610	1282	748	624	1550	739	746	252	1780	1267	272	258	164	844	1200	1298	630		740	1668	910
Duluth, Minn.	1515	1191	1202	1265	899	1119	1486	992	1135	1007	468	749	808	1335	1149	1038	411	740		1577	259
El Paso, Tex.	253	444	1471	2095	1386	1304	2414	1920	1622	836	1396	1561	1736	1724	646	730	1166	1668	1577		1667
Fargo, N. Dak.	1605	1281	1372	1435	640	1289	1656	1162	876	1097	638	919	978	1513	1239	1128	501	910	259	1667	
Houston, Tex.	925	634	856	1517	1755	718	1933	1554	1991	1205	1205	1110	1370	1110	264	1099	1002	1368	1413	827	1503
Indianapolis, Ind.	1430	1056	585	691	1462	503	962	468	1692	1161	184	109	283	681	951	1154	542	303	652	1500	822
Jacksonville, Fla.	1819	1466	350	794	2226	438	1210	1190	2462	1877	1083	840	1100	280	1096	1811	1301	1098	1551	1764	1721
Kansas City, Mo.	887	559	890	1198	1051	737	1469	975	1287	702	451	616	791	1111	517	636	221	723	632	945	722
Knoxville, Tenn.	1556	1183	197	545	1849	254	961	737	2085	1460	574	296	553	293	903	1454	880	551	1042	1549	1212
Los Angeles, Calif.	889	1216	2285	2908	1452	2118	3244	2750	1216	1302	2227	2370	2555	2538	1460	1353	1954	2499	2309	814	2092
Louisville, Ky.	1463	1090	474	696	1583	392	1052	558	1809	1194	295	114	374	581	861	1188	614	372	763	1508	933
Memphis, Tenn.	1135	761	420	967	1535	253	1382	938	1771	1186	527	494	754	673	481	1120	645	752	1031	1128	1121
Miami, Fla.	2185	1832	716	1160	2592	804	1576	1556	2828	2243	1449	1206	1466	646	1462	2177	1667	1464	1917	2130	2087
Mobile, Ala.	1369	1016	353	1029	1958	266	1444	1191	2194	1569	917	747	1007	607	646	1481	988	1005	1374	1292	1464
Nashville, Tenn.	1374	1000	288	761	1634	205	1177	745	1870	1245	446	301	561	509	720	1238	664	559	914	1367	1084
New Orleans, La.	1229	876	493	1154	1924	355	1569	1280	2160	1447	921	836	1096	747	506	1341	1039	1094	1425	1152	1515
New York, N.Y.	2216	1866	862	187	2186	986	229	396	2416	1903	908	755	571	701	1635	1934	1266	648	1376	2310	1546
Oklahoma City, Okla.	648	274	907	1454	1394	740	1743	1249	1631	845	794	880	1065	1160	236	739	565	1031	976	718	1066
Omaha, Nebr.	1015	754	1025	1284	896	892	1506	1012	1132	507	488	752	828	1246	712	538	145	760	500	1140	590
Philadelphia, Pa.	2124	1775	771	95	2094	894	321	415	2330	1811	816	664	479	610	1543	1842	1174	644	1285	2190	1454
Pittsburgh, Pa.	1776	1427	806	328	1747	797	668	260	1983	1463	468	316	131	772	1291	1494	826	296	937	1834	1107
Portland, Oreg.	1849	1837	2798	3030	961	2665	3217	2723	725	1266	2199	2470	2539	3019	2227	1372	1918	2505	1820	2002	1601
Richmond, Va.	2038	1664	579	155	2140	735	570	550	2370	1840	862	581	544	360	1385	1833	1220	708	1330	2031	1500
St. Louis, Mo.	1190	816	612	920	1310	479	1202	708	1546	921	284	338	523	833	711	914	340	489	726	1223	816
St. Paul, Minn.	1363	1039	1130	1193	882	1047	1414	920	1112	855	396	677	736	1263	997	886	259	668	152	1425	242
Salt Lake City, Utah	985	973	2051	2310	669	1906	2532	2038	433	519	1514	1778	1854	2272	1343	570	1171	1786	1526	1238	1309
San Antonio, Tex.	870	617	1066	1720	1739	928	2125	1631	1975	1189	1208	1247	1447	1320	271	1083	1009	1413	1420	617	1510
San Francisco, Calif.	1209	1537	2718	3059	1418	2551	3281	2787	1182	1268	2263	2527	2603	2971	1930	1374	1920	2535	2275	1284	2058
Seattle, Wash.	2031	2019	2824	2937	903	2691	3159	2665	667	1448	2141	2422	2481	3045	2394	1554	1944	2413	1762	2184	1503
Spokane, Wash.	1726	1714	2514	2628	593	2381	2849	2355	357	1143	1831	2112	2171	2735	2084	1249	1634	2103	1452	1979	1193
Tucson, Ariz.	565	756	1783	2407	1698	1616	2726	2232	1718	1148	1708	1873	2048	2036	958	1042	1478	1980	1889	312	1979
Washington, D.C.	2047	1690	638	38	2043	761	454	434	2273	1759	764	544	427	476	1410	1790	1122	592	1233	2056	1403
Wichita, Kans.	721	347	986	1401	1236	819	1681	1187	1472	686	663	819	1003	1239	408	580	433	935	844	791	934

wing Travel Distances (Short Line) Between
lroad Centers of the United States in Statute Miles

	Jacksonville, Fla.	Kansas City, Mo.	Knoxville, Tenn.	Los Angeles, Calif.	Louisville, Ky.	Memphis, Tenn.	Miami, Fla.	Mobile, Ala.	Nashville, Tenn.	New Orleans, La.	New York, N.Y.	Oklahoma City, Okla.	Omaha, Nebr.	Philadelphia, Pa.	Pittsburgh, Pa.	Portland, Oreg.	Richmond, Va.	St. Louis, Mo.	St. Paul, Minn.	Salt Lake City, Utah	San Antonio, Tex.	San Francisco, Calif.	Seattle, Wash.	Spokane, Wash.	Tucson, Ariz.	Washington, D.C.	Wichita, Kans.
0	1819	887	1556	889	1463	1135	2185	1369	1374	1229	2216	648	1015	2124	1776	1849	2038	1190	1363	985	870	1209	2031	1726	565	2047	721
5	1466	559	1183	1216	1090	761	1832	1016	1000	876	1866	274	754	1775	1427	1837	1664	816	1039	973	617	1537	2019	1714	756	1690	347
5	350	890	197	2285	474	420	716	353	288	493	862	907	1025	771	806	2798	579	612	1130	2051	1066	2718	2824	2514	1783	638	986
1	794	1198	545	2908	696	967	1160	1029	761	1154	187	1454	1284	95	328	3030	155	920	1193	2310	1720	3059	2937	2628	2407	38	1401
2	2226	1051	1849	1452	1583	1535	2592	1958	1634	1924	2186	1394	896	2094	1747	961	2140	1310	882	669	1739	1418	903	593	1698	2043	1236
3	438	737	254	2118	392	253	804	266	205	355	986	740	892	894	797	2665	735	479	1047	1906	928	2551	2691	2381	1616	761	819
2	1210	1469	961	3244	1052	1382	1576	1444	1177	1569	229	1743	1506	321	668	3217	570	1202	1414	2532	2125	3281	3159	2849	2726	454	1681
3	1190	975	737	2750	558	938	1556	1191	745	1280	396	1249	1012	415	260	2723	550	708	920	2038	1631	2787	2665	2355	2232	434	1187
2	2462	1287	2085	1216	1809	1771	2828	2194	1870	2160	2416	1631	1132	2330	1983	725	2370	1546	1112	433	1975	1182	667	357	1718	2273	1472
4	1877	702	1460	1302	1194	1186	2243	1569	1245	1447	1903	845	507	1811	1463	1266	1840	921	855	519	1189	1268	1448	1143	1148	1759	686
4	1083	451	574	2227	295	527	1449	917	446	921	908	794	488	816	468	2199	862	284	396	1514	1208	2263	2141	1831	1708	764	663
9	840	616	296	2370	114	494	1206	747	301	836	755	880	752	664	316	2470	581	338	677	1778	1247	2527	2422	2112	1873	544	819
3	1100	791	553	2555	374	754	1466	1007	561	1096	571	1065	828	479	131	2539	544	523	736	1854	1447	2603	2481	2171	2048	427	1003
1	280	1111	293	2538	581	673	646	607	509	747	701	1160	1246	610	772	3019	360	833	1263	2272	1320	2971	3045	2735	2036	476	1239
1	1096	517	903	1460	861	481	1462	646	720	506	1635	236	712	1543	1291	2227	1385	711	997	1343	271	1930	2394	2084	958	1410	408
4	1811	636	1454	1353	1188	1120	2177	1481	1238	1341	1934	739	538	1842	1494	1372	1833	914	886	570	1083	1374	1554	1249	1042	1790	580
2	1301	221	880	1954	614	645	1667	988	664	1039	1266	565	145	1174	826	1918	1220	340	259	1171	1009	1920	1944	1634	1478	1122	433
3	1098	723	551	2499	372	752	1464	1005	559	1094	648	1031	760	644	296	2505	708	489	668	1786	1413	2535	2413	2103	1980	592	935
2	1551	632	1042	2309	763	1031	1917	1374	914	1425	1376	976	500	1285	937	1820	1330	726	152	1526	1420	2275	1762	1452	1889	1233	844
0	1764	945	1549	814	1508	1128	2130	1292	1367	1152	2310	718	1140	2190	1834	2002	2031	1223	1425	1238	617	1284	2184	1979	312	2056	791
2	1721	722	1212	2092	933	1121	2087	1464	1084	1515	1546	1066	590	1454	1107	1601	1500	816	242	1309	1510	2058	1503	1193	1979	1403	934
7	975	781	972	1641	996	616	1341	503	855	363	1703	500	976	1612	1426	2491	1435	921	1261	1607	210	2111	2656	2348	1139	1478	672
	935	518	388	2272	111	491	1301	769	298	858	811	782	654	719	371	2427	690	240	580	1680	1164	2429	2325	2015	1775	653	721
5		1175	547	2578	824	691	366	472	637	612	981	1178	1330	890	1052	3148	640	917	1479	2344	1185	2989	3129	2819	2076	756	1257
8	1175		818	1776	552	484	1541	926	602	873	1329	343	195	1237	889	1968	1197	278	480	1206	788	1970	1954	1644	1257	1160	212
8	547	818		2363	277	422	913	520	216	609	732	909	953	640	609	2726	482	540	970	2001	1174	2720	2715	2405	1861	507	988
2	2578	1776	2363		2306	1942	2944	2106	2181	1966	3082	1490	1809	2991	2643	1188	2845	2032	2157	783	1431	470	1370	1556	502	2906	1563
1	824	552	277	2306		380	1190	658	187	747	869	867	687	778	430	2460	695	274	691	1713	1133	2462	2486	2176	1820	658	755
1	691	484	422	1942	380		1057	394	239	394	1153	487	679	1062	810	2496	903	305	879	1653	753	2298	2438	2128	1440	929	566
1	366	1541	913	2944	1190	1057		838	1003	978	1347	1544	1696	1256	1418	3514	1006	1283	1845	2710	1551	3355	3495	3185	2442	1122	1623
9	472	926	520	2106	658	394	838		471	140	1215	871	1062	1124	1063	2872	932	648	1222	1988	713	2553	2861	2551	1604	991	1053
8	637	602	216	2181	187	239	1003	471		560	948	726	738	856	617	2511	697	324	842	1892	992	2537	2537	2227	1679	723	805
8	612	873	609	1966	747	394	978	140	560		1355	742	1068	1264	1152	2732	1072	699	1273	1848	573	2436	2900	2590	1464	1115	913
1	981	1329	732	3082	869	1153	1347	1215	948	1355		1592	1396	91	439	3107	341	1051	1304	2422	1906	3171	3049	2739	2586	225	1532
2	1178	343	909	1490	867	487	1544	871	726	742	1592		538	1501	1153	2131	1390	542	824	1247	507	1811	2293	1987	1030	1424	172
4	1330	195	953	1809	687	679	1696	1062	738	1068	1396	538		1304	956	1773	1333	414	348	1026	983	1775	1799	1489	1452	1252	407
9	890	1237	640	2991	778	1062	1256	1124	856	1264	91	1501	1304		348	3015	250	959	1212	2330	1815	3079	2957	2647	2494	133	1440
1	1052	889	609	2643	430	810	1418	1063	617	1152	439	1153	956	348		2668	413	611	865	1982	1535	2731	2610	2300	2146	296	1092
7	3148	1968	2726	1188	2460	2496	3514	2872	2511	2732	3107	2131	1773	3015	2668		3095	2187	1803	884	2498	718	182	368	1690	3025	1971
0	640	1197	482	2845	695	903	1006	932	697	1072	341	1390	1333	250	413	3095		919	1258	2359	1645	3108	3003	2693	2343	117	1400
0	917	278	540	2032	274	305	1283	648	324	699	1051	542	414	959	611	2187	919		574	1440	924	2189	2213	1903	1572	882	481
0	1479	480	970	2157	691	879	1845	1222	842	1273	1304	824	348	1212	865	1803	1258	574		1374	1268	2123	1745	1435	1737	1161	692
0	2344	1206	2001	783	1713	1653	2710	1988	1892	1848	2422	1247	1026	2330	1982	884	2359	1440	1374		1614	821	1066	790	1285	2278	1087
4	1185	788	1174	1431	1133	753	1551	713	992	573	1906	507	983	1815	1535	2498	1645	924	1268	1614		1901	2666	2356	929	1681	679
9	2989	1970	2720	470	2462	2298	3355	2553	2537	2436	3171	1811	1775	3079	2731	718	3108	2189	2123	821	1901		900	1086	972	3028	1884
5	3129	1954	2715	1370	2486	2438	3495	2861	2537	2900	3049	2293	1799	2957	2610	182	3003	2213	1745	1066	2666	900		310	1872	2906	2139
5	2819	1644	2405	1556	2176	2128	3185	2551	2227	2590	2739	1987	1489	2647	2300	368	2693	1903	1435	790	2356	1086	310		2291	2596	1829
5	2076	1257	1861	502	1820	1440	2442	1604	1679	1464	2586	1030	1452	2494	2146	1690	2343	1572	1737	1285	929	972	1872	2291		2368	1103
3	756	1160	507	2906	658	929	1122	991	723	1115	225	1424	1252	133	296	3025	117	882	1161	2278	1681	3028	2906	2596	2368		1363
1	1257	212	988	1563	755	566	1623	1053	805	913	1532	172	407	1440	1092	1971	1400	481	692	1087	679	1884	2139	1829	1103	1363	

Glossary of Map Terminology

A

Altitude. The height of an object or elevation above a given level.

Antarctic Circle. The geographic parallel of 66°33′ S., enclosing the area within which the sun is continuously above the horizon on December 22, and below the horizon on June 21.

Antipodes. Two places on the surface of the globe diametrically opposite to each other, i.e., North Pole and South Pole; England and the Antipodes Is.

Archipelago. A group of islands more or less adjacent to each other and arranged in groups covering portions of the sea.

Arctic Circle. The geographic parallel of 66°33′ N., enclosing the area within which the sun is continuously above the horizon on June 21, and below the horizon on December 22.

Atlas. A bound collection of maps. First used in this sense by Mercator in the 16th century.

Atmosphere. Ocean of air surrounding the earth.

Atoll. A coral island in the form of a ring, more or less continuous, around an interior lagoon.

Autumnal Equinox. The time when the overhead sun crosses the Equator on its apparent migration from north to south, or about September 23, and the length of day and night is approximately the same in all latitudes.

Axis. The straight line passing through the center of the earth, about which the earth rotates.

Azimuth. A great circle direction, or the angle measured clockwise between any meridian and an intersecting great circle.

Azimuthal Projection. A map projection on which the directions of all lines radiating from a central point or pole are the same as the directions of the corresponding lines on the sphere. When centered on one of the poles, sometimes called a "polar projection."

B

Bank. An elevation of the ocean bottom above which the water is relatively shallow but sufficient for navigation.

Basin. Area drained by a river and its tributaries.

Bay. A penetration of the sea into the coast. A bay is usually very much wider in the middle than at the entrance.

Bayou. A sluggish watercourse, usually the outlet of a lake or of a river through its delta.

Butte. A conspicuous, isolated hill or mountain.

C

Calms, Belt of. A zone on either side of the Trade Winds where calms of long duration prevail.

Canal. An artificial watercourse.

Canyon. A deep gorge or ravine through which a river flows.

Cape. A point of land projecting into a body of water.

Cartography. The art or science of making maps.

Central Meridian. The vertical meridian of a map projection around which the map is centered.

Climate. The aggregate weather conditions of a given region over a long period of time.

Co-Latitude. The difference between the latitude of a place and 90°, or its distance in degrees from one of the poles of the earth.

Conformal Projection. A map projection on which all small or elementary figures upon the surface of the earth retain true shape, the meridians and parallels being at right angles to one another.

Conic Projection. A map projection which can be imagined as drawn on the surface of a cone. The meridians appear as straight lines along which the parallels, as concentric circles, may be spaced in such a way as to give some desired quality, such as conformality or equal area.

Continent. One of the main continuous bodies of land on the earth's surface. The number of continents considered to exist varies with usage from five to seven, i.e., America (North and South); Eurasia (Europe and Asia); Africa; Antarctica; and Australia.

Continental Divide. The height of land which separates the streams flowing into one ocean from those flowing into another.

Continental Shelf. The zone of the continental margin extending from the shore line to the depth, usually about 100 fathoms or 200 meters, where there is a marked or rather steep descent toward the ocean depth.

Contour Line. A line drawn on a map to indicate points of the same height or depth.

Coordinates, Geographical. The intersecting lines of latitude and longitude which determine the geographical position of any given place.

Cultural Feature. Any man-made feature of the earth's surface shown on a map.

Cylindrical Projection. A map projection produced by projecting the geographic meridians and parallels onto a cylinder which is tangent to the surface of a sphere, and then developing the cylinder into a plane.

D

Degree. A unit of measurement equal to 1/360 of a circle. A degree of latitude on the earth's surface is roughly equivalent to 69 statute miles. A degree of longitude varies in length but is always equivalent to about 4 minutes of time.

Delta. The tract of land formed by the deposit of silt at the mouth of a river.

Doldrums. The equatorial belt of calms and variable winds.

Downs. Certain hilly districts in southern England underlain by chalk and hence unforested.

E

Eastern Hemisphere. Usually considered in cartography to be half of the earth extending from pole to pole between 20° W. and 160° E., including continents of Eurasia, Africa, and Australia.

Elevation. The vertical distance of a point above or below a reference surface, usually mean sea level.

Equal Area Projection. A map projection on which a constant ratio of areas is preserved; that is, any given part of the map bears the same relation to the area on the sphere which it represents, as the whole map bears to the entire area represented.

Equator. The great circle around the earth equidistant from the poles.

Equatorial Current. Westward drift of surface water on either side of Equator in Trade Wind belts.

Estuary. The coastal section of a river which is to a greater or lesser extent invaded by the sea and subject to tidal influence.

F

Fathom. A unit of measurement used for soundings, equal to 1.83 meters or 6 feet.

Firth. A long arm of the sea, partially landlocked.

Fjord. A narrow arm of the sea between high lands.

G

Geodesy. Investigation of scientific questions connected with the shape and dimensions of the earth.

Geographic Center. That point on which any area would balance if it were a plate of uniform thickness. The geographic center of the conterminous United States is at latitude 39° 50′ longitude 98° 35′, in the eastern part of Smith County, Kansas.

Geography. The scientific description and explanation of the earth's regions.

Glacier. A field or body of land-formed ice moving slowly down a mountainside or valley.

Globe. A spherical map of the earth or heavens.

Gnomonic Projection. A perspective map projection on a plane tangent to the surface of a sphere, having the point of projection at the center of the sphere. It is the only map projection on which all great circles represented are straight lines.

Great Circle. The line of intersection of the surface of a sphere and any plane which passes through the center of the sphere.

Great Circle Direction. The great circle direction of point A from point B is the angle, measured clockwise from true North, formed by the meridian of point B and the great circle passing through points A and B. See Azimuth.

Great Circle Distance. The distance between any two points, measured either in degrees or miles, along the great circle connecting them.

Greenwich Civil Time. Mean solar time for the Greenwich Meridian, counted from midnight.

Gulf Stream. The warm current which flows out of the Gulf of Mexico through the Straits of Florida and northward through the Atlantic Ocean until it merges with the West Wind Drift.

H

Hachures. Lines used in shading elevations on a map to outline them and to indicate slope.

Hemisphere. Any half of the earth's surface. See Northern, Southern, Eastern, Western, Land, and Water Hemisphere.

Horizon. The line at which the earth and sky appear to meet.

Horse Latitudes. Zones of high atmospheric pressure with calms and variable breezes, which border the polar edges of the Trade Wind areas.

Hydrography. The science of measuring and studying oceans, seas, rivers, and other waters, with their marginal land areas, especially for the purpose of aiding navigation. As a map feature, the pattern of rivers, oceans, etc. shown on a map.

I

Ice Cap. An ice sheet of vast extent covering the topographic features of a continental land mass.

Inclination of the Earth. The tilt of the earth's axis in relation to the plane of the earth's orbit. The angle of inclination is 23½° from vertical.

International Date Line. The line extending from pole to pole along the 180th meridian, with local variations, where each new calendar day begins with the passing of the midnight hour. Travelers crossing the line going west must advance their calendar one day, while those going east must retard the calendar one day.

Interrupted Map Projection. A projection in which the pattern of meridians and parallels is interrupted or broken so that certain areas may be centered upon different central meridians.

Isthmus. A narrow strip of land with water on both sides connecting two larger bodies of land.

K

Kilometer. A unit of length; 1,000 meters; 3,280.84 feet; approximately ⅝ of a mile.

L

Land Hemisphere. That half of the earth, centered near Nantes, France, which includes the greatest possible land area.

Latitude. The angular distance in degrees of a point on the earth north or south of the Equator.

Longitude. The angular distance (degrees) of a place east or west of the Prime Meridian.

M

Magnetic Declination. From any given place, the angle of magnetic North from true North.

Magnetic Poles. The two locations representing the poles of unlike magnetism belonging to the earth as a magnetized body. The **North Magnetic Pole** is currently located at approximately 73°N. Lat. and 100°W. Long. on Prince of Wales Island. The **South Magnetic Pole** is currently located at approximately 71°S. Lat. and 149°E. Long. in Antarctica.

Map. A graphic representation, on a plane, of certain selected features of a part or the whole of the earth's surface.

Map Grid. The framework of parallels and meridians by means of which map features are located.

Map Projection. A network of lines representing parallels of latitude and meridians of longitude, derived by geometrical construction or mathematical analysis.

Map Scale. The relationship which exists between a distance on a map and the corresponding distance on the earth. It may be expressed as an equivalence, one inch equals 16 statute miles; as a fraction or ratio, 1:1,000,000; or as a bar graph subdivided to show the distance which each of its parts represents on the earth.

Mean Solar Time. Also called Mean Time. Time measured by the daily motion of a fictitious body called the "mean sun." Since the apparent sun travels in the ecliptic with a variable motion, it cannot be used to measure time, and the "mean sun," supposedly moving uniformly in the Celestial Equator, is used.

Mercator Projection. A conformal projection on which the meridians and parallels are shown as parallel straight lines at right angles to one another, the divisions of latitude being expanded north and south of the Equator in the same proportion as the divisions of longitude have been lengthened by projection. On this projection a line of constant bearing, or rhumb line, is represented by a straight line.

Meridian. A great circle on the earth's surface which passes through the terrestrial poles.

Mesa. A flat-topped mountain or hill, usually bounded on at least one side by a steep cliff.

Meter. A unit of length equivalent in the United States to exactly 39.37 inches.

Monsoon. A periodic, seasonal movement of air from land to water and vice versa.

Moraine. A mound or ridge of unstratified rock material deposited by a glacier.

N

Nadir. Point in the heavens diametrically opposite to the Zenith, or point directly under observer.

Nautical Mile. A unit commonly used for measuring distances at sea; the length of a minute of latitude; 1,853 meters or 6,080 feet.

Northern Hemisphere. That half of the earth north of the Equator.

North Pole. The end or pole of the earth's axis pointing toward the star Polaris.

O

Ocean. A vast expanse of salt water bordered by the continents. The oceans are usually considered to be four in number: Pacific, Atlantic, Indian, and Arctic.

Ocean Current. A specific portion of any ocean moving in a definite direction. It may also be called a stream or drift.

Oceanography. The science of the oceans, their forms, physical features, and phenomena.

Orbit of the Earth. Curve which earth describes in the heavens as it revolves around the sun.

P

Parallels. Small circles on earth's surface, or lines on a map, perpendicular to axis of the earth, marking latitude north or south of Equator.

Physical Map. A map in which natural regions and physical features are emphasized by the use of different colors.

Planet. A celestial body revolving around the sun in a nearly circular orbit, such as the earth.

Plateau. Elevated area of relatively level land.

Polar Ice Pack. The entire area of thick and closely packed polar ice, more than one year old.

Polar Projection. One in which the meridians appear as straight lines radiating from the pole and the parallels of latitude as concentric circles with the pole as center.

Political Map. A map in which political divisions and boundaries are emphasized through use of color.

Prime Meridian. The meridian on the earth's surface from which longitude is measured, generally the meridian of Greenwich, England.

Projection. Any method of delineating on a plane surface the whole or a part of the surface of the earth, including parallels of latitude and meridians of longitude. See Azimuthal, Conformal, Conic, Cylindrical, Equal Area, Gnomonic, Mercator, and Polar Projections.

R

Reef. A rocky or coral elevation in the ocean bottom, which may show above water at times.

Revolution. The movement of the earth around

the sun. One complete revolution of the earth requires 365 days, 5 hours, 48 minutes, 46 seconds.

Rhumb Line. A line which makes equal angles with all the meridians it crosses.

Roaring Forties. A term used by sailors to describe the stormy regions between 40° and 50° from Equator in northern and southern oceans.

Rotation. Movement of the earth around its axis. One complete rotation determines length of one day.

S

Savanna. Originally, an extensive treeless plain, but now more frequently used to mean a tropical landscape of scattered trees and extensive grasslands.

Sea. A mass of salt water more or less confined by portions of the continent or by chains of islands, and forming a basin distinct from the oceans.

Sea Level. The level of the surface of the sea considered at any moment at a given place.

Small Circle. Any circle on a sphere smaller than a great circle. Thus, all parallels on a globe or map except the Equator.

Solar System. The sun and all celestial bodies revolving around it, together with their satellites.

Solar Time. Also called true solar time. Time measured by the apparent daily motion of the sun.

Solstice. The time at which the overhead sun is at its greatest distance from the Equator. In the Northern Hemisphere the summer solstice occurs about June 21, and the winter solstice about December 22.

Southern Hemisphere. That half of the earth south of the Equator.

South Pole. The opposite end of the earth's axis from the North Pole.

Standard Parallel. A parallel of latitude which is used as a control line in the computation of a map projection, and is, therefore, true to scale.

Statute Mile. A unit of distance generally used in measurements on land, and equal to 5,280 feet.

Steppe. The grassy plains of Russia.

Strait. A relatively narrow waterway between two larger bodies of water.

T

Temperate Zones. The two belts or zones of the earth lying between Tropics and Polar Circles.

Time. The measurable aspect of duration based upon the happening of periodic events, such as: the rotation of the earth (day), the revolution of the moon around the earth (month), and the revolution of the earth around the sun (year). See Greenwich Civil Time, Mean Solar Time, Solar Time.

Time Zone. A belt or zone, extending from north to south across a country, which is given a designated time by law. The United States has four standard time zones, namely: Eastern, Central, Mountain, and Pacific.

Topography. The features of the actual surface of the earth, considered collectively as to form. A single feature, such as a mountain or valley, is called a topographic feature.

Torrid Zone. A term formerly used to describe the belt or zone of the earth's surface bounded by Tropic of Cancer and Tropic of Capricorn. Better geographical form today is "Tropical Zone."

Trade Winds. The regular easterly winds which prevail over the oceans on either side of the Equator to about 30° north and south latitudes.

Transverse Projection. A map projection which is turned 90° from its usual orientation, and consequently is centered upon some great circle other than a meridian.

Tropic. A line on a map or globe, usually broken or dotted, marking the limit reached by the overhead or vertical sun in its apparent annual migration. The northern line is called the **Tropic of Cancer,** and the southern line the **Tropic of Capricorn.** Both are about 23½° from the Equator.

Tundra. The marshy, treeless plains of northern Asia and northern North America.

Twilight. The periods of partial daylight after sunset and before sunrise, when light from the sun is reflected from the atmosphere overhead.

Typhoon. A violent, destructive storm similar to a hurricane, that occurs in the western Pacific Ocean.

V

Vernal Equinox. The date when the overhead sun crosses the Equator on its apparent migration from south to north, or about March 21, and the length of day and night is approximately the same in all latitudes.

Volcano. A more or less conical hill or mountain from which, when active, steam, gases, ashes, or molten rocks are ejected.

W

Water Hemisphere. That half of the earth centered near New Zealand which includes the greatest possible water area.

Westerlies. The prevailing winds of the middle latitudes, that is, between 30° and 60° in north and south latitudes.

Western Hemisphere. Usually considered in cartography to be that half of the earth extending from pole to pole between 160° E. and 20° W., thus including the Americas and Greenland.

West Wind Drift. A general term applied to the eastward movement of oceanic water under the influence of the westerly winds.

Z

Zenith. The point in the celestial sphere directly over a given point on the earth.

Metric Conversion Chart

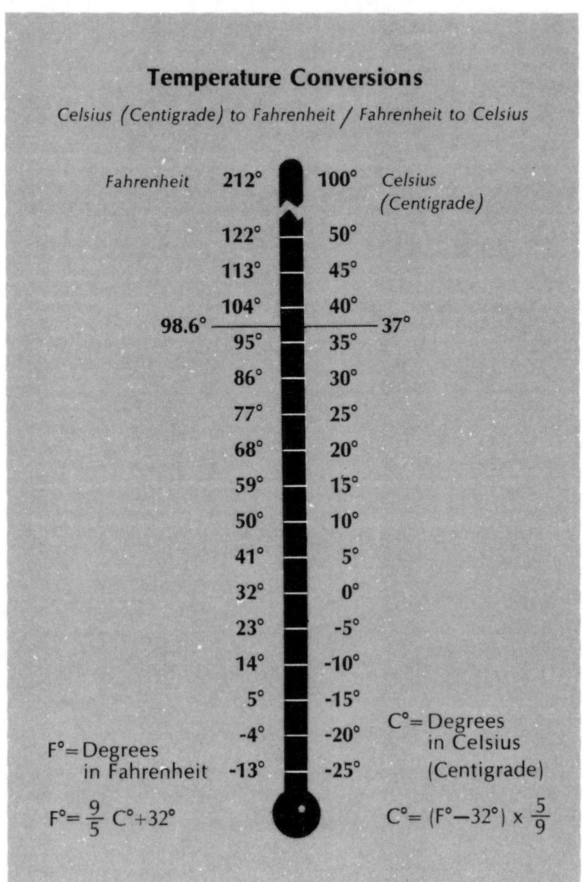

Length

1 inch	=	2.54 centimeters
1 foot	=	.305 meter
1 yard	=	.914 meter
1 mile	=	1.609 kilometers
1 nautical mile	=	1.151 statute miles
1 nautical mile	=	1.852 kilometers
1 meter	=	1.094 yards
1 kilometer	=	.621 mile

Volume

1 cubic inch	=	16.387 cubic centimeters
1 cubic foot	=	.028 cubic meter
1 cubic yard	=	.765 cubic meter
1 cubic meter	=	1.308 cubic yards

Weight

1 ounce	=	28.35 grams
1 pound	=	.454 kilogram
1 long ton	=	1.016 metric tons
1 gram	=	.035 ounce
1 kilogram	=	2.2 pounds

Area

1 square inch	=	6.452 square centimeters
1 square foot	=	.093 square meter
1 square yard	=	.836 square meter
1 acre	=	.405 hectare
1 square mile	=	2.59 square kilometers
1 square kilometer	=	.386 square mile
1 hectare	=	2.471 acres
1 square meter	=	1.196 square yards

Capacity

1 U.S. fluid ounce	=	2.957 centiliters
1 U.S. liquid pint	=	.473 liter
1 U.S. liquid quart	=	.946 liter
1 U.S. gallon	=	3.785 liters
1 U.S. gallon	=	.833 British gallon
1 liter	=	1.057 U.S. liquid quarts

Mathematical Formulae

Diameter of Circle: Circumference divided by 3.1416

Circumference of Circle: Diameter multiplied by 3.1416

Area of Circle: Square of the radius multiplied by 3.1416 or square of the diameter multiplied by .7854

Area of Triangle: Multiply base by .5 altitude

Area of Parallelogram: (including rectangle) Base multiplied by altitude

Surface Area of Sphere: Square of the diameter multiplied by 3.1416

Volume of Sphere: Cube of the diameter multiplied by .5236

Volume of Prism or Cylinder: Area of base multiplied by altitude

Volume of Pyramid or Cone: Area of base multiplied by ⅓ of the altitude

Amount of Simple Interest

Principle multiplied by rate (of interest) multiplied by time (in terms of years or fractions thereof)

Abbreviations

lmin	administered
fg	Afghanistan
fr	Africa
la	Alabama
lb	Albania
lg	Algeria
lsk	Alaska
lta	Alberta
m	American
m. Sam	American Samoa
nd	Andorra
ng	Angola
nt	Antarctica
rc	Arctic
ch	archipelago
rg	Argentina
riz	Arizona
rk	Arkansas
tl. O.	Atlantic Ocean
us	Austria
ustl	Australia, Australian
ton	autonomous
z. Is	Azores Islands
a	Bahamas
arb	Barbados
. C.	British Columbia
el	Belgium, Belgian
hu	Bhutan
s. Arch	Bismarck Archipelago
ngl	Bangladesh
ol	Bolivia
ots	Botswana
r	British
az	Brazil
ru	Brunei
ul	Bulgaria
ur	Burma
alif	California
am	Cameroon
an	Canada
an. Is	Canary Islands
en. Afr. Rep	Central African Republic
en. Am	Central America
	county
ol	Colombia
olo	Colorado
on	Congo
onn	Connecticut
nt	continent
. R.	Costa Rica
. V.	Cape Verde
yp	Cyprus
zech	Czechoslovakia
.C.	District of Columbia
el	Delaware
en	Denmark
p	dependency, dependencies
pt	department
st	district
v	division
ji	Djibouti
om. Rep	Dominican Republic
	Ecuador
g	Egypt
ng	England
quat. Gui	Equatorial Guinea
th	Ethiopia
ur	Europe
alk. Is	Falkland Islands
ed	Federation
n	Finland
a	Florida
r	France, French
. Gu	French Guiana
a	Georgia
am	Gambia
er., Fed. Rep. of	Federal Republic of Germany
er. Dem. Rep	German Democratic Republic
ib	Gibraltar
Grc	Greece
Grnld	Greenland
Guad	Guadeloupe
Guat	Guatemala
Guy	Guyana
Hai	Haiti
Haw	Hawaii
Hond	Honduras
Hung	Hungary
I	Island
I.C	Ivory Coast
Ice	Iceland
Ill	Illinois
incl	includes, including
Ind	Indiana
Indian res	Indian reservation
Indon	Indonesia
I. of Man	Isle of Man
Ire	Ireland
is	islands
isl	island
Isr	Israel
It	Italy
Jam	Jamaica
Jap	Japan
Kam	Kampuchea
Kans	Kansas
Ken	Kenya
Kor	Korea
Kuw	Kuwait
Ky	Kentucky
La	Louisiana
Leb	Lebanon
Le. Is	Leeward Islands
Leso	Lesotho
Lib	Liberia
Liech	Liechtenstein
Lux	Luxembourg
Mad	Madagascar
Mad. Is	Madeira Islands
Mala	Malaysia
Man	Manitoba
Mart	Martinique
Mass	Massachusetts
Maur	Mauritania
Md	Maryland
Medit	Mediterranean
Mex	Mexico
Mich	Michigan
Minn	Minnesota
Miss	Mississippi
Mo	Missouri
Mong	Mongolia
Mont	Montana
Mor	Morocco
Moz	Mozambique
mtn	mount, mountain
mts	mountains
mun	municipality
N.A.	North America
nat. mon	national monument
nat. park	national park
N.B	New Brunswick
N.C	North Carolina
N. Cal	New Caledonia
N. Dak	North Dakota
Nebr	Nebraska
Nep	Nepal
Neth	Netherlands
Nev	Nevada
Newf	Newfoundland
N.H	New Hampshire
Nic	Nicaragua
Nig	Nigeria
N. Ire	Northern Ireland
N.J	New Jersey
N. Mex	New Mexico
Nor	Norway, Norwegian
N.S	Nova Scotia
N.W. Ter	Northwest Territories
N.Y	New York
N.Z	New Zealand
occ	occupied area
Okla	Oklahoma
Om	Oman
Ont	Ontario
Oreg	Oregon
Pa	Pennsylvania
Pac. O	Pacific Ocean
Pak	Pakistan
Pan	Panama
Pap. N. Gui	Papua New Guinea
Par	Paraguay
par	parish
P.D.R. of Yem	Yemen, People's Democratic Republic of
P.E.I	Prince Edward Island
pen	peninsula
Phil	Philippines
Pol	Poland
pol. dist	political district
pop	population
Port	Portugal, Portuguese
poss	possession
P.R	Puerto Rico
pref	prefecture
prot	protectorate
prov	province, provincial
pt	point
Que	Quebec
reg	region
rep	republic
res	reservation, reservoir
R.I	Rhode Island
riv	river
Rom	Romania
S. A	South America
S. Afr	South Africa
Sal	El Salvador
Sask	Saskatchewan
Sau. Ar	Saudi Arabia
S.C	South Carolina
Scot	Scotland
S. Dak	South Dakota
Sen	Senegal
S.L	Sierra Leone
Sol. Is	Solomon Islands
Som	Somalia
Sov. Un	Soviet Union
Sp	Spain, Spanish
St., Ste	Saint, Sainte
Sud	Sudan
Sur	Suriname
Swaz	Swaziland
Swe	Sweden
Switz	Switzerland
Syr	Syria
Tan	Tanzania
Tenn	Tennessee
ter	territories, territory
Tex	Texas
Thai	Thailand
Trin	Trinidad & Tobago
trust	trusteeship
Tun	Tunisia
Tur	Turkey
U.A.E	United Arab Emirates
Ug	Uganda
U.K	United Kingdom
Ur	Uruguay
U.S	United States
Va	Virginia
Ven	Venezuela
Viet	Vietnam
Vir. Is	Virgin Islands
vol	volcano
Vt	Vermont
Wash	Washington
W.I	West Indies
Win. Is	Windward Islands
Wis	Wisconsin
W. Sah	Western Sahara
W. Sam	Western Samoa
W. Va	West Virginia
Wyo	Wyoming
Yugo	Yugoslavia
Zimb	Zimbabwe

Reference Map Index

This universal index includes in a single alphabetical list all important names that appear on the reference maps. Each place name is followed by its location, the map index key, and the page number of the map.

State locations are given for all places in the United States. Province and country locations are given for all places in Canada. All other place name entries show only country locations.

The index reference key, always a letter and figure combination, and the map page number are the last items in each entry. Because some places are shown on both a main map and an inset map, more than one index key may be given for a single map page number. Reference also may be made to more than a single map. In each case, however, the index key *letter and figure* precede the map page number to which reference is made. A lowercase key letter indicates reference to an inset map which has been keyed separately.

Each major and minor political division is followed by both a descriptive term (co., dist., region, prov., dept., state, etc.), indicating political status, and by the country in which it is located. United States counties are listed with state locations; all other divisions are given with country references.

The more important physical names that are shown on the maps are listed in the index. Each entry is followed by a descriptive term (bay, hill, range, riv., mtn., isl., etc.) to indicate its nature.

Country locations are given for all names except features entirely within a state of the United States or province of Canada, in which case this division is given.

Some names included in the index were omitted from the maps because of scale size or lack of space. These entries are identified by an asterisk (*), and reference is given to the approximate location on the map.

A long name may appear on the map in a shortened form, with the full name given in the index. The part of the name not on the map then appears in italics, thus: St. Gabriel *-de-Brandon*.

The system of alphabetizing used in the index is standard. When more than one name with the same spelling is shown, place names are listed *first* and political divisions *second*.

A

B

C

Carlinville, Ill. D4 156
Carlisle, Ark. C4 147
Carlisle, Eng. C5 102
Carlisle, Iowa C4 158
Carlisle, Ky. B5 160
Carlisle, Pa. F7 179
Carlisle, co., Ky. f8 160
Carl Junction, Mo. D3 167
Carloforte, It. E2 107
Carlos Casares, Arg. B4 126
Carlow, Ire. D3 102
Carlow, co., Ire. *D3 102
Carlsbad, Calif. F5 148
Carlsbad, N. Mex. C6 146
Carlstadt, N.J. h8 172
Carlton, Oreg. B3, h11 178
Carlton, co., Minn. D6 165
Carlyle, Sask., Can. H4 137
Carlyle, Ill. E4 156
Carmagnola, It. B1 107
Carman, Man., Can. E2 138
Carman, hill, Pa. C6 179
Carmanville, Newf., Can. D4 142
Carmarthen, Wales E4 102
Carmarthen, co., Wales *E4 102
Carmaux, Fr. E5 103
Carmel, Calif. D3 148
Carmel, Ind. E5 157
Carmel, N.Y. D7 173
Carmel, mtn., Isr. B3 113
Carmelo, Ur. E1 128
Carmel Valley, Calif. *D3 148
Carmel Woods, Calif. *D3 148
Carmen, Par. E4 127
Carmen de Patagones, Arg. C4 126
Carmi, Ill. E5 156
Carmichael, Calif. *C3 148
Carmichaels, Pa. G2 179
Carmona, Sp. D3 106
Carnarvon, Austl. D1 123
Carnduff, Sask., Can. H5 137
Carnegie, Okla. B3 177

D

E

F

G

H

I

J

K

L

M

N

O

P

Q

R

S

T

U

V

W

Westmoreland City, Pa. *F2 179
Westmorland, Calif. F6 148
Westmorland, co., N.B., Can. C5 141
Westmorland, co., Eng. *C5 102
Westmount, Que., Can. *D4 140
West Mystic, Conn. D9 150
West Newton, Pa. F2 179
West New York, N.J. h8 172
West Nyack, N.Y. *D7 173
Weston, Ont., Can. m14 139
Weston, Conn. E3 150
Weston, Mass. g10 163
Weston, Mo. B3, h10 167
Weston, Ohio A2 176
Weston, W. Va. B4 185
Weston, co., Wyo. C8 187
Weston-Super-Mare, Eng. E5 102
West Orange, N.J. B4 172

X-Y-Z

Photo Credits: *p. 7,* Dr. Georg Gerster/John Hillelson; *p. 20,* United States Geological Survey; *p. 38,* National Aeronautics and Space Administration; *p. 58,* Colour Library International; *p. 92,* Tony Duffy/All Sport; *p. 98,* Ray Atkeson; *p. 204,* Robert Frerck/Odyssey.

Acknowledgment: "Gazetteer of the World" reprinted, with permission, from *The Webster's Desk Encyclopedia,* published by Outlet Book Co., Inc., New York.